SOUTHEASTERN MICHIGAN PIONEER FAMILIES

Especially Lenawee County

AND

New York Origins

Compiled by

Helen F. Lewis

KiNSHiP

60 Cedar Heights Road
Rhinebeck, New York 12572

Compiled by:
Helen F. Lewis
1567 Nassau Circle
Tavares, FL 32778
April 15, 1994
copyright Helen F. Lewis 1994

ISBN 1-56012-130-0

KiNSHiP

INTRODUCTION

Settlement of Michigan accelerated rapidly after the completion of the Erie Canal in 1825. That same year, construction was begun on a road headed for Chicago. In the 1830s, land was selling for $1.25 an acre, and eager land seekers from New York and New England, as well as immigrants from Great Britain and Germany poured into the Territory. The area was easily accessible by water or overland through Pennsylvania and northern Ohio.

Lenawee County was formed in 1822 when Michigan was still a Territory. In the 1830 census of the Territory of Michigan, there were only about 258 heads of families enumerated in Lenawee Co. In 1835, Hillsdale County was formed from a portion of Lenawee. By the 1840 census, the population of Lenawee Co. was 17,889, which indicates the rapid influx of these settlers during that 10 year period. Fulton & Lucas Cos, Ohio border Lenawee on the south, and there were some early boundary changes between these counties. Michigan had become a State in 1837.

The book *Portrait and Biographical Album of Lenawee Co., Mich.*, Chapman Brothers, Chicago, 1888, provides the nucleus of the Michigan families noted in this book. The Album, out of print for many years, contains over 1200 pages, and buried in the biographical sketches were hundreds of references to connecting families.

Only the name of the subject was indexed in the above book and none of the connecting families appeared in that index, making it virtually impossible to locate them. I have gleaned only the family information such as names, dates, and places, eliminating all the flowery prose, rewrote it in the format explained following, and placed all the surnames in alphabetical order. Connecting families are cross-referenced and their family data entered under that surname. In many cases, I fleshed out the family record with entries from the 1850 Federal Census of Lenawee Co. The above Album was published in 1888, therefore it provided not only the names of ancestors and descendants of these settlers, but names of their children's spouses and where they migrated from Lenawee Co. Children of these settlers moved all over Michigan, and the United States.

By far the largest number of these families were from New York State. There were also some New England families who came directly, but many had a generation or more reside first in New York before moving further west. Many of these families proudly recorded their Colonial and Revolutionary ancestry in the Album. Lenawee County also had a good representation of families from England, Ireland, and Germany, who also carefully recorded their family origins.

My husband, Edwin C. Lewis, had a Great-Great Grandfather, John Finn, who was in Lenawee Co., Mich. as early as 1840. Among his children was Julia A. who married John Ormsby. They were the parents of Carrie A., mentioned following.

My husband's Great Grandparents, James and Sarah E. (Blackmar) Lewis, were residents of Addison, Lenawee Co., but they were not there until the late 1880s, so cannot be counted among the pioneer families. However, Sarah was the daughter of John & Mary (Southworth) Blackmar, and was believed to have had relatives who had settled earlier in Lenawee Co. James & Sarah are buried in Hillside Cemetery, Addison. Their son, William Alvin, was born 10 Dec. 1878, and he married Carrie A. Ormsby, mentioned above, and they resided in Lenawee County when their eldest son, Alvin James, was born on 25 Jan. 1901. William and Carrie are buried in Dover Cemetery, Lenawee Co. Alvin J. married in Jackson Co. to Hazel L. Brown, and they were residing in Clayton, Lenawee Co., when my husband, Edwin C., was born in 1924. Therefore, I have a great interest in this area of Michigan. I dedicate this book to the memory of my Father-in-Law, Alvin James Lewis, who died 5 September 1989.

SAMPLE ENTRY & EXPLANATION

ARCHER[1], WILLIAM D.[2], son of JOHN (preceding). was born in Wayne Co., NY. He married 17 Oct. 1848 to NEUBELIA (HIGBEE)[3], daughter of Gad C.[4] (also see), in Palmyra, Wayne Co., NY. They removed to Palmyra Twp., Lenawee Co., Mich. She died 17 May 1867. Children: 1. ORSON H.[5] (PalmyraTwp.[6]); 2. HENRY C. (Dallas, TX). William D. married second in Mar. 1872 to CAROLINE E. (CALKINS)[3], daughter of Lorentus[4] (also see). Son: 3. BAYARD T.[5] Ref: PB&A-Len pg. 542-3 & portrait of farm[7].

Explanation:

(1). Surname under which this entry appears.

(2). All given names of the subject surname are in Upper Case. In this case, there is an entry for his father alphabetically preceding William D.

(3). Maiden name of wife in parentheses.

(4). Name of wife's father under which further information about wife is noted.

(5). Given names of children of the subject surname are in Upper Case.

(6). Data in parentheses following the children's names is information about that child that was current at the time the Album was published (1888). In many cases, it is where they resided by that date, names of spouses, etc.

(7). Reference: In this case, *Portrait & Biographical Album of Lenawee Co., Mich.*, Pg. #, and included was a portrait of the farm of William D. Archer.

Pioneer Families of Southeastern Michigan

- A -

ABBOTT, AARON born ca. 1832, NY, was listed in the 1850 census of Adrian Twp., Lenawee Co., Mich. Note this name in the household of Ezra & Emily Abbott, following.

ABBOTT, ABBIE (See Peter McLouth)

ABBOTT, DANIEL C. & wife, CATHERINE (BURCH), were born in Cayuga Co., NY. They moved to Fairfield Twp., Lenawee Co., Mich. ca. 1851, and he died there Oct. 1880, and she died 8 Oct. 1868. Of seven children 3 survived in 1888: 1. LOVINA (m. Philander Savage, Adrian Twp.); 2. HIRAM B. (following); 3. ORRIN L. (Addison, Mich.). Ref: PB&A-Len pg. 354-7.

ABBOTT, DARIUS was listed in the 1840 census index of Dover Twp., Lenawee Co., in close proximity to EZRA (following).

ABBOTT, ELEANOR (See Samuel W. Hagerman)

ABBOTT, EZRA born ca. 1800, and wife, EMILY (TUTTLE), born ca. 1805, both born NY, came from Oneida Co., NY to Dover Twp., Lenawee Co., Mich. in Oct. 1835. They remained there until 1860, then moved into Adrian, where he died in 1861, and she was residing in 1888. Children: 1. NANCY (m. Harley D. Foster, also see); 2. AARON b. ca. 1827 (Clayton, Mich.); 3. GEORGE L. b. ca. 1829 (d. Dover Twp. 1870); 4. ORMAN b ca. 1833 (Lansing, Mich.); 5. EZRA (following); 6. OLIVE b. ca. 1842 (m. A. Amos? J. Fisk; she d. 1859 Dover Twp.); 7. ELON b. ca. 1845 (d. 10 Jan. 1885); 8. JEROME b. ca. 1847 (d. 13 Sept. 1885, Ingham Co., Mich.); 9. OSCAR (following). Ref: P&BA-Len 640-1.

ABBOTT, EZRA, son of EZRA (preceding), married SARAH D. (THURBER), daughter of Norman H. (also see). Ezra died 20 Dec. 1886. Children: 1. DORA L. (d. young); 2. NORMAN D. (d. young); 3. LORA B. Ref: P&BA-Len 248-9.

ABBOTT, HIRAM B., son of DANIEL C. (preceding), was born 27 Dec. 1830 in Niles, Cayuga Co., NY; and moved with parents in 1851 to Fairfield Twp., Lenawee Co., Mich. He married JULIETTE (WOOD) in Royalton, Ohio on 14 Dec. 1854, and settled in Franklin Twp., Lenawee Co. Children: 1. SELLICK G. b. 27 Sept. 1855; 2. DORLISKA S. (m. Franklin Fox; she d. 13 Sept. 1884, age 25, Fairfield Twp.). Ref: P&BA-Len pg. 354-7 with portrait.

ABBOTT, JAMES was born ca. 1826, New York, and is listed in the 1850 census of Dover Twp., Lenawee Co., Mich.

ABBOTT, JOHN & wife, CLARISSA (SIZER), moved from New York to Huron Co., Ohio, where he died age 63; and she died age 84. Known daughter, JULIA A., m. Anson Sizer (also see) in New York and moved ca. 1834 to Huron Co., Ohio. Ref: P&BA-Len pg. 767-8.

ABBOTT, JONATHAN was born ca. 1787, and wife, NANCY, was born ca. 1801, both in New Jersey. In the 1850 census of Fairfield Twp., Lenawee Co., Mich., they listed in their household the following all born NY: HENRY, age 22; RHODA A., age 18; WATSON, age 16; BETSEY E., age 14; GEORGE, age 13; MARTHA, age 11; JONATHAN, age 8. Note: SINCLAIR & WILLIAM, following, may also be related.

ABBOTT, ORPHA, age 65, born New Hampshire, is listed in the 1850 census of Cambridge Twp., Lenawee Co., Mich.

ABBOTT, OSCAR, son of EZRA & EMILY (preceding), was born Oneida Co., NY on 2 Feb. 1835; and moved with parents to Dover Twp., Lenawee Co., Mich. He married 11 June 1859, Hudson Twp., Lenawee Co., to CATHERINE (BARTHOLOMEW), daughter of Abraham (also see), and settled in Dover Twp. Children: 1. ALICE L.; 2. GEORGE E.; 3. DELLA. P&BA-Len pg. 640-1.

ABBOTT, RHEUMMA L. born Thetford, Vt. ca. 1805, married first to Horace Fenton[3] (also see); and second to Bigelow C. Fenton.

ABBOTT, SINCLAIR born ca. 1830, NY, was listed in the 1850 census of Fairfield Twp., Lenawee Co., MIch. (Note JONATHAN, preceding).

ABBOTT, THEODORE was born ca. 1807, New Hampshire, and his wife, ELECTA (GILLETT), daughter of John (also see), was born 1811 in Sempronius, Cayuga Co., NY. They settled before 1840 in Adrian Twp., Lenawee Co., Mich. He died 5 June 1868; and she died 5 Oct. 1858. In 1850 census, they were listed Rome Twp., Lenawee Co. with the first 3 children: 1. LUCY L. b. 2 Oct. 1835 (m. Hayden W. Maynard, also see); 2. THANKFUL I. age 13 (m. James H. Filkins, Hillsdale Co., Mich.); 3. MOSES EDGAR age 9 (m. Juliette Dailey, Rome Twp.); 4. JOHN M. (m. Ida Shepherd, dau. of James H., also see); 5. THEODORE W. (m. Delilah Lohr, Hudson Twp. Ref: P&BA-Len pg. 764-5.

ABBOTT, WILLIAM was born ca. 1823, and his wife, LAVINA (STUCK), was born ca. 1825, both in NY. They moved from New York in 1846, and were in the 1850 census of Fairfield Twp., Lenawee Co., Mich. listing MARY P., age 2; MARCELLUS E., age 1/12. Known daughter, NANCY (b. after 1850; m. William Anderson, also see). William died in 1856, and Lavina lived in Weston, Mich. in 1888. (They were listed 2 doors from Jonathan in 1850 census).

ACKER, GERRY (See Henry J. Wirt)

ACKER, HANNAH born Schoharie Co., NY married before 1800 to Jacob Reasoner (also see). Ref: P&BA-Len 1017-8.

ACKER, JACOB was born ca. 1803, and married in Penn. to ELIZABETH (SHILEY), both born there. They moved to Seneca Co., NY, where known daughter, LAVINA, married in 1851 to George Garling[2] (also see). Ref: P&BA-Len 1026-7.

ACKER, MARGARET (See Joseph Every)

ACKLES, DIANTHA of Ontario Co., NY was first wife of Edwin A. Baker (also see); and her sister, URSULA, was his second wife. Ref: P&BA-Len pg. 632-3.

ACKLEY, GEORGE L. married EMMA (NEGUS), daughter of Charles (also see). They resided in Otsego Co., Mich. in 1888. Children: 1. ZEANNA H.; 2. JOHN E. Ref: P&BA-Len 573-4.

ADAIR, ALEXANDER & wife, ? (McKEE), probably of Montgomery Co., NY, were parents of JANET born 1800 who married Robert Liddel (also see). Ref: P&BA-Len pg. 745-6.

ADAIR, ESTHER was born ca. 1820 in New Hampshire, and is in the 1850 census of Madison Twp., Lenawee Co., Mich. in the home of Lewis Taylor. It may be she listed again in Rome Twp., Lenawee Co., (age 29, b. NY?) in Nial Southard household.

ADAM, CHARLES H., son of JOHN J. (following), born in Detroit, Mich. 31 Oct. 1844; married in Adrian, Lenawee Co. in 1871 to MARY E. (REDFIELD), daughter of Asil (also see) She died Sept. 1885 in Adrian. Children: 1. JOHN H.; 2. MINNIE. Ref: P&BA-Len pg. 292-3.

ADAM, JOHN J., son of ROBERT (following), was born in Paisley, Scotland 30 Oct. 1807. He came first to Baltimore, MD or Philadelphia, PA. He taught for a time in Crawford, PA. In 1827, he came to Franklin Twp., Lenawee Co., Mich.; and resided also for a time in Detroit, Mich. He married in Aug. 1838 to ARMENIA (BRADLEY), daughter of William (also see). They lived in Franklin Twp., Lenawee Co., in the 1850 census, and in 1854 in Tecumseh, Lenawee Co., where he resided in 1888. She died 8 July 1870 in Tecumseh. Children: CHARLES H. (preceding); (ARMENIA) MINNIE B. b. 25 Nov. 1846 (m. Thomas Adamson, Tecumseh). John J. married second on 5 Nov. 1873 to Mrs. CORNELIA M. (BRADLEY) WOIMPLE, sister of Armenia, and widow of John Woimple. Ref: P&BA-Len pg. 292-3 & 465-6 (with portrait).

ADAM, ROBERT of Paisley, Scotland married October 1804 to MARY (CRICHTON) of Dumfriesshire; he died Paisley in 1809. After his death, she moved to Closeburn Parish where she remained. Sons: 1. Dr. THOMAS C. (lived in Wilkes Barre, PA for a time then moved to Lenawee Co., Mich.); 2. JOHN J. (preceding). Ref: P&BA-Len pg. 465-6.

ADAMS, ABIGAIL (See Jonathan Wyman)

ADAMS, AMOS, age 23, born NY, was listed in the 1850 census of Woodstock Twp., Lenawee Co., Mich. in a McCarty household.

ADAMS, DAVID W. born ca. 1815, and wife, RUTH E., born ca. 1812, both in NY, were listed in the 1850 census of Medina Twp., Lenawee Co., Mich. with Fanny M. Ruggles, age 18, b. NY; and Charles Cogswell, age 8, b. Mich., in the household.

ADAMS, EBER born ca. 1807, and wife, ANNA, born ca. 1815, both in NY, were listed as hotel keepers in the 1850 census of Adrian Twp., Lenawee Co., Mich. with MARIA, age 18; JOHN J., age 15, both b. NY.

ADAMS, FRANCIS H. Rev. born ca. 1812, and wife, SARAH M., born ca. 1817, both in NY, were listed in the 1850 census of Madison Twp., Lenawee Co., Mich. with CHARLES F., age 1?, b. Mich., in their household.

ADAMS, HENRY (See Isaiah C. Miller)

ADAMS, HIRAM born ca. 1799, VT? (place illegible), and wife, ELIZABETH, born ca. 1803, NY, were listed in the 1840 census index of Tecumseh Twp., Lenawee Co., Mich. (adjacent to ISAAC; & PETER R.); and in the 1850 census with LOUIS?, age 8, b. Mich., in their household.

ADAMS, HORACE born ca. 1820, NY, was listed in the 1850 census of Rome Twp., Lenawee Co., Mich. in a Luther household.

ADAMS, ISAAC born ca. 1802, Penn., and wife, MARY, born ca. 1811, Mass., were listed in the 1840 census index of Tecumseh Twp., Lenawee Co., Mich. (adjacent to PETER R.); and in the 1850 census with OSCAR, age 22; PETER, age 19; HELEN, age 18; RUFUS, age 17; MARY, age 16; CORDELIA, age 13, all b. Penn.; and ROVENA, age 10; JOHN, age 3; FRANCINA, age 1, all b. Mich., in their household.

ADAMS, J. (See Jabez Briggs). There was a JOSEPH, age 15, born NY, listed in the 1850 census of Woodstock Twp., Lenawee Co.

ADAMS, LEWIS B. born ca. 1813, and wife, CAROLINE, born ca. 1818, both in NY, were listed in the 1850 census of Madison Twp., Lenawee Co., Mich. with WILLIAM, age 13; JOSEPH, age 12; EMELINE, age 10; CAROLINE, age 8; LYDIA, age 5; LEWIS, age 2, all b. NY, in their household.

ADAMS, LOUISA Mrs. was daughter of Ira Holloway (also see).

ADAMS, LUCAS, son of SAMUEL (following), born ca. 1806, married MARY (BAKER), daughter of Elisha (also see). Lucas was listed in the 1840 census index in Bedford Twp., Monroe Co., Mich. He died 24 May 1895, age 89y/1m/8d; and Mary died 11 Jan. 1891, aged 78y/19d. Known sons, ELISHA B., b. ca. 1838, d. 9 Jan. 1851, aged 13y/10m; CHARLES b. ca. 1837, d. 26 May 1868, aged 31y/11m (buried with parents in same cemetery as Samuel). **ADAMS, LURA A.** born ca. 1817, Conn., was listed in the 1850 census of Rollin Twp., Lenawee Co., Mich. with MARTHA J., age 9; WILLIAM W., age 6; WELTHA, age 4; CHARLES, age 1, all b. Mich., in the household of Nathan Rice.

ADAMS, OLIVE E. of Medina Twp., Lenawee Co., Mich. married William C. Bennett on 1 Jan. 1858 in Tecumseh.

ADAMS, OSCAR G. born ca. 1830, and wife, HANNAH, born ca. 1829, both in NY, were listed in the 1850 census of Tecumseh Twp., Lenawee Co., Mich.

ADAMS, PETER R., son of RUFUS (following), was born 10 Feb. 1805, Tioga Co., PA; and married in 1829 possibly in Ohio to CORDELIA (WALLER), daughter of David (also see). In May 1830, they moved to Detroit, Mich., and then to Tecumseh, Lenawee Co. Children: 1. PETER W. b. 1834, Mich. (may be he m. Clara M. Fessenden of Shelby, NY 23 Oct. 1855); 2. ELIZA M. b. ca. 1848 (m. Col. W. C. Fitzsimmons; she d. 20 Apr. 1878); 3. MARY C. (m. John D. Schull, Tecumseh). Ref: P&BA-Len pg. 1063-4.

ADAMS, RUFUS, son of ISAAC, moved from Connecticut to Tioga Co., PA. His wife was MARY (ROBERTS), a native of Livingston Co., NY. Rufus died ca. 1812, Tioga Co., PA. Known son, PETER R. (preceding); also note ISAAC (preceding). Ref: P&BA-Len pg. 1063-4.

ADAMS, SAMUEL born 7 May 1761, served in the Revolutionary War. His wife was ANNA (STONE) born 1761. He died 7 Sept. 1847; and she died June 1838; both buried in an unnamed cemetery located "2 miles from the Ohio line, at the corner of Sterns Rd. & Lewis Ave." The records are in a book <u>Tombstone inscriptions in Lenawee Co., Mich.</u> by the Northwestern Ohio Genealogical Soc. However, your compiler was unable to pinpoint this location on a Lenawee Co. map; and as there is a Sterns Rd. in Monroe Co., Mich. that appears to be about that distance from the Ohio line, and ends on the Lenawee/Monroe Co. line, it is apparently actually in Monroe Co. Son, LUCAS, preceding, also buried there.

ADAMS, WILLIAM was born ca. 1788 in New Jersey, and is listed in the 1850 census of Rollin Twp., Lenawee Co., Mich., with wife(?), LODUSKY, born ca. 1815 in Connecticut. In the household were Charles L. Post,

Pioneer Families of Southeastern Michigan

age 13; Clarissa A. Post, age 11; Jane Post, age 7, all born NY (possibly step-children? Grandchildren?)

ADAMSON, THOMAS (See John J. Adam & George Heesen)

ADLUM, CATHARINE (See Joseph Whitacre)

AINSWORTH, LUCINDA (See Abel Perry)

ALBAIN, JOHN, possibly son of ROBERT (following), was born in Canada, and came with parents to Monroe Co., Mich. as a child. He married before 1838 to ANN J. (KELLOGG), born Ireland, and remained in Monroe Co. Known daughter, MARTHA, b. 25 Aug. 1838, Monroe Co., m. Stephen P. Bailey (also see). Ref: P&BA-Len pg. 822-3.

ALBAIN, ROBERT settled in Monroe Twp., Monroe Co., Mich. by 1830. In the 1830 census he counted males: 2 (15-20); 1 (20-30); 1 (40-50) & females: 1 (10-15); 1 30-40); 1 (40-50). In the 1840 census index, he was listed as "Alban." Note JOHN (preceding).

ALCHIN, THOMAS born ca. 1823, England, married MARY S. (TOWN), daughter of Dr. Nathan (also see), and was listed in the 1850 census of Rollin Twp., Lenawee Co., Mich. with CORNELIA G., age 1, b. Mich., in their household.

ALDRICH also see ALDRIDGE

ALDRICH, ABNER was born in Rhode Island and moved to Ontario Co., NY at age 17, where he married EMILY (HENDERSON) who was born NY. They removed to Green Creek Twp., Sandusky Co., Ohio. Of 11 children 10 grew to maturity. Known son: #3. LYMAN H. (following). Ref: P&BA-Len pg. 1039-40.

ALDRICH, EUNICE (See John Morton, Sr.)

ALDRICH, EVALINE (See John B. Valentine)

ALDRICH, LYDIA (See Benjamin B. Fisk)

ALDRICH, LYMAN H., son of ABNER (preceding), married in Green Creek Twp., Sandusky Co., Ohio on 13 May 1847 to MARY (LYBARKER), daughter of Henry (also see). In 1848, they moved to Royalton, Fulton Co., Ohio; and in 1850 to Seneca Twp., Lenawee Co., Mich. Children: 1. EDGAR D. (m. Olive Bickford); 2. HENRY A. (m. Louisa A. Dull); 3. VIOLA (m. Felch Hayward, son of Henry[4], also see); 4. NANCY (d. infancy); 5. ALICE (d. age 18, Seneca Twp.); 6. AMELIA (d. age 23, Seneca Twp.). Ref: P&BA-Len pg. 1039-40.

ALDRICH, PHILIP W., son of SILAS (following), born 16 Oct. 1845, married CLARISSA (HUTCHINS). They settled in Rome Twp., Lenawee Co., Mich. Children: 1. EDITH M. b. 22 July 1869 (m. Cassius Miles, Arbor Springs, Mich.); 2. LUCY E. b. 28 Feb. 1872; 3. GEORGE L. b. 8 Apr. 1874; 4. ELMER A. b. 18 Apr. 1878. Ref: P&BA-Len 1092-3.

ALDRICH, SILAS, son of WELCOME (following), was born 12 May 1824, Wallingford, Rutland Co., VT, and moved with parents to Rome Twp., Lenawee Co., Mich. He married first 24 Sept. 1844 to LUCY (ROBERTS), daughter of Philip (also see). She died there 6 Mar. 1855, leaving 4 children: 1. PHILIP W. (preceding); 2. PHEBE R.(ROSILLA) b. 19 Aug. 1847 (m. A. P. Keith, Adrian); 3. SILAS L. b. 24 Jan. 1849 (m. Sadie McKay; lived Coffey Co., KS); 4. MELISSA C. b. 31 May 1851 (d. 20 Nov. 1858). Silas married second to CHARITY (ROBERTS), sister of Lucy, on 31 May 1856. Ref: P&BA-Len pg. 1092-3.

ALDRICH, WELCOME, son of SILAS[1] (who moved with wife, MEHITABLE, from New Hampshire to Rutland Co., VT in 1806), was born 28 Dec. 1796 in Richmond, NH, and moved with parents to Vermont. He married 15 Feb. 1815, Wallingford, VT to PHEBE (DOTY), daughter of Isaac (also see). They removed in 1835 to Rome Twp., Lenawee Co., Mich. She died 3 July 1876; and he died 13 Sept. 1883. In the 1850 census of Rome Twp., they listed COMMODORE P., age 20, b. VT. Known son, SILAS (preceding). Ref: P&BA-Len pg. 1092-3.

ALDRICH, WILLIAM was born 1803 in Canada, and his wife, ROXANNA, was born ca. 1809 in Vermont. In the 1850 census of Cambridge Twp., Lenawee Co., Mich., they listed MARTHA, age 18, b. NY (m. Peter Onsted, also see); MATILDA, age 9; MARIETTA, age 6; MILO, age 1, last 3 b. Mich. Ref: P&BA-Len Pg. 1100-1.

ALDRIDGE also see ALDRICH

ALDRIDGE, VIOLA (See LYMAN H. ALDRICH, preceding)

ALEXANDER, C. D. Y. (See Stephen Allen)

ALEXANDER, DAVID, son of NELL (following), was born 2 Feb. 1811 in Windham Co., Conn., and moved with his parents in 1813 to Wayne Co., NY. He married MARY ANN (HOWELL or HULL). They removed to Rollin Twp., Lenawee Co., Mich. in 1857. He died Jan. 1880. Children: 1. HARRIET b. 20 Aug. 1841 (m. S. M. Burgess); 2. GEORGE N. b. 7 Oct. 1843 (served Co. H., Mich. Lt. Art., & 6th Reg. Heavy Art., Civil War; went to Seattle, WA); 3. FRANCIS "FRANK" (following); 4. WILLIAM P. b. 12 Aug. 1851 (m. Ada Hardy, Rollin Twp.). Ref: P&BA-Len Pg. 944-5 & 973-4.

ALEXANDER, FRANCIS "FRANK," son of DAVID (preceding), born 20 May 1849, moved with parents to Rollin Twp., Lenawee Co., Mich. He married 8 Aug. 1874 to ELIZABETH D. (GREEN), daughter of Orson (also see) and settled in Rollin Twp. Daughter, SARAH A., b. 5 Dec. 1880. Ref: P&BA-Len Pg. 973-4.

ALEXANDER, JAMES was born ca. 1804, NY, and his wife, LYDIA, was born ca. 1801, Maryland. In the 1850 census of Franklin Twp., Lenawee Co., Mich., they listed MORTIMER, age 22; RACHEL, age 20; & OSCAR, age 6, all born NY.

ALEXANDER, NELL moved from Windham Co., Conn. to Wayne Co., NY in 1813. He died there at age 57; and his wife died at age 71. Known son, DAVID (preceding). Ref: P&BA-Len 973-4.

ALEXANDER, WILLIAM H. born ca. 1820, and wife, NANCY S., born ca. 1822, both in NY, in the 1850 census of Seneca Twp., Lenawee Co., Mich., listed HARMON S., age 11; WILLIAM, age 9; NANCY S., age 7; FRANCES A., age 5; ANDREW, age 3, all born NY.

ALGER, EZRA & wife, HARRIET (COLES), were natives of Connecticut, who after their marriage moved to Lewis Co., NY. In 1832, they moved to Rochester, NY; and 1836 to Cook Co., Ill. She died in 1842; and he afterwards went to Walworth Co., Wis. He returned to Cook Co., and then about 1868 removed to Fairfield Twp., Lenawee Co., Mich. where he died 1 Apr. 1877.

There were 3 daughters and 2 sons. Known son, ORLANDO H. (following). Ref: P&BA-Len Pg. 1087-8.

ALGER, ORLANDO H., son of EZRA (preceding), was born 23 Dec. 1824, Lewis Co., NY, and moved with his parents to Cook Co., Ill. He married there to SALLY (HIGGINS), daughter of Isaac (also see). They moved to Fairfield Twp., Lenawee Co., Mich. in 1865. Children: 1. CLARENCE A. b. 20 Aug. 1855; 2. ADELBERT (d. age 3); 3. EMERY P. (m. Mary Furman); 4. AUGUSTUS C. (d. age 3); 5. HERBERT O. (m. Alida White; had children, Harley C. & Fern R.); 6. BEATRICE; 7. LAFAYETTE (d. child); 8. PEARL (d. child). Ref: P&BA-Len Pg. 1087-8.

ALLBRING, AMOS R. (See Thomas Chandler)

ALLEN, A. H. born ca. 1808, and wife, MARIA, born ca. 1807, NY, both in NY, were listed in the 1850 census of Seneca Twp., Lenawee Co., Mich. with AUSTIN W., age 16; MARTHA A., age 14, both b. NY; and MARY J., age 10; LORENZO M., age 8, both b. Mich., in their household. May be he listed in the 1840 census index of Medina Twp., adjacent to an "A" (Note ARTEMUS, following).

ALLEN, ADELINA who died 22 Aug. 1853 had parents who were pioneers of Lenawee Co., Mich. (See Henry C. Christman).

ALLEN ALVIN was born ca. 1815 in VT, and in the 1850 census of Medina Twp., Lenawee Co., Mich., he listed in his household Delinda Hutchins, age 40, b. VT; George Hutchins, age 8; & Mary Hutchins, age 2, both born Mich. Note JOSEPH L., following.

ALLEN, AMZI born ca. 1813, Mass., and wife, SUSAN J., born ca. 1808, NY, were listed in the 1850 census of Raisin Twp., Lenawee Co., Mich. with Joseph Gibbons, age 53, b. Penn., in their household.

ALLEN, ARTEMUS was born ca. 1801, and his wife, LUCINDA, was born ca. 1815, both in NY. In the 1850 census of Medina Twp., Lenawee Co., Mich., they listed HARRIET, age 15, b. NY; ERVIN, age 8; HELEN, age 11, both born Mich. May be he listed as "A." in the 1840 census index of Medina Twp. Note A. H. (preceding).

ALLEN, BENJAMIN F. was listed in the 1840 census index of Tecumseh Twp., Lenawee Co., Mich.

ALLEN, BENJAMIN S., son of STEPHEN (following), was born 22 Dec. 1822 in Seneca Co., NY, and moved to Lenawee Co., Mich. with his parents. He married 27 Mar. 1856 to SARAH (ALLEN), who was born 4 Aug. 1822, Seneca Co., NY, & settled in Madison Twp., Lenawee Co., Mich. Daughter, LETTA N. (m. Frank Welsh). Ref: P&BA-Len pg. 831-2.

ALLEN, BENJAMIN W. born ca. 1803, NJ, and wife, ESTHER, born ca. 1805, Penn., were listed in the 1840 census index of Dover Twp., Lenawee Co., Mich.; and in the 1850 census with JOHN B., age 19, b. NJ; and EDWARD T., age 7, b. Mich., in their household.

ALLEN, C. E. (male), age 16, and probably sister, CORNELIA, age 11, both born Ohio, were listed in the 1850 census of Madison Twp., Lenawee Co., Mich. in the household of Charles N. Parsons and wife, OLIVE, age 20, b. Ohio, possibly another sister?

ALLEN, CHARLES born ca. 1805, and wife, ANNA, born ca. 1814, Ireland, were listed in the 1850 census of Franklin Twp., Lenawee Co., Mich. with CHARLES, age 8; ANN, age 6, both b. NY; and CORNELIA, age 4; ROSETTA, age 2, both b. Mich., in their household. Also see DANIEL, listed next door in 1850.

ALLEN, CHARLES married ELMA (GRIFFITH), daughter of Cyrus (also see), and settled in Dover Twp., Lenawee Co., Mich. Known child, LESLIE C. Ref: P&BA-Len pg. 1034-5.

ALLEN, CLARA R. (See James B. Wells)

ALLEN, CORODON born ca. 1822, NY, and wife, ALMIRA, born ca. 1822, Mich., were listed in the 1850 census of Blissfield Twp., Lenawee Co., Mich. with NORMAN, age 3, b. Mich., in their household.

ALLEN, DANIEL born ca. 1796, and wife, BETSEY, born ca. 1794, both in NY, were listed in the 1850 census of Palmyra Twp., Lenawee Co., Mich. with SEYMOUR, age 17; JULIA, age 16, both b. NY, in their household.

ALLEN, DANIEL born ca. 1818, NY, and wife, HARRIET, born ca. 1819, Mass., were listed in the 1850 census of Franklin Twp., Lenawee Co., Mich. with SAMUEL, age 7, b. NY; LYMAN, age 3; ASHLEY (male), age 1, all b. Mich.; and Sarah M. Horton, age 20, b. Mass., in their household. Listed next door to CHARLES, also see, in the 1850 census.

ALLEN, DANIEL R. born ca. 1800, Mass., and wife, ANN, born ca. 1800, NY, were listed in the 1850 census of Franklin Twp., Lenawee Co., Mich. with HENRY, age 25; GEORGE, age 22, both b. Mass.; and CLASTINA, age 19, b. NY; and JAMES, age 11, b. Mich., in their household.

ALLEN, EBENEZER Col. was a relative of General Ethan Allen of Revolutionary fame. Col. Ebenezer & wife, LYDIA, were residents of Tinmouth, Rutland Co., VT, and known daughter, EUNICE, was born 7 Apr. 1779 in Tinmouth (m. William Luther, also see). Ref: P&BA-Len pg. 884-5.

ALLEN, ELISHA was born in Charleston, Montgomery Co., NY on 26 June 1786; and wife, ELIZABETH, was born 28 Mar. 1785. They lived in Jefferson Co., NY where he died 13 Apr. 1873; and she died 20 Oct. 1865. Of 10 children, 4 were living in 1888. Known daughter, CLARA, married in 1844 to Charles G. Stowers (also see). Ref: P&BA-Len pg. 384-5.

ALLEN, EMILY was listed head of household in the 1840 census index of Tecumseh Twp., Lenawee Co., Mich. Note BENJAMIN F.; & TRISTAM.

ALLEN, ERASMUS DARWIN was born 3 May 1823 in Farmington, Ontario Co., NY, son of ? & ? (EDDY) ALLEN, and he came to Medina Twp., Lenawee Co., Mich. in 1849, and was in business with his brother (possibly JOHN, age 21, who was in his household in 1850 census). Erasmus married in June 1846 to MARIA (McOMBER). Listed in their household in the 1850 census of Medina Twp. was AUGUSTUS, age 2, b. NY (relationship not known). Also in the home was Sarah McOmber, age 14, b. NY. They went to Nebraska ca. 1857, but returned to Morenci, Mich. ca. 1859. He died 28 Feb. 1885, Morenci. No children were named in the sketch. Ref: P&BA-Len pg. 1064-6.

ALLEN, ETHAN was a lineal descendant of Ethan of Revolutionary fame. Ethan and wife, CYNTHIA (BLANDEN), moved from Vermont to Tecumseh, Lenawee Co., Mich. where they remained. Known daughter, HELEN born ca. 1824, VT (m. Aaron

Pioneer Families of Southeastern Michigan

Norcross[2], also see). LEMUEL born ca. 1837, Mich., in household of Aaron & Helen in 1850 census is probably son of Ethan. Ref: P&BA-Len pg. 264.

ALLEN, ETHAN born ca. 1808, and wife, SALLY, born ca. 1810, both in NY, were listed in the 1840 census index (adjacent to G. W., following) of Seneca Twp., Lenawee Co., Mich.; and in the 1850 census with no family in the household.

ALLEN, ETHAN born ca. 1817, and wife, MARGARET, born ca. 1818, both in NY, were listed in the 1850 census of Cambridge Twp., Lenawee Co., Mich. with ELIZABETH, age 11; MARY, age 9, both b. NY; and CAROLINE, age 4, b. Mich., in their household.

ALLEN, EUNICE (See William Luther)

ALLEN, FANNIE (See James Green)

ALLEN, FRANKLIN was born ca. 1818, and his wife, ANNA A., was born ca. 1819, both in NY. In the 1850 census of Medina Twp., Lenawee Co., Mich., they listed MARIAH, age 12; CYRUS, age 8; ALICE, age 5; GEORGE, age 11/12, all born NY.

ALLEN, FRANKLIN (See Aaron Whitacre)

ALLEN, G. W. was listed in the 1840 census index of Seneca Twp., Lenawee Co., Mich., adjacent to ETHAN, preceding.

ALLEN, GEORGE W., probably son of DANIEL (preceding), married ELIZA (WHELAN), daughter of William (also see), Franklin Twp., Lenawee Co., Mich. Ref: P&BA-Len pg. 458-9.

ALLEN, GEORGE W. Jr., son of GEORGE W. Sr. (following), was born 20 Nov. 1840, Franklin Twp. Lenawee Co., Mich. He married 23 Dec. 1870 to CYNTHIA (McCLURE), who was born 6 July 1854, London, Ontario, Canada (See McClure). Children: 1. IRENA F.; 2. LEON R.; 3. NINA A.; 4. EARLE R. Ref: P&BA-Len pg. 230.

ALLEN, GEORGE W., Sr. was born ca. 1807 in Massachusetts, and came to Franklin Twp., Lenawee Co., Mich. in 1832. He married there in 1834 to IRENA (WHELAN) who was born 1811 in Monroe Co., Mich. to a family who settled there in 1830s (See Eli Whelan). In the 1850 census of Franklin Twp., listed in the household were MELLINA?, age 15; ADELINE, age 13; GEORGE W. Jr. (preceding); MYRA, age 3; AUGUSTA, age 1/12, all born Mich. Ref: P&BA-Len pg. 230. In the 1850 census, they are listed next door to JOHN R., also see.

ALLEN, HANNAH (See Miles P. Morton)

ALLEN, HARRIET, age 15, born NY, was listed in the 1850 census of Madison Twp., Lenawee Co., Mich. in a Babcock household.

ALLEN, HENRY was listed in the 1840 census index of Adrian Twp., Lenawee Co., Mich.

ALLEN, HENRY G. born ca. 1816, NJ, and wife, PRUDENCE?, born ca. 1824, NY, were listed in the 1850 census of Seneca Twp., Lenawee Co., Mich. with ELIZA B., age 7; CHARLES B., age 4; JOHN H., age 1, all b. Mich., in their household.

ALLEN, HENRY V. born ca. 1802, NJ, and wife, ELIZABETH, born ca. 1815, Mass., were listed in the 1850 census of Woodstock Twp., Lenawee Co., Mich. with MORTIMER, age 12, b. NY, all listed in a Jackson household.

ALLEN, HOWARD M. born ca. 1818, NY, and wife, CATHARINE, born ca. 1819, Canada, were listed in the 1850 census of Ogden Twp., Lenawee Co., Mich. with WILLIAM, age 13; GEORGE, age 11, both b. Canada; and ELIZA J., age 9; MARY A., age 7; LORETTA, age 5; ALEXANDER, age 1, all b. Mich., in their household.

ALLEN, IRA B. born ca. 1825, NY, and wife, JANE, born ca. 1830, Canada, were listed in the 1850 census of Palmyra Twp., Lenawee Co., Mich. with IRA B., age 2; HANNAH A., age 3/12, both b. Mich., in their household.

ALLEN, ISRAEL born Connecticut, and wife, MARGARET (BARKER), born Mass., lived in Litchfield Co., Conn. before moving to Pennsylvania. They sold in Penn. after the War of 1812, and moved to Bethany, Genesee Co., NY. In 1857, they came to Lenawee Co., NY to live with son, Oliver. Three known of 8 children: AUORILLA b. Litchfield Co., Conn. (unmarried); REUBEN (m. Elizabeth Leet, lived Allegan Co., Mich.); OLIVER b. 17 Aug. 1817, Genesee Co., NY (unmarried). Ref: P&BA-Len pg. 222.

ALLEN, JAMES was listed in the 1840 census index of Medina Twp., Lenawee Co., Mich.

ALLEN, JAMES born ca. 1805, and wife, MARY, born ca. 1813, both in NY, were listed in the 1850 census of Cambridge Twp., Lenawee Co., Mich. with SARAH, age 10; ORANGE, age 8; MARILLA, age 4, all b. Mich., in their household. May be he listed in the 1840 census index, note preceding.

ALLEN, JAMES was listed in 1840 census index of Rome Twp., Lenawee Co., Mich. He was not listed in 1850, however, note RHODA, following. LYMAN & RUSSELL (following) were adjacent to James in the 1840 census index.

ALLEN, JAMES of Ann Arbor, Mich. (See Jacob D. Ayers).

ALLEN, JAMES, age 21, born Mass., and ROSETTA, age 20, born NY, were listed in the 1850 census of Adrian Twp., Lenawee Co., Mich. in a hotel.

ALLEN, JAMES C. born ca. 1816, Virginia, and wife, MARTHA, born ca. 1814, NY, were listed in the 1850 census of Tecumseh Twp., Lenawee Co., Mich. with MARY, age 7/12, b. Mich., and Lafayette Kelly, age 18, b. Mich., in their household.

ALLEN, JAMES P. was listed in the 1840 census index of Franklin Twp., Lenawee Co., Mich.

ALLEN, JANE (WILLIAMS) - See Thomas Williams.

ALLEN, JOHN was listed in the 1840 census index of Seneca Twp., Lenawee Co., Mich.

ALLEN, JOHN born ca. 1790, Rhode Island, and wife, SARAH, born ca. 1796, NJ, were listed in the 1840 census of Raisin Twp., Lenawee Co., Mich.; and in the 1850 census with WILLIAM, age 23; ELIZABETH, age 18, both b. NY, in their household.

ALLEN, JOHN born ca. 1829, NY (See ERASMUS DARWIN, preceding).

ALLEN, JOHN born ca. 1812, and wife, NANCY, born ca. 1816, both in NY, were listed in the 1850 census of Ridgeway Twp., Lenawee Co., Mich. with WILLIAM H., age 13; ELIZA J., age 10; MARY E., age 6; ELIZABETH, age 5; ARMINDA, age 3; EMELINE, age 1, all b. Mich., in their household.

ALLEN, JOHN H. born ca. 1790, Mass., and wife, PHEBE, born ca. 1799, NY, were probably they listed as John in the 1840 census index of Macon Twp., Lenawee Co., Mich.; and in the 1850 census with MATILDA, age 19; DANIEL, age 17, both b. Canada; and MAHALA, age

14; LUKE?, age 8, both b. Mich.; and Mary Swick, age 7, b. Mich., in their household.

ALLEN, JOHN, Jr. was born 20 Oct. 1774 in New England, and settled in White Creek, Washington Co., NY at an early day. He married ROSANNA (STEWART) who was born 1 July 1782, and died at age 35. He died at age 84, White Creek. Known son, JOSEPH S. (preceding). Ref: P&BA-Len pg. 1198-1200. Note: In French's Gazeteer of New York State, JOHN & EBENEZER ALLEN were early settlers of White Creek, NY.

ALLEN, JOHN R. born ca. 1790, Mass., was in the 1850 census of Franklin Twp., Lenawee Co., Mich., with wife, HARRIET, age 51, b. NY; and in the household is ELIJAH, age 13, b. Mich. They are next door to GEORGE W. It is probably this JOHN listed in the 1840 census index of Franklin Twp.

ALLEN, JOHN W., son of STEPHEN (following), was born 18 Jan. 1830 in Seneca Co., NY, and came to Madison Twp., Lenawee Co., Mich. with his parents. In 1851, he went to California, but returned in 1854. He married in Apr. 1862 to MARTHA (TENBROOK), probably daughter of Garrett (also see); but she died after 6 months. He married second in Seneca Co., NY to MARY (VAN DUYN), born 28 Mar. 1837. They settled in Madison Twp., Lenawee Co. Son, WILLIAM W. S. b. 16 Nov. 1869. Ref: P&BA-Len pg. 1018-9.

ALLEN, JOHN W., son of JOSEPH S. (following), was born ca. 1833 in VT, and came with parents to Rollin Twp., Lenawee Co., Mich. He married 15 Mar. 1860 to MARY J. (NEWCOMB), daughter of Bethuel of Prairie du Sac, Wis. They settled in Rollin Twp. Children: 1. STELLA A. b. 10 Oct. 1861 (m. C. C. Fuller); 2. GRACE R. b. 5 May 1865; 3. BERTHA H. b. 18 Feb. 1868; 4. MAUDE E. b. 4 Mar. 1870, d. 24 Aug. 1872; 5. LIZZIE L. b. 17 May 1876. Ref: P&BA-Len pg. 1198-1200.

ALLEN, JOSEPH S., son of JOHN, Jr. (preceding), was born 5 Aug. 1805 in Washington Co., NY; and his wife, LUCINDA (ROBBINS), was born 31 1806 in Shaftsbury, VT. In 1834, they moved from Vermont to Rollin Twp., Lenawee Co., Mich. She died 28 Apr. 1870; and he died 25 Apr. 1883. Two of 5 children died infancy. Children: 1. JOHN W. (preceding); 2. DAVID H. b. 30 May 1838, Mich. (m. Melissa A. Page, daughter of Nicholas Amos, also see); 3. HASSAN D. b. ca. 1843 (d. 2 Feb. 1865, result of injuries received in Civil War). Ref: P&BA-Len pg. 1198-1200.

ALLEN, JULIA A. born ca. 1824, NY, of Ridgeway Twp., Lenawee Co., Mich., married John Pocklington (also see). Her parents (names not given) both died in Ridgeway Twp.

ALLEN, LEVI born ca. 1807 in Vermont, and wife, SARAH, born ca. 1811 in New Jersey, were listed in the 1850 census of Medina Twp., Lenawee Co., Mich., with ELIZABETH, age 17; GEORGE A., age 16, both b. NY; LYMAN, age 14; WEALTHY A., age 12; HENRY, age 8, preceding 3 b. Ohio; and ADALINE, age 6; ELEANOR, age 1, both born Mich., in their household.

ALLEN, LORRIN born ca. 1814, place not known, and wife, CLARINDA, born ca. 1824, Canada, were listed in the 1850 census of Ridgeway Twp., Lenawee Co., Mich. with JOHN, age 7; DANIEL, age 6; EDWARD, age 5, all b. Canada, in their household.

ALLEN, LYMAN born ca. 1801, and wife, LAURA, born ca. 1804, both in NY were in the 1840 index census of Rome Twp., Lenawee Co., Mich.; and in the 1850 census with CHARLES, age 25; CALEB, age 18, both b. NY; LAURA, age 14; DANIEL, age 4, both b. Mich., in the household. (Note JAMES & LEVI, preceding, & RHODA, following).

ALLEN, MARIA (See Orlando Brown)

ALLEN, MARY A. of Macon & Tecumseh Twps, Lenawee Co., Mich. (See Isaac Collins). Ref: P&BA-Len pg. 192-3.

ALLEN, MASON was born ca. 1830, born NY, was listed in the 1850 census of Rome Twp., Lenawee Co., Mich., with wife, CYNTHIA, age 19, married within the year, in the household of John Conner (perhaps Cynthia is daughter of this household?)

ALLEN, NATHAN of Monroe Co., NY was a direct descendant of Ethan Allen of Ticonderoga fame. Nathan and wife, MARY, were parents of HARRIET who married first to ? Doty, and married second to Levi R. Pierson (also see). Ref: P&BA-Len pg. 705-6.

ALLEN, RACHEL (See Lewis Goodwin)

ALLEN, RHODA (Mrs.?) was born ca. 1780 in NY, and was listed in the 1850 census of Rome Twp., Lenawee Co., Mich. in the household of William Barrus and his wife, MARY (ALLEN), possibly daughter of Rhoda. See JAMES who was in Rome Twp. in 1840.

ALLEN, ROBERT moved from Seneca Co., NY to Jefferson Twp., Hillsdale Co., Mich. in 1855. He later moved to Reading Twp. where he died. His known daughter, EMILY, born in Seneca Co., NY married John Velie Munger (also see). Ref: P&BA-Len pg. 816-7.

ALLEN, RUSSELL born ca. 1801, and wife, SUSANNA, born ca. 1805, both in NY, were listed in the 1840 index census of Rome Twp., Lenawee Co.., Mich.; and in the 1850 census with ADALINE, age 16, b. NY; RUSSELL Jr., age 12; HENRY, age 9; MARSHALL, age 5, last 3 b. Mich., in the household. Also note JAMES; LYMAN & RHODA, preceding.

ALLEN, SARAH Mrs. was listed head of household in the 1840 census index of Clinton, Lenawee Co., Mich.

ALLEN, SILAS L., son of STEPHEN (following), was born 16 July 1828 in Romulus, Seneca Co., NY, and came with parents to Madison Twp., Lenawee Co., Mich. He married 19 Nov. 1856 to EMMA (DAVIS), daughter of Joshua (also see). They lived in Seneca Twp., then Hudson Twp., Lenawee Co., where Emma died 25 Sept. 1872 leaving 4 children: 1. EMMA L. (m. J. Jerome Travis, Clinton, MIch.); 2. STANLEY G. (Kansas City, KS); 3. CHARLES D. (Hudson Twp.); 4. MARIAN. Silas L. married second on 8 July 1875 to BERNICE (BURR), daughter of Lonsen R. (also see). Children: 5. WALTER P.; 6. LEIGH. Ref: P&BA-Len pg. 1034-5.

ALLEN, SPENCER, and wife, SOPHIA, of Macedon, Wayne Co., NY, were the parents of MARY ANN who married first to Darius Cole, and second to Elvin C. Cole (see both). Ref: P&BA-Len pg. 556-7.

ALLEN, STEPHEN, son of SILAS, was born 21 Dec. 1795 in Morristown, NJ, and remained there until age 10 when he moved with his parents to Seneca Co., NY. He married DEBORAH (SUTTON), daughter of Benjamin & Mary who had moved from NJ to Seneca Co., NY. Stephen & Deborah came first to Dover Twp., Lenawee Co., Mich. in 1836, and afterwards moved to Madison Twp. Deborah died 6 Apr. 1877, Madison Twp. Of 9 children, known were: 1. BENJAMIN S. (preceding); 2. MARY (m. Elihu B. Pond, Ann Arbor, Mich.); 3.

Pioneer Families of Southeastern Michigan

ESTHER b. ca. 1828 (m/1 C.D.Y. Alexander who d. 1860, m/2 James A. Bayless, Kansas City, MO); 4. SILAS L. (preceding); 5. JOHN W. (preceding); 6. GILBERT T. b. ca. 1832 (d. 20 July 1858, age 27); 7. LOUISA C. b. ca. 1834 (m. James Bayless, she d. 1874, MO); 8. PHOEBE b. ca. 1836 (d. Feb. 1854, age 17). Ref: P&BA-Len pg. 336-7; 1018-9; 1034-5.

ALLEN, THEODORE born ca. 1812, NY, and MARY, born ca. 1817, West Indies, were listed in the 1850 census of Franklin Twp., Lenawee Co., Mich. with HENRY, age 14, b. Mich.; and ADELINE, age 9; MARCUS, age 6; HANNAH, age 4; EMILY, age 2, all b. Ohio, in their household.

ALLEN, THOMAS B., probably son of TIMOTHY (of Madison Twp., following). born ca. 1827, and wife, MARY A., born ca. 1827, both in NY, were listed in the 1850 census of Madison Twp., Lenawee Co., Mich., with CYRUS, age 1, b. Mich., in their household.

ALLEN, TIMOTHY born ca. 1779, and wife, NANCY, born ca. 1796, both in New Jersey, were listed in the 1850 census of Franklin Twp., Lenawee Co., Mich. with MARGARET, age 20, b. NJ, all listed in the household of Lafayette Wells and wife, CLARY, age 23, b. NJ, probably another daughter of Timothy. Note: In the 1840 census index, there was a TIMOTHY in Grass Lake, Jackson Co., Mich.

ALLEN, TIMOTHY born ca. 1787, NY, was listed in the 1850 census of Madison Twp., Lenawee Co., Mich. with THOMAS B., age 23 (preceding) and family in his household.

ALLEN, TRISTAM born ca. 1803, Mass., and wife, ELIZABETH, born ca. 1812, NY, were listed in the 1840 census index of Tecumseh Twp., Lenawee Co., Mich.; and in the 1850 census with DAVID, age 19; SUSAN, age 15, both b. NY; and FREDUS, age 14; CORNELIA, age 12; MARY, age 10; ALBERT, age 8; ANN, age 5; PHEBE, age 2, all b. Mich., in their household.

ALLEN, TRISTIAM, age 16?, born Rhode Island, was listed in the 1850 census of Tecumseh Twp., Lenawee Co., Mich. in a Murray household.

ALLEN, WILLIAM (See James Lanning)

ALLEN, WILLIAM born ca. 1798, and wife, HANNAH, born ca. 1790, with FRANCES, age 21; WILLIAM, age 18, both b. Mass., were listed in the 1850 census of Woodstock Twp., Lenawee Co., Mich. in a Horton household.

ALLEN, WILLIAM born ca. 1822, and wife, HARRIET, born ca. 1828, both in Ohio, were listed in the 1850 census of Franklin Twp., Lenawee Co., Mich. with MILES, age 4, b. Mich., in their household.

ALLEN, WILLIAM born ca. 1822, and wife, SARAH, born ca. 1824, both in NY, were listed in the 1850 census of Blissfield Twp., Lenawee Co., Mich. with HARRIET, age 5; HENRY, age 3; MARIA, age 1, all b. Mich., in their household. Note DANIEL, preceding.

ALLIS, EDWARD P., son of SOLOMON (following), was born 9 Feb. 1819 in Franklin Co., Mass. He moved in 1844 to Rome Twp., Lenawee Co., Mich. He married HANNAH (JENNINGS). daughter of Zera (also see) on 2 Apr. 1851, Hudson Twp. Children: 1. ELLIOTT W.; 2. LUCIUS F. (following); 3. MARY. Ref: P&BA-Len pg. 329-30.

ALLIS, LUCIUS F., son of EDWARD P. (preceding), was born 11 July 1857 in Rome Twp., Lenawee Co., Mich. He married SAMANTHA (GANDER), daughter of David (also see) and settled in Madison Twp. Children: 1. EDWARD D.; 2. ARTHUR L. Ref: P&BA-Len pg. 329-30.

ALLIS, SOLOMON, son of LUCIUS (who settled in Conway, Franklin Co., Mass. 1764), was born in Franklin Co., Mass. He married ANNA B. (DICKINSON), and he died there in 1823; and she died in 1863. Known son, EDWARD P. (preceding). Ref: P&BA-Len pg. 329-30.

ALLISON, SARAH J. (See John TenBrook)

ALVERSON, C. A. (See Josiah Hawley)

ALVORD, JOSIAH born ca. 1780, and wife, LYDIA, age 72, were both born in Mass., and in the 1850 census of Fairfield Twp., Lenawee Co., Mich., they listed son, MARSHALL (following) & family and Jane C. Beals, age 12; Clarissa Shumway, age 16 (See Mrs. Lydia Shumway) in the household.

ALVORD, MARSHALL W., son of JOSIAH (preceding), born ca. 1813 in Mass., and his wife, LEAH B., age 33, b. NY, and children, CORDELIA, age 6; LUCY, age 4; LYDIA H., age 1, all b. Mich., were listed in Josiah's household in the 1850 census of Fairfield Twp., Lenawee Co., Mich.

ALVORD, MARY A., age 65, born Conn., was listed in the 1850 census of Palmyra Twp., Lenawee Co., Mich. in the household of Volney & Lorina Spaulding.

AMBROSE, WILLIAM W. married JANE (GILMORE), daughter of Lyman (also see) probably in Washtenaw Co., Mich. They had a known son, Dr. AMBROSE L. of Hanover, Jackson Co., Mich. Ref: P&BA-Len pg. 896-8.

AMES, ?, of the Ames Family who came on the "Mayflower," married in New London, Conn. to Jeremiah Page who came to America in 1765.

AMES, BISHOP, son of ELIAS, was born in Rensselaerville, Albany Co., NY. Some time after 1800, he moved with his parents to Cayuga Co., NY. He married ALMIRA (TICHENOR), daughter of Joseph in Cayuga Co., NY. They later settled in Groton, Tompkins Co., NY. Of 11 children, 9 grew to maturity. Known son, #4. BISHOP H. (following). Ref: P&BA-Len pg. 536-7.

AMES, BISHOP H., son of BISHOP (preceding), was born 15 Feb. 1821, Cayuga Co., NY; and he married in 1843 to DELIA (MURRAY), daughter of Edward (also see). In 1844, they removed to Franklin Twp., Lenawee Co., Mich.; later moved to Somerset Twp., Hillsdale Co., but by 1865 returned to Hudson Twp., Lenawee Co. Children: 1. Infant (d. unnamed); 2. IDA (m. John C. McCowan, also see); 3. HENRY B. (m. INEZ AMES, had ch: Emily A.; & Fern; note Inez in family of CHARLES HENRY, following); 4. EMILY M. (m. Prof. J. W. Mauk; she d. 26 Apr. 1879). Ref: P&BA-Len 536-7.

AMES, CHARLES, son of PETER (following), was born 1799 in Petersham, Mass. He married 10 Apr. 1823 in Geneva, NY to SARAH S. (BALL), daughter of Nathan (also see). In 1833, they removed to Pittsford, Hillsdale Co., Mich., but returned to Geneva, Ontario Co., NY in 1847, and remained 4 years, before returning to Pittsford. He died in 1874, and she died in 1869.

Youngest son, EDWIN W., b. 3 Feb. 1836 in Hillsdale Co., Mich., resided in Hudson Twp., Lenawee Co., Mich. in 1888, possibly unmarried. Ref: P&BA-Len pg. 986-7.

AMES, CHARLES HENRY, son of CLARK (following), was born Hillsboro Co., NH, 26 Apr. 1835; and came with parents to Hudson Twp., Lenawee Co., Mich. He married 20 Apr. 1859 to HARRIET C. (BUSH), daughter of Eli (also see). They resided in Hudson Twp. Children: 1. H. ELIZA; 2. FRANK H.; 3. INEZ M. (Note INEZ who m. HENRY B. in family of BISHOP H., preceding). Ref: P&BA-Len pg. 582-3.

AMES, CLARK, son of PETER (following), was born 12 May 1794 in Petersham, Mass. He removed to Francestown, NH, and married first to SARAH (HUBBARD) who was born 14 Nov. 1804 in New Hampshire. He came to Hudson Twp., Lenawee Co., Mich. in 1837, then returned to New Hampshire and brought his wife & 4 children to Michigan in 1838. Sarah died in Hudson Twp. 11 Aug. 1841. Children: 1. SARAH FRANCES b. 30 Oct. 1827 (m. William Brown, Hudson Twp.); 2. ORLANDO SCOTT b. 23 Apr. 1831 (to Independence, IA); 3. WILLIAM HENRY (d. infancy); 4. CHARLES HENRY (preceding); 5. LIZZIE (MARY? in census) b. 16 Aug. 1837 (m. Harvey J. Griffes). Clark married second on 21 June 1842 to DELIA (WHITTIER) born 29 July 1802; died 13 Feb. 1884. Children: 6. ANNA MARIA b. 6 Feb. 1844 (m. William Porter, Hillsdale Co., Mich.); 7. AUGUSTUS b. 15 Dec. 1846, Hudson Twp. (to Osceola Co., Mich.). Ref: P&BA-Len pg. 582-3.

AMES, EZRA, son of PETER (following), was born 30 Nov. 1813 in Petersham, Worcester Co., Mass. After his parents died, he lived for a time with an uncle, but later went to Francestown, NH and lived with his brother. He came to Michigan first on 6 Sept. 1833 with his brothers, settling at Pittsford, Hillsdale Co., Mich. He returned to New Hampshire in 1834, and in 1838 returned to Michigan. He married first on 7 Sept. 1839 to SUSAN (LEWIS) who was born 10 Apr. 1815, Francestown, NH. He moved to Hudson, Mich. in 1842. Susan died 31 Dec. 1847. Three children, but only mentioned was GEORGE F. b. ca. 1841, Mich., who was the only survivor in 1888 (lived Sheridan, Montcalm Co., Mich.). SUSAN M. b. ca. 1847 (was in household in 1850 census). Ezra married second on 30 Aug. 1849 to LUCY (MOON) who was born Niagara, NY on 27 May 1822. She died 20 Aug. 1887. Son, CHARLES R. (Buffalo, NY). Ref: P&BA-Len pg. 1015-6. Note: Alice Moon in their household in 1850 may be Lucy's sister?

AMES, FLORA (See Samuel Hoyt)

AMES, JULIA was born ca. 1832 in Ohio, and was listed in the 1850 census of Madison Twp., Lenawee Co., Mich. in the household of Charles Parsons whose wife, Olive, was age 20, also b. Ohio.

AMES, PETER was a native of Framingham, Mass. who moved to Petersham at an early date (prior to 1794). He married SUSAN (CLARK). He died there in 1816, and she died in 1814. Known children: 1. CLARK (preceding); 2. CHARLES; 3. EZRA (preceding). Ref: P&BA-Len pg. 582-3. Also note WILLIAM B. (following).

AMES, PETER was born in 1792, and his wife, LOUISA, was born ca. 1797, both born Penn. In the 1850 census of Macon Twp., Lenawee Co., Mich., they listed JOHN, age 30; & CAROLINE, age 25 (handicapped person).

AMES, WILLIAM B. was born ca. 1809, Mass., and his wife, MARIAH, was born ca. 1811 in New Hampshire. They were listed in the 1850 census of Hudson Twp., Lenawee Co., Mich.

AMINGTON, MERCY A. (See Daniel Chittenden)

AMMERMAN, MARGARET (See E. E. Underwood)

ANDERSON, BENJAMIN & wife, ANN, resided in Sussex Co., NJ, probably originally from Philadelphia, PA, as daughter, MARGARET, was born 12 Aug. 1788, Philadelphia. Margaret married Elias Kinney (also see). Ref: P&BA-Len pg. 512-3.

ANDERSON, ELIZABETH (See John Mawdsley)

ANDERSON, GORAM, native of Sweden, & wife, MARIA (EARL), native of NY, came to Kent Co., Mich. She died 26 Aug. 1873, and he resided in Sparta, Kent Co. in 1888. Children; 1. WILLIAM H.; 2. IDA C.; 3. EMMA J. (m. James W. Ash, also see); 4. LIZZIE V. Ref: P&BA-Len pg. 1070-2.

ANDERSON, H. VIOLA (See Cicero Torrey)

ANDERSON, HENRY was born ca. 1834 in Michigan and in the 1850 census of Madison Twp., Lenawee Co., Mich., was in the household of George Payne.

ANDERSON, JOHN (See William L. Rogers)

ANDERSON, JOHN C. was born ca. 1811 in Scotland. He came to NY and married first ALMYRA (GRIFFITH) born ca. 1820, NY. They came first to Madison Twp., Lenawee Co., Mich., and were listed in the 1850 census with ELIZABETH, age 7; WILLIAM (following); JOHN, age 4; ALBERT, age 2, all born Mich. There were 7 children. They later moved to Adrian Twp.; and then to Fulton Co., Ohio where he died in 1861. Ref: P&BA-Len pg. 1023.

ANDERSON, JOSIAH was born ca. 1801 in NY, and his wife, JANE, was born ca. 1802 in Pennsylvania. In the 1850 census of Madison Twp., Lenawee Co., Mich., they listed JAMES M., age 15; & MARY A., age 12, both born NY.

ANDERSON, JULIA (See Beriah H. Lane)

ANDERSON, MATTIE (See John A. Townsend)

ANDERSON, NANCY was born ca. 1825 in NY, and was listed in the 1850 census of Madison Twp., Lenawee Co., Mich. in the home of Jacob & Mary Hunt.

ANDERSON, WILLIAM was born ca. 1806, and his wife, ELIZA, was born ca. 1811, both in NY. In the 1850 census of Madison Twp., Lenawee Co., Mich., they listed JOSEPH W., age 17; WILLIAM H., age 14; SUSANNAH, age 14; SARAH, age 11; DANIEL, age 9, all born NY; & SAMUEL, age 2, born Mich.

ANDERSON, WILLIAM & wife, ELIZA (GETTY), of The-Craig, Co. Antrim, Ireland, came to Macon Twp., Lenawee Co.., Mich. in 1866, and he died soon after arrival; & and she still resided in Macon Twp., age 68, in 1888. Known daughter, JENNIE, b. The-Craig, Ireland, 30 July 1848 m. Thomas Murphy (also see). Ref: P&BA-Len pg. 510-11.

ANDERSON, WILLIAM, son of JOHN C. (preceding), was born 5 Sept. 1844 in Madison Twp., Lenawee Co., Mich. He married on 6 Apr. 1876 to NANCY (ABBOTT), daughter of William (also see). Children: 1.

FLORENCE (d. infancy); 2. WEBSTER S.; 3. LAVERN W.; 4. JOHN; 5. FREDERICK. Ref: P&BA-Len pg. 1023.

ANDREWS, EDWIN P. Dr., son of JUSTICE (following), was born 26 Aug. 1826 in Plymouth, Wayne Co., Mich. He married 14 May 1851 in Lenawee Co. to SARAH M. (WISNER), daughter of Rev. William G. (also see), and settled in Adrian, Mich. Children: 1. EDWIN H. b. 22 Feb. 1853; 2. Dr. FRANK E. b. 25 Jan. 1857; 3. CLARENCE B. b. 14 Jan. 1860; 4. FRED B. b. 20 Apr. 1862; 5. HARRY W. b. 27 Mar. 1871. Ref: P&BA-Len pg. 1118-9.

ANDREWS, HANNAH (See Judson Fellows)

ANDREWS, JUSTICE, son of JOHN J., was born 26 Sept. 1801 in Stillwater, Saratoga Co., NY. In 1806, he moved with his parents to Steuben, Orleans Co., NY. He married 21 Aug. 1825 to Mrs. DEBORAH (BUTTERFIELD) LARD, who was born 26 Nov. 1801 in Amherst, NH. In 1826, they removed to Plymouth Twp., Wayne Co., Mich.; 1847 to Fairfield Twp., Lenawee Co.; and 1862 to Adrian. He died 14 Sept. 1878, and she died 11 Mar. 1878. Three sons, only 2 named in sketch: 1. Dr. EDWIN P. (preceding); 2. ERWIN H. b. ca. 1829 (in household in 1850 census). Ref: P&BA-Len pg. 1118-9.

AMDREWS, LUCY (See Michael Moran)

ANDREWS, MARGARET (See Edward Clark)

ANDREWS, MARTHA Mrs. was daughter of Levi & Anna (Howe) Fowler (also see).

ANDREWS, MARY (See Azariel Smith)

ANDREWS, THERON (See Joseph Patterson)

ANDREWS, WILLIAM J. was born 12 June 1827, Leicestshire, England, and came to the US in 1850 and settled in Ridgeway Twp., Lenawee Co., Mich. He married 24 Oct. 1855, Ridgeway Twp., to ELIZABETH (PILBEAM), also born England. Children: 1. AMANDA (d. age 16); 2. MARY A. (m. Andrew Jackson, also see). Elizabeth died in 1859, and he married second on 19 Mar. 1860 to ELIZABETH (BURNETT), daughter of John (also see). Children: 3. ORIN P. (d. age 3 mo.); 4. WILLIAM J. Ref: P&BA-Len pg. 277-8.

ANGELL, DAVID & wife, MARY H., were parents of LENA born 21 Feb. 1865, who married Edwin J. Shepherd (also see). Ref: P&BA-Len pg. 616-7.

ANGELL, EZEKIEL was born in Rhode Island, and his wife, CYNTHIA (BROWN), was born in 1800 in Mass. After their marriage, they settled in Herkimer Co., NY. He died 24 Feb. 1868, age 68; and she died in 1886. Of 9 children, 8 lived to maturity, and known son, HENRY A. (following), was born Newport, NY 14 Sept. 1826. Ref: P&BA-Len pg. 393-4.

ANGELL, GEORGE A. born ca. 1815, and wife, MARY A., age 24, both b. England, were listed in the 1850 census of Medina Twp., Lenawee Co., Mich. with JOSEPH, age 13, b. NY; and ANN M., age 1/12, b. Mich., all in the household of James S. Daws. Also listed was JAMES, age 29, also b. England, probably brother of George.

ANGELL, HENRY A., son of EZEKIEL (preceding), married 4 Oct. 1849 to ADELIA S. (SIZER) & moved from Herkimer Co., NY to Adrian, Lenawee Co., Mich. in 1853. Adopted daughter, MAGGIE, m. E. Russell, Chicago, Ill. Ref: P&BA-Len pg. 393-4, & portrait.

ANGELL, JAMES born ca. 1821, England (See GEORGE A., preceding).

ANGELL, JASON, probably son of JOHN (following), was born ca. 1819, and wife, LUCINDA, was born ca. 1820, both b. NY. In the 1850 census of Ogden Twp., Lenawee Co., Mich., they listed MARY, age 7; SARAH, age 6; RUTH, age 2, all born Mich., and the family was listed in the household of JOHN (following).

ANGELL, JOHN was born ca. 1776 in Rhode Island, and wife, SARAH, was born ca. 1783 in NY. In the 1850 census of Ogden Twp., Lenawee Co., Mich. they listed in their household JASON (preceding) & his family.

ANGELL, MARIA (Mrs.?) was born ca. 1814 in NY, and was head of household in the 1850 census of Ogden Twp., Lenawee Co., Mich., near JOHN, & in her household was CAROLINE, age 12, b. Mich.

ANGLE, MATILDA (See Samuel Hoyt)

ANSELUS, MARGARET (See Albert Maples)

ANTHONY, JANE (See John Wemple)
ANTHONY, MARY C. (See John Mawdsley)

APPLEBY, ETTA (See Augustus Bradish)
APPLEBY, JACOB, & wife, MARY (PECK), of Erie Co., Penn., had 6 children: 1. ELSIE M. b. 18 Apr. 1825, Erie Co. (m. Augustus W. Bradish, also see); 2. ROSETTA; 3. NANCY; 4. WILLIAM; 5. JOHN; 6. JULIUS. Ref: P&BA-Len pg. 310-11.

APPLEGATE, THOMAS S. born 8 June 1838, England, came to Utica, NY with his parents who later moved to Rome, NY. He came to Adrian, Lenawee Co., Mich. in 1865. He married HARRIET M. (SINCLAIR), daughter of Daniel D. (also see). Ref: P&BA-Len pg. 915-6.

APPLETON, ISAAC of Dublin, NH, was father of SARAH, born 5 Mar. 1790, Dublin, NH (m. James B. Todd, also see); & of SAMUEL of Boston, Mass. Ref: P&BA-Len 915-6.

APPLETON, JAMES (See Thomas Chandler)

ARCHER, JACOB was born ca. 1819, and wife, NANCY, was born ca. 1821, both in NY. In the 1850 census of Hudson Twp., Lenawee Co., Mich., they listed AMELIA A., age 5, b. NY.

ARCHER, JAMES was born in Ireland, and came to the US where he married before 1800 in Washington Co., NY to MARY (ENGLISH) who was born in Mass. They remained in Washington Co., NY. Known son, JOHN (following). Ref: P&BA-Len pg. 542-3.

ARCHER, JOEL was born ca. 1817 in Penn., and wife, SARAH, was born ca. 1818 in NY. In the 1850 census of Medina Twp., Lenawee Co., Mich., they listed HENRY, age 12; ELIZABETH, age 10; ANGELINE, age 8; LYDIA A., age 6; CHARLES, age 3, all born NY.

ARCHER, JOHN, son of JAMES (preceding), born Washington Co., NY, moved to Wayne Co., NY before 1819, and married there to AXIE (WARREN), daughter of Samuel (also see). About 1824 they moved to Macedon, NY. Known son, WILLIAM D. (following). Ref: P&BA-Len 542-3.

ARCHER, WILLIAM D., son of JOHN (preceding), was born 8 May 1819 in Wayne Co., NY. He married 17 Oct. 1848 to NEUBELIA (HIGBEE), daughter of Gad C. (also see) in

Palmyra, NY. They removed to Palmyra Twp., Lenawee Co., Mich. She died 17 May 1867. Children: 1. ORSON H. (Palmyra Twp.); 2. HENRY C. (Dallas, TX). William D. married second in Mar. 1872 to CAROLINE E. (CALKINS), daughter of Lorentus S. (also see). Son, 3. BAYARD T. Ref: P&BA-Len pg. 542-3 & farm portrait.

ARCHER, WILLIAM D. of Wayne Co., NY married Mrs. LOSINA (PARKER) LAPHAM, daughter of Joshua (also see) & widow of Nelson Lapham of Wayne Co., NY. William D. apparently died prior to 1879, as she married that year to Samuel White (also see) as her 3rd husband. Ref: P&BA-Len 784-5.

ARCHIBALD, CHRISTINA of Scotland (See Peter King).

ARCHIE, ABIGAIL (See Samuel Linn)

ARMITAGE, WILLIAM, son of ISAAC (who had come from England & died in Penn.), was born in NY, and moved as an infant to Philadelphia with his parents. He married PHILINDA (VINCENT), daughter of Clark (also see) in Penn. In 1865, they removed to Deerfield village, Lenawee Co., Mich., where they lived in 1888. Known daughter, JENNIE, b. 16 Feb. 1852, Spring Creek, Warren Co., Penn., m. Robert Edgar Burnett (also see). Ref: P&BA-Len pg. 603-4.

ARMSTRONG, ALMARIN K., son of WILLIAM (from England to America at an early date), was born ca. 1810 probably in Monroe Co., NY. He married LUCINDA (JERRELLS), daughter of Ebenezer (also see). They came to Rome Twp., Lenawee Co., Mich. after 1840; and he died in 1873. Children: 1. JAMES b. 10 Aug. 1838, Monroe Co., NY; 2. CARRIE L. b. 18 Mar. 1859, Rome Twp. Lucinda married second to Theodorick Luther (also see). Ref: P&BA-Len pg. 587-8.

ARMSTRONG, MARGARET JOSEPHINE (See James Whitney)

ARMSTRONG, MARTHAR was born ca. 1787 in England, and his wife, SALLY, was born ca. 1891 in Conn. They are listed in the 1850 census of Hudson Twp., Lenawee Co., Mich., next door to (son?), RANSOM, age 27, b. NY (with wife, SUSAN K., age 29, b. NY).

ARMSTRONG, PELEG was born ca. 1785 in Conn., and was listed in the 1850 census of Cambridge Twp., Lenawee Co., Mich. with LUCY, age 30; HARRIET, age 28; LYDIA, age 26; LUCRETIA, age 24, all b. Conn. in his household.

ARMSTRONG, PHOEBE (See Joseph C. Tenant)

ARMSTRONG, WILLIAM was born ca. 1810 in Penn., and his wife, ELIZA, was born ca. 1816 in NY. In the 1840 census index, they were listed in Adrian, Lenawee Co., Mich.; and in 1850 census listed CHARLES, age 12; THOMAS; age 10; JOHN, age 8; JAMES, age 8 (twin?); MARY, age 4; MATILDA, age 9/12, all born Mich. Also listed was Elizabeth Wiltsey, age 68, b. NJ.

ARNER, Mrs. was a daughter of John F. Schreder.

ARNER, JACOB was born ca. 1820 in Penn., and listed with him in the 1850 census of Ridgeway Twp., Lenawee Co., Mich., was wife, ELLEN, age 20, married within the year. They were in the household of Oliver Miller.

ARNER, PETER was listed in the 1840 census index of Macon Twp., Lenawee Co., Mich.

ARNOLD, AMY (See Job Burleson)

ARNOLD, BARZILLA was born ca. 1803, and wife, HANNAH, was born ca. 1806, both in New Jersey. In the 1850 census of Fairfield Twp., Lenawee Co., Mich., they listed LEVI, age 22, born NY; LYDIA, age 11; LUCY D., age 8; RACHEL, age 4, last 3 b. Mich. (Note HIRAM; JACOB W.; ROBERT B.; JOHN; & LEVI, following, for possible family connection).

ARNOLD, DARIUS was born ca. 1797 in NY, and it may be he listed in Salem, Washtenaw Co., Mich. in the 1840 census index. In the 1850 census of Dover Twp., Lenawee Co., he is listed in the household of ROBERT (following).

ARNOLD, EDWARD was born ca. 1814 in NY, and is head of household in the 1850 census of Adrian Twp., Lenawee Co., Mich. with the following listed: (wife?) CLARISSA, age 19, b. VT; and EUNICE A., age 13; HARRISON, age 11; LUCINA M., age 6; SABRA, age 3, all born Mich. Note JACOB, following.

ARNOLD, ELIZABETH ANN was listed head of household in the 1840 census index of Tecumseh Twp., Lenawee Co., Mich.

ARNOLD, HIRAM & wife, SALLY (ELY), both born NY, settled in Chautauqua Co., NY after their marriage. He died there in 1851; and she was living there in 1888, age 77. Of 5 sons, the youngest was HIRAM D. (following). Ref: P&BA-Len pg. 583-4.

ARNOLD, HIRAM D., son of HIRAM (preceding), was born 13 May 1850 in Chautauqua Co., NY. He married 23 Apr. 1874 to PHOEBE L. (WILBUR), daughter of Thomas (also see) of Fairfield Twp., Lenawee Co., Mich. and they settled in Fairfield Twp. Children: 1. CHARLIE E.; 2. CARLTON G. Ref: P&BA-Len pg. 583-4.

ARNOLD, JACOB was listed in the 1840 census index of Adrian Twp., Lenawee Co., Mich. Note EDWARD, preceding.

ARNOLD, JACOB W. was born ca. 1819, and his wife, SARAH E., was born ca. 1828, both in NY. In the 1850 census of Fairfield Twp., Lenawee Co., Mich., they listed ROBERT H., age 5; & FRANCES E., age 1/12, both b. Mich.

ARNOLD, JOHN was born ca. 1779 in New Jersey, and wife, ABIGAIL, was born ca. 1788 in Nova Scotia. They are listed in the 1850 census of Seneca Twp., Lenawee Co., Mich., with no family (in 1840 census index they were adjacent to LEVI).

ARNOLD, LEVI was listed in the 1840 census index of Seneca Twp., Lenawee Co., Mich. Note given name in family of BARZILLA.

ARNOLD, PHEBE (See Turner Crane)

ARNOLD, ROBERT, probably son of DARIUS (preceding), was born ca. 1822, and wife, ESTHER, was born ca. 1829, both in NY. In the 1850 census of Dover Twp., Lenawee Co., Mich., they listed CLEMINA, age 3, b. Mich.; and also in the household was DARIUS, age 53, b. NY.

ARNOLD, ROBERT B. was born ca. 1811 in NY, and wife, CLARISSA, was born ca. 1816 in Mass. He is listed in the 1840 census index of Fairfield Twp., Lenawee Co., Mich. adjacent to BARZILLA, preceding. In the 1850

Pioneer Families of Southeastern Michigan

census of Fairfield Twp., they listed LYMAN, age 8, born Mich.

ARNOLD, WILLIAM was born ca. 1831 in Penn., and is listed in the 1850 census of Franklin Twp., Lenawee Co., Mich. Note William "Arold," following.

ARTHUR, NANCY (See Isaac Higgins)

AROLD, WILLIAM (See George Traben; also note ARNOLD, WILLIAM, preceding).

ASH, AZIAH H., son of WILLIAM (following), was born 12 Mar. 1836, Raisin Twp., Lenawee Co., Mich. He married first to LUCINDA (KNEELAND). daughter of Abner (also see), and had children, EMMA & FRANK (both d. young). He married again on 10 Aug. 1872 to EMELINE (JOHNSON), daughter of Nicholas (also see). Children: CORA (d. age 9); ORRI I. (d.infancy); FRANK b. 10 Aug. 1873; FREDDIE E. b. 15 Apr. 1877. Ref: P&BA-Len pg. 211-2.

ASH, EDWIN married ADELINE (FARST), daughter of Isaac (also see). They settled in Medina Twp., Lenawee Co., Mich. Children: 1. MARY A.; 2. NELLIE C. (deceased before 1888); 3. EDITH L. Ref: P&BA-Len pg. 997-8.

ASH, JAMES born ca. 1822 in England, and wife, MARTHA A., born ca. 1826, NY, were listed in the 1850 census of Rollin Twp., Lenawee Co., Mich., with HANNAH, age 6; HARRIET, age 4; EMILY, age 2, all born Mich., in the household.

ASH, JAMES W., son of WILLIAM (following), was born 28 July 1857. He married EMMA (ANDERSON), daughter of Goram (also see) in 1881 in Kent Co., Mich. They settled in Raisin Twp., Lenawee Co., Mich. Children: ERNEST b. 18 Mar. 1882; CLYDE J. b. 22 Mar. 1884; PEARL G. b. 26 Feb. 1886. Ref: P&BA-Len 1070-2.

ASH, JOHN born ca. 1812, England, and wife, ESTHER, born ca. 1819, NY, were listed in the 1850 census of Raisin Twp., Lenawee Co., Mich. with MARY, age 13; PHEBE, age 10; SARAH J., age 8; PELEG, age 5; WING, age 4; MARTHA J., age 5/12, all born Mich.

ASH, WILLIAM born ca. 1811, Yorkshire (or Lincolnshire), England, came to the US in 1831; and lived in Adrian & Raisin Twp.s, Lenawee Co., Mich. until 1833, when he went to New York. He was in Raisin Twp. in 1836. He married 3 times, first to ESTHER (WESTGATE), daughter of Sylvanus (also see). Following the birth of 5 children, she died 14 Dec. 1843 (or 7 Dec. 1844). Following 3 in household in 1850 census. Eldest son, AZIAH H. (preceding); LOVINA b. ca. 1839; PAULINA b.ca. 1841. He married before 1850 to HARRIET (HOUGHTBY), daughter of John (also see). She died 26 Oct. 1874. William died 13 July 1880, age 70, in Raisin Twp. Probably children of he & Harriet in household in 1850: ADALINE b. ca. 1848; EMELINE b. 15 Jan. 1850 (m. Abner Gallaway, also see); CLARA A.; HARRIET C.; JAMES W. (preceding); CHLOE J.; SOPHIE E. Third marriage wife's name not known. Ref: P&BA-Len pg. 220 & 1070-2.

ASHBILL, FLORENCE D. (See Henry Ragless)

ASHDOWN, GEORGE, age 14; & brother, JAMES, age 12, both b. Mich., were listed in the 1850 census of Rome Twp., Lenawee Co., Mich. in the household of Mrs. Anna Wickham (who is probably their mother). It may be Anna listed as a "Miss Ashtown" in the 1840 census index of Rome Twp., and afterwards married Wickham?

ASHLEY, CHARLES (See Justus Cooley)

ASHLEY, ELIZA born ca. 1823, Mass., was listed in the 1850 census of Blissfield Twp., Lenawee Co., Mich. in the home of Harrison Munson.

ASHLEY, GEORGE born ca. 1784, Mass., was listed in the 1850 census of Tecumseh Twp., Lenawee Co., Mich. in the household of John Gregg. It may this George who was listed in the 1840 census index of Adrian Twp. Also note HARRY.

ASHLEY, HARRY was listed in the 1840 census index of Tecumseh Twp., Lenawee Co., Mich.

ASHLEY, JOHN & wife, SARAH (RAWSON), were natives of England who came to Utica, NY where they remained. Eight children, only known son, #5. WILLIAM (following). Ref: P&BA-Len pg. 1078-9.

ASHLEY, JOSEPH born ca. 1810, New Hampshire, and wife, DELINDA L., born ca. 1821, NY, were listed in the 1850 census of Rollin Twp., Lenawee Co., Mich., with WARREN A., age 12; FRANCES M., age 10; HELEN J., age 6; CASSIUS M., age 3; ABIGAIL, age 1, all born Mich., in the household.

ASHLEY, LOUISA (See Amos A. Kinney)

ASHLEY, SARAH S. born ca. 1813, Mass., was listed with children MARY J., age 7; & JULIAETE A., age 4, both b. Mich., in the 1850 census of Adrian Twp., Lenawee Co., Mich. in the household of James Penniman (age 72, b. Mass).

ASHLEY, WILLIAM, son of JOHN (preceding), born 2 Jan. 1828, Utica, NY, came to Hudson, Lenawee Co., Mich. where he married 13 Sept. 1860 to MARGARET (BRYANT), daughter of John (also see). He died 29 Sept. 1879. Of 7 children, 6 following survived in 1888: 1. MARY (m. A. G. Hartle, Newaygo Co., Mich.); 2. JESSE A. (m. Altha V. Smith, Dover Twp.); 3. CHARLES B.; 4. MYRTLE M.; 5. EDNA M.; 6. IRA W. Ref: P&BA-Len pg. 1078-9.

ATCHISON, POLLY (See Nehemiah Hall & William Buell)

ATEN also see AUTEN

ATEN, CATHERINE (See Israel Baker Maxwell)

ATEN, GARRETT was born ca. 1786, and wife, ELIZABETH (HENDERSHOTT), was born ca. 1786, both in Penn., and after their marriage settled in Jersey, Penn. They later moved to Groveland, Livingston Co., NY where 5 sons & 3 daughters were born. They came to Tecumseh Twp., Lenawee Co., Mich. before 1840. He died in Macon Twp., age 90 yrs. Known children: MARGARET (m. A. W. Ellis, also see); then in household in 1850 census: JACKSON, age 25; HENRY, age 21, both b. NY; CHARLES, age 17; & GARRY, age 10 (grandson?), both b. Mich. Note that JOHN, MATHIAS A., & PETER, all following, may be additional sons?

ATEN, JOHN born ca. 1824, and wife, BEDA?, b. ca. 1825, both in NY, were listed in the 1850 census of Tecumseh Twp., Lenawee Co., Mich. with COMMODORE, age 1, b. Mich. in the household.

ATEN, MATHIAS, possibly son of GARRET (preceding), born ca. 1812, and wife, MARY, age 34, both b. Penn., were listed in the 1850 census of Tecumseh Twp., Lenawee Co., Mich. with THOMAS, age 13; PATIENCE, age 12; WILLIAM, age 6, all b. NY, in the household.

ATEN, PETER, possibly son of GARRET (preceding), born ca. 1804, and wife, MARY, b. ca. 1810, both in Penn., were listed in the 1850 census of Tecumseh Twp., Lenawee Co., Mich. with APSMANDA, age 22; SIMON, age 20, both b. NY (possibly this is "Simeon" of Tecumseh who m. Thankful Bradley of Franklin 16 Oct. 1855); & FRANCES, age 17; JOHN, age 15; JAMES, age 13, last 3 born Mich., in their household.

ATKINSON, BETSEY (See Joseph Thompson)

ATWELL, HERMAN (See John Iveson[2])
ATWELL, PHENA (See Allen Burr)

ATWOOD, LUCIUS was listed in the 1840 census index of Seneca Twp., Lenawee Co., Mich., and was the only one of this surname in Lenawee Co. It is POSSIBLY his family listed in the 1850 census of Seneca Twp., with CHARLES, age 18, listed as head of household; and with him, HANNAH, age 41, b. NY, probably his mother, and siblings, EMILY, age 19, b. NY; MARTHA, age 16; MELISSA, age 9; EUNICE, age 5; last 3 born Mich.

ATWOOD, MARY (See Abraham Lowe)

ATWOOD, RODNEY & wife, LOUISE (AYERS), were natives of Perry, Wyoming Co., NY, who in 1853 removed to Hudson Twp., Lenawee Co., Mich. She died in Mar. 1862. He moved to Pentwater, Mich., where he died in 1866. Four sons & four daughters; known daughter, HELEN, b. 7 Mar. 1833, Perry, NY (m. Levi L. Stockwell, also see). Ref: P&BA-Len pg. 727-8.

ATWOOD, SETH, son of WILLIAM (from England who d. NY), was b. 1811 in Romulus, NY. He married JANE A. (HOOD), daughter of John (also see). They removed to Rome Twp., Lenawee Co., Mich. in 1837. He died before 1845. Children: 1. SOPHIA b. ca. 1836 (m. Clark Raymond, Adrian); 2. ESTHER b. ca. 1837 (m. Charles F. Finch, Adrian); 3. GEORGE G. b. 19 Aug. 1838 (unmarried, lived with mother 1888); 4. LEVI R. b. ca. 1841 (d. age 18). Jane A. married second to Isaac Raymond (also see) before 1846. Note: In the 1850 census, Jane A. Raymond was head of household, with her Atwood children in her household. Ref: P&BA-Len pg. 188 & 1068-9.

AUCHMOODY, MAGDALIA (See Garrett F. Harris)

AULLS, RUHAMA (See Rufus Raymond)

AUSTIN, AUGUSTINE born ca. 1819, and wife, MARIA E., b. ca. 1825, both b. NY, were listed in the 1850 census of Seneca Twp., Lenawee Co., Mich. with JAMES B., age 6; JACOB, age 3; MARTHA A., age 1, all born Mich.
AUSTIN, CHARLES was listed in the 1840 census index of Rome Twp., Lenawee Co., Mich.
AUSTIN, HARRIET was born ca. 1835, NY, and is listed in the 1850 census of Ridgeway Twp., Lenawee Co., Mich. in a Demott household.
AUSTIN, ISAAC S. was born ca. 1805 in Maine, and went to Vermont, and later to Steuben Co., NY. He married LOUISA (PIERCE), daughter of Daniel (also see). They moved in 1840 to Palmyra Twp., Lenawee Co., Mich., and were listed in the 1850 census of Blissfield Twp., with PHILETUS, age 19; CHARITY, age 18; MARIA b. 20 Feb. 1833, Steuben Co., NY (in Barret household in 1850 census; m. Charles H. Kendrick, also see); PHEBE O., age 14, all b. NY; & WILLIAM, age 9; CAROLINE, age 5, both b. Mich. in their household. Ref: P&BA-Len pg. 933-4.

AUSTIN, JAMES L. was born ca. 1790, and his wife, HANNAH, was born ca. 1793, both in Rhode Island. They are listed in the 1840 census index of Adrian, Lenawee Co., Mich.; and in the 1850 census, they had in their household Charles W. Sheffield, son of William (also b. Rhode Island, moved to Utica, NY) & Mary E. (Carpenter) Sheffield. Charles W. was a "nephew" of this household.

AUSTIN, JONATHAN W. was born ca. 1805, Salem, Mass., and wife, LYDIA (MOORE), was born ca. 1805 in Bradford, VT, where they married. About 1830, the moved to Fairfield Twp., Lenawee Co., Mich. and purchased land, but returned to Vermont for a brief time. They later moved to Seneca Twp., Lenawee Co., then to Dover Twp., where he died 9 Sept. 1864; and she died 30 July 1871. Children: 1. LOUISE (d. young); 2. ROSWELL M. (d. young); 3. INFANT died; 4. LYDIA E. (m. A. F. Brown, Chicago, Ill.); 5. ADELINE b. ca. 1833, VT (m. Hiram Bovee, Gratiot Co., Mich.); 6. ANN M. b. 18 Aug. 1840, Dover Twp. (m. Darwin H. Warren, also see). Ref: P&BA-Len pg. 423-4.

AUSTIN, LEANDER born ca. 1806, and wife, CONTENT, born ca. 1812, both in NY, were listed in the 1850 census of Cambridge Twp., Lenawee Co., Mich. with ABIGAIL, age 14; EDMUND?, age 13; OLIVE, age 10; HELEN, age 8; LEANDER (or Leman), age 5, all b. NY, in the household. Also listed was Edmund Redfield, age 77, b. Conn.

AUSTIN, MARY (See Oramon Tuttle, Jr.)

AUSTIN, REUBEN was listed in the 1840 census index of Seneca Twp., Lenawee Co., Mich. Perhaps unrelated in the 1850 census of Seneca Twp., Lenawee Co., Mich. in the household of other families are PATIENCE, age 4; & HARRIET, age 4/12, both b. Mich. Also note AUGUSTINE, preceding.

AUSTIN, SAMUEL and wife, LYDIA (RAILSBACK), were parents of ELEANOR M. (m. John Jones, also see). It may this Samuel listed in the 1840 census index of Macon Twp., Lenawee Co., Mich. Ref: P&BA-Len pg. 270-1.

AUSTIN, SILAS born 1804, and wife, HANNAH, born 1804, both in NY, were listed in the 1850 census of Macon Twp., Lenawee Co., Mich. with NATHAN, age 21; GEORGE, age 19; LORETTA, age 18; JOHN, age 16; JONAS, age 14; CALVIN, age 12; SARAH, age 10; PHILIP W., age 8; JAMES W., age 3, all b. NY, & ELIZABETH, age 3/12, b. Mich., were in the household Note: SILAS, age 19, listed in another household in the 1850 census may belong to this family.

AUSTIN, WILLIAM was a veteran of the War of 1812, in which he served with 2 of his sons. He died in Genesee Co., NY. Known daughter, SUSAN(NAH) m. Jared Calkins (also see) before 1812. Ref: P&BA-Len pg. 1171-2.

Pioneer Families of Southeastern Michigan

AUSTIN, WILLIAM was listed in the 1840 census index of Hudson Twp., Lenawee Co., Mich.

AUTEN also see ATEN
AUTEN, PAUL born 1798 in NY, & wife, HARRIET, born ca. 1793 in New Jersey, were listed in the 1850 census of Ridgeway Twp., Lenawee Co., Mich., with McCAN, age 24; JEHIEL, age 22; DANIEL, age 19, all b. NY; & NORMAN, age 17; SUSAN, age 13, both b. Ohio, in the household.
AUTEN, TIB (See James Smith)

AVERILL, SUSAN (See John Greenleaf)

AVERY also see EVERY
AVERY, AARON, age 17, b. ca. 1833, Mich., was listed in the 1850 census of Madison Twp., Lenawee Co., Mich. in the Scofield household.
AVERY, ANN (See Obadiah Gore of Sheshequin, Bradford Co., Penn.)
AVERY, ASAHEL D. born ca. 1817, NY, and wife, LUCY A., born ca. 1822, VT, were listed in the 1850 census of Adrian Twp., Lenawee Co., Mich. with ORRIN A., age 7; AMOS, age 5; JOHN F, age 2, all b. NY, and BETSEY J., age 2/12, b. Mich. in their household.
AVERY, CYNTHIA of Sandusky Co., Ohio (See Hiram Haff).
AVERY, CYRUS born ca. 1777, and wife, NANCY, born ca. 1781, both in Conn., were listed in the 1850 census of Hudson Twp., Lenawee Co., Mich. with GEORGE W. (following); & CHARLES F., age 40, b. Conn., in their household
AVERY, DANIEL born ca. 1802, and wife, BETSEY A., born ca. 1810, both in NY, were listed in the 1850 census of Raisin Twp., Lenawee Co., Mich. with JAMES, age 16; OSCAR, age 15; ORVILLE, age 12; AMBROSE L., age 10, all b. NY, and CAROLINE E., age 5, b. Mich., in their household.
AVERY, GEORGE W., son of CYRUS (preceding), born ca. 1816, and wife, SARAH M., age 36, both b. Conn., were listed in the 1850 census of Hudson Twp., Lenawee Co., Mich. with EUGENE E., age 4; FANNY B., age 5/12, both b. Mich., all in the household of CYRUS.
AVERY, JOHN born ca. 1813, and wife, PARMELIA, born ca. 1812, both in NY, were listed in the 1850 census of Adrian Twp., Lenawee Co., Mich. with FRANCES, age 14; AMELIA, age 12; EDELIA A., age 9; RUTH E., age 7, all b. NY; and HELEN V., age 2, b. Mich.; and ELECTA, age 50, b. NY, in their household.
AVERY, JONATHAN born ca. 1817, and wife, PHEBE, born ca. 1814, both in NY, were listed in the 1850 census of Adrian Twp., Lenawee Co., Mich. with ALFRED, age 11; JAMES, age 8; AMELIA, age 6, all b. Ohio; and NELSON, age 6/12, b. Mich., in their household.
AVERY, MANERVA Mrs. born ca. 1812, NY, was listed head of household in the 1850 census of Fairfield Twp., Lenawee Co., Mich. with MORRIS M., age 19, b. NY; and ELIZABETH M., age 11; ORRIN J., age 8; HARRIET, age 5; ALONZO E., age 4/12, all b. Mich., in their household.
AVERY, WILLIAM W. born ca. 1793, and wife, MARTHA, born ca. 1798, both in NY, were listed in the 1850 census of Tecumseh Twp., Lenawee Co., Mich.

AYERS also see AYRES
AYERS, JACOB D. was born 7 Feb. 1798 in Essex Co., NJ, and his wife, MARY A., was born August 1795 in Newark, NJ. They married in Essex Co., and remained there until 1836, when they moved to Jackson Co., Mich. He died 5 May 1871. Children: 1. MARY J. (m. James Allen of Ann Arbor, Mich.); 2. FRANCES (m. James Allen, as 2d wife); 3. ABBIE D. (Arkansas); 4. DANIEL B. (unmarried). Ref: History of Jackson Co., Mich., pg. 992-3.
AYERS, JOHN V.(?) born 1796, and wife, NANCY, born 1800, both in New Jersey, were listed in the 1850 census of Macon Twp., Lenawee Co., Mich. with JOHN W., age 25; LESTER B., age 17, born b. NY; and ADELINE, age 11; CATHERINE, age 8, both b. Mich., in the household. (There was a JOHN B. listed in the 1840 census index of Saline Twp., Washtenaw Co., Mich.)
AYERS, JOHN, son of SEPTIMUS (following), was born ca. 1822 in Oneida Co., NY, and came with parents to Fairfield Twp., Lenawee Co., Mich. He married in 1852 to AMANDA J. (PORTER), and settled in Fairfield Twp. Two children, not named in sketch, were deceased before 1888, those suviving: 1. ALBERT J.; 2. LYDIA E. (m. Charles F. Morse); 3. GEORGE W. b. 7 Dec. 1854 (unmarried 1888). Ref: P&BA-Len pg. 1045.
AYERS, JULIUS, probably another son of SEPTIMUS (following), was listed adjacent in the 1840 census of Fairfield Twp., Lenawee Co., Mich.; and in the 1850 census listed wife, MARY H., age 34, b. NJ; & NANCY, age 9; SEPTIMUS, age 7; WILLIAM S., age 4; HARRIET S., age 10/12, all b. Michigan, in his household.
AYERS, LOREN, born ca. 1816, Mass., & wife, SALLY, b. ca. 1830, NY, were listed in the 1850 census of Fairfield Twp., Lenawee Co., Mich. Note SEPTIMUS, following.
AYERS, LOUISE (See Rodney Atwood)
AYERS, MATILDA (See Joshua W. Lawton)
AYERS, RUSSELL was born ca. 1828 in NY, and was listed in the 1850 census of Blissfield Twp., Lenawee Co., Mich. in the Carpenter household.
AYERS, S. C. Dr. and wife, JULIA (JEWELL), moved from Ohio to Seneca Twp., Lenawee Co., Mich. ca. 1868. In 1874, they settled in Fairfield Twp. He died Weston, Mich. on 18 Jan. 1885, and she was still living in 1888. Known daughter, ISABELLA, b. 7 Dec. 1860, Spring Hill, Ohio (m. Prof. William E. Tripp, also see). Ref: P&BA-Len pg. 665.
AYERS, SEPTIMUS was born ca. 1787 and wife, ISABEL, was born ca. 1788, both in Mass.; and lived in Oneida Co., NY by 1822. He was listed in the 1840 census index of Fairfield Twp., Lenawee Co., Mich.; and in the 1850 census of Adrian Twp., they listed in the household JOHN (preceding); and LAURA, age 22, b. NY. Also note JULIUS; LOREN; & STEPHEN.
AYERS, SETH was listed in the 1840 census index of Seneca Twp., Lenawee Co., Mich.
AYERS, STEPHEN was listed in the 1840 census index of Fairfield Twp., Lenawee Co., Mich. It is probably he who is listed in the 1850 census of Adrian Twp., Lenawee Co., age 32, b. NY, with wife, LUCY, age 27, b. Mass; and WILLIAM, age 6, b. Mich. in the household. Note SEPTIMUS, preceding.
AYERS, W. F. (See Luke N. Damon)
AYERS, WILLIAM was listed in the 1840 census index of Blissfield Twp., Lenawee Co., Mich. Note RUSSELL, preceding.

AYRES also see AYERS

AYRES, ABRAHAM was born ca. 1800, England, and his wife, BETSEY, was born ca. 1818 in Ireland. It is probably he listed in the 1840 census index of Franklin Twp., Lenawee Co., Mich. as "Abram;" as they are listed in the 1850 census of Franklin Twp.

AYRES, ANDREW born ca. 1805, and wife, RUTH, born ca. 1822,

both in England, were probably they listed in the 1840 census index of Cambridge Twp., Lenawee Co., Mich.; and they are listed there in the 1850 census with LYDIA, age 3, b. Mich. in their household.

AYRES, BENJAMIN born ca. 1814, and wife, MARY, born ca. 1805, both in England, are probably they listed in the 1840 census index of Franklin Twp., Lenawee Co., Mich.; and are listed in the 1850 census of Cambridge Twp., Lenawee Co., Mich., with HANNAH, age 19; WILLIAM, age 12; ANDREW, age 10, all born Mich.

AYRES, JOHN born ca. 1806, England, and wife, HARRIET, born ca. 1824, NY, were listed in the 1850 census pf Cambridge Twp., Lenawee Co., Mich. with ANSON, age 5; MELVILLE, age 3; JOHN, age 4/12, all born Mich., in the household

AYRES, JUNIUS of Adrian, Lenawee Co., Mich., married ANNE PRESALA (DREW) of Dover Twp. on 11 Dec. 1853.

- B -

BABCOCK, ANN born ca. 1799, NY, was listed as head of household in the 1850 census of Woodstock Twp., Lenawee Co., Mich., with AUGUSTUS, age 22; & GEORGE, age 12, both b. NY, in her household. Please note WILLIAM of Woodstock Twp., following.

BABCOCK, CHARLES married MARY (TUTTLE), daughter of Oramon, Jr. (also see). Children: EDITH; TRACY; HERVEY; MEDORA. Mary was a widow before 1888.

BABCOCK, GEORGE was listed in the 1840 census index of Clinton Twp., Lenawee Co., Mich.

BABCOCK, HARRY, son of REUBEN (following), married in Genesee Co., NY to CALISTA D. (FORDHAM), daughter of Hezekiah (also see). She died in 1875, age 57, in Jackson Co., Mich.; and he was living in Branch Co., Mich. in 1888. Known daughter, ELIZA J., b. 18 June 1849, Genesee Co., NY (m. Jeremiah Wilsey, also see, Woodstock Twp., Lenawee Co.) Ref: P&BA-Len pg. 752-3.

BABCOCK, HIRAM, born ca. 1810, and wife, E----, age 34, both born NY, were listed in the 1850 census of Dover Twp., Lenawee Co., Mich. with EUNICE E., age 13; DAVID B., age 12; ANGELINE, age 5; WILLIAM, age 2, all b. Mich., in their household.

BABOCK, HIRAM born ca. 1811, and wife, SARAH E., born ca. 1808, both in NY, were listed in the 1850 census of Rollin Twp., Lenawee Co., Mich. with MARY J., age 8, b. Mich., in their household. Note: HIRAM, probably b. after 1850, who m. Orilla Wood, daughter of Charles (also see), may belong to this family. BABCOCK, JOHN is listed in the 1840 census index of Medina Twp., Lenawee Co., Mich.

BABCOCK, LABAN (See William Underwood)

BABCOCK, LOUISA MARIA Mrs. was the daughter of William Sickly (also see). Ref: P&BA-Len pg. 1132-3.

BABCOCK, NANCY was born ca. 1814 in NY, and is listed in the 1850 census of Madison Twp., Lenawee Co., Mich.

BABCOCK, REBECCA (See Clark Rogers)

BABCOCK, REUBEN was probably he written as "Badcock" in the 1800 censns index of Rensselaer Co., NY. Reuben died in Genesee Co., NY, aged 87 years. Known son, HARRY, b. 14 Jan. 1815, Rensselaer Co., NY (preceding). Ref: P&BA-Len pg. 752-3.

BABCOCK, SARAH C. (See Nicholas Houghtalin)

BABCOCK, SOLOMON was a native of Herkimer Co., NY, and married EMELINE in Jan. 1829 in Seneca Co., NY, and moved to Bridgewater, Washtenaw Co., Mich. in Sept. 1836. He died in Oct. 1864, near Clinton, Mich.; and she resided with known son, WILLIAM F. (following) in 1888; also had a known daughter, LUCY. Ref: History of Jackson Co., Mich., pg. 993.

BABCOCK, WILLIAM was listed in the 1840 census index of Woodstock Twp., Lenawee Co., Mich. Note, ANN, preceding, wife?

BABCOCK, WILLIAM born ca. 1824, VT, and wife, MARIAN, born ca. 1825, NY, were listed in the 1850 census of Seneca Twp., Lenawee Co., Mich., with ABRAM, age 7; SARAH, age 4, both born NY; & ANSON, age 2, b. Mich., in the household.

BABCOCK, WILLIAM F., son of SOLOMON (preceding), was born Nov. 1832, Seneca Co., NY, and moved with his parents to Washtenaw Co., Mich., where he married in Aug. 1855 to CALPERNA (RANDALL), daughter of Russel (also see). They resided near Norvell, Jackson Co., Mich. Three children died infancy. Ref: History of Jackson Co., Mich., pg. 993.

BACHMAN, JOHN married a daughter of George Miller (also see). Ref: P&BA-Len pg. 939-40.

BACK, ERASTUS, son of JUDAH (following), was born in Chaplin, Windham Co., Conn. About 1835, with his wife, ANNIE (FLINT), also born Conn., and 5 children, moved to Bridgewater, Williams Co., Ohio, where he died in 1845; and she died at almost 90 years of age. Children: 1. CHRISTIANA (m. Joseph Foster, Windham Co., Conn.); 2. SALLY (m. Chandler Holt, Bridgewater, O.); 3. GILBERT; 4. EMELINE (m. Philo Holt; she d. Conn.); 5. WILLIAM (Doniphan Co., KS); 6. GEORGE H. (following); 7. JOSEPH (Bridgewater, O.). Ref: P&BA-Len pg. 768-70.

BACK, GEORGE H., son of ERASTUS (preceding), was born ca. 1820, Chaplin, Conn., and moved with his parents to Ohio at age 15. He married 26 Feb. 1845 to ALMIRA (DAVIS), daughter of Ethan (also see), and settled first in Bridgewater, Ohio. They remained until 1851, then moved to Blissfield Twp., Lenawee Co., Mich. Of their 6 children, ALICE (m. M. L. White); MIRON A.; & ELMER, were deceased by 1888; and EMELINE (m. George Davenport, also see); CLARK (Blissfield Twp.); AARON (Roscommon, Mich.) were living in 1888. Ref: P&BA-Len pg. 768-70.

BACK, JUDAH was born in Connecticut, and was a Lieutenant in the Revolutionary War. He married PRISCILLA (GATES). and they lived out their lives in Chaplin, Windham Co., Conn. Known son, ERASTUS (preceding). Ref: P&BA-Len pg. 768-70

BACKUS, ANSON was born in Lee, Mass., and married there to HANNAH (TOWN), daughter of Robert. Soon afterwards, they moved to Herkimer Co., NY, and about 1836 to Orleans Co., NY. She died at age 78, & he died in 1865 at age 83. There were 9 children; known son #6. ANSON (following) b. 25 July 1818, Herkimer Co., NY. Ref: P&BA-Len pg. 1213-4.

BACKUS, ANSON, son of ANSON (preceding), was age 18 when his parents moved to Orleans Co., NY from Herkimer Co., NY. As an adult, he lived for a time in Adrian, Lenawee Co., Mich., and in Sandusky Co., Ohio, but returned to New York. He had married in Ohio to Mrs. LETITIA (WILSON) THOMS in 1842. They lived for 25 years in Hillsdale Co., Mich., but then moved to Adrian, Lenawee Co. Letitia died in March 1886. They had one daughter, MARY J. (m. Capt. J. H. Fee, Adrian). Ref: P&BA-Len pg. 1213-4.

BACKUS, HANNAH (See John Brounell)

BACOME, MARY (RAYMOND), born 1846, was daughter of Isaac Raymond (also see).

BACON, A. R., probably son of JAMES (following), was born ca. 1808 in NY, and is listed in the 1850 census of Rollin Twp., Lenawee Co., Mich., 2 doors from James, with wife, AMY, age 34, b. NY; and STEWART P., age 5/12, b. Mich., in the household.

BACON, ASAHEL was born ca. 1799 in NY, and is listed in the 1850 census of Riga Twp., Lenawee Co., Mich.

BACON, ASAPH born ca. 1799, and wife, SARAH, born ca. 1805, both in NY, were listed in the 1850 census of Riga Twp., Lenawee Co., Mich., and in their household were AMOS, age 18; JESSE, age 15; EMORY, age 14; SARAH, age 10, all b. NY; & HANNAH, age 3, b. Mich. IRA, following, was listed in household next door, and is probably another son.

BACON. CHARLES C. married ANNA E. (MAYNARD), daughter of David T. (also see) of Huron Co., Ohio. Known daughter, FANNY L., married Don C. Hoag, Adrian, Lenawee Co., Mich. After death of Charles C., Anna E. married second to Dr. Francis Grandy (also see). Ref: P&BA-Len pg. 576-7.

BACON, HENRY was born ca. 1805 in Mass., and wife, ELIZABETH, was born ca. 1815 in NY. He is listed in the 1840 census index of Tecumseh Twp., Lenawee Co., Mich.; and in 1850 they listed in their household ALEXANDER, age 7; PIERPOINT, age 5, both b. Mich.

BACON, IRA, age 23, with wife, ADELIA, age 17, both b. NY, were listed in the 1850 census of Riga Twp., Lenawee Co., Mich. in the household of Roswell W. Knight, next door to ASAPH (preceding).

BACON, JAMES, born ca. 1778, VT, and wife, EUNICE, b. ca. 1785, Mass., were listed in the 1850 census of Rollin Twp., Lenawee Co., Mich., with SARAH J., age 25, b. NY, in the household. Also see A. R. (preceding).

BADCOCK see BABCOCK

BADGER, SUSANNAH (See Ezekiel Sanford)

BAER, JOHN A., son of PETER (following), was born 18 July 1827, Fayette, Seneca Co., NY, and moved to Fulton Co., Ohio with his parents. He married CHARLOTTE (WHITE) on 13 Aug. 1848, and they settled probably after 1850 in Medina Twp., Lenawee Co., Mich. She died 14 Sept. 1865. Children: 1. JAMES L. (Dakotas); 2. ELIZABETH (d. infancy); 3. HARRIET (d. age 2); 4. SARAH (d. age 16); 5. ALICE (m. Mitchell, Munson, Mich.); 6. MARTHA (m. William Lifort, Medina Twp.); 7. WILLIAM; 8. GIDEON; 9. SUSANNA (m. Scott Sturtevant, Morenci, Mich.); 10. ROSE ANN (m. John Williamson, Canada). John A. married second to Mrs. CATHARINE A. (GEORGE) HULBON, daugher of Abraham George, and widow of Gideon Hulbon (see both). Daughter, 11. ROSA. Ref: P&BA-Len pg. 841-2.

BAER, PETER was born 17 Apr. 1804, Lehigh Co., Penn., and moved as an infant to Berks Co., Penn. He married first 6 Feb. 1825 to MARY (SMITH), daughter of Abraham (also see). About 1847, they moved to Fulton Co., Ohio, and Mary died shortly following. Children: 1. SAMUEL S. (LaPorte Co., IN); 2. JOHN A. (preceding); 3. ELIZABETH A. (Fayette, Fulton Co., O.); 4. PETER L. (Medina Twp.); 5. SOPHIA; 6. BENJAMIN (m. Louvisa Whiting, dau. of Hiram, also see, & d. young man); 7. LYDIA ANN (Medina Twp.); 8. LAVINA (Morenci, Mich.); 9. JANE (Medina Twp.). Peter married second Mrs. Elmira (WOOLSEY) WHITING, dau. of Nathaniel W. Woolsey, and widow of Hiram S. Whiting (see both). Ref: P&BA-Len pg. 841-2.

BAGERLY, JOHN, born ca. 1813, Maryland, was listed in the 1850 census of Dover Twp., Lenawee Co., Mich., in an Austin household.

BAGERLY, TYSON & wife, SARAH (BELL), were natives of Maryland who had moved to New York where they had married. He died about 1822 & Sarah moved to Michigan in 1857, and died in Seneca Twp., Lenawee Co., Mich. in 1876, aged 86. There were 2 sons & 4 daughters, Known #5. CATHERINE b. 12 July 1820, Wayne Co., NY (m/1 Robert Sloan; m/2 Seth B. Sayres (see both). Ref: P&BA-Len pg. 1188-90.

BAILEY also see BALEY

BAILEY, ALFRED was born 26 Aug. 1808 in Wayne Co., NY; and his wife, CELINDA (WHITE), was born 25 Nov. 1817 in Washington Co., NY; and they married in Niagara Co., NY. On 8 May 1845, they moved to Fairfield Twp., Lenawee Co., Mich. He died there 10 Nov. 1869; and she died 14 Mar. 1879, Blissfield Twp. at home of a son. Children: 1. LYDIA S. b. ca. 1838; 2. WARREN A. (following); 3. MYRON Z. b. ca. 1844. Ref: P&BA-Len pg. 985-6.

BAILEY, ALSON was listed in the 1840 census of Fairfield Twp., Lenawee Co., Mich.

BAILEY, BENDIAH, born ca. 1815, and wife, LOUISA, born ca. 1820, both in NY, were listed in the 1840 census index of Palmyra Twp., Lenawee Co., Mich. (adjacent to NATHAN, following); and in the 1850 census of Fairfield Twp. with JARED, age 12; HIRAM, age 10; ELIZABETH, age 8; NATHAN, age 6; MARIA, age 4; MATILDA, age 2, all born Mich. in their household.

BAILEY, EBENEZER was the father of POLLY who married Daniel Camp (also see). Ebenezer was the 4th in descent from a John Bailey who came in Colonial time to Scituate, Mass. Ref: P&BA-Len pg. 1193-5.

BAILEY, ELIJAH B., son of NATHANIEL (who was a pioneer of Geauga Co., Ohio from Tompkins Co., NY & d. Montville, O.), was born in Tompkins Co., NY, and married AURELIA W. (FENTON), daughter of Ambrose Fenton (also see) of Ashtabula Co., Ohio. Known daughter, FLORENCE A. (m. George W, Fenton, also see). Ref: P&BA-Len pg. 711-2.

BAILEY, ELISHA was listed in the 1840 census index of Hudson Twp., Lenawee Co., Mich. Also note W. B.; & PHEBE (following).

BAILEY, ELIZABETH (See Benjamin G. Graves)

BAILEY, GEORGE, born ca. 1817, Penn., and wife, CAROLINE M., born ca. 1816, NY, were listed in the 1850 census of Madison Twp., Lenawee Co., Mich. with STELLA, age 12; GEORGE H., age 10; ROBERT N., age 8; NEWTON A., age 6, all b. NY; and EMILY E., age 1, b. Mich., in their household.

BAILEY, NATHAN born ca. 1784, and wife, LUCY, born ca. 1790, both in NY, were listed in the 1840 census index of Palmyra Twp., Lenawee Co., Mich.; and in the 1850 census with CHARLES, age 22; JOHN, age 21, both b. NY, in their household. Note BENDIAH, preceding.

BAILEY, NATHAN A., son of PASCHAL D. (following), was born 20 May 1840 in Adrian Twp., Lenawee Co., Mich. He married 1 Oct. 1868 to LYDIA (MAPES), daughter of Wilson (also see); and lived first in Adrian Twp., then in Franklin Twp., eventually returning to Adrian Twp. Children: 1. MARY A. b. 15 July 1870; 2. MYRTIE E. b. 22 June 1872; 3. ARTHUR M. b. 13 Jan. 1874. Ref: P&BA-Len pg. 1019-20.

BAILEY, NORTON H., son of PETER H. (following), married 29 Aug. 1877 in Jackson, Mich. to IDA (HARDING), who was born in Ypsilanti, Mich. In 1883, they moved to Morenci, Lenawee Co., Mich. Children: 1. FLORENCE; 2. BONELLA (d. age 3 yrs). Ref: P&BA-Len pg. 1128-9.

BAILEY, PASCHAL D. married in Oneida Co., NY to MARY ANN (ROWLEY), and moved to Adrian Twp., Lenawee Co., Mich. before 1838. They had known children: 1. CAROLINE b. ca. 1838, Mich. (m. Eli Havens, Adrian); 2. NATHAN A.(AARON), preceding; 3. ELNORA J. b. ca. 1848 (m. Robert Sloan); 4. HERMAN (Franklin Twp.). Ref: P&BA-Len pg. 1019-20.

BAILEY, PETER H. and wife, JANE (WEATHERWAX), were born in the Mohawk Valley of NY. They had moved by 1857 to Saline, Washtenaw Co., Mich. There were 3 sons & 1 daughter; known son, NORTON H. (preceding) b. 11 Apr. 1857, Saline, Mich. Ref: P&BA-Len pg. 1128-9.

BAILEY, PETER L. (See John R. Clark)

BAILEY, PHEBE was born ca. 1790 in Rhode Island, and was head of household in the 1850 census of Hudson Twp., Lenawee Co., Mich., with IRENA, age 34; JACOB, age 32; ALONZO, age 19, all b. NY in her household. Note ELISHA (preceding); & W. B. (following).

BAILEY, ROBERT M., son of Rev. T. H. (following), was born 12 Dec. 1826 in Newbury, VT. He married 6 Mar. 1850 to SUSAN (PIERCE), daughter of John (also see). (Note: In the 1850 census of Madison Twp., Lenawee Co., Mich., he listed wife, CORNELIA, age 26, b. NY, in his household??). His wife died leaving 2 children, AMELIA; & MARCUS M. (m. Dunreath Thompson). Robert M. married second to JANE (STRONG), daughter of Selden of Mass. She died in 1878; and Robert M. afterwards married her cousin, LAURA M. (STRONG). Ref: P&BA-Len pg. 1168.

BAILEY, SAMUEL and wife, JOANNA, came to Lenawee Co., Mich. from NY. (May be they in Madison Twp., Lenawee Co., in 1840 census index). She was said to have died in New York? Children: 1. STEPHEN P. b. 30 Nov. 1816 (following); 2. OLIVER b. ca. 1821, NJ? (to Nebraska); 3. JANE b. ca. 1823, NJ. Apparently Samuel had married again to MEHITABLE, b. ca. 1788, NJ, as she is listed as head of household in the 1850 census of Madison Twp., Lenawee Co., Mich., with the above named children listed in her household, ages as shown, spelled "Baley." Ref: P&BA-Len pg. 822-3. Note: in the 1840 census index, JOSEPH BALEY is listed adjacent.

BAILEY, SAMUEL was listed in the 1840 census index of Dover Twp., Lenawee Co., Mich.

BAILEY, SARAH "SALLY" (See John Osterhout)

BAILEY, STEPHEN P., son of SAMUEL (preceding), came to Lenawee Co., Mich. with his parents in 1836. He married in Monroe Co., Mich. on 17 Apr. 1862 to MARTHA (ALBAIN), daughter of John (also see). Stephen P. died 23 Dec. 1886, Lenawee Co. Children: 1. JOHN; 2. JOANNA (m. Hiram Church, Jackson, Mich.); 3. STEPHEN; 4. SAMUEL; 5. IRA; 6. ASA; 7. ADA; 8. OLIVER; 9. MARTHA J. (d. infancy); 10. CLARENCE; 11. GEORGE; 12. MARTHA. Ref: P&BA-Len pg. 822-3 with portrait.

BAILEY, T. H. Rev. was born in Vermont, and was father of ROBERT M. Also note THADDEUS, following, who may be same man.

BAILEY, THADDEUS was listed in the 1840 census index of Madison Twp., Lenawee Co., Mich.

BAILEY, WARREN A., son of ALFRED (preceding), was born 14 Sept. 1839, Niagara Co., NY, and came to Fairfield Twp., Lenawee Co., Mich. with his parents. He married 13 June 1861 to LORETTA A. (WHITE), in Madison Twp. They resided in Fairfield Twp. Children: 1. WARREN L; 2. BYRON C.; 3. JAMES B. Ref: P&BA-Len pg. 985-6.

BAILEY, WILLIAM D. born ca. 1811, and wife, DORLISKA A., born ca. 1822, both in NY, were listed in the 1850 census of Madison Twp., Lenawee Co., Mich., with JAMES, age 8; PHEBE, age 5; JONATHAN, age 2, all b. Mich., in the household. Also in the household was ELIZA J., age 28, b. NY, all spelled "Baley."

BAILEY, W. B. was listed in the 1840 census index of Hudson Twp., Lenawee Co., Mich. Note ELISHA, & PHEBE, preceding.

BAIRD, MARY (See Christopher Forncrook)
BAIRD, POLLY (See John Sutfin)

BAKER, AARON was listed in the 1840 census index of Fairfield Twp., Lenawee Co., Mich. with ALVA; BENJAMIN; BENJAMIN G.; CALEB M.; JOHN; MOSES; & ORAN (ORRIN) listed adjacent (following).

BAKER, ACHILLES, born ca. 1826, Penn., and wife, AGNES, b. ca. 1829, NY, were listed in the 1850 census of Fairfield Twp., Lenawee Co., Mich., with DOLLY, age 4; ADAM, age 2, & WILLIAM, age 1/12, all b. Mich., in the household.

BAKER, ALBERT M. was born in Eden, Erie Co., NY; and married in Buffalo, NY in August 1837 to SARAH (KEELER), who was born 1817, and they came to Adrian Twp., Lenawee Co., Mich. in 1838. He died 20 July 1860, and she was still living in 1888, age 71, with son, DELOS M. (following). Ref: P&BA-Len pg. 294.

BAKER, ALONZO was listed in the 1840 census index of Adrian Twp., Lenawee Co., Mich.

BAKER, ALVA, possibly son of MOSES (following), born ca. 1814, and wife, MARTHA A., born ca. 1819, both in NY, were listed in the 1850 census of Fairfield Twp., Lenawee Co., Mich., with BENNET C., age 13; PHEBE A., age 10; DELAND G., age 4, all b. Mich., in the household.

BAKER, ANDREW was listed in the 1840 census index of Rome Twp., Lenawee Co., Mich. adjacent to JOSEPH W.; LYMAN W.; & NORMAN C. (see all). It may be he listed in the 1850 census of Adrian Twp., Lenawee Co., Mich., age 46, b. Rhode Island, with wife, LYDIA, born ca. 1820, VT. Also listed were SARAH M., age 7; JOHN W., age 4; MARY J., age 1, all b. Mich.

BAKER, APPOLOS & wife, LUCY (CHURCH), were born in Mass., and moved to Erie Co., NY, where he died in 1823. She lived with her daughter, Fila, until her death in 1848, when she was "buried next to her husband in Orleans, Ontario Co., NY." Known children: Mrs. FILA (BALCOM) MURRAY; & CLARISSA A. b. 1815 (m. Justus Cooley, also see). Ref: P&BA-Len pg. 593-4.

BAKER, BENJAMIN, born ca. 1811, & wife, EMILETTA, born ca. 1812, both in NY, were listed in the 1850 census of Fairfield Twp., Lenawee Co., Mich., with STEPHEN H., age 14; GEORGE W., age 13; HARRIET E., age 8; FRANCIS B., age 1, all b. Mich., in the household.

BAKER, BENJAMIN, born ca. 1813, and wife, AMANDA, born ca. 1816, both in NY, were listed in the 1850 census of Fairfield Twp., Lenawee Co., Mich., with IRA, age 8; DAVID, age 6; VOLINA, age 3; CHARLOTTE, age 4/12, all b. Mich., in the household. Also in the household was Hannah Runnels, age 70, b. NY (mother of Amanda??).

BAKER, BETSEY, born ca. 1791, Mass., was head of household in the 1850 census of Adrian Twp., Lenawee Co., Mich., with a child, David S. Hoag, age 9, b. Mich., in her household.

BAKER, C. D. (See Benjamin P. Perry)

BAKER, CALEB M., born ca. 1809, and wife, LOWINA?, born ca. 1813, both in New York, were listed in the 1850 census of Fairfield Twp., Lenawee Co., Mich. with ASAHEL, age 15, b. NY; SARAH, age 12; MELISSA, age 11; MARTHA A., age 7; ESTHER, age 6; MARY J., age 5; ELIZABETH, age 3; WILLIAM, age 2, all b. Mich., listed in the household.

BAKER, CAROLINE (See Richard Robinson); also note Caroline in household of CHARLES R., following.

BAKER, CHARLES R., born ca. 1820, England, and wife, PHILENDA, born ca. 1823, NY, were listed in the 1850 census of Rome Twp., Lenawee Co., Mich. with EDWIN, age 6; CAROLINE, age 4; GEORGE, age 2, all b. Mich., in their household.

BAKER, DANIEL D. was born ca. 1822, and wife, ANN (WHITFIELD), born ca. 1823, both in NY, & had 5 children. In the 1850 census of Fairfield Twp., Lenawee Co., Mich. they listed the first 2; CHARLES H., age 33; & EDWARD, age 4/12. Known daughter, NETTIE, b. 20 Aug. 1853 (m. Lewis C. Fitts, also see). Ref: P&BA-Len pg. 867-8.

BAKER, DAVID was listed in the 1840 census index of Adrian Twp., Lenawee Co., Mich.

BAKER, DELOS M., son of ALBERT M. (preceding), was born 26 May 1838 in Buffalo, NY, and came to Adrian Twp., Lenawee Co., Mich. with his parents. He married first on 27 Jan. 1863 to JULIA (BLOUNT), of Milwaukee, Wisc.; and she died 1881, leaving no children. He married second to MARY K. (GOODMAN), daughter of Eleazer & Mahala Goodman of Glen Falls, NY. Son, ALBERT G. Ref: P&BA-Len pg. 294.

BAKER, DORA (See Alonzo James)

BAKER, EDWIN A., son of MILES (following), was born near Hopewell, Ontario Co., NY; and married first in Ontario Co. to DIANTHA (ACKLES), who was born there. They moved first to Wayne Co., NY, where they remained until ca. 1855, then moved to Jackson Co., Mich., where Diantha died shortly following, leaving daughter, 1. EMMA (m. Christopher Hutchins, Hudson Twp., Lenawee Co., Mich.). Edwin A. married second in Jackson Co. to URSULA (ACKLES), sister of Diantha, and remained there for 8 years before moving to Rome Twp., Lenawee Co., Mich. Afterwards, they moved to Wayne Co., NY where Ursula died. Children: 2. ALICE L. (m. William Vivian, Burlington, IA); 3. ETTA E.; 4. CHARLES. About 1870, the family returned to Dover Twp., Lenawee Co., Mich. Edwin A. married third to ELLA (CAPRON), daughter of Ebenezer (also see). She died 9 Feb. 1888, Rome Twp. Children: 5. MUSA P.; 6. EDWIN A. Ref: P&BA-Len pg. 632-3.

BAKER, ELEAZER, born ca. 1802, Rhode Island; and wife, HANNAH H., born ca. 1812, NY, were listed in the 1850 census of Adrian Twp., Lenawee Co., Mich. with JEROME D., age 13, b. Mich., in their household. Also note ANDREW (preceding).

BAKER, ELISHA, born Canada, was the son of a Baptist Minister who had moved to Canada (where he died). After the War of 1812, Elisha moved to Steuben Co., NY, where he died in June 1819. His wife, RUTH AMELIA (DAVID), was born in Vermont, and had moved to Canada with her parents. After Elisha's death, she moved to Shelburne, VT where she married again. She spent her last years in Monroe Co., Mich. with her childfren, and died age 88y/3m, buried with daughter, MARY, who was born ca. 1813 (m. Lucas Adams, also see, Bedford Twp., Monroe Co., Mich.). Known son, GEORGE ANSON (following). Another daughter went to Cleveland, Ohio; and a son went to Danville, Ohio. Ref: P&BA-Len pg. 767-8.

BAKER, EXPERIENCE M. was born ca. 1808 near Manchester, Ontario Co., NY, and married there to Uriah Decker (also see). In the 1850 census of Adrian Twp., Lenawee Co., Mich., they were listed next door to NORTON BAKER (also see). She may be another daughter of JOSEPH M. (following).

BAKER, GEORGE ANSON, son of ELISHA (preceding), was born 5 Feb. 1819, Jersey, Steuben Co., NY; and moved to Cleveland, Ohio in 1834 with a married sister. About 1835, he lived in Bedford Twp., Monroe Co., Mich.; and between 1840-1845 lived in Salisbury, VT, Danville, Ohio, Fitchville & Richmond in Huron Co., Ohio, & Lorain Co., Ohio. He married on 29 Mar. 1843 to MARY M. (SIZER), daughter of Anson (also see) of Huron Co., Ohio. By 1850, they were in Monroe Co., Mich., and about 1852 went to California. In 1867 they settled in Blissfield Twp., Lenawee Co., Mich. Daughter,

CARRIE M. (m. Rev. Nathan N. Clark). Ref: P&BA-Len pg. 767-8.

BAKER, ISAAC, born ca. 1822, & wife, ALMEDA A., born ca. 1829, both in NY, were listed in the 1850 census of Dover Twp., Lenawee Co., Mich. with DAVID, age 8/12, b. Mich., in their household. Also note LORIN, JOSIAH, SAMUEL, & WILLIAM of Dover Twp., following.

BAKER, JESSE, born ca. 1816, and wife, AMANDA, born ca. 1829, both in NY, were listed in the 1850 census of Fairfield Twp., Lenawee Co., Mich., with MARY A., age 1; & MARY??, age 1, both b. Mich. in their household. Also listed was SARAH, age 13, b. Mich.

BAKER, JOHN, possibly son of MOSES (following), was born ca. 1798 in Mass., and his wife, POLLY, was born ca. 1801 in Canada; and they were in the 1850 census of Fairfield Twp., Lenawee Co., Mich. with LYDIA A., age 16; CHLOE I., age 15; LEVI, age 13; HORACE L., age 11; JOHN, age 8, all b. Mich. Also in the household were Allen White, age 22, with wife, Cynthia, age 18, born NY; & Ezekiel Smith, age 71, b. Mass. (possibly father of Polly). Note NATHANIEL, following.

BAKER, JOHN S., born ca. 1820, and wife, RUTH, born ca. 1826, both in NY, were listed in the 1850 census of Fairfield Twp., Lenawee Co., Mich., with ALONZO, age 5; REBECCA P., age 1, both b. Mich., in their household.

BAKER, JOSEPH[1] of Narragansett Bay in 1680 was the ancestor of Joseph Baker of Mass. & NY. Joseph[1] had among his children sons, JOSEPH & DAVID, both of whom married a Chase.

BAKER, JOSEPH, a descendant of JOSEPH[1], was born in Mass., and married EXPERIENCE (MARTIN); and settled first in Rutland Co., VT, where he died at age 60. Among children: JOSEPH M. (following). Ref: P&BA-Len pg. 303-4.

BAKER, JOSEPH F., son of JOSEPH M. (following), was born Manchester, Ontario Co., NY on 19 June 1819. He married first to CYNTHIA M. (DEWEY), daughter of Col. Edmond B. (also see), and she died 15 Oct. 1857 in Rome Twp., Lenawee Co., Mich. leaving three children, among them EDMOND. Joseph F. married second to Mrs. ANNA (DEWEY) TEACHOUT, sister of Cynthia, and widow of Alonzo Teachout (also see). Daughter, CYNTHIA JOANNA, b. 10 Jan. 1866, Adrian (d. 17 Feb. 1875). They resided in Adrian Twp. Ref: P&BA-Len pg. 303-4.

BAKER, JOSEPH M., son of JOSEPH (preceding), was born 19 Feb. 1780 in North Adams, Mass., and moved with his father to Rutland Co., VT. He moved as a young man to Ontario Co., NY, and married on 27 Dec. 1801 to SALLY (CRUTHERS), daughter of John (also see), at Phelps, NY. They moved to Palmyra, Wayne Co., NY; and in 1833 to Bedford Twp., Monroe Co., Mich. in a family group of 14 persons that included grandchildren. They moved to Rome Twp., Lenawee Co., Mich. before 1840, and he died 27 May 1872, age 93, in Rome Village; and she died in 1875. There were 6 sons & 5 daughters. Known children: NORTON (following); JOSEPH F. (preceding); SALLY F. b. 18 June 1819, NY (twin of Joseph F.; m. Charles L. Thomas, also see). Ref: P&BA-Len pg. 303-4; 957-8; & 1085-6. Also note ANDREW; LYMAN W.; NORMAN C.; & EXPERIENCE M. (who m. Uriah Decker, and was next door to Norton in the 1850 census), all preceding.

BAKER, JOSIAH, born ca. 1789, Mass., and wife, DEBORAH, born ca. 1789, Rhode Island, were probably they listed in the 1840 census index of Madison Twp., Lenawee Co., Mich. In the 1850 census of Dover Twp., Lenawee Co., Mich., they listed ROSCO?, age 32; ROSINA, age 2-?; RUTH A., age 22; JOHN D., age 20, all born NY. Also note LORIN; ISAAC; SAMUEL; & WILLIAM in Dover Twp.

BAKER, LEVI W., son of SAMUEL (following), was born 17 Aug. 1835 in Macedon, Wayne Co., NY, and came with parents to Dover Twp., Lenawee Co., Mich. He married 3 Dec. 1857 to MARTHA (CRATER), daughter of Matthias (also see). Son, ANDREW S., born 3 July 1870. Ref: P&BA-Len pg. 927.

BAKER, LORIN, born ca. 1815, and wife, AMANDA, born ca. 1819, both in NY, were listed in the 1850 census of Dover Twp., Lenawee Co., Mich., with RILEY, age 12, b. Ohio; LUCIUS, age 10; CYRUS, age 8; MARTHA J., age 5; NELSON, age 2, last 4 b. Mich., in their household. Also note ISAAC; JOSIAH; SAMUEL; & WILLIAM in Dover Twp.

BAKER, LYMAN W. (See JOSEPH M., preceding) was born ca. 1804, NY, and married 11 Feb. 1830 to ASENATHA L. (WARNER) who was born 12 July 1813, Phelps, Ontario Co., NY; and they settled in Rome Twp., Lenawee Co., Mich. in 1833. She died 12 Apr. 1856. Children: 1. ORRA C. b. ca. 1833, NY (m. B. C. Knowles, Adrian Twp.); 2. LYDIA J. b. ca. 1835, Mich. (m. George H. Lane, Rome Twp.); 3. RALPH P. (following). Lyman W. married second on 22 Oct. 1856 to JERUSHA T. (HINCKLEY), daughter of Benjamin (also see). She died in Rome Twp. in 1883. Children: 4. LYMAN W. Jr.; 5. SAMUEL H.; 6. DOUGLAS S.; 7. GRACE A. (deceased before 1888); 8. LEE H. Ref: P&BA-Len pg. 541-2.

BAKER, MARY (See Benjamin D. Osborn)

BAKER, MELFORD (See Benjamin Hornbeck)

BAKER, MILES born in Ontario Co., NY, and his wife, DELINDA (MALTBY), born in VT, settled in Ontario Co., NY where they remained. Four sons & 3 daughters, of whom 5 survived in 1888, 2 in Michigan & 3 in NY, names not stated. Known son, EDWIN A. (preceding). Ref: P&BA-Len 632-3.

BAKER, MOSES was born ca. 1777, and his wife, LUCINDA, was born ca. 1784, both in Mass. In the 1850 census of Fairfield Twp., Lenawee Co., Mich., they lived adjacent to JOHN; ORRIN; & ALVA, as noted here (sons?). In the 1840 census index, Fairfield Twp., adjacent were AARON; ALVA; BENJAMIN; CALEB M.; JOHN; & ORRIN. SALLY, born ca. 1816, NY, who married Joseph Deland (also see), and lived close by in 1850, may be also related.

BAKER, NATHAN born ca. 1811; & wife, NANCY, born ca. 1808, both in NY, were listed in the 1850 census of Rome Twp., Lenawee Co., Mich. with EDWIN P., age 16; ELIZA M., age 13; NANCY L., age 9, all b. NY, in their household.

BAKER, NATHANIEL born ca. 1824, and wife, POLLY, born ca. 1830, both in NY, were listed in the 1850 census of Fairfield Twp., Lenawee Co., Mich. next door to JOHN (preceding), and listed CHARLES H., age 1, b. Mich.; and Laura Cook, age 18, b. NY in their household.

Pioneer Families of Southeastern Michigan

BAKER, NORMAN C. (See JOSEPH M.) born ca. 1804, and wife, HARRIET (ROBINSON), born ca. 1810, both in NY, settled in Rome Twp., Lenawee Co., Mich. before 1838. In the 1850 census of Rome Twp., they listed HIRAM, age 12; FRANKLIN, age 10; MIRA (MYRA?), age 6; LASIRA b. 3 Mar. 1847 (m. Asel Cure, also see); MARTIN, age 1, all b. Mich. Ref: P&BA-Len pg. 840-1

BAKER, NORTON, son of JOSEPH M. (preceding), was born 9 Dec. 1802, Manchester, Ontario Co., NY; and married 12 Sept. 1830 to ALMEDA (HOWLAND), daughter of Jonathan (also see). They accompanied his father & family to Lenawee Co., Mich., and settled in Adrian Twp. Children: 1. SARAH M. (m. Dr. Willard Perkins, Franklin, Lenawee Co.); 2. ISAAC H. b. ca. 1832 (d. 3 Apr. 1852, age 19); 3. ELLEN L. b. ca. 1836 (m. George Gambee, Adrian); 4. LOIS A. b. ca. 1837 (d. 12 Mar. 1852, age 16); 5. (MARY) EMELINE b. ca. 1840 (m. George Hunt, Rome Twp.); 6. ROXANNA I. b. ca. 1841 (d. 2 Apr. 1852, age 11); 7. LEWIS C. b. 18 Feb. 1844; 8. FRANCIS "FRANK" I. b. ca. 1846 (d. 2 June 1862, age 17); 9. ALMEDA b. ca. 1848 (d. 16 Feb. 1852, age 4); 10.AVA. Ref: P&BA-Len pg. 957-8.

BAKER, ORRIN, possibly a son of MOSES (preceding), born ca. 1801, and wife, MELINDA, born ca. 1811, both in NY, were listed in the 1850 census of Fairfield Twp., Lenawee Co., Mich., with CYNTHIA B., age 16; CATHERINE E., age 12; ZACHARIAH T., age 4/12, all b. Mich., in their household. Also listed were Henry Clark, age 27, with wife, Sarah (Baker?), age 25, both b. NY, and daughter Lydia Clark, age 1, b. Mich.

BAKER, RALPH P., son of LYMAN W. (preceding), was born ca. 1837, Mich., and married 4 Dec. 1858 in Rome Twp., Lenawee Co., to ARISTEEN (PHELPS), daughter of Philo P. (also see). By 1888, they lived in Rome Center. Children: 1. ROSA P. (m. J. Purchis, Eaton Co., Mich.); 2. CYNTHIA M. (d. Oct. 1879, age 20); 3. ALMA C. (m. George Fuller, Franklin Co., Mich.); 4. HELEN M. (m. Charles Spangle, Rome Twp.); 5. ASENATH W.; 6. DAISY B. Ref: P&BA-Len pg. 541-2.

BAKER, REBECCA (See Thomas Chandler)

BAKER, RIENGE (See Fernando C. Beaman)

BAKER, SALLY (Note MOSES, preceding; & see Joseph Deland).

BAKER, SAMUEL was born ca. 1811, and his wife, CHARLOTTE (MILLS), was born ca. 1818, both in NY. After marrying, they settled in Wayne Co., NY, and remained until 1840, when they removed to Lenawee Co., Mich. It is probably he in the 1840 census index of Dover Twp., and he died there 5 Oct. 1870; and she died 22 Oct. 1868. Sons, AMOS W. b. ca. 1835, NY; & LEVI W. (preceding). Ref: P&BA-Len pg. 927. Also note ISAAC; JOSIAH; LORIN; & WILLIAM in Dover Twp. in 1850.

BAKER, SARAH (See John Eddy)

BAKER, THOMAS was listed in the 1840 census index of Adrian Twp., Lenawee Co., Mich., and was probably father of ESTHER born 1 Apr. 1828 in England (m. Michael McAdam, also see); & THOMAS, JR. b. ca. 1822, England, listed in the 1850 census of Adrian Twp., with wife, LYDIA, age 30, b. NY. Ref: P&BA-Len pg. 668-9.

BAKER, WILLIAM was born 4 Dec. 1784, Berkshire Co., Mass.; and he married SARAH (WHEELER), born 2 Jan. 1794. They moved to Ft. Ann, Washington Co., NY. Six children, known son, WILLIAM, (following). Ref: P&BA-Len pg. 931-2. (Note: There was a M. S. BAKER in Hudson Twp., Lenawee Co., Mich. in 1840 census index).

BAKER, WILLIAM, son of WILLIAM (preceding), was born 21 Oct. 1818, Ft Ann, NY, and came to Michigan in 1837 to join an older brother. In 1841, he settled in Hudson Twp., Lenawee Co., Mich. He married 11 July 1843 to DELORA (OSBORN), daughter of John (also see). Children: 1. GAMALIEL (1st, d. age 4); 2. JOHN M.; 3. GAMALIEL (2d, m. Emma Elliott, Hudson Twp.). Ref: P&BA-Len pg. 931-2 with portrait.

BAKER, WILLIAM, born ca. 1823, and wife, LOGINA?, born ca. 1817, both in NY, were listed in the 1850 census of Dover Twp., Lenawee Co., Mich. with ALTHA V., age 6; MARSELL J., age 3. both born Ohio, in their household.

BAKEWELL, AGNES (See Lewis Sanford)

BALCOM, FILA - Mrs. Fila (Balcom) Murray was called the daughter of Appolos Baker, also see.

BALDIN, AMY (See Samuel Howd)

BALDWIN, CHARLES H., born ca. 1813, and wife, ELECTA A., born ca. 1819, both in NY, were listed in the 1850 census of Medina Twp., Lenawee Co., Mich., with AURILLA, age 6; EDWARD R., age 4, both born Mich., in their household.

BALDWIN, CHARLES M. was born 28 Feb. 1806, and his wife, MARTHA K. (MITCHELL), was born 1 Feb. 1816, both in Mass. (Berkshire Co.?) They married on 24 July 1834. It may be they listed in the 1840 census index of Avon Twp., Oakland Co., Mich. They moved to Fairfield Twp., Lenawee Co., and by 1850 to Medina Twp. He died 3 Apr. 1852, and she died 17 Aug. 1864. Children: 1. EMMA LOUISE; 2. CLARISSA ORPHELIA b. 3 Apr. 1837, Mich.; 3. CYRUS MITCHELL b. ca. 1839 (served Civil War, Co. A., 18th Mich. Inf.; lived Morenci, Mich.); 4. Infant d. unnamed; 5. NELSON b. ca. 1842; 6. EDGAR E. b. ca. 1846; 7. CHARLES EROTUS b. ca. 1849. Ref: P&BA-Len pg. 789-90. Note: Due to proximity in 1850 census of Medina Twp., Charles M. may be brother of ESTHER E. who m. Noah K. Green, also see.

BALDWIN, DEXTER W., born ca. 1813, and wife, ELECTA M., born ca. 1816, both in Mass., were listed in the 1850 census of Madison Twp., Lenawee Co., Mich. with MARY A., age 17; ELLEN, age 14, both b. Mass.; & LOWELL M., age 9, b. Mich., in their household.

BALDWIN, ELIAS J., born ca. 1798, and wife, OLIVE?, b. ca. 1802, both in Mass., were probably he listed as "E. J." in the 1840 census index of Seneca Twp., Lenawee Co., Mich.; and in 1850 had in their household SAMUEL, age 20; LUCIUS, age 18; LUCY A., age 16, all b. Mass.; and HARRIET P., age 13; EMMA, age 7, both b. Mich. Note: S. A. BALDWIN of Adrian m. Mary (James) of Tecumseh, 6 Oct. 1856. Was this Samuel?

BALDWIN, ESTHER E. was born 14 Aug. 1807, Berkshire Co., Mass; and married there to Noah K. Green (also see); and moved to Medina Twp., Lenawee Co., Mich. before 1835. Also see CHARLES M.

BALDWIN, HARVEY I., son of ISAAC (following), was born 15 Oct. 1828, Litchfield, Conn., and moved with his parents to Westfield, Medina Co, Ohio. He married 16 Oct. 1848 to CATHARINE (MILLER) who was born 25 Jan. 1830, NY. They moved about 1855 to Cambridge Twp., Lenawee Co., Mich. She died 13 June 1856. Children: 1. CHARLES b. Westfield, O.; 2. WILLIAM b. Mich. Harvey I. married second on 3 Sept. 1857 to EMILY (MILLER, born NY, 25 Jan. 1835; and she died 19 Aug. 1887. Daughter, 3. CORA C. Ref: P&BA-Len pg. 628-9.

BALDWIN, HENRY born ca. 1826, Canada, and is listed in the 1850 census of Madison Twp., Lenawee Co., Mich. Also see JOHN.

BALDWIN, ISAAC was born in Litchfield, Conn, son of a man who had settled there from England before the Revolution. He married SARAH (GILLETTE), daughter of Asa of Litchfield. In 1840, they moved to Westfield, Medina Co., Ohio; and in 1867, to Allegan Co., Mich. where he died in 1880, and she died in 1881. Five sons, known son, #2. HARVEY I. (preceding). Ref: P&BA-Len pg. 628-9.

BALDWIN, J. W. (See Nelson Bradish)

BALDWIN, JOHN, born ca. 1786, NY, and wife, MATILDA, born ca. 1799, Canada, may be they listed in the 1840 census index of Washtenaw Co., Mich. In the 1850 census of Madison Twp., Lenawee Co., Mich., they listed JOHN, age 19, b. NY; MATILDA, age 18?; ABIGAIL, age 17; CLARISSA, age 15, last 3 b. Mich.

BALDWIN, MILLICENT (See Simon D. Wilson)

BALDWIN, PHILO and wife, BETSEY (HOPKINS), were parents of LOUISA M. who m. John M. Cary (also see).

BALDWIN, SAMUEL D. was born in Mass., and he settled in Palmyra Twp., Lenawee Co., Mich. by 1840. Known daughter, MERCY, m. Dr. Charles W. Stocum, also see, in Apr. 1860, Seneca Twp. Ref: P&BA-Len pg. 602-3.

BALDWIN, WILLIAM, born ca. 1801, and wife, DELIA, born ca. 1798, both in Conn., are listed in the 1850 census of Tecumseh Twp., Lenawee Co., Mich. (probably they in the 1840 census index).

BALEY also see BAILEY

BALEY, GEORGE W., son of JOSEPH (following), came to Dover Twp., Lenawee Co., Mich. with his parents. He married there in 1847 to MARY E. (BRADFORD) of Wayne Co., Mich. She died 2 July 1848, leaving a son, JOSEPH. George W. married second on 7 July 1864, Adrian, to MARY C. (PONTIUS), daughter of Henry (also see). They resided in Dover Twp. Son, JOHN C. Ref: P&BA-Len pg. 1089-90.

BALEY, HENRY, probably son of TRUSTIN (following), was born ca. 1829 in VT, and his wife, LYDIA, was born ca. 1832, Mich. They were listed in the 1850 census of Adrian Twp., Lenawee Co., Mich., shown married within that year. In their household was Mary Gould, age 29, b. NY.

BALEY, HIRAM S. was born ca. 1824, NY, and was listed as head of household in the 1850 census of Dover Twp., Lenawee Co., Mich., with SALLY, age 66, b. VT, probably mother, and DANIEL B., age 26; TRUMAN E., age 23, both b. NY, also listed.

BALEY, JOSEPH was born ca. 1793, Penn., and his wife, OLIVE (BURGESS), was born June 1795 in Orange Co., NY. She died Romulus, Seneca Co., NY on 10 Feb. 1836; and he afterwards moved to Michigan. He died 4 Nov. 1844 (1884?), Dover Twp., Lenawee Co., Mich. Children: 1. GEORGE W. (preceding) b. 13 Oct. 1821, Romulus, NY; 2. LOUISA P. b. 31 Oct. 1823, Romulus (m. Martin P. Stockwell, also see); 3. CINDERELLA (m. N. P. Ellis, Iowa); 4. WILLIAM P. (d. NY); 5. HENRY (Wisconsin); 6. A. JUDSON (d. Dover Twp., age 8 or 9). Ref: P&BA-Len pg. 215-7 & 1089-90.

BALEY, LUTHER R., age 6, b. Mich., was listed in the 1850 census of Dover Twp., Lenawee Co., Mich. in the household of Marvin & Celinda Cleveland.

BALEY, TRUSTIN, born ca. 1805, and wife, EUNICE, born ca. 1807, were listed In the 1850 census of Adrian Twp., Lenawee Co., Mich., with SIMEON, age 18; GEORGE, age 16; LORENZO, age 13; WESLEY, age 11; LYDIA, age 9, all b. NY; and TRUSTIN, JR., age 2, b. Mich. HENRY (preceding), probably son of Trustin, age 21, was listed next door. Also note HIRAM S.

BALIS also see BALUSS

BALIS, SAMUEL, born ca. 1797, and wife, MARY, born ca. 1801, both in NY, were probably they listed as "Bailes" in the 1840 census index of Dover Twp., Lenawee Co., Mich.; and in the 1850 census, they listed ANDREW H., age 23; JONATHAN, age 21; JANE A., age 18, all b. NY; & JAMES A., age 16; OPHELIA, age 14; SAMUEL M., age 12; BENJAMIN, age 10, all b. Mich.

BALL, JOEL, born ca. 1800, NJ, and wife, MARGARET, born ca. 1804, NY, were listed in the 1850 census of Ridgeway Twp., Lenawee Co., Mich. with MARGARET, age 17, b. NY; LUCINDA, age 14; ISAAC, age 12; HENRY, age 10; EDWARD, age 7; MARY J., age 5 STEPHEN, age 2, all b. Mich., in their household.

BALL, JONATHAN[2], son of NATHANIEL[1], was born ca. 1804, NY; and he married JULIA A. (TINGLEY), daughter of Samuel, Sr. (also see), probably in Seneca Co., NY. In 1833, they removed to Rollin Twp., Lenawee Co., Mich. He died 18 Dec. 1866, age 62; and she died 31 Dec. 1873, age 65. Known children: 1. NATHANIEL[3] (following) b. ca. 1836, Mich.; 2. WILLIAM H. b. ca. 1839 (Rollin Twp.). Ref: P&BA-Len pg. 591.

BALL, MARTIN was born ca. 1830, NY, and was probably related to JONATHAN (preceding), as he was listed in the household of Julia's brother, Samuel Tingley, in the 1850 census of Adrian Twp., Lenawee Co., Mich.

BALL, NATHAN was from Mass., and went first to Vermont, and then to Ontario Co., NY. He married JANE (SMITH) who was born 1767 in Mass. He died in 1826 in Geneva, NY; and she came to Pittsford Twp., Hillsdale Co., Mich., where she died age 92. Known daughter, SARAH S. (m. Charles Ames, also see). Ref: P&BA-Len pg. 986-7. Note resemblance to NATHANIEL[1] (following).

BALL, NATHANIEL[1] was a Revolutionary soldier who died in New York state. He was the father of JONATHAN[2] (preceding) b. ca. 1804. Ref: P&BA-Len pg. 591.

BALL, NATHANIEL[3], son of JONATHAN[2] (preceding), was born in Seneca Co., NY, and came with his parents to Rollin Twp., Lenawee Co., Mich. He married 1 FEb. 1860 to R. J. (CUMMINS), daughter of James (also see), and they settled in Rollin Twp. Children: 1. JONATHAN W. b. 7 Feb. 1865 (to Ionia Co., Mich.); 2.

LUVINA b. 11 Feb. 1867; 3. MARTIN T. b. 24 June 1868 (m. Dora Bennett, dau. of Roswell, also see); 4. NELLIE b. 15 Jan. 1870 (m. Justin Curtis, son of Robert, also see); 5. JULIA b. 20 Nov. 1872 (d. 1875). Ref: P&BA-Len pg. 591.

BALLARD, NANCY (See James Day)

BALLARD, SARAH (See Frederick Harsh)

BALUSS also see BALIS

BALUSS, CORNELIUS W., son of an early settler of Wayne Co., NY, was born there in 1816; and married in 1837 to SARAH (DURKEE) who was born 1818, and they moved to Medina Twp., Lenawee Co., Mich. In 1839, they moved to Fairfield Twp.; and in the 1850 census, they are listed with 5 of their 6 children, all born Mich.: PHINEAS, age 15; CORNELIUS, age 12; HAMILTON, age 10 (went to Wayne Co., Mich.); DANIEL D., age 5 (following); HORACE, age 2 Sarah died in 1854, and Cornelius married again and had 2 more children, names not stated. Ref: P&BA-Len pg. 773-4.

BALUSS, DANIEL D., son of CORNELIUS W. (preceding), was born 23 Mar. 1845 in Fairfield Twp. He married 17 Jan. 1869 to AMANDA (HOUGHTBY), daughter of William (also see) of Ogden Twp. They settled in Ogden Twp. Children: 1. ARTHUR D.; 2. FRED C.; 3. JOHN W.; 4. GRACE S.; 5. HARRY. Ref: P&BA-Len pg. 773-4.

BALZMIER, ELIZABETH (See Henry H. Samsen)

BANCROFT, CLARA (See Addison Ganun)

BANCROFT, CORNELIUS, son of NELEY (following), came to Rome Twp., Lenawee Co., Mich. with his parents. He married 27 May 1855 to HARRIET M. (MOORE), daughter of William C. (also see), and settled in Rome Twp. Children: 1. WILLIAM W. b. 30 Feb. 1856 (m. Emma L. Thompson, dau. of Ebenezer, also see); 2. HENRIETTA L. (d. 22 July 1858); 3. ELLA J. (d. 21 Feb. 1860, infancy); 4. MARY E. b. 3 Oct. 1860 (m. John H. Wells, son of Gideon L., also see); 5. ROSA E. b. 25 Mar. 1863 (m. George E. Barnett, Boston, Mass.); 6. WALLACE G. b. 15 May 1865; 7. HERBERT O. b. 15 May 1867; 8. SARAH A. b. 14 Aug. 1869; 9. GEORGE L. b. 6 May 1873. Ref: P&BA-Len pg. 738-9.

BANCROFT, JAMES and wife, JANE, were parens of FLORA who married Ralph T. Pope, son of Arnold (also see) in Palmyra Twp., Lenawee Co., Mich. Ref: P&BA-Len pg. 578-9.

BANCROFT, JOSEPH Capt., son of MOSES, was a Revolutionary soldeer from Mass., and lived in Auburn, Worcester Co., Mass., where known son, NELEY (NEALY?), following, was born 22 May 1799.

BANCROFT, NELEY (NEALY?), son of Capt. JOSEPH (preceding), married in Mass. on 1 Nov. 1827 to SALLY "SALLY" (STONE) who was born in Bennington, VT on 6 Apr. 1800. They moved to Lockport, Niagara Co., NY, where they remained until 1835, then moved to Rome Twp., Lenawee Co., Mich. She died 9 Mar. 1852. Known son, CORNELIUS (preceding) was born 27 Aug. 1830, Lockport, NY. Neley married second on 4 Dec. 1852 to ANN (MOORE), a native of Orange Co., VT. He died 7 July 1870. Ref: P&BA-Len pg. 738-9.

BANGS, ALANSON, son of JOSEPH (following), was born 25 Sept. 1801 in Stamford, Delaware Co., NY; and married there 15 Dec. 1824 to MARY (MACKEY), daughter of Uriyon (also see). In 1825, they moved to Tecumseh Twp., Lenawee Co., Mich., but soon afterwards settled in Raisin Twp. Children: 1. JOSEPH b. 16 Nov. 1827 (d. 18 Jan. 1832); 2. BETSEY b. 11 Oct. 1829 (m. George W. Haight, Jackson, Mich.); 3. URIYON F. b. 20 Jan. 1831 (d. 8 Aug. 1842); 4. HULDAH M. b. 31 Aug. 1834 (m. Edward L. Russell, Raisin Twp.); 5. HANNAH J. b. 3 May 1836 (d. 12 Mar. 1837); 6. ALANSON B. b. 23 Oct. 1838 (following); 7. JOHN F. b. 4 May 1840 (d. 8 Aug. 1842); 8. MARY ELLEN b. 14 Nov. 1843 (d. 27 Oct. 1850). In the 1850 census of Raisin Twp., mother, HULDAH, age 65, is in the household. Alanson died 5 Feb. 1873. Ref: P&BA-Len pg. 910-11.

BANGS, ALANSON B., son of ALANSON (preceding), married 9 May 1866 in Tecumseh, Mich. to ALMEDA M. (COLLER), daughter of Thomas (also see), and settled in Raisin Twp. Children: 1. MONTELLO; 2. ARTHUR A. Ref: P&BA-Len pg. 910-11.

BANGS, JOHN, probably son of JOSEPH (following), was born 26 Mar. 1805 in Stamford, Delaware Co., NY, and married BETSEY, who was born ca. 1815, NY. In the 1850 census of Raisin Twp., Lenawee Co., Mich., they listed HARRIET, age 12; WILLIAM H., age 10; CHARLES W., age 8; CLARISSA A., age 5; FRANCIS A., age 3, all born Mich. Known daughter, MARY JOSEPHINE, b. 12 Feb. 1851, Raisin Twp. (m. Michael Smeltzer, also see). John died 25 Mar. 1869. Ref: P&BA-Len pg. 1059-60.

BANGS, JOSEPH was born 25 Apr. 1777, Stamford, Delaware Co., NY, and his wife, HULDAH (SILLIMAN), was born ca. 1785 in Conn. They moved to Tecumseh Twp., Lenawee Co., Mich., where he died 7 Jan. 1848. Known son, ALANSON (preceding); and probably also JOHN, preceding. Ref: P&BA-Len pg. 910-11.

BARBER, ELIJAH, born ca. 1808, and wife, MARY, born ca. 1807, both in NY, were listed in the 1850 census of Rome Twp., Lenawee Co., Mich. with AMELIA, age 18; ALFRED, age 16; OLIVE, age 13, all b. NY; & JOHN, age 7; CYRUS, age 5; EDWARD, age 2, last 3 b. Mich., in their household.

BARBER, JOHN, born ca. 1794, and wife, LAURA, born ca. 1800, both in Mass., were probably they listed in the 1840 census index of Adrian Twp., Lenawee Co., Mich.; and in the 1850 census, they listed HARRIET D., age 27, b. NY (m. Norman Geddes, also see). Note: In the 1840 census index, also listed were SYDNEY, Adrian Twp.; & TIMOTHY in Madison Twp.

BARBER, MARGARET C. born in 1808 in Catlin, Chemung Co., NY, had apparently came to Mich. with parents before 1838; & married Cornelius S. Randolph (also see). Ref: P&BA-Len pg. 397-8.

BARBER, SIMON, born ca. 1795, NY, was listed in the 1850 census of Palmyra Twp., Lenawee Co., Mich.

BARCH, CATHARINE (See Michael Linderman)

BARDWELL, SARAH J. (See David M. Blair)

BARGER, NELLIE (See James Welch)

BARHYDT, JEROME, of Holland descent, was listed in Albany Co., NY in 1800, and most likely in the area later in Schenectady Co. Known daughter, ELEANOR (m. Daniel Ketchum, also see, in Schenectady Co., NY). Ref; P&BA-Len pg. 359-60.

BARKER, ISAAC was born ca. 1788, Mass., and wife, HULDAH, was born ca. 1792, Rhode Island, and it is probably they listed in the 1840 census index of Seneca Twp., Lenawee Co., Mich.; and in the 1850 census, they listed PHILINDA, age 24; VINING?, age 22, both b. NY. Next door in census was ORION (following).

BARKER, JAMES, born ca. 1811, and wife, MARTHA, born ca. 1812, both in NY, were listed in the 1850 census of Adrian Twp., Lenawee Co., Mich., with CORDELIA, age 15, b. NY; MELISSA, age 10; WILLIAM, age 10?; ORSON, age 5; ERVIN, age 3; ELLEN, age 1, last 5 b. Mich.

BARKER, MARGARET (See Israel Allen)

BARKER, NEWMAN was listed in the 1840 census index of Clinton, Lenawee Co., Mich.

BARKER, ORION, probably son of ISAAC (preceding), was born ca. 1816, NY, and his wife, CATHARINE L., was born ca. 1817 in Mass, and in the 1850 census of Seneca Twp., Lenawee Co., Mich., they listed OLIVER P., age 5; EDGAR L., age 3, both b. Mich. in their household.

BARKER, ROSA E. (See John T. Colegrove)

BARKER, RUTH married in 1790 in Dutchess Co., NY to John Green (also see). Ref: P&BA-Len pg. 948-50.

BARKER, WILLIAM was listed in the 1840 census index of Ogden Twp., Lenawee Co., Mich.

BARKER, WILLIAM C. (See John Young)

BARKLEY, CHARLOTTE E. (See Pharis Sutton)

BARLOW, DANIEL (See Ezra Sanford)
BARLOW, LUCY (See John Blodgett)

BARNABY, AMBROSE, and wife, SALOME (TAYLOR), moved from Ithaca, Tompkins Co., NY to Raisinville, Monroe Co., Mich. before 1840. He died there at age 64; and she died age 54. Known daughter, HARRIET, born 15 July 1823, Ithaca, NY m. George W. Clark (also see). Ref: P&BA-Len pg. 818-9. Note: In the 1850 census of Ithaca, NY, there is an ALONZO born 1810, VT; and also there was an AMBROSE who d. Fredonia, Chautauqua Co., NY in 1829.

BARNARD (female) of Franklin Co., Mass. married Ebenezer Fisk (also see).

BARNARD, LUCIEN (LUCIUS?), born ca. 1805, and wife, Rebecca G., born ca. 1810, both in NY, settled in Palmyra Twp., Lenawee Co., Mich. before 1840; and in the 1850 census listed AUGUSTUS H., age 16; HARRIET A., age 15, both b. NY; & ELLEN S., age 9, b. Mich. in their household.

BARNARD, MIRIAM (See Cpt. William Perry)

BARNES, ABBIE was born in Conn., and married Oramon Tuttle, Sr., son of Noah, in Camden, Oneida Co., NY. Note: Early settlers in Camden, NY with Noah Tuttle, were BENJAMIN BARNES, SR.; BENJAMIN, JR.; & PHILIP, probably related to Abbie.

BARNES, BURTON S., son of HARMON (following), was born 19 Sept. 1844, Lapeer Co., Mich. He married 14 Feb. 1867, Tecumseh, Lenawee Co., Mich. to LOUISA M. (GILBERT), daughter of George (also see), and settled in Adrian, Mich. Children: 1. BERTIE; W. NETTIE; 3. LOUIS S. Ref: P&BA-Len pg. 429-30.

BARNES, C. W. was listed in the 1840 census index of Seneca Twp., Lenawee Co. Mich.

BARNES, ELIZA of Carroll Co., MD (See Joshua Grimes).

BARNES, ETHER was born ca. 1786 in NY, and by a first marriage had son, ETHER (following). He married second after 1839 to Mrs. FREELOVE (BROMLEY) SEELEY, born 1798, VT, widow of Jonathan Seeley (also see) of Seneca Twp., Lenawee Co., Mich. They resided in Medina Twp., where he died in 1866. Ref; P&BA-Len pg. 864.

BARNES, ETHER, son of ETHER (preceding), was born ca. 1824, and his wife, EVALINE, was born ca. 1832, both in NY, and in the 1850 census of Medina Twp., Lenawee Co., Mich. listed daughter, CHLOE, age 1, b. Mich., all in the household of father.

BARNES, FRANK (See William TenBroeck Schermerhorn)

BARNES, HARMON & wife, EMELINE, from Vermont, settled in Lapeer Co., Mich. before 1844. Known son, BURTON S. (preceding). Ref; P&BA-Len pg. 429-30.

BARNES, JENNIE of Seneca Twp., Lenawee Co., Mich., (possibly a daughter of C. W.??), married Andrew A. Russell (also see). Ref: P&BA-Len pg. 380-3.

BARNETT, GEORGE E. (See Cornelius Bancroft)

BARNETT, JOHN came from near St. Thomas, Upper Canada, to Dundee, Monroe Co., Mich. in 1851. His wife was JANE (RICE), who had married first in Canada to Moses Cowen (See Demon Cowen). John died shortly after moving to Michigan.

BARNEY, MIRIAM (See Amos Noyes)

BARNHART, WILLIAM, son of JACOB (who had come from Germany to New Jersey), was born in Burlington Co., NJ. He married SARAH (BROWN), and in 1810, moved to Wayne Co., NY. Six children, known daughter, MARY, b. 9 Jan. 1800, Burlington Co., NJ (m. John Eddy, also see). Ref; P&BA-Len pg. 659-60.

BARR, SAMUEL of Bedford, New Hampshire was the father of CHARLOTTE, born 8 Jan. 1810, Bedford (m. Josiah Stowell, also see, as his 3rd wife). Ref: P&BA-Len pg. 1072-3.

BARRAGER, LUCINDA (See Abner Hoag)

BARRIS, JOHN (See John Barrus)

BARRETT, (Given name not stated) of Williamstown, Berkshire Co., Mass., and wife, moved to Bennington Co., VT in 1818; and he died there in 1828. In 1830, his wife moved with the family back to Williamstown. About 1833, they removed to Blissfield Twp., Lenawee Co., Mich. Nine children, only known, SEYMOUR (following), b. 12 Feb. 1815, Williamstown. Ref: P&BA-Len pg. 584-5. Note: BENJAMIN; & HENRY (following) may also be sons. The following appears to be this family: In the 1850 census of Blissfield Twp., in the household of Albert Bliven, age 25, b. Ohio, and wife, JANE M. (Barrett?, age 25, b. VT), were also

Pioneer Families of Southeastern Michigan

CHLOE BARRETT, age 65, born Mass., with ROYAL, age 26; BENJAMIN, age 21 (following), both b. VT; also a MINERVA?, age 7, b. Mich. In the household next door, was CHARLES, age 18, b. NY.

BARRETT, ARMON born ca. 1807, Ohio, and wife, NANCY, born ca. 1817, Ireland, were listed in the 1850 census of Riga Twp., Lenawee Co., Mich. with MARY J., age 12; EMILY, age 11; DAVID, age 7, all b. Canada; & JANES, age 6; ISRAEL, age 4; JOHN, age 2, all b. Mich., in their household.

BARRETT, BENJAMIN, son of unknown (preceding), was born ca. 1829, VT, and it is probably he who married 14 July 1851 to CAROLINE (WATSON), also b. NY, in Adrian, Lenawee Co., Mich. Benjamin was killed when the locomotive in which he was the engineer was hit by a falling tree. Children: 1. HERBERT; 2. SEYMOUR (d. young); 3. ANNA; 4. ALMA b. 17 Oct. 1853, Blissfield (m. George L. Hoxsie, also see); 5. SEYMOUR (2d); 6. LAURA. Ref: P&BA-Len pg. 219-20.

BARRETT, CHRISTOPHER born ca. 1790, and wife, ANN, born ca. 1792, both in England, were listed in the 1850 census of Raisin Twp., Lenawee Co., Mich. with CHRISTOPHER, age 12, b. Mich., in their household. Also note WILLIAM (following).

BARRETT, GAIUS was a native of Conn., and a pioneer to Stillwater, Oneida Co., NY, where he died over age 90. Known daughter, LAURA, b. Conn. (m. Orrin or Owen Morrison, also see, Oneida Co., NY.

BARRETT, HENRY born ca. 1816, NY, and wife, EMELINE, born ca. 1828, Mass., were listed in the 1850 census of Blissfield Twp., Lenawee Co., Mich., with LUCY, age 3, in the household of SEYMOUR (following).

BARRETT, ISRAEL born ca. 1809, and wife, SALLY, born ca. 1820, both in NY, were "pioneers of Blissfield Twp., Lenawee Co., Mich.; and in the 1850 census of Blissfield, listed DAVID, age 11; EMILY, age 9; EDWARD, age 7; ALICE, age 8/12, all b. Mich. Known daughter, JENNIE (b. after 1850? m. John William Brown, also see, in Dec. 1869.) Ref: P&BA-Len pg. 989-90.

BARRETT, JONAS born ca. 1811, and wife, MARGARET, born ca. 1815, both in NY, were listed in the 1850 census of Macon Twp., Lenawee Co., Mich., with MARIA, age 14; EMILY, age 11; JOHN, age 8. all b. NY; & SIBLY? (male), age 3/12, b. Mich. in their household.

BARRETT, SEYMOUR, son of Unknown (preceding), was born ca. 1815 in Mass., and he brought his mother & 8 brothers & sisters to what is now Blissfield Twp., Lenawee Co., Mich. from Mass. in 1833. He married 9 Dec. 1840 in Blissfield to SOPHIA (PARKER), daughter of Ira. In the 1850 census, HENRY (preceding) and his family were in the household. Ref: P&BA-Len pg. 584-5.

BARRETT, WILLIAM born ca. 1815, England, and wife, SALLY A., born ca. 1821, NJ, were listed in the 1850 census of Macon Twp., Lenawee Co., Mich. with WILLIAM, age 16; ELLEN, age 10; JACOB, age 8; MARY, age 3; CHARLES H., age 5/12, all b. Mich. in their household.

BARROW, JAMES of Blissfield, Mich. (See John L. Knapp).

BARRUS, DELLENCE (DELANCY), probably son of WILLIAM[1], was born ca. 1801, NY, and came to Lenawee Co., Mich. before 1836. He married probably in Rome Twp. to EMILY (SMITH), daughter of David (also see), born ca. 1820, NY. The sketch stated he died in 1849, but that is apparently an error, as he is listed in the 1850 census of Rome Twp., with the following in the household: LEROY, age 14; HARRIET A., age 11 (m. 1859 to Charles Teachout, also see); LUTHER, age 7; LUKE, age 5; ESTHER E., age 3; HEPSEY, age 1, all b. Mich. Ref: P&BA-Len pg. 853-4.

BARRUS, JOHN born ca 1785, and wife, HANNAH, born ca. 1785, both in New Jersey, are listed in the 1850 census of Macon Twp., Lenawee Co., Mich., possibly as "Barris," as it is difficult to read.

BARRUS, WILLIAM[1] Rev. came to Lenawee Co., Mich. at an early date, and it was either he or son, WILLIAM[2] (following), listed in the 1840 census index of Rome Twp., adjacent to DELLENCE (preceding). He and his wife moved to Dane Co., Wisc. where he died at age 75.

BARRUS, WILLIAM[2], son of WILLIAM[1] (preceding), was born ca. 1813, New Hampshire, and married MARY A. (ALLEN), born ca. 1811, NY, probably daughter of Rhoda Allen (age 70, b.NY), who was in their household in the 1850 census of Rome Twp., Lenawee Co., Mich. They also listed CELIA, age 13; & JULIA b. 22 Aug. 1839 (m. Marshall Reed, also see). In 1888, they moved to Adrian. Ref: P&BA-Len pg. 1191-2.

BARTHOLOMEW, ABRAHAM & wife, JANE (HAUVER), moved from New York to Dover Twp., Lenawee Co., Mich. in 1855. Only child, CATHERINE, born 4 Sept. 1843, Cayuga Co., NY (m. Oscar Abbott, also see). Ref: P&BA-Len pg. 640-1.

BARTHOLOMEW, ALBERT J. was born in Madison Co., NY; and married there to NANCY (SMITH), who was born Hartford, Conn.; and they remained until 1854, then moved to Jefferson Co., Wisc. He died in 1868; and she died 24 Jan. 1888, Whitewater, Wisc. Known son, S. J. (following). Ref: P&BA-Len pg. 286-7.

BARTHOLOMEW, S. J., son of ALBERT J. (preceding), was born 22 June 1840 in Madison Co., NY, and moved to Wisconsin with his parents, where he served in the Civil War. He married 6 July 1870 to EMILY (MORRISON), daughter of Orrin (also see); and in 1873, moved to Pottawottamie Co., IA. In 1880, they removed to Riga Twp., Lenawee Co., Mich. Children: 1. JOHN C.; 2. LOUISA W. Ref: P&BA-Len pg. 286-7.

BARTLETT, ABRAHAM came to Connecticut from England in Colonial times; and married SUBMIT (EVITS). They later moved to West Stockbridge, Mass. where they remained. Known son, ISAAC A. (following). Ref: P&BA-Len pg. 1165-7.

BARTLETT, CATHARINE married Amos Miller & moved from Moravia, Cayuga Co., NY to Bridgewater, Washtenaw Co., Mich. in 1837. Ref: P&BA-Len pg. 1003-4.

BARTLETT, ELLIE (See John S. Clark)

BARTLETT, ISAAC A., son of BRAHAM (preceding), went with his parents at age 10 from Conn. to Mass. He served in the Revolutionary War. He married MELINDA (CAMP), daughter of John (also see); and they lived first in West Stockbridge, Mass., and after the birth of 9 children, removed to Augusta, Oneida Co., NY. They remained for a time, then moved to Madison Co., NY; and afterwards to Pompey Hill,

Onondaga Co., NY; then in 1844 to Peterboro, Madison Co., NY. He died there in Mar. 1847, and she died in Nov. 1848. Children: 1. JOHN C. (d. LaGrange Co., Ind.); 2. EUNICE (m. Isaac Jackson, d. Augusta, NY); 3. MELINDA (m. Luther Howe, Ft Wayne, Ind.); 4. RUTH (m. J. G. Curtis, Peterboro, NY); 5. SARAH (m/1 Charles Crane; m/2 Dr. Wm. Bradley, Greece, Monroe Co., NY); 6. ABRAHAM (d. Syracuse, NY); 7. ACHSAH (unmarried); 8. ELIZABETH (unmarried); 9. PHEBE (m. Wm. J. Curtis, Pompey Hill, NY); 10. ISAAC A. Jr. b. 12 June 1809, Augusta, NY (visited Mich. several times, finally settled in Ogden Twp., Lenawee Co., Mich. ca. 1862, unmarried). Ref: P&BA-Len pg. 1165-7.

BARTLETT, PHINEAS born ca. 1811, married MARY ANN (ROY), and resided in Washtenaw Co., Mich. by 1842. In 1868, they moved to Woodstock Twp., Lenawee Co., Mich., where she died at age 63; and he was still living in 1888, age 77. Known daughter, MABEL, b. Sept. 1842, Washtenaw Co., Mich. (m. William Davison, also see). Ref: P&BA-Len pg. 613-4.

BARTLETT, SAMUEL of Vermont was the father of MARY who was born in 1779 & married Samuel Hoyt (also see). Ref: Pioneer & Patriot Families of Bradford Co., Penn., by C. F. Heverly, 1913.

BARTLETT, THOMAS and wife, CATHARINE, were parents of LOUIS born 26 Apr. 1812 (See William Hood).

BARTOW, ALICE C. (See Thomas B. Eddy)

BASCOM, GEORGE D., b. ca. 1810, and wife, SARAH S. (TAYLOR), b. ca. 1814, both in Vermont, married in Raisin Twp., Lenawee Co., Mich. on 1 May 1836. In the 1850 census of Adrian Twp. Lenawee Co., Mich., they listed LUCRETIA, age 13; HARRIET T., age 10 (m. Andrew Hood, also see); JULIA L., age 9; GEORGE E., age 7; LUCY S., age 5; MARY J., age 2, (and mother of Sarah), Hannah Taylor, age 70, b. Mass., in their household. Ref: P&BA-Len pg. 188-9.

BASS, POLLY was the granddaughter of JONATHAN who was a Minute Man at Lexington and served in the Continental Army during the Revolution from Mass. Polly married Dr. Consider H. Stacey (also see).

BASSETT, ALBERT, probably son of NATHANIEL (following), was born ca. 1817, and wife, MARY, was born ca. 1821, both in NY, and in the 1850 census of Madison Twp., Lenawee Co., Mich., they listed HELEN M., age 1/12, b. Mich.

BASSETT, ARTEMAS, son of WILLIAM (following), was born 19 June 1782 in Uxbridge, Mass. (census said RI?), and moved with his parents to New Hampshire. He married there on 28 Mar. 1805 to SARAH (HARKNESS), daughter of Nathan (also see). They were Quakers. They moved from New Hampshire to Starksboro, VT, and before 1850, moved to Adrian Twp., Lenawee Co., Mich. He died age 77, and she died age 85. There were 2 sons & 4 daughters, known son, NATHAN H. (following). Ref: P&BA-Len pg. 1147-8. Also note ERASTUS (following).

BASSETT, EBENEZER, born ca. 1821, NY, was listed in the 1850 census of Madison Twp., Lenawee Co., Mich. He may relate to NATHANIEL (following).

BASSETT, ERASTUS, born ca. 1811, and wife, EMELINE, born ca. 1821, both in NY, were listed in the 1850 census of Hudson Twp., Lenawee Co., Mich. with FRANCIS M., age 12; ANNE M., age 10, both b. NY; & MARY M., age 7; BENJAMIN F., age 5; ERASTUS M., age 2, last 3 b. Mich., in their household.

BASSETT, LYDIA (See Fletcher Sizer)

BASSETT, NATHAN H., son of ARTEMAS (preceding), born 3 Mar. 1812, Cheshire Co., NH, moved to VT with his parents. He came to Medina, Lenawee Co., Mich. in 1833, and he married 15 Sept. 1836 to ADELIA (WEBB), probably daughter of Ezekiel (also see). In 1850, they were in Hudson Twp., Lenawee Co., Mich., and in 1855, they moved to Adrian Twp. Children: 1. WILLIAM J. b. Sept. 1837 (d. 16 Aug. 1869, Indian Terr.); 2. ALBERT H. b. 15 Sept. 1842 (m. Hallie James, dau. of Asa, lived Illinois); 3. EDGAR A. b. 29 Aug. 1844 (m. Drum, Ashland, Dak.); 4. FRANCIS M. b. 21 Nov. 1849 (d. 16 Aug. 1855). Ref: P&BA-Len pg. 1147-8.

BASSETT, NATHANIEL, born ca. 1786, and wife, MARY, born ca. 1787, both in NY, were listed in the 1850 census of Madison Twp., Lenawee Co., Mich., with GEORGE, age 23, b. NY; & CHARLES, age 20, b. Mich. in the household. Adjacent was ALBERT (preceding); also note EBENEZER. Ref: P&BA-Len pg. 1147-8.

BASSETT, WILLIAM & wife, MARGERY, moved from Mass. to New Hampshire, and they were parents of ARTEMAS (preceding). Ref: P&BA-Len pg. 1147-8.

BATEMAN, ABRAHAM, son of DANIEL (following), was born ca. 1818, England, and married there in 1842 to RACHEL (RATHBUN) who was born in Yorkshire, ca 1808; and they came to the US in May of 1850. They were in Ridgeway Twp., Lenawee Co., Mich. in the 1850 census. She died in Franklin Twp. in 1868, age 60. He married second to Mrs. ELIZABETH (CURTIS) LIGDEN, daughter of Samuel and widow of James (see both). No children were mentioned. Ref: P&BA-Len pg. 747-8.

BATEMAN, ALFRED, born ca. 1801, and wife, SAMANTHA, born ca. 1803, both in VT, were listed in the 1850 census of Adrian Twp., Lenawee Co., Mich. with FRANCIS, age 22, b. VT; CAROLINE, age 20; MARCUS, age 18; ANALIZA, age 12; ABIGAIL, age 10; ROLLIN, age 6, all b. NY, in the household.

BATEMAN, DANIEL & wife, ANN (HEIRST), were natives of Leeds, England, & he died there age 56, and she died age 44. Of 10 children, 2 d. infancy, names not stated. Known son, ABRAHAM (preceding). Ref: P&BA-Len pg. 747-8.

BATEMAN, THOMAS, born ca. 1813, and wife, ELIZABETH, born ca. 1815, possibly both born Kentucky (difficult to read), were in the 1850 census of Blissfield Twp., Lenawee Co., Mich. with CHRISTOPHER, age 16; ANN, age 14; JANE, age 11; MARY, age 9, all born KY; and NANCY, age 7; WILSON, age 6; MARTHA, age 4; JEPTHA, age 6/12, all born Mich., in the household.

BATES, ALTHERIA (See John Hatter)
BATES, AURILLA (See RUTH ERILLA, dau. of WINSLOW, following).
BATES, CALEB, son of DANIEL (following), was born 8 Nov. 1821, Erie Co., NY. He married in Cattaraugus Co., NY in 1844 to MALINTHA (POWELL), daughter of

Pioneer Families of Southeastern Michigan

Stephen (also see), and removed to Rome Twp., Lenawee Co., Mich. Children: 1. DANIEL P. b. 17 July 1845 (m. Emily Stearns; d. 23 Feb 1887); 2. JULIET b. 13 Oct. 1846 (m. Ervin Sayers, also see); 3. ELNORA P. (m. Wm. H. Hood, Rome Twp.). Ref: P&BA-Len pg. 551-2.

BATES, DANIEL, son of STEPHEN (following), was born 8 Aug. 1800 in Pownal, VT, and moved with parents to Otsego Co. & Erie Co., NY. He married 11 Oct. 1818 to PRISCILLA (COLE), daughter of Peleg (also see). In 1835, they moved from Clarence, Erie Co., NY to Rome Twp., Lenawee Co., Mich. He died 13 Jan. 1877, age 77y/6mo; and she was living in 1888 in Woodstock Twp. with a daughter, Mrs. Rexford. Nine children, those known: Eldest, WINSLOW (following); CALEB (preceding); PHEBE D. b. 29 Dec. 1828, Erie Co., NY (m. Zebulon Watson, also see); DAUGHTER (m. Rexford, Woodstock Twp., she may be one of them named below). In the 1850 census of Rome Twp., in their household was EPHRAIM, age 17; SOPHIA, age 14, both b. NY; MARTHA, age 11; MARIETTE, age 6, both b. Mich. Ref: P&BA-Len pg. 551-2; 567-8; 1124-5.

BATES, FIDELIA (See Charles Ford)

BATES, FRANKLIN of Tecumseh, Lenawee Co., Mich., married MATILDA (McCULLEY) of Raisin Twp., in Blissfield, 11 Apr. 1852.

BATES, HARRISON, born ca. 1817, and wife, ELIZA, born ca. 1818, both in NY, were listed in the 1850 census of Rome Twp., Lenawee Co., Mich., with ALTHURA, age 6; & SUSAN, age 2, both b. Mich., in their household.

BATES, JAMES C., son of JOHN H. (following), born ca. 1820, and wife, DIANTHA, born ca. 1823, both in NY, were listed in the 1850 census of Rome Twp., Lenawee Co., Mich., with PERRY W., age 6; MARTIN C., age 4; CAROLINE, age 1/12, all b. Mich., in their household.

BATES, JOHN H. was born ca. 1777 in Rhode Island, and his wife, CHARLOTTE, was born ca. 1782, Mass., and they resided in New York before coming to Rome Twp., Lenawee Co., Mich. before 1840. In the 1850 census, they were in the household of son, JAMES C. (preceding); probably son, PERRY W. (following).

BATES, JOHN T. married CAROLINE H. (THOMPSON) in Cortland Co., NY, and she died there in 1863, age 37. Known daughter, ATLANTA A., born 5 Nov. 1853, Cortland Co. (m. James Updike, Jr. also see). John T. married second to SALINE (COYLE) and they moved to Tecumseh, Lenawee Co., Mich., where he died 31 July 1877, age 63. She returned to Homer, NY, where she resided in 1888. Ref: P&BA-Len pg. 249-50.

BATES, P. P. (See David S. Mather)

BATES, PERRY W., probably son of JOHN H. (preceding), born ca. 1818, NY, and wife, ESTHER, born ca. 1831, NY, were listed in the 1850 census of Rome Twp., Lenawee Co., Mich., 2 doors from Daniel C., with MARY, age 1, b. Mich., in the household.

BATES, PHILIP M., son of WINSLOW (following), was born 6 Oct. 1849, Rome Twp., Lenawee Co., Mich. He married EMILY (SMITH), daughter of David, Jr. (also see) on 25 Dec. 1872 in Rome Twp. Daughter, FLORENCE M., b. 12 Jan. 1874. Ref: P&BA-Len pg. 554-5.

BATES, PHINEAS. born ca. 1815, Ohio?, was listed as head of household in the 1850 census of Ogden Twp., Lenawee Co., Mich., with ABIGAIL, age 60, probably his mother, also b. Ohio, in the household. There was a man by this name listed in the 1840 census index of Milford Twp., Oakland Co., Mich.

BATES, STEPHEN, son of FRANCIS (whose father came from England to Rhode Island), was born in Rhode Island; and he served in the Revolution. He married PHEBA, and after the War, they first went to VT, and then to Lisbon, Otsego Co., NY. In 1811, they removed to Newstead, Erie Co., NY, where he died in 1850, age 85; and she died age 75. Known son, DANIEL (preceding). Ref: P&BA-Len pg. 551-2 & 567-8. Also note JOHN (preceding).

BATES, VANILLA (See Elijah Kilburn)

BATES, WINSLOW, son of DANIEL (preceding), married LUCINA (SWEET), daughter of Philip (also see) on 5 Apr. 1843, Rome Twp., Lenawee Co., Mich. Children: 1. d. infancy; 2. LYDIA P. b. 4 Apr. 1845 (m. Henry Pearson, Adrian); 3. MARY E. b. 15 Feb. 1848 (m. Oliver H. Beach, Rome Twp.); 4. PHILIP M. (preceding); 5. E. MADORA b. 4 June 1852 (m. Fred A. Knight, Rome Twp.); 6. DANIEL W. b. 27 Oct. 1854 (m. Ella Lapham); 7. RUTH ERILLA b. 7 Feb. 1857 (m. Seymour Kuney, son Christian, also see). Ref: P&BA-Len pf. 554-5 & 567-8.

BATTERSON, T. J. (See Ephraim Wilder)

BATTEY, MARY, age 75, born Mass., was listed in the 1850 census of Raisin Twp., Lenawee Co., Mich. in household of Elijah Brownell (also see).

BAXTER, MARTHA of Troy, Bradford Co., Penn. (See Jeremiah Wilsey).

BAY. DANIEL was born ca. 1802, and wife, CATHARINE (BIDDLE), was born ca. 1805, both in Wurtemburg, Germany, where they married. He served 8 yrs. in the German Army. About 1832, after the birth of 2 children, they came to Baltimore, MD, and in 1833, moved to Blissfield Twp., Lenawee Co., Mich. In 1834, they moved to Ogden Twp.; and in the 1850 census of Ogden Twp., his name was spelled "Bye." He died 11 Feb. 1877, age 75, and she died 9 July 1886, age 82. Children: 1. CALEB (served Mexican & Civil War, lived Baltimore, MD); 2. JACOB b. ca. 1833 (went to Calif. in 1852 served Civil WAr, 4th Calif. Cav., killed by Indians); 3. SOPHIA b. ca. 1836; 4. DANIEL b. ca. 1838; 5. BARBARA b. ca. 1840 (m. Clark Boone, Blissfield Twp.); 6. FREDERICK (following); 7. WILLIAM b. ca. 1848 (Ogden Twp.). Ref: P&BA-Len pg. 755-6.

BAY, FREDERICK, son of DANIEL (preceding), was born 12 Feb. 1843, Ogden Twp., Lenawee Co., Mich., and enlisted 16 Apr. 1861 in the Adrian Cadets, Co. K., 1st Mich. Inf. He also served Co. C., 18th Mich. Inf. He married 17 Nov. 1866 to ATHALEEN (BRADLEY), daughter of Adam (also see). She died in 1872, leaving a daughter, 1. LORA. Frederick married second 17 Oct. 1874 to ELEANOR E. (FARR), daughter of Sylvester (also see). Children: 2. ALENA A.; 3. MARION E.; 4. ELEANOR E.; 5. FREDERICK B.; 6. ETHELBERT S. Ref: P&BA-Len pg. 755-6.

BAYLESS also see BALIS & BALUSS
BAYLESS, JAMES A. (See Stephen Allen)

BAYLOR J. H. (See Van Rensselaer J. Osborn)
BAYLOR, MARTIN E. married MARIA LYDIA (WELCH), daughter of James (also see); had children MAUD E.; EARL. They lived in Rensselaer, Ind.

BEACH also see BEECH
BEACH, AMOS, born ca. 1810, and wife, SALLY, born ca. 1807, both in NY, were listed in the 1840 census index of Rome Twp., Lenawee Co., Mich.; and in the 1850 census listed ADONIRAM A., age 19; LUCRETIA, age 17; ISAAC I., age 15, all b. NY; and JOHN W., age 13; OLIVER H., age 10; ANALIZA, age 4, last 3 born Mich.
BEACH, ELIZABETH, born Ontario Co., NY, married there to ? Russell (also see) who was born 30 Aug. 1803, Ontario Co. Ref: P&BA-Len pg. 660-2.
BEACH, GEORGE born ca. 1825, and wife, BETSEY, born ca. 1825, both in NY, were listed in the 1850 census of Medina Twp., Lenawee Co., Mich. with NEWTON, age 1, b. Mich. in the household.
BEACH, HESTER, born 8 Oct. 1810, Rockland Co., NY, married 25 Nov. 1832 to John R. Gurnee (also see). Ref: P&BA-Len pg. 954-5.
BEACH, HIGHLAND (HILAND) was born ca. 1785, and it is probably he listed as "Hilan" in the 1840 census index of Lasalle Twp., Monroe Co., Mich. He was in Fairfield Twp., Lenawee Co., Mich. in the 1850 census, and listed MARIA, age 38, b. Maryland; LOYAL B., age 14; WILLIAM, age 12; JAMES, age 8; ANNA M., age 2, all b. Mich. HIGHLAND (following) probably related.
BEACH, HIGHLAND born ca. 1823, and wife, ALMEDA, born ca. 1831, both in Mich., were listed in the 1850 census of Hudson Twp., Lenawee Co., Mich. with FRANCES, age 2; KATE, age 1, both b. Mich., in their household.
BEACH, IRENE (See Charles H. Kendrick)
BEACH, MARIETTA MATILDA Mrs. of Livingston Co., Mich. was the daughter of Jesse Maxson (also see) of Pittsford Twp., Hillsdale Co., Mich. Ref: P&BA-Len pg. 1155-6.
BEACH, NILES C. born ca. 1823, NY, and wife, DELILAH B., born ca. 1827, Rhode Island, were listed in the 1850 census of Hudson Twp., Lenawee Co., Mich. with EMMA A., age 1/12, b. Mich.; and JANE, age 23, b. NY, in their household.
BEACH, OLIVER H. (See Winslow Bates)
BEACH, REUBEN (age 3?) and wife, ROSA? M., born ca. 1825, both born NY, were listed in the 1850 census of Hudson Twp., Lenawee Co., Mich. with MARY M., age 15; MARTHA, age 11; ALBERT R., age 10; GEORGE, age 9; JAMES, age 5, all born NY, in the household.
BEACH, ROSWELL was born ca. 1795, NY, and wife, ANN (KING), was born ca. 1810 in Ohio. They moved from Ohio in 1839, and were listed in the 1850 census of Hudson Twp., Lenawee Co., Mich. with MARIAH, age 20; LOUISA b. 8 July 1831, Erie Co., Ohio (m/1 John Kesler; m/1 Abraham Lerch, also see); ELTON, age 14, all b. Ohio; and GEORGE, age 7; BYRON, age 3, both b. Mich., in the household. Ref: P&BA-Len pg. 1032-3. Also note NILES & REUBEN, preceding.
BEACH, SIDNEY born ca. 1815 in NY was listed in the 1850 census of Madison Twp., Lenawee Co., Mich.

BEACHMAN, HORACE K. (See John R. Gurnee)

BEADLE, ABRAHAM died in Middletown, Orange Co., NY, age 90 yrs.; and it may be he listed in the 1800 census index of Ulster Co., NY. Known daughter, NANCY, b. 1803, Delaware Co., NY (m. Silas Landon, also see). Ref: P&BA-Len pg. 367-8.

BEAGLE also see BIGLE
BEAGLE, BARBARA, born ca. 1831, Germany, was listed in the 1850 census of Adrian, Lenawee Co., Mich. in the household of the Howard family; and it is probably she listed again, age 20, in the 1850 census of Madison Twp.
BEAGLE, CATHARINE, age 30, born Germany, was listed in the 1850 census of Adrian Twp., Lenawee Co., Mich., adjacent to GEORGE (following), possibly as head of household (entry is not clear). Also see JOHN, following.
BEAGLE, CAROLINE, age 14, born Penn., was listed in the 1850 census of Adrian Twp., Lenawee Co., Mich., in a Cornell household. See HENRY, following.
BEAGLE, CHRISTIANA, age 11, born Penn., was listed in the 1850 census of Adrian Twp., Lenawee Co., Mich. See HENRY, following.
BEAGLE, CHRISTOPHER was born ca. 1809, Germany, and settled first in Maryland, then moved to Blissfield, Lenawee Co., MIch. in 1836. By first marriage had children: 1. CAROLINE b. ca. 1830, MD (m. Charles Myers, Adrian); 2. CATHARINE C. b. 28 Dec. 1833, Baltimore, MD (m. FREDERICK G. BEAGLE, following); 3. JUSTINA (m. John Brooker, South Bend, Ind.); 4. MARY b. ca. 1839. Christopher married again and had 7 children, names not stated. Ref: P&BA-Len pg. 1198-9.
BEAGLE, FREDERICK G., son of GEORGE (following), was born 11 Feb. 1834, Baden, Germany, and came to the US with his parents. He married in Lenawee Co., Mich. to CATHERINE C. (BEAGLE), daughter of CHRISTOPHER (preceding) of Adrian. Children: 1. CATHERINE (m. D. P. Wheeler, East Saginaw, Mich.); 2. CHARLES L. (Detroit); 3. ELLA (d. 3 May 1876, age 18); 4. IDA (m. Dr. G. G. Mosher, Kansas City); 5. MARY; 6. FREDERICK (Jackson, Mich.; 7. BURTON H. (Kalamazoo, Mich.) Ref: P&BA-Len pg. 1197-8.
BEAGLE, GEORGE born ca. 1809, and wife, BARBARA, born ca. 1809, were natives of Baden, Germany, and came to the US in 1847, and almost immediately came to Lenawee Co., Mich. In the 1850 census of Madison Twp., Lenawee Co., Mich. they listed LEWIS, age 11; BARBARA, age 8; JOHN, age 6; CATHERINE, age 2. Known son, FREDERICK G., was listed in another household in 1850. Ref: 1197-8.
BEAGLE, HENRY born ca. 1810, and wife, ELIZABETH, born ca. 1812, both in Germany, were listed in the 1850 census of Adrian Twp., Lenawee Co., Mich. with MARY, age 10; ROSA, age 7; CHARLOTTE, age 5, all b. Penn., in the household. Note: CHRISTIANA, & CAROLINE, preceding.
BEAGLE, JOHN born ca. 1815, Germany, was listed in the 1850 census of Adrian Twp., Lenawee Co., Mich., in a household adjacent to GEORGE, preceding. Next to him is CATHARINE (preceding), age 30, also b. Germany, entry not clesr whether it is same household.

BEAL also see BEALS

Pioneer Families of Southeastern Michigan

BEAL, JOSEPH born ca. 1782, Mass., was listed in the 1850 census of Rollin Twp., Lenawee Co., Mich. in the household of Alanson Eddy, and wife, Lucretia (who was b. ca. 1812, NY, possibly a daughter of Joseph?).

BEAL, MARTHA was born 1808, NY (See Americus Smith). Note: They were listed a few doors from PORTER (following) in the 1850 census of Rollin Twp., Lenawee Co., Mich.

BEAL, MARTHA (See Walden Wing)

BEAL, PORTER was born ca. 1819, NY and his wife, SUSAN A. (BROWNELL), was born ca. 1823, Mass. They settled in Rollin Twp., Lenawee Co., Mich. before the 1840 census; and in the 1850 census listed MELVINA A., age 9; ELMIRA B. b. 11 July 1842 (m. Amos R. Cole, also see); JUDSON, age 3, all born Mich. Ref: P&BA-Len pg. 556-7.

BEAL, SILAS of Tecumseh, Lenawee Co., Mich., married ANGELINE E. (MALLERY) of Macon, in Franklin Twp. on 6 May 1858.

BEAL, WILLIAM, born ca. 1806, and wife, RACHEL, was ca. 1812, both in NY, came to Rollin Twp., Lenawee Co., Mich. by 1831. In the 1850 census of Rollin Twp., they listed WILLIAM J., age 17; JOSEPH O., age 15; MARY C. b. 27 Oct. 1848 (m. Oliver C. McLouth, also see), all born Mich. Ref: P&BA-Len pg. 1141.

BEAL, WARREN H., probably b. after 1850 (See Thomas F. Moore).

BEALS also see BEAL

BEALS, CALEB was born Plainfield, Mass., and married in Adams, Mass. to LYDIA (SHERMAN), daughter of Kelly of Berkshire Co. They moved to Moriah, Essex Co., NY where they remained for 16 years, then moved to western NY. In 1834, they removed to Adrian, Lenawee Co., Mich. He may have died prior to 1850, however one record said 1851, & another said 1855, Litchfield, Mich. while visiting a daughter. In the 1850 census of Dover Twp., Lenawee Co., Mich., Lydia, age 68, b. Mass., was listed in the household of Marvin E. Palmer, and wife, Phebe L. (b. ca. 1822, NY, possibly dau. of Lydia?). Lydia died in Mass., while on a visit, but was buried in Oakwood Cem., Lenawee Co., Mich. Of 7 children, 6 lived to maturity. Eldest son, KELLY S. (following); known daughter, SAMANTHA M. (m/1 9 June 1842 to Reuben Wheeler; m/2 Charles Dunham, see both). Ref: P&BA-Len pg. 214-5 & 842-3.

BEALS, DEBORAH (See Hezekiah Ford)

BEALS, KELLY S., son of CALEB (preceding), born 17 Apr. 1812 on Green Mountain in Mass., married in Adrian, Lenawee Co., Mich. on 21 Apr. 1836 to ADELINE M. (HATHAWAY), daughter of Jeptha (also see). They settled in Rollin Twp., Lenawee Co., Mich. Three children died young, only WILLIAM HENRY lived to age 5. Ref: P&BA-Len pg. 214-5.

BEALS, MARY (See Ebenezer Davenport)

BEALS, SAMUEL of Wayne Co., NY (See James Patrick).

BEAMAN, ELIJAH & wife, THANKFUL (NICHOLS), were residents of Lancaster, Mass. when known son, JOSHUA (following), was born. Elijah was the grandson of GAMALIEL who had settled Dorchester, Mass. Ref: P&BA-Len pg. 201-2.

BEAMAN, JOSHUA, son of ELIJAH (preceding), born Lancaster, Mass., remained there until 1787, then moved to Chester, VT. He married in 1791 to HANNAH (OLCOTT), daughter of Timothy (also see). Before 1814, they moved to Chautauqua or Franklin Co., NY. Fourteen children, known son, FERNANDO C. (following). Ref: P&BA-Len pg. 201-2.

BEAMAN, FERNANDO C., son of JOSHUA (preceding), born 28 June 1814, Chautauqua Co., NY., married 10 May 1841 in Brockport, NY to MARY (GOODRICH), daughter of Ira (also see). Fernando C. died 27 Sept. 1882, Adrian, Lenawee Co., Mich. Children: 1. MARY A. b. 4 Mar. 1842, Adrian (m. Rienzi Baker); 2. EDWARD C. b. 12 Mar. 1845 (d. 5 July 1846, Adrian); 3. ROSCOE W. b. 18 July 1847 (d. 31 Aug. 1877, Chicago, IL.) Ref: P&BA-Len pg. 201-2.

BEAN, ALONZO (See William W. Tilton)

BEARDWOOD, ANNA (See John Iveson[1])

BEATTIE, JAMES and wife, CATHARINE (BROADFOOT), of Galloway, Scotland, were parents of ANN born 12 July 1831, Galloway, who came alone to the US in 1854 to marry Robert Sloan (also see). Ann married second to William King (also see). Ref: P&BA-Len pg. 977.

BECKER, MARY L. (See Capt. Charles R. Miller)
BECKER, SARAH M. (See Samuel Nash)

BECKEY, MARSHALL N. (See Josiah Carpenter)

BECKLEY, ARDIN born ca. 1808, Conn., and wife, MARTHA, born ca. 1811, NY, were listed in the 1850 census of Madison Twp., Lenawee Co., Mich. with BETSEY, age 18; EZRA, age 16; DANIEL, age 14; CLARISSA, age 12, all born Ohio; and MARILLA, age 8; EMILY, age 7, both b. Mich., in their household.

BECKLEY, CHRISTOPHER & wife, ELIZABETH (BIGLE. also see BEAGLE), were born in Baden, Germany. After the birth of 3 children, they came to New York City. They later came to Macon Twp., Lenawee Co., Mich. and made their home with son, JOHN (following). Christopher died in 1868, age 89, and she died in 1865, age 75. Ref: P&BA-Len. pg. 325.

BECKLEY, JOHN, son of CHRISTOPHER (preceding), was born 25 Oct 1825, New York City. He came to Macon Twp., Lenawee Co., Mich. where he married MARGARET (SCHREYER), daughter of Frederick J. (also see). No children listed. Ref: P&BA-Len pg. 325.

BECKWITH, MARIA (See Benjamin Hornbeck)

BEDELL, A. B. (See Henry F. Townsend)

BEDELL, ABRAHAM born in France, came to America with French troops under General D'Estaing during the Revolution and remained, settling in Sussex Co., NJ, where he married POLLY (OSBORNE). They lived out their lives there. Known sons, JACOB (following); ABRAM b. ca. 1797 (lived with Jacob in Hector, Tompkins Co., NY in 1850 census). Ref: P&BA-Len pg. 753-4.

BEDELL, ALVA E., son of ZACHARIAH (following), born 17 Oct. 1852, Luzerne Co., Penn., came with his parents to Woodstock Twp., Lenawee Co., Mich. where he married 31 Dec. 1874 to BETSEY B. (WHEATON), daughter of Peter M. (also see). They settled in

Woodstock Twp. Known children: 1. BERTHA R. b. 22 Apr. 1876; 2. JAMES M. b. 14 Sept. 1880; 3. MILFRED A. b. 29 Oct. 1887. Ref: P&BA-Len p g. 601-2.

BEDELL, AUGUSTINE, son of JACOB (following), was born 1 May 1823, Sussex Co., NJ, and came alone to Tecumseh, Lenawee Co., Mich. in 1851. He married in 1854 in Cambridge Twp, Lenawee Co., Mich. to ADENIA (ONSTED), daughter of John (also see), and settled there. Daughter, EDITH A. (m. John Watters). Ref: P&BA-Len pg. 753-4.

BEDELL, DAVID, born ca. 1808, NY?, and wife, HANNAH, born ca. 1810, NJ, were listed in the 1850 census of Seneca Twp., Lenawee Co., Mich. with SUSANNA, age 21; PHEBE E., age 18; JOHN, age 16; LEWIS, age 14; CATHERINE, age 12, all b. NJ; amd SARAH E., age 10; CHARLES, age 4; LOUISA M., age 2; ROSETTA, age 1/12, last 4 b. Mich., in their household.

BEDELL, ELIZABETH H. (See James P. Hawley)

BEDELL, JACOB, son of ABRAHAM (preceding), was born 1787 in New Jersey; and he served in the War of 1812. His first wife died leaving 3 children. He married second to ELIZABETH (OHOUT), who died ca. 1826/7 leaving son, AUGUSTINE (preceding). Jacob moved to Hector, Tompkins Co., NY where he was listed in the 1850 census, age 63. In the household was Lydia Kirkpatrick (daughter?), age 27, with a son, Oscar, age 9. Also in the household was ABRAM, age 59, b. NJ. Jacob died in 1876, age 93, Tompkins Co., NY.

BEDELL, JOHN & wife, CATHERINE, were natives of New Jersey who moved to Penn., where they remained. Known son, ZACHARIAH (following). Ref: P&BA-Len pg. 601-2.

BEDELL, LEWIS H. Dr., son of ZACHARIAH (following), was born 14 June 1842, Rawson Twp., Luzerne Co., Penn.; and married there on 1 Nov. 1867 to OCTAVIA (BURR), daughter of John (also see). They moved to Morenci, Lenawee Co., Mich. Children: 1. LAURA G. b. 29 July 1869 (m. John W. McGee); 2. DOLLY b. 4. July 1877. Ref: P&BA-Len pg. 604-7.

BEDELL, WILLIAM & wife, CATHARINE (LEPPER), moved from near Utica, Oneida Co., NY to Ashtabula Co., O. after 1821, and remained there. Known daughter, SUSAN ADELINE, b. 8 June 1821, Utice (m. Galusha Case, also see). Ref: P&BA-Len pg. 911-2. Note: In the History of Ashtabula Co., Ohio, there is a HENRY, born 4 Sept. 1818, Amsterdam, Montgomery Co., NY, son of WILLIAM & MARGARET who had come to Orwell, Ashtabula Co. ca. 1842, with a family of 7 children.

BEDELL, ZACHARIAH, son of JOHN (preceding), born 14 June 1812, Sussex Co., NJ, moved to Rawson Twp., Luzerne Co., Penn. He married MARGARET (DRAKE), daughter of Jacob (also see). They removed to Woodstock Twp., Lenawee Co., Mich. He died in 1878, age 66; and she was still living in Woodstock in 1888. Known son, 1. Dr. LEWIS H. (preceding); 2. ALVA E. (preceding). Ref: P&BA-Len pg. 601-2 & 604-7.

BEDFORD, WILLIAM married first SARAH (ISLEY); and apparently married second to her sister, ANN (ISLEY), both daughters of William (also see). They resided in Evansville, Ind. Ref: P&BA-Len pg. 746-7.

BEEBE, CLARK born 1798, and wife, DOLLY, born ca. 1799, both in NY, were listed in the 1850 census of Franklin Twp., Lenawee Co., Mich. with WILLIAM, age 14; CHARLES, age 11; SARAH, age 9, all b. Mich., in their household.

BEEBE, DESIAH (See Peleg Joslyn)

BEEBE, FISKE (See William Whelan)

BEEBE, GEORGE of Waterford, Conn. accompanied Henry Manwaring (also see) to Fulton Co., Ohio in 1856. Note PAUL, following.

BEEBE, GIDEON born ca. 1806, Penn. and wife, BETSEY A., born ca 1815, Conn., were listed in the 1850 census of Hudson Twp., Lenawee Co. Mich. with HIRAM M., age 19; LEWIS M., age 10; CORNELIA G., age 8; HARRIET, age 4, all b. Mich., in their household.

BEEBE, LEVI M. of Franklin Twp., Lenawee Co., married NANCY (DEYO) of Adrian on 4 Dec. 1856.

BEEBE, LUCRETIA (See Dr. John D. Tripp)

BEEBE. MARTHA (See Joseph Kellogg)

BEEBE, PAUL and wife, MARY (ROGERS), were natives of Waterford, Conn. Known daughter, EUNICE (m. Isaac Manwaring, also see, before 1820). Ref: P&BA-Len pg. 922-4. Note GEORGE, preceding.

BEEBE, SOPHIA (See Thompson Halstead)

BEECH also see BEACH

BEECH, MARY M. (See John Hancock Carleton)

BEECHER, CYNTHIA D. (See Rev. Philo Tower)

BEECHER, SARAH was a native of Conn. and married Joseph Sperry (also see) before 1800; and she was a cousin of Rev. Lyman Beecher, father of Henry Ward Beecher. She resided in New Haven Conn., until after the death of her husband. She was a widow for 40 years; and died at the home of a son in Parkman, Ohio.

BEECHER, WILLIAM (See Gabriel Todd)

BEERS, CHARLES W. born ca. 1797, NY, and wife, KEZIAH, born ca. 1800, NJ, were listed in the 1840 census index of Adrian Twp., Lenawee Co., Mich. as "Bears." In the 1850 census, they listed STEPHEN age 19, b. NY (may be he who m. Mary Hood, daughter of William, also see, lived Adrian, then Nebraska); & MARY J., age 16; JOHN, age 12, both born Mich.

BEERS, DANIEL born ca. 1824, NY, was listed in the 1850 census of Medina Twp., Lenawee Co., Mich.

BEERS, HENRY and wife, MARGARET (McMURTY), of New Jersey may be they listed in the 1800 census index of Cayuga Co., NY. Known daughter, NANCY, b. Morristown, NJ (m. John Hood, also see, of Northumberland Co., Penn., and went to Orleans Co., NY ca. 1819); and possbily CATHERINE b. NJ or NY (m. Amsey L. McConnel, Orleans Co., NY, also see). Ref; P&BA-Len pg. 455-6.

BEERS, JABEZ A. was listed in the 1840 census index of Rome Twp., Lenawee Co., Mich.; and was not listed in 1850, though there was a MARY, age 11, b. Mich. listed in Rome Twp. in the household of Charles & Sarah Sly.

BEERS, JEPTHA W., probably son of CHARLES W. (preceding), was born ca. 1821, and his wife, LUCY A., was born ca. 1824, both in NY, and they listed in the 1850 census of Adrian Twp., Lenawee Co., Mich. CHARLES A., age 3; & HELEN J., age 2 (note NELLIE J., following), both b. Mich.

Pioneer Families of Southeastern Michigan

BEERS, NELLIE J. of Tecumseh, Lenawee Co., Mich. married Lavern I. Bidwell in Tecumseh in May 1866. This is probably same as HELEN J., in household of JEPTHA (preceding).

BEERS, STEPHEN (See William Hood) Also note CHARLES W., preceding.

BEEVERS, BENJAMIN was born ca. 1819, and wife, ELIZABETH (LEE), was born ca. 1824, both in Yorkshire, England, where they married and remained till after the birth of first 2 children. They came to Raisin Twp., Lenawee Co., Mich. by 1849. Of 12 children, some died young. Those known: 1. MARY A. b. ca. 1842; 2. WILLIAM b. 5 Nov. 1846; 3. ANN ELIZABETH b. 18 July 1849; 4. SARAH b. 6 May 1851 (m. Charles E. Dubois, also see); 5. ANNA b. 10 Jan. 1855; 6. GEORGE b. 23 Aug. 1856; 7. JANE b. 16 July 1857; 8. CAPITOLA b. 13 Apr. 1859; 9. HARRIET E. b. 8 July 1862 (See Hattie, following); 10. LEONA b. 15 Nov. 1869. Ref: P&BA-Len pg. 387-8.

BEEVERS, HATTIE, probably HARRIET in family of BENJAMIN, preceding (See David B. Osterhout).

BELAND, JOHN^1 and wife, THEODORA (KRENSENG), were natives of Bavaria, Germany where they remained. He died at age 63, and she died at age 98. Of 7 children, 6 remained in Bavaria. Son, #3. JOHN^2 b. 7 Nov. 1823 (following). Ref: P&BA-Len pg. 658-9.

BELAND, JOHN^2, son of JOHN^1, came alone to the US in 1853, and settled first in Mercer Co., Penn. where he married on 21 Apr. 1854 to CATHARINE (DENNINGER) who was born on 7 Sept. 1829, Bavaria, and had sailed on the same ship as John. That same year, they moved to Macon Twp., Lenawee Co., Mich. Children: 1. MAGGIE (m. John Gettz, also see); 2. EVA; 3. ANNA; 4. LIZZIE; 5. HENRY (m. Ida Martin, Macon Twp.); 6. FREDERICK (prob. he who m. Ida B. Martin, dau. of Michael J.); 7. ADAM; 8. JOHN W. Ref: P&BA-Len pg. 658-9.

BELCHER, ALFRED, son of ENOCH (following), was born 1 June 1822, Genesee Co., NY, and came to Mich. in 1833 with his parents. He married ca. 1850 to MARY A. (ROCKWELL), daughter of Hiram (also see) in Rollin Twp., Lenawee Co. He served in the Civil War in the Mechanic Corps. They settled in Rollin Twp. Children: 1. SALEM M. b. 15 Feb. 1851; 2. ELLEN A. b. 10 Mar. 1853 (m. Henry Page, Burlington, Coffey Co., KS); 3. JAMES b. 12 June 1855 (m. Celia Payne); 4. STEPHEN J. b. 28 Mar. 1866 (m. Dora Snyder). Ref: P&BA-Len pg. 969-70.

BELCHER, ANDREW was born 16 Mar. 1816, NY, and he married in Hudson Twp., Lenawee Co., Mich. on 4 Jan. 1852 to CATHERINE ANN (DITMARS), daughter of William V. (also see). Andrew died 9 Oct. 1857 in Hudson Twp. Children: 1. WILLIAM V. b. 2 Mar. 1854 (m. Ellen Johnson, Nebraska); 2. JOHN A. b. 19 Apr. 1857 (went to Colorado). Catherine Ann married second to Levi Jennings (also see). Ref: P&BA-Len pg. 533-4.

BELCHER, BENJAMIN born ca. 1823, Penn. and wife, ALMIRA, born ca. 1824, NY, were listed in the 1850 census of Raisin Twp., Lenawee Co., Mich. with CORDELIA, age 4; CORNELIA, age 4, both b. NY; & ELIZA A., age 1, b. Mich., in the household

BELCHER, ENOCH was born ca. 1789, Conn., and went to Genesee Co., NY as a young man. He served in the War of 1812 (and his father, name not stated, was said to have served in the Revolution). He married ELIZABETH "BETSEY" (BENNETT) who was born ca. 1790 in NY. In 1833, they moved to Adrian Twp., Lenawee Co., Mich.; and in 1834 to Rollin Twp. where she died at age 75. There were 9 children, only known: JOHN (following); ALFRED (preceding); & ASAPH b. ca. 1831 (in Enoch's household 1850 census of Rollin Twp.) A son, name not stated, lived in Indiana; and a daughter lived Woodbridge, Hillsdale Co., Mich. in 1888. Ref: P&BA-Len pg. 969-70 & 987-9. Also see HENRY, following.

BELCHER, HENRY, possibly son of ENOCH (preceding), born ca. 1812, and wife, ELVIRA, born ca. 1820, were listed adjacent to Enoch in the 1840 census index of Rollin Twp., Lenawee Co., Mich.; and in the 1850 census listed LUCY, age 10; ROENA, age 8; JOHN, age 6; WILLIAM, age 4; SARAH J., age 2; HIRAM, age 3/12, all born Mich., in their household.

BELCHER, ILEY (See Abial Lewis)

BELCHER, JOHN, son of ENOCH (preceding), was born 1818 in Verona, NY, and moved to Lenawee Co., Mich. with parents. He married on 3 Dec. 1847 to LUCENA (VAN AKIN), daughter of Hiram (also see), and they settled in Hudson Twp., Lenawee Co., Mich. where he died in 1860. Children: 1. THOMAS W. b. ca. 1843 (to Indianapolis, Ind.); 2. HOMER D. (Kent Co., Mich.); 3. CLARIE; 4. MARY (d. age 3 mos); 5. HARRY (d. age 14 mos); 6. JOHN HERBERT (d. age 10 yrs). Lucena married second to Samuel King (also see). Ref: PBA-Len pg 987-8.

BELCHER, PHEBE Mrs., born ca. 1812, NY, was head of household in the 1850 census of Hudson Twp., Lenawee Co., Mich., with EZRA, age 13; BETSEY A., age 11; SALLY C., age 9; JESSE B., age 7, all b. Mich., in her household.

BELDING, ABIGAIL (See Samuel Reynolds)

BELDING, CONSIDER was a pioneer of Ontario Co., NY, and was father of ESTHER who married Joel Whitney (alse see). Ref: P&BA-Len pg. 823-4.

BELL, ABIGAIL (See Obed Hervey, Jr.)

BELL, GEORGE L. (See Jessiah Westerman)

BELL, JONATHAN G. was born Cumberland, England and married there first to ANNA (SMITH) who died during their voyage to Canada, leaving 2 daughters. He married again in Canada to FRANCES (ROACH) who was born Cumberland, England in 1818. They moved to Portage Co., Ohio before 1851, and moved in 1855 to Seneca Twp., Lenawee Co., Mich. There were 7 sons; known son, JOSEPH R. (following). Ref: P&BA-Len pg. 976.

BELL, JOSEPH R., son of JONATHAN G. (preceding), was born 22 Dec. 1851 in Portage Co., Ohio, and moved with parents to Seneca Twp., Lenawee Co., Mich. He married 1 Jan. 1874 to MARY ANN (HAYWARD), daughter of Stephen (also see) of Seneca Twp. No children were listed. Ref: P&BA-Len pg. 976.

BELL, SARAH (See Tyson Bagerly)

BEMANDIEFER, ALLIE (See Robert Sloan)

BEMANDIFFER, MARY (See Eli E. Munn)

BEMIS, ABEL, born Vermont, and wife, ESTHER (CUMMINGS), born NY, were early settlers to Springfield, Lucas Co., Ohio. There were 10 children. She died 11 Oct. 1869, Whiteford, Monroe Co., MIch. at home of a son; and he died 20 Oct. 1873 at the home of daughter, MARIA b. 7 Jan. 1835, Springfield, Ohio (m. Henry Manwaring, also see). Known sons: JOSEPH (d. Civil War); WILLIAM (d. Civil War); CHARLES (served Civil War; afterwards lived in Whiteford, Monroe Co., Mich.). Ref: P&BA-Len pg. 922-4.

BEMISH, DORA (See Joseph E. Exelby)

BENEDICT, DANIEL, of Warwick, Orange Co., NY, had a will made 9 May 1822, & probated 10 Jan. 1823, that named wife, MARY; & sons: JOHN; JAMES; WOLLIS (WALLACE?); BENJAMIN; DANIEL; & THOMAS; & daughters: RUTH; HANNAH SMITH; MARY BLAUVELT; & RACHEL. Also mentioned was grandson, JAMES B. Sons, John & James were Executors, and witnesses were Ezra Sanford, Ezra S. Doty & James Burt. Note resemblance to JOHN, following.

BENEDICT, ISAAC and wife, SUSAN (SANFORD), came from Canada to Dover Twp., Lenawee Co., Mich. ca. 1854, where they remained about 25 years, and Susan died there. Children: JOHN C.; 2. LOUISA M. (m. Spencer H. Foster, also see); 3. HIRAM; 4. SARAH. Isaac married second to CORDELIA (CURTIS) of Oakland Co., Mich.

BENEDICT, JOHN, (See DANIEL, preceding) was born 7 Dec. 1787 in Warwick, Orange Co., NY, and he married there to PHEBE (TAYLOR) who was born 23 Oct. 1792 in New Jersey. They later moved to Steuben Co., NY; and then in 1854 to Raisin Twp., Lenawee Co., Mich. to join known son, JOHN W. (following). Ref: P&BA-Len. pg. 300-1.

BENEDICT, JOHN W., son of JOHN (preceding), was born Warwick, Orange Co., NY, and moved with parents to Steuben Co., NY, where he married 14 Apr. 1847 to LAURINDA (WOLCOTT), daughter of Kalep (also see). In 1852, they moved to Raisin Twp., Lenawee Co., Mich., and in 1864 to Tecumseh, Mich. Children: 1. GEORGE J. b. 4 Nov. 1851 (to Harper, KS); 2. CHARLES M. b. 23 Sept. 1854 (Tecumseh Twp.); 3. FRANK H. b. 26 June 1858 (Harper, KS); 4. RHODA M. b. 14 Oct. 1867. Ref: P&BA-Len pg. 300-1.

BENFER, GEORGE was born in Penn.; and he married MARY (DUFFY) and in 1830, after the birth of 4 children, they moved to Spencer Twp., Medina Co., Ohio. Known daughter, CLARISSA, b. 24 May 1824, Centre Co., Penn. (m. Jeremiah T. Newton, also see). Ref: P&BA-Len pg. 771-2

BENHAM, SAMUEL (See Rev. Paul Shepherd)
BENHAM, ZADIA B. (See Prosper J. Wheeler)

BENNETT, AARON (See John Johnson)

BENNETT, ALMIRA (See William Sutfin)
BENNETT, AMANDA (See Orville Woodworth)
BENNETT, ARNOLD (See Levi Jennings)
BENNETT, BENJAMIN H. born ca. 1814, and wife, REBECCA, born ca. 1815, both in NY, were listed in the 1850 census of Adrian Twp., Lenawee Co., Mich. with SAMUEL S., age 9; CHARLES T., age 7; both b. NY; & JAMES F., age 5; BENJAMIN, age 1, both b. Mich., in the household.

BENNETT, DAVIS D., son of MATTHEW (following), was born 25 Mar. 1808 in Tioga Co., NY (now Chemung Co.). He came alone to Michigan in 1828, but returned to Orleans Co., NY in 1829, where he married MALINDA (HAGAMAN) who was born 1809. They settled in Adrian, Lenawee Co., Mich. in 1830; and moved later to Fairfield Twp. Children (ages from 1850 census, Fairfield): 1. ELIZABETH H. b. 27 Oct. 1830, Adrian (m. John T. Mead, also see); 2. NANCY, age 17 (m. Cornelius Quick, also see); 3. CATHARINE, age 16; 4. MARY, age 14; 5. ALVIRA, age 12; 6. ANDREW J., age 10; 7. STILLMAN W. (following); 8. HELEN M., age 2; 9. ADDIE? E., age 6/12, all b. Mich. Davis D. married second to Mrs. REBECCA BAKER in Fairfield (at home of Charles Livesay) on 26 Jan. 1861. Ref: P&BA-Len pg. 535-6 & 1140-1.

BENNETT, ELIZABETH (See Enoch Belcher)
BENNETT, ERASTUS was listed in the 1840 census index of Palmyra Twp., Lenawee Co., Mich.
BENNETT, FRANCIS born ca. 1806, NY, and wife, ADELINE, born ca. 1819, Penn., were listed in the 1850 census of Fairfield Twp., Lenawee Co., Mich. with AMANDA A., age 11; NELSON, age 9; MARY, age 7, all b. NY; & HENRY, age 3, b. Mich., in the household.
BENNETT, GEORGE E., son of JOHN A. (following), married HELEN E. (MAXWELL), daughter of John O. (also see). Known children: LYNN M.; & J. DEWITT. Ref: P&BA-Len pg. 971-2.
BENNETT, GEORGE L. (See John G. Mason)
BENNETT, GEORGE W. born ca. 1819, Ohio, and wife, SARAH H., born ca. 1823, NY, were listed in the 1850 census of Adrian Twp., Lenawee Co., Mich. with EMMA A., age 3, born Mich. in the household. Also listed was MARY J., age 16, b. Ohio, possibly sister of George W.?
BENNETT, GERSHOM, son of MOSES (following), was born 6 Apr. 1782 in NY, and married ca. 1804 in Luzerne Co., Penn. to DORCAS and lived in Tioga Co., NY by 1816; and possibly also went afterwards to Ohio. They settled in Seneca Twp., Lenawee Co., Mich. before 1840. Known sons: STODDARD C. (following); & GEORGE (per family records of Eleanor Russell of Jackson, Mich.) In the 1850 census of Seneca Twp., Gershom, age 67, listed in the household, Harley Ford, age 23, and wife, Catharine Ford, age 23 (daughter of Gershom?), and Ellen D. Ford, age 1. After 1850, Gershom was said to have married POLLY M.
BENNETT, GERSHOM B., son of MATTHEW (following, was born 2 Jan. 1823, Shelby, Orleans Co., NY. He married in Rollin Twp., Lenawee Co., Mich. on 23 Oct. 1845 to MARIA (RAWSON), daughter of Theodore (also see). Children: 1. Rev. ELBERT R. b. 21 Mar. 1848 (m. Gertrude Mills, Grand Rapids, Mich.); 2. EMMA M. b. 19 Jan. 1852 (m. Rev. Stephen D. Whitmore, also see); 3. GEORGE L. b. 22 Dec. 1859 (m. Stella D. Mason, dau.

John G., also see); 4. EDSON J. b. 11 June 1861 (d. 19 Sept. 1865). Ref: P&BA-Len pg. 649-50.

BENNETT, GUY C. was listed in the 1840 census index of Adrian Twp., Lenawee Co., Mich.

BENNETT, HIRAM was listed in the 1840 census index of Rollin Twp., Lenawee Co., Mich. Also note MATTHEW.

BENNETT, JAMES of Carpenter Point, NY (See Simeon Westfall).

BENNETT, JEREMIAH, a Revolutionary soldier from New Jersey, married NANCY (RANDOLPH), and they moved first to Ontario Co., NY & then to Orleans Co. NY, where he died at age 75. (Note: There was a JEREMIAH listed in the militia of Upper Stoe Creek, Cumberland Co., NJ in 1793). Known son, MOSES (following). Ref: P&BA-Len pg. 1072.

BENNETT, JOEL, son of MOSES (following), was born 3 June 1790 in Pennsylvania. He married in Elmira, NY to MERCY (WINKLER), daughter of John (also see), and after their marriage, they rafted down the Ohio River to the Kentucky shore opposite Portsmouth. They later moved to Columbus, Ohio, and then Miami Co., Ohio. Before 1840, they removed to Hudson Twp., Lenawee Co., Mich., where she died in 1843. Joel, age 60, was listed in the 1850 census of Hudson Twp., in the household of son, JOHN T. (following); with daughter, NANCY, age 19, b. Ohio, also in the household (Nancy m. Luther Warner, also see, as his 3rd wife). Joel made his home with his children until his death on 3 Feb. 1865. Ref: P&BA-Len pg. 932-3.

BENNETT, JOHN born ca. 1810, and wife, LOUISA, born ca. 1814, were listed in the 1850 census of Rome Twp., Lenawee Co., Mich., with MILES, age 16; LUCRETIA, age 14; MELISSA, age 12; LOIS, age 8; with entire family shown born Conn.

BENNETT, JOHN A., son of Rev. MOSES (following), was born 17 Mar. 1830 in Scioto Co., Ohio, and came to Rollin Twp., Lenawee Co., Mich. with his parents. He married 28 Apr. 1853, Rome Twp., to RHODA M. (SMITH), daughter of Joseph (also see), and they settled in Cambridge Twp. Children: 1. GEORGE E. (preceding); 2. EUGENE T. (m. Frances L. Thompson); 3. ELIZABETH M. (m. Eugene Turner, Woodstock Twp.); 4. J. WILLIAM. Ref: P&BA-Len pg. 758-9.

BENNETT, JOHN T., son of JOEL (preceding), born ca. 1817, and wife, SARAH, born ca. 1826. both in NY, were listed in the 1850 census of Hudson Twp., Lenawee Co., Mich., with EDWIN D., age 5; JULIA A., age 3; HORACE E., age 1, all b. Mich., in their household. Father, JOEL, preceding, was also listed.

BENNETT, JONATHAN and wife, MARY, apparently moved from Washington Co., NY to Westmoreland, Oneida Co., NY. Known daughter, LUCY R., b. 10 Feb. 1814, Salem, Washington Co., NY (m. Henry F. Townsend, also see). Ref: P&BA-Len pg. 511-2.

BENNETT, JOSEPH R., son of MATTHEW (following), was born 18 May 1819, Shelby, Orleans Co., NY, and came to Rollins Twp., Lenawee Co., Mich. with his parents. He married there 3 Apr. 1839 to NANCY J. (ROWLEY) of Hudson, Mich., who was born 1824, Onondaga Co., NY. She died 18 Apr. 1880. Children: 1. HELEN M. b. ca. 1842 (m. Maj. S. E. Graves, also see); 2. (EUDORA) DORA E. b. ca. 1847. In the 1850 census of Madison Twp., Lenawee Co., Mich., in addition to above, he listed EUNICE, age 24; NANCY, age 20, both b. Ohio; and ALMA A., age 14, b. Mich., possibly sisters of Joseph R. Ref: P&BA-Len pg. 981-2.

BENNETT, LESTER C. born ca. 1805, Penn., and wife, BETSEY A., born ca. 1817, NY, were listed in the 1850 census of Rollin Twp., Lenawee Co., Mich., with GENNETT (Janette?), age 10; AMELIA, age 6, both b. Mich., in their household. Note MATTHEW, following.

BENNETT, LEVI was a resident of Rollin Twp., Lenawee Co., Mich. in the 1840 census index. Also note MATTHEW, following.

BENNETT, LEWIS R., born ca. 1824, Ohio, was listed in the 1850 census of Madison Twp., Lenawee Co., Mich.

BENNETT, MARCUS was born 5 May 1810, NY, and he worked on the Erie Canal, and lived in Niagara Co., NY where he married first in 1836 to OLIVE (ODELL). He purchased land in Monroe Co., Mich. (now part of Lucas Co., O.) in 1834. Olive died in Ohio on 19 Jan. 1839, leaving a daughter, 1. SALLIE (m. C. M. C. Cook, Lansing, Mich.). Marcus married again on 22 June 1841, Niagara Co., NY to EMELINE (LUSK) who was born 28 Dec. 1814, Bloomfield, Ontario Co., NY. They were in Ohio until 1866, when they removed to Madison Twp., Lenawee Co., Mich. Children: 2. PERRY (killed Civil War, Co. F., 14th Ohio Inf.); 3. ALANSON (Adrian, Mich.); 4. LYMAN b. 25 May 1847 (m. 2 Nov. 1871, Emma Grant, Adrian; had dau., Bessie). Ref: P&BA-Len pg. 782-3.

BENNETT, MARY Mrs., age 40, was listed head of household in the 1850 census of Medina Twp., Lenawee Co., Mich., with ELI, age 21; JOSEPH, age 12; JOHN, age 6, all born Ohio; and also LYDIA, age 70, b. NY (mother-in-law?), in her household.

BENNETT, MATTHEW, son of MOSES (following), was born in 1778, Orange Co., NY, and moved with parents to Wilkes Barre, Luzerne Co., Penn. He married there to NANCY (BRACE) who was born ca. 1787 in Saratoga Co., NY. In 1805, they removed to Tioga Co., NY; and in 1816 to Genesee Co., NY, in an area now in Orleans Co. About 1832, they removed to Rollin Twp., Lenawee Co., Mich., where she died; and he afterwards went to Fairfield Twp. where he died in 1863. Ten children; known sons: DAVIS D. (preceding); 2. JOSEPH R. (preceding); 3. GERSHOM B. (preceding). Daughter, DEBORAH, age 19, listed in household in 1850 census of Rollin Twp. In the household of Joseph R. were POSSIBLY additonal children of Matthew: EUNICE, age 24; NANCY, age 20. both b. Ohio; ALMA A., age 14, b. Mich. Also note LESTER C. (preceding); & MOSES D. (following). Ref: P&BA-Len pg. 535-6; 649-50; 981-2.

BENNETT, MATTHEW M., son of MOSES D. (following), enlisted in 1862 in Co. I., 6th Mich. Art., during Civil War. He married in Morenci, Mich. to SARAH (GREELEY), daughter of Noah (also see). No children listed. Ref: P&BA-Len pg. 1051-2.

BENNETT, MILES (See Chancy Rowlson)

BENNETT, MOSES was born ca. 1755, and married about 1777 in Orange Co., NY to ELIZABETH (or MARY) WOOD. They moved before 1795 to Luzerne Co., Penn.; and later to Scioto Co., Ohio, where he died after 1820; and she died ca. 1830. Children: 1. MATTHEW b. 1778, Warwick, NY (preceding); 2. SARAH "SALLY" b. 5 Dec. 1781 (m. Joseph Scott); 3. GERSHOM b. 6 Apr. 1782 (preceding); 4. EUNICE b. 17 Feb. 1785 (m. Joseph

Rickey); 5. OLIVE b. 25 Apr. 1786 (m. James McDaniel); 6. Rev. MOSES (following); 7. REBECCA b. bef. 1790; 8. JOEL (preceding); 9. JOSIAH b. 31 Mar. 1795 (m. Susan Shoemaker); 10. HOSEA b. 16 May 1802; 11. THOMAS. Ref: Family records of Eleanor Russell of Jackson, Mich.; and P&BA-Len pg. 932-3.

BENNETT, MOSES Rev., son of MOSES (preceding), was born 6 Sept. 1787, NY, and married there to ELIZABETH "BETSEY" (WINKLER), and they removed to Scioto Co., Ohio. About 1835, they moved to Rollin Twp., Lenawee Co., Mich., where he died 3 Sept. 1844, age 57. She died 10 May 1877, Greenville, Montcalm Co., Mich. at the home of a son. There were 6 sons & 5 daughters. In the 1850 census of Rollin Twp., Betsey, age 57, was listed as head of household with her known children #8. JOHN A. b. 17 Mar. 1830; 9. ASAHEL, age 18; 10. GEORGE C., age 15, all b. Ohio; & 11. THADDEUS C., age 13, b. Mich. in her household. Also listed were John Chittenden, age 24, b. Ohio, with wife, Ellen (daughter of Moses?), age 24, b. Ohio, and child, Judson, age 2., b. Mich. Note: Betsey married second to John Greenleaf (also see) after 1850. Ref: P&BA-Len pg. 932-3.

BENNETT, MOSES, son of JEREMIAH (preceding), born 18 Oct. 1795, NJ. married EDITH (COLLINS) who was born 30 Mar. 1797, NJ. They removed to New York (probably Ontario & Orleans Cos.) after their marriage. He served in the War of 1812. In 1868, they removed to Hillsdale Co., Mich. where he died at age 88; and she died in 1872, age 75. There were 10 children, one dying infancy. Known son, ROSWELL (following). Ref: P&BA-Len pg. 1072.

BENNETT, MOSES D. (See MATTHEW, preceding) was born ca. 1811, and his wife, PRUDENCE (JONES), was born ca. 1813, both in NY, and they were listed in the 1850 census of Hudson Twp., Lenawee Co., Mich. with MATTHEW (preceding) b. 25 July 1838, Hudson Twp.; DANIEL A. b. ca. 1841; DARWIN J. b. ca. 1850, in their household. Moses D. died in 1875, age about 60?; and she was still living in 1888, Hudson Twp. Ref: P&BA-Len pg. 1051-2.

BENNETT, NATHANIEL CARPENTER, son of MOSES (not noted here) of Otsego Co., NY, was born 28 Dec. 1824, Maryland, NY. He married in 1846 to REBECCA (MYERS), daughter of Ephraim (also see) of Otsego Co. They lived in Albany, NY; ca. 1856 in Ossian, Iowa; and then in Columbia, Boone Co., MO. They settled in Riga Twp., Lenawee Co., Mich. Adopted son, JOHN M. (m. Anna Durham, had children Thaddeus & Artie May). Ref: P&BA-Len pg. 503-4.

BENNETT, ROSWELL, son of MOSES & EDITH (preceding), was born 14 Sept. 1815, Ontario Co., NY. By first marriage (wife's name not stated) had children: 1. BENJAMIN R. (Rollin Twp.); 2. GEORGE S.; 3. LEWIS. Roswell married on 31 Dec. 1854 to MARY J. (HODGES), daughter of Rodman (also see), and settled in Palmyra Twp., Lenawee Co., Mich. by 1856, and in 1863 in Rollin Twp. Children (order of birth not given): deceased before 1888, EDWIN O.; ELLEN M.; LYDIA G.; those surviving, FLORENCE M. (m. Henry Kemberling, Detroit, Mich.); MARY E. (m. John Darling, Woodstock Twp.); DORA A. (m. Martin T. Ball), son of Nathaniel³, also see); EDWIN R. Ref: P&BA-Len pg. 591 & 1072.

BENNETT, REUBEN born ca. 1781, NY, was listed in the 1850 census of Tecumseh Twp., Lenawee Co., Mich. in the household of Nehemiah & Lydia Morse (also see), and she was age 34, b. NY, possibly his daughter; and in the household next door was ALMIRA (BENNETT), age 37, b. NY, with husband William Sutfin (also see), possibly also daughter of Reuben.

BENNETT, STILLMAN W., son of DAVIS D. (preceding), was born 30 July 1842 in Fairfield Twp., Lenawee Co., Mich. He married 16 Jan. 1868 to MARY L. (LIVESAY), daughter of James (also see). They resided in Adrian in 1888. Children: 1. ARTHUR LIVESAY b. 1 Apr. 1871; 2. FLORENCE b. 20 Jan. 1881. Ref: P&BA-Len pg. 535-6.

BENNETT, STODDARD C., son of GERSHOM (preceding), was born 29 June 1816, Tioga Co., NY, and his wife, (Sarah) ELIZABETH T. (CAVENDER), was born ca. 1821, New Hampshire. He was listed as "S. C." in the 1840 census index of Seneca Twp., Lenawee Co., Mich.; and in the 1850 census of Medina Twp., Lenawee Co., Mich., listed children: WILLIAM C. b. 24 June 1839 (following); ROSMAN D. b. 27 Dec. 1843, both b. Mich., in the household; (Eleanor Russell of Jackson, Mich. provided the balance of children's names) MARY R. b. 28 Aug. 1848; & GERSHOM JUDSON.

BENNETT, WILLIAM of Hamburg Twp., Livingston Co., Mich., had wife, ESTHER (SANFORD), daughter of Ezra (also see).

BENNETT, WILLIAM C. of Seneca Twp., Lenawee Co., Mich. married in Tecumseh, on 1 Jan. 1858 to OLIVE E. (ADAMS), of Medina Twp. Possibly same man as following??

BENNETT, WILLIAM C.. son of STODDARD C. (preceding), married in June 1864 to WELTHIA E. (BURT), daughter of Hiram A. He died 15 Aug. 1876, Canandaigua, Mich.; and she died 1930 in Medina, Mich., and both buried in Canandaigua. Children: 1. IMOGENE b. 26 May 1871 (m. Sylvester P. Huff); 2. ROSA b. 28 May 1865; 3. LILLY IRENE b. 25 Dec. 1866; 4. FRANK b. 27 Aug. 1868; 5. JUDSON A. b. 15 Nov. 1872. Ref: Family records of Eleanor Russell of Jackson, Mich.

BENSON, ELIZABETH (See Joseph Hoxsie)
BENSON, MARY G. (See William W. Luck)

BENTLY, CALEB of Rhode Island was the father of MARY who married Lonsen R. Burr (also see) of Fairport, Monroe Co., NY. Ref: P&BA-Len pg. 1034-5.

BENTLY, EZEKIEL was a Revolutionary soldier. (It may be he with Rhode Island service, with widow, ANNA, listed in the RW Pension Appllications, #W10407). Ezekiel moved from Rhode Island to Orleans Co., NY where he died at age 90. Known daughter, ELIZABETH, b. 20 July 1796, RI, married probably in Orleans Co., NY to Moses Bugbee (also see). Ref: P&BA-Len pg. 974-5.

BENTON, ELISHA listed in the 1840 census index of Ogden Twp., Lenawee Co., Mich., sold land in 1848 in Ogden Twp. to John Houghtby; and does not appear in the 1850 census.

BENTON, JOSIAH H. Rev. born ca. 1817, Vermont, and wife, MARTHA, born ca. 1822, New Hampshire, were listed in the 1850 census of Tecumseh Twp., Lenawee Co.,

Pioneer Families of Southeastern Michigan

Mich. with JOSIAH, age 7; MARTHA, age 4; MARY, age 2, all b. VT, in their household.

BERDAN, DAVID, b. ca. 1807, & wife, HARRIET (CANNON), b. ca. 1807, both in NY, came to Macon Twp., Lenawee Co., Mich. by 1833. David died 3 Oct. 1881, age 71; and Harriet died in 1874. Known daughter, VIANA, b. 11 June 1833 (1838?), Macon Twp. (m. Francis H. Whiting, also see). In the 1850 census of Macon Twp., in their household was WILLSON H., age 19; ANDERSON, age 16, both b. NY; & FRANCES V. (This may be VIANA??), age 12; ORANGE F., age 8; ELLEN J., age 7, last 3 b. Mich. Ref: P&BA-Len pg. 353-4.

BERRY, AMBROSE S. was born ca. 1814, NY, and he married LUCY (HART), daughter of Joseph (also see). He was listed in the 1840 census index of Adrian Twp., Lenawee Co., Mich., and was listed in the 1850 census in Madison Twp. Listed in his household were LANKFORD G., following, probably brother, with the following children BENJAMIN H., age 8; ALICE, age 4; MARY, age 1, exact relationship not known.

BERRY, ELECTA (See John Bixby)

BERRY, JAMES born 1814, England, and wife, JULIA A., born 1819, NY, were listed in the 1850 census of Adrian Twp., Lenawee Co., Mich., with MARY A., age 14, b. NY; and JULIA A., age 10; ELLA A., age 4; CLARA E., age 1, all b. Mich. in the household. SUSETTE R. (b. after 1850) who married George A. Wilcox (also see) may be another daughter.

BERRY, LANKFORD G., born ca. 1812, NY, was listed in the 1850 census of Madison Twp., Lenawee Co., Mich. in the household of brother, AMBROSE S. (preceding).

BERRY, PRUDENCE (See Dr. Henry Wyman)

BERT, SARAH (See John H. Carpenter)

BEST, ANNIE (See Adam Van Tuyle)
BEST, CATHERINE (See John W. Clapper)

BETTS, SARAH (BRESIE) Mrs. (See William Bresie)

BEVIER was also called BOVIER
BEVIER, JEREMIAH and wife, LYDIA (VAN CUREN), of Ulster Co., NY, were parents of SARAH J. born there 8 Jan. 1830 (m/1 William Drake; m/2 Johannes LaFever, see both). Jeremiah died in Ulster Co., NY. Ref: P&BA-Len pg. 1046-9.

BEYL, REGINA (See Samuel Lerch)

BICKFORD, AZARIAH moved from Maine to Ontario Co., NY, where he married PHILENA (PERKINS) in the 1820s. There were 5 sons and 4 daughters. Those mentioned: LYMAN (New York); MARCUS (Iowa); DELIA (New York); HARLOW (Iowa); & HOMER (following). Ref: P&BA-Len 1158-9.

BICKFORD, HOMER, son of AZARIAH (preceding), was born 20 Dec. 1834, East Bloomfield, Ontario Co. NY; and married there to EMILY (WATKINS), daughter of Marshall (also see). They resided in Newark and Macedon, NY. In 1876, they moved to Raisin Twp., Lenawee Co., Mich. Children: 1. CARRY P. b. 5 Mar. 1860 (d. 9 Oct. 1864); 2. WILLARD C. b. 28 July 1862 (d. 9 Oct. 1864); 3. FANNY E. b. 27 July 1865 (d. 3 Nov. 1866). Ref: P&BA-Len pg. 1158-9.

BICKFORD, OLIVE (See Lyman H. Aldrich)

BIDDLE, CATHARINE born 1805, Germany (See Daniel Bay).
BIDDLE, ISRAEL & wife, MARTHA (LOWRY), of Montour, Penn. were parents of MARY L. b. ca. 1802 (m. Robert Richart, also see).
BIDDLE, MARTHA (See Richard B. Gillespie[3])
BIDDLE, MARY ANNA (See David S. Stephens)
BIDDLE, SARAH (See Josephus White)

BIDWELL, ALONZO F. of Coldwater, Mich. married EMELINE (CONKLING) of Raisin Twp., Lenawee Co., Mich. on 1 June 1853.
BIDWELL, ASA was born ca. 1778, and his wife, EUNICE (UNDERWOOD), was born ca. 1781, probably in Conn. In 1819, they moved from Colebrook, Conn. to Livingston Co., NY where they remained. Eight sons and 3 Daughters, names not stated. Known son, #6. BIRDSEY J. (following). Ref: P&BA-Len pg. 825-6.
BIDWELL, BIRDSEY J., son of ASA (preceding), was born 14 Sept. 1810, Colebrook, Litchfield Co., Conn., and moved with his parents to Livingston Co., NY. In 1838, he moved to Tecumseh Twp., Lenawee Co., Mich. He married in Feb. 1842 to ELIZABETH A. (CUSHING), daughter of Samuel (also see). Children: 1. LAMONT C. b. ca. 1844 (to Harper Co., KS); 2. LAVERN I. b. ca. 1846 (m. Nellie J. Beers, May 1866). Ref: P&BA-Len pg. 825-6.
BIDWELL, CHARLES born ca. 1822, and wife, ELIZA, born ca. 1828, both in Conn., were listed in the 1850 census of Adrian Twp., Lenawee Co., Mich. Mary Kip, age 47, born Germany, was in the household.
BIDWELL, ERASTUS was listed in the 1840 census index of Adrian Twp., Lenawee Co., Mich.
BIDWELL, FLEMING B. was listed in the 1840 census index of Adrian Twp., Lenawee Co., Mich.
BIDWELL, GEORGE born ca. 1833, Mich., was listed in the 1850 census of Tecumseh Twp., Lenawee Co., Mich., in the household of David & Olive Brooks.
BIDWELL, GEORGE L. born ca. 1817, NY, was listed in the 1850 census index of Adrian, Lenawee Co., Mich. in a hotel.
BIDWELL, GERSHOM born ca. 1801, and wife, ANN, born ca. 1810, both in Penn., were listed in the 1850 census of Tecumseh Twp., Lenawee Co., Mich., with MARTHA, age 6, b. Mich., in their household.
BIDWELL, IRA born ca. 1804, and wife, CLARISSA, born ca. 1810, both in Conn., were in Adrian Twp., Lenawee Co., Mich. by the 1840 census; and in 1850, they listed LOUISA, age 17; HENRY, age 15, both b. NY; and ALBERT, age 10, b. Mich., in the household.
BIDWELL, LYDIA (See John B. Peebles)
BIDWELL, NORMAN born ca. 1819, Conn., was listed in the 1850 census of Adrian, Lenawee Co., Mich. in a hotel.
BIDWELL, SETH settled in Brighton Twp., Livingston Co., Mich. in 1835. Early Land records of Livingston Co., Mich. give his origins as Livingston & Orleans Cos, NY.
BIDWELL, STEPHEN born ca. 1828, NY, was listed in the 1850 census of Tecumseh Twp., Lenawee Co., Mich. in the Powell household.

BIGELOW, CHARLES of Toledo, Ohio married FRANCES E. (STINSON), daughter of Rev. Hiram K. (also see) at Adrian, Lenawee Co., Mich. on 15 Apr. 1851.

BIGELOW, DANIEL P. Maj. & wife, BETSEY (KNIGHT) of Barre, Orleans Co., NY were parents of HARRIET P. (m. George W. Moore, also see, as his 2d wife.) Ref: P&BA-Len pg. 1000-2.

BIGELOW, PAMELIA (See James Halladay, Sr.)

BIGELOW, WILLIAM and wife, SUSANNA N., moved from Waltham, Mass. to Hanover, NH. Known daughter, BETSEY (ELIZABETH?) born 28 Apr. 1783, Waltham (m. 1806, Simeon Dewey, also see). Ref: P&BA-Len gp. 1101-2.

BIGLE also see BEAGLE
BIGLE, ELIZABETH (See Christopher Beckley)

BILLINGTON, WILSON was born ca. 1806, NY, and came to Franklin Twp., Lenawee Co., Mich. where he married JULIA (WHELAN) who was born ca. 1824, NY. He died in Franklin Twp. 18 May 1874, age 68; and she was still living in 1888 in Tipton, Mich. In the 1850 census of Franklin Twp., given name looked like "Nelson," age 40, listed children ALVIRA, age 6; ALONSO?, age 4; LORENZO, age 4 (m. Rosetta Whelan, dau. of William, also see); LAURA b. 11 Apr. 1848 (m. Ervin Whelan, Jr., also see). Ref: P&BA-lEN PG. 637-8.

BILLS, HIRAM and wife, VIRTUE, moved from Conn. to Vermont before 1810, and she died there in 1840. Known son, PERLEY (following). Ref: P&BA-Len pg. 1159-60.

BILLS, PERLEY, son of HIRAM (preceding), was born 5 June 1810, Wilmington, VT. At age 19, he went to Honesdale, Penn.; returned to VT; went to Medina Co., O. and again returned to VT. In 1837, he moved to Tecumseh Twp., Lenawee Co., Mich. He married 8 Nov. 1838 to CAROLINE (BROWN), daughter of Isaac (also see) of Tecumseh. Children: 1. FREDERICK H. b. ca. 1841; w. OSCAR P. b. ca. 1843; 3. CAROLINE b. ca. 1846 (m. Gen. Lemuel Savier, St. Louis, Mich.); 4. MARY H. b. ca. 1847 (m. Lt. Col. Nathan Church, Ithaca, Mich.); 5. Dr. HARRIET B.; 6. CHANDLER D. Ref: P&BA-Len pg. 1159-60.

BINGHAM, ANN (See Samuel DePuy & Ira Ladd)
BINGHAM, JENNIE (See George Sheeler)
BINGHAM, RIAL Capt. enlisted in the Revolution in Hartford, Conn. After the war, he was said to have received Bounty land near what is now Syracuse, NY (Onondaga Co.). It should be noted, however, that there is no man by this name in the RW Pensions Applications index for bounty land, so name may have been different. In the 1800 census index of NY, there is a "Regal Bingham" listed in Onondaga Co. Known daughter, ELIZABETH, born Conn., married John A. Vrooman (also see). Ref: P&BA-Len pg. 792-3.

BINN, ALTHA (See John Cheever)

BINNS, CHARLES D. (See Lewis Sanford)
BINNS, CHESTER married NETTIE M. (ROGERS), daughter of John C. (also see), and had children: BERTHA & CARL.

BIRCH also see BURCH
BIRCH, ETHRO was listed in the 1840 census index of Blissfield Twp., Lenawee Co., Mich. Also note MORRIS.
BIRCH, JAMES see BURCH, JAMES
BIRCH, MORRIS was listed in the 1840 census index of Blissfield Twp., Lenawee Co., MIch.

BIRD, BENJAMIN of Broome Co., NY married MARIA (MERCHANT), and he died there in 1825 in the prime of life. Known son, CHARLES G., born 30 Aug., 1820, Windsor, NY (following). Maria married second to William Moore (also see). Ref: P&BA-Len pg. 1172-3.

BIRD, BURTIS was born ca. 1807, NJ, and his wife, MARY A. (BODINE), was born NY. They moved before 1837 to Macon Twp., Lenawee Co., Mich., and she died there on 1 July 1839. In the 1850 census of Macon Twp., he listed (second wife?), MARY, age 29, b. NY; and SARAH A., age 21, b. NY; & MARY E. b. 14 Oct. 1837, Macon Twp. (m. George V. Osgood, also see); CHARLES, age 8; HELEN, age 5; HA---(male), age 2. Also in the household was SAMUEL, age 40, b. NJ, probably a brother. Ref: P&BA-Len pg. 581-2.

BIRD, CHARLES E. (See George Lane)
BIRD, CHARLES G., son of BENJAMIN (preceding), came to Adrian Twp., Lenawee Co., Mich. in 1831 with his family. He married on 30 Dec. 1847 to MARY A. (HOOD) in Adrian Twp., and settled in Adrian, Mich. Children: 1. MARTIN A.; 2. CHARLES H.; 3. JOHN H. Ref: P&BA-Len pg. 1172-3.

BIRD, CHAUNCEY was born ca. 1778, Conn., and his wife, LYDIA, was born ca. 1797, Mass. Note: This may be Mrs. Lydia (Morse) Caniff (also see) who was said to have married second to John Bird (following).

BIRD, EBENEZER, age 61, born Mass., was listed in the 1850 census of Madison Twp., Lenawee Co., Mich.

BIRD, GEORGE born ca. 1819, and wife, HARRIET, born ca. 1823, both in NY, were listed in the 1850 census of Adrian Twp., Lenawee Co., Mich. with TERRY, age 2, b. Mich., in the household.

BIRD, JOHN was said to have married Mrs. LYDIA (MORSE) CANNIFF, widow of John Canniff (also see) and settled in Clayton, Lenawee Co., Mich. However, note CHAUNCEY (preceding) & REUBEN (following).

BIRD, JOHN M. was called a "neighbor" of Henry F. Townsend in Dover Twp., Lenawee Co., Mich. in 1835. In the 1850 census of Dover Twp., he was born ca. 1810, Conn., and wife, SARAH, was born ca. 1809, VT, with JULIA A., age 12; & MARY E. (age illegible), in the household.

BIRD, JOHN M., born ca. 1818, Penn., and wife, LORINDA, born ca. 1817, NY, were listed in the 1850 census of Madison Twp., Lenawee Co., Mich. with SARAH J., age 4; CHARLES H., age 1, both b. Mich., in the household. Also listed was Abba Pope, age 60, b. NY; and Ezra Pope, age 38, b. NY, possibly Lorinda's mother & brother??

BIRD, KELSEY born ca. 1789, NJ, and wife, SARAH, born ca. 1792, Penn., were listed in the 1850 census of Raisin Twp., Lenawee Co., Mich. In their household, relationship not known, were Sarah Colier, age 26, with children, Sarah E., age 2, and Freeman, age 1, possibly their daughter & grandchildren?

Pioneer Families of Southeastern Michigan

BIRD, LOREN A. born ca. 1820, and wife, EUNICE, born ca. 1820, both in NY, were listed in the 1850 census of Madison Twp., Lenawee Co., Mich. with HIRAM, age 7, b. NY; & MARY, age 2, b. Mich., in their household.

BIRD, REUBEN E. born ca. 1812, and wife, CAROLINE, born ca. 1825, both in NY, were listed in the 1850 census of Hudson Twp., Lenawee Co., Mich. with CHAUNCEY N., age 1, in the household. Note: They were listed next door to the Canniff family, see JOHN M., preceding.

BIRD, SAMUEL born ca. 1810, NJ (See BURTIS, preceding).

BIRD, WILLIAM & wife, LUCRETIA (STANTON) who was born 29 July 1802, NY, moved from NY to Palmyra Twp., Lenawee Co., Mich. William died 9 Feb. 1846, and she died in July 1875. Of 6 children, 4 grew to maturity. In her household in the 1850 census of Palmyra Twp., were CHARLES M., age 14, b. NY; MARY E., age 12; ALMENA J., age 9 (m. Chester J. Corbett, also see); ARTHUR, age 7, b. Mich. Ref: P&BA-Len pg. 350.

BIRDSELL, WILLIAM (See Conrad L. Lowe)

BIRDSEY, POLLY (See Chancellor Hyde)

BISBEE, CLARISSA (See William Mitchell)

BISCO, LOIS (See Milton Foote)

BISHOFF, CHRISTIAN of Preston, W. Va., was father of MARY (m. John G. Heckert, also see). Ref: P&BA-Len pg. 1108-9.

BISHOP, DAVID moved from New Haven Co., Conn. to Paris, Oneida Co., NY. Known daughter, PARNEL, born 1789 in Branford, Conn. (m. John Townsend^2, also see). Ref: P&BA-Len pg. 511-2.

BISHOP, HARRIET born Utica, NY in 1812 (See Thomas Hendryx).

BISHOP, MARY of Lyme, Conn. married Joseph Keeney (also see) and went to LeRoy, Genesee Co., NY in 1814. Ref: P&BA-Len pg. 1060-3.

BISSEL also see BISSELL

BISSEL, THEODORE married CYNTHIA (SPAFFORD), daughter of Abner (also see), and he died before 1870, probably in Tecumseh Twp., Lenawee Co., Mich. Cynthia married second to William W. Tilton (also see).

BISSELL also see BISSEL

BISSELL, ANSON from Huron Co., Ohio purchased land in Springport, Jackson Co., Mich. in 1836.

BISSELL, EDWARD from Niagara Co., NY purchased land in Liberty Twp., Jackson Co. Mich. in 1836.

BISSELL, JOHN M. was listed in the 1840 census index of Adrian Twp., Lenawee Co., Mich.

BISSELL, LEVI born ca. 1826, and wife, MARY, born ca. 1827, England, were listed in the 1850 census of Tecumseh Twp., Lenawee Co., Mich.

BITELY, JOHN^1 was born in Germany and came first to New Jersey, and later moved to near Ft. Ticonderoga, NY. He moved to Monroe, NY, where he died in 1817. Known son, PETER^2 (following). Ref: P&BA-Len pg. 991-2. Note: There was a JOHN BITELEY, with wife, MARTHA, with NY service, listed in the Rev. War. Pension Applications #R872 (rejected).

BITELY, JOHN^3, son of PETER^2, was born 10 July 1812, Monroe, NY. In 1836, he prospected for land as far west as Chicago, but returned to Palmyra Twp., Lenawee Co., Mich. He married in 1840 to PERMELIA (SMALLEY), daughter of James (also see). He served in Co. F., 7th Mich. Cav. in the Civil War. Permelia died in Oct. 1876. Children: 1. PHEBE J. b. 20 Feb. 1842 (d. 1864); 2. WILLIAM b. ca. 1843 (served Civil War as Mechanic & Civil Engr.); 3. MARTHA b. ca. 1845 (m. Jerome DeBar; 4. EUNICE b. ca. 1846 (m. Reuben Hill); 5. JAMES b. ca. 1848 (poss. d. 1864?); 6. JOHN b. ca. 1849. Ref: P&BA-Len pg. 991-2.

BITELY, PETER^2, son of JOHN^1, was born in NJ, and moved with parents to NY. He served in the Revolution (Note: This is questionable, possibly should be JOHN^1, preceding). He married MARTHA (McDONALD) who was born in Albany, NY, and settled in Monroe, NY where they remained until 1831, and then moved to Madison Co., NY. In 1838, they moved to Michigan and joined son, JOHN^3 (preceding) where they remained, apparently deceased before 1850. Children: 1. POLLY; 2. SALINE; E. EUNICE; 4. SYLVIA; 5. JOHN (preceding); 6. NANCY; 7. AMOS; 8. WILLIAM; 9. WALTER. Ref: P&BA-Len pg. 991-2.

BITTER, LOUISA (See Henry H. Samsen)

BIXBY, ALONZO FOSTER, son of DAVID (following), born 6 July 1819, Batavia, NY, came to Adrian Twp., Lenawee Co., Mich. with parents. As an adult, he went to Canandaigua, Mich., and LaGrange, Texas, but had returned to Adrian Twp. by 1846. He married 19 Oct. 1851 to EMMA L. (KEENEY), daughter of Joseph (also see). In 1850, they both resided in the household of Jane McDonald. After their marriage, they settled in Adrian Twp. He died 18 Apr. 1870. Children; 1. DAVID ALONZO b. 24 Sept. 1854; 2. WILLIAM KEENEY b. 2 Jan. 1857 (m. Lilliam B. Tuttle; had children Sidney T. & Emma S.); 3. MINNIE E. b. 16 Oct. 1858 (m. William Holland Samson, also see); 4. GEORGE SPOFFORD b. 23 Apr. 1863 (d. age 3y/3mo); 5. FRED FOSTER b. 9 Aug. 1866. Ref: P&BA-Len pg. 1021-2.

BIXBY, DAVID, son of SAMUEL (following), was born 1783 in Sutton, Mass. He married 9 Apr. 1811 to LAURA (FOSTER), daughter of Abel (also see), and lived first in Charlton, Mass., then moved about 1815 to Batavia, Genesee Co., NY, and afterwards to Albion, NY. They moved to Adrian Twp., Lenawee Co., Mich. in 1827. Known daughter, ELLEN MARIA (m. William Augustus Whitney, also see). Only son, ALONZO FOSTER (preceding). In the 1850 census of Adrian Twp., Lenawee Co., Mich., they listed LAURA JANE, age 15, b. Mich., possibly granddaughter, in the household. David died 4 Jan. 1865; and she died 12 Apr. 1882, age 87. Ref: P&BA-Len pg. 1021-2. Also see JOHN (following).

BIXBY, JOHN born ca. 1816, and wife, ESTHER, born ca. 1822, both died in 1896, and are buried in the Mills Cemetery, Franklin Twp., Lenawee Co., Mich. Buried with them is MERION, 1847-1924, with wife ELECTA (BERRY) 1847-1928.

BIXBY, SAMUEL was born Sutton, Worcester co., Mass. in 1712, the first white child born there. He married ANNA (CHASE). He died there at age 97, and she died at age 104. Known son, DAVID (preceding). Ref: P&BA-Len pg. 1021-2.

BLACKMAN, WESTERN of Napoleon, Jackson Co., Mich. married ELLEN M. (BLAIR) of Franklin Twp., Lenawee Co., Mich. 21 Apr. 1853.

BLACKMAR, CHARLES and wife, ELEANOR (ELLEN/HELENA? RICE) who was born ca. 1790, moved from Wales, Erie Co., NY to Ohio in 1826, and to Cambridge Twp., Lenawee Co., Mich. in 1829. (There was a Charles "Blackman" listed in the 1830 census of Lenawee Co., Mich. Territory, but ages didn't seem correct. Note S. BLACKMAR, following). Charles died 24 Aug. 1834. She is probably the "Helena," age 60, b. NY, listed in the 1850 census of Cambridge Twp. in the household of son(?), CLINTON (following). Known daughter, ALZINA b. 25 May 1810, Erie Co. NY (m. Ezra F. Blood, also see). Known son, WILLIAM S. (following). Ref: P&BA-Len pg. 819-20 & History of Jackson Co., Mich., pg. 962-3. Also note CHARLES, following.

BLACKMAR, CHARLES born ca. 1822, NY, was listed in the 1850 census of Woodstock Twp., Lenawee Co., Mich.

BLACKMAR, CLINTON A., probably son of CHARLES (preceding), was born ca. 1825, NY, with mother, HELENA (ELEANOR?), age 60, b. NY, in the household. Also listed were MARINDA, age 24, b. Ohio, and ALBERT, age 9/12, b. NY. Note: They are listed in the 1850 census 3 doors from WILLIAM S. (following).

BLACKMAR, JOHN married MARY JANE (SOUTHWORTH) who was born 16 Feb. 1818. In 1852, they were living in Erie Co., Penn., apparently moved to Lenawee Co., Mich. Children: 1. SEVERUS WILLIAM b. 3 Apr. 1838 (d. Civil War, Battle of Chancellorville); 2. HENRIETTA b. 12 Mar. 1840 (m. Dewey); 3. child b. 19 July 1841; 4. ELIZA JANE b. 12 Feb. 1842 (m. Buchanan); 5. MARY LOUISE b. 16 Aug. 1844 (m. Orin Nickly); 6. ALAN; 7. JOHN ALVA ADELBERT b. 13 Sept. 1850; 7. SARAH EMELINE b. 24 Apr. 1852, Erie Co., Penn. (m. James Lewis, also see). Ref: Bible Rec. of Lewis Family.

BLACKMAR, S. was listed in the 1830 census of Lenawee Co., Territory of Michigan, with males 1 15-20; 1 20-30; 1 40-50; and females 1 20-30; 1 60-70. (Possibly CHARLES is the male 40-50?)

BLACKMAR, WILLIAM S., son of CHARLES (preceding), was born 24 Feb. 1814, Wales, Erie Co., NY. He moved with his parents to Ohio, and then to Cambridge Twp., Lenawee Co., Mich. where he is listed in the 1840 census index. He married first in 1844 to CATHARINE (LOUCKS) who died in 1847 leaving 2 children: 1. OCTAVIA b. ca. 1844 (m. W. H. Loomis); 2. HOWARD (d. 1847). William S. married before 1850 to PYRA (PATIRA? BLAIR) born 1827, NY, who died leaving children: 3. ELLEN (m. C. Richards); 4. CHARLES (d. 1854). William S. married in 1857 to CHRISTIANA (BULKIN) and they had 4 children, and two were deceased, names not stated, surviving were: 5. ANNA; 6. WILLIAM S. The family had nmoved to Brooklyn, Jackson Co., Mich. in 1857, and then Napoleon where he resided in 1881. Ref: History of Jackson Co., Mich., pg. 962-3.

BLAIN, JOSEPH and wife, AGNES (McINTYRE), both born England, moved to Canada about 1832 and settled in Montreal, and he died that year of Cholera; and she died 1872, Toronto. Known son, JOSEPH H. (following). Ref: P&BA-Len pg. 275-6.

BLAIN, JOSEPH H., son of JOSEPH (preceding), was born 26 Feb. 1824, Liverpool, England, and came to Canada with his parents. He married ca. 1857 to CATHERINE (VanEVERY) at St. Catherines, Canada. She lived in Lincoln Co., near Niagara Falls, Canada. They moved to Adrian, Lenawee co., Mich. in 1862. There were 6 children, 2 of whom were born in Toronto, and 4 following were still living in 1888: 1. JOSEPH M. (Puget Sound); 2. ABRAHAM L. (Ft. Wayne); 3. AGNES M.; 4. KATIE L. Ref: P&BA-Len pg. 275-6.

BLAIN, LEAH married in 1833 in Seneca Co., NY to Joseph Hagaman (also see).

BLAINE, SARAH (See Pharis Sutton)

BLAIR, CHARLES born ca. 1802, and wife, SARAH, born ca. 1810, both in NY, were listed in the 1850 census of Franklin Twp., Lenawee Co., Mich. with DANIEL, age 20 (see DANIEL C., following), b. NY; & MARY, age 15; JOSEPHINE, age 6, both b. Mich., in their household.

BLAIR, DANIEL C., probably son of CHARLES (preceding), married on 20 Apr. 1852 in Franklin Twp., Lenawee Co., Mich. to MARY E. (MILLS), daughter of Philo C. (also see). They moved to Napoleon, Jackson Co., Mich. Children: 1. HATTIE; 2. HERBERT; 3. CHARLES; 4. NELLIE P. (m. Wood?); 5. MINNIE; 6. BERTHA. Ref: P&BA-Len pg. 1060-3.

BLAIR, DAVID was born in Mass., and wife, TEMPERANCE (DeKAY), was born Penn., and they lived in Sodus, Wayne Co., NY before 1828. He was said to be a "cripple," and she died there in 1840 as a young woman leaving 4 sons & 1 daughter. Known sons, DAVID M. b. 4 Dec. 1828, Sodus, NY (following); JAMES b. 11 Mar. 1833, Sodus, NY (following). Ref: P&BA-Len pg. 849-50.

BLAIR, DAVID M., son of DAVID (preceding), helped care for the family after the death of his mother. He married in Seneca Co., NY to LUCINDA (CLARK) who was born in Ohio in 1830. About 1850, they went to Gorham Twp., Ohio, and in 1855 to Morenci, Mich. Lucinda died 6 July 1879. Children: 1. WARREN; 2. LUCY A.; 3. GEORGE (m. Sarah J. Bardwell; had sons, David M.; Jessie L; & Clarence); 4. ELLEN (may be same ELLEN M., following); 5. ERNEST M. (Ashland, Wis.). David M. married second on 22 Oct. 1879 to Mrs. ELLEN N., widow of James Page (also see). Ref: P&BA-Len pg. 849-50.

BLAIR, ELLEN M. (note DAVID M., preceding) of Franklin Twp., Lenawee Co., Mich. married Western Blackman of Napoleon, Jackson Co., MIch. on 21 Apr. 1853.

BLAIR, JAMES, son of DAVID (preceding), was age 7 when his mother died, and he went to Seneca Co., NY to live with another family. He married first to AGNES N. (FERGUSON) who died in Rochester, NY leavng a daughter: 1. ANNIE. James married second to LUCINDA (ORAM) in Canada. In 1866, they settled in

Pioneer Families of Southeastern Michigan

Morenci, Mich. Children: 2. CHARLES; 3. LILLY M. (m. Fred Fisk, son of Daniel, also see); 4. FRANK. Ref: P&BA-Len pg. 850.

BLAIR, PYRA/PATIRA (See William S. Blackmar)

BLAKE, ALEXANDER born ca. 1814, NY, and wife, SUSAN, born ca. 1823, Conn., were listed in the 1850 census of Medina Twp., Lenawee Co., Mich. with OPHELIA, age 3; JANE, age 1, both b. Mich., in the household.

BLAKE, CHARLES (See Samuel Hopkins, son of Levi)

BLANCHARD, CHARLES, son of JOHN W. (following), was born 27 June 1835 in Oakland Co., Mich. After the death of his parents, he lived with an uncle, Horace Garlick, and was in that household in the 1850 census of Medina Twp., Lenawee Co., Mich. He married 10 Apr. 1855, Medina Twp., to CLARISSA OPHELIA (BALDWIN), daughter of Charles M. (also see), and settled there. Children: 1. LURA EMMA; 2. CHARLES EROTUS (m. Mary Maybin, Morenci, Mich.); 3. ERNEST W.; 4. CYRUS M. (Ft. Scott, KS); 5. WILLARD A.; 6. ETHEL W.; 7. WALTER M.; 8. EFFIE E.; 9. BESSIE O.; 10. RENA M.; 11. ROSCOE W. Ref: P&BA-Len pg. 789-90.

BLANCHARD, ETTA (See Charles Perry)

BLANCHARD, JOHN was listed in the 1840 census index of White Lake Twp., Oakland Co.,Mich., a "pensioner," age 77 yrs. (b. ca. 1763). Note JOHN W., following, possibly son.

BLANCHARD, JOHN W., possibly son of JOHN (preceding), was born ca. 1800, NY, and came to Oakland Co., Mich. with his father. He married there to PHEBE who was born ca. 1805, NY; and she died in 1846, and he died in 1848. Children: 1. LEWIS M.; 2. MARSHALL (following); 3. CHARLES (preceding); 4. ELIZABETH. Ref: P&BA-Len pg. 789-90.

BLANCHARD, LEVI, born ca. 1819, NY, possibly son of NATHAN (following), was listed next door to Nathan in the 1850 census of Medina Twp., Lenawee Co., Mich. He listed wife, SALLY A., b. ca. 1825, NY, and JANETTE, age 4; ALMOND, age 2, both b. Mich., in the household.

BLANCHARD, MARSHALL (SeeRoswell H. Hicks). Note this name in the family of JOHN W., preceding.

BLANCHARD, NATHAN born ca. 1784, Mass., and wife, POLLY, born ca. 1790, NY, were listed in the 1850 census of Medina Twp., Lenawee Co., Mich. with CALVIN, age 42; LEWIS, age 27; HARLOW, age 23, all b. NY, in the household. Listed next door was LEVI (preceding).

BLANCHARD, REUBEN born ca. 1814, and wife, LUCINDA, born ca. 1818, both in NY, were listed in the 1850 census of Riga Twp., Lenawee Co., Mich., with no family in their household.

BLANCHARD, STEPHEN S. was born ca. 1773 in Mass. In the 1830 census of the Michigan Territory, he was listed age 50-60; and had a female 40-50, and two 15-20 in the household. It may be he listed in the 1840 census index of Plymouth, Wayne Co., Mich. In the 1850 census of Hudson Twp., Lenawee Co., Mich. he was age 77, and was listed in the household of Joshua & Mary Kinney.

BLANCHARD, STILLMAN was born ca. 1796 in Vt, and his wife, LUCY, was born ca. 1809, Conn. In the 1830 census of Michigan Territory, Lenawee Co., he listed 3 males 30-40; 1 20-30; 1 5-10; and females 1 20-30; 1 15-20; 1 under 5. In the 1850 census of Tecumseh Twp., Lenawee Co., he listed DARILLA?, age 21; JULIA, age 16; FRANCES, age 12; EMMA, age 8; CHARLES, age 6, all b. Mich., in the household.

BLANDON, CYNTHIA (See Ethan Allen)

BLINN, HARRIET M. (See Charles Burridge)

BLISS, ALMON L. born ca. 1832, Mich., wa listed in the 1850 census of Blissfield Twp., Lenawee Co., Mich. Probably this is "A. L." who married ALMIRA (GOFF), daughter of Sewell S. (also see) after 1850, Blissfield Twp.

BLISS, E. K. (See George Sisson, son of Cook)

BLISS, HARVEY was listed in the 1830 census of Lenawee Co., Mich. Territoy with males: 1 under 5; 1 5-10; 1 10-15; 1 40-50; & females: 1 5-10; 1 10-15; 1 40-50. In the 1840 census index of Blissfield Twp, Lenawee Co., Mich. he was adjacent to WILLIAM (following). MARTHA, following, possibly his wife?? ALMON; HARVEY; HIRAM; & WILLIAM W., may be sons??

BLISS, HARVEY born ca. 1830, Mich., was listed in the 1850 census of Blissfield Twp., Lenawee Co., Mich. with JULIA A., age 17, b. NY (possibly his wife), in the household of Calvin Hagaman.

BLISS, HIRAM born ca. 1823, and wife, LOVICA, born ca. 1823, both in NY, were listed in the 1850 census of Blissfield Twp., Lenawee Co., Mich. with DANIEL, age 6; ALMON(D), age 5, both b. Mich., in their household.

BLISS, LUCINDA (See Calvin Burnham)

BLISS, MARTHA born ca. 1778 was listed in the 1850 census of Macon Twp., Lenawee Co., Mich. in the household of Samuel & Sarah Fuller (mother of Sarah??). Also note HARVEY, preceding.

BLISS, WILLIAM W., born ca. 1817, Mich.?, and wife, ELIZABETH, born ca. 1818, NY, were listed in the 1840 census index of Blissfield Twp., Lenawee Co., Mich.; and in the 1850 census listed WILLIAM J., age 9; CHARLES M., age 1, both b. Mich. in their household. Note HARVEY, preceding.

BLIVEN, ALBERT H., son of SAMUEL (following), born 13 May 1825, Lee, Mass. (or Ohio), came to Michigan with his parents. He married JANE M., born ca. 1827, VT. He died 29 July 1855, Blissfield Twp., Lenawee Co., Mich. In the 1850 census of Blissfield Twp., they listed CHARLES F., age 4/12, b. Mich. in the household, as well as Chloe Barrett (also see), age 65, with other Barrett children (Jane may be another daughter). Ref: P&BA-Len pg. 785-6.

BLIVEN, GEORGE W., son of SAMUEL (following), was born 16 Mar. 1821, Great Barrington, Mass. He came to Michigan with his parents, and married 13 May 1854 to ANNA E. (GOODALE), daughter of Hiram (also see) of Deerfield Twp., Lenawee Co. Children: 1. ALICE J. (m. Haskell Warren, Beadle Co., Dak.); 2. EDWARD G.; 3. CORA J. (m. William Sisson, Adrian Twp.); 4. EGBERT B. (d. age 7 mos); 5. LUCY J. E.; 6. AGNES MABEL b. 20 Dec. 1865 (m. Charles B. Phillips, Jr., Toledo, O.; she d. 14 Mar. 1886, and son, Kenneth L., lived with grandparents.) Ref: P&BA-Len pg. 785-6.

BLIVEN, JONATHAN and wife, AMY (BLIVEN), were natives of Westerly, RI. Daughter, MARY, born 11 June 1795, Westerly (m. SAMUEL (following).

BLIVEN, SAMUEL, son of GEORGE (a Revolutionary soldier of Westerly, RI), was born 28 Feb. 1792, Westerly. He was a Seaman, and the served as a Minute Man in the War of 1812 from Conn., and was later a Pensioner. He married 1 Feb. 1818 to MARY (BLIVEN), daughter of JONATHAN (preceding). They lived in Berkshire Co., Mass, and then about 1819 moved to Cleveland, Ohio. In 1833, they moved to Blissfield Twp., Lenawee Co., Mich. She died in 1846, but he was still living in 1888, over age 95. Children: 1. GEORGE W. (preceding); 2. JOSEPH F. b. 1 Apr. 1823; 3. ALBERT H. (preceding); 4. SAMUEL M. b. 8 Jan. 1832, Ohio (d. San Francisco, CA); 5. MARY A. b. 8 Apr. 1839, Blissfield Twp.; 6 & 7 son & daughter d. infancy. Ref: P&BA-Len pg. 785-6.

BLODGETT, ISAIAH and wife, MARGARET, were parents of BETSEY who married Hezekiah Fordham (also see) in Genesee Co., NY by 1818. Ref: P&BA-Len pg. 752-3.

BLODGETT, JOHN and wife, LUCY (BARLOW), of Clarkston, Monroe Co., NY were parents of 8 children. Known daughter, ALTHEA A. (m/1 Joseph Bordwell; m/2 George W. Moore, see both). Ref: P&BA-Len pg. 1000-2.

BLODGETT, URI Mrs. of Coldwater, Mich. was the daughter of Charles Marble (also see).

BLOOD, BETSEY (See Lewis Nickerson)

BLOOD, EZRA F. was born 28 Oct. 1798, Deering, Hillsboro Co., NH; and served in the War of 1812. At age 21, he went to Brownville, Jefferson Co., NY. In 1824, in the company of 14 men, some with families, he came to Tecumseh Twp., Lenawee co., Territory of Michigan. He married 12 Jan. 1830 to ALZINA (BLACKMAR), daughter of Charles (also see). He died 18 Feb. 1887, Tecumseh Twp., and she was still living there in 1888. Children: 1. MARY JANE (d, infancy); 2. MARY A. b. ca. 1832 (m. Jacob Talman, Mt. Morris, NY); 3. CHARLES H. b. ca. 1837 (Tecumseh Twp.); 4. WILLIAM A. b. ca. 1840 (d. Andersonville Prison, Civil War); 5. LEROY C. (m. Frances E. Conkling, daughter of Hudson W., also see); 6. ORVILLE O. (Tecumseh Twp.). Ref: P&BA-Len pg. 819-20.

BLOOD, HIRAM H. born ca. 1814, New Hampshire, and wife EMELINE, born ca. 1815, VT, were listed in the 1850 census of Seneca Twp., Lenawee Co., Mich. with HIRAM H., age 12; ELSA J., age 9; LODAMA, age 8, all b. NH; and ELLEN J., age 3, b. Mich. in the household.

BLOOD, LEONARD P. born ca. 1824, and wife, LUCINDA, born ca. 1825, both in NY, were listed in the 1850 census of Seneca Twp., Lenawee Co., Mich. (adjacent to HIRAM H., preceding) with LEONARD N., age 6; JAMES H., age 3; & MARSHALL W., age 1, all b. Mich., in the household.

BLOOMER, ANN (See Roswell Henry)

BLOUNT, JULIA E. (See Delos M. Baker)

BLUE, MARY (See Peter Van Vleet, Jr.)

BOARDMAN, SALLY (See Joseph Meech)

BODINE, ABRAHAM W. born ca. 1810, Penn., and wife, SARAH, born ca. 1828, England, were listed in the 1850 census of Cambridge Twp., Lenawee Co., Mich. with MARY, age 1, b. Mich., in their household. Note: There was an ABRAHAM & WILLIAM listed in the 1840 census index of Genesee Co., Mich. Also see JOHN, following.

BODINE, FRANCES (See Henry Nichols)

BODINE, JOHN, born ca. 1786, NJ, and wife, JANE, born ca. 1800, Penn., were listed in the 1850 census of Cambridge Twp., Lenawee Co., Mich. with HIRAM, age 18, b. NY, in their household.

BODINE, JOHN born ca. 1820, and wife, SALLY ANN, born ca. 1822, both in NY, and it may be he listed in the 1840 census index of Franklin Twp., Lenawee Co., Mich. In the 1850 census of Franklin Twp., they listed ESTELLA, age 3, b. Mich. in the household.

BODINE, MARY A. (See Burtis Bird)

BODINE, PETER of Ovid, Seneca Co., NY was the father of MARGARET born 18 July 1808 (m. James Lanning, also see). Ref: P&BA-Len pg. 797-8. Note: There was a "Pierre Bodin" listed in the 1840 census index of Bedford Twp., Monroe Co., Mich.

BODINE, PHEBE (See Abraham Latourrette)

BODKIN, THOMAS was listed in the 1840 census index of Dundee Twp., Monroe Co., Mich., and is most likely the first husband of MARY A. (FRAMPTON). Mary married again before 1850 to Joseph Pilbeam (also see), and the following BODKIN children were listed in the household in the 1850 census of Ridgeway Twp., Lenawee Co., Mich.: 1. ELIZABETH, age 20; 2. MARIA, age 18; 3. SARAH A., age 13, all b. NY; and MARGARET, age 11; EMILY, age 8, both b. Mich. In 1888, Mary A. was living with her daughter, Mrs. Margaret Caswell in Milan Twp., Monroe Co., Mich.

BOGERT, PETER, ca. 1799, New Jersey, was the son of a Revolutionary soldier who had come from Germany just prior to the War. He settled before 1840 in Adrian Twp., Lenawee Co., Mich. In the 1850 census of Adrian Twp., listed were wife, SYLVA, age 45, b. NJ; and children: JOHN, age 15, b. NY; ADELIA, age 12; PETER, JR., age 4, both b. Mich.; and ADELAIDE, born 3 Jan. 1850, Adrian (called "SALLY," in census, age 6/12; m. Dwight Snedeker, also see). Ref: P&BA-Len pg. 372-3. Note: In the 1840 census index of Adrian were CORNELIUS; E. C. V.; ISAAC; & THOMAS, spelled "Boget." In the list of Revolutionary Pension applications is a CORNELIUS "BOGART," NJ, #BLWt.8151.100, among others.

BOGERT, CYNTHIA Mrs., age 40, born Canada, was head of household in the 1850 census of Adrian Twp., Lenawee Co., Mich. with ATWATER, age 16, b. NY; ELISHA, age 13; BENJAMIN F., age 9, both b. Mich., in her household. Note, preceding, the men who were listed in Adrian Twp. in 1840 census index.

BOHEN, ANN G. (See Thomas Rinehart) Note that name may also be spelled BOHAN/BOHON.

BOIES, DAVID of Mass. was a descendant of a French Huguenot family named DeBoies who had come to America at an early date. Among his children were

Pioneer Families of Southeastern Michigan

Rev. ARTEMUS (of Philadelphia, Penn.); Judge JOSEPH (of Washington Co., NY); & LEMUEL (following). Ref: P&BA-Len pg. 748-9.

BOIES, HENRY M., son of LEMUEL (following), was born ca. 1820, Mass., and wife, MARGARET A., was born ca. 1830, NY, and they were listed in the 1850 census of Hudson Twp., Lenawee Co., Mich. with FRANK H., age 3, b. Mich. in the household. Also listed was JOHN K. (following).

BOIES, JOHN K., son of LEMUEL (following), was born 6 Dec. 1828, Blandford, Hampden Co., Mass. He went to Oberlin, Ohio in 1845, and to Hudson Twp., Lenawee Co., Mich. by 1846. In 1850, he was listed in the household of HENRY M., preceding. He married first on 22 Oct. 1852 to SARAH AMELIA (SPEER) who was born 1832, Palmyra, Wayne Co., NY, and she died 5 Jan. 1870. Children: 1. EVA A. b. 4 Nov. 1853 (m. Frederick A. Wing); 2. CLARA E. b. 16 July 1857 (m. Herman V. C. Hart, Adrian); 3. JOHN HENRY b. 16 July 1864. John K. married second on 26 Aug. 1875 to MARY (COLTON), daughter of Rev. T. G. Colton of Hudson. Child: 4. BESSIE b. ca. 1880. Ref: P&BA-Len pg. 748-9.

BOIES, LEMUEL, son of DAVID (preceding), married in 1813 in Blandford, Hampden Co., Mass. to EXPERIENCE (KEEP), daughter of Samuel (also see). He died in Blandford, and she afterwards moved to Westfield, Mass. Known sons: HENRY M.; & JOHN K. (both preceding). Ref: P&BA-Len pg. 748-9.

BOLLES, FREDERICK E. and wife, SARAH A., settled in Chelsea, Washtenaw Co., Mich. before 1840. Known daughter, FRANCES E. (m. 4 Apr. 1864 Capt. Henry N. King, also see). Ref: P&BA-Len pg. 592-3.

BOLTON, HELEN (See Richard Pelham)
BOLTON, SARAH (See Joseph Pilbeam)

BONFOEY, HANNAH married first to Hosea Treat, and second to Obediah Platt (See Treat Family). Ref: P&BA-Len pg. 1167-8.

BOODY, DANIEL was born VT, and his wife, MARY (SEVEY), was born in New Hampshire. They settled first in Quebec, Canada, and later moved to Rochester, NY, Delphi, Ind., back to Rochester, and then to Allegany Co., NY. In 1872, they moved to Coldwater, Mich. where he died 25 Oct. 1876. Two sons and 2 daughters. Known son, ROBERT P. (following); and daughter (who m. A. D. Collins, Fulton Co., Ohio). Ref: P&BA-Len pg. 1007-8.

BOODY, ROBERT P., son of DANIEL (preceding), was born 17 Oct. 1834, Orleans Co, VT (near Canadian border). He later lived in Rochester, NY and Allegany Co., NY; and then moved to Chesterfield, Fulton Co., Ohio. He married on 19 Dec. 1858 to EMILY M. (KINSMAN), daughter of Adnah B. (also see). They moved to Morenci, Lenawee Co., Mich. in 1883. No children were listed. Ref: P&BA-Len pg. 1007-8.

BOOHER, FRED was listed in the 1840 census index of Kalamazoo, Kalamazoo Co., Mich.

BOOHER, JACOB was born ca. 1792, Switzerland. He came to Washtenaw Co., Mich. where he married MARGARET (SNYDER) who was born ca. 1802 in Wurtemburg, Germany. They settled in Cambridge Twp., Lenawee Co., Mich. before 1835. He died 1 Oct. 1870; and she died 16 July 1870. There were 4 daughters, 1 died young. 1. CATHARINE M. b. 19 Apr. 1835 (m. Sinon Shultis, also see); 2. HANNAH b. ca. 1840 (m. Jefferson Louden, also see); 3. MARY b. ca. 1841 (m. Brainard). Ref: P&BA-Len pg. 993-4 & 1150-1.

BOONE, CLARK (See Daniel Bay)

BOOTH, BELDEN married in Clinton, Lenawee Co., Mich. to SALLIE A. (WRIGHT), daughter of Elijah (also see). Belden died before 1842, and she married second to Rancelier Mills (also see). Ref: P&BA-Len pg. 1086-7.

BOOTH, PHILA M. (See George Bowen)

BORDEN see BORDON

BORDINE, ANN (See Harmon Vedder)
BORDINE, CHRISTINA? Mrs., age 59, b. NY, was listed head of household in the 1850 census of Dover Twp., Lenawee Co., Mich. with JACOB, age 17; & DANIEL, age 15, in her household.
BORDINE, DAVID born ca. 1822, and wife, LORETT, born ca. 1827, both in NY, were listed in the 1850 census of Dover Twp., Lenawee Co., Mich. with ELMA? J., age 6; & DAVID, age 4, both b. NY, in the household.

BORDON, BETSEY (See Watson Hanchett)

BORDWELL, JOSEPH married ALTHEA (BLODGETT), daughter of John (also see) on 29 Apr. 1852. He died in Albion (probably Barre), Orleans Co., NY on 17 June 1877. Children: 1. JOSEPH N. (m. Mina Cramer, Rochester, NY); 2. MARY A. (d. infancy); 3. ADA M. (d. infancy); 4. JOHN B. (Albion, NY). Althea married second to George W. Moore (also see). Ref: P&BA-Len pg. 1000-2.

BORICK, JACOB N. married MARY ANN (SLOAN), daughter of Robert (also see). Children: 1. DELLA; 2. WILLIE; 3. KATIE; 4. EMMA; 5. LULU.

BORNOIR, DAVID (See Wilber West)

BORTON, JOSEPH (See George W. Stephenson)

BOSS, GEORGE S. of Ridgeway Twp., Lenawee Co., Mich. was uncle to MARY I., whom he raised. Mary married Warren J. Holdridge (also see).

BOUGHTON, GUY C., son of NATHAN, was born in Stockbridge, Berkshire Co., Mass.; and moved with his father to Grafton, Lorain Co., Ohio in 1818. He married HARRIET (SPRAGUE), daughter of David (also see), and in 1854 they moved to Norwich, Huron Co., Ohio, where he died that same year. She died in 1885. Known daughter, ACHSAH (m. Ira Holloway, also see). Ref: P&BA-Len pg. 1139-40.

BOVEE, ABRAM born ca. 1813, and wife, SARAH, born ca. 1817, both in NY, were listed in the 1850 census of Hudson Twp., Lenawee Co., Mich. (next to Matthias) with MARY, age 10; FRANCIS, age 11; DAVID, age 7, all b. Mich., in their household.

BOVEE, CHARLES born ca. 1832, NY, was listed in the 1850 census of Fairfield Twp., Lenawee Co., Mich.

BOVEE, EMMA (See James H. Shepherd)

BOVEE, HIRAM (See Jonathan Austin)

BOVEE, JACOB born ca. 1807, and wife, ESTHER, born ca. 1808, both in NY, were listed in the 1850 census of Dover Twp., Lenawee Co., Mich. with ELISHA, age 20; ELIJAH, age 19; EZRA, age 17, all b. NY; and ALBERT, age 15; ARTHUR, age 12; HAMILTON, age 9; MYRON, age 5; LUCY A., age 7; ESTHER, age 4; HULDAH, age 1, all b. Mich., in their household.

BOVEE, JOHN born ca. 1800, NY, and wife, ELECTA, born ca. 1807, Canada, were listed in the 1850 census of Dover Twp., Lenawee Co., Mich. with HENRY, age 25; AARON, age 23; LEVI, age 21; IRA, age 16, all b. NY; and LORENZO, age 23; DAVID, age 11; CHARLES, age 6, all b. Mich., in the household.

BOVEE, MATTHIAS born ca. 1803, and wife, MARIAH, born ca. 1810, both in NY, were listed in the 1850 census of Hudson Twp., Lenawee Co., Mich. with MARTHA, age 18; MINERVA, age 16; both b. NY; and ANDREW, age 13; GROSVENOR, age 10, both b. Mich., in the household.

BOVEE, MILO of Dover Twp. (See Isaac Warren)

BOVEE, PETER born ca. 1815, and wife, MARY, born ca. 1824, both in NY, were listed in the 1850 census of Hudson Twp., Lenawee Co., Mich. with ELIZA J., age 9; ANGELINE, age 6; JAMES H., age 8/12, all born Mich., in their household.

BOVIER, see BEVIER

BOWEN, CATHERINE Mrs. born ca. 1806, NY, was listed in the 1850 census of Madison Twp., Lenawee Co., Mich. in the household of Henry Withuwar?, age 77, b. NY. With her were apparently her children, HENRY, age 13, b. NY; GEORGE, age 12; SILAS, age 10; HIRAM, age 8; JANE A., age 4, all b. Mich.

BOWEN, GEORGE was born ca. 1790, Mass., and served in the War of 1812. He married in Bristol, Ontario Co., NY to PHILA (PHILOMILA? BOOTH) who was born ca. 1798, Conn., and they moved to Monroe Co., NY. About 1836, they moved to Tecumseh, Lenawee Co., Mich. Known sons: NATHANIEL K. (following); GEORGE N. (following). LOREN, age 21, b. NY, in the 1850 census in another household may relate to this family. Ref: P&BA-Len pg. 1038-9.

BOWEN, GEORGE (See George M. Lewis)

BOWEN, GEORGE N., son of GEORGE (preceding), born ca. 1813, and wife, ALMYRA, born ca. 1815, were listed in the 1850 census of Tecumseh Twp., Lenawee Co., Mich. with JEROME, age 3, b. Mich., and his parents, preceding, and William Spaulding, age 25, b. Ohio, in their household.

BOWEN, GEORGE W. Dr. (See Joshua W. Thurber)

BOWEN, HENRY and wife, SARAH (CAMBREN), came to Michigan in 1830; and by 1857 resided in Adrian, Lenawee Co. Known son, HENRY C. (following). Ref: P&BA-Len pg. 514.

BOWEN, HENRY born ca. 1808, Mass., married first (poss. in Otsego Co., NY) to ? (COUNROD), daughter of Peter (also see). She died leaving 8 children. In the 1850 census of Franklin Twp., Lenawee Co., Mich., he listed CYNTHIA, age 17; HENRY, age 16; NORMAN?, age 15; LEVI, age 13; POLLY, age 12; BENONI, age 10; FRANKLIN, age 9; JOSEPH, age 7, all b. NY. He married again ca. 1851 in Cherry Valley, NY to her sister, Mrs. LUCINDA (COUNROD) STEARNS, widow of Willard Stearns[1] (also see). Lucinda died 3 Feb. 1879, Adrian, Mich. Ref: P&BA-Len pg. 615-6.

BOWEN, HENRY C., son of HENRY & SARAH (preceding), was born 28 Mar. 1857, Adrian, Lenawee Co., Mich. He married in 1883 to LOUISE (WIES), daughter of Stephen (also see). Daughter, OLGA, born 13 Mar. 1887. Ref: P&BA-Len pg. 514.

BOWEN, JANES married LOUISE (WHIPPLE) of Adrian, Lenawee Co., Mich. on 10 Apr. 1853.

BOWEN, MALVIN (See Thomas C. Isley)

BOWEN, NATHANIEL K., son of GEORGE, was born 15 Feb. 1810, Bristol, Ontario Co., NY, and married there first to SOPHIE (PHILLIPS) who was born in Bristol in 1814. She died in 1840 in Clinton Twp., Lenawee Co., Mich. leaving sons, JEREMIAH (deceased before 1888); GEORGE b. ca. 1840 (m. Abbie M. Frost, Clinton Twp.). Nathaniel married in Clinton Twp. in 1842 to ELIZABETH (SPAULDING) who was born in Seneca Co., NY in 1815 (she had gone as a child to near Akron, Ohio, and afterwards to Macon Twp., Lenawee Co.). Children: 3. DANIEL E. b. ca. 1846 (m. Mary Gillett, had children, Zella I. & Roy E., lived Dundee, Monroe Co., Mich.); 4. DEWITT C. (m. Miss Clyde Stewart, Adrian). Ref: P&BA-Len pg. 1038-9.

BOWERMAN, ABIGAIL Mrs., age 50, born NY, was head of household in the 1850 census of Raisin Twp., with MOSES, age 24, b. NY in her household. JOHN, age 26, (following) listed next door, may be a son.

BOWERMAN, CHARLES E., son of SAMUEL (following), was born 27 Aug. 1845, Raisin Twp., Lenawee Co., Mich.; and he married there 13 Oct. 1864 to FRANCES A. (WILSON, also see Thomas). Children: 1. ALMA L. b. 3 May 1870; 2. HARVEY E. b. 11 Sept. 1872; 3. HARRY A. b. 7 Feb. 1881; 4. BESSIE L. b. 19 Aug. 1884. Ref: P&BA-Len pg. 195.

BOWERMAN, DOROTHY married James Hathaway (also see), a Quaker, in Berkshire Co., Mass. Ref: P&BA-Len pg. 657-8.

BOWERMAN, JEMIMA (See William Gallaway)

BOWERMAN, JOHN born ca. 1824, NY, and wife, MARY A., born ca. 1829, NY, married within the year, were listed in the 1850 census of Raisin Twp., Lenawee Co., Mich. next door to ABIGAIL, preceding, possibly his mother.

BOWERMAN, JOSEPH born ca. 1811, NY, was listed as head of household in the 1850 census of Raisin Twp., Lenawee Co., Mich. with ADA ANN, age 19, b. NY; PELEG, age 16; GEORGE, age 14; JOSEPH M, age 12; ISAAC, age 10; STEPHEN, age 8 (may be he m. Nancy Haviland, dau. of Peleg, also see); EPHRAIM, age 6; ABIGAIL, age 5, PHILISTIA, age 3, last 6 b. Mich., in the household.

BOWERMAN, MOSES Jr., son of MOSES Sr. (following), was born 27 Nov. 1811, Providence, Saratoga Co., NY. He married 9 Feb. 1831, Royalton, Niagara Co., NY, to ZILPHA (HAVILAND), daughter of Charles (also see), and they moved to Raisin Twp., Lenawee Co. Mich. in 1832. Children: 1. EUNICE (d. young); 2. MARTHA b.

Pioneer Families of Southeastern Michigan

ca. 1833 (d. age 22); 3. EUNICE 2d b. ca. 1836; 4. CORDELIA ANN (d. age 3); 5. ROSALINDA b. ca. 1840 (d. age 45); 6. MARY b. ca. 1844 (d. age 43); 7. ESTHER b. ca. 1837 (m. Solomon Dye, Nebraska); 8. MOSES b. ca. 1839 (m. Rocina Haviland, See Peleg C.; to Summit City, Mich.); 9. NANCY b. ca. 1842 (m. James Kennedy); 10. LOUISA b. ca. 1846 (m. James Starm, Raisin Twp.); 11. SARAH b. ca. 1848 (m. Charles Widney, Louisiana); 12. ELLEN J. (m. Orlando Westgate). Ref: P&BA-Len pg. 322-4.

BOWERMAN, MOSES Sr. was born in Mass., and moved with his second wife, EUNICE (DEXTER) to Saratoga Co., NY and afterwards to Royalton, Niagara Co., NY where he died in 1823. Eunice remained in Niagara Co., NY until ca. 1832, then moved to Raisin Twp., Lenawee Co., Mich. with her family. Known son, MOSES, Jr. (preceding). Ref: P&BA-Len 322-4. In the 1840 census index, EUNICE is listed as head of household adjacent to JOSEPH (preceding); JOSHUA; LEVI, SAMUEL (following); possibly additional sons of Moses, Sr.

BOWERMAN, NILES of Raisin Twp., Lenawee Co., Mich. married MARY (WEST), daughter of Benjamin (also see) who was born in either Dutchess Co., NY or Norwich, Oxford Co., Canada. Note ISAAC BEAGLE BOWERMAN, father of WILLIAM, following.

BOWERMAN, SAMUEL, possibly son of MOSES, Sr. (preceding), was born ca. 1814, a "native of Saratoga Co., NY," whom also lived in Niagara Co., NY. He married DORCAS (WESTGATE, see Jeremiah), and settled in Raisin Twp., Lenawee Co., Mich. They were Quakers. She died 11 Apr. 1865, and he died in 1880. There were 11 children, those following in the 1850 census of Raisin Twp., all born Mich.: 1. AMY, age 15; 2. JANE, age 12; 3. ELVIRA, age 9; 4. LOVINA, age 7; 5. LOVISA (twin), age 7; 6. CHARLES E. b. 27 Aug. 1845 (preceding); 7. MARY A., age 3. Ref: P&BA-Len pg. 195.

BOWERMAN, WILLIAM was born Norwich, Oxford Co., Canada, 22 Jan. 1836, son of ISAAC BEAGLE. Following ancestry was given: An ancestor came from Germany and settled in Dutchess Co., NY, and had son, JOHN^1, who was father of JOHN^2 who died Bay of Quinte, Canada and had son, JOHN^3 who was born in Dutchess Co., NY, who married MARY (BEAGLE), and went to Canada. JOHN^3 had son, ISAAC BEAGLE, born 1812, Canada, who married MARY (WEST), daughter of Levi (also see), and became parents of WILLIAM. William came to Lenawee Co., Mich. and lived with relatives. He married 30 June 1861 to LYDIA (INGERSOLL), daughter of Reuben S. & Olivia I. Children: 1. MARY; 2. MAGGIE L.; 3. LIZZIE E.; 4. CHARLES B.; 5. RALPH A.; BESSIE J. Ref: P&BA-Len pg. 965-6.

BOWMAN, DIANTHA born 31 July 1817, Claremont, NH, married at Jonesville, Hillsdale Co., Mich. to Harley J. Olds (also see). Ref: P&BA-Len pg. 1072-3.

BOWMAN, DORCAS (See George Kayner & Jeremiah Westgate)

BOYCE, GEORGE - There were 2 men by this name in Lenawee Co., Mich. in the 1850 census. One, age 27, b. NY, in Medina Twp.; and one, age 22, b. England, in Ridgeway Twp.

BOYCE, JAMES, born 1813, and wife, ELIZABETH, born ca. 1821, both in Ireland, were listed in the 1850 census of Adrian Twp., Lenawee Co., Mich. with FREDERICK I., age 9; ELIZABETH, age 5, both b. NY; and EMMA, age 3; ALICE, age 1, both b. Mich., in their household.

BOYCE, JAMES T., son of JOHN (following), was born 10 Sept. 1836, Co. Antrim, Ireland, and came to Tecumseh Twp., Lenawee Co., Mich. with his parents ca. 1854. He married in 1868 to ESTHER (KYLE), daughter of Robert (also see). By 1877, they were living in Macon Twp. Of 9 children, 7 survived: 1. MAGGIE (m. Onie Curry, Milan, Monroe Co., Mich.); 2. MARY "MAMIE" (m. Arthur Underwood, son of William, also see); 3. ROBERT; 4. WILLIAM (m. Etta Craig, Republic, KS); 5. CARRIE; 6. MAUDE L.; 7. VERNA G. Ref: P&BA-Len pg. 704-5.

BOYCE, JOHN was born ca. 1795, Co. Antrim, Ireland, and married there to JANE (TILFORD). About 1847, they sailed to Baltimore, MD; and about 1854 came to Tecumseh Twp., Lenawee Co., Mich. They afterwards lived in Clinton, Mich., where he died in June 1873, age 78. She was still living in 1888, age 72, in the home of son, SAMUEL; another son, JAMES T. (preceding). Ref: P&BA-Len pg. 704-5.

BOYD, ARCHIBALD R., son of JAMES, Jr. (following), was born 10 Aug. 1858, Raisin Twp., Lenawee Co., Mich. He married 1 Jan. 1882 to ELLEN "ELLA" R. (HOLDRIDGE), daughter of Horace (also see). Children: 1. LAWRENCE K.; 2. JAMES CARROLL. Ref: P&BA-Len pg. 416-9.

BOYD, DAVID married in Ireland to ROSA (BOYD), where he died; and Rosa afterwards came to Macon Twp., Lenawee Co., Mich. to the home of daughter, MARGARET (m. JOHN BOYD, following). Rosa died 7 Sept. 1875, age 88. Ref: P&BA-Len pg. 685-6.

BOYD, JAMES, Jr., son of JAMES, Sr. (following), was born ca. 1810, Ireland, and came to Raisin Twp., Lenawee Co., Mich. from Livingston Co., NY. He married 3 Feb. 1853, Raisin Twp., to NANCY (RICHARD), daughter of Archibald (also see). James Jr. died 23 Dec. 1880, but she was still living in Tecumseh, Mich. in 1888, over age 60. Children: 1. ROBERT M. (following); 2. JAMES (Tecumseh); 3. ARCHIBALD R. (preceding); 4. JENNIE (m. Dr. R. B. House, Springfield, O.). Ref: P&BA-Len pg. 526-7.

BOYD, JAMES, Sr. was born in Co. Antrim, Ireland (of Scottish ancestry), and had come to America and settled in Livingston Co., NY where he died in 1820. Known son, JAMES, Jr. (preceding). Ref: P&BA-Len pg. 526-7. Also note, ROBERT, following.

BOYD, JOHN, son of SAMUEL, Jr. (following), was born 11 Jan. 1830 in Co. Antrim, Ireland. He came to Livingston Co., NY in 1848 with other family members. He moved to Macon Twp., Lenawee Co., Mich. in 1853, and he married 9 Feb. 1857 in Tecumseh to MARGARET (BOYD), daughter of DAVID (preceding). Children: 1. THOMAS; 2. MARGARET. Ref: P&BA-Len pg. 685-7.

BOYD, ROBERT came to America in 1818 (1828?) in the company of William Colvin (also see) and Fulton Jack all from Co. Antrim, Ireland. He prospected for land in 1830 in Raisin Twp., Lenawee Co., Mich. In the 1850 census of Raisin Twp., there is a ROBERT, age 43, b. Ireland, who would seem too young to have come to

America in 1818. His wife, SARAH, was age 36, b. Ireland, and they were 2 doors from William Colvin (who was age 60). Robert had in his household Jane Richard, age 34, b. Ireland (See Archibald Richard).

BOYD, ROBERT was born in Co. Antrim, Ireland in January 1831, and he married there in Nov. 1850 to MARY (PRESTON) who was born in 1831. They came to America in 1852, and settled in Tecumseh, Lenawee Co., Mich., and later in Raisin Twp. Nine children, of whom WILLIAM; ALFRED; DAVID; & ADDIE died in 1865 of Diptheria, and a daughter, ELIZA, died young. Surviving were EMMA (m. James Smith, Franklin Center); WILLIAM 2d?; MAGGIE; & FRED. Ref: P&BA-Len pg. 934-5.

BOYD, ROBERT M., son of JAMES, Jr. (preceding), was born in Raisin Twp., Lenawee Co., Mich. 1 Nov. 1853; and married on 4 Mar. 1884 to ANNA M. (BROWN), daughter of James W. (also see). Known daughter, LEORA J. Ref: P&BA-Len pg. 526-7.

BOYD, SAMUEL, Jr., son of SAMUEL, Sr. (following), married in Co. Antrim, Ireland to JANE (KYLE). They later followed their children to Livingston Co., NY. Known son, JOHN (preceding). Ref: P&BA-Len pg. 685-7.

BOYD, SAMUEL, Sr. of Country Antrim, Ireland married JANE (CARSON) who was of Scottish ancestry. They remained there. Known son, SAMUEL, Jr. (preceding). Ref: P&BA-Len pg. 685-7.

BOYD, THOMAS was born in Co. Antrim, Ireland in 1830, son of WILLIAM & JANE (PRESTON) who remained in Ireland. Thomas came first to Quebec, Canada; but shortly afterwards went to Vermont, then to Livingston Co., NY. In 1851, he moved to Raisin Twp., Lenawee Co., Mich., and then to Tecumseh Twp. He married MARGARET (CALHOUN), daughter of Robert (also see) in Lenawee Co. Children: 1. ESTHER A. (m. Wallace Tilden); 2. FANNY (m. Chester Haynes, Tecunseh village); 3. MAGGIE; 4. HATTIE (m. Arthur Dibble, Adrian); 5. WALLACE LAVERN. Ref: P&BA-Len pg. 301-2.

BOYED also see BOYD
  BOYED, SAMUEL (See Thomas Lee)

BOYER, ANNA M. was born ca. 1793, Cayuga Co., NY (See Henry Smith). Note: There was a JOHN in the 1800 census index, Cayuga Co., NY.

BOYER, LAVINA was born ca. 1790, Penn. (See Hebron Camburn).

BOYER, THOMAS and wife, SARAH, were parents of DEBORAH (m. James Knox^2, also see, in 1847 in Fairfield Twp., Lenawee Co., Mich., and d. in 1849); and EMELINE b. near Elmira, then Tioga Co., NY (m. James Knox^2, as 2d wife). Ref: P&BA-Len. pg. 588.

BRACE, NANCY (See Matthew Bennett)

BRADFORD, MARY E. (See George W. Baley)

BRADISH, AUGUSTUS W., son of CALVIN^1 (following), was born 24 Jan. 1815, Macedon, Wayne Co., NY, and came to Madison Twp., Lenawee Co., Mich. in 1831 with parents. He married 13 Apr. 1847 to ELSIE M. (APPLEBY), daughter of Jacob (also see). Children: 1. CAROLINE A.; 2. CLARENCE M.; 3. HERBERT H. (m. Etta Appleby, Fairfield Twp.); 4. CARROLL E. (m. Addie Spauldidng, Madison Twp.); 5. WILLIAM R.; 6. JOSEPHINE E.; 7. FRANK A. (m. Alice Harwood); 8. MARY E. Ref: P&BA-Len pg. 310-11.

BRADISH, CALVIN^1 was born in Mass., and his wife, NANCY (POST), was born Long Island, NY. They settled first in Macedon, Wayne Co., NY; and then in 1831 moved to Madison Twp. Lenawee Co., Mich. She died in 1839, and he died 17 Sept. 1851. Children: 1. MENTHA M.; 2. CURRAN (following); 3. NELSON (following); 4. SARAH; 5. LUTHER b. ca. 1808 (m. Rachel, b. 1810, NJ, lived Madison Twp.); 6. CALVIN (following); 7. JOHN; 8. HANNAH b. ca. 1820, NY (lived with Amanda 1850 census, Madison Twp.); 9. AUGUSTUS W. (preceding); 10. AMANDA C. b. 31 Jan. 1818, Macedon (m. Melvin T. Nickerson, also see); 11. MYRON W.; 12. NORMAN F. b. 25 Aug. 1822 (following). By 1888, the only surviving children were Augustus, Amanda, & Norman). Ref: P&BA-Len pg. 310-11.

BRADISH, CALVIN^2, son of CALVIN^1, was born 27 Dec. 1808, Wayne Co., NY, and came with parents to Madison Twp., Lenawee Co., Mich. He married MARY (JENNINGS), daughter of Daniel (also see). Children: 1. HORACE C.; 2. ORIN H.; 3. CHARLES C. (following). Ref: P&BA-Len pg. 395.

BRADISH, CHARLES C., son of CALVIN^2 (preceding), was born 28 Sept. 1845, Madison Twp., Lenawee Co., Mich., and married 23 Feb. 1871 to ELIZA (ENGLISH), daughter of Richard (also see), who died 13 June 1874. He married second on 17 Feb. 1876 to CHLOE (SANFORD) born in Wayne Co., NY, and she died 2 Feb. 1877, Madison Twp. The married third to CARRIE (SANFORD) on 28 June 1882; had children: 1. EDITH M.; 2. STANLEY S. Ref: P&BA-Len 395.

BRADISH, CHLOE was born 1 Apr. 1775, Hardwick, Mass., married Gain Robinson (also see) and moved to Wayne Co., NY. Ref: P&BA-Len pg. 1103-4.

BRADISH, CURRAN, son of CALVIN^1, was born ca. 1806 in Wayne Co., NY. He married RHODY S. (COMSTOCK) born 1805, Wayne Co., NY, and they moved to Madison Twp., Lenawee Co., Mich. in 1830. He died in 1869, and she died in 1870, Adrian Twp. Children: 1. HELEN E. b. 22 Sept. 1830 (m. Stephen Carpenter, also see). Those following from 1850 census of Madison Twp. 2. THERESA A., age 18; DARIUS C., age 16; CALVIN S., age 24; NANCY A., age 12; SARAH M., age 10; ADDSON C., age 9; CHARLES P., age 3, all b. Mich. Ref: P&BA-Len pg. 357-8.

BRADISH, MYRON W., son of NELSON (following), was born 20 Apr. 1830, Madison Twp., Lenawee Co., Mich. (1st child born in Twp.). In 1856, he went to California, but returned by 1859. He married MARTHA E. (DENNISON), daughter of Stephenson (also see) on 17 Jan. 1867. Children: 1. NORAH BELLE; 2. NINA BLANCHE; 3. NELLIE BEATRICE. Ref: P&BA-Len pg. 493-4.

BRADISH, NELSON, son of CALVIN^1 (preceding), was born ca. 1803, Wayne Co., NY. He married in Sodus, NY on 8 May 1828 to PHEBE (WILSON) born 1803, Rockland Co., NY. They settled in Madison Twp., Lenawee Co.,

Pioneer Families of Southeastern Michigan

Mich. before 1830. In 1860, they retired to Adrian, Mich.; and he died 6 May 1875, and she died 11 Apr. 1880. Children: 1. MYRON W. (preceding); 2. CULLEN (this may be WILLIAM b. ca. 1833 listed in household in 1850 census, deceased by 1888); 3. ANNE E. b. ca 1835 (m. J. W. Baldwin, Madison Twp.); 4. WARNER C. b. ca. 1837 (d. Civil War of illness); 5. MARY C. b. ca. 1844 (m. Joseph B. Dennison, see Stephenson); 6. Infant who died. Ref: P&BA-Len pg. 493-4.

BRADISH, NORMAN F., son of CALVIN[1] (preceding), married CAROLINE (CATON), daughter of John (also see) on 7 Oct. 1845, Madison Twp., Lenawee Co., Mich. Children: 1. MENTHA A. b. 11 Sept. 1846 (d. 23 Jan. 1852; 2. HELEN A. b. 23 Jan. 1849 (d. 1 Aug. 1851); 3. RUSSELL N. b. 22 Feb. 1852 (m. Jennie Spaulding, Madison Twp.); 4. MENTHA AMANDA (m. George B. Horton, also see); 5. MAGGIE A. b. 25 May 1862 (d. 18 Feb. 1864). Ref: P&BA-Len pg. 975-6. & 990-1.

BRADISH, ROWENA born 30 Sept. 1786, Cummington, Mass., married John Comstock (also see). Ref: P&BA-Len pg. 648-9.

BRADISH, WILLIAM and wife, REBECCA (WARREN), were parents of EMMA JANE born 22 Mar. 1835, Macedon, Wayne Co., NY (m. John S. Johnson (after 1861) in Medina Twp., Lenawee Co.). Ref: P&BA-Len pg. 1008-9.

BRADLEY, ADAM, probably son of WILLIAM (following), born ca, 1812, NY, settled in Franklin Twp., Lenawee Co., Mich. by 1840. His wife, ALMIRA, was born ca. 1811, New Hampshire. In the 1850 census of Franklin Twp., the listed WINCHESTER, age 13; ELMER, age 11; ATHALENE, age 8 (m. Frederick Bay, also see); JOHN, age 1, all born Mich.

BRADLEY, EBER and wife, HANNAH (WHITNEY), of Milan, Monroe Co., Mich. were parents of JULIA A. b. 3 Jan. 1840 (m. J. F. Gilmore, also see). Ref: P&BA-Len pg. 896-8.

BRADLEY, GRACE (See Willard F. Day)

BRADLEY, LETTIE (See Aaron Norcross[2])

BRADLEY, PATTIE (See Timothy Lewis)

BRADLEY, ROBERT J. born ca. 1822, NY, and wife, LAURA W., born ca. 1821, VT, were listed in the 1850 census of Adrian Twp., Lenawee Co., Mich. with WILLIAM F., age 6; HORACE B., age 3; GEORGE B., age 10/12, all born Mich., in their household.

BRADLEY, SCHUYLER (See Cyrenus Sanford)

BRADLEY, THOMAS[1] was born in Dublin, Ireland of English descent, and came to America in Colonial times and settled near Braintree, VT, where he died. Known son, THOMAS[2] (following). Ref: P&BA-Len pg. 577-8.

BRADLEY, THOMAS[2], son of THOMAS[1] (preceding), born ca. 1772, near Braintree, VT, married ABIGAIL (DAKE) there, and afterwards removed to Painesville, Lake Co., Ohio; and then about 1831 to Elyria, Lorain Co., Ohio. She died in Elyria in 1856, but he removed to Blissfield Twp., Lenawee Co., Mich. where he died in 1876, age 94. Known daughter, JULIA, b. 2 Nov. 1827, Painesville, O. (m. Porter M. Weylie, also see). Ref: P&BA-Len pg. 577-8.

BRADLEY, WILLIAM Deacon born ca. 1788, Conn., and wife, MARTHA, born 1788, NY, moved from Orleans Co., NY to Franklin Twp., Lenawee Co., Mich. in 1834. Known daughters: CLARA A. (m. Austin Love, also see); ARMENIA b. 7 Mar. 1817, Barre, NY (m. John J. Adam, also see); CORNELIA b. 8 Mar. 1822, Barre, NY (m/1 John Woimple; m/2 John J. Adam in 1873 as 2d wife). Others following were in the household in the 1850 census of Franklin Twp.: MARTHA, age 20; MARY, age 18; THANKFUL, age 15 (probably she who m. Simeon Aten, son of Peter, also see), all b. NY. Ref: P&BA-Len pg. 465-6. Note: Note ADAM (preceding), & WILLIAM, Jr. (following) whom may also be sons.

BRADLEY, WILLIAM, Jr., probably son of WILLIAM (preceding), was born ca. 1821, and wife, URSILLA, was born ca. 1821, both in NY, and were listed in the 1850 census of Franklin Twp., Lenawee Co., Mich. with FRANK, age 1, b. Mich. in the household.

BRADNER, BENJAMIN, son of COLVILL (following), and wife, CHARITY (MILLS), daughter of Micah (also see), were born and married in Orange Co., NY. She died in Warwick, Orange Co., NY 31 July 1837, age 47. Known sons: COE G. b. 17 July 1818 (d. 17 Feb. 1863, Warwick); ELEAZER MILLS; & JAMES W. (following). Benjamin married second to MARY (SLY); and married third to ELIZABETH (DEMOREST). Ref: P&BA-Len pg. 1114-8.

BRADNER, COLVILL of Warwick, Orange Co., NY had will dated 17 Feb. 1802, and proved 29 Mar. 1802. Mentioned were wife, ANNA; sons: JAMES; JOHN; BENJAMIN (preceding); COLVILL; COE; SAMUEL; and daughters: JULIA; POLLY; MARGARET; CHRISTIANN VANDEVORT; SARAH MINTHORN. Executrix was wife, ANNA; and witnesses were William Wisner; Abraham Chandler; Benjamin S. Hoyt. Ref: Early Wills of Orange Co., NY, by OCGS.

BRADNER, JAMES W., son of BENJAMIN (preceding), was born 4 Oct. 1821, Warwick, Orange Co., NY, and married in Blooming Grove to JANE A. (THORN). In 1859, they moved to Clinton Twp., Lenawee Co., Mich. She died 29 Sept. 1863, leaving 6 children (1 deceased before 1888, name not stated). 1. ALBERT (Steuben Co., Ind.); 2. HENRY (Washington Terr.); 3. COE G.; 4. EDGAR; 5. HATTIE (m. C. N. Greene, Bridgewater, Mich.). James W. married again on 28 July 1864 to MARY E. (PLUMB), daughter of Seth G. (also see). Children: 6. SETH B.; 7. MARY P. Ref: P&BA-Len pg. 1114-8 with portrait.

BRAGG, CHESTER married IDA MAY (TUTTLE), daughter of Oramon, Jr. (also see). Children: MAUDE A.; EDDIE; EARL; EUNICE MAY.

BRAIDS, AGNES (See James Knox)

BRAINARD, MARY (BOOHER) Mrs. was the daughter of Jacob Booher (also see) of Cambridge Twp., Lenawee Co., Mich. Ref: P&BA-Len pg. 993-4.

BRAINARD, WILLIAM, born ca. 1823, NY, and wife, SARAH A., born ca. 1827, both in NY, were listed in the 1850 census of Rollin Twp., Lenawee Co., Mich., with SARAH M., age 1, b. Mich. in the household.

BRAMBLE, CLEMENT, son of MOSES (following), born Manlius, NY, married ELIZABETH (PRINDLE) who was born Orange co., NY, and settled in Seneca Co., NY. Four sons and 3 daughters. Known children: ELIZABETH (m. Ira Kelly, also see); JEHIAL H. (following). Ref: P&BA-Len pg. 491-2 & 676-7.

BRAMBLE, JEHIAL H., son of CLEMENT (preceding), was born 23 June 1817, Lodi, Seneca Co., NY. After the death of his father, he lived with relatives in Steuben Co., NY. He married ca. 1847 to ANNA (WIXSON), daughter of Reuben (also see). He prospected for land in Ohio and Michigan, and then in 1850 brought his family to Macon Twp., Lenawee Co., Mich. They later moved to Franklin Twp., and about 1879 moved to Tecumseh, Mich. Children: 1. ELIZABETH (m. Benjamin F. DePuy/DePugh, also see); 2. PHEBE (d. age 24; 3. MINNIE (d. age 20); 4. CLEMENT H. b. 21 Oct. 1861 (m. Nellie E. Heath, dau. of L. H., also see). Ref: P&BA-Len pg. 676-7.

BRAMBLE, JOHN G., born ca. 1805; and wife, ABIGAIL, born ca. 1808, were listed in the 1840 census index of Macon Twp., Lenawee Co., Mich.; and in the 1850 census of Ridgeway Twp., listed SUSAN A., age 18; SALLY A., age 15, both b. NY, in the household.

BRAMBLE, MOSES was a native of Maryland who sent to Seneca Co., NY at an early date and remained there. Known son, CLEMENT (preceding). Ref: P&BA-Len pg. 676-7.

BRAMLEY, SARAH S. (See Rev. William P. Wastell)

BRANAGAN, ANN (See Patrick Hogan)

BRASHEARS, DORA (See John Maynard)

BRASIE also see BRAZEE; BREESE; BRESIE
BRASIE, LUCETTA (See Samuel Conklin)

BRAZEE also see above.
BRAZEE, HENRY, son of JOHN^2 (following), was born 21 May 1833, Ontario Co., NY, and came to Adrian Twp., Lenawee Co., Mich. with his parents. He married 31 Dec. 1861 to MARIA (McCONNEL), daughter of Matthew B. (also see). They lived first in Barry Co., Mich.; then after 20 years, moved to Adrian Twp., Lenawee Co., Mich. (also owning in Wayne Co., Mich.). Children: 1. IDA M.; 2. HOMER; 3. MARK R.; 4. EMMA; 5. BERTHA; 6. ELLA; 7. MAUD. Ref: P&BA-Len pg. 908-9.

BRAZEE, JOHN^1 and wife, CATHERINE, were natives of the Mohawk Valley, and moved to Ontario Co., NY where they were among the first settlers. Known son, JOHN^2 (following). Ref: P&BA-Len pg. 908-9. Note: There was a JOHN C. listed 1800 census index, Delaware Co., NY. The Brazee family was said to descend from a Frenchaman who had come with Gen. Lafayette during the Revolution.

BRAZEE, JOHN^2, son of JOHN^1 (preceding), born 20 Mar. 1800, Mohawk Valley of NY, moved with his parents to Ontario Co., NY where he married HANNAH (SAYLES), daughter of Francis (also see). They lived first in Perrinton, Ontario Co. (Monroe Co.?), NY; then in 1825 removed to Adrian Twp., Lenawee Co., Mich. She died in Mar. 1878, and he died 18 Feb. 1879. Nine children. Known son, HENRY (preceding); and the following in their household in the 1850 census of Adrian Twp.: NORMAN, age 15; SYLVESTER, age 13; MARY, age 10; MOSES, age 9. Ref: P&BA-Len pg. 908-9.

BRAZEE, MARIA married John Sheldon (also see) before 1816 in Livingston Co., NY.

BREARS, MARY (See John Stephenson)

BREEN, ANNA (See John Moriarity)

BREERS, ANN (See E. G. Mills)

BREESE also see BRASIE; BRAZEE; BRESIE
BREESE, LEANDER born ca. 1830, NY, was listed in the 1850 census of Tecumseh Twp., Lenawee Co., Mich. in Keyser household.

BREESE, MARIA (See John A. Miller)

BRENINGSTALL, ABRAHAM and wife, MARY ANN, were pioneers of Oneida Co., NY. They removed to Dundee, Monroe Co., Mich. in 1836. Known daughter, ROSETTA C., b. 1824, Oneida Co., NY (m. Morgan Parker, also see). Ref: P&BA-Len pg. 599-600.

BRESIE also see BREESE; BRAZEE
BRESIE, CLARISSA (See John S. Kinney). Note NICHOLAS, following.
BRESIE, NICHOLAS (Note BRAZEE family) was born in the Mohawk Valley of NY, and married NAOMI (CASE), daughter of Leonard (also see), a native of Hebron, Washington Co., NY. They settled in Livingston Co., NY, where they raised 5 daughters and 3 sons. Known son, WILLIAM (following). Also note that CLARISSA (preceding) was from Livingston Co., NY, and also went to Tecumseh Twp., Lenawee Co., Mich. Ref: P&BA-Len pg. 799-800.

BRESIE, WILLIAM, son of NICHOLAS (preceding), was born 25 Apr. 1817, Livingston Co., NY. He married MARY A. (JOHNSON), daughter of Eli (also see), on 20 Mar. 1839, and they lived in Livingston Co., NY; Cleveland, O.; and finally Tecumseh Twp., Lenawee Co., Mich. Children: 1. WILLIAM R. (Decatur, Ill.); 2. ELIZABETH (m. John Crowell); 3. SARAH (m/2 Betts); 4. AMANDA (d. age 3). Ref: P&BA-Len pg. 799-800.

BREWER, HORACE was born 13 Aug. 1816, Hartford, Conn. (census said NY?); and came to Tecumseh Twp., Lenawee Co., Mich. in 1837. He married on 4 Nov. 1841 to MARIA (KETCHAM), daughter of Isaac H. (also see). In the 1850 census of Tecumseh Twp., they listed GEORGE, age 7; ALBERT L., age 5 (prob. he who m. Harriet L. Hamilton, dau. of Dr. Increase S., also see); CHARLES, age 3; MARIA, age 4/12. Ref: P&BA-Len pg. 313-4.

BREWER, IDA (See John Johnson, son of John)
BREWER, JOHN born ca. 1799, and wife, ANNA, born ca. 1805, both in NY, were listed in the 1840 census index of Rome Twp., Lenawee Co., Mich.; and in the 1850 census of Rome Twp. listed DANIEL M., age 9; & MARIAM E., age 5, both b. Mich. in the household.

BREWER, JOSEPH was born in Hartford, Conn., and moved to Livingston Co., NY. He later moved to Michigan. Known daughter, FANNIE F., b. Livingston Co., NY (m. Homer L. Stewart, also see). Ref: P&BA-Len pg. 1110-1.

BREWSTER, CALEB born ca. 1784, and wife, DEBORAH, born ca. 1788, both in NY, were listed in the 1840 census

Pioneer Families of Southeastern Michigan

index of Clinton Twp., Lenawee Co., Mich.; and in the 1850 census of Tecumseh Twp. with ALMIRA, age 20, b. NY; and Fredus Himes, age 14, b. Mich., in their household.

BREWSTER, CLINTON and wife, CLARA, were natives of NY who settled probably in Clinton Co., Mich. Known daughter, CLARINDA F., married William H. Mather (also see).

BREWSTER, JULIET C. (See Nathan Florance)

BREWSTER, MICHAEL M. married Mrs. Mary Lane, both of Clinton, Lenawee Co., Mich., on 14 Jan. 1852.

BREWSTER, RUSSELL born ca. 1809, and wife, ANN MARIA, born ca. 1819, both in Ohio, were listed in the 1850 census of Tecumseh Twp., Lenawee Co., Mich. with GEORGE, age 8, b. Ohio, in their household.

BRIDGE, MARY (See Robert I. Dowling)

BRIDGE, SAMUEL born ca. 1816, England, and wife, ELLEN, born ca. 1816, Ireland, were listed in the 1850 census of Cambridge Twp., Lenawee Co., Mich., adjacent to WILLIAM (following).

BRIDGE, WILLIAM born ca. 1810, England, and wife, ABIGAIL (CLARK), born ca. 1812, Vermont, married in Cambridge Twp., Lenawee Co., Mich., and in the 1850 census listed JEROME, age 11; ELIZABETH b. 27 Aug. 1841 (m. John B. Dowling, also see); JAMES, age 3; GEORGE, age 2, in their household.

BRIGGS, ALBERT & wife, JULIA (BRINK), were parents of CORA who married James O. Wheaton (See Peter M. Wheaton).

BRIGGS, CAROLINE Mrs. married second in 1858 to George B. Niedhammer (also see) in Adrian, Lenawee Co., Mich.

BRIGGS, CHARITY (See William H. Day)

BRIGGS, CYRUS (See Gideon Bryan)

BRIGGS, DAVID born ca. 1826, NY, was listed in the 1850 census index of Madison Twp., Lenawee Co., Mich.

BRIGGS, ELIZA (See David Wood)

BRIGGS, JABEZ, son of JOHN (following), was born 28 June 1817 in Moravia, Cayuga Co., NY, and came to Michigan with his parents. He married 26 May 1839 to EMELINE A. (DRAKE), daughter of Simon of Hillsdale Co., Mich. They settled first in Scipio Twp., Hillsdale Co., Mich.; but by 1850 had joined his father in Woodstock Twp., Lenawee Co. They afterwards resided in Jonesville, Hillsdale Co.; and ca. 1858 in Somerset, Mich. In 1861, they returned to Woodstock Twp., Lenawee Co. Children: 1. AUGUSTA A. b. 4 July 1840, Hillsdale Co. (m. J. Adams, Cleveland, O.); 2. ALBERT D. b. 14 Jan. 1843 (m. Liveria Reed, Adams Co., Nebr., see Stephen W. Reed); 3. ADELAIDE (twin of Albert; d. 2 Sept. 1843); 4. CLARISSA A. b. 21 Dec. 1844 (d. 10 Aug. 1846); 5. CLARISSA A.(2d) b. 3 Apr. 1847 (d. 16 Sept. 1849); 6. JOHN R. b. 16 May 1849 (d. 24 Mar. 1851); 7. CECELIA P. b. 9 Sept. 1851 (m. G. C. Windle; d. 6 Apr. 1873); 8. JOHN S. b. 6 Nov. 1853 (m. Belle Swarthout, Hudson, Mich.); 9. FRANK J. b. 13 Jan. 1856 (m. Ada Nicholl, Woodstock Twp.). Ref: P&BA-Len pg. 824-5.

BRIGGS, JAMES born ca. 1785, NY, and wife, MARIA, born ca. 1784, NJ, were listed in the 1850 census of Fairfield Twp., Lenawee Co., Mich. with JOEL, age 36; JAMES WEBB, age 20., b. NY; and CATHARINE, age 9; STEPHEN, age 5, & JAMES, age 1, all b. Mich. (last 3 possibly grandchildren), in their household.

BRIGGS, JOEL was born ca. 1801, and wife, HANNAH, was born ca. 1807, both in NY, were listed in the 1850 census of Seneca Twp., Lenawee Co., Mich. with NATHAN, age 16, b. NY; DANIEL, age 9; & LOUIS, age 6, last 2 b. Mich., in their household.

BRIGGS, JOHN, son of THOMAS & MARY (who were Quakers born ca. 1760), was born 1 Jan. 1785, near Easton, Washington Co., NY; and he served in the War of 1812. He married TRIPHENA (ST JOHN) who was born in Stillwater, NY (then Washinton Co., now Saratoga Co.). They went to Moravia, Cayuga Co., NY; and then about 1833, moved to Hillsdale Co., Mich., and ca. 1840 to Woodstock Twp., Lenawee Co., Mich. She died at age 50; and he died 6 Oct. 1875. There were 5 sons & 3 daughters. Known sons, JABEZ (preceding); & SMITH (following). Ref: P&BA-Len pg. 824-5 & 1173-4.

BRIGGS, MAHALA (See George Worthring of Orleans Co., NY)

BRIGGS, RUTH (See William Wilber)

BRIGGS, SARAH (See Chester Buck)

BRIGGS, SMITH, son of JOHN (preceding), was born 22 Dec. 1825, Moravia, Cayuga Co., NY, and came to Mich. in 1833 with his parents. At age 11, he became a stage driver, and in 1839 went to Auburn, NY. He married in 1842 in Seneca Falls, NY to LAURA (JONES), daughter of Thomas (also see). In 1845, they lived in Burlington, VT; and later in Albany, NY. About 1877, they moved to Jackson, Mich. where she died 14 Aug. 1880; and he afterwards went to Woodstock Twp., Lenawee Co. Children: 1. LAURA JOSEPHINE b. 14 Mar. 1844, NY (m. Charles A. Hoyt, Butte, Mont.); 2. FRANCIS E. b. 14 Mar. 1847, Burlington, VT (Woodstock Twp.); 3. MARY W. b. 12 Aug. 1859, Albany, NY (d. 12 Apr. 1860); 4. GRACE E. b. 11 Jan. 1866, Albany, NY. Ref: P&BA-Len pg. 1173-4.

BRIGGS, WILLIAM (spelled "Brigs" in census) born ca. 1793, and wife, RUTH, born ca. 1803, both in NY, were listed in the 1850 censu of Dover Twp., Lenawee Co., Mich. with DAVID, age 24; JAMES, age 21; GEORGE, age 18; EUGENIA, age 16; CHARLOTTE, age 12; MARY, age 9; WALTER, age 6, all b. NY, in their household.

BRIGHAM, MARTHA E. Mrs. was the daughter of Zibra Corbett (also see).

BRIGHT, ADA (See Cyrus Griffith)

BRIGHTMAN, BENJAMIN was born 20 Sept. 1763, Mass. Known sons: SAMUEL (following); HENRY (killed by pirates off coast of Matanzas). Ref: P&BA-Len pg 1120-1.

BRIGHTMAN, SAMUEL, son of BENJAMIN (preceding), was born 8 Nov. 1794, Mass., and was a Sea Captain early in life; but by 1832 settled in Ontario Co., NY. He had married in Mass. to PHEBE (MARBLE), daughter of Charles (also see); and moved to Bloomfield, Ontario Co., NY. In 1844, they moved to Hudson Twp., Lenawee Co., Mich., where he died 26 Jan. 1849. In the 1850 census of Hudson Twp., Phebe was head of household with the following listed: 1. HENRY, age 22; 2. FRANCIS M., age 20, both b. Mass; 3. LUCIA b. 8 Oct.

1832, Bloomfield, NY (m. Peter V. Smith, also see); 4. CAROLINE, age 15; 5. MARY A.; 6. BENJAMIN, age 12, last 4 b. NY. Ref: P&BA-Len pg. 1120-1.

BRINK, BENJAMIN (See James E. Rounds)
BRINK, JULIA (See Albert Briggs)

BRISCO also see BRISCOE
BRISCO, JOHN born ca. 1782, Conn, was listed in the 1850 census of Rome Twp., Lenawee Co. MIch. in the household of Ferris Sutton and wife, Hannah (age 40, b. Conn.)

BRISCOE also see BRISCO
BRISCOE, LOIS (See Milton Foote)

BRISTOL, MEHITABLE (See Daniel Eldredge)
BRISTOL, WILLARD (See Edward Roberts)

BRITTAIN also see BRITTEN; BRITTON
BRITTAIN, ABRAM born ca. 1809, and wife, CATHARINE, born ca. 1813, both in NY, were listed in the 1850 census of Madison Twp., Lenawee Co., Mich. with HENRIETTA, age 16; HELEN, age 13; JOHN, age 11; JANE E., age 9; JOSEPH, age 3, all b. NY, in their household.
BRITTAIN ABRAHAM W. born ca. 1810, Penn., and wife, HARRIET (CRANE), born ca. 1824, NY, were listed in the 1850 census of Adrian Twp., Lenawee Co., Mich. with ANN M. (MARIE) b. 12 Dec. 1843, Adrian (m/1 to Kent; m/2 Charles Kayner, also see); AMERICUS, age 5; HENRY, age 1, both b. Mich., in their household.
BRITTAIN, CHARLES (See John L. Knapp)
BRITTAIN, NATHAN born ca. 1810, Mass., and wife, ELOISE, born ca. 1816, VT, were listed in the 1850 census of Adrian Twp., Lenawee Co., Mich. with ELOISE, age 11; GERTRUDE, age 8; FRANK, age 1, all b. NY, in their household.

BRITTEN also see BRITTAIN; BRITTON
BRITTEN, RICHARD R. was born ca. 1812, and wife, ELLEN (COLLINS), was born 1818, both in NY. They settled before 1840 in Pittsford, Hillsdale Co., Mich. where he died in 1875; and she lived in 1888, at age 70. Known daughter, IDA, b. 12 Dec. 1852, Pittsford (m. Thomas J. Curtis, also see). Ref: P&BA_Len pg 555-6. Note: In the 1840 census index of Pittsford, Hillsdale Co., adjacent were ABRAM; JACOB; & NATHANIEL.

BRITTON also see BRITTAIN; BRITTEN
BRITTON, BENKINS??, born ca. 1818, Penn., and wife, JANE, born ca. 1821, NY, were listed in the 1850 census of Hudson Twp., Lenawee Co., Mich. with LOUISA M., age 8; WILLIAM H., age 5; MARY J., age 4; & JOHN? B. (male), age 2, all b. Mich. in the household.
BRITTON, JOHN Sr. was born ca. 1806, Yorkshire, England, and married there to SARAH (COATS) born ca. 1810 (See Francis Coats, probably brother, with mother, Maria). After the birth of 4 children, they came to the US in 1850, and settled in Ridgeway Twp., Lenawee Co., Mich. and were counted that year in the census. Known sons, JOHN (following); & CHARLES b. ca. 1846, England. John Sr. died in 1875, age 68; and his wife was still living in 1888, age 82?. Next door in the 1850 census was (probably daughter) JANE b. ca. 1826, Yorkshire (m. Daniel Wiggins, also see) with JOHN & CHARLES, above, in their household.
BRITTON, JOHN Jr., son of JOHN Sr. (preceding), was born 6 Feb. 1833, Yorkshire, England and came to Ridgeway Twp., Lenawee Co., Mich. with parents. He married 25 Mar. 1855 to SARAH A. (OSTERHOUT), daughter of Flower (also see). He served in Co. F., 26th Mich. Inf., Civil War. He was associated with the C. I. & N Railroad and as a result the station of Britton was named for him. Children: 1. ZORA (d. infancy); 2. WILLIAM (m. Eliza Curtis); 3. MORRIS D. (Milan, Mich.); 4. CARRIE E. Ref: P&BA-Len pg. 902-3.
BRITTON, KELLY born ca. 1827, and wife, ELIZABETH, born ca. 1824, both in NY, were listed in the 1850 census of Hudson Twp., Lenawee Co., Mich., with RILEY, age 9, b. NY; ANN A., age 4; & JAMES, age 1, both b. Mich., in their household. LEWIS, following, was listed next door.
BRITTON, LEWIS born ca. 1825, and wife, POLLY A., born ca. 1827, were listed in the 1850 census of Hudson Twp., Lenawee Co., Mich. with GEORGE, age 5; MILO, age 2, both b. Mich. in the household. Note KELLY, preceding.
BRITTON, WILLIAM (See Hiram A. Curtiss)

BROADFOOT, CATHARINE (See James Beattie)

BROCAW, OPHELIA (See Levi C. Richmond)

BROCKELBANK, JOHN B. was born in Ontario Co., NY, son of an early pioneer of Canandaigua. He married CHLOE (SANGER), a native of Mass. She died in 1852, age 55; and he died in 1877, over age 80, both in Canandaigua, NY. Five sons & 2 daughters. #3. ELECTA A. b. 28 July 1821 (m. Charles Negus, also see). Ref: P&BA-Len pg. 573-4.
BROCKELBANK, MARY born Mass. married James Eaton, Sr. (also see).

BROCKWAY, AUSTIN was listed in the 1840 census index of Palmyra Twp., Lenawee Co., Mich.
BROCKWAY, EDWIN born ca. 1808, NY, and wife, LOVINA, born ca. 1820, Ohio, were listed in the 1850 census of Palmyra Twp., Lenawee Co., Mich. with LOUIS M., age 11; HARLEY T., age 9; GEORGE H., age 7; CHARLES O., age 5, all b. Mich.; and listed last, SAPHRONA, age 18, b. Mich., who seems too old to be a child of Lovina.
BROCKWAY, ELISHA A. born ca. 1828, Ohio, and wife, JANE, born ca. 1828, NY, were listed in the 1850 census of Ogden Twp., Lenawee Co., Mich. with EDGAR M., age 1/12, b. Mich.; and WILLIAM H., age 13, b. Mich. (who is too old to be their child). Note the WILLIAM H. who was listed in the 1840 census index of Ogden Twp., possibly father of this family??
BROCKWAY, EMELINE (Mrs.) born ca. 1815, NY, was listed as head of household in the 1850 census of Palmyra Twp., Lenawee Co., Mich. with EUNICE, age 14, b. Ohio; ELISHA, age 7; HORACE, age 4; PHEBE, age 4, all b. Mich., in her household. Note AUSTIN (preceding); & WILLIAM H. (following), who were listed in 1840 census index.
BROCKWAY, ERASTUS (See WATSON, following) was born 13 Apr. 1802, probably in Livingston Co., NY, and

Pioneer Families of Southeastern Michigan

moved as a young man to Erie Co., NY. He married first to MARY (COWELL) and they lived first in Ohio; then about 1835 moved to Lenawee Co., Mich. It may be he listed "Eusebius" in the 1840 census index of Palmyra Twp. They settled in an area now in Ogden Twp. Mary died 30 Apr. 1845 leaving children: 1. CLARK b. 23 June 1832 (d. 12 Oct. 1832); 2. OLIVER W. b. 5 May 1833 (served Civil War, 18th Reg., Mich. Vol.; d. 22 May 1864, Andersonville Prison); 3. MARTIN B. b. ca. 1835, Ohio (served 4th Reg., Mich. Vol., Civil War; in Andersonville for 21 mos); 4. BESSIE (ANN?) b. ca. 1837, Mich. (m. James Gilliand, Adrian); 5. MATTHEW W. (served Civil War, 15th Ohio Reg., lost a leg; lived Ogden Twp.); 6. ALONZO b. ca. 1843 (listed in household in 1850, not named in sketch). Erastus married second 11 Dec. 1845 to SARAH "SALLY" ANN (TEEPLE), daughter of Peter (also see). She died 29 July 1851 leaving children: 7. WILLIAM SMITH b. ca. 1847; 8. NORMAN C.; 9. ERASTUS Jr. (following). Erastus married third to ELIZABETH (TEEPLE), sister of Sally Ann. A child died infancy. Ref: P&BA-Len pg. 757-8.

BROCKWAY, ERASTUS, son of ERASTUS (preceding), was born 1 June 1851; and he married in 1873 to LOETTA (LUKE), daughter of John C. (also see). They settled in Ogden Twp., Lenawee Co., Mich. Children: 1. LUCIEN; 2. PEARLY. Ref: P&BA-Len pg. 757-8.

BROCKWAY, GEIUS (GAIUS?) was listed in the 1840 census index of Clinton Twp., Lenawee Co., Mich.

BROCKWAY, HENRY born ca. 1819, Ohio, and wife, DRUSILLA, born ca. 1820, NY, were listed in the 1850 census of Ogden Twp., Lenawee Co., Mich. with AMELIA, age 7; LEWIS, age 4; ORVILLA M., age 3; ALMINA, age 1/12, all b. Mich., in their household.

BROCKWAY, JOSEPH born ca. 1826, and wife, SOPHIA, born ca. 1831, both in Ohio, were listed in the 1850 census of Ogden Twp., Lenawee Co., Mich.

BROCKWAY, STEPHEN D. born ca. 1836, NY, was listed in the 1850 census of Fairfield Twp., Lenawee Co., Mich.

BROCKWAY, WATSON[1] who settled in Lynn, Conn. in Colonial times was the progenitor of ERASTUS (preceding). Watson had descendants WILLIAM[2,3,4]. WILLIAM[4] died in Lynn, Conn., but two of his sons, names not stated, went to what is now Lima, Livingston Co., NY (formed in 1802 from Ontario Co., NY). In the 1800 census index of Ontario Co., NY were BURBEN & GIDEON, possibly one the father of ERASTUS, preceding. Ref: P&BA-Len pg. 757-8.

BROCKWAY, WILLIAM born ca. 1823, and wife, MARY J., born ca. 1831, both in NY, were listed in the 1850 census of Ogden Twp., Lenawee Co., Mich. with Mary Holmes, age 68, b. NY, in the household (mother-in-law??). This William seems to be too young to be WILLIAM H., following.

BROCKWAY, WILLIAM H. was listed in the 1840 census index of Ogden Twp., Lenawee Co., Mich. Note this given name in household of ELISHA A. (preceding).

BROMLEY, FREELOVE S. (See Jonathan Seeley & Ether Barnes)

BROOKER, JOHN (See Christopher Beagle)

BROOKS, GEORGE H., son of JAMES (following), was born 12 Sept. 1836, Seneca Co., NY. He married first in NY in Jan. 1860 to ELIZABETH (SWICK) who died after 8 months of marriage. He married again in 1864 to MARY (WATROUS), daughter of John. They settled in Medina Twp., Lenawee Co., Mich. Children: 1. ELIZABETH (d. young); 2. ELIZABETH 2d; 3. JENNIE; 4. NELLIE. Ref: P&BA-Len pg. 629.

BROOKS, JAMES and wife, JANE (SEBRING), were natives of New Jersey who had gone at a young age to Seneca Co., NY where they were married. (His father was a General, and her father a Lt. in the War of 1812, neither name stated). James died in 1863, age 61; and she died in 1886, age 78, in Seneca Co., NY. Nine children. Known son, #7. GEORGE H. (preceding). Ref: P&BA-Len pg. 629.

BROOKS, JOSEPH born ca. 1817, and wife, MARY, born ca. 1823, both in NY, were listed in the 1850 census of Woodstock Twp., Lenawee Co., Mich. with CHARLOTTE, age 7; CATHARINE?, age 4; PHOEBE, age 1, all b. Mich., in the household.

BROOKS, MAGGIE (MARGARET) See Rancelier Mills.

BROOKS, MARY (See James Mayne)

BROOKS, MERCHANT was the son of JOSEPH & ? (ROLLIN). (Joseph & wife remained in Delaware Co., NY). Merchant married MARY (EVERY, b. 1800), daughter of Joseph Every (also see) in Delaware Co., NY. They settled in Woodstock Twp., Lenawee Co., Mich. ca. 1835. In the 1850 census of Woodstock Twp., Mary is head of household with 5 sons listed: 1. URIAH, age 24; 2. WILLIAM HENRY (following), age 22; 3. EVERY, age 18; 4. ANGELLUS, age 14, all b. NY; and AUGUSTUS, age 12, b. Mich. Known daughters: MARGARET (m. Nelson Kelley, probably Columbia Twp., Jackson Co., Mich.); ANGELECK (m. Jefferson White, prob. son of Walter, also see; Clarklake, Jackson Co. Mich.); PHEBE b. ca. 1821, Delaware Co., NY (m. Garrett F. Harris, also see). Ref: P&BA-Len pg. 739-40.

BROOKS, WILLIAM HENRY, son of MERCHANT (preceding), was born 14 Apr. 1832, Delaware Co., NY (1850 census said age 22?). He married 4 July 1856 to DEBORAH (DEAN), daughter of Harvey (also see). They settled in Woodstock Twp., Lenawee Co., Mich. Children: 1. MERCHANT D. b. 27 Mar. 1856 (m. Emma Nicholson); 2. STELLA I. b. 4 Oct. 1858 (m. Percy Kelley); 3. HOPKINS b. 2 June 1863 (m. Clara Kelley); 4. SHIRLEY b. 29 June 1872 (d. 11 Dec. 1879). Ref: P&BA-Len pg. 1175-6.

BROSS, ELIZABETH "BETSEY" (See Levi Russell)

BROUNELL also see BROWNELL

BROUNELL, JOHN and wife, HANNAH (BACKUS) moved ca. 1783 from New York to Osnabruck, Stormont Co., Canada. Known daughter, BETSEY, born Osnabruck (m. John C. Hogaboam (also see). Ref: P&BA-Len pg. 1105-6.

BROUWER also see BROWER
BROUWER, JACOB was father of EMMA F. (See John W. Davis).

BROWER also see BROUWER
BROWER, ARCHIBALD was born 13 Feb. 1805, Dutchess Co., NY; and went to Seneca Twp., Lenawee Co. Mich. in 1833. He married there to JULIA A. (MILLETT) of

Fairfield Twp., and it was the first marriage in Seneca Twp. Known children: 1. ALMA J. b. ca. 1835 (m. Willett); 2. ELIAS b. 31 Mar. 1837 (following); 3. WILLIAM H. b. ca. 1839; 4. SARAH ANN b. ca. 1842; 5. JAMES A. b. ca. 1846; 6. JOHN J. b. ca. 1844. Also listed in the household in the 1850 census of Seneca Twp., was REBECCA, age 76, b. NY, probably his mother. One of his children was said to have gone to Missouri, and another to Iowa, names not stated. Ref: P&BA-Len pg. 1009-10.

BROWER, ELIAS, son of ARCHIBALD (preceding), married on 10 Feb. 1865, Seneca Twp., Lenawee Co. Mich. to SARAH J. (KINER), daughter of Conrad (also see), and they settled in Seneca Twp. Children: 1. HENRY (m. Mina VanSickle, Weston, Mich., had son, Ray Henry); 2. FRANK; 3. OLIVE; 4. BURT; 5. ROSA (deceased by 1888); 6. LOUISA; 7. CLARENCE E.; 8. LAWRENCE. Ref: P&BA-Len pg. 1009-10.

BROWN, A. F. (See Jonathan Austin)

BROWN, ABNER, son of Jonathan (b. 1741, served in Revolution in Conn.), was born 27 Aug. 1781, Conn. He married HANNAH (COOK) born 20 May 1780 (census said b. VT, but sketch said b. Conn.). They moved first to Otsego Co., NY, and then to Washtenaw Co., Mich. in 1836; and 1845 to Adrian Twp., Lenawee Co. In the 1850 census of Adrian Twp., they were listed in household of known son, BENAJER (BENAJAH?), following. Abner died age 85, and she died age 71. Ref: P&BA-Len pg. 1208-9.

BROWN, ABRAHAM born ca. 1785, England, was listed in the 1850 census of Adrian Twp., Lenawee Co., Mich. in the household of John Sheffer and wife, Charlotte (who was age 34, b. England).

BROWN, ALBERT (See Harvey Shelden)

BROWN, BENAJER (BENAJAH?), son of ABNER (preceding), was born 2 Sept. 1805, Otsego Co. NY. He married 5 Nov. 1828 to SALLIE (STONE), daughter of Lewis (also see). They lived in Orleans Co., NY, then moved to Washtenaw Co., Mich. in 1836, and Adrian Twp., Lenawee Co. in 1845. Son, JAMES L. (following) was listed in census as "LEWIS." Also in the household in 1850 were parents.

BROWN, CALVIN F. born ca. 1808, and wife, MARY, born ca. 1810, both in Maine, were listed in the 1850 census of Adrian Twp., Lenawee Co., Mich. with CHARLES, age 18; EDWIN, age 16; ROSANNA, age 13; WILLIAM, age 10, all b. Maine; and MARY E., age 4, b. Mich., in their household.

BROWN, CARRIE (See Peter Kishpaugh)

BROWN, CHARLES, son of SOLOMON (following), was born 8 Jan. 1808, Cayuga Co., NY; where he remained until 1830, then went to Genesee, Livingston, & Wyoming Cos., NY. He married first in Cattaraugus Co., NY to PAULINA (WALKER) who was born & died in New York. About 1851, he went to Wisconsin, and about 1852 to Medina Twp., Lenawee Co., Mich. He married after 1866 to Mrs. ELIZABETH B. (STANLEY) FARNSWORTH, daughter of Benjamin M., and widow of Charles G. (see both). No Brown children were named. He retired to the village of Medina ca. 1882. Ref: P&BA-Len pg. 780-1.

BROWN, CYNTHIA of Herkimer Co., NY (See Ezekiel Angell).

BROWN, DAVID born ca. 1819, Mass., and wife, HARRIET P., born ca. 1825, NY, were listed in the 1850 census of Medina Twp., Lenawee Co., Mich. with SARAH, age 6; NANCY P., age 2, both b. Mich., in the household. Note LEWIS, following.

BROWN, EDMUND BURRIS (See James Whitney)

BROWN, ELIAS born ca. 1791, and wife, MELORA, born ca. 1793, both in NY, were listed in the 1850 census of Adrian Twp., Lenawee Co., Mich. with SAMUEL, age 25; MELORA E., age 17; WILLIAM L., age 15, all b. NY, in their household.

BROWN, ELIZABETH b. Derbyshire, England (See Thomas O. Turner).

BROWN, ELVINA Mrs. (See Thomas Tunison)

BROWN, F. D. (See George W. Carter)

BROWN, FRANCIS was born ca. 1803, Newburg, Orange Co., NY. His father died when he was 4 years old, and at age 16 was apprenticed to a cabinet maker. He afterwards served in the U.S. Marine service for 4 years, 9 months; and after discharge, went to Streetsboro, Ohio, then to Hudson Twp., Summit Co., Ohio where he remained until 1848. He married LUCETTA (JOHNSON) who was born Ohio. They went to Medina, Ohio; and then in 1853 went to Blissfield Twp., Lenawee Co., Mich. He died in 1883, age 80. Children: 1. JOHN WILLIAM (following); 2. MARY (m. Dr. Edwin Turner; d. in Blissfield Twp.); 3. HENRY B. (Coldwater, Mich.); 4. FRANKIE (d. age 6); 5. LORIN (d. age 2). Ref: P&BA-Len pg. 989-90.

BROWN, G. R. (See Morgan Parker)

BROWN, GEORGE C. (See Jesse B. Odell)

BROWN, HANNAH (See Ebenezer Mead)

BROWN, IDA (See Frederick H. Corwin)

BROWN, ISAAC and wife, REBECCA, moved from Mass. to Michigan in 1837 (and possibly Illinois). In the 1850 census of Tecumseh Twp., Lenawee Co., Mich. he was age 58, b. New Hampshire, & his (second?) wife was listed as ELECTA, age 57. b. Mass. In their household was Harriet Parmenter, age 36, b. Mass. Known daughter, CAROLINE, b. 17 Apr. 1817, Charlmont, Mass. (m. Perly Bills, also see). Ref: P&BA-Len pg. 1159-60.

BROWN, JAMES L.(LEWIS), son of BENAJAH (preceding), was born 7 Sept. 1831 in Orleans Co., NY, and came to Michigan with parents. He married in Adrian Twp., Lenawee Co. to MARIA (MATIS), daughter of Garrett (also see) on 26 May 1853. Children: 1. CHARLES L. b. 31 Mar. 1854 (m. Barbara Zaler); 2. MARY L. b. 23 Oct. 1855 (m. W. Lewis); 3. EDWARD H. (m. Mary G. Mapes); 4. GEORGE D. b. 29 Nov. 1860 (m. Ella Mapes); 5. ALICE E. b. 3 Dec. 1864 (m. George Stewart); 6. BURT b. 8 Feb. 1867; 7. NELLIE b. 14 Apr. 1869; 8. BLANCHE E. b. 30 Aug. 1875 (d. age 11 mo); 9. ALVORD M. b. 6 Aug. 1877. Maria died 30 Mar. 1881. James L. married second to ELLE M. (BROWN), daughter of ORLANDO (following). Ref: P&BA-Len pg. 1208-9.

BROWN, JAMES W. & wife, SARAH (SEYMOUR), moved from Orange Co., NY to Raisin Twp., Lenawee Co., Mich. Known daughter, ANNA M. (m. Robert M. Boyd, also see). James & Sarah moved to Ford Co., Kansas. Ref: P&BA-Len pg. 526-7.

BROWN, JANE (See Benjamin B. Fisk)

BROWN, JEREMIAH was born 2 May 1789, Vermont, and he served in the War of 1812. He married MARY

Pioneer Families of Southeastern Michigan

(WATERMAN) who was born 21 Apr. 1796 (census said b. NJ). They moved to near Ticonderoga, NY, but returned to Vermont. About 1840, they moved to Rome Twp., Lenawee Co., Mich., and about 1848 to Woodstock Twp.; then Cambridge Twp. briefly before going to Hennipin Co., Minn. She died there 18 Jan. 1864; and he afterwards returned to Addison, Lenawee Co., Mich. where he died at age 85. There were 6 children. Known son, Dr. WILLIAM (following); & daughter, ESTHER (m. Roberts; d. 2 July 1874, Addison, Mich.) and following in household in the 1850 census of Woodstock Twp: NANCY b. ca. 1827; JOHN b. ca. 1833; JOB b. ca. 1835. Ref: P&BA-Len pg. 964-5.

BROWN, JOHN WILLIAM, son of FRANCIS (preceding), was born 7 Apr. 1841, Streetsboro, Ohio and came to Blissfield Twp., Lenawee Co., Mich. with parents. He served in Co. B., 11th Mich. Inf. during the Civil War. He married in Dec. 1869 to JENNIE (BARRETT), daughter of Israel (also see), and the settled in Blissfield Twp. Children: 1. MABEL; 2. EDWARD. Ref: P&BA-Len pg. 989-90.

BROWN, K. N. married MARGARET (SMITH) in Monroe Co., NY, and after the birth of 7 children, moved to Bridgewater, Washtenaw Co., Mich. He died there in 1874, age 74; and she died in 1883, age 80. Known son, SOLOMON (following). Note: There was a KINNER W. listed in Washtenaw Co., Mich. in the 1840 census index.

BROWN, LEWIS born ca. 1820, Mass., and wife, MARY M., born ca. 1827, NY, were listed in the 1850 census of Medina Twp., Lenawee Co., Mich. with ROSANA E., age 5; & ORVILLE R., age 3. both b. Mich., in their household.

BROWN, MARTHA (See John Forbes)

BROWN, MARY (See Isaac Holmes; John DeCamp; & James Smith)

BROWN, NANCY (See Philip Wareham[3])

BROWN, ORLANDO and wife, MARIA (ALLEN), were parents of ELLE M. born 5 Sept. 1838, Lucas Co., Ohio (m. JAMES L., preceding). Orlando & Maria remained in Ohio.

BROWN, PHINEAS was a Revolutionary soldier. (May be he Phinheas Brown, Mass. service, Pension application #W5905, widow, HULDAH). He died in Royalton, Fulton Co., Ohio in 1842; and was grandfather of HANNAH b. NY (m. John Warner, also see). Note: There were 2 PHINEAS in NY in 1800 census index, 1 in Greene Co. & 1 in Oneida Co.).

BROWN, RUSSELL & wife, CLARA, were natives of Mass. He died in Warwick, Mass., but she died in Adrian, Lenawee Co., Mich. Known daughter, CLARA, born 1 Jan. 1852, Warwick, Mass. (m. James Farrar, also see). Ref: P&BA-Len pg. 259-60.

BROWN, SAMUEL of Mass. was a Lt. in the Revolutionary War and was wounded at Bunker Hill. He died 7 years later as a result of his injuries. Known daughter, CATHERINE, born ca. 1768, Mass. (m. Darius Kimball, also see). Ref: P&BA-Len pg. 779-80.

BROWN, SAMUEL came to Lenawee Co., Mich. from Rochester, NY with his parents. He married RHODA (KNAPP), also from Rochester, NY. Known son, L. S. born 26 Oct. 1860, Raisin Twp. Ref: P&BA-Len pg. 327.

BROWN, SARAH (See William Barnhart)

BROWN, SOLOMON & wife, SARAH (McCRACKEN) were believed to be from Mass., and they settled after their marriage in Venice, Cayuga Co., NY. It is probably they listed in the 1800 census index of Cayuga Co., NY. He died there, and she afterwards moved to Wyoming Co., NY, but returned to Venice. Six sons & 6 daughters. Known son, #9. CHARLES b. 8 Jan. 1808 (preceding). Ref: P&BA-Len pg. 780-1.

BROWN, SOLOMON, son of K. N. (preceding), was born 22 July 1824, Monroe Co., NY and moved with his parents to Bridgewater, Mich. He married in Fayette Co., Ind. to SARAH (McILWAIN) whose parents had moved from South Caroline to Indiana at an early date. Sarah died in Clinton, Lenawee Co., Mich. in 1879. Children: 1. CALISTA; 2. FRANCIS E.; 3. LOU A.; 4. IDA; 5. CARRIE (m. John L. Kishbaugh). Solomon married second to JANE A. (LIDDELL). Ref: P&BA-Len pg. 328-9.

BROWN, SUSAN (See Henry Kuney)

BROWN, SUSANNA b. ca. 1793, Mass. (See Jacob Rogers).

BROWN, WILLIAM (See Clark Ames)

BROWN, WILLIAM Dr., son of JEREMIAH (preceding), came with his parents to Rome Twp., Lenawee Co., Mich. He married 6 Mar. 1842 to SARAH TEMPERANCE (CHURCH) in Hudson Twp. She was born 28 Jan. 1832, Lyons, NY. He practiced with Dr. Case, and later Dr. Spalding of Adrian. In 1850, they were listed in the census of Woodstock Twp. She died in Addison, Mich. on 6 Sept. 1880. Children: 1. SARAH F. b. 28 Nov. 1842 (m. William Kline; he d. 30 Jan. 1880, leaving her with 4 children); 2. JEREMIAH b. 22 Apr. 1845 (m. Ann Van Vleet); 3. DAY b. 4 July 1849. Ref: P&BA-Len pg. 964-5.

BROWN WILLIAM H. was born in Palmyra, NY, and he married in Maumee, Ohio to JULIA (FLYNN) who was born ca. 1823, Co. Kerry, Ireland. (She came to the US in 1837). They remained there for a time, then moved to Adrian, Lenawee Co., Mich. He died 14 Apr. 1875, and she was still living in Adrian in 1888. Known children (ages from 1850 census): 1. MARY b. 12 May 1843, Adrian (m. Thomas Gahagan, also see); 2. EDWARD b. ca. 1845; 3. CATHARINE b. ca. 1847; 4, JULIA A. b. ca. 1850. Ref: P&BA-Len pg. 903-4.

BROWNELL also see BROUNELL

BROWNELL, ELIJAH born ca. 1807, Mass.,and wife, PHEBE, born ca. 1805, RI. were listed in the 1840 census index of Raisin Twp., Lenawee Co., Mich.; and in the 1850 census with WALTER E., age 19; CHARLES L., age 15; MILTON, age 12; FRANKLIN, age 12; ELIZABETH, age 9, all b. Mich.; and MARY BATTEY, age 75, b. Mass. in the household. JOSEPH, age 17, b. Mich., in another household may relate to this family.

BROWNELL, JOHN born ca. 1797, Mass., and wife, MARY, born ca. 1803, VT, were listed in the 1840 census index of Madison Twp., Lenawee Co., Mich.; and in the 1850 census with CHARLES, age 22, b. VT; LUCINDA, age 17, b. NY; and MARY, age 14; ALBERT, age 11, both b. Mich., in their household.

BROWNELL, SANDS born ca. 1811, Rhode Island, and wife, HANNAH, born ca. 1809, Ohio, were listed in the 1840 census index of Rollin Twp., Lenawee Co., Mich.; and in the 1850 census of Adrian Twp. with JAMES R., age 11; PHEBE S., age 8; ROBY, age 6; DAVID T., age 2, all b. Mich., in the household.

BROWNELL, SUSAN born ca. 1823, Mass. (See Porter Beal).
BROWNELL, THOMAS born ca. 1805, Rhode Island, and wife, AMELIA, born ca. 1812, England, were listed in the 1840 census index of Rollin Twp., Lenawee Co., Mich.; and in the 1850 census with SOPHIA A., age 14; THOMAS Jr., age 13; JOHN, age 11; ADALINE, age 8; LAURA J., age 5; ARTHUR T., age 3; ROBY A., age 6/12, all b. Mich., in the household. MARY E., age 19, b. Mich., in another household, may relate to this family.

BRUNDOW, ANNA (See John Rhinemiller)

BRYAN, GIDEON was born ca. 1791, Waterbury, Conn.; and he married MALINDA (WARNER), b. ca. 1797 in Conn. They moved in 1816 to Tioga Co., Penn.; and in 1818 to Tompkins Co., NY. About 1830, they moved to Raisin Twp., Lenawee Co., Mich.; and he died in Adrian in 1860. There were 7 sons & 4 daughters, 1 dying infancy (name not stated). 1. SAMUEL (following); 2. MARY b. ca. 1818, NY (m. Ellery Sisson, also see); 3. WARNER (prob. he who m. Mrs. Mary J. Niblack of Tecumseh in Ridgeway Twp., 25 Feb. 1855); 4. NELSON (Neosho Co. KS); 5. GILBERT b. ca. 1832, Mich. (Brown Co., KS); 6. TILLOTSON (Hillsdale Co. Mich.); 7. ALMIRA (m. Cyrus Briggs; deceased by 1888); 8. CLARISSA b. ca. 1829, NY (m. David Slayton, Franklin Twp. Note: This is probably David Slater in the household in 1850); 9. EDWIN b. ca. 1836 (d. age 40); 10. GEORGE b. ca. 1840 (Macon Twp.). Ref: P&BA-Len pg. 296-7. In Gideon's household in the 1850 census of Raisin Twp., also listed was JAMES K., age 5; & ALSON E., age 3, both b. Mich., probably grandchildren.

BRYAN, SAMUEL, son of GIDEON (preceding), was born 3 Aug. 1815, Waterbury, Conn., and came to Raisin Twp., Lenawee Co., Mich. with his parents. He married LAURA (SMITH) in 1844; and she died in 1856. In 1850 they were listed in the census in Tecumseh Twp., Lenawee Co., with first 3 children in the household: 1. NEWTON, age 4 (Raisin Twp.); 2. OSCAR, age 1 (Kansas); 3. DELILAH, age 1/12 (m. O. V. Fitch, Raisin Twp.); 4. WALLACE (Kansas); 5. LAURA (m. William Schofield). Samuel married second in 1858 to MARIA (SCOUT), daughter of William (also see). Ref: P&BA-Len pg. 296-7. In the 1850 census EDWARD, age 13, b. Mich., in Samuel's household, may be the same as EDWIN in Gideon's household.

BRYANT, AMELIA (See Christian Kuney)
BRYANT, AMOS born ca. 1782, NJ, and wife, ANNA, born ca. 1791, NY, were probably they listed in the 1840 census index of Wheatland, Hillsdale Co., Mich. In the 1850 census of Rollin Twp., Lenawee Co., Mich., they listed LEVI, age 39; WILLIAM (following); NATHANIEL, age 28; LORANA, age 25; AARON, age 20; DANIEL, age 17, all b. NY, in their household.
BRYANT, DANIEL and wife, MARY (PHILLIPS), natives of New Jersey, moved to Seneca Co., NY, where she died 23 Apr. 1870; and he was still living in 1888 in Varick, NY, age 88. Known daughter, CORDELIA, born 6 Oct. 1827, Varick, NY (m. David Pontius, also see). Ref: P&BA-Len pg. 687.
BRYANT, JOHN was born ca. 1800, Leeds, England, and came to the US at age 25. He married in Scottsville, Monroe Co., NY to MARGARET (WATSON), daughter of William (also see). About 1836, they moved from Wheatland, NY to Dover Twp., Lenawee Co., Mich. He died in 1856, and she was still living in 1888. Children: 1. SAMUEL (following); 2. WILLIAM W. b. ca. 1834 (m. Elizabeth Smith, Dover Twp.); 3. JOHN (following); 4. MARGARET b. 28 Aug. 1838 (m. William Ashley, also see); 5. WALLACE (following); 6. ALEXANDER b. ca. 1842 (m. Elizabeth Holmes; McLean Co., Ill.); 7. WINFIELD S. b. ca. 1844 (Greenwood Co., KS); 8. GEORGE b. ca. 1846 (m. Emma Leacox, Dover Twp.); 9. CHARLES THOMAS b. ca. 1848 (m. Hannah Holmes, McLean Co., Ill.); 10. HELEN M. b. ca. 1805 (d. age 3-1/2 yrs.) Ref: P&BA-Len pg. 766-7; 817-8; 1074-5; & 1078-9.
BRYANT, JOHN, son of JOHN (preceding), born 18 Sept. 1835, Monroe Co., NY, came to Dover Twp., Lenawee Co., Mich. with parents. He married on 12 Nov. 1863 to SOPHRONIA (VEDDER), daughter of Harman (also see). They lived on a farm that was in both Dover & Seneca Twps. Children: 1. HELEN M. b. 19 July 1865; 2. FRANK E. b. 10 Sept. 1866; 3. IDA M. b. 20 June 1871; 4. RALPH J. b. 21 Dec. 1879. Ref: P&BA-Len pg. 1075-6.
BRYANT, JOHN H. born ca. 1804, NY. is probably he listed in the 1840 census index of Franklin Twp., Lenawee Co., Mich. In the 1850 census of Franklin Twp., he was head of household with CAROLINE, age 25; AUSTIN, age 21; LEVI, age 20; THEODOSIA, age 17, all b. NY; and AMANDA, age 12; MARYETTE, age 10; MARGARET, age 8; MARTHA, age 8, last 4 b. Mich., in his household.
BRYANT, MARY (See Henry W. Burke)
BRYANT, SAMUEL, son of JOHN (preceding), was born 22 July 1833, Wheatland, Monroe Co., NY, and came to Lenawee Co., Mich. with parents. He married 24 Oct. 1866 to HELEN M. (JOHNSON), daughter of David M. (also see) in Medina Twp.; and they settled in Dover Twp. Children: 1. ELMER C.; 2. STANLEY; 3. CLIFFORD (d. infancy); 4. GRACE; 5. ALICE. Ref: P&BA-Len pg. 766-7.
BRYANT, WALLACE, son of JOHN (preceding), was born ca. 1840, Dover Twp., Lenawee Co., Mich. He married in Seneca Twp. on 25 Dec. 1866 to CAROLINE (TUTTLE), daughter of Oramon, Jr. (also see). Son, ERNEST J., b. ca. 1873. Ref: P&BA-Len pg. 817-8.
BRYANT, WILLIAM, probably son of AMOS (preceding), was born ca. 1821, and wife, SARAH, was born ca. 1832, both in NY, and were listed in the 1850 census of Rollin Twp., Lenawee Co., Mich. (next door to AMOS, preceding), with GEORGE, age 1, b. Mich. in the household.

BUCHANAN, MARY (See John Ladd)
BUCHANAN, NELSON (See David M. Johnson)

BUCK, ALLEN (See Dr. John D. Tripp)
BUCK, CHARLES H. born ca. 1828, and wife, EMILY, born ca. 1830, both in NY, were listed in the 1850 census of Rome Twp., Lenawee Co., Mich. in the household of Nathan Baker.
BUCK, CHESTER and wife, SARAH (BRIGGS), of Vermont, moved to Oneida Co., NY before 1824. In 1852, they removed to Adrian, Lenawee Co., Mich.; and later to Plymouth, Ind. where he died 13 Jan. 1872. Sarah returned to Adrian and lived with a daughter, Mrs. C. B. Johnson (given name not stated), where she died 12

Pioneer Families of Southeastern Michigan

May 1876. Daughter, WEALTHY ANN, b. 17 Dec. 1824, Whitesboro, Oneida Co., NY (m. Richard H. Kinney, also see). Probably a son, CHESTER C. born ca. 1836, NY (lived with Wealthy Ann in 1850 census Seneca Twp.) Ref: P&BA-Len pg. 532-3. Note: Chester is probably descendant of WILLIAM^1 b. 1658 who came from England with 9 sons. A descendant, DANIEL^5 b. 28 Feb. 1738, with wife Ann (Denton), who moved from New Milford, Conn. to Woburn, Mass., and then to Vermont; married second to Olive (Stevens), and afterwards moved to Great Bend, Penn., had 16 children, among them 6 sons, ICHABOD; BENJAMIN; ENOCH; DANIEL; ISRAEL; & SILAS.

BUCK, ELLA M. (See Ira Goodsell)

BUCK, FRANCIS J. born ca 1818, and wife, ALZEBA, born ca. 1828, both in NY, were listed in the 1850 census of Madison Twp., Lenawee Co., Mich. with no family in the household.

BUCK, GEORGE born ca. 1814, and wife, HARRIET, born ca. 1822, both in NY, were listed in the 1840 census index of Dover Twp., Lenawee Co., Mich.; and in the 1850 census of Dover Twp., listed LUMAN, age 12; LYMAN, age 7; FRANKLIN, age 5; HELEN, age 3; CYRUS, age 4/12, all b. Mich., in their household.

BUCK, HENRY born ca. 1791, NY, was listed in the 1840 census index of Palmyra Twp., Lenawee Co., Mich.; and in the 1850 census was alone in the household.

BUCK, IRA was listed in the 1840 census index of Adrian Twp., Lenawee Co., Mich.

BUCK, MARIA was born ca. 1832, Ohio, and was listed in the 1850 census of Adrian Twp., Lenawee Co., Mich. in the household of Joseph Warner.

BUCK, SAMUEL settled in Blissfield Twp., Lenawee Co., Mich. by 1827. He married MARGARET (FRARY), daugher of David (also see); and Samuel died before 1830. They are probably parents of LUCINDA, b. ca. 1827, Mich. Margaret married second before 1850 to Sewell S. Goff of Blissfield Twp., and in the 1850 census, Lucinda was listed in their household.

BUCKLEY, JOHN came from England in 1777, and settled in eastern NY. Daughter, ANNIE, married in 1815 in Oneida Co., Ny to Josephus Weter. Ref: P&BA-Len pg. 283-4.

BUDLONG, DANIEL, born ca. 1769, RI, lived in Utica, NY in 1812, and moved to Tully, NY about 1815; and later to Cortland, NY. He moved to Genoa, Cayuga Co., NY; and then to Adrian, Lenawee Co., Mich. in 1835; and Daniel was living in household of Lanson G. in 1850, age 81. Known children: 1. LONSON G. (following); 2. ALFRED WELLS; 3. SARAH ANN b. 21 Feb. 1812, Utica, NY (m. Abel Whitney, also see); 4. ALMIRA M. b. ca. 1814, NY (lived with Sarah Ann, 1850 census, Adrian Twp.). Ref: P&BA-Len pg. 186.

BUDLONG, ELISHA born ca. 1814, Rhode Island, and wife, EVELINE, born ca. 1824, NY, were listed in the 1850 census of Madison Twp., Lenawee Co., Mich. with ARTHUR, age 4; FLORENCE, age 6/12, both b. Mich., in the household.

BUDLONG, LONSON G. born ca. 1802, NY, was listed as head of household in the 1850 census of Adrian Twp., Lenawee Co., Mich. with CALISTA, age 54, b. NY; and DANIEL (father), age 81, born Rhode Island, in his household.

BUELL, ORLANDO F. born ca. 1824, and wife, SARAH D., born ca. 1826, both in NY, were listed in the 1850 census of Madison Twp., Lenawee Co., Mich. with SHELDON, age 22, b. NY in the household. Laura Clisby?, age 68, born Conn., in the household, possibly mother-in-law?

BUELL, SARAH of Conn., and Genesee Co., NY (See Samuel Smith).

BUELL, WILLIAM born ca. 1796, Canada, married Mrs. POLLY (ATCHISON) HALL, born ca. 1794, Conn, widow of Nehemiah (also see) in Monroe Co., NY. They moved before 1840 to Madison Twp., Lenawee Co., Mich.; and then to Quincy, Branch Co., Mich., where she died ca. 1860. Ref: P&BA-Len pg. 569-70.

BUGBEE, DANIEL, possibly son of MOSES (following) born ca. 1812, and wife, SYLVIA, born ca. 1816, both in NY, were listed in the 1850 census of Rome Twp., Lenawee Co., Mich. with STEPHEN, age 21; JAMES H., age 17; LUCY A., age 13, in their household. There is a man with this name in the 1840 census index of Hillsdale Co. Mich., adjacent to ELIAS.

BUGBEE, ELIAS was listed in the 1840 census index of Hillsdale Co., Mich. adjacent to DANIEL, preceding.

BUGBEE, MOSES was born 22 June 1787, Mass., and wife, ELIZABETH (BENTLY), daughter of Ezekiel (also see) was born 30 July 1796, Rhode Island; and they settled after their marriage in Orleans Co., NY. About 1829, they moved to the Mich. Territory, and about 1830 to what is now Adrian Twp., Lenawee Co., Mich. He died there 19 Apr. 1869, and she died 26 Feb. 1875. They had 7 sons. Known son, STEPHEN (following); and probably DANIEL (preceding). Also in Moses' household in the 1850 census were ANDREW J., age 18; and WILLIAM, age 16. Ref: P&BA-Len pg. 974-5.

BUGBEE, SILAS born ca. 1826, Vt, and wife, ELIZABETH, born ca. 1829, NY, were listed in the 1850 census of Rollin Twp., Lenawee Co., Mich. with CATHARINE, age 5/12, b. Mich. in the household.

BUGBEE, STEPHEN, son of MOSES (preceding), was born 23 May 1831, Michigan, and married 28 Dec. 1847 to ALMIRA (SANDERS), daughter of Jacob (also see). They settled in Adrian Twp., Lenawee Co., Mich. Children: 1. MARY b. 7 Oct. 1848 (m. R. R. George, Rome Twp.); 2. JACOB N. b. 7 Sept. 1853 (to Colorado); 3. JOHN E. b. 26 Aug. 1862; 4. FRANK C. b. 28 Nov. 1864 (Rome Twp.); 5. MINNIE M. b. 7 May 1869. Ref: P&BA-Len pg. 974-5.

BUHL, ROSANNA (See Michael Schmidt)

BULKIN, CHRISTIANA (See William S. Blackmar)

BULLEN, MARY (See Ezekiel Smith)

BULREES, JOHN of Canandaigua, Ontario Co., NY was father of ANN (m. William Service, also see). Ref: P&BA-Len pg. 445.

BUMP also see BUMPUS

BUMP, ALBERT H., son of BARTLETT (following), was born 29 Jan. 1818, Chatham, Columbia Co., NY. He moved with his parents to Wayne Co., NY; and then to Palmyra Twp., Lenawee Co., Mich. where he reamined until age 21, then went to Wheatland Twp., Hillsdale Co., Mich. He married first in Wheatland Twp. in Nov. 1842 to FANNY (HAWKINS), daughter of John (also see), where they remained until 1870, then moved to Medina Twp., Lenawee Co. She died in 1871 leaving 6 children: 1. BARTLETT H. (Wheatland Twp.); 2. GEORGE H. (Hudson Twp., Lenawee Co.); 3. ALBERT H. Jr. (Hudson Twp.); 4. MAY E. (m. Denison, Muskegon, Mich.); 5. EMMA (m. Trumbull, Hudson Twp.); 6. ELLEN (m. Helmie, Wheatland Twp.) Albert H. married again on 13 Aug. 1872 to Mrs. REBECCA A. (NICHOLS) SMITH, daughter of Lev, and widow of Thomas C. (see both). About 1883, they settled in Hudson Twp., Lenawee Co. Ref: P&BA-Len pg. 940-1.

BUMP, BARTLETT, son of BENJAMIN (following), moved as a young man from Greenfield, Saratoga Co., NY to Chatham, Columbia Co., NY; and he served in the War of 1812. He married afterwards to MARY (SWIFT) who was born in Conn., and they remained until 1825, then moved to Wayne Co., NY. In March of 1833 they moved to Palmyra Twp., Lenawee Co., Mich., and resided with George Crane. In 1837, they removed to Wheatland, Hillsdale Co., Mich. where they remained. He died in Aug. 1887, age 87. Children: 1. ALBERT H. (preceding); 2. BARBARA A. (m. J. F. Taylor, Wheatland Twp.); 3. CHARLES (Toledo, O.); 4. BENJAMIN F. (Wheatland Twp.). Ref: P&BA-Len pg. 940-1.

BUMP, BENJAMIN was a native of New England who was a pioneer settler to Greenfield, Saratoga Co., NY. It is probably he written as "Bumpus" in the 1800 census index of Saratoga Co. He died there. Known son, BARTLETT (following). Ref: P&BA-Len pg. 940-1.

BUMP, JOHN born ca. 1810, Conn, and wife, SAR--ITA?, born ca. 1821, NY, were listed in the 1840 census index of Medina Twp., Lenawee Co., Mich.; and in the 1850 census listed SOPHIA E., age 14; MARY J., age 13, both b. NY; and JOHN J., age 10; SARAH J., age 7, both b. Mich., in their household.

BUMPUS also see BUMP

BUMPUS, URSON married 19 Mar. 1858 in Stockton, Portage Co., Wisc. to MARIAN M. (WILSON), daughter of Marvin L. (also see). Urson was killed in the Civil War on 22 May 1863. Son, MARVIN. Marian married second to Peter Gussenbauer (also see), of Fairfield Twp., Lenawee Co., Mich.. Ref: P&BA-Len pg. 566-7.

BUNNELL, HANNAH (See Caleb Mead[4])

BURCH also see BIRCH
BURCH, CATHERINE (See Daniel C. Abbott)
BURCH, CHARLES born ca. 1810, and wife, MARGARET, born ca. 1809, both in NY, were listed in the 1850 census of Macon Twp., Lenawee Co., Mich. with JOHN, age 20; STEPHEN, age 17, both b. NY; and GEORGE, age 13; ADELBERT, age 8; ALONZO, age 6?, all b. Mich., in the household.
BURCH, EDMUND was born ca. 1776/1780 in Dutchess Co., NY; and he married there to LOVISA (VAN SCOY, possibly VAN SCOYCK). It may be he listed in the 1800 census index of Chenango Co., NY as "Birch." They moved from Chenango Co. possibly first to New Jersey, and then to Adrian Twp., Lenawee Co., Mich. where they were listed in the 1850 census. She died at age 45, and he died in 1853, age 77. There were 6 sons & 5 daughters. Known daughter, JULIA A., born 2 July 1833, (sketch said b. NJ, but census said b. NY), lived for a time in Ohio (m. Cyrus Griffith, also see, Madison Twp., Lenawee Co., Mich. in 1855). Ref: P&BA-Len pg. 1033-4. Also see EBSEN, following.

BURCH, EBSEN, probably son of EDMUND (preceding), and wife, SOPHRONIA (ROOT), lived first in Chenango Co., NY after their marriage. In 1844, they removed to Fulton Co., Ohio; and in 1854 to Madison Twp., Lenawee Co., Mich. He died 2 Apr. 1869, age 64; and she died 9 Aug. 1853, age 46. Six children. Known daughter, ADARESTA b. 14 May 1844, Chenango Co., NY (m. Lazarus G. Elliott, also see). Ref: P&BA-Len pg. 888-9.

BURCH, JAMES was born ca. 1830, NY, and was listed in the 1850 census of Blissfield Twp., Lenawee Co., Mich. Note ETHRO & MORRIS BIRCH.

BURCH, L. C. was listed in the 1840 census index of Dover Twp., Lenawee Co., Micn

BURCH, LEVI A. was born ca. 1834, Mich., and is listed in the 1850 census of Rome Twp., Lenawee Co., Mich.

BURDICK, BELINDA (See John Newitt)

BURGES, WILLIAM born ca. 1810, England, and wife, NANCY, born ca. 1813, NY, were listed in the 1850 census of Adrian Twp., Lenawee Co., Mich. with ELIZA, age 11; ALMON C., age 6, both b. NY; and HANNAH E., age 1, b. Mich., in their household.

BURGESS, DAVID was listed in the 1840 census index of Adrian Twp., Lenawee Co.. Mich.; and in the 1850 census of Adrian Twp., was age 57 (or 61), b. Maine, with wife, ELIZABETH, born ca. 1793, NJ. Also in their household was Elizabeth Leyres, age 34.

BURGESS, OLIVE (See Joseph Baley)
BURGESS, S. M. (See David Alexander)

BURHAM, FIDELIA (WHITING) of Milan, Monroe Co., Mich. (See George Whiting).

BURK also see BURKE
BURK, JOHN B. (See Edward Clark)
BURK, MAGDALENA (See George Uloth)

BURKE, female married Moses McCollum (also see).
BURKE, HENRY W., son of JOSEPH (following), was born 17 Oct. 1828, Tioga Co., NY, and came to Hillsdale Co., Mich. with parents. He married 17 Dec. 1854 to LOUISA E. (JEWELL), daughter of John M. (also see), and they settled first in Hillsdale Co., and by 1867 in Rome Twp., Lenawee Co., Mich. Children: 1. HERBERT E. b. 26 Oct. 1856 (m. Mary Bryant); 2. CHARLOTTE ANN b. 17 Dec. 1857 (m. J. Ryder, Rome Twp., Lenawee Co.); 3. JOSEPH b. 19 Jan. 1862 (m. Eva Cane); 4. HENRY ELMER b. 7 Apr. 1864; 5. CATHARINE E. b. 31 Jan. 1867, Lenawee Co. (m. Fred D. Southard). Ref: P&BA-Len pg. 813-4.

BURKE, JOSEPH was born in Tioga Co., NY; and wife, CATHARINE (DAVENPORT), was born in Tompkins Co., NY. They lived in Tioga Co., NY until about 1835,

Pioneer Families of Southeastern Michigan

then removed to Hillsdale Co., Mich. where he died at age 75; and she died at age 68. Eleven children. Known son, HENRY W. (preceding). Ref: P&BA-Len pg. 813-4.

BURLESON, CHARLES, son of JOB (following), was born in Macon Twp. The sketch gave his birthdate as 8 Sept. 1837, but in the 1850 census he was listed as age 5. He married SUSAN (LARZELERE), daughter of Hiram (also see), and they settled in Macon Twp., Lenawee Co., Mich. Childen: 1. GEORGE; 2. LILBURN; 3. BENJAMIN. Ref: P&BA-Len pg. 815-6.

BURLESON, JOB was born ca. 1803, NY, and came to Michigan in 1832. He married AMY (ARNOLD), born NY, in Macon Twp., Lenawee Co., Mich. She died in Macon Twp.; and he died in Apr. 1881, age 78. In the 1850 census of Macon Twp., he listed ELISA, age 13; JEREMIAH, age 11; ICHABOD, age 10?; TIMOTHY, age 7; CHARLES (preceding); STEPHEN, age 3, all b. Mich. Listed last was ANN, age 38, b. NY (this may be AMY??). Ref: P&BA-Len pg. 815-6.

BURNAM see BURNHAM

BURNETT, JAMES, son of THOMAS (following), was born in Shaftsbury, VT. He married JEANETTE (EDGAR), daughter of James (also see), and in 1800 they moved to Washington Co., NY. He was killed there in 1805, thrown by a horse. Known son, ROBERT (following). Ref: P&BA-Len pg. 590-1.

BURNETT, JOHN & wife, MARY (See John Bushnell).

BURNETT, JOHN was born ca. 1775, and wife, ELIZABETH (HORTON), was born ca. 1791, both in Yorkshire, England, and they came to the US by 1850, and settled in Macon Twp., Lenawee Co., Mich. A son lived in Canada, named not stated; and known daughter, ELIZABETH b. Sept. 1822, England (m. William J. Andrews, also see). In the 1850 census of Macon Twp., John listed in his household ROBERT, age 39; HENRY, age 31; WILLIAM, age 25; JOHN, age 13; JANE, age 23; SARAH, age 17, all b. England. (It may be SARAH, age 17, b. England, counted again in the 1850 census of Raisin Twp.). Ref: P&BA-Len pg. 277-8.

BURNETT, JOHN McCLELLAND, son of ROBERT (following), was born 4 Sept. 1849, Deerfield Twp., Lenawee Co., Mich. He married 27 Apr. 1872 to ADDIE R. (KILBURN), daughter of Elijah (also see) in Deerfield Twp. Children: 1. NELSON b. 19 Nov. 1874; 2. MARIAN b. 29 Aug. 1881. Ref: P&BA-Len pg. 642.

BURNETT, ROBERT, son of JAMES (preceding), born ca. 1802 in Vermont, went to Washington Co., NY with parents, and married in 1830 to AMELIA (PRATT) born ca. 1805. They remained until 1835, then moved to Deerfield Twp., Lenawee Co., Mich. He died 6 Feb. 1856, and she died 16 Jan. 1872, Deerfield Twp. Children: 1. MARIAN b. ca. 1833 (m. William Kedzie, Adrian); 2. SARAH (d. infancy); 3. JANE b. ca. 1837 (d. age 18); 4. MARY b. ca. 1839 (m. Carlton M. Ellis, also see); 5. DANIEL b. ca. 1841 (Monroe Co., Mich.); 6. JANES b. ca. 1843 (Fargo, SD); 7. ROBERT EDGAR (following); 8. JOHN McCLELLAND (preceding). Ref: P&BA-Len pg. 590-1.

BURNETT, ROBERT EDGAR, son of ROBERT (preceding), was born 13 May 1846, Deerfield Twp., Lenawee Co., Mich. He married 14 Aug. 1872 to JENNIE (ARMITAGE), daughter of William (also see) and settled in Deerfield Twp. Known child, MAUD E. b. 18 Nov. 1879. Ref: P&BA-Len pg. 603-4.

BURNETT, SAMUEL born ca. 1821, and wife, MARGARET, born ca. 1825, both in Ohio, were listed in the 1850 census of Hudson Twp., Lenawee Co., Mich.

BURNETT, THOMAS was born in Dumfriesshire, Scotland, and settled in Shaftsbury, VT during Colonial times. Known son, JAMES (preceding). Ref: P&BA-Len pg. 590-1.

BURNHAM, A. B. (See Ephraim Hall)

BURNHAM, BENJAMIN F. born ca. 1843, NY?, was listed in the 1850 census of Blissfield Twp., Lenawee Co., Mich. in a household a few doors from EMERY (following).

BURNHAM, CALVIN and wife, LUCINDA (BLISS), had lived in Franklin Co., Mass., and moved to Summerfield Twp., Monroe Co., Mich. by 1840. Daughter, OLIVE C., born 29 Dec. 1821, Montague, Franklin Co., Mass. (m. Lysander Ormsby, also see, in Monroe Co., Mich.) Ref: P&BA-Len pg. 306-7. Note: In the 1840 census index, listed adjacent to Calvin in Summerfield Twp. was OBADIAH; & WARREN in Whiteford Twp., Monroe Co.

BURNHAM, EMERY born ca. 1832, Mass., was listed in the 1850 census of Blissfield Twp., Lenawee Co., Mich. in the household of Jason Heminway (also see) and wife, Nancy (b. 1827, Mass., perhaps she was a Burnham?)

BURNHAM, JAMES born ca. 1837, Mich., was listed in the 1850 census of Blissfield Twp., Lenawee Co., Mich. in a Ferguson household.

BURNHAM, JONATHAN was listed in the 1840 census index of Blissfield Twp., Lenawee Co., Mich. (There was a man by this name in St. Clair Co., Mich. in the 1830 census of the Michigan Territory, age 30-40; and females 1 under 5; 2 5-10; 1 10-15; 1 20-30; 1 30-40).

BURNHAM, JULIA born ca. 1824, NY, was head of household in the 1850 census of Blissfield Twp., Lenawee Co., Mich. with JANE E., age 14; ABNER J., age 4; HIRAM F., age 2, all b. Mich., in the household.

BURNHAM, LAURA born ca. 1842, Mich., was listed in the 1850 census of Blissfield Twp., Lenawee Co., Mich., in a Colyer household.

BURNHAM, MOSES was listed in the 1840 census index of Blissfield Twp., Lenawee Co., Mich.

BURR, ALLEN, son of LINDEN (following), was born 22 Feb. 1810, Brownsville, Oneida Co., NY, where he grew to his majority. He came to Palmyra Twp., Lenawee Co., Mich. in 1831; then returned to Wayne Co., NY in 1832 and married PHEBE (ATWELL). They returned to Palmyra Twp., where she died in 1834, leaving sons, THOMAS b. ca. 1832; & CALEB b. ca. 1834 (d. Sept. 1836, age 2). Allen married second to ELIZA (PARKER), daughter of William of Rhode Island. In the 1850 census of Palmyra Twp., Eliza, age 34, b. RI, was listed head of household. Children: 1. BENJAMIN F. (d. 18 Feb. 1841, age 3); 2. THERON L. (following); 3. CHARLES A. (served Civil War; lived Neosho, MO); 4. RENA E. (m. Marvin Saxton, Missouri); 5. ORLANDO (d. result of being in Libby Prison, Civil War); 6. LOUISA b. ca. 1846; 7. BETSEY b. ca. 1848 (married & lived Newton, MO). Ref: P&BA-Len pg. 230-1.

BURR, CHARLES R. (See Dr. Alexander W. Seger)

BURR, ISAIAH born ca. 1810, NY, was listed in the 1850 census of Ogden Twp., Lenawee Co., Mich. with HARRIET, age 20, b. NY, in the household.

BURR, JOHN, son of RICHARD (who d. Ohio, age 64), was a native of NY. He married NAOMI (HOUSS), and they moved to Darke Co., Ohio about 1840. About 1850, they moved to Palmyra Twp., Lenawee Co., Mich.; and in 1867 to Cambridge Twp. He died there at age 74, and she was living there in 1888. Known daughter, OCTAVIA, born Aug. 1850, Darke Co., O. (m. Dr. L. H. Bedell, 1 Nov. 1867, also see). Ref: P&BA-Len pg. 604-5.

BURR, LINDEN was born in Rhode Island and he an wife, ? (ALLEN), were early settlers to Oneida Co., NY; and afterwards Wayne Co., NY where he died at age 80; and she preceded him. Son, ALLEN (preceding). Ref: P&BA-Len 230-1.

BURR, LONSEN R., son of ZERA (who had moved from Conn. to Monroe Co., NY), of Fairport, Monroe Co., NY, married MARY (BENTLEY), daughter of Caleb Bently (also see). They later moved to Adrian, Lenawee Co., Mich. Known daughter, BERNICE (m. Silas L. Allen on 8 July 1875, as second wife). Ref: P&BA-Len pg. 1034-5.

BURR, THERON L., son of ALLEN (preceding), married 11 Feb. 1864 to HARRIET (WILSON), daughter of Cornelius of NY, born 13 Feb. 1839. She had come to Michigan ca. 1860 with an uncle. Children: 1. ALLEN A. V. b. Feb. 1865 (to Nebraska); 2. MATTIE L. b. 11 May 1866 (Hudson, Mich.); 3. HOMER O. b. 3 Oct. 1869; 4. CHARLES E. b. 12 Oct. 1872; 5. DELPHINE b. 11 Oct. 1875; 6. ADA A. b. 13 May 1879. Ref: P&BA-Len pg. 230-1.

BURRIDGE, CHARLES, son of WILLIAM (following), was born 5 Jan. 1837, London, England, and came with parents to the US. As a young man, he went to Kentucky, but returned to Tecumseh, Lenawee Co., Mich. He married in July 1867 to HARRIET M. (BLINN) of Tecumseh. Children: 1. WALTER C.; 2. MARY L.; 3. CHARLES. Ref: P&BA-Len pg. 1196-7.

BURRIDGE, WILLIAM and wife, LOUISA (STEELE), were natives of London, England, and they married there and became parents of 10 children. In 1852, when youngest son, CHARLES (preceding), was age 15, they removed to the US, and settled first in Richland Co., Ohio; and soon afterwards went to White Pigeon & Constantine, Mich. After a brief stay, they settled in Lenawee Co., Mich. Ref: P&BA-Len pg. 1196-7.

BURROUGHS, C. S. married JENNIE V. (LANCASTER), daughter of F. D. (also see). Known son, FRANK.

BURROUGHS, EDSON (See Levi L. Stockwell)

BURROUGHS, LAVINA (See Aaron Phillips)

BURROUGHS, SOPHIA (HUFF) Mrs. married second to John P. Silvers (also see).

BURTON, ALBERT G., son of GEORGE (following), was born 9 May 1824, Vernon, Oneida Co., NY, and came with parents to Clinton Twp., Lenawee Co., Mich. He married in 1852 to HARRIET (SEYMOUR) who died leaving son, GEORGE (Chicago, Ill.). Albert G. married second to JANE E. (ROLAND), and she died in 1863, leaving children: HATTIE; & KATE. He married again to MARGARET C. (SMITH). Children: CARLTON S. (Chicago, Ill.); JULIA (d. 1884, age 17); CHRISTINE; WILLIAM. Margaret died 22 Feb. 1881; and he was still living in 1888. Ref: P&BA-Len pg. 320-1.

BURTON, GEORGE was born 1797 in Norwich, VT, and moved ca. 1812 to Madison Co., NY; and later to Oneida Co., NY. He married CHARLOTTE (LOCKWOOD) who was born in Madison Co., NY. In 1835, they removed to Clinton Twp., Lenawee Co., Mich. He died in Clinton village in 1873, and she died in 1883, age 80. Four sons & 4 daughters. It stated that only ALBERT G. (preceding), and 3 daughters, names not stated, were living in 1888. Note: George had a brother, MINOR, of Clinton, NY mentioned in the sketch. Ref: P&BA-Len pg. 320-1.

BUSH, ANNA (See Dr. Charles Farnsworth, Hillsdale, Mich.)

BUSH, ELI, son of ELI (who d. in NY), was born in Barre, Orleans Co., NY. He married EVALINE (HARD), a narive of Vermont. They moved to Wisconsin in 1846, and in 1855 to Pittsford Twp., Hillsdale Co., Mich. He died in Oct. 1872; and Eveline went to Nebraska and lived with a son, where she died in Feb. 1887. Known daughter, HARRIET (m. Charles Henry Ames, also see). Ref: P&BA-Len pg. 582-3.

BUSHNELL, JOHN & wife, MARY, of Chesterfield, Mass. were parents of MARY b. ca. 1782 (m. Joseph Rice, also see). It should be noted that Mary Bushnell was called daughter of John & Mary "Burnett," so there is uncertainty as to which name is correct. Ref: P&BA-Len pg. 598-9.

BUSSEY, ELIZABETH (See Theodore Rawson)

BUTLER, AUGUSTA, age 17, born NY, was listed in the 1850 census of Adrian Twp., Lenawee Co., Mich.

BUTLER, BENJAMIN F. was a resident of Ogden Twp., Lenawee Co., Mich. in 1847.

BUTLER, C. W. Dr. (See Henry H. Wilcox)

BUTLER, DAVID was listed in the 1840 census index of Palmyra Twp., Lenawee Co., Mich., and was not listed in 1850. Possibly related in the 1850 census of Palmyra Twp. was ORRIN, age 22, b. NY. In a Jacobs household in 1850 census of Palmyra Twp., was ELIZABETH, age 24, b. NY, with children DAVID, age 3, b. Mich.; & LETTA, age 2, b. Ohio.

BUTLER, EMMA J. (See Edgar E. Underwood) Note: There was an EMMA, age 24, b. NY, listed in the 1850 census of Tecumseh Twpo., Lenawee Co., Mich.

BUTLER, HANNAH, a woman of color, age 50, born North Caroline, was listed as head of household in the 1850 census of Tecumseh Twp., Lenawee Co., Mich., with GEORGE, age 12; ELIZABETH, age 7, both b. Mich., in her household

BUTLER, NATHAN was listed in the 1840 census index of Tecumseh Twp., Lenawee Co., Mich.

BUTLER, OLIVER born ca. 1802, and wife, EMMA, born ca. 1806, both in Maine, were listed in the 1850 census of Ogden Twp., Lenawee Co., Mich. with ALBION, age 15; HELEN, age 11; WILLIAM H., age 7, all b. Canada; and Henry Horselander, age 26, b. NY, with wife, MARY A. (probably daughter of Oliver), age 18, b. Canada (married within the year), in their household.

BUTLER, SILAS of Lanesboro, Mass. was the father of ADAH ANN (m. Reuben Humphrey (also see) before 1829).

Pioneer Families of Southeastern Michigan

Silas died in North Adams, Mass. at age 92. Ref: P&BA-Len pg 941-2.

BUTLER, WILLIAM (See Philip S. DePuy)

BUTLER, WILLIAM A. born ca. 1818, NY; and wife, RUTH, born ca. 1819, Canada, were listed in the 1850 census of Dover Twp., Lenawee Co., Mich. with DAVID, age 4; JONATHAN, age 3; NATHAN, age 11/12, all b. Mich.; as well as Philinda Harris, age 10; Levi Harris, age 8 (possibly step-children), both b. Mich., in his household. Note DAVID & NATHAN, preceding.

BUTRICK, JOSEPHINE M. (See Sylvester Kemp)

BUTTERFIELD, DEBORAH was born 26 Nov. 1801, Amherst, NH (according to sketch, but census said b. VT). She married first to ? Lard; and then married on 21 Aug. 1825, Steuben, Orleans Co., NY to Justice Andrews (also see). Ref: P&BA-Len pg. 1118-9.

BUTTERFIELD, SARAH (See Moses Marsh)

BYCE, JOHN T. (See Lembarger)

- C -

CADMAN, JOHN Dr. born ca. 1804, and wife, HANNAH N., born ca. 1803, were listed in the 1850 census of Madison Twp., Lenawee Co., Mich. with CHARLES C., age 14; JOHN W., age 12; ROSAMOND D., age 10, all b. NY; and JAMES P., age 9, b. Mich., in the household. Note: Hannah N. is probably NANCY, daughter of Joseph Keeney (also see), who m. a Cadman and resided in Lenawee Co.

CADMUS, ABRAHAM was born in NJ, son of RICHARD[1], possibly from Essex Co., NJ, where an Abraham was listed in the militia in 1793. He married JOHANNA (VAN VLEET), born ca. 1801, NY, and they lived in Lodi, Seneca Co., NY. In 1833, they moved to Macon Twp., Lenawee Co., Mich., where he soon afterwards died as a result of being frozen. Known children: 1. MARY A. b. ca. 1822, NY (m. James M. Miller, also see); 2. PETER (d. young man in Macon Twp.); 3. RICHARD (following); 4. JOHN (Raisin Twp.). Johanna married second before 1850 to Simeon Davidson (also see); and died at home of a daughter in Clinton Co., Mich. at age 70. Ref: P&BA-Len pg. 331-3. Note: May be Johanna listed as "Hannah" in the 1840 census index of Macon Twp., adjacent to WILLIAM (following).

CADMUS, RICHARD[1] of New Jersey moved to Lodi, Seneca Co., NY. He remained there until quite elderly, and then came to Macon Twp., Lenawee Co., Mich. to join son, ABRAHAM (preceding), where he died. Other known children, WILLIAM, b. ca. 1800, NJ (lived with Deborah 1850 census of Macon Twp.); DEBORAH b. ca. 1802, Middlesex Co., NJ ("dau. of Richard," m. Daniel Clarkson, also see). Ref: P&BA-Len pg. 331-3; 467-8; 970-1. Note: In 1778-1780, there was a number of persons of this surname in Newark, Essex Co., NJ.

CADMUS, RICHARD, son of ABRAHAM (preceding), was born 27 Aug. 1823, Lodi, Seneca Co., NY, and moved with parents to Macon Twp., Lenawee Co., Mich. He married 12 Aug. 1845 to ELIZABETH (RUSSELL), daughter of Asa (also see), and settled in Ridgeway Twp., Lenawee Co. by the 1850 census. She died 26 Mar. 1875, Macon Twp. Children: 1. WALLACE PETER b. ca. 1847 (m. Mary Haight, see Stephen P.; had son, Herbert); 2. HANNAH AUGUSTA b. 22 Jan. 1849 (m. Guernsey P. Waring, also see); 3. HELEN A. or "ELLA" (m. Guernsey P. Waring, as 2d wife). Ref: P&BA-Len pg. 331-3.

CADMUS, WILLIAM was listed in the 1840 census index of Macon Twp., Lenawee Co., Mich. adjacent to HANNAH (See ABRAHAM, preceding).

CAHILL, MARY (See Cornelius Murty)

CAIN also see CANE/KANE

CAIN, JOHN, son of PATRICK & MARY, was born 2 Apr. 1819, Genesee Co., NY, and came to Adrian Twp., Lenawee Co., Mich. in 1837, and afterwards to Rollin Twp., where he married Nov. 1842 to SOPHIA (MARLOTT), daughter of John (also see). They lived in Fairfield Twp. in 1850 census. Children: 1. Name not stated, d. infancy; 2. JAMES O. b. ca. 1843; 3. CHARLES (m. Margaret Stuck, had son, John; Fairfield Twp. Sophia died in 1857, age 34, Fairfield Twp., and he married again in 1858 to ANN (SCOVILLE). She and an infant died in 1859. He married on 17 June 1860 to PATIENCE (SPRAGUE), daughter of Amasa (also see). Ref: P&BA-Len pg. 333-4.

CAIN, LYDIA born ca. 1798, Virginia, was listed in the 1850 census of Woodstock Twp., Lenawee Co., Mich. with no family.

CAIRNS, JAMES R., son of WILLIAM (following), was born 28 Aug. 1832, Seneca Falls, NY, and came with parents to Tecumseh Twp., Lenawee Co., Mich. He married 19 Aug. 1855 to EMILY A. (GREENLEAF), daughter of John (also see) in Jackson Co., Mich. He served in the Civil War as a 1st Lt., Co. B., 9th Mich. Cav., under Col. James I. David. They lived in Franklin Twp., Lenawee Co. until 1882, then moved to Raisin Twp. Children: 1. JENNIE (m. R. S. Wilson, Flowerfield, Mich.); 2. ELLSWORTH W. (Albion, Mich.); 3. DORA B. (twin of Nora); 4. NORA D.; 5. SADIE U.; 6. ARTHUR (deceased by 1888); 7. FLORENCE H. (deceased by 1888); 8. Infant, name not stated, deceased. Ref: P&BA-Len pg. 288-9.

CAIRNS, ROBERT was born in Scotland and came to the US in Colonial times. He married ELIZABETH (WOOD) on 11 May 1786. He died in 1797 in Seneca Co., NY, and she died there 8 Feb. 1812. Children: 1. JOHN b. 1787 (killed in Penn. falling from tree); 2. NELLIE b. 1789 (d. Mich.); 3. WILLIAM (following); 4. MARY W. b. 1793; 5. JEANETTE b. 1796; 6. ROBERT b. 1798 (d. Mich.)

CAIRNS, ROBERT, son of WILLIAM (following), was born 23 July 1819, Seneca Co., NY, and came with his parents to Tecumseh Twp., Lenawee Co., Mich. He married 27 Dec. 1852 to ALVIRA (RUNDELL) of Franklin Twp. Only child, M. ALICE, d. 27 Dec. 1880. Ref: P&BA-Len pg. 806-7. Note: In the 1850 census of Tecumseh Twp., he was listed, age 31, head of household, with HARRIET, age 22 (sister?), both b. NY, in the household.

CAIRNS, WILLIAM, son of ROBERT (preceding), was born ca. 1791, NY, and married on 26 Jan. 1815 in Seneca Co., NY to ABIGAIL (WILSON) who was born ca. 1795, NY. In 1836 they moved to Monroe Co., Mich.; and in 1838 to Tecumseh Twp., Lenawee Co. He died in 1840, but it is probably he listed in the 1840 census index of Clinton, Lenawee Co. There were 11 children, of whom

3 died in Seneca Co., NY. Abigail died 29 Jan. 1878, age 83, in White Pigeon, Mich. at home of known daughter, MARY E.(ELLEN) who was b. 1827 (m. William Seekel, also see). HARRIET, age 22, b. NY, who was in household of William in 1850, may be another daughter. Known sons: JAMES R. (preceding); ROBERT (preceding); WILSON b. ca. 1817, NY (m. Miranda, born ca. 1822, NY, listed in Tecumseh Twp. in 1850 census, no family). Ref: P&BA-Len pg. 288-9 & 806-7.

CALHOUN, ROBERT, and wife, ESTHER, were natives of Ireland, where he died. Esther came to Michigan and died in Nov. 1878 at home of her known daughter, MARGARET, whom had come to the US in 1848 and married Thomas Boyd (also see) after 1851. Ref: P&BA-Len pg. 301-2.

CALKINS, ASHLEY born ca. 1829, NY, was listed in the 1850 census of Palmyra Twp., Lenawee Co., Mich.

CALKINS, EPHRAIM born ca. 1824, and wife, REBECCA C., born ca. 1826, both in NY, were listed in the 1850 census of Dover Twp., Lenawee Co., Mich. with DIANA, age 7, b. NY; and AUGUSTUS, age 5; SUSAN J., age 2, both b. Mich., in their household. Note: There was a man by this name in the 1840 census index of Macomb Co., Shelby Twp., Mich. who was probably an older man.

CALKINS, JAMES born ca. 1817, Nova Scotia, and wife, KEZIA, born ca. 1820, NY, were listed in the 1850 census of Adrian Twp., Lenawee Co., Mich. with MARY L., age 2-1/2, b. Mich., in the household.

CALKINS, JARED born ca. 1788 was born either in NY or Vt. He was orphaned and bound out, but ran away to Sackett's Harbor, Jefferson Co., NY. He lived variously in Jefferson and Cayuga Cos., NY. He married SUSANNAH (AUSTIN), daughter of William (also see), born ca. 1792, Vermont. About 1814, they lived in Macedon, Wayne Co., NY; and later in Genesee Co., NY. In 1836, they removed to Rives Twp., Jackson Co., Mich. and before 1840 to Raisin Twp., Lenawee Co. In the 1850 census they were in Palmyra Twp., Lenawee Co. with DARIUS, age 11, b. Mich. (grandson?) in the household. Jared died at age 81; and she died in Monroe Co., Mich. Known sons: A. B. (Petersburg, Mich.); LORENTUS S. (following). Ref: P&BA-Len pg. 1171-2.

CALKINS, JOHN was born ca. 1779, NY, and wife, DEBORAH, was born ca. 1781, Conn. They were listed in the 1850 census of Raisin Twp., Lenawee Co., Mich. in the household of Timothy & Jerusha Mitchell, also see. Also note JARED, preceding.

CALKINS, LORENTUS S., son of JARED (preceding), was born 23 Aug. 1812, Cayuga Co., NY. He married in Apr. 1836 to SOPHIA (HOLLISTER), daughter of Amazi (also see). They came first to Jackson Co., Mich. and settled later in Palmyra Twp., Lenawee Co. She died 13 Oct. 1882. Children (ages from 1850 census of Palmyra Twp.): 1. ANN, age 12 (m. George Jones, Palmyra Twp.); 2. (CAROLINE) ELIZA, age 8 (m. William D. Archer, Palmyra Twp.); 3. HARRISON, age 5 (m. Phebe Walters); 4. NANCY J., age 5/12; 5. HARRIET E. (m. Clarence E. Judson, also see); 6. WILLARD; 7. FILURA (& followinn children mentioned as deceased by 1888); 8. GEORGE L.; 9. DAVID; 10. SAMUEL L. Ref: P&BA-Len pg. 751-2 & 1171-2.

CALKINS, MATTHIAS settled in Jackson Co., Mich. by 1842.

CALKINS, SARAH R. (See Ira H. Remington)

CALKINS, WILLIAM was born 17 Oct. 1799, NY, and settled in Napoleon, Jackson Co., Mich. He had 7 children by his first wife, names not stated. He married second to Mrs. KEZIAH (BRACE) ELDRED, widow of J. C. William died in 1879 in Napoleon.

CALKINS, WILLIAM A. born ca. 1824, and wife, RHODA S., born ca. 1828, both b. NY, were listed in the 1850 census of Palmyra Twp., Lenawee Co., Mich. with HENRIETTA, age 1, b. Mich., in their household.

CAMBREN, SARAH (See Henry Bowen)

CAMBURN, ALMON, probably son of WILLIAM (following), born ca. 1823, NY, and wife, ESTHER, born ca. 1830, Mich., were listed in the 1850 census of Franklin Twp., Lenawee Co., Mich. with ELLEN, age 3, b. Mich., in their household.

CAMBURN, ELWIN M., son of JOHN (following), was born 25 Jan. 1845, Macon Twp., Lenawee Co., Mich. He married 4 Mar. 1878 to ALMIRA "MIRA" (SMITH), daughter of Rev. Herman C. (also see), and settled in Macon Twp. Children: 1. BESSIE F. b. 25 Jan. 1880; 3. ERNEST b. 24 Mar. 1884. Ref: P&BA-Len pg. 1010-11.

CAMBURN, ESTELLA (See Solomon Wolf)

CAMBURN, HARMON (See Eleazer Holdridge)

CAMBURN, HEBRON was born ca. 1784, New Jersey, and wife, LAVINA (BOYER), was born ca. 1790, Penn.; and they married 1 Apr. 1810, Monmouth Co., NJ. They moved to Macon Twp., Lenawee Co., Mich. in 1836. Known son, JOHN (following) & others from 1850 census of Macon Twp. in Hebron's household: HENRY, age 36; HEBRON, age 26; JAMES, age 22; LOUIS S., age 20; DAVID, age 16, all b. NJ. Note: In 1790, there was a JOSEPH Jr. & NATHAN in Stafford, Monmouth Co., NJ; and in 1793, there were ROBERT; NATHANIEL; & WILLIAM Jr. listed in the militia of Stafford, NJ.

CAMBURN, IRA H. born ca. 1815, and wife, PATTY, born ca. 1817, both in NY, were listed in the 1850 census of Franklin Twp., Lenawee Co., Mich. with SOPHRONIA, age 10, b. Mich. in their household.

CAMBURN, JACOB H., possibly son of WILLIAM (following), born ca. 1824, and wife, ELEANOR, born ca. 1826, both in NY, were listed in the 1850 census of Franklin Twp., Lenawee co., Mich. with THOMAS, age 4/12, b. Mich., in their household.

CAMBURN, JAMES W. born ca. 1804, and wife, HANNAH, born ca. 1803, both in NY, were listed in the 1850 census of Seneca Twp., Lenawee Co., Mich. with WILLIAM R., age 23; JOSEPH F., age 23; ALVA B., age 19; MARY A., age 17, all b. NY; and SARAH, age 16; LORANA, age 13; MIRON W., age 10; IRA M., age 1, HARRIET AUSTIN, age 4/12, all b. Mich., in the household.

CAMBURN, JAMES I? born ca. 1826, and wife, LORINDA, born ca. 1828, both in NY, were listed in the 1850 census of Seneca Twp., Lenawee Co., Mich. with SARAH, age 4; MINERVA, age 2; HANNAH, age 1, all b. Mich., in their household.

CAMBURN, JOHN born ca. 1812, and wife, MARGARET, born ca. 1818, both in NY, were listed in the 1850 census of Seneca Twp., Lenawee Co., Mich. with HANNAH A., age 13; SALLY A., age 11; MARGARET A., age 4; JOHN J., age 1, all b. Mich., in their household.

CAMBURN, JOHN, son of HEBRON (preceding), was born ca. 1821, Barnegat, NJ, and came to Lenawee Co., Mich. with parents. He married ELIZABETH (MORGAN), born 1825, daughter of Charles (also see). They were listed in the 1850 census of Macon Twp., Lenawee Co., with ELWIN (preceding); & CHARLES W., age 3, in their household. John died in 1872, age 51; and Elizabeth was living in 1888, age 63, with son, Elwin. Ref: P&BA-Len pg. 1010-11.

CAMBURN, JOSEPH born ca. 1795, NJ, and wife, ROXANNA, born ca. 1800, Mass., were listed in the 1850 census of Franklin Twp., Lenawee Co., Mich. with GEORGE, age 30; SARAH, age 18, both b. NJ; and FREELOVE, age 24, b. Mich.?; RUTH, age 16; HARRIET, age 13; THOMAS, age 11; AMY, age 9; PHELETIA, age 7; EUGENE, age 3, all b. Mich., in their household. (Note: In Monmouth Co., NJ marriage records, a JOSEPH m. Mary Carr, 20 Sept. 1810.)

CAMBURN, LEVI Rev. was born in New Jersey of Scottish ancestry. He married in NJ, and afterwards moved to Lockport, Niagara Co., NY. His wife died in NY; and he died in 1842 in Hillsdale Co., Mich. Known son, WILLIAM (following). Ref: P&BA-Len pg. 299-300. Also note ALMON & JACOB H. (preceding).

CAMBURN, REBECCA born ca. 1799, died 27 Jan. 1840, age 41 yrs., is buried in the Mills Cem., Franklin Twp., Lenawee Co., Mich. Also buried there, relationship not known, is ALBERT who died 24 Oct. 1904, with wife, ELVIRA, who died 20 Nov. 1883, aged 54y/2m/9d.

CAMBURN, RILEY born ca. 1828, NY, was listed in the 1850 census of Seneca Twp., Lenawee Co., Mich.

CAMBURN, T. M.(MASON?), son of WILLIAM (following), was born 6 Sept. 1835 in Franklin Twp., Lenawee Co., Mich. He married 3 Apr. 1860 to ELIZABETH B. (MILLS), daughter of E. G. (also see). She died 5 Apr. 1875. Children: 1. WILLIAM E. (m. Nancy Crane, Franklin Twp.); & 2. ELMA S. T. M. married second to JENNIE (MILLS), sister of Elizabeth B. Ref: P&BA-Len pg. 299-300.

CAMBURN, WILLIAM, son of LEVI (preceding), was born ca. 1795, NJ, and moved to Lockport, Niagara Co., NY with parents. He married SABRINA (HILL); and he served in the War of 1812 from NY. In 1831, he moved to Tecumseh Twp., Lenawee Co., Mich.; and afterwards to Franklin Twp. He died 7 Apr. 1872; and his wife died in 1849, age 52. There were 16 children, including 2 sets of twins and 1 set of triplets. Listed in William's household in the 1850 census of Franklin Twp.: LEVI, age 22; MARTHA, age 20; MARGARET, age 20, all b. NY; and JULIA ANN, age 17; T. M. (Mason?, age 14, preceding); MELISSA, age 11; WILLIAM, age 8, all b. Mich. ALMON, age 27 (preceding), was next door; and also note JACOB H. Ref: P&BA-Len pg. 299-300.

CAMBURN, WILLIAM C., born ca. 1811, NJ, and wife, RACHEL, born ca. 1819, NY, were listed in the 1850 census of Franklin Twp., Lenawee Co., Mich., with CHARLES, age 9; ANNETTE, age 8, both b. Mich., in their household. Note JOSEPH, preceding.

CAMP, AMBROSE was born ca. 1818, and wife, PHEBE (MILLS), was born ca. 1823, and they were natives of Wayne Co., NY where they married. They removed to Dover Twp., Lenawee Co., Mich. before 1843. He died in Hillsdale Co., Mich. while visiting a nephew; and she died in Medina Twp., Lenawee Co. in the home of her daughter. Three children, those known following from the 1850 census of Dover Twp.: 1. HARRIET M. b. ca. 1843 (prob. she m. Joshua P. Tolford, son of Hugh, also see); 2. JEROME (following). Also in the household was SAMUEL, age 22, b. NY, probably brother of Ambrose. Ref: P&BA-Len pg. 920-1. Note DANIEL, following.

CAMP, DANIEL, son of ISAAC (following), was born ca. 1784, Conn., and he migrated as a young man to Canada. He was drafted in the British Army in 1812, but refused to serve, and deserted and fled to Syracuse, NY. He married POLLY (BAILEY), daughter of Ebenezer (also see). They lived in Port Bay, Wayne Co., NY until 1837, then removed to Deerfield Twp., Lenawee Co., Mich. (listed in Blissfield Twp. in 1840 census index); also purchasing land in Barry Co., Mich. He died 11 Nov. 1848, age 64, Deerfield Twp; and she, age 61, b. Mass., resided with son, Isaac, in the 1850 census of Blissfield Twp.; and she died age 78. Known son, ISAAC (following); known daughter, SUSAN, b. 19 Aug. 1827, Port Bay, NY (m. Mark A. Cannon, also see). Ref: P&BA-Len pg. 1193-5.

CAMP, HENRY C. born ca. 1808, Con., was listed in the 1850 census of Tecumseh Twp., Lenawee Co., Mich. in an Inn.

CAMP, ISAAC Dr. was Scottish by birth, and a physician who served in the Revolutionary War. After the war he settled in Conn. where he remained. Known son, DANIEL (preceding). Ref: P&BA-Len pg. 1193-5.

CAMP, ISAAC of Virginia was the father of JEMINA who married in 1803 to Rev. Joseph Tharp of Muskingum Co., Ohio (also see).

CAMP, ISAAC, son of DANIEL (preceding), born ca. 1820, NY, was head of household in the 1850 census of Blissfield Twp., Lenawee Co., Mich. with mother, POLLY, age 61, b. Mass; and SUSAN, age 13, b. NY, in the household.

CAMP, JAMES born ca. 1800, and wife, POLLY, born ca. 1807, both in NY, were probably they listed in the 1840 census of Dover Twp., Lenawee Co.; and in the 1850 census with MARYETTE, age 18, b. NY; and JAMES, age 16; RUHANA, age 6, both b. Mich., in their household. Also note JOSEPH, following.

CAMP, JEROME, son of AMBROSE (preceding), was born 20 Sept. 1844, Dover Twp., Lenawee Co., Mich. He lived in Lenawee Co. all of his life except for 2 years in West Toledo, Ohio. They moved to Fairfield Twp. in 1887. Childen: 1. LEVI B. b. ca. 1869; 2. OMAR A. b. ca. 1881. Ref: P&BA-Len pg. 920-1.

CAMP, JOHN and wife, EUNICE (COE), were parents of MELINDA born in Durham Co., Conn. (m. Isaac A. Bartlett, a Revolutionary veteran, also see, in West Stockbridge Mass.). Ref: P&BA-Len pg. 1165-7.

CAMP, JOHN born ca. 1783, Mass., and wife, ANNA?, born ca. 1790, NY, were listed in the 1850 census of Seneca Twp., Lenawee Co., Mich. with SYLVESTER, age 28; & CHESTER, age 24, both b. NY, in their household.

CAMP, JOSEPH born ca. 1788, and wife, MARY, born ca. 1807, both in NY, were listed in the 1840 census index of Dover Twp., Lenawee Co., Mich.; and in the 1850 census listed RACHEL, age 20; HENRY, age 16, both b. NY; and JOSEPH, age 13; SARAH J., age 8; AMY A., age 3, all b. Mich. in the household.

CAMP, ROBERT born ca. 1816, Ireland, and wife, POLLY, born ca. 1822, NY, were listed in the 1850 census of Palmyra Twp., Lenawee Co., Mich. with WARREN, age 7; ALMON, age 3; ELISHA, age 2, all b. Mich., in their household.

CAMPBELL, ABIJAH was listed in the 1840 census index of Franklin Twp., Lenawee Co., Mich.

CAMPBELL, CHARLOTTE, age 30, born NY, was listed in the 1850 census of Adrian Twp., Lenawee Co., Mich.

CAMPBELL, DILLON born ca. 1796, NY, was head of household in the 1850 census of Medina Twp., Lenawee Co. Mich. with ROBERT, age 15, b. NY in the household, and in the household next door was MALINDA, age 9, b. Ohio.

CAMPBELL, ELIZA E. (See Daniel E. Hull)

CAMPBELL, EVA (See Elliott Gray)

CAMPBELL, HANNAH (See Job Cook & John Queal)

CAMPBELL, HARRY was listed in the 1840 census index of Tecumseh Twp., Lenawee Co., Mich. adjacent to ISAIAH, following.

CAMPBELL, HUGH born ca. 1814, and wife, NANCY, born ca. 1814, both in Ireland, were listed in the 1850 census of Raisin Twp., Lenawee Co., Mich. with JAMES, age 12; JOHN, age 9; ROBERT W., age 7; JOSEPH R., age 5; THOMAS, age 3; GEORGE A., age 1, all shown b. NY, in their household.

CAMPBELL, ISAIAH, born ca. 1777, NY, was listed in the 1840 census index of Tecumseh Twp., Lenawee Co., Mich., adjacent to HARRY; and in the 1850 census of Tecumseh Twp. with no family.

CAMPBELL, J. W. was listed in the 1840 census index of Seneca Twp., Lenawee Co., Mich.

CAMPBELL, JAMES was born ca. 1788, and wife, BRIDGET (HOEY), was born ca. 1795, both in Co. Louth, Ireland. In 1832, they came to the US, and settled first in Livingston Co., NY; and in 1836 moved to Medina Twp., Lenawee Co., Mich. where they remained. Known children: 1. PATRICK; 2. PETER (following); 3. JAMES (following). Ref: P&BA-Len pg. 900 & 904-5.

CAMPBELL, JAMES, son of JAMES (preceding), was born 17 Mar. 1827, Co. Louth, Ireland and came to Medina Twp., Lenawee Co., Mich. with parents. He married 18 Sept. 1852 to MARY (FLYNN), daughter of Michael (also see) and settled in Medina Twp. He died 8 Aug. 1885, and she survived him. Children: 1. WILLIAM (Toledo, O.); 2. LIZZIE (Marion Co., Ind.); 3. ELLA (m. James H. Davitt, East Saginaw, Mich.); 4. AGNES; 5. ISABELLA; 6. ANNA; 7. ALICE; 8. CHARLES; 9. GEORGE; 10. ROBERT. Ref: P&BA-Len pg. 990.

CAMPBELL, JOHN S., age 23, b. Canada, was listed in the 1850 census of Ridgeway Twp., Lenawee Co., Mich.

CAMPBELL, JOHN born ca. 1822, and wife, NANCY, born ca. 1825, both in Ireland, were listed in the 1850 census of Raisin Twp., Lenawee Co., Mich.

CAMPBELL, MARTHA (See Michael Fiser)

CAMPBELL, PETER, son of JAMES (preceding), was born ca. 1825 in Co. Louth, Ireland, and moved with his parents to NY and Medina Twp., Lenawee Co., Mich. He lived about 2 years in Ohio, but returned to Medina Twp., where he married in 1854 to MARGARET (KENNEDY). She died 27 Nov. 1866 leaving 3 children: 1. VICTOR E. (m. Mary Russell; Springfield, MO); 2. PETER V. (Chicago, Ill.); 3. MAY (m. Fitzpatrick; Hudson Twp.) Peter married again to ROSE (MURTEY), daughter of Cornelius (also see). They had 9 children, 1 dying infancy, name not stated. 4. MATTIE; 5. JOHN J.; 6. LOUIS; 7. FRANK; 8. EDITH; 9. BURT; 10. CLARA; 11. LEO. Ref: P&BA-Len pg. 904-5.

CAMPBELL, THOMAS married after 1827 in Butler Co., Penn. to Mrs. MARGARET (HAMILTON) CLEMENT who was born Nov. 1798, Ireland, the widow of Andrew Clement (also see). They started for Michigan about 1832, but he died during a Winter layover in Toledo, Ohio. Known daughter, LETITIA, born ca. 1832, Penn. (m. Prof. Foster, Ypsilanti, Mich.). It is probably Margaret in the 1850 census of Blissfield Twp., Lenawee Co., Mich. listed as Margaret White, age 51, b. Ireland with LETTA, age 18, b. Penn. in the household.

CAMPBELL, WILLIAM was listed in the 1840 census index of Rollin Twp., Lenawee Co., Mich.

CAMPBURN see CAMBURN

CAMPSE D. (See Michael Mulzer)

CANBURR, FANNIE (See McClure)

CANE also see CAIN/KANE

CANE, EVA (See Henry W. Burke)

CANFIELD, ASAHEL and wife, JERUSHA (HAMLIN), of Durham, NY were parents of HARRIET (m. Charles Dunham 23 Dec. 1835, also see). Ref: P&BA-Len pg. 842-3.

CANFIELD, ELIZABETH (See Ira Stewart)

CANFIELD, SAYRES born ca. 1798, and wife, SARAH, born ca. 1809, both in NY, were listed in the 1840 census index of Rome Twp., Lenawee Co., Mich. adjacent to SILAS & SILAS C. (following); and were in the 1850 census of Rollin Twp., Lenawee Co. with LUCINDA, age 23; JOHN, age 19; ELIZABETH, age 16, all b. NY; and EZRA, age 13; LOUISA, age 11; ALONZO, age 9; NATHANIEL, age 7; HARVEY, age 2, all b. Mich., in the household.

CANFIELD, SILAS & SILAS C. were listed in the 1840 census index of Rome Twp., Lenawee Co., Mich., but neither are listed in 1850.

CANFIELD, SYLVESTER accompanied the Wilson Wood family from Orleans Co., NY to Lenawee Co., Mich. by 1836 (not listed 1840 census index).

CANNIFF, ENOS, son of JOHN (following), was born 11 Feb. 1822, Knowlesville, Orleans Co., NY and came to Hillsdale Co., Mich. with his mother; but went back to NY. He married 15 May 1842 to LUCY B. (ESTES), daughter of Sylvanus (also see). They located first in Richfield, and then in Hudson Twp., Lenawee Co., Mich. In 1883, they lived for a time in the west while he was a postal clerk on the rail line between Granger, Wyo. and Huntington, Ore.; and also was Deputy Postmaster in Weiser, Ida. before returning to Hudson, Mich. Children: 1. EMMA b. ca. 1849 (m. W. W. Carter, Hudson, Mich.); 2. IDA (m. W. H. Tower, Union City, Mich.); 3. ALENA; 4. ROSA (Union City, Mich.). Ref: P&BA-Len pg. 1200.

CANNIFF, JOHN was among the first to buy land from the Holland Purchase Co.; and lived in Knowlesville

Pioneer Families of Southeastern Michigan

(Ridgeway), Orleans Co., NY. He married LYDIA (MORSE), possibly daughter of Enos (also see). John supervised the building of the Erie Canal through that area, and died of drowning in Ashtabula Co., Ohio in 1830. After his death, Lydia remained in NY for a time, then purchased in Wheatland Twp., Hillsdale Co., Mich.; and lived in 1839 in Pittsford with son, STEPHEN. Other known children: ENOS (preceding); & probably LEWIS (following); & possibly MATILDA, b. ca. 1826, NY in LEWIS' household in 1850 census. Lydia married second after 1839 to Stephen Bird (also see). Ref: P&BA-Len pg. 1200.

CANNIFF, LEWIS, probably son of JOHN (preceding), born ca. 1820, NY, was listed in the 1850 census of Hudson Twp., Lenawee Co., Mich. with WILLIAM H., age 2; LADORA A., age 2, both born Mich., and listed last, MATILDA, age 24, b. NY, exact relationship not known.

CANNON, FREDERICK, probably son of GEORGE (following), was born ca. 1828, England, and was listed in the 1850 census of Blissfield Twp., Lenawee Co., Mich. with (wife?) CHARLOTTE, age 19, b. NY, in his household.

CANNON, GEORGE was born ca. 1796, Buckinghamshire, England, and married there to ANN (SAUNDERS) born ca. 1798. After the birth of 9 children, they came to the US in 1837; and went immediately from NY to Blissfield Twp., Lenawee Co., Mich. They remained there till 1864, then moved into to village of Blissfield, where he died in 1871, age 75; and she died in 1883. There were 12 children. Known son, MARK A. (following); and listed in George's household in the 1850 census: BENJAMIN, age 20; JOSEPH, age 14; SUSANNAH, age 10; JAMES, age 6. Ref: P&BA-Len pg. 1193-4. Also note FREDERICK, PHILIP, & WILLIAM, as there were no other Cannon families in Lenawee Co. in 1850.

CANNON, HARRIET born ca. 1807, NY (See David Berdan).

CANNON, MARK A., son of GEORGE (preceding), was born 11 Oct. 1821, Buckinghamshire, England and came to Blissfield Twp., Lenawee Co., Mich. with parents. He married 17 Nov. 1850 to SUSAN (CAMP), daughter of Daniel (also see). Children: 1. GEORGE (resident of Canada); 2. DELLA (m. Allen McKee, Danville, KY); 3. FRANK E. (lived Louisville, KY); 4. WINFIELD b. 22 Nov. 1854 (d. 13 May 1878); 5. EARL. b. 19 Apr. 1863 (d. 7 Sept. 1863). Ref: P&BA-Len pg. 1194-5.

CANNON, PHILIP, probably son of GEORGE (preceding), was born ca. 1825, England, and was living in another household in the 1850 census of Madison Twp., Lenawee Co., Mich.

CANNON, WILLIAM, probably son of GEORGE (preceding), was born ca. 1831, England, and was living in another household in the 1850 census of Blissfield Twp., Lenawee Co., Mich.

CAPRON, EBENEZER A. born ca. 1817, NY, and wife, SARAH (YOUNGS), see Davis Youngs, born ca. 1824, Penn., were in the 1850 census of Seneca Twp., Lenawee Co., Mich. with SABRA A., age 6; & ELLA F. b. 3 Nov. 1848 (m. Edwin A. Baker, also see), both b. Mich., in their household. Ebenezer was still living in 1888 in Seneca Twp., but Sarah preceded him in death. Ref: P&BA-Len pg. 632-3.

CARD, AUGUSTUS born ca. 1801, Rhode Island, and wife, POLLY, born ca. 1804, NY, were listed in the 1840 census index of Hudson Twp., Lenawee Co., Mich.; and in the 1850 census with LEWIS, age 18; BETSEY A., age 22, both b. NY, in their household.

CARD, CHARLES R. born ca. 1803, and wife, HANNAH, born ca. 1803, both in England, were listed in the 1840 census index of Franklin Twp., Lenawee Co., Mich.; and in the 1850 census of Franklin Twp. with WILLIAM, age 15 (d. 4 Sept. 1863, age 27y/6m/17d, in Civil War); FANNY, age 12, both b. NY; and HESTER, age 7; JOHN F., age 5 (m. Charlotte A.; she d. 15 July 1893, he d. 1921); JESSE, age 3 (d. 4 Sept. 1850), last 3 b. Mich., in their household. Charles R. died 2 Aug. 1874, aged 71y/5m/24d; and Hannah died 24 Jan. 1875, aged 71y/5m/18d. They and the children noted with death dates were buried in Mills Cemetery, Franklin Twp. Note: MARY ANN, age 17, b. NY, in the 1850 census of Franklin Twp., in household of John Main (See FRANCES, following), may relate to this family.

CARD, JOB was listed in the 1840 census index of Dover Twp., Lenawee Co., Mich.

CARD, FRANCES born 21 Sept. 1804, England (See John Main).

CARD, RICHARD J., age 8/12, b. Mich., was listed in the household of Newman and Olive Perkins in the 1850 census of Hudson Twp., Lenawee Co., Mich.

CARD, WEDEN? born ca. 1797, Conn., and wife, JULIA A., born ca. 1808, Mass., were listed in the 1850 census of Dover Twp., Lenawee Co., Mich. with LOVICA A., age 22; MINERVA, age 21, both b. Mass.; and W. S. (male), age 18; CICERO, age 16, both b. NY, in their household.

CARD, WILLIAM born ca. 1775, died 31 Dec. 1845, age 70 yrs, was buried in the Mills Cemetery, Franklin Twp., Lenawee Co., Mich. It is probably he listed in the 1840 census index of Franklin Twp., adjacent to WILLIAM, Jr. (following). Note CHARLES R. (listed adjacent in the 1840 census index); & FRANCES (preceding).

CARD, WILLIAM born ca. 1810, England, and wife, HARRIET, born ca. 1819, NY, were listed in the 1850 census of Franklin Twp., Lenawee Co., Mich. with MARY, age 10; MARTHA, age 8; HARRIET, age 6; VIOLETTA, age 4, all b. Mich., in their household. William died 26 Feb. 1889, age 79y/5m/25d, and is buried in the Mills Cemetery, Franklin Twp. This is probably WILLIAM, Jr. listed in the 1840 census index of Franklin Twp.

CAREY also see CARY

CAREY, MARY (See Oramon Tuttle, Jr.)

CAREY, STEPHEN born ca. 1795 and wife, MARY, born ca. 1798, both in NY, were listed in the 1850 census of Woodstock Twp., Lenawee Co., Mich. with THOMAS, age 20; STEPHEN, age 19; MARY, age 15, all b. NY; and FRANKLIN, age 12, b. Mich. in the household.

CAREY, WALTER born ca. 1816, and wife, MALISSA, born ca. 1822, both in NY, were listed in the 1850 census of Woodstock Twp., Lenawee Co., Mich. with ALBERT, age 3, b. Mich. in their household.

CARLETON also see CARLTON

CARLETON, JOHN HANCOCK, son of JESSE (who c. 1818, Bath, Grafton Co., NH), was born 16 Oct. 1802, Grafton,

NH. He went first to Canada, and then about 1830 to Wayne Co., Mich. He married there to CELESTIA ELVIRA (SMITH), daughter of Daniel (also see). In 1835, they moved to Hudson Twp., Lenawee Co. He died there 9 Feb. 1872; and she afterwards lived both in Hudson Twp., and in Brooklyn, NY. Children: 1. HENRY b. ca. 1834 (m. Mary Beech; served Civil War, Co. A., 18th Vol. Inf., d. in Selma, Ala. Prison); 2. MARY A. b. ca. 1836 (m. Addison Kidder; she d. 1861); 3. ALMIRA b. ca. 1840 (m. Heman Goodrich; she d. Aug. 1872); 4. HARRISON (d. infancy); 5. WILLIAM M. b. ca. 1846. Ref: P&BA-Len pg. 838-40.

CARLTON, HENRY J., son of LEONARD (following), was born 20 Mar. 1831 in Cattaraugus Co., NY. He married in Toledo, Ohio on 17 May 1853 to SARAH E. (WOOD), daughter of George (also see). They moved to Raisin Twp., Lenawee Co., Mich. Child, name not stated, died infancy. Ref: P&BA-Len pg. 447-8.

CARLTON, JACOB was a pioneer settler of Genesee Co., NY. Known daughter, LOUISA, born ca. 1802, NY (m. Cook Sisson, also see). Ref: P&BA-Len pg. 811-2.

CARLTON, LEONARD born in NY, married there to DIANA (HOWARD). They moved to Monroe Co., Mich. in 1836; and in 1853 to Raisin Twp., Lenawee Co. He died 8 Sept. 1878; and she died 4 Apr. 1878. Known son, HENRY J. (preceding). Ref: P&BA-Len pg. 447-8.

CARNEY, GEORGE, son of JOHN (who had come from Ireland to Livingston Co., NY), was born ca. 1812, Dansville, Livingston Co., NY. He married there to ELISA born ca. 1814, NY. About 1845, they moved to Tecumseh Twp., Lenawee Co., Mich. In the 1850 census of Tecumseh Twp., they listed JOHN, age 14; JAMES (following); ISADORA, age 3, all b. NY. In 1881, they returned to Sparta, Livingston Co., NY. Ref: P&BA-Len pg. 803-4.

CARNEY, JAMES, son of GEORGE (preceding), was born 23 Apr. 1837, Livingston Co., NY and came to Tecumseh Twp., Lenawee Co., Mich. with parents. He served in the Civil War with the Mich. Cavalry; was taken prisoner, and was in both Libby & Andersonville prisons. He married 16 July 1865 to MARY E. (McCOMB), daughter of William (also see). They lived in Coldwater, Mich., and in 1870 lived in Ashtabula Co., Ohio. In 1875, they returned to Ogden Twp., Lenawee Co., Mich. Only child, DORA A., was born 13 May 1866 (m. Sterry A. Johnson, son of William J., also see). Ref: P&BA-Len pg 803-4.

CARPENTER, ABNER born ca. 1814, and wife, AMANDA, born ca. 1821, both in NY, were listed in the 1840 census index of Rome Twp.; and in the 1850 census of Madison Twp., Lenawee Co., Mich. with LURA, age 13; LAURA, age 10; PHEBE, age 8; ALBINA, age 5; WARREN, age 3, all b. NY, in the household. Note SAMUEL, following.

CARPENTER, ABRAM, son of Rev. JAMES (following), born ca. 1810, NY and wife, JULIA, born ca. 1807, both in NY, were listed in the 1840 census index of Fairfield Twp., Lenawee Co., Mich.; and in the 1850 census of Fairfield Twp. (in household of Rev. James) with children, GEORGE, age 13; FRANKLIN, age 8; SHELDON, age 5, all b. Mich.

CARPENTER, ASENATH married Parker Wyman (also see). Also note CLEMENT[7], (following). Ref: P&BA-Len pg. 1020-1.

CARPENTER, BASSETT C., born ca. 1817, and wife, SARAH, born ca. 1820, both in NY, were listed in the 1850 census of Fairfield Twp., Lenawee Co., Mich. with CYRUS, age 6; JOHN, age 3; ELEANOR, age 1, all b. Mich., in their household. Bassett may be "Rassett," son of JOHN H., following.

CARPENTER, BEACH N., probably son of SMITH (following), was born ca. 1827, NY, and was listed in the 1850 census of Fairfield Twp., Lenawee Co., Mich., next door to SMITH, with wife, ROBY, age 20, b. NY, in the household.

CARPENTER, BENJAMIN, son of Rev. JAMES (following), was born 1 June 1807 near Elmira, NY, and moved with his parents to Shelby, Orleans Co., NY where he married 13 Jan. 1828 to ELIZA M. (WICOX), daughter of Silas (also see). He entered for land in Fairfield Twp., Lenawee Co., Mich. in 1832; and remained there until 1855, then moved to Madison Twp. Thirteen children, of whom 5 sons served in the Civil War. All known children following, except SILAS B., age 17, b. NY, were listed in the household in the 1850 census: ABRAM S., age 15; #5. LUCRETIA M. b. 29 Sept. 1837 (m. Henry Ragless, also see); THOMAS J., age 10; JEROME B., age 8; CHARLES A., age 6; WILLIAM H., age 4; BENJAMIN C., age 4/12. Ref: P&BA-Len pg. 523-4.

CARPENTER, BETSEY (See Francis A. Howard)

CARPENTER, CHARLES (See Samuel Lewis)

CARPENTER, CHARLES born ca. 1825, and wife, RICTYNA?, age 20, were listed in the 1850 census of Fairfield Twp., Lenawee Co., Mich. with no family shown. Note: He may be CHARLES, son of JOHN H., following.

CARPENTER, CLEMENT[7], son of GREENWOOD[6] (See EZRA[5], following) was born 10 Oct. 1781. He married ELIZABETH (GILMORE), daughter of Robert of Londonderry, NH. About 1808, they settled in Potsdam, St. Lawrence Co., NY; and he died there 1 May 1860, and she died 20 Mar. 1863. Large family, those known: (Eldest son) GUY b. 1809 (went to Blissfield Twp., listed there 1840 census index, died 1849, age 40); DAVID (following); ROBERT B. (Potsdam, NY); JOEL (following); ZELINDA (m. 1844 to Dr. Henry Wyman, also see). Ref: P&BA-Len pg. 1202-3. Also see ASENATH, preceding.

CARPENTER, DAVID[8], son of CLEMENT[7] (preceding), was born 19 Apr. 1815, Potsdam, NY. In 1836, he went to Toledo, Ohio. He married on 22 May 1837 to THIRZA (PEASE) who was born in Chittenden, VT on 19 May 1812. In 1838, they removed to Blissfield Twp., Lenawee Co., Mich. She died there 22 Dec. 1839. He married second to MAY L. (ELLIS) who was born 3 Oct. 1822, Potsdam, NY and died 15 Jan. 1848, Blissfield Twp. He married third to HEPSIBETH (WORTH), see John Worth for Ancestry, on 16 Aug. 1848, and they were listed in the 1850 census of Blissfield Twp. One son, GUY DAVID, born 15 Oct. 1877. Ref: P&BA-Len pg. 837. Note: In the 1850 census, he listed Swift Pearce, age 5, b. Mich. in the household.

CARPENTER, DAVID married Mrs. JUDITH (WILBER) PARKS, daughter of William (also see), and widow of David (who d. in Johnstown, Fulton Co., Ohio). They settled in Madison Twp., Lenawee Co., Mich., where

Pioneer Families of Southeastern Michigan

they remained. Ref: P&BA-Len pg. 875-6. Also see SAMUEL of Madison Twp. (following).

CARPENTER, ELIHU born ca. 1798, and wife, ANNA (VARNEY), born ca. 1800, were natives of Addison Co., Vermont, who went to Erie Co., NY. In 1837, they moved to Raisin Twp., Lenawee Co., Mich. Known children: JOSEPH (following); & youngest child, STEPHEN (following). Ref: P&BA-Len pg. 357-8.

CARPENTER, EZRA^5 - The following ancestry was provided for this family. In 1563, a Coat of Arms was granted to WILLIAM$_2$ of Cobham, Surrey, England. His son, WILLIAM^2 came to Weymouth, Mass. about 1633, and died in 1658 in Rehoboth. His son, WILLIAM^3, born 1631, England, had come to Mass. with his parents; and by a second wife, name not stated, had son, NATHANIEL^4, born 1666, d. 1754 in Attleboro, Mass. Nathaniel^4 lived Rehoboth, and also Boston, Mass., and afterwards went to Cheshire Co., NH, and died in Walpole, NH in 1785. He was the father of EZRA^5 born ca. 1730, who married ELIZABETH (GREENWOOD), daughter of Rev. Thomas of Rehoboth, Mass. They lived first in New Hampshire, but moved to Bunker Hill (Charleston, now Boston) about 1750; then moved later back to Swanzey, NH where he died in 1814. Known son, GREENWOOD^6, born ca. 1752, married in 1780 to ? (SUMNER), daughter of Rev. Clement Sumner. Greenwood served in the Revolution. About 1803, they moved to Potsdam, St. Lawrence Co., NY, where he died in 1843, aged about 91. Known son, CLEMENT^7 (preceding). Ref: P&BA-Len pg. 1202-3. Also note EZRA, following.

CARPENTER, EZRA, and wife, LUCY, of Mass. were parents of ESTHER, born Mass., who married Andrew Coryell (also see) in Seneca Co., NY by 1822. Ref: P&BA-Len pg. 982-3 & 1029-30.

CARPENTER, FREDERICK born ca. 1831, NY, was listed in the 1850 census of Fairfield Twp., Lenawee Co., Mich. (Note BENJAMIN of Fairfield Twp.) It is probably he listed again in household of SMITH, following.

CARPENTER, GEORGE was listed in the 1840 census index of Raisin Twp., Lenawee Co., Mich.

CARPENTER, HENRY born ca. 1790, and wife, SARAH, born ca. 1784, both born in NJ, were listed in the 1840 census index of Rome Twp., Lenawee Co., Mich.; and in the 1850 census were next door to HENRY J. (following). Note JOHN M., following.

CARPENTER, HENRY J., probably son of HENRY (preceding), born ca. 1817, NJ, and wife, ZUBA, born ca. 1821, NY, were listed in the 1850 census of Rome Twp., Lenawee Co., Mich. with JOSEPH, age 8; BENJAMIN, age 6; DANIEL, age 4, all b. Mich., in their household (next door to HENRY, preceding).

CARPENTER, HIRAM born ca. 1830, NY, is listed in the 1850 census of Fairfield Twp., Lenawee Co., Mich. and may actually be CHARLES H., son of JOHN H., following.

CARPENTER, JACKSON of Woodstock Twp., Lenawee Co., Mich. married SARAH (ROWLSON), daughter of Chauncey (also see). Sarah died 23 Dec. 1878, leaving daughter, SARAH. Also note JOSIAH, following.

CARPENTER, JAMES Rev. was born 1785, Orange Co., NY; and married CATHARINE (STRIKER), born ca. 1785, NY. They lived near Elmira (then Tioga, now Chemung Co.), NY until about 1810, then moved to Shelby, Orleans Co., NY. In 1833, they moved to Fairfield Twp., Lenawee Co., Mich., where he died in 1857. Known children: 1. BENJAMIN (preceding); 2. ABRAM (preceding); 3. SARAH C. b. 18 July 1815, Shelby, NY (m. William Weatherby, also see); 4. LYDIA b. 4 Nov. 1817, Shelby (m. Sheldon Wyman in Fairfield Twp., also see); 5. JAMES K. (following). Ref: P&BA-Len pg. 459-60; 523-4; 1020-1. Also note REUBEN, & WILLIAM S., following.

CARPENTER, JAMES (See Jesse B. Odell)

CARPENTER, JAMES C., son of SAMUEL (following), born ca. 1824, was listed in the 1850 census of Madison Twp., Lenawee Co., Mich. (in household of Samuel) with wife, CORDELIA, age 20, both b. NY, and HANNAH, age 6/12, b. Mich.

CARPENTER, JAMES K., son of Rev. JAMES (preceding), was probably he listed in the 1840 census index of Fairfield Twp., Lenawee Co., Mich. adjacent to Rev. JAMES.

CARPENTER, JOEL^8, son of CLEMENT^7 (preceding), born 3 Sept. 1818, Potsdam, NY, married there on 12 Oct. 1842 to THEODOCIA A. They moved to Blissfield Twp., Lenawee Co., Mich. and she died 7 Dec. 1843. He married again to MINERVA L. (MEAD), daughter of Darius Mead (also see), who died 12 Mar. 1852, leaving children: 1. CLEMENT b. 23 Mar. 1848, Toledo, Ohio; 2. CARRIE F. b. 6 Aug. 1850; 3. MINERVA E. (d. infancy). Joel married third to LUCY (GILMORE), daughter of Asa (also see) of Tecumseh. She died 3 Oct. 1861 leaving a son, 4. GUY D. b. 23 Sept. 1861 (d. 4 Mar. 1864). On 14 Jan. 1864, Joel married ESTHER C. (NEWTON), daughter of E. (probably Ezra) of Blissfield. Ref: P&BA-Len pg. 1202-3.

CARPENTER, JOHN born ca. 1795, NY, was listed in the 1850 census of Palmyra Twp., Lenawee Co., Mich. with ELIZABETH, age 23; SYDNEY, age 21; & SARINA?, age 16, all b. NY, in his household.

CARPENTER, JOHN born ca. 1826, NY, and wife, MARY, born ca. 1829, Penn., were listed in the 1850 census of Fairfield Twp., Lenawee Co., Mich. with LABAN, age 3; ROBERT, age 1, (note following), both b. Mich., in the household. Note: In the census was next door to REUBEN, following.

CARPENTER, JOHN H., son of JOSHUA & SARAH (BERT) whom remained in NY, was born ca. 1791, NY, and married there to ELIZABETH (COOK), daughter of Moses (also see), born ca. 1796, Conn.; and then came from near Elmira, NY to Madison Twp., Lenawee Co., Mich. in 1831; and later moved to Fairfield Twp. (probably he listed in the 1840 census index of Fairfield Twp. as "John A.") He died in Fairfield Twp. on 3 July 1874; and she died in June 1866. Children: 1. RASSET (probably BASSET C., preceding); 2. PHEBE; 3. EUNICE N. b. May 1822, Elmira (m. Norman H. Thurber, also see); 3. CHARLES H. (This may be HIRAM, age 20, listed in household next door in 1850 census); 4. DANIEL B. b. ca. 1827, NY; 5. AARON W.; 6. ELSIE A. b. ca. 1832, Mich.; 7. MARTHA W. b. ca. 1836, Mich. Ref: P&BA-Len pg. 248-9.

CARPENTER, JOHN M. born ca. 1805, NJ, and wife, MARY A., born ca. 1815, NY, were listed in the 1840 census index of Seneca Twp., Lenawee Co., Mich. (as "J. M."); and in the 1850 census of Seneca Twp. with JOHN, age 8; ELIAS, age 5; COMFORT, age 2; LYDIA, age 11/12, all b. Mich., in their household.

CARPENTER, JOHN R. born ca. 1807, and wife, AMANDA, born ca. 1814, both in NY, were listed in the 1850 census of Adrian Twp., Lenawee Co., Mich. with ROMANDA, age 14; SARAH, age 11; LYDIA, age 9; NAOMI, age 8; MARTHA, age 4; MARQUIS D. L., age 1, all b. Mich., in their household.

CARPENTER, JOHN V. was listed in the 1840 census index of Fairfield Twp., Lenawee Co., Mich.; and may be one of the men listed previously.

CARPENTER, JOSEPH was listed in the 1850 census of Dover Twp., born ca. 1791, Conn., with no family.

CARPENTER, JOSEPH born ca. 1803, NH, and wife, PERSILLA, born ca. 1818, NY, were listed in the 1850 census of Blissfield Twp., Lenawee Co., Mich. with JULIA, age 18; JAMES, age 17; JUDSON, age 15, all b. NY; and ANN, age 14; JANE, age 11; ROLLIN, age 9, all b. Mich., in their household. It may be this Joseph listed as Joseph P. in the 1840 census index of Blissfield Twp. See CLEMENT for possible relationship.

CARPENTER, JOSEPH, probably son of ELIHU (preceding), was born ca. 1819, VT, and wife, MARY H. (HARKNESS?), born ca. 1829, NY, were listed in the 1850 census of Raisin Twp., Lenawee Co., Mich. with ELMIRA, age 9; MALVINA, age 4, both b. Mich.; and Mary Harkness, age 63, b. NY, in their household.

CARPENTER, JOSEPH H., born ca. 1796, NJ, and wife, SARAH, born ca. 1800, NY, were listed in the 1840 census index of Cambridge Twp., Lenawee Co., Mich.; and in the 1850 census with CHARLES, age 19; CATHARINE, age 15; both b. NY; and HOPE, age 12; ROSETTA, age 11; SARAH, age 8; LAVINA, age 4, all b. Mich., in their household.

CARPENTER, JOSIAH, son of URIAH (following), was born 17 Nov. 1801, Berkshire Co., Mass., and moved to Greenfield, Saratoga Co., NY. He married there 11 Jan. 1828 to NANCY (HARKNESS), daughter of Nathan (also see). In 1836, they moved to Woodstock Twp., Lenawee Co., Mich., where she died 3 Nov. 1851. Children: 1. ANNA A. b. 28 Sept. 1829, Greenfield, NY; 2. MANSON (following); 3. NATHAN H. b. 21 Jan. 1833, Monroe Co., Mich.; 4. HANNAH A. b. 8 May 1835 (m. Philip Kelley); 5. URIAH b. 14 Apr. 1838, Woodstock Twp. Josiah married second on 21 Nov. 1852 to CLARISSA A. (PRATT). Children: 6. ALBERT b. 16 Aug. 1853 (d. 7 Aug. 1884, left wife and child); 7. NANCY A. b. 4 Feb. 1857 (m. Marshall N. Beckey, Salina, KS). Josiah died 13 Apr. 1887 in Monroe Co., Mich. at home of Nathan. Ref: P&BA-Len pg. 612-3.

CARPENTER, LOUISA (See Oliver Griffin)

CARPENTER, MANSON, son of JOSIAH (preceding), was born 2 Oct. 1830, Saratoga Co., NY, and moved with his parents to Woodstock Twp., Lenawee Co., Mich. He married on 9 May 1862 to ANN E. (JOHNSON), daughter of Thomas (also see). Son, JOHN J. b. 3 June 1864 (to Brown Co., Dak.). Ref: P&BA-Len pg. 612-3.

CARPENTER, MARY (See Joseph C. Newell)

CARPENTER, MARY C. (See William Sheffield)

CARPENTER, MOSES born ca. 1827, and wife, SARAH, born ca. 1828, both in NY, were listed in the 1850 census of Fairfield Twp., Lenawee Co., Mich. with no family.

CARPENTER, REUBEN T. (See Rev. JAMES, preceding) born ca. 1818, NY and wife, ROSANA, born ca. 1829, Ireland, were listed in the 1850 census of Fairfield Twp., Lenawee Co., Mich. with LEWIS, age 2; LORENZO, age 7/12, both b. Mich., in their household. Note: They were next door to JOHN in the census.

CARPENTER, ROBERT married EVELYN G. (WARREN), daughter of Jesse H. (also see) in Madison Twp., Lenawee Co., Mich. Children: GRACE; & MERTA. Note JOHN, preceding, with son, ROBERT.

CARPENTER, SAMUEL born 1779, and wife, POLLY, born ca. 1790, both in NY, were probably they listed in the 1840 census index of Madison Twp., Lenawee Co., Mich.; and in the 1850 census listed JAMES C., age 26 (preceding, with family); & ANDREW, age 18, b. Mich. in their household. Also note ABNER & DAVID, preceding.

CARPENTER, SARAH (See Luther Warren). Also note HENRY, preceding.

CARPENTER, SMITH born ca. 1797, and wife, PHEBE, born ca. 1807, both in NY, were listed in the 1850 census of Dover Twp., Lenawee Co., Mich. with FREDERICK G., age 19; ANDREW J., age 17; LUCINDA M., age 12, all b. NY; and ALPHEUS, age 3, b. Mich., in their household; and next door BEACH N. (also see).

CARPENTER, STEPHEN, son of ELIHU (preceding), born 7 Apr. 1827, Starksboro, VT, came with parents to Raisin Twp., Lenawee Co., Mich. He married 28 Jan. 1852 to HELEN E. (BRADISH), daughter of Curran (also see). They were Quakers. Nine children, of whom 5 died young; & 4 were living in 1888, names not stated. A son, STEPHEN E., died age 6 yrs.

CARPENTER, URIAH was born 1769 in Smithfield, RI. he married CONTENT (SLACK), daughter of Baker (also see). About 1790, they removed to Adams, Mass., where he died in 1829, and she died in 1840. Eight children, only known son, JOSIAH (preceding). Ref: P&BA-Len pg. 612-3.

CARPENTER, WILLIAM S. born ca. 1803, and wife, SARAH, born ca. 1807, both in NY, were probably they listed in the 1840 census index of Fairfield Twp., Lenawee Co., Mich.; and in the 1850 census of Seneca Twp., they listed WILLIAM, age 25; MORDICAI, age 22; MARTIN?, age 15, all b. NY; and LAMIRAH?, age 14; JOHN, age 12; PETER, age 10; SARAH, age 8; PHEBE, age 6; GARRET, age 2, all b. Mich., in their household.

CARSKADDON, JAMES and wife, SUSAN (HAYES), settled first in Clinton Co., Penn; and he died there. She moved to Medina Twp., Lenawee Co., Mich. Children: 2 sons (names not stated); and daughter, LAVINA, born 1 Nov. 1821, Clinton Co., Penn. (m. Isaac D. Packer, also see). Ref: P&BA-Len pg. 671-2.

CARSON, ALONZO MARSHALL, son of WILLIAM S. (following), was born 20 July 1829, Seneca, Ontario Co., NY; and as an adult went to Cleveland, Ohio where he was living in 1851. He moved to Newark, Ohio, and then to Hudson Twp., Lenawee Co., Mich. in 1852. He married 22 Sept. 1852 to B. JENNIE (PECK), daughter of Ira (also see). Children: 1. BELL (to Grayling, Crawford Co., Mich.; 2. OLIN (d. infancy); 3. MAY (d. age 22). Ref: P&BA-Len pg. 832-4.

CARSON, ANNA (See Aaron Whitacre)

CARSON, JAMES was born in Penn. and was a pioneer settler to Farmington, Ontario Co., NY, where he died ca. 1815. Known son, WILLIAM S. (following). Ref: P&BA-Len pg. 832-4.

Pioneer Families of Southeastern Michigan

CARSON, JANE (See Samuel Boyd, Jr.)

CARSON, WILLIAM S., son of JAMES (preceding), was born Sept. 1808, Farmington, NY, and was "bound out" at age 12 in Seneca, NY. He married there to ANGELINE BURLINGAME (COLWELL), daughter of Daniel (also see). He prospected for land in Mich. in 1835, then returned to NY where he remained until 1860, then came to Hudson Twp., Lenawee Co., Mich. to join son, ALONZO MARSHALL (preceding). William S. died in 1862. Ref: P&BA-Len pg. 832-4.

CARTER, ANSON born ca. 1792, and wife, ZILPHA (GILLETT), born ca. 1798, both in NY, moved from Junius, Seneca Co., NY to Hudson Twp., Lenawee Co., Mich. by 1850. There were 8 children, and those following are from the 1850 census of Hudson Twp.: GEORGE W. (following); WILLIAM, age 18; NANCY, age 13; IRA, age 10; HENRY, age 8, all b. NY. Ref: P&BA-Len pg. 812-3.

CARTER, ASEL was born New England ancestry; and he served in the War of 1812, and died in VT over age 85. Known daughter, CLARISSA, born 1808, VT (m. Hiram Cure, also see in NY ca. 1827). Ref: P&BA-Len pg. 840-1.

CARTER, CYRUS B. born ca. 1806, Mass., and wife, AMYRA?, born ca. 1809, NY, were listed in the 1840 census index of Franklin Twp., Lenawee Co., Mich.; and in the 1850 census with ANN ELISA, age 8; FIDELIA, age 5; CHARLES, age 2, all b. Mich., and listed last, CYRUS, age 20, b. NY, in their household.

CARTER, ELI born ca. 1788, and wife, SARAH, born ca. 1793, both in NJ, were listed in the 1840 census index of Macon Twp., Lenawee Co., Mich.; and in the 1850 census with JOSEPH, age 29; REBECCA, age 24; ENOS, age 17, all b. NJ; and JOHN, age 13; WILLIAM, age ?, both b. Mich., in their household. Note MICHAEL, following.

CARTER, GEORGE W., son of ANSON (preceding), came to Hudson Twp., Lenawee Co., Mich. with his parents. He married 1 Jan. 1857 to MARY D. (PRATT), daughter of Jesse (also see). Children: 1. ALICE A. b. Nov. 1857 (m. F. D. Brown; she d. Oct. 1881); 2. BELLE; 3. ARTHUR; 4. EFFIE MAY; 5. GEORGE W.; 6. EDNA. Ref: P&BA-Len pg. 812-3.

CARTER, GERRY was listed in the 1840 census index of Seneca Twp., Lenawee Co., Mich.

CARTER, GULIELMUS b. ca. 1807, Mass., and wife, LETSY, b. ca. 1806, NY, were listed in the 1840 census index of Tecumseh Twp., Lenawee Co., Mich., and in the 1850 census with LETSY ANN, age 21, b. NY; & CATHARINE, age 14, b. Mich. in the household.

CARTER, JOEL H. born ca. 1821, with wife, SARAH A., born ca. 1831, both in NY, were listed in the 1850 census of Seneca Twp., Lenawee Co., Mich. with SUSAN, age 64, born Conn. (probably mother) in the household. Note GERRY, preceding.

CARTER, LEVI was listed in the 1840 census index of Tecumseh Twp., Lenawee Co., Mich. not far from MEHITABLE, following.

CARTER, MARCUS born ca. 1774, with wife, LUCY, born ca. 1773, both in Conn., were listed in the 1840 census index of Franklin Twp., Lenawee Co., Mich.; and also in the 1850 census.

CARTER, MEHITABLE was listed in the 1840 census index of Tecumseh Twp., Lenawee Co., Mich. not far from LEVI, preceding.

CARTER, MICHAEL born ca. 1822, NJ, and wife, MARTHA, born ca. 1827, NY, were listed in the 1850 census of Macon Twp., Lenawee Co., Mich. with PHEBE B., age 1, b. Mich., in their household. Also note ELI, preceding.

CARTER, NICHOLAS born ca. 1810, RI, and wife, MARY A., born ca. 1816, NY, were listed in the 1850 census of Madison Twp., Lenawee Co., Mich. with TUNIS J., age 15 (m. Martha Daniels, dau. of Augustus F., also see); & JANE E., age 9, both b. NY, in their household.

CARTER, NORMAN B. born ca. 1801, Conn., and wife, MENTHA M., born ca. 1800, NY, came to Ogden Twp., Lenawee Co., Mich. in 1836. In the 1850 census of Ogden Twp., they listed RUSSELL C., age 18, b. NY; and AMANDA D. born 10 Oct. 1834, Ashford, Cattaraugus Co., NY (m. John G. Mason, also see). Ref: P&BA-Len pg. 199.

CARTER, PETER was listed in the 1840 census index of Franklin Twp., Lenawee Co., Mich. Also note MARCUS & CYRUS, preceding.

CARTER, RICHARD was listed in the 1840 census index of Palmyra Twp., Lenawee Co., Mich.

CARTER, TRUMAN, born ca. 1823, and wife, ALMA, born ca. 1827, NY, were listed in the 1850 census of Seneca Twp., Lenawee Co., Mich.

CARTER, URI born ca. 1804, Mass., and wife, FANNY, born ca. 1811, NH, were listed in the 1840 census index of Adrian Twp., Lenawee Co., Mich.; and in the 1850 census of Tecumseh Twp., with LUCY, age 19, b. NY, in the household.

CARTER, W. W. (See Enos Canniff)

CARTER, WILLIAM was born in New Haven, Conn., and he married MARY (STEWART) born in NY, and they settled in the "Holland Purchase," NY. They moved to Lorain Co., Ohio; and then to Norwalk, Ohio. She died in Lorain Co., O., and he died in Michigan. Known daughter, NANCY (m. Henry L. Hurlburt, also see). Ref: P&BA-Len pg. 416.

CARY also see CAREY

CARY, JOHN M. was born 20 Mar. 1810, Oneida Co., NY, and after the death of his father, was bound out at age 13 to an uncle, but ran away at age 19. He married at age 23 in Cayuga Co., NY to FANNY (HOPKINS), daughter of Ira (also see), and they went first to Lysander, Onondaga Co., NY. They afterwards lived in many parts of the country, including Penn., Virginia, Racine, Wis. & Montgomery Co., Ohio, but settled finally in 1864 in Madison Twp., Lenawee Co., Mich. Children: 1. IRA (Nebraska); 2. ELIZABETH (m. Benjamin Latham, Moville, IA). He married second to LOUISA M. (BALDWIN), daughter of Philo (also see). Daughter, 3. BESSIE M.; 4. Child name not stated deceased by 1888. Ref: P&BA-Len pg. 191-2.

CARY, NATHANIEL (CORY?) born ca. 1808, NY, and wife, BETSEY, born ca. 1810, Maine, were listed in the 1850 census of Madison Twp., Lenawee Co., Mich. with NATHAN, age 16; CATHARINE, age 15, both b. NY; GEORGE M., age 10; JAMES H., age 8; FRANCIS E., age 1, all b. Mich., in their household.

CARY, NELLIE (See William Underwood)

CASE, AARON (Note ABRAHAM^6, following) was born ca. 1787 near Hartford, Conn., and married ? (ROBERTS) who died in Conn. at age 35. He with his sons moved afterwards to near Windsor, Ashtabula Co., Ohio; and then to Cambridge Twp., Lenawee Co., Mich. Known sons: GALUSHA; & HERMAN (both following). Ref: P&BA-Len pg. 911-2. Note: AARON N. is listed in the 1840 census index of Windsor, Ashtabula Co., O.; and in 1850 only GALUSHA and HELEN are listed in Windsor, O.

CASE, ABRAHAM^6, son of PHILIP^5 (following), was born 28 Dec. 1761 in Hartford Co., Conn. and moved with his father to Hebron, NY. He married there to RUTH (PRESTON), daughter of Othneil, and they settled in North Hebron. Children: 1. NAOMI b. 20 May 1785; 2. AARON b. 2 July 1786 (note resemblance to preceding); 3. WILLIAM b. 5 July 1788 (m. Polina Roblee); 4. RUTH b. 8 July 1791. His wife, Ruth, died 2 Sept. 1791; and he married again in 1792 to NAOMI (PRESTON), sister of Ruth, and she died in 1849. Children: 5. LEONARD (following); 6. ANNA b. 8 Aug. 1795 (m. Daniel Woodward, Sr.); 7. HIRAM b. 9 July 1797 (m. Polly Woodward); 8. NAAMAN b. 6 Apr. 1799; 9. DANIEL b. 30 Mar. 1801; 10. ELIZABETH b. 8 Aug. 1803 (m. Roswell Temple; she d. 6 Feb. 1895; 11. PHILANDA b. 19 Jan. 1805; 12. ABRAHAM b. 7 Aug. 1806 (m. Lydia Allen; 13. JASPER b. 4 Mar. 1807; 14. MERRITT b. 1 Dec. 1810.

CASE, ALBA J., son of GALUSHA (following), was born 13 Nov. 1851, Windsor, Ashtabula Co., Ohio; and he married on 7 Apr. 1874 to ELLA J. (LOOMIS), daughter of Sereno (also see) of Windsor. They settled in Cambridge Twp., Lenawee Co., Mich. Son, GUY L. Ref: P&BA-Len 911-2.

CASE, ALICE (See Ethan Davis)

CASE, BANIN born ca. 1790, NY, and wife, BETSEY, born ca. 1800, VT, were listed in the 1840 census index of Ogden Twp., Lenawee Co., Mich.; and in the 1850 census with CHAPMAN, age 15; & CHRISTIAN, age 6, both b. NY, in their household. Note: It may be this same BETSEY, and CHRISTY, listed again in the household of (son?) CLINTON (following) in the 1850 census. CHARLES & ISAAC (following) may also be sons. There was a "Benning Case" listed in 1830 census index of Perrysburg. Cattaraugus Co., NY.

CASE, CATHERINE (See Ephraim Wilder)

CASE, CHARLES born ca. 1820, and wife, BEULA?, born ca. 1829, both in NY, were listed in the 1850 census of Ogden Twp., Lenawee Co., Mich. Note BANIN, preceding.

CASE, CLINTON born ca. 1824, and wife, GERINA?, born ca. 1831, both in NY, were listed in the 1850 census of Ogden Twp., Lenawee Co., Mich. and in the household were BETSEY, age 48, b. NY; and CHRISTY (male), age 6, b. NY, and they may be the same that were listed in household of BANIN (preceding, father of Clinton?).

CASE, EDWARD born ca. 1824, and wife, MATILDA, born ca. 1827, both in NY, were listed in the 1850 census of Tecumseh Twp., Lenawee Co., Mich. and in their household was CYNTHIA, age 26, b. NY, possibly sister?

CASE, EPHRAIM was a native of Dutchess Co., NY where he remained and died at age 95. Known daughter, MARY b. 18 May 1790 (m. Jacob Lapham, also see). Ref: P&BA-Len pg. 1212-3.

CASE, GALUSHA, son of AARON (preceding), was born 19 Nov. 1817 near Hartford, Conn. In 1833, he and brother, HERMAN (following), went to Ashtabula Co., Ohio to prospect for land; returned to Conn. and moved their father and family to Ashtabula Co. He married ca. 1836 to SUSAN (BEDELL), daughter of William of Ashtabula Co. They went to Texas for about 3 years, and then about 1866 moved to Cambridge Twp., Lenawee Co., Mich. In 1884, he moved to Detroit, Mich. and died there 28 June 1886. Children: 1. Dr. WILLIAM N. (of Marengo, Calhoun Co., Mich.); 2. MARTIN E. (Franklin Twp., Lenawee Co.); 3. ALBA J. (preceding); 4. OVID M. (Detroit, Mich.); 5. LELAND (Detroit, Mich.); 6. CATHERINE (1888 lived Detroit with mother). Ref: P&BA-Len pg. 911-2.

CASE, HARVEY born ca. 1824, and wife, LUCY A., born ca. 1822, both in NY, were listed in the 1850 census of Riga Twp., Lenawee Co. Mich. with JANE, age 1, b. Mich., in the household.

CASE, HERMAN (written "Harmon"), son of AARON (preceding), born ca. 1818, Conn., and wife, PAULINA, born ca. 1812, NY, were listed in the 1850 census of Cambridge Twp., Lenawee Co., Mich. with LAURA, age 5, b. Ohio; and DOREMUS, age 1, b. Mich., in the household.

CASE, ISAAC born ca. 1810, and wife, NANCY, born ca. 1817, both in NY, were listed in the 1850 census of Ogden Twp., Lenawee Co., Mich. with LOUISA, age 10, b. Mich., in the household.

CASE, L. S. was listed in the 1840 census index of Rome Twp., Lenawee Co., Mich.

CASE, LEONARD^7, son of ABRAHAM^6 (preceding), was born 18 July 1793 in Hebron, Washington Co., NY. He married POLLY (LYMAN); and he died there 20 Dec. 1840. Known daughter, NAOMI (m. before 1817 to Nicholas Bresie (also see) and settled in Livingston Co., NY.) Ref: P&BA-Len pg. 799-800.

CASE, LUCINDA born Richland Co., Ohio (See Wm. J. Johnson).

CASE, PHILIP^5, son of TIMOTHY^4 (RICHARD^3;JOHN^2;WILLIAM^1), was born in 1732, probably in Simsbury or Hartford Co., Conn. He married in 1758 to LYDIA (SOVERIL). He settled near Hebron, Washington Co., NY before 1776; and he served in the Revolution. He died in 1814. Known son, ABRRAHAM^6 (preceding).

CASEY, CATHERINE A. (See Philip Wareham^3)

CASEY, LYMAN of York, Livingston Co., NY was the father of LAURA E. b. ca. 1822, NY (m. Norman Geddes, also see, in 1848, Lenawee Co., Mich.)

CASSON, SUSAN M. (See Roland R. Hill)

CASWELL, CLARISSA was born ca. 1833, NY, and was listed in the 1850 census of Fairfield Twp., Lenawee Co., Mich. in household of another family. Note RICHARD, following.

CASWELL, JNO was listed in the 1840 census index of Macon Twp., Lenawee Co., Mich.

CASWELL, MARGARET Mrs. (See Bodkin, Mary A.)

CASWELL, MARGARET (See Christopher Treadway)

Pioneer Families of Southeastern Michigan

CASWELL, RICHARD was listed in the 1850 census of Fairfield Twp., Lenawee Co., Mich. in the household of another family. Note CLARISSA, preceding.

CATLIN, ANNA (See Edwin Smith)
CATLIN, ELIZA (See James Green)
CATLIN, L. (See James Green)

CATON, JOHN and wife, ELIZABETH (LOBDELL), were natives of Palmyra, NY, and she died there in 1827, and he moved to New Jersey. Children: WILLIAM; SAMUEL L.; ELIZABETH; JOHN D.; CAROLINE M. b. 30 Sept. 1826, Palmyra, NY (m. Norman F. Bradish, also see). Ref: P&BA-Len pg. 975-6.

CATON, JOHN born ca. 1820, and wife, CHRISTINE, born ca. 1827, both in NY, were listed in the 1850 census of Madison Twp., Lenawee Co., Mich. with SAMUEL, age 2, b. Mich., in the household. They were in the household of Erasmus W. Payne, age 40, and wife, Casiah (Keziah?), age 35, both b. NY.

CATON, MATTHEW born ca. 1819, and wife, MARY, born ca. 1812, both in Ireland, were listed in the 1850 census of Blissfield Twp., Lenawee Co., Mich. with MARY A., age 11; ELIZA, age 9; ELLEN, age 5; GEORGE, age 4; JOHN, age 2, all b. Mich., in their household.

CATON, PHEBE (Mrs.?) born ca. 1818, Penn., was listed with a child, GEORGE W., age 7, b. Mich., in the household of Stephen Northrup, age 67, b. Conn., & wife, Phebe, age 54, b. NY, in the 1850 census of Fairfield Twp., Lenawee Co., Mich.

CAWLEY, FRANKLIN was born in Penn., and moved in 1835 to Seneca Twp., Lenawee Co., Mich. near Morenci. He married 20 Sept. 1842 in Lake Co, Ohio to SUSAN H. (DAY), daughter of James (also see), and they settled in Morenci, Mich. Six children of whom 2 died infancy (names not stated): 1. FRANK E. (m. Sarah C. Scofield, dau. of Silas A., also see; Morenci); 3. ANNA C. (m. Watson C. Crabbs, Toledo, O.); 2. SARAH L.; 4. PERLEY F. (m. Luella Rorick, Fayette, O.) Ref: P&BA-Len pg. 977-8. Note: Susan H. married second to Joseph Hagaman (also see).

CERROW, JOSEPH born ca. 1795, and wife, RACHEL, born ca. 1796, both in NY, came to Dover Twp., Lenawee Co., Mich. before 1840; and in the 1850 census of Dover Twp. listed LYMAN, age 22; RANSOM, age 19 (following); RACHEL, age 16; all b. NY, in the household. Next door was SIDNEY (following).

CERROW, RANSOM, probably son of JOSEPH, married ALVIRA (LUTHER), daughter of Theodorick (also see) of Rome Twp., and it may be she who died 6 Aug. 1860 (sketch was unclear). It is probably he who married ELIZABETH (LEFFERTS), daughter of Hiram (also see), in Dover Twp. He died in 1866. Elizabeth married second to John Forbes (as his 3rd wife) in Dover Twp. Ref: P&BA-Len pg. 344-5 & 587-8.

CERROW, SIDNEY, son of JOSEPH (preceding), born ca. 1817, NY, and wife, ANN, born ca. 1819, both in NY, were listed in the 1850 census of Dover Twp., Lenawee Co., Mich. with EDGAR, age 6; & LUSINA?, age 3, both b. Mich., in their household.

CHADLER, ASENATH (Chandler?; See Adnah Kinsman)

CHAFFEE, ALLEN B. born ca. 1804, and wife, ABIGAIL, born ca. 1810, both in NY, were listed in the 1840 census index of Adrian Twp., Lenawee Co., Mich. (spelled "Chapee"); and in the 1850 census with JOSEPH H., age 19; AMELIA, age 14; AMI B., age 12; JARVIS A., age 9; JACOB O., age 7; SARAH A., age 2, all b. Mich., in their household. In the 1840 census index, there was an "Orry Chapee" listed nearby.

CHAFFEE, ADELIA (See Walter Robinson)

CHAFFEE, FRANCIS born ca. 1830, NY, was listed in the 1850 census of Adrian Twp., Lenawee Co., Mich. in the household of Warner F. Comstock (Note JEROME, following).

CHAFFEE, JARVILLA (See Walter Robinson)

CHAFFEE, JEROME B. born ca. 1825, NY, married MARIAN B. (COMSTOCK), daughter of Warner B. (also see). In the 1850 census of Adrian Twp., Lenawee Co., Mich., they listed JULIA, age 18, b. NY (sister?); and HORACE, age 1, b. Ind. Marian died 11 Nov. 1857, Adrian Twp. He was said to have gone to Colorado. P&BA-Len pg. 494-5 & 648-9. Note WARREN, following.

CHAFFEE, LYMAN born ca. 1829, NY and wife, MARY (LUTHER), daughter of Theodorick (also see), age 18, both b. NY, were listed in the 1850 census of Adrian Twp., Lenawee Co., Mich. with ORIENT (male), age 2/12, b. Mich., in their household.

CHAFFEE, ORRY? was listed in the 1840 census index of Adrian Twp., Lenawee Co., Mich. not far from ALLEN B., preceding.

CHAFFEE, WARNER F. either age 51 or 57, born VT, and wife, HANNAH, age 57, born Conn., were listed in the 1850 census of Adrian Twp., Lenawee Co., Mich. with OSCAR, age 20; & AMANDA, age 18, both b. NY, in their household.

CHAFFEE, WARREN born ca. 1797, VT, was listed in the 1850 census of Adrian Twp., Lenawee Co., Mich. with (wife?) MALINDA, age 33; SARAH A., age 15; MARY E., age 8, all b. NY; and ELIZABETH E., age 7; CORWIN, age 6; JARVE?, age 3; CAROLINE, age 1, all born Ind.; and also Oliver Munn, age 75, b. NY, in the household.

CHALONER, CHARLES A., eldest of the 4 children of CHARLES J. & ELIZA (LATHAM) who remained in England, was born 22 May 1829, London, England. He married there to DIANA (MOON) of Staffordshire, and settled first in Wolverhampton, Staffordshire. In Jan. 1858, they sailed from Liverpool to New York City, and after spending a few months in Canada, moved to Adrian, Lenawee Co., Mich. Children: 1. ANNIE E.; 2. WILLIAM H.; 3. ROSA E.; 4. LAURA L.; 5. CHARLES J. (d. age 2-1/2). Ref: P&BA-Len pg. 480-1.

CHAMBERLAIN, CHARLES married in Cleveland, Ohio to ROSETTA (MARKS), daughter of Nehemiah (also see). They moved to Dallas Co., Iowa, where he died 6 Jan. 1856. Son, CHARLES D. (m. Estella Tryon, Bedford IA). Rosetta married second to Addison P. Halladay (also see) of Adrian, Lenawee Co., Mich. Ref: P&BA-Len pg. 456-7.

CHAMBERLAIN, DAVID P. Dr. born ca. 1827, and wife, LOUISA, born ca. 1827, both in NY, were listed in the

1850 census of Hudson Twp., Lenawee Co., Mich. with ELLA G., age 2, b. Mich., in their household.

CHAMBERLAIN, ICHABOD Cpt., a Revolutionary soldier. (See Elijah Curtis, Jr.).

CHAMBERLAIN, MOSES S. born ca. 1798, NY, and wife, DA--MISS?, age 33, b. Canada, were listed in the 1850 census of Blissfield Twp., Lenawee Co., Mich. with JAMES, age 11; JOANNA, age 9; JANE, age 6, all b. Ohio; and JANET, age 5; JULIA A., age 9/12, both b. Mich., in their household.

CHAMBERLAIN, PHILONSO born ca. 1804, and wife, CYNTHIA, born ca. 1800, both in NY, were listed in the 1850 census of Woodstock Twp., Lenawee Co., Mich. with WILLIAM, age 21; JAMES, age 19; LEWIS, age 17; EUNICE, age 15, all b. NY; and AUGUSTUS, age 13; ALVIRA?, age 10; MARION, age 7, all b. Mich., in the household.

CHAMBERLAIN, NANCY (See John Diver)

CHAMBERLIN see CHAMBERLAIN

CHAMBERS, CHARLES (See William L. Rogers)

CHAMBERS, JAMES born ca. 1803, NY, and wife, MABILLA?, born ca. 1806, both in NY, were listed in the 1850 census of Macon Twp., Lenawee Co., Mich. with RACHEL, age 16; SAMUEL, age 15; LENORA, age 13; WILLIAM, age 10; ARCHIBALD, age 9; JAMES, age 7; JOHN, age 6; CULVER, age 3, all b. NY, in their household.

CHAMBERS, W. (See William L. Rogers)

CHAMBERS, THOMAS born ca. 1823, and ANNA A., born ca. 1823, both in NY, were listed in the 1850 census of Fairfield Twp., Lenawee Co., Mich. with WALTER, age 9; JANE, age 7; CHARLES, age 7; CLARA, age 4; JULIA, age 2, all b. Mich., in their household.

CHAMPENOIS, WILLIAM A. born ca. 1807, Westchester Co., NY married there first to ALICE (CORNELL) who died in 1833 leaving children: 1. CHARLES A. b. ca. 1832; ALICE b. ca. 1833, NY (m. Henry Read, also see). William A. married second to MARY E., born ca. 1810, NY, and they were listed in the 1850 census of Rome Twp., Lenawee Co., Mich. with children above and LEROY, age 10; ARTHUR, age 7; JANE, age 4; MORRIS, age 2, all b. Mich., in their household. Note: The early ancestry of this family is noted in <u>Westchester Patriarchs</u>, by Norman Davis, Heritage Books, 1988.

CHANDLER, ASENATH (See Asenath Chadler)

CHANDLER, CHARLES born ca. 1805, NY, and wife, ELISA, born ca. 1805, Conn., were listed in the 1840 census index of Clinton Twp., Lenawee Co., Mich. (adjacent to HENRY); and in the 1850 census of Tecumseh Twp. with CHARLES, age 12; MARY, age 9; ABIGAIL, age 6; SAMUEL, age 3; WILLIAM, age 1/12, all b. Mich., in their household.

CHANDLER, DAVID was born ca. 1779, Vermont, and his wife, COMFORT (GILMAN), was born ca. 1782 in New Hampshire. They apparently lived first in New Hampshire, then moved to near Lockport, Niagara Co., NY, where he died in 1827, age 48. She later moved to Ridgeway Twp., Lenawee Co., Mich. where she died in Apr. 1866, age 84, at the home of daughter, Miranda. Nine children, those known: SAMUEL (following); MIRANDA b. 4 Mar. 1825, Pendleton, Niagara Co. NY (m. John Iveson, also see). Ref: P&BA-Len pg. 1084-5.

CHANDLER, E. C. (See Asaph K. Porter)

CHANDLER, GEORGE F., son of THOMAS (following), was born 9 Dec. 1836, E. Kent, England, and came to the US in 1854 with parents and lived for a time in Wayne Co., NY. He lived in Ohio for a time, finally in Sylvania, Lucas Co., Ohio in 1861. He served in the Civil War from Ohio. He married 18 Feb. 1865 to AUGUSTA (DOLPH), daughter of Abda (also see) in Sylvania. They afterwards settled in Riga Twp., Lenawee Co., Mich. Children: 1. CLINTON C.; 2. ALBERT(A) R. (m. Julia Gibbs, dau. of Thomas, also see); 3. MILLIE R. (m. 24 Nov. 1881 William H. Gibbs, son of Thomas, also see); 4. BERNARD W.; 5. FRANK G.; 6. CHARLES D.; 7. MERLE H.; 8. KENNETH O. Ref: P&BA-Len pg. 389-90.

CHANDLER, HANNAH (See Joshua Beaman)

CHANDLER, HENRY was a descendant of Ann & William Chandler of Roxbury, Mass. He and wife, SALLY (MUNGER), lived in Coventry, Chenango Co., NY, and he died there in 1869. She afterwards came to Clinton Twp., Lenawee Co., Mich., where she died in 1875, age 80, at the home of daughter, MILANCY b. 29 Jan. 1820, Coventry, NY (m. Philip S. DePuy, also see). Ref: P&BA-Len pg. 1214-6. Note CHARLES, preceding, & HENRY, following.

CHANDLER, HENRY born ca. 1810, NY, and wife, PHILINA, age 40, b. Conn., were listed in the 1840 census index of Clinton Twp., Lenawee Co., Mich. (adjacent to CHARLES, preceding); and in the 1850 census of Tecumseh Twp. with ADELADE, age 17; & WINTHROP, age 14, both b. Mich., in their household. Note HENRY, preceding.

CHANDLER, JOSEPH N. born ca. 1807, and wife, LUCINDA, born ca. 1805, both in VT, were listed in the 1850 census of Adrian Twp., Lenawee Co., Mich. with LAURA J., age 13, b. Ohio, in the household.

CHANDLER, SAMUEL, probably son of DAVID (preceding), born ca. 1807, VT, and wife, MARTHA, born ca. 1811, England, were listed in the 1850 census of Ridgeway Twp., Lenawee Co., Mich. with DAVID, age 18, b. NY; & SARAH J., age 5, b. Mich., all in the household of John Iveson & wife, MIRANDA (CHANDLER), daughter of DAVID.

CHANDLER, SAMUEL Dr. of Washtenaw Co., Mich. (See Joseph S. Kies).

CHANDLER, THOMAS born ca. 1806, Penn., and wife, JANE M., born ca. 1814, NY, were listed in the 1850 census of Raisin Twp., Lenawee Co., Mich. with MERRITT, age 6; WILLIAM, age 5; GEORGE, age 3, all b. Mich., in the household. Note: CAROLINE, age 7, b. Mich. in a Holdridge household may relate to this family.

CHANDLER, THOMAS[4], son of GILES[3] (THOMAS[2];GILES[1]), was born 21 Feb. 1807, Kent, England, where he married REBECCA (BAKER). They came to the US in May 1854 on the "Christiana" with 4 of their 6 children, and settled first in Wayne Co., NY. About 1863, they moved to Riga Twp., Lenawee Co., Mich., where he died 1 June 1886. Children: 1. FANNY (m. Thomas West, Australia); 2. CHARLOTTE (m. James Appleton, Ramsgate, England); 3. GEORGE F. (preceding); 4. THOMAS G. (following); 5. HANNAH (m. John Stiggins, Wayne Co., NY); 6. HARRIET (m.

Pioneer Families of Southeastern Michigan

Amos P. Allbring). Ref: P&BA-Len pg. 389-90 & 483-5.

CHANDLER, THOMAS G., son of THOMAS[4] (preceding), born 8 Aug. 1838, Kent, England, came to the US with his parents. He moved from Wayne Co., NY to Fulton Co., Ohio, and then Sylvania, Lucas Co., Ohio, and also taught school in Monroe Co., Mich. He came to Riga Twp., Lenawee Co., Mich. and married on 10 Oct. 1860 to ROSE E. (COMSTOCK), daughter of Giles (also see). He served in the Civil War. Children: 1. LOTTIE; 2. DANA G. (m. Iley Lewis, daughter of Adelbert, also see); 3. NAMA R. Ref: P&BA-Len pg. 483-5.

CHANDLER, WILLIAM A. born ca. 1823, Penn., was head of household in the 1850 census of Macon Twp., Lenawee Co., Mich. with MARGARET L, age 17?, b. Penn.; & WINFIELD, age 5, b. Mich.; DAVID, age 3, both b. Mich., in the household.

CHAPIN, CLARISSA. Mrs. (daughter of Zibra Corbett, also see).

CHAPMAN, DORASTUS?, born ca. 1794, and wife, MARY, b. ca. 1790, were listed in the 1850 census of Madison Twp., Lenawee Co., Mich. with no family. Note: WILLIAM born ca. 1830, Mich., in another household may relate.

CHAPMAN, HANNAH (See Lowry Newell)

CHAPMAN, JONATHAN born ca. 1812, and wife, CAROLINE, born ca. 1825, both in NY, were listed in the 1850 census of Fairfield Twp., Lenawee Co., Mich. with OPHELIA, age 4; CAROLINE, age 7, both b. Mich., in their household.

CHAPMAN, LOVINA (See Ansel Witherell, Sr.)

CHAPMAN, MATTIE E. born 8 May 1876 was the adopted daughter of Reuben Sayers[2] (also see). Ref: P&BA-Len pg. 1054-5.

CHAPMAN, SARAH born 14 Mar. 1791, Conn, married 1818 in Erie Co., O. to Dr. Richard P. Christophers (also see).

CHAPMAN, SARAH Mrs. (daughter of William Sickly, also see). Ref: P&BA-Len pg. 1132-3.

CHAPMAN, SUSAN (JOSELYN) Mrs. born ca.1815, NY, married first to Chapman and had child, SELIAH b. ca. 1837, Mich.; and married second 23 Sept. 1847 in Canton, Wayne Co., Mich. to Russell Lewis of Superior Twp., Washtenaw Co., Mich. Ref: P&BA-Len pg. 1080-1.

CHARLES, WILLIAM (See Abraham Cramer)

CHARLTON, ANN born England, came to America as a child and married here Jesse Stretch (also see).

CHASE, ? female (See Samuel H. Thurber)
CHASE, ADELINE born Palmyra, Wayne Co., NY m. George A. Hathaway (also see).
CHASE, ALICE (See Ingurson Haviland)
CHASE, ANNA of Sutton, Mass. (See Samuel Bixby).
CHASE, JESSE (See Edwin Pickford)
CHASE, LEVI C. Rev., son of LEVI H. (following), born 17 July 1843, Raisin Twp., Lenawee Co., Mich., married SARAH A. (CODDINGTON), daughter of John (also see), on 31 Mar. 1864, Adrian Twp. Child: ELBERT J. b. 26 May 1871.
CHASE, LEVI H. born ca. 1807, Providence, Saratoga Co., NY, married in Niagara Co., NY on 24 Oct. 1826 to ANNA (HAVILAND), born ca. 1808, NY. In 1833, they moved to Raisin Twp., Lenawee Co., Mich. Though reared a Quaker, he became a Baptist Minister. He died 5 Oct. 1877, age 71. Anna lived with son, Franklin N., in 1888, at age 80. In the 1850 census of Raisin Twp., Levi H. listed the following in his household: 1. ELIZA J. b. 26 Dec. 1827 (m/1 Coffin, see Eliza Coffin, and m/2 Hulett West, also see); 2. PHEBE, age 20; 3. SALLY A., age 18, all b. NY; 4. DANIEL H., age 17 (m. Elizabeth Montague, see Montague); 5. AMZI, age 15; 6. EMILY, age 13; 7. ARTEMAS, age 11; 8. CATHERINE L., age 9; 9. LEVI C., age 7 (preceding); 10. FRANKLIN I (N?)., age 5, last 7 b. Mich. Ref: P&BA-Len pg. 350-2. Note: See James Haviland, possibly father of Anna. Also note ALICE (preceding).
CHASE, P. B. (See Alanson Woolsey)
CHASE, SELLICK born ca. 1820, and wife, LETTICE (probably nee' FLEMING), born ca. 1823, both in NY, were listed in the 1850 census of Rollin Twp., Lenawee Co., Mich. with MARIA, age 5; ROSENE, age 1, both b. Mich., in the household. Also listed were James Fleming, age 63, b. Penn., possibly father of Lettice?

CHATFIELD, ABI age 9, b. Mich., was listed in the household of a different family in the 1850 census of Rome Twp., Lenawee Co., Mich.
CHATFIELD, ALMINA J., age 10, b. Mich., was listed in the household of a different family in the 1850 census of Raisin Twp., Lenawee Co., Mich.
CHATFIELD, ELI was listed in the 1840 census index of Raisin Twp., Lenawee Co., Mich.; not listed in 1850.
CHATFIELD, JOSIAH was listed in the 1840 census index of Raisin Twp., Lenawee Co., Mich.; not listed in 1850. There was a child, JOSIAH, age 7, b. Mich., listed in another household in 1850 census of Raisin Twp.
CHATFIELD, LYMAN born ca. 1805, Conn., and wife, ELIZABETH, age 31, b. NY, were listed in the 1850 census of Raisin Twp., Lenawee Co., Mich. with DAVID, age 3, b. Mich. in their household. Note that some of the children listed preceding may belong to this family?? Also it was probably Lyman listed as "Simon" in the 1840 census index of Raisin Twp., adjacent to JOSIAH & ELI, preceding.
CHATFIELD, ROSA (See John H. Todd)
CHATFIELD, STERLING, age 16; and HENRY, age 14, both b. Ohio, were listed in household of a different family in the 1850 census of Medina Twp., Lenawee Co., Mich.

CHEENY see CHENEY

CHEEVER, JACOB was born ca. 1790, and wife, RACHEL (RICE), was born ca. 1794, both in NY, and both reared in Jefferson Co., NY where they married. He served in the War of 1812, After the birth of their children, they moved to Penn. & Ohio; and then in 1837 to Ridgeway Twp., Lenawee Co., Mich. Children: JACOB Jr. (following); & probably NATHAN (following); and they listed in the 1850 census of Ridgeway Twp.: JAMES, age 27; JOHN (following); WILFORD, age 20, all b. NY. Also in the household was CAROLINE, age 8, b. Mich., probably a granddaughter. Rachel died in 1853, age 60; and he died in Aug. 1859 (sketch said age 84, probably 69?). Ref: P&BA-Len pg. 982-3.

CHEEVER, JACOB Jr., son of JACOB (preceding), was born ca. 1816, and wife, LAURA, was born ca. 1822, NY, and they were in the 1850 census of Ridgeway Twp., Lenawee Co., Mich. with CHARLOTTE, age 10; LEANDER, age 4; ELEANOR, age 2; PHILANDER, age 5/12, all b. Mich., in their household.

CHEEVER, JOHN, son of JACOB (preceding), was born 9 Jan. 1826, Champion, NY, and moved with his parents to Ridgeway Twp., Lenawee Co., Mich. He married 8 Mar. 1851 to CATHERINE (CORYELL), daughter of Andrew (also see); and they lived first in Macon Twp., then moved to Ridgeway Twp. There were 12 children, and 4 were deceased by 1888. Those deceased were DAVID A. d. 1879; SARAH MALONA d. 18 Aug. 1880; JAMES E. 1st; JAMES E. 2d. Surviving were MARTHA (m. John Wiggins, Macon Twp.); MARY A.; ANDREW (m. Altha Binn, Ridgeway Twp.); OLIVE; WILLIAM; KEAN; EUGENE (twin of Kean); JAMES E. 3rd. Ref: P&BA-Len pg. 982-3.

CHEEVER, NATHAN, probably son of JACOB (preceding), born ca. 1820, and wife, MARGARET, born ca. 1826, both in NY, were listed in the 1850 census of Ridgeway Twp., Lenawee Co., Mich. with EMELINE, age 3; NANCY, age 1, both b. Mich., in the household.

CHENEY, ALFORD was listed in the 1840 census index of Rome Twp., Lenawee Co., Mich. (spelled "Cheeny).

CHENEY, ALPHEUS[3], son of JOHN[2] (following), was born in Turnbridge, VT, and moved with his parents to Fairfield Twp., Lenawee Co., Mich. He moved to Lucas Co., Ohio where he married EUGENIA (DeMOTT), daughter of Ellison (also see). Known daughter, EVA (m. George F. Wotring, also see, on 17 Oct. 1886). Ref: P&BA-Len pg. 1104-5.

CHENEY, DUDLEY was listed in the 1840 census index of Tecumseh Twp., Lenawee Co., Mich. (spelled "Cheeney).

CHENEY, JERVIS (probably son of JOHN[1] (following), born ca. 1804, VT, and wife, SALLY, born ca. 1807, NY, were listed in the 1840 census index and 1850 census of Ogden Twp., Lenawee Co., Mich.

CHENEY, JOHN[1] was born 1765, New Hampshire, and he married there in 1788 to LUCY (FINCH), born there in 1770. They lived in Vermont by 1802; and then in 1803 removed to Scipio, Cayuga Co., NY; and in 1809 to Parma, Monroe Co., NY. She died in 1810, and he died in 1840 in Parma. Ten children, those known, JOHN[2] (following); and probably JERVIS (preceding). Ref: P&BA-Len pg. 781-2.

CHENEY, JOHN[2], son of JOHN[1] (preceding), born ca. 1803, Turnbridge, VT, and only lived with his parents till age 7. He married in NY on 1 Jan. 1827 to LOUISA (FINCH), daughter of Asahel, Sr. (also see). They lived in Parma, NY in 1829, and in 1833 removed to Madison Twp., Lenawee Co., Mich. They moved to Fairfield Twp. in 1847; and he was still living there in 1888. Children: 1. EDWARD b. 9 July 1828, Rochester, NY (d. 24 Mar. 1863 of disease serving in Civil War); 2. EVELYN F. b. ca. 1832, Parma, NY; 3. GEORGE P. b. ca. 1834, Madison Twp. (d. 15 Sept. 1864, age 20); 4. DELFINA A. b. ca. 1836 (m. William Jenkins; she d. 17 Apr. 1879, Ogden Twp.); 5. ALPHEUS b. ca. 1838 (preceding); 6. CULLEN T. b. ca. 1840 (Fairfield Twp.); 7. JOHN N. b. ca. 1842 (Ogden Twp.); 8. DEWITT B. b. ca. 1844 (d. 7 Apr. 1864, age 19); 9. WILLIAM H. (following). Ref: P&BA-Len pg. 781-2.

CHENEY, WILLIAM H., son of JOHN[2] (preceding), wa born 12 July 1847; and he married 1 Nov. 1874 to HARRIET (WALKER), daughter of Seth (also see). They lived in Ogden & Fairfield Twps., Lenawee Co., Mich. Children: 1. ORA L.; 2. ARA; 3. ASA (twin of ARA); 4. DELLA A. Ref: P&BA-Len pg. 781-2.

CHILDS, AUGUSTUS W. born ca. 1814, and wife, AMYTIS?, born ca. 1822, both in NY, were listed in the 1850 census of Hudson Twp., Lenawee Co., Mich. with AUGUSTUS O., age 6; DELORA, age 4; MARION, age 1, all b. Mich., in the household.

CHILDS, DANIEL was listed in the 1840 census index of Madison Twp., Lenawee Co., Mich. not far from OLIVER, following.

CHILDS, DAVID was listed in the 1840 census index of Rome Twp., Lenawee Co., Mich.

CHILDS, EDWIN (See John H. Todd)

CHILDS, IRENE (See David Gander)

CHILDS, OLIVER was listed in the 1840 census index of Madison Twp., Lenawee Co., Mich. Also note DANIEL, preceding.

CHILDS, RACHEL (See Chester Hutchinson)

CHIPMAN, ELAN and wife, REBECCA, were parents of DELIA born in Malone, Franklin Co., NY (m. Marvin M. Maxson, also see, in Apr. 1865.) Ref: P&BA-Len pg. 1155-6.

CHITTENDEN, DANIEL and wife, MERCY (AMINGTON), moved from NY to Madison Twp., Lenawee Co., Mich. before 1836, and he died aged 44 years. There were 2 sons and 5 daughters. (She apparently married again to a Marsh, as she was head of household in the 1850 census of Dover Twp., Lenawee Co., Mich., listed as Mercy Marsh, with the following Chittenden children in her household): SEYMOUR, age 20 (may be counted again in Madison Twp., with wife?, MARGARET, age 18, in his household); MATILDA, b. ca. 1835 (m. Andrew J. Van Sickle); HARLOW, age 6, b. Mich. Also in the household was Cynthia Marsh, age 4; Marian Marsh, age 1, both b. Mich. Ref: P&BA-Len pg. 208. Note: HULDAH, age 10, b. Mich., listed in another household may also belong to this family.

CHITTENDEN, FOSTER B. born ca. 1821, NY, and wife, BETSEY, born ca. 1826, Ohio, were in the 1850 census of Rollin Twp., Lenawee Co., Mich. with JUDSON L., age 2, b. Mich., all in the household of Betsey Bennett, age 57, b. NY.

CHITTENDEN, JESSE B. and wife, MARY (EASTLAND), were natives of Cayuga Co., NY; and the lived in Bethany, Genesee Co., NY in 1839. He died in 1875, NY, and she afterwards moved to Palmyra Twp., Lenawee Co., Mich. where she was living in 1888. Known daughter BESSIE M. b. 3 Aug. 1839, Bethany, NY (m. George R. Cochrane, also see). Ref: P&BA-Len pg. 1170-1.

CHITTENDEN, OLIVE born ca. 1811, NY, was listed in the 1850 census of Adrian Twp., Lenawee Co., Mich. in the household of Henry Hart.

CHRISLER probably CHRYSLER

Pioneer Families of Southeastern Michigan

CHRISLER, DELLA (See Bethuel Newcomb)

CHRIST, MAGDALENA (See Martin Keusch[1])

CHRISTMAN, JOHN and wife, JANE (DeCOW), moved from Niagara Co., NY to Ohio ca. 1835; and then to Washtenaw Co., Mich. in 1838, and settled in Gratiot Co., Mich. in 1868. Jane was born ca. 1812, Canada, and died 1886 in Michigan. John was still living in 1888, age 80 yrs. Known son, HENRY C. (following). Ref: P&BA-Len pg. 200-1.

CHRISTMAN, HENRY C., son of JOHN (preceding), was born 2 Aug. 1830, Niagara Co., NY, and moved with his parents to Michigan. He married first to ADELINA (ALLEN) on 1 Dec. 1852, and she died 22 Aug. 1853. He married second to SUSAN E. (HINES), daughter of George (also see). Henry served in the Civil War in Co. M., 1st Regt. Engineers & Mechanics. They resided in Rome Twp., Lenawee Co., Mich. Known daughter, MARY L. (m. William A. Teachout, also see). Ref: P&BA-Len pg. 200-1.

CHRISTOPHERS, RICHARD P. Dr. was born 22 Feb. 1793, and his wife, SARAH (CHAPMAN), was born 14 Mar. 1791, both in Conn. They married in 1818 in Erie Co., Ohio. where he was a pioneer physician (then Huron Co., O.) He died near New London, Ohio on 16 Aug. 1829; and she died 8 Mar. 1854, Bellevue, Ohio at the home of her children. There were 4 sons and 1 daughter. Known son, JOHN b. 6 Dec. 1822, Huron Co., O. (came to Medina Twp., Lenawee Co., Mich. in 1844 with Charles C. Morse, and was listed in his household in 1850 census). Ref: P&BA-Len gp. 936-7.

CHRONKLITE, PHILIP S. born ca. 1810, and wife, MARY, born ca. 1811, both in NY, were listed in the 1850 census of Tecumseh Twp., Lenawee Co., Mich. with PERMILLA, age 8; ELLEN, age 6; ELIAS, age 4; NANCY, age 6?; ADELINE, age 2, all b. Mich., in their household.

CHURCH, ANN of Chilton, Berkshire, England married Joseph Hopkins (also see). Ref: P&BA-Len pg. 539-40.

CHURCH, DEBORAH (See James D. Manchester)

CHURCH, HARLOW B. born ca. 1815, and wife, ANN, born ca. 1825, both in NY, were listed in the 1850 census of Franklin Twp., Lenawee Co., Mich.

CHURCH, HIRAM of Jackson, Mich. (See Stephen P. Bailey).

CHURCH, HIRAM born ca. 1817, NY, and wife, RUBY, born ca. 1825, Conn., were listed in the 1850 census of Rome Twp., Lenawee Co., Mich. with JOHN J., age 8; GEORGE C., age 6; LOUISA, age 5; MILTON O., age 3, all b. Mich., in their household.

CHURCH, LUCY (See Appolos Baker)

CHURCH, NATHAN Lt Col. (See Perly Bills)

CHURCH, OLIVER born ca. 1822, and wife, HENRIETTA, born ca. 1820, both in NY, were listed in the 1850 census of Dover Twp., Lenawee Co., Mich. with ELIZABETH, age 2, b. Mich., in the household.

CHURCH, OLIVER S. born ca. 1784, Conn., and wife, FLORINDA, born ca. 1789, NY, were listed in the 1840 census index of Madison Twp., Lenawee Co., Mich.; and were in the 1850 census with WILLIAM, age 22, b. NY; and Florinda Butts, age 30 (possibly a daughter); and Elizbeth Butts, age 12, b. Mich. in their household.

CHURCH, OLIVER born ca. 1822, and wife, HENRIETTA, born ca. 1820, both in NY, were listed in the 1850 census of Dover Twp., Lenawee Co., Mich. with ELIZABETH, age 2, b. Mich., in their household.

CHURCH, REUBEN born ca. 1818, and wife, SARAH, born ca. 1818, both in NY, were listed in the 1850 census of Rollin Twp., Lenawee Co., Mich. with CORNELIA, age 4; FRANKLIN, age 1, both b. Mich., in their household.

CHURCH, SAMUEL (See Austin Wilcox)

CHURCH, SARAH TEMPERANCE born 28 Jan. 1823, Lyons, NY, married on 6 Mar. 1842 in Hudson Twp., Lenawee co., Mich. to Dr. William Brown (also see). Ref: P&BA-Len pg. 964-5.

CHURCH, WILLARD was listed in the 1840 census index of Dover Twp., Lenawee Co., Mich.

CHURCH, WILLIAM born ca. 1827, NY, was listed in the 1850 census of Rollin Twp., Lenawee Co., Mich., a student in household of Dr. Daniel Tims. (Note: May be he also in household of OLIVER S.; Also see George W. Stephenson).

CHURCHILL, ERASTUS born ca. 1818, Mass., and wife, NANCY, born ca. 1826?, NY, were listed in the 1850 census of Hudson Twp., Lenawee Co., Mich. with WILLIAM, age 11; NANCY, age 9; LAURA, age 7, all b. Ohio; and RUTH, age 6; SYLVANUS, age 4, both b. IA (Indiana or Iowa?); and ERASTUS, age 2, b. Mich., in their household.

CHURCHILL, JOHN and wife, ANNIE (HEWITT), of Beaver Creek, VT, were parents of NANCY who married James Nicholson[2] (also see). Ref: P&BA-Len pg. 557-8.

CLAFLIN, INCREASE was a Revolutionary soldier from Mass.; and was father of SALLY b. ca. 1785, Mass. (m. John Stimson, also see).

CLAGHORN, SARAH married Ephraim Green (also see) in 1790 in Palmyra, NY.

CLAPP, DEVILLA? M. born ca. 1801, and wife, DOROTHY, born ca. 1808, both in NY, were listed in the 1850 census of Raisin Twp., Lenawee Co., Mich. with HANNAH M., age 8; OTIS, age 6, both b. Mich., in their household.

CLAPP, HENRY was listed in Dutchess Co., NY in the 1800 census index; and was said to have died in Wayne Co., NY. Known daughter, MELLE, b. Dutchess Co. (m. William Mitchell, also see). Ref: P&BA-Len pg. 579-80.

CLAPP, MARIA (See Lewis Quick)

CLAPPER, JOHN W. born ca. 1788, and wife, CATHERINE (BEST), were both natives of Columbia Co., NY. They removed to Madison Twp., Lenawee Co., Mich. about 1844, and she died there in 1849. Known daughter, MARGARET, b. 24 June 1826 (m. Anthony Poucher, also see). John W. married second to MARY, born ca. 1803, NY, and they were listed in the 1850 census of Palmyra Twp., Lenawee Co., Mich. They later moved to Clinton Co., Iowa where he died 14 Oct. 1856. Ref: P&BA-Len pg. 735-6. Note PETER, following.

CLAPPER, PETER born ca. 1825, and wife, JANE A., born ca. 1832, both in NY, were listed in the 1850 census of Madison Twp., Lenawee Co., Mich. with John Fitch, age 79, b. Mass.; and HARRIET, age 11, b. Mich. in their household.

CLARK, A. C. (See Philip H. Kells; also see George S. Stranahan)

CLARK, ABIGAIL (See William Bridge)

CLARK, ALLIE (See John W. Ormsby)

CLARK, ANSON came from Monroe Co., Mich. to Adrian, Lenawee Co., Mich. by 1834 (mentioned in James Whitney sketch). Ref: P&BA-Len pg. 184.

CLARK, ANTONY married JANE E. (SANFORD), daughter of John (also see) in Cohoctah, Livingston Co., Mich. in 1834.

CLARK, BARZILLAI, son of HARDING (a Revolutionary soldier who was one of Washington's Rangers), was born 31 July 1780, Hartford, Conn. In 1786, the family moved to Hudson, NY; and then to Pompey, NY. In 1807, they settled in Ontario Co., NY. Barzillai married 24 Apr. 1808 to PATIENCE (LEACH), daughter of Timothy (also see). In 1836, they moved to Adrian Twp., Lenawee Co., Mich.; and he died in 1847. In the 1850 census, Patience was age 61, living in household of son, John. She died 26 Jan. 1878, Adrian. Children: 1. ELIHU L. (following); 2. JOHN R. (following). Ref: P&BA-Len pg. 774-5.

CLARK, CECIL born ca. 1799, VT, and wife, LUCY, was born ca. 1790, NY, were listed in the 1850 census of Ridgeway Twp., Lenawee Co., Mich. with HEZEKIAH, age 25, b. NY, in their household.

CLARK, CHESTER and wife, ANNA, had known daughter, SAMANTHA L. b. 27 Aug. 1810, Otisco, Onondaga Co., NY (m. Jonathan L. Hoyt, also see). Ref: History of Jackson Co., Mich., pg. 766.

CLARK, CLARA (See Joshua Waring)

CLARK, CLARISSA of Chenango Co., NY (See Middleton Tackabery).

CLARK, EDWARD, son of THOMAS (following), born 22 Mar. 1818, Homer, NY, went at age 15 to Hamilton, Madison Co., NY where he remained 5 years, then went to Syracuse, NY. He married 4 Jan. 1841 to LOUISA (FORNCROOK), daughter of Christopher (also see). They lived first in Skaneateles, NY, and then moved to Fulton Co., Ohio. About 1858, they moved to Morenci, Lenawee Co., Mich. Children: 1. JAMES F. (m/1 Margaret Andrews; m/2 Ella Sinclair); 2. MARY M. (m. Dudley C. Henion); 3. EDWARD R. (d. age 2); 4. WILLIS E. (m. Elizabeth Mason); 5. KATE L. (m. John B. Burk). Ref: P&BA-Len pg. 1148-9.

CLARK, ELIHU L., son of BARZILLAI (preceding), born ca. 1811, NY, and wife, ISABELLA, born ca. 1810, Maine, were listed in the 1850 census of Madison Twp., Lenawee Co., Mich. with DEWIT C., age 13; CASSIUS?, age 6; ELIHU L., age 4; ISABELLA M., age 1, all b. Mich., in their household.

CLARK, ELIPHALET and wife, MARGARET (ELDRIDGE), were natives of Dutchess Co., NY. They resided in Groton, Tompkins Co., NY before 1818. They came to Tecumseh Twp., Lenawee Co., Mich. in 1829, and about 1831 removed to Raisinville, Monroe Co., Mich, where he died. Known son, GEORGE W. (following). Note: In Landmarks of Tompkins Co., NY, by J. H. Selkreg, 1894, there is the following biographical sketch. JESSE CLARK, a Capt. in the Revolution, and wife, SARAH (FOOTE), shortly after the War moved to Groton, Tompkins Co., NY. Children listed: ELI; CYNTHIA; SALLY; MILLIE; JESSE; JOHN; CHARLES; ALMA; TRYPHEN; RUTH (b. ca. 1802, m. Sabin; to LaPorte Co., Ind.). No proof it is this family except similarity of name, date, and place.

CLARK, GEORGE & wife, ANN, of Princeton, NJ were parents of ALMIRA (m. Robert Street (also see). Ref: P&BA-Len pg. 578-9. CLARK, GEORGE W., son of ELIPHALET (preceding), born 24 Apr. 1818, Groton, Tompkins Co., NY, moved with his parents to Michigan. He married first to CHARLOTTE (YOUNGLOVE) who died leaving son, 1. GEORGE (to Dakotas). George W. married again in Feb. 1844 at Raisinville, Monroe Co. Mich. to HARRIET (BARNABY), daughter of Ambrose (also see). They moved to Ridgeway Twp., Lenawee Co., Mich. They had 6 children, and 1 died prior to 1888 (name not stated): 2. CHARLES (m. Mary Kliblinger, Elkhart, Ind.); 3. WILLIS (m. Clara Wilberham; Britton, Mich.); 4. AMBROSE (m. Sarah Helm; Elkhart, Ind.); 5. CLARA (m/1 Gilbert Waring, son of Joshua, also see, who d. 1874; m/2 Robert Hauseman); 6. HATTIE (m. J. R. Miller; Colorado). Ref: P&BA-Len pg. 818-9.

CLARK, GEORGE W., son of ZACHARIAH & LEFA (of New England parentage), came to Michigan in 1830. He married MARY (OSBORN); and he died 3 July 1836, leaving her with 2 children: SARAH M. b. 14 May 1833, Detroit; 2. Son, name not stated, d. age 31, Woodstock Twp., Lenawee Co., Mich. Mary married second to Stephen Turrell; and 3rd to Hiram Johnson (see both). Ref: P&BA-Len pg. 1132-5.

CLARK, HENRY born ca. 1817, and wife, ESTHER, born ca. 1806, both in England, were listed in the 1850 census of Ridgeway Twp., Lenawee Co., Mich. with THOMAS, age 17, b. NY; GEORGE, age 16; WILLIAM, age 9, both b. Ohio; and ESTHER A., age 5, b. Mich., in their household.

CLARK, HENRY born ca. 1823, with wife, SARAH, b. ca. 1825, both in NY, with LYDIA, age 1, b. Mich., were listed in the 1850 census of Fairfield Twp., Lenawee Co., Mich. in the household of Orrin Baker (possibly Sarah's father?).

CLARK, JOHN R, son of BARZILLAI (preceding), born 4 Sept. 1822, Ontario, Ontario Co., NY (in area now Walworth, Wayne Co.) He moved to Adrian Twp., Lenawee Co., Mich. with parents. He lived in Madison Twp., and in Adrian; and married 8 Apr. 1846 to EMILY E. (WADSWORTH), daughter of Joseph E. (also see). Four children, 2 died infancy (names not stated): 1. HELEN M. b. 1 June 1848 (m. Peter L. Bailey; she d. 30 Oct. 1873); 2. MARIA ISABELLA b. 16 Sept. 1865, Madison Twp. Ref: P&BA-Len pg. 774-5.

CLARK, JOHN born ca. 1795, and wife, SARAH, born ca. 1794, both in Vermont, were listed in the 1850 census of Tecumseh Twp., Lenawee Co., Mich. with LAURA, age 22 (m. Dr. Albert Tuttle, also see); SARAH, age 19; FLETCHER?, age 18, all b. VT, in their household. Also note THADDEUS, listed 2 doors away, brother??

CLARK, JOHN S. born 1819, Dummerston, VT, was said to be a son of a brother (name not stated) of THADDEUS (following), probably JOHN (preceding). He came to

Clinton, Lenawee Co., Mich. in 1840; and married LOUISA (SKINNER), daughter of Allen (also see). (Louisa was a niece of Catharine Ryan, wife of THADDEUS, as Catherine was her mother's sister). They settled in Clinton Twp., and he died in 1883. Children: 1. KATE; 2. ALBERT E.; 3. JOHN F. (m. Jane E. Newcomb; children, Louis L. & Hazel H.; lived Grosse Pointe, Mich.); 4. CHARLES F. (m. Ellie M. Bartlett). Ref: P&BA-Len pg. 900-1.

CLARK, LUCINDA born ca. 1830, Ohio (See David M. Blair).

CLARK, LYDIA born ca. 1800, Hampshire Co., Mass., married Alvin Whitmarsh (also see) as his first wife; and she was a sister of NAOMI (following).

CLARK, NAOMI M. born ca. 1803, Hampshire Co., Mass., married Alvin Whitmarsh (also see) as 2nd wife, after death of her sister, LYDIA (preceding), his 1st wife.

CLARK, NATHAN N. Rev. married CARRIE M. (BAKER), daughter of George Anson (also see) and had children: HARLAND G.; & MIAL V. Ref: P&BA-Len pg. 767-8.

CLARK, NOAH born ca. 1787, and wife MARY (HARKNESS), moved from (Orleans Co.?) NY to Manchester Twp., Washtenaw Co., Mich. She died there in July 1862; and he afterwards moved to Franklin Twp., Lenawee co., Mich., where he died 9 Sept. 1870, age 87. Known daughter, MARY S. b. 22 Feb. 1824, Carlton, Orleans Co., NY (m. Ansel Witherell, also see, in 1844, Franklin Twp., Lenawee Co., Mich.) Ref: P&BA-Len pg. 886-7.

CLARK, POLLY (See Daniel Jennings)

CLARK, RHODA (See S. Wells Graves)

CLARK, SARAH (See Peter Ames)

CLARK, SEYMOUR S. born ca. 1819, NY, was reared in Genesee Co., NY. In 1839, he came to Adrian, Lenawee Co., Mich., but returned to Genesee Co., NY where he married on 2 Nov. 1845 to ELIZA A. (SMITH), daughter of John (also see). They moved to Adrian, Lenawee Co., and then to Madison Twp. before 1850; and to Palmyra Twp. ca. 1855. In the 1850 census of Madison Twp., THURZA, age 70, b. NY, probably his mother, was in their household. They moved to Hillsdale Co. Mich. where he died 16 Mar. 1861. No children were listed. His wife, Eliza A, married second to a John Phillips (also see). Ref: P&BA-Len pg. 699-700.

CLARK, STACY (See George S. Stranahan)

CLARK, THADDEUS born ca. 1781, and wife, CATHARINE (RYAN), born ca. 1796, both in Vermont, came to Clinton, Lenawee Co., Mich. in 1831, bringing wife's niece, Louisa Skinner (m. JOHN S., preceding); and John Tyrrell (See John Terryl). Ref: P&BA-Len pg. 900-1.

CLARK, THOMAS was born in Vermont, and wife, RHODA (KINNEY), was born in New Hampshire; and they resided in Homer, Cortland Co., NY by 1818. They had 9 children, and 5 sons and 2 daughters (names not stated) grew to maturity. Known son, EDWARD (preceding). Ref: P&BA-Len pg. 1148-9.

CLARK, WILLIAM of Rollin Twp., Lenawee Co. Mich. (See Levi Jennings).

CLARKE, HANNAH (See Thomas Nichols)

CLARKE, S. (See David Wood)

CLARKE, W. H. (See Simon D. Wilson)

CLARKSON - From Middlesex Co. (NJ) Heirs to Estates, 1780-1870, by V. A. Brown, are the following notes which seem to pertain to the family following. JAMES was in Woodbridge, Middlesex Co., NJ as early as 1709. ROBERT & JEREMIAH served in the Revolution from Middlesex Co; and in 1778-1780, JEREMIAH; JOHN; & ROBERT are listed in Woodbridge; and LEVINUS at New Brunswick, Middlesex Co. In 1793, ABEL (exempted); JAMES; & JEREMIAH were listed in Woodbridge militia (men 18-45 yrs old). In the estate records of Middlesex Co., NJ: ROBERT of Woodbridge died intestate, April 1786, and mentioned are heirs (children): ABEL; PHEBE; MARY; MARGARET; ROBERT; EXPERIENCE; and mentioned is property "adjoining JOHN." JEREMIAH had an estate dated 5 Sept. 1822 that mentioned heirs "children of son, ISAAC." CLARKSON, ABIGAIL born between 1794/1802 in Middlesex Co., NJ married there to Stephen P. E. Martin (also see) and moved to Lodi, Seneca Co., NY; and then to Macon Twp., Lenawee Co., Mich. Ref: P&BA-Len pg. 970-1.

CLARKSON, DANIEL b. ca. 1801, Woodbridge, Middlesex Co., NJ, went as a young man to Lodi, Seneca Co., NY; and he married there to DEBORAH (CADMUS), b. ca. 1802/8, daughter of Richard (also see). After the birth of 5 children, they moved to Macon Twp., Lenawee Co., Mich. in 1831. He died in July 1869, and she died in Jan. 1870, age 62? Children following were listed in their household or adjacent in the 1850 census of Macon Twp.: 1. RICHARD (following); 2. JOHN (following); 3. CLARISSA, age 23; 4. JAMES, age 21, all b. NY; 5. WILLIAM, age 14; 6. JOSEPHINE b. 8 Apr. 1838 (m. Leroy Mead, also see); 7. HENRIETTA, age 8; 8. THOMAS, age 5; 9. EMMA, age 4, last 5 b. Mich. William Cadmus, age 50, probably brother of Deborah, was also in the household. Ref: P&BA-Len pg. 467-70.

CLARKSON, JOHN, son of DANIEL (preceding), born ca. 1825, and wife, MARY A., born ca. 1822, both in NY, were listed in the 1850 census of Macon Twp., Lenawee Co., Mich., with DEBORAH, age 8, b. Mich., in their household.

CLARKSON, RICHARD, son of DANIEL (preceding), was born 28 May 1823, Lodia, Seneca Co., NY, and came to Macon Twp., Lenawee Co., Mich. with parents. He married 3 Nov. 1853 to MARY M. (OSGOOD), daughter of John (also see); and they settled in Macon Twp. Children: 1. MINNIE E. (d. age 2 wks); 2. MARGARET J.; 3. MARTHA E.; 4. ELLA S. (m. John M. Pennington). Ref: P&BA-Len pg. 467-8.

CLARSON, THOMAS (See Aaron R. Tufts)

CLAY, BRADBURY S. Rev. and wife, MARY (RAYMER), moved from Seneca Co., NY to Adrian, Lenawee Co., Mich. in 1839. They also lived in Indiana & Illinois at various times. Known son, FRANK W. (following). Ref: P&BA-Len pg. 866-7.

CLAY, FRANK W., son of Rev. BRADBURY (preceding), was born 24 May 1837, Farmer Village, Seneca Co., NY. He married AMELIA C. (HICKOX) of Rochester, NY in Dec. 1862 (she was a native of Avon Springs, NY). They settled in Adrian, Lenawee Co., Mich. Children: 1. RIAL; 2. GERALDINE. Ref: P&BA-Len pg. 866-7.

CLAY, HENRY born ca. 1834, Mich.?, was listed in the 1850 census of Adrian Twp., Lenawee Co., Mich. in the household of William Seward Wilcox (and his wife, SARAH CLAY). Note BRADBURY, preceding.

CLAY, SAMUEL born ca. 1814, England, and wife, FANNY, born ca. 1823, NH, were listed in the 1850 census of Adrian Twp., Lenawee Co., Mich. with no family.

CLAY, SARAH F. born ca. 1824, NY, married William Seward Wilcox (also see), and in their household in the 1850 census of Adrian Twp., was HENRY (preceding).

CLAYTON, ISABELLE (See William Grove)

CLAYTON, MARY (See Charles H. Smith)

CLAYTON, PHEBE born ca. 1832, Canada, was listed in a hotel in the 1850 census of Adrian Twp., Lenawee Co., Mich.

CLEMENSEN, EVELINE (See Mathew H. Kerr)

CLEMENT also see CLEMENTS

CLEMENT, ANDREW born in Co. Antrim, Ireland (of Scottish descent), and wife, MARGARET (HAMILTON). born in Nov. 1798, Co. Down, Ireland (also of Scottish descent), came to the US about 1820 with 2 children, and settled in Butler Co., Penn. He died in 1827, leaving her with 7 children (names not stated). Those known: JAMES (d. 8 Mar. 1839, age 21); WILLIAM (following); ANDREW (d. 1870, Adrian, Mich.); JOHN B. (following). Margaret married again to Thomas Campbell (also see) in Butler Co., Penn., and about 1832, they started for Michigan, and during a Winter layover in Toledo, O., Thomas died. Margaret and her children afterwards continued on to Palmyra Twp., Lenawee Co., Mich. Margaret apparently married again, as she was listed in the 1850 census of Palmyra Twp. as Margaret White, age 51, b. Ireland, with her daughter, Letitia Campbell, age 18, b. Penn. in her household. Ref: P&BA-Len pg. 950-1.

CLEMENT, ELEANOR (See James Eaton, Sr.)

CLEMENT, FREEMAN was born ca. 1780, and died 7 Sept. 1819, aged 39y/10m/5d, and is buried in the Mills Cemetery, Franklin Twp., Lenawee Co., Mich., adjacent to JAMES & REBECCA (following).

CLEMENT, GEORGE W., probably son of JAMES (following), born ca. 1812, and his wife, ANN (NANCY) b. ca. 1815, both in NY, were listed in the 1850 census of Franklin Twp., Lenawee Co., Mich., with MARIETTA, age 11; ALMA, age 4 (bur. in Mills Cem., d. 30 Sept. 1850, age 1(4?)y/11m/16d.); DIANTHA, age 2 (d. 16 Jan. 1856, age 7y/1m/16d); FRANKLIN, age 3/12; & also in the Mills Cem., ADELPHIA (d. Jan. 1853, age 3y/11m). George W. died in 1863; and Nancy Ann died in 1901, both buried in Mills Cem. with the children noted above.

CLEMENT, JAMES born ca. 1774, and died 15 Apr. 1844, age 70 yrs. He is buried in the Mills Cemetery, Franklin Twp., Lenawee Co., Mich., adjacent to REBECCA, assumed to be his wife (no dates). In the 1850 census of Franklin Twp., Rebecca is age 69, b. Mass., listed in the household of JAMES M. (following). GEORGE W. (preceding) was listed next door. Also note FREEMAN, preceding.

CLEMENT, JAMES M., probably son of JAMES (preceding), born ca. 1815, and wife, MARY, born ca. 1820, both in NY, were listed in the 1850 census of Franklin Twp., Lenawee Co., Mich. with REBECCA, age 7; HARRIET, age 6; MILTON, age 4; IRA, age 8/12, all b. Mich.; as well as REBECCA (mother), in their household. Additional children in the records of the Mills Cemetery, Franklin Twp., were ANDREW J. (d. 11 Feb. 1849, age 13y/15d); and ELLEN I. b. 19 Mar. 1855 (d. 3 Aug. 1855). It is probably James M. as "J. M." with a GAR marker (no dates) also buried there.

CLEMENT, JOHN B., son of ANDREW (preceding), born 3 Oct. 1825, Butler Co., Penn., came to Michigan with his mother. He married PRUDENCE E. (GRAY), daugher of Jonathan (also see). They settled in Ogden Twp., Lenawee Co., Mich. Children: 1. GEORGE b. ca. 1847 (m. Martha Ross; Edwards Co., KS); 2. JOHN b. ca. 1850 (d. 1871); 3. EMMA (m. Silas Gordan; Edwards Co., KS); 4. ANDREW (m. Della Hogland; Edwards Co. KS); 5. IDA J. (m. Frederick Gray; Ogden Twp.); 6. WILLIAM (m. Nellie McIntosh; Topeka, KS); 7. EDWIN b. 27 Dec. 1860 (d. 12 July 1863); 8. MARY (m. Edward Theed; Englewood, Ill.); 9. ROLLIN; 10. MINNIE. Ref: P&BA-Len pg. 950-1.

CLEMENT, PETER born ca. 1795, and wife, LUCINDA, born ca. 1809, both in NY, were listed in the 1850 census of Madison Twp., Lenawee Co., Mich. with ELI, age 21, b. RI; PHILINDA, age 21, b. NY (probably wife of Eli?); SARAH, age 16; PETER, age 9, all b. NY; and JANE, age 6/12, b. Mich., in their household.,

CLEMENT, WILLIAM, probably son of ANDREW (preceding), was born ca. 1820, Penn., and wife, JOANNA, was born ca. 1818, NY. in the 1850 census of Ogden Twp., Lenawee Co., Mich. they listed LOUISA, age 9; MARGARET, age 7; ANNA, age 5; WILLIAM, age 3; FRANCES, age 1, all b. Mich., in their household. William was said to have died 17 May 1886, Kansas. Note: JOHN B., preceding, was next door in the 1850 census.

CLEMENTS also see CLEMENT

CLEMENTS, ARTHUR born ca. 1813, and wife, MARY, born ca. 1825, both in Ireland, were listed in the 1850 census of Tecumseh Twp., Lenawee Co., Mich. with SARAH ANN, age 9; JOHN, age 4, both b. Ireland, in their household. There is an ARTHUR, age 8, b. Ireland, listed in another household who may relate to this family.

CLEVELAND, AARON (See ? Van Pelt)

CLEVELAND, DAVID was a descendant of Moses Cleveland who came on the Mayflower; and he resided in Ontario, Canada when his wife died. He removed to Washtenaw Co. Mich. by 1840. He died in Jackson Co., Mich, at age 84. Known daughter, DELIA JANE, born May 1807, Ontario, Canada (m. John L. Tuttle, also see, in Ann Arbor, Mich.). Ref: P&BA-Len pg. 373-4. Note MARY A., following.

CLEVELAND, DAVID born ca. 1812, and wife, PHEBE, born ca. 1815, both in NY, were listed in the 1840 census index of Dover Twp., Lenawee Co., Mich.; and in 1850 census with SYNTHA A. age 10; HARRIET A., age 8; ELIJAH D., age 6; J. H. W. (male), age 4, all b. Mich., in their household. Note JAMES & M. (following).

CLEVELAND, DELLA (See Benjamin Converse)

CLEVELAND, JAMES was listed in the 1840 census index of Dover Twp., Lenawee Co., Mich. adjacent to DAVID

Pioneer Families of Southeastern Michigan

(preceding); and M. (following). Note Mrs. SARAH, following.

CLEVELAND, JOHN & wife, ALMIRA (LOOMIS) born ca. 1807, Penn., married in Livingston Co., NY. In 1830, they removed to Raisin Twp., Lenawee Co., Mich. He died in 1842, and she died in 1884, age 83? Eight children, 2 deceased by 1842 (names not stated). Almira was head of household in the 1850 census of Raisin Twp. with WHITING "White" (following); JEROME, age 22, b. NY; & EDWARD, age 18; SOPHIA, age 14; JAMES, age 12, all b. Mich., in her household. Ref: P&BA-Len pg. 378-9.

CLEVELAND, JOSEPH H. born ca. 1811, and wife, JULIA A., born ca. 1814, both in NY, were listed in the 1840 census index of Adrian Twp., Lenawee Co., Mich.; and in the 1850 census with WILLIAM H., age 18; MARY S., age 17; CHARLES M., age 13; LUCINDA R., age 11; GEORGE S., age 7, all b. Mich., in their household.

CLEVELAND, M. (MARVIN, following?) was listed in the 1840 census index of Dover Twp., Lenawee Co. Mich.

CLEVELAND, MARVIN born ca. 1822, and wife, CELINDA, born ca. 1822, both in NY, were listed in the 1850 census of Dover Twp., Lenawee Co., Mich.

CLEVELAND, MARY A. (See William J. Tuttle)

CLEVELAND, NORMAN born ca. 1818, and wife, HANNAH, born ca. 1818, both in NY, were listed in the 1850 census of Dover Twp., Lenawee Co., Mich. with WILLIAM, age ?, b. Ohio; HENRY CLAY, age 6; IRA H., age 1; and MARY A., age 10, all b. Mich., in their household.

CLEVELAND, SAMUEL was listed in the 1840 census index of Seneca Twp., Lenawee Co., Mich.

CLEVELAND, SARAH Mrs. born ca. 1800, NY, was head of household in the 1850 census of Dover Twp., Lenawee Co., Mich. with DARWIN, age 27, NY; IRA, age 19, b. Ohio; SUSAN, age 12; TEMPERANCE, age 6, both b. Mich.; and Horace Eaton, age 22, b. NY; & Mary Eaton, age 16, b. Ohio; Nathan Reed, age 25; Elizabeth Reed, age 22, both b. Ohio, in her household. Note JAMES, preceding.

CLEVELAND, WHITING "WHITE," son of JOHN (preceding), was born 8 July 1826, Groveland, NY, and came to Lenawee Co., Mich. with his parents. He married in Brooklyn, Mich. on 20 Oct. 1863 to Mrs. HARRIET (PLANK) LEMBARGER, daughter of Robert Plank (also see), whose husband had died in the Civil War (See Lembarger). They settled in Tecumseh Twp., Lenawee Co., Mich. Children: GRANT (twin of Brant); 2. BRANT (d. infancy); 3. DON CARLTON. Ref: P&BA-Len pg. 378-9.

CLEVELAND, WILLIAM born ca. 1811, VT; and wife, LURINDA, b. ca. 1809, NY, were listed in the 1850 census of Tecumseh Twp., Lenawee Co., Mich., with JOHN, age 6; JANET, age 3; EDWARD, age 2, all b. Mich., in their household.

CLINE, CORNELIUS (See James Whitney)

CLOSSER, PERRY (See Morgan Parker)

COAH, ALICE (See Henry L. Hurlburt)

COATS, CHARLES was listed in the 1840 census index of Madison Twp., Lenawee Co., Mich.

COATS, D. C. was listed in the 1840 census index of Medina Twp., Lenawee Co., Mich.

COATS, ELEANOR born ca. 1797, NY, was listed in the 1850 census of Adrian Twp., Lenawee Co., Mich. in the household of Benjamin & Mary (b. 1815, NY) Mulholland, possibly mother of Mary?

COATS, FRANCIS born ca. 1801, England, and wife, HENRIETTA, born ca. 1814, Ireland, were listed in the 1840 census index of Macon Twp., Lenawee Co., Mich.; and in the 1850 census of Ridgeway Twp. with HENRY L., age 18, b. England; and MARIA, age 84, b. England (probably his mother), in their household. Note: SARAH, born ca. 1810, England, who m. John Britton, Sr. (also see) was listed next door in the 1850 census, probably a sister.

COATS, MARY (See Levi Corey)

COBB, HULDAH (See Hezekiah Ford[4])

COCHRAN, ? was father of THOMAS (Alden, NY); REBECCA (m. Richard Thornton, Toledo, O.); OLIVE ANN b. ca. 1821 (m/1 Shelby; m/2 Samuel Cook, also see, and moved from Erie Co., Penn. to St. Joseph Co., Mich.). Ref: P&BA-Len pg. 719-20.

COCHRAN, JONATHAN born ca. 1807, NH, and wife, AMARYLLIS, born ca. 1816, Conn., were listed in the 1850 census of Palmyra Twp., Lenawee Co., Mich. with WILLIAM S., age 8; SARAH J., age 5; MARY W., age 2; HARRIET, age 1/12, all b. Ohio, in the household.

COCHRAN, JANET of Londonderry, NH (See John Moore[1])

COCHRANE, DAVID born Co. Cavan, Ireland (of Scottish descent), married there to LYDIA (YOUNG). In 1845, they came to the US and settled first in Brockport, NY; where she died in 1857. He went to Rochester, NY in 1861, and died there in 1869. Children: 1. LYDIA A. (m. William Unger, NYC); 2. GEORGE R. (following). Ref: P&BA-Len pg. 1170-1.

COCHRANE, GEORGE R., son of DAVID (preceding), was born 18 Feb. 1841, Co. Cavan, Ireland and came to the US with his parents. After the death of his mother, he lived with an uncle in Genesee Co., NY. He enlisted in 1863 in Co. G., 8th NY Artl, and lost an arm. After the war, he settled first in Batavia, NY, and then Rochester, NY. He married 29 Nov. 1865, Bethany, NY to BESSIE M. (CHITTENDEN), daughter of Jesse B. (also see). In 1868, they moved to Palmyra Twp., Lenawee Co., Mich.; and afterwards in Blissfield and Adrian; finally returning to Palmyra Twp. Children: 1. LILLY b. 1869; 2. WILLIAM b. 1871; GEORGE b. 1877. Ref: P&BA-Len pg. 1170-1.

CODDING, WILLIAM A. born ca. 1814, NY, and wife, MARIAH (LUTHER), daughter of Theodorick (also see), were listed in the 1850 census of Dover Twp., Lenawee Co., Mich. with JULIA A., age 9; CHARLOTTE, age 7; ANGELINE, age 6; ANDREW J., age 3; THEODORICK, age 1, all b. Mich., in their household. They may have gone to St. Joseph Co., Mich. at a later date.

CODDINGTON, ALVAH born ca. 1808, & wife, BARBARA (SWICK), born ca. 1810, both in NY, came from Tompkins Co., NY and settled first in Washtenaw Co.,

Mich., and later in Bath Twp., Clinton Co., Mich., and then returned to NY for a few years. He died 18 June 1882, age 84?, at home of son in Lenawee Co., Mich.; and she had died 13 Mar. 1876 in Tompkins Co., NY. There were 2 daughters (names not stated), and 1 son. In the 1850 census of Hector, Tompkins Co., NY, they listed PHIDELIA, age 17; ANSEL P. (following); also listed was MONORCA, age 70, b. NY, probably his mother, in their household. Ref: P&BA-Len pg. 1012-5.

CODDINGTON, ANSEL P., son of ALVAH (preceding), born 19 Oct. 1835, Tompkins Co., NY, was reared in Clinton Co., Mich. He went to school at Stearkey Seminary, Yates Co., NY. He enlisted in Co. G., 109th NY Inf., during the Civil War, and became a Lt. in the Commissary Dept. He married in Seneca Co., NY to MARY M. (KELLY) who was born there, and they moved to Tompkins Co., NY where she died in 1877. Children: 1. ALVAH J.; 2. ANNA C.; 3. SARAH L.; 4. BARBARA E.; 5. EDGAR A. Ansel married again in Oct. 1877 to FANNY (TEETER), daughter of John (also see), and they moved to Tecumseh Twp., Lenawee Co., Mich. Ref: P&BA-Len pg. 1012-5.

CODDINGTON, JOHN born ca. 1810, and wife, ANNE (DEMUND), born ca. 1808, both in NY, came to Seneca Twp., Lenawee Co., Mich. before 1840. He died in 1852. Known children: 1. SARAH A. b. ca. 1843 (m. Levi C. Chase, also see); 2. PETER b. ca. 1846. Ref: P&BA-Len pg. 350-2.

CODY, JOHN (See Samuel Lewis)

COEN, JOHN of Columbia Co., NY was father of MARY (m. Peter Schutz, also see).

COE, EUNICE (See John Camp)
COE, HANNAH (See Halsted Gurnee)
COE, JAMES, age 13, b. Ohio, was listed in the 1850 census of Adrian Twp., Lenawee Co., Mich. in the Henry & Louisa Smith household.
COE, JOHN M. born ca. 1803, NY, and wife, MARIA A., born ca. 1806, Mass., were listed in the 1840 census index of Rome Twp., Lenawee Co., Mich.; and in the 1850 census with MELVINA, age 16; ELIZA L., age 14; ELLEN M., age 11; ANNA A., age 8, all b. Mich., in their household.
COE, JONATHAN was listed in the 1840 census index of Macon Twp., Lenawee Co., Mich.
COE, WILLIAM was listed in the 1840 census index of Raisin Twp., Lenawee Co., Mich.

COFFIN, ELIZA Mrs. was the daughter of Levi H. Chase (also see). Her children were LEVI F. (m. Hattie L. Stevenson); DANA (m. Stella Wells, Blissfield Twp., Lenawee Co., Mich); MARY A. (m. Edward Isely, son of Thomas C., also see, of Blissfield Twp.); HERBERT (d. age 14); OWEN (d. age 22); ANNA (d. age 21.) The given name of her first husband was not stated; but she married second to Hulett West, per the sketch of his brother, Wilber West, in which he incorrectly called her the "widow of Levi H. Chase." Ref: P&BA-Len pg. 504.
COFFIN, ELIZABETH born ca. 1785, NY, married first to ? Warner, and married second to John Lagore (also see).
COFFIN, WATERMAN born ca. 1783, and wife, LOVE, born ca. 1787, both in Mass., were listed in the 1840 census index of Raisin Twp., Lenawee Co., Mich.; and in the 1850 census with CHARLES, age 22, b. NY; and probably grandchildren, ALBERT, age 2; HARRIS, age 6/12, both b. Mich., in their household.

COGGSWELL also see COGSWELL
COGGSWELL, R. S. and wife, LYDIA P. (STRETCH), were parents of IDA E. born Palmyra, Wayne Co., NY (m. Dayton Parker, MD, also see). Ref: P&BA-Len pg. 599-600.

COGSWELL also see COGGSWELL
COGSWELL, CHARLES born ca. 1842, Mich., was listed in the 1850 census of Medina Twp., Lenawee co., Mich. in the household of David W. Adams.
COGSWELL, E. H. (See Isaiah C. Miller)
COGSWELL, HENRY and wife, CAROLINE (HAYES), of Springville, Erie Co., NY, were parents of SARAH C. b. Springville, NY (m. Lemuel James Morse, May 1875, Medina Twp., Lenawee Co., Mich.). Ref: P&BA-Len pg. 898-9.
COGSWELL, MERIBAR, age 58?, born NY, was listed in the 1850 census of Rollin Twp., Lenawee Co., Mich. in the household of Edward & Eveline Birdsell.
COGSWELL, WILLIAM H. born ca. 1813, VT, and wife, MARGARET, born ca. 1816, NJ, were listed in the 1850 census of Hudson Twp., Lenawee Co., Mich. with EMILY, age 14, b. NY, in their household.

COLBATH, HIRAM C., son of SAMUEL (following), was born 8 Jan. 1823, Sodus, Wayne Co., NY. He moved with his parents to Monroe Co., Mich., and in 1838, moved to Rome Twp., Lenawee Co., Mich. He married 22 Jan. 1846 to HANNAH ELIZABETH (OWEN), daughter of Charles (also see); and she died 11 Sept. 1867 leaving 5 children (names not stated). Known son, #3. SEYMOUR (following). They were listed in the 1850 census of Rome Twp. with EDWARD, age 16, probably brother of Hiram, in their household. Hiram married second to CORDELIA (HATTER), daughter of John, on 25 Feb. 1869. Ref: P&BA-Len pg. 862-3.
COLBATH, SAMUEL was born 27 Dec. 1788, Maine, and he married 21 Sept. 1816 to SALLIE (LEWIS) who was born 11 Feb. 1794, Conn. They removed to Wayne Co., NY; and in 1832 to Monroe Co., Mich., where he died 22 July 1837. Ten children (names not stated). Known sons, HIRAM C. (preceding); and EDWARD, b. ca. 1834, NY (in Hiram's household in 1850). Also EDGAR, b. ca. 1830, NY, in 1850 census of Tecumseh Twp. may relate to this family. Ref: P&BA-Len pg. 862-3.
COLBATH, SEYMOUR A., son of HIRAM C. (preceding), married 2 Sept. 1868 to NANCY A. (TRIM), daughter of Ira (also see). They resided in Rome Twp., Lenawee Co., Mich. Children: 1. WILLIAM E. b. 25 Oct. 1869; 2. HIRAM I. b. 29 Nov. 1871; 3. LEILA G. b. 25 Apr. 1875; 4. GEORGE b. 20 June 1879. Ref: P&BA-Len pg. 862-3.

COLE, AARON is listed in the 1800 census index of Cayuga Co., NY. Note DANIEL, following.
COLE, AARON H., son of DANIEL (following), was born 26 Feb. 1813, Covert, Seneca Co., NY. As an adult, he went to Ohio and Indiana where he taught school, and then returning to NY married LYDIA (RAPPLEYE), daughter of William (also see). In 1835, they moved to Spencer,

Lucas Co., Ohio; and in 1849 to Maumee city. In 1856, they moved to Genesee Co., Mich. and remained 3 yrs, then returned to Ohio. They moved to Adrian, Lenawee Co., Mich. in 1866, and he died 27 Oct. 1867. Children: 1. HARRIET C. (m. Rev. H. B. Taft; she d. 1868, Salem, Washtenaw Co., Mich.); 2. WILLIAM R. (to Dallas, TX); 3. MINER T. (following); 4. ADONIRAM J. (d. Fulton Co., O., age 17); 5. FRANK M.; 6. RALPH T. (Mobeetie, TX); 7. GEORGE I. (Toledo, O.) Ref: P&BA-Len pg. 228-30.

COLE, ALFRED born ca. 1822, and wife, MATILDA, born ca. 1828, both in NY, were listed in the 1850 census of Fairfield Twp., Lenawee Co., Mich. with GEORGE, age 2, b. NY; and CHARLES A., age 2/12, b. Mich., in the household. Also see BENJAMIN, following.

COLE, AMOS R., son of ELVIN C. (following), was born 19 May 1839, Seneca Co., NY. He went as an adult to Mt. Vernon, Iowa; and then to DeKalb Co., Ill. He served in the Civil War in Co. L., 8th Ill. Cav. He came to Rollin Twp., Lenawee Co., Mich. and married ELMIRA B. (BEAL), daughter of Porter (also see). Children: 1. SUSAN L. b. 27 Aug. 1865 (m. L. Llewellyn Harkness, son of John U., also see, 4 Mar. 1885); 2. CELIA O. b. 20 Feb. 1868 (m. Edward M. Rawson, son of Henry H., also see; Rollin Twp.); 3. ELVIRA R. b. 5 Sept. 1872; 4. DeWITT b. 7 Jan. 1874. Ref: P&BA-Len pg. 556-7.

COLE, BENJAMIN born ca. 1812, and wife, LOUISA, born ca. 1814, both in NY, were listed in the 1850 census of Fairfield Twp., Lenawee Co., Mich. HIRAM, age 17; MARY, age 15, both b. NY; and ALANSON, age 10, b. Mich. ALFRED (preceding) was listed next door in the census.

COLE, CYRUS A. born ca. 1826, and wife, EMILY, born ca. 1829, both in NY, were listed in the 1850 census of Franklin Twp., Lenawee Co., Mich. with GEORGE, age 2; and ANGELINE, age 2/12, both b. Mich., in their household.

COLE, DANIEL born 23 Dec. 1779, Conn., and wife, SARAH (HOPKINS) born 10 Sept. 1781, lived in Putnam Co., NY before moving to Covert, Cayuga Co. (later Seneca Co.), NY. It may be he listed in Dutchess Co. in the 1800 census index (as Putnam was formed from Dutchess in 1812), though there is also a man by this name listed in Tioga Co., NY. Known children: ANNA b. 10 July 1803 (m. Thomas Tunison, also see); & AARON H. (preceding). Ref: P&BA-Len pg. 228-30; 514-5.

COLE, DANIEL born ca. 1801, NY, and HANNAH, born ca. 1810, VT, were listed in the 1850 census of Palmyra Twp., Lenawee Co., Mich. with MARY A., age 16, b. NY; & ELIZABETH, age 14; ORRIN, age 11, all b. Mich., in the household. Also in his household were SALMON, age 47; MILO, age 28; LAFAYETTE, ag 23, all b. NY, relationships not known.

COLE, DARIUS of Rollin Twp., Lenawee Co., Mich. married MARY ANN (ALLEN), daughter of Spencer (also see), and died after 1843. Mary Ann married second to ELVIN C., following. Ref: P&BA-Len pg. 556-7.

COLE, DAVID of Erie Co., NY was the father of LYDIA (m. Philip Sweet). David was apparently a brother of JOB, as Lydia was called a "niece of JOB" who was "a cousin of PELEG" (following). There was a DAVID listed in the 1800 census index of Otsego Co., NY. Ref: P&BA-Len pg. 567-8.

COLE, EDWIN W. born ca. 1814, and wife, MARY A., born ca. 1825, both in NY, were listed in the 1850 census of Fairfield Twp., Lenawee Co., Mich. with HASCHELL?, age 11; NATHAN, age 9; URSULA? (female), age 6; PORTER?, age 5; RACHEL; age 4/12, all b. Mich., in their household. Note: It is probably he in the 1840 census index of Fairfield Twp. listed as EDMUND W., adjacent to EVRY (following)

COLE, ELECTA (See Nathan Myers)

COLE, ELECTA married first to William Watson (also see) before 1827, Erie Co., NY. Son, Zebulon Watson married Phebe D. Bates, daughter of Daniel Bates and wife, PRISCILLA (COLE). Electa may be a daughter of PELEG (following)? Also see DAVID (preceding).

COLE, ELIZA, born ca. 1810, was head of household in the 1850 census of Palmyra Twp., Lenawee Co., Mich. She listed in her household IRA, age 19; S----(male), age 17; SILAS, age 9; MONROE, age 6, all b. Mich. Note JAMES & JOHNSON (following); and DANIEL (preceding).

COLE, ELMER, son of LEWIS (following), born 4 Dec. 1812, Hector, NY, married LUCRETIA (SMITH) born 4 Dec. 1812, Delaware Co., NY, and before 1844 settled in Rollin Twp., Lenawee Co., Mich. Known sons: OGDEN (following); JOHN R. b. ca. 1847. Ref: P&BA-Len pg. 594-5.

COLE, ELVIN C., son of LEWIS (following), was born 4 Dec. 1812, Hector, Tompkins Co., NY. He went to Monroe Co., NY for a time; then married 7 Mar. 1837 to LYDIA (TUNISON), daughter of Philip (also see) of Seneca Co., NY. She died in Covert, Seneca Co., NY 17 Dec. 1843. Known children: 1. AMOS R. (preceding); 2. LEWIS b. ca. 1843. Elvin C. moved to Rollin Twp., Lenawee Co., Mich. where he married second to Mrs. MARY ANN (ALLEN) COLE, daughter of Spencer, and widow of DARIUS (preceding). Known children: 3. DARIUS b. ca. 1846; 4. ELVIN Jr. b. ca. 1850 (d. young?); 5. ALLEN (to Clinton C., Mich.) Mary Ann died 2 May 1852. Elvin C. married again to ELVIRA L. (DAYTON), of Rollin Twp. Children: 6. EMMA C. b. 21 July 1853 (m. John C. Schneider, Rollin Twp.); 7. ELVIN D. (following). Ref: P&BA-Len pg. 556-7; & 610-1.

COLE, ELVIN D., son of ELVIN C. (preceding), born 28 Feb. 1861, married 9 Mar. 1881 to ALICE E. (RICE), daughter of Freeman (also see). Son, RAY F. b. 13 Sept. 1885. Ref: P&BA-Len pg. 610-1.

COLE, EVRY was listed in the 1840 census index of Fairfield Twp., Lenawee Co., Mich. adjacent to EDWIN W. (preceding); and close to BENJAMIN (preceding). Note EZRA, following.

COLE, EZRA born ca. 1807, and wife, ANGELINE, born ca. 1810, both in NY, were listed in the 1850 census of Fairfield Twp., Lenawee Co., Mich. with ORVILLE P., age 21, b. NY; and LYDIA, age 17; LOUIS, age 16, both b. Ohio; and HARRIET, age 14; SARAH, age 11; DANIEL, age 10; JANE, age 8; MATILDA, age 4; JOHN, age 1, all b. Mich., in their household. Probably SAMANTHA P., born ca. 1830, NY, is another daughter (m. Cornelius Quick, also see, resided next door in the 1850 census). Note EVRY, preceding, perhaps this was EZRA?

COLE, FREDERICK born ca. 1812, NY, was listed in the 1850 census of Madison Twp., Lenawee Co., Mich. in the Upton household.

COLE, JAMES was listed in the 1840 census index of Palmyra Twp., Lenawee Co., Mich. Note ELIZA (preceding).

COLE, JAMES came to Lenawee Co., Mich. to live with daughter, ABBIE, born NY (married James T. Finch, as his 3rd wife, of Rome and Adrian Twps, and resided in Adrian Twp., Lenawee Co., Mich.) James died in Adrian, age 83, at home of Abbie. Ref: P&BA-Len pg. 621-2.

COLE, JANE (See John TenBrook)

COLE, JOB (See DAVID, preceding)

COLE, JOHN born ca. 1798, and wife, MARY, born ca. 1808, both in New Jersey, were listed in the 1850 census of Seneca Twp., Lenawee Co., Mich. with ELEANOR, age 18; EMILY, age 15; JOHN, age 13, all born NY, in their household.

COLE, JOHNSON born ca. 1833, NY, was listed in the 1850 census of Palmyra Twp., Lenawee Co., Mich. in the household of a Crane family. Note JAMES & ELIZA (preceding).

COLE, LAFAYETTE (See DANIEL, preceding)

COLE, LEWIS was a pioneer to Cayuga Co., NY (it may be he listed in the 1800 census index of Essex Co., NY with an AMOS, adjacent). He married HANNAH (ROGERS) who died in 1813, probably in Hector, Tompkins Co., NY, leaving 6 children (all names not stated). Known son, ELVIN C. (preceding); ELMER (twin of Elvin C., preceding). Lewis married again to FANNIE (HAZEN) and had 3 children (names not stated). Ref: P&BA-Len pg. 556-7; & 610-2. Also note DARIUS, preceding.

COLE, LUCY (See Zalman L. Goodsell)

COLE, MARVIN born ca. 1824, and wife, ABIGAIL, born ca. 1824, both in NY, were listed in the 1850 census of Adrian Twp., Lenawee Co., Mich. with no family.

COLE, MILO (See DANIEL, preceding)

COLE, MINER T., son of AARON H. (preceding), was born 3 July 1839, Spencer Twp., Lucas Co., Ohio. He served in the Civil War. He married MARY J. (TAYLOR), daughter of William (also see); and they settled in Palmyra Twp., Lenawee Co., Mich. Children: 1. HATTIE; 2. HARLEY L.; 3. FLORENCE; 4. MARY. P&BA-Len pg. 228-30.

COLE, OGDEN, son of ELMER (preceding), born 16 Mar. 1844, Rollin Twp., Lenawee Co., Mich.; married there on 10 Oct. 1863 to HANNAH H. (HAWKINS), daughter of John R. (also see). Children: 1. ELMER E. b. 9 Apr. 1865; 2. ROSA A. b. 22 Aug. 1876; 3. MINNA E. b. 6 Mar. 1883. Ref: P&BA-Len pg. 594-5.

COLE, PELEG, born ca. 1759, Providence, RI., removed to Otsego Co., NY (probably he listed Otsego Co. in 1800 census index). He may have lived in Vermont before moving to Rome Twp., Lenawee Co., Mich., probably to join his children. His mother was a Winslow, descendant of a Mayflower family. Known daughter, PRISCILLA b. 4 Dec. 1801, Otsego Co., NY (m. Daniel Bates, also see). WINSLOW, following, is probably a son; and ELECTA (preceding, who m. William Watson) is probably a daughter? Ref: P&BA-Len pg. 551-2. Also note DAVID (preceding).

COLE, SALMON born ca. 1804, NY, was listed in the household of DANIEL (preceding) 1850 census of Palmyra Twp., Lenawee Co., Mich. It is probably he listed as SOLOMAN in the 1840 census index of Palmyra Twp.

COLE, SARAH b. ca. 1800, Dutchess Co., NY (See Sylvester King). Also note DANIEL, preceding.

COLE, THIRZA b. ca. 1790 married Lewis Porter (also see) in Covert, Seneca Co., NY.

COLE, WILLIAM F. amd wife, EMILY J., wer parents of LIZZIE C. born 24 Sept. 1837 (m. Michael P. Long, also see, 1866, Adrian, Lenawee Co., Mich

COLE, WINSLOW, probably son of PELEG (preceding), born ca. 1793, VT, and wife, BETSEY, born ca. 1805, NY, were listed in the 1840 census index of Rome Twp., Lenawee Co., Mich.; and in the 1850 census with DIADAMA, age 15; DAVID, age 14, both b. NY; and LYSANDER, age 11; PHILANDER, age 11; DANTHFORD, age 9; LARKEN? (male), age 7; ORPHEUS F., age 5, all b. Mich., in their household.

COLEBURN, CHARLOTTE born ca. 1786, NY, married Charles Ellis (also see), and in the 1850 census of Tecumseh Twp., Lenawee Co., Mich., they listed SUSANNAH, age 88, b. NY, probably her mother, in their household.

COLEGROVE, ANNIS (See Benjamin Hornbeck)

COLEGROVE, AVANDER H., son of BENJAMIN (following), born ca. 1818, NY?, and his wife, HARRIET, born ca. 1819, NY, were listed in the 1850 census of Medina Twp., Lenawee Co., Mich. with son, HENRY, age 4, b. Mich., and Emily Baker, age 17; Jacob Baker, age 14; both b. Mich., and Martha Wheeler, age 16, b. NY, in their household.

COLEGROVE, BEEDER? born ca. 1822, and wife, HARRIET, born ca. 1820, both in NY, were listed in the 1850 census of Adrian Twp., Lenawee Co., Mich. with ANDREW H., age 4; ANNA H., age 1, both b. Mich., in their household.

COLEGROVE, BENJAMIN was born ca. 1788, Plainfield, Windham Co., Conn.; and wife, LUCY (GARLIC), was born Lanesboro, Berkshire Co., Mass. They married ca. 1814 and afterwards moved to McKean Co., Penn. The four eldest sons left Penn., and Benjamin later followed to Lenawee Co., Mich., and he was living in Medina Twp. by the 1850 census, and Lucy was apparently deceased. He moved to Morenci, Mich. where he died 4 Apr. 1875, age 88. Children: 1. AVANDER H. (preceding); 2. MARY A.; 3. HENRY G. (following); 4. JOHN T. (following); 5. ALONZO B.; 6. NAOMI G. b. ca. 1832, Penn.; 7. TRUMAN D. b. ca. 1839, Penn. (d. 1862 of Typhoid in Civil War). Ref: P&BA-Len pg. 952-3; & 1119-20.

COLEGROVE, BENJAMIN M., son of JOHN T. (following), was born 11 Nov. 1857, Medina Twp., Lenawee Co., Mich. He married on 20 Jan. 1878 to FRANCES (RICE), daughter of Philip (also see), and settled in Medina Twp. Children: CLARK E.; 2. SYLVANUS J.; 3. PHILIP. Ref: P&BA-Len pg. 952-3.

COLEGROVE, HENRY G., son of BENJAMIN (preceding), was born 30 Apr. 1819, Norwich Twp., McKean Co., Penn.; and came to Medina Twp., Lenawee Co., Mich. in 1843. He returned to Clearfield, Penn. where he married on 22 May 1844 to HARRIET (COLEMAN), and they returned to Medina Twp. Children: 1. HERMAN b. ca. 1846 (m. Gettie VanWort); 2. COLEMAN b. ca. 1850 (d. before 1888). In the 1850 census, they were listed next door to Benjamin.

Pioneer Families of Southeastern Michigan

COLEGROVE, HOLDEN born ca. 1799, and wife, LUCY, born ca. 1797, both in Rhode Island, were listed in the 1850 census of Madison Twp., Lenawee Co., Mich. with ALONZO, age 26; & ELLEN, age 20, both b. NY, in their household.

COLEGROVE, JOHN T., son of BENJAMIN (preceding), was born 22 May 1820, Norwich Twp., McKean Co., Penn.; and came to Medina Twp., Lenawee Co., Mich. He married S(SARAH) HORTENSA (HOLMES), daugher of Benjamin (also see) on 25 Aug. 1846. Children: 1. OTTIS b. ca. 1849 (m. Rosa E. Barker, had children: Vining B.; Viola H.); 2. BENJAMIN M. (preceding). Ref: P&BA-Len pg. 952-3.

COLEGROVE, WARREN born ca. 1826, NY, was listed in the 1850 census of Adrian Twp., Lenawee Co., Mich. See HOLDEN (preceding).

COLEMAN, BENJAMIN M. born ca. 1801, and wife, ANNA, born ca. 1800, both in Mass., were listed in the 1840 census index of Raisin Twp., Lenawee Co., Mich.; and in the 1850 census with OBED M., age 12; SAMUEL, age 10, both b. Mich., in their household.

COLEMAN, BENJAMIN F. born ca. 1807, NY, and wife, PHILENA, born ca. 1805, NH, were listed in the 1850 census of Adrian Twp. with BENJAMIN F. Jr., age 13; FRANCES M., age 11, both b. NY, in their household.

COLEMAN, FRANKLIN born ca. 1836, NY, was listed in the 1850 census to Madison Twp., Lenawee Co., Mich. in a Park household.

COLEMAN, HARRIET (See Henry G. Colegrove)

COLEMAN, HARVEY was listed in the 1840 census index of Franklin Twp., Lenawee Co., Mich.

COLEMAN, HENRY born ca. 1793, Mass., and wife, ELIZA, born ca. 1808, NY, were listed in the 1850 census of Rome Twp., Lenawee Co., Mich. with NANCY C., age 22; SOPHRONA, age 21, ALANSON, age 15, all b. Mass.; & ALVIN H., age 1, b. Mich. (m. Mary Richardson, dau. of James M., also see), in their household. COLEMAN, JOHN (See John Monahan^2)

COLES also see COLE

COLES, HARRIET born Conn. (See Ezra Alger).

COLLAR also see COLLER

COLLAR, GEORGE, born ca. 1825, NY, was listed in the 1850 census of Madison Twp., Lenawee Co., Mich. (may be he listed again in household of JOSHUA D., following).

COLLAR, JOSHUA D. born ca. 1792, Rhode Island, and wife, HANNAH, born ca. 1798, NY, were listed in the 1840 census index of Adrian Twp., Lenawee Co., Mich.; and in the 1850 census of Adrian Twp. with GEORGE W., age 23; CORDELIA, age 21; EMELINE R., age 18; all b. NY; and ANN, age 12 b. Mich., in their household.

COLLER also see COLLAR

COLLER, CHRISTIAN G. born ca. 1824, NY, was listed as head of household in the 1850 census of Tecumseh Twp., Lenawee Co., Mich., with (wife?) SARAH, born ca. 1830, NY; and CATHARINE (mother?), age 46, b. Penn., in the household.

COLLER, JAMES born ca. 1821, NY, and wife, AMANDA, born ca. 1827, Penn., were listed in the 1850 census of Macon Twp., Lenawee Co., Mich. with SARAH, age 1, b. Mich., in the household.

COLLER, JESSE B. born ca. 1798, NJ, and wife, SARAH, born ca. 1800, Penn., were listed in the 1840 census index of Macon Twp., Lenawee Co., Mich.; and in the 1850 census with CATHARINE, age 24; LESTER, age 18; ELI, age 15, all b. NY; and Phebe Rice, age 68, b. VT, in the household. Also possibly their children: ROSINA (m. Michael Hendershott, also see, Macon Twp., July 1834); & JAMES (preceding). Ref: P&BA-Len pg. 390-3.

COLLER, LEWIS born ca. 1828, NY, is listed in the 1850 census of Tecumseh Twp., Lenawee Co., Mich. It is probably he who married on 17 Feb. 1852 to ISABELLA A. (MILLER) of Tecumseh; and it may be he of Tecumseh who married SARAH A. (ARTMAN) of Sparta, Livingston Co., NY on 5 Apr. 1855. Note CHRISTIAN, preceding.

COLLER, PETER born ca. 1826, NY, was listed in the 1850 census of Tecumseh Twp., Lenawee Co., Mich. Note CHRISTIAN G., preceding.

COLLER, THOMAS married MARGARET (HENDERSHOTT) and resided in Lenawee Co., Mich. He died ca. 1849 as a young man, leaving known daughter, ALMEDA M. b. ca. 1846 (m. Alanson B. Bangs, also see). Margaret married again to Samuel S. Henry (also see). Ref: P&BA-Len pg. 910-1.

COLLIER see COLLER & COLYER

COLLINS also see COLLONS

COLLINS, A. D. of Fulton Co., Ohio married a daughter of Daniel Boody (also see). Ref: P&BA-Len pg. 1007-8.

COLLINS, ALLEN, son of ISAAC (following), born 26 Aug. 1843, Macon Twp., Lenawee Co., Mich.; married in Macon Twp. on 6 Oct. 1869 to AUGUSTA (MAPLES), daughter of Albert (also see). They settled first in Tecumseh Twp.; but moved in 1875 to Macon Twp. Children: 1. AGNES J.; 2. NINA E.; 3. LEROY M.; 4. ISAAC W. Ref: P&BA-Len pg. 513-4.

COLLINS, CHARLES born ca. 1821, and wife, CLARA, born ca. 1822, both in England, were listed in the 1850 census of Madison Twp., Lenawee Co., Mich. with REBECCA C., age 7, b. NY, in their household. Note JOHN b. England, following.

COLLINS, EDITH born 30 Mar. 1797, NY (See Moses Bennett, son of Jeremiah).

COLLINS, ELI (possibly son of JAMES, following) born ca. 1815, NJ, and wife, MARY A., born ca. 1826, NY, were listed in the 1850 census of Macon Twp., Lenawee Co., Mich. with JOHN, age 3; JAMES, age 1, both b. Mich., in their household.

COLLINS, ELIZABETH M. b. Chester, Mass. (See Amandas Sizer).

COLLINS, ELLEN (See Richard R. Britten)

COLLINS, HANNAH, probably born in Monmouth Co., NJ, married Gabriel Mills (also see) in 1827, and moved to Macon Twp., Lenawee Co., Mich. Ref: P&BA-Len pg. 473-4 & 1053-4.

COLLINS, ISAAC, son of JAMES (following), was born ca. 1813, Monmouth Co., NJ, and moved to Macon Twp., Lenawee Co., Mich. at age 18. He married MARY A. (ALLEN) born ca. 1823, Prince Edward Island, Canada (who had come with her parents to Macon Twp.) There were 6 children, names not all stated. Those listed in the 1850 census of Macon Twp.: 1. (JAMES) ALBERT b. 2 Dec. 1841 (m. Abbie J. Harriott, dau. of William, also see); 2. ALLEN (preceding); 3. SOPHIA b. ca. 1846; 4. CHARLES E. b. 20 Sept. 1848, Macon Twp. (unmarried). After Isaac's death, Mary A. married Andrew Wilson of Tecumseh. Ref: P&BA-Len pg. 192.

COLLINS, JAMES born ca. 1783, NJ, married in New Jersey, where his first wife (name not stated) died; and he came to Macon Twp., Lenawee Co., Mich. in 1831. He returned to New Jersey and married again (name not stated), and brought her Macon Twp.; and in the 1850 census of Macon Twp., he was head of household with RACHEL, age 38; ELIZABETH, age 43; JAMES, age 23, all b. NJ; and Amy Dillingham (perhaps another daughter), age 43, b. NJ with 3 children (See Dillingham). Known son by 1st marriage, ISAAC (preceding); and probably ELI (preceding); JOSEPH & SAMUEL (following); and possibly HANNAH (preceding). James died in 1864, Macon Twp. Ref: P&BA-Len pg. 192.

COLLINS, JAMES born ca. 1810, VT (See JOHN, b. Vt, following)

COLLINS, JAMES born ca. 1806, NY (See WILLIAM, following).

COLLINS, JOHN born ca. 1815, & JAMES born ca. 1810, both b. VT, were listed in the 1850 census of Rollin Twp., Lenawee Co., Mich. in the household of Joseph S. Allen (also see).

COLLINS, JOHN born ca. 1820, England, was listed in the 1850 census of Hudson Twp., Lenawee Co., Mich. Note CHARLES, preceding.

COLLINS, JOSEPH, probably son of JAMES, born ca. 1808, NJ, was listed adjacent to James in the 1840 census index of Macon Twp., Lenawee Co., Mich.; and in the 1850 census listed wife, ELIZABETH "BETSEY" (WHEELER), daughter of James (also see); and MARY, age 8; JAMES E., age 7; JOHN A., age 6; WHEELER M., age 4; SARAH M., age 2, all b. Mich., in his household.

COLLINS, MARY A. came to Lenawee Co., Mich. in 1854 with her parents (names not stated), both natives of NY, and her mother died in 1886; and her father was residing in Adrian in 1888. Mary A. married Richard C. Fuller (also see). Ref: P&BA-Len pg. 365-6.

COLLINS, MORGAN L. was listed in the 1840 census index of Adrian Twp., Lenawee Co., Mich.

COLLINS, SAMUEL, possibly son of JAMES (preceding), was born ca. 1820, NJ; and his wife, MARY J., was born ca. 1831, NY, and they were in the 1850 census of Macon Twp., Lenawee Co., Mich. with SOPHIA, age 2, b. Mich., in the household.

COLLINS, SIMEON born ca. 1820, and wife, PHEBE, born ca. 1826, both in NY, were listed in the 1850 census of Rollin Twp., Lenawee Co., Mich. with EDWARD, age 3/12, b. Mich., in the household.

COLLINS, WILLIAM born ca. 1810, NY, and wife, JERUSHA, born ca. 1816, VT, were listed in the 1850 census of Madison Twp., Lenawee Co., Mich. with CAROLINE E., age 9, b. VT; and HENRY E., age 6; EDWARD F., age 2, both b. Mich.; and JAMES, age 44, b. NY, probably his brother, in their household.

COLLONS also see COLLINS

COLLONS, JOHN (See Samuel Hopkins, son of Levi)

COLLUM, JONATHAN was listed in the 1840 census index of Macon Twp., Lenawee Co., Mich. with MATTHIAS & WILLIAM, adjacent, and none of them appear in the 1850 census.

COLTON, T. G. Rev. of Hudson, Lenawee Co., Mich. was father of MARY (m. John K. Boies, also see, as 2nd wife).

COLVIN, ABRAM born ca. 1814, and wife, ANGELINA, born ca. 1813, both in NY, were listed in the 1850 census of Palmyra Twp., Lenawee Co., Mich. with ANNE M., age 5; LUCY I., age 3, both b. Mich., in the household. Also see GEORGE & ISAAC A., following.

COLVIN, GEORGE born ca. 1808, NY, and wife, MARY ANN, born ca. 1816, Mass., were listed in the 1840 census index of Palmyra Twp., Lenawee Co., Mich.; and in the 1850 census with WILLIAM H., age 15; ELIZABETH, age 12; SARAH C., age 4; FREEMAN R., age 9/12, all b. Mich., in their household. Note JOHN who was adjacent in the 1840 census index of Palmyra Twp.

COLVIN, HOSEA born ca. 1807, and wife, SOPHIA, born ca. 1814, both in England, were listed in the 1850 census of Madison Twp., Lenawee Co., Mich. with HANNAH, age 18; TEYPHINA?, age 16, both b. NY; and CATHARINE, age 9; CHARLES, age 7, ELIZABETH, age 5, all b. Ohio, in their household.

COLVIN, ISAAC A. born ca. 1805, NY, and wife, ELIZABETH (CRANE) moved from Palmyra, NY to Madison Twp., Lenawee Co., Mich. before 1834. They moved to Pittsfield, Hillsdale Co., Mich. in 1837, but returned to Palmyra Twp. by 1847. Apparently they also lived in Hudson, Mich. as Elizabeth died there. He married before 1850 to NANCY (TUCKER), born ca. 1806, NY. They were listed in the 1850 census of Palmyra Twp. with the following children in the household (not known which wife is mother): 1. PHILA b. ca. 1828; 2. GEORGE b. ca. 1829; 3. LYDIA b. ca. 1832, all b. NY; 4. JOHN (following); 5. HARVEY b. ca. 1841; 6. DELORA b. ca. 1846, Mich. Isaac A. was said to have gone "west" and was never heard from again. Nancy died in 1884, Hudson, Mich. Ref: P&BA-Len pg. 193.

COLVIN, JAMES B., son of WILLIAM (following), was born 5 May 1826, Groveland, Livingston Co., Mich.; and he came to Raisin Twp., Lenawee Co., Mich. with his parents. He married HARRIET A. (TILTON), daughter of William (also see) on 27 Jan. 1856, and settled in Raisin Twp. Children: 1. JOSEPHINE L. b. 25 Sept. 1857; 2. HERBERT J. b. 12 Oct. 1860; 3. NORA B. b. 27 June 1870. Ref: P&BA-Len pg. 687-8

COLVIN, JOHN was listed in the 1840 census of Palmyra Twp., Lenawee Co., Mich. adjacent to GEORGE (preceding); and near NEHEMIAH (following).

COLVIN, JOHN born ca. 1815, Ireland, and wife, DINA, age 27, b. NY, were listed in the 1850 census of Raisin Twp., Lenawee Co., Mich. with PASCHAL P., age 6; JOHN R., age 5; MARY J., age 4, all b. Mich.; and Jacob W. Parker, age 4, b. Mich., in their household.

COLVIN, JOHN, son of ISAAC A. (preceding), b. 2 Apr. 1834, Madison Twp., Lenawee Co., Mich., married on 17 Nov. 1864 to ELLEN M. (LIVESAY), daughter of James (also see), in Adrian. Children: 1. JAMES H. b. 15 Sept. 1866; 2. BESSIE D. b. 17 May 1873. Ref: P&BA-Len pg. 193.

COLVIN, PHILANDER born ca. 1819, Virginia, is listed in the 1850 census of Raisin Twp., Lenawee Co., Mich.

COLVIN, WILLIAM born 4 Mar. 1791, Co. Antrim, Ireland, came to the US in 1818 in the company of Robert Boyd

Pioneer Families of Southeastern Michigan

and Fulton Jack, leaving behind his wife, LETITIA (SMITH), daughter of James (also see); but she joined him in 1820. They lived first in Groveland, Livingston Co., NY, but he prospected for land in Michigan in 1830. In 1832, the family moved to Raisin Twp., Lenawee Co., Mich. In the 1850 census, they were in separate households; he was listed alone in Raisin Twp., and she was in the household of daughter, Mary Potter in Tecumseh Twp. She died 5 Dec. 1878; and he died 6 Oct. 1879. Children (1st 3 b. Ireland): 1. JOHN b. 15 Dec. 1814 (to Ionia Co., Mich.); 2. JEANETT b. 15 June 1817 (m. Jacob Snyder, Macon Twp.); 3. MARY b. 15 July 1819 (m. John Potter; eventually to Oakland, CA); 4. MARGARET JANE b. 6 Sept. 1822, Brighton, NY (m. Hugh McConnell, also see); 5. WILLIAM b. 19 Feb. 1824, Groveland, NY (Larned, Pawnee Co., KS); 6. JAMES B.(preceding); 7. ELIZABETH b. 6 Feb. 1829, Raisin Twp.; 8. CAROLINE N. b. 1 May 1831. Ref: P&BA-Len pg. 687-8. (Note ELISA, age 6, b. Mich. was in the household with Letitia in 1850, possibly a granddaughter.)

COLWELL, CALVIN C., son of DANIEL^3 (following), born 15 Jan. 1830, came with his parents from Ontario Co., NY to Michigan. He lived in Wheatland, Hillsdale Co., Mich. until age 16, the moved to Hudson Twp., Lenawee Co. Mich., and lived with his uncle JOHN (following). He served in the Civil War in Berdan's Sharpshooters, Co. C. He married 5 Dec. 1867 to MARGARET (VANDEMARK), daughter of Henry (also see), and settled in Hudson Twp. Children: 1. CRIFF; 2. MAUD A. Ref: P&BA-Len pg. 820-2.

COLWELL, DANIEL^1 and wife, MERCY (HOPKINS), were born in Rhode Island, and she died there. He was a pioneer to Sempronius, Cayuga Co., NY, where he died at age 95. Known son, DANIEL^2 (following). Ref: P&BA-Len pg. 820-1 & 823-4.

COLWELL, DANIEL^2, son of DANIEL^1 (preceding), born Rhode Island, came as a young man with his father to NY, and married in Richfield, Otsego Co., NY to THANKFUL (PAYNE) also born Rhode Island (but had come at age 10 with parents to NY). About 1801, after the birth of 2 children, they moved to near Seneca Castle, Ontario Co., NY. He died there at age 45. They had 12 children (all names not stated). Known children: JOHN (following); DANIEL (following); ANGELINE BURLINGAME (m. William S. Carson, also see); CHRISTOPHER b. ca. 1815 (m. Catherine b. 1820, NY, Hudson Twp. in 1850 census); WILLIAM G. (mother lived with him in Ontario Co., NY); OLIVER S. (following). Thankful married again to Nathan Whitney in Seneca Castle, NY, whom she survived, and she died at age 85. Ref: P&BA-Len pg. 820-1 & 823-4.

COLWELL, DANIEL, son of DANIEL^2 (preceding), was born ca. 1804, Seneca Castle, Ontario Co., NY. He married CYNTHIA (SANDERSON), daughter of Deacon Sanderson of Barre, NY, and they settled first in Barre. In 1836, they removed to Rome Twp., Lenawee Co., Mich. He sold out and moved to Hillsdale Co., Mich. where he died in 1840, age 36. Known son, CALVIN C. (preceding). Cynthia married again and remained in Hillsdale Co. Ref: P&BA-Len pg. 820-2.

COLWELL, JOHN, son of DANIEL^2 (preceding), born ca. 1803, and wife, HULDAH, born ca. 1801, both in NY, were listed in the 1850 census of Hudson Twp., Lenawee Co., Mich. with LUCY, age 14; and nephew, CALVIN C. (son of Daniel, preceding), in their household. John died 30 Apr. 1860, age 57; and she died in 1882, age 82, Hudson Twp.

COLWELL, OLIVER S., son of DANIEL^2 (preceding), was born 13 June 1820, and remained in Seneca Castle, NY until 1841, then came to Hudson Twp., Lenawee Co., Mich. He returned to NY where he married on 2 Sept. 1841 to SYBIL (WHITNEY), daughter of Joel^2 (also see). They settled in Hudson Twp., Lenawee Co., Mich. near brother, JOHN (preceding). Children: 1. WILLIAM G. b. ca. 1843 (served in Civil War in Berdan's Sharpshooters; later to Lawrence, KS); 2. MARTHA "MATTIE" b. ca. 1845 (m. J. J. Wood; she d. age 38, Hudson, Mich.); 3. LIBBIE M. (m. Clarence E. Root, Flint, Mich.); 4. son (name not stated, d. infancy). Ref: P&BA-Len pg. 823-4.

COLYER also see COLLER

COLYER, WILLIAM born ca. 1810, England, and wife, OLIVE E., born ca. 1820, NY, were listed in the 1850 census of Blissfield Twp., Lenawee Co., Mich. with WILLIAM HENRY (following); JOHN W., age 3; CLARENCE R., age 2, all b. Mich., and Laura Burnam, age 8, b. Mich., in their household.

COLYER, WILLIAM HENRY, son of WILLIAM (preceding), born 6 May 1843, Blissfield Twp., Lenawee Co., Mich., married there on 25 Oct. 1863 to MARY E. (VANDYNE), daughter of George (also see). William H. served in the 11th Mich. Inf. during the Civil War. The lived in Blissfield Twp. Children: 1. GEORGE OTIS; 2. ADA BLANCHE; 3. CLARENCE WILLIAM; 4. CASSIUS M.; 5. CLIFFORD HENRY. Ref: P&BA-Len pg. 1151.

COMBS, HENRY P. Dr., son of JOHN (following), was born 19 June 1820, Onondaga Co., NY. He came to Lenawee Co., Mich., and studied in Adrian, and also in Cleveland, Ohio. In 1850, he was residing in Rome Twp., Lenawee Co., Mich. in home of his future father-in-law. He married in 1858 to LUCY A. (SHARER), daughter of David (also see), and they settled in Rome Twp. Children: 1. JOHN H. b. 20 Dec. 1861 (m. Nellie E. Williams, had dau., Alice E.); 2. ALICE E. b. 1872 (d. 1872). Ref: P&BA-Len pg. 960-1.

COMBS, JOHN was born ca. 1799, New Hampshire, and went to Onondaga Co., NY at an early date. He married there in 1816 to MARIA S. (PLATT), daughter of Henry S. (also see). John died at age 34. Known son, Dr. HENRY P. (preceding). Maria married second to Joseph Rhodes (also see). Ref: P&BA-Len pg. 960-1.

COMFORT, AARON born ca. 1800, and wife, ANN, born ca. 1803, both in Penn., were listed in the 1840 census index of Raisin Twp., Lenawee Co., Mich.; and in the 1850 census of Raisin Twp. with JANE, age 22; WOOLSTON, age 16; MOSES, age 14, all b. Penn., in their household. ELWOOD, age 28, b. Penn., listed in another household in Raisin Twp.; and JONATHAN J., age 20, b. Penn., listed in a household in Ridgeway Twp., probably belong to this family.

COMFORT, MARY (See Silas Odell)

COMFORT, SALLY (See Philip DePuy)

COMPTON, AMANDA b. ca. 1806, VT, & reared In Wayne Co., NY (See Ira Packard).

COMPTON, ELMER came from NY to Fairfield Twp., Lenawee Co., Mich. before 1840. He married EXPERIENCE (EDDY), daughter of Abraham (also see); and he died in 1850 while visiting in NY state. She married second to Dr. Francis Grandy (also see). Ref: P&BA-Len pg. 576-7. Note JOHN, following, only family listed in Fairfield Twp., Lenawee Co. in 1840.

COMPTON, JOHN born ca. 1797, and wife, MARY, born ca. 1799, both in NJ, apparently lived in NY prior to 1830, and were listed in the 1840 census index of Fairfield Twp., Lenawee Co. Mich. In the 1850 census they listed CELINA, age 20, b. NY, in their household.

COMSTOCK, ADDISON J., born ca. 1803, NY, was listed in the 1830 census of Lenawee Co., Territory of Mich., with males: 2 20-30; & females 2 20-30 & 1 under 5 (obviously two families). In the 1840 census index of Adrian Twp., Lenawee Co., Mich. he was listed adjacent to JARED & WARNER (following); and in the 1850 census listed wife, SARAH, born ca. 1806, NY; and ISAAC D., age 16; DARIUS E., age 13; CHARLES H., age 10; ADDISON J., age 4; SARAH E., age 1, all b. Mich. Listed last in their household, relationships not known, were PHEBE, age 25; DARIUS, age 22, both b. NY. Note DARIUS, following.

COMSTOCK, ALLEN born ca. 1821, and wife, SARAH, born ca. 1815, both b. NY, were listed in the 1850 census of Tecumseh Twp., Lenawee Co., Mich. with EMELINE, age 1, b. Mich., in their household.

COMSTOCK, ALMOT (See James L. EnEarl)

COMSTOCK, ANNA born ca. 1782, NJ, was listed in the 1850 census of Raisin Twp., Lenawee Co., Mich. in the household of Artemus & Phebe Dean.

COMSTOCK, CALVIN B. born ca. 1822, and wife, FANNA M., born ca 1826, both in NY, were listed in the 1850 census of Raisin Twp., Lenawee Co., Mich. with FRANCIS O., age 1, b. Mich., all in the household of Sylvenus & Esther Westgate.

COMSTOCK, DARIUS, son of NATHAN (following), was listed in the 1830 census of Lenawee Co, Mich. Territory, with males: 1 60-70; 5 20-30; 2 15-20; 1 under 5; females: 1 40-50; 2 20-30; 1 5-10. He was listed in the 1840 census index of Raisin Twp.; but was not listed in the 1850 census. Note ADDISON J., preceding.

COMSTOCK, DAVID born ca. 1784, Rhode Island, was listed in the 1850 census of Ogden Twp., Lenawee Co., Mich. in the household of Isaac Thomas, age 32, and wife, Elizabeth A., age 28, both b. Ohio (Elizabeth may be a Comstock?). Also note ESAH & JASPER, following.

COMSTOCK, EDWIN born ca. 1817, and wife, EMELINE, born ca. 1828, both in NY, were listed in the 1850 census of Adrian Twp., Lenawee Co., Mich. with ALICE, age 2, b. Mich, and (mother?) SALLY, age 69, b. NY, in their household.

COMSTOCK, ESAH? (See DAVID, preceding) born ca. 1813, NY, and wife, MARY, born ca. 1819, VT, were listed in the 1850 census of Ogden Twp., Lenawee Co., Mich. with ALFRED, age 9, b. Ohio; MARY, age 6; ANDREW, age 4; HENRY, age 4/12, all b. Mich., in their household. He was next door to DAVID in 1850 census.

COMSTOCK, GILES, son of SALMON (preceding), was born 5 Aug. 1817, Cooperstown, Otsego Co., NY; and he moved to Sylvania, Lucas Co., Ohio, where he married ELECTA E. (VROOMAN), daughter of John A. (also see). They were pioneers to Whiteford, Monroe Co., Mich. Known daughter, ROSE E., born 13 May 1844, Monroe Co., Mich. (m. Thomas G. Chandler, also see). Ref: P&BA-Len pg. 483-5. Note: In the 1840 census index, there was a BETSEY listed in Summerfield, Monroe Co., Mich.

COMSTOCK, HORACE W., son of WARNER M. (following), was born 19 Dec. 1825, Lockport, Niagara Co., NY. He married FANNY (COMSTOCK), daughter of JARED (following). No children's names stated. Ref: P&BA-Len pg. 648-9.

COMSTOCK, JARED was born ca. 1798, Mass., and wife, CATHERINE (HALL), born ca. 1796, Conn., moved from Niagara Co., NY to Adrian Twp., Lenawee Co., Mich. in 1835. They settled in Raisin Twp., Lenawee Co., Mich.; and went to Palmyra Twp. in 1846, then returned to Raisin Twp. before 1850. He died in 1865; and she died in 1882, age 84, at the home of a daughter. Children (all names not stated): Known daughter, MARY b. 22 Dec. 1828, Niagara Co., NY (m. Thomas Underwood, also see). Following were in Jared's household in 1850 census: JOSEPH b. ca. 1823; ABIGAIL, age 22, NATHAN, age 18, all b. NY; ALBERT, age 13, b. Mich.; known daughter, FANNY b. 28 Dec. 1842, Raisin Twp. (m. HORACE W., preceding). Ref: P&BA-Len pg. 537-8 & 648-9. Note NATHAN, following.

COMSTOCK, JASON of Cambridge, Washington Co., NY had moved before 1790 to Sunderland, Rutland Co., & Burlington, VT. He died while making a journey to market from VT to Troy, NY. Five children, all names not stated. The eldest son, THOMAS (following). Ref: P&BA-Len pg. 413-4. Note: In the 1800 census index of Washington Co., NY were listed: DANIEL; JOSHUA; ROSWELL; & SAMUEL.

COMSTOCK, JASPER born ca. 1811, NY, and wife, FANNY, born ca. 1816, Penn, were listed in the 1850 census of Ogden Twp., Lenawee Co., Mich. with HULDAH, age 12; LUCETTA, age 11; NATHAN, age 8; DAVID, age 7, all b. Ohio; and ELBRIDGE, age 4; CHARLES, age 1, both b. Mich., in their household. Also note DAVID, & ESAH, preceding.

COMSTOCK, JOB S. was listed in the 1830 census of Lenawee Co., Mich. Territory, with males: 1 30-40; 1 10-15; 1 5-10; 1 under 5; females: 1 30-40; 1 10-15; 1 5-10; 1 under 5, in the household. He resided in Rome Twp., Lenawee Co., Mich. in 1835, and was in the 1840 census index.

COMSTOCK, JOHN, son of NATHAN (following), was born 1774(8?), Mass. He married in 1801 to ROWENA (BRADISH) who was born 30 Sept. 1786, Cummington, Mass. They moved first to Ontario Co., NY; and were the first settlers to Lockport, Niagara Co. NY with his brothers, ZENO & DARIUS (preceding). In 1830, they moved to Palmyra Twp., Lenawee Co.., Mich., and later to Raisin Twp., where he died in 1851; and she died 8 Feb. 1870.

In the 1850 census, their ages were listed as 72 & 62, respectively, and in the household were MARY J., age 25; CHARLES V., age 32, both b. NY. Known son, WARNER M. (following). Ref: P&BA-Len pg. 648-9.

Pioneer Families of Southeastern Michigan

COMSTOCK, JOHN T. born ca. 1808, and wife, RHOENA, born ca. 1809, both in NY, were listed in the 1850 census of Rollin Twp., Lenawee Co., Mich. with ELIZABETH, age 17, b. NY; & EDNA, age 14; AMY, age 12; CHARITY, age 4, all b. Mich., in their household. Note: It is probably this daughter, CHARITY C., who m. John U. Harkness, probably son of Gideon (also see). Ref: P&BA-Len pg. 765-6. Note SAMUEL, following.

COMSTOCK, LAURISON A., born ca. 1826, and wife, HARRIET, born ca. 1833, both in NY, listed in the 1850 census of Raisin Twp., Lenawee Co., Mich. between JOHN & PEACE (following). It may be he listed as "LOTT," same age, with wife, HARRIET, same age, listed in the 1850 census of Palmyra Twp.

COMSTOCK, MILO was counted in the 1830 census of Lenawee Co., Mich. Territory with males: 1 30-40; 1 10-15; 1 under 5; & females: 1 30-40; 2 5-10 in the household. He was listed in the 1840 census index adjacent to JOHN & DARIUS (preceding).

COMSTOCK, NATHAN moved from Mass. to Farmington, Ontario Co., NY in 1788. His known sons: JOHN (preceding); ZENO; & DARIUS (preceding). Also note RHODY S. (following), who named a son, Darius C.; and JARED (preceding). Note: In the 1800 census index of Ontario Co., NY were listed (2) NATHAN; KILLIUS?; DARIUS; OTIS; & SAMUEL

COMSTOCK, NATHAN was listed in the 1830 census of Lenawee Co., Mich. Territory, with males: 1 20-30; 1 15-20; females: 1 20-30; 2 under 5, in the household. There was an "N" listed in Ypsilanti Twp., Washtenaw Co., Mich. in the 1840 census index. Also there was a child, NATHAN, age 3, born Mich., listed in the household of Erastus & Cynthia C. Aldridge in the 1850 census.

COMSTOCK, NOAH B. born ca. 1789, NY, and wife, SOPHIA, born ca. 1805, Penn., settled in Blissfield Twp., Lenawee Co., Mich. in 1835. In the 1850 census of Palmyra Twp., Lenawee Co., Mich., the listed AMELIA, age 15; MORTIMER, age 11; MARY A., age 13; & HARRISON, age 6, all b. Mich., in their household.

COMSTOCK, NOAH born ca. 1815, NY, and wife, LAURA, born ca. 1825, Ohio, were listed in the 1850 census of Blissfield Twp., Lenawee Co., Mich. with HELEN, age 7; ALICE age 6, both b. Mich., in their household.

COMSTOCK, PEACE (Mrs.), age 51, b. NY, was listed as head of household in the 1850 census of Raisin Twp., Lenawee Co., Mich. with CALEB, age 19; PERRY, age 15; WILLIAM, age 11; HELEN, age 6, all born Mich., in her household.

COMSTOCK, RHODY S. born ca. 1850, NY (See Curran Bradish).

COMSTOCK, SALMON (SOLOMON) was born in 1760 in Cooperstown, Otsego Co., NY and remained there. Known son, GILES (preceding). Ref: P&BA-Len pg. 483-5. Note: In the 1800 census index of Otsego Co., NY, there were (2) SOLOMON; BENAJAH; HEMAN; ISRAEL; LUTHER; & WILLIAM listed.

COMSTOCK, SAMUEL born ca. 1805, and wife, RHODA, born ca. 1807, both in NY, were listed in the 1840 census index of Rollin Twp., Lenawee Co., Mich.; and in the 1850 census of Rollin Twp. listed JARED, age 22; FARTHINGILL, age 20, both b. NY; & ELMARINDA, age 18; MATILDA, age 15; HENRIETTA, age 13; ADDISON, age 6, all b. Ohio. Also note SUSANNA, listed adjacent to Samuel in the 1840 census index. Note NATHAN, preceding.

COMSTOCK, STEPHEN born ca. 1819, Ohio, was head of household in the 1850 census of Rollin Twp., Lenawee Co., Mich. with BETSEY (probably mother), age 59, b. VT, in his household.

COMSTOCK, SUSANNA was head of household in the 1840 census index of Rollin Twp., Lenawee Co., Mich. adjacent to SAMUEL (preceding).

COMSTOCK, THOMAS, son of JASON (preceding), born 6 Oct. 1790, VT, after the death of his father, lived with his grandparents in Cambridge, Washington Co., NY, where he married on 5 Feb. 1814 to LUCY (SMITH), daughter of Sanford (also see), b. ca. 1793, NY, and they moved to Vermont. About 1816, they removed to Chautauqua Co., NY; and about 1834 to Lenawee Co., Mich. (not listed in the 1840 census index; there is an "I" listed in Adrian Twp., possibly an indexing error?). They were listed in the 1850 census of Palmyra Twp.; and he died there in 1872 at the home of a daughter. Known children: 1. SANFORD S. (d. 1835, Palmyra Twp.); 2. SENECA T. (d. 1835, Palmyra Twp.); 3. CHARLOTTE M. b. Harmony, NY (m. Edwin Underwood, also see). Ref: P&BA-Len pg. 413-4.

COMSTOCK, URIAS (this may be Darius?) lived in Raisin Twp., Lenawee Co., Mich. in 1831; and William Ash resided with him. Ref: P&BA-Len pg. 211.

COMSTOCK, WALTER was listed in the 1830 census of Monroe Co., Mich. Territory with males: 1 40-50; 1 10-15- 1 under 5; females: 1 30-40; 1 15-20; 2 10-15 in the household.

COMSTOCK, WARNER M., son of JOHN (preceding), was born 8 Sept. 1802 in Ontario Co., NY; and he married on 7 Jan. 1825 to MARY M. (PERRY), daughter of Capt. William (also see). They moved to Adrian Twp., Lenawee Co., Mich. in 1836. She died 14 Jan. 1876, Adrian. Children: 1. HORACE W. (preceding); 2. MARIAN B. b. 28 Sept. 1829 (m. Jerome B. Chaffee, also see); 3. ELLEN R. b. 26 Dec. 1832 (m. Jonathan F. Seymour, Adrian); 4. ALMIRA S. b. 1 Jan. 1835 (m. Alfred H. Wood, also see); and 2 daughters (names not stated) died infancy. Ref: P&BA-Len pg. 494-5 & 648-9.

CONDITT, BENJAMIN (or Condict?) born ca. 1813, NJ, and wife, MIRIAM M., born ca. 1827, NY, were listed in the 1850 census of Madison Twp., Lenawee Co., Mich. with JAMES, age 1, b. Mich.; and HIRAM (following) in their household.

CONDITT, E. A. (See Oren E. Green)

CONDITT, HIRAM born ca. 1821, NJ, and wife, FRANCES, age 26, born NY, were listed in the household of BENJAMIN (preceding).

CONE, JOSEPH (See John Dubois)

CONE, MARY J. (See Benjamin I. Laing)

CONGER, DAVID married RACHEL (WILBER) and they first resided in Rutland Co., VT., and after the birth of 8 children (all names not stated) they moved to Erie Co., NY, where he died in 1823, age 45; and she died in 1855. Known son, GEORGE (following). Ref: P&BA-Len pg. 217-8.

CONGER, GEORGE, son of DAVID (preceding), was born in Rutland Co., VT and moved with his parents to Erie

Co., NY. He married there to ELIZA (HOAG) who was born in NY. They removed to Clinton Twp., Lenawee Co., Mich in 1861; where Eliza died in 1865, age 45, leaving son, STEPHEN (following). George married second to Mrs. FRANCES (RICHARDSON) MALLARD who was born in 1820, NY. Ref: P&BA-Len pg. 217-8.

CONGER, JOHN born ca. 1818, NY, and wife, LOUISA, born ca. 1821, NY, were listed in the 1850 census of Madison Twp., Lenawee Co., Mich. with CHARLOTTE, age 9, b. NY; and CLARENCE, age 3; LOUISA A., age 6/12, both b. Mich., in their household.

CONGER, STEPHEN, son of GEORGE (preceding), married MARY E. (MISER) in Tecumseh Twp., Lenawee Co., Mich., where he died a young man, leaving children: 1. GEORGE S. (m. Anna Staiger); 2. FRANK H.; 3. ADA E.; 4. NOEL E. Mary E. married again to Norman Mattison of Tecumseh Twp. Ref: P&BA-Len pg. 217-8.

CONKHITE, JENNIE (See William Ladd)

CONKLIN was spelled variously, CONCKLIN; CONKLING in the census, so the following are listed as they were spelled in the census, sometimes they were spelled differently in the listing of the same household.

CONKLIN, ABIAH (See Daniel Underhill)

CONKLIN, AUGUSTUS born ca. 1823, and wife, REBECKA, born ca. 1826, both in NY, were listed in the 1850 census of Dover Twp., Lenawee Co., Mich. with DIANA, age 7?, b. NY; & SUSAN J., age 6?; EPHRAIM, age 4, both b. Mich., in their household.

CONKLIN, CHARLES B. (See Horatio F. Pope)

CONKLIN, ERASTUS born ca. 1815, and wife, MARY A., born ca. 1815, both in NY, were listed in the 1850 census of Hudson Twp., Lenawee Co., Mich. with WILLIAM H., age 14; NANCY A., age 8, both b. Mich., in their household.

CONKLIN, ESTHER was the daughter of a man who came from France to NY and served in the American Revolution. He had lived near Poughkeepsie, NY; and afterwards moved to Norwalk, Ohio where he died. Esther married Nathan Shaw (also see). Ref: P&BA-Len pg. 1094-5.

CONKLIN, HENRY was listed in the 1840 census index of Cambridge Twp., Lenawee Co., Mich. Note ISAAC, following.

CONKLING, HUDSON W., son of SAMUEL G. (following), was born 24 Dec. 1821, Middletown, Orange Co., NY, and came to Raisin Twp., Lenawee Co., Mich. with his parents. He married CAROLINE (GRAY), daughter of Hugh (also see). The moved in to Tecumseh by 1888. Four children (all names not stated), first 2 listed in 1850 census: 1. FRANCES E. b. ca. 1843 (m. Leroy C. Blood, son of Ezra F., also see; to Lansing, Mich.); 2. DEWITT C. b. ca. 1847 (deceased before 1888); 3. SARAH J. (m. Joseph B. Van Ness). Ref: P&BA-Len pg. 293-4.

CONKLIN, ISAAC was born ca. 1786, and wife, JANE b. ca. 1788, of Sparta, Sussex Co., NJ, were parents of ELIZABETH b. 30 Sept. 1809, Sparta (m. Peter Onsted, also see). They were listed in the 1850 census of Cambridge Twp., Lenawee Co., Mich. Ref: P&BA-Len pg. 1100-1.

CONCKLIN, JOHN D. born ca. 1810, and wife, NANCY, born ca. 1811, both in NY, were listed in the 1850 census of Adrian Twp., Lenawee Co., Mich. with CHARLES, age 12, b. Mich., in the household. Note: There was a John D. listed in Eaton Co., Mich. in the 1840 census index.

CONKLIN, MERRITT E., son of SAMUEL (following), was born 2 Apr. 1835, Livingston Co., NY, and came to Raisin Twp., Lenawee Co., Mich. in 1861; and moved to Tecumseh in 1878. He married 30 Nov. 1864 to JULIA A. (STEARNES), daughter of Alpheus (also see). Children: 1. NELLIE E.; 2. HATTIE E.; 3. CLARENCE A. Ref: P&BA-Len pg. 827.

CONKLING, NATHANIEL of Goshen, Orange Co., NY had a will dated 1 Dec. 1815, and probated 16 Jan. 1816, Liber F, pg.11. Named were wife, MARTHA; Sons: ENOS; JOSHUA; NATHANIEL (d. 1812); and SAMUEL (note Samuel G., following); and daughters: MARY; HELEN (m. JOSEPH CONKLING). Also mentioned were BENJAMIN (deceased, with relationship not given); and grandchildren: Children of Nathaniel: MARGARET GREGG; ANNA COLEMAN; NATHANIEL; ELIZABETH & CHRISTIAN; and grandson, son of Samuel: COE. Witnesses were DAVID CONKLING; James I. Smith; Daniel Poppino; Exex.: Sons, ENOS & JOSHUA.

CONKLING, RICHARD born ca. 1824, and wife, HULDAH, born ca. 1829, both in NY, were listed in the 1850 census of Hudson Twp., Lenawee Co., Mich.

CONCKLIN, ROYAL born ca. 1826, NY, and wife, JANE A., born ca. 1833, Canada, were listed in the 1850 census of Adrian Twp., Lenawee Co., Mich.

CONKLING, SAMUEL (note NATHANIEL, preceding) was born 11 Apr. 1797, Orange Co., NY; and married there to JULIA A. (CORVIN), born 1800. In 1833, they removed to Raisin Twp., Lenawee Co., Mich.; where she died in 1876. He died in Tecumseh in 1883. There were 5 sons and 7 daughters, and 4 daughters died infancy, with 4 sons & 1 daughter surviving in 1888, names not stated. Known son, HUDSON W. (preceding); and the following were in Samuel's household in the 1850 census of Raisin Twp.: ARMINDA, age 24; SAMUEL L., age 22; EMELINE, age 21 (m. Alonzo F. Bidwell, Coldwater, Mich., 1 June 1853), all b. NY; and JOHN, age 13; DELIA, age 7, both b. Mich. Ref: P&BA-Len pg. 293-4.

CONKLIN, SAMUEL was born Livingston Co., NY and married there to LUCETTA (BRASIE). They remained until 1869, then moved to Tecumseh Twp., Lenawee Co., Mich. He died 29 Apr. 1877, age 68; and she died 12 Aug. 1877, age 64. Four sons and 6 daughters, names not stated. Known son, MERRITT E. (preceding). Ref: P&BA-Len pg. 827.

CONKLIN, WILLIAM was listed in the 1840 census index of Raisin Twp., Lenawee Co., Mich. (Also see Thomas Tumison).

CONLEY, ANNA married Watson C. (or Weston C.) Crabbs. Her name may be Anna Cawley.

CONNER also see CONNOR

CONNER, GEORGE born ca. 1808, and wife, MARGARET, born ca. 1828, both in Germany, were listed in the 1850 census of Riga Twp., Lenawee Co., Mich. with CATHARINE, age 4/12, b. Mich. in their household.

CONNER, JOHN born ca. 1804, and wife, OLIVE, born ca. 1807,

Pioneer Families of Southeastern Michigan

both in NY, were listed in the 1850 census of Rome Twp., Lenawee Co., Mich. with ELIZABETH, age 12, b. NY; and MARY A., age 9; GEORGE, age 6, both b. Mich., in their household.

CONNER, SALLIE (See Henry Keyser)

CONNERY also see CONREY
CONNERY, WILLIAM married Mrs. CLARA (FARST) GEORGE, daughter of Isaac Farst, and widow of Reuben George (see both). They probably lived in Dodge City, KS. Children: 1. A. BERNICE; 2. CLARA ELIZABETH. Mrs. Connery died 7 Aug. 1880. Ref: P&BA-Len pg. 997-8.

CONNOR also see CONNER
CONNOR, MARY of Co. Kerry, Ireland (See James Moriarty)
CONNOR, STEPHEN (See Alonzo James)

CONOVER, DENNIS of Steuben Co., NY was father of JENNIE who married Chauncey M. Crego (also see) of Columbia Twp., Jackson Co. Mich.

CONREY also see CONNERY
CONREY, HENRY born ca. 1798, Mass., and wife, AMY, born ca. 1801, Conn., were listed in the 1850 census of Hudson Twp., Lenawee Co. Mich. with GEORGE W., age 18; AMY, age 15; HENRY, age 13, all born VT; and WILLIAM, age 9, b. Mich., in their household. Note WILLIAM CONNERY, preceding.

CONSAUL, J. M. married ADELAIDE B. (MORSE), b. ca. 1842, daughter of Charles C. (also see) of Medina Twp., Lenawee Co., Mich. Known children: CHARLES F.; FRED M.

CONSAULES, MARTHA (See Benjamin D. Osborn)

CONVERSE, AMASA P., son of EPHRAIM (following), born ca. 1812, and wife, HARRIET, born ca. 1817, both in Mass., were listed in the 1850 census of Medina Twp., Lenawee Co., Mich. with HARRIET M., age 11; NELSON J., age 4, both b. Mich., in their household.
CONVERSE, BENJAMIN, son of EPHRAIM (following), was born 29 Oct. 1813, Belchertown, Mass., and moved with his parents to Northampton, Mass. He remained until 1834, then with brother, AMASA, went to Medina Twp., Lenawee Co., Mich.; and then returned after 2 years. In 1840, he returned to Medina Twp. where he lived the rest of his life, except for 2 years that he went back to Mass. He married first in Brattleboro, VT to ELIZABETH (PLUMLEY), a native of Mass. She died 1 Aug. 1847, Medina Twp., leaving son, LEWIS H. (following). Benjamin married again in Enfield, Mass. to MARY (TYLER); and had one son, HERBERT S. (m. Della Cleveland; Ionia, Mich.). Ref: P&BA-Len pg. 1207-8.
CONVERSE, EPHRAIM, son of JAMES (following), was born 1 Dec. 1779, Brookfield, Mass., and his wife, LUCY (PRATT), was born 11 July 1778, Belchertown, Mass. They lived first in Belchertown, and afterwards in Northampton, where they remained until 1851 then moved to Medina Twp., Lenawee Co., Mich. He died 7 Nov. 1867; and she died 13 Oct. 1876. There were 6 sons and 2 daughters (all names not stated). Known sons: AMASA P. (preceding); & #5. BENJAMIN (preceding); and JAMES (following). Ref: P&BA-Len pg. 1207-8.
CONVERSE, ERASTUS born ca. 1823, NY, was listed in the 1850 census of Adrian Twp., Lenawee Co., Mich.
CONVERSE, JAMES born 11 May 1750, Brookfield, Mass., married PHEBE (PERKINS) born 25 Jan. 1753, Bridgewater, Mass. They remained in Mass. Known son, EPHRAIM (preceding). Ref: P&BA-Len pg. 1207-8.
CONVERSE, JAMES, son of EPHRAIM (preceding), born 1808, Mass., and wife, HULDAH, born ca. 1806, NY, were listed in the 1850 census of Medina Twp., Lenawee Co., Mich. with EPHRAIM P., age 19; LUCY M., age 18; SARAH S., age 16; EBENEZER P., age 14; JAMES C., age 12; HULDAH A., age 10, all b. Mass., in their household.
CONVERSE, LEWIS H., son of BENJAMIN, born 12 Sept. 1846, married on 18 Dec. 1867 to HARRIET I. (HALL), daughter of John L. (also see). Children: 1. CHARLES L.; 2. CARRIE E.; 3. LENA E. Ref: P&BA-Len pg. 1207-8.
CONVERSE, MARTIN born ca. 1824, NY, was listed in the 1850 census of Hudson Twp., Lenawee Co., Mich.
CONVERSE, REBECCA was born 1769, Windham Co., Conn., and married Noah Green, Sr. (also see). Ref: P&BA-Len pg. 914-5.

COOK, BENET born ca. 1816, Mass., and wife, SEREPTA, born ca. 1819, NY, were listed in the 1850 census of Palmyra Twp., Lenawee Co., Mihc. with HANNAH, age 9; THOMAS, age 7; EMIRILLA, age 5; ANDREW, age 4, all b. Mich., in their household.
COOK, BENJAMIN born ca. 1789, and wife, NANCY, born ca. 1795, both b. NY, were listed in the 1850 census of Raisin Twp., Lenawee Co., Mich. with EDWARD, age 13, b. NY, in the household.
COOK, CASPER (See Israel Schreder)
COOK, EDWIN, son of JOB (following), was born 30 Nov. 1812, Hadley, Mass. He married 4 Feb. 1834 to LOVICA C. (SEYMOUR), daughter of Horace (also see); and they moved to Avon, Livingston Co., NY; then to Kendall, Orleans Co., NY and lived at Holley, NY. In May 1851, they moved to Franklin Twp., Lenawee Co., Mich. She died there 10 Oct. 1875. Children: 1. SARAH S. b. 16 Mar. 1837 (m/1 Edward W. Turner; m/2 F. J. Smith; she d. 1 Nov. 1868, Franklin Twp.); 2. SUSAN R. b. 3 May 1839 (d. 2 Apr. 1857); 3. HENRY D. b. 13 Nov. 1842 (d. 22 May 1844); 4. EDWIN CLARENCE b. 19 May 1855 (m. Effie Pawsen, Franklin Twp.). Edwin married second to Mrs. CHARLOTTE (TILLYAR) OSBORN, daughter of William, and widow of Richard (see both). Ref: P&BA-Len pg. 352-3.
COOK, EMMA (See Edwin A. Knowles)
COOK, HENRY, age 12, born NY, was listed in the 1850 census of Madison Twp., Lenawee Co., Mich. in a Thompson household.
COOK, HERMAN born ca. 1813, and wife, CATHARINE, b. ca. 1824, both in NY, were listed in the 1850 census of Macon Twp., Lenawee Co., Mich. with ANN C., age 10; LEONARD S., age 6, both b. NY; & MARY A., age 4; CASPER C., age 1, both b. Mich., in their household.
COOK, HIRAM born ca. 1812, and wife, CATHARINE, born ca. 1817, both in NY, were listed in the 1850 census of Macon Twp., Lenawee Co., Mich. with ALVA? B., age 11; SUSAN A., age 4; JOHN K., age 3, all b. NY; MYRTAS?, age 1. b. Mich., in their household.

COOK, JOANNA Mrs. born ca. 1798, NJ, was head of household in the 1850 census of Raisin Twp., Lenawee Co., Mich. with LEWIS H., age 27, b. NY, in her household.

COOK, JOB was born in Mass; and married HANNAH (CAMPBELL) in Hadley, Mass. He died in 1820 at age 40. She died in Franklin Twp., Lenawee Co., Mich. at the home of a daughter. Known children: 1. EDWIN (preceding); 2. MARTHA D. (m. Turner, Franklin Twp.). Ref: P&BA-Len pg. 352-3.

COOK, JOHN B. born ca. 1824, NY, was listed in the 1850 census of Madison Twp., Lenawee Co., Mich.

COOK, LAURA born ca. 1832, NY, was listed in the 1850 census of Fairfield Twp., Lenawee Co., Mich., in the household of Nathaniel Baker, age 26, and wife, Polly, age 20.

COOK, LUTHER P. born ca. 1821, and wife, HARRIET M., born ca. 1825, both in NY, were listed in the 1850 census of Adrian Twp., Lenawee Co., Mich. with MARTIN E., age 6, b. Ohio, all in the household of Russel Hervey.

COOK, MOSES and wife, PHEBE (PERKINS), were parents of ELIZABETH, born ca. 1796, Conn., who married John J. Carpenter (also see) and settled in Fairfield Twp., Lenawee Co., Mich.

COOK, PARDON W. born ca. 1816, and wife, HARRIET, born ca. 1821, both in NY, were listed in the 1850 census of Fairfield Twp., Lenawee Co., Mich. with ELDRIDGE F., age 7, b. Ohio; and MARTHA E., age 4, b. Mich., in their household.

COOK, RICHARD B. born ca. 1821, Conn., and wife, CORNELIA, born ca. 1828, NY were listed in the 1850 census of Cambridge Twp., Lenawee Co., Mich. with JAMES, age 4; EDWARD, age 2, both born Mich., in their household. In addition there was H.?(male), age 23, ANN, age 21, and ORRIN (father?), age 71, all b. Conn.

COOK, SAMUEL was listed in the 1840 census index of Franklin Twp., Lenawee Co., Mich.

COOK, SAMUEL and wife, OLIVE ANN (COCHRAN), moved from Pennsylvania to St. Joseph Co., Mich. about 1860. She died in Mishawaka, Ind. in 1869, age 48; and he was still living in 1888 in St. Joseph Co., Mich. Known children: ADA O. b. 14 June, Erie Co., Penn. (m. Charles D. Wood, also see); JENNIE P. (m. J. O. Lendah., Denver, CO). Note: Olive Ann had son, Elus M. Shelby (also see), by first marriage. Ref: P&BA-Len pg. 719-20.

COOK, SARAH A. born ca. 1818, NY, was listed in the 1850 census of Cambridge Twp., Lenawee Co., Mich, with a child, ELLEN, age 7, b. NY, both in the household of John & Henrietta Smith. COOK, STEPHEN born ca. 1797, NY, and wife, ELIZABETH, born ca. 1798, NJ, were listed in the 1850 census of Adrian Twp., Lenawee Co., Mich.

COOK, WILLIAM born ca. 1823, Mass., was listed in the 1850 census of Adrian Twp., Lenawee Co., Mich. in a hotel.

COOKE, TEMPERANCE (See George Eddy)

COOLEY, CALEB C. born ca. 1808, and wife, PHEBE, born ca. 1820, both in VT, were listed in the 1850 census of Hudson Twp., Lenawee Co., Mich. with PHEBE J., age 9; RUPERT C., age 6, both b. Mich., in their household.

COOLEY, FANNIE born between 1801 & 1808, NY, was a sister of THOMAS M. (following), and she married Artemus Wilder (also see). Ref: P&BA-Len pg. 967-8.

COOLEY JOHN born ca. 1801, Mass, and wife, JULIA A., age 42, b. NY, were listed in the 1850 census of Seneca Twp., Lenawee Co., Mich. with no family. The "old John Cooley farm" was mentioned in the sketch of JUSTUS of Medina Twp. (following).

COOLEY, JUSTUS, son of LEONARD, was born 9 Feb. 1810 near Phelpstown, Ontario Co., NY. He married 4 Apr. 1833 to CLARISSA (BAKER), daughter of Appolos (also see); and they removed to Medina Twp., Lenawee Co., Mich. (It may be he listed in the 1840 census index of Fayette Twp., Hillsdale Co., Mich.) They resided in Medina Twp. in the 1850 census with children #1-3 & 5-10 in the household (Caroline apparently deceased): 1. MARY JANE b. ca. 1833 (m. Jason King, Gratiot Co., Mich.); 2. WILLIAM HENRY b. ca. 1835, NY; 3. ORLANDO b. ca. 1836, Mich.; 4. CAROLINE ; 5. SARAH b. ca. 1839; 6. JUSTUS b. ca. 1841 (m. Eliza Stytes, Gratiot Co. Mich.); 7. HERMAN b. ca. 1844 (m. Alice Sullen; Dakotas); 8. LUCY I. b. 25 Dec. 1845 (m. Edgar Alonzo Perry, also see); 9. RENSSELAER b. ca. 1847; 10. MILES b. ca. 1849 (m. Emma Wilson, Beadle Co.,Dak.); 11. CLARA B. (m. Charles Ashley, Medina Twp.); 12. JAMES. Orlando, Caroline, Rensslaer, & James deceased before 1888. Ref: P&BA-Len pg. 593-4.

COOLEY, LEONARD and wife, IRENA, were born and married in Mass.; but lived near Phelpstown, Ontario Co., NY ca. 1810, and eventually moved to Erie Co., NY. By 1842, they moved to Ann Arbor, Washtenaw Co., Mich. (Note: In the 1840 census index, there is a LEONARD & LEONARD, Jr. in Lodi, Washtenaw Co. Mich.) There were 4 sons and 2 daughters (all names not stated). Known son, #4. JUSTUS (preceding). Also note JOHN (preceding). Ref: P&BA-Len pg. 593-4.

COOLEY, THOMAS M. born ca. 1824, and wife, MARY E., born ca. 1829, both in NY, were listed in the 1850 census of Adrian Twp., Lenawee Co., Mich. with EUGENE, age 6/12, b. Mich., all in the household of David & Betsey Horton. (Note FANNIE, preceding).

COOMER, N. V. married ELLEN A. (OSGOOD), daughter of Josiah (also see), and they moved to Isabella Co., Mich. Children: 1. MARY FLORENCE; MARTHA VIOLET; MABEL L.; EVA L. Ref: P&BA-Len pg. 1040-1.

COONRAD also see COUNROD
COONRAD, ELVA (See Amos A. Kinney)

COOPER, GEORGE born ca. 1828, NY, and wife, HELEN, born ca. 1832, NY, were listed in the 1850 census of Seneca Twp., Lenawee Co., Mich. 2 doors from JONAS B. (following).

COOPER, H. C. (See Solomon Jeffords)

COOPER, HARRISON V.? born ca. 1826, NY, was listed in the 1850 census of Medina Twp., Lenawee Co., Mich. in the Charles Baldwin household.

COOPER, JONAS B. born ca. 1800, and wife, JULIA, born ca. 180, both in Mass., were listed in the 1850 census of Seneca Twp., Lenawee Co., Mich. with LUCY, age 10, b. Ohio; EUGENE, age 4, b. Mich., in their household. GEORGE (preceding) was 2 doors away in census.

COOPER, JOSEPH L, born ca. 1810, and wife, LOUISA, born ca. 1812, place not given, were listed in the 1850 census

Pioneer Families of Southeastern Michigan

of Adrian Twp., Lenawee Co., Mich. with FRANCES L., age 6, b. Mich., all listed in a hotel.

COOPER, MARY (See Thomas Lupton)

COOPER, NATHANIEL born ca. 1811, and wife, PARMELIA, born ca. 1813, both in NY, were listed in the 1850 census of Adrian Twp., Lenawee Co., Mich. with SALLY, age 17; HIRAM W., age 15, both b. Ohio; and PHEBE A., age 11; LYMAN, age 7; MARY A., age 1, all b. Mich., in their household.

COOPER, PORTER born ca. 1802, and wife, SARAH, born ca. 1806, both in Mass., were listed in the 1850 census of Medina Twp., Lenawee Co., Mich. with MARCY M., age 21; CHARLES, age 18, both b. Mass.; & ELIJAH, age 16; LUCY, age 11; EPHRAIM, age 9, all b. Ohio; and MARY, age 7, b. Mich., in their household.

COOPER, SARAH (See Col. Edmond B. Dewey)

COPPINS, ANNA J. (See Nicholas Amos Page)

CORBETT also spelled CORBET

CORBETT, CHESTER J., son of CLARK E. (following), was born 16 July 1833, NY, and moved to Illinois, and then to Palmyra Twp., Lenawee Co., Mich. with his parents, where he married on 16 Apr. 1861 to ALMENA J. (BIRD), daughter of William (also see). He served in the Civil War. Son, CLARK W. b. 8 Sept. 1873. Ref: P&BA-Len pg. 350.

CORBETT, CLARK E., son of ZIBA (or ZIBRA), born ca. 1801, NY, apparently lived in Illinois ca. 1839, and then moved to Palmyra Twp., Lenawee Co., Mich. In the 1850 census of Palmyra Twp., he listed in his household: LUCY, age 25; CHESTER (preceding), both b. NY; EMMA, age 11, b. Illinois; & ZINA, age 5; LUCIUS, age 4; CYRUS, age 2, all b. Mich. Ref: P&BA-Len pg. 350.

CORBETT, EMERY E., son of ZIBRA (following), born ca. 1817, NY; and wife, MARIA C., born ca. 1829, Mich., were in the 1850 census of Palmyra Twp., Lenawee Co., Mich. with MYRON E., age 6; ALMYRA, age 5; HENRY, age 4, all b. Mich., and also ZIBA, age 66, b. VT, in their household.

CORBETT, WILLIAM M., son of ZIBRA (following), was born 22 May 1826, Villanova, Chautauqua Co., NY; and moved with his parents to Palmyra Twp., Lenawee Co., Mich. After the death of his mother, he lived in Monroe Co., Mich. with W. G. Powers. He married 25 June 1850 to SUSAN CLOTILDA (SPALDING), daughter of Obediah (also see). In 1854, they moved to Blissfield Twp., Lenawee Co., Mich. The first 2 children were born in Monroe Co., and the rest in Blissfield Twp. Children: 1. ROLLIN S. b. 28 Apr. 1851 (d. 30 Sept. 1862); 2. WILLIAM P. b. 27 Mar. 1853 (to Riga Twp.); 3. MARY E. b. 4 Nov. 1854 (d. 17 Sept. 1862); 4. LIZZIE M. b. 23 Apr. 1856 (m. Hudson Orr); 5. FRANK B. b. 4 Apr. 1858 (to Toledo, O.); 6. ADDIE L. b. 17 May 1862 (d. 24 Mar. 1864); 7. BURTON O. b. 25 Feb. 1866; 8. MATTIE B. b. 4 Aug. 1867; 9. SUSAN M. b. 26 Jan. 1871; 10. ANNA C. b. 3 Apr. 1872. Ref: P&BA-Len pg. 1178-80.

CORBETT, ZIBA (ZIBRA?) born 1785, (in VT per census, NY per sketch), served as a Capt. in the War of 1812. He married in 1810 to EMMA (NOBLE), and they first lived in Villanova, Chatauqua Co., NY. About 1835, they removed to Palmyra Twp., Lenawee Co., Mich. She died there 16 Apr. 1840, and in 1850, Ziba lived in the household of son, EMERY (preceding). He died 28 Apr. 1859. Known children: 1. CLARK E. (preceding); 2. CLARISSA A. (m. Chapin, Osseo, Hillsdale Co., Mich.); 3. CELESTIA ANN b. 3 Apr. 1814, Villanova, NY (m. Rollin Robinson, also see); 4. EMERY P. (preceding); 5. MARIA (m. Hubbard, Ogden Twp., Lenawee Co.); 6. MARY E. (m. Powers, Cleveland, O.); 7. WAYNE A. (Bay City, Mich.); 8. MARTHA E. (m. Brigham); 9. WILLIAM M. (following). Ref: P&BA-Len pg. 1103-4 & 1178-80.

CORBIN, HORACE was born Charleston, NH, and moved to Tioga Co., NY where he married on 8 Jan. 1824 to FRANCES (WRIGHT), daughter of Thomas (also see). Horace died in 1828. Children: 1. WILLIAM (following); 2. HORACE (Plymouth, Ind.). Frances married second to Eben Dunham (also see). Ref: P&BA-Len pg. 375-6.

CORBIN, WILLIAM born 30 July 1825, Nichols, Tioga Co., NY, moved in 1843 to Dundee, Monroe Co., Mich. He married on 20 Dec. 1849 to ELIZA ANN (DREW), daughter of William (also see). They settled in Adrian, Lenawee Co., Mich. Children (4 deceased by 1888, names not stated): 1. MARY M. (m. Frank A. Douglas, Houghton, Mich.); 2. ALICE E. (m. R. P. Humphrey; Sioux Falls, Dak.); 3. EDWARD A. (Chicago, Ill.) Ref: P&BA-Len pg. 375-6.

COREY, LEVI born ca. 1789, Maine; and wife, MARY (COATS b. VT). lived in Niagara Co., NY. In 1836, they moved to Franklin Twp., Lenawee Co., Mich.; and in 1841 to Clinton, Mich. Mary died in 1837 leaving 6 sons & 2 daughters (names not stated) except LUCY b. 1 Nov. 1829, Alcott, NY; & in his household in 1850 were SAMUEL, age 16; ZEBULON, age 15, b. Mich. Levi married second to MARY (RICHARDSON) born ca. 1814, VT. They had 1 son & 3 daughters (names not stated). They were listed in the 1850 census of Tecumseh Twp., Lenawee Co., Mich. with last 3 children, above, and WILLIAM, age 7; CAROLINE, age 5; FRANCES, age 2, all b. Mich, in their household. Elizabeth Ellitson, age 43, b. Maine; and Samuel Ellitson, age 15, b. NY, were also in the household. Levi died in March 1874, age 86; and MARY was living with a daughter in 1888. Ref: P&BA-Len pg. 368-9. Note: CALVIN, age 23, listed in the 1850 census of Tecumseh Twp. in a different household may also relate to this family.

COREY, NATHANIEL (spelled "Cory") was born ca. 1808, NY; and his wife, BETSEY, was born ca. 1810, Maine, and they are listed in the 1850 census of Madison Twp., Lenawee Co., Mich. with NATHAN, age 16; CATHARINE, age 15, both b. NY; and GEORGE M., age 10; JAMES H., age 8; FRANCIS E., age 1, all b. Mich., in their household.

CORNELIUS, WILLIAM of Dutchess Co., NY possibly went to Ontario Co., NY before moved to Clinton, Lenawee Co., Mich. in 1841. Known daughter, MARY J. b. 16 Mar. 1824, Dutchess Co. (m. Henry H. Rawson, also see). Ref: P&BA-Len pg. 684-5.

CORNELL, ALICE (See William A. Champenois)

CORNELL, ASA born ca. 1812, NY, and wife, FRANCES, born ca. 1822, both in NY, were listed in the 1850 census of Adrian Twp., Lenawee Co., Mich. with ELLEN, age 5; CHARLES, age 3; both b. Mich., and Caroline Beagle, age 19, b. Germany, in their household.

CORNELL, CHARLES born ca. 1806, NY, and wife, HANNAH, born ca. 1804, Conn., were listed in the 1850 census of Rome Twp., Lenawee Co. Mich. with ESTHER C., age 18, b. NY; and ALBERT W.; RAMSON R., age 12, both b. Mich., in the household.

CORNELL, ELIZABETH Mrs. born ca. 1792, Penn., was head of household in the 1850 census of Palmyra Twp., Lenawee Co., Mich. with ALICE, age 11, b. NY; & ARLETTA, age 10; ADETHEAN, age 7; ALANSON, age 6; ALZINA, age 5; JAMES, age 1, all b. Mich., in her household.

CORNELL, SARAH (See James Sands)

CORNES, W. H. (See Dr. Leonard G. Hall)

CORNISH, VILITIA (See Archer Crane)

CORNVILLE, GEORGE L. (See John Henry)

CORNWELL, ARIEL and wife, NARY ANN (RATHBONE), of Liberty Twp., Jackson Co., Mich. were parents of M. A. (MARY ANN?) who married Aaron B. Sutfin (also see) as his 3rd wife.

CORSON, MARY (See William Taylor)

CORVIN, JULIA A. (See Samuel Conkling)

CORWIN, FREDERICK H. born 13 Sept. 1818, Suffolk Co., NY, moved about 1834 with his parents to Niagara Co., NY. He married on 13 Nov. 1847, Royalton, to LOUISA J. (TREADWELL). In 1853, they removed to Ogden Twp., Lenawee Co., Mich., and about 1871 into the village of Fairfield. Children: 1. EMERSON b. ca. 1850; 2. PARKER; 3. LIBBIE (m. Nicholas Wotring in 1877, Fairfield Twp.); 4. CHARLES (m. Ida Brown of York Co., Nebr. and moved to Furnas Co., Nebr.); 5. GRACE b. ca. 1860 (m. William R. Porter, Fairfield Twp.); 6. (adopted) LILLIE b. ca. 1874. Ref: P&BA-Len pg. 894.

CORYELL, ? (HAUSE) Mrs. was the daughter of Sanford Hause, also see.

CORYELL, ANDREW, son of DAVID (following), was born in Dec. 1800, New Jersey. He moved with parents to Seneca Co., NY. He married ESTHER (CARPENTER), daughter of Ezra (also see); and they settled first in Seneca Co., NY, then moved to Steuben Co., NY. By 1826, they moved to Washtenaw Co., Mich. (near what is now Ann Arbor), and built the first frame home in the area. They afterwards moved to Monroe Co., Mich., returned to Washtenaw Co., and then by 1836 to Jackson Co., Mich. It may be he listed in the 1840 census index of Macon Twp., Lenawee Co., Mich.; and in 1841, they settled in Ridgeway Twp. He died in 1883. Known children (all but Ezra from 1850 census of Ridgeway Twp.): 1. EZRA C. (following); 2. DAVID, age 22; 3. CATHARINE b. 24 Feb. 1832, Monroe Co., Mich. (m. John Cheever, also see); 4. ANDREW JR., age 15; 5. WILLIAM L., age 12; 6. SARAH E., age 10; 7. JOHN, age 8, all b. Mich. Ref: P&BA-Len pg. 982-3 & 1029-30.

CORYELL, DAVID of New Jersey moved from Seneca Co., NY to Michigan in the 1820s. He died in 1838 in Ridgeway Twp., Lenawee Co., Mich. Known son, ANDREW (preceding). Note: In the 1840 census index of Macon Twp., Lenawee Co., in addition to ANDREW, there was also JOHN; & in Dundee, Monroe Co., Mich. WILLIAM I.

CORYELL, EZRA C., son of ANDREW (preceding), was born 1 August 1822, Romulus, Seneca Co., NY, and moved with his parents to Michigan. He married in 1843 to JOANNA (HARDING), who died in 1885. He married again to LYDIA M. (HAIGHT), daughter of Salmon L. (also see). No children listed. Ref: P&BA-Len pg. 1029-30. Note: Abel Harding, age 12, b. NJ, was in the household in 1850.

COTRELL also see COTTRELL
COTRELL, LUCY (See James Rogers)

COTTRELL note COTRELL preceding.
COTTRELL, LAWRENCE went from Lenawee Co., Mich. went overland to California in 1852 (See Edgar Alonzo Perry).
COTTRELL MARY A. (See Henry Williamson)

COUDER see KUDER

COUNROD also see COONRAD
COUNROD, PETER of Otsego Co., NY had daughter (name not stated) who married Henry Bowen (also see); and a daughter, LUCINDA, who married first to Willard Stearnes (also see), and married second to Henry Bowen as his 2nd wife. Ref: P&BA-Len pg. 615-6.

COUPPLE, ELIZABETH (See Charles McCarbery)

COURTWRIGHT, MARY (See Simon Gilson)
COVERT - In the Gazeteer of New York State, by French, in Lodi, Seneca Co., NY are the following notes: ABRAHAM came from New Jersey, with son, ABRAHAM A., in 1790. TEUNIS arrived in 1794 (possibly he in the militia of Bridgewater, Somerset Co., NJ in 1793). In Lodi in 1793, there were weddings of ABRAHAM A. & CATHARINE (COVERT) COVERT; & JANE & Enoch Stewart.

COVERT, ANDREW born ca. 1819, and wife, MARY, born ca. 1825, both in NY, were listed in the 1850 census of Madison Twp., Lenawee Co., Mich. with ELIZABETH, age 5; & CHARLES H., age 3, both b. Mich., and Jane Bortles, age 36, b. NY; & Sidney Beach, age 35, b. NY, in their household.

COVERT, ANNA married Dennis Van Duyn (also see) probably in Somerset Co., NJ and moved to Seneca Co., NY in 1804.

COVERT, CHARITY married John Kelley (also see) in Seneca Co., NY.

COVERT, JANE, age 51, born NY, is listed in the 1850 census of Palmyra Twp., Lenawee Co., Mich. in the household of Peter C. & Margaret Vanwey?

COVERT, MAGDELENA born 12 June 1779, NJ, married in Lodi, Seneca Co., NY to William Osgood (also see). Ref: P&BA-Len pg. 1040-1.

COVERT, REBECCA (See Jacob Emons)

COVILLE, ASAHEL H. born ca. 1809, and wife, MARGARET, born ca. 1804, both b. NY, were listed in the 1850 census of Ridgeway Twp., Lenawee Co., Mich. with WARREN, age 13; HARRIET, age 11; WILLIAM R., age 8, all b. Mich., in their household.

COVILLE, GEORGE W. born ca. 1796, Mass, and wife, HANNAH, born ca. 1800, NY, were listed in the 1850 census of Ridgeway Twp., Lenawee Co., Mich. with DANIEL H., age 19; ANNIS, age 17, both b. NY; & SARAH, age 7, b. Mich., in their household.

COVILLE, HIRAM born ca. 1827, NY, with wife, MARY H., age 19, b. VT, with HARRIET E., age 1, b. Mich., were listed in the 1850 census of Hudson Twp., Lenawee Co., Mich. in the household of Charles S. Shaw (possibly father of Harriet E.?)

COVILLE, JAMES (See Franklin F. Palmer)

COVILLE, JOHN S. born ca. 1827, NY, was listed in the 1850 census of Tecumseh Twp., Lenawee Co., Mich.

COVILLE, WILLIAM born ca. 1821, and wife, ELIZABETH, born ca. 1831, both in NY, were listed in the 1850 census of Ridgeway Twp., Lenawee Co., Mich. (2 doors from ASAHEL, preceding) with MARY J., age 1, b. Mich., in their household.

COWELL, AM-- born ca. 1800, Conn., and wife, EMILY, born ca. 1810, NY, were listed in the 1850 census of Ogden Twp., Lenawee Co., Mich. with MICHAEL, age 20; JOSEPH, age 18; ALFRED, age 16; WILLIAM, age 13; REBECCA, age 11; KEZIAH, age 8, all b. Ohio; and CLEMINCE, age 6; SALLY, age 3, both b. Mich., in the household.

COWELL, EDMOND born ca. 1810, and wife, THANKFUL, born ca. 1809, both in NY, were listed in the 1850 census of Ogden Twp., Lenawee Co., Mich. with AMASA, age 8; BRADLEY, age 7; WILLIAM, age 4, all b. Mich., and Edward Gilbert, age 18; Susanna Gilbert, age 14; Eliza Gilbert, age 14, all b. Mich. (possibly stepchildren??).

COWELL, ERASTUS C., born ca. 1813, NY, and wife, HANNAH, born ca. 1822, Ohio, were listed in the 1850 census of Ogden Twp., Lenawee Co., Mich. with SARAH A., age 8; JERUSHA M., age 7; ELLEN S., age 5; ESTHER C., age 1, all b. Ohio, in the household.

COWELL, MARY (See Erastus Brockway)

COWELL, SMITH born ca. 1799, and wife, RUTH, born ca. 1805, both in NY, were listed in the 1850 census of Fairfield Twp., Lenawee Co., Mich. with EMELINE, age 6, b. Mich. in the household. JOSHUA, age 15, b. Ohio, in a different household may also relate to this family.

COWEN, DEMMON, son of MOSES (following), born 13 Mar. 1838, near St. Thomas, Upper Canada, came to Dundee, Mich. with his parents. He married there to MARY (FRIEDT), born Penn. of German parents (who also came to Mich.) Demmon moved to Ridgeway Twp., Lenawee Co. in 1857. He served in Co. K, 11th Mich. Inf., Civil War. Children: 1. CAROLINE (m. William Frayor, Ridgeway Twp.); 2. SUSAN; 3. JOHN H. Ref: P&BA-Len pg. 247-8 with portrait.

COWEN, HENRY M. born ca. 1819, Penn., and wife, SARAH ANN, born ca. 1822, NY, were listed in the 1850 census of Ridgeway Twp., Lenawee Co., Mich. with WILLIAM, age 7; JOHN, age 5, both b. NY; & ELIZABETH, age 3, b. Mich.; and Garner Green, age 17, b. NY, in their household.

COWEN, MOSES married JANE (RICE) and lived near St. Thomas, Upper Canada to Dundee, Monroe Co., Mich., where he died. Known son, DEMMON (preceding). Jane married again to John Barnett (also see) and they moved to Dundee, Monroe Co., Mich. in 1851. Ref: P&BA-Len pg. 247-8.

COX, CHARLES, probably son of MICAJAH (following), born ca. 1820, and wife, HANNAH, born ca. 1824, both in NY, were listed in the 1850 census of Medina Twp., Lenawee Co., Mich. with LEVI, age 6; HARVEY, age 4, both b. Mich., in their household.

COX, JANE (See Isaac Van Winkle)

COX, JOHN born ca. 1800, Penn., was listed in the 1850 census of Ridgeway Twp., Lenawee Co., Mich. with MARY A., age 17; CHARLES, age 14; THEODORE, age 10; THOMAS, age 8; WILLIAM, age 5, all b. Mich., in his household. LEWIS, age 18, b. Penn., in a different household may also relate to this family. Note SARAH, following.

COX, MARTHA (See George W. Farst)

COX, MICAJAH born ca. 1796, Maine, and wife, PHEBE, born ca. 1801, NY, were listed in the 1850 census of Medina Twp., Lenawee Co., Mich. with MARTIN H., age 26. b. NY; and EMILY, age 13, b. Mich. in the household. Next door was CHARLES (preceding).

COX, SARAH born ca. 1829, Penn., was listed in the 1850 census of Tecumseh Twp., Lenawee Co., Mich. She may relate to JOHN (preceding). (May be she who m. Joseph W. Gray, also see).

COX, WILLIAM born ca. 1815, and wife, HANNAH, born ca. 1819, both in NY, were listed in the 1850 census of Franklin Twp., Lenawee Co., Mich. with MARYETTE, age 10; CAROLINE, age 5, both b. Mich., in their household.

COY, ELIAS born ca. 1827, NY, ws listed in the 1850 census of Rome Twp., Lenawee Co., Mich.

COY, WILLIAM was a resident of Medina Twp., Lenawee Co., Mich. in 1835. He was listed in the 1840 census index adjacent to JUSTICE.

COYLE, SALINA (See John T. Bates)

CRABB also see CRABBS

CRABB, ISAAC Rev. born ca. 1798, NY, and wife, ELIZABETH, born ca. 1793, Ireland, were listed in the 1850 census of Madison Twp., Lenawee Co. Mich.

CRABBS also note CRABB

CRABBS, ABRAHAM and wife, PRISCILLA, of Springfield, Jefferson Co., Ohio were parents of 5 children (all names not stated). Known son, Rev. JOHN (following). Ref: P&BA-Len pg. 1211.

CRABBS, JOHN Rev., son of ABRAHAM, was born 22 Oct. 1823, Springfield, Ohio; and married in Ashland Co., Ohio to SUSAN (ILGER), daughter of Jacob (also see). They moved to Morenci, Lenawee Co. Mich. in 1855. Children: 1. WATSON C. (m. Anna Cawley, dau. of

Franklin, also see; resided Toledo, O.); 2. WILLIAM W. (following); 3. JOHN C. (m. Minerva Packer); 4. JENNIE M. (m. Lewis M. Rorick, Morenci). Ref: P&BA-Le pg. 1211.

CRABBS, WESTON C. (may be WATSON C. in family above). CRABBS, WILLIAM W., son of Rev. JOHN (preceding), was born 29 Oct. 1848, Savannah, Ashland Co., Ohio. He moved to Morenci, Mich. from Ohio about 1883; and he married on 29 Apr. 1886 to GEORGIA M. (PERKINS), who was born 5 Dec. 1863 in Kalamazoo, Mich. Known daughter, HAZEL. Ref: P&BA-Len pg. 1149.

CRAIG, ETTIE (See James T. Boyce)

CRAIG, ROBERT born ca. 1805, NY, and wife, RHODA, born ca. 1807, Ohio, were listed in the 1850 census of Palmyra Twp., Lenawee Co., Mich. with ROBERT, age 20; HIRAM, age 18; CALVIN, age 14, all b. Ohio; and RHODA, age 10; FRANKLIN, age 6, both b. Mich., in their household.

CRAIG, ROSE A. born Co. Antrim, Ireland (See John H. Wilson).

CRAIG, SAMUEL married MARTHA (REASONER), daughter of Benjamin (also see). Children: 1. OSEMUS; 2. DIANA; 3. EDMUND; 4. EDWIN. Ref: P&BA-Len pg. 1017-8.

CRAIN also see CRANE

CRAIN, CATHERINE (See John Eddy)

CRAIN, SARAH (See Sylvanus Kinney)

CRAMER, ABRAHAM, son of CONRAD (following), born ca. 1808, NY, married 28 Nov. 1835 to SARAH ANN (STERLING). They moved to Rome Twp., Lenawee Co., Mich. in 1836, and in 1838 to Medina Twp. She died 28 Oct. 1849. Children: 1. EDWIN C. b. ca. 1837 (m. Jane Ann Wilcox, Medina Twp.); 2. MARY ANN b. ca. 1840 (m. William Charles, Bangor, Mich.); 3. GEORGE W. b. ca. 1841 (m. Jane DeLong, Hillsdale Co., Mich.); 4. WELLINGTON S. b. ca. 1845; 5. LORENZO L. b. ca. 1849. Abraham married again before the 1850 census to MARY A. (HARRIS) in Hillsdale Co., born ca. 1825, Ohio. She died 6 May 1887, Medina Twp. Ref: P&BA-Len pg. 1152-5.

CRAMER, CONRAD & wife, ELIZABETH, were residents of NY state, where she died of Cholera at age 45; and he died in 1872. Known children: NANCY (m. Wilder, lived Perryville, NY, and father died at her home); ABRAHAM (preceding). Ref: P&BA-Len pg. 1152-5. Note: In the 1800 census index, there were 2 CONRAD listed, one in Herkimer Co., and 1 in Montgomery Co., NY.

CRAMER, JUDITH (See Micajah Willitts)

CRAMER, MINA (See Joseph Bordwell)

CRANDALL, CYRUS born ca. 1824, and wife, EMMA?, born ca. 1826, both in NY, were listed in the 1850 census of Rome Twp., Lenawee Co., Mich. with (mother?) LYDIA A., age 46; ORSON, age 18 (following), both b. NY; and LUCY, age 6, b. Mich., in their household. Note: There was a DAVID listed in the 1840 census index of Rome Twp., possibly father of Cyrus?

CRANDALL, H. (See John Landon)

CRANDALL, JAMES born ca. 1760, Rhode Island, a Quaker, moved to Ghent, Columbia Co., NY where he died in 1845, age 85. Known daughter, ELIZABETH (m. Worth, See John Worth family). Ref: P&BA-Len pg. 837.

CRANDALL, ORSON (See CYRUS, preceding) born ca. 1832, NY, is probably he who married CLARISSA (JENNINGS), daughter of Levi (also see) and was said to have gone to Riley, Mich. by 1888.

CRANDALL, WILLIAM born ca. 1808, Rhode Island, and wife, REBECCA, born ca. 1813, NY, were listed in the 1840 census index of Rollin Twp., Lenawee Co., Mich.; and in the 1850 census of Rollin Twp. with ELIZABETH, age 19; CAROLINE, age 16; LAURA, age 13; HENRY, age 12, all b. NY; & CHARLES, age 10; EDWIN, age 7; THEODORE, age 1, all b. Mich., in their household.

CRANE also see CRAIN

CRANE, ALBERT born ca. 1815, Mass., and wife, DOVEY, born ca. 1817, NY, were listed in the 1850 census of Madison Twp., Lenawee Co., Mich. with MARIA A., age 11?, b. Mich., in the household. Also note PHEBE, following.

CRANE, ALFORD (Alfred?) born ca 1805, and wife, CATHARINE (LEONARD), born ca. 1815, both in NY, moved from Monroe Co., NY to Madison Twp., Lenawee Co., Mich. in 1836. In the 1850 census of Madison Twp., they listed ALVIRA, age 19; ALBERT, age 17, both b. NY; and HENRY, age 14; WILLIAM, age 11; ALFORD, age 7; MARY, age 5; MARTHA A., age 1 (m. Horatio L. Wilson, also see), all b. Mich., in their household. Ref: P&BA-Len pg. 1006-7.

CRANE, AMBROSE born ca. 1790, Conn., and wife, JANE, born ca. 1805, NY, were listed in the 1840 census index of Franklin Twp., Lenawee Co., Mich.; and in the 1850 census of Madison Twp. listed ASA, age 20; ADELINE, age 7; ELDAH? (female), age 1, all b. Mich. AMBROSE, age 38, b. NY, listed in the 1850 census of Adrian Twp. probably relates to this family.

CRANE, AMOS R. (probably son of ELIJAH, following) of Raisin Twp., Lenawee Co., Mich. married JANE (GRANDY), daughter of Edmund (also see). Children: 1. CHARLES H. b. 28 Nov. 1853; 2. DORCAS J. b. 14 Jan. 1856 (m. R. G. Gidley, Gratiot Co., Mich., had son, John); 3. MATTIE A. b. 30 Nov. 1869. After Amos died, Jane married again after 1874 to John Landon (also see). Ref: P&BA-Len pg. 367-8.

CRANE, ARCHER was the descendant of a New England family who had moved to New York at an early date. He married VILITIA (CORNISH) and they lived in Onondaga Co., NY until 1829, then removed to Wayne Co., NY. Known sons, JAMES K. (following); EDWIN D. (following). Ref: P&BA-Len pg. 1204-6.

CRANE, BENJAMIN was listed in the 1840 census index of Madison Twp., Lenawee Co., Mich.; and it is probably he, age 38, and wife, ANNE E., born ca. 1818, both born NY, in the 1850 census of Madison Twp. with GEORGE, age 3, b. Mich. in their household. Note GEORGE (following).

CRANE, CALVIN and wife, JANE (ELLIOTT), were natives of Preston Co., West Virginia. He served in the War of 1812. She died 25 Feb. 1886. Known daughter, MARY A. b. 3 Apr. 1836, Preston Co., W. Va. (m. Capt. Jehu F. Wotring, also see). Ref: P&BA-Len pg. 1107-8.

Pioneer Families of Southeastern Michigan

CRANE, CALVIN, son of GEORGE (following), was born 25 Dec. 1816, Palmyra, Wayne Co., NY. He moved to Palmyra Twp., Lenawee Co., Mich. with his parents, and he married 7 Feb. 1844 to DEBORAH (POWER), daughter of Arthur (also see). They settled in Palmyra Twp., and later moved to Adrian. Son, ARTHUR P. b. 7 July 1846, Palmyra Twp. (to Toledo, O.) Ref: P&BA-Len pg. 370-2 with portrait.

CRANE, CALVIN H., son of GEORGE L. (following), was born 20 May 1842, Madison Twp., Lenawee Co., Mich. He married 11 Apr. 1866 at Rose, Wayne Co., NY to JENNIE (MIRRICK), daughter of George W. (also see). She died 30 Nov. 1871, leaving a son, GEORGE H. b. 25 Nov. 1871. Calvin H. married second on 24 July 1878 to Mrs. EMMA (LIVERMORE) KELLOGG, daughter of James, and widow of Lewis B. (see both). Ref: P&BA-Len pg. 966-7.

CRANE, CHARLES (See Isaac A. Bartlett)

CRANE, EDWIN D., son of ARCHER (preceding), was born 14 May 1812 in Onondaga Co., NY. He moved with his parents to Wayne co., NY; and married 22 May 1831 to SARAH B. (KEYES), daughter of James (also see) of Sodus, Wayne Co. They resided there until 1837, then moved to Freedom Twp., Washtenaw Co., Mich. About 1839, they removed to Genesee Co. Mich.; and in 1842 to Blissfield, Lenawee Co., Mich. In 1864, they moved to Adrian, where he died 14 Feb. 1867; and Sarah B. died 20 June 1884. Children: 1. MAHLON D. (to Dakota); 2. JAMES K. (following); 3. CHARLES E. (Knox Co., Ind., where he d. 16 June 1887); 4. HELEN M. (m. John D. Smead; she d. Blissfield, 20 Dec. 1882).

CRANE, ELIZABETH (See Isaac A. Colvin) Note GEORGE & TURNER (following).

CRANE, ELIJAH born ca. 1787, NY, and his wife, MARY, born ca. 1786, Conn., were listed in the 1840 census index of Raisin Twp., Lenawee Co., Mich.; and in the 1850 census of Raisin Twp., were next door to son?, AMOS R. (preceding). MATHEW was adjacent in the 1840 census index.

CRANE, GEORGE was born in March 1783, Mass., and he married CHARITY (LINCOLN), daughter of Benjamin (also see), born 7 Aug. 1782, Bristol, Mass. They were Quakers. They moved first before 1810 to Palmyra, Wayne Co., NY; and in 1833 removed to Palmyra Twp., Lenawee Co., Mich. He died 17 Apr. 1856, and she died 21 Sept. 1863. Children: 1. PHILA P. (d. young); 2. ELIZABETH W. (may be she m. Isaac A. Colvin, also see); 3. ROWENA C.; 4. GEORGE L. (following); 5. BENJAMIN L.; 6. CALVIN (preceding); 7. CLARISSA P. b. ca. 1827, NY. Ref: P&BA-Len pg. 370-2.

CRANE, GEORGE L., son of GEORGE (preceding), was born 20 Nov. 1810, Palmyra, NY; and moved to Palmyra Twp., Lenawee Co., Mich. with his parents. He married 1 Oct. 1835 to LEAH (RAMSDELL), daughter of Gideon (also see) at Perrinton, Monroe Co., NY; and they settled in Madison Twp., Lenawee Co., Mich. Children: 1. LUCY R. b. 24 Sept. 1837 (m. John F. Jones, Adrian); 2. CALVIN H. (preceding). Ref: P&BA-Len pg. 636-7.

CRANE, HANNAH (See Sylvanus Kinney)

CRANE, HARRIET (See A. W. Brittain)

CRANE, JAMES K., son of EDWIN D. (preceding), was born 8 Mar. 1834, Sodus, Wayne Co., NY; and at age 8 came from Washtenaw Co., Mich. to Blissfield, Lenawee Co., Mich. with his parents. He married 27 Mar. 1856 to CYNTHIA A. (SPERRY), daughter of Enoch (also see). He served in Co. F., 26th Mich. Inf., Civil War, finishing as a 1st Lt. Children: 1. DWIGHT H. b. 1 Apr. 1857 (resided San Francisco, CA); 2. CYNTHIA A. b. 2 May 1859; 3. MYRA A. b. 18 Mar. 1861; 4. J. ALFRED b. 16 Aug. 1863; 5. EDMUND B. b. 19 July 1866; 6. HELEN A. b. 20 Jan. 1870. Ref: P&BA-Len pg. 1204-6.

CRANE, JESSE born ca. 1807, NH, and wife, AUGUSTA, born ca. 1817, Ohio. were listed in the 1850 census of Madison Twp., Lenawee Co., Mich. with ECKFORD? L., age 13, b. Ohio; & CUTLER A., age 10; ACT-? M. (female), age 8, both b. Mich., in their household. Note: They were listed next door to GEORGE L.; and 2 doors from BENJAMIN (preceding).

CRANE, LAFAYETTE born ca. 1824, NY, was listed in the 1850 census of Tecumseh Twp., Lenawee Co., Mich.

CRANE, LILLA (See Addison P. Halladay)

CRANE, MARY "POLLY" (See Stimpson Harvey)

CRANE, NANCY (See T. M. Camburn)

CRANE, NATHAN L. born ca. 1827, NY, and wife, ANN, born ca. 1830, Mich., were listed in the 1850 census of Raisin Twp., Lenawee Co., Mich. with MARY J., age 3/12, b. Mich., in the household. Note ELIJAH, preceding.

CRANE, SALMON (See SOLOMON)

CRANE, SILAS - There were 2 listed in the 1840 Lenawee Co. census index; one was listed in Madison Twp., adjacent to BENJAMIN & TURNER; and one in Adrian Twp.

CRANE, SOLOMON was born ca. 1776, Vermont, and was listed in the 1850 census of Tecumseh Twp., Lenawee Co., Mich. in the household of Calvin & Mary Snell (she was age 34, b. Penn., possibly daughter, as she named a son, Solomon). Note LAFAYETTE (preceding); & SOLOMON (following).

CRANE, SOLOMON (written "Salmon") born ca. 1814, and wife, HARRIET, born ca. 1818, both in NY, were listed in the 1850 census of Tecumseh Twp., Lenawee Co., Mich. with THEODORE, age 6; CHARLES, age 2; HENRY, age 8/12, all b. Mich., in their household.

CRANE, TURNER & wife, PHEBE (ARNOLD), were natives of Mass. who went at an early date to New Hampshire. They moved to Macedon, Ontario Co. (now Wayne Co.), NY where they remained until 1832, then moved to Madison Twp., Lenawee Co. Mich., where he died (before 1850). There were 8 sons and 3 daughters (names not stated). Known daughter, #4. CLARISSA C.(Caroline) b. 13 Dec. 1819, NH (m. John L. Hall, also see). In the 1850 census of Madison Twp., Phebe, age 55?, was head of household with HIRAM, age 28; STINSON?, age 24; ASA, age 22; WILLIAM, age 18, all b. NY; and EDWIN?, age 16; HARRISON?, age 14, both b. Mich., in her household. Note: In the 1840 census index of Lenawee Co., Turner was listed adjacent to BENJAMIN & SILAS (preceding). Also see JESSE (preceding).

CRANE, W. H. Mrs. is a daughter of Daniel Ketchum (also see).

CRATER, MATTHIAS was born in New Jersey, and his wife, DEBORAH (SHIPPY), was born in Vermont; and after their marriage they settled in Wayne Co., NY. He died 20 June 1854; and she afterwards went to Rock Co., Wisc. where she died 27 Dec. 1871. Only child,

MARTHA b. 29 Sept. 1840, Arcadia, Wayne Co., NY (m. Levi W. Baker, also see). Ref: P&BA-Len pg. 927.

CRAW, PRUDENCE D. (See Peter Hathaway)

CRAWFORD, ABRAM born ca. 1806, and wife, LYDIA, born ca. 1810, both in NY, were listed in the 1840 census index of Rollin Twp.; and in the 1850 census of Hudson Twp. with LUCINDA age 12; ADELINE, age 9; CELINDA, age 7; EMMA J., age 3, all b. Mich., in their household. Note HIRAM, following.

CRAWFORD, CELESTA (See John M. Jewell)

CRAWFORD, DELIA (See Levi C. Richmond)

CRAWFORD, ELIZABETH born ca. 1832, NY, was listed in the 1850 census of Rome Twp., Lenawee Co., Mich.

CRAWFORD, HIRAM was listed in the 1840 census index of Rollin Twp., Lenawee Co., Mich. adjacent to ABRAM, preceding. There was a LESTER, age 16, b. NY, in the 1850 census of Rollin Twp. who may relate to this family.

CRAWFORD, JOHN born ca. 1807, NY, was listed in the 1850 census of Tecumseh Twp., Lenawee Co., Mich.

CRAWFORD, MARGARET (See Robert Gardner)

CRAWFORD, RANSOM P. born ca. 1807, NY, and wife, MARY W., born ca. 1800, NJ, were listed in the 1850 census of Medina Twp., Lenawee Co., Mich. with IRA, age 20; CYNTHIA J., age 17; GEORGE, age 14; MATILDA, age 12; JUDITH B., age 8, all b. Mich., in their household. Note: It may be this Ransom listed in the 1840 census index of Hillsdale Co., Mich.

CREGO, CHAUNCEY M., son of RICHARD (following), was born 2 Aug. 1835, Erie Co., NY and moved with his parents to Columbia Twp., Lenawee Co., Mich. He married 14 Dec. 1861 to JENNIE (CONOVER), daughter of Dennis of Steuben Co., NY. Daughter, NORA (d. 1864). Jennie died in 16 July 1865. Chauncey married again to DELIA (WYMAN), daughter of Jonas (also see). Children: DENNIS M.; WALTER L.; ADDIE; MAY; EDITH A.; MAGGIE E.; CORA. Ref: History of Jackson Co., Mich. pg. 792.

CREGO, HENRY J., son of RICHARD (following), was born 19 July 1823, Clarence, Erie Co., NY, and came to Columbia Twp., Jackson Co., Mich. with his parents. He married LYDIA A. (RUSSELL) born 6 Feb. 1828. Children: (1 deceased, name not given): CHAUNCY C.; ELVA L (m. W. S. Knapp, Kansas); EMMA A. (m. G. E. Jones); HERMAN H.; OMER P.; ARTHUR J.; CARRIE A.; MATTIE J. History of Jackson Co., Mich., pg. 940.

CREGO, RICHARD was a native of Herkimer Co., NY; and he married on 6 June 1813 to MARTHA (GALLUP); and they moved to Erie Co., NY. (Note: It may be he in the 1800 census index of Columbia Co., NY). In 1835, they removed to Columbia Twp., Jackson Co., Mich. where they remained. There were 8 sons & 1 daughter (names not stated). Known sons, HENRY J. (following); JOHN; ERASTUS; SOLOMON G. (following); CHAUNCEY M. (preceding); HARVEY. Ref: P&BA-Len pg. 241-2; History of Jackson Co., Mich., pg. 792. Note: ABRAHAM who had wife, Charity, and died 1869, Jackson Co., Mich. may relate to this family.

CREGO, RULIFF was listed in the 1840 census index of Woodstock Twp., Lenawee Co., Mich.

CREGO, SOLOMON F., son of RICHARD (preceding), was born 10 July 1826, Erie Co., NY, and moved to Jackson Co., Mich. with his parents. He married DIANA F. (RUSS), daughter of Nathaniel (also see). Solomon died 23 Sept. 1866, Jackson Co. Children: 1. LEVI b. 3 Sept. 1850 (d. age 3 mo.); 2. FRANCES A. b. 17 Oct. 1852 (d. 13 July 1868); 3. CORA A. b. 16 Aug. 1855 (d. 7 Nov. 1879); 4. CLARA A. b. 7 Mar. 1859 (d. 16 Dec. 1876); 5. H. C. b. 7 Feb. 1864 (d. 12 Sept. 1866). Diana F. married again to Henry N. Skeels (also see). Ref: P&BA-Len pg. 241-2.

CRICHTON, MARY (See Robert Adam)

CRIM, ANGELINE (See John Forbes)

CRIPPIN, JENETTE C. (See Benjamin B. Fisk)

CRISSEY, ANNA D. born ca. 1835, NY, was the daughter of E. A. of Astoria, Long Island and she was listed in the 1850 census of Madison Twp., Lenawee Co., Mich. in the household of Norman & Laura Geddes. Anna married Samuel E. Hart (also see).

CRISSEY, CALEB (See Thomas Tunison)

CRIST see CHRIST

CROCKETT, ALEXANDER born ca. 1828, NY, was in the 1850 census of Ogden Twp., Lenawee Co., Mich. in household of NATHANIEL (following), possibly not a son of that household?

CROCKETT, EMILY born ca. 1835, Mich., was listed in the 1850 census of Fairfield Twp., Lenawee Co., Mich. and may relate to the families in Ogden Twp.

CROCKETT, JOHN, son of NATHANIEL (following), born 29 July 1826, NY, came to Ogden Twp., Lenawee Co., Mich. with parents. He married on 12 Mar. 1855 to PAULINE (POTTER), daughter of Mowry S. (also see), and settled in Ogden Twp. Children: 1. ELMA; 2. HATTIE; 3. NORA; 4. GLADYS; 5. ORRIN; 6. WILLIAM. Ref: P&BA-Len pg. 672-5.

CROCKETT, NATHANIEL born ca. 1798, Maine, was orphaned at an early age, and at age 13 went to Wayne Co., NY with relatives. He married there in 1823 to MARY (WHITE), daughter of William (also see), born Maine, 1805. In 1836, after the birth of 7 children, they moved from NY to Ogden Twp., Lenawee Co., Mich. In 1857, they moved to Delaware Co., Iowa where he died in 1875, and she afterwards returned to Ogden Twp. and died at home of son, David. There were 11 children (all names not stated). From the sketches & the 1850 census of Ogden Twp. are the following: 1. THIRZA b. 29 Aug. 1824, Huron, Wayne Co., NY (m. Levi Eddy, also see); 2. JOHN (preceding); 3. WILLIAM b. ca. 1828; 4. LYDIA b. 22 Nov. 1830, Huron, NY (m. Elisha Eddy, also see); 5. ROSELLA b. ca. 1832; 6. WILLARD (following); 7. MARY A. b. ca. 1836 (m. Harvey Shelden, also see); 8. DAVID b. ca. 1842; 9. JULIA E. b. ca. 1847 (m. William H. Marshall, also see). Ref: P&BA-Len pg. 659-60; 672-5; 864-5; & 993.

CROCKETT, ROBERT born ca. 1800, and wife, MARY, born ca. 1805, both in Maine, were listed in the 1850 census of Ogden Twp., Lenawee Co., Mich. with SARAH, age 16; SAMUEL, age 13, both b. Maine; & ANGELINE, age

Pioneer Families of Southeastern Michigan

11; CAROLINE, age 11; LEVI, age 7, all b. Mich., in their household.

CROCKETT, WILLARD, son of NATHANIEL (preceding), born 1 Dec. 1834, Wayne Co., NY, moved with his parents to Ogden Twp., Lenawee Co., Mich. In 1853, he went to California; but returned by 1859. He married in Ogden Twp. to HANNAH E. (RICE), daughter of Samuel L. (also see). Children: 1. ADDIE; 2. JENNIE; 3. ALVA; 4. CLARA; 5. CASSIUS; 6. RUSSELL. Ref: P&BA-Len pg. 662.

CROMAN, SARAH (See John Haas)

CROMMER, CHRISTOPHER C. (See Jonathan E. Ingersoll)
CROMMER, HARRISON (See Jonathan E. Ingersoll)

CROSBY, CHARLES born in Conn., and wife, ABIGAIL (FAIRBANKS), born in Mass., moved to Ypsilanti, Washtenaw Co., Mich., whre he died. She died in Morenci, Lenawee Co., Mich., at home of daughter, RACHEL b. 9 Dec. 1810, Thompson, Conn. (m. Hiram Wakefield, also see). ABIGAIL F. who married Dennis Wakefield (also see), brother of Hiram, may be another daughter.

CROSS, DARIUS was born ca. 1815, Rowe, Mass., and came as a young man to Madison Twp., Lenawee Co., Mich. He married LUCRETIA (RANNEY) born ca. 1819, Buckland, Mass. They lived in Madison Twp. all except 4 years that they lived in Palmyra Twp. There were 5 daughters & 1 son (names not stated). Known children: 1. EDWIN R. (following); 2. RUTH A. b. ca. 1842 (m. GEORGE CROSS, Barry Co., Mich.); 3. ELLAH A. b. ca. 1846; 4. CORA. Ref: P&BA-Len pg. 1024-5.

CROSS, EBENEZER born ca. 1811, and wife, NANCY, born ca. 1812, both in Mass., were listed in the 1840 census index of Fairfield Twp., Lenawee Co., Mich.; and in the 1850 census listed CANDIS, age 12; WILLIAM, age 7; JEDU?, age 4; OLIN; age 1, all b. Mich., in their household. JANE, age 16, b. Mass, in an Ayers household, may relate to this family.

CROSS, EDWIN R., son of DARIUS (preceding), was born 20 July 1840 in Madison Twp., Lenawee Co., Mich.; and he married 1 Jan. 1866 to SUSAN (PATEE), daughter of William (also see) in Steuben Co., Ind. They settled in Madison Twp. Son, JAPETH. Ref: P&BA-Len pg. 1024-5.

CROSS, GEORGE of Barry Co., Mich. (See DARIUS, preceding).

CROSS, JAPETH born ca. 1810, NY, and wife, SARAH, born ca. 1816, NY, were listed in the 1840 census index of Adrian Twp., Lenawee Co., Mich., and in the 1850 census of Adrian Twp., listed Clarissa Bartlett, age 55, b. NY, in the household.

CROSS, MICHAEL born ca. 1811, and wife, MARGARET, born ca. 1810, both in Ireland, were listed in the 1850 census of Medina Twp., Lenawee Co., Mich. with EDWARD, age 2, b. Mich., in their household.

CROSS, SAMUEL born ca. 1804, and wife, SARAH, born ca. 1802, both in NY, were listed in the 1850 census of Dover Twp., Lenawee Co., Mich. with DAVID, age 19; POLLY A., age 17; SAMUEL, age 13; ESTHER, age 9, all b. NY, in their household.

CROSWELL, CHARLES M. was born 31 Oct. 1825, Newburg, Orange Co., NY; and came with an uncle to Adrian, Lenawee Co., Mich. in 1837. In the 1850 census of Adrian Twp., he resided in the household of Jane McDonald (age 63, b. NY). He married LUCY M. (EDDY), daughter of Morton (also see). Charles M. was prominent in politics, and became Governor of Michigan in 1876. Children: 1. CHARLES MORTON b. 30 May 1861; 2. HATTIE; 3. LUCY ELIZABETH. Ref: P&BA-Len pg. 1206-7.

CROUNSE, JACOB and wife, HENRIETTA (VAN VALKENBURG) of Schoharie Co., NY were parents of BARBARA (m. John W. Winne, also see).

CROUSE, ADAM was born in Germany and served in Napoleon's army. He came to the US and settled in Birmingham, Erie Co., Ohio. Known son, CASPER (following). Ref: P&BA-Len pg. 1161-2.

CROUSE, CASPER, son of ADAM (precding), lived at Brownhelm, Lorain Co., Ohio and afterwards at Birmingham, Erie Co., Ohio. Known daughter, MARY b. 18 May 1850, Brownhelm, O. (m. William H. Kurtz, also see). Ref: P&BA-Len pg. 1161-2.

CROUT, ANN born 25 Feb. 1811, Ontario Co., NY married Levi Jennings (also see).

CROUT, LUTHER, age 19; SELAR W., age 17, both b. NY; and LYMAN L., age 14, b. Mich., were listed in the 1850 census of Rollin Twp., Lenawee Co., Mich., next door to Levi Jennings (See ANN, preceding).

CROVER, AMANDA (See Dennis Wakefield)

CROWE, E. T. (See John W. Tolford)

CROWELL, JOHN (See William Bresie)

CRUMMEY also see CRUMMERY
CRUMMEY, ELIZABETH (See Orson Green)

CRUMMERY note CRUMMEY preceding.
CRUMMERY, JOHN born ca. 1807, and wife, MARGARET, born ca. 1808, both born Ireland, were listsed in the 1850 census of Hudson Twp., Lenawee Co., Mich. with ESTHER, age 14; MARY J., age 13; EDWARD, age 12; CATHARINE, age 10; JOHN, age 9; ELIZABETH, age 7; DAVID, age 6; THOMAS, age 5; WILLIAM, age 2, all b. NY, in their household.

CRUTHERS, JAMES born ca. 1780, and wife, ELIZABETH, born ca. 1788, both in NY, were listed in the 1850 census of Cambridge Twp., Lenawee Co., Mich. with LAURA, age 24; BETSEY, age 19; JAMES, age 16, all b. NY, in their household.

CRUTHERS, JOHN and wife, BETSEY, of Phelps, Ontario Co. NY were parents of SALLIE, born 1778 in Half Moon (Saratoga Co.), NY who married in 1800 to Joseph M. Baker (also see). Note: There was a ROBERT in 1800 census index of Rensselaer Co., NY.

CULBERTSON spelled CULVERTSON in census.

CULBERTSON, ANDREW born ca. 1780, and wife, MARGARET, born ca. 1790, both in Penn., were listed in the 1850 census of Ridgeway Twp., Lenawee Co., Mich.

CULBERTSON, CHARLES W., probably son of JOHN (following), was born ca. 1820, Penn. He married DEBORAH (GOHEEN), daughter of John (also see), born ca. 1825, NY. In the 1850 census of Tecumseh Twp., Lenawee Co., Mich. they listed EDWARD, age 4; JOHN, age 2, both b. Mich., in their household. Note CHARLES W., following, possibly another son.

CULBERTSON, CHARLES W. (See Morgan M. Florance)

CULBERTSON, JOHN born ca. 1794, Penn., was listed in the 1840 census index of Tecumseh Twp., Lenawee Co., Mich.; and in the 1850 census of Tecumseh listed CHRISTIANNE, age 22; ELLEN, age 20., both b. NY; and MARY, age 16; JOHN, ae 13, both b. Mich., in his household. CHARLES W., preceding, was next door, probably another son.

CULVERSTON see CULBERTSON

CUMMING, M. J. (See Henry Matthews)

CUMMINGS, ALONZO born ca. 1817, NH, and wife, ANN M., born ca. 1817, NY, were listed in the 1850 census of Adrian Twp., Lenawee Co., Mich. with LAVINA A., age 7, b. NY; LYMAN (SYMAN?), age 2, b. Mich., in their household.

CUMMINGS, ESTHER (See Abel Bemis)

CUMMINS, JAMES was born in Orange Co., NY and he married LUVINIA (ROBISON) who died in NY on 25 Oct. 1844. He moved to Ionia, Mich. in 1862, where he died at age 76. Seven children (names not stated). Known daughter, R. J. b. 25 Jan. 1834, Lansing, Tompkins Co., NY (m. Nathaniel Ball[3], also see). Ref: P&BA-Len pg. 591.

CUMMINS, JOHN born ca. 1797, and wife, ESTHER, born ca. 1800, both in England, were listed in the 1850 census of Tecumseh Twp., Lenawee Co., Mich.

CUMMINS, THOMAS born ca. 1820, England, and wife, WILLOMINA, born ca. 1826, Penn., were listed in the 1850 census of Tecumseh Twp., Lenawee Co., Mich. with CHARLES, age 4; JOHN, age 2, both b. Mich., in their household.

CURE, ASEL, son of HIRAM (following), was born 17 Apr. 1832, Orleans Co., NY. At age 12, he worked on the Great Lakes as a seaman, and worked at that for over 21 years. However, it appears to be listed as "Asahel," age 18, in the 1850 census of Rome Twp., Lenawee Co., Mich. in his father's household. He married on 8 Jan. 1867 in Adrian to LASIRA (BAKER), daughter of Norman (also see) of Rome Twp., and they settled on a farm in Rome Twp. that extended into Cambridge Twp. Children: 1. CLERA b. 10 Apr. 1873; 2. JENNIE P. b. 3 Mar. 1879; 3. CHANNING b. 24 Mar. 1887. Ref: P&BA-Len pg. 840-1.

CURE, CATHARINE born ca. 1793, Greene Co., NY, married Ransom Thomas and lived in Penfield, Monroe Co., NY; and in Rome & Adrian Twps., Lenawee Co., Mich. Ref: P&BA-Len pg. 1085-6. Note JOHN, following.

CURE, GEORGE, probably son of JOHN (following), born ca. 1817, and wife, HARRIET, born ca. 1827, both in NY, were listed in the 1850 census of Rollin Twp., Lenawee Co., Mich. with BENJAMIN F., age 5; MARY A., age 3; ELEANOR, age 1, all b. Mich., in their household.

CURE, HIRAM, son of JOHN (following), born ca. 1804, NY, worked on the Erie Canal until about a year after his marriage (ca. 1827) in NY to CLARISSA (CARTER), daughter of Asel (also see); and they were in Orleans Co., NY ca. 1832. They moved to Adrian Twp., Lenawee Co. Mich., then moved to Rollin Twp. before 1850, where Clarissa died at age 56. He afterwards moved to Rome Twp. where he died. Known children: 1. LINAS A. (served Mexican War; died a Seaman during "Dr. Kane's expedition to the Polar Seas."); 2. MALVINA b. ca. 1831; 3. ASEL (preceding); 4. LUCRETIA b. ca. 1836, preceding all b. NY; and 5. MINERVA b. ca. 1840; 6. HIRAM W., born ca. 1845, last 2 b. Mich.

CURE, JOHN came from Germany to New York before 1793. There was a man by this name in Greene Co., NY in the 1800 census index. He was said to have had a home in Vermont per sketch. He married ELEANOR, also b. Germany, and she died in New York at age 81. John came to Adrian, Lenawee Co., Mich. and died at "an advanced age." Known son, HIRAM (preceding). Ref: P&BA-Len pg. 840-1. Also note CATHARINE, GEORGE, MARIA, & MARTIN.

CURE, MARIA born 4 Oct. 1804, Saratoga Co., NY married Leander Wood (also see) and lived Orleans Co., NY before moving to Mich. Note JOHN, preceding.

CURE, MARTIN (See JOHN, preceding) born ca. 1813, and his wife, LYDIA, born ca. 1819, both in NY, were listed in the 1840 census index of Rome Twp., Lenawee Co., Mich. as "Cune;" and were listed in the 1850 census of Rome Twp. with ADELIA, age 13; DOLLY, age 9; GEORGE, age 7; JAMES, age 5; HELEN, age 2, all b. Mich., in their household.

CURRIER, HANNAH (See Hugh Tolford)

CURRIER, JAALA? was listed in the 1840 census index of Clinton Twp., Lenawee Co., Mich. Note SARAH E. (following).

CURRIER, SARAH E. Mrs.? born ca. 1804, Conn., was head of household in the 1850 census of Tecumseh Twp., Lenawee Co., Mich., with OSCAR D. S., age 14, b. NY; and M. K. Ogden, age 27, Ambrosia Ogden, age 22; James Knapp, age 25; Lydia Knapp, age 20, all b. NY in her household.

CURRY, JAMES born ca. 1798, England, and wife, POLLY, born ca. 1807, NY, were listed in the 1850 census of Macon Twp., Lenawee Co., Mich. with WILLIAM, age 17; SARAH, age 14; SAMUEL, age 12; JANE, age 6; CATHARINE, age 3; HENRY, age 1, all b. NY, in their household.

CURRY, JOHN B. born ca. 1809, and wife, ABBY ANN, born ca. 1820, both in NY, were listed in the 1850 census of Tecumseh Twp., Lenawee Co., Mich. with GEORGE W., age 11. b. Mich. in their household. Also there were Asahel Sanford (also see), and wife, Abby, perhaps in-laws?

CURRY, MARGARET of Ireland (See James Moreland[1])

CURRY, OLIVER (See John Dubois)

CURRY, ONIE (See James T. Boyce)

Pioneer Families of Southeastern Michigan

CURTIS also see CURTISS

CURTIS, ADDIE born after 1850 (See Jonathan Rowley).

CURTIS, AUGUSTUS E. (See Burton Kent)

CURTIS, CHARILLA married 25 Jan. 1818, Saratoga Co. NY, to James L. Rogers (also see). Ref: P&BA-Len pg. 647-8.

CURTIS, CHESTER (See Samuel Lewis)

CURTIS, CLARISSA (See Philip Salsbury)

CURTIS, CORDELIA of Oakland Co. Mich. married Isaac Benedict (also see) of Dover Twp., Lenawee Co., Mich. as his second wife. Her parents (names not stated) went from Oakland Co. Mich. to Hitchcock Co., Nebr.

CURTIS, DAVID, son of Rev. STEPHEN (following), born 9 Feb. 1802, Cambridge, Washington Co., NY, moved with his parents to Otsego Co., NY. He moved first to Cayuga Co., NY, but returned to Otsego Co. He married CHARLOTTE (ST JOHN) who was born 17 Oct. 1807, Chagrin Village, Ohio (census said b. NY). About 1840, they removed to Hudson Twp., Lenawee Co., Mich. She died 10 Jan. 1876. Children (ages from 1850 census of Hudson Twp.): 1. STEPHEN W. (following); 2. 2. MARY A., age 15; 3. EVELINE, age 11; 4. CORNELIA, age 10; 5. CORDELIA, age 10 (twin); 6. ELIZABETH, age 8, all b. NY; and 7. JULIA, age 6, b. Mich. Note: CHARLOTTE F., age 16, b. NY, in the household of a Howe family may relate to this family. Ref: P&BA-Len pg. 696-7.

CURTIS, DAVID A. born ca. 1820, and wife, MARY J., born ca. 1824, both in NY, were listed in the 1850 census of Seneca Twp., Lenawee Co., Mich. with ALONZO, age 3/12, b. Mich., in their household.

CURTIS, DAVID A. Rev. (See Eben Dunham)

CURTIS, E. W. born ca. 1818, and wife, LUCY M., born ca. 1821, both in NY, were listed in the 1850 census of Dover Twp., Lenawee Co., Mich. with MARCUS A., age 7, b. NY, in their household.

CURTIS, EDWARD, son of SAMUEL (of England, who remained there), was born in England, and came as a young man to the US and lived first in Oneida Co., NY; and in 1835 came to Rome Twp., Lenawee Co., Mich. where he died at age 32. He had married SUSANNAH (SMITH) born 1810, England, who had come with her parents to the US and settled in Jackson Co., Mich. After his death, she was living in the household of (his brother?), WILLIAM (following), with her children, ages as shown: ROBERT b. 5 Feb. 1832, Oneida Co.; 2. REBECCA, age 13; 3. PERLEY, age 9; 4. THOMAS, age 7 (Note THOMAS J., following); 5. ORLANDO, age 6; 6. ELIZA, age 2, last 5 b. Mich.

CURTIS, ELIJAH of Ontario Co., NY died there at age 65. His wife (name not stated) came to Mich. and died at age 88 at the home of a son in Genesee Co., Mich. Known daughter, RACHEL (m. Jacob Teachout^2 born ca. 1784). Ref: P&BA-Len pg. 961-2. Note: This may be same man as ELIJAH SR. (following), as there were several Teachout families also in Saratoga Co., NY in 1800.

CURTIS, ELIJAH W. (Sr.) was born 1760, Conn., and enlisted in the Revolution at age 15. He received Bounty Lad in Galway, Saratoga Co., NY, where he settled, and he died at Saratoga Springs at age 75. Known son, ELIJAH W. (Jr.), following. Ref: P&BA-Len pg. 251-2. Probably he in the 1800 census index of Saratoga Co., NY.

CURTIS, ELIJAH W. (Jr.), son of ELIJAH W. (preceding), married _?_ (CHAMBERLAIN), daughter of Capt. Ichabod (also a Rev. soldier) probably in Saratoga Co., NY. He moved to Michigan ca. 1851 and died a few months later. Known son, GEORGE H. (following). Ref: P&BA-Len pg. 251-2. Note: There was an ELIJAH listed in the 1840 census index of Novi, Oakland Co. Mich.

CURTIS, GEORGE C. born ca. 1817, VT, and wife, PERCES?, born ca. 1822, Mass., were listed in the 1850 census of Adrian Twp., Lenawee Co., Mich.

CURTIS, GEORGE H., son of ELIJAH W. (Jr., preceding), was born 23 Mar. 1835, Saratoga Spring, NY. He served as a Lt. in Co. B., 2d New Jersey Inf., Civil War. He came to Mich. in 1851, and settled first in Rome Twp., Lenawee Co., Mich., and afterwards in Adrian. He married HARRIET E. (DUTTON), daughter of William (also see). Children: 1. FANNY L.; 2. MAMIE; 3. WILLIAM WHEELER; 4. GEORGE OSCAR; 5. JAMES E.; 6. EVA; 7. ETHEL. Ref: P&BA-Len pg. 251-2.

CURTIS, J. G. of Peterboro, NY (See Isaac A. Bartlett). See WILLIAM following.

CURTIS, JOHN born ca. 1824, and wife, ELMIRA, born ca. 1825, both in Ohio, were listed in the 1850 census of Palmyra Twp., Lenawee Co., Mich. with LEWIS E., age 3, b. Ohio; CYNTHIA A., age 6/12, b. Mich., in their household.

CURTIS, NEWMAN born ca. 1824, and JANE, born ca. 1830, both in NY, were listed in the 1850 census of Rome Twp., Lenawee Co., Mich. in the household of Isaiah Teachout. Note ELIJAH of Ontario Co., NY, preceding.

CURTIS, ROBERT, son of EDWARD (preceding), born 5 Feb. 1832, Oneida Co., NY, came to Rome Twp., Lenawee Co., Mich. with his parents. He married there in 1857 to MAHALA (MYERS), daughter of Nathan (also see). Children: 1. NATHAN b. 25 Apr. 1859 (m. Lillian Slocum); 2. GEORGE E. b. 22 Oct. 1860 (d. 6 Jan. 1872); 3. CORA M. b. 23 Nov. 1862 (m. Bert Short, Cambridge Twp.); 4. LILIBURN L. b. 10 Jan. 1865; 5. JUSTIN R. b. 29 Dec. 1868 (m. Nellie Ball, dau. of Nathaniel^3, also see); 6. ADA M. b. 20 July 1872; 7. LEE O. b. 26 Sept. 1874; 8. OCTA N. b. 23 May 1876. Ref: P&BA-Len pg. 591 & 835-6.

CURTIS, SAMUEL and wife, SARAH (LEWIS), were natives of England. They had 15 children (names not stated), and a son came to the US (note EDWARD, preceding); and also daughter, ELIZABETH b. 1817, East Kent, England (m/1 James Ligden; m/2 Abraham Bateman, also see.) Ref: P&BA-Len pg. 747-8. Also see WILLIAM, with whom EDWARD resided in the 1850 census of Rome Twp., Lenawee Co. Mich.

CURTIS, SARAH (See Jonah Miller)

CURTIS, SHADY (See John Howell)

CURTIS, STEPHEN of Mass. (See William Ladd)

CURTIS, STEPHEN Rev. of New England lived first in Washington Co., NY and then in Otsego Co., NY. He married POLLY (LOOMIS). He died in 1837 after returning from a visit to Michigan. Eight children (names not stated). Known son, DAVID (preceding). Ref: P&BA-Len pg. 696-7.

CURTIS, STEPHEN W., son of DAVID (preceding), born 17 Mar. 1831, Ira, Cayuga Co., NY, moved with his parents to Lenawee Co., Mich.; and married in Sept. 1857 in Hudson Twp. to JEANNETTE (LADD), daughter of John (also see). She died 18 Feb. 1866, age 34, leaving 2 children: 1. ADALINE (m. A. D. Rowley, Hudson Twp.); 2. GEORGE W. (Hudson Twp.). Stephen W. married again on 19 Feb. 1868 to MARTHA J. (SUTTON), daughter of John D. (also see). Children: 3. WILLIAM J.; 4. FRED M. b. 25 Feb. 1873 (d. Dec. 1873); 5. JOHN. Ref: P&BA-Len pg. 696-7.

CURTIS, THOMAS J. (See EDWARD, preceding) was born 24 Aug. 1842, Rome Twp., Lenawee Co., Mich. He served in the Civil War, Co. K., 4th Mich. Inf. He married IDA (BRITTEN), daughter of Richard R. (also see), 12 Dec. 1868, Pittsford, Hillsdale Co., Mich. They lived first in Pittsford, then moved to Rome Twp., Lenawee Co., Mich. Children: 1. WILLARD R. b. 30 May 1870, Pittsford; 2. MANELLA b. 6 Feb. 1874, Rome Twp.; 3. RAY R. b. 29 Nov. 1879; 4. GLENN b. 10 June 1884; 5. GAIL b. 1 Apr. 1886. Ref: P&BA-Len pg. 555-6.

CURTIS, WILLIAM was born ca. 1818, England, and is listed as head of household in which EDWARD (preceding) and family were living in the 1850 census of Rome Twp. They may be sons of SAMUEL (preceding).

CURTIS, WILLIAM J. of Pompey Hill, NY (See Isaac A. Bartlett). Also see J. G. (preceding).

CURTISS also see CURTIS

CURTISS in the 1800 census index of Columbia Co., NY were AMAZIAH; DANIEL; JAMES; ROSANNA; SAMUEL; SAMUEL A.; SAMUEL JR.; SELDEN. Note CHARLES O., following.

CURTISS, CHARLES O., born 6 Dec. 1785, Columbia Co., NY, went to Paris, Oneida Co., NY, where he married HANNAH (HAMMOND). She died at age 40. They had known children: LYMAN (following); HIRAM A. (following); JULIA b. 27 Nov. 1818 (lived with Hiram in 1888). Charles O. married twice more, and he had a total of 17 children (names not stated). He died at age 83 in Paris, NY. Ref: P&BA-Len pg. 976-7; 992-3.

CURTISS, HIRAM A., son of CHARLES O. (preceding), was born 17 June 1816, Paris, Oneida Co., NY. He married in 1842 to LYDIA (HULL), daughter of Benjamin (also see); and they moved that year to Ridgeway Twp., Lenawee Co., Mich. She died 21 Apr. 1887. Of their 5 children, 3 died young (as follows): HANNAH J. d. 12 Apr. 1845, age 2yr/9da; CHARLES E. d. 13 Mar. 1851, age 2yr/3mo; GEORGE W. d. age 1yr/2mo. Surviving were WILLIAM H. (m. Elizabeth Zeluff); ELIZA (m. William Britton, Britton, Mich.). Ref: P&BA-Len pg. 976-7.

CURTISS, LYMAN A., son of CHARLES O. (preceding), was born 17 Mar. 1814, Paris, NY. He married there to POLLY (DUNHAM), daughter of Aaron (also see). They moved to Ridgeway Twp., Lenawee Co., Mich. in 1839, where they remained. Childen: 1. L. MILTON; 2. DARIUS J. (m. Margaretta Gibson); 3. MARY A.; 4. SAMANTHA J.; 5. SARAH A.; 6. ANN O. (deceased before 1888). Ref: P&BA-Len pg. 992-3.

CURTISS, MYRON A. born ca. 1812, and wife, JULIANN, born ca. 1820, both in NY, were listed in the 1850 census of Tecumseh Twp., Lenawee Co., Mich. with CHARLES F., age 6; and ELISA, age 4, both b. Mich., in their household.

CUSHING, SAMUEL and wife, DORCAS (DANILES/DANIELS?), moved from Vermont to Michigan. Known daughter, ELIZABETH A. (m. Birdsey J. Bidwell, also see, 1842, in Tecumseh Twp., Lenawee Co. Mich.)

CUSHMAN, THEODORA (See Erastus Knight)

CUTSHAW - Four young men of this family were said to have gone to California in 1852 by ship, in the company of several other young men from Lenawee Co., Mich. (See Marvin A. Packard). Ref: P&BA-Len pg. 890-1.

CUTSHAW, J. B. born ca. 1822, Ohio, and wife, DIANEY P., born ca. 1826, NY, were listed in the 1850 census of Adrian Twp., Lenawee Co., Mich. with BYRON, age 6; and LEMUEL, age ?, both b. Mich., in their houshold.

CUTLER, LUCY (See Samuel Day)

- D -

DAGGETT, MARIA Mrs. (written in census as "Daget") born ca. 1808, NY, was listed in the 1850 census of Madison Twp., Lenawee Co., Mich. with MARIA, age 10, b. NY, was in the household of Ebenzer F. Gleason.

DAGGETT, RUFUS and wife, ESTHER (DEXTER), moved from Rhode Island to Chenango Co., NY where they remained. Eleven children (names not stated). Known daughter, SALLIE b. 14 July 1815, RI (m. George W. Stephenson, also see). Ref: P&BA-Len pg. 884-5.

DAILEY also see DALEY; DALLEY; DALY

DAILEY, JOHN see JOHN DARBY

DAILEY, JULIETTE (See Theodore Abbott)

DAILEY, MICHAEL born ca. 1805, and wife, MARY, born ca. 1805, both in Ireland, were listed in the 1850 census of Blissfield Twp., Lenawee Co., Mich. with JAMES, age 23; JOHN, age 16; MICHAEL, age 12, all b. Canada; and WILLIAM, age 4, b. Mich., in their household.

DAILEY, PATRICK born ca. 1810, and wife, MARGARET, born ca. 1810, both in Ireland, were listed in the 1850 census of Blissfield Twp., Lenawee Co., Mich. with HUGH, age 19, b. NY, in their household.

DAKE, ABIGAIL (See Thomas Bradley[2])

DALEY also see DAILEY; DALLEY, DALY

DALEY, LYMAN born ca. 1820, NY, and wife, LUSANY, born ca. 1824, Ohio, were listed in the 1850 census of Ridgeway Twp., Lenawee Co., Mich. with WARREN, age 4; DANIEL, age 1, both b. Ohio; and Lucy Palmer, age 33, b. NY, with children Emily, age 11; Jerome, age 9; Lavina, age 6, all b. Ohio.

DALEY, WILLIAM born ca. 1790, NY, was listed in the 1850 census of Raisin Twp., Lenawee Co., Mich.

DALLEY also see DAILEY; DALEY, DALY

DALLEY, JULIUS and wife, MARGARET (WILLETT), of Readington, Hunterdon Co., NJ lived out their lives there, he dying in 1850, and she in 1823. Known daughter, MARIA b. 13 May 1814 (m. James Lanning, also see, in Raisin Twp., Lenawee Co., Mich.) Note: Maria was said to have come to Michigan from New Jersey with "sister-in-law, ELIZABETH DALLEY." Ref: P&BA-Len pg. 797-8.

DALY, HENRY F., son of HENRY (b. Washington Co., NY), was born Lockport, Niagara Co., NY. He married on 20 Apr. 1834 to MARIE (McCAMBER) who was born Rose,

Pioneer Families of Southeastern Michigan

Wayne Co., NY. They came first to Michigan in 1850, then went to Wisconsin, Illinois, and Colorado, returning to Adrian, Lenawee Co., Mich. by 1852. He was still living in 1888, age 59. Children: 1. HENRY; 2. JOSEPHINE b. 24 May 1856 (m. George H. Oram, also see); 3. EVA; 4. EDWIN; 5. THAD B.; 6. LINNIE. Ref: P&BA-Len pg. 645-6.

DAMON, ALBERT born ca. 1822, and wife, HARRIET, born ca. 1824, both in NY, were listed in the 1850 census of Adrian Twp., Lenawee Co., Mich. with FRANCIS E., age 4; EMMA, age 2, both b. Mich., in their household.

DAMON, LUKE, son of LUTHER (following), was born 19 Feb. 1822, Fitzwilliam, NH, and married there 13 Nov. 1843 to ESTHER I. (WALES), daughter of Jacob (also see). They moved to Adrian Twp., Lenawee Co., Mich. in 1853. Known daughter, EDWINA, b. 28 Jan. 1848 (m. W. F. Ayers, Adrian). Ref: P&BA-Len pg. 460-1.

DAMON, LUTHER & wife, SYBIL (FISK) were natives of New Hampshire; and he died in Fitzwilliam at age 49. She died in Dana, Mass. at age 84. Five sons and 6 daughters (names not stated). In 1888, one child lived in VT; 2 in New Hampshire; & known son, LUKE (preceding). Ref: P&BA-Len pg. 460-1.

DANCER, HARRIET E. (See William Davison)

DANIELS also see DANILES

DANIELS, ALBERT C. of Fulton Co., Ohio (See Cyrenus Sanford).

DANIELS, AMOS born ca. 1787, Conn., and wife, NANCY, born ca. 1798, NY, were listed in the 1840 census index of Cambridge Twp., Lenawee Co., Mich., and in the 1850 census listed ALBERT, age 33; GEORGE, age 25; RICHARD, age 25; CALVIN, age 23, all b. NY, in their household.

DANIELS, ANDREW P. born ca. 1810, Maine, and wife, MARTHA, born ca. 1821, NY, were listed in the 1850 census of Adrian Twp., Lenawee Co., Mich. with ALVIRA N., age 5; ASA B., age 3, both b. Mich., and RICHARD, age 37, b. Maine (brother?), in their household.

DANIELS, AUGUSTUS F., son of GEORGE (following), was born 12 Mar. 1815, Hillsboro, NH. He moved to Rensselaer Co., NY. He married first in NY to MARY (RANNEY) who was born ca. 1816 in Ashfield, Franklin Co., Mass. In 1838, they moved to Medina Twp., Lenawee Co., Mich.; and in 1842 to Madison Twp.; and 1845 to Adrian, but returned to Madison Twp. by 1850, where Mary died in 1878. Children: 1. MARTHA b. ca. 1838, Mich. (m. Tunis J. Carter, Seneca Twp.); 2. GEORGE b. ca. 1850 (m. Mrs. Louise Taylor, Morenci, Mich.); 3. FREDINO (m. Mary Riter, Cambridge Twp.). Augustus married again on 7 Mar. 1880 to Mrs. LORETTA L. (HOWARD) SAMMONS, daughter of Francis (also see), and widow of John F. Sammons, son of Sampson (also see). Ref: P&BA-Len pg. 362-3. Note: In the 1840 census index, Augustus was listed adjacent to EBENEZER & DANIEL R. (following).

DANIELS, CHARLES born ca. 1820, NY, was listed in the 1850 census of Rome Twp., Lenawee Co., Mich.

DANIELS, DANIEL R. born ca. 1807, and wife, MATILDA, born ca. 1811, both in NY, were listed in the 1840 census index of Medina Twp., Lenawee Co., Mich.; and in the 1850 census of Hudson Twp. with WALAND E., age 10; MARY J., age 3; ARCHIBALD, age 1, all b. Mich.; and LEMUEL, age 44, b. NY (brother?), in their household.

DANIELS, DAVID I. (See John Phillips)

DANIELS, EBENEZER born ca. 1805, and wife, LAURA, born ca. 1818, both in NY, were listed in the 1840 census index of Medina Twp., Lenawee Co., Mich.; and in the 1850 census of Hudson Twp. with HARRIET, age 3, b. Mich.; and Ann Hamilton, age 11, b. Mich. (See Dr. Increase S. Hamilton), in their household.

DANIELS, ELIZABETH (See John M. Osborn; and see Zenus Roberts)

DANIELS, ELIZABETH E. born ca. 1829, England, and JABEZ J., age 19, b. Mich., were listed in the 1850 census of Medina Twp., Lenawee Co., Mich. They may be related to THOMAS (following).

DANIELS, EZEKIEL M. born ca. 1820, VT, and wife, ANN, born ca. 1825, NY, were listed in the 1850 census of Medina Twp., Lenawee Co., Mich. with ROBERT E., age 4; EZEKIEL, age 1, both b. Mich., in their household.

DANIELS, GEORGE and wife, NANCY (SMITH), were natives of New Hampshire, who remained there. There were 12 children (names not stated) of whom 6 lived to maturity; and in 1888 there were 3 surviving, including known son, AUGUSTUS F. (preceding). Ref: P&BA-Len pg. 362-3.

DANIELS, HARRIET R. married in 1842, possibly in Medina Twp., Lenawee Co., Mich. to Dr. Increase S. Hamilton (as second wife), and settled in Tecumseh. Note EBENEZER & DANIEL R.

DANIELS, HARRISON, probably son of JAMES (following), was born 4 Apr. 1810; and his wife, SYLVIA (HADLEY), was born 26 May 1809, and are listed in the 1840 census index of Franklin Twp., Lenawee Co., Mich. (apparently elsewhere in 1850). He died 9 July 1896, and she died 27 Aug. 1879, and they sre buried in the Mills Cemetery, Franklin Twp. Buried with them are JEFFERSON b. 27 Jan. 1847 (d. 27 Feb. 1868); EDWIN b. 3 Mar. 1841 (d. 27 Oct. 1841), probably not a complete list of children.

DANIELS, J. B. (See Marshall Reed)

DANIELS, JAMES born ca. 1781, New Hampshire, and wife, JULIA, born ca. 1792, VT, were listed in the 1840 census index of Franklin Twp., Lenawee Co., Mich., and in the 1850 census listed in the household SABRINA, age 9, place of birth not legible (possibly a grandchild). James died 27 Dec. 1850, age 70y/4m/16d; and Julia died 11 Dec. 1857, aged 63y/8m/1d, both buried in Mills Cemetery, Franklin Twp. See HARRISON (preceding).

DANIELS, JEANINE (See Lucius Lilley)

DANIELS, LEMUEL A. (See DANIEL R., preceding)

DANIELS, LYMAN was listed in the 1840 census index of Adrian Twp., Lenawee Co., Mich., but not in 1850.

DANIELS, MINERVA (See James Whitney)

DANIELS, RICHARD (See ANDREW P., preceding)

DANIELS, SAMUEL was listed in the 1840 census index of Palmyra Twp., Lenawee Co., Mich., but not listed in 1850.

DANIELS, THOMAS was born ca. 1825, England, and his wife, ELIZABETH, was born ca. 1832, NY, and they are listed in the 1850 census of Hudson Twp., Lenawee Co., Mich. Note ELIZABETH E. (preceding) & JABEZ J.

DANILES also see DANIELS

DANILES, DORCAS (See Samuel Cushing)

DARBY, CELIA (See John Forbes)

DARBY, JOHN born ca. 1784, and wife, FANNY, born ca. 1787, both in NY, were listed in the 1850 census of Franklin Twp., Lenawee Co., Mich. shown as married within the year(?). (Note: However, due to the extremely poor penmanship in that census, much was hard to read; and this name was indexed under "DAILEY," though it appeared to your compiler to be "DARBY.") Listed in their household were ABRAHAM, age 35; WILLIAM, age 21; CATHARINE, age 16, all b. NY; and children: AMANDA, age 9; CHARLES, age 7, possibly "Daily," both b. Mich. Albert H. Briggs, age 13, b. Mich. was also listed.

DARBY, LUCRETIA born Washington Co., NY (See John Lagore)

DARBY, PATRICK born ca. 1810, Ireland, was listed in the 1850 census of Seneca Twp., Lenawee Co., Mich.

DARLING, BENJAMIN born ca. 1794, and wife, EDITH, born ca. 1794, both in New Hampshire, were listed in the 1840 census index of Woodstock Twp., Lenawee Co. Mich.; and in the 1850 census with SALVADOR, age 22, b. NY; and THOMAS, age 17; ELIZABETH, age 13; GEORGE, age 11, all b. Ohio, in their household.

DARLING, ENOCH born ca. 1824, and wife, AURILLA, born ca. 1831?, both b. in NY, were listed in the 1850 census of Hudson Twp., Lenawee Co., Mich. with EDWIN, age 6, b. Mich., in their household.

DARLING, GEORGE W. (See James K. Jeffrey)

DARLING, HECTOR was listed in the 1840 census index of Tecumseh Twp., Lenawee Co., Mich.

DARLING, HENRY born ca. 1810, Conn, and wife, MATILDA, born ca. 1813, NY, were listed in the 1850 census of Macon Twp., Lenawee Co., Mich. with MARY E., age 12, b. Ohio; and JAMES M., age 7; JULIA F., age 5; JOHN H., age 3; NOYES/MAYER?, age 5/12, all b. Mich., in their household.

DARLING, JOHN (b. ca. 1860s?; see Roswell Bennett).

DARLING, MARCELLUS born ca. 1820, and wife, ADELIA, born ca. 1826, both in NY, were listed in the 1850 census of Rome Twp., Lenawee Co., Mich. with no family.

DARLING, N. A. Dr. of Ann Arbor, Mich. married MARY A. (GILMORE), daughter of Lyman (also see); and he died and Mary A. resided with her father in Macon Twp., Lenawee Co., Mich. in 1888.

DARLING, R. P. (See John Wilson)

DARLING, ROANDEL? born ca. 1818, Vermont, and wife, MINERVA, born ca. 1822, NY, were listed in the 1850 census of Woodstock Twp., Lenawee Co., Mich. with LEGRAND, age 3; PHILENA, age 2, both b. Mich., in their household. Note: BENJAMIN, preceding.

DARLINGTON, ISRAEL born ca. 1808, Penn., and wife, ANNA, born ca. 1813, VT, were listed in the 1850 census of Woodstock Twp, Lenawee Co., Mich. with ELISA, age 2, b. Mich., and Henry Tibbits, age 6, both b. Mich. in their household. Note: In the 1850 census, John Iveson was 2 doors away, see OLIVER (following).

DARLINGTON, OLIVER (See John Iveson)

DAVENPORT, CATHARINE born Tompkins Co., NY (See Joseph Burke).

DAVENPORT, CORNELIUS born ca. 1805, NJ, and wife, CAROLINE, born ca. 1805, NY, were listed in the 1840 census index of Macon Twp., Lenawee Co., Mich.; and in the 1850 census listed LAWRENCE, age 22; HUMPHREY, age 20; CALVIN, age 18, all b. NY; and SARAH L., age 15; HANNAH, age 12; ABRAHAM, age 10; LYMAN C., age 7, all b. Mich., in their household.

DAVENPORT, EBENEZER snd wife, MARY (BEALS), both born Rhode Island, married there, and about 1821 moved to Wayne Co., NY, and then to Yates Co., but returned to Wayne Co. where they remained. Nine children of whom 8 lived to maturity (names not stated). Known son, PARDON T. (following). Ref: P&BA-Len pg. 984-5.

DAVENPORT, GEORGE W., son of PARDON T. (following), was born 31 Dec. 1845, Blissfield Twp., Lenawee Co., Mich., and married EMELINE (BACK), daughter of George H. (also see). Children: 1. NELLIE M.; 2. HARRY C. Ref: P&BA-Len pg. 984-5.

DAVENPORT, JOHN born ca. 1816, NY, is probably he listed in the 1840 census index of Franklin Twp., Lenawee Co., Mich.; and in the 1850 census with children: MARY, age 10; WILLIAM, age 9; EDWARD, age 7; ALSE? (female), age 5; EDGAR, age 2, all b. Mich. in his household.

DAVENPORT, JOHN born ca. 1801, Mass., and wife, AZUBAL, born ca. 1800, Penn., were listed in the 1850 census of Hudson Twp., Lenawee Co., Mich. with GEORGE W., age 7, b. Mich., in their household. Note: SIMON, age 15, b. Mich., in the household of Highland Beach, and wife, Almeda (age 19, b. NY), may relate to this family.

DAVENPORT, PARDON T., son of EBENEZER (preceding), was born 10 Mar. 1815, Tiverton, RI, and moved with his parents to Wayne Co., NY. In 1835, he moved to Blissfield Twp., Lenawee Co., Mich.; and on 28 Nov. 1838 married FRANCES MARIA (WARREN) in Dover Twp. She was born 20 Feb. 1818, Farmington, Ontario Co., NY (See Samuel Warren). They settled in Blissfield Twp. Son, GEORGE W. (preceding). Ref: P&BA-Len pg. 984-5.

DAVID, RUTH AMELIA (See Elisha Baker)

DAVIDSON, AMERICUS born ca. 1833, NY, was listed in the 1850 census of Rome Twp., Lenawee Co., Mich. in household of Benjamin & Maria Luther.

DAVIDSON, FRANK (FRANCISCO), son of SIMEON (following), born ca. 1839, married 26 Mar. 1862 to ELIZABETH (LACOCK), daughter of Henry (also see), and they settled in Tecumseh Twp., Lenawee Co., Mich. Children: 1. GEORGE S.; 2. LOANNA M.; 3. GUY J. Ref: P&BA-Len pg. 883-4.

DAVIDSON, GEORGE (probably son of PETER, following) born ca. 1827, NY, and wife, JULIETTE, b. ca. 1832, both in NY, were listed in the 1850 census of Tecumseh Twp., Lenawee Co. Mich.

DAVIDSON, HELEN born ca. 1831, VT, was listed in the 1850 census of Tecumseh Twp., Lenawee Co., Mich. in the Dayton household. Note LYMAN (following).

DAVIDSON, LYMAN born ca. 1808, VT, and wife, MARANDA, born ca. 1815, Mass., were listed in the 1850 census of Palmyra Twp., Lenawee Co., Mich. with CORDELIA, age 20, b. NY; HENRY, age 23, b. Mich.?;

CHARLES, age 9, b. Ohio; and FREDERICK, age 7; HELEN, age 3, both b. Mich., in their household. Note HELEN, preceding. Also, CAROLINE, b. ca. 1832, Ohio, in 1850 census of Macon Twp., in household of Osborn family, may relate to this family. DAVIDSON, PETER born ca. 1807, and wife, LUCRETIA, born ca. 1808, both in NY, were listed in the 1850 census of Tecumseh Twp., Lenawee Co. Mich. with GEORGE (preceding) listed next door.

DAVIDSON, SIMEON born ca. 1804, NY, married first to CERENA (MILLER), daughter of Isaiah (also see), in 1829 in Lodi, Seneca Co., NY. About 1832, they moved to Macon Twp., Lenawee Co., Mich. Children: 1. GEORGE W. (d. child); 2. CLARISSA (d. child); 3. MINOR M. b. ca. 1832; 4. JEHIEL b. ca. 1836; 5. FRANCISCO (FRANK) b. ca. 1839. Simeon married again before 1850 to Mrs. JOHANNA "HANNAH" (VAN VLEET) CADMUS born ca. 1810, NY, widow of Abraham Cadmus (also see). They later moved to Tecumseh, Mich. Ref: P&BA-Len pg. 331-3.

DAVIS, ABIGAIL (See James Keyes)

DAVIS, AMOS born ca. 1815, and wife, SARAH, born ca. 1818, both in NY, were listed in the 1850 census of Tecumseh Twp., Lenawee Co., Mich. with ABBA, age 2, b. Mich., in the household.

DAVIS, ARVILLA (NIBLACK) - See John Niblack.

DAVIS, ASA and wife, POLLY, natives of Mass., moved to New York before 1802, and remained there. Known daughter, POLLY C. b. 18 Oct. 1803 (m. John Morton^2, also see,). Note: In the 1800 census index, there were 2 men named ASA, one in Oneida Co., and one in Otsego Co. NY.

DAVIS, BETSEY (See Jonathan Knowles)

DAVIS, CATHARINE (See William Osborn)

DAVIS, CHARLES was listed in the 1840 census index of Palmyra Twp., Lenawee Co., Mich.

DAVIS, COLLINS born ca. 1802, and wife, ARVILLA, born ca. 1820, both in NY, were listed in the 1850 census of Tecumseh Twp., Lenawee Co., Mich. with IRENE, age 7; GEORGE, age 4, both b. Mich.; and Elisa Britton, age 22, b. NY, in their household. DELIA, age 16, b. Mich., in a Crowder household may relate to this family.

DAVIS, EBENEZER born ca. 1800, Mass., and wife, EUNICE, born ca. 1812, NY, were listed in the 1850 census of Franklin Twp., Lenawee Co., Mich. with CHARLES, age 16; ESTELLA, age 8; HELEN, age 1, all b. Mich., in their household.

DAVIS, ETHAN, born in Conn., moved to Monroe Co., NY with his parents (names not stated). He married ALICE (CASE), who was born in NY, and they moved to Dundee, Monroe Co., Mich. before 1840 (Note: In the 1840 census index he was listed as Ethan Jr.); and they both died in Petersburg, Monroe Co. Known daughter, ALMIRA (m. George H. Back, also see). Ref: P&BA-Len pg. 768-70.

DAVIS, HIRAM L. born ca. 1809, and wife, LYDIA, born ca. 1821, both in NY, were listed in the 1850 census of Adrian Twp., Lenawee Co., Mich. with MARY, age 16; ANN, age 11, both b. Canada; and ANNAMARIA, age 7, b. NY, in their household. They were listed next door to LEWIS (following).

DAVIS, ISAAC born ca. 1803, and wife, AMELIA (VAN OSTRAND), born ca. 1802, both in NY, were listed in the 1850 census of Palmyra Twp., Lenawee Co., Mich. with ISAAC W., age 22, b. NY; and all following b. Mich.: HANNAH, age 16; WILLIAM, age 13; JULIA A., age 11; JONATHAN, age 9; SARAH H. b. Nov. 1843 (m. Merritt H. Higby, also see). Ref: P&BA-Len og. 1100. Also see CHARLES & POLLY.

DAVIS, JANE (See Ephraim Weylie)

DAVIS, JOHN PARSON was born Long Island, NY, son of a Revolutionary Officer (name not stated), and was of Welsh descent. He was an early settler of Montgomery Co., NY, where he died. Known son, RAMUS (following). Ref: P&BA-Len pg. 268-9.

DAVIS, JOHN W., son of RAMUS (following), was born 5 Sept. 1843, Amsterdam, NY. He married EMMA F. (BROUWER), daughter of Jacob, on 27 Oct. 1868. He served in the Civil War. Two children (names not stated) were deceased before 1888. Ref: P&BA-Len pg. 268-9.

DAVIS, JOSEPH born ca. 1787, Conn., was listed in the 1850 census of Adrian Twp., Lenawee Co., Mich. in the household of (son?) GEORGE, age 33, b. NY. Also in the household were JANE, age 25; ELIZA, age 22, both b. NY, relationships not known. Note HIRAM L.; & LEWIS.

DAVIS, JOSEPH born ca. 1823, and wife, OLIVE, born ca. 1824, both in NY, were listed in the 1850 census of Madison Twp., Lenawee Co., Mich. with FRANK A., age 4/12, b. Mich., in their household.

DAVIS, JOSHUA b. 1807, NY, and his wife, SOPHIA (WILLIAMS), born ca. 1811, Conn. moved to first to Ohio, then before 1850 to Franklin Twp., Lenawee Co., Mich. where they listed in the census EMMA, age 15, b. Ohio (m. 19 Nov. 1856, Seneca Twp., Lenawee Co., Mich. to Silas L. Allen, also see); STANLEY, age 13; CHARLES, age 11, both b. NY?; and URSULA, age 8; MAXWELL, age 6; MANNING, age 4, all b. Mich. Ref: P&BA-Len pg. 1034-5.

DAVIS, LEWIS born ca. 1812, and wife, SALLY A., born ca. 1822, both in NY, were listed in the 1850 census of Adrian Twp., Lenawee Co., Mich. with JOSEPH, age 12, b. NY; and RUDLANDUS?, age 2, b. Mich., in their household. Also there were Stephen Mosier, age 25, and Elizabeth A. Mosier, age 22, both b. NY. Note JOSEPH, preceding; and in the 1850 census they were next door to HIRAM L (preceding).

DAVIS, LOREN born ca. 1824, with wife, SUSAN, born ca. 1832, both in NY, were listed in the 1850 census of Hudson Twp., Lenawee Co., Mich. witn Jacob Rice, age 23, b. NY, in their household.

DAVIS, LYMAN E. Rev. (See Andrew J. Hood)

DAVIS, MATHIAS L., son of PHINEAS (following), was born 19 May 1833, Spencer, Medina Co., Ohio. In 1854, he moved to Williams Co., Ohio; and in 1855 moved to Morenci, Lenawee Co., Mich. He married on 23 Mar. 1856, Morenci, to JANE (HAUSE), daughter of Peter (also see). He served in Co. F., 4th Inf., during the Civil War. In 1875, they moved to Dover Twp. Children: 1. ALONZO (d. age 3); 2. FRANK (m. Amanda Deline, Gratiot Co., Mich.); 3. CORA (d. 1865, age 3); 4. PRESTON S.; 5. ULYSSES S.; 6. CARY A. Ref: P&BA-Len pg 343-4.

DAVIS, PHINEAS, son of JOHN (a Revolutionary soldier), was born in Vermont. He married ELIZABETH (LANE), daughter of Mathias (also see); and they settled in New York (Note: There was a Phineas in Herkimer Co., NY in the 1800 census index). He served in the War of 1812 from NY; and in 1829, they moved to Medina Co., Ohio. He died in 1843; and his wife came to Morenci, Mich. in 1856 to live with only son, MATHIAS L. (preceding). There were also 9 daughters (names not stated). Ref: P&BA-Len pg. 343-4.

DAVIS, POLLY Mrs. born ca. 1784, Conn. was listed head of household in the 1850 census of Palmyra Twp., Lenawee Co., Mich. (Note CHARLES, preceding). She listed FREDERICK, age 21; GRADNER, age 16, both b. NY; and (Mrs.) Nancy Shumway, 26, b. NY, with children Mary, age 4, & Levi, age 3, both b. Mich., relationship not known, in her household.

DAVIS, PROSPER born ca. 1817, NY, and wife, MARY, born ca. 1821, Germany, were listed in the 1850 census of Blissfield Twp., Lenawee Co., Mich. with VICTORIA, age ?; and LORENZO, age 1, both b. Mich., in their household.

DAVIS, RAMUS, son of JOHN PARSON (preceding), was born 1 Jan. 1807, Montgomery Co., NY (which later became Fulton Co.). Ramus married HARRIET (WEMPLE), daughter of John (also see), also born Montgomery Co., NY, and they moved in 1838 to Mishawaka, Ind. for 2 years. They returned to Amsterdam, NY; then moved to Eldridge, Onondaga Co., NY from whence they moved to Palmyra Twp., Lenawee Co., Mich. in 1863. He died 21 July 1877, and his wife was surviving in 1888. Children: 1. SUSIE J. (d. 1871); 2. RAMUS B. (served Civil War, lived Riga Twp., Lenawee Co., and Dundee, Monroe Co., Mich.); 3. JOHN W. (preceding); 4. THEOPHILUS A. (following). Ref: P&BA-Len pg 225-6 & 268-9.

DAVIS, SARAH (See Noah Green, Sr.)

DAVIS, SELINA Mrs. born ca. 1822, Ohio, was head of household in the 1850 census of Adrian Twp., Lenawee Co., Mich. with SIMON, age 7; CORNELIA, age 5, both b. Ohio; and PARLEY, age 1, b. Mich., in her household.

DAVIS, SYLVIA (See Jacob Rogers)

DAVIS, THEOPHILUS A., son of RAMUS (preceding), was born 7 Feb. 1849, Montgomery Co., NY, and married CLARA (TOOKER), daughter of Ira on 8 Feb. 1874. Children: 1. MINNIE A.; 2. RAMUS T.; 3. ELLA M.; 4. THEOPHILUS. Ref: P&BA-Len pg. 268-9.

DAVIS, THOMAS born ca. 1811, North Carolina, and wife, HANNAH, born ca. 1826, NY, noted as "Black," had HARRIET, age 1, b. Mich. in their household.

DAVIS, WILLIAM born ca. 1816, and wife, CLARISSA, born ca. 1815, both in Virginia, were listed as "Black."

DAVISON, JOHN born England, came to the US in 1810, and located first in Syracuse, NY. He married ELIZABETH (DOUGLAS), and in 1820, they moved to Niagara Co., NY, and 1823 to Erie Co., NY, where he died at age 75. Elizabeth later came to Woodstock Twp., Lenawee Co., Mich. and died at home of son, WILLIAM (following). There were 5 children (all names not stated). Ref: P&BA-Len pg. 613-4.

DAVISON, WILLIAM, son of JOHN (preceding), was born 8 Nov. 1836, Erie Co., NY. He married there in 1855 to HARRIET E. (DANCER). In 1858, they removed first to Lenawee Co., Mich. and then in 1860 to Jackson Co., Mich. In 1861, they returned to Erie Co., NY; but later returned to Woodstock Twp., Lenawee Co., Mich. Children: 1. LORENZO D. b. 13 Sept. 1856; 2. CORA D. b. 15 Aug. 1859. Harriet died, and William married again to (MAGDALENA) "LANY" (HARRIS), daughter of Garrett F. (also see), and she died leaving son: 3. CASSIUS b. 25 Oct. 1879. William married third to MABEL (BARTLETT), daughter of Phineas (also see), and had son, 4. WILLIE D. b. 6 Nov. 1884. Ref: P&BA-Len pg. 613-4.

DAVITT, HUGH, son of MICHAEL (following), was born 1810, Ireland; and he married in 1842 to MARY (DONNELLY), daughter of John (also see) of Co. Mayo. In 1847, with one child, they came to New York City, and afterwards to Macedon, Wayne Co., NY. In 1854, they moved to Medina Twp., Lenawee Co., Mich. Children: 1. JOHN b. Ireland (to Dakota); 2. PATRICK (d. Ireland); 3. ROSA (m. Michael Tierney, Chicago, Ill.); 4. HARRIET ANN (m. Walter Wright, Hudson Twp.); 5. JAMES (Saginaw); 6. LIZZIE A.; 7. THOMAS; 8. KATIE H.; 9. CLARA; 10. WILLIAM (d. Dakota); 11. MICHAEL (deceased by 1888); 12. MARY (d. NY). Ref: P&BA-Len pg. 1042-3.

DAVITT, JAMES H. (Note JAMES, son of HUGH, preceding. Also see James Campbell).

DAVITT, MICHAEL & wife, BRIDGET (SCANLAN) lived out their lived in Ireland. She died in 1838. Known son, HUGH (preceding). Ref: P&BA-Len pg. 1042-3.

DAWES also see DAWS

DAWES, HIRAM born ca. 1806, and wife, MARY, born ca. 1810, both in NY, were listed in the 1840 census index of Adrian Twp., Lenawee Co., Mich.; and in the 1850 census with EDWARD, age 20; LEWIS, age 18; GEORGE, age 17; MARY, age 15, all b. Canada; and MELISSA, age 13; EMILY J., age 8; MELLVILLE, age 5; ANSON, age 2; FRANCIS, age 7/12, all b. Mich., in their household.

DAWES, JAMES born ca. 1813, Ireland, was listed in the 1850 census of Hudson Twp., Lenawee Co., Mich.

DAWS also see DAWES

DAWS, JAMES S. born ca. 1813, Mass., and wife, ALBINA S., born ca. 1821, NY, were listed in the 1840 census index of Medina Twp., Lenawee Co., Mich.; and in the 1850 census with ADELAID, age 6; MARIAM, age 2, both b. Mich., in their household. Also in the household were George A. Angell (also see) and family.

DAWS, JOHN was born ca. 1803, and wife, ELECTA, was born ca. 1805, both in Mass., and they were listed in the 1840 census index of Medina Twp., Lenawee Co., Mich.; and in the 1850 census with STEPHEN T., age 17, b. Mass.; and SARAH M., age 13; HARLAND P., age 3, both b. Mich., in their household. Next door was NEWTON (following); and also see POLLY (following).

DAWS, LYDIA (See Moses Negus)

DAWS, NEWTON was born ca. 1811, and wife, CLARA, was born ca. 1822, Mass., and they were listed in the 1850 census of Medina Twp., Lenawee Co., Mich. with CHARLES B., age 4; FRANKLIN H., age 2, both b. Mich., in their household.

POLLY DAWS, age 75, born Mass., was listed in the 1850 census of Medina Twp., Lenawee Co., Mich. in the household of Stephen and Dorothy Shaw (age 44, b.

Pioneer Families of Southeastern Michigan

Mass.). She may be mother-in-law. They were listed next door to JOHN (preceding).

DAWSON, HENRY F. (See Samuel Hopkins, son of Levi)

DAY, ASA born ca. 1789, and wife, MARY, born ca. 1790, both in NY, were listed in the 1850 census of Madison Twp., Lenawee Co., Mich. with ELIZABETH, age 24, b. NY, in their household. Theodore Taylor, age 34, b. RI, and wife, Lydia, age 32, b. NY were also in the household.

DAY, JAMES and wife, NANCY (BALLARD), were natives of Thompson, Conn. He died in Conn., though the family had lived both in Mass. & Conn. There were 5 sons and 4 daughters (names not stated). Known daughter, #4. SUSAN H. b. 12 Feb. 1815, Conn. (m/1 Franklin Cawley; m/2 Joseph Hagaman, see both). Nancy married again to Abel C. Ely of Lake Co., Ohio, and they afterwards moved to Morenci, Lenawee Co., Mich. Ref: P&BA-Len pg. 977-8.

DAY, JAMES B., son of WILLIAM H. (following), born 2 Mar. 1844, Fairfield Twp., Lenawee Co., Mich., married SUSAN W. (HAGAMAN), daughter of Samuel W. (also see) in Jackson Co., Mich., and they settled in Fairfield Twp. No children mentioned. Ref: P&BA-Len pg. 451-2.

DAY, NELSON born ca. 1837, Mich., was listed in the 1850 census of Palmyra Twp., Lenawee Co., Mich. in the household of Nelson & Ruth Goodrich.

DAY, RACHEL (See Samuel Ormsby)

DAY, RODNEY N. born ca. 1818, NY, and wife, SARAH, born ca. 1820, England, were listed in the 1850 census of Tecumseh Twp., Lenawee Co., Mich. with FRANCIS, age 10; CHARLES, age 7; WALLACE, age 4; WILLIAM, age 2, all b. Mich., in their household. Also see WILLIAM C. (following).

DAY, SAMUEL was born 23 June 1781, Chesterfield, Cheshire Co., NH; and he married LUCY (CUTLER), born 29 Sept. 1782, same place. About 1834, they moved to Lenawee Co., Mich. and then before 1840 to Pittsford, Hillsdale Co., Mich. He died there in 1856, age 75. Children: 1. WARREN b. 16 May 1812 (d. Hudson Twp., Lenawee Co. 1885); 2. WILLIAM b. 5 May 1815 (d. Civil War with Mich. Inf.); 3. WILLARD F. (following); 4. MARY A. b. 23 Oct. 1819 (d. age 22); 5. WILSON L. b. 12 July 1821 (lived Pittsford, Hillsdale Co.); 6. WINSLOW H. (Hudson Twp.); 7. FANNY A. (m. Augustus Kent, Hudson Village, Mich.). Ref: P&BA-Len pg. 678-9.

DAY, SAMUEL born ca. 1820, NJ?, and wife, ELIZABETH H., born ca. 1823, NY, were listed in the 1850 census of Madison Twp., Lenawee Co., Mich. with CHARLES, age 5, b. NY?, all in the household of Josiah Anderson.

DAY, WILLARD F., son of SAMUEL (of NH, preceding), was born 14 Sept. 1817, Cheshire Co., NY; and he moved to Michigan with his parents. He married 19 Mar. 1861 to ELIZA H. (HOLCOMB), daughter of Chancy (also see) in Hillsdale Co., Mich. They lived first in Hillsdale Co., but moved to Hudson Twp., Lenawee Co., Mich. about 1864. They retired to Hudson Village. Children: 1. GEORGE W. b. 27 Feb. 1862 (d. age 16); 2. WILLARD F. Jr. (m. Grace Bradley, Toledo, O.) Ref: P&BA-Len pg. 678-9.

DAY, WILLIAM C. born ca. 1813, VT, and wife, SARAH, born ca. 1820, NH, were listed in the 1850 census of Tecumseh Twp., Lenawee Co., Mich., in the household of RODNEY N. (preceding).

DAY, WILLIAM H. born ca. 1818, and wife, CHARITY (BRIGGS), born ca. 1814, both in NY, settled in Fairfield Twp., Lenawee Co., Mich. by 1840. He was killed falling a tree in 1850, and she died in 1858. There were 4 daughters and 2 sons (all names not stated). In the 1850 census the following were listed: 1. MARY b. ca. 1838; 2. AUGUSTA b. ca. 1842; 3. JAMES B. (preceding); 4. THOMAS b. ca. 1846; ISABELLA b. ca. 1850, all b. Mich. Ref: P&BA-Len pg 451-2.

DAYTON, ELVIRA L. born 2 June 1826, Van Buren, Onondaga Co., NY was daughter of a family who had moved from Middletown, Rutland Co., VT to Van Buren, NY (parents names not stated). Her mother died 21 July 1837, Van Buren, NY, and her father afterward came to Rollin Twp., Lenawee Co., Mich. where he died 1 Oct. 1869, age 63. Elvira L. married there on 2 May 1852 to Elvin C. Cole (also see) as his 3rd wife. Ref: P&BA-Len pg. 610-11.

DAYTON, HELIM M. born ca. 1801, and wife, CHARLOTTE, born ca. 1804, both in NY, settled in Clinton Twp., Lenawee Co., Mich. by 1840 (written as "Belim" Dayton); and were listed in the 1850 census of Tecumseh Twp., with Helen Davidson, age 19, b. VT, in the household. EDWARD, age 12, b. Mich., in the 1850 census of Tecumseh Twp. in the household of Joseph & Permelia Richard may relate.

DAYTON, MARIETTA born Rensselaer Co., NY married Jesse Maxson (also see). Ref: P&BA-Len pg. 1155-6.

DEAN, ARTEMIS born ca. 1821, and wife, PHEBE A., born ca. 1825, both in NY, were listed in the 1850 census of Raisin Twp., Lenawee Co., Mich. with MARY A., age 3; JULIA A., age 1, both b. Mich., and next door were Edmund Grandy and wife, DORCAS (DEAN), following.

DEAN, BA--SON born ca. 1824, and wife, SOPHIA, born ca. 1824, both in NY, were listed in the 1850 census of Riga Twp., Lenawee Co., Mich. with ANSEL, age 3; JOSEPHINE, age 1, both b. Mich., in their household.

DEAN, CARRIE S. (See Francis L. Ganun)

DEAN, CHARLES born ca. 1806, Conn, and wife, ELEANOR, born ca. 1806, NY, were listed in the 1850 census of Hudson Twp., Lenawee Co., Mich. with GEORGE, age 16; HARRIET M., age 10; SUSAN M., age 8, all b. NY; and CHARLES H., age 5, b. Mich., in their household. LESTER (following) was next door.

DEAN, DORCAS born ca. 1785, NY (See Edmund Grandy). Also see ARTEMIS (preceding).

DEAN, E. B. born ca. 1819, and wife, ABIGAIL H., born ca. 1819, both in NY, were listed in the 1850 census of Raisin Twp., Lenawee Co., Mich. with CHARLES W., age 6/12, b. NY?, all in the household of Wing & Cynthia Chase, perhaps in-laws?

DEAN, HARVEY born ca. 1804, Delaware Co., NY, married POLLY (EVERY) born ca. 1808, Putnam Co., NY. In 1848, they moved to Woodstock Twp., Lenawee Co., Mich., where he died in 1878. There were 5 children (all names not stated). In the 1850 census they listed 1. CORDELIA b. ca. 1832; 2. DEBORAH b. 26 June 1837, Delaware Co., NY (m. William Henry Brooks, also see);

3. ABIGAIL b. ca. 1839; 4. MARY b. ca. 1843. Ref: P&BA-Len pg. 1175-6.

DEAN, HEMAN H. born ca. 1807, and wife, LUCY, born ca. 1807, both in VT, were listed in the 1840 census index of Madison Twp., Lenawee Co., Mich., and in the 1850 census with ISAIAH, age 21; AUGUSTUS, age 18, both b. VT; & LUCINDA, age 16; ALBERT, age 13, both b. NY; and CAROLINE, age 11, b. Mich., in their household.

DEAN, ISAAC born ca. 1771, and wife, ABIGAIL, born ca. 1781, both in Conn., were listed in the 1850 census of Adrian Twp., Lenawee Co., Mich. with DORCAS, age 42, b. NY, in their household. See ISAAC A., following.

DEAN, ISAAC A., probably son of ISAAC (preceding), born ca. 1812, and wife, SOPHIA, born ca. 1813, both in NY, were listed in the 1850 census of Adrian Twp., Lenawee Co., Mich. with ALBERT E. age 1, b. Mich., in the household.

DEAN, JAMES born Ireland, came to NY, and then moved to Whiteford Twp., Monroe Co. Mich. by 1840, where he remained. Known daughter, HANNAH (m. James Leonardson, also see, before 1834 in Lucas Co., Ohio). Ref: P&BA-Len pg. 1136-8.

DEAN, LESTER P., probably son of CHARLES (preceding), born ca. 1830, NY, and wife, FRANCES A., born ca. 1830, Maine, were listed in the 1850 census of Hudson Twp., Lenawee Co., Mich.

DEAN, OMER? S. born ca. 1798, and wife, LYDIA, born ca. 1808?, NY, were listed in the 1850 census of Seneca Twp., Lenawee Co., Mich. with WILLIAM C., age 19, b. NY, and ANN? C., age 14?, b. Mich. (this was almost illegible) in the household.

DEAN, ORRIN born ca. 1813, Conn., and wife, TRYPHENA, born ca. 1810, VT, were listed in the 1850 census of Hudson Twp., Lenawee Co., Mich with ELLEN, age 9; HARRIET, age 8; both b. Mich., and ESTHER, age 32, b. NY (sister?), in their household.

DEAN, SAMUEL born ca. 1816, and wife, RUBY, born ca. 1822, both in NY, were listed in the 1850 census of Woodstock Twp., Lenawee Co., Mich. with WALTER, age 8; GEORGE, age 1; SAMUEL, age 4/12, all b. Mich., in their household.

DEAN, SARAH (See Dr. Gideon Tiffany)

DeBAR, JEROME (See John Bitely)

DeBOIES see BOIES

DeCAMP, DENNIS born ca. 1796, and wife, PRUDENCE, born ca. 1796, both in New Jersey, were listed in the 1840 census index of Palmyra Twp., Lenawee Co., Mich.; and in the 1850 census with no family in the household.

DeCAMP, ELIAS born ca. 1833, NY, was listed in the 1850 census of Seneca Twp., Lenawee Co., Mich. in a Stevenson household.

DeCAMP, JOHN & wife, MARY (BROWN), of Northamptonshire, England were parents of ANN who married Thomas C. Isley (also see).

DeCAMP, PERMELIA was born ca. 1829, NY, and was listed in the 1850 census of Seneca Twp., Lenawee Co., Mich. in a Russ household.

DECK, BETSEY (See Andrew Fabrique)

DECKER, ALEXANDER Dr. born ca. 1820, and wife, ANGELINE, born ca. 1826, both in NY, were listed in the 1850 census of Madison Twp., Lenawee Co., Mich. with ALTHA H., age 3/12, b. Mich., in their household.

DECKER, CLARK W., son of URIAH (following), was born 17 May 1838, Adrian Twp., Lenawee Co., Mich. he served in the Civil War, leaving as a Lt. from the 11th Mich. Cav. He married 14 Oct. 1865 to EMELINE "EMMA" (HALSTED), daughter of John (also see) of Rome Twp., Lenawee Co. In 1868, they moved from Rome Twp. to Adrian, where they were residing in 1888. Children: 1. ZOE; 2. LEON E. Ref: P&BA-Len pg. 315-6.

DECKER, DANIEL had a daughter, JANE, who married James Van Akin (also see) of Monroe Co., Penn.

DECKER, HANNAH, age 55, b. NY, was listed in the 1850 census of Hudson Twp., Lenawee Co., Mich. in the household of Philip Hubble and wife, Mary (age 25, b. NY). Possibly Hannah was mother of Mary?

DECKER, HARLEY born ca. 1826, and wife, MARINDA, born ca. 1828, both b. in NY, were listed in the 1850 census of Adrian Twp., Lenawee Co., Mich. with JASPER R., age 2, OLIVE R., age 2/12, both b. Mich., in the household. WALTER, age 16, b. NY, listed in the household next door may relate to this family.

DECKER, HENRY E. born ca. 1810, and wife, ESTHER, born ca. 1822, both in NY, were listed in the 1850 census of Franklin Twp., Lenawee Co., Mich. with ELIZABETH, age 3, b. Mich. in their household.

DECKER, JOHN born Penn. was the father of CHARITY who married Fred K. Tiffany (also see) of Canada. Ref: P&BA-Len pg. 407-8.

DECKER, URIAH born 24 Oct. 1805, Columbia Co., NY, and wife, EXPERIENCE (BAKER), born 1808 near Manchester, Ontario Co. NY, moved to Adrian Twp., Lenawee Co., Mich. in 1833. He died in Dec. 1885, and she was still living in Adrian Twp. in 1888. (All children's names not stated). Known daughter, SALLY A.(ADELINE) b. 12 Apr. 1830, Manchester, NY (m. William Wood, also see). In Uriah's household in the 1850 census were: JOSEPH, age 17; SYDNEY, age 16; IRINA, age 14; CLARK W. (preceding); ISABELLA, age 10; ALZORA (male), age 6; EDWARD N., age 3; EDWIN N., age 3, last 7 b. Mich. Ref: P&BA-Len pg. 315-6 & 1146-7.

DECKER, WALTER (See HARLEY, preceding)

DECKER, WILLIAM born ca. 1833, Ohio, was listed in the 1850 census of Dover Twp., Lenawee Co., Mich. in the William Baker household.

DeCOW, JANE (See John Christman)

DeGRAFF, CORNELIUS, son of PETER (who d. Old Paltz, Ulster Co., NY), born 22 Apr. 1814, Old Paltz; married 11 Feb. 1836 to CATHARINE (VAN WEY), daughter of Henry (also see). In 1844, they removed to Palmyra Twp., Lenawee Co., Mich. In the 1850 census of Palmyra Twp., his wife was listed as MARY, age 38, b. NY. Children listed were MARY, age 16; SARAH, age 10; PETER, age 9 (following), all b. NY. Lucy Sage, age 7/12, relationship not known, was also in the household. Ref: P&BA-Len pg. 763.

DeGRAFF, PETER, son of CORNELIUS (preceding), was born 12 Dec. 1841, Ulster Co., NY, and he moved to

Pioneer Families of Southeastern Michigan

Michigan with his parents. He married in Sept. 1861 to MELISSA F. (HILL), daughter of Ebbin S. (also see). He served in Co. F., 7th Mich. Cav., Civil War. They settled in Palmyra Twp., Lenawee Co., Mich. Children: 1. CARRIE B.; 2. DEANE C. Ref: P&BA-Len pg. 763.

DeGREENE, RALPH N. & wife, HENRIETTA (NESS), of Yorkshire, England, remained there and he died at Walton, age 68, and she died age 63. Known son, RICHARD (following). Ref: P&BA-Len pg. 657-8. Also note MARGARET, following.

DeGREENE, MARGARET married Richard Sorby (also see). Ref: P&BA 1058-9.

DeGREENE, RICHARD, son of RALPH N. (preceding), was born Oct, 1813, Yorkshire, England, and came to the US at age 23, and settled in Rollin Twp., Lenawee Co., Mich. He married in 1842 to ELIZABETH A. (HATHAWAY), daughter of James (also see). Children: 1. NORMAN b. 1843 (d. 1851); 2. ALBERT b. 1847 (d. age 23, leaving 2 children); 3. EMMA (EMILY E.) b. 1850 (m. Edwin Wilson); 4. MARY (m. John Sorby, also see). Ref: P&BA-Len pg. 657-8 & 1058-9.

DeKAY, TEMPERANCE (See David Blair)

DeLAMATER, JOHN L. (See Abram Sanford)

DeLAND, CHARLES V. was born 25 July 1828, North Bloomfield, Mass., and came with parents to Jackson, Jackson Co., Mich. on 21 May 1830. He went to E. Saginaw, Mich. as an adult. Ref: History of Jackson Co., Mich., pg. 142. Note WILLIAM R. (following)

DeLAND, IRA born ca. 1790, Conn., and wife, MARY, born ca. 1786, NJ, were listed in the 1850 census of Fairfield Twp., Lenawee Co., Mich. They were next door to WILLIAM, following. In the 1840 census index, the name was written as "Delane" and in the 1850 census as "Delon."

DeLAND, JOSEPH born ca. 1813, and wife, SALLY (BAKER), born ca. 1816, both b. NY, settled in Fairfield Twp., Lenawee Co., Mich. He died 15 Mar. 1879, and she was living in Fairfield Twp. in 1888. Known children (1st 3 ages per census): 1. MARY A., age 13 (d. age 14); 2. CHARLES G., age 10; 3. ALBERT, age 8; 4. MARTIN (following); 5. SALINA A. b. 13 Aug. 1847, Fairfield Twp. (m. William W. Wyman, also see). Ref: P&BA-Len pg. 694 & 1020-1.

DeLAND, MARTIN, son of JOSEPH (preceding), was born 25 Jan. 1845, Fairfield Twp., Lenawee Co., Mich., married 4 July 1869 to CARRIE (SMITH), daughter of William (also see), and they settled in Fairfield Twp. Children: 1. EMERY A. (d. infancy); 2. FOREST; 3. ORLANDO S.; 4. ERNEST R. (d. infancy); 5. VERNON C. Ref: P&BA-Len pg. 694.

DeLAND, WILLIAM was born 1827, and wife, MERCY J., born ca. 1826, both in NY, were listed in the 1850 census of Fairfield Twp., Lenawee Co., Mich., with MYRON, age 5; MARGARET, age 4; JAMES E., age 3, all b. Mich., in their household.

DeLAND, WILLIAM R. was born 20 July 1795, Mass., and settled in Jackson, Jackson Co., Mich. 27 May 1830. His wife, MARY G., was born 1802, Caroline, NJ. JAMES S., b. 10 Nov. 1835, Jackson, is probably a son; and also see CHARLES V. (preceding). Ref: History of Jackson Co., Mich., pg. 142.

DELANE, IRA See Ira DeLand

DELANEY, JULIA (See Philip Wareham[3])

DELANO, LUCINDA E. (See Marvin L. Winslow)

DeLAPP, RICHARD of Franklin Twp., Lenawee Co., Mich. married JULIA (MORSMAN), daughter of Herman (also see). Son, IRVING T.

DELINE, ABRAM born ca. 1811, NY, and wife, NELLY?, born ca. 1818, VT, were listed in the 1840 census index of Dover Twp., Lenawee Co., Mich., and in the 1850 census with ALZINA, age 11; IRA W., age 7; CELESTIA, age 6; SARAH, age 3, all b. Mich., in their household.

DELINE, AMANDA (See Mathias L. Davis)
DELINE, IDA M. (See Aaron R. Tufts)
DELINE, ISAAC born ca. 1806, and wife, ORRILLA?, born ca. 1807, both in NY, were listed in the 1840 census index of Dover Twp.; and in the 1850 census with ALBERT, age 17; ORRILA, age 15, both b. NY; and TELIDIA?, age 12; ESTHER A., age 11; EDGAR, age 9; WESLEY, age 8; ELERY A., age 6, all b. Mich., in their household.

DELINE, LEVI J. (See Darwin H. Warren)
DELINE, WILLIAM born ca. 1808, and wife, ESTHER, born ca. 1816, both in NY, were listed in the 1840 census index of Dover Twp., Lenawee Co., Mich.; and in the 1850 census with ALONZO, age 18; ANDREW, age 15, both b. NY; and EDWIN, age 10; HENRY, age 8; CYNTHIA, age 6; WELLINGTON, age 3; ERVIN, age 1, all b. Mich., in their household.

DeLONG, GORDON was listed in the 1840 census index of Adrian Twp., Lenawee Co., Mich. In the 1850 census of Adrian Twp., in the household of John Pierson & wife, Eliza, there was an ANN E., age 4, b. Mich. (perhaps a stepchild), who may relate to Gordon?.

DeLONG, JANE (See Abraham Cramer)
DeLONG, JOSEPH born ca. 1826, NY, was listed in the 1850 census of Medina Twp., Lenawee Co., Mich.

DEMING, DANIEL H. born ca. 1804, Conn, and wife, MARY J., born ca. 1814, NY, were listed in the 1850 census of Dover Twp., Lenawee Co., Mich., with ERASTUS H., age 7; JULIA A., age 2, both b. Mich., in their household. Note JULIA, and HARRIET, both following.

DEMING, DANIEL born ca. 1806, NY, was listed in the 1850 census of Adrian Twp., Lenawee Co., Mich. with OPHELIA, age 17, b. NY; PHIDEALUS (male), age 15, b. Ohio; ALBERT, age 9; GEORGE H., age 5; WILLIAM H., age 4/12, last 3 b. Mich., in his household.

DEMING, HANNAH (See William Dix)
DEMING, HARRIET possibly b. after 1850 married Edwin Nichols, son of Henry (also see) of Dover Twp., Lenawee Co., Mich.

DEMING, JULIA (See Fleming McMath)
DEMING, JOHN W. born ca. 1806, and wife, MARY, born ca. 1818, both b. NY, were listed in the 1850 census of Franklin Twp., Lenawee Co., Mich. with DESIAH, age 11; LAURA, age 8; MARY, age 7, all b. Mass.; FREDUS,

age 4, b. Ohio; JOSEPH, age 9/12; JOHN, age 9/12, (twins?), born Mich., in their household. MARY, age 66, b. Mass., was listed in the household, see LUMAN Sr, (following).

DEMING, LUMAN (Sr.?) was listed in the 1840 census index of Franklin Twp., Lenawee Co., Mich., with LUMAN (Jr.), following. In the 1850 census, in the household of JOHN W. (preceding), was MARY, age 66, b. Mass., who may be wife of Luman, Sr.?

DEMING, LUMAN (Jr.?) born ca. 1810, NY, and wife, MARY, born ca. 1812, Mass., were listed in the 1840 census index of Franklin Twp., Lenawee Co., Mich; and in the 1850 census as "LAMEN," with EDWIN, age 15; WAITE, age 12; LEYSTER, age 8; JESSE, age 5; HARRIET (note preceding), age 4, all b. Mich., in their household.

DEMMING, JULIA A. (See Cyrenus Sanford)

DeMOTT, ABRAM born ca. 1797, and wife, JANE (HOGARTH), born ca. 1800, both in NY, came from Lodi, Seneca Co., NY to Ridgeway Twp., Lenawee Co., Mich. ca. 1844; and were listed there in the 1850 census. After being in the mercantile business, they returned to New York. Four children (names not stated) lived to maturity. Known children: 1. WILLIAM b. ca. 1832, Lodi, NY (served Civil War, Co. K., 3d Mich. Cav., probably unmarried); 2. GEORGE (Tecumseh Twp.); 3. CHARLES (following).

DeMOTT, CHARLES, probably son of ABRAM (preceding), was born 1821, and wife, ZELINDA C., was born ca. 1823, both in NY, and were listed in the 1850 census of Ridgeway Twp., Lenawee Co., Mich. (2 doors from ABRAM), with SARAH H., age 3, b. Mich., in their household.

DeMOTT, ELLISON and wife, (name not stated), were natives of NY who first moved to Lucas Co., Ohio and then Toledo, Ohio. Known daughter, EUGENIA (m. Alpheus Cheney, b. 1838, also see). Ref: P&BA-Len pg. 1104-5.

DEMUND also see DEMUNN
DEMUND, ANNE (See John Coddington)

DEMUNN also see DEMUND
DEMUNN, PETER born 4 May 1764, died 15 Jan. 1815; and wife, MARGARET A., born 3 June 1764, died 9 Mar. 1846. Known daughter, MARY L., born NJ, married Jacob Drake (also see). Ref: P&BA-Len pg. 601-2. Note: In 1793, there was a Peter "Demond" in Hardwick, Sussex Co., NJ, and one in Somerset Co., NJ, in the militia.

DENIGER, CAROLINE (See John G. Miller)

DENISON also see DENNISON
DENISON, CATHERINE (See Cornelius McFall)
DENISON, DAVID of Monroe Co., Mich. married JOHANNA born Westport, NY. Children: 1. JANE (deceased beofre 1888); 2. CARRIE E. David died Monroe Co., Mich., and Johanna married again to John Dubois (also see). Ref: P&BA-Len pg. 314-5.

DENNINGER, CATHARINE (See John Beland[2])

DENNIS, DAVID B. born ca. 1817, NY, and wife, SARAH P., born 1824, Mass., were listed in the 1850 census of Adrian Twp., Lenawee Co., Mich. with HENRY H., age 4; CHARLES, age 2, both b. Mich., in their household.

DENNIS, ELIAS and wife, ADELINE (STEPHENS), were natives of New England, who settled in Farmington, Ontario Co., NY. They came to Michigan in 1827, and were listed in the 1830 census of Lenawee Co., Mich. Territory with males: 1 under 5; 1 5-10; 2 20-30; 1 50-60; females: 2 under 5; 1 5-10; 1 20-30. They lived in Adrian, where they both died. Five children (names not stated): Known daughter, #3. ANN D. b. 18 Sept. 1821, Farmington, NY (m. Charles Mitchell (also see). Ref: P&BA-Len pg. 920. Note Stephenson Dennison.

DENNISON also see DENISON
DENNISON, JOHN born ca. 1820, NY, was listed in the 1850 census of Madison Twp., Lenawee Co., Mich.
DENNISON, MAY E. Mrs. was the daughter of Albert Humphrey Bump (also see). The Dennisons went to Muskegon, Mich. by 1888. Ref: P&BA-Len pg. 940-1.
DENNISON, NANCY (See Joshua W. Lawton)
DENNISON, STEPHENSON born 5 June 1806, and wife, MARTHA (MASON), born 26 June 1810, married on 8 Mar. 1827, Farmington, Ontario Co., NY, and soon afterwards moved to Fairfield Twp., Lenawee Co., Mich. She died 9 Apr. 1853, and he died 31 Mar. 1880 at home of a daughter. Children: 1. LYDIA S.; 2. BERNARD M.; 3. STEPHEN A.; 4. JOSEPH B. b. ca. 1836 (m. Mary C. Bradish, dau. of Nelson, also see; Benton Harbor, Mich.); 5. ORIN D. b. ca. 1838 (Berrien Co., Mich.); 6. ERASTUS M. (d. infancy); 7. JOHN S. b. ca. 1844 (to Grand Rapids, Mich.); 8. (MARY) ADA b. ca. 1839 (d. age 18); 9. MARTHA A. b. 19 Oct. 1846, Fairfield Twp. (m. Myron W. Bradish (also see). Ref: P&BA-Len pg. 493-4.
Note: ALMON, age 17, b. NY, in a Livesay household, may be same as STEPHEN A.

DePUY also known as DePUGH & DEPEW
DePUY FAMILY - SAMUEL[1] was a descendant of a BENJAMIN who had come from France and settled in Ulster Co., NY; and at an early date SAMUEL[1] removed to Cayuga Co., NY (In the 1800 census index of Cayuga Co. spelled "DePugh" were ABRAHAM; BENJAMIN; DAVID; PHILIP (see following); & SAMUEL). He had a known son, BENJAMIN[2] who married SARAH (HORNBECK) and resided in Cayuga Co. and were parents of known son: BENJAMIN[3]. BENJAMIN[3] had known son: SAMUEL[4] (following).

DePUY, BENJAMIN F.[5], son of SAMUEL[4] (following), born 25 Feb. 1841, Livingston Co., NY and moved with his parents to Macon Twp., Lenawee Co., Mich. He married on 18 Nov. 1886 to ELIZABETH (BRAMBLE), daughter of Jehiah H. (also see), of Franklin Twp., and she died 12 Mar. 1868. He married again on 7 Aug. 1872 to SARAH ALMEDA (SPARLING), daughter of Joseph (also see). They lived in Macon Twp., Lenawee Co., Mich. Daughter, BRUNELLA, b. 28 July 1876. Ref: P&BA-Len pg. 895-6.

DePUY, EDWIN (See Justus Lowe)
DePUY, PHILIP (See DePUY FAMILY, preceding), born 24 Apr. 1774, married on 18 Jan. 1798, Orange Co., NY, to SALLY (COMFORT) born 2 Aug. 1778. They were

Pioneer Families of Southeastern Michigan

pioneers to Owasco, Cayuga Co., NY; and in 1831, they moved to Mt. Morris, Livingston Co., NY where he died 8 Oct. 1839, and she died 5 Oct. 1837. Four sons and six daughters (names not stated). Known children: ELEANOR (m. Smith); PHILIP S. (following). Ref: P&BA-Len pg. 302-3 & 1214-6.

DePUY, PHILIP S., son of PHILIP (preceding), was born 21 Nov. 1817, Owasco, Cayuga Co., NY, and moved with his parents to Mt. Morris, NY, where he married 31 Dec. 1837 to SARAH J. or MARIA J. (SMITH) born Cayuga Co., NY. She died 29 June 1844, Mt. Morris, NY. Children: 1. HARRIET ELIZABETH (m. William Butler; d. Mason, Ingham Co., Mich.); 2. HARRISON SMITH (d. 13 June 1862 of illness during service in Civil War, age 19). Philip S. married again in Nunda, Livingston Co., NY, to MILANCY (CHANDLER), daughter of Henry (also see). Children: 3. JOSEPHINE M. b. 13 Dec. 1845 (m. John Hendershott, Tecumseh, Mich.); 4. FAYETTE b. 21 Nov. 1847 (m. Carrie Updike); 5. WELLINGTON b. 20 Aug. 1849 (m. Ella A. Reynolds, Allegan Co., Mich.); 6. E. CORA b. 11 Aug. 1851; 7. ROSELLE b. 25 Sept. 1853 (m. Thomas Taber, Madison, Wisc.); 8. EMMA b. 1 Aug. 1858 (m. Ozen Keith; d. 1882). Ref: P&BA-Len pg. 1214-6.

DePUY, SAMUEL[4], son of BENJAMIN[3] (preceding), born Cayuga Co., NY, married in Livingston Co., NY to ANN (BINGHAM) born New Jersey. In 1852, they moved to Macon Twp., Lenawee Co., Mich. He died 7 Mar. 1872; and she died 27 Sept. 1874, age 67. Six children (names not stated). Known son, BENJAMIN F.[5] (preceding).

DE RAN, DENNIS and wife, CATHERINE, of Sandusky Co., Ohio were parent of LIBBIE born 11 Apr. 1844, Sandusky Co. (m. Edwin Haff (also see). Ref: P&BA-Len pg. 921-2.

DERBYSHIRE, DANIEL, son of JAMES (following), was born 8 July 1784, Saratoga Co., NY. He married FANNY (MOSHER) born 2 May 1788, and they lived in Cortland Co., NY ca. 1821. She died 9 Aug. 1849, Onondaga Co., NY; and he died 4 Jan. 1856, Rollin Twp., Lenawee Co., Mich. Known son, WILLIAM (following). Ref: P&BA-Len pg. 642-3.

DERBYSHIRE, JAMES was the son of WILLIAM (following). He became a Quaker, and moved from Saratoga Co. to Madison Co., NY where he died. Known son, DANIEL (preceding). Ref: P&BA-Len pg. 642-3.

DERBYSHIRE, WILLIAM married in Westchester Co., NY to ? (KNAPP). (Note: In the 1800 census index of Westchester Co., NY, there was a William "Derbyshar," and Daniel "Darbyshore.") He was said to have been a Revolutionary soldier. Four children (names not stated). Known son, JAMES (preceding). Ref: P&BA-Len pg. 642-3.

DERBYSHIRE, WILLIAM, son of DANIEL (preceding), was born 16 Nov. 1821, Cortland Co., NY. He married first on 22 Apr. 1851 to ROSANNA (WOOD) who was born 20 Dec. 1830, Madison Co., NY. They moved to Rollin Twp., Lenawee Co., Mich., where she died 19 Dec. 1861. He married again on 10 Sept.1862 to Mrs. MARIA (NEWITT) WOOD, daughter of John, and widow of Charles (see both). Children: 1. DANIEL Z. b. 28 Oct. 1863, Rollin Twp. (m. Della Lyons 1886); 2. WILLIAM N. b. 18 Aug. 1867; 3. GLENN B. b. 12 Jan. 1874; 4. PAUL b. 11 Feb. 1876. Ref: P&BA-Len pg. 642-3.

DERSHAM, ABRAHAM V., son of SAMUEL (following), was born 26 June 1830, White Deer Twp., Union Co., Penn. He went to Lockport, Niagara Co., NY where he married SUSAN M. (STAHLER), daughter of Henry (also see). They moved to Erie Co., NY; and then back to Willamsport, Penn. About 1864, they removed to Seneca Co., Ohio; and about 1866 to Palmyra Twp., Lenawee Co., Mich. Children: 1. MARGARET (d. infancy); 2. HENRY (Niagara Co., NY); 3. EUGENE (Palmyra Twp.); 4. LILLIE; 5. IDA M.; 6. CARRIE; 7. JULIA (d. age 3-1/2 yrs). Ref: P&BA-Len pg. 836-7.

DERSHAM, SAMUEL son of JACOB (from Germany to Union Co., Penn.), was born in Penn. and resided in both Union & York, Cos.; and married in Penn. to SUSAN (SHETLY). He died in 1838; and she died in 1864, age 80. Eleven children (names not stated). Known son, ABRAHAM V. (preceding). Ref: P&BA-Len pg. 836-7.

DESERMIA, F. A. married HELEN E. (TEACHOUT), daughter of George W.[5] (also see); had known daughter, BEULAH A. They lived Onsted, Mich. in 1888.

DEWEY, CHARLES H. Capt., son of SIMEON (following), was born 25 July 1823, Concord, NH, and moved with parents to New York. They later moved to Tecumseh, Lenawee Co., Mich. About 1840, he went to Virgil, Cortland Co., NY; and returned in 1841 to Tecumseh. He married 30 Mar. 1843 in Cambridge Twp. to ELVIRA (MOULTON), daughter of Dr. Arba N. (also see). They resided in Cambridge Twp., and finally in Cambridge Junction. During the Civil War, he was a recruiter for the State. Children: 1. MALINDA P. b. ca. 1844; 2. (OLE)ANDER S. b. ca. 1846; 3. WARREN C. b. ca. 1850 (to NYC); 4. ELIZA M.; 5. CHARLES A. Ref: P&BA-Len pg. 1101-2.

DEWEY, CONRAD & wife, RACHEL (McNEIL) were residents of Cumberland Co., Penn. where they remained. There were 8 children (names not stated), except RACHEL b. 29 Feb. 1808 (m. Philip Wareham[3], Penn, also see.). Ref: P&BA-Len pg. 939-40.

DEWEY, EDMOND B. Col. & wife, SARAH (COOPER), of Manchester, Ontario Co., NY, were parents of known daughters: ANNA b. 19 Dec. 1822 (m/1 Alonzo Teachout, m/2 Joseph F. Baker, as 2d wife.); CYNTHIA M. b. 29 Jan. 1828, Manchester (m. Joseph F. Baker). Ref: P&BA-Len pg. 303-4.

DEWEY, EMELINE of Ontario Co., NY (m. Philo P. Phelps, also see). Ref: P&BA-Len pg. 541-2.

DEWEY, FRANCIS A., son of SIMEON (following), born 25 Feb. 1811, New Hampshire, moved to Three Rivers, Quebec, Canada with his parents. He moved with them to Buffalo, Erie Co., NY, and to Tecumseh, Lenawee Co., Mich. He drove stage between Detroit, Ypsilanti, and Monguagon, Mich. In 1834, he settled in Cambridge Twp., Lenawee Co. He married there to MARY ANN (SMITH), daughter of Isaac (also see) on 25 Oct. 1836. Children: 1. JANE b. 27 Aug. 1837 (d. 10 Feb. 1855); 2. GEORGE H. b. 10 Jan. 1839 (m. Mary Alice Queal, dau. of William, also see, lived Cambridge Twp.); 3. JOHN W. b. 17 Mar. 1841 (lived Cambridge

Twp.); 4. ALBERT F. b. 15 Apr. 1843; 5. FRANKLIN S. b. 27 Mar. 1845 (to Alpena, Mich.); 6. ISAAC S. b. 8 Apr. 1848. Mary Ann died 15 Sept. 1852; and Francis A. married again on 27 Jan. 1853 to Mrs. MARIE S. (HOXIE) SMITH, daughter of Julius Hoxie (also see). She died 14 Sept. 1863; and he married third on 15 Jan. 1863 to HARRIET (SMITH), sister of Mary Ann. Children: 7. MARY J. b. 10 Dec. 1863; 8. LYSTER H. b. 14 Mar. 1865; 9. IRVING A. b. 31 Mar. 1870. Ref: P&BA-Len pg. 877-8.

DEWEY, HIRAM D., son of SAMUEL (following), was born ca. 1802, and his wife, SARAH A. (LINSLEY), was born ca. 1806, both in NY. After their marriage, they moved to Chautuaqua Co., NY. About 1841, they removed to Madison Twp., Lenawee Co., Mich. There were 5 children, amd 3 grew to maturity (names not stated). In the 1850 census of Palmyra Twp., they listed LAGRANGE H. (HIRAM L., following); LOUISE, age 17; CAROLINE, age 15, all b. NY; and SARAH E., age 6, b. Mich., in their household. Ref: P&BA-Len pg. 846-7.

DEWEY, IRA born ca. 1801, NY, and wife, BETSEY A., born ca. 1811, Conn., were listed in the 1840 census index of Dover Twp., Lenawee Co., Mich.; and in the 1850 census of Fairfield Twp., they listed EDWARD, age 18, b. NY; and MARVIN, age 16; SEYMOUR, age 14; IRA, age 12; SAMUEL, age 10; WESLEY, age 8; ANDREW, age 4; SARAH J., age 2, all b. Mich., in their household.

DEWEY, LAGRANGE H. (HIRAM L.), son of HIRAM D. (preceding), was born 17 June 1830, Oneida Co., NY; and he came to Lenawee Co., Mich. with his parents. He married 6 Nov. 1856 to CHARITY A. (WINES), daughter of Surrajah (also see). They settled in Palmyra Twp. Children: 1. LAFAYETTE L. b. 21 Nov. 1858; 2. ELLA (m. George Nichols, Coldwater, Mich.). Ref: P&BA-Len pg. 846-7.

DEWEY, LORENZO born ca. 1802, Ohio, and wife, AMANDA, born ca. 1816, Mich., were listed in the 1840 census of Tecumseh Twp., Lenawee Co., Mich. In the 1850 census they listed ALVIRA, age 16; ANTENICON (female), age 13; LORENZO, age 11; DEGARMO?(male), age 10; ALPHONSE, age 8; ELIZABETH, age 5, all b. Mich.

DEWEY, LUCINDA (See Samuel Warren)
DEWEY, MARTHA E. (See George A. Ingall)
DEWEY, SAMUEL was born 1763, and was a drummer boy in the Revolutionary War, and was a prisoner of the Indians for 3 years. He resided in NY, but moved to Hillsdale Co., Mich. where he died. Known son, HIRAM D. (preceding). Note: There was a SAMUEL listed in Medina Twp., Lenawee Co. in the 1840 census index.

DEWEY, SIMEON was born 7 Oct. 1784 in Hanover, NY, and he married there in 1806 to BETSEY (BIGELOW), daughter of William (also see). They moved first to Three Rivers, Quebec, Canada, and then about 1826 to Buffalo, NY; and then in 1829 to Tecumseh Twp., Lenawee Co., Mich. They moved after 1850 to Monroe Co., Mich. where he died 1 Apr. 1863. Seven children (names not stated). Known sons: FRANCIS A. (preceding); #7. Capt. CHARLES H. (preceding). Ref: P&BA-Len pg. 877-8 & 1101-2.

DEWEY, W. M. was listed in the 1840 census index of Seneca Twp., Lenawee Co., Mich.

DEWITT, CORNELIUS Cpt. was a Revolutionary soldier, and the father of ELIZABETH (m. James Hornbeck, Sussex Co., NJ, also see). Ref: P&BA-Len pg. 563-4. Note: In the records of the Dutch Ref. Church of Kingston, NY is a CORNELIUS bpt. 27 Jan. 1745, son of CORNELIUS & SARAH (HORNBECK) of Rochester, NY. This "Dutch" family of Ulster Co., NY had lines whom settled in Montague & Wantage, Sussex Co., NJ. There is a CORNELIUS DEPUY DEWITT, with NY service, and widow, MARGARET, in the Rev. War. Pension Applications, #W19173 (widow"s) & BLWt-28615-160-55 (Bounty Land), no proof it is this same man. In 1778-1780, listed in Sussex Co., NJ were ABRAHAM; BARNET; ISAAC SR. & JR; JACOB; MOSES; PETER; & SAMUEL.

DEWITT, NANCY (See Edwin J. Wilcox)
DEWITT, SARAH (See Samuel Hinkley)

DEXTER, ESTHER (See Rufus Daggett)
DEXTER, EUNICE (See Moses Bowerman, Sr.)
DEXTER, MERIBAH b. 16 Aug. 1770, New Bedford, Mass. (See Henry Jennings).

DEYO, NANCY of Adrian, Lenawee Co., Mich. married Levi M. Beebe of Franklin Twp. on 4 Dec. 1856.

DIBBLE, ANDREW was a resident of Delaware Co., NY before 1800, and moved to Genesee Co., NY. Known daughter, CLARISSA b. 4 May 1801, Delaware Co. (m. Capt. Stephen P. Hall, also see, on 1 June 1822, Genesee Co.) Ref: P&BA-Len pg. 1130-2.

DIBBLE, ARTHUR (See Thomas Boyd)
DIBBLE, FRANCIS, possibly son of NATHAN (following), born ca. 1820, and wife, BATHSHEBA, born ca. 1825, both in NY, were listed in the 1850 census of Ridgeway Twp., Lenawee Co., Mich. with POLLY, age 7; JAMES, age 5; GEORGE, age 3, all b. Mich., in their household.

DIBBLE, ISAIAH born ca. 1800, Conn. was listed in the 1840 census index of Hudson Twp., Lenawee Co., Mich,; and in the 1850 census with NOAH, age 28; EDMUND, age 11; RANDLE, age 5; ABRAM, age 3; EDWARD, age 7; EDWIN, age 8, all b. Mich., in his household.

DIBBLE, JONAH born ca. 1803, and wife, ANNA, born ca. 1805, both in NY, were listed in the 1850 census of Ridgeway Twp., Lenawee Co., Mich. with no family.

DIBBLE, MOSES born ca. 1824, and wife, LOISA, born ca. 1826, both in NY, were listed in the 1850 census of Franklin Twp., Lenawee Co., Mich. with ADELINE, age 5; EVELINE, age 4; ELISA, age 2, all b. Mich., in their household.

DIBBLE, NATHAN born ca. 1794, and wife, POLLY C., born ca. 1792, both in NY, were listed in the 1850 census of Ridgeway Twp., Lenawee Co., Mich. with JOHN, age 23; CHANCEY, age 20, both b. NY, in their household. Also see FRANCIS, preceding.

DIBBLE, SARAH (See David Mitchell)
DIBBLE, STEPHEN V. (See David B. Osterhout)

DICKINSON, ANNA B. (See Solomon Allis)
DICKINSON, JOHN born ca. 1827, and wife, HARRIET L., born ca. 1829, both in NY, were listed in the 1850 census of Adrian Twp., Lenawee Co., Mich.
DICKINSON, JULIUS C. Dr. born ca. 1823, NY, and wife, JANE, born ca. 1825, VT, were listed in the 1850 census

Pioneer Families of Southeastern Michigan

of Hudson Twp., Lenawee Co., Mich. with THOMAS, age 8/12, b. Mich., in their household.

DICKINSON, PERMELIA born 18 Jan. 1796, Conn. (See John Hammond).

DICKINSON, SWIFT born ca. 1814, and wife, JANE, born ca. 1815, both in England, were listed in the 1850 census of Cambridge Twp., Lenawee Co., Mich. with LANGLEY, age 13, b. England, and BYRON, age 8/12, b. Mich., in their household.

DICKSON, ISAAC D. was a native of Wayne Co., NY whose father (name not stated) had come from Penn. Isaac D. died in Wayne Co., NY, but his wife was living in Livingston Co., Mich. in 1888, age 88. Known daughters: SABRINA b. 29 Sept. 1826, Wayne Co. (m. Jacob A. Harder, also see); SALLIE b. ca. 1832 (m. William L. Rogers, also see, as a 2nd wife). Ref: P&BA-Len pg. 529-30.

DICKSON, SALLIE (See Cornelius Scott)

DICKSON, THOMAS was listed Tecumseh Twp., Lenawee Co., Mich. in the 1840 census index.

DIEWY also see DEWEY

DIEWY, MARTHA E. (See George A. Ingall)

DILLINGHAM, AMY Mrs. born ca. 1807, NJ, was listed in the 1850 census of Macon Twp., Lenawee Co., Mich. with EDWIN, age 19, b. Ohio; and ALBERT, age 8; ELIZABETH, age 6, both b. Mich., all in the household of James Collins (also see), perhaps father of Amy?

DILLINGHAM, JEPTHA was listed in the 1840 census index of Seneca Twp., Lenawee Co., Mich. (not listed in 1850).

DILLINGHAM, JOSEPH born ca. 1834, NY, was listed in the 1850 census of Madison Twp., Lenawee Co., Mich. in the Harvey household.

DILLINGHAM, MARY (See Arthur Power)

DILLINGHAM, PHILIP born ca. 1836, Mich., was listed in the 1850 census of Palmyra Twp., Lenawee Co., Mich. in Underwood household.

DILLINGHAM, SARAH (See Ansel C. Lambert)

DILLON, SARAH A. (See James Henry Thorn)

DINGLE, ANNA E. (See Michael Karcher)

DINGS, JOHN, son of PETER (following), came from NY to Riga Twp., Lenawee Co., Mich. in 1850, with wife, ELIZABETH (ROCKAFELLER) who was born in Columbia Co., NY, daughter of Teal (also see). Known daughter, ELLA b. 5 July 1856 (m. Conrad Ickler, also see). Ref: P&BA-Len pg. 266-7.

DINGS, PETER came from NY to Lenawee Co., Mich. Known son, JOHN (preceding). Ref: P&BA-Len pg. 266-7. Note: There was a JOHN listed in Columbia Co., NY in the 1800 census index.

DISBROW, JESSE was born Conn. and died at sea at age 26. His wife, ABIGAIL (TAYLOR), moved afterwards to eastern NY, where she lived to age 97. Known daughter, REBECCA, b. 1805, Conn. (m. John Ladd, also see). Ref: P&BA-Len pg. 519-20.

DISBROW, JOEL was listed in the 1840 census index of Medina Twp., Lenawee Co., Mich.

DISBROW, JOHN born ca. 1832, NY, was listed in the 1850 census of Raisin Twp., Lenawee Co., Mich. in the household of Alva Raymond.

DISBROW, LODOWICK born ca. 1829, and wife, AMELIA, born ca. 1835, were listed in the 1850 census of Ogden Twp., Lenawee Co., Mich., shown married within the year.

DISBROW, POLLY (See Benjamin West)

DITMARS, WILLIAM V. was born 4 Mar. 1810, and his wife, CATHERINE ANN (PETTY), was born 2 Feb. 1811, both in New Jersey. They moved to Lenawee Co. by 1842. He died 5 Oct. 1865, and she died 30 July 1876. In the 1850 census of Hudson Twp., Lenawee Co., Mich. they listed: ELIZABETH, age 16; CATHERINE ANN b. 1 Apr. 1835, near Trenton, NJ (m/1 Andrew Belcher, m/2 Levi Jennings, see both); JULIETT, age 9, b. NY; WILLIAM R., age 4, b. Mich. Ref: P&BA-Len pg. 533-4. Note: In New Jersey in 1793, listed for the militia of Reading, Hunterdon Co., NJ were WILLIAM; JOHN; & JOHN, Jr.

DIVER, ANDREW (possibly son of JOHN^1, following) was born in Canada, and moved to Mich. while it was still a Territory. He is listed in the 1830 census of Monroe Co., with males: 1 5-10; 1 30-40; females: 1 under 5; 3 5-10; 1 40-50. Andrew died in Monroe Co., Mich. Known son, JOHN (following). Ref: P&BA-Len pg. 379-80.

DIVER, ASA, possibly son of JOHN, following), married HARRIET C. (TENANT), daughter of Joseph C. (also see).

DIVER, JOHN^1 was listed in the 1830 census of Monroe Co., Mich. Territory with a male age 60-70; and female age 50-60. Note ANDREW (preceding).

DIVER, JOHN, son of ANDREW, was born in Monroe Co., Mich. He married NANCY (CHAMBERLAIN) also a native of Monroe Co., is probably they listed in the 1840 census index of Monroe, Monroe Co. They remained there until 1864, then moved to Deerfield Twp., Lenawee Co., Mich. Known daughter, SARAH, b. 1 Apr. 1851, Monroe Co. (m. Danford Tenant, also see). Ref: P&BA-Len pg. 379-80. Also see ASA, preceding.

DIX, WILLIAM and wife, HANNAH (DEMING), were natives of Conn. who had settled in NY. They moved to Pittsfield Twp., Washtenaw Co., Mich. by 1840, where they lived most of their lives; but died in Dover Twp., Lenawee Co. at the home of known daughter, JULIA b. ca. 1816, Oneida Co., NY (m. Conrad Holmes, also see). Ref: P&BA-Len pg. 212-3.

DODGE, CARPENTER was born ca. 1830, Mich., and was listed in the 1850 census of Madison Twp., Lenawee Co., Mich.

DODGE, CYNTHIA (See David Morrison)

DODGE, CYRUS P., probably son of JESSE (following), born ca. 1803, and wife, POLLY, born ca. 1807, both in NY, were listed in the 1850 census of Madison Twp., Lenawee Co., Mich. with LUCY, age 16, b. NY; and PERMELIA, age 12; SARAH, age 10; BETSEY, age 7; LYDIA A., age 4, all born Mich., in their household.

Also note CARPENTER, & HARRIET listed in other households.

DODGE, DAVID A. of Adrian, Lenawee Co., Mich. married 20 July 1865 to HELEN L. (MILLS), daughter of Philo C. (also see) of Franklin Twp. He served in Co. I, 18th Mich. Inf. during Civil War. Known children: MAMIE E. b. 18 Oct. 1857; 2. LOUISE FRANCES b. 2 Mar. 1875. Ref: P&BA-Len pg. 1060-3.

DODGE, GEORGE born ca. 1800, NH, and wife, ELIZA, born ca. 1806, b. NY, were listed in the 1840 census index of Rome Twp., Lenawee Co., Mich.; and in the 1850 census with HENRY W., age 16, b. NY; and WILLIAM S., age 13, b. Mich., in their household.

DODGE, HARRIET was born ca. 1835, Mich., and was listed in the 1850 census of Madison Twp., Lenawee Co., Mich.

DODGE, HIRAM - There were 2 men listed by this name in Lenawee Co., Mich., one in Clinton Twp., and one in Palmyra Twp.

DODGE, JACOB born ca. 1805, and wife, ELSY, born ca. 1808, both born NY, were listed in the 1850 census of Cambridge Twp., Lenawee Co., Mich. with LEVI, age 23; JANE, age 20; CATHARINE, age 17; NANCY, age 14; HANNAH, age 11; LAURAETT?, age 10; DORCAS, age 7, all b. NY; and CHARLES, age 6; JAMES F., age 1, both b. Mich., in their household.

DODGE, JESSE born ca. 1775, Mass., and wife, SARAH, born ca. 1777, Conn., were listed in the 1850 census of Madison Twp., Lenawee Co., Mich. next door to CYRUS P. (preceding).

DODGE, JOSHUA T. was listed in the 1840 census index of Tecumseh Twp., Lenawee Co., Mich.

DODGE, LEWIS Dr. born ca. 1812, and wife, LOVINA, born ca. 1815, both in NY, were listed in the 1850 census of Madison Twp., Lenawee Co., Mich. with MARY, age 11; JOHN, age 6; FRANCIS, age 4; LEWIS H., age 1, all b. Mich., in their household.

DODGE, LUCRETIA (See Thomas Kinney)

DODGE, THOMAS F. Dr. born ca. 1806, VT, was probably he listed in the 1840 census index of Adrian Twp., Lenawee Co., Mich., and in 1850 he listed LUCINDA, age 23; JOHN, age 11; ARTEMICIA, age 8; JOSEPHINE, age 7; THOMAS, age 2, all b. Mich., in his household.

DODGE, WILLIAM born ca. 1797, and wife, LUCY, born ca. 1806, both in NY, is probably they listed in the 1840 census index of Adrian Twp., Lenawee Co., Mich.; and in 1850 census with ELIZABETH, age 15; ORISSA, age 10; ROSAMOND, age 8, all b. Mich., in their household.

DODGE, WINSLOW (spelled "Doge" in census) born ca. 1810, and wife, HARRIET, born ca. 1838, both in NY, were listed in the 1850 census of Cambridge Twp., Lenawee Co., Mich. with THERESA, age 14; ALFRED, age 12; ISAAC, age 10; JOSHUA, age 8, all b. NY, in their household.

DOLPH, ABDA and wife, AMELIA (PORTER), moved from NY to Sylvania, Lucas Co., Ohio in 1846. Amelia died there in Mar. 1879. Known daughter, AUGUSTA, b. & Mar. 1848, Sylvania (m. George F. Chandler, also see). Ref: P&BA-Len pg. 389-90.

DOLPH, ELIZABETH (See Elisha Hinsdale)

DOLPH, WIRA (See Cornelius Gilson)

DONELSON, NANCY (See Thomas Johnson)

DONNELLY, JOHN and wife, ROSE (GALLAGHER), of Co. Mayo, Ireland died there, she in 1881, age 82; and he in 1882, age 86. There were 10 children (names not stated). Known children: MARY (m. Hugh Davitt, also see); PATRICK (following). Ref: P&BA-Len pg. 1045-6.

DONNELLY, PATRICK, son of JOHN (preceding), was born 15 Feb. 1828, Ireland, and sailed for St. John, Brunswick, Canada on 7 July 1849. He went first to Macedon, Wayne Co., NY; and then to Medina Twp., Lenawee Co., Mich. He married on 14 Feb. 1860 to ANN (HOWLEY), daughter of Michael (also see), and they settled in Medina Twp. Children: 1. MARY ELLEN (m. William Murray, Medina Twp.); 2. ROSE ANN (m. Ed Kelly); 3. JOHN; 4. HENRY; 5. PATRICK HENRY; and 2 children died infancy (names not stated). Ref: P&BA-Len pg. 1045-6.

DONNELSON, ELIZABETH (See William Graves)

DOREMUS, ANNA (See John V. Hoagland)

DORIELL, WILLIAM was born in 1822 in Milan Twp., Monroe Co., Mich. He married ELIZABETH "BETSEY" (HITCHINGS), daughter of Joseph (also see). He died in 1859. Four children (names not stated). Known daughter, DORA b. Aug. 1853 (m. Daniel T. Hall, also see). Betsey married again to William Pilbeam (also see). Ref: P&BA-Len pg. 1145 & 1049-50.

DORMOYER, CATHARINE (See Abraham George)

DORR, W. H. (See Peter Kishpaugh)

DOTY also see DOUGHTY

DOTY, ABIGAIL, age 54, born NY, was listed in the 1850 census of Fairfield Twp., Lenawee Co., Mich. in an Abrams household.

DOTY, ALVAN, son of BENJAMIN (following), born ca. 1789, Saybrook, Conn., moved to Greene Co., NY with his parents, and married on 11 Nov. 1807, Durham, NY, to MALINDA (VERGIL), daughter of Asel/Asahel (also see). They settled first in the Catskill Mountains, but about 1835 moved to Raisin Twp., Lenawee Co., Mich. He died 2 Dec. 1866, aged 78; and she died 20 July 1880, aged almost 92. Nine children (all names not stated). Known children: DAVID (following); and in Alvan's household in 1850: HENRY b. ca. 1815; EUNICE b. ca. 1833; WILLIAM E. (following). Note: AMELIA, age 31, also in household may be a wife of Henry, or another daughter?? Ref: P&BA-Len pg. 234-5.

DOTY, BENJAMIN was a Revolutionary soldier who moved from Conn. to Greene Co., NY where he remained. He had known son, ALVAN (preceding). Note: In the 1800 census index, there is a BENJAMIN; BENJAMIN JR.; EDWARD; ELIJAH listed in Greene Co., NY.

DOTY, DAVID, son of ALVAN (preceding), born ca. 1810, and wife, CATHARINE M. "MARIA", born ca. 1815, were listed in the 1850 census of Raisin Twp., Lenawee Co., Mich. next door to Alvan, with SAMUEL B., age 5, b. Mich., in their household (They were counted again in the 1850 census of Cambridge Twp.)

Pioneer Families of Southeastern Michigan

DOTY, FANNY, age 20, b. NY, was listed in the 1850 census of Hudson Twp., Lenawee Co., Mich. in a Boies household.

DOTY, FERRISS was listed in the 1840 census index of Franklin Twp., Lenawee Co., Mich. He was not listed in 1850, however, the following family may relate to him. SALINDA, age 43, born NY, listed head of household, with HARVEY, age 19; HESTER, age 15, both b. NY; and MAILA, age 13; WILLIAM, age 10; PLEURA?, age 8; RICHARD, age 4, all b. Mich., in her household.

DOTY, G. M. (See Calvin Town of Jackson Co., Mich.).

DOTY, HARRIET Mrs. was the daughter of Nathan Allen (also see). Harriet married first to Doty, and married second to Levi R. Peirson (also see) of Hudson, Lenawee Co., Mich. Ref: P&BA-Len pg. 709-10.

DOTY, ISAAC and wife, LUCINDA, of Wallingford, Rutland Co., VT, were parents of PHEBE b. 30 Sept. 1798, Wallingford (m. Welcome Aldrich, also see). Ref: P&BA-Len pg. 1092-3.

DOTY, ISAAC was listed in the 1840 census index of Rome Twp., Lenawee Co., Mich.

DOTY, JANE, age 16, born VT, was listed in the 1850 census of Hudson Twp., Lenawee Co., Mich. in a Hall household.

DOTY, JOHN J., son of LYDIA? (following), born ca. 1814, and wife, LYDIA B., born ca. 1817, both in NY, were listed in the 1850 census of Raisin Twp., Lenawee Co., Mich. with MARY W., age 13; SUSAN, age 6; CHARLES, age 1, all b. Mich., in their household.

DOTY, LYDIA (Mrs.) born ca. 1793, NY, was listed as head of household in the 1840 census index of Raisin Twp., Lenawee Co., Mich., and in the 1850 census with DAVID, age 35; MARY, age 22, both b. NY, in her household. JOHN J. (preceding) was listed next door.

DOTY, WILLIAM E., son of ALVAN (preceding), born 17 Dec. 1830, Greene Co., NY, moved with parents to Raisin Twp., Lenawee Co., Mich., and married CAROLINE M. (RAYMOND) born 20 Apr. 1829, Steuben Co., NY (who had come with parents, names not stated, to Raisin Twp. where they both died). Children: 1. HENRY; 2. WILLIE R.; 3. LINNIE S.; 4. HATTIE (m. George G. Haskell); 5. CARRIE; 6. STANLEY E.; 7. EVA. Ref: P&BA-Len pg. 234-5.

DOTY, ZEBULON born ca. 1810, Penn., was listed in the 1840 census index of Clinton Twp., Lenawee Co., Mich.; and in the 1850 census of Tecumseh Twp. with wife, HELENA?, born ca. 1810, NJ, Mich. and Laura Scofield, age 17, b. Mich., in their household.

DOUGHTY also see DOTY

DOUGHTY, HENRY born ca. 1802, and wife, SARAH, born ca. 1797, both in NY, were listed in the 1840 census index of Ogden Twp., Lenawee Co., Mich.; and in the 1850 census of Palmyra Twp. with EDWARD, age 14, b. Penn. in their household.

DOUGLAS, ALEXANDER was listed in the 1840 census index of Hudson Twp., Lenawee Co., Mich.

DOUGLAS, DANIEL died in NY, and his wife, HANNAH, afterwards came to Van Buren Twp., Wayne Co., Mich. where she died at age 62. Known daughters: ELIZABETH b. 18 Mar. 1814 (m. Orson Green, also see); CLEMENZA b. ca. 1821 (m. Orson Green, as 2nd wife.)

DOUGLAS ELIZABETH (See John Davison; and see Alanson Woolsey).

DOUGLAS, FRANK A. (See William Corbin)

DOUGLAS, GEORGE born ca. 1828, Mass., and HENRY, age 20, b. Mass., were listed in the 1850 census of Hudson Twp., Lenawee Co., Mich. in the household of John Rice and wife, Minerva (born ca. 1814, Mass.). Note ALEXANDER, preceding.

DOW, E. E. (See Robert G. Marhsall)

DOWLING, JOHN B., son of ROBERT I. (following), was born 2 Oct. 1835, Somersetshire, England; and came with parents to Cambridge Twp., Lenawee Co., Mich. at age 3. He married 15 Oct. 1861, Adrian, to ELIZABETH (BRIDGE), daughter of William (also see). They settled in Franklin Twp. Children: 1. WILLIS R.; 2. EUGENE R.; 3. IRA H.; PERLEY; 5. ALBA. Ref: P&BA-Len pg. 406-7.

DOWLING, P. H. (See Theodorick Luther)

DOWLING, ROBERT I. born ca. 1805, and wife, MARY (BRIDGE), born ca. 1810, natives of Somersetshire, England, came to Cambridge Twp., Lenawee Co., Mich. in 1838. He died 18 Sept. 1883, age 76; and she died 25 Dec. 1873. In the 1850 census of Cambridge Twp., they listed: 1. JOHN B. (preceding); 2. ELIZABETH, age 13, b. England; 3. GEORGE, age 11; 4. RICHARD, age 9; 5. WILLIAM, age 7; 6. ISAAC, age 5; 7. LUCINDA, age 3, last 5 b. Mich. Ref: P&BA-Len pg. 406-7.

DOWNE, WILLIAM B. (See Henry Pontius)

DOWNEY, LAURA (See Solomon Steele)

DOWNS, HENRY P., son of REUBEN (following), was born 1 Nov. 1829, Holland Purchase, Ripley, Chautauqua Co., NY, and moved to Michigan with his parents. He married first to CALISTA (MORGAN), daughter of Charles (also see). She died 1 Dec. 1881, Clinton, Lenawee Co., Mich. Five children, first 4 died young: FLORA S.; JENNIE M.; WILLIE H.; HARRY M. Surviving son, FRANK E. (Clinton, Mich.). Henry P. married second to Mrs. FRANCES M. (SHAW) WITHAM born in Lynn, Mass. (See Witham). Ref: P&BA-Len pg. 347-8.

DOWNS, JULIUS D. born ca. 1819, and wife, ORILLA?, born ca. 1822, both in NY, were listed in the 1850 census of Tecumseh Twp., Lenawee Co., Mich. with CHARLES, age 9; DELIA, age 1, both b. Mich., in their household.

DOWNS, L. Mrs. was listed as head of household in the 1840 census index of Clinton, Lenawee Co., Mich.

DOWNS, REUBEN was born in Dutchess Co., NY, and after the early death of his father (name not stated), he lived in Oneida Co., NY. (Note: The 1800 census index of Dutchess Co., NY listed a MARY). Reuben married in Augusta, Oneida Co. to SOPHRONIA (WAKELY), a native of Bennington Co., VT, and they moved to Lockport, NY. Before 1829, they moved to Holland Purchase, Chautauqua Co. In 1831, they moved to Bridgewater, Washtenaw Co., Mich., where Reuben died in 1835. Four children, 2 deceased before 1888 (names not stated): 1. MARY E. (m. Samuel St. John; 2. HENRY P. (preceding). After Reuben's death, Sophronia married Jacob Ward; and after his death, married Deacon Charles Morgan (also see). She died in Macon Twp., Lenawee Co., Mich. at age 65. Ref: P&BA-Len pg. 347-8. Note: There was a JOHN D. in the 1840 census index of Washtenaw Co., Mich.

DOYLE, ELLEN (See James Gahagan)

DRAKE, ALEUDA (See John Galloway)
DRAKE, ALVIN T. born ca. 1821, and wife, ANNA, born ca. 1821, both in Canada, were listed in the 1850 census of Palmyra Twp., Lenawee Co., Mich. with ELIZABETH, age 8; LEAH J., age 5; JAMES B., age 3; WILLIAM M., age 3, all b. Canada; and PETER, age 1/12; JOSHUA, age 1/12, born in Mich., in their household. (JOSHUA, following, was next door in census).
DRAKE, AMANDA (See James Patrick)
DRAKE, ELIAS Dr. born ca. 1803, and wife, JANE B., born ca. 1811, both in NY, were listed in the 1850 census of Dover Twp., Lenawee Co., Mich. with LUDLOM C., age 11; ELIZA J., age 9. both b. Mich., in their household.
DRAKE, ELISHA born ca. 1811, and wife, IRENA, born ca. 1815, both in Mass., were listed in the 1850 census of Ogden Twp., Lenawee Co., Mich.
DRAKE, ELIZABETH (See Abram Knapp)
DRAKE, JACOB & wife, MARY L. (DEMUNN), daughter of Peter (also see), were born born in New Jersey, and moved to Penn. (possibly Luzerne Co.) where they both died. Known daughter, MARGARET b. 28 Apr. 1813, NJ (m. Zachariah Bedell, also see). Ref: P&BA-Len pg. 601-2.
DRAKE, JOHN B. born ca. 1812, and wife, CLARISSA, born ca. 1814, both in NJ, were listed in the 1850 census of Cambridge Twp., Lenawee Co., Mich. with SARAH, age 16; ELIZABETH, age 8; LYDIA, age 7; ANTHONY, age 4; EMILY, age 2, all b. Mich., in their household.
DRAKE, JOSHUA C. born ca. 1817, Canada, and wife, ELIZABETH, b. 1819, NY, were listed in the 1850 census of Palmyra Twp., Lenawee Co., Mich. with ALVIN T., age 11; JOHN W., age 10; THOMAS, age 8; JAMES, age 6; JOSHUA C., age 4, all b. Canada; and EDWAY, age 2, b. Mich., in their household. (Next door to ALVIN T., preceding, in the census).
DRAKE, NATHANIEL P. was listed in the 1840 census index of Tecumseh Twp., Lenawee Co., Mich.
DRAKE, RILEY V. born ca. 1835, NY, was listed in the 1850 census of Rollin Twp., Lenawee Co., Mich. in a Sutliff household.
DRAKE, SALLY ANN (SARAH?) born Sussex Co., NY married 16 Apr. 1842 to Isaac C. Gunn (also see).
DRAKE, SIMON & wife, CLARISSA (SIMMONS), were natives of Conn. who lived in Genesee Co., NY by 1822. About 1834, they removed to Scipio Twp., Hillsdale Co., Mich., where he died at age 60, and she died at age 65. Eight children (names not stated). Known daughter, EMELINE A., b. 12 July 1822, Genesee Co., NY (m. Jabez Briggs, also see). Ref: P&BA-Len pg. 824-5.
DRAKE, STEPHEN born ca. 1826, NY, was listed in the 1850 census of Cambridge Twp., Lenawee Co., Mich.
DRAKE, WILLIAM married in Ulster Co., NY to SARAH J. (BEVIER), daughter of Jeremiah (also see). They afterwards moved to Rochester, Sangamon Co., Ill. He died in 1860, and she returned to Ulster Co., NY. Children: 1. MARIE (m. John Stonecker, Blissfield Twp., Lenawee Co., Mich.) 2. BENJAMIN F. (Palmyra Twp., Lenawee Co.). Sarah J. married second to Johannes LeFever (also see). Ref: P&BA-Len pg. 1046-9.
DRAKE, WILLIAM L. born ca. 1823, and wife, EMILY, born ca. 1830, both in NY, were listed in the 1850 census of Rome Twp., Lenawee Co., Mich. with MARY E., age 2/12, b. Mich. in their household.

DRAPER, DOW (See Jacob B. Smith)
DRAPER, MARY b. ca. 1836, England, was listed in the 1850 census of Madison Twp., Lenawee Co., Mich. in a Griffith household.
DRAPER, PRUDENCE Mrs. was listed in the 1850 census of Cambridge Twp., age 32, b. England, with ELI, age 17; CATHARINE, age 14, both b. Mich., all in the household of Firth & Ann Reed, also b. England.

DREW, ABIGAIL (See Thomas Tabor)
DREW, ANNE PRESALLA (Priscilla? See Junius Ayres).
DREW, DELOSS born ca. 1827, NY, was listed in the 1850 census of Adrian, Lenawee Co., Mich. in a hotel.
DREW, LIBBEUS born ca. 1820, NY, and wife, JULIA, born ca. 1825, VT, were listed in the 1850 census of Tecumseh Twp., Lenawee Co., Mich. with Julia D. Green, age 8, b. Mich., and Mary Thomas, age 31, b. NY, in the household.
DREW, WILLIAM & wife, MARGARET, moved to Clarkson, Monroe Co., NY to Somerfield, Monroe Co., Mich. in 1831. They moved to Dundee, Monroe Co., Mich. where Margaret was living in 1888, age 87. Known daughter, ELIZA ANN b. 10 Mar. 1827, Clarkson, NY (m. William Corbin, also see). Ref: P&BA-Len pg. 375-6.
DREW, WILLIAM born ca. 1810, Conn, and wife, HANNAH, born ca. 1811, NY, were listed in the 1850 census of Adrian Twp., Lenawee Co., Mich. with James H. Carroll, age 22, and wife, Mary E., age 19, b. NY, in their household.

DREWRY also see DRURY
DREWRY, ELIHU born ca. 1795, VT, and wife, PRISCILLA, born ca. 1806, NY, were listed in the 1850 census of Madison Twp., Lenawee Co., Mich. with BETSEY, age 17, b. NY, in the household.

DRIGS see DRIGGS
DRIGS, JEHIAL was listed in the 1840 census index of Branch Co., Mich. Note BARBARA, following.

DRIGGS, BARBARA (written "Drigs") born 1810, NY, was listed as head of household in the 1850 census of Madison Twp., Lenawee Co., Mich., with LEANDER, age 18; HIRAM, age 15; ALFRED, age 13; RILEY, age 11; ANN A. age 5, all b. Mich., in her household. Note SAMUEL E., following.
DRIGGS, EDWIN, son of JOSEPH (following), was born 21 Jan. 1834, Elyria Twp., Lorain Co., Ohio. He married 8 Oct. 1866 to MAGGIE (HASTINGS), daughter of Robert (also see) of Erie Co., Ohio. In 1866, they moved to Adrian, Lenawee Co., Mich. from Elyria, Ohio. Children: 1. HUGH H. b. 25 Nov. 1867; 2. CHARLES E. b. 31 May 1870; 3. HARRY A. b. 13 July 1872; 4. GRACIE B. b. 6 Apr. 1876; 5. CARL L. b. 23 Nov. 1887. Ref: P&BA-Len pg. 756-7.

Pioneer Families of Southeastern Michigan

DRIGGS, ELISHA born 1 Feb. 1760, may be he listed in the 1800 census index of Dutchess Co., NY. He went to Otsego Co., NY ca. 1800. He was killed 2 July 1813 in the Battle of Ft. Meigs during the War of 1812. Known son, JOSEPH (following). Ref: P&BA-Len pg. 756-7.

DRIGGS, JOSEPH, son of ELISHA (preceding), was born 28 July 1800, Otsego Co., NY. He was a drummer boy in the War of 1812, and acompanied his father to Ft. Meigs. He married CORNELIA (PIERSON), daughter of William (also see). In 1833, they moved to Elyria, Lorain Co., Ohio; and in 1863 moved to Rome Twp., Lenawee Co., Mich., and she died 30 Oct. 1879. In 1881, he moved into Adrian, where he died in July 1883. Children: 1. WILLIAM (Elyria, O.); 2. EDWIN (preceding); 3. JOHN (Kalamazoo Co., Mich.); 4. CORNELIA (m. Small; Reading, Hillsdale Co., Mich.); 5. CHARITY C. (d. Adrian, Mich.). Ref: P&BA-Len pg. 756-7.

DRIGGS, SAMUEL E. was listed in the 1840 census index of Woodstock Twp., Lenawee Co., Mich. Note BARBARA, preceding.

DRIVER, MARY ELLA (See Richard H. Kinney)

DROWN, APPOLOS, son of SAMUEL & CYNTHIA (TURNER), was born 22 Sept. 1802, Victor, Ontario Co., NY. He married 24 Dec. 1824 to LYDIA B. (EATON), daughter of Capt. James, Sr. (also see) of Canandaigua, NY. In 1827, he and his father-in-law, went to Tecumseh Twp., Lenawee Co., Mich. to prospect for land. He returned to Canandaigua, NY and remained until 1829, then moved his wife and 3 children to Lenawee Co.. They lived in Tecumseh Twp., Medina Twp., & finally in Adrian, where he died 4 Mar. 1875, age 72. She died ca. 1883, age 80. Known children (from 1850 census of Medina Twp.): 1. JANE (m. Alvin D. Rice, also see); 2. GEORGE A. b. ca. 1827, NY; 3. OSCAR A. b. ca. 1835; 4. ADELIA M. b. ca. 1836; 5. CAROLINE B. b. ca. 1837; 6. SARAH A. b. ca. 1839; 7. MARY E. b. ca. 1842; 8. NELLIE M. (m. Edward A. Milliken, Jr., also see), all b. Mich. Mary A. Eaton, age 74, b. NH, was also in the household. Ref: P&BA-Len pg. 598-9 & 899-900.

DROWN, JAMES (See John L. Hall)

DRURY also see DREWRY
DRURY, SUSAN (See Alvah Fuller)

DUBOIS, ALEXANDER and wife, SUSAN (GRIER), of Co. Antrim, Ireland, moved with 6 children to Quebec, Canada; and then to Ogdensburg, St. Lawrence Co., NY, where they remained. Known son, JOHN (following). Ref: P&BA-Len pg. 314-5.

DUBOIS, CHARLES R., son of JOHN (following), was born 12 Nov. 1849, Ridgeway Twp., Lenawee Co., Mich. and married 3 Mar. 1871 to SARAH (BEEVERS), daughter of Benjamin (also see). Children: 1. ERNEST; 2. MARY ELIZABETH. Ref: P&BA-Len pg. 387-8.

DUBOIS, GIDEON of Greenfield, Saratoga Co., NY, said to be of "German descent," was the father of NELLIE (m. William Dunham, also see, ca. 1800). Ref: P&BA-Len pg. 842-3.

DUBOIS, HANNAH of Ulster Co., NY (See Andrew LeFever).

DUBOIS, JOHN, son of ALEXANDER (preceding), was born ca. 1820 in Co. Antrim, Ireland, and came with his parents to Canada, then St. Lawrence Co., NY. He married first to MARY (OSTERHOUT), daughter of John (also see), possibly in Seneca Co., NY. They settled in Ridgeway Twp. in 1845, and she died there. Children: 1. (MARY) ELIZABETH b. ca. 1846 (m. George W. Smith, also see); 2. CHARLES R. (preceding); 3. EMMA (m. Ebenezer Price, also see). 3. EVA (m. Joseph Cone, Monroe Co., Mich.). John married second to Mrs. JOHANNA DENISON, widow of David (also see); and she died in 1875, age 37, leaving children: 6. OLLIE (m. Oliver Curry, Milan Twp., Monroe Co., Mich.); 7. FRED. John married again to MARIA (McFALL), daughter of Cornelius (also see), and had son: 8. JOHN. Ref: P&BA-Len pg. 314-5.

DUFFY, MAY (See George Benfer)

DULL, LOUISA A. (See Lyman H. Aldrich)

DUNBAR, JANE (See Thomas Wilbur)
DUNBAR, MARGARET (See John Rainey)

DUNHAM, AARON and wife, MEHITABLE (WOOD), were natives of Mass., where they married, and then moved to Onondaga Co., NY. They later moved to Birmingham, Ohio where he died; and she afterwards went to Lansing, Mich. where she died. Known daughter, POLLY, b. 1916, Black River area of Onondaga Co., NY (She went at age 12 to to live with an uncle, J. DUNHAM, in Oneida Co., NY where she m. Lyman A. Curtiss, also see). Ref: P&BA-Len pg. 992-3.

DUNHAM, CHARLES, son of WILLIAM (following), born 11 Aug. 1812, Brockville, Canada, married 23 Dec. 1835, probably in Saratoga Co., NY, to HARRIET (CANFIELD), daughter of Asahel (also see) of Durham, NY. In 1838, they removed to Bristol, Ontario Co., NY; and also lived in Monroe Co., NY. They also lived in Pittsford, NY, and Cayuga Co., NY before moving to near Ypsilanti, Washtenaw Co., Mich. She died there 3 Mar. 1867. There were 6 children, 2 deceased before 1888 (names not stated). 1. ASAHEL C; 2. ADDIE M. (m. W. H. Yost, Kansas City); 3. HATTIE (m. W. M. Ellsworth, Sandusky, O.); 4. CHARLES A. (Kansas City). In 1869, Charles moved to Hudson, Lenawee Co., Mich. He married again 27 Oct. 1869 to Mrs. SAMANTHA (BEALS) WHEELER, daughter of Caleb, and widow of Reuben (see both). Ref: P&BA-Len pg. 842-3.

DUNHAM, EBEN married probably in Nicholas, Tioga Co., NY to Mrs. FRANCES (WRIGHT) CORBIN, daughter of Thomas; and widow of Horace (see both). In 1863, the moved to Petersburg, Monroe Co., Mich., and she died there in Mar. 1886, age 79. Children: 1. JAMES W. (Petersburg, Mich.); 2. ELLEN J. (m. Rev. David A. Curtis; 3. EDWIN A. (d. Civil War); and 3 others (names not stated), deceased before 1888. Ref: P&BA-Len pg. 375-6.

DUNHAM, CATHERINE (See James Patterson)
DUNHAM, JOHN E., born ca. 1802, Conn., and wife, EMILY, borh ca. 1808, Mass., were listed in the 1850 census of Tecumseh Twp., Lenawee Co., Mich. with HARRIET, age 17; GEORGE, age 16; CHARLES, age 14, all b. NY, in their household.

DUNHAM, WILLIAM, son of EPHRAIM (who came from Holland to Saratoga Co., NY and died Waterford, ca. 1820), was born Half Moon (now Waterford), NY. He married NELLIE (DUBOIS), daughter of Gideon (also see). In December of 1811, they moved to Brockville, Canada, but were forced to flee during the War of 1812, and they returned to Half Moon, NY. He died at North Bristol, NY while visiting a son in 1845; and she died in 1878, East Bloomfield, NY, age 96yrs, 7 mos., while visiting a daughter. Nine children (names not stated). Known son, #5. CHARLES (preceding). Ref: P&BA-Len pg. 842-3.

DUNN, CHARLES W., son of JEFFERSON (following), was born 24 Nov. 1834, Wayne Co., Mich. (where his mother was visiting from Lenawee Co.). He was reared in Fairfield Twp., Lenawee Co., Mich. He married 1 Jan. 1862 to MARY J. (SANFORD), daughter of Osbourn/Isburn (also see). No children were listed. Ref: P&BA-Len pg. 922.

DUNN, JEFFERSON (possibly ROBERT JEFFERSON) and wife, ADELIA (MORRIS) who was born ca. 1805, were both natives of NY, who came to Wayne Co., Mich. early in their marriage. In 1833, they moved to Fairfield Twp., Lenawee Co., Mich. He died 24 June 1838. (Note: It may be she listed as "Delilah" as head of household in the 1840 census index of Seneca Twp.) Children: 1. SABRA (d. age 13); 2. CHARLES W. (preceding); 3. JOHN W. (twin of Charles, killed at age 10 being thrown from a wagon); 4. ROBERT J. b. ca. 1838. Ref: P&BA-Len pg. 922. Adelia married second to Nelson Smith (also see) and they were listed in the 1850 census of Fairfield Twp. with CHARLES & ROBERT J. in the household. Note: In the 1840 census index, Wayne Co., Mich., there were listed BARBARA; CRANDELL; GEORGE W.; JAMES at Livonia; DUNCAN A. at Van Buren; MICHAEL at Romulus; SAMUEL at Plymouth; WILLIAM in Detroit; JAMES H. & JOHN in Ham(tramyck?); JOHN at Nankin.

DUNN, RICHMOND was listed in the 1840 census index of Macon Twp., Lenawee Co., Mich.

DuPUGH, BENJAMIN F. (See Benjamin F. DePuy)

DURHAM, ANNA (See Nathaniel C. Bennett)

DURKEE, SARAH (See Cornelius W. Baluss)

DURKEES, MATILDA (See John L. Hamilton)

DUSENBURY, POLLY (See John Maloney)

DUTCHER, ADAM was born ca. 1790, NY, and was listed in the 1840 census index of Tecumseh Twp., Lenawee Co., Mich., and in the 1850 census listed RACHEL, age 40, b. NY, in his household.

DUTCHER, ANDROS born ca. 1805, and wife, MARY, born ca. 1809, were listed in the 1850 census of Medina Twp., Lenawee Co., Mich. with ANDROS, age 15, b. NY; SARAH, age 5, b. Ohio; THOMAS J., age 1, b. Mich., and Francis A. Crouch, age 23, b. NY, and Rachel Crouch, age 17, b. NY, married within the year (Rachel possibly daughter of Andros?).

DUTCHER, CHARLES (See Henry Nichols)

DUTCHER, ELLEN (See John M. Payne)

DUTCHER, JOSEPH Dr. born ca. 1803, and wife, ELIZA, born ca. 1810, both in NY, were listed in the 1850 census of Rome Twp., Lenawee Co., Mich. with ELIZA M., age 16; JOSEPH, age 13; SYLVIA J., age 10; WILLIAM H., age 7; MARY L, age 5, all b. NY, in their household.

DUTTON, WILLIAM born ca. 1813, NH, and wife, HARRIET (THOMAS), born ca. 1822, NY, moved to Adrian Twp., Lenawee Co., Mich. from Lyndeboro, Hillsborough Co., NH before 1850. He died 30 Nov. 1884; and she was said to have died 12 July 1843? (but this seems to be an error, as he listed wife, Harriet, in the 1850 census, possibly d. 1883?) Known children from 1850 census: 1. HARRIET E. b. 15 June 1843, Mich. (m. George H. Curtis, also see); FRANCES W. b. ca. 1848. Ref: P&BA-Len pg. 251-2.

DUYREE, ELIZABETH (See Rancelier Mills)

DUYREE, JOHN born ca. 1816, and wife, LOVIZA, born ca. 1828, both in NY, were listed in the 1850 census of Hudson Twp., Lenawee Co., Mich. with MARY A., age 5; SALLY E., age 2; CELESTIA, age 1, all b. Mich., in their household.

- E -

EARL also see EARLE
EARL, MARIA E. (See Rancelier Mills)

EARLE, ALVAN D. born ca. 1820, Ohio, and wife, MELISSA, born ca. 1826, NY, were listed in the 1850 census of Rome Twp., Lenawee Co., Mich. with DELOSS S., age 3; CHARLES D., age 7/12, both b. Mich., in their household.

EARLE, CHARLES (See William Lagore). Also note CHARLES D., in household of ALVAN D., preceding.

EARLE, ELIJAH (called "Earles"), son of JOHN (following), born 15 Feb. 1805, Lakes, NY, came first to Adrian, Lenawee Co., Mich. in 1834, accompanying the Maloney family. He married there to MARY (MALONEY), daughter of John (also see) who was born 1818, NY. They returned to Monroe Co., NY before 1836; and to Palmyra Twp., Lenawee Co., Mich. in 1842, where they were living in the 1850 census. They moved to Ogden Twp.; and then to Blissfield, Mich. where they lived in 1888. Known children from census: 1. REBECCA b. 10 Apr. 1836, Mendon, NY (m. James Nicholson, also see); 2. CATHARINE b. ca. 1841, NY; 3. POLLY b. ca. 1846, Mich. Ref: P&BA-Len pg. 557-8.

EARLE, JOHN born in Greenbush, Rensselaer Co., NY, moved to Lake (Chautauqua Co.?), NY where he married REBECCA (WHITE) before 1805. He later moved to Monroe Co., NY where they died. Known son, ELIJAH (preceding). Ref: P&BA-Len pf. 557-8.

EARLE, MERCY born ca. 1770, NJ, was listed in the 1850 census of Raisin Twp., Lenawee Co., Mich. in the household of Laing and Abba (age 56) Smith, both b. NJ, possibly Mercy is mother of Abba?

EARLES see EARLE

EAST, CHARLES (See John Henry)

Pioneer Families of Southeastern Michigan

EAST, JAMES and wife, JANE (FENSEM), were reared and married at Boxmore (near London), England. In 1851, they came to the US and settled in Macon Twp., Lenawee Co., Mich. He died in Jan. 1882, age 76, and she was living in 1888, age 81. Known children: CHARLES; & ELLEN b. 10 Nov. 1834, Boxmore (m. Thomas Lee, also see). Ref: P&BA-Len pg. 807-8.

EASTLAND, MARY (See Jesse B. Chittenden)

EASTLICK, DAVID married a daughter of George Miller (also see). Ref: P&BA-Len pg. 939-40.

EASTMAN, LOIS (See Simeon Sheldon)

EATON, CAROLINE (See Caroline Caton, dau. of John).

EATON, CHRISTOPHER born ca. 1811, and wife, ELEANOR, born ca. 1817, both in NY, were listed in the 1850 census of Ridgeway Twp., Lenawee Co., Mich. with MARY, age 13; SARAH, age 11; ALBERT, age 8; JAMES H., age 7; GEORGE, age 5; OSCAR, age 3; QUINCY, age 8/12, all b. Mich., in their household.

EATON, DAVID and wife, ELEANOR (CLEMENT), were natives of Mass. Known son, JAMES (following). David had 3 brothers, SAMUEL, JOSEPH, & JONATHAN; and SAMUEL served in the Revolution at age 16. Ref: P&BA-Len pg. 471-2.

EATON, EDWIN MD[4], son of JACOB O.[3] (following), was born 6 Nov. 1849, Wilton, Franklin Co., Maine. About 1873-6, he lived in Lewiston, ME. He married 18 Nov. 1874 to JENNIE (McFARLAND), daughter of David (also see) of Wales, ME. About 1876, they moved to Clayton, Lenawee Co., Mich., and about 1886 to Hudson. No children were listed. Ref: P&BA-Len pg. 827-8.

EATON, EMERY F., age 5, b. Ill., was listed in the 1850 census of Medina Twp., Lenawee Co., Mich. in the household of David & Saphronia Wilber.

EATON, HORACE born ca. 1828, NY, and wife, MARY, born ca. 1834, Ohio, were listed in the 1850 census of Dover Twp., Lenawee Co., Mich., married within the year, in the household of Sarah Cleveland, perhaps mother of Mary.

EATON, HORACE B., son of JAMES C. (following), was born 9 Oct. 1843 in Raisin Twp., Lenawee Co., Mich. He married 11 Nov. 1869 to SARAH A. (WARING), daughter of Daniel (also see). In 1882, they lived in Tecumseh Twp. Children: 1. JOSEPH O.; 2. MARY A.; 3. AGNES L. Ref: P&BA-Len pg. 471-2.

EATON, JACOB O.[3], son of NATHAN[2] (following), was born in East Kingston, NH. He moved first to Haverhill, Mass., and then to Wilton, ME. He married there to ELIZABETH J. (FLETCHER), daughter of Abner of Wilton. They settled near East Dixfield, and eventually retired into the town. Known twin sons, Dr. EDWIN[4] (preceding); and one who became a dentist and resided in Livermore, ME. Ref: P&BA-Len pg. 827-8.

EATON, JAMES, son of DAVID (preceding), born in Mass., married there to MARY (BROCKELBANK) who was born ca. 1776, New Hampshire. They moved to Vermont, and then in 1802 to Ontario Co., NY. In 1828, they moved to Raisin Twp., Lenawee Co., Mich. Known son, JAMES C. (following); and known daughter, LUCY b. 23 July 1799, VT (census said b. NH; m. Appolos Drown, also see). Mary, age 74, b. NH, was living in the household of Lucy in the 1850 census of Medina Twp. Ref: P&BA-Len pg. 471-2 & 598-9.

EATON, JAMES C., son of JAMES (preceding), was born May 1808, Canandaigua, Ontario Co., NY. He moved to Raisin Twp., Lenawee Co., Mich. with his parents. He married in 1834 to SARAH J. (WHEELER), daughter of James (also see). He died 18 Nov. 1853, and 2 children (names not stated) were deceased before him. Known children: 1. JAMES W. b. 1837 (to India); 2. AMANDA M. b. ca. 1839 (m. John H. Waring, son of Daniel, also see); 3. CHARLES H. b. 27 May 1840 (d. 1869); 4. HORACE B. b. ca. 1844 (preceding); 5. JULIA D. b. ca. 1847; 6. PHILURA A. b. ca. 1849; J. CLEMENT. Ref: P&BA-Len pg. 471-2. Note: MARY, mother of James C., was listed again in the 1850 census of Raisin Twp. in his household, age 76, b. NH.

EATON, JEMIMA born ca. 1824, NY; and HIRAM, age 16; JOHN B., age 10, both b. NY; and FRANCIS, age 4, b. Mich., were listed in the 1850 census of Rome Twp., Lenawee Co., Mich. in the household of Horatio Larabee, age 22, and wife, Mary, age 18, both b. NY, married within the year, and also in their household was Mary Berry, age 73, b. NY.

EATON, MERCY ANN (See John Osborn)

EATON, NATHAN[2], son of NATHAN[1], both of whom were born in East Kingston, NH (descendants of a man, name not stated, who had settled in New Hampshire in Colonial times, and had brothers go to NY and Canada). Known son, JACOB O.[3] (preceding). Ref: P&BA-Len pg. 827-8.

EATON, SILAS born ca. 1798, and wife, ELIZA, born ca. 1802, both in NY, were listed in the 1850 census of Hudson Twp., Lenawee Co., Mich. with STEPHEN A., age 24, b. NY; and RANSOM, age 11, b. Mich., in their household. Also listed were Lafayette A. Lagore (also see), age 25, and wife, Charlotte M., age 23, b. Mass.

EATON, STEPHEN born ca. 1824, NY, was listed in the 1850 census of Adrian Twp., Lenawee Co., Mich. in a hotel. There was an H. U., age 20, b. NY, listed in another hotel in the 1850 census of Adrian Twp.,

EBBITT, MARY (See A. W. Ellis)

ECCLES, DANIEL, son of DANIEL, was born Co. Tyrone, Ireland and moved first to Lambton Co., Ontario, Canada; then to Iona, Canada. He married SUSAN (LUCKHAM). He died 1 Mar. 1866, and she was still living in Iona in 1888. Five children (names not stated). Known son, ROSINGRAVE M. (following). Ref: P&BA-Len pg. 666-7.

ECCLES, ELIZA born ca. 1830, and MARY, born ca. 1832, both in Ireland, and CHARLES, born ca. 1834, NY, were listed in the 1850 census of Madison Twp., Lenawee Co., Mich. in the household of Elizabeth Rider, age 77, b. Ireland.

ECCLES, ROSINGRAVE M., MD, son of DANIEL (preceding), was born 3 Mar. 1858, Elgin Co., Ontario, Canada. He moved to Blissfield Twp., Lenawee Co., Mich. in 1876. He married CARRIE HELEN (PRITCHARD) of London, Canada. They resided in Blissfield, where she died 6 Jan. 1884. Daughter, MABEL. Ref: P&BA-Len pg. 666-7.

EDDY, ?, married probably in Mass. to SARAH (BAKER), moved at an early date to Wayne Co., NY. They were parents of JOHN (following); & probably ASA b. 1805, NY (listed in Blissfield Twp. in 1850 census).

EDDY, ABRAHAM is probably "Abram" listed in the 1840 census index of Madison Twp., Lenawee Co., Mich. Known daughter, EXPERIENCE (m/1 Elmer Compton who d. 1850; m/2 Dr. Francis Grandy, also see). Ref: P&BA-Len pg. 576-7.

EDDY, ALANSON born ca. 1817, and wife, LUCRETIA, born ca. 1812, both in NY, were listed in the 1850 census of Rollin Twp., Lenawee Co., Mich. with MARION L., age 5, b. Mich.; and probably also SARAH V., age 3, b. Mich. (who was dittoed after Joseph Beal, age 68, b. Mass., possibly father of Lucretia.)

EDDY, ALBINA (See Warren Gilbert, also note HIRAM S., following).

EDDY, ASA born ca. 1806, NY (See JOHN, following).

EDDY, AUGUSTUS, Rev. was the brother of (name not stated) who married an Allen and resided in Farmington, Ontario Co., NY (See Erasmus Darwin Allen).

EDDY, CALEB from Vermont settled near Canandaigua, Ontario Co., NY where known daughter, LUCY married Caleb Smith (b. 1776, also see). Ref: P&BA-Len pg. 579-80.

EDDY, CROWELL, son of JOHN (of NJ following), was born 6 Apr. 1811, Morristown, NJ. He moved to Schuyler Co., NY; and in 1832 to Erie Co., Ohio. He married there to MARY A. (SPEARS) born 3 Feb. 1817, Monroe Co., NY (whose parents, names not stated, had moved from Penfield, NY to Erie Co.) In 1845, they settled in Franklin Twp., Lenawee Co., Mich. She died Mar. 1885, age 68. Children: 1. CATHERINE b. ca. 1838, Ohio; 2. HENRY H. b. ca. 1841, Ohio (to Vinton, IA); 3. CHARLES b. ca. 1843, Ohio (d. age 22 while returning from Civil War); 4. EDWIN b. ca. 1844, Ohio (Manchester Twp., Washtenaw Co., Mich.) 5. GEORGE W. (WILLIAM? b. ca. 1847, Mich.; to Vinton, IA); 6. AMELIA b. ca. 1848 (d. 6 Mar. 1857, age 8); 7. HORACE G. (Vinton, IA); 8. JAMES C. (Vinton, IA); 9. JOHN (Akron, Col.); 10. LIBBIE S. Ref: P&BA-Len pg. 273-4.

EDDY, ELISHA, son of JOHN (of Mass. following), was born 22 Apr. 1824, Wayne Co., NY, and moved to Blissfield Twp., Lenawee Co., Mich. with his parents. He married in Oct. 1851 to LYDIA (CROCKETT), daughter of Nathaniel (also see). They lived first in Blissfield Twp., then moved to Ogden Twp. About 1882, they returned to Blissfield Twp. Children not mentioned. Ref: P&BA-Len pg. 659-60.

EDDY, ELON (male) was born ca. 1794, NY, and was listed in the 1850 census of Ridgeway Twp., Lenawee Co., Mich. in the household of Fenner & Phebe Palmer.

EDDY, GEORGE was born in Penn., and wife, TEMPERANCE (COOKE), was born in NY; and they lived first in Utica, NY, then moved to Perinton, and later to Pittsford, Monroe Co., NY. They moved last to Erie Co., Ohio where he died in 1869, and she died in 1863. Children: 1. GEORGE C. (served Civil War, died Milan, O. of resulting illness); 2. SAMUEL M. (served Civil War; lived Cleveland, O.); 3. THOMAS B. (following); 4. WILLIAM H. (d. 1865, Civil War of illness). Ref: P&BA-Len pg. 218-9.

EDDY, HIRAM S. born ca. 1812, VT, and wife, MARGARETTA, born ca. 1817, NY, were listed in the 1840 census index of Fairfield Twp., Lenawee Co., Mich.; and in the 1850 census with HELEN, age 11; PARLEY J., age 7; ALBINA, age 5, all b. Mich.; and ZEPHANIAH, age 28, b. NY, in their household.

EDDY, JOHN was a native of New Jersey, and it may be he listed in the militia of Morristown, NJ in 1793. He married CATHERINE (CRAIN), Morristown; and they remained there until after the birth of first 6 children. They removed to Reading, Schuyler Co., NY where their last 5 children were born. There were 7 sons and 4 daughters (names not stated). He died at age 58. Known son, CROWELL (preceding). Ref: P&BA-Len pg. 273-4.

EDDY, JOHN, son of (name not stated, preceding) & SARAH (BAKER), was born in 1798, Mass., and moved with his parents to Wayne Co., NY during its early settlement. He married there to MARY (BARNHART), daughter of William (also see). In 1832, they removed to Blissfield Twp., Lenawee Co., Mich., where he died in Apr. 1849, age 51. Mary was listed as head of household in the 1850 census of Riga Twp. Known sons: LEVI (following); #2. ELISHA (preceding). The following were in the household in 1850: ANDREW, age 20; MOSES, age 11, both b. NY; MARY, age 8; JULIA, age 4, both b. Mich. Ref: P&BA-Len pg. 659-60. ASA, age 44, b. NY, was also in the household in 1850, probably brother of JOHN.

EDDY, LEVI, son of JOHN (of Mass., preceding), was born 7 July 1822, Wayne Co., NY, and moved with his parents to Blissfield Twp., Lenawee Co., Mich. He married in 1845 in Riga Twp. to THIRZA (CROCKETT), daughter of Nathaniel (also see), and they settled in Riga Twp. Children: 1. JOHN b. ca. 1849; 2. CELESTIA b. ca. 1850; 3. WILLIAM; 4. LORINDA (m. Harvey Honsinger). Ref: P&BA-Len pg. 864-5.

EDDY, MORTON born ca. 1807, Mass., and wife, WEALTHY, born ca. 1805, NY, were early settlers to Adrian Twp., Lenawee Co., Mich.; and were in the 1850 census of Madison Twp., Lenawee Co., Mich. with LUCY M., age 19 (m. Charles M. Crosswell, also see); HIRAM C., age 17; GEORGE, age 16; ORVILLE, age 13; EUGENE, age 7, all b. NY; and EMILY A., age 5, b. Mich., in their household.

EDDY, SAMUEL born ca. 1807, Penn., and wife, AXY, born ca. 1809, NY, were listed in the 1850 census of Hudson Twp., Lenawee Co., Mich. with GRAHAM S., age 18; MORTON S., age 16; NELSON B., age 14; ELIZA M., age 12. all b. NY, in their household.

EDDY, THOMAS B., son of GEORGE (preceding), born 21 July 1839, Perinton, Monroe Co., NY, married ELIZABETH (HATHAWAY) on 27 Dec. 1859 in Milan, Ohio. They came to Dover Twp., Lenawee Co., Mich. in 1883. Children: 1. WALTER H. (m. Alice Bartow, Rome Twp., Lenawee Co.); 2. FRANCES E.; 3. DECKIE M.; 4. CLARA E.; 5. ALICE S.; 6. ANNA L.; 7. ELSIE E.; 8. THOMAS H. Ref: P&BA-Len pg. 218-9.

EDDY, THOMAS? C. born ca. 1812, and wife, DIANTHA? P., born ca. 1819, both in NY, were listed in the 1850 census of Ogden Twp., Lenawee Co., Mich. with LUCY A., age 7; POLLY A., age 1, both b. Mich., in their household.

EDDY, WILLIAM H. was listed in the 1840 census index of Macon Twp., Lenawee Co., Mich.

Pioneer Families of Southeastern Michigan

EDDY, ZEPHANIAH (See HIRAM S., preceding).

EDDY, ZILPHA of Rutland Co., VT and Niagara Co., NY (See Samuel S. Round). Ref: P&BA-Len pg. 1017-8.

EDGAR, JAMES and wife, MARY (WELLS), were of Scottish birth and were probably residents of Shaftsbury, VT where daughter JEANNETTE married before 1800 to James Burnett (also see). Ref: P&BA-Len pg. 590-1.

EDGAR, WILLIAM R. (See George Lane)

EDWARDS, ALFRED (See William Knight)

EDWARDS, ANDREW was listed in the 1840 census index of Clinton Twp., Lenawee Co., Mich.

EDWARDS, ASA G. was listed in the 1840 census index of Franklin Twp., Lenawee Co., Mich. adjacent to CALVIN & RICHARD (following).

EDWARDS, CALVIN was listed in the 1840 census index of Fairfield Twp., and another in Franklin Twp., probably one of them is the same as following. In Franklin Twp., there was an ASA G.; & RICHARD (following) listed adjacent. See SARAH (following).

EDWARDS, CALVIN born ca. 1809, VT, and his wife, CLARISSA, born ca. 1811, NY, were listed in the 1850 census of Tecumseh Twp., Lenawee Co., Mich. with HARRIET, age 20; LUCY, age 18, both b. NY; and CHARLES, age 16 (following); ISRAEL, age 13 (probably he who m. Sarah Sheeler, dau. of George, also see); MARY, age 11; EDNA, age 7; MORRIS, age 5; FRANCES, age 1, all b. Mich., in their household.

EDWARDS, CHARLES (probably son of CALVIN, preceding) had wife, MARY E. (SMITH), daughter of Robert. Mary E. married second to D. W. Love (See Robert Smith & D. W. Love).

EDWARDS, CLARINDA of Seneca Twp., Lenawee Co., Mich. married Andrew A. Russell (also see).

EDWARDS, DANIEL S. born ca. 1807, and wife, CAROLINE, born ca. 1808, both in NY, were listed in the 1840 census index of Adrian Twp., Lenawee Co., Mich.; and in the 1850 census with BYRON, age 12; SARAH E., age 9; ALFRED, age 6; JAMES H., age 5; ANAWINES? (female), age 2, all b. Mich., in their household.

EDWARDS, DAVID born ca. 1828, NY lived in household of Appolos Drown in the 1850 census of Medina Twp., Lenawee Co., Mich.; and he married there to MARY (WILLIAMS), daughter of Thomas (also see). Children: 1. ELLEN J. (m. E. C. Palmer, Hudson Twp., had daughter, Eva May); IDA (deceased before 1888). David died in the Civil War, and Mary married second to Benjamin D. Osborn (also see). Ref: P&BA-Len pg. 1077-8.

EDWARDS, ISRAEL born ca. 1794, Rhode Island, was listed in the 1850 census of Medina Twp., Lenawee Co., Mich., alone.

EDWARDS, JULIA M., age 21, and MARY, age 12, both b. NY, were listed in the 1850 census of Madison Twp., Lenawee Co., Mich. in the household of Harlow & Jane B. Milliken.

EDWARDS, RANDOLPH D. M. born ca. 1829, and (wife?), ELECTA ANN, born ca. 1832, both in NY, were listed in the 1850 census of Franklin Twp., Lenawee Co., Mich. with BELWIDA?, age 15, b. Mich. (sister?) in their household. Probably relate to RICHARD, following.

EDWARDS, RICHARD born ca. 1797, and wife, SARAH, born ca. 1798, both in NJ, were listed in the 1850 census of Franklin Twp., Lenawee Co., Mich. with NATHANIEL, age 28, PHOEBE, age 23, both b. NY; and SE-ING?(male), age 17; ELIJAH, age 13, both b. Mich., in their household. See RANDOLPH, preceding; also note CALVIN, preceding.

EDWARDS, SARAH born ca. 1798, NY, was listed in the 1850 census of Franklin Twp., Lenawee Co., Mich. with no family. Note ASA G. & CALVIN, preceding, who were in Franklin Twp. in 1840 census index.

EFLAND, AMANDA (See Montague)

EGBERT, JAMES moved from Penn. to Illinois; and then to Hillsdale Co., Mich. where he died at age 72. Known daughter, LYDIA, b. 20 Dec. 1793, Penn. (m. Jacob Sanders, also see). Ref: P&BA-Len pg. 974-5.

EGGLESTON, BRADFORD born ca. 1808, and wife, HARRIET, born ca. 1809, both in NY, were listed in the 1850 census of Adrian Twp., Lenawee Co., Mich. with JAMES, age 16; ELIZA, age 9, both b. NY; and ALBERT, age 1, b. Mich., in their household.

EGGLESTON, JAMES born 1 Jan. 1798, Pittsfield, Rutland Co., VT, married LYDIA who was born 14 Mar. 1805, Ware, VT. He died in Sept. 1863; and she died in 1876. Known daughter, OLIVE L. (m. Dr. Alexander W. Seger, also see. 11 Oct. 1859, Rome Twp., Lenawee Co., Mich.). Ref: P&BA-Len pg. 1114-7.

ELA, DAVID and wife, NANCY (FISHER), daughter of Samuel (also see) of Londonderry, NH, had known daughter, LOIS, b. 1 Apr. 1788 (m. Richard Kent², also see).

ELA, SAMUEL of Derry, NH was the father of SALLIE born 2 June 1786, Derry (m. Stephen Reynolds, also see, and she d. Sept. 1861). Ref: P&BA-Len pg. 297-9.

ELDREDGE also see ELDRIDGE

ELDREDGE, DANIEL¹ was born 25 Feb. 1745, Mass., and he married _?_ (WARNER), daughter of Col. Seth. They supposedly settled in Conn. He had a known son, DANIEL² (following). Note: There was a Daniel "Elridge," with Mass. service, with wife, Phebe, Rev. Pension Appl. #W24116; no proof it is he.

ELDREDGE, DANIEL², son of DANIEL¹ (preceding), born 7 Feb. 1772, moved from Conn. to Vermont as a young man. He married at Sandgate, VT to MEHITABLE (BRISTOL). They moved that year to near Auburn, Cayuga Co., NY, and it may be he listed in the 1800 census index of Cayuga Co., NY as "Eldridge." He was a Capt. in the War of 1812. Known sons: Dr. H. D.; Col. NATHANIEL BUEL (following). Ref: P&BA-Len pg. 937-8.

ELDREDGE, NATHANIEL BUEL Col. & Dr., son of DANIEL² (preceding), was born 28 Mar. 1813, Auburn, NY. He studied medicine under his brother, Dr. H. D., and attended Medical School at Fairfield, NY. About 1837, he moved to Milford Twp., Oakland Co., Mich. where he had a practice until 1843. He married on 21 Apr. 1839 to JEANNETTE (PATTEN), daughter of George (also see). They moved in 1843 to Lapeer, Mich. where he had a practice with Dr. DeLaskie Miller. He served in the Civil War as a Major in the 7th Inf., and Lt. Col. in the 11th Inf. In 1865, they moved to Adrian,

Lenawee Co., Mich. There were 7 sons & 4 daughters (all names not stated). Those mentioned: 1. LANSINGH B. (Major in 4th Mich. Cav., Civil War); 2. LEWIS T.; 3. DAN B.; 4. GEORGE H.; 5. JOHN B.; 6. DAVID D.; 7. LOUISA A.; 8. ELLA (m. William P. Smith, Ionia Co., Mich.). Ref: P&BA-Len pg. 937-8.

ELDRIDGE also see ELDREDGE
ELDRIDGE, ALBERT born ca. 1835, NY, was listed in the 1850 census of Macon Twp., Lenawee Co., Mich. in household of Peter Vandeventer.
ELDRIDGE, CLARK was listed in the 1840 census index of Madison Twp., Lenawee Co., Mich.
ELDRIDGE, MARGARET (See Eliphalet Clark)
ELDRIDGE, SYLVESTER was listed in the 1840 census index of Madison Twp., Lenawee Co., Mich.

ELIGER, ELIZABETH (See Lazarus Griffith)

ELLIOTT, ADEN born ca. 1801, NY, and wife, PHEBE (GRIFFITH), probably daughter of Lazarus (also see), were reared and married in Chenango Co., NY. They moved to Fairfield Twp., Lenawee Co., Mich. ca. 1834; and moved to near Morenci, Seneca Twp. before 1850. He died 20 Mar. 1869, and she died 22 June 1867. Children's names not stated. All following were in the household in the 1850 census: 1. BURRITT, age 23, b. NY; 2. LAZARUS G. (following); 3. SPAULDING, age 13; 4. HANNAH, age 11; 5. MARIA, age 5; 6. JOHN, age 8/12, last 4 b. Mich. Ref: P&BA-Len pg. 888-9.
ELLIOTT, ALBERT born ca. 1813, and wife, POLLY, born ca. 1810, were listed in the 1850 census of Dover Twp., Lenawee Co., Mich. with NANCY W., age 18; HENRY M., age 16, both b. NY; and NELSON, age 12; ERASTUS, age 10; MARANDA, age 6; MARILLA, age 2, all b. Mich., in their household.
ELLIOTT, DANIEL born ca. 1818, and wife, CLARINDA, b. ca. 1824, both in NY, were listed in the 1850 census of Cambridge Twp., Lenawee Co., Mich. with SALLY RICE?, age 30, b. NY; and listed last ELIZABETH, age 1, b. Mich.
ELLIOTT, ELIZABETH (See John Ripley)
ELLIOTT, EMMA (See William Baker)
ELLIOTT, FRANCIS was listed in the 1840 census index of Dover Twp., Lenawee Co., Mich. Note SILAS, following.
ELLIOTT, GEORGE was listed in the 1840 census index of Clinton, Lenawee Co., Mich.
ELLIOTT, JANE (See Calvin Crane of Preston Co., W. Va.)
ELLIOTT, LAZARUS G., son of ADEN (preceding), was born 7 Oct. 1833 (on Lake Erie, Ohio, during family's trip from NY to Mich.). He was reared in Fairfield & Seneca Twps., Lenawee Co., Mich. He married ADARESTA (BURCH), daughter of Esben (also see). They settled in Madison Twp. Children: 1. ADELPHA (d. age 9 wks); 2. FREDERICK (d. age 7 wks); 3. ERNEST (m. Myra Fenton, Madison Twp.); 4. BURT; 5. ELFREY; 6. FORD; 7. FRANK; 8. GEORGE. Ref: P&BA-Len pg. 888-9.
ELLIOTT, SILAS, age 14; ADELINE, age 11; FIDELIA, age 7, were listed in the 1850 census of Dover Twp., Lenawee Co., Mich. in the household of James Martin (age 36, b. England) and wife, Mary, age 45, b. NY. These Elliott children may be step-children? Note FRANCIS, preceding.
ELLIOTT, SMITH born ca. 1795, and wife, PHILATTA, born ca. 1799, both in NY, were listed in the 1840 census index of Rome Twp., Lenawee Co., Mich.; and in the 1850 census with GEORGE, age 14, b. NY (note GEORGE, in household of WILLIAM J., following, possibly same person); and LANSING, age 11; JULIA, age 9, both b. Mich., in their household.
ELLIOTT, WILLIAM J. born 1826, NY, and wife, JULIA A., born ca. 1830, Mich., were listed in the 1850 census of Madison Twp., Lenawee Co., Mich. with GEORGE, age 14 (brother?), b. NY, all in the household of Hannah Edmund, age 63, b. NY.

ELLIS, ABNER W., son of CHARLES (following), was born 7 Nov. 1821, Benton Center, Yates Co., NY, and came to Tecumseh Twp., Lenawee Co., Mich. with his father. He married in Jan. 1844 to MARGARET (ATEN), daughter of Garret (also see); and they moved to Macon Twp. Children: 1. HULDAH (d. young); 2. CARRIE (d. young); 3. CLAYTON b. ca. 1846 (m. Elizabeth Lightfall, Pennington Corners, Mich.); 4. ALMEDA b. ca. 1849 (m. John Sones, Macon Twp.); 5. LIBBY (m. William Esterbrook, Franklin Twp.); 6. CHARLES (m. Mary Ebbitt); 7. GARRET D. (m. Elfa Thomas); 8. MARTHA (m. C. Hendershott, d. 1888, Clinton Twp.). Ref: P&BA-Len pg. 348-9.
ELLIS, ALEXANDER born ca. 1811, Scotland, and wife, JANE, born ca. 1815, NY, were listed in the 1850 census of Tecumseh Twp., Lenawee Co., Mich. with JANE, age 13; GEORGE, age 12; JOHN, age 9; MARY ANN, age 7; ALICE, age 3, all b. Mich., in their household.
ELLIS, ALICE J. (See Rancelier Mills)
ELLIS, AZARIAH born ca. 1815, and wife, PHEBE A., born ca. 1814, were listed in the 1850 census of Ridgeway Twp., Lenawee Co., Mich. with EZRA L., age 10; EMOTT, age 7, both b. NY; MONTGOMERY, age 4; SARAH M., age 9/12, both b. Mich., in their household.
ELLIS, BENJAMIN G. Dr. born ca. 1794, and wife, ABIGAIL, born ca. 1794, both in Conn., were listed in the 1850 census of Tecumseh Twp., Lenawee Co., Mich. with ABBY, age 24; CORNELIA, age 22; BENJAMIN, age 15, all b. NY; and also Fanny Wilson, age 28, b. NY, in the household may be another daughter.
ELLIS, CARLTON M., son of WILLIAM (son of ZIBA, following), was born 21 Dec. 1829, Potsdam, St. Lawrence Co., NY. He married on 22 Nov. 1865, Petersburg, Monroe Co., Mich., to MARY (BURNETT), daughter of Robert Sr. (also see). They resided in Blissfield Twp., Lenawee Co., Mich. Known child: CLARA L. b. 11 Dec. 1871. Ref: P&BA-Len pg. 590-1.
ELLIS, CHARLES, son of WILLIAM (following), born ca. 1791, Yates Co., NY, married CHARLOTTE (COLEBURN) born ca. 1786, NY. After the birth of 8 children (names not stated), they moved to Clinton Twp., Lenawee Co., Mich. She died in 1856, and he died in 1865, Macon Twp., where he was living with son, ABNER W. (preceding). They were listed in the 1850 census of Tecumseh Twp. with SYLVESTER, age 30; JEMIMA, age 25, both b. NY; and ISABELLA, age 11, b. Mich.; and Susannah Coleburn, age 88, born NY, probably mother of Charlotte, in their household. Ref: P&BA-Len pg. 348-9.

Pioneer Families of Southeastern Michigan

ELLIS, CHARLES K. born ca. 1822, and wife, SARAH, born ca. 1828, both in NY, were listed in the 1850 census of Tecumseh Twp., Lenawee Co., Mich.

ELLIS, FANNIE married first to ? Wilson; and married second to Leander Fisk (See Benjamin B. Fisk).

ELLIS, GEORGE B. born ca. 1815, and wife, LUCY, born ca. 1820, both in NY, were listed in the 1850 census of Tecumseh Twp., Lenawee Co., Mich. with CHARITY, age 16; LUCY, age 14; ROBERT, age 12, all b. NY, in their household.

ELLIS, HIRAM D., age 23, b. NY, was listed in the 1850 census of Madison Twp., Lenawee Co., Mich.

ELLIS, KATIE (See John W. Tolford)

ELLIS, LETITIA, born ca. 1775, NY, was listed in the 1850 census of Rollin Twp., Lenawee Co., Mich. in the household of Rufus & Abigail (b. ca. 1805, NY) Herman. She is probably mother of Abigail, as they named a daughter, Letitia.

ELLIS, LEWIS born ca. 1828, NY, and wife, ELIZABETH, born ca. 1827, Penn., were listed in the 1850 census of Madison Twp., Lenawee Co., Mich.

ELLIS, MATTHEW born ca. 1821?, and wife, MARY, born ca. 1822?, both in NY, were listed in the 1850 census of Macon Twp., Lenawee Co., Mich. with FRANCIS, age 9; PANAM-O? (female), age 7, both b. Mich., in their household.

ELLIS, MAY L. born 3 Oct. 1822, Potsdam, St. Lawrence Co., NY (m. David Carpenter, also see, Blissfield Twp., Lenawee Co., Mich.) Note resemblance to WILLIAM, son of ZIBA.

ELLIS, N. P. (See Joseph Baley)

ELLIS, NATHAN born ca. 1796, and wife, PHEBE, born ca. 1795, both in NY, were listed in the 1850 census of Ridgeway Twp., Lenawee Co., Mich. with CAROLINE, age 14, b. NY; and Ruliff Sebring (also see), age 74, b. NJ, in their household.

ELLIS, WILLIAM was born in Ireland, and came to America and settled in Benton Center, Yates Co., NY, where he died. He married JEMIMA (FENTON). Known son: CHARLES (preceding). Ref: P&BA-Len pg. 348-9.

ELLIS, WILLIAM, son of ZIBA (following), was born in Springfield, Mass., and moved with his parents to Vermont; and then at age 10 to St. Lawrence Co., NY. He married MARY A. (SHERMAN) who was born Hinesburg, VT. They settled first in Potsdam, NY; and then in 1854 moved to Blissfield, Lenawee Co., Mich. She died 18 July 1878, and he died 10 Jan. 1876. Known son: CARLTON M. (preceding). Ref: P&BA-Len pg. 590-1. Also see MAY L., preceding.

ELLIS, WILLIAM born ca. 1820, NY, was listed in the 1850 census of Tecumseh Twp., Lenawee Co., Mich. with MARTHA, age 60?, b. NY, in his household.

ELLIS, ZIBA was a seaman in New Bedford, Mass. at an early day. He moved first to Vermont, and then was a pioneer to St. Lawrence Co., NY, where he died. Known son: WILLIAM (preceding). Ref: P&BA-Len pg. 590-1.

ELLSWORTH, ALEXANDER, son of RICHARD (following), was born 6 Feb. 1811, Penn. He married LYDIA (HAND), daughter of Nehemiah (also see). In 1836, they moved to Woodstock Twp., Lenawee Co., Mich. where she died 16 July 1839. Known daughter, ELIZA A. b. 31 Dec. 1837 (lived with Nehemiah Hand in 1850 census; m. John J. Patterson, son of Joseph, also see). In the 1850 census, Alexander had wife, SARAH, age 24, b. NY, and in the household were CHARLES, age 6 (probably he who m. Mary L. Patterson, dau. of Joseph, also see); LYDIA, age 5; WARREN, age 2; ALBERT, age 1, all b. Mich. Ref: P&BA-Len pg. 715-6.

ELLSWORTH, CLARK born ca. 1821, NY, and wife, LYDIA, born ca. 1821, Canada, were listed in the 1850 census of Woodstock Twp., Lenawee Co., Mich. with THOMAS, age 4, b. Canada, and FRANCES, age 2, b. Mich., in their household.

ELLSWORTH, RICHARD & wife, MARGARET, came to Woodstock Twp., Lenawee Co., Mich. at an advanced age and died at the home of known son, ALEXANDER (preceding). Ref: P&BA-Len pg. 715-6.

ELLSWORTH, W. M. (See Charles Dunham)

ELSEY, WILLIAM b. England had known daughter, SARAH A. (See George Lane).

ELY, ABEL C. married Mrs. NANCY (BALLARD) DAY born ca. 1780s, widow of James (also see), in Lake Co., Ohio; and they afterwards moved to Morenci, Lenawee Co., Mich. Ref: P&BA-Len pg. 977-8.

ELY, SALLY (See Hiram Wilbur)

EMBURY, ELIZA (See Edward Jenkins)

EMERSON, JESSE married ELBRA (PATTEE) in western NY, and after Jesse's death, she married Earl Whitmore (also see).

EMERSON, JOHN born ca. 1794, and wife, BETSEY, born ca. 1793, both in VT, were listed in the 1850 census of Tecumseh Twp., Lenawee Co., Mich. with ELIZABETH, age 16, b. Canada, in their household.

EMERY, BENJAMIN P., son of JESHURUN (following), born 13 Aug. 1828, Cattarugus Co., NY, came with parents to Adrian Twp., Lenawee Co., Mich. He married in 1852 to CATHARINE (MILES), daughter of William (also see). She died 5 Feb. 1864. Children: 1. LYDIA b. 25 Feb. 1853 (to Jackson, Mich.); 2. WILLIAM J. b. 2 Feb. 1855 (to Ottawa Co., Mich.); 3. JERMAINE B. b. 4 Jan. 1857 (to Washtenaw Co., Mich.); 4. BERTHA E. b. 12 Oct. 1858 (m. C. D. Baker, Adrian); 5. IDA M. b. 18 Jan. 1862; 6. MILES (d. age 8 mos). Benjamin P. married again to EMILY M. (MILES), daughter of Ira L. (also see). Children: 7. BEAMEN b. 21 Jan. 1866; 8. BENJAMIN P. b. 29 Dec. 1867; 9. KITTIE M. b. 18 Sept. 1868; 10. ELEANOR A. b. 8 Feb. 1871; 11. GERTRUDE M. b. 27 Sept. 1873; 12. ALICE M. b. 1 Mar. 1875. Ref: P&BA-Len pg. 411-2.

EMERY, PHEBE, born ca. 1825, NY, was listed in the 1850 census of Madison Twp., Lenawee Co., Mich. in the household of Thomas & Martha Ramsdell.

EMERY, JESHURUN, son of EZEKIEL (a Revolutionary soldier who died in Maine), was born 2 Jan. 1788, Kennebec, Maine. He moved about 1818 to Ontario Co., NY and married there in 1822 to ELIZABETH (PIERSON), daughter of Henry (also see). About 1822, they moved to Cattarugus Co., NY; and in 1830 to Adrian Twp., Lenawee Co., Mich. In 1834, they moved to what is now Rome Twp., but returned to Adrian Twp. in 1836. He died 6 May 1848; and she died 14 June 1873. Seven children (names not stated). In the 1850 census, Elizabeth, age 56, b. NJ?, was living in the household of known son, BENJAMIN P. (preceding); and with her was WILLIAM, age 16, b. Mich. Note PHEBE, preceding, possibly related.

EMONS see EMMONS

EMMONS, FRED B. (See Isaac C. Gunn)

EMMONS, JACOB was born ca. 1800 in Farmersville, Seneca Co., NY (census said b. Penn.); and he married REBECCA (COVERT) born ca. 1803, NJ, probably in Seneca Co., NY. They moved about 1835 to Macon Twp., Lenawee Co., Mich. He died 20 Dec. 1867; and she died in 1868. Six children (names not stated; those following were in the 1850 census of Macon Twp.): 1. RUTH, age 18, b. NY; and 2. CATHARINE, age 15; 3. LOUISA, age 13; 4. SUSAN, age 11, all b. Mich.; 5. WILLIAM P. b. 12 Mar. 1845, Macon Twp. (census said age 7?; m. in 1879 Sophie Smith, daughter of James, also see). Ref: P&BA-Len pg. 430-1. JOHN, age 20, b. NY, listed in the 1850 census of Raisin Twp., is possibly the other child.

EnEARL, JAMES L. born ca. 1824, and wife, ALMOT J. (COMSTOCK), born ca. 1825, married in Franklin Twp., Lenawee Co., Mich., but moved to Raisin Twp. by the 1850 census. She died there in 1853. Known daughter, KATE E. b. 9 June 1850, Raisin Twp. (m. C. W. Luce, also see). James L. married twice more (names not stated). Ref: P&BA-Len pg. 246-7.

EnEARL, WILLIAM born ca. 1831, NY, was listed in the 1850 census of Raisin Twp., Lenawee Co., Mich.

ENGELL, JACOB born in Germany, came to Lenawee Co., Mich. where daughter, JOHANNA, married in Adrian Twp. in 1844 to Samuel Tingley (also see).

ENGLEHART, DOROTHEA (See George Miller)

ENGLISH, CLARA (See Rancelier Mills)

ENGLISH, CYNTHIA J., age 13; FRANCIS, age 11; ELIZA, age 9; MERCY, age 6, all b. Mich., were listed in the 1850 census of Madison Twp., Lenawee Co., Mich. in a George Torban household.

ENGLISH, ELLEN, age 9, b. Mich., was listed in the 1850 census of Dover Twp., Lenawee Co., Mich. in a Graham household.

ENGLISH, JOHN was listed in the 1840 census index of Adrian Twp., Lenawee Co., Mich., and it may be he age 45, with no family in the 1850 census. (He was the only one of this surname in Lenawee Co. in 1840 census index.)

ENGLISH, MARY born Mass. (See James Archer).

ENGLISH, RICHARD born ca. 1813, NY, and wife, CATHARINE, born ca. 1824, Ireland, were listed in the 1850 census of Madison Twp., Lenawee Co., Mich. with ANN, age 5; ELIZA W., age 3 (m. Charles C. Bradish, also see); MARY, age 2/12, all b. Mich., and ELIZA, age 68, born Ireland (mother?).

ENSIGN, DANIEL born ca. 1787, Conn., was listed in the 1850 census of Tecumseh Twp., Lenawee Co., Mich. in the household of James and Huldah Page (also see).

ERKSKINE, FRANCIS (See William Whelan)

ESKEL, ANNA MARIE (See John Ungemach)

ESTELINE, ALZINA (See James E. Rounds)
ESTELINE, SEYMOUR (See James E. Rounds)

ESTERBROOK, JOSEPH (See James B. Wells)
ESTERBROOK, WILLIAM (See A. W. Ellis)

ESTES, BENJAMIN and wife, SARAH (KIRBY), were Quakers from Mass. who moved to Kennebec, Maine; and then to Wheatland, Monroe Co., Mich. Known daughter, DEBORAH b. ca. 1803, Maine (m. Libni Kelley, also see). Ref: P&BA-Len pg. 1216-7.

ESTES, ELIJAH born ca. 1800, and wife, JERUSHA, born ca. 1807, both in Mass., were listed in the 1840 census index of Raisin Twp., Lenawee Co., Mich.; and in the 1850 census with CHARLES H., age 13, b. Mass.; JAMES E., age 10; CAROLINE E., age 8; WILLIAM W., age 6; EVERETT, age 4, all b. Mich., in their household. Probably son, ELIJAH H. born ca. 1833, Mass., was listed in the 1850 census of Raisin Twp., Lenawee Co., Mich. in a Hayward household.

ESTES, PHILIP was listed in the 1840 census index of Madison Twp., Lenawee Co., Mich.

ESTES, ROBERT (See William Ladd)

ESTES, RUFUS born ca. 1805, Mass., was listed in the 1850 census of Cambridge Twp., Lenawee Co., Mich., with MYRON, age 1, b. Mich. in the household.

ESTES, SYLVANUS and wife, RUTH (RAMSDELL), were natives of Mass., and pioneer settlers of Lenawee and Hillsdale Cos., Mich. In the 1840 census index, he was listed in Pittsford, Hillsdale Co. Known daughter, LUCY B., b. Mass. (m. Enos Canniff, also see, on 15 May 1842.)

EURITT, ANNA married on 14 June 1849 to Butler Treat (also see), however, in the 1850 census his wife's name was shown as LUCINA??

EVANS, ADELIA, age 7, b. Mich., was listed in the 1850 census of Rome Twp., Lenawee Co., Mich. in the household of Daniel R. & Hannah Griffin.

EVANS, GEORGE W. born ca. 1821, Mass., and wife, MARY A., born ca. 1823, NY, were listed in the 1850 census of Rollin Twp., Lenawee Co., Mich. with HENRY, age 13, b. Mass. (brother?), in their household.

EVANS, JAMES K., age 5, b. Mich., was listed in the 1850 census of Rome Twp., Lenawee Co., Mich. in the household of Nial & Mary Southard.

EVANS, JOHN born ca. 1819, Mass., and wife, CORNELIA, born ca. 1818, NY, were listed in the 1850 census of Hudson Twp., Lenawee Co., Mich. with EUNICE A., age 2; SYLVESTER B., age 1, both b. Mich., in their household.

EVANS, JOHN born ca. 1813, NY, and wife, CHLOE, born ca. 1820, Penn., were listed in the 1850 census of Hudson Twp., Lenawee Co., Mich. with SARAH E., age 9; LUCY J., age 5, both b. NY, and JAMES B., age 1/12, b. Mich., in their household.

EVANS, JEREMIAH born ca. 1821, Ohio, and wife, ELLEN, born ca. 1821, Penn., were listed in the 1850 census of

Pioneer Families of Southeastern Michigan

Madison Twp., Lenawee Co.. Mich. with EVAN, age 7; GEORGE, age 6; ABSALOM, age 3, all b. Ohio, in their household.

EVANS, LESTER born ca. 1794, Conn., and wife, ABIGAIL, born ca. 1800, Canada, were listed in the 1840 census index of Rome Twp., Lenawee Co., Mich.; and in the 1850 census with ELIZABETH, age 22; ALVAN, age 20; LOVISA A., age 15, all b. NY; and JANE, age 11; WESLEY, age 7, both b. Mich., in their household.

EVANS, LUTHER was listed in the 1840 census index of Rollin Twp., Lenawee Co., Mich. See GEORGE W., preceding.

EVANS, MUSGROVE was a mail carrier between Tecumseh, Lenawee Co. and Ypsilanti, Washtenaw Co., Mich. in 1830.

EVANS, TAMAR ELIZABETH (See Daniel Mickley)

EVERETT, AMEY (See Alvin D. Rice)

EVERETT, AUGUSTUS Dr. born ca. 1813, NY, and wife, PERMILLA, born ca. 1815, Penn., were listed in the 1850 census of Tecumseh Twp., Lenawee Co., Mich. with ROBERT, age 10; AMELIA, age 1, both b. NY, in their household.

EVERETT, JAMES born ca. 1815, and wife, POLLY, born ca. 1817, both in NY, were listed in the 1850 census of Ogden Twp., Lenawee Co., Mich. with MARY A., age 8; MYRON D., age 5; JULIA A., age 2; ELLEN A., age 1/12, all b. Mich., in their household.

Note: There was a JAMES in Ypsilanti, Washtenaw Co., Mich. in 1840 census index.

EVERITT, MARY (See Peter Quick)

EVERY also see AVERY

EVERY - In the History of Jackson Co., Mich., pg. 780, it states that JOHN, REUBEN; GEORGE; & URIAH settled in the southern part of Columbia Twp., Jackson Co., Mich. in 1835. In the 1840 census index of Jackson Co., listed were CORRENTUA; GEORGE; JOHN; JOSEPH; REUBEN; & URIAH, Columbia Twp.; and LORICA in Springport. In the 1800 census index of Delaware Co., NY were ISAAC; JOHN; JOSEPH (following); & URIAH.

EVERY, CARRINGTON (written Avery) born ca. 1823, and wife, MARY, born ca. 1823, both in NY, were listed in the 1850 census of Woodstock Twp., Lenawee Co., Mich. with ALSON? (male), age 5; RINALDO?, age 3, both b. Mich., in their household.

EVERY, JACOB was listed in the 1840 census index of Woodstock Twp., Lenawee Co., Mich. (See Garrett F. Harris).

EVERY, JOSEPH and wife, MARGARET (ACKER), lived in Delaware Co., NY in 1800, and moved to Jackson Co., Mich. in 1835; and Woodstock Twp., Lenawee Co. in 1837, where they both died at advanced ages. (Joseph was said to have brought his mother to Woodstock Twp., where she died at age 99; your compiler was unable to located them in the 1850 census of Woodstock Twp.; and it may be he listed in the 1840 census index of Columbia Twp., Jackson Co. adjacent to CORRENTUA; GEORGE; JOHN; REUBEN; & URIAH; also there was LORICA in Springport, Jackson Co.) Note CARRINGTON, preceding; and JOSEPH, following.

EVERY, JOSEPH born ca. 1826, NY, and wife, ELIZABETH, born ca. 1829, Penn., were listed in the 1850 census of Woodstock Twp., Lenawee Co., Mich. with S--MUS? (female), age 5; REBECCA, agd 2, both b. Mich., in their household.

EVERY, MIRAN (MYRON? See David Smith, Jr.)

EVERY, POLLY born ca. 1808, Putnam Co., NY (m. Harvey Dean, also see). Ref: P&BA-Len pg. 1175-6.

EVITS, SUBMIT (See Abraham Bartlett)

EXELBY, GEORGE was born ca. 1805 in England, and came to Ridgeway Twp., Lenawee Co., Mich. in 1831. He married MARY (THACKRAY) who was born ca. 1808, Yorkshire, England. He died 18 Apr. 1861, result of a wagon accident; and she died in 1880, at home of son, George. Ten children (names not stated) but in their household in the 1850 census of Ridgeway Twp. were: 1. HANNAH, age 17; 2. JOSEPH P. E. (following); 3. GEORGE (following); 4. JANE A., age 13; 5. JOHN (following); 6. SARAH b. 4 Jan. 1844 (m. Edgar R. Wells, also see); 7. JESSE, age 3; 8. ELIZABETH, age 6/12.

EXELBY, GEORGE, son of GEORGE (preceding), was born 8 Mar. 1836, Ridgeway Twp., Lenawee Co., Mich., and married in the Fall of 1862 to ANN (PALMER), daughter of Fenner (also see). They remained in Ridgeway Twp. until 1887, then moved into Britton, Mich. Children: 1. WALTER M. (m. Jane Gibson, had son, Allen); 2. EDGAR (m. Sophrina "Phrenie" Underwood, dau. of William, also see); 3. ELLA. Ref: P&BA-Len pg. 330-1.

EXELBY, JOHN, son of GEORGE (preceding), was born 9 Mar. 1840, Ridgeway Twp., Lenawee Co., Mich., and married 21 Nov. 1860 to MARY (McCAM) born 4 June 1843, Ontario, Canada (whose parents, names not stated, had come from Ireland to Canada). He served in the Civil War. In 1866, they moved from Ridgeway to Clinton Twp., but later returned to Ridgeway. About 1872, they moved to Juniata, Adams Co., Nebr. They returned to Mich. in 1879, and he operated a hotel at Britton; and they moved to Detroit in 1888. Children: ALPHORIA; HENRY L.; & CARRIE (all died young); and surviving were FREDERICK; SULLIVAN; & ANNA M. Ref: P&BA-Len pg. 477-8.

EXELBY, JOSEPH E. born 14 Oct. 1834, married on 18 Nov. 1854 in Ridgeway Twp., Lenawee Co., Mich. to LETITIA (LINN), daughter of Samuel (also see). They remained there until 1883, when they moved into Britton, Lenawee Co., Mich. Children: 1. EDWARD (d. age 2); 2. EVA (d. age 3); 3. CORNELIUS (m. Dora Bemish who d. 1885, dau., Dora); 4. WESLEY (m. Ida Wiggins, probably dau. of Daniel, also see); 5. CLARENCE; 6. EVERETT; 7. LEONARD. Ref: P&BA-Len pg. 461-2.

- F -

FABER, WILLIAM (See Franz Joseph Mitchell)

FABRIQUE, ANDREW born ca. 1811, and wife, BETSEY (DECK), moved from Herkimer Co., NY to Edinboro, Erie Co., Penn., where she died in 1839, leaving known daughter, MARY C. b. 13 Sept. 1836, Herkimer Co., NY (m. Chancey R. Fuller, also see). Andrew married again (name not stated); and they moved to Clinton, Lenawee Co., Mich. where he was living in 1888, age 77. Ref: P&BA-Len pg. 343. Note: In the 1800 census index, there was a LEWIS in Herkimer Co., NY.

FABRIQUE, JOHN was listed in the 1840 census index of Albion, Calhoun Co., Mich.

FAELBANK, PHILIP born 11 Nov. 1813, and wife, MARGARET (NEINBORN) born 24 Jan. 1825, were natives of Germany, who came to the US in 1850, and settled first in Sandusky, Ohio. They afterwards moved to Black Swamp, Ohio, where they resided in 1888. Children: 1. CAROLINE; 2. MARGARET b. 16 Nov. 1847 (m. Christ Walter, also see); 3. CHRISTIAN; 4. HENRY; 5. ANDREAS; 6. CATHERINE; 7. EMMA; 8. CHARLES; 9. PHILIP. Ref: P&BA-Len pg. 626-7.

FAIRBANKS, ABIGAIL (See Charles Crosby)

FAIRBANKS, JEWELL? born ca. 1812, Mass., and wife, ACHSAH P., born ca. 1816, NH, were listed in the 1850 census of Palmyra Twp., Lenawee Co., Mich. with CHARLES D., age 11; ELIZABETH P., age 8, both b. Ill., and MARY E., age 3, b. Ohio, in their household.

FANCHER, ELIZABETH was the daughter of S. (note SYLVANUS, following) and was born in Warwick, Orange Co., NY. She married David S. Mather (also see). Note: BETSEY is the nickname for Elizabeth.

FANCHER, SYLVANUS of Warwick, Orange Co., NY had a will dated 2 Mar. 1826, and probated 23 Oct. 1828, Liber H, pg. 467. Mentioned was wife, SARAH; Sons: HENRY; DAVID; WILLIAM SMITH; JAMES; and daughters: SALLY; REBECKAH; DEBORAH; BETSEY (note preceding); HANNAH (deceased). Granddaughters (daughters of Hannah), Sarah & Eleanor. Exec were Wife, Sarah, John Pelton, & David Fancher. Witnesses: Sally Christie, Jane Wood, & John I. Christie.

FANNING, THOMAS (See Thomas S. Weter)

FARLING, JOHN born ca. 1784, and wife, MARY, born ca. 1780, both in Rhode Island, were listed in the 1850 census of Raisin Twp., Lenawee Co., Mich. (written "Farlin"), next door to Briggs West who married POLLY (FARLING), born ca. 1817, NY, possibly daughter of John.

FARNSWORTH, CHARLES Dr. born 18 Feb. 1802, Hawley, Franklin Co., Mass., married ANNA (BUSH) on 14 Sept. 1828. They removed to New York, and then to Ohio. In 1837, they settled in Somerset Twp., Hillsdale Co., Mich., where they remained. Nine children (names not stated), except FRANCES b. 13 Aug. 1838, Somerset, Mich. (m. John C. Rogers, also see). Ref: P&BA-Len pg. 647-8.

FARNSWORTH, CHARLES G. born ca. 1810, Mass., and wife ELIZABETH B. (STANLEY), daughter of Benjamin (also see) probably married in New Hampshire. In 1839, they settled in Medina Twp., Lenawee Co., Mich., and he died there in 1866. Children: 1. ELIZABETH F. b. ca. 1834, NH (m. L. P. Wilkins; she d. 1860, Medina Twp.); 2. EDMUND G. b. ca, 1836, NH (m. Mary J. Roosa, probably dau. of Simon, also see, Medina Twp.).

Elizabeth B. married second to Charles Brown, also see, son of Solomon. Ref: P&BA-Len pg. 780-1.

FARR, ELIZA (See Jacob McConnell)

FARR, SYLVESTER and wife, JULIA, natives of New York, were parents of ELEANOR E. b. 16 May 1855 (m. Frederick Bay, also see, of Ogden Twp., Lenawee Co., Mich.)

FARR, TRUMAN born ca. 1806, and wife, MARGARET, born ca. 1810, NY, were listed in the 1850 census of Tecumseh Twp., Lenawee Co., Mich. with MARY, age 18; HORACE, age 16, both b. NY; and EDWARD, age 13; DE--AS(male), age 10, both b. Mich., in their household.

FARRAH, THOMAS born ca. 1783, and wife, MARY (TEMPLE), born ca. 1798, both born England, settled first in NY, and then in Raisin Twp., Lenawee Co., Mich. in 1838. He died there 20 Jan. 1852, and she died 1 Oct. 1872. Six children (names not given), except eldest, JANE b. England (m. 10 Jan. 1844 to John Patterson, also see). In the 1850 census of Raisin Twp., in Thomas' household were: JOHN, age 28; HANNAH, age 23, both b. England; and THOMAS, age 14, b. NY. Ref: P&BA-Len pg. 388-9. Note Nicholas Temple.

FARRAR, ALLEN, son of SAMUEL (following), born ca. 1826, Ohio, and wife, ALMIRA, born ca. 1821, NY, were listed in the 1850 census of Rollin Twp., Lenawee Co., Mich. with MARY, age 7, b. Mich., in the household.

FARRAR, DANIEL born Nov. 1783, New Hampshire, married in Fitzwilliam, NH to SENA (MELLEN), daughter of Daniel (also see); and moved to Troy, NH, where they remained. Three sons & 4 daughters, names not stated, of whom 6 lived to maturity. Known son, #6. JAMES (following). Ref: P&BA-Len pg. 259-60.

FARRAR, JAMES, son of DANIEL (preceding), was born 29 June 1820, Troy, Cheshire Co., NH; and married CLARA (BROWN), daughter of Russell (also see). They moved to Adrian, Lenawee Co., Mich. in 1853, and had a store with Damon. Children: (2 died young, names not stated); & IDA R. (m. T. M. McFarland, Cambridge, Ohio). Ref: P&BA-Len pg. 259-60.

FARRAR, SAMUEL born ca. 1798, New Jersey, and wife, MARY, born ca. 1802, Scotland, were listed in the 1850 census of Rollin Twp., Lenawee Co., Mich. adjacent to sons: WILLIAM b. ca. 1822, Ohio (m. Almira, b. ca. 1833, NY); JOHN b. ca. 1824, Ohio (m. Rusha, b. ca. 1827, NY); ALLEN (preceding); ANDREW J. b. ca. ?, Ohio (m. Susannah, b. ca. 1833, Mich.). In Samuel's household in 1850 were NANCY, age 16; RICHARD, age 13; ELIZA J., age 7, all born Ohio.

FARST, AARON, son of ISAAC (following), born 31 July 1837, Seneca Co., NY, moved with his parents to Medina Twp., Lenawee Co., Mich. He married first to SARAH (BUMP); and married second to MARY (MOORE). Children (not stated which wife was mother): 1. JOHN R.; 2. FRANK W.; 3. ROYAL E. Ref: P&BA-Len pg. 997-8.

FARST, GEORGE and wife, CATHARINE (PONTIUS), were natives of Northumberland Co., Penn., and they moved after their marriage to near Fayette, Seneca Co., NY. There were 4 sons & 5 daughters (names not stated). About 1851, they moved with known son, ISAAC

Pioneer Families of Southeastern Michigan

(following) to Medina Twp., Lenawee Co., Mich. Ref: P&BA-Len pg. 997-8.

FARST, GEORGE W., son of ISAAC (following), born 1 Oct. 1846, Seneca Co., NY, moved with parents to Medina Twp., Lenawee Co., Mich. He married MARTHA (COX). Children: 1. ISAAC; 2. HATTIE; 3. ROSS EARL. Ref: P&BA-Len pg. 997-8.

FARST, ISAAC, son of GEORGE (preceding), born 21 July 1813, Seneca Co., NY, married on 2 Dec. 1834 to SARAH (KEEFER), daughter of Frederick (also see). After the birth of all but their youngest child, they moved in 1851 to Medina Twp., Lenawee Co., Mich. Children: 1. CHARLES b. 29 Mar. 1836 (d. 30 July 1840); 2. AARON (preceding); 3. HANNAH B. b. 25 Feb. 1839 (d. 23 Apr. 1840); 4. ADELINE b. 9 Apr. 1834 (m. Edwin Ash, also see); 5. CLARA b. 1 Oct. 1844 (m/1 Reuben George; m/2 Wm. Connery, see both); 6. GEORGE W. (preceding); 7. OLIVE b. 12 Oct. 1851 (m. Delilah Stiles, Seneca Twp.); 8. JOHN G. b. 1 May 1856 (m. Hattie Layman, Medina Twp.). Ref: P&BA-Len pg. 997-8.

FARWELL, HIRAM was born in Wheatland Twp., Monroe Co., NY.
He married there to MARGARET (SKINNER) who was born in Canada on her "Grandfather's (Ebenezer's) farm." They moved after 10 years to Gorham Twp., Fulton Co., Ohio. Children: 1. PHILA (m. Charles Perry, also see, in 1844, Ohio; resided Medina Twp., Lenawee Co.); 2. EDWIN; 3. DOLLY A.; 4. ELIZABETH; 5. DAVID; 6. JANE; 7. AMANDA (had a twin, unnamed, d. infancy); 8. ELLEN; 9. SCOTT (a twin brother, d. infancy). Ref: P&BA-Len pg. 652-3.

FEATHERLY, ISAAC settled in Nankin, Wayne Co., Mich. before 1840.

FEATHERLY, JOHN was a pioneer settler of Canton Twp., Wayne Co., Mich. with brother-in-law, Nicholas Stansell. John had a known son, FREDERICK (who had a known daughter, JULIA A., who m. William H. H. Van Akin, also see). Ref: P&BA-Len pg. 607-8.

FEDERMAN, WILLIAM (See Lysander Ormsby)

FEE, J. H. Capt. (See Anson Backus)

FELLOWS, HIRAM N., son of JUDSON (following), was born 7 Sept. 1818, Brutus, Cayuga Co., NY; and at age 17, moved to Medina Twp., Lenawee Co., Mich. (Note: There was a man by this name in the 1840 census index of Troy, Oakland Co., Mich.) He married in 1841 to (SARAH) MARIE (PERRY), daughter of Abel (also see) of Medina Twp. They settled in Medina Twp., and then moved about 1851 to Rome Twp., and later to Hudson Twp. He died 17 Aug. 1876. Nine children (names not stated) of whom only Abel P. & Grant were surviving in 1888. First 3 listed were in the household in the 1850 census: 1. ABEL P. b. 11 Dec. 1843; 2. ERVIN K. b. ca. 1847; 3. HENRY G. b. ca. 1849; 4. GRANT b. 13 Apr. 1865, Hudson Twp.

FELLOWS, JAMES B. born ca. 1815, Mass., and wife, HARRIET, born ca. 1826, Penn., were listed in the 1850 census of Rollin Twp., Lenawee Co., Mich. with JOSEPHINE M., age 1; ADONIS, age 1/12, both b. Mich., in the household.

FELLOWS, JUDSON and wife, HANNAH (ANDREWS), lived in Ira, Cayuga Co., NY in 1818. There were 6 children (names not stated). Known son, HIRAM N. (preceding). Ref: P&BA-Len pg. 926-7. Note: There was a JOSEPH listed in the 1800 census index of Tioga Co., NY.

FELTON, BENJAMIN K. lived in Tecumseh Twp., Lenawee Co., Mich. before 1840.

FELTON, MARY may be FULTON? (See Russell Skeels).

FELTON, MARY C. born 2 Jan. 1830, Clarence Hollow, Erie Co., NY, married first to ? Vaughn (also see), and married second to Welcome V. Fisk (also see).

FELTON, WILLIAM born ca. 1776, Mass., and wife, MEHITABLE, born ca. 1777, Conn., were listed in the 1850 census of Rome Twp., Lenawee Co., Mich. in the household of Roswell Hale.

FENSEM, JANE (See James East)

FENTON, AMBROSE and wife, BETSEY (NICHOLS), of Morgan Twp., Ashtabula Co., Ohio had known daughter, AURELIA W., b. Ashtabula Co. (m. Elijah B. Bailey, also see). Ref: P&BA-Len pg. 711-2.

FENTON, BIGELOW C. (See SETH^2, & HORACE^3, following).

FENTON, GEORGE born ca. 1819, and wife, ELIZA ANN, born ca. 1829, both in NY, were listed in the 1850 census of Tecumseh Twp., Lenawee Co., Mich. with FRANCIS, age 2; GEORGE, age 6/12, both b. Mich., in their household.

FENTON, GEORGE W.^{4}, son of HORACE^3, born 6 Apr. 1845, Pittsford Twp., Hillsdale Co., Mich. came to Hudson Twp. with his parents. He married FLORENCE A. (BAILEY), daughter of Elijah B. (also see). They resided in Hudson Village, Lenawee Co. Children: 1. HORACE S. b. 2 July 1876; 2. CHARLES A. b. 22 July 1878. Ref: P&BA-Len pg. 711-2. Note AMBROSE, preceding.

FENTON, HORACE^3, son of SETH^2 (following), was born 6 Oct. 1804 near Rutland, Vermont. He went first to Buffalo and Batavia, NY, but returned to VT. He married there on 4 Feb. 1827 to RHEUEMMA L. (ABBOTT) born Thetford, VT. About 1837, they removed to Pittsford Twp., Hillsdale Co., Mich., and then on 25 Oct. 1847 to Hudson Village, Lenawee Co. He died 9 Apr. 1876. Known children (all but Mary listed in household in 1850 census): 1. HORACE S. b. ca. 1830; 2. FLORA b. ca. 1833; 3. JOHN b. ca. 1837, all b. VT; 4. GEORGE W. (preceding); 5. MARY A. (m. Lyon). Ref: P&BA-Len pg. 711-2. Note: Rheuemma married second to BIGELOW C. FENTON, and died 14 Jan. 1887, Granville, Bradford Co., Penn.

FENTON, JEMIMA (See William Ellis)

FENTON, MYRA (See Lazarus G. Elliott)

FENTON, SETH^2, son of JOHN^1 (who came from England to New England in Colonial times), was Captain of a company of Vermont Dragoons; and married on 1 Dec. 1803 to JANE (KEELER). About 1839, they moved from VT to Granville, Bradford Co., Penn. She died there 2 June 1855; and he died 20 Dec. 1858. Eleven children (names not given). Known sons: HORACE (preceding); SETH W. (following). Ref: P&BA-Len pg. 711-2. Note BIGELOW C., preceding.

FENTON, SETH W.[3], son of SETH[2] (preceding), born ca. 1805, VT, and wife, NANCY, born ca. 1806, NY, were listed in the 1850 census of Madison Twp., Lenawee Co., Mich. with FRANCIS, age 21, b. VT; FLORA I., age 19, b. NY; HELEN, age 10; SARAH, age 9, last 2 born Mich., in their household.

FERGUSON a number were spelled FURGUSON.

FERGUSON, ABRAHAM (spelled "Furguson") born ca. 1797, and wife, SARAH, born ca. 1799, both in NY, were listed in the 1850 census of Rome Twp., Lenawee Co., Mich., with STEPHEN, age 21, JAMES H., age 17, both b. NY; LUCY A., age 13, born Mich., in their household. Note JEREMIAH, following.

FERGUSON, AGNES N. (See James Blair)

FERGUSON, CALEB born ca. 1830, NY was listed in the 1850 census of Medina Twp., Lenawee Co., Mich. in the household of William & Hannah Reynolds, with ALICE, age 15, also b. NY, possibly sister of Caleb.

FERGUSON, CASE born ca. 1804, and wife, MELINDA, born ca. 1804, both in NY, were listed in the 1850 census of Hudson Twp., Lenawee Co., Mich. with RICHARD G., age 20; MARY E., age 19; ESTES, age 17; ADELINE, age 15; PERRY, age 13; CHARLES, age 8, all b. NY; and JAMES, age 1, b. Mich., in their household.

FERGUSON, GEORGE, son of JOHN (following), was born 16 Sept. 1786, Perthshire, Scotland, and came to America in 1788 with his father. He was reared in Jackson, Washington Co., NY. He married ELEANOR (GILLESPIE), daughter of Cornelius (also see). In 1833, after the birth of 7 children (names not stated), they moved to Blissfield, Lenawee Co., Mich., and afterwards to Deerfield Twp. She died there 16 Mar. 1842, age about 60; and he died 4 Jan. 1867. Known children (in household in 1850 census of Blissfield Twp.): GEORGE (following); ALEXANDER, age 34; JAMES, age 26; JANE, age 23; & NANCY, age 22, all b. NY. Ref: P&BA-Len pg. 635-6.

FERGUSON, GEORGE, probably son of GEORGE (preceding), born ca. 1814, NY, and wife, JANE, born ca. 1828, both in NY, were listed in the 1850 census of Blissfield Twp., Lenawee Co., Mich. next door to GEORGE (preceding), with ANGUS, age 3; DELILA, age 1, both b. Mich., in their household.

FERGUSON, GEORGE born ca. 1822, NY, was listed in the 1850 census of Blissfield Twp., Lenawee Co., Mich.

FERGUSON, GEORGE, age 12, b. Mich., was listed in the 1850 census of Fairfield Twp., Lenawee Co., Mich. in the household of Solomon Force (also see). Children "dittoed" after George were Harriet, age 9; Catharine, age 6, possibly Force children? Note family of HENRY of Fairfield Twp., following.

FERGUSON, HELEN, age 9, and AMY, age 7, both born Mich., were listed in the 1850 census of Adrian Twp., Lenawee Co., Mich. in the household of Samuel and Ellen Nichols.

FERGUSON, HENRY, son of JOHN (nothing more stated), was the father of SARAH born 1776 (m. Nathaniel Moore[4], also see, 14 Mar. 1800, Peterboro, NH). Ref: P&BA-Len pg. 1000-2.

FERGUSON, HENRY (spelled Furguson) born ca. 1787, and wife, SARAH, born ca. 1788, both b. NY, were listed in the 1850 census of Fairfield Twp., Lenawee Co., Mich. In their household was Thomas H. Laverty, age 28, and wife, Janet, age 21, both b. NY. Probably children of Henry were: ORRY; HIRAM; HENRY JR., JAMES H.; JOSEPH, all following.

FERGUSON, HENRY JR., probably son of HENRY (of Fairfield Twp. preceding) born ca. 1824, and wife, LYDIA, born ca. 1828, both in NY, were listed in the 1850 census of Fairfield Twp., Lenawee Co., Mich. with MARTHA J., age 1, b. Mich., in the household.

FERGUSON, HENRY H. (See Cornelius Knapp)

FERGUSON, HIRAM, probably son of HENRY (of Fairfield Twp., preceding), born ca. 1814, and wife, MARIA, born ca. 1822, both in NY, were listed in the 1850 census of Fairfield Twp., Lenawee Co., Mich. with MARY A., age 12; EMELINE, age 10; WILLIAM, age 8; MATILDA, age 2; ARLENA, age 9/12, all b. Mich., in their household (adjacent to JOSEPH & HENRY, Jr.).

FERGUSON, JAMES H., born ca. 1828, NY, was listed in the 1850 census of Fairfield Twp., Lenawee Co., Mich. in an Aldrich household.

FERGUSON, JEREMIAH born ca. 1814, and wife, MATILDA, born ca. 1816, both in NY, were listed in the 1850 census of Rome Twp., Lenawee Co., Mich. with Betsey A. Hopkins, age 11; and Howard Hopkins, age 8, both b. NY, (stepchildren??), in their household.

FERGUSON, JOHN was born Scotland, and came to America in 1788, and was a pioneer settler near Jackson, Washington Co., NY. Known son, GEORGE of Blissfield Twp. (preceding). Ref: P&BA-Len pg. 635-6.

FERGUSON, JOHN was born in Aberdeen, Scotland, and married CAROLINE (SHUFFLEBOTHAM), daughter of George (also see) born Manchester, England. John died in Manchester on 31 Apr. 1848, at age 30. Caroline came to Tecumseh, Lenawee Co., Mich. in 1850 with her children. 1. EMMA; 2. MARIA b. 6 Apr. 1842, Manchester, England (m. Granville Mills, also see); 3. FREDERICK A. Caroline married again to David Hatch of Macon Twp., where they both died. Ref: P&BA-Len pg. 473-4.

FERGUSON, JOHN (spelled Furguson) born ca. 1815, and wife, HARRIET, born ca. 1831, both in NY, were listed in the 1850 census of Adrian Twp., Lenawee Co., Mich. with ALLEN, age 3, JANE, age 3/12, both b. Mich., in their household.

FERGUSON, ORRY born ca. 1808, and wife, CYNTHA M., born ca. 1808, both in NY, were listed in the 1850 census of Fairfield Twp., Lenawee Co., Mich. with HENRY E., age 18; and LUCY J., age 13, both b. Mich., in the household.

FERGUSON, PHEBE born ca. 1832, NY, was listed in the 1850 census of Madison Twp., Lenawee Co., Mich. in the household of Abram Brown.

FERGUSON, WILLARD born ca. 1804, Mass., and wife, LYDIA, born ca. 1814, VT, were listed in the 1840 census index of Cambridge Twp., Lenawee Co., Mich. (as "Furgison"); and in the 1850 census with JAMES, age 14, b. NY; and WILLARD, age 12; ERASTUS, age 10; WALTER, age 8; WALLACE, age 6; LYDIA, age 4; MARY, age 2; ANDREW, age 5/12, all b. Mich., in their household. Note: There was a WALLACE "FURGASEN" listed in the 1840 census index of Washtenaw Co., Mich.

FERRIS, GEORGE (See James E. Rounds)

Pioneer Families of Southeastern Michigan

FESSENDEN, CLARA M. of Shelby, NY married Peter W. Adams on 23 Oct. 1855, Tecumseh, Lenawee Co., Mich. (See Peter Adams).

FESSENDEN, ELIAS born ca. 1832, NY, was listed in the 1850 census of Raisin Twp., Lenawee Co., Mich.

FESSENDEN, KITTIE E. (See William R. Wilson)

FETTON, WILLIAM born ca. 1776, Mass., and wife, MEHITABLE, born ca. 1777, Conn., were listed in the 1840 census index of Rome Twp., Lenawee Co., Mich.; and in the 1850 census were in the household of Roswell & Priscilla Hale (also see).

FETTERMAN, HENRY (See Wilbur West)

FIELD, CHARLES FREDERICK, son of JOHN (following), was born 23 Sept. 1851, Manchester, Washtenaw Co., Mich. He married 31 Dec. 1879 to KATIE (KIES), daughter of Joseph S. (also see). They resided first in Clinton, Mich., and then Tecumseh, Lenawee Co. No children were listed. Ref: P&BA-Len pg. 681-2.

FIELD, JAMES born ca. 1790, Mass., and wife, MARY A., born ca. 1815, NY, were listed in the 1850 census of Adrian Twp., Lenawee Co., Mich. with JAMES JR., age 19 b. NY; and HENRY, age 12; MARY, age 10; CATHARINE, age 6; EDWARD, age 5, all b. Mich., in their household.

FIELD, JOEL (See Harley D. Foster)

FIELD, JOHN and wife, ALCY J., moved from Wayne Co., NY to Manchester, Washtenaw Co., Mich. where known son, CHARLES FREDERICK (preceding) was born. Ref: P&BA-Len pg. 681-2.

FIELD, PLINNY born ca. 1783, Mass., and wife, BETSEY, born ca. 1781, Conn., were listed in the 1850 census of Tecumseh Twp., Lenawee Co., Mich. with CHRISTOPHER, age 40; SARAH, age 35; & ACHSAH, age 29 (listed "insane"), all b. NY; and Harriet Gillett, age 32, b. NY (also listed "insane.")

FIELD, ROBERT & wife, ABIGAIL (SUTTON), of Long Island were parents of SARAH born ca. 1730 (m. Isaac Underhill, see Underhill family).

FILKINS, JAMES H. (See Theodore Abbott)

FINCH, ASAHEL Sr. was born 4 Dec. 1755, Catskill, (Greene Co.) NY. He married ELIZABETH born 1 Aug. 1778, Durham, NY. They moved to Ogden, Monroe Co., NY, and later to Waukesha, Wisc. She died in Milwaukee in 1845. Known children: ASAHEL Jr. (operated a store with Skeels, Adrian, in 1830s; may be he in the 1840 census index of Albion, Calhoun Co., Mich.); LOUISA b. ca. 1807, NY (m. John Cheney[2], also see). Ref: P&BA-Len pg. 781-2.

FINCH, CATHERINE M. born ca. 1841, Mich., was listed in the 1850 census of Raisin Twp., Lenawee Co., Mich. in the Birdsell household.

FINCH, DANIEL G. was listed in the 1840 census index of Tecumseh Twp., Lenawee Co., Mich.; and in the 1850 census of Adrian Twp., Lenawee Co., Mich, there was a DANIEL G., age 8; AND JOHNSON, age 9, listed in the household of Elijah Vandegriff (also see), connection, if any, to the elder Daniel G. not known. Also see JOSEPH H. & WILLIAM T.

FINCH, JAMES T., son of PHILETUS (following), was born 16 Jan. 1814, Orange Co., NY, and moved with his parents to Steuben Co., NY. After the death of his parents, he went to Yates Co., NY and lived with an uncle. He married ca. 1837 to EMELINE (HALSTED), daughter of John (also see) in Yates Co. He had come first in 1836 to Rome Twp., Lenawee Co., Mich., then returned to New York. He brought his family to Rome Twp., where Emeline died 22 Jan. 1846. Children: 1. CHARLES b. 30 Aug. 1838 (prob. he who m. Esther Atwood, dau. of Seth, also see); 2. JOHN b. 5 Mar. 1840 (served in Civil War; afterwards to Mt. Phillips, KS); 3. PHILETUS b. 17 Jan. 1842 (served Civil War; afterwards to Calif.); 4. EMELINE b. 24 Aug. 1845 (m. Clark Decker, Adrian). James T. married again on 12 Sept. 1848 to SUSAN A. (HOOD) who was born ca. 1827, NY. She died in Sept. 1852, Rome Twp.; and James moved about 1853 to Adrian Twp. Children: 5. LORAN C. "CASS" b. 17 Sept. 1849 (to Oscela Co., Mich.); 6. son d. infancy. James T. married again to ABBIE (COLE), daughter of James (also see). Ref: P&BA-Len pg. 621-2.

FINCH, JOSEPH H. was listed in the 1840 census index of Adrian, Lenawee Co., Mich. Note DANIEL G. & WILLIAM T.

FINCH, LUCY born 1770, New Hampshire (See John Cheney[1])

FINCH, O. V. (See Samuel Bryan)

FINCH, PHILETUS born Orange Co., NY, married ELIZABETH (PADDOCK); and they removed to Steuben Co., NY by 1828. She died in 1830, age 40; and he died there over age 80. Six sons and one daughter (names not stated). Known son, JAMES T. (preceding). Ref: P&BA-Len pg. 621-2.

FINCH, S. J. (spelled "Finche") was listed in the 1840 census index of Hudson Twp., Lenawee Co., Mich.

FINCH, WILLIAM T. was listed in the 1840 census index of Tecumseh Twp., Lenawee Co., Mich. adjacent to DANIEL G. (also see).

FINGER, HENRY[1] and wife, ELIZABETH (IMHOF), were natives of Hesse-Cassel, Germany, where they remained. Nine children, of whom 6 survived (names not stated.) Known sons, CHRISTOPHER (came to US in 1844, lived Boston, Mass.); HENRY[2] (following). Ref: P&BA-Len PG. 706 & 709.

FINGER, HENRY[2], son of HENRY[1] (preceding), was born 6 June 1837, Willersforf, Hesse-Cassel, Germany. He sailed from Bremen on 26 Apr. 1857. He married in Oct. 1859 to CATHARINE ELIZABETH (UNGEMACH), daughter of John (also see) and they lived in New York City. In 1876, they removed to Riga Twp., Lenawee Co., Mich. Children: 1. CHRISTOPHER H.; 2. WILLIAM C.; 3. JOHN; 4. HENRY (d. age 4 yrs). Ref: P&BA-Len pg. 706 & 709.

FINGER, JACOB[1], son of JOHN (probably a descendant of the Dutch & German families who were first settlers at Taghanick, NY), was a native of Taghanick, Columbia Co., NY. He married there to CHRISTIANA (TRAVER) and remained there. Known son, JACOB[2] (following). Ref: P&BA-Len pg. 658.

FINGER, JACOB[2], son of JACOB[1] (preceding), was born 17 Mar. 1820, Taghanick, NY; and married MARIA (SCHUTZ) on 7 Nov. 1840. They lived variously in Dutchess Co., Rensselaer Co., NY and New Jersey. In 1866, they removed to Riga Twp., Lenawee Co., Mich. Children: FRANKLIN b. 28 Nov. 1842, Columbia Co., NY (served Civil War, 7th NY Heavy Artl; d. 14 Aug.

1864); MARGARET L. (m. Adelbert Lewis, son of Abial, also see); & ELLIS. Ref: P&BA-Len pg. 658.

FINN, JOHN born ca. 1812, England, and wife, MARY, born ca. 1813, (place not given in census) came to Rollin Twp., Lenawee Co., Mich. In the 1850 census of Rollin Twp., Lenawee Co., Mich. they listed AMY, age 17; SAMUEL, age 15; JULIA A. b. 3 Feb. 1840 (m. John W. Ormsby, also see); ZILPHA, age 8; WILLIAM H., age 6; JOHN R., age 4; MARY E., age 2/12, all born Mich., in their household. Note: There was a John "Fin" listed in the 1840 census index of Madison Twp., Lenawee Co., Mich.

FINZEL, MARGARET (See Michael Mulzer)

FISER, MICHAEL AND wife, MARTHA (CAMPBELL), lived in Seneca Co., Ohio, and Martha died there in 1851; but he was still living there in 1888. Known daughter, FANNY b. 5 Feb. 1844, Seneca Co., Ohio (m/1 Joseph Garwood; m/2 Edwin Smith (also see). Ref: P&BA-Len pg. 430-1.

FISHER, C. C. (See Charles W. Sheffield)
FISHER, BENJAMIN born ca. 1828, NY (See WILLIAM, following).
FISHER, CATHARINE, age 13, and ANNA, age 7, both b. NY, were listed in the 1850 census of Medina Twp., Lenawee Co., Mich. in an Ingersoll household.
FISHER, ELIZABETH Mrs. born ca. 1808, Canada, was head of household in the 1850 census of Blissfield Twp., Lenawee Co., Mich. with HENRY, age 11; ALONZO, age 9; ANDREW, age 4, all b. Mich., in the household.
FISHER, GEORGE, probably son of JOEL (following), born 1814, and wife, LUCINA, born ca. 1824, both in NY, were listed in the 1850 census of Palmyra Twp., Lenawee Co., Mich. with JOEL, age 10; PHEBE, age 7; MARY, age 4, all b. NY; and CHARLES, age 1, b. Mich., in their household.
FISHER, HENRY born ca. 1808, and wife, ALMIRA, born ca. 1810, both in NY, were listed in the 1850 census of Rome Twp., Lenawee Co., Mich. with EMILY, age 12; ELIZA J., age 10, both b. NY, in their household.
FISHER, JOEL born ca. 1780, Mass., was listed in the 1850 census of Palmyra Twp., Lenawee Co., Mich. in the household of probably son, NELSON (following). Also see GEORGE (preceding).
FISHER, JOHN^1 was born ca. 1784, Mass., and married in Franklin, Mass. to ELIZABETH (HULL) born ca. 1786. After the birth of 11 children (names not stated), in Mar 1836, with the surviving 9 children, they removed to Clinton Twp., Lenawee Co., Mich. He died 5 May 1863, age 79; and she died 3 May 1862. Known son, JOHN^2 (following); and also in the 1850 census of Tecumseh Twp. in their household was SARAH, age 18 (probably she who m. 1 Jan. 1852 to P. J. Allen, Tecumseh). Ref: P&BA-Len pg. 504-5.
FISHER, JOHN^2, son of JOHN^1 (preceding), was born 4 Aug. 1829, Charlemont, Franklin Co., Mass., and came with parents to Clinton Twp., Lenawee Co., Mich. He married in Tecumseh Village on 14 Feb. 1854 to RACHEL (HAMPTON), daugher of Isaac (also see). She died 14 Feb. 1868. Children: 1. WILLIAM F.; 2. ELLEN R.; 3. CHARLES H. (d. age 24). John^2 married again in Kalamazoo, Mich. on 31 July 1868 to Mrs. ZORAIDA A. (HENDERSON) HOOD, daughter of R. H. Henderson (also see), and they resided in Tecumseh. Ref: P&BA-Len pg. 504-5 with portrait of farm.
FISHER, JOHN (or Jonathan, listed "Jno") was listed in the 1840 census index of Franklin Twp., Lenawee Co., Mich. adjacent to PLINY (following).
FISHER, LORINDA (See Charles Strong)
FISHER, LUCIA O. (See Henry T. Luce)
FISHER, MICHAEL born ca. 1816, and wife, LAU--?, born ca. 1816, both in Germany, were listed in the 1850 census of Madison Twp., Lenawee Co., Mich. with no family.
FISHER, NELSON, probably son of JOEL (preceding), born ca. 1809, and wife, ELIZA, born ca. 1810, both in NY, were listed in the 1840 census index of Palmyra Twp., Lenawee Co., Mich.; and in the 1850 census with CAROLINE, age 18; WILLET, age 16, both b. NY, and JOEL (preceding), age 70, b. Mass., in their household.
FISHER, SAMUEL born in Ireland in 1721 of Scottish ancestry, came to America in 1740. Known daughter, NANCY (m. David Ela (also see) of Londonderry, NH). Ref: P&BA-Len pg. 297-9.
FISHER, PLINY was born Mass., and married LOVISA (GATES), born in Penn. (census said b. 1809, NY?), and they settled in Otsego Co., NY. They came to Franklin Twp., Lenawee Co., Mich. where he was listed in the 1840 census index as Plinney Fisher, Jr. In the household in the 1850 census of Franklin Twp. were: CAROLINE, age 18, b. NY; DELIA A. b. 15 Apr. 1834, Otsego Co., NY (m. D. W. Love, also see); and GEORGE, age 11; WILLIAM, age 9, both b. Mich. Ref: P&BA-Len pg. 252-3. Note: In the 1840 census index, there was "JNO" listed adjacent.
FISHER, THERINA (See Curtice W. Stockwell)
FISHER, W. R. (See Levi Hopkins)
FISHER, WILLIAM born ca. 1797, and wife, SARAH (HIGGS), born ca. 1800, both in England, came to the US in 1834(6?). They lived in Tecumseh, Lenawee Co., Mich. in 1840; but in the 1850 census were listed in Macon Twp. with WILLIAM C. (following); HARRIET, age 24, both b. England; EMMA J., age 11; HENRY, age 9; EDWIN, age 6, both b. Mich., in their household. Ref: P&BA-Len pg. 359. BETSEY, age 18, b. England, in the 1850 census of Tecumseh Twp., probably relates to this family.
FISHER, WILLIAM born ca. 1824, NY, was listed as head of household in the 1850 census of Adrian Twp., Lenawee Co., Mich. with PERMELIA, age 55, b. NJ, probably his mother, and probably siblings, MATILDA, age 30, MARY A., age 24; CAROLINE, age 20; BENJAMIN, age 22, all b. NY, in the household.
FISHER, WILLIAM C., son of WILLIAM (preceding born England), was born 7 Jan. 1830, England, and came to the US with his parents. He married in Tecumseh to ABBIE (MURRAY), daughter of A. (See Alonzo). William C. died 10 May 1879. There was an adopted daughter (name not stated). Ref: P&BA-Len pg. 359.

FISK, A. J. (See Ezra Abbott; and also note JABEZ, following)
FISK, BENJAMIN B. was born in Conn., and married there in 1816 to LYDIA (ALDRICH). After the birth of the first 2 children, they moved to York, Livingston Co., NY. He died 28 Sept. 1823 of Typhoid; and it appears to be Lydia listed in the 1840 census index of Clinton,

Pioneer Families of Southeastern Michigan

Lenawee Co., Mich. Children: 1. CYRUS B. (d. 1846); 2. LEANDER b. ca. 1822, NY (m. Mrs. Fannie (Ellis) Wilson, Oakland, CA); 3. WELCOME V. (following); 4. HORACE A. (m. Jane Brown, Bridgewater, Washtenaw Co., Mich.); 5. Gen. CLINTON B. (m. Jenette C. Crippen on 1 Feb. 1850, Coldwater, Mich.; to Seabright, NJ); 6. BENJAMIN W. (d. 1840 young). Lydia married second to William Smith of Jackson Co., Mich.; and married third to Rev. Robert Powell whom she survived. She died at age 83 in home of son, Horace A. Ref: P&BA-Len pg. 339-40. Also see JOHN W., following.

FISK, DANIEL, son of JABEZ (following), was born 1 Feb. 1825, Chemung Co., NY. He married in Sept. 1852 in Seneca Twp., Lenawee Co., Mich. to ELIZABETH (QUICK), daughter of Lewis (also see) of Chemung Co., NY. Children: 1. FRED M. (m. Lilly M. Blair, Morenci, Mich; had dau., Rena May; to California); 2. CARRIE M. (Detroit, Mich.); 3. HARRY J. (Seneca Twp.). Ref: P&BA-Len pg. 1041-2.

FISK, DORCAS, age 24, b. NY, was listed in the 1850 census of Adrian Twp., Lenawee Co., Mich.

FISK, EBENEZER^1 married ? (BARNARD) and lived in Franklin Co., Mass., where he died at age 91. Known son, EBENEZER^2 (following). Ref; P&BA-Len pg. 334-5. Also note JABEZ, following, as another son went to Lenawee Co. before EBENEZER^2.

FISK, EBENEZER^2, son of EBENEZER^1 (preceding), was born ca. 1785, Franklin Co., Mass.; and married HANNAH (TERRELL) born Abington, Mass. He died in 1847, age 62; and she died in Franklin Co. at age 82. There were 7 sons & 2 daughters (names of only the 5 surviving in 1888 stated): 1. DANIEL (Newburyport, Mass.); 2. ISAAC (Franklin Co., Mass.); 3. EBENEZER (following); 4. FRANK? (female, Mrs. Mather); 5. CHARLOTTE (m. Slate; Mass.). Ref: P&BA-Len pg. 334-5.

FISK, EBENEZER^3, son of EBENEZER^2 (preceding), was born 28 Aug. 1815, Franklin Co., Mass. He followed a brother to Lenawee Co. in 1838, but then returned to Mass. until 1841. He married 18 Nov. 1841, Adrian Twp., Lenawee Co., Mich. to ELIZABETH (SMEAD), daughter of Rufus (also see). Children: 1. RUFUS H. b. 17 Aug. 1844 (m. Elizabeth Cordelia Harder, Adrian); 2. EBENEZER (1848-1849); 3. EDWARD P. b. 14 Nov. 1848 (m. Frances P. Poucher, dau. of Abraham, also see, had dau., Anne Laura); 4. HERMAN S. b. 3 Aug. 1853; 5. ANNA E. b. 19 Sept. 1856 (m. Clarence Frost, Adrian). Ref: P&BA-Len pg. 334-5.

FISK, ELI D., age 26, b. NY, was listed in the 1850 census of Medina Twp., Lenawee Co., Mich.

FISK, ELVIRA. age 19, born NY, was listed in the 1850 census of Hudson Twp., Lenawee Co., Mich.

FISK, HENRY born ca. 1826, and wife, SARAH J., born ca. 1832, both in NY, were listed in the 1850 census of Franklin Twp., Lenawee Co., Mich. in the Graves household.

FISK, HENRY M. born ca. 1812, Mass., and wife, MATILDA T., born ca. 1825, NY, were listed in the 1850 census of Medina Twp., Lenawee Co., Mich. with Alice M. Humphrey, age 12, b. Mich. in the household.

FISK, JABEZ born ca. 1794, Mass. (See EBENEZER^1). He served in the War of 1812; and moved to Chemung Co., NY where he married CATHERINE (TENBROOK) born Chemung Co. In 1833, they removed to Madison Twp., Lenawee Co., Mich. In 1847, they moved to Dover, Mich. where he died in 1867, age 73. His wife died in 1870, age 73. There were 10 sons and 3 daughters (all names not stated, some of following from 1850 census). Known children: REBECCA b. 19 Aug. 1822, Tioga Co., NY (m. Joshua W. Thurber, also see); #5. DANIEL b. 1 Feb. 1825; GARRET b. ca. 1826; JOSEPH b. ca. 1827; JACKSON b. ca. 1830; AMOS b. ca. 1832, all born NY; and WILLIAM born ca. 1834; MARGARET b. ca. 1836; LYMAN b. ca. 1840; JAMES b. ca. 1844, last 4 b. Mich. Note: AMOS is probably "A. J." who married Olive Abbott, dau. of Ezra of Dover Twp.) Ref: P&BA-Len pg. 408-9 & 1041-2.

FISK, JOHN T. born ca. 1821, NY, and wife, MARTHA, born ca. 1828, VT, were listed in the 1850 census of Madison Twp., Lenawee Co., Mich. with AUGUSTA, age 4; FRANKLIN, age 1, both b. Mich., in their household.

FISK, JOHN W. born ca. 1810, and wife, HARRIET, born ca. 1810, both in NY, were listed in the 1850 census of Hudson Twp., Lenawee Co., Mich. with PAUL C., age 17, b. NY; OPHELIA, age 15; FIDELIA A., age 14; CORNELIA, age 13; MARY E, age 11; LEANDER, age 6, last 4 b. Mich.; and also listed were Harriet M. Brown, age 18, and Marian? J. Brown, age 16, both b. NY, possibly step-children? See BENJAMIN (preceding).

FISK, SYBIL (See Luther Damon)

FISK, WELCOME V., son of BENJAMIN B. (preceding), was born 29 June 1823, York, Livingston Co., NY. He probably accompanied his mother to Clinton Twp., Lenawee Co., Mich. where he married AMANDA (VAUGHN), who was born ca. 1829, Varysburg (Sheldon, Wyoming Co.), NY. Children: 1. LEANDER D. (d. age 16 mos); 2. FRANK (m. Nellie Meyer, Newton, IA); 3. GRACE (m. Porter C. Smith, son of Jacob B., also see); 4. LEANDER D. 2d (m. Almeda Ross; d. Apr. 1884, San Francisco, CA). Welcome V. married again in 1866 to Mrs. MARY C. (FELTON) VAUGHN (See Vaughn); and she died 18 June 1887. Ref: P&BA-Len pg. 339.

FITCH, CHARLES (See George Sisson)

FITCH, ERASTUS born ca. 1812, NY, and wife, HARRIET, born ca.1820, England, were listed in the 1850 census of Blissfield Twp., Lenawee Co., Mich. with SALLY A., age 8; RACHEL, age 2, both b. Mich., in their household.

FITCH, HESTER Mrs. (See John Morton, Jr.)

FITCH, JAMES and wife, PAMELIA, were early settlers of Rome Twp., Lenawee Co., Mich. (listed in 1840 census index). Known daughter, HARRIET E. (m. Alfred A. Miller, also see, on 2 Apr. 1873). Ref: P&BA-Len pg. 1162-5.

FITCH, JOHN born ca. 1771, Mass., was listed in the 1850 census of Madison Twp., Lenawee Co., Mich. in the household of Peter Clapper.

FITCH, OTIS B. married SARAH THANKFUL (HUME), daughter of Roderick R. (also see) of Medina Twp., Lenawee Co., Mich. They moved to Fort Wayne, Ind. Known children: 1. JESSE HUME; 2. ALICE MAY; 3. GRACE AURELIA; 4. RODERICK WILLIAM. Ref: P&BA-Len pg. 924-5.

FITCH, WILLIAM married on 9 Oct. 1760, Conn., to ALTIE (WHEELER). Known daughter, MARGARET, b. 7 Nov.

1763 (m. Philip Reed, also see, and went to Ontario Co., NY). Ref: P&BA-Len pg. 1191-2.

FITTS, ANDREW was born in Worcester, Mass. and moved with parents to Oxford, Mass. He married RUTH (PIKE) born Charlton, Mass, and they settled in Oxford where they remained. Ten children (names not stated). Known son, HARRISON (following). Ref: P&BA-Len pg. 953-4.

FITTS, CHARLES (See Edwin D. Pierson)

FITTS, HARRISON, son of ANDREW (preceding), was born 13 Mar. 1815, Oxford, Worcester Co., Mass. He moved to Wayne Co., NY; and married in 1844 to NANCY E. (HOUSTON) born Madison Co., NY. They lived in Ontario Co., NY, and moved about 1851 to Somerset, Hillsdale Co., Mich. In 1860, the moved to Rollin Twp., Lenawee Co., Mich., and also had a business in Jackson Co., Mich. In 1881, they settled in Blissfield, Lenawee Co. Children: 1. RUTH (m. A. Heath, Hanover Center, Mich.); 2. VERNELIA A. (m. Jerome Segar; d. Rome, Mich.); 3. LEWIS C. (following); 4. CHARLES H. (Blissfield, Mich.); 5. SARAH (m. G. T. Greenshaw, Jackson Co., Mich.); 6. AUSTIN; 7. FRANK. Ref: P&BA-Len pg. 867-8 & 953-4.

FITTS, LEWIS C., son of HARRISON (preceding), was born 5 Mar. 1849, Ontario Co., NY. He moved to Lenawee Co., Mich. with his parents, and he married on 31 Mar. 1881, Rollin Twp., to NETTIE (BAKER), daughter of Daniel (also see). Known son, HARRY b. 10 Jan. 1882. Ref: P&BA-Len pg. 867-8. See MOLLY following.

FITTS, MOLLY (spelled "Fitz") born ca. 1777, Mass., was listed in the 1850 census of Rome Twp., Lenawee Co., Mich. in the household of Labius H. Goodrich, and wife, Sally (who was age 46, b. Mass., daughter of Molly??). Note that Sally named a son, Lewis C.

FITZMYER, MARY (See George V. Osgood)

FITZPATRICK, ANN born ca. 1790, Ireland, was listed in the 1850 census of Medina Twp., Lenawee Co., Mich. Also see THOMAS, followiong.

FITZPATRICK, MAY (CAMPBELL) Mrs., born after 1850, was the daughter of Peter Campbell (also see) of Medina Twp., Lenawee Co., Mich.

FITZPATRICK, SAMUEL born ca. 1816, and wife, HANNAH, born ca. 1825, both in Ireland, were listed in the 1850 census of Hudson Twp., Lenawee Co., Mich.

FITZPATRICK, THOMAS born ca. 1805, and wife, MARY A., born ca. 1813, both in Ireland, were listed in the 1850 census of Medina Twp., Lenawee Co., Mich. (2 doors from ANN, preceding; and Peter Campbell was one of the households between them; note MAY, preceding).

FITZSIMMONS, THOMAS of Tecumseh Twp., Lenawee Co., Mich. was the father of HELEN m. (m. George Griswold, also see).

FITZSIMMONS, W. C. Col. (See Peter R. Adams)

FLANDERS, LUCINDA (See Abner Kneeland)

FLEMING, CHARLES was listed in the 1840 census index of Adrian Twp., Lenawee Co., Mich.

FLEMING, JAMES, son of JOHN (following), was born ca. 1787, Lycoming, Penn. He married MARTHA (?); and they lived in Romulus, Seneca Co., NY by 1812. They moved to Rome Twp., Lenawee Co., Mich. by 1840; and Martha was apparently deceased before the 1850 census. Known daughter, JANE b. 12 June 1812, Romulus, NY (m. William K. Parker, also see). Also, probably LETTICE b. ca. 1823, NY (m. Sellick Chase, also see, as James lived in their household in the 1850 census of Rollin Twp.) MARTHA, age 25, b. NY (m. Wilson Matthews, may also be a daughter, as Martha A. Parker, granddaughter of James, was living with them in the 1850 census. Also note JARVIS, JOHN & JESSE (following).

FLEMING, JARVIS, possibly son of JAMES (preceding), born ca. 1812, and wife, CATHARINE A., born ca. 1816, both in NY, were listed in the 1850 census of Adrian Twp., Lenawee Co., Mich. with THADDEUS C, age 14; WILLIAM H., age 12; LETTICE A., age 10; ROBERT, age 8; AUGUSTUS, age 6, all b. NY, in their household.

FLEMING, JEPTHA W. born ca. 1809, and wife, LUCY G., born ca. 1819, both in NY, were listed in the 1850 census of Rome Twp., Lenawee Co., Mich. with WILLIAM W., age 7, b. Mich., in their household.

FLEMING, JESSE born ca. 1812, and wife, SUSAN, born ca. 1817, both in NY, were listed in the 1850 census of Rome Twp., Lenawee Co., Mich. with Albert Waggoner, age 6, b. Mich., and Mary McConnell, age 19, b. NY, in their household. In the 1840 census index he was adjacent to JAMES, preceding.

FLEMING, JOHN was born in Chester Co., Penn., and was a descendant of ROBERT who came from Paisley, Scotland to Canada at an early date. John went to Lycoming Co., Penn. where son, JAMES (preceding) was born in 1787. Ref: P&BA-Len pg. 884-5.

FLEMING, JOHN, possibly son of JAMES (preceding), born ca. 1819, and wife, NANCY, born ca. 1820, both in NY, were listed in the 1850 census of Rome Twp., Lenawee Co., Mich. with JANE, age 9 (probably she who m. Erastus S. Hawks, also see); GEORGE, age 8; DENTON, age 1; MILLARD F., age 5/12, all b. Mich. John died at age 76; and his wife, died at age 71.

FLEMING, JOHN (spelled "Flemming") born ca. 1802, Penn., and wife, CHLOE, born ca. 1809, Ohio, were listed in the 1850 census of Woodstock Twp., Lenawee Co., Mich. with WILLIAM, age 19; EMILY, age 17; FRANKLIN, age 14; JOHN, age 10, all b. Ohio; and CHLOE, age 6, b. Mich., in their household.

FLEMING, JOHN T. born ca. 1807, NY, and wife, ELIZABETH, born ca. 1809, New Jersey, may be they listed in the 1840 census index of Rome Twp., Lenawee Co., Mich.; and in the 1850 census were listed with MARIAN H., age 16; JOSEPHA J., age 14, both b. NY, in their household.

FLEMING, SAMUEL born ca. 1794, and wife, PHEBE, born ca. 1795, both in NY, were listed in the 1840 census index of Adrian Twp., Lenawee Co., Mich., and in the 1850 census listed MARTHA, age 31; JEPTHA, age 19, both b. NY, in their household. Also note CHARLES; JEPTHA; & JAMES, preceding.

FLEMING, WILLIAM was listed in the 1840 census index of Tecumseh Twp., Lenawee Co., Mich. There was a WILLIAM, age 19, b. Mich., listed in the 1850 census of Madison Twp., in the household of Abel & Elizabeth Palmer.

Pioneer Families of Southeastern Michigan

FLETCHER, ABNER of Wilton, ME was the father of ELIZABETH H. who married Jacob O. Eaton (also see) before 1849.

FLETCHER, ALFRED born ca. 1816, and wife, RHODA M. (PENOYER), born ca. 1815, both in NY, came from Ontario Co., NY to Michigan (there is a man by this name in the 1840 census index of Putnam Twp., Livingston Co., Mich.) They were listed in the 1850 census of Fairfield Twp., Lenawee Co. with ANN E. b. 14 June 1836, Ontario Co., NY (m/1 George Kendall; m/2 Cyrenus Sanford, see both); WILLIAM, age 12, b. NY; ELLEN M., age 2, b. Mich., in their household. Ref: P&BA-Len pg. 804-5.

FLETCHER, JEMIMA (See Samuel Underwood)

FLETCHER, JESSE, age 11, born Mich., was listed in the 1850 census of Blissfield Twp., Lenawee Co., Mich. in a White household. Note WILLIAM of Blissfield Twp., following.

FLETCHER, ORPHA born ca. 1815, NY, was listed in the 1850 census of Blissfield Twp., Lenawee Co., Mich. in a Blevins household. Note WILLIAM of Blissfield Twp., following.

FLETCHER, RUSSELL of Wayne Co., NY reared Betsey H. Scott, daughter of Lemuel (also see).

FLETCHER, WILLIAM was listed in the 1840 census index of Blissfield Twp., Lenawee Co., Mich. Note ORPHA & JESSE, preceding.

FLETCHER, WILLIAM born ca. 1814, and LURILLA, born ca. 1830, both in NY, were listed in the 1850 census of Riga Twp., Lenawee Co., Mich.

FLINN see FLYNN

FLINT, ANNIE born Conn. (See Erastus Back).

FLINT, JACOB born ca. 1816, and wife, ANN, born ca. 1809, both in England, were listed in the 1850 census of Woodstock Twp., Lenawee Co., Mich. with WILLIAM, age 7; LEWIS, age 6; ANNA, age 4; JOHN, age ?, all b. Mich., in their household.

FLINT, MARY (See Ezekiel Smith)

FLOCKTON, ALICE (See John Smith)

FLORANCE also see FLORENCE

FLORANCE, MORGAN M., son of NATHAN (following), was born 11 June 1828, Middlesex, Yates Co., NY. After the death of his father, he was reared by Augustus Montgomery (also see) with whom he came to Mich. in 1833. About 1842, he lived with his mother and stepfather, possibly in Eaton Co., Mich., but was in the household of the Montgomerys in the 1850 census of Ridgeway Twp., Lenawee Co. He married JULIET H. (TOBEY), daughter of Thomas (also see). Children: 1. FLOYD G. (m. Eva Kelley, Holloway, Mich.); 2. FANNIE E. (m. Charles W. Culbertson, Ridgeway Twp.); 3. THOMAS T.; 4. MONTIE R.; 5. VOLNA E. (deceased before 1888). Ref: P&BA-Len pg. 681.

FLORANCE, NATHAN was born in France in 1799, and he came to America, where he married JULIET C. (BREWSTER). They lived in Middlesex, Yates Co., NY, where he died in 1833, age 34. Five children (names not stated), except MORGAN M. (preceding). Juliet C. married again and moved to Charlotte, Eaton Co., Mich., where she died June 1856. Ref: P&BA-Len pg. 681.

FLORENCE also see FLORANCE

FLORENCE, ANSAH (See I. H. Schreder)

FLORENCE, EMELINE born ca. 1823, NY, was listed in the 1850 census of Macon Twp., Lenawee Co., Mich. in the household of John & Mary A. Clarkson (also see).

FLYNN, JULIA born Co. Kerry, Ireland, came to the US in 1837, and married in Maumee, Ohio to William Brown (also see).

FLYNN, MICHAEL born ca. 1801, Ireland, had come to the US, where he married ELIZABETH (MANNIX), born ca. 1809, Ireland (who had come to the US at age 16). They settled first in Utica, NY, and in 1841 moved to Hudson Twp., Lenawee Co., Mich. Children: 1. MARY b. ca. 1830, Utica (m. James Campbell, also see); 2. ELIZABETH b. ca. 1831 (m. Edward Gray, Hudson Twp.); 3. JOHN b. ca. 1835 (became a Sea Captain). Ref: P&BA-Len pg. 900.

FOGLESONG, JESSE (See George Frederick Harsh)

FOLGER, ELIZABETH (See John Worth family) and her brother, WALTER, were Quakers, and a grandniece & nephew of Benjamin Franklin.

FOLLETT, HENRY was born 2 July 1776, and wife, SARAH (KELLEY), was born 2 July 1792. They lived in Bennington, VT, and some time after 1817 moved to Huron Co., Ohio. Known daughter, SARAH b. 24 Apr. 1817, Bennington Co., VT (m. Charles C. Morse, also see). Ref: P&BA-Len pg. 898-9.

FOLLETT, LEWIS was listed in the 1840 census index of Adrian Twp., Lenawee Co., Mich.

FOLLETT, ZUBA (female) born ca 1806, VT, was listed in the 1850 census of Adrian Twp., Lenawee Co., Mich. in the household of Russell and Eunice Lyman (also see).

FOLSOM, MARY (See Ezekiel Ladd[1])

FOOT also see FOOTE

FOOT, ELIZA born ca. 1829, NY, married first to Warren S. White (also see). In their household in the 1850 census of Fairfield Twp., they listed PHEBE, age 60, b. Ohio, possibly mother of Eliza. After the death of Warren S. White, Eliza married Seth B. Sayres (also see). Note LUTHER, following.

FOOT, LUTHER was listed in the 1840 census index of Fairfield Twp., Lenawee Co., Mich.

FOOTE also see FOOT

FOOTE, CHARLES born ca. 1830, NY, was listed in the 1850 census of Adrian Twp., Lenawee Co., Mich. in a Rogers household.

FOOTE, DAVID and wife, MARY, were natives of Ireland who came to America in 1798. They lived in Schenectady, NY; then located in Ovid, Seneca Co., NY, where she died in 1851, and he died in 1855. Known daughter, MARY JANE, b. Schenectady (m. William H. Osborne, also see). Ref: P&BA-Len pg. 421-2.

FOOTE, ELLERY (spelled Elery?) born ca. 1822, and wife, LYDIA A., born ca. 1828, both in NY, were listed in the

1850 census of Dover Twp., Lenawee Co., Mich. in the household of Philip & Polly Smith (possibly parents of Lydia A.), with MARYETTE, age 8/12, b. Mich.

FOOTE, FREDERICK (See Valentine Wenzel)

FOOTE, JAMES born ca. 1802, and wife, ESTHER, born ca. 1810, both in NY, were listed in the 1850 census of Seneca Twp., Lenawee Co., Mich. with SARAH, age 18; MARGARET, age 13, both b. NY; and JOSIAH, age 5, b. Mich., in their household.

FOOTE, JOHN J. born ca. 1815, and wife, OLIVE J., born ca. 1825, Ohio, were listed in the 1850 census of Palmyra Twp., Lenawee Co., Mich. with SARAH, age 7; NATHAN, age 4; ELLEN, age 2, all b. Mich., and Amanda Robin, age 12, b. Ohio, in their household.

FOOTE, MILTON was born Conn., and he married LOIS (BISCO or BRISCOE). They lived in Cayuga Co. or Chautauqua Co., NY before removed to Madison Twp., Lenawee Co., Mich. in 1830 (in 1840 he was listed in Adams Twp., Hillsdale Co.). He died either in Rome Twp., Lenawee Co. or in Hillsdale Co., Mich. (two different versions given). She died in Adrian in 1883, age 95. There were 5 sons & 5 daughters (all names not stated). Known daughters: HANNAH M. b. 18 Dec. 1809, Newtown, Conn. (m. Pharis Sutton in NY); ABBIE b. Cayuga Co., NY (m/1 Alonzo Moore; and m/2 in 1867 to Sylvanus Kinney, also see). Ref: P&BA-Len pg. 223-4 & 251-2. Note: In the 1840 census index there were JAMES & JOHN M., possibly sons, adjacent to Milton in Adams Twp., Hillsdale Co. FOOTE, PETER H. born ca. 1803, and wife, LORANA, age 36?, both born NY, were listed in the 1840 census index of Palmyra Twp., Lenawee Co., Mich.; and were in the 1850 census of Dover Twp. with JAMES M., age 24, b. NY; and LAURA, age 15; ELIZA, age 14; EMERY, age 12; PERCILLA, age 11; ORRIN, age 8; SINTHA (CYNTHIA?), age 6; ZEBINA, age 4, all b. Mich., in their household.

FORBES, ALEXANDER was born in Herkimer Co., NY, and married there to BETSEY (KESSLER). (Note: This area of Herkimer Co. is probably now Montgomery Co.) He died there, but Betsey went to Cayuga Co., NY where she remained. There were 5 sons and 5 daughters (names not stated). Known son, #2. JOHN (following). Ref: P&BA-Len pg. 344-5.

FORBES, JOHN, son of ALEXANDER (preceding), born 1 Mar. 1808, Palatine Church (now Montgomery Co.), NY, married ANGELINE (CRIM) born ca. 1813, NY. They moved to Dover Twp., Lenawee Co., Mich. in 1835. Children (First 8 were in the household in 1850 census): 1. ELIZABETH b. ca. 1831 (m. Richard McKenzie, Hudson Twp.); 2. TIMOTHY b. ca. 1833 (m. Mary E. Jones, Clayton, Mich.); 3. DANIEL b. ca. 1834 (m. Martha Brown, Hudson Twp.); 4. ALVIRA b. ca. 1836 (m. William W. Herron; Ohio); 5. POLLY b. ca. 1838 (m. Eugene Terwilliger, Wexford, Mich.); 6. ANGELINE b. ca. 1841 (d. age 20); 7. MARY J. b. ca. 1843 (m. Henry Ruloff, d. Hudson Twp.); 8. WILLIAM J. b. ca. 1847 (d. of Typhoid, Civil War); 9. JOHN W. (d. age 6); 10. JOHN E. (m. Celia Darby, Hudson Twp.). John's wife, Angeline, died 16 July 1867, and he married again to Mrs. MARY PERKINS, widow of John T., and she died in Hudson Twp. He married third to Mrs. ELIZABETH (LEFFERTS) CERROW, daughter of Hiram, and widow of Ransom (see both). Ref: P&BA-Len pg. 344-5.

FORCE, HENRY born ca. 1817, NY, and wife, MARY A., born ca. 1822, Ireland, were listed in the 1850 census of Fairfield Twp., Lenawee Co., Mich. with MARGETA?, age 6; JOHN N., age 5; ANNA, age 4, ALBERT, age 2; ALONZO, age 1, all b. Mich., in their household. Note: Listed 2 doors from MARGARET (FORCE) SALSBURY, wife of D. C. (also see).

FORCE, HIRAM S. born ca. 1814, NY, and wife, MARIA L., born ca. 1820, Ireland, were listed in the 1850 census of Medina Twp., Lenawee Co., Mich. with SARAH M., age 1, b. Mich. in the household.

FORCE, JANE, age 15, b. Mich., is listed in the 1850 census of Madison Twp., Lenawee Co., Mich. in an Aldrich household. It may be she listed again in Adrian Twp. in a Merrick household.

FORCE, MARGARET born ca. 1824, NY, married D. C. Salsbury (also see). In the 1850 census of Fairfield Twp., she was listed 2 doors from HENRY (preceding). Note SOLOMON, following.

FORCE, SOLOMON born ca. 1792, and wife, CATHARINE, born ca. 1808, both in NY, were listed in the 1840 census index of Adrian Twp., Lenawee Co., Mich.; and were in the 1850 census of Fairfield Twp., with JOSEPH, age 9; SOLOMON JR, age 3; JAMES, age 1, all b. Mich. With the children there is a George Furgurson, age 12, b. Mich., and then dittoed after him are HARRIET, age 9; CATHARINE, age 6, which are either Force or Furgurson?? As Solomon was the only person of this surname in Lenawee Co. in 1840, JANE, & MARGARET, preceding, may relate to this family.

FORD, ANNIE (See Nathaniel Smith^1).

FORD, ANSEL^5, son of HEZEKIAH^4 (following), was born 27 June 1788 in Cummington, Mass., and married there on 7 June 1807 to DEBORAH (TOWER) born 16 July 1786. Children: 1. DEBORAH b. 15 Aug. 1807 (d. same); 2. CHARLES (following); 3. HOSEA b. 4 Apr. 1810 (d. 27 Oct. 1867); 4. OTIS b. 5 Jan. 1812 (d. 2 Jan. 1886); 5. AMOS b. 6 Dec. 1813 (d. 28 July 1877); 6. LUCIUS b. 9 Nov. 1815; 7. ALMINA b. 11 Mar. 1817 (d. 1 Sept. 1846); 8. FRANKLIN b. 7 Mar. 1819 (d. Aug. 1821); 9. CYRUS b. 18 Mar. 1821 (d. 24 Aug. 1868); 10. ANNA b. 27 Nov. 1824 (d. 27 Feb. 1886); 11. DELIA b. 29 Apr. 1827; 12. DARIUS b. May 1829 (d. same); 13. FRANKLIN b. 4 Dec. 1831. The family remained in Mass. until 1841, then moved to Toledo, Ohio, and later to Gorham, Fulton Co., Ohio. He died in Ohio 21 Dec. 1858, and she died 1 Aug. 1869. Ref: P&BA-Len pg. 1136-8. Note: In the 1830 census of Saline Twp., Washtenaw Co., Mich. there was an ANSEL, age 30-40, listed, with only a male 10-15 in the household.

FORD, CHARLES^6, son of ANSEL^5 (preceding), was born 22 Jan. 1809, Cummington, Mass.; and married on 20 May 1835 to FIDELIA (BATES) born 4 July 1813, Cummington. They lived in Windsor, VT in 1849; and in the Fall of 1850, followed his father to Ohio. The following Spring they settled in Richfield Twp., Lucas Co., Ohio. His wife died 21 May 1879, but Charles was still living in 1888. Children: 1. LEVI B. (following); 2. GEORGE F. (following); 3. EUGENE F. b. 5 Apr. 1841 (m. Pamelia Wilson, Riga Twp.); 4. LUCIUS L. b. 24 Oct.

Pioneer Families of Southeastern Michigan

1843; 5. LOVINA B. b. 31 Oct. 1848 (m. John Leonardson, son of James, also see); 6. CHARLES D. b. 24 July 1853 (d. 23 May 1854); 7. ELLEN M. b. 8 May 1858 (m. Squire Garnsey, Toledo, O.). Ref: P&BA-Len pg. 1136-8.

FORD, EDWIN was listed in the 1840 census index of Rome Twp., Lenawee Co., Mich.

FORD, ELIZA B. Mrs. born ca. 1811, Mich.?, was head of household in the 1850 census of Adrian Twp., Lenawee Co., Mich. with WILLIAM T., age 18; MARY, age 15; SAMANTHA, age 8, all b. Mich. in her household.

FORD, EPHRAIM born ca. 1800, Mass., and wife, D--A, born ca. 1800, NY, were listed in the 1840 census index of Woodstock Twp., Lenawee Co., Mich.; and in the 1850 census with JEFFERSON, age 18; EZEKIEL, age 16(10?), both b. NY; and AMOS, age 9; ALTHA?, age 21, born NY, in their household.

FORD, GEORGE F.[7], son of CHARLES[6] (preceding), was born 2 Mar. 1838, Cummington, Mass.; and moved with his parents to Lucas Co., Ohio. He served in Co. A., 84th Ohio Inf., & Co. A., 189th Ohio Inf., in the Civil War. He married 14 Nov. 1861 to SARAH H. (WALTERS), daughter of John (also see). They settled in Riga Twp., Lenawee Co., Mich. with adjoining property in Lucas Co., Ohio. Children: 1. FLORENCE F.; 2. CHARLES R. (Riga Twp.); 3. GEORGE W.; 4. WILLIE B.; 5. VERNE E.; 6. BESSIE; 7. CHINA A. Ref: P&BA-Len pg. 809-10.

FORD, HARLEY born ca. 1826, and wife, CATHERINE, born ca. 1827, both b. NY, with ELLEN D., age 1, b. Mich., were listed in the 1850 census of Seneca Twp., Lenawee Co., Mich. in the household of Gershom Bennett (also see).

FORD, HARRIET, age 29, born VT, was listed in the 1850 census of Hudson Twp., Lenawee Co., Mich. in a Sherwood household.

FORD, HEZEKIAH[1] was born in 1688, Abington, Mass., of Scottish parentage. He married in 1712 to RUTH (WHITMARSH). Known son, HEZEKIAH[2] (following).

FORD, HEZEKIAH[2], son of HEZEKIAH[1] (preceding), born 1713, Abington, Mass., married in 1734 to DEBORAH (BEALS). They moved from Abington to Cummington, Hampshire Co., Mass. on 20 June 1774, and he died in 1775. Known son: HEZEKIAH[3] (following).

FORD, HEZEKIAH[3], son of HEZEKIAH[2] (preceding), born 1735, Abington, Mass.; married ca. 1759 to ? (FISHER). They remained there until 20 June 1774, then moved to Cummington. Hezekiah served in the French & Indian War, and the Revolution. He died 8 Feb. 1826. Known children: HEZEKIAH[4] (following); AMOS; & 2 daughters (names not stated). Ref: P&BA-Len pg. 1136-8.

FORD, HEZEKIAH[4], son of HEZEKIAH[3] (preceding), was born 29 Dec. 1759, Abington, Mass., moved with his parents to Cummington. He had some service during the Revolution. He married HULDAH (COBB) on 23 Jan. 1787. Children: 1. ANSEL (preceding); 2. DARIUS b. 16 May 1790 (d. 6 Apr. 1859); 3. CYRUS (twin of Darius; d. 13 Apr. 1864); 4. OTIS b. 22 Mar. 1793 (d. 2 Oct. 1795); 5. HANNAH b. 2 Nov. 1796 (d. next day); 6. DELIA b. 22 Feb. 1798 (d, 3 July 1798); 7. OTIS 2d b. 26 Apr. 1799 (d. 28 Aug. 1801); 8. ROXY b. 9 Oct. 1802 (d. young); 9. LEWIS b. 20 Feb. 1806. On 3 Oct. 1842, Hezekiah[4] went to Cleveland, O. to lived with son, Cyrus, and died 19 Dec. 1848, East Cleveland. Ref: P&BA-Len pg. 1136-8.

FORD, LEVI B.[7], son of CHARLES[6] (preceding), was born 19 Mar. 1836, Cummington, Mass. He moved with his parents to Lucas Co., Ohio, where he married on 12 Apr. 1863 to NANCY (LEONARDSON), daughter of James (also see). They settled in Riga Twp., Lenawee Co., Mich. Children: 1. DORRANCE b. 23 Jan. 1864; 2. JAMES B. b. 16 Mar. 1867; 3. JAY L. b. 4 June 1871; 4. IVEY L. b. 22 Dec. 1878. Ref: P&BA-Len pg. 1136-8.

FORD, RICHARD born ca. 1824, and wife, JULIANE, born ca. 1828, both in NY, were listed in the 1850 census of Tecumseh Twp., Lenawee Co., Mich. with ADELADE, age 5; RICHARD, age 4/12, both b. Mich.; and LURY (female), age 25. b. NY, in their household.

FORDHAM, HEZEKIAH and wife, BETSEY (BLODGETT), daughter of Isaiah (also see), were parents of CALISTA D. b. 21 Nov. 1818, Genesee Co., NY (m. Harry Babcock, also see). Ref: P&BA-Len pg. 752-3.

FORNCROOK, CHRISTOPHER and wife, MARY (BAIRD), were natives of Montgomery Co., NY who moved to Lysander, Onondaga Co., NY. There were 6 sons and 3 daughters (names not stated). Known daughter, #3. LOUISA b. 1 Oct. 1821, Lysander, NY (m. Edward Clark, also see). Ref: P&BA-Len pg. 1148-9.

FOSTER, A. Rev. (See Asa Osborn)

FOSTER, ABEL was born 1769, Mass., and married there to NANCY (TUCKER). Known daughter, LAURA b. 1795, Mass. (m. David Bixby, also see). Ref: P&BA-Len pg. 1021-2.

FOSTER ASA was listed in the 1840 census index of Rollin Twp., Lenawee Co., Mich.

FOSTER, AUSTIN born ca. 1830, Ohio, and NORMAN, age 13, were listed in the 1850 census of Rollin Twp., Lenawee Co., Mich. in the Stephen Comstock household.

FOSTER, BETSEY (See Dr. R. H. Henderson)

FOSTER, CHARLES H. (See James Page)

FOSTER, CHARLOTTE born ca. 1830, NY, was listed in the 1850 census of Palmyra Twp., Lenawee Co., Mich. in the Ransom Stewart household.

FOSTER, DANIEL born ca. 1795, NY, settled in Dover Twp., Lenawee Co., Mich. in 1835. He may have lived for a time in Medina Co., Ohio. In the 1850 census of Dover Twp., Lenawee Co., Mich., wife, LOVINA, was shown age 40, born NY, and RICHMOND N., age 15; MARION, age 12; CAROLINE A., age 10; MARTIN S., age 3, all b. Mich. Note: If Lovina's age was correct, she may be a second wife, as she seems young to be the mother of some of these children. Also, HARLEY D. (following), may also be a son of Daniel. There is a DANIEL, born ca. 1819, NY, Ohio, in the 1850 census of Seneca Twp., in household of Amos Kinney, whom may relate.

FOSTER, DOLLY (See Roswell Perry)

FOSTER, EMILY Mrs. was born ca. 1809, Conn., and is listed as head of household in the 1850 census of Franklin Twp., Lenawee Co., Mich., with DANETTE, age 13, b. NY; and MARY, age 9, b. Mich., in her household.

FOSTER, HARLEY D., possibly son of DANIEL (preceding), was born ca. 1821, NY, and apparently lived for a time in Medina Co., Ohio. He came to Dover Twp., Lenawee Co., Mich. in 1835 with his parents. He married 17 Oct. 1843 to NANCY (ABBOTT), daughter of Ezra (also see). They settled in Seneca Twp. (listed there 1850 census), and at retirement moved to Clayton, Mich. Children: 1. SPENCER H. (following); 2. MARY N. (m. Joel Field, Jackson, Mich.); 3. GEORGE S. (Clayton, Mich.). Ref: P&BA-Len pg. 865-6.

FOSTER, JACOB D. born ca. 1795, and wife, PHEBE, born ca. 1795, both in NY, were listed in the 1850 census of Rollin Twp., Lenawee Co., Mich. with SARAH A., age 26; ABIGAIL J., age 24; WILLIAM P., age 18; LIBIUS H., age 16, all born NY. (possibly related to ASA, preceding?)

FOSTER, JAMES (See Samuel Lewis)

FOSTER, JOHN born ca. 1802, and wife, MARY, born ca. 1805, both in New Jersey, were listed in the 1850 census of Hudson Twp., Lenawee co., Mich. with ALBERT, age 22; SARAH J., age 20, both b. NY; and MARGARET, age 12; FRANKLIN, age 9, both b. Mich., in their household.

FOSTER, JOHN born ca. 1807, and wife, JANE, born ca. 1800, both in Ireland, were listed in the 1850 census of Rollin Twp., Lenawee Co., Mich. with JOHN M., age 17; MARIA, age 15, both b. NY; and ESTHER, age 11; DANIEL, age 8, both b. Mich., in their household. There is a DANIEL, age 30, b. Ireland, listed in the 1850 census of Rollin Twp., with no family, who may be related.

FOSTER, JOHN R. born ca. 1802, VT, and wife, CHARITY (PHILLIPS) born ca. 1807, Mass., settled first in Orleans Co., NY. About 1833, they removed to Medina Twp., Lenawee Co., Mich., and were the first to buy Government land in the township. Children: 1. JOHN REED; 2. MARY C. b. ca. 1828, NY (m. Josiah Osgood, also see); 3. CHLOE P.; 4. AUGUSTUS W.; 5. HENRY b. ca. 1837 (first white child b. in twp.; d. in Civil War, Co. D., 18th Mich. Inf.); 6. MARTHA B. b. ca. 1842; 7. GEORGE R. b. ca. 1848; 8. IRA H. Ref: P&BA-Len pg. 1040-1.

FOSTER, JOSEPH of Conn. (See Erastus Back).

FOSTER, JOSEPH W., age 30, SOPHIA C., age 22; CATHARINE, age 20; MARY, age 18; LOUISA, age 14; AMANDA, age 12, all born Ohio; and an ABIGAIL, age 46? (40?), b. Ohio, were all listed in the 1850 census of Woodstock Twp., Lenawee Co., Mich. in the household of Francis Challender.

FOSTER, L. W. (male) born ca. 1807, VT, was listed in the 1850 census of Tecumseh Twp., Lenawee Co., Mich. (may relate to SPENCER F., following).

FOSTER, LETITIA Mrs. (See Andrew Clement)

FOSTER, M. L. (See Asaph K. Porter)

FOSTER, NANCY (Mrs.) born ca. 1814, NY, was head of household in the 1850 census of Cambridge Twp., Lenawee Co., Mich. with MARY, age 4; ZACHARIAH, age 2, both b. Mich., in the household.

FOSTER, PHEBE (See Reuben N. Turner)

FOSTER, PLUMA C. (See Thomas Fox)

FOSTER, RICHARD born ca. 1783, New Hampshire, was listed in the 1850 census of Palmyra Twp., Lenawee Co., Mich. with EMELINE, age 22, b. Penn. in the household.

FOSTER, RICHARD N. born ca. 1813, and wife JANE, born ca. 1823, both in NY, were listed in the 1850 census of Hudson Twp., Lenawee Co., Mich. with MILTON, age 6; SALLY A., age 3, both b. Mich., in their household.

FOSTER, SAMUEL born 15 Apr. 1788. He lived in Schoharie Co., NY; and married POLLY (TEN EYCK). They moved to Russia, Herkimer Co., NY, where she died. He remained until 1833, then moved to Elton, Madison Co., NY, and died in 1846. Known son, ASA b. 18 Sept. 1816, Russia, NY (as a young man went to Onondaga & Wayne Cos., NY; and in 1866 moved to Blissfield Twp., Lenawee Co., Mich. No family mentioned). Ref: P&BA-Len pg. 814-5.

FOSTER, SPENCER F. born ca. 1809, VT, and wife, EUNICE, born ca. 1813, NY, were listed in the 1850 census of Tecumseh Twp., Lenawee Co., Mich. Note JOHN R. & L. W., preceding.

FOSTER, SPENCER H., son of HARLEY D. (preceding), was born 30 Oct. 1844, Dover Twp., Lenawee Co., Mich., and moved to Seneca Twp. with his parents. He married 12 Sept. 1867 to LOUISA M. (BENEDICT), daughter of Isaac (also see), and they settled in Dover Twp. About 1870, they moved to Butler Co., Kans.; and in 1874 to Ingham Co., Mich. By 1877, they lived in Clayton, Lenawee Co., Mich. Children: 1. ELLSWORTH D.; 2. FRED H.; 3. CLAIR B. Ref: P&BA-Len pg. 865-6.

FOSTER, STACY was born ca. 1831 in Mich. (note WILLIAM, following). He is listed in the 1850 census of Adrian Twp., Lenawee Co., Mich.

FOSTER, WILLIAM born ca. 1781, Conn, and wife, PHEBE, born ca. 1792, NY, were listed in the 1840 census index of Adrian Twp., Lenawee Co., Mich.; and in the 1850 census of Madison Twp. with CORDELIA, age 25, b. NY; SOPHRONA S., age 20; EMELINE, age 17, both b. Mich., in their household. Also there was Lydia Mann, age 82, b. Mass., possibly mother of Phebe??

FOWLE, ELIZABETH (See Isaac L. Kniffen)

FOWLER, A. and wife, LYDIA (GUILD), of Steuben Co., NY were parents of MARY A. b. June 1819 (m. Jairus P. Slayton, also see). Ref: P&BA-Len pg. 431-2.

FOWLER, EMILY of Steuben Co., NY married Salmon L. Haight (also see). Ref: P&BA-Len pg. 1029-30.

FOWLER, HORACE, brother of LEVI (following), settled in Cohocton, Steuben Co., NY in 1806 (per French's, Gazeteer of NY State). Horace married SUSAN (HOWE), sister of Anna (wife of LEVI). It is probably he, "from Steuben Co., NY," listed in 1836 in the early land records of Jackson Co., Mich. He was listed in the 1840 census index of Hanover, Jackson Co., Mich.

FOWLER, JOSHUA from Coshocton Co., Ohio settled in Jackson Co., Mich. ca. 1836.

FOWLER, JUSTUS[1] came from NY to Liberty Twp., Jackson Co., Mich., where he died 19 May 1858, age 90. He had known son, JUSTUS[2] (following). (There was a JUSTUS & LEVI adjacent in the 1800 census index of Onondaga Co., NY).

FOWLER, JUSTUS[2], son of JUSTUS[1] (preceding), was born 26 Mar. 1810, Fabius, Onondaga Co., NY. He moved to Liberty Twp., Jackson Co., Mich. in 1838. He married at Tully, NY in 1839 to FLORY M. (LAKE), and they settled in Liberty Twp., Jackson Co., Mich. Sons: 1. HENRY H. b. 30 Mar. 1840 (served 14th Mich. Cav., Civil War, killed at Murfreesboro, Tenn.); 2. CHARLES W. b. 17 Sept. 1842. Flory M. died 2 Dec. 1847; and

Pioneer Families of Southeastern Michigan

Justus married again on 12 Dec. 1848 to OLIVE R. (MINER), daughter of Anderson (also see). Sons: 3. CLARK R. b. 9 Dec. 1850; 4. FRANK W. b. 20 Jan. 1853. Ref: History of Jackson Co., Mich., pg. 1066.

FOWLER, LEVI born 16 June 1774; and he married ANNA (HOWE). It may be he in the 1800 census index of Onondaga Co., NY adjacent to JUSTUS. About 1836, they moved to Liberty Twp., Jackson Co., Mich., where he died in FEb. 1842, age 67. Anna went to Jonesville, Hillsdale Co., Mich. where she died at home of daughter, Martha. Children: 1. TEMPERANCE; 2. ELECTA; 3. EMELINE; 4. CAROLINE; 5. DELIA; 6. MARTHA (m. Anderson, lived Hillsdale Co.); 7. JAMES; 8. JOHN; 9. WILLIAM H. (following); 10. ABIGAIL C.; 11. THANKFUL; 12. MARY J.; 13. SALOME ANN. Ref: P&BA-Len pg. 1106-7.

FOWLER, LEVI born ca. 1803, was a native of Steuben, Oneida Co., NY. Levi prospected for land in Adrian Twp., Lenawee Co., Mich. in 1834. With wife, SALLY (IVES), born 1813, NY, they came to Lenawee Co. shortly afterwards, but returned to NY because of illness. They returned to Adrian Twp. in 1846, where he died 6 Nov. 1886, and Sally survived him. (Children listed in the 1850 census): 1. HENRY F. b. ca. 1834; 2. HORACE S. b. ca. 1836, NY; 3. ALMA M. b. ca. 1846, Mich. (m. Thomas J. Harris, also see). Ref: P&BA-Len pg. 197. Note HORACE, preceding. Also, there was a LEVI listed in the 1800 census index of Oneida Co., NY.

FOWLER, NOAH R. born ca. 1829, NY, was listed in the 1850 census of Adrian Twp., Lenawee Co., Mich. in the household of William Carroll; and with him was HANNAH, age 15, relationship not known.

FOWLER, RAYFUL born ca. 1784, Conn., and wife, HANNAH, born ca. 1792, NY, were listed in the 1850 census of Palmyra Twp., Lenawee Co., Mich. with HARRIET B., age 17; SUSANNAH?, age 15; THOMAS R., age 21, all b. NY, in their household.

FOWLER, WILLIAM H., son of LEVI (& ANNA, preceding), was born 17 Mar. 1824, Cohocton, Steuben Co., NY, and came to Jackson Co., Mich. with his parents. He married in Liberty Twp., Jackson Co. on 26 Nov. 1848 to MARY J. (ROOT), daughter of Chauncey (also see). They remained there until about 1857, then moved to Ridgeway Twp., Lenawee Co., Mich. Children: 1. IDA A.; 2. CHARLES L.; 3. EVA E. Ref: P&BA-Len pg. 1106-7.

FOX, ABRAM was listed in the 1840 census index of Palmyra Twp., Lenawee Co., Mich. with CHARLES R. listed adjacent.

FOX, ANN born ca. 1800, Mass., was head of household in the 1840 census index of Tecumseh, Lenawee Co., Mich.; and in the 1850 census of Franklin Twp. with MORRIS, age 25; and ANN, age 19, both b. Mass., in her household.

FOX, CHARLES (See Franz Joseph Mitchell)

FOX, CHARLES R. was listed in the 1840 census index of Palmyra Twp., Lenawee Co., Mich. with ABRAM listed adjacent.

FOX, FRANKLIN (See Hiram B. Abbott)

FOX, JEROME, age 11, and MYRON, age 8, both b. Mich., were listed in the household of Nathan Blanchard in Medina Twp., Lenawee Co., Mich.

FOX, MASTIN? born ca. 1823, and wife ANNA, born ca. 1826, both in NY, were listed in the 1850 census of Palmyra Twp., Lenawee Co., Mich. with THADDEUS, age 3,; SAPHRONA, age 2/12, both b. Mich., in their household.

FOX, SILAS born ca. 1805, Mass., was listed in the 1840 census index of Blissfield Twp., Lenawee Co., Mich.; and in the 1850 census of both Palmyra Twp., and Adrian Twp., with no family.

FOX, THOMAS born ca. 1823, England, and wife, PLUMA C. (FOSTER), born ca. 1830, NY, were listed in the 1850 census of Hudson Twp., Lenawee Co., Mich. with CLARISSA (CLARA) A., b. ca. 1850 (m. Henry J. Wirt, also see). Ref: P&BA-Len pg. 717-8.

FRAMPTON, MARY A. BODKIN (See Joseph Pilbeam)

FRANCISCA, ISABELLA (ROBINSON) Mrs. married in Canton, Wayne Co., NY to Adam Mott (also see).

FRANCISCO, ABIGAIL born ca. 1768, VT, was listed in the 1850 census of Adrian Twp., Lenawee Co., Mich. in the household of Samuel & Ellen Nichols.

FRANKLIN, AMOS and wife, CYNTHIA (McKINNEY) born ca. 1807, Penn., moved from Bradford Co., Penn. to Seneca Twp., Lenawee Co., Mich. in 1835. He died in 1844, and she died in 1871. There were 5 children (names not stated), but Cynthia was listed in the 1850 census of Seneca Twp. with GEORGE b. ca. 1836 (prob. he who m. Ruth Welch, dau. of James, also see; had dau., Cora Belle; Weston, Mich.); REBECCA, age 13; JULIA, age 8; BENJAMIN C. (following). Ref: P&BA-Len pg. 997.

FRANKLIN, BENJAMIN C., son of AMOS (preceding), was born 5 Nov. 1842, Seneca Twp., Lenawee Co., Mich.; and he married there on 21 Aug. 1881 to CLARA I. (NEGUS), daughter of Moses (also see) and settled in Seneca Twp. Known son, E. CLYDE. Ref: P&BA-Len pg. 997.

FRANKLIN, ELISHA was listed in the 1840 census index of Seneca Twp., Lenawee Co., Mich., adjacent to AMOS & JOHN.

FRANKLIN, JOHN (son of ELISHA??) born ca. 1812, and wife, LUCY L., born a. 1819, both in NY, are probably they listed in the 1840 census index of Seneca Twp., Lenawee Co., Mich. (adjacent to ELISHA & AMOS); and in the 1850 census (2 doors from CYNTHIA, note AMOS, preceding) with JANE, age 12; ELBRIDGE, age 10; LUTHER, age 8; SUSAN, age 5; LYDIA, age 2; ELISHA, age 1/12, all born Mich., in the household.

FRANTZ, ADA (See Josiah Osgood)

FRANTZ, PHILIP (spelled Frants) born ca. 1814, Penn., and wife, MARY, born ca. 1817, NY, were listed in the 1850 census of Tecumseh Twp., Lenawee Co., Mich. with HELEN, age 7, b. NY; and Louis Cook, age 3, b. Mich.; Sary (Sarah?) Cook, age 6, b. NY (step-children??), in the household.

FRARY, BENJAMIN born ca. 1820, Mich., and wife, JANE, born ca. 1827, NY, were listed in the 1850 census of Blissfield Twp., Lenawee Co., Mich. with ELLEN, age 3; JOHN, age 6/12, both b. Mich., in their household.

FRARY, DAVID was a "pioneer settler of Blissfield Twp., Lenawee Co., Mich.," but it may be he listed by 1840 in York, Washtenaw Co., Mich. Known daughters, MARGARET (m/1 Samuel Buck; m/2 Sewell S. Goff, see both); & LUCY b. 5 Feb. 1820, Mich. (m. Sewell S. Goff, as 2nd wife). Note, BENJAMIN & STEPHEN, possibly sons of David.

FRARY, ELISHA born ca. 1781, Mass., was listed in the 1850 census of Adrian Twp., Lenawee Co., Mich. with SUBMIT, age 35, b. VT, and MARY A., age 19, b. NY, in the household.

FRARY, NORMAN T. born ca. 1829, NY, is listed in the 1850 census of Madison Twp., Lenawee Co., Mich.

FRARY, STEPHEN born ca. 1815, and wife, LOUISA, born ca. 1820, were listed in the 1840 census index of Blissfield Twp., Lenawee Co., Mich.; and in 1850 with HENRY, age 5, b. Mich., in their household.

FRASIER see FRAZIER

FRAVER, MARGARET (See Russel Nichols)

FRAYOR, WILLIAM (See Demmon Cowen)

FRAZIER, JOHN served in the Revolutionary War, possibly from Rhode Island. He died in Middlefield, Otsego Co., NY. Known son, STEPHEN (following). Ref: P&BA-Len pg. 948-50.

FRAZIER, MARCUS L., son of SAMUEL (following), was born 11 Jan. 1826, Scriba, Oswego Co., NY; and moved with parents to Hudson Twp., Lenawee Co., Mich. He returned to NY where he married 5 May 1850 to SARAH E. (GREENE), daughter of Ambrose, also see, and also note MARTHA, following). In 1851, they moved to German Flats, Herkimer Co., NY, where they remained until 1865, then returned to Hudson Twp., Lenawee Co., Mich. Children: 1. NELSON E.; 2. MARY E.; 3. ELMER E. Ref: P&BA-Len pg. 948-50.

FRAZIER, MARTHA born 21 Feb. 1801, Schodack, Rensselaer Co., NY, married in German Flats, Herkimer Co., NY to Ambrose Greene (also see). Ref: P&BA-Len pg. 948-50. Note MARCUS L., preceding.

FRAZIER, SAMUEL, son of STEPHEN (following), was born 1802, probably Cobleskill, NY. He moved to German Flats, Herkimer Co., NY with his parents. He married LYDIA (YOUNG), daughter of Samuel (also see). They later moved to Scriba, Oswego Co., NY, and in 1833 to Royalton, Niagara Co., NY. In 1835, he prospected for land near Chicago, Ill., but returned to NY and moved his wife and 7 children (names not stated) befoe 1840 to near Salem, Washtenaw Co., Mich. In 1844, they moved to Hudson, Lenawee Co., Mich.; and about 1852 moved to Goshen, Ind. where he apparently remained. His wife, after his death, lived in Lenawee Co. for a time with son, Marcus, but died at the home of a daughter, Mrs. Coon, in Goshen, Ind. Known children (those with ages shown from 1850 census of Hudson Twp.): STEPHEN D., age 27; MARCUS L. (preceding); WILLIAM C., age 19; CLARISSA A, age 14, all b. NY; and MARIAH T., age 10; MARY A., age 8, both b. Mich. Ref: P&BA-Len pg. 948-50.

FRAZIER, STEPHEN, son of JOHN (preceding), was born in Rhode Island, and moved to Boston, Mass. He married RUTH (TORREY), daughter of John (also see) of Williamston, Mass. They may have lived for a time in New Jersey; but later lived in Cobleskill, Schoharie Co., NY; and then in 1805 moved to German Flats, Herkimer Co., NY. He died there in Mar. 1845 and she died in Jan. 1857, age 87. Known son, SAMUEL (preceding). Also note WILLIAM (following).

FRAZIER, WILLIAM (note STEPHEN, preceding) born ca. 1800, NJ, and wife, SARAH, born ca. 1808, NY, were listed in the 1850 census of Hudson Twp., Lenawee Co., Mich. with JOHN M., age 19; GEORGE M., age 18; RICHARD, age 16, all b. NY; and ELIZABETH, age 13; SARAH, age 8; WILLIAM, age 9/12, all b. Mich., in their household.

FREDERICK, ALEX is listed in the 1840 census index of Washtenaw Co., Mich.

FREDERICK, HARRIET was the daughter of a family (parents names not stated, note ALEX, preceding) who had settled at an early date near Bridgewater, Washtenaw Co., Mich.; and afterwards in Clinton Twp., Lenawee Co., Mich. where her parents died. Harriet married there 9 June 1833 to Denis Lancaster (also see). Ref: P&BA-Len pg. 662-3.

FREEMAN, ALEXANDER born ca. 1808, and wife, HANNAH M. born ca. 1820, both in NY, were listed in the 1850 census of Madison Twp., Lenawee Co., Mich. with JOHN H., age 13; HARRIET M., age 12, both b. Ohio; and CHARLES A., age 10; LUCY, age 8; ALBERT B., age 7; ALONZO, age 6; AMBROSE, age 4; ALEXANDER, age 8/12, all b. Mich., in their household.

FREEMAN, CHARLES was listed in the 1840 census index of Macon Twp., Lenawee Co., Mich.

FREEMAN, EMELINE (SMITH) Mrs. had married first to ? Freeman; and married second to Constant Rowley (also see).

FREEMAN, EMILY (See Russell Lewis)

FREEMAN HARROP (See Thomas S. Weter)

FREEMAN, JOSEPH was listed in the 1840 census index of Madison Twp., Lenawee Co., Mich.

FREEMAN, WILLIAM (son of WILLIAM who died in Attleboro, Mass. in 1804), was born 10 Mar. 1796, Attleboro. He married in 1818 to BETSEY (THAYER) of Taunton, Mass. In 1842, they removed to Palmyra Twp., Lenawee Co., Mich., where she died 5 Apr. 1848. He apparently moved before 1850 to Ogden Twp. Nine children (names not stated). Known children (those with ages from 1850 census of Ogden Twp.): 1. WILLIAM B. (BRADFORD, following); 2. GEORGE b. ca. 1828, Mass (in another household in Palmyra Twp. in 1850); 3. JULIA b. ca. 1825; 4. EDWIN N. b. ca. 1830; 5. FRANCIS E. b. ca. 1837; 6. RUEL A. b. ca. 1838, all preceding b. Mass.; and 7. SAMUEL J. b. ca. 1842, Mich. Ref: P&BA-Len pg. 668-9.

FREEMAN, WILLIAM (BRADFORD), son of WILLIAM (preceding), born ca. 1820, Mass., and wife, NANCY A., born ca. 1817, NY, were listed in the 1850 census of Ogden Twp., Lenawee Co., Mich. (next door to WILLIAM) with Phila A. Harvey, age 10?, and Nancy F. age 6, both b. Mich., in their household.

FRIEDT, MARY (See Demmon Cowen)

FRISBEE, EDWARD (See John Ladd)

Pioneer Families of Southeastern Michigan

FRISBIE, MARY (See James Whitney)

FROST, CLARENCE (See Ebenezer Fisk[3])

FROST, HIRAM, probably son of NATHAN (following), born ca. 1810, NY, and wife, NANCY, born ca. 1811, Conn., were listed in the 1850 census of Tecumseh Twp., Lenawee Co., Mich. with SAMUEL, age 7; PHILANDER, age 5; ABBY, age 2, all b. Mich., in their household (next door to NATHAN).

FROST, NATHAN born ca. 1782, Mass., was listed in the 1850 census of Tecumseh Twp., Lenawee Co., Mich., next door to HIRAM (preceding).

FROST, REBECCA born ca. 1826, NY, was listed in the 1850 census of Tecumseh Twp., Lenawee Co., Mich. in George Green household.

FROST, WILLIAM born ca. 1785, Mass., and wife, MARY, born ca. 1808, NY, were listed in the 1850 census of Tecumseh Twp., Lenawee Co., Mich. with Sarah Tompkins, age 18, b. NY in their household.

FRY, BARBARA (See Christian Schnierla)

FRY, SOPHIA born ca. 1822, Penn., was listed in the 1850 census of Medina Twp., Lenawee Co., Mich. in the Jacob Smith household.

FULLER, ALVAH and wife, SUSAN (DRURY), were natives of Herkimer Co., NY who moved to Erie Co., Penn., where they married. He died in 1855, and she died in Edinboro, Penn. in 1888, age 76. Known son, CHANCY R. (following). Ref: P&BA-Len pg. 343.

FULLER, C. C. (See John W. Allen, son of Joseph S.)

FULLER, CHANCY R., son of ALVAH (preceding), was born 15 Nov. 1834, Springfield, Erie Co., Penn. He married in Penn. on 3 July 1855 to MARY C. (FABRIQUE), daughter of Andrew (also see). They moved to Clinton, Lenawee Co., Mich. in 1861. Daughter: CLARA A. Ref: P&BA-Len pg. 343.

FULLER, CLARK B. born ca. 1819, New Hampshire, and wife, SUSANNAH, born ca. 1833, NY, were listed in the 1850 census of Franklin Twp., Lenawee Co., Mich. with NEWELL, age 5/12, b. Mich., in their household (next door to GEORGE, following; also note JARVIS, 2 doors away).

FULLER, EUNICE Mrs. born ca. 1789, Mass., was head of household in the 1850 census of Madison Twp., Lenawee Co., Mich. with JOHN, age 23; LUCY, age 20; LOUISA, age 24, all b. NY, in her household. Note: JOHN listed in the 1840 census index of Madison Twp., possibly husband of Eunice?

FULLER, GAIN, probably son of JOHN (of Mass., following), born ca. 1820, and wife, CYNTHIA, age 34, both b. NY, were listed in the 1850 census of Ogden Twp., Lenawee Co., Mich. with BYRON, age 9; GAIN, age 6; MARGARET, age 4; MARY, age 1, all b. Mich., in the household of JOHN.

FULLER, GEORGE born ca. 1808, VT, and wife, BETSEY, born ca. 1811. Rhode Island, were listed in the 1840 census index of of Franklin Twp., Lenawee Co., Mich.; and in the 1850 census with DELOS, age 8, b. Mich. in their household. Note CLARK B. & JARVIS who were listed adjacent.

FULLER, GEORGE possibly born after 1850, Franklin Twp., Lenawee Co., Mich. (See Ralph P. Baker).

FULLER, GEORGE P., age 7, born Mich., was listed in the 1850 census of Madison Twp., Lenawee Co., Mich. in the household of Rial & Mary H. Niles.

FULLER, HIRAM P. born ca. 1797, and wife, SARAH, born ca. 1808, both in NY, were listed in the 1850 census of Seneca Twp., Lenawee Co., Mich. with BULA (BEULAH?), age 21; MORRIS, age 17; RUDEE, age 14; SARAH, age 13; J---CENT (male), age 11; ACHSAH A., age 9, all b. NY; and CASH D., age 5; FRANCIS, age 2; CASSIUS M., age 4, all b. Mich., and Louisa Gould, age 25, b. NY, perhaps another daughter?

FULLER, JARVIS born ca.1808, VT, and wife, SALLY born ca. 1814, NY, were listed in the 1840 census index of Franklin Twp., Lenawee Co., Mich.; and in the 1850 census with CLARK, age 15; HARRIET, age 14; FRANCES, age 12; CHARLES, age 10; BENJAMIN, age 8; ARAFEM? (male), age 6; CYNTHIA, age 4; AMANDA, age 3; HARVY?, age 1, all b. Mich., in their household. Note GEORGE & CLARK B., preceding.

FULLER, JEFFERSON born ca. 1812, and wife, MARY A., born ca. 1818, both in NY, were listed in the 1850 census of Seneca Twp., Lenawee Co., Mich. with ARTHUR J., age 13, b. NY; JOHN J., age 11, b. Mich., and Patience Austin, age 4, b. Mich., in their household.

FULLER, JOHN born ca. 1783, Mass., and wife, MARGARET, born ca. 1787, NY, were listed in the 1850 census of Ogden Twp., Lenawee Co., Mich. with son, GAIN (preceding) & family in their household.

FULLER, JOHN born ca. 1807, and wife, BETSEY, born ca. 1804, both in NY, were listed in the 1850 census of Hudson Twp., Lenawee Co., Mich. with JOHN P., age 21; LOUISA, age 19, both b. NY, in their household.

FULLER, JOHN (See Jonathan Hare)

FULLER, JOHN, age 22, b. NY, was listed in the 1850 census of Madison Twp., Lenawee Co., Mich. Note in the household of EUNICE, may be same JOHN? Note: There was a JOHN in Madison Twp. in the 1840 census index.

FULLER, JULIA (See Henry L. Hurlburt)

FULLER, LEWIS, son of NATHANIEL, of Dutchess Co., NY, moved to Monroe Co., NY at age 24. He married there first to ? (WILLIAMS) who died 2 years later. He married second to CHLOE (LEE), daughter of Thomas (also see) of Batavia, NY. In 1835, they moved to Calhoun Co., Mich., and in 1851 to Hillsdale Co. In 1857, they moved to Lenawee Co., but returned to Hillsdale Co., where he died 27 June 1887. Known daughter, MARTHA (m. Nathaniel Lane, also see). Ref: P&BA-Len pg. 1098-1100.

FULLER, MARTIN and wife, MARTHA (LAWRENCE), were born in NY, but moved to Cramahe, Ontario, Canada before 1833, and remained there. Eleven children (names not stated, except youngest): RICHARD C. (following). Ref: P&BA-Len pg. 365-6.

FULLER, MARY J., age 18, born NY, was listed in the 1850 census of Adrian Twp., Lenawee Co., Mich. in a Spalding household.

FULLER, NATHAN was listed in the 1840 census index of Seneca Twp., Lenawee Co., Mich.

FULLER, PHILO C. was listed in the 1840 census index of Adrian Twp., Lenawee Co., Mich.

FULLER, RICHARD C., son of MARTIN (preceding), was born 16 Apr. 1833, Cramahe, Ontario, Canada. He moved to Orleans Co., NY, then to Ohio. In 1871, he moved from Toledo, Ohio to Fairfield Twp., Lenawee Co., Mich. He married first in Vigo Co., Ind. to MARY (SHOWALTER), who died in Medina Twp., Lenawee Co. in 1863. Daughter: 1. KATE M. T. (to Minneapolis, Minn.) Richard C. married again in Adrian to MARY A. (COLLINS) born in NY, who had come with her parents to Lenawee Co. in 1854. Children: 2. MARTIN A.; 3. FRANCIS A.; 4. CARRIE; 5. MARTHA; 6. ELGIN. Ref: P&BA-Len pg. 365-6.

FULLER, ROBERSON G. was listed in the 1840 census index of Ogden Twp., Lenawee Co., Mich.

FULLER, SALLY (SARAH?), age 16, and JAMES FULLER, age 15, both b. Mich., were listed in the 1850 census of Seneca Twp., Lenawee Co., Mich. in the household of Alson & Samantha Bailey. Note NATHAN, preceding.

FULLER, SAMUEL born ca. 1807, and wife, SARAH, born ca. 1811, both in NY, were listed in the 1840 census index of Macon Twp., Lenawee Co., Mich.; and in the 1850 census with ADISON H. (female?), age 20, b. NY; and HARRIET M., age 14; MARTHA S., age 10; CHARLES F., age 8; SARAH A., age 5; ATWOOD S., age 3; EMELINE, 2/12, all b. Mich., and also Martha Bliss, age 72, b. NY (possibly mother of Sarah??)

FULLER, SAMUEL H. was listed in the 1840 census index of Madison Twp., Lenawee Co., Mich.

FULLER, STEPHEN, age 17, born NY, was listed in the 1850 census of Raisin Twp., Lenawee Co., Mich. in a Horton household. FULLER, THOMAS was listed in the 1840 census index of Palmyra Twp., Lenawee Co., Mich., adjacent to WILLIAM.

FULLER, WILLIAM was listed in the 1840 census index of Palmyra Twp., Lenawee Co., Mich., adjacent to THOMAS.

FULLER, WILLIAM, age 14, b. Mich., was listed in the 1850 census of Palmyra Twp., Lenawee Co., Mich. in the household of Apollos Anthony.

FULLER, WILLIAM was listed in the 1840 census index of Fairfield Twp., Lenawee Co., Mich.

FULLER, WILLIAM, age 9, born NY, was listed in the 1850 census of Rollin Twp., Lenawee Co., Mich. in an Aldridge household.

FULLMER, ELSTEN (See Benjamin Laur)

FULTON, MARY, daughter of William (of Mass. & VT), may be "Felton." (See Russell Skeels).

FULTON, MARY (See Roderick R. Hume)

FURGUSON see FERGUSON

FURMAN, ADDIE (See Mathew H. Kerr)
FURMAN, D. J. (See Hugh Tolford)
FURMAN, MARY (See Orlando H. Alger)

- G -

GAGE, ANDREW born ca. 1817, and wife, MARY, born ca. 1821, both in NY, were listed in the 1850 census of Adrian Twp., Lenawee Co., Mich. with SOLOMON H., age 3; MARY E., age 1, both b. Mich., in their household.

GAGE, DAVID born ca. 1795, Mass., and wife, ELIZABETH, born ca. 1800, New Hampshire, was listed in the 1840 census index of Hudson Twp., Lenawee Co., Mich.; and in the 1850 census with MARIAH P., age 20, b. NY, in their household, a few doors away from DAVID (following).

GAGE, DAVID, probably son of DAVID (preceding), born ca. 1819, NH, and wife, ELOUIS A., born ca. 1820, NY, were listed in the 1850 census of Hudson Twp., Lenawee Co., Mich. with LOVEL H., age 7; CLARISSA C., age 6; FRANKLIN H., age 3; GEORGE A., age 6/12, all b. Mich., in their household.

GAGE, GILBERT born ca. 1801, NY, married ABISHA (WILBER), daughter of William (also see) possibly in Albany Co., NY. They moved to Dover Twp., Lenawee Co., Mich. by 1835. They were listed in the 1850 census of Dover Twp. with Amanda Richardson, age 41, Mary Richardson, age 16, Jeremiah Richardson, age 6, all b. NY, in their household. Note WALTER, possibly related; also note GILBERT (See Aaron Phillips).

GAGE, JOHN probably of Cheshire Co., NH, was father of SALLY born before 1800 (m. Samuel H. Thurber, also see).

GAGE, TIMOTHY born ca. 1820, and wife, MARGARET, born ca. 1820, both in NY, were listed in the 1850 census of Woodstock Twp., Lenawee Co., Mich. with NANCY, age 3, b. Mich., in the household.

GAGE, WALTER born ca. 1815, and wife, PHEBE, born ca. 1825, both in NY, were listed in the 1850 census of Dover Twp., Lenawee Co., Mich. with ANTOINETTE, age 8; SALLY A., age 4; ELIAS, age 10/12, all b. Mich., in their household. Note GILBERT, preceding.

GAHAGAN, JAMES born ca. 1802, and wife, ELLEN (DOYLE), born ca. 1810, were natives of Co. Westmeath, Ireland. They married there 13 Feb. 1829, and remained until 3 July 1834 when they sailed for New York City. They settled first in Leroy, Genesee Co., NY. About 1837, they purchased in Medina Twp., Lenawee Co., Mich.; and he returned to NY until 1837, then moved the family to Michigan. They later moved into Hudson, Mich. where she died 13 Feb. 1879, and he died 10 Mar. 1881. Children (ages from 1850 census of Medina Twp.): 1. THOMAS (following); 2. JOHN, age 18; 3. MARY, age 17; 4. JAMES, age 15; 5. ELLEN (HELEN?), age 12; 6. MARGARET, age 9; 7. PETER, age 8; 8. DANIEL A., age 7; 9. JOSEPH P., age 4; 10. MICHAEL, age 3; 11. FRANCIS, age 1. Ref: P&BA-Len pg. 903-4.

GAHAGAN, THOMAS, son of JAMES (preceding), was born in May 1830, Co. Westmeath, Ireland; and came to the US with his parents. He lived in Genesee Co., NY, and then Medina Twp., Lenawee Co., Mich. until 1855, when he went by ship to California. He remained about 6 years, then returned to Hudson Twp., Lenawee Co., Mich. He married on 5 May 1862 to MARY (BROWN), daughter of William (also see). They settled in Medina Twp. Children: 1. JOHN W.; 2. FRANCIS J.; 3. JOSEPH P.; 4. ELLEN M.; 5. JAMES F.; 6. DANIEL; 7. THOMAS E.; 8. GEORGE MOORE; 9. MARY A.; 10. WILLIAM E. Ref: P&BA-Len pg. 903-4.

GALE, I. R. (See Martin P. Stockwell)
GALE, LUCRETIA B. (See William J. Wilber)

GALLAGHER, ROSA/ROSE (See John Donnelly)

GALLAWAY, ABNER, son of STEPHEN (following), born 29 Dec. 1848, Raisin Twp., Lenawee Co., Mich., married on

Pioneer Families of Southeastern Michigan

9 Feb. 1870 to EMELINE (ASH), daughter of William (also see). Children: 1. MATTIE b. 12 Oct. 1875; 2. HARVEY b. 4 June 1886. Ref: P&BA-Len pg. 220-1.

GALLAWAY, ALMON born ca. 1816, NY, married CALISTA A. (KNOWLES), daughter of Jonathan (also see). In the 1850 census of Adrian Twp., Lenawee Co., Mich., they listed DAVID A., age 12, b. Ohio; and DUANE C., age 6, b. Mich., in their household.

GALLAWAY, D. S. (See Eliathah Stockwell)

GALLAWAY, JOHN, son of Capt. JAMES of Palmyra, Wayne Co., NY, married in Wayne Co. to ALEUDA (DRAKE). They moved ca. 1820 to near Pontiac, Oakland Co., Mich.; and by 1840 to Raisinville, Monroe Co., Mich., where they both died. Known daughter, ELIZABETH, b. 11 Aug. 1833, near Pontiac (m. Edwin A. Knowles, also see). Ref: P&BA-Len pg. 426-9.

GALLAWAY, STEPHEN, son of WILLIAM (following), was born 8 Apr. 1827, Washington Co., NY. He married on 26 Dec. 1846 to MARIA (HOAG), daughter of Abner I. (also see). Known son: ABNER (preceding). In the 1850 census of Raisin Twp., Lenawee Co., Mich., his mother, JEMIMA, age 63, born Conn., was also in his household.

GALLAWAY, THOMAS and wife, ARUBA, of Palmyra, NY were parents of HARRIET G. (m/1 ? King; m/2 Samuel E. Hart, also see). Ref: P&BA-Len pg. 290-1.

GALLAWAY, WILLIAM, (son of THOMAS born Ireland, d. Washington Co., NY), born 8 Apr. 1775, Rensselaer Co., NY, moved with parents to Washington Co., NY. He married first ELIZABETH (HAXTON) and had 3 children (names not stated); married second to MARTHA (MACOMBER) and had 9 children (names not stated); and both wives died in Washington Co., NY. He married third to JEMIMA (BOWERMAN) born 1787, Conn., and had 2 children, and only the youngest child, STEPHEN (preceding) was named in sketch. William died in Washington Co., NY; and Jemima afterwards came to Raisin Twp., Lenawee Co., Mich. where she died in Jan. 1856, age 67, at home of Stephen. Ref: P&BA-Len pg. 220-1.

GALLIGAN, BRYAN settled in Northfield, Washtenaw Co., Mich. before 1840. Known daughter, ANN (m. William M. Johnson, also see, in 1860). Ref: P&BA-Len pg. 927-31.

GALLUP, EZEKIEL born ca. 1787, VT, and wife, PERMELIA, came from Melbourne, Canada to Medina Twp., Lenawee Co., Mich. before 1840. Known daughter, PERMELIA, b. 15 Mar. 1827 (m. Richard H. Osborn, also see). Also see FREDERICK, following. In the 1850 census of Medina Twp., Ezekiel, age 63, listed a wife, REBECCA, age 57, b. Mass. In the household were ZELOTUS, age 25; WILLIAM, age 22 (probably same listed in household of Frederick); FRANKLIN, age 20; ELMAR?, age 18, all b. Canada; and MARIA S., age 17?, b. NY; NANCY E., age 13, b. Canada, and ELISHA, age 23, b. NY; Polden Golden (female), age 38, b. Canada, and Carlos Golden, age 11, b. Mich. Ref: P&BA-Len pg. 530-1. Also see GEORGE B., in household of GEORGE, following.

GALLUP, FREDERICK (probably son of EZEKIEL, preceding) born ca. 1824, Canada, and wife MARIA, born ca. 1826, NY, were listed in the 1850 census of Medina Twp., Lenawee Co., Mich. with WILLIAM, age 21, b. Canada, probably brother (listed again in household of Ezekiel), in their household.

GALLUP, GEORGE born ca. 1815, VT, and wife, ALMIRA, born ca. 1807, NH, were listed in the 1850 census of Medina Twp., Lenawee Co., Mich. with (relationship not known) GEORGE B., age 24; EDWIN, age 14; CAROLINE, age 9; HARRIET, age 8, all b. Canada; and CAMELIA, age 3, b. Mich. in their household. Note EZEKIEL, preceding.

GALLUP, MARTHA (See Richard Crego; and note that GARDNER J. & WILLIAM GALLUP settled in Columbia Twp., Jackson Co., Mich. at same time as Richard Crego.)

GALLUP, WARREN born ca. 1823, NY, and wife, MARY, born ca. 1827, Ohio, were listed in the 1850 census of Woodstock Twp., Lenawee Co., Mich. with FRANKLIN, age 4, b. Mich., in their household.

GAMBEE also see GAMBER

GAMBEE, CHARLES married EMMA (PONTIUS), daughter of Henry (also see). Note CHARLES in household of DANIEL & LYDIA, following.

GAMBEE, DANIEL was born in Penn. (possibly Berks Co., see JACOB, following); and he married first to SARAH (GAMBEE) also born Penn. They settled in Varick, Seneca Co., NY where Sarah died. Children: 1. JOHN (following); 2. GIDEON (following); 3. SUSAN; 4. DANIEL; 5. WASHINGTON; 6. WILLIAM; 7. ELIZA; 8. FRANCES; 9. GEORGE (note GIDEON, following); 10. LAVINA; 11. SARAH; 12. MARY; 13. CATHERINE. Daniel married again to LYDIA (SHIRK) and they removed to Akron, Ohio where he died. Ref: P&BA-Len pg. 726-7. *Note: In the sketch (following) note strong resemblance to this family.

GAMBEE, DANIEL and wife, LYDIA (KAISER) were born in Seneca Co., NY. In 1840, (note JACOB, following), they moved to Reed Twp., Seneca Co., Ohio, where he died 29 Mar. 1884. In 1888, she was living in Ionia, Mich. Eight children, 2 died infancy (names not stated): 1. MARY; 2. JACOB C. (following); 3. CHARLES (see preceding); 4. SARAH A.; 5. SAMUEL (note following); 6. CHRISTINA A. Ref: P&BA-Len pg. 366.

GAMBEE, DANIEL, born ca. 1824, and wife, CECILIA, born ca. 1831, both in NY, were listed in the 1850 census of Dover Twp., Lenawee Co., Mich., married within that year.

GAMBEE, GIDEON G., probably son of DANIEL & SARAH (preceding), born ca. 1819, and wife, ARMINDA, born ca. 1827, both in NY, were listed in the 1850 census of Adrian Twp., Lenawee Co., Mich. with GEORGE D., age 23, probably brother, in the household.

GAMBEE, JACOB born 11 July 1784, Berks Co., Penn., married MARY C. (GAMBER) born 26 Jan. 1791, Berks Co. They settled in Fayette, Seneca Co., NY. He died 22 Feb. 1868; and she died 9 Mar. 1865. Children: 1. MARY E.; 2. DANIEL (note preceding); 3. GEORGE; 4. Twin of George, name not stated; 5. JACOB; 6. JOHN; 7. MARY C.; 8. REBECCA; 9. JESSE; 10. SUSANNA b. 25 Apr. 1825 (m/1 Reuben Kuney; m/2 Jacob Reed, also see); 11. JOHN B.; 12. SARAH A. Ref: P&BA-Len pg. 845-6.

GAMBEE, JACOB C., son of DANIEL & LYDIA (preceding), was born 30 Nov. 1838, Seneca Co., NY. He moved to

Ohio with his parents, and served in the Civil War first in Hoffman's Battalion, and then in Co. D., 128th Ohio Inf. In April 1866, he moved to Lenawee Co., and married on 31 Dec. 1868 in Dover Twp. to DEBORAH (SUTTON), daughter of Pharis (also see). No children listed in sketch. Ref: P&BA-Len pg. 366.

GAMBEE, JOHN, son of DANIEL & SARAH (preceding), was born 25 Dec. 1816, Varick, NY; and married in Fayette on 4 Jan. 1849 to SARAH (PONTIUS), daughter of Henry (also see). He visited Michiggan in 1853, and the following Spring moved his family to Dover Twp., Lenawee Co. Only child: EDWIN P. (m. Ella Hoxter, dau. of Hezekiah, also see). Ref: P&BA-Len pg. 726-7.

GAMBEE, SAMUEL born ca. 1813, and wife, MARY, born ca. 1814, both in Penn., were listed in the 1850 census of Medina Twp., Lenawee Co., Mich. with LUCINDA, age 17, b. Penn.; and HANNAH, age 14; SUSANNAH, age 12; MARY, age 10; SARAH A., age 9; WILLIAM L., age 8, all born Ohio; and ERASTUS, age 4, b. Mich., in their household. Note DANIEL & LYDIA, preceding.

GAMBEE, SAMUEL B. (See Alonzo Teachout)

GAMBER also see GAMBEE

GAMBER, JOHN and wife, ELIZABETH (WARNER), were natives of Penn. who moved to Seneca Co., NY. Children: 1. HENRY; 2. MARGARET; 3. ELIZABETH; 4. SARAH; 5. MARY A. b. ca. 1816 (m. Christian Kuney, also see); 6. JOHN; 7. GEORGE. Ref: P&BA-Len pg. 420-1.

GAMBER, MARY (See Jacob Gambee)

GAMBLE, MARGARET (See David Service)

GAMBOL, FREDERICK (See Joseph W. Gray)

GAMBY see GAMBEE

GANDER, DAVID born 1818, Franklin Co., Ohio, married 26 May 1842, Putnam Co., Ohio to SUSANNAH (HAMPSHIRE) daughter of John (also see). They remained there for a time, then moved to Allen Co., Ohio; and in 1866 removed to Madison Twp., Lenawee Co., Mich. He died 7 July 1880. Eleven children, of whom 8 survived in 1888 (names of deceased not stated): 1. MARTHA E. (m. Ebenezer Hunt, Cherokee Co., KS); 2. LOUISA (m. Edward Reed, Madison Twp.); 3. SAMUEL (m. Irene Childs, Madison Twp.); 4. PETER W. (m. Sophia Saunders, Dover Twp.); 5. SAMANTHA (m. Lucius F. Allis, also see, Madison Twp.); 6. MARIA E.; 7. DOROTHY E. (m. George F. Smith, Dover Twp.); 8. ANNIE A. Ref: P&BA-Len pg. 457-8.

GANNON, HANNAH (See Garrett Tenbrook)

GANUN (sometimes called GANUNG & spelled GANOUNG in census; the spelling GANONG/GENUNG was prevalent in Dutchess Co., NY.)

GANUN, ADDISON, son of NATHAN (following), born 3 Mar. 1861. He moved with parents to Palmyra Twp., Lenawee Co., Mich. He married CLARA (BANCROFT) and settled in Blissfield Twp., Lenawee Co. Children: 1. WILLIAM L.; 2. ETHEL; 3. ELEAZER H. Ref: P&BA-Len pg. 321-2.

GANUN, FRANCIS L., son of NATHAN (following), married CARRIE S. (DEAN) and lived in Blissfield Twp., Lenawee Co., Mich. Children: 1. MABEL L.; 2. LILLIE M.; 3. OLIVER D.; 4. ELSIE. Ref: P&BA-Len pg. 321-2.

GANUN, LEWIS, son of JEREMIAH, was born in Putnam Co., NY. He married MARY Z. (KNIFFIN), and they moved after a few years to Fairfield Co., Conn. where they lived out their lives. Children: 1. BELINDA (twin of following); 2. EMELINDA (m. Newman Worden, Fairfield, Conn.); 3. NATHAN (following); 4. NEWMAN. Ref: P&BA-Len pg. 321-2.

GANUN, NATHAN, son of LEWIS (preceding), was born 15 Sept. 1838 in Putnam Co., NY. He married in Westchester Co., NY on 23 Dec. 1857 to JANE A. (REYNOLDS) born 16 Feb. 1837. They later moved to Berea, Ohio; and then in 1866 to Palmyra Twp., Lenawee Co., Mich. Children: 1. FRANCIS L. (preceding); 2. ADDISON (preceding); 3. NEWMAN J. b. 7 Mar. 1863 (m. Ella Jones); 4. MALVINA A. b. 7 July 1865. Ref: P&BA-Len pg. 321-2.

GANUN, PERSES (spelled Ganoung) born ca. 1799, and wife, SUSANNE, born ca. 1806, both in NY, were listed in the 1850 census of Macon Twp., Lenawee Co., Mich. with MARTHA, age 14; MARY, age 12; SARAH, age 10; PHEBE, age 8; ISAAC, age 5, all born NY, and Adams Marshall, age 20, b. NY, in their household.

GARDNER, ASA born ca. 1802, NY, and wife, LYDIA, born ca. 1801, Mass., were listed in the 1850 census of Tecumseh Twp., Lenawee Co., Mich. with LYDIA, age 51, b. NY; and LYDIA A., age 23, b. NY, in their household.

GARDNER, DAVID? married ELIZABETH (SOOP), daughter of Abram & Maria of the Mohawk Valley of New York. They apparently went to Madison, Wisc., as nephew, Abram Wing (also see), son of William & Maria (Soop) Wing, lived there with them in 1850. Ref: P&BA-Len pg. 1156-7.

GARDNER, DAVID born ca. 1818, Ireland, and wife, SARAH, born ca. 1809, NY, were listed in the 1850 census of Medina Twp., Lenawee Co., Mich. with JULIA, age 6; GERSHOM B., age 1, b. Mich. in their household.

GARDNER, ELSIE born 1799, NY, married in Herkimer Co., NY to ? Jones (See James J. Jones). Ref: P&BA-Len pg. 995-6. Note DAVID, preceding, as Herkimer Co. was part of Mohawk Valley of NY.

GARDNER, JOHN born Conn., died in Syracuse, NY. His wife (name not stated) died in Owego, Tioga Co., NY. Known daughter ROWENA (m. before 1820, Skaneateles, Onondaga Co., NY to Horace Munn, also see). Ref: P&BA-Len pg. 1057-8.

GARDNER, JOHN born ca. 1806, and wife, MARY, born ca. 1820, both in Penn., were listed in the 1850 census of Seneca Twp., Lenawee Co., Mich. with WILLIAM, age 16; JOSEPHINE, age 9; WASHINGTON, age 7, all b. Penn., in their household.

GARDNER, JOHN S., age 25, b. NY, was listed in the 1850 census of Fairfield Twp., Lenawee Co., Mich. in a Baker household.

GARDNER, LOUISA (See Cyrenus Sanford)

GARDNER, POLLY "MARY?" (See Andrew Pletcher)

GARDNER, ROBERT and wife, MARGARET (CRAWFORD), first lived in Columbia, Penn., and then moved to Lycoming Co. Later they moved to Williams

Pioneer Families of Southeastern Michigan

Co., Ohio. Four sons and 5 daughters (names not stated, except): #6. RACHEL b. 2 Apr. 1817, Columbia Co., Penn. (m. Aaron Whitacre, also see). Ref: P&BA-Len pg. 476-7.

GARDNER, THOMAS C. born ca. 1820, and SARAH A., born ca. 1810, both in NY, were listed in the 1850 census of Adrian Twp., Lenawee Co., Mich. with CLEANTHA E., age 7; SARAH A., age 5; HAMLINE J., age 3; RHODA, age 8/12, all b. Mich., in their household.

GARLIC also see GARLICK
GARLIC, LUCY (See Benjamin Colegrove; and also note HORACE GARLICK, following)

GARLICK see GARLIC, preceding.
GARLICK, BENJAMIN born ca. 1818, and wife, MARY J., born ca. 1832, both in NY, were listed in the 1850 census of Seneca Twp., Lenawee Co., Mich. with DEWIT C., age 5, b. Mich., in their household.

GARLICK, ELI of Lanesboro, Mass. had known daughter, HARRIET, born 18 Apr. 1824 (m. there Stephen M. Mead^8, also see). Ref: P&BA-Len pg. 941-2.

GARLICK, HORACE born ca. 1807, and wife, OLIVE, born ca. 1800, both in NY, were listed in the 1850 census of Medina Twp., Lenawee Co., Mich. with LUCY A., age 14; OLIVE A., age 12, both b. Mich., in their household. Also in the household was Charles Blanchard (also see), age 16, a "nephew."

GARLICK, LAMON? W. born ca. 1815, Conn., and wife, ANNA, born ca. 1816, NY, were listed in the 1850 census of Adrian Twp., Lenawee Co., Mich. with HENRY, age 13; AMELIA M., age 10; DANIEL, age 8, all b. NY; and ADELBERT, age 4/12, b. Mich., in their household.

GARLING, GEORGE^1 was born in Germany, and married there to BARBARY (MILLER). About 1827, after the birth of 4 children, they came to the US, and settled first in Pennsylvania. He died there in 1845; and she died in NY. Children: 1. LENA; 2. GEORGE (following); 3. PHILLIP; 4. FREDERICK; 5. LUCY; 6. JOHN; 7. HENRY; 8. ELIZA; & 2 died infancy (names not stated). Ref: P&BA-Len pg. 1026-7.

GARLING, GEORGE^2, son of GEORGE^1 (preceding), was born 28 Jan. 1820, Germany, and came to the US with his parents. He moved from Pennsylvania to New York where he married in 1851 to LAVINA (ACKER), daughter of Jacob (also see) in Seneca Co., NY. In 1854, they moved to Medina Twp., Lenawee Co., Mich. Children: 1. WILLIAM P. (m. Esther Scott, Medina Twp., children, Olivia & GArtha); 2. JACOB H. (d. age 3); 3. IDA E. (m. Abel L. Perry, son of Charles, also see); 4. GEORGE W. (m. Mary Lance, Medina Twp.); 5. ELMER E. Ref: P&BA-Len pg. 453.

GARLOCK see GARLICK

GARNSEY, J. H. (See Robert G. Marshall)
GARNSEY, SQUIRE (See Charles Ford^4)

GARWOOD, JOSEPH married in Seneca Co., Ohio to FANNY (FISER), daughter of Michael (also see). Two children (names not stated) died infancy. After the death of Joseph, Fanny married again to Edwin Smith (also see) as his 3rd wife. Ref: P&BA-Len pg. 430-1.

GASTEN also see GASTON
GASTEN, ANNIE (See William Gregg)

GASTON also see GASTEN, preceding.
GASTON, HENRY born ca. 1802, and wife, MARY, born ca. 1804, both in Mass., were listed in the 1850 census of Woodstock Twp., Lenawee Co., Mich. with GEORGE, age 18, b. NY; and LOISA, age 15; ALVIRA, age 13, both b. Mass., in their household.

GATES, ALVAH born ca. 1794, Conn., and wife, MARTHA, born ca. 1796, Mass. were listed in the 1850 census of Tecumseh Twp., Lenawee Co., Mich. with ALMIRA, age 9; GEORGE, age 6; ANNA, age 4; MARTHA, age 1, all b. Mich., in their household (possibly grandchildren?).

GATES, AMOS M., born ca. 1798, NY, and wife, SOPHIA, born ca. 1804, NJ, were listed in the 1850 census of Rollin Twp., Lenawee Co., Mich. with DELOSS, age 21; ARAMANTHA, age 17, both b. NY; and GEORGE L., age 6, b. Mich., in their household. Note: Sophia is probably a second wife, and was the widow of George Hines (also see), as also in the household were children Jane Hines, age 16, b. NJ; and Susan Hines, age 14, b. NY. Therefore she is not the mother of the first two Gates children listed.

GATES, GEHIAL (JEHIEL?) born ca. 1814, VT, and wife, ADALINE, born ca. 1821, NH, were listed in the 1850 census of Adrian Twp., Lenawee Co., Mich. with LENORA, age 9, born Mich., in their household.

GATES, HENRY C. was listed in the 1840 census index of Rome Twp., Lenawee Co., Mich.

GATES, JOHN born ca. 1819, NY, and wife MARTHA (WILSEY), daughter of Jeremiah^2 (also see) born ca. 1825, Troy, Bradford Co., Penn., were listed in the 1850 census of Tecumseh Twp., Lenawee Co., Mich. with CHARLOTTE, age 60, (mother of John?), born NY, in their household.

GATES, LOVISA (See Pliny Fisher)
GATES, PRISCILLA (See Judah Back)

GAUMER, CHARLES (See William Service)

GEDDES, JAMES^1 came from Scotland to Pennsylvania in 1752. He had 3 known sons: PAUL; WILLIAM; & SAMUEL. Son, PAUL^2 had known daughter, ELIZABETH^3; and son, SAMUEL^2 had son, SAMUEL^3 (following) who married cousin, ELIZABETH^3. Ref: P&BA-Len pg. 1030-1

GEDDES, NORMAN^4 Judge, son of SAMUEL^3 (following), was born 14 Apr. 1823, Livonia, Livingston Co., NY, and came to Michigan with his parents. He married 9 Oct. 1848 to LAURA E. (CASEY), daughter of Lyman (also see) of York, Livingston Co., NY. They settled in Madison Twp., Lenawee Co., Mich. She died 21 Apr. 1851, leaving a son: 1. FREDERICK L. Norman married again to HARRIET D. (BARBER), daughter of John (also see). She died 30 Apr. 1857, leaving children: 2. HERBERT (to Colorado); 3. HARRIET E. (m. W. N. VanBrunt, Adrian). Norman married third on 15 Sept. 1859 to JANE M. (TERRY), daughter of Isaac of

Royalton, Niagara Co., NY. Children: 4. ADA (d. 1 Apr. 1864, age 4); 5. CLIFTON b. ca. 1868. Ref: P&BA-Len pg. 1030-1.

GEDDES, PAUL[4], possibly son of SAMUEL[3] (following), was listed in the 1840 census index of Cambridge Twp., Lenawee Co., Mich. adjacent to SAMUEL[3].

GEDDES, SAMUEL[3], son of SAMUEL[2] (See JAMES[1], preceding), was born in Penn., and married 7 Oct. 1802 in Northumberland Co. to his cousin, ELIZABETH[3], daughter of PAUL[2] (See JAMES[1], preceding). They moved to Livonia, Livingston Co., NY before 1818; and to Niagara Co., NY ca. 1833. In 1835, they moved to Cambridge Twp., Lenawee Co., Mich. He died there in 1848, and she died in 1865. Elizabeth, age 71, born Penn., was head of household in the 1850 census of Cambridge Twp., with JAMES, age 41, b. Penn.; and WILLIAM (& wife, following) in her household. Also had known sons, NORMAN[4] and probably PAUL[4], preceding.

GEDDES, WILLIAM[4], son of SAMUEL[3] (preceding), born ca. 1818, NY, and wife, CAROLINE, born ca. 1816, were listed in the household of mother, ELIZABETH, in the 1850 census of Cambridge Twp., Lenawee Co., Mich. Anna E. Wickham was said to have made her home with William & Caroline ca. 1866.

GEHRIG, GEORGE came to the US from Switzerland in 1848, and he eventually settled in Morenci, Mich. Known daughter, SUSAN, born ca. 1843, Switzerland (m. Andrew Stephenson, also see, as 2nd wife in 1877). Ref: P&BA-Len pg. 861-2.

GEHRINGER see GERINGER

GELISPA also see GILLESPIE
GELISPA, ELIZA, age 22, b. NY, was listed in the 1850 census of Madison Twp., Lenawee Co., Mich.

GEORGE, ABRAHAM and wife, CATHARINE (DORMOYER), had known daughter, CATHARINE A. (m/1 Gideon Hulbon; and m/2 after 1865 to John A. Baer, see both, in Medina Twp., Lenawee Co., Mich.) Ref: P&BA-Len pg. 841-2.
GEORGE, EUNICE (See John Lester)
GEORGE, HARVEY born ca. 1824, NH, was listed in the 1850 census of Rollin Twp., Lenawee Co., Mich.
GEORGE, MERIBAH (See Simeon Root[2])
GEORGE, MILES (written "Georgia?") born ca. 1784, Conn., and wife, LETTE?, born ca. 1791, NY, were listed in the 1850 census of Rollin Twp., Lenawee Co., Mich.
GEORGE, MILLAR (prob. b. after 1860, see McKinzey Seeley).
GEORGE, R. R. (See Stephen Bugbee)
GEORGE, REUBEN married CLARA (FARST), daughter of Isaac (also see) born 1 Oct. 1844. Known son, FRANK (may have gone to Dodge City, KS). After Reuben's death, Clara married again to William Connery (also see). Ref: P&BA-Len pg. 997-8.

GEORGIA see GEORGE

GERINGER, MARY A. (See John C. Odell)

GERWELL, NANCY (See George Wolf)

GETTY, ELIZA b. ca. 1820, Ireland, married there to William Anderson (also see).
GETTY, JAMES and wife, MATTIE M., natives of Ireland, settled in Ridgeway Twp., Lenawee Co., Mich., where she died. He afterwards moved to Deerfield Twp. Known daughter, ELIZA J. (m. William Underwood, also see, who was b. 8 Aug. 1843).

GETTZ, JOHN married MAGGIE (BELAND), daughter of John[2] (also see) born ca. 1855. They moved to Saginaw, Mich. She died 28 Aug. 1884. Children: 1. FREDERICK; 2. HENRY. Ref: P&BA-Len pg. 658-9.

GIBBS, ALPHONSO T. born ca. 1812, NY, and wife, MARY, born ca. 1815, England, were listed in the 1840 census index of Cambridge Twp., Lenawee Co., Mich.; and in the 1850 census of Woodstock Twp. with WILLIAM, age 13, b. NY; and JOHN, age 9; ROBERT, age 6, both b. Mich., in their household.
GIBBS, ELINDA, age 26, b. NY, was listed in the 1850 census of Adrian Twp., Lenawee Co., Mich.
GIBBS, JAMES H. born ca. 1816, and wife, LOUISA, born ca. 1815, both in NY, were listed in the 1850 census of Cambridge Twp., Lenawee Co., Mich. with JAMES, age 7; THOMAS, age 5, both b. Mich., in their household.
GIBBS, JULIUS was listed in the 1840 census index of Palmyra Twp., Lenawee Co., Mich. adjacent to NATHAN (following).
GIBBS, NATHAN born ca. 1799, VT, and wife, ANNA, born ca. 1807, NY, were listed in the 1840 census index of Palmyra Twp., Lenawee Co., Mich.; and in the 1850 with MARTHA, age 13; GAINS, age 5, both b. Mich., and Sarah A. Ranger, age 23, b. NY, and dittoed after her CLARISSA H., age 2, b. Mich., either "Ranger" or "Gibbs?" Note: JULIUS was adjacent in 1840 census.
GIBBS, ROXEY M., age 1, b. Mich., was listed in the 1850 census of Adrian Twp., Lenawee Co., Mich. in a Collar household.
GIBBS, SILAS H. born ca. 1822, and wife, ADELINE, born ca. 1827, both in NY, were listed in the 1850 census of Palmyra Twp., Lenawee Co., Mich. with SARAH M., age 2; SOLOMON J., age 1, both b. Mich., and Henry Worden, age 5, (stepchild?), b. Mich., in their household.
GIBBS, THOMAS of Sylvania, Lucas Co., Ohio was the father of the following known children: WILLIAM H. (m. Millie R. Chandler, dau. of George F.); JULIA (m. Albert R. Chandler, son of George F., also see). Ref: P&BA-Len pg. 389-90.

GIBSON, CHARLES, age 22, born NY, was listed in the 1850 census of Hudson Twp., Lenawee Co., Mich. in a Leisering household.
GIBSON, JANE (See George Exelby[2])
GIBSON, MARGARETTA (See Lyman A. Curtiss)
GIBSON, MARY (See John Hamilton)
GIBSON, MARYETTE (See Francis Hawley)

GIDLEY, R. G. (See Amos R. Crane)

GIFFORD, BYRON born ca. 1821, and wife, HARRIET, born ca. 1829, both in NY. were listed in the 1850 census of Medina Twp., Lenawee Co., Mich. with FOSTER A.,

Pioneer Families of Southeastern Michigan 137

age 7; AMERIGO?, age 5; GEORGE, age 2, all b. NY, in their household.

GIFFORD, GEORGE E., probably son of STEPHEN (following), born ca. 1815, NY, and wife, SARAH, born ca. 1816, NJ, were listed in the 1850 census of Ridgeway Twp., Lenawee Co., Mich. with HENRY, age 5, b. Ind.; and JOHN, age 3; GEORGE W., age 1, both b. Mich., in their household.

GIFFORD, LAURA (See Moses Plues)

GIFFORD, LINAS born ca. 1810, and wife, ANNA, born ca. 1807, both in NY, were listed in the 1850 census of Blissfield Twp., Lenawee Co., Mich. with LEVI?, age 17, b. NY; and CHARLES, age 12; ELIZA A., age 10; EMILY, age 8; MARTHA, age 2; JAMES, age 1, all b. Mich., in their household. Note: It is probably he listed in the 1840 census index of Dundee Twp., Monroe Co., Mich. adjacent to a HENRY & JEREMIAH L.

GIFFORD, LUCY, age 16, b. NY, was listed in the 1850 census of Madison Twp., Lenawee Co., Mich. May be she in household of STEPHEN, following.

GIFFORD, STEPHEN was listed in the 1840 census index of Macon Twp., Lenawee Co., Mich.; and in the 1850 census of Ridgewa Twp., age 59, born Conn., and wife, ABIGAIL, age 56, born Mass., with ELISHA, age 18; LUCY A., age 15, both b. NY; and listed next door is GEORGE E. (preceding) and family.

GILBERT, CHARLES B. born ca. 1810, Conn., was listed in the 150 census of Rome Twp., Lenawee Co., Mich. with JOHN R., age 5; EDGAR M., age 3, both b. NY, in his household.

GILBERT, ELIAS[1] was a Revolutionary soldier from Conn., and he married twice (wives' names not stated). He had 9 children by second marriage, but only eldest son, ELIAS[2] (following) was named in sketch. Elias[1] went to Davenport, Iowa with Elias[2], and died there at age 95. Ref: P&BA-Len pg. 694-5.

GILBERT, ELIAS[2], son of ELIAS[1] (preceding), was born 29 Nov. 1776, Hartford, Conn., and married there to POLLY (STEELE) who was born there in 1781. They removed to Richmond, Ontario Co., NY, where she died at age 34, leaving children: 1. POLLY; 2. AMANDA; 3. MARIETTA; 4. WARREN (following). ELIAS[2] apparently married again (name of wife not known) and had children: 5. THEODOSIA; 6. ANN E. Ref: P&BA-Len pg. 694-5.

GILBERT, FRANK W. (See William B. White)

GILBERT, FREDERICK born ca. 1811, and wife CHRISTANY, born ca. 1810, both in Germany, were listed in the 1850 census of Madison Twp., Lenawee Co., Mich. with FREDERICK, age 13, b. Maryland; and JOHN, age 9; WILLIAM, age 6; MARGARET, age 2; MICHAEL, age 1/12, all b. Mich., in their household.

GILBERT, GEORGE and wife, SUSAN, of Tecumseh Twp., Lenawee Co., Mich. had known daughter, LOUISA M. born 9 July 1844 (m. Burton S. Barnes, also see). Ref: P&BA-Len pg. 429-30.

GILBERT, JAMES born ca. 1810, and wife, MARY, born ca. 1803, both in England, were listed in the 1850 census of Blissfield Twp., Lenawee Co., Mich. with CATHARINE, age 14; WILLIAM, age 11, both b. Canada, and another WILLIAM, age 1/12, b. Mich., in the household. Note MARY J., following.

GILBERT, LUCINDA born ca. 1815; died in Sandusky, Ohio in 1847, age 32. (See William Lagore; and note TRUMAN, following.)

GILBERT, LUCRETIA H., age 17; WALTER, age 12; MARY, age 7, were listed in the 1850 census of Hudson Twp., Lenawee Co., Mich. in the Bradley Harrington household.

GILBERT, MARY J. born ca. 1831, England, was listed in the 1850 census of Adrian Twp., Lenawee Co., Mich. in the household of Phineas & Susan F. Peck (also see).

GILBERT, SALLY "SARAH?" (See John Wooldridge)

GILBERT, SARAH Mrs., age 60, born NY, was head of household in the 1850 census of Ogden Twp., with WILLIAM, age 22, b. NY listed.

GILBERT, THERON C. was listed in the 1840 census index of Cambridge Twp., Lenawee Co., Mich.

GILBERT, TRUMAN, born in Conn., was the son of a man (name not stated) who came from England and died in Conn. Truman removed to Ohio, where he married JANE (McKELVEY). He died in Sandusky, Ohio at age 79, and she had died at age 44. Nine children, names not stated, except: WARREN (following). Ref: P&BA-Len pg. 553-4.

GILBERT, WARREN, son of TRUMAN (preceding), born 1 Sept. 1821, Greenfield Twp., Huron Co., Ohio, married MINERVA (ROOT), daughter of Simeon[2] (also see). They settled in Rome Twp., Lenawee Co., Mich. by 1859. Children: 1. ADELBERT W. b. 8 Jan. 1845 (d. infant); 2. FRANK S. b. 1 Nov. 1847 (m. Isabella Nye, Cleveland, O.); 3. AUSTIN B. b. 6 May 1849 (m. Emma Sanders, Saginaw, Mich.); 4. CHARLES W. b. 21 Dec. 1851 (m. Esther McMath, dau. of Fleming, also see). Ref: P&BA-Len gp. 553-4.

GILBERT, WARREN[2], son of ELIAS[2] (preceding), was born 3 Apr. 1822, Richmond, Ontario Co., NY. He came to Michigan in 1843, and lived Grand River, Clinton Co., Mich. before moving to Rome Twp., Lenawee Co. (by 1850). He married in 1845 to ALMIRA M. (REED), daughter of Wheeler (also see). Children: 1. WILLIAM GOODELL b. 18 Apr. 1846 (m. Albina Eddy; he d. 26 Mar. 1884); 2. THEODOSIA (EMILY T.) b. ca. 1849 (m. William M. Sheppard, also see); 3. FRANK W. (m. Mary White, dau. of Wm., Rome Twp.). Ref: P&BA-Len pg. 694-5.

GILE also see GILES

GILE, JUDA (See Henry Green[1])

GILES, ? General, had known daughter, LOUISA (m. 1826 in Mich. to Jacob Lane, also see, settled in Blissfield Twp., Lenawee Co., Mich. Note GEORGE, following).

GILES, GEORGE was listed in the 1830 census of Lenawee Co., Mich. Territoy, written as "Gile." He counted males: 2 under 5; 1 5-10; 1 15-20; 1 20-30; 1 40-50; and females: 1 10-15 & 1 30-40. It is probably he in the 1840 census index of Blissfield Twp., Lenawee Co., Mich. Probably his family were GEORGE (head of household) born ca. 1817, DANIEL born ca. 1829, LUCINDA F., born ca. 1834, all b. Mich. in the 1850 census of Blissfield Twp., Lenawee Co., Mich. JAMES, JOHN & WILLIAM, following, probably also related.

GILES, JAMES was listed in the 1840 census index of Blissfield Twp., Lenawee Co., Mich. adjacent to GEORGE.

GILES, JOHN born ca. 1810, and wife, HARRIET, born ca. 1815, both in NY, were listed in the 1850 census of Blissfield Twp., Lenawee Co., Mich. with HARRIET, age 10; EDGAR, age 7; DANIEL, age 3. all b. NY, in their househod.

GILES, WILLIAM G. born ca. 1821, Mich., and wife, PERMELIA, born ca. 1825, NY, were listed in the 1850 census of Blissfield Twp., Lenawee Co., Mich. with WILLIAM A., age 7; CHARLES H., age 4, both b. Mich., in their household.

GILLIAND, JAMES (See Erastus Brockway)

GILLESPIE also see GELISPA

GILLESPIE, BROWN[1] came from the North of Ireland as a young man with his family and settled in Steuben Co., NY, where he remained. Known son, RICHARD B.[2] (following). Ref: P&BA-Len pg. 1123-4.

GILLESPIE, CORNELIUS and wife, MARY (THOMPSON), of Argyle, Washington Co., NY had a known daughter, ELEANOR b. ca. 1782, Argyle, NY (m. George Ferguson, also see). Ref: P&BA-Len pg. 635-6.

GILLESPIE, CORNELIUS was listed in the 1840 census index of Stockbridge Twp., Ingham Co., Mich.

GILLESPIE, RICHARD B.[2] Maj., son of BROWN[1] (preceding), was born ca. 1792 (sketch says b. Steuben Co., NY, and census b. Ireland). He married first to MARGARET (GRAY) and settled in Livingston Co., NY. He served in the War of 1812. Margaret died there leaving children: 1. MARIA; 2. JANE. Richard B. married again to CLARINDA (ROBERTS) born ca. 1808, NY. They moved by 1835 to Clinton Twp., Lenawee Co., Mich. He died 16 June 1870; and she died 1 July 1880, age 70? Children: 3. MARGARET b. 22 Mar. 1820, Sparta, Livingston Co., NY (m. I. H. Schreder, also see); 4. GUSTAVUS b. ca. 1830, NY; 5. JOHN b. ca. 1832; 6. ANN b. ca. 1833; 7. RICHARD B. (following); 8. WILLIAM b. ca. 1838. Ref: P&BA-Len pg. 227-8 & 1123-4.

GILLESPIE, RICHARD B.[3], son of RICHARD B.[2] (preceding), was born 29 Dec. 1835, Clinton Twp., Lenawee Co., Mich. He married first on 23 Dec. 1864 to MARTHA (BIDDLE) born 1841, Macon Twp (Note: There is a Gerhsom Bidwell in the 1850 census of Tecumseh Twp., with a daughter, Martha, age 6). They resided for 2 years in Raisin Twp., and then settled in Clinton Twp. She died 10 Oct. 1868, and had a child (name not stated) that preceded her. Richard B. married again to LUCY A. (RECTOR), daughter of John I. (also see); and had children: 1. GARLAND R.; 2. GRACE E.; 3. ORA B.; 4. JENNIE P. Ref: P&BA-Len pg. 1123-4.

GILLETT also see GILLETTE

GILLETT, AUSTIN, son of JOHN (following), born 1 Jan. 1816, Auburn, Cayuga Co., NY, came to Rome Twp., Lenawee Co., Mich. in 1838; and he married on 11 Oct. 1846 to ELIZA (VAN AUKEN), daughter of Lewis (also see) of Washtenaw Co., Mich. In May 1872, they moved to Adrian, Mich. In the 1850 census, they listed (relationship not known) JULIAN F., age 5; and they had known daughter, EMMA J. Ref: P&BA-Len pg. 486-7.

GILLETT, CORNELIA A., age 22, b. NY, was listed in the 1850 census of Hudson Twp., Lenawee Co., Mich.

GILLETT, DANIEL born ca. 1806, NY, was listed as head of household in the 1850 census of Tecumseh Twp., Lenawee Co., Mich. with the family of Nancy Badger listed in his household. A few doors away, in the household of Plinny Field, is HARRIET, age 42, b. NY, apparently "Insane," and possibly daughter of Plinny? She may relate to Daniel?

GILLETT, JOHN born in Conn., moved as a young man to NY where he married LOIS (GRIFFIN). They settled first in Cayuga Co., NY; and later moved to Monroe Co., Mich. (it may be they in the 1840 census index of Summerfield, Monroe Co.) Children: 1. DANIEL; 2. JOHN; 3. GILBERT (possibly he in Madison Twp., Lenawee Co. in 1840 census index); 4. ELECTA b. 1811, Sempronius, NY (m. Theodore Abbott, also see); 5. LUCY; 6. AUSTIN (preceding); 7. EPHRAIM; 8. CHAUNCEY; 9. BENJAMIN G.; 10. DEWITT C. Ref: P&BA-Len pg. 486-7.

GILLETT, LUCRETIA (See Dudley Worden)
GILLETT, MARY (See Nathaniel K. Bowen)
GILLETT, ZILPHA (See Anson Carter)

GILLETTE also see GILLETT, preceding.
GILLETTE, ASA of Litchfield, Conn. had known daughter, SARAH (m. Isaac Baldwin, also see). Ref: P&BA-Len pg. 628-9.

GILLETTE, PETER (See Joseph Atkinson Thompson)

GILLIS, ANNA (See Anthony McCurran)

GILMAN, COMFORT born ca. 1782, New Hampshire (See David Chandler).

GILMORE, ASA was born ca. 1802, Mass., and it is probably he listed in the 1830 census of Lenawee Co., Michigan Territory; and in the 1840 census index of Tecumseh Twp. In the 1850 census, there was a wife, SUSAN, age 40, b. NY; and ADDISON, age 19; HENRY, age 16; LUCY M., age 12 (m. Joel Carpenter, also see); JOSEPH, age 10; AUGUSTINA, age 6, all born Mich. Susan may not have been the mother of these children, as also listed in the household was Elizabeth Lacock, age 10, daughter of Henry & Susan Lacock (also see); so Susan was probably widow of Henry.

GILMORE, CALVIN was listed in the 1840 census index of York Twp., Washtenaw Co., Mich. adjacent to LYMAN & ROBERT, following.

GILMORE, CHARLES H. born ca. 1815, VT, and wife, RUTH A., born ca. 1820, Mass., were listed in the 1840 census index of Blissfield Twp., Lenawee Co., Mich.; and in the 1850 census with CHARLES, age 9; ARTHUR, age 3, both b. Mich., in their household.

GILMORE, CHARLES born ca. 1800, NY, and wife, DIANEY, born ca. 1810, VT, were listed in the 1840 census index of Rome Twp., Lenawee Co., Mich.; and in the 1850 census with SAMUEL N., age 19; JANE, age 15, both b. NY; and HENRY, age 11, b. Mich., in their household.

GILMORE, J. F., son of LYMAN (following), was born 17 Mar. 1841 in York Twp., Washtenaw Co., Mich., and moved with his father in 1857 to Macon Twp., Lenawee Co. He served in the Civil War in Co. G., 4th Mich. Inf. He married in Jan. 1867 to JULIA A. (BRADLEY), daughter of Eber (also see) in Milan, Monroe Co., Mich. They settled in Macon Twp., Lenawee Co. Seven children (1 deceased before 1888, name not stated): 1. CLARENCE; 2. FRANK; 3. LULU; 4. ALTA; 5. JULIA; 6. RAY. Ref: P&BA-Len pg. 896-8.

GILMORE, JOHN born ca. 1792, Ireland, and wife, POLLY, born ca. 1798, NY, were listed in the 1850 census of Raisin Twp., Lenawee Co., Mich. with JOHN, age 17; JAMES, age 15, both b. NY; and MARTHA, age 10, b. Mich., in their household. Note SAMUEL, following.

GILMORE, LYMAN, son of ROBERT (following), was born in VT, and moved with parents as a child to Steuben Co., NY. In 1832, they moved to York Twp., Washtenaw Co., Mich.; but he returned to Steuben Co., NY where he married ALMEDA (HERENDEEN), daughter of Thomas (also see). They lived in York Twp., Washtenaw Co., Mich. until 1857, then moved to Macon Twp., Lenawee Co. She died there in Dec. 1873, age 59. Children: 1. MARY A. (m. Dr. N. A. Darling; he d. Ann Arbor, Mich., she then resided with father in Macon Twp.); 2. J. F. (preceding); 3. JANE (m. William W. Ambrose); 4. EDWIN A. (d. age 4). Ref: P&BA-Len pg. 896-8.

GILMORE, ROBERT of Londonderry, NH, had known daughter, ELIZABETH (m. before 1803 to Clement Carpenter, also see, and settled in Potsdam, St. Lawr. Co., NY).

GILMORE, ROBERT, of "New England ancestry," lived in Vermont, and afterwards in Steuben Co., NY. He removed to York Twp., Washtenaw Co., Mich., where he was the first to take up Government land. He died at an advanced age in Wayne co., Mich. Known son, LYMAN (preceding); and also note CALVIN. Ref: P&BA-Len pg. 896-8.

GILMORE, SAMUEL born ca. 1825, and wife, CHRISTIAN A., born ca. 1824, both in NY, were listed in the 1850 census of Raisin Twp., Lenawee Co., Mich. with EDA E., age 9/12, b. Mich., in their household.

GILSON, CORNELIUS, son of JEREMIAH A. (following), was born 13 Jan. 1829, Brownville, Jefferson Co., NY. He moved first ca. 1850 to near Elmore, Ottawa Co., Ohio. He married there 8 Nov. 1853 to ESTHER MARIA (SMITH), daughter of Jonathan (also see). In 1879, they moved to Blissfield Twp., Lenawee Co., Mich. Children: 1. ALICE (m. Wira Dolph, Blissfield Twp.); 2. OPHELIA b. 10 Sept. 1854 (d. 12 Sept. 1871); 3. CORNELIA b. 17 Dec. 1855 (d. 24 Feb. 1875); 4. HATTIE M.; 5. WILLIAM (m. Kate Howland, dau. of Dr. Howland, Blissfield Twp.); 6. JAMES EDGAR. Ref: P&BA-Len pg. 723-4.

GILSON, JEREMIAH A. was born Albany Co., NY, and moved as a young man to Jefferson Co., NY. He married MARY (VAN CURLEY) who was born in the Mohawk Valley of NY. About 1851, they removed to near Elmore, Ottawa Co., Ohio, where she died in Feb. 1860. Eleven childen of whom 9 grew to maturity (names not stated, except): CORNELIUS (preceding). Ref: P&BA-Len pg. 723-4.

GILSON, JOSEPH was listed in the 1840 census index of Medina Twp., Lenawee Co., Mich. He was not listed in the 1850 census, however, in Medina Twp. were MARY E., age 16, & EDGAR A., age 13, both b. Mich., listed in the household of Alex B. & Augusta Collison (perhaps stepchildren??)

GILSON, SIMON and wife, MARY (COURTWRIGHT), moved from Penn. to Hillsdale Co., Mich. (in Adams Twp. in 1840 census index). They later moved to Tomah, Wisc., where he died. Known daughter, AMANDA, born Wayne Co., Mich. (m. William W. Jackson, also see). Ref: P&BA-Len pg. 788-9. Note: The 1840 census index of Wayne Co., Mich. lists a DAVID in Livonia; and GEORGE in Sumpter Twp.

GLASER, AUGUST, son of ERNEST (following), was born 29 Feb. 1836 in Baden, Germany. He came to the US and went first to Sandusky Co., Ohio with brother, WILLIAM. He married there in 1857 to CHRISTIANA (SHETLER) who was born in Wurtemburg, Germany. August served in the Civil War in Co. D., 128th Ohio Inf. After the war, they moved to Riga Twp., Lenawee Co., Mich. Christiana died in 1870, leaving children: 1. LOUIS; 2. WILLIAM; 3. GEORGE. August married on 10 Sept. 1871 to Mrs. BARBARA (TAGSOLD) MILLER, daughter of John; and widow of John; had children: 4. THEODORE; 5. ALMA; 6. AGNES; 7. CARRIE. Ref: P&BA-Len pg. 959-60.

GLASER, ERNEST of Baden, Germany died there in 1836; and his wife died in 1841. Known sons: WILLIAM (came to the US); AUGUST (preceding).

GLASGOW, MARY (See William McComb)

GLAZIER, EUNICE was born ca. 1830, Ohio, and was listed in the 1850 census of Blissfield Twp., Lenawee Co., in the household of Elisha Smith. Dittoed after her is CZARINA, age 1, b. NY. GLAZIER, WALKER born 16 June 1789, and wife, CORNELIA, born 1 Apr. 1791, moved from Peekskill, Westchester Co., NY to Covert Seneca Co., NY. Known daughter, RACHEL, born 10 May 1818, Peekskill, NY (m. Asaph K. Porter, also see). Ref: P&BA-Len pg. 702-3.

GODDARD, CAROLINE, age 7, born Ill., was listed in the 1850 census of Tecumseh Twp., Lenawee Co., Mich. in the household of
Isaac Brown.

GODDARD, FRANCIS, age 8; JAMES, age 6; LETER? (male), age 4, all b. NY, were listed in the 1850 census of Madison Twp., Lenawee Co., Mich. in a Hulbert household.

GODDARD, JULIA ANN (See Fenner Palmer)

GODDARD, LUCY A. (spelled "Godard") born ca. 1828, NY, was listed in the 1850 census of Adrian Twp., Lenawee Co., Mich. in the household of George Seger.

GODDARD, LYMAN died of Yellow Fever in the War of 1812. Known daughter, AMANDA (m/1 Henry Hoagland, also see; m/2 Samuel Willis.) Ref: P&BA-Len pg. 377-8.

GODDARD, RUFUS was listed in the 1840 census index of Rome Twp., Lenawee Co., Mich.

GODFREY, ELIZABETH born Lincolnshire, England (See John Houghtby).

GODFREY, WILLIAM born ca. 1815, Mass., and wife, JANE E., born ca. 1823, NY, were listed in the 1850 census of Adrian Twp., Lenawee Co., Mich. with MORTIMER, age 6; ROSELLA A., age 2, both b. Mich., in their household.

GOFF, ALVIN born ca. 1814, and wife, FRANCES, born ca. 1820, both in Mass., were listed in the 1850 census of Palmyra Twp., Lenawee Co., Mich. with GERTRUDE J., age 4; ALICE, age 2, both b. Mich., in their household. Note SALLY & TIMOTHY, following.

GOFF, HUMPHREY born ca. 1820, NY, was listed in the 1850 census of Palmyra Twp., Lenawee Co., Mich. Note SALLY & TIMOTHY, following.

GOFF, LESLIE T., son of SEWELL S. (following), was born 1 Apr. 1845, Blissfield Twp., Lenawee Co., Mich. He married first on 10 Apr. 1866 to CARRIE D. (KELLOGG), dau. of Rev. Kellogg. Children: 1. LUCY MABEL (m. W. W. Smith); 2. WILLIAM HERBERT. Leslie T. & Carrie were divorced; and he married again on 28 Jan. 1878 to CLARA A. (LaBOUNTY), daughter of Chauncey (also see). Son: 3. CHARLES b. 20 July 1881. Ref: P&BA-Len pg. 934-5.

GOFF, SALLY was listed head of household in the 1840 census index of Palmyra Twp., Lenawee Co., Mich. Note TIMOTHY B., following.

GOFF, SEWELL S. was born in Royalston, Mass. on 29 Jan. 1811. He moved to Lewiston, NY; and then in 1829 to Blissfield Twp., Lenawee Co., Mich. He married by 1830 to Mrs. MARGARET (FRARY) BUCK, daughter of David, and widow of Samuel (see both). Margaret died 31 May 1839. Children: 1. WARNER W. b. ca. 1831; 2. ALMIRA b. ca. 1833 (m. A. L. Bliss, Adrian, Mich.); 3. SEWELL (d. infancy). Sewell S. married again to LUCY (FRARY), sister of Margaret. Children: 4. PHILANDER K.; 5. LESLIE T. (preceding); 6. JOHN A. b. ca. 1848 (to St. Marys, Mich.) Ref: P&BA-Len pg. 934-5. Note STILMAN, as this is probably Sewell S., as that is the name listed in 1830 & 1840 census. Also note TIMOTHY B.

GOFF, STILMAN is probably SEWELL S., preceding. In the 1830 census of Lenawee Co., Michigan Territory, he was age 15-20 (Sewell was 19); and wife was age 15-20 (probably Margaret); and a female child under 5 is probably Lucinda Buck, daughter of Margaret, who was living in Sewell's household in the 1850 census of Blissfield Twp.

GOFF, TIMOTHY B. was listed in the 1830 census of Lenawee Co., Michigan Territory, adjacent to WILLARD, following. Timothy listed males: 2 under 5; 1 5-10; 2 10-15; 1 30-40; and females: 1 5-10; 1 10-15; 1 40-50. He is not listed in 1840, but note SALLY, preceding.

GOFF, WILLARD was born ca. 1797, Mass., and was listed in the 1830 census of Lenawee Co., Michigan Territory, with another male 5-10; and females: 1 20-30; 1 under 5; and 1 60-70. In 1830, Willard was listed adjacent to TIMOTHY B.; and in the 1840 census index was listed near STILMAN (SEWELL). He was listed in the 1850 census of Blissfield Twp., Lenawee Co. with HESTER A., age 21; NEWELL H., age 19; NELSON W., age 13; LUCETTA I., age 7; SARAH A., age 5; JASPER W., age 3; NANCY M., age 15 (listed last), all born Mich., in his household.

GOHEEN, E. WELLS, son of JOHN (following), was born 16 Nov. 1822, Groveland, Livingston Co., NY, and moved with his parents in 1831 to Tecumseh Twp., Lenawee Co., Mich. He married 13 Mar. 1859 in Saline, Washtenaw Co., Mich. to CHARLOTTE (NIBLACK), daughter of John (also see) born ca. 1826, NY. Six children (1 died infancy, name not stated): 1. FRANK b. ca. 1850 (went "West"); 2. FREMONT (m. Sophia Talbor, Ingham Co., Mich.); 3. PATIENCE; 4. LILLIE; 5. FRED. Ref: P&BA-Len pg. 287-8.

GOHEEN, EDWARD, a native of Wales, came to America about the time of the Revolution. He married CHRISTIANA (ROUP), probably in Penn. They resided in Northumberland Co., Penn. for a time, but moved to Groveland, Livingston Co., NY, where he died at age 36. His widow came to Michigan with son, JOHN (following), and died in 1845. Ref: P&BA-Len pg. 287-8.

GOHEEN, JOHN, son of EDWARD (preceding), was born in 1794/6, Northumberland Co., Penn., and moved with parents to Groveland, NY. He married there to ELIZABETH (HEADLY) born 1797 (and reared by Roup family). Note: In the 1850 census, her age was given as 47, b. Penn. They moved to Tecumseh Twp., Lenawee Co., Mich. in 1831, and after 1850 to Clinton Twp. He died in 1866; and she died in 1881. Children: 1. E. WELLS (preceding); 2. DEBORAH b. ca. 1825 (m. Charles W. Culbertson, also see); 3. LYDIA b. ca. 1827, NY; 4. JOHN V. (following); 5. CHARLES b. ca. 1833, Mich.; 6. MIRANDA b. 27 Mar. 1835 (operated farm with brother, John V. in 1888); 7. DELINDA (AMANDA in 1850 census, twin of Miranda?). Four were still living in 1888 (names not stated). Ref: P&BA-Len pg. 287-8 & 643-4.

GOHEEN, JOHN V., son of JOHN (preceding), born 12 Oct. 1829, Groveland, NY, moved to Lenawee Co., Mich. with his parents. He married 11 Oct. 1883 to ESTHER (MURPHY), daughter of John (also see). No children listed in sketch. Ref: P&BA-Len pg. 643-4.

GOLDSBOROUGH, NERINA E. Mrs. (husband's given name not stated) was the daughter of Charles C. Morse (also see) and had known children: FAY M; & ALICE S.

GOODALE also see GOODALL & GOODELL

GOODALE, HIRAM, son of NATHAN (following), was born 4 Oct. 1800, Fabius, Onondaga Co., NY; and moved with his parents to Madison Co., NY where he remained until age 14, then went to Monroe Co., NY, and then Baldwinsville, Onondaga Co., NY. He married there to SARAH E. (KEENE), daughter of Samuel B. (also see). In 1845, they moved to Deerfield Twp., Lenawee Co., Mich. (Note: Couldn't locate them in 1850 census? Perhaps came in 1854?) He died 5 May 1856. Known daughter, ANNE E. (m. George W. Bliven, also see). After the death of Hiram, Sarah E. married Joseph C. Tenant (also see) of Blissfield Twp.; and she died in Deerfield Twp. 28 Aug. 1866. Ref: P&BA-Len pg. 785-6.

GOODALE, NATHAN was a native of "New England;" and he married ? (MATTOON). He served in in the War of 1812, and became a pensioner. They lived in Onondaga and Madison Cos., NY. His wife died in 1813, and he died in 1823. Known son, HIRAM (preceding). Ref: P&BA-Len pg. 785-6.

GOODALL, HENRY, age 40, born NY, was listed in the 1850 census of Blissfield Twp., Lenawee Co., Mich. in a Hemingway household.

Pioneer Families of Southeastern Michigan

GOODELL also see GOODALE

GOODELL, ABNER was born ca. 1817, Maine, and wife, CLARISSA, born ca. 1821, Canada, were listed in the 1850 census of Fairfield Twp., Lenawee Co., Mich. with HIRAM M., age 2; and MARY A., age 10/12, both b. Mich., in their household.

GOODELL, GEORGE born ca. 1821, and wife, PHEBE, born ca. 1830, both in NY, were listed in the 1850 census of Fairfield Twp., Lenawee Co., Mich. with ALMOND, age 2, b. Mich., in the household.

GOODELL, ISRAEL born ca. 1815, Maine, and his wife, BETSEY, born ca. 1825, NY, were listed in the 1850 census of Fairfield Twp., Lenawee Co., Mich. with JOSEPH, age 20, b. NY, in their household.

GOODELL, JOHN, born ca. 1826, Maine, was listed in the 1850 census of Madison Twp., Lenawee Co., Mich. in a Crane household.

GOODELL, JONAS was listed in the 1840 census index of Rome Twp., Lenawee Co., Mich.

GOODENOUGH also see GOODNOW

GOODENOUGH, CAROLINE, age 6, born Mich., was listed in the 1850 census of Rollin Twp., Lenawee Co., Mich. in the household of Andrew and Delilah Darrow, perhaps a stepchild?

GOODMAN, ELEAZER and wife, MAHALA, of Glen Falls, NY, has known daughter, MARY K. (m. Delos M. Baker, also see).

GOODMAN, ROSANNA (See Henry Pontius)

GOODNOW also see GOODENOUGH

GOODNOW, GEORGE (See John Phillips)

GOODRICH, DANIEL born in 1752, and wife, BETHIAH (SHEPHERD), born in 1759, were early settlers of Wells, VT, where he died 2 June 1826; and she died 24 Mar. 1826. They had a large family (all names not known). Daughter, VIANA (m. Raymond Hotchkiss, d. 20 Apr. 1804, age 23, Wells, VT.); & sons: ROSWELL (m. Abigail Blossom); HALSEY (m. Julia Lawrence); GEORGE (nothing further noted in book, however see following). Ref: Wells, VT, 20 Years, by Grace P. Wood, 1955. Note: Also described was a DAVID who had come to Granville, VT from Glastonbury, Conn., and afterwards to Wells, VT.

GOODRICH, DWIGHT A. (See I. H. Schreder)

GOODRICH, GEORGE, possibly son of DANIEL (preceding), married CLAMANIA (LEE) who was born 16 June 1790 in Wells, VT; and they moved to Williston, VT. About 1836, they moved to Pittsford Twp., Hillsdale Co., Mich. He died 2 June 1850, and she died 13 Dec. 1863. Known daughter, ELIZA, born 22 Feb. 1814, Williston, VT (m. Sylvester Kenyon, also see, and moved to Hudson Twp., Lenawee Co., Mich.) Ref: P&BA-Len pg. 816-7.

GOODRICH, HEMAN (See John Hancock Carleton)

GOODRICH, HORACE was listed in the 1830 census of Lenawee Co., Michigan Territoy, with males: 1 under 5; 2 5-10; 1 10-15; 1 20-30; 1 40-50; female: 1 30-40.

GOODRICH, IRA and wife, FEAR (POTTER), had known daughter, MARY (m. Fernando C. Beaman, also see). Ira died at age 40 in Rochester, NY, and his wife died in Brockport, NY. Ref: P&BA-Len pg. 201-2.

GOODRICH, IRA born ca. 1795, and wife, SALLY, born ca. 1801, both in NY, were listed in the 1830 census of Lenawee Co., Michigan Territory, adjacent to THOMAS (following). They listed males: 1 under 5; 1 20-30; and females: 2 5-10; 1 15-20; 1 20-30. They were listed in the 1850 census of Tecumseh Twp., Lenawee Co., Mich., with son, GEORGE, age 23, born Mich., listed next door as head of a household, with (probably their other children) SANFORD, age 19; SARAH, age 13, all b. Mich.; and CHARLOTTE, age 23, b. NY, listed last, relationship not known.

GOODRICH, LABIUS H. born ca. 1807, VT, and wife, SALLY, born ca. 1804, Mass., were listed in the 1850 census of Rome Twp., Lenawee Co., Mich. with ALMIRA, age 17, b. VT; and LEWIS C., age 4, b. Mich.; and Molly Fitz (Fitts?), age 73, b. Mass. (mother-in-law?), in their household.

GOODRICH, NELSON born ca. 1811, and his wife, RUTH, born ca. 1818, both in Mass., were listed in the 1850 census of Palmyra Twp., Lenawee Co., Mich. with ESTHER, age 9; JAMES, age 7; JOHN, age 11, all b. Mich., and Nelson Day, age 13, b. Mich.; and Milo Stearns, age 24, b. Mass., in their household.

GOODRICH, THOMAS born ca. 1774, and wife, BETSEY, born ca. 1785, both in Mass., were listed in the 1830 census of Lenawee Co., Michigan Territory, with males: 1 15-20; 1 20-30; 1 40-50; and females: 1 under 5; 2 10-15; 1 15-20; 1 20-30; 1 40-50. IRA (preceding) was adjacent in the 1830 census. Thomas & Thomas Jr. were both listed in the 1840 census index of Tecumseh Twp.; and in the 1850 census they were listed next door to THOMAS (Jr.?) (following).

GOODRICH, THOMAS, probably son of THOMAS (preceding), born ca. 1807, and wife, CELESTIA, born ca. 1818, both in NY, were listed in the 1850 census of Tecumseh Twp., Lenawee Co., Mich. with WEBSTER, age 14; ELEANOR, age 10; MARY, age 8; HENRY CLAY, age 7, all b. Mich., in their household.

GOODSELL, FRANKLIN and wife, NANCY, were from Portland, Chautauqua Co., NY. Known daughter, LUCY, born 20 Sept. 1846, Portland, NY (m. James Burt Reed on 25 Feb. 1863, Fairfield Twp., Lenawee Co., Mich.)

GOODSELL, IRA, son of ZALMAN L. (following), born 13 Sept. 1832, Portland, Chautauqua Co., NY, moved to Erie Co., Ohio about 1850 (at age 18). About 1854, he moved to Ogden Twp., Lenawee Co., Mich. where he remained about 3 years. He married there on 12 Dec. 1855 to ELIZABETH C. (PHILLIPS), daughter of Alanson (also see). They later moved to Jasper, Lenawee Co., Mich. Son, ARTHUR A. (m. Ella M. Buck, Jasper, Mich.). Ref: P&BA-Len pg. 968-9.

GOODSELL, ZALMAN L. was born by 1793, and reared in Columbia Co., NY. He married LUCY (COLE) and they settled in Hillsdale, Columbia Co., NY; and later moved to Portland, Chautauqua Co., NY. She died there 10 May 1843, age 50. In 1857, he moved to Ogden Twp., Lenawee Co., Mich., and then to Adrian, and last to Madison Twp. He died 6 Apr. 1873. Six sons and 3 daughters lived to maturity (names not stated), 2 died infancy. Known son: #8. IRA (preceding). Ref: P&BA-Len pg. 968-9. Note FRANKLIN, preceding.

GOODSPEED, ABNER (See William Ladd)

GOODWIN, JOHN was born in Virginia, and he served in the Revolutionary War at age 15; and was a seaman until age 35. He settled in Turner, Maine where he married ? (YEATTEN/YEATON), daughter of Stephen. She died ca. 1813. Known son, LEWIS (following). Ref: P&BA-Len pg. 1011-2. Note: There is a JOHN with Va. Revolutionary service in the Pension Applications, #S8587, no proof it is this man.

GOODWIN, LEWIS, son of JOHN (preceding), was born 15 Aug. 1808, Oxford, Maine. After the death of his mother, he made his home with her brother, Stephen Yeatten, till age 15. In 1835, he went to NY, and about 1837 to Clinton, Lenawee Co., Mich. He married in 1850 to RACHEL (ALLEN), and settled in Ogden Twp., Lenawee Co. Children: 1. GEORGE b. 4 May 1851; 2. ORRA b. 26 Nov. 1854; 3. MELISSA b. 16 Aug. 1857; 4. WALLACE b. 23 June 1860 (deceased bef. 1888); 5. ELIZABETH b. 17 June 1863; 6. IDA b. 20 Apr. 1865 (deceased bef. 1888); 7. JOHN b. 20 June 1868 (deceased by 1888). Ref: P&BA-Len pg. 1011-2.

GOODWIN, SETH and wife, POLLY, were resident of Detroit, Mich. in 1870. (There was a man by this name in Colon, St. Joseph Co., Mich. in 1840 census index). Known daughter, CYNTHIA b. 28 June 1850, Royal Oak, Mich. (m. Augustus W. Slayton, also see, Tecumseh, Mich.) Ref: P&BA-Len pg. 549-50.

GORDAN also see GORDON
GORDAN, SILAS (See John B. Clement)

GORDON, JOHN J. (spelled Gorden) was listed in the 1840 census index of Franklin Twp., Lenawee Co., Mich.

GORDON, SAMUEL (spelled Gorden) was listed in the 1840 census index of Adrian Twp., Lenawee Co., Mich.

GORE, MOSES was listed in the 1840 census index of Medina Twp., Lenawee Co., Mich.

GORE, OBADIAH and wife, ANN (AVERY), of Sheshequin, Bradford Co., Penn. were parents of WEALTHY ANN born 1767 (m. Col. John Spalding, also see) in Sheshequin). Ref: P&BA-Len pg. 1178-80.

GORHAM, SHUBAEL and wife, POLLY, were parents of SALLY born 4 July 1818, Elbridge, Onondaga Co., NY (m. Cyrenus Whaley, also see). Ref: P&BA-Len pg. 998-9.

GOTHAM, MATTIE (See John L. Knapp)

GOULD, A. J. born ca. 1815, and wife, HANNAH, born ca. 1813, both in NY, were listed in the 1850 census of Seneca Twp., Lenawee Co., Mich. with LYDIA P., age 8; MARY, age 5, both b. Mich., in their household.

GOULD, JAMES B. born ca. 1830, and wife, MARY, age 23, both born NY, were listed in the 1850 census of Macon Twp., Lenawee Co., Mich. with FRANCIS, age 1, b. Mich. in the household.

GOULD, JOHN was listed in the 1840 census index of Medina Twp., Lenawee Co., Mich.

GOULD, JOHN born ca. 1808, and wife, ROSEANN, born ca. 1811, both in NY, were listed in the 1840 census index of Seneca Twp., Lenawee Co., Mich.; and in the 1850 census with RAWELL?, age 8; DAVID, age 6, both b. Mich., in their household.

GOULD, LOUISA, age 25, born NY, was listed in the 1850 census of Seneca Twp., Lenawee Co., Mich. in a Fuller household.

GOULD, MARIA (See Noah Greeley)

GOULD, MARY, age 29, born NY, was listed in the 1850 census of Adrian Twp., Lenawee Co., Mich. in a Baley household.

GOULD, SAMUEL born ca. 1806, Conn., and wife, ELIZABETH, born ca. 1810, NY, were listed in the 1840 census index of Franklin Twp., Lenawee Co., Mich.; and in the 1850 census with CATHARINE, age 19; DAVID, age 15, both b. NY; and SUSAN, age 8; NANCY, age 1/12, both b. Mich., in their household.

GOULD, THOMAS B. born ca. 1812, and wife, PARMILLA, born ca. 1808, both in NY, were listed in the 1850 census of Macon Twp., Lenawee Co., Mich. with JAMES, age 20; PHOEBE, age 18 (may be she listed again in 1850 census of Tecumseh Twp., Scofield household); LEWIS, age 14; CINDERILLA?, age 12; SMITH, age 11; GEORGE, age 10; MARILLA, age 8, all b. NY; and SIMON, age 6; THOMAS, age 4; CHARLES, age 2, all b. Mich., in their household.

GOULD, WILLIAM D., age 31, born NY, was listed in the 1850 census of Seneca Twp., Lenawee Co., Mich. in a Kinney household.

GRAGG also see GREGG
GRAGG, ANN (See David Service)

GRAHAM, SARAH C. (See George A. Ingall)

GRANDY, ALGERNON S., son of Dr. FRANCIS (following), married IDA (WARRING), and settled in Fairfield, Lenawee Co., Mich. Children: 1. CHARLES F. (d. age 2); 2. WALTER H.; 3. HELEN; 4. BESSIE; 5. ARTHUR; 6. GOLDIE. Ref: P&BA-Len pg. 576-7.

GRANDY, BENJAMIN, possibly son of EDMUND (following), born ca. 1810, NY, and wife, ANNA, born ca. 1814, Conn., were listed in the 1850 census of Raisin Twp., Lenawee Co., Mich. with JAMES, age 15; PARKER, age 6; NANCY, age 2, all b. NY, in their household.

GRANDY, EDMUND born ca. 1782, New Hampshire, moved with his family to New York about 1795, and married there to DORCAS (DEAN), born ca. 1785, NY. They lived first near Glen Falls, (Warren Co.) NY; and later in Montgomery Co., then Wayne Co., NY. About 1848, they moved to Raisin Twp., Lenawee Co., Mich. There were 11 sons, and 4 daughters (names not stated), and 7 were still living in 1888. They both died in Raisin Twp., he in 1856 and she in 1858, both about age 74. Known son, #12. Dr. FRANCIS M. (following); known daughter, JANE (m/1 Amos R. Crane; m/2 John Landon, see both). Edmund had in his household in the 1850 census of Raisin Twp.: PHEBE, age 37; ANNA, age 34; GEORGE, age 27; ENOS, age 22; JOSEPH, age 17, all b. NY. BENJAMIN (preceding) is probably another son. Ref: P&BA-Len pg. 367-8 & 576-7.

Pioneer Families of Southeastern Michigan

GRANDY, FRANCIS M. Dr., son of EDMUND (preceding), was born 31 Dec. 1826, Root, Montgomery Co., NY. He married in Adrian, Lenawee Co., Mich. on 11 July 1852 to Mrs. EXPERIENCE (EDDY) COMPTON, daughter of Abraham, and widow of Elmer (see both). She died at their home in Fairfield leaving son, 1. ALGERNON S. (preceding). Dr. Francis married again to Mrs. ANNA (MAYNARD) BACON, daughter of David T., and widow of Charles C. (see both). Children: 2. FRANK M. b. 5 Nov. 1871; 3. AGNES E. b. 26 Aug. 1873 (d. 30 Oct. 1877); 4. VICTOR A. b. 20 May 1879. Ref: P&BA-Len pg. 576-7.

GRANGER, ALICE married Thaddeus King (also see) of Suffield Co., Conn. He was a Capt. in the American Revolution. She was from a prominent family, and mentioned were her brothers, ELIJAH, GIDEON, and FRANCIS of Suffield, Conn. Ref: P&BA-Len pg. 520-1.

GRANGER, WILLIS born 14 Jan. 1861 (See Luther McRobert).

GRANT, ABRAM J. (or T.?) born ca. 1811, and wife, JANE, born ca. 1812, both in NY, were listed in the 1840 census index of Dover Twp., Lenawee Co., Mich. (as "A. J."); and in the 1850 census with GEORGE, age 13; ELLEN C., age 12; MARY A., age 9; AUGUSTA L., age 3, all b. Mich., in their household. Note JOHN S., following.

GRANT, ALEXANDER was listed in the 1840 census index of Seneca Twp., Lenawee Co., Mich.

GRANT, ELIZABETH (See Nathaniel Moulton)

GRANT, EMMA (See Marcus Bennett)

GRANT, JOHN C. born ca. 1820, and wife, WEALTHY, born ca. 1819, were listed in the 1850 census of Dover Twp., Lenawee Co., Mich. with SINTHA (CYNTHIA?) M., age 7; CHARLES G., age 5, both b. Mich., in their household. They were 2 doors from JOHN S. (following).

GRANT, JOHN S. born ca. 1788, and wife, PHEBE, born ca. 1791, both born NJ (almost illegible), were listed as "J. S." in the 1840 census index of Dover Twp., Lenawee Co., Mich.; and in the 1850 census with DARIUS, age 19, b. NY, in their household. Also see ABRAM T. & JOHN C., preceding.

GRANT, WILLIAM born ca. 1821, and wife, SARAH, born ca. 1822, both in Maine, were listed in the 1850 census of Woodstock Twp., Lenawee Co., Mich. with WILLIAM, age 7, b. ME; and HANNAH, age 3, b. Mich.; and Sarah Lovejoy, age 19, b. ME, in their household.

GRAVES, AMOS (See Eleazer Holdridge)

GRAVES, ARNOLD T., son of WILLIAM (following), was born 19 Feb. 1834, Schoharie Co., NY; and lived with parents in Oneida Co., NY, and came with them to Adrian Twp., Lenawee Co., Mich. in 1839. He married on 21 Oct. 1861 to JANE (RICHMOND), daughter of Otis (also see) at Manchester, Washtenaw Co., Mich. They resided in Cambridge Twp., Lenawee Co. Children: 1. MATTIE A.; 2. CHARLES C.; 3. WILLIE C.; 4. ANNA B. Ref: P&BA-Len pg. 531-2.

GRAVES, BENJAMIN F. was born 19 May 1839, Charlotte, Chautauqua Co. NY. He went first to Warren Co., Penn. in 1859. He served in the Civil War from Ohio, reaching rank of Captain. He lived Titusville, Penn.; but married in June 1864 to ELIZABETH (BAILEY) at Warsaw, Wyoming Co., NY. They settled in Warsaw, NY in 1868, and in 1871 moved to Big Rapids, Mecosta Co., Mich. She died in Mar. 1876. Children: 1. CLINTON B.; 2. BENTON F.; 3. FLORENCE E. Benjamin F. married again in June 1877 to ELIZABETH (KINNEY), daughter of Samuel (also see). In 1879, they moved to Adrian, Lenawee Co., Mich. Ref: P&BA-Len pg. 502-3.

GRAVES, CAROLINE (called a "spinster?") born ca. 1817, Conn., was listed head of household in the 1850 census of Tecumseh Twp., Lenawee Co., Mich. with CAROLINE, age 8; GEORGE, age 6, both b. Mich. in her household.

GRAVES, CAROLINE Mrs. born ca. 1820, NY, was listed as head of household in the 1850 census of Dover Twp., Lenawee Co., Mich. with BURRITT, age 10; ALBERT H., age 2, both b. Mich., in the household. Note STEPHEN WELLS, following, listed 2 doors away.

GRAVES, FRANCIS born ca. 1822, Mass., and wife, ROXANA, born ca. 1826, NY, were listed in the 1850 census of Adrian Twp., Lenawee Co., Mich. with ELMIRA, age 2; ADELIA, age 6/12, both b. Mich., in their household.

GRAVES, GEORGE L. (See William H. Osborne)

GRAVES, JOB born ca. 1800, Mass., and wife LAURA (WITHERELL), daughter of Ansel Sr. (also see), settled in Franklin Twp., Lenawee Co., Mich. by 1837. In the 1850 census of Franklin Twp., they listed LAURA, age 13; MARY, age 4, both b. Mich., and Henry Fisk, age 24, b. NY, and wife Sarah J., age 18, b. Mich. (possibly she is another daughter?), in their household.

GRAVES, JOEL born ca. 1774, Mass., lived in Schoharie Co., NY before 1807, and was a lumberman in the Catskill Mountains. He was said to have died at the home of a relative in Rochester, NY at age 87, but in the 1850 census of Tecumseh Twp., Lenawee Co., Mich., age 76, was in the household of son, WILLIAM (following). Joel married twice (wives' names not stated), but William was a son of first marriage. Ref: P&BA-Len pg. 531-2.

GRAVES, RHODA, age 10, born Mich., was listed in the 1850 census of Ridgeway Twp., Lenawee Co., Mich. in the household of Abijah Russell.

GRAVES, S. E. Maj. married HELEN M. (BENNETT), daughter of Joseph R. (also see). She died 6 June 1883. Son, WALTER J. Ref: P&BA-Len pg. 981-2.

GRAVES, SAMUEL B. born ca. 1777, VT, and wife, REBECCA, born ca. 1778, Conn., were listed in the 1840 census index of Raisin Twp., Lenawee Co., Mich.; and in the 1850 census in the household of WILLIAM M. (following).

GRAVES, STEPHEN WELLS born 1791, Harrington, Litchfield Co., Conn., married RHODA (CLARK) born 1793, Burlington, Conn. They moved to Cayuga Co., NY, where they remained until 1835, then moved to Clayton, Lenawee Co., Mich. She died 28 Feb. 1837, Dover Twp.; and he died 2 Aug. 1854. Known children: (NANCY) LUCINDA (m. George Merrick, also see, d. May 1882, Adrian); LORENZO (d. 9 Jan. 1849, Clayton); ELVIRA b. 18 Oct. 1821, Harrington, Conn. (m. Bradley Shaw, Jr., also see). Ref: P&BA-Len pg. 237-8. Note: In the 1850 census of Dover Twp., Stephen W., age 58, was listed with the following in his household (perhaps family of Lorenzo?): CYNTHIA, age 27, b. NY; RHODA A., age 3; DELILAH R., age 1, both b. Mich. Note

RHODA (preceding), who may relate to this family. CAROLINE, listed 2 doors away in Dover Twp., may relate; and also the CAROLINE in Tecumseh Twp.

GRAVES, WILLIAM, son of JOEL (preceding), was born 25 Mar. 1807 in Schoharie Co., NY; and married there to ELIZABETH (DONNELSON), of a Quaker family, born 16 May 1807, Schoharie Co. They removed to Oneida Co., NY; and then in 1839 moved to Adrian, Lenawee Co., Mich. He died 19 Mar. 1867; and she afterwards lived in Ypsilanti, Washtenaw Co., Mich. with a daughter, until her death on 18 Sept. 1887. In the 1850 census of Tecumseh Twp., they listed SARAH, age 20; ARNOLD T. (preceding); MATILDA, age 15; GEORGE, age 12; CHARLES, age 10, all b. NY; and SARAH, age 8; WILLIAM, age 5, both b. Mich. Father, Joel, age 76, b. Mass., was also in the household. Ref: P&BA-Len pg. 531-2.

GRAVES, WILLIAM born ca. 1823, and wife, LUCINDA, born ca. 1824, both in NY, were listed in the 1850 census of Palmyra Twp., Lenawee Co., Mich. with MADISON M., age 1, b. Mich., all in the household of Benjamin Slade (possibly in-laws?). It may be this Madison Graves who was the foster son of Benjamin Kelly (also see), a Quaker family.

GRAVES, WILLIAM M., probably son of SAMUEL B. (preceding), born ca. 1810, VT, and his wife, SARAH M., born ca. 1812, Conn., were listed in the 1850 census of Adrian Twp., Lenawee Co., Mich. with OSCAR H., age 18; MARY J., age 16, both b. NY; and WILLIAM H., age 13; SAMUEL E., age 11; MARTHA C., age 8, all b. Mich., in their household, as well as SAMUEL B. & wife, (preceding).

GRAY, CHARLES born ca. 1820, VT, and wife, JANE, born ca. 1825, NY, were listed in the 1850 census of Palmyra Twp., Lenawee Co., Mich. with NELSON, age 8, b. Penn.; and MILES, age 7; AUGUSTUS, age 2; EDWIN, age 3/12, all b. Mich., in their household.

GRAY, EDWARD married ELIZABETH (FLYNN) who was born ca. 1831, daughter of Michael, also see, and settled in Hudson Twp., Lenawee Co., Mich. Ref: P&BA-Len pg. 900.

GRAY, ELLIOTT, son of JOSEPH W. (following), was born 11 May 1833, Raisin Twp., Lenawee Co., Mich. He married on 22 June 1852 to ELIZA (GUTHRIDGE) born Black Rock, NY of Irish descent. He served in Co. B, 7th Mich. Cav., in the Civil War. Children: 1. JOSEPH E. (m. Eva Campbell, Tecumseh Twp.); 2. ALICE (m. Joseph Rynd, Fairfield Twp.); 3. MELLA ANN; 4. MARY E. Ref: P&BA-Len pg. 448-9.

GRAY, ELLIOTT M., born ca. 1808, and wife, MARY ANN, born ca. 1811, both in Mass., were listed in the 1840 census index of Tecumseh Twp., Lenawee Co., Mich.; and in the 1850 census with WILLIAM, age 15; ELLEN, age 14, both b. Mass.; and ELLIOTT, age 12, b. NY; and MARIAN, age 6; CHARLES, age 1, both b. Mich., in their household. THANKFUL, following, was listed nearby in 1840.

GRAY, ERASTUS born ca. 1822, and wife, SARAH, born ca. 1824, both in NY, were listed in the 1850 census of Fairfield Twp., Lenawee Co., Mich. with MALVINA, age 8; GEORGE O., age 6; LUCY, age 4, all b. Mich., in their household.

GRAY, HORACE born ca. 1808, and wife, ABIGAIL, born ca. 1812, both in Conn., were listed in the 1850 census of Macon Twp., Lenawee Co., Mich. with MARY J., age 17; GEORGE, age 15, both b. Conn.; and IRA, age 12, b. Mich., in their household.

GRAY. HUGH born ca. 1790, Penn., and wife, MARY (SINCLAIR), born ca. 1792, Ireland, were listed in Raisin Twp., Lenawee Co., Mich. by the 1840 census; and in the 1850 census with HUGH M. B., age 22, b. NY in their household. Known daughter, CAROLINE, born ca. 1826, NY (m. Hudson W. Conkling, also see) Ref: P&BA-Len pg. 293-4.

GRAY, JAMES of Penn., died in Portsmouth, Ohio, and had known daughter, MARGARET (m. William McCormick, also see).

GRAY, JAMES born ca. 1805, NY, was listed in the 1850 census of Tecumseh Twp., Lenawee Co., Mich. in an Inn.

GRAY, JONATHAN born ca. 1787, Dutchess Co., NY was reared there. He was an early settler to Yates Co., NY. He married SALLIE (ROBERTSON), daughter of Calvin (also see) of Steuben Co., NY. About 1833, they removed to Allegany Co., NY; and in 1838 to Ogden Twp., Lenawee Co., Mich. He died in 1860, and she died in Apr. 1879. In the 1850 census of Ogden Twp., they listed known son, CALVIN b. ca. 1814, NY, and SALLY M., age 16, b. NY. Known daughter, PRUDENCE b. 20 Jan. 1828, Dundee, Yates Co., NY (m. John B. Clement, also see). Ref: P&BA-Len pg. 950-1.

GRAY, JOSEPH W. born ca. 1805, VT (per 1850 census), was called a "native of Jefferson Co., NY," and married before 1830 to NELLA (KITCHAM), daughter of Jacob (also see) in Tecumseh Twp., Lenawee Co., Mich. They settled by 1830 in Raisin Twp., Lenawee Co., Mich. In the 1850 census of Raisin Twp., they were listed with only Maria & Eliza in the household. Children: 1. JANE (d. age 16); 2. FRANCES b. ca. 1831 (m. Samuel Helm, also see); 3. ELLIOT (preceding); 4. MARIA b. ca. 1836 (m. Frederick Gambol, Tecumseh Twp.); 5. ELIZA A. b. ca. 1840 (m. Milton Ross, Addison, Mich.); 6. ALBERT (d. child). Nella died (after 1850), and Joseph W. married again to SARAH (COX). He died in 1885, and she was still living on the homestead in 1888. Children: 7. WILLARD; 8. JOHN; 9. NELLIE. Ref: P&BA-Len pg. 448-9.

GRAY, LUCY born ca. 1808, NY, is listed in the 1850 census of Tecumseh Twp., Lenawee Co., Mich. in the household of Salmon & Harriet Crane. Note THANKFUL, following.

GRAY, MARGARET (See Henry Pelham; & Richard B. Gillespie)

GRAY, MARY (See William Tillyar)

GRAY, PARLY (See Clark Vincent)

GRAY, SYLVESTER born ca. 1826, Penn., was listed in the 1850 census of Palmyra Twp., Lenawee Co., Mich.

GRAY, THANKFUL was listed in the 1840 census index of Tecumseh Twp., Lenawee Co., Mich. Note ELLIOTT M., & LUCY, preceding.

GRAY, THOMAS born ca. 1820, Conn., and wife, LUCY A., born ca. 1821, NJ, were listed in the 1850 census of Macon Twp., Lenawee Co., Mich. with PHARA (male), age 7; JANE, age 4; FRANK, all 9/12, all b. Mich., in their household.

Pioneer Families of Southeastern Michigan

GRAY, WALTER, born ca. 1827, and wife, **CHRISTINA**, born ca. 1830, both in NY, were listed in the 1850 census of Blissfield Twp., Lenawee Co., Mich. with DANIEL, age 7/12, b. Mich. in their household.

GRAY, WILLIAM (spelled "Grey") was listed in the 1840 census index of Rome Twp., Lenawee Co., Mich.

GREELEY, BRAINARD (See George W. Stephenson)

GREELEY, NOAH born ca. 1799, New Hampshire, was a second cousin of Horace Greeley. Noah married MARIA (GOULD), born ca. 1813, NY, and in 1837, they removed to Seneca Twp., Lenawee Co., Mich. He died in Morenci, Mich. in 1874, age 74; and she died in 1859, age 49, Seneca Twp. Children (ages shown from 1850 census): 1. LOUISA J., age 18; 2. NOAH G., age 15; 3. LODEMA A., age 13, all b. NY; and 4. CHARLES E., age 11; 5. GEORGE W., age 9; 6. SARAH M. b. 14 May 1843, Seneca Twp. (m. Matthew Bennett, also see); 7. HARRIET E., age 3; 8. ORPHA & 9. EFFA (twins), age 2/12, all b. Mich. Ref: P&BA-Len pg. 1051-2.

GREELEY, WILLIAM L. born ca. 1814, and wife, **ELIZABETH**, born ca. 1819, Mass., were listed in the 1850 census of Adrian Twp., Lenawee Co., Mich. with WILLIAM H., age 5, b. Mich., in the household.

GREEN also see GREENE following.

GREEN, ALEXANDER born ca. 1822, NY, and wife, **ABIGAIL**, born ca. 1820, Mass., were listed in the 1850 census of Tecumseh Twp., Lenawee Co., Mich. with GEORGE, age 5; EDGAR, age 2, both b. Mich., in the household.

GREEN, ALMIRA (See Samuel Hoyt)

GREEN, ARTHUR C. (See Joseph M. Hunt)

GREEN, BENJAMIN F. Dr. born ca. 1803, Conn., and probably wife, **LAVINIA**, born ca. 1795, NY, were listed in the 1840 census index of Tecumseh Twp., Lenawee Co., Mich., and in the 1850 census of Adrian Twp. with Catherine E. Owens, age 21, b. NY, and Charles W. Owens, age 4/12, b. Mich., in the household.

GREEN, DANIEL B. was listed in the 1840 census index of Tecumseh Twp., Lenawee Co., Mich.

GREEN, DAVID was listed in the 1840 census index of Tecumseh Twp., Lenawee Co., Mich.

GREEN, DEBORAH (See John S. Wells)

GREEN, G. OLIN (See Eleazer Holdridge)

GREEN, EBENEZER was a Revolutionary soldier from the Mohawk Valley of NY. Known daughter, MARY, born 9 June 1783 (m. Maj. Philo Mills, also see, and settled in Franklin Twp., Lenawee Co., Mich.) Ebenezer was a descendant of a JOHN who had left the Mass. Colony with Roger Williams and founded the Colony of Rhode Island. Ebenezer and 3 of his brothers served in the Revolution, and mentioned was brother, JOSEPH, who had enlisted at age 15, and had lived until 1852. Note: There is an EBENEZER with NY service, with wife, PRISCILLA, in the Revolutionary War Pension Applications, #W23164, no proof it is the same man.

GREEN, EPHRAIM born in Thompson, Windham Co., Conn., moved to Palmyra, Ontario (now Wayne) Co., NY at age 20. He married there in 1790 to SARAH (CLAGHORN). He was Capt. of Militia in the War of 1812. She died in Ontario Co., NY at age 63. There were 5 sons and 4 daughters (only one name stated): ORSON (following). Ref: P&BA-Len pg. 944-5. Also note NELSON, following.

GREEN, FRANKLIN I. born ca. 1822, and wife, **SARAH**, born ca. 1823, both in NY, were listed in the 1850 census of Madison Twp., Lenawee Co., Mich.

GREEN, FREEBORN born ca. 1790, Rhode Island, and wife, **RACHEL**, born ca. 1797, NY, were listed in the 1840 census index od Franklin Twp., Lenawee Co., Mich.; and in the 1850 census next door to NOBLE K. (following).

GREEN, GEORGE S. born ca. 1815, VT, and wife, **IRENE**, born ca. 1816, NY, were listed in the 1840 census index of Clinton, Lenawee Co., Mich.; and in the 1850 census of Tecumseh Twp., Lenawee Co. with ELIZABETH, age 13; BRADLEY, age 10; WESLEY, age 8; WILLIAM, age 6; ANN ELISA, age 5; ANNABELLE, age 3, all b. Mich., in their household. Note NATHANIEL S. (following).

GREEN, GEORGE W., son of NATHANIEL S. (following), was born 14 Mar. 1838, Clinton, Mich., and married on 25 Oct. 1860 to MARY E. (TOWNSEND), daughter of Joseph. They settled in Brooklyn, Jackson Co., Mich. Children: 1. GEORGE E.; 2. CHARLES T.; 3. LEON S.; 4. CLARK. Ref: History of Jackson Co., Mich., pg. 796 (spelled "Greene.")

GREEN, HENRY[1] came from Greenwich, England in 1629, and was among the founders of the Salem Colony, Mass. His name was spelled "Greene" originally, but later generations dropped the "e." He had 11 children, only one mentioned was HENRY[2] who married JUDA (GILE), and afterwards moved to Windham Co., Conn. Henry[2] had 8 children, and only one mentioned was HEZEKIAH[3] (following). Ref: P&BA-Len pg. 914-5.

GREEN, HEZEKIAH[3], son of HENRY[2] (See HENRY[1], preceding), was born 12 Nov. 1733, Windham Co., Conn. (He was a cousin of General Nathaniel Green of Revolutionary fame). Hezekiah married in 1755 to ALICE (LEAVENS) of Windham Co., and they remained there until 1780, then moved to Berkshire Co., Mass. She died in 1796, and he died there, age 92. Eight children, names not stated, except: NOAH, Sr. (following). Ref: P&BA-Len pg. 914-5.

GREEN, JAMES born ca. 1792, and wife, **ELEANOR**, born ca. 1800, both in NY, were listed in the 1850 census of Madison Twp., Lenawee Co., Mich. with HENRY, age 24; SARAH, age 20; HANNAH, age 18, all b. NY; and listed last, LOUIZA, age 26, b. NY; and children, JANE, age 2/12, & ALBERT, age 9, both b. Mich., in their household.

GREEN, JAMES (son of JACOB & RACHEL (PALMER), both of whom remained in Ireland) was born in Co. Antrim, Ireland in 1809. He married there on 3 May 1830 to ELIZA (McCONNELL) born 26 June 1814. In 1831, they came to the US, and settled first in Clinton Co., Mich. for 6 years; then lived near Toledo, Ohio. In 1838, they settled in Fairfield Twp., Lenawee Co., Mich. There were 10 children. Four died young, namely RACHEL; JACOB; ROBERT; & WILLIAM (1st). The survivors (except George) following were in the household in the 1850 census: ELIZA b. 1838, Ohio (m. Edwin Smith, also see); JAMES H. (following); SYLVESTER b. ca. 1842 (m/1 L. Catlin; m/2 Eliza Catlin who d. 6 Sept. 1887); RACHEL S. b. ca. 1845 (m. Richard Miller, Tuscola, Mich.); WILLIAM E. b. ca. 1849 (m. Amelia Smith); GEORGE (m. Fannie Allen). Ref: P&BA-Len pg. 430-1.

GREEN, JAMES C. born ca. 1810, VT, and wife, **LYDIA**, born ca. 1810, NY, were listed in the 1850 census of Palmyra

Twp., Lenawee Co., Mich. with WILLIAM, age 18; CAROLINE, age 14, both b. NY; and AUGUSTA, age 9; LYDIA S., age 3, both b. Mich., in the household.

GREEN, JAMES H., son of JAMES (of Fairfield Twp., preceding), was born 28 Feb. 1840, Fairfield Twp., Lenawee Co., Mich. He prospected in California, but returned to Fairfield Twp., where he married on 1 Mar. 1867 to CLARISSA (SALSBURY), daughter of D. C. (also see). Children: 1. HARTIE E.; 2. FLORENCE C.; 3. JAMES B.; 4. BESSIE; 5. BERT. Ref: P&BA-Len pg. 457.

GREEN, MARTHA S. (male) born ca. 1804, Conn., and wife, SOPHIA, born ca. 1804, VT, were listed in the 1850 census of Tecumseh Twp., Lenawee Co., Mich. with MA--SEE? (female), age 14, b. VT; and GEORGE, age 12; CHARLES, age 10, both b. Mich., in their household.

GREEN, NATHANIEL S. was a native of Northfield, VT, who came to Michigan in 1834 and settled in Clinton, Lenawee Co., Mich. (Not listed in 1840 census index, however there were 2 NATHANS in Washtenaw Co. There was a SHUBAEL R. in Clinton in 1840 census index). Ref: History of Jackson Co., Mich., pg. 796 (spelled Greene.") Note GEORGE S., preceding.

GREEN, NELSON born ca. 1803, and wife, MELISSA, born ca. 1800, both in NY, were listed in the 1850 census of Rollin Twp., Lenawee Co., Mich. with SARAH W., age 23; MARY J., age 21; WILLIAM, age 19; ALZORA, ae 17; NELSON A., age 16; JAMES L., age 14; ELIAS, age 12; BETSEY E., age 9, all b. NY, in their household. Note EPHRAIM, preceding.

GREEN, NOAH, Sr.^{4}, son of HEZEKIAH^3 (preceding), was born 20 Aug. 1761, Windham Co., Conn., and he served in the Revolution (There was a Noah with Conn. service, Rev. Pension Appl. #S29840). He married in 1791 to REBECCA (CONVERSE) who was born 1769, Windham Co., Conn. Noah Sr. had a total of 14 children (names not stated) by 3 wives, of whom 5 lived to maturity. Rebecca died in 1803. Known son, OREN (d. 1841 on Steamer, "Erie," during a fire). Noah, Sr. married again to SARAH (DAVIS) of Windham Co., Conn., and they moved to Berkshire Co., Mass. before 1808. She died in 1815. Known son, NOAH K.^{5} (following). Noah Sr. married third to BETSEY (HARWOOD) of Hampshire Co., Mass. Known daughter, HARRIET (m. ? Warren, lived Wauwatosa, Wisc. in 1888). Ref: P&BA-Len gp. 914-5.

GREEN, NOAH K.^{5}, son of NOAH, Sr.^{4} (preceding), was born 24 Dec. 1808, Berkshire Co., Mass. He married there to ESTHER E. (BALDWIN) who was born 14 Aug. 1807. Shortly afterwards, ca. 1835, they moved to Medina Twp., Lenawee Co., Mich. Noah K. served on the County Board of Supervisors, and from 1850-1863 in the State Legislature. He died 8 May 1886. Children: 1. OREN E. (following); 2. NOAH T. b. ca. 1838; 3. GEORGE D. b. ca. 1842; 4. HENRY E. b. ca. 1850. Ref: P&BA-Len pg. 914-5.

GREEN, NOBLE K., probably son of FREEBORN (preceding), born ca. 1821, and wife, JANE?, born ca. 1833, both in NY, were listed in the 1850 census of Franklin Twp., Lenawee Co., Mich. with SALLY, age 75, b. NY, in the household (next door to FREEBORN).

GREEN, OREN E.^{6}, son of NOAH K.^{5} (preceding), born 14 Nov. 1835, was the second baby born in Medina Twp., Lenawee Co., Mich. He married in 1859 to LUCY (ROGERS), daughter of James (also see) in Hillsdale Co., Mich. They settled in Medina Twp. Children: 1. ALICE F. (m. Prof. E. A. Conditt, Delta, Ohio); 2. AGNES L. (m. W. F. Smith; Hosking, Dak.); 3. LURA A.; 4. GEORGE R. (d. age 1); 5. GEORGE W. Ref: P&BA-Len pg. 914-5.

GREEN, ORSON, son of EPHRAIM (preceding), was born in Palmyra, Ontario (now Wayne) Co., NY. On 10 Apr. 1833, he came to Mich. to prospect for land, then returned to Cattaraugus Co., NY. He married 5 Feb. 1834 to ELIZABETH (DOUGLAS), daughter of Daniel (also see). They came to Rollin Twp., Lenawee Co., Mich. before 1837. She died 25 Feb. 1850, age 36. Children: 1. DANIEL D. b. 27 Nov. 1836 (d. 25 Jan. 1848); 2. EPHRAIM C. b. 18 Jan. 1838 (m. Elizabeth Crummey); 3. SARAH M. b. 27 Nov. 1840; 4. ELIZABETH D. b. 5 Feb. 1850 (m. Francis Alexander, dau. of David, also see). Orson served in the State Legislature in 1859 and 1871-5. Orson married again on 23 Feb. 1863 to CLEMENZA (DOUGLAS), sister of Elizabeth. She died on 24 Aug. 1871, age 50. Ref: P&BA-Len pg. 944-5.

GREEN, POLLY (See Stephen P. Haight)

GREEN, SARAH (See Appolos Long)

GREEN, SHUBAEL R. was listed in the 1840 census index of Clinton Twp., Lenawee Co., Mich.

GREEN, THERISA of Erie Co., NY (See Lemuel C. P. Vaughan).

GREENE also see GREEN

GREENE, AMBROSE^1 was born 9 Apr. 1746, Suffolk Co., Long Island, NY. He married before 1770 to GULAELMA (LESTER), and they lived in Dutchess Co., NY by 1770. They removed to Rensselaer Co., NY in 1775; and in 1795 moved to Danube, Herkimer Co., NY. He died 29 Aug. 1837, and she died 1 June 1826. Known son, JOHN^2 (following). Ref: P&BA-Len pg. 948-50. Note: In the 1800 census index of Herkimer Co., NY under "Greene" there were ABRAHAM; CALEB; (2) JOHN; JOHN C.; JOSEPH; JOSIAH; SILAS; & WILLIAM.

GREENE, AMBROSE^3, son of JOHN^2 (following), was born 18 Sept. 1791, Schodack, Rensselaer Co., NY, and moved with parents to Daube, Herkimer Co. He married there to DIMMIS (SKEELS) in 1815, and she died in 1816. He married again to MARTHA (FRAZIER) born 21 Feb. 1801, Schodack, NY. They settled in German Flats, Herkimer Co., NY. He died 7 June 1863, and she died 24 Apr. 1842. Known daughter, SARAH E. b. 8 July 1827, German Flats (m. Marcus L. Frazier, also see). Ref: P&BA-Len pg. 948-50.

GREENE, C. N. (See James W. Bradner)

GREENE, D. B. married ALMIRA N. (MILLS), daughter of Maj. Philo Mills (also see); and they moved to Ypsilanti Twp., Washtenaw Co., Mich. Note the DANIEL B. GREEN in Tecumseh Twp., Lenawee Co. in 1840.

GREENE, JOHN^2, son of AMBROSE^1 (preceding), was born 17 Apr. 1770, Dutchess Co., NY; and married there to RUTH (BARKER) in 1790. They moved to Danube, Herkimer Co., NY. She died there in June 1850, and he died in Dec. 1851. Known son, AMBROSE^3 (preceding). Ref: P&BA-Len pg. 948-50.

GREENLEAF, CHARLES W., son of JOHN (following), was born 29 Jan. 1832, Mexico, Oswego Co., NY. He came to Cambridge Twp., Lenawee Co., Mich. with his parents.

He married on 5 July 1856 to ANN M. (SHEELER), daughter of George (also see). They settled in Cambridge Twp. Children: 1. GEORGE W. (m. Ida A. Kane; 2 children, Ethel M. & Bessie A., Rome Twp.); 2. CAKVALLO L. (m. Lizzie Rise, had son, Mindret C.). Ref: P&BA-Len pg. 550-1.

GREENLEAF, JOHN born New Hampshire married in Paris, Oneida Co., NY on 2 Apr. 1818 to SUSAN (AVERILL) born 1799, Conn. They were in Mexico, Oswego Co., NY in 1832. In 1836, they removed to Cambridge Twp., Lenawee Co., Mich. where he died in May 1872; and she died 11 Feb. 1857. Seven children were born in Oneida Co., NY and one died there (names not stated). The following known children from the 1850 census of Cambridge Twp.: 1. CHARLES W. (preceding); 2. HARRIET E. b. ca. 1834 (m. Henry Pulver, also see); 3. EMILY A. b. 24 Mar. 1838, Cambridge Twp. (m. James R. Cairns, also see). It is probably this John who married again to Mrs. ELIZBETH (WINKLER) BENNETT, widow of Rev. Moses (also see) in Cambridge Twp. Ref: P&BA-Len pg. 288-9 & 550-1.

GREENLEAF, WILLIAM A. born ca. 1823, and wife, EVALINE, born ca. 1825, both in NY, were listed in the 1850 census of Rome Twp., Lenawee Co., Mich. with HOBERT H., age 5, b. Mich., in the household.

GREENSHAW, G. T. (See Harrison Fitts)

GREENWOOD, THOMAS Rev. of Rehoboth, Mass. had known daughter, ELIZABETH (m. Ezra Carpenter[5], born 1698).

GREGG also see GRAGG

GREGG, EMILY (See James B. Wells)

GREGG, JOHN born ca. 1787, Mass., was listed in the 1850 census of Tecumseh Twp., Lenawee Co., Mich. with SARAH, age 90, born Conn. (mother?), and ALMIRA, age 58, b. Mass.; and George Ashley, age 66, b. Mass., in his household.

GREGG, MAGGIE (See Thomas Lee)

GREGG, SAMUEL born ca. 1791, New Hampshire, and wife, RHODA, born ca. 1796, Mass. were listed in the 1840 census index of Medina Twp., Lenawee Co., Mich.; and in the 1850 census with ROLLIN R., age 21; SARAH L., age 18; CAROLINE, age 16, all b. NY, in their household.

GREGG, WILLIAM, son of ANDREW & NANCY (LINTON) who were of Scottish ancestry, was born 1832, Co. Antrim, Ireland. He married there to MARGARET (STEWART), daughter of Samuel & Ellen (Linton). Both sets of their parents died in Ireland. In 1866, after the birth of 4 children, William & Margaret came to the US and settled in Macon Twp., Lenawee Co., Mich. Children: 1. ANGIE (m. William Nectell, Canada; d. 1866, leaving dau., Margaret); 2. ROBERT J.; 3. ANDREW (m. Annie Gasten); 4. SAMUEL; 5. THOMAS; 6. WILLIAM. Ref: P&BA-Len pg. 205-6.

GREGORY, NATHANIEL M. (See Samuel Lewis)

GREYTRAX, ? married ELIZA (NORTON) in Livingston Co., NY; and she died in Groveland, NY in 1834. He came to Genesee Co., Mich., where he was living in 1888 at "an advanced age." Known daughter, SARAH b. 16 Aug. 1825, Livingston Co., NY (m. James Kimball, also see). Ref: P&BA-Len pg. 779-80. Note: There was a Sylvanus "Greatrase" in Albany Co., NY in 1800 census index.

GRIBBEN, CAROLINE Mrs. was the daughter of Ira Holloway (also see).

GRIER, SUSAN (See Alexander Dubois)

GRIFFES, HARVEY J. (See Clark Ames)

GRIFFIN, CATHERINE (See Michael Hogan)

GRIFFIN, DANIEL born ca. 1811, and wife, HANNAH, born ca. 1810, both in NY, were listed in the 1850 census of Rome Twp., Lenawee Co., Mich. with GILBERT, age 13 (probably he who m. Wealthy Landon, dau. of John, also see); BERTLEY, age 8, both b. Mich., in their household. Note: It is probably Daniel listed as "D. R." in the 1840 census index of Rome Twp.

GRIFFIN, HARVEY probably b. after 1850 (See Elliot R. Kilbury).

GRIFFIN, LOIS (See John Gillett)

GRIFFIN, OLIVER and wife, LOUISA (CARPENTER), were natives of Mass.; and they settled before 1817 near Kingsbury, Washington Co., NY. In 1836, they removed to Columbia Twp., Jackson Co., Mich.; and then to Mason, Ingham Co., Mich. He died in 1874, age 90; and she died in 1846, age 52. Known sons: J. C. b. 1 Mar. 1817, Kingsbury, NY (lived Jackson Co., Mich.); R. F. (lived Ingham Co., Mich.); and known daughters: EMILY b. 30 Sept. 1811 (m. Charles L. Hawley, also see); AMELIA M. b. 18 May 1825 (m. Henry Hawley, also see). Ref: History of Jackson Co., Mich., pp. 144 & 976.

GRIFFING, RUTH (See Daniel Johnson)

GRIFFITH, ABNER born ca. 1795, NY, was listed in the 1850 census of Seneca Twp., Lenawee Co., Mich. with ORSON, age 20; LOVICA, age 16, both b. Ohio; and GEORGE, age 14; ALONZO, age 10, both b. Mich., in his household. Also see RILEY, listed next door in 1850 census.

GRIFFITH, ALMYRA (See John C. Anderson)

GRIFFITH, ANDREW was listed in the 1840 census index of Medina Twp., Lenawee Co., Mich. Note GEORGE, following.

GRIFFITH, CYRUS, son of LAZARUS, born 27 Aug. 1826, Chemung Co., NY, and moved with his parents to Madison Twp., Lenawee Co., Mich. He married 3 July 1855 to JULIA A. (BURCH), daughter of Edmund (also see), and they settled in Madison Twp. Children: 1. ETHELINDA (d. age 2); 2. THERON; 3. ESBEN (m. Ada Bright, Nebraska); 4. ELMA (m. Charles Allen, also see); 5. MAY; 6. SARAH. Ref: P&BA-Len pg. 1033-4.

GRIFFITH, GEORGE was listed in the 1840 census index of Medina Twp., Lenawee Co., Mich. Note ANDREW, preceding.

GRIFFITH, GEORGE S. born ca. 1826, and wife, LORINDA, born ca. 1829, both in NY, were listed in the 1850 census of Madison Twp., Lenawee Co., Mich. with MATILDA, age 50, b. NY (relationship not known), in their household.

GRIFFITH, JAMES, age 13, born NY, was listed in the 1850 census of Fairfield Twp., Lenawee Co., Mich. in a James Knox household; also note JOHN, age 11, following, 2 doors away. (Also see John Hendryx).

GRIFFITH, JOHN born ca. 1818, and wife, ELTHIN?, born ca. 1829, both in NY, were listed in the 1850 census of Madison Twp., Lenawee Co., Mich. with HENRY, age 1, b. Mich., in the household. See LAZARUS, following.

GRIFFITH, JOHN, age 11, born NY., was listed in the 1850 census of Fairfield Twp., Lenawee Co., Mich., in the household of Charles E. Mickly, 2 doors from JAMES, age 13, preceding.

GRIFFITH, JOSEPH born ca. 1812, and wife, PHEBE A., born ca. 1824, both in NY, were listed in the 1850 census of Fairfield Twp., Lenawee Co., Mich. with HULDAH, age 5; FLORENCE A., age 3; and EMELINE, age 1, all b. Mich., in their household.

GRIFFITH, LAZARUS was born ca. 1778/80, and wife, ELIZABETH (ELIGER), daughter of a Revolutionary soldier (name not stated), was born ca. 1785/7, both born in Dutchess Co., NY. They had both moved with parents to Chemung Co., NY, where they married. They moved to Madison Twp., Lenawee Co., Mich. in 1833 (probably he written as "L. A." in the 1840 census index). She died in 1853, age 66; and he died in 1860, age 82. There were 5 daughters and 4 sons (names note stated). Probably a daughter, PHEBE b. 1805 (following); and in the 1850 census of Madison Twp., Lazarus, age 70, and Elizabeth, age 65, listed youngest son, CYRUS (preceding) in the household. JOHN, preceding, was 3 doors away in the census; and also note LEWIS, following, who was listed about 6 doors away.

GRIFFITH, LEWIS born ca. 1806 was listed in the 1850 census of Madison Twp., Lenawee Co., Mich. with CHARLES, age 15; JAMES, age 13; JOHN, age 10; SUSAN, age 8; HARRIET, age 6; GEORGE, age 3, all b. Mich., in his household. See LAZARUS, preceding.

GRIFFITH, LYMAN (See Jeremiah Wilsey²)

GRIFFITH, MARY P., born ca. 1797, Wales, was listed head of household in the 1840 census index of Tecumseh Twp., Lenawee Co., Mich.; and in the 1850 census with THEOPHILUS, age 22, b. NY, in her household.

GRIFFITH, PHEBE born 1805, NY, married Aden Elliot (also see), and as she named a son. Lazarus G., is probably a daughter of LAZARUS, preceding.

GRIFFITH, RHODA (See Rufus Scofield)

GRIFFITH, RILEY (possibly son of ABNER, preceding) born ca. 1815, and wife, LUCY A. P., born ca. 1817, both in NY, were listed in the 1850 census of Seneca Twp., Lenawee Co., Mich. with DEWANE C., age 12; MARY E., age 10; REBECCA, age 7; THEODORE E., age 7/12, all b. Mich., in their household (next door to ABNER)

GRIMES, DENNIS O., son of JOSHUA (following), was born 9 May 1833, Carroll Co., Maryland. He lived for a time in Erie Co., Ohio, and Indiana. He married on 3 Sept. 1863 to SARAH J. (MULLENIX), daughter of Samuel (also see), of Erie Co., Ohio; and settled in Rome Twp., Lenawee Co., Mich. by 1864. Children: 1. ALBERT L. b. 4 June 1864; 2. JOSEPH J. b. 3 Aug. 1866; 3. GEORGE W. b. 12 Aug. 1874; 4. FRANCES N. b. 1879 (d. age 3 mos). Ref: P&BA-Len pg. 524-5.

GRIMES, JOSHUA, son of BARSEL (who was b. England and d. Maryland), was born in Carroll Co., Maryland. He married there to ELIZA (BARNES); and he died there at age 65; and she was residing there in the home of a daughter in 1888. Known son, DENNIS O. (preceding). Ref: P&BA-Len pg. 524-5.

GRISWOLD, ASA born ca. born ca. 1822, and wife, MARY A., born ca. 1829, both in NY, were listed in the 1850 census of Hudson Twp., Lenawee Co., Mich.

GRISWOLD, CHARLES, son of THOMAS (following), born ca. 1819, and wife, ABBY, born NY, was listed in the 1850 census of Tecumseh Twp., Lenawee Co., Mich. with VIRGINIA, age 6; GEORGE, age 2, both b. Mich., and BETSEY (mother, see THOMAS), in their household.

GRISWOLD, DAVID moved from Conn. to Southport, (then Montgomery Co., later Tioga Co.) Chemung Co., NY by 1778 (listed in Tioga Co., NY 1800 census index). It may be he with NY served with widow, JANE, in the Revolutionary pension applications #W1754, & BLWt 11085-160-55. Known son, THOMAS (following). Ref: P&BA-Len pg. 267-8.

GRISWOLD, GEORGE, son of THOMAS (following), born ca. 1823, NY, married in Tecumseh Twp., Lenawee Co., Mich. to HELEN M. (FITZSIMMONS), daughter of Thomas (also see). In the 1850 census they had no children as yet in the household. Children: 1. HATTIE ESTELLE (d. age 4 yrs); ISABEL F. (m. William Waldron, also see); 3. ALICE E. Ref: P&BA-Len pg. 267-8.

GRISWOLD, PHILANDER born ca. 1836, NY, was listed in the 1850 census of Hudson Twp., Lenawee Co., Mich. in a Palmer household.

GRISWOLD, THOMAS, son of DAVID (preceding), was born 22 Feb. 1790, Southport, NY; and served in the War of 1812. He married BETSEY (WEIR), daughter of John, Esq. (also see). In 1825, they moved to Tecumseh Twp., Lenawee Co., Mich. He died 15 Oct. 1836; and she died Dec. 1871. There were 4 sons and 3 daughters (all names not stated). In the 1850 census, Betsey, age 53, b. NY, was in the household of known son, CHARLES (preceding); with BENJAMIN, age 24, b. NY; and SALLY ANN, age 19; JOHN, age 16, both b. Mich.; and son, GEORGE (preceding) was listed next door. Ref: P&BA-Len pg. 267-8.

GRISWOLD, WILLIAM at an early date moved from New England to Eaton, Madison Co., NY. Known daughter, SARAH (m. Justus Root, also see, before 1828). Ref: P&BA-Len pg. 697-8.

GROSS, SUSAN born Penn. (See L. D. Heath).

GROVE, WILLIAM and wife, ISABELLE (CLAYTON), were natives of New Jersey, who remained there until after the birth of all their children. They moved to Ovid, Seneca Co., NY, where he died in 1873, and she died 1863. Known daughter, ALICE D. b. 24 Mar. 1820 (m. Franklin Osborn, also see). Ref: P&BA-Len pg. 261-2.

GROVER, LEONARD was a native of Vermont, who moved in 1837 to Lucas Co., Richfield Twp., Ohio. He died there on 15 May 1861, and his widow married again (name of husband not stated) and moved to Riga Twp.,

Pioneer Families of Southeastern Michigan

Lenawee Co., Mich. Known daughter, BETTIE M. (m. Jessiah Westerman, also see). Ref: P&BA-Len pg. 276-7.

GUIETT, ANN (See John Millson)

GUILD, LYDIA (See A. Fowler)

GULL, HENRY (See John H. Van Pelt)

GULLICK, DELILAH married first to _?_ Hathaway; and second to Ira Rogers (also see). Ref: P&BA-Len pg. 1177-8.

GUNDERMAN, JACOB and wife, CLARISSA, moved from New Jersey to Lodi, Seneca Co.,NY; and he died there in 1845, and she died in 1874. Known daughter, SARAH M. b. ca. 1826, NY (m. Aaron K. Waldron, also see). Ref: P&BA-Len pg. 1066-7.

GUNN, ISAAC C., son of JACOB (following), was born 27 Oct. 1819, Sussex Co., NJ. He was bound out at age 8, but returned home at age 15. He married on 16 Apr. 1842 to SALLY ANN (DRAKE), also born Sussex Co. They moved to Huron Co., Ohio, where she died in 1849, leaving 5 children (all names not stated). Known daughter, MARY E. (m. Levi Mering). Isaac C. married again to MARY E. (WEDGE), daughter of Squire (also see). They later moved to Woodstock Twp., Lenawee Co., Mich. (after 1850). There were 10 children, all names not stated, just those following who survived in 1888: RHODA b. 27 Oct. 1852, Ohio (m. Samuel Hogue); ALTHA b. 7 July 1857 (m. Fred B. Emmons); ALICE (twin of Altha; m. A. F. Wood); CHARLES E. b. 7 June 1859, Woodstock Twp. (to LaClede, MO); T. B. b. 3 Aug. 1861. Ref: P&BA-Len pg. 945-6.

GUNN, JACOB and wife, MARY (OGDEN), were reared and married in Sussex Co., NJ. About 1845, they removed to Montrose, Penn., where they both died at age 67. Thirteen children (names not stated, except): ISAAC C. (preceding). Ref: P&BA-Len pg. 945-6.

GUNN, LUCY born 25 Dec. 1776, NY (See Thomas Jones).

GUNSOLUS, ELLA (See Henry H. Tabor)

GURLEY, THOMAS and wife, JANE, were born Ireland, and came to the US and settled first in Albany, NY. They moved to Huron Co., Ohio. where he died in 1872, and she died in Jan. 1868. Two sons and 5 daughters, and only name stated was MATILDA b. 18 Dec. 1821 (m. Henry L. Hurlburt, also see, in Ohio). Ref: P&BA-Len pg. 416.

GURNEE, HALSTED married HANNAH (COE) in 1802 in Rockland Co., NY. He died there at age 47; and she died in SenecaCo., NY at age 57. Known son, JOHN R. (following). Ref: P&BA-Len pg. 954-5.

GURNEE, JOHN R., son of HALSTED (preceding), was born 9 Jan. 1805, Rockland Co., NY. He went at age 15 to Orange Co., NY to work, and then to Hempstead, NY, and later to Bloomfield, NJ. After the death of his father, he operated the farm in Rockland Co., NY till the fall of 1831, when he went first to Lenawee Co., Mich. He returned to NY, where he married on 25 Nov. 1832 to HESTER (BEACH), born 8 Oct. 1810, Rockland Co., and they moved to Adrian Twp., Lenawee Co., Mich. where all their children were born. 1. MARY b. ca. 1834 (d. 17 Sept. 1871, Chicago, Ill.); 2. HELEN M. b. ca. 1838 (m. W. R. King, Chicago, Ill.); 3. LUCY b. ca. 1840 (m. Horace K. Beachman, Williamsburg, Mich.); 4. FRANCES b. ca. 1843 (d. 27 July 1857); 5. ELLA b. ca. 1847 (m. E. G. Savage, had dau., Grace). Ref: P&BA-Len pg. 954-5.

GUSSENBAUER, GEORGE and wife, BARBARA (MAURER), were born in Germany, and came to the US, and settled in Monroe Co., Mich. in 1839. They operated a hotel, and remained there. Seven children (all names not stated, except): #3. PETER (following). Ref: P&BA-Len pg. 566-7.

GUSSENBAUER, PETER, son of GEORGE (preceding), was born 10 June 1842, Monroe, Mich. He married first in Fairfield Twp., Lenawee Co. to ELIZA J. (RATHBUN), daughter of Rufus H. (also see). Eliza died there 25 Jan. 1864, leaving known son, JOHN R. Peter married again on 5 May 1864 to Mrs. MARIAN M. (WINSLOW) BUMPUS, daughter of Marvin L., and widow of Urson (see both). Ref: P&BA-Len pg. 566-7 & 802-3.

GUTHRIDGE, ELIZA (See Elliott Gray)

- H -

HAAS, ALPHEUS F., son of JOHN (following), born 21 Oct. 1845, Brooklyn, Jackson Co., Mich. He served in the Civil War. On 15 Oct. 1868, he married MARY (TOLCHARD) born 1848, Geneva, NY. They settled first in Hudson, Lenawee Co., and then moved in 1880 to Adrian. Son, LOUIS T. b. 1873. Ref: P&BA-Len pg. 226-7.

HAAS, JOHN born ca. 1811, Germany, married SARAH (CROMAN), born ca. 1811, Penn., both of whom had come to Michigan early in their lives. They married in Washtenaw Co., Mich. where they remained for 10 years, then moved to Jackson Co., and after 6 years (by 1850) to Hudson Twp., Lenawee Co. (Note: There was a John "Hass" in Columbia Twp., Jackson Co. Mich. in 1840 census index). She died in 1852, and he afterwards went to Fremont, Nebraska where he died in the Spring of 1883. There were 3 sons and 3 daughters, names not stated (except Alpheus) and others following are from the 1850 census of Hudson Twp.: 1. ALVINA A., age 14; 2. CHRISTINA, age 13; 3. MARY C., age 11; 4. ALPHEUS F. (preceding); 5. JOHN W., age 1. Ref: P&BA-Len pg. 226-7.

HACKETT, CHARLES (See David Pearson)
HACKETT, WALTER (See John P. Schwab)

HADLEY, HANNAH (See John Newton)
HADLEY, SADIE (See Henry H. Rawson)
HADLEY, SYLVIA (See Harrison Daniels)

HAFF, CORNELIA M. Mrs. was the daughter of Thomas C. & Rebecca A. (Nichols) Smith (also see). The Haffs resided in Clinton Co., NY in 1888.

HAFF, EDWIN, son of HIRAM (following), was born 7 Mar. 1840 in Sandusky Co., Ohio; and served in Co. F., 49th Ohio Inf., becoming a Lieut., during the Civil War. He married 22 Dec. 1868, Clyde, Ohio to LIBBIE (DE RAN), daughter of Dennis (also see), and settled in Medina Twp., Lenawee Co., Mich. Children: 1. GEORGE M.; 2. LENNIE; 3. BELLE. Ref: P&BA-Len pg. 921-2.

HAFF, HIRAM and wife, CYNTHIA (AVERY), natives of NY, moved to Sandusky Co., Ohio by 1840. Known son, EDWIN (preceding). Ref: P&BA-Len pg. 921-2.

HAGAMAN also see HAGERMAN

HAGAMAN, ABIGAIL born 1805, NY, was head of household in the 1850 census of Fairfield Twp., Lenawee Co., Mich. with LYDIA, age 17; ELIZABETH, age 16, both b. NY; and HOVERT?, age 13; MILA, age 11; SARAH H., age 8, all b. Mich., in her household (listed in census between IRA J. & JOHN W., following) Note THOMAS, following, husband of Abigail??

HAGAMAN, CALVIN born ca. 1813, and wife, ASELATH?, age 33, both b. NY, were listed in the 1850 census of Blissfield Twp., Lenawee Co., Mich. with no family.

HAGAMAN, EDGAR S., son of IRA J. (following), was born 25 Jan. 1844; married on 5 Oct. 1865 to ALMYRA (THURBER), daughter of Robert G. (also see). In 1867, they removed to Jasper Co., Iowa, and returned on 5 Mar. 1875 to Fairfield Twp., Lenawee Co., Mich. In 1882 they moved to Weston, Mich. No children were listed. Ref: P&BA-Len pg. 1044-5.

HAGAMAN, FRANCIS born ca. 1821, NY, was listed in the 1850 census of Fairfield Twp., Lenawee Co., Mich. in the household of Henry Smith (a few doors from SAMUEL W.). Francis may be another son of JOHN S.?

HAGAMAN, IRA J., son of JOSEPH S. (following), was born ca. 1816, Shelby, Orleans Co., NY, and came to Adrian Twp., Lenawee Co., Mich. with his parents. He married in Adrian on 23 Mar. 1838 to ELIZABETH (PADDOCK), daughter of Nathan (also see). They settled in Fairfield Twp. He died 14 Feb. 1886; and she was surviving in 1888. Children: 1. MARY A. b. 18 Jan. 1839 (m. Lewis P. Mead, Jasper Co., IA); 2. EDGAR S. (preceding); 3. EDSON B. (twin of Edgar); 4. JOSEPH b. 29 Oct. 1854. Ref: P&BA-Len pg. 1044-5.

HAGAMAN, JOHN I. born ca. 1800, and wife, SALLY, born ca. 1800, both in NY, were listed in the 1850 census of Fairfield Twp., Lenawee Co., Mich. with SMITH, age 22; CALVIN, age 19, both b. NY; and DEBORAH H., age 12; ISAIAH S., age 10; TENNY? A. (female), age 9; JOHN, age 6, all b. Mich., in their household.

HAGAMAN, JOHN S. born ca. 1777, New Jersey, probably moved to Seneca Co., NY. In the 1850 census of Fairfield Twp., Lenawee Co., Mich. he was in the household of SAMUEL W. (following). Also note FRANCIS (preceding). Note: In the militia of Somerset Co., NJ in 1793, were a number of "Hagamon" men listed, including a JOHN.

HAGAMAN, JOHN W. born ca. 1825, and wife, JANE, born ca. 1829, both in NY, were listed in the 1850 census of Fairfield Twp., Lenawee Co., Mich. with CHARLOTTE, age 2; and ALONA, age 6/12, both b. Mich., in their household (next door to ABIGAIL, preceding).

HAGAMAN, JOSEPH S. born ca. 1783, married Mrs. ELIZABETH (STOUT) WALDRON born ca. 1788, both born New Jersey; and afterwards went to Seneca Co., NY. They moved to Adrian Twp., Lenawee Co., Mich. in June 1832. Known son, IRA J. (preceding). and JOSEPH (following) possibly another son; and in the 1850 census of Fairfield, Joseph S. listed in his household: MATILDA, age 25; CAROLINE, age 20, both b. NY. Ref: P&BA-Len pg. 977-8 & 1044-5.

HAGAMAN, JOSEPH, possibly son of JOSEPH S. (preceding), was born 18 Mar. 1816, Varick, Seneca Co., NY. He married first in 1833 to LEAH (BLAIN), daughter of Samuel (also see). She died 4 Oct. 1863 in Morenci, Mich. He married again on 7 Sept. 1864 to Mrs. SUSAN (DAY) CAWLEY, daughter of James, and widow of Franklin (see both). No children listed. Ref: P&BA-Len pg. 977-8.

HAGAMAN, MELINDA (See Davis D. Bennett)

HAGAMAN, SAMUEL T. was listed in the 1850 census of Ogden Twp., Lenawee Co., Mich., age 32, born NY, with no family.

HAGAMAN, SAMUEL W., son of JOHN S. (preceding), was born ca. 1812; and his wife, ELEANOR (ABBOTT) was born ca. 1813, New Jersey. They moved from Seneca Co., NY to Fairfield Twp., Lenawee Co., Mich. in 1835, but returned to NY for about a year. It is probably they in the 1840 census index of Fairfield Twp.; and in the 1850 census father, JOHN S. was also in the household. Samuel W. died 19 Feb. 1882, and Eleanor died 2 Oct. 1885. Children: 1. JOHN S. b. ca. 1833; 2. ELIZABETH b. ca. 1836; 3. SARAH b. ca. 1838, all b. NY; 4. SUSAN E. b. 5 Feb. 1850, Fairfield Twp. (m. James B. Day, also see). Ref: P&BA-Len pg. 451-2.

HAGAMAN, THOMAS (spelled "Hagerman") was listed in the 1840 census index of Fairfield Twp., Lenawee Co., Mich. Note ABIGAIL, preceding. Note: There was a THOMAS listed in Cayuga Co., NY in the 1800 census index (Seneca formed from part of Cayuga).

HAGERMAN also see HAGAMAN

HAGERMAN, JOHN J. (See William H. Osborne). Note John S. in household of Samuel W. Hagaman.

HAGHAN, CHARLES (See William Kendrick)

HAHN, JOHN married a daughter (given name not stated) of George Miller (also see). Ref: P&BA-Len pg. 939-40.

HAIGHT, ALLEN was listed in the 1840 census index of Raisin Twp., Lenawee Co., Mich. He was not listed in the 1850 census, however, SARAH, age 49, b. NY, may be his wife, and she was listed in the household of GEORGE W., born ca. 1827, probably a son. Also in the household were ELVIRA, age 14; NEWTON, age 12; WILLIAM H., age 9 (may be he who served in Civil War from Jackson Co.) SOPHRONA, age 16, b. NY, in another household in the 1850 census of Raisin Twp., may also relate to this family.

HAIGHT, BENJAMIN was listed in the 1840 census index of Adrian Twp., Lenawee Co., Mich.

HAIGHT, CALEB born ca. 1783, NY, and wife, ALMINA, born ca. 1795, Conn., were listed in the 1850 census of Medina Twp., Lenawee Co., Mich. with Betsey Tabor, age 4, in their household.

HAIGHT, DAVID born ca. 1800, and wife, AVIS, born ca. 1804, both in NY, were probably they listed as "D" in the 1840 census index of Adrian Twp., Lenawee Co., Mich.; and in the 1850 census listed HIRAM, age 26; STEPHEN, age 23; ELIZA M., age 19; MARY A., age 17, all b NY; and CHARLES, age 14; PHEBE J., age 12; HORACE, age 10; GEORGE, age 6; MATTHEW L., age 2, all b. Mich., in their household.

HAIGHT, DAVID M. born ca. 1816, and wife, ADALIZA M., born ca. 1825, both in NY, were listed in the 1850 census of Seneca Twp., Lenawee Co., Mich. with KAZIAH? (female), age 6; JUNIUS? R., age 4; ROSELLA, age 2, all b. Mich., and (sister?) ELIZA, age 18, born NY, in their household.

HAIGHT, GEORGE W. born ca. 1827, NY (See ALLEN, preceding) is probably he who married after 1850 to BETSEY (BANGS), daughter of Alanson (also see), and later moved to Jackson Co., Mich.

HAIGHT, REUBEN was born ca. 1834, NY, and was listed in the 1850 census of Madison Twp., Lenawee Co., Mich. Note DAVID, preceding.

HAIGHT, SALMON L. and wife, EMILY (FOWLER), came from Steuben Co., NY, and it is probably they listed as "S. L." in the 1840 census index of Saline, Washtenaw Co., Mich. Known daughter, LYDIA M. (m. Ezra C. Coryell, also see, in Lenawee Co.) Ref: P&BA-Len pg. 1029-30. Note: There was a "W. T." also listed in the 1840 census index of Saline Twp., Washtenaw Co., Mich.

HAIGHT, SOPHRONA born ca. 1834, NY, was listed in the 1850 census of Raisin Twp., Lenawee Co., Mich. in a Raymond household. Note ALLEN, preceding.

HAIGHT, STEPHEN P. and wife, POLLY (GREEN), were from Steuben Co., NY. Polly died in Cass Co., Mich.; and he afterwards was living in 1888 in Ridgeway Twp., Lenawee Co., Mich. Known daughter, MARY b. Canisteo, Steuben Co., NY (m. Wallace P. Cadmus, see Richard.) Ref: P&BA-Len pg. 331-2. Note: There was a JOSEPH in Volinia Twp., Cass Co., Mich. in the 1840 census index.

HAILEY see HALEY

HAINES see HANES & HAYNES

HAIR also see HARE

HAIR, ABRAHAM born ca. 1807, and wife, SUSANNAH, born ca. 1810, both in Penn., were listed in the 1840 census index of Adrian Twp., Lenawee Co., Mich.; and in the 1850 census of Tecumseh Twp. with GEORGE, age 19; WILLIAM, age 18; CHARLES, age 16; SARAH, age 13, all b. Penn; and SAMUEL, age 10, b. Ohio; and HIRAM, age 8; MARGARET, age 5; ALBERT, age 2, all b. Mich., in their household.

HALE, GARDNER born ca. 1820, and wife, BETSY, born ca. 1825, both in NY, were listed in the 1850 census of Medina Twp., Lenawee Co., Mich. with MARY A., age 7, b. NY; and LEVI P., age 3, b. Mich., in their household.

HALE, ISRAEL & wife, AMANDA (OLDS), were from Mass., and moved to Mich. in 1866, settling first in Shiawassee Co., and then moved to Ohio. About 1881, they moved to Seneca Twp., Lenawee Co., Mich. where they resided in 1888. Daughter, MARY F. b. 7 Dec. 1848, Norwich, Mass. (m. Martin Odell, also see). Ref: P&BA-Len pg. 422.

HALE, ROSWELL born ca. 1823, and wife, PRISCILLA, born ca. 1832, both in NY, were listed in the 1850 census of Rome Twp., Lenawee Co., Mich. with William Fetton, age 74, b. Mass., and Mahitable Fetton, age 73, b. Conn., in their household.

HALEY, WILLIAM born ca. 1811, and wife, MARY (RUSSELL), BORN CA. 1817, were both natives of Co., Kildare, Ireland. They settled in Hudson Twp., Lenawee Co., Mich. by 1838. In the 1850 census, they listed (all b. Mich.): 1. THOMAS, age 12; 2. ELIZABETH, b. May 1842 (m. John Monahan[3], also see, Hudson Twp.); 3. WILLIAM, age 8; 4. SUSAN, age 7; 5. JOHN, age 4; 6. TERSA (TERESA?), age 2. Ref: P&BA-Len pg. 1109-10.

HALL, ABEL and wife, CATHERINE (PAUL), of Gorham, Fulton Co., Ohio, were parents of SUSAN (m. George W. Woodworth, also see). The Halls died in Fulton Co.

HALL, ABNER born ca. 1755, Dedham, Mass., was a Revolutionary soldier; and he married MARY (JACKSON) of Newtown, Mass. in 1775. They removed to Sudbury, VT, where he died in 1841; and she preceded him. There were 7 sons and 5 daughters (names not stated), and the 11th child & 6th son was EPHRAIM (following). Ref: P&BA-Len pg. 253-4.

HALL, ADELAIDE (See Thomas J. Pilbeam)

HALL, ALFRED D., son of Capt. STEPHEN H. (following), was born 6 Jan. 1824, Byron, Genesee Co., NY, and moved with parents to Albion, Calhoun Co., Mich. He married there 9 Sept. 1851 to EMILY A. (TODD), daughter of James B. (also see). They moved to Tecumseh, Lenwawee Co., Mich. in 1854. She died 21 Feb. 1862 leaving children: 1. DANIEL T. (following); 2. SARAH A. b. 27 Dec. 1854 (m/1 E. J. Stevenson, also see; m/2 William H. Wiggins as 3rd wife). Alfred D. married again on 15 Feb. 1865 to ENGELINE (HEESEN), daughter of Rudolph (also see). Children: 3. FRANK H. b. 22 July 1866; 4. GEORGE E. b. 16 June 1868 (d. 20 Apr. 1869); 5. WILLIAM E. b. 15 May 1870; 6. RACHEL N. b. 5 Dec. 1872; 7. EMILY E. b. 15 Feb. 1875. Ref: P&BA-Len pg. 1049-50; 1069-70; 1130-2.

HALL, AUSTIN G., son of EDMUND (following), was born 6 Apr. 1839, Raisin Twp., Lenawee Co., Mich. He married on 4 Apr. 1868 to LAURA A. (WILDER), daughter of Artemus (also see). They settled first in Tecumseh, but about 1873 settled in Raisin Twp. Children: ARTHUR A.; & a child (name not stated) deceased before 1888. Ref: P&BA-Len pg. 967-8.

HALL, BENJAMIN was a native of Conn. who moved (possibly by 1800) to Cooperstown, NY, and then to Genesee Co., NY. Known son, Capt. STEPHEN P. (following). Ref: P&BA-Len pg. 1130-2.

HALL, CAROLINE (See Jeremiah Lockwood[3])

HALL, CATHERINE (See Jared Comstock)

HALL, CHARLES D., son of MATTHIAS (following), was born 3 Nov. 1851, Lorain Co., Ohio; and married in Adrian, Lenawee Co., Mich. in 1875 to ALICE A. (McLOUTH), daughter of Lewis (also see). Children: 1. LOUISA BELL b. 13 May 1880; 2. CHARLES ARTHUR b. 21 Feb. 1882; 3. EDWIN M. b. 29 Oct. 1885. Ref: P&BA-Len pg. 243-4.

HALL, CLARK born ca. 1809, and wife, HARRIET, born ca. 1810, both in NY, were listed in the 1840 census index of Raisin Twp., Lenawee Co., Mich.; and in the 1850 census with SAMANTHA, age 17; HOSEA, age 15; SALONA, age 5, all b. Mich., in their household.

Also note EDMUND; REUBEN; & JONATHAN, possibly brothers?

HALL, DANIEL T., son of ALFRED D. (preceding), was born 15 May 1852, Calhoun Co., Mich. He married DORA (DORIELL), daughter of William, and they resided in Tecumseh village, Lenawee Co., Mich. Children: 1. ALFRED D.; 2. CLARE D.; 3. OSCAR S. Ref: P&BA-Len pg. 1049-50.

HALL EDMUND, son of EDMUND, was born 20 Feb. 1807, Pompey, NY. He came from Steuben Co., NY in 1835, as a single man, to Raisin Twp., Lenawee Co., Mich. He married on 10 Feb. 1836 to LUCRETIA (RAYMOND), a Quaker, daughter of Rufus (also see). They were listed in the 1840 census index of Raisin Twp. as "Edwin;" and in the 1850 census with the following children: 1. JAMES J. b. ca. 1837; 2. AUSTIN G. (preceding); 3. RUFUS R. b. ca. 1840; 4. RUHAMA b. ca. 1842 (m. James T. Lane). Ref: P&BA-Len pg. 967-8 & 1043-4.

HALL, E. P. was listed in the 1840 census index of Medina Twp., Lenawee Co., Mich.

HALL, EPHRAIM, son of ABNER (preceding), was born 20 Jan. 1810, Sudbury, VT. He came to Detroit, Mich. in 1833; and then moved to Deerfield, Lenawee Co., Mich. He married at Middleport, Niagara Co., NY to MARY A. (SMITH) who was born 30 Dec. 1818, Sudbury, VT. They settled in Deerfield, Mich. They were listed in the 1840 census index of Blissfield Twp., Lenawee Co., Mich.; and in the 1850 census there. She died 30 Aug. 1881, Denver, Col., where she had gone shortly before for her health. Children: 1. MARY E. (d. infancy); 2. WALTER G. b. 9 Aug. 1840 (d. young); 3. HELEN J. b. 16 Sept. 1841 (m. A. B. Burnham, Louisville, KY; he d. 24 July 1887, and family went to Denver, Col.); 4. ADA A. b. 27 Oct. 1845 (m. Neal McQuarie, Deerfield); 5. HERVEY G. b. 27 Dec. 1854 (to Louisville, KY); 6. FLORENCE A. Ref: P&BA-Len pg. 253-4.

HALL, GEORGE born ca. 1795, Conn., was listed in the 1850 census of Blissfield Twp., Lenawee Co., Mich. with ALMIRA, age 22, b. NY; CELIA M., age 6, and LUCINDA, age 1, both b. Mich. in the household. Note GEORGE, JR. (following).

HALL, GEORGE Jr. was born ca. 1824, Mass., and was listed in the 1850 census of Blissfield Twp., Lenawee Co., Mich. with no family in the household. Note GEORGE, preceding.

HALL, HARVEY and wife, SARAH (HULL) were parents of OLIVE b. 29 Dec. 1803, Conn. (m. John Hood, Jr., also see, in Erie Co., Penn.). Ref: P&BA-Len pg. 1172-3.

HALL, HENRY was listed in the 1840 census index of Palmyra Twp., Lenawee Co., Mich.

HALL, HENRY C., son of Dr. LEONARD G. (following), was born 4 Apr. 1841, Hudson Twp., Lenawee Co., Mich. In 1859, he went to California, and later to New York City. He returned to Hudson where he married on 24 Dec. 1870 to M. JOSEPHINE (HEMANS), daughter of Enoch (also see). No children listed. Ref: P&BA-Len pg. 918-20.

HALL, HUDSON B. was listed in the 1840 census index of Tecumseh Twp., Lenawee Co., Mich.

HALL, JOHN was listed in the 1840 census index of Clinton, Lenawee Co., Mich. adjacent to WILLIAM A. (following).

HALL, JOHN[3] was the son (the 10th child and youngest) of RICHARD[2]. (Richard[2] was son, and 2nd child, of JOHN[1] who was an original settler of Basking Ridge, NJ). John[3], who probably went to Penn., was the father of MOSES[4] (following). Ref: P&BA-Len pg. 341-2.

HALL, JOHN L., son of NEHEMIAH (following), was born 14 Dec. 1813, Parma, Monroe Co., NY. He came first to Medina Twp., Lenawee Co., Mich. in 1835, purchased land but didn't settle. In 1836, he went to Illinois, and lived in Farmington & Rock Island. He returned to Lenawee Co. where he married on 28 Jan. 1841 to CLARISSA C. (CAROLINE? CRANE), daughter of Turner (also see) of Madison Twp. They settled in Medina Twp. Children: 1. CAROLINE b. ca. 1842 (m. James Drown, also see); 2. HARRIET I. b. ca. 1849 (m. Lewis H. Converse); 3. PHEBE (m. John B. Spooner). Ref: P&BA-Len pg. 569-70.

HALL, JONATHAN was born ca. 1804, Conn., and wife, LYDIA, was born ca. 1816, NY, and they were listed in the 1840 census index of Macon Twp., Lenawee Co., Mich.; and in the 1850 census of Raisin Twp. with SARAH M., age 14; LUCY V., age 11; MARY E., age 7; MELVIN, age 2/12, all b. Mich., in their household. Note: They were 2 doors from REUBEN. Also see EDMUND, preceding. HALL, JOSEPH E. born ca. 1810, Conn., and wife, SARAH ANN, born ca. 1811, both in Conn., were listed in the 1840 census index of Tecumseh Twp., Lenawee Co., Mich., and in the 1850 census in the household of Caroline Graves, also see.

HALL, LEONARD G. Dr. was born 7 Aug. 1806, Duanesburg, Schenectady, NY (son of a man who had moved from Mass. to Duanesburg before 1806, then that year moved to Cold Brook, Herkimer Co., NY). Leonard G. first went to St. Catharine's, Canada, to work, but returned to Fairfield, Herkimer Co., NY where he obtained his medical degree. In 1834, he removed to Rollin Twp., Lenawee Co., Mich., and resided with Daniel Rhodes. He married 12 Oct. 1839 to NANCY K. (WELLS), daughter of Daniel (also see); and moved in 1840 to Hudson, Lenawee Co. She died 12 Oct. 1853; and he died 29 Oct. 1877, Hudson. Children: 1. HENRY C. (preceding); 2. JOHN W. b. ca. 1843 (to Detroit, Mich.); 3. IONE C. b. ca. 1845 (m. Dr. A. R. Smart, Toledo, O.); 4. INEZ F. b. ca. 1847 (m. W. H. Cornes, Hudson). Ref: P&BA-Len pg. 918-20.

HALL, MARY Mrs. (See George Price)

HALL, MATTHIAS and wife, SOPHIA (HOPKINS), were natives of NY, who settled in Lorain Co., Ohio. She died in 1857, and Matthias afterwards moved to Lansing, Mich. where he died at age 78. Five sons and 3 daughters (names not stated). Known son, CHARLES D. (preceding). Ref: P&BA-Len pg. 243-4.

HALL, MOSES[4], son of JOHN[3] (preceding), went before 1800 from Penn. to Ontario Co., NY as a young man. He had a known daughter, JANE, b. 25 Apr. 1809, Geneva, NY (m. John Humphrey, also see). Moses died over age 70 in Willamsport, Penn. at the home of a son. Ref: P&BA-Len pg. 341-2 & 470-1.

HALL, MOSES was listed in Battle Creek, Calhoun Co., Mich. in 1840 census index. Note MOSES, preceding.

HALL, NATHANIEL and wife, BELINDA, apparently lived in Canada ca. 1801; and later in Isle LaMotte, Grand Isle Co., VT. Known daughter, AMELIA b. 29 Apr. 1801, Lower Canada (m. Theodorick Luther, also see). Ref: P&BA-Len pg. 587-8.

Pioneer Families of Southeastern Michigan

HALL, NEHEMIAH and wife, POLLY (ATCHISON), were natives of New England who settled in Monroe Co., NY after their marriage (before 1813). He died there a young man. Children: 1. POLLY (m. Allen Washburne); 2. BEZALLEL (d. Illinois); 3. LYMAN D. (to Oregon); 4. JOHN L. (preceding). Polly married again to William Buell (also see) and died in Quincy, Branch Co., Mich. Ref: P&BA-Len pg. 569-70.

HALL, OTHNIEL born ca. 1810 was listed in the 1840 census index of Clinton, Lenawee Co., Mich.; and in the 1850 census of Tecumseh Twp. with OTHNIEL, age 15; JOSEPH, age 3; FRANCES, age ?, all b. Mich., in his household. Also note JOHN; & JOSEPH E.

HALL, OZRO? born ca. 1820, and wife, MARIA, born ca. 1826, both in NY, were listed in the 1850 census of Madison Twp., Lenawee Co., Mich. with no family.

HALL, PHILO born ca. 1815, NY, and wife, CAROLINE, born ca. 1823, Penn., were listed in the 1850 census of Medina Twp., Lenawee Co., Mich. with WARREN, age 9; JANE, age 7, both b. NY; and ALFRED, age 5; HELEN, age 4; DAVID, age 1, all b. Mich., in their household.

HALL, PRINCE BRYANT and wife, ABIGAIL, moved from Mass. to Vermont. They may have moved later to Chenango Co., NY. Known daughter, EVELINA S, b, & June 1797, St. Albans, VT (m. Dobson Page, also see, probably in Chenango Co.)

HALL, REUBEN married CONTENT (WELLS), daughter of John S. (also see) and resided in NY. Ref: P&BA-Len pg. 454-5.

HALL, REUBEN L. born ca. 1806, and wife, ABBA, born ca. 1810, both born Conn., were listed in the 1840 census index of Raisin Twp., Lenawee Co., Mich.; and in the 1850 census listed WILLIAM H., age 15; EMMA A., age 13; MORRIS S., age 11; FRANCIS E., age 9; MARY S., age 6; FRANCES W., age 3; ANNA R., age 1, all b. Mich., in their household (near to JONATHAN, preceding).

HALL, STEPHEN P. Capt., son of BENJAMIN (preceding), born 15 Dec. 1797, New London, Conn., moved with parents to Genesee Co., NY. He married there on 1 June 1822 to CLARISSA (DIBBLE), daughter of Andrew (also see). In 1845, they moved to Albion, Calhoun Co., Mich. He became a Captain in the State Militia. There were 4 sons and 4 daughters (names not stated). He died 4 Mar. 1861; and she was living in 1888 in Reed City, Osceola Co., Mich. with known daughter, FRANCES J. (m. Dean). They also had known son, ALFRED D. (preceding). Ref: P&BA-Len pg. 1130-2.

HALL, THOMAS born ca. 1800, England, was listed in the 1850 census of Ridgeway Twp., Lenawee Co., Mich. with JOHN, age 20; JAMES, age 18; ABEL, age 16; JANE, age 14, all b. NY, in his household.

HALL, THOMAS born ca. 1807, and wife, MARY, born ca. 1815, both in England, were listed in the 1850 census of Tecumseh Twp., Lenawee Co., Mich. with JAMES, age 12, b. England, and MARY ANN, age 5/12, b. Mich., in their household.

HALL, WHITMAN born ca. 1810, Mass., and wife, JULIA, born ca. 1816, NY, were listed in the 1850 census of Hudson Twp., Lenawee Co., Mich. with OSCAR, age 18, b. Mass.; BRIGGS C., age 15; JAMES A., age 13; LUCY A., age 10; FRANCIS W., age 7; FREDERICK J., age 5, all born Ohio; and THOMAS A., age 3; CELESTIA E., age 6/12, both b. Mich., in their household.

HALL, WILLIAM A. born ca. 1810, and wife, MARY, born ca. 1818, were listed in the 1840 census index of Clinton, Lenawee Co., Mich.; and in the 1850 census of Tecumseh Twp., Lenawee Co. with EMIBELL?, age 7; CHARLOTTE, age 4; WILLIAM, age 1, all b. Mich., in their household. Note: They were adjacent to JOHN (preceding) in the 1840 census index.

HALLADAY, ABRAM (spelled HOLLADAY) was listed in the 1840 census index of Medina Twp., Lenawee Co., Mich.

HALLADAY, ADDISON P., son of JAMES, Sr. (following), was born 1 Nov. 1827, Ontario Co., NY; and married there to MARY E. (HOWLAND) who was born Mass. (See Thomas J. Howland). They removed first to Brooklyn, Jackson Co., Mich.; and after 6 years to Clinton Twp., Lenawee Co., Mich. Son, HORACE (m. Lilla Crane, Manchester, Ontario Co., NY.) Mary E. died, and Addison P. married again to Mrs. ROSETTA (MARKS) CHAMBERLAIN, daughter of Nehemiah, and widow of Charles (see both). Children: 2. CEBERT M. (m. Rachel Post); 3. OSCAR H.; 3. HERMAN. Ref: P&BA-Len pg. 456-7.

HALLADAY, JAMES Jr., son of JAMES, Sr. (following), was born 22 Jan. 1832, Manchester, Ontario Co., NY. He moved with his parents to Michigan, and he married on 19 Feb. 1873 in Clinton Twp., Lenawee Co., Mich. to SARAH (RICHMOND), daughter of Levi C. (also see). Children: 1. ALICE; 2. RALPH A. Ref: P&BA-Len pg. 244.

HALLADAY, JAMES, Sr. was born in Ontario Co., NY. He married PAMELIA (BIGELOW). They moved to Bridgewater, Washtenaw Co., Mich. in 1863. He died 28 Dec. 1880, age 82, Bridgewater, and she was still living there in 1888, age 83, with a daughter (name not stated). There were 7 children, and only names stated: ADDISON P.; and JAMES, Jr. (both preceding). Ref: P&BA-Len pg. 244.

HALSEY, male, (given name illegible) age 10, b. Mich. was listed in the 1850 census of Adrian Twp., Lenawee Co., Mich. in a Ludlum household. Note that MILTON, following, was the only one of this surname listed in the 1840 census index in Lenawee Co.

HALSEY, EMMA (See Charles Raynor)

HALSEY, MILTON N. born ca. 1810, and wife, OCTAVIA, born ca. 1820, both in NY, were listed in the 1840 census index of Adrian Twp., Lenawee Co., Mich.; and in the 1850 census with MILTON G., age 1, b. Mich., in their household.

HALSTEAD also see HALSTED

HALSTEAD, ELIZA, age 25, born NY, was listed in the 1850 census of Tecumseh Twp., Lenawee Co., Mich. in the household of Abraham & Amanda Jones.

HALSTEAD, THOMPSON and wife, SOPHIA (BEEBE), were natives of NY who settled in Cuba, Allegany Co., NY. She died there 27 Nov. 1850, and he was still living there in 1888. Known daughters: 1. NANCY b. 19 June 1846, Cuba, NY (m. Isaac Newton Warren, also see, in Clayton, Mich.); 2. ELIZABETH A. (d. infancy). Ref: P&BA-Len pg. 522-3.

HALSTED also see HALSTEAD

HALSTED, ANN born ca. 1829, NY, was listed in the 1850 census of Madison Twp., Lenawee Co., Mich. in a Merick household. Note MARIA, following.

HALSTED, DAVID W. was listed in the 1840 census index of Rome Twp., Lenawee Co., Mich. adjacent to those following who were in Rome Twp.

HALSTED, EDWARD born ca. 1815, and wife, ELIZA, born ca. 1816, both in NY, were listed in the 1840 census index of Rome Twp., Lenawee Co., Mich.; and in the 1850 census with ALONZO, age 13, b. NY; and MELISSA b. 6 Nov. 1838 (m. William Hood, also see); CAROLINE, age 6; MARIA, age 3; OLIVER, age 1, all b. Mich., in their household.

HALSTED, ELIZABETH "BETSEY" was born in Aug. 1804, possibly in Greene Co., NY, and married Leonard Reynolds (also see) possibly in Yates Co., NY. They settled in Rome Twp., Lenawee Co., Mich. by 1840. Ref: P&BA-Len pg. 1085-6. Note JOHN, following.

HALSTED, EMMA of Rome Twp., Lenawee Co., Mich. (See Clark W. Decker).

HALSTED, JACOB born ca. 1796, and wife, ELIZABETH, born ca. 1800, both in NY, were listed in the 1840 census index of Rome Twp., Lenawee Co., Mich.; and in the 1850 census with ELIZABETH A., age 21; REUBEN, age 15; OLIVER, age 12, all b. NY; and EDWIN W., age 10; MARGARET, age 9; ANAZLIA, age 7, all b. Mich., in their household. Also note JACOB W., following, probably he listed as Jacob Jr. in 1840 census index.

HALSTED, JACOB W. born ca. 1817, is probably he listed as Jacob Jr. in the 1840 census index (note JACOB, preceding), and wife, JANE, born ca. 1820, both in NY, were listed in the 1850 census of Rome Twp., Lenawee Co., Mich. with MYRON, age 6; LUCINDA, age 5; ELIZABETH, age 2, all b. Mich., in their household.

HALSTED, JEROME born ca. 1807, and wife, ABBY, born ca. 1808, both in NY, were listed in the 1840 census index of Rome Twp., Lenawee Co., Mich.; and in the 1850 census with EMELINE, age 5; NEHEMIAH, age 1, both b. Mich., in their household (2 doors from PETER & EDWARD.

HALSTED, JOHN moved from Yates Co., NY to Rome Twp., Lenawee Co., Mich. in 1837. He died in Rome Twp. at age 82 (before 1850). Known daughter, EMELINE b. 30 Sept. 1808 (m. James T. Finch, also see). Ref: P&BA-Len pg. 621-2. Note MARY, in the household of PETER, following.

HALSTED, LEWIS M. born ca. 1822, and wife, ELSINA, born ca. 1821, both in NY, were listed in the 1850 census of Rome Twp., Lenawee Co., Mich. with CHLOE A., age 2, b. Mich., in their household (next door to PETER, following).

HALSTED, MARIA was born ca. 1816, NY, and was listed in the 1850 census of Madison Twp., Lenawee Co., Mich. in a Hunt household. Note ANN, preceding.

HALSTED, PETER born ca. 1822, NY, was listed as head of household with mother(?), MARY, age 65, b. NY, in the household in the 1850 census of Rome Twp., Lenawee Co., Mich. LEWIS M. was listed next door, and JEROME 2 doors away.

HALSTED, SAMUEL born ca. 1779, and wife, PHEBE, born ca. 1782, both in NY, were listed in the 1840 census index of Rollin Twp., Lenawee Co., Mich. and in the 1850 census with Frederick Hare, age 48; Betsey Hare, age 49; and Martin Hare, age 20, all b. NY, in their household.

HALSTED, THOMAS born ca. 1815, and wife, MARY, born ca. 1817, both in NY, were listed in the 1840 census index of Rome Twp., Lenawee Co., Mich.; and in the 1850 census with OLIVER, age 10; ALBERT, age 7; LEVI, age 4; HUDSON, age 1, all b. Mich., in their household.

HAM, CHRISTINA (See James Winters)

HAMBROOK, HATTIE Mrs. was the daughter of Ira Holloway (also see).

HAMILTON, ABRAM, son of WILLIAM (following), moved about 1822 with his parents from Chenango Co., NY to Erie Co., Ohio (an area now in Huron Co.) He married there before 1829 to ADELINE (WILLIAMS), and they lived in Milan Twp., Huron Co., and later moved to York Twp., Sandusky Co., Ohio. She died in 1832. Known daughter, LOUISA A. b. 11 Mar. 1829 (m. J. William Whitaker, also see). In 1853, the family moved to Dover Twp., Lenawee Co., Mich. Abram married again to ELEANOR (SWIFT) KINNEY. She died June 1883; and he died in Sept. 1885. Ref: P&BA-Len pg. 854-5.

HAMILTON, ALVIN born ca. 1805, Mass., and wife, PHEBE D., born ca. 1823, NY, were listed in the 1850 census of Hudson Twp., Lenawee Co., Mich. with MARY, age 2, b. Mich.; and Lucy A. Hide, age 6, b. Mich. (stepchild?); John Luther, age 28; Eugene Luther, age 1, in their household.

HAMILTON, ARCHELAUS born ca. 1806, and wife, ESTHER A., born ca. 1814, both in New Jersey, were listed in the 1850 census of Raisin Twp., Lenawee Co., Mich. with JOSEPH C., age 9; PALMER, age 6; WILLIAM, age 2, all b. Mich., in their household.

HAMILTON, BEMIS born ca. 1795, Mass., and wife, SARAH, born ca. 1804, Conn., may be they listed in the 1840 census index of Napoleon Twp., Jackson Co., Mich. In the 1850 census of Rome Twp., Lenawee Co. they listed ALBERT, age 18, b. NY; SYLVESTER, age 14, b. Ohio; SOPHIA, age 11; HENRY, age 8, both b. Mich., in their household.

HAMILTON, INCREASE S. Dr., son of OBADIAH (following), was born 5 Jan. 1809 in Cummington, Mass., and moved with parents to New York. He married first in 1834 to SARAH B. (WHEELER). In 1835, they moved to Canandaigua, Lenawee Co., Mich., and then to Tecumseh. She died 17 Oct. 1841 in Medina village, Mich., leaving children: 1. ANN FRANCES b. ca. 1839 (d. age 20); 2. SARAH B. b. ca. 1842 (d. age 34). Increase S. married again in 1842 to HARRIET R. (DANIELS) born ca. 1816, NY, and they resided in Tecumseh Twp. in the 1850 census (Note that daughter, Elizabeth, was said to have been born NY in 1845?). Harriet died in Tecumseh in 1872. Children: 3. ELIZABETH A. b. ca. 1845, NY (d. before 1888); 4. HARRIET L. b. ca. 1847, Mich. (m. A. L. Brewer, d. bef. 1888, leaving a child). Increase S. married third to ANN E. (WHITE), daughter of Thomas (also see). Ref: P&BA-Len pg. 1076-7.

HAMILTON, JOHN was born in Ireland, and came to Pennsylvania where he married MARY (GIBSON) who

Pioneer Families of Southeastern Michigan

was also born Ireland. They settled in Butler Co., Penn., where he died 29 Jan. 1852. She later came to Riga Twp., Lenawee Co., Mich. where she died 16 Nov. 1881. Known daughter, SARAH (m. Lemuel McCormick, also see). Ref: P&BA-Len pg. 327-8.

HAMILTON, JOHN L., son of OBADIAH (following), was born 1 June 1797, Cheshire Co., Mass. He married first on 16 Oct. 1824 to MATILDA (DURKEES), and they went to Orleans Co., NY; and apparently also to Perinton, Monroe Co., NY. She died 28 June 1832. Three children, only one name stated: SAMUEL M. (following). In 1834, the family moved to near Akron, Summit Co., Ohio, where John L. married again (wife's name not stated). In 1837, they moved to Lenawee Co., Mihc.; and in 1840 to Columbia, Whitley Co., Ind. They returned to Seneca Twp., Lenawee Co., in 1850, and it is probably he, age 52, b. Mass., listed in the census, with wife, SALLY, age 62, born Mass. After retiring, John L. made his home with son, Samuel M., where he died 25 July 1866. Ref: P&BA-Len pg. 398-9.

HAMILTON, MARGARET (See Andrew Clement)

HAMILTON, MARY, age 37, born Canada, probably the wife of a son of OBADIAH (following), was head of household in the 1850 census of Medina Twp., Lenawee Co., Mich. with LUCINA, age 19; OBADIAH, age 16; DUDLEY R., age 12; ESTHER, age 9, all b. NY; and JOSEPH W., age 6, b. Mich., in her household.

HAMILTON, OBADIAH was born in Pelham, Mass., and he served in the Revolution. He married LUSANAH (RICHARDSON), of Cummington, Mass., and they remained there until about 1818, then went to Northampton; and afterwards moved to Fairport (Perinton), Monroe Co., NY. Also was believed to have moved to Orleans Co., NY where he died in Sept. 1829. Seven children (names not stated). Known children: JOHN L. (preceding); & possibly "S." (listed in 1840 census index of Medina Twp., Lenawee Co., possibly husband of MARY, preceding?); and youngest son, Dr. INCREASE S. (preceding) with whom Lusannah resided after coming to Lenawee Co. Ref: P&BA-Len pg. 398-8 & 1076-7.

HAMILTON, S. was listed in the 1840 census index of Medina Twp., Lenawee Co., Mich. Note MARY & OBADIAH, both preceding.

HAMILTON, SAMUEL M., son of JOHN L. (preceding), was born 24 Dec. 1826, Perinton, Monroe Co., NY, and came to Madison Twp., Lenawee Co., Mich. with his parents in 1835. He removed to Whiteside, Ill. in 1845, and in 1847 returned to Ogden Twp., Lenawee Co., Mich. He married on 21 Aug. 1853 to NANCY (NASH), daughter of Samuel (also see). In 1869, they removed to Saline Co., Kansas, but returned to Palmyra Twp., Lenawee Co., Mich. in 1877. Children: 1. NATHAN A. S. b. 1 Aug. 1854, Ogden Twp.; 2. EVLYN b. 18 May 1859; 3. INA A. b. 20 May 1866. Ref: P&BA-Len pg. 398-9.

HAMILTON, SARAH born ca. 1830, NY, was listed in the 1850 census of Madison Twp., Lenawee Co., Mich.

HAMILTON, WILLIAM came to America as a child from Scotland, and his parents died during the voyage. He was reared near Esopus, Ulster Co., NY. He lived later in Chenango Co., NY; but about 1822, removed to Erie Co., Ohio (area now in Huron Co.). He later moved to York Twp., Sandusky Co., Ohio. Known son, ABRAM (preceding). Ref: P&BA-Len pg. 854-5.

HAMLIN, AARON S. born ca. 1803, Canada, was listed in the 1840 census index of Dover Twp., Lenawee Co., Mich., and in the 1850 census with wife, MARIAN, age 38, born NY; MALVINA, age 18; CHARLES, age 15, both b. NY; and HEMAN, age 13; ROSANA, age 9; LUCINA, age 6, all b. Mich., in their household.

HAMLIN, CHARLES born ca. 1820, and wife, ELIZABETH, born ca. 1829, both in NY, were listed in the 1850 census of Hudson Twp., Lenawee Co., Mich. with EDGAR V., age 6, b. NY; ASA L., age 4; HARRIET E., age 3, both b. Mich.; and PATTY, age 72, b. Mass. (nother?), in their household.

HAMLIN, CHAUNCEY, age 15, born NY, was listed in the 1850 census of Medina Twp., Lenawee Co., Mich. in a Sloan household.

HAMLIN, ELSIE (See Aaron Whitacre)

HAMLIN, HIRAM born ca. 1812, Canada, and wife, ALMEDA, born ca. 1818, NY, were listed in the 1840 census index of Medina Twp., Lenawee Co., Mich. (adjacent to LUMAN, following); and in the 1850 census with HARRISON, age 9; ASHER, age 7; SARAH, age 5, all b. Mich., in their household.

HAMLIN, JERUSHA (See Asahel Canfield)

HAMLIN, LUMAN born ca. 1794, Canada, and wife, CHRISTIANA, born ca. 1812, NY, were listed in the 1840 census index of Medina Twp., Lenawee Co., Mich.; and in the 1850 census with SARAH E., age 16; LUTHER, age 12, both b. NY; and ROYAL, age 9 (probably he who m. Lucy D. Wilson, dau. of Simon D., also see, and d. 1882); LUCINDA, age 6; LYDIA, age 4, all b. Mich., in their household. Note: Adjacent to HIRAM in 1840.

HAMLIN, PERRY born ca. 1825, NY, married ELIZA (WOOD), daughter of David (also see), possibly in Fulton Co., Ohio. They moved to Fairfield Twp., Lenawee Co., Mich. where they were listed in the 1850 census with BETSEY, age 8/12, b. Mich., in their household. They resided later in Morenci, Mich.

HAMLIN, RICHARD was born ca. 1805, Ireland, and was listed in the 1850 census of Medina Twp., Lenawee Co., Mich.

HAMMOND, BENJAMIN was born ca. 1799, NY, and wife, JANE, was born ca. 1802, place not legible in the 1850 census of Cambridge Twp., Lenawee Co., Mich. There was a notation "insane" after Benjamin, so it may be this Jane who was listed as head of household in the 1840 census index of Cambridge Twp. In the 1850 census they listed GEORGE, age 13; MARY, age 7, possibly born Mich. (illegible).

HAMMOND, HANNAH born ca. 1791, Rhode Island, was listed in the 1850 census of Tecumseh Twp., Lenawee Co., Mich. in the household of Donald Lattimore, age 49, b. Conn., and wife, Bersheba, born ca. 1800, NY.

HAMMOND, HANNAH of Oneida Co., NY (See Charles O. Curtiss).

HAMMOND, JOHN was born 18 Aug. 1791, Long Island, NY; and he married in Cortland Co., NY to PERMELIA (DICKINSON) who was born 18 Jan. 1796, Conn. They removed to Mich. in 1838 (in the 1840 census index there is a man by this name in Rollin Twp., Lenawee Co.,; Augusta Twp., Washtenaw Co.; and Green Oak Twp., Livingston Co.) In 1841, they settled in Ransom,

Hillsdale Co., Mich. He died there in 1881, and she died 3 Nov. 1838 (probably 1883?). Known daughter, MARIA b. 15 June 1824, Freetown, Cortland Co., NY (m. Jonathan E. Ingersoll, also see). Ref: P&BA-Len pg. 740-3.

HAMMOND, SYMOR?, age 20, born NY, was listed in the 1850 census of Tecumseh Twp., Lenawee Co., Mich.

HAMPSHIRE, JOHN and wife, ELIZABETH, were born in Penn., and after their marriage moved to Perry Co., Ohio, and afterwards in Putnam Co., Ohio, where they died. Known daughter, SUSANNAH b. 22 June 1828, Perry Co., O. (m. David Gander, also see). Ref: P&BA-Len pg. 457-8.

HAMPTON, CHARLES D. Dr. born ca. 1821, and wife, CORNELIA, born ca. 1825, both in NY, were listed in the 1850 census of Medina Twp., Lenawee Co., Mich. with GEORGE, age 2, b. Mich., and CLARISSA A., age 22?, b. NY (sister?), in their household.

HAMPTON, DUDLEY, age 20, born NY, was listed in the 1850 census of Tecumseh Twp., Lenawee Co., Mich.

HAMPTON, ISAAC and wife, ALMERA (HEWITT), were early settlers to Lenawee Co. from NY; and resided in Tecumseh village ca. 1854. He died in Illinois, and she died in NY at advanced ages. Known daughter, RACHEL b. 1832 (m. John Fisher[2], also see). Note JAMES, following.

HAMPTON, ISAAC H., son of JAMES, was born ca. 1815, NY, and he moved to Tecumseh Twp., Lenawee Co., Mich. He married HARRIET N. (MILLS), daughter of Maj. Philo (also see). In the 1850 census of Tecumseh Twp., they were in household of James, with FRANCES, age 11; and a child (possibly MARION?, name & gender illegible), age 5, both b. Mich. listed.

HAMPTON, JAMES born ca. 1776, NY, was listed in the 1840 census index of Tecumseh Twp., Lenawee Co., Mich. (near ISAAC); and in the 1850 census with ISAAC H. (preceding) and family in his household. Note JAMES B., following.

HAMPTON, JAMES B. born ca. 1811, and wife, ESTHER, born ca. 1816, both in NY, were listed in the 1850 census of Franklin Twp., Lenawee Co., Mich. with FRANCIS, age 13; EUSINA, age 11; CHARLES, age 8; ELISHA, age 6; SALMON, age 3, all b. Mich., in their household.

HAMTON see HAMPTON

HANCHETT, WATSON was born in 1804 near Syracuse, NY; and married there in March 1833 to BETSEY (BORDON). In 1834, they removed to Medina Co., Ohio, and he died there at age 52; and she died at age 42. Nine children, names not stated, except ANN J. b. 28 Nov. 1836, Medina Co., O. (m. George W. Rudesill, also see). Ref: P&BA-Len pg. 618-9.

HANCOCK, JOHN and wife, CHARLOTTE (LAPHAN), were parents of EMILY C. born Utica, NY (m. Dayton Parker, MD, also see, on 18 Nov. 1869, possibly in Dundee, Monroe Co., Mich.). Ref: P&BA-Len pg. 599-600.

HAND, EBENEZER was listed "Hands" in the 1840 census index of Tecumseh Twp., Lenawee Co., Mich., not far from EDWARD (following).

HAND, EDMUND born ca. 1813, possibly son of HOLLAND (following), born ca. 1813, and wife, HARRIET, born ca. 1815, both in Mass., were listed in the 1840 census index of Macon Twp., Lenawee Co., Mich.; and in the 1850 census with JOSEPHINE, age 12; HORACE, age 9; HOWARD, age 5; HERMAN, age 1; HELEN, age 1 (m. Joseph W. Osborne, also see). He died in 1884, and Harriet lived with a son in 1888 on the family farm. Ref: P&BA-Len pg. 1025-6.

HAND, EDWARD born ca. 1814, and wife, CAROLINE A., born ca. 1820, both in NY, were listed in the 1840 census index of Tecumseh Twp., Lenawee Co., Mich.; and in the 1850 census with NANCY, age 11, b. NY; and MARY, age 1, b. Mich., in their household. Also see EBENEZER, preceding.

HAND, HENRY born ca. 1814, NY, and wife, MARY, born ca. 1819, Scotland, were listed in the 1850 census of Cambridge Twp., Lenawee Co., Mich. with JONATHAN, age 4; WILLIAM, age 1, both b. Mich., in their household.

HAND, HOLLAND born ca. 1779, and wife, CHARLOTTE, born ca. 1785, both in Mass., were listed in the 1840 census index of Macon Twp., Lenawee Co., Mich. as "HOLLABIRD." They were probably parents of EDMUND, preceding; and in the 1850 census of Macon Twp. listed JOSEPH (following, and his family), and SAMUEL, age 32, b. Mass., in the household.

HAND, JOSEPH, son of HOLLAND (preceding), born ca. 1815, Mass., and wife, CAROLINE, born ca. 1820, NY, were listed in the 1850 census of Macon Twp., Lenawee Co., Mich. (in the household of Holland) with children: ERASMUS D., age 8; JESSE, age 8/12, both born Mich.

HAND, NEHEMIAH born 12 Apr. 1788, New Jersey, and wife, ELIZABETH "BETSY" (ROBINSON), born 27 Feb. 1796, Rhode Island, may have lived for a time in NY & Pennsylvania. In 1835, they removed to Woodstock Twp., Lenawee Co., Mich. He died there 27 Mar. 1869, and she died 3 Apr. 1879. In the 1850 census of Woodstock Twp., they had granddaughter, Elisa A. Ellsworth, age 12, b. Mich., in their household. Children: 1. LYDIA b. 14 July 1814 (m. Alexander Ellsworth, also see); 2. ELIZA ANN b. July 1819 (d. 28 Aug. 1819); 3. LEONARD R. b. 26 Mar. 1828 (d. 13 July 1844). Ref: P&BA-Len pg. 715-6.

HANDGEN, JOHN (See Halsey Lewis)

HANDLEY, JOHN (See Joseph P. Lee)

HANDY, MICHAEL was a native of Vermont, and known daughter, LUCRETIA b. 11 Mar. 1810, VT (m. John Landon, also see, in NY). Ref: P&BA-Len pg. 367-8.

HANES also see HAYNES
HANES, BETSEY (See Philip Wareham[1])
HANES, JASON born ca. 1811, Canada, and wife, JULIANA, born ca. 1821, NY, were listed in the 1850 census of Cambridge Twp., Lenawee Co., Mich. with JOEL, age 12; MARY, age 9; JANE, age 5; ABIGAIL, age 3, all b. Mich., in their household. Note: See JOSIAH HAYNES.

HANLON, PETER and wife, SUSAN (JOHNSON), were natives of Co. Fermanagh, Ireland, and came to the US and settled first near Rochester, NY. They later moved

Pioneer Families of Southeastern Michigan

to Milan Twp., Monroe Co., Mich. Known daughter, ROSA b. 8 June 1843, Rochester, NY (m. Charles Shaler, also see). Ref: P&BA-Len pg. 641. Also note SUSAN, following.

HANLON, SUSAN (See Jacob Masten)

HANNIBAL, LYDIA (See Peter S. Terpeney)
HANNIBAL, MARY J. (See Franklin F. Palmer)

HANNON, NORCHE (See William Ladd)

HARD, EVALINE (See Eli Bush)

HARDEE see HARDY

HARDER, ELIZA CORDELIA (See Ebenezer Fisk^3)
HARDER, GEORGE I. born ca. 1803, Columbia Co., NY (son of parents, names not stated. who remained in Columbia Co., and the mother lived till age 90), married on 6 Nov. 1825 to CATHERINE (TATOR) born 8 Feb. 1807, Columbia Co. Catherine died there 22 Mary 1829 leaving children: 1. JACOB A. (following); 2. GEORGE L. b. 29 Apr. 1829 (d. 17 Aug. 1830). George I. married again on 25 June 1831 to ANNA (WHITEMAN) of Columbia Co. In 1833, they moved to Wayne Co., NY. Anna died leaving children: 3. CATHERINE N. b. 19 Dec. 1833 (m. P. B. Porter, Oswego Co., NY, she d. 18 July 1887, Lenawee Co., Mich.); 4. SALLIE N. b. 29 Dec. 1836 (d. 8 June 1839); 5. JOHN H. b. 2 Nov. 1838 (lived Adrian Twp.). George I. married third on 27 Feb. 1842 to H. E. (MOORE) born 5 Dec. 1817. He died in Fairville, NY at age 65; and she was still living there in 1888. Ref: P&BA-Len pg. 529-30.
HARDER, GERTRUDE (See Benjamin F. Houghtalin)
HARDER, JACOB A., son of GEORGE I. (preceding), was born 16 Apr. 1827, Columbia Co., NY, and moved with parents to Wayne Co. NY. He married on 24 Sept. 1849 to SABRINA (DICKSON), daughter of Isaac (also see). About 1864, they moved to Ohio, and about 1865 to Adrian Twp., Lenawee Co., Mich. Children: 1. GEORGE E. b. 15 June 1859 (d. 27 Sept. 1860); 2. JESSIE E. b. 23 May 1864 (m. Cassius M. Knowles, also see). Ref: P&BA-Len pg. 529-30.

HARDING, ABEL (possibly HARDY?) born ca. 1800, and wife, LYDIA, born ca. 1803, both in NY, were listed in the 1850 census of Palmyra Twp., Lenawee Co., Mich. with LAUREN (male), age 27, b. NY, in their household. Note: They were 3 doors from SOLOMON, following.
HARDING, IDA (See Norton H. Bailey MD)
HARDING, JOANNA was born ca. 1816, New Jersey. She married in Lenawee Co., Mich. in 1843 to Ezra C. Coryell (also see). In the 1850 census of Ridgeway Twp., they listed in their household ABEL, age 12, b. NJ, relationship not known, possibly stepson?. Note the given name, Abel, in the following family.
HARDING, SOLOMON was born ca. 1808, NY, and wife, HANNAH, was born ca. 1818, Ohio. In the 1850 census of Palmyra Twp., Lenawee Co., Mich. they listed MARINDA, age 12; ABEL, age 10; JAMES, age 7; ELIZA, age 5; BENJAMIN, age 3, all b. Ind.

HARDY, ABEL see ABEL HARDING, preceding.

HARDY, ADA (See David Alexander)
HARDY, CONSTANTINE born ca. 1806, Mass., and wife, GULIELMA, born ca. 1815, NY, were listed in the 1850 census of Adrian Twp., Lenawee Co., Mich. with STEPHEN, age 6; MARVIN S., age 3, both b. Mich., in their household.
HARDY, IRA, probably son of ISRAEL (following), born ca. 1810, New Hampshire, and wife, SUSAN, born ca. 1813, NY, were listed in the 1840 census index of Franklin Twp., Lenawee Co., Mich., and in the 1850 census with CHARLES, age 9; ALOISA, age 7; BENJAMIN, age 5; SARAH, age 3, all b. Mich.; and ISRAEL (following), in their household.
HARDY, ISRAEL born ca. 1785, New Hampshire, was listed in the 1840 census index of Franklin Twp., Lenawee Co., Mich. as "Hardey," but as Hardee in the 1850 census where he was listed in the household of IRA (preceding).

HARE also see HAIR
HARE - From American Ancestry, Vol. I, City of Albany, by Thomas P. Hughes. This family was believed to have descended from a Dutch family named Har or Hur. DANIEL D. of this family, born ca. 1768, married ELIZABETH (GRAHAM) and moved from Dutchess Co., NY to Esperance, (probably then Albany Co., now Schoharie Co.), NY. Note: In the 1800 census index, the name was spelled "Hair," and listed in were DANIEL; HENRY; JACOB; NICHOLAS (note following); & WIILIAM.
HARE, AMOS was listed in the 1840 census index of Ogden Twp., Lenawee Co., Mich.
HARE, ANNA, age 60, born NY, was listed in the 1850 census of Madison Twp., Lenawee Co., Mich. in a Knapp household.
HARE, ANNIS, age 15 (female), born Mich., was listed in the 1850 census of Palmyra Twp., Lenawee Co., Mich.; and it may be she listed again as age 17, in the 1850 census of Madison Twp., born NY. Note ANNA, preceding.
HARE, DANIEL, age 21, born NY, was listed in the 1850 census of Madison Twp., Lenawee Co., Mich.
HARE, EUNICE (See Aaron Whitacre)
HARE, FREDERICK born ca. 1802, and wife, HANNAH, born ca. 1801, NY, both in NY, were listed in the 1850 census of Rollin Twp., Lenawee Co., Mich. with MARTIN, age 20, b. NY, all in the household of Samuel Halsted (also see).
HARE, GEORGE, son of NICHOLAS (following), married probably before 1800 in Schenectady Co., NY to WEALTHY (WOOD) who was born in Albany Co., NY. Four children (names not stated, except): #3. JONATHAN (following). Ref: P&BA-Len pg. 729-30.
HARE, HANNAH, born Dutchess Co., NY, married Andrew Torbron (also see). Note HARE, preceding.
HARE, JANE, age 21, born NY, was listed in the 1850 census of Dover Twp., Lenawee Co., Mich. in the household of Lester and Sintha (Cynthia?) Leonard.
HARE, JONATHAN, son of GEORGE (preceding), born 13 June 1804, Schenectady Co., NY, married there in 1835 to MARTHA (MORRISON), daughter of David (also see). They removed to Dover Twp., Lenawee Co., Mich. by 1844. In the 1850 census of Dover Twp., the wife of Jonathan is written as "MATILDA," age 32, born NY. They also lived in Raisin Twp., and also in Branch Co., Mich. before finally settling in Blissfield Twp.,

Lenawee Co. Children: 1. CYNTHIA b. ca. 1836 (m. Daniel B. Nichols); 2. AMANDA M. b. ca. 1838; 3. CATHARINE A. b. ca. 1840 (d. age 28); 4. ADELINE (SARAH?) b. ca. 1842 (d. age 28); 5. CHLOE b. ca. 1846 (m. John Fuller, Blissfield Twp.); 6. DANIEL H. (d. age 16). Ref: P&BA-Len pg. 729-30.

HARE, MARION (See John H. Tingley[3])

HARE, NICHOLAS was possibly born in Gotham, Columbia Co., NY (whose father had come from England, and was an early settler of Duanesburg (then Albany, now Schenectady Co., NY). In the sketch Nicholas was called the father of GEORGE (preceding), and grandfather of JONATHAN (preceding). However, this may be an error, as in JONATHAN'S household in the 1850 census of Dover Twp., was NICHOLAS, age 65, b. NY, therefore, he may actually be father of JONATHAN. Note: There was NICHOLAS "HAIR" listed in the 1840 census index of Bedford Twp., Monroe Co., Mich.

HARKNESS, DANIEL W. born ca. 1825, and wife, SARAH A., born ca. 1828, both in NY, were listed in the 1850 census of Raisin Twp., Lenawee Co., Mich. with MIRIAN, age 3, born Mich., in their household.

HARKNESS, DAVID was listed in the 1840 census index of Henrietta Twp., Jackson Co., Mich. There was a man by this name in the 1800 census index of Chenango Co., NY. Note MARY & DAVID, JR. (both following).

HARKNESS, DAVID, JR. was listed in the 1840 census index of Raisin Twp., Lenawee Co., Mich. adjacent to GIDEON (following); and was not listed in the 1850 census. However, note SARAH M. (following).

HARKNESS, GIDEON born ca. 1811, and wife, ELIZABETH, born ca. 1812, both in NY, were listed in the 1840 census index of Raisin Twp., Lenawee Co., Mich. adjacent to DAVID, JR. (preceding). In the 1850 census of Rollin Twp., they were listed with CATHERINE, age 12; JOHN (see JOHN U., following), age 10; LINDLEY (following), age 8, all b. Mich., in their household.

HARKNESS, JOHN U., probably son of GIDEON (preceding), born ca. 1840, Lenawee Co., Mich., married in 1862 to CHARITY C. (COMSTOCK), probably daughter of John T. (also see), and lived in Rollin Twp. Children: 1. LINA; 2. BEULAH; 3. LLEWELLYN b. 26 Feb. 1864, Rollin Twp. (m. Susan L. Cole, daughter of Amos R., also see, on 4 Mar. 1885). Ref: P&BA-Len pg. 765-6.

HARKNESS, LINDLEY R., probably son of GIDEON (preceding), born ca. 1842, Lenawee Co., Mich., married MARY E. (PATTERSON), daughter of John (also see) and they moved to Elkhart, Ind. Children: 1. FREDDIE L.; 2. JENNIE E. Ref: P&BA-Len pg. 388-9.

HARKNESS, MARY born ca. 1787, NY, was listed in the 1850 census of Raisin Twp., Lenawee Co., Mich. in the household of Joseph W. Carpenter (also see) and wife, Mary H. (age 28, b. NY, possibly daughter of Mary?)

HARKNESS, NATHAN and wife, SUSANNAH, of Richmond, NH, were parents of SARAH born ca. 1780, NH (m. Artemas Bassett, also see). Ref: P&BA-Len pg. 1147-8. Note: Artemas & Sarah were listed in the 1850 census of Adrian Twp., Lenawee Co., Mich., and next door was RICHARD (following), probably related?

HARKNESS, NATHAN born 24 Feb. 1769, married RUTH (KELLEY) born 19 Apr. 1768, Mass. They resided in Greenfield, Saratoga Co., NY, where he died 13 Mar. 1817, and she died 14 Mar. 1837. Known daughter, NANCY b. 24 Feb. 1796, NY (m. Josiah Carpenter, also see, in Saratoga Co., NY and moved to Woodstock Twp., Lenawee Co., Mich.) Ref: P&BA-Len pg. 612-3. Also probably a son, NATHAN, following, who was listed next door to Josiah Carpenter in 1850.

HARKNESS, NATHAN, probably son of NATHAN & RUTH (preceding), born ca. 1806, and wife, CATHARINE, born ca. 1807, both in NY, were listed in the 1840 census index of Woodstock Twp., Lenawee Co., Mich.; and in the 1850 census with JEREMIAH, age 16; RUTH, age 4, both shown b. NY, in their household (next door to Josiah & Nancy (Harkness) Carpenter).

HARKNESS, RICHARD born ca. 1820, and wife, DEBORAH, born ca. 1823, both in NY, were listed in the 1850 census of Adrian Twp., Lenawee Co., Mich. with MARY C., age 6; and DEBORAH R., age 1, both b. Mich., in their household. (Listed in census next door to Artemas & SARAH (HARKNESS) Bassett, probably related).

HARKNESS, SARAH M. born ca. 1816, NY, was listed as head of household in the 1850 census of Tecumseh Twp. with DAVID, age 11, and MARY, age 6, in her household. Note DAVID JR. & MARY (both preceding).

HARKNESS, WILLIAM born ca 1821, and wife, BETSEY, born ca. 1822, both in NY, were listed in the 1850 census of Rollin Twp., Lenawee Co., Mich. with DAVID, age 3; EDWIN J., age 1, both b. in Mich., in their household. Note DAVID, preceding.

HARLOW, F. M. (See Gilbert M. Pettys)

HARLOW, LEVI was listed in the 1840 census index of Woodstock Twp., Lenawee Co., Mich.

HARMON, SALLY born 6 July 1799, Richmond, Ontario Co., NY (m. James B. Wells, also see, and moved to Franklin Twp., Lenawee Co., Mich.).

HARMON, EBENEZER born ca. 1809, and wife, SALLY, born ca. 1813, both in NY, were listed in the 1840 census index of Macon Twp., Lenawee Co., Mich.; and in the 1850 census with LURA?, age 16. b NY; and JAMES, age 13; ANSON, age 11, both b. Mich., in their household.

HAROLD, ANNIE G. (See Michael Karcher)

HARPER, SARAH A. (See James Seeley)

HARRINGTON also see HERRINGTON
HARRINGTON, ADDIE E. (See William H. Marshall)
HARRINGTON, BRADLEY born ca. 1798, VT, and wife, MARY, born ca. 1809, NY, were listed in the 1850 census of Hudson Twp., Lenawee Co., Mich. with MORLEY, age 19; HENRY, age 11, SARAH, age 7, all b. NY; and NATHANIEL, age 5; ALZADA, age 2, both b. Mich., and also possibly stepchildren: Lucretia H. Gilbert, age 17; Walter Gilbert, age 12; Mary Gilbert, age 7, all b. Mich.; and also Clarissa Wadsworth, age 15, b. Mich., in their household. In another household next door was BRADFORD, age 28, b. NY, probably related.

HARRINGTON, D. S. (See Seymour Mead[7])

Pioneer Families of Southeastern Michigan

HARRINGTON, MARTHA born 12 Mar. 1777 (m. Anthony Howd, also see, and lived Cazenovia, now Madison Co., NY by 1816).

HARRINGTON, SAMANTHA born ca. 1810, NY, was head of household in the 1850 census of Medina Twp., Lenawee Co., Mich. with MARTHA, age 15; ALMOND, age 13, both b. NY; and EUDORAH, age 3, b. Mich., in her household.

HARRIOTT, MATILDA, possibly daughter of ROBERT (following), of Macon Twp., Lenawee Co., Mich. (m. Jerome E. Travis, also see).

HARRIOTT, ROBERT born ca. 1790, and wife, SARAH, born ca. 1800, both in New Jersey, were listed in the 1840 census index (spelled "Herriott") of Macon Twp., Lenawee Co., Mich.; and in the 1850 census with ROBERT F., age 26; PHEBE I., age 23; G. W. (male), age 21; SARAH L., age 19; EDWARD, age 17, all b. NY; and CAROLINE M., age 12, b. Mich., in their household. Note: Caroline M. may be Matilda, preceding.

HARRIOTT, WILLIAM and wife, SARAH H. (SANFORD), natives of NY, settled in Saline, Washtenaw Co., Mich. where known daughter, ABBIE J. was born 15 Aug. 1846 (m. Albert Collins, son of Isaac, also see). Ref: P&BA-Len pg. 1067-8.

HARRIS, ABIGAIL born ca. 1786, NY, was listed in the 1850 census of Cambridge Twp., Lenawee Co., Mich. in the household of John Holland and wife, Maria (age 33, b. NY).

HARRIS, ABRAM born 13 Feb. 1783, and wife, POLLY (WALDRON), born 23 Sept. 1776, were natives of Ulster Co., NY. They moved to near Fort Wayne, Ind., where he died at age 59, and she died at age 67. Six children (names not stated, except): GARRET F. (following). Ref: P&BA-Len pg. 739-40.

HARRIS, AMAZIA (male), age 18, born Ohio, was listed in the 1850 census of Medina Twp., Lenawee Co., Mich.

HARRIS, GARRET F., son of ABRAM (preceding), born 19 July 1813, Ulster Co., NY, married 2 Jan. 1836 to MAGDALIA (AUCHMOODY), and they removed to Woodstock Twp., Lenawee Co., Mich. She died there 15 Aug. 1840, age 21, leaving two children: 1. ABRAM (ABRAHAM) b. 8 Dec. 1837, Woodstock Twp. (m. Mary Hewitt, probably dau. of Merrit, also see, Clinton Co., Mich.); 2. MARY b. 3 July 1839 (m. Jacob Every, also see, Jackson Co., Mich.) Garret married again to PHEBE (BROOKS), daughter of Merchant (also see). Children: 3. Daughter (d. infancy); 4. MAGDALENA "LANY" b. 5 Mar. 1843 (m. William Davison, also see, & d. 16 Apr. 1881); 5. WESSEL D. b. 16 Apr. 1846 (m. Nellie Turner); 6. MERCHANT B. b. 5 Mar. 1849 (m. Olive Nichols); 7. WILLIAM HENRY b. 6 Nov. 1851 (m. Eliza Swarthout); 8. ELMA E. b. 26 June 1855 (m. James Horton); 9. SOPHRONIA b. 16 Oct. 1858 (m. F. Peterson); 10. LORA b. 9 Mar. 1864 (m. Edith Sanford). Ref: P&BA-Len pg. 613-4 & 739-40.

HARRIS, ISAAC born ca. 1815, and wife, MARY, born ca. 1815, place of birth unknown, listed as "black," were in the 1850 census of Adrian Twp., Lenawee Co., Mich. with SARAH, age 8, b. Mich. in the household.

HARRIS, JAMES born ca. 1812, and wife, HANNAH, born ca. 1817, both in NY, were listed in the 1850 census of Franklin Twp., Lenawee Co., Mich. with HARRIET, age 14; MELISSA, age 10; SARAH, age 7; DAVID, age 3, all b. Mich., in their household

HARRIS, MARILLA was listed in the 1840 census index of Tecumseh Twp., Lenawee Co., Mich.

HARRIS, MARY A. (See Abraham Cramer)

HARRIS, PHILINDA, age 10, and LEVI, age 8, both b. Mich., were listed in the 1850 census of Dover Twp., Lenawee Co., Mich. in the household of William A. & Ruth Butter, possibly stepchildren.

HARRIS, POLLY H. (See Hiram M. Higby)

HARRIS, THOMAS J., son of WALTER (following), born 7 Mar. 1839, Homer, Calhoun Co., Mich., served in the Civil War. He married in August 1867 to ALMA (FOWLER), daughter of Levi (also see). They lived mostly in Adrian Twp., Lenawee Co., Mich. Children: 1. EUGENE b. 17 May 1868; 2. ELMER T. b. 15 Dec. 1869; 3. GEORGE N. b. 16 Feb. 1875; 4. FRANK J. b. 8 Oct. 1877; 5. Child b. 16 Apr. 1886. Ref: P&BA-Len pg. 195-7.

HARRIS, WALTER, son of ISAAC (born in England), born in 1803, Shaftsbury, VT, married THANKFUL (LOOK), daughter of Thomas (also see). They moved to Hanover, Jackson Co., Mich. about 1835; then lived about 5 years in Cleveland, Ohio; then returned to Coldwater, Mich. where they remained. Known children: 1. THOMAS J. (preceding); 2. GEORGE W. (served in Civil War; retired to Georgia). Ref: P&BA-Len pg. 195-7.

HARRIS, WILLIAM born ca. 1811, and wife, ELIZA, born ca. 1815, both in England, were listed in the 1840 census index of Rome Twp., Lenawee Co., Mich.; and in the 1850 census with EDMUND, age 13; EMILY E., age 11; CHARLES, age 10; FREDERICK, age 6; MARY, age 4; JOSEPH, age 1, all b. Mich., in their household.

HARRISON, ALBERT J. born ca. 1809, Conn., and wife, MARY, born ca. 1807, NY, were listed in the 1840 census index of Palmyra Twp., Lenawee Co., Mich.; and in the 1850 census with ELIZABETH J., age 16; LUTHER R., age 14; ANDREW J., age 10; ALFRED C., age 9, all b. Mich., in their household. In the 1840 census index were adjacent to JERUSHA & LUTHER B. (both following).

HARRISON, ALMON(D) born ca. 1802, and wife, ELIZA D., born ca. 1810, both in Mass., were listed in the 1840 census index of Blissfield Twp., Lenawee Co., Mich. (adjacent to SOLOMON, following); and in the 1850 census with DANIEL, age 16; CLEMENT, age 14; JOEL, age 12; GERTRUDE, age 8; WYMAN, age 6; DWIGHT, age 3, all b. Mich., in the household.

HARRISON, ANN of Yorkshire, England (See John Taylor).

HARRISON, DAVID, probably son of MATTHEW (following), born ca. 1827, and wife, ELIZABETH, born ca. 1823, both in England, wee listed in the 1850 census of Ridgeway Twp., Lenawee Co., Mich. with JAMES, age 1, and MATTHEW (following), in their household.

HARRISON, HANNAH (See John Niblack)

HARRISON, JERUSHA was listed in the 1840 census index of Palmyra Twp., Lenawee Co., Mich. adjacent to ALBERT (preceding) & LUTHER B. (following).

HARRISON, JOHN and wife, SARAH (WRIGHT), both born Yorkshire, England, came to the US in 1830, and settled in Tecumseh Twp., Lenawee Co., Mich. (where he was listed in the 1840 census index). She died in 1833; and he died in 1865. Known daughter, MARY ANN b. 17 Apr. 1811, Yorkshire, England (m. Daniel Waring, also see). It is probably JOHN, age 71, b. England, listed in the household of Daniel Waring in the 1850 census of Tecumseh Twp., as John "Addison."

HARRISON, JOSEPH born ca. 1802, and wife, NANCY, born ca. 1806, both in NY, were listed in the 1850 census of Madison Twp., Lenawee Co., Mich. with ADELINE, age 19, b. NY; and HENRY, age 16; ANN, age 6, both b. Mich., in their household. Note: There was a JOSEPH in Washtenaw Co., Mich. in the 1840 census index.

HARRISON, LUTHER B. born ca. 1805, and wife, MARY E., born ca. 1810, both in Conn., were listed in the 1840 census index of Palmyra Twp., Lenawee Co., Mich.; and in the 1850 census with RACHEL, age 18, b. Conn.; and SIMEON, age 12; WILLIAM, age 9; HARRIET, age 4, all b. Mich., in their household. Note ALBERT & JERUSHA, both preceding.

HARRISON, MATTHEW was born ca. 1790, England, and is listed in the 1850 census of Ridgeway Twp., Lenawee Co., Mich. in the household of DAVID (preceding). Also note WILLIAM, following.

HARRISON, REBECCA born 8 Apr. 1792, Vermont, married Aaron Seger (also see). Her father (given name not stated) came from London, England in Colonial times, settled in Vermont where he served in the American Revolution. Her mother was Rebecca (Keeler). Ref: P&BA-Len pg. 1114-7.

HARRISON, SOLOMON (SALMON) born ca. 1809, and wife, FRANCES, born ca. 1820, both in Mass., were listed in the 1840 census index of Blissfield Twp., Lenawee Co., Mich. (adjacent to ALMON, preceding); and in the 1850 census of Palmyra Twp. with GERTRUDE J., age 4; ALICE, age 2, both b. Mich., in their household.

HARRISON, WILLIAM born ca. 1816, and wife, ELIZABETH, born ca. 1820, both b. England, were listed in the 1850 census of Ridgeway Twp., Lenawee Co., Mich. Note MATTHEW, preceding.

HARSH, FREDERICK (son of a pioneer family of near Aurora, Preston Co., then Virginia) was a native of Maryland, and settled with his family in Preston Co., Va. He married there to SARAH (BALLARD). There were 12 children (all names not stated). Known children: SARAH (m. Jacob Wotring, also see); & GEORGE FREDERICK (following). Ref: P&BA-Len pg. 734-5.

HARSH, GEORGE FREDERICK, son of FREDERICK (preceding), was born 1823, Preston Co., West Virginia. He married there to ANN SALOME (RUDOLPH), daughter of John (also see). After the Civil War, they moved to Ogden Twp., Lenawee Co., Mich. He died in Feb. 1870. Children: 1. J. LUTHER (Ogden Twp.); 2. JOHN G.; 3. SARAH P. (m. M. L. Wilt, Palmyra Twp.); 4. EMMA E. (m. Jesse Foglesong, Ogden Twp.); 5. JESSE W. (Ogden Twp.); 6. MARTHA R.; 7. LYDIA A.; 8. BURTON F.; 9. LENARD C. (deceased by 1888); 10. ANNGELETTA E. (deceased by 1888). Ref: P&BA-Len pg. 1023-4.

HARSH, LUTHER (See John Houghtby, and note J. LUTHER, in family of GEORGE FREDERICK, preceding).

HART, ERASTUS (See John Maynard)

HART, HARVEY, son of JABEZ (who settled in Ontario Co., NY before 1800), was born probably in Ontario Co., NY; and he married MARY (JACKSON) who was born Perinton, Monroe Co., NY. Known son, JOHN (following). Ref: P&BA-Len pg. 844-5.

HART, HENRY born ca. 1818, and wife, JANE, born ca. 1818, both in NY, were listed in the 1850 census of Adrian Twp., Lenawee Co., Mich. with JOSEPH C., age 7; HENRY C., age 3; JANE C., age 3/12, all b. Mich., in their household.

HART, HERMAN V. C. born ca. 1784, and wife, MIRIAM, born ca. 1795, both in NY, were listed in the 1850 census of Adrian, Lenawee Co., Mich. with ENOCH L., age 35; MARIA, age 29; FREDERICK, age 23; FRANCES, age 19; HERMAN V. C. JR., age 16 (m. Clara E. Boies, dau. of John K., also see); WILLIAM, age 14, all b. NY, in their household.

HART, JOHN born ca. 1811, and wife, EMILY, born ca. 1811, both in NY, were listed in the 1840 census index of Cambridge Twp., Lenawee Co., Mich.; and in the 1850 census with MARY, age 9; EVELYN, age 5; HELEN, age 3, all b. Mich., in their household.

HART, JOHN, son of HARVEY (preceding), born ca. 1813, Victor, Ontario Co., NY, married on 17 Feb. 1835 to ELVIRA (LADD), daughter of John (also see). In 1837, they moved to Adrian, Lenawee Co., Mich., then to Wheatland, Hillsdale Co., Mich. About 1839, they went to Royalton, Niagara Co., NY, but returned about 1844 to Hudson Twp., Lenawee Co., Mich. He died there 15 Dec. 1880; and she was living on the home farm in 1888 with son, Albert. Children: 1. LLEWELYN (following); 2. MARIAN E. b. ca. 1847; 3. ALBERT b. 16 Aug. 1851 (served Co. A., 72d Ohio Inf., Civil War; unmarried, operated farm with mother & sister). Ref: P&BA-Len pg. 778-9 & 844-5.

HART, JOHN (See James K. Jeffery)

HART, JOSEPH born 20 Nov. 1773, Berlin, Conn., moved with parents to Durham, Greene Co., NY. He married there on 3 May 1798 to LUCY (KIRTLAND) of Saybrook, Conn. In 1812, they moved to Albion, Orleans Co., NY, where he died 22 July 1853. There were 10 children (mentioned were those following): B. K. (lived Alton, Ill.); LUCY H. b. ca. 1814, NY (m. Ambrose S. Berry, also see); Daughter (m. Lankford G. Berry); LOVICA H. b. ca. 1814 (m. Orange M. Rood, also see); and the youngest, SAMUEL E. (following). Ref: P&BA-Len pg. 290-1. Note: There was an ELIHU listed in the 1800 census index of Greene Co., NY.

HART, LLEWELYN, son of JOHN (preceding), was born 29 Sept. 1840, Royalton, Niagara Co., NY, and came to Lenawee Co., Mich. with his parents. He married in Nov. 1882 to MARY S. (JACKSON), daughter of William W. (also see) in Addison, Mich. Known son, CARROLL. Ref: P&BA-Len pg. 788-9.

HART, LUCIUS, age 5, born Mich., was listed in the 1850 census of Palmyra Twp., Lenawee Co., Mich. in the household of Lydia Clark.

HART, MARION (See Silas Marshall)

HART, PETER A. born ca. 1825, NY, was listed in the 1850 census of Medina Twp., Lenawee Co., Mich.

HART, PHILANDER born ca. 1809, and wife, EUNICE, born ca. 1803, both in VT, were listed in the 1840 census index of Woodstock Twp., Lenawee Co., Mich.; and in the 1850 census with CAROLINE, age 21, IRA, age 18, both b. Penn.; and SARAH, age 14, b. Mich., in their household.

HART, SAMUEL E., son of JOSEPH (preceding), was born 13 Aug. 1823, Albion, Orleans Co., NY. He came to Adrian, Lenawee Co., Mich. in 1840 to live with his sister (the Berrys); and in the 1850 census resided with sister, LOVICA, in Madison Twp. He married on 7 Oct. 1852 to ANNA D. (CRISSEY), daughter of E. A. of Astoria, Long Island, and settled in Adrian. Children: 1. OTHO S. b. 9 Jan. 1856; 2. KATE ELIZABETH b. 21 Aug. 1861. After the death of Anna, Samuel E. married Mrs. HARRIET G. (GALLOWAY) KING, daughter of Thomas (also see), at Palmyra, NY. Son, 3. CHARLES G. b. 6 June 1873, Adrian. Ref: P&BA-Len pg. 290-1.

HART, SAMUEL P. born ca. 1824, Ohio, and wife, ELIZA A., born ca. 1825, NY, were listed in the 1850 census of Hudson Twp., Lenawee Co., Mich. with FRANCELIA? B., age 4; SALLY A., age 3, both b. Ohio, in their household.

HART, WILLIAM (See Richard H. Kinney)

HART, ZALMON born ca. 1823, and wife, ELIZABETH, born ca. 1828, both in NY, were listed in the 1850 census of Palmyra Twp., Lenawee Co., Mich. with ADALADE, age 3; EDWIN, age 1, both b. Mich., in their household.

HARTLE, A. G. (See William Ashley)

HARTMAN, JONATHAN and wife, ELIZA (SCHISLER), of Mill Creek, Alvordton, Williams Co., Ohio, were parents of 3 sons and 3 daughters (given names not stated). Known daughter, MARY b. 1 June 1866 (m. Winfield Scott, also see). Ref: P&BA-Len pg. 697.

HARVEY also see HERVEY

HARVEY, BARZILLA J., son of STIMPSON (following), born ca. 1809, and wife, NANCY, born ca. 1810, both in NY, were listed in the 1840 census index of Palmyra Twp., Lenawee Co., Mich.; and in the 1850 census with ABIGAIL, age 14; JAMES B., age 6, both b. Mich., in the household.

HARVEY, CORNELIUS born ca. 1812, New Hampshire, and wife, MARY, born ca. 1814, Penn., were listed in the 1840 census index of Adrian Twp., Lenawee Co., Mich.; and in 1850 census of Rome Twp. with the following (in this order) in their household: JAMES, age 8; OLIN? M., age 6, both b. Mich.; James Hampton, age 9; Malinda Hampton, age 6, both b. Ohio; and Alvira Hampton, age 5, born Mich., and listed last, LEWIS, age 10, b. Mich. HARVEY, DAVID S., son of STIMPSON (following) was listed in the 1840 census index of Ogden Twp., Lenawee Co., Mich. He is not listed in 1850, and was said to be deceased before 1888. However, in the 1850 census of Ogden Twp. were PHILA C., age 10; NANCY F., age 6, both b. Mich., listed in the household of William B. and Nancy A. Freeman. These children may be children of DAVID S., and stepchildren of William Freeman?

HARVEY, GEORGE C., son of STIMPSON (following), born ca. 1807, and wife, REBECCA, born ca. 1807, both born Mass., were listed in the 1850 census of Palmyra Twp., Lenawee Co., Mich. with STIMPSON G., age 13; HELEN R., age 7, both b. Mich., in their household.

HARVEY, JOHN C., son of STIMPSON (following), born 22 Oct. 1820, Farmington, Ontario Co., NY, moved to Lenawee Co., Mich. with his mother. He married on 29 Apr. 1845 in Madison Twp. to MARY A. (UNDERWOOD), daughter of Edward (also see). They were listed in the 1850 census of Madison Twp. with no children listed, so probably all 5 children following were born after 1850. DAVID J.; MARY L.; & CLARA E. (all died young); and surviving were ANNA MARIA; CORNELIA P. Ref: P&BA-Len pg. 415-6.

HARVEY, STIMPSON born 30 Apr.1780, and wife, MARY "POLLY" (CRANE) born 17 Apr. 1787, both born Mass., moved before 1820 to Farmington, Ontario Co., NY. He died there on 2 Mar. 1828. Before 1840, Polly and 4 sons moved to Lenawee Co., Mich., and settled first in Palmyra Twp., and by 1840 in Madison Twp. (where she was listed head of household in the 1840 census index). Children: 1. GEORGE C. (preceding); 2. BARZILLA J. (preceding); 3. DAVID S. (preceding); 4. JOHN C. (preceding); 5. HARRISON (d. young in NY). Ref: P&BA-Len pg. 415-6.

HARWOOD, ALICE (See Augustus Bradish)
HARWOOD, BETSEY (See Noah Green, Sr.)
HARWOOD, WASHINGTON born ca. 1812, Mass., and wife, LAURA, born ca. 1813, VT, were listed in the 1850 census of Madison Twp., Lenawee Co., Mich. with SUSAN A., age 11; ROSETTA, age 9, both b. NY; and HENRY D., age 7; LAURA M., age 4, both b. Mich., in their household.

HASKELL, GEORGE G. (See William E. Doty)

HASTINGS, ROBERT and wife, MAGGIE (JOHNSON), of Erie Co., Ohio, had known daughter, MAGGIE (MARGARET?) b. 15 Nov. 1847, Erie Co. (m. Edwin Driggs, also see). Ref: P&BA-Len pg. 756-7.

HASTINGS, SYLVENUS born ca. 1817, and wife, SALLY, born ca. 1824, both in NY, were listed in the 1850 census of Tecumseh Twp., Lenawee Co., Mich. with CLARISSA, age 5; WILLIS, age 3, both b. Mich., in their household.

HATCH, DAVID of Macon Twp., Lenawee Co., Mich. married Mrs. CAROLINE (SHUFFLEBOTHAN) FERGUSON, widow of John Ferguson (also see). Ref: P&BA-Len pg. 473-4.

HATHAWAY, ASHER born ca. 1799, NY, and (probably second?) wife, DELIA E. (note DELILAH, following), born ca. 1815, NY, were listed in the 1850 census of Dover Twp., Lenawee Co., Mich. with DOLPHUS A., age 22 (note that Delia is too young to be mother of Dolphus); PHEBE M., age 16, both b. NY; and ASHER L., age 12; JOHN G., age 10; DELIA A., age 8; JAMES H., age 6; CHARLES, age 4; ROLLIN, age 2, all b. Mich., in their household. Note BENJAMIN & JACOB, both following.

HATHAWAY, BENJAMIN born ca. 1812, and wife, DELANA, born ca. 1820, both in NY, were listed in the 1850 census of Dover Twp., Lenawee Co., Mich. with EMILY, age 16; BENJAMIN, age 12, both b. NY; and DANIEL, age 9; JO (male), age 1/12, both b. Mich., in their household (2 doors from ASHER, preceding). Also see JACOB, following.

HATHAWAY, DAVID was listed in the 1840 census index of Adrian Twp., Lenawee Co., Mich.

HATHAWAY, DELILAH (GULLICK) Mrs. (See Ira Rogers)

HATHAWAY, GEORGE A., son of HIRAM (following), was born ca. 1808, Palmyra, Wayne Co., NY, and married there to ADELINE (CHASE) born ca. 1818, NY. In 1832, they removed to Palmyra Twp., Lenawee Co., Mich.; and in the 1850 census were listed in Madison Twp., but may have returned to Palmyra Twp. At retirement, they moved into Blissfield village where he died in Dec. 1883, and she died in 1885. Children: 1. GEORGIANNA (d. age 10); 2. EDWARD b. ca. 1841 (to Arkansas); 3. HERBERT B. (following); 4. MAY N. b. ca. 1849 (d. 1875, age 22?). Ref: P&BA-Len pg. 925-6.

HATHAWAY, HERBERT B., son of GEORGE A. (preceding), was born 20 Jan. 1845, Palmyra Twp., Lenawee Co., Mich. He served in Co. E., 18th Mich. Inf. during the Civil War, and afterwards served in the regular army in Kansas, Colorado, New Mexico, and Wyoming. He married in Oct. 1872 to SARAH (SPAULDING) of Lewiston, Niagara Co. NY. They lived in Palmyra Twp., Lenawee Co.; and also in Benton Co., Ind., and Kentucky. In 1875, they resided in Allegan Co., Mich., but in 1879 settled in Blissfield village, Lenawee Co. Children: 1. MAUD; 2. MAY; 3. HOPE; 4. GEORGE. Ref: P&BA-Len pg. 925-6.

HATHAWAY, HIRAM was born in Mass., and was among the early settlers of Palmyra, Wayne Co., NY. His wife, name not stated, lived to age 102. Known son, GEORGE A. (preceding). Ref: P&BA-Len pg. 925-6.

HATHAWAY, JACOB born ca. 1814, and wife, ELIZA, born ca. 1815, both in NY, were listed in the 1840 census index of Dover Twp., Lenawee Co., Mich.; and in the 1850 census with SINTHIA, age 15; IRENA, age 12, both b. NY; and CATHERINE, age 4; JOSEPHINE, age 1/12, both b. Mich., in their household. (In the 1840 census index, listed near BENJAMIN, preceding.)

HATHAWAY, JAMES was born ca. 1787, Berkshire Co., Mass., and married there to DOROTHY (BOWERMAN) born ca. 1794, Mass., and they were Quakers. They moved in 1834 to Rollin Twp., Lenawee Co., Mich. He died at age 68, and she died at age 86. Known daughter, ELIZABETH (m. 1842, Rollin Twp., to Richard DeGreene, also see); and in James' household in the 1850 census of Rollin Twp.: ORVILLE P., age 20, b. Mass. Ref: P&BA-Len pg. 657-8. Note: In the 1840 census index of Rollin Twp., were listed adjacent to WILLIAM (following).

HATHAWAY, JEPTHA born ca. 1778, Rhode Island, and he married NANCY, and they lived in Mass. Known daughter, ADELINE b. 26 Nov. 1806, Mass. (m. Kelly S. Beals, also see). In the 1850 census of Adrian Twp., Lenawee Co., Mich., they were living in the household of Kelly & Adeline Beals.

HATHAWAY, PETER born Philadelphia, Penn., and wife, PRUDENCE D. (CRAW), born VT, settled in Milan, Erie Co., Ohio. He died there, and Prudence moved to Dover Twp., Lenawee Co., Mich. with daughter, Elizabeth. Children: 1. EDWARD; 2. JOSEPH; 3. Name not stated; 4. ELIZABETH b. 15 Feb. 1838 (m. Thomas B. Eddy, also see). Ref: P&BA-Len pg. 218-9.

HATHAWAY, PHILIP born ca. 1787, and wife, NANCY, born ca. 1790, both born Mass., were listed in the 1840 census index of Macon Twp., Lenawee Co., Mich.; and in the 1850 census of Ridgeway Twp. with BETSY A., age 25; SYDNEY, age 23; JAMES, age 20, all b. NY; and CHARLES, age 7, born England (grandcild?), in their household.

HATHAWAY, WILLIAM born ca 1811, Mass., and wife, SALLY A., born ca. 1816, NY, were probably they in the 1840 census index of Madison Twp., Lenawee Co., Mich., (adjacent to JAMES, preceding); and were in the 1850 census with no children.

HATHAWAY, WILLIAM R. born ca. 1810, and wife, MARY, born ca. 1814, both in NY, were listed in the 1850 census of Madison Twp., Lenawee Co., Mich. with CHARLES, age 10, b. NY; and OSCAR, age 4, b. Mich., in their household.

HATHEWAY, GILBERT of New Baltimore, Macomb Co., Mich. had known daughter, ISABELLE H. b. 18 Jan. 1851 (m. Adolph Wheeler, also see). Ref: P&BA-Len pg. 480-1.

HATTER, JOHN and wife, ALTHERIA (BATES), lived in Newfane, Niagara Co., NY when she died on 29 Apr. 1841. He died in 1851. Known daughter, CORDELIA (m. Hiram C. Colbath, also see). Ref: P&BA-Len pg. 862-3.

HAUSE also see HOUSE

HAUSE, BELINDA (See James Updike, Sr.)

HAUSE, LINA (See Levi L. Stockwell)

HAUSE, LYMAN E., son of SANFORD (following), born 21 Dec. 1841, Ridgeway Twp., Lenawee Co., Mich., served in the Civil War. He married first on 17 Feb. 1866 at Ida Station, Monroe Co., Mich., to EMMA (POCKLINGTON) born 1846, Yorkshire, England. (Note: This is probably Emeline Pocklington, daughter of William, also see, who lived 2 doors away in the 1850 census of Ridgeway Twp.) She died 23 Sept. 1875. Children: 1. WILLIAM S.; 2. IRVA; 3. EMMA b. 23 Sept. 1875. Lyman E. married again to CAROLINE (KNIFFEN), daughter of Isaac L. (also see). Children: 4. CLARENCE. Ref: P&BA-Len pg. 475-6.

HAUSE, MORRIS B. born ca. 1828, NY, was listed in the 1850 census of Tecumseh Twp., Lenawee Co., Mich., written possibly as "House."

HAUSE, PETER and wife, ANNA (TREXLER), from Greenville, Mercer Co., Penn. moved to Seneca Twp., Lenawee Co., Mich. in 1852. He died in 1873, and she was still living there in 1888. Known daughter, JANE b. 28 Sept. 1835, Greenville, Penn. (m. Mathias L. Davis, also see). Ref: P&BA-Len pg. 343-4.

HAUSE, SANFORD born ca. 1806, and wife, LYDIA (SWARTHOUT), born ca. 1808, both in NY, came to Macon Twp., Lenawee Co., Mich by the 1840 census (listed as "House.") In the 1850 census, they were listed in Ridgeway Twp. He died on 15 Feb. 1885. Known daughter, HANNAH, born ca. 1826, near Rochester, NY (m. William Pilbeam, also see); and those in the household of Sanford in the 1850 census were: WILLIAM, age 20, b. NY; and MARTHA, age 15; ELMAR, age 14; AMANDA, age 12; LYMAN E. (following), all b. Mich. One daughter (given name not stated) m. a Coryell. Ref: P&BA-Len pg. 475-6 & 1145.

HAUSEMAN, ROBERT (See George W. Clark)

HAUVER, JANE (See Abraham Bartholomew)

Pioneer Families of Southeastern Michigan

HAVEN also see HAVENS

HAVEN, ASA of Chenango Co., NY, had known daughter, POLLY (m. Andrew Stephenson, also see). Ref: P&BA-Len pg. 861-2.

HAVENS, CLARKSON, age 7, born Mich., was listed in the 1850 census of Tecumseh Twp., Lenawee Co., Mich. in a Scofield household.

HAVENS, HENRY born ca. 1821, and wife, MARY, born ca. 1825, both in NY, were listed in the 1850 census of Medina Twp., Lenawee Co., Mich. with MARY M., age 3, b. Mich., in their household (2 doors from FRANCIS; and see S. H., following).

HAVENS, J. G. was listed in the 1840 census index of Dover Twp., Lenawee Co., Mich.

HAVENS, JAMES was listed in the 1840 census index of Madison Twp., Lenawee Co., Mich.

HAVENS, JOHNSON L., age 1, born NY?, was listed in the 1850 census of Adrian Twp., Lenawee Co., Mich. in the household of Daniel L. and Elizabeth Johnson, possibly grandparents.

HAVENS, PETER was listed in the 1840 census index of Somerset Twp., Hillsdale Co., Mich., adjacent to PETER, JR. (following), with the notation "penioner, age 78y." Note: there was a JACOB & THOMAS L. in Moscow Twp., Hillsdale Co., Mich. 1840.

HAVENS, PETER (Jr.), probably son of PETER (preceding), and wife, HANNAH (HAVENS), were born in Pultney, NY; and moved to Somerset Twp., Hillsdale Co., Mich. in 1838. Children: 1. ANDREW J.; 2. HORACE A.; 3. BENJAMIN; 4. PHEBE b. 17 Oct. 1833, Pultney, NY (m. Silas Marshall, also see); 5. ELIZA C.; 6. HANNAH D. Ref: P&BA-Len pg. 1088-9.

HAVENS, S. H. was listed in the 1840 census index of Medina Twp., Lenawee Co., Mich. He was not listed in 1850, but in that census was FRANCIS, age 43, born VT, head of household, with SALLY, age 74, born Mass., in the household.

HAVENS, SAMUEL born ca. 1797, New Jersey, and wife, SARAH A., born ca. 1806, NY, were listed in the 1840 census index of Seneca Twp., Lenawee Co., Mich.; and in the 1850 census with SAMUEL, age 26; AARON, age 25; SALLY A., age 22; JOSEPH, age 19; ANNA, age 16; HIRAM, age 14, all b. NY; and HENRY, age 11; ALMIRA, age 9; JOHN, age 4, all b. Mich., in their household.

HAVENS, SARAH, age 19, born NY, was listed in the 1850 census of Madison Twp., Lenawee Co., Mich. in a Niles household.

HAVENS, STEPHEN born ca. 1799, NJ, and wife, MARY, born ca. 1812, NY, were listed in the 1840 census index of Cambridge Twp., Lenawee Co., Mich.; and in the 1850 census of Adrian Twp. with PHILIP W., age 21; MERCY A., age 17, both b. NY; and CHARLES H., age 13; ELI V., age 11; WILLLIAM F., age 8; MARY J., age 6; GEORGE, age 2, all b. Mich., in their household.

HAVENS, THOMAS born ca. 1778, NJ, was probably he listed in the 1840 census index of Macon Twp., Lenawee Co., Mich.; and in the 1850 census of Ridgway Twp., age 72, in the household of James C. and Matilda Frear.

HAVILAND, ANNA born ca. 1804, probably in Saratoga Co., NY, married on 24 Oct. 1826 to Rev. Levi H. Chase (also see). Ref: P&BA-Len pg. 350-2. In the 1850 census of Raisin Twp., listed next door to the Chases were JAMES & SAMUEL (both following).

HAVILAND, CHARLES born ca. 1778, Conn., a Quaker Minister, married ESTHER (MOSHER), and lived first in Saratoga Co., NY and then in Niagara Co., NY till 1833, when they removed to Raisin Twp., Lenawee Co., Mich. She died there 10 Jan. 1840. There were 12 children (names not stated). Probably a son, ISAAC (following, next door in 1850 census); & possibly CHARLES; ELI C.; IRA (all following); and known daughter, #10. ZILPHA b. 9 Jan. 1812, Providence, Saratoga Co., NY (m. Moses Bowerman, Jr., also see). In the 1850 census of Raisin Twp., Charles listed a wife, SARAH, age 65, born Mass. He died 17 Dec. 1856. Ref: P&BA-Len pg. 322-4. Also note SENECA, following.

HAVILAND, CHARLES, possibly son of CHARLES (preceding), born ca. 1819, and wife, ERVILLA, born ca. 1824, both in NY, were listed in the 1850 census of Raisin Twp., Lenawee Co., Mich. with LYDIA, age 9; NANCY, age 7; SARAH, age 5; ALVIRA, age 3; SENECA, age 7/12, all b. Mich., in their household. (Listed next door to IRA, following, in the census).

HAVILAND, DANIEL born ca. 1815, and wife, LUCINDA, born ca. 1826, both in NY, were listed in the 1850 census of Raisin Twp., Lenawee Co., Mich. with ASA M., age 15; EDWIN, age 13; SARAH, age 8; PHEBE, age 3, all born Mich., in their household.

HAVILAND, DANIEL born ca. 1828, and wife, MARY, born ca. 1831, were listed in the 1850 census of Raisin Twp., Lenawee Co., Mich. with no family.

HAVILAND, ELI C., possibly son of CHARLES (preceding), born ca. 1811, and wife, SUSANNA, born ca. 1824, both in NY, were listed in the 1850 census of Raisin Twp. (next door to Moses Bowerman, note CHARLES, preceding) with ISAAC J., age 6; WILLIAM H., age 3; CHRISTIAN R., age 1, all b. Mich., in their household.

HAVILAND, ELIZABETH (KAYNER) - See George Kayner.

HAVILAND, HULDAH W. born ca. 1823, NY, was listed in the 1850 census of Adrian Twp., Lenawee Co., Mich. and may relate to the families in Raisin Twp.

HAVILAND, INGURSON, son of JAMES (following), was born in Dutchess Co., NY and moved with parents to Saratoga Co., NY, where he married ALICE (CHASE) born ca. 1787, NY. In 1821, they moved to Royalton, Niagara Co., NY; and in 1834 to Raisin Twp., Lenawee Co., Mich., where he died soon following. In the 1850 census of Raisin Twp., she was age 63, living in household of son, PELEG C. (following). She died 4 Jan. 1851. Eleven children (given names not stated). Known daughter, ESTHER. Ref: P&BA-Len pg. 498.

HAVILAND, IRA born ca. 1815, and wife, SARAH, born ca. 1826, both in NY, were listed in the 1850 census of Raisin Twp., Lenawee Co., Mich. with CHARLES N., age 1, born Mich., in their household (next door to CHARLES & ERVILLA, preceding).

HAVILAND, ISAAC, probably son of CHARLES (preceding), born ca. 1805, and (second?) wife, MARGARET, born ca. 1821, both in NY, were listed in the 1850 census of Raisin Twp., Lenawee Co., Mich. (next door to CHARLES) with ELI, age 16; NELSON, age 15; ARTEMAS, age 13; ENNICE (EUNICE?), age 11; CHANCY, age 9; ISAAC, age 5; ESTHER, age 3; ADALINE, age 3; RANSELAR, age 7; SUSAN I., age 6;

FRANKLIN, age 1, all b. Mich., in their household. Note: If Margaret's age is correct, she seems too young to be mother of some of these children.

HAVILAND, JAMES and wife, MARTHA (INGURSON), moved from Dutchess Co., NY to Saratoga Co., NY at an early date, where they remained. Known son, INGURSON (preceding). Also note JAMES, following.

HAVILAND, JAMES (note JAMES, preceding) born ca. 1795, and wife, SUSANNA, born ca. 1795, both in NY, were listed in the 1850 census of Raisin Twp., Lenawee Co., Mich. with PHILO D., age 26; JAMES JR., age 23; JARED C., age 19; SUSAN C., age 17, all b. NY; and EDITH N., age 15, b. Mich., in their household. Also listed was Edith White, age 87, b. Mass., who MAY be mother of Susanna.

HAVILAND, PELEG C., son of INGURSON (preceding), born 26 Mar. 1813, Providence, Saratoga Co., NY; moved to Niagara Co., NY and Raisin Twp., Lenawee Co., Mich. with his parents. He married on 14 June 1836 to LAURA (SLADE), daughter of Lawton (also see), in Niagara Co., NY, and they settled in Raisin Twp., Lenawee Co. Children (all b. Mich.): 1. HIRAM b. ca. 1838; 2. JOHN; 3. HULDA b. ca. 1841 (m. Thomas Savage, Adrian Twp.); 4. ROCINA (ROXANA) b. ca. 1843 (m. Moses Bowerman, Jr., to Grand Traverse Co., Mich.); 5. NANCY b. ca. 1847 (m. Stephen Bowerman, Raisin Twp.); 6. PHEBE b. ca. 1849; 7. EMERSON (m. ELLA HAVILAND). Ref: P&BA-Len pg. 498. (Note: In 1850 census were 2 doors from WING, following.)

HAVILAND, PHEBE (See Charles Kayner) Note PHEBE in the households of DANIEL (preceding) and WING (following).

HAVILAND, SAMUEL born ca. 1799, and wife, PHEBE, born ca. 1803, both in NY, were listed in the 1850 census of Raisin Twp., Lenawee Co., Mich. with IRA, age 23; ANNA, age 20; LEONARD, age 18, all b. NY; and MINERVA, age 14; JULIA, age 12; MARY, age 10, all b. Mich., in their household.

HAVILAND, SENECA, possibly son of CHARLES (preceding), born ca. 1823, and wife, MARY S., born ca. 1825, were listed in the 1850 census of Raisin Twp., Lenawee Co., Mich. with ELIZA J., age 4; JACOB S., age 7/12, both b. Mich., in their household.

HAVILAND, WING born ca. 1808, and wife, BETSEY, born ca. 1813, both in NY, were listed in the 1850 census of Raisin Twp., Lenawee Co., Mich. with PHEBE A., age 15; LAURA, age 14, both b. NY; and LYMAN, age 12; JACOB, age 7; CYNTHIA, age 6; ULISSA (MELISSA?), age 5; CHLOE A., age 1, all b. Mich., in their household. (Listed 2 doors from PELEG C. in 1850 census).

HAWKINS, ALONZO was listed in the 1840 census index of Adrian Twp., Lenawee Co., Mich.

HAWKINS, BENJAMIN was listed in the 1840 census index of Madison Twp., Lenawee Co., Mich.

HAWKINS, DELIA, age 18, born Mich., was listed in the 1850 census of Madison Twp., Lenawee Co., Mich. in a Young household.

HAWKINS, ERASTUS born ca. 1786, Conn., and wife, PATTY, born ca. 1790, VT, were listed in the 1840 census index of Franklin Twp., Lenawee Co., Mich.; and in the 1850 census of Madison Twp. were listed in the household of Jacob W. & Mary Hunt (b. ca. 1820, NY, daughter??)

HAWKINS, GEORGE was listed in the 1840 census index of Hudson Twp., Lenawee Co., Mich.

HAWKINS, GEORGE born ca. 1812, Rhode Island, and wife, EMILY, born ca. 1815, Conn., were probably they listed (as GEORGE B.) in the 1840 census index of Adrian Twp., Lenawee Co., Mich.; and were in the 1850 census of Adrian Twp. with EUNICE, age 14; JAMES, age 10, both b. Conn.; and ASHAEL, age 8; EMILY A., age 2; GEORGE JR., age 4/12, all b. Mich., in their household.

HAWKINS, GEORGE V. (Note JOHN, following) born ca. 1816, England, and wife, RACHEL, born ca. 1825, NY, were listed in the 1850 census of Medina Twp., Lenawee Co., Mich. with EDWIN, age 4?; EDWARD, age 4, both b. Mich., in their household.

HAWKINS, JOHN and wife, ELIZABETH (VAUGHN), came to the US in 1833 from Oxford, England, and settled first near Rochester (Michigan?) where he died. Elizabeth died in Hillsdale Co., Mich. at the home of known daughter, FANNY b. 1818, Oxford, England (m. Albert Humphrey Bump, also see). Ref: P&BA-Len pg. 940-1. Also note GEORGE V. (preceding), and JOHN R. & RICHARD (both following).

HAWKINS, JOHN HENRY, son of JOHN R. (following), born 6 Feb. 1843, Rollin Twp., Lenawee Co., Mich., married there on 31 Dec. 1865 to MEHITABLE (MONIER), daughter of Robert (also see). Children: 1. NELLIE M. b. 5 May 1877; 2. JOHN R. b. 26 July 1881; 3. Infant (d. unnamed); 4. HERBERT H. (d. age 4 wks). Ref: P&BA-Len pg. 730-1.

HAWKINS, JOHN R. (note JOHN, preceding) was born 1809, Oxford, England, and came to the US in 1830 and in 1834 settled in Rollin Twp., Lenawee Co., Mich. He married HANNAH T. (HAYWARD), daughter of Henry (also see) born 1810, NY. He died in 1882, age 73, and she died in 1881, age 72. Six children (given names not stated, following from 1850 census of Rollin Twp.): 1. MARY A. b. ca. 1835; 2. ROSANA b. ca. 1837; 3. JOHN HENRY b. 6 Feb. 1843 (preceding); 4. HANNAH H. b. 14 May 1845 (m. Ogden Cole, also see, Rollin Twp.); 5. JAMES b. ca. 1847. Ref: P&BA-Len pg. 594-5 & 730-1.

HAWKINS, JOSEPH born ca. 1820?, VT, was head of household in the 1850 census of Hudson Twp., Lenawee Co., Mich. with ELIZABETH, age 37; and JOSEPH, age 15, both b. VT in his household.

HAWKINS, LOREN, age 19, born England, was listed in the 1850 census of Blissfield Twp., Lenawee Co., Mich. in a Hubbard household.

HAWKINS, MARTHA (See James Oliver)

HAWKINS, RICHARD (note JOHN, preceding) born ca. 1816, England, and wife, ADALINE, born ca. 1824, NY, were listed in the 1850 census of Medina Twp., Lenawee Co., Mich. with no family.

HAWKINS, WILLIAM A. was listed in the 1840 census index of Clinton, Lenawee Co., Mich.

HAWKS, AARON moved from Mass. to Adrian Twp., Lenawee Co., Mich. about 1837, and died there age 60 (possibly before 1840); and his wife, given name not stated, died there at age 72. Known son, JOHN A. (following). Ref: P&BA-Len pg. 255-6.

HAWKS, ANNA (See Rufus Smead)

HAWKS, ERASTUS SHELDON, son of JOHN A. (following), born 9 Mar. 1836, Adrian Twp., Lenawee Co., Mich., served in Co. F., 4th Mich. Cav. during Civil War. He

Pioneer Families of Southeastern Michigan

married first to ? (HAWLEY) and had children: 1. JOHN H.; 2. ESTELLA M. His wife died in 1876, and he married second to JANE J. (FLEMING), daughter of John. Ref: P&BA-Len pg. 255-6.

HAWKS, JOHN A., son of AARON (preceding), born July 1809, Franklin Co., Mass., married 2 May 1833 to LAVINA (SMEAD), daughter of Rufus (also see), and settled in Adrian Twp., Lenawee Co., Mich. Children: 1. ERASTUS SHELDON (preceding); 2. ELECTA F. b. 30 Apr. 1838 (d. 1 Nov. 1863); 3. FREDERICK A. b. 27 Mar. 1841 (d. 27 May 1884); 4. ALVIN A. b. 19 Apr. 1847 (went to Wyoming Territory). Ref: P&BA-Len pg. 255-6. Note: In the 1850 census of Raisin Twp., it may be daughter, Electa F., listed again in the household of Isaac Randall and wife, Electa, age 68, b. Mass. Perhaps Electa, age 68, was the widow of Aaron, and married again?

HAWLEY, ? (Wife of Erastus Sheldon Hawks, also see).

HAWLEY, ASHLEY was listed in the 1840 census index of Adrian Twp., Lenawee Co., Mich.

HAWLEY, B. PERRY, son of JAMES P. (following), born 15 July 1837, Baltimore, NY, came as an adult to Jackson Co., Mich. He married on 18 Jan. 1861 to MARY R. (HAWLEY), daughter of CHARLES L. (following). Children: 1. ERWIN; 2. ARTHUR; 3. HOMER. Ref: History of Jackson Co., Mich., pg. 979.

HAWLEY, CHARLES L., son of LYMAN (following) born 9 May 1811, Leyden, Lewis Co., NY, came to Napoleon Twp., Jackson Co., Mich. with parents. He married EMILY (GRIFFIN), daughter of Oliver (also see), and settled in Napoleon Twp. Known daughter, MARY R. b. 19 Jan. 1838 (m. B. PERRY HAWLEY, preceding). Ref: History of Jackson Co., Mich., pg. 979.

HAWLEY, CHAUNCEY born 26 Sept 1797, Granby, Conn., moved at an early date to Hartford, Washington Co., NY. They moved to Napoleon Twp., Jackson Co., Mich. ca. 1832. He died 31 Mar. 1880, Napoleon. Known son, JAMES P. b. 25 Sept. 1828, Hartford, NY (d. 3 July 1876, age 48, Napoleon). Ref: History of Jackson Co., Mich., pg. 144 & 978-9 Adjacent to CHARLES & LYMAN in 1840 census index of Napoleon, Jackson Co., Mich.

HAWLEY, FRANCIS, son of WILLIAM (following), born 19 Feb. 1840, Lenawee Co., Mich., married on 3 July 1867 to MARYETTE (GIBSON) born 17 July 1849. They settled in Liberty Twp., Jackson Co., Mich. Children: 1. EFFIE M. b. 9 May 1871; 2. OTTO F. b. 19 May 1873; 3. MATTIE A. b. 22 July 1880; 4. Child (d. 30 Oct. 1856; 5. Child d. 3 Dec. 1877. Ref: History of Jackson Co., Mich., pg. 942-3.

HAWLEY, HENRY, possibly son of LEVI (following), born ca. 1803, Ohio?, and wife, MARY A. (THOMAS), born ca. 1819, NY, settled in Adrian Twp., Lenawee Co., Mich. by 1835. He died in 1870, and she died 1873, probably in Adrian. Known children (following in household in 1850 census of Adrian Twp.): 1. ELEANOR b. ca. 1835; 2. CATHERINE b. ca. 1837; 3. LEVI (following); 4. CHARLES b. ca. 1842 (d. Andersonville prison, Civil War, 19 Sept. 1864); 5. EMELINE b. ca. 1844; 6. WILLIAM b. ca. 1846; 7. MARCELLINE b. ca. 1849.

HAWLEY, HENRY, son of LYMAN (following), born 26 Mar. 1813, Leyden, Lewis Co., NY, moved to Napoleon Twp., Jackson Co., Mich. with parents. He married AMELIA M. (GRIFFIN), daughter of Oliver, also see. Only son, WALLACE A. b. 11 Mar. 1848 (m. Mary E. Russell on 10 Jan. 1871, & d. 30 May 1871). Ref: History of Jackson Co., Mich., pg. 979.

HAWLEY, JAMES from Lenawee Co., Mich. purchased land in 1832 in Columbia Twp., Jackson Co., Mich. (Note: May be JAMES P., following).

HAWLEY, JAMES P., called a "native of Conn.," was reared in NY, and he married there to NANCY (VANSTYKE), and lived in Baltimore, Greene Co., NY. They had known son, B. PERRY (preceding). It is probably this James P. with a second? wife, ELIZABETH H. (BEDELL), who had son, FRANK J. b. 25 June 1848, Greene Co., NY. In 1860, James P. moved to Jackson Co., Mich. where he died in April 1866. His wife survived him and lived in Napoleon with son, Frank. Ref: History of Jackson Co., Mich., pg. 979. Is James P. a brother of CHAUNCEY, preceding?

HAWLEY, JOHN (See William L. Rogers)

HAWLEY, JOSEPH settled in Waterloo, Jackson Co., Mich. probably after 1840.

HAWLEY, JOSIAH born 6 Sept. 1830 near Rochester (Ulster Co.), NY, came to Adrian Twp., Lenawee Co., Mich. in 1832 with his parents (names not stated, note ASHLEY, preceding). He married 14 Dec. 1854 to JANE (SNYDER). Children: 1. LINA; 2. LILLIE (m. C. A. Alverson); 3. HARRIET.

HAWLEY, JUSTUS from Cayuga Co., NY purchased land in Sandstone Twp., Jackson Co., Mich. in 1836.

HAWLEY, LEVI born ca. 1770, Conn., and wife, OLIVE (PAYNE), born ca. 1775, Rhode Island, lived in Seneca, Ontario Co., NY, and moved by 1840 to Rome Twp., Lenawee Co., Mich. He died there on 7 May 1852, age 82, and Olive died 4 Jan. 1853. In 1850, they were listed in the census in the household of son, NELSON (following). Known daughter, EMELINE b. 11 June 1814, Seneca, Ontario Co., NY (m. David Smith, Jr., also see). Also note HENRY (preceding), LEVI & WILLIAM (both following). Ref: P&BA-Len pg. 994-5.

HAWLEY, LEVI, possibly son of LEVI (preceding), born ca. 1817, and wife, POLLY R., born ca. 1820, both in NY, were listed in the 1850 census of Hudson Twp., Lenawee Co., Mich. with ALMOND W., age 6; ELMYRA, age 5; L. D. V., age 6/12, all b. Mich., in their household.

HAWLEY, LEVI, son of HENRY (preceding), born 30 Dec. 1838, Adrian Twp., Lenawee Co., Mich., married on 23 Oct. 1863 to MARIAM (HOOD), daughter of Moses G. (also see). Levi served in the Civil War in Co. H., 11th Mich. Cav.

HAWLEY, LYDIA, age 50, born NY, was listed in the 1850 census of Hudson Twp., Lenawee Co., Mich. in the household of Diadema Cavender. Note WILLIAM, following.

HAWLEY, LYMAN born 8 Dec. 1787, Granby, Conn, married JERUSHA born 5 Jan. 1788, Conn. They moved to Leyden, Lewis Co., NY before 1811. By 1840, they moved to Napoleon Twp., Jackson Co., Mich. He died 20 Apr. 1875, age 88, and she died in 1848, age 62. Known children: 1. CHARLES L. (preceding); 2. HENRY (preceding). Ref: History of Jackson Co., Mich., pg. 979.

HAWLEY, NELSON, probably son of LEVI (preceding), born ca. 1811, and wife, SALLY, born ca. 1817, both in NY, were listed in the 1850 census of Rome Twp., Lenawee

Co., Mich. with WALLACE, age 12; WILLIAM, age 4, both b. Mich., and parents, LEVI & OLIVE, in their household.

HAWLEY, NEWTON? born ca. 1807, and wife, SARAH, born ca. 1816, both in NY, were listed in the 1850 census of Seneca Twp., Lenawee Co., Mich. with EMILY, age 12; EDEN, age 9; HENRY, age 7; HARRIET, age 5, all b. Mich., in their household.

HAWLEY, RUANAH born ca. 1812, NY, was listed as head of household with JOSEPHINE, age 15; ELISHA, age 14; MATILDA, age 11; LUCINDA, age 6, all b. Mich., in her household. Note ASHLEY, preceding.

HAWLEY, WILLIAM and wife, LOWENA (SMITH), were early settlers to Lenawee Co. It may be he listed in the 1840 census index of Hudson Twp., Lenawee Co., Mich. Known daughter, LUCINDA B. (m. Lafayette Ladd, also see, on 12 Apr. 1868, Adrian). Ref: P&BA-Len pg. 519-20.

HAWLEY, WILLIAM and wife, MELANIE (SALES), settled in Rollin Twp., Lenawee Co., Mich. as early as 1832. It may be he listed in the 1840 census index of Rome Twp., Lenawee Co. Known son, FRANCIS (preceding). Ref: History of Jackson Co., Mich., pg. 942-3.

HAXTON, ELIZABETH (See William Gallaway)

HAYDEN, EMILY, age 8, born Mich., was listed in the 1850 census of Dover Twp., Lenawee Co., Mich. in a Johnson household.

HAYDEN, HEZEKIAH born 6 June 1777, Hartford, Conn., married in Oct. 1802 to HANNAH (HAYDEN), daughter of ISAAC (following). They resided in Springfield, Otsego Co., NY, where he died in June 1823, and she died in August 1823. Twelve childen (only following are known): HENRY A. (to Jackson, Mich.); 2. ALBERT (d. of Cholera enroute to Calif. goldfields); #10. WILLIAM (following). Ref: P&BA-Len pg. 548-9.

HAYDEN, ISAAC and wife, LUCY, of Windsor, Conn. were parents of known daughter, HANNAH b. 10 Dec. 1778, Windsor (m. HEZEKIAH, preceding). Possibly son, ALBERT (d. Tecumseh, 10 Apr. 1877, called "Uncle" of WILLIAM, following, taken to Windsor, Conn. for burial).

HAYDEN, WILLIAM, son of HEZEKIAH (preceding), born 25 Mar. 1819, Springfield, Otsego Co., NY, after the death of his parents, went to Genesee Co., NY and was reared by an uncle. He went to California during the Gold Rush. He settled in Jackson, Mich. in 1851; and later to Tecumseh, Lenawee Co., Mich. where he married on 18 Dec. 1856 to SARAH M. (HOSMER), daughter of Alonzo (also see). Children: 1. EMILY M. (d. 2 Aug. 1863, age 6); 2. WILLIAM H.; 3. ALBERT S.; 4. CLARA B.; 5. LIZZIE F.; 6. MABEL; 7. LEVI C.; 8. J. MARVIN. Ref: P&BA-Len pg. 548-9.

HAYES also see HAYS
HAYES, CAROLINE (See Henry Cogswell)
HAYES, SUSAN (See James Carskaddon)

HAYNES, ABNER was listed in the 1840 census index of Macon Twp., Lenawee Co., Mich. as "Hanes."
HAYNES, CHESTER A. (See Thomas Boyd)
HAYNES, JOHN W. Rev. born ca. 1802, England, and wife, ANN, born ca. 1835, Mass., were listed in the 1850 census of Hudson Twp., Lenawee Co., Mich. with CHARLES E., age 14, b. Mass., and THOMAS E., age 2, born Canada, in their household.

HAYNES, JOSIAH born ca. 1809, VT, and wife, LOVISA (LAVIRA?), born ca. 1821, Ohio, were listed (spelled "Hanes") in the 1840 census of Cambridge Twp., Lenawee Co., Mich.; and in the 1850 census with MARY, age 12, SETH, age 9; JANE, age 2, all b. Mich., in their household. Note JASON HANES.

HAYNES, LEVI born ca. 1809, and wife, CATHERINE, born ca. 1815, both in NY, were listed in the 1840 census (spelled "Hanes") of Macon Twp., Lenawee Co., Mich.; and in the 1850 census with ANNETTE, age 12; MATILDA, age 10; MARY A., age 7; CHARLES, age 5; JOHN, age 2, all b. Mich., in their household.

HAYS also see HAYES
HAYS, ELLEN born Co. Wexford, Ireland (See Thomas Wickham).

HAYWARD also spelled "HAYWOOD" in the 1840 census index for some of these families. Note: In old records, this name was also written HEYWOOD, and was later altered to HOWARD.

HAYWARD, HENRY^2, son of STEPHEN^1 (following), was born 12 July 1787, Cummington, Mass., and moved with parents to Ontario Co., NY where he married ELIZABETH (WILLITTS), daughter of Micajah (also see). In 1831, he purchased land in Livingston Co., Mich., but returned to New York. In 1833, they moved to Hudson Twp., Lenawee Co.,Mich.; and in 1834 to Seneca Twp. (where he is listed in the 1840 census index as "Haywood." He died there 26 Jan. 1842, age 64, and she died 13 Aug. 1849, age 66. Known daughter, HANNAH T. b. ca. 1810, NY (m. John R. Hawkins, also see). Known sons, STEPHEN (following); MICAJAH (following). Ref: P&BA-Len pg. 913-4 & 998-9. Also note HENRY C.; HORATIO; MARY ANN (all following).

HAYWARD, HENRY^4, son of STEPHEN^3 (following), born 24 Mar. 1840, Seneca Twp., Lenawee Co., Mich., married on 24 May 1859 to HELEN (WHALEY), daughter of Cyrenus (also see), and settled in Seneca Twp. Children: 1. FELCH (m. Viola Aldrich, dau. of Lyman H., also see, had daughter, Millie); 2. ARLETTA (m. D. M. Hough, also see); 3. RALPH B.; 4. ROBERT; 5. STEPHEN; 6. JANE; 7. REUBEN. Ref: P&BA-Len pg. 998-9.

HAYWARD, HENRY C. (possibly son of HENRY^2, preceding) born ca. 1812, and wife, JANE, born ca. 1820, both in NY, were listed in the 1850 census of Seneca Twp., Lenawee Co., Mich. with PETER S., age 2, b. Mich., in their household.

HAYWARD, HORATIO (possibly son of HENRY^2, preceding) born ca. 1820, and wife, ELIZABETH M., born ca. 1821, both in NY, were listed in the 1850 census of Seneca Twp., Lenawee Co., Mich.with EDGAR D., age 8; MELISSA D., age 6, both b. Mich., in their household.

HAYWARD, JOEL was listed in the 1840 census index of Blissfield Twp., Lenawee Co., Mich. Note JOHN M., following.

HAYWARD, JOHN D. born ca. 1824, and wife, MINERVA, born ca. 1824, both in NY, were listed in the 1850 census

Pioneer Families of Southeastern Michigan

of Tecumseh Twp., Lenawee Co., Mich. with JOHN, age 2; and HARRIET, age 1, both b. Mich., in their household.

HAYWARD, JOHN M. born ca. 1809, New Hampshire, may be he listed in the 1840 census index of Blissfield Twp., Lenawee Co., Mich. as JOHNSON M. In the 1850 census of Blissfield Twp., he listed wife, ELIZABETH J., age 23, born Canada, and EMOGENE, age 3; JOHN H., age 1; WILLIAM J., age 1, all b. Mich., in the household. Also note JOEL, preceding.

HAYWARD, MARY ANN married on 17 June 1834, Farmington, Ontario Co., NY to Amos A. Kinney (also see). Note HENRY^2 (preceding).

HAYWARD, MICAJAH^3, son of HENRY^2 (preceding), born 18 Jan. 1816, Farmington, Ontario Co., NY, came to Seneca Twp., Lenawee Co., Mich. in 1833 with parents. He married 12 May 1839 to PHILA (SANGER), daughter of Benjamin (also see), and settled in Seneca Twp. He died 10 Apr. 1887. Children: 1. BETSEY b. ca. 1844 (m. Silas W. Morris, also see); 2. ROSWELL JAMES b. ca. 1845 (m. Eva Potter, children: Harry P & Micajah); 3. JUDITH P. b. ca. 1845 (m. John Nelson, also see); 4. EFFA J. b. ca. 1848 (m. William M. Wiley, also see); 5. OLIVE ANN (m. Jonathan Salsbury, Seneca Twp.). Ref: P&BA-Len pg. 913-4.

HAYWARD, NANCY, age 15; DANIEL D., age 4; MARY E., age 1, were listed in the 1850 census of Seneca Twp., Lenawee Co., Mich. in the household of Abram Varnum, and wife, Julia (age 38, b. NY), and may be stepchildren in that household. They are 2 doors from MICAJAH, and may relate to the family of Henry^2. It should be noted that Daniel D. & Mary E. were "dittoed" after Nancy, and MAY actually have been meant to be named Varnum?

HAYWARD, ORLANDO M. (note THEODORE, following) born ca. 1826, and wife, CORNELIA, born ca. 1828, both in NY, were listed in the 1850 census of Dover Twp., Lenawee Co., Mich. with BYRON, age 5; EMILY, age 3; HELEN, age 5/12, all b. Mich., in their household.

HAYWARD, SHUREBIAH? T. (note THEODORE, following) born ca. 1821, and wife, MARY K., born ca. 1824, both in NY, were listed in the 1850 census of Dover Twp., Lenawee co., Mich.

HAYWARD, STEPHEN^1 of Cummington, Mass. was a Lt. in the Continental Army. He married HANNAH (TRACEY) and they had known son, HENRY^2 (preceding). Ref: P&BA-Len pg. 998-9.

HAYWARD, STEPHEN born ca. 1777, New Jersey, was listed in the 1850 census of Ridgeway Twp., Lenawee Co., Mich. in the household of son, STEPHEN R. (following).

HAYWARD, STEPHEN^3, son of HENRY^2 (preceding), was born ca. 1814, and moves with his parents to Seneca Twp., Lenawee Co., Mich. He married in Jan. 1837 to SARAH JANE (SANGER), daughter of Benjamin (also see), and settled in Seneca Twp. (spelled "Haywood" in 1840 census index). In the 1850 census they listed WILLIAM, age 8; MYRON C., age 5; MARY A., age 3; RHODA, age 1, all b. Mich., in their household. Ref: P&BA-Len pg. 998-9.

HAYWARD, STEPHEN R., son of STEPHEN (of NJ, preceding), born ca. 1810, and wife, POLLY, born ca. 1816, both in NY, were listed in the 1840 census index of Raisin Twp., Lenawee Co., Mich., and in the 1850 census of Ridgeway Twp., with MARTHA, age 11; HULDAH, age 9; RACHEL, age 7; HANNAH, age 6; RICHARD, age 2; STEPHEN, age 2/12, all b. Mich., in their household.

HAYWARD, THEODORE born ca. 1791, Mass., and wife, CHARLOTTE, born ca. 1795, Conn., were probably they listed in the 1840 census index of Dover Twp., Lenawee Co., Mich. (spelled "Haywood.") In the 1850 census of Dover Twp., they listed CHARLES, age 17; SARAH T., age 19, both b. NY, in their household. Also note ORLANDO M.; SHUREBIAH T. (preceding). They are probably parents of ADELINE J. b. 17 Sept. 1817, Farmington, Ontario Co., NY (m. Charles E. Mickley, also see). If so, the sketch states that her father died on 15 May 1872, Royalton, Ohio, and her mother died 1 Apr. 1869, Dover Twp. Ref: P&BA-Len pg. 1122-3.

HAYWARD, WILLIAM (note STEPHEN of NJ, preceding) born ca. 1822, and wife, IRENA, born ca. 1823, both in NY, were listed in the 1850 census of Raisin Twp., Lenawee Co., Mich. with MINOR C., age 8, b. NY; and ALMEDA M., age 6, b. Ohio; and WILLIAM, age 1, b. Mich., in their household.

HAYWOOD see HAYWARD

HAYWOOD, FELCH (See HAYWARD, HENRY^4, for son, FELCH)

HAYWOOD, JASPER (spelled Hawood) was listed in the 1830 census of Lenawee Co., Mich., Mich. Territory, with only he age 20-30 listed.

HAZARD, J. L. (See George Lane)

HAZEN, FANNIE (See Lewis Cole)

HAZEN, OBADIAH born ca. 1825, Ohio, and wife, SARAH, born ca. 1832, NY, were listed in the 1850 census of Adrian Twp., Lenawee Co., Mich.

HAZEN, SILAS born ca. 1797, Conn., and wife, DELILAH, born ca. 1808, NY, were listed in the 1850 census of Rollin Twp., Lenawee Co., Mich. with SARAH M., age 10, b. Mich., in their household. Note: There were men by this name in the 1840 census index of Superior Twp., Washtenaw Co., and Bruce Twp., Macomb Co., Mich.

HEADLY, ELIZABETH (See John Goheen)

HEAGY, MARGARET (See Daniel Heck)

HEATH, A. (See Harrison Fitts)

HEATH, CHESTER born ca. 1799, Conn., and wife, ANNA, born ca. 1812, VT, were listed in the 1850 census of Woodstock Twp., Lenawee Co., Mich. with CHARLES, age 15, b. NY; and CHARLOTTE, age 11/12, b. Mich., in their household.

HEATH, L. D. born NY, and wife, SUSAN (GROSS), born Penn., lived in Spring Lake, Ottawa Co., Mich., where known daughter, NELLIE E. b. 14 July 1866 (m. Clement H. Bramble, also see). Ref: P&BA-Len pg. 725-6.

HEATHERTON, JOSEPH (See William Ladd)

HECK, DANIEL and wife, MARGARET (HEAGY), lived near Carlisle, Penn. and had 6 children and the only given name listed was the eldest, JOHN A. b. 16 Aug. 1830,

Penn. John A. and a brother moved to Adrian, Lenawee Co., Mich. by 1874. Ref: P&BA-Len pg. 482.

HECK, CATHERINE (See George Traben)

HECKERT, ANNA M. (See John Rudolph)

HECKERT, DAVID B., son of JOHN G. (following), born 8 Sept. 1833, Preston Co., W. Va., moved to Ogden Twp., Lenawee Co., Mich. in 1855. He married 12 Nov. 1858 to MARGARET E. (HILE), daughter of Peter (also see) and settled in Ogden Twp. Children: 1. DORA A. (m. Howard E. Lour 30 Oct. 1887); 2. ESTHER MAY. Ref: P&BA-Len pg. 1108-9.

HECKERT, JOHN G., son of PETER (who moved from Penn. to Preston Co., W. Va.), was born in Preston Co. He married first to MARY (BISHOFF), daughter of Christian, and she died in 1842 leaving 6 children (only following listed): DAVID B. (preceding). John G. married again to JULIA (WAGNER) with whom he had 5 children (given names not stated), and she died in Preston Co., W. Va. He joined son, David B., in Ogden Twp., Lenawee Co., Mich.; and married LUCY A. (HILE) who died in Ogden Twp., leaving 1 child (name not stated). Ref: P&BA-Len pg. 1108-9.

HECKERT, JOHN PETER, son of SOLOMON (following), born 20 Feb. 1828, near Aurora, W. Va., married on 30 Dec. 1856, in Preston Co., W. Va. to MARTHA ELLEN (PORTER) born 7 Aug. 1837 near Frostburg, MD. They moved to Ogden Twp., Lenawee Co., Mich. in 1865. She died 29 July 1879. Children: 1. MARY E.; 2. ALBERT W.; 3. HANNAH B.; 4. JOHN S.; 5. WILLIAM F.; 6. EDWARD W.; 7. Infant who d. unnamed. Ref: P&BA-Len pg. 1180.

HECKERT, SOLOMON, son of PETER (note JOHN G., preceding), was born in Preston Co., W. Va., and married there to MARIA (NINES), daughter of Christian. They remained there till 1869, then moved to Ogden Twp., Lenawee Co., Mich. Known son, JOHN PETER (preceding). Ref: P&BA-Len pg. 1180.

HECOX see HICKCOX

HEDGES, RHODA (See Kalep Wolcott)

HEESEN, GEORGE, son of RUDOLPH (following), born 12 Mar. 1829, Dinxperlo, Province of Gelderland, Holland, came to the US with his parents. He moved from Cleveland, Ohio to Grand Rapids, Mich. for a time, but returned to Cleveland. He married there in 1858 to ANGELINE (NYLAND), daughter of Anthony (also see), and they settled in Tecumseh, Lenawee Co., Mich. on 19 Apr. 1858. Children: 1. NELLIE (m. Thomas Adamson, Tecumseh, Mich.); 2. DELIA (m. John L. Trann, St. Louis); 3. RUDOLPH; 4. HANNAH; 5. ALFRED J. Ref: P&BA-Len pg. 856-7.

HEESEN RUDOLPH, son of ANDREW (of Holland), and wife, PETRONELLA (TAUTE), were natives of Suderwick (near Buchold), Jerrinkhoff, Province to Gelderland, Holland, apparently lived at Dinxperlo. They came to the US in 1846, and settled first in Baltimore, MD, and then Youngstown, Ohio, and later to Cleveland, Ohio. She died in Cleveland on 4 July 1859/60. He afterwards moved to Tecumseh, Lenawee Co., Mich., where he died on 17 Apr. 1861, age 61, at the home of a daughter. There were 3 sons and 2 daughters, all of whom moved to Tecumseh, Mich. Those known: GEORGE (preceding); HANDRENA (m. John H. Nyland, also see); ENGELINA b. 19 Apr. 1838 (m. Alfred D. Hall, also see). Ref: P&BA-Len pg. 856-7 & 1130-2.

HEIRST, ANN (See Daniel Bateman)

HELM, DANIEL born ca. 1815, Penn., and wife, JANE, born ca. 1819, Ireland, were listed in the 1850 census of Tecumseh Twp., Lenawee Co., Mich. with ELIZABETH, age 7; SAMUEL, age 6, both b. Mich., in their household. Note PARMELIA & SAMUEL (following).

HELM, HOLMES born ca. 1812, and wife, CLARISSA, born ca. 1818, both in NY, were listed (as "Helms") in the 1840 census index of Medina Twp., Lenawee Co., Mich.; and in the 1850 census with VICTORY, age 11, b. NY; and CHARLES, age 8; MARTIN, age 6; ARAMITTA, age 1, all b. Mich., in their household.

HELM, JAMES W. born ca. 1817, NY, and wife, PHEBE, born ca. 1827, Conn., were listed in the 1850 census of Adrian Twp., Lenawee Co., Mich. with JAMES W., age 2; LYDIA P., age 2/12, both b. Mich., in their household.

HELM, MARY born ca. 1830, Mich., was listed in the 1850 census of Tecumseh Twp., Lenawee Co., Mich., 2 doors from DANIEL (preceding). Note PARMELIA, following.

HELM, PARMELIA born ca. 1794, New Jersey, was listed as head of household in the 1840 census index of Tecumseh Twp., Lenawee Co., Mich. In the 1850 census she was listed, age 56, b. NJ, in the household of SAMUEL (following). Also note MARY & DANIEL, preceding.

HELM, SAMUEL (note PARMELIA, preceding) born ca. 1826, Penn., married in Tecumseh Twp., Lenawee Co., Mich. to FRANCES (GRAY), daughter of Joseph W. (also see) born ca. 1831, Michigan. In the 1850 census of Tecumseh Twp., they listed only PARMELIA (preceding) in their household.

HELM, SARAH (See George W. Clark)

HELM, VICTOR H. was listed in the 1840 census index of Adrian Twp., Lenawee Co., Mich. (written "Helms").

HELMIE, ELLEN Mrs. was the daughter of Albert Humphrey Bump (also see), and the Helmies resided in Wheatland Twp., Hillsdale Co., Mich.

HELMS see HELM

HEM, MARGARET (See William Sheeler[1])

HEMANS, ENOCH and wife, ELIZABETH, of Jackson Co., Mich., had known daughter, M. JOSEPHINE (m. Henry C. Hall, also see, 24 Dec. 1870 in Hudson, Lenawee Co., Mich.)

HEMINGWAY also see HEMINWAY
HEMINGWAY, RUFUS was listed in the 1840 census index of Adrian Twp., Lenawee Co., Mich.

HEMINOVER, ELIZABETH (See Peter M. Wheaton)
HEMINOVER, LOUISE (See Peter M. Wheaton)

Pioneer Families of Southeastern Michigan

HEMINWAY also see HEMINGWAY

HEMINWAY, JASON born ca. 1811, NY, was listed in the 1840 census index of Blissfield Twp., Lenawee Co., Mich.; and in the 1850 census he listed wife, NANCY, born ca. 1827, Mass. (As some of the following appear too old to be children of Nancy, perhaps she was a second wife?) In the household were CHARLOTTE, age 14, b. NY; and JASON, age 9; TRUMAN, age 6; MARIAM, age 3, all b. Mich., and also Emery Burnham, age 18, b. Mass.

HEMINWAY, LORA (See Norman B. Pierce)

HEMLER, JAMES C. and wife, MARY, had known daughter, ALICE B. b. 28 Jan. 1853, Utica, Licking Co., Ohio (m. 18 Jan. 1887 to John Johnson, also see, in Burbank, Wayne Co., Ohio). Ref: P&BA-Len pg. 585-7.

HEMPHALE also see HEMPHILL

HEMPHALE, LOIS born Saratoga Co., NY, came to Lenawee Co., with parents "as a child" and married David Woodward (also see). Note: It is probably she written as "Hemphill," age 14, born NY, in the 1850 census of Franklin Twp., Lenawee Co., Mich. in an Easterbrook household.

HEMPHILL, JERUSHA was listed in the 1840 census index of Franklin Twp., Lenawee Co., Mich. (Note LOIS HEMPHALE, preceding).

HEMPHILL, SARAH (See James B. Wells)

HENDEE, AUGUSTA M. (See Solomon M. Newton)

HENDERSHOTT, ALVAH born ca. 1813, Penn., and wife, RACHEL, born ca. 1814, NY, were listed in the 1850 census of Tecumseh Twp., Lenawee Co., Mich. with DEWITT, age 7; ROSEANN, age 6; REBECCA, age 4; ADELBERT, age 2, all b. Mich., in their household.

HENDERSHOTT, CALEB (note WILLIAM, following) born Apr. 1806, Jersey Twp., Northumberland Co., Penn., came to Clinton Twp., Lenawee Co., Mich. in 1832 with is parents. He married in 1834/5 to ELIZABETH (SHIPMAN) who had come to Michigan with parents. They were listed in the 1840 census index of Tecumseh Twp. She died in 1849. In the 1850 census of Tecumseh Twp., in his household were SARAH, age 17; THOMAS, age 14; EVAN, age 11; ROXANA, age 8; CYRUS (See J. C. following); CHARLES, age 3, all b. Mich. CHARLOTTE, age 25, b. NY, was also in the household. Caleb died on 1 Apr. 1886. Ref: P&BA-Len pg. 683-4.

HENDERSHOTT, DEBORAH born ca. 1821, NY, was head of household in the 1850 census of Tecumseh Twp., Lenawee Co., Mich. with JACOB, age 6; JOHN, age 6; SALLY ANN, age 3; ROBERT, age 2, all b. Mich., in her household. Note GEORGE & HENRY, following.

HENDERSHOTT, ELIZABETH born 1786, Penn. (See Garret Aten).

HENDERSHOTT, EVAN and wife, MARGARET (McBRIDE), moved from Northumberland Co., Penn. to Clinton Twp., Lenawee Co., Mich. ca, 1868. Known daughter, HENRIETTA b. 25 Apr. 1845, Penn. (m. "J. C." CYRUS, following). Ref: P&BA-Len pg. 683-4.

HENDERSHOTT, C. (See A. W. Ellis)

HENDERSHOTT, GEORGE was listed in the 1840 census index of Macon Twp., Lenawee Co., Mich. adjacent to HENRY, RALPH, & WILLIAM (all following). He is not listed in the 1850 census. Note DEBORAH, preceding.

HENDERSHOTT, HENRY was listed in the 1840 census index of Macon Twp., Lenawee Co., Mich. adjacent to GEORGE, RALPH & WILLIAM. Note DEBORAH, preceding.

HENDERSHOTT, J. C. (probably CYRUS), son of CALEB (preceding), was born 28 Nov. 1844, Tecumseh Twp., Lenawee Co., Mich., and married HENRIETTA (HENDERSHOTT), daughter of EVAN (preceding) on 6 May 1873. Children: 1. BLANCHE (d. young); 2. ROSCOE C.; 3. ELMER. Ref: P&BA-Len pg. 683-4.

HENDERSHOTT, JOHN born ca. 1788, Penn., was listed in the 1850 census of Macon Twp., Lenawee Co., Mich. next door to RALPH (following).

HENDERSHOTT, JOHN married JOSEPHINE (DePUY), daughter of Philip S. (also see) born 1845, in Tecumseh Twp., Lenawee Co., Mich. Note JOHN in household of RALPH (following).

HENDERSHOTT, MARGARET born ca. 1825, NJ, married first to Thomas Coller (also see); and he died before 1850 and she married second to Samuel S. Henry (also see), Tecumseh Twp., Lenawee Co., Mich.

HENDERSHOTT, MARTIN (See MICHAEL, following)

HENDERSHOTT, MARY born ca. 1831, NY, was listed in the 1850 census of Tecumseh Twp., Lenawee Co., Mich. in a Benaway household.

HENDERSHOTT, MICHAEL, son of WILLIAM (following), born 8 June 1805, Jersey Twp., Northumberland Co., Penn., moved at age 18 to Livingston Co., NY. He married first to ROSINA (COLLER), probably daughter of Jesse B. (also see). In the 1850 census of Macon Twp., he lists a wife, LUCINDA, age 27, born NY. Children: 1. WILLIAM H. b. ca. 1841 (to Leslie, Ingham Co., Mich.); 2. JOHN T. b. ca. 1841, twin? (Tecumseh Twp.); 3. JESSE b. ca. 1842; 4. CATHERINE b. ca. 1845 (m. MARTIN HENDERSHOTT); 5. SARAH LOUISA b. ca. 1848 (m. Cassius M. Mills, Macon Twp.); 6. GEORGE (Macon Twp.); 7. EVA (m. ?, Dunkirk, Ohio); 8. MICHAEL (to Minnesota); 9. ELMER E. (Physician, Dunkirk, Ohio). Ref: P&BA-Len pg. 390-3.

HENDERSHOTT, PATRICK born ca. 1827, Penn, and wife, MARGARET (JOHNSON?), born ca. 1828, Scotland were listed in the 1850 census of Franklin Twp., Lenawee Co., Mich. with LAURA, age 2/12, b. Mich.; and Alexander Johnson (also see) in their household.

HENDERSHOTT, RALPH (note JOHN, preceding), born ca. 1807, and wife, JULIA, born ca. 1814, both in Penn., were listed in the 1850 census of Macon Twp., Lenawee Co., Mich. with ISAIAH, age 15; ISRAEL, age 14; ELISA, age 13; MARY, age 10; HALSEY?, age 8; ROBERT, age 6; JOHN, age 4; JULIA A., age 2; RALPH, age 4/12, all b. Mich., in their household. (JOHN was listed next door)

HENDERSHOTT, SHERWOOD born ca. 1828, NY, was listed in the 1850 census of Tecumseh Twp., Lenawee Co., Mich.

HENDERSHOTT, WILLIAM born ca. 1780, and wife, MARY (KITCHEN), born ca. 1779, both in Penn., came to Macon Twp., Lenawee Co., Mich. by 1840 to live near their son, MICHAEL (preceding). In the 1850 census of Macon Twp., they listed in their household (probably grandchildren) HARRIET, age 13; REBECCA, age 8; both b. Mich. Note: In the 1840 census index, listed with WILLIAM in Macon Twp. were GEORGE, HENRY, & RALPH; and listed in Tecumseh Twp. were CALEB & JOHN (all preceding).

HENDERSON, ASAHEL (ASAEL) born ca. 1809, and wife, MARIA, born ca. 1810, both in NY, were listed in the 1850 census of Madison Twp., Lenawee Co., Mich. with PURLETTE (male), age 10; PRELETTE (female), age 10; ELEANOR, age 5; CHARLES C., age 3; CONRAY G., age 3; ADIA, age 3; DETROIT (male), age 2, all b. Mich., in their household.

HENDERSON, DAVID born ca. 1810, Mich.?, and wife, MARIA, born ca. 1817, NY, were listed in the 1840 census index of Tecumseh Twp., Lenawee Co., Mich.; and in the 1850 census with CHARLES, age 12, b. Mich., in their household.

HENDERSON, EMILY married in Ontario Co., NY to Abner Aldrich (also see) and moved to Green Creek Twp., Sandusky Co. Ohio. Ref: P&BA-Len pg. 1039-40.

HENDERSON, HELEN M., age 6, born Ohio, was listed in the 1850 census of Fairfield Twp., Lenawee Co., Mich. in a Williams household.

HENDERSON, JAMES born ca. 1814, Canada, and wife, CELESTIA, born ca. 1817, NY, were listed in the 1850 census of Hudson Twp., Lenawee Co., Mich. with VANRENSELAER, age 14; EUSIL (male), age 8; HALSEY H., age 6, all b. Ohio, in their household.

HENDERSON, JANET born 1819, Inverness, Scotland, married Douglad Moore (also see) in Middlesex Co., Ontario, Canada.

HENDERSON, JOEL, age 21, born NY, was listed in the 1850 census of Palmyra Twp., Lenawee Co., Mich. in a Crane household. There was another, age 25, b. NY, perhaps same man, listed in the 1850 census of Madison Twp., Lenawee Co., Mich. in Haskell household.

HENDERSON, JONATHAN born ca. 1809, and wife, ELECTA, born ca. 1810, were listed in the 1840 census index of Fairfield Twp., Lenawee Co., Mich.; and in the 1850 census of Ogden Twp. with JONATHAN, age 18, b. NY; and ALMA, age 13; CAROLINE, age 10; JULIA, age 8; HENRY, age 2, all b. Mich., in their household. Note THOMAS, following.

HENDERSON, PHILO, age 12, born Mich., was listed in the 1850 census of Fairfield Twp., Lenawee Co., Mich. in a Hill household.

HENDERSON, R. H. Dr. born NY, and wife, BETSEY (FOSTER), born Mass., settled in Lockport, Niagara Co., NY where 9 of their 10 children (names not stated) were born. In 1835, they moved to near Ann Arbor, Washtenaw Co., Mich. He died in Aug. 1838, and in the 1840 census index, Betsey was listed in Lodi Twp., Washtenaw Co. She died in Ann Arbor. Known daughter, ZORAIDA b. 17 June 1832 (m. first to ? Hood; m/2 John Fisher of Tecumseh, Lenawee Co., Mich., also see). Ref: P&BA-Len pg. 504-5.

HENDERSON, STEPHEN A. born ca. 1822, NY, and wife, JULIA A., born ca. 1827, Canada, were listed in the 1850 census of Madison Twp., Lenawee Co., Mich. with JOHN, age 4; EPHRAIM, age 2, both b. Mich., in their household.

HENDERSON, THOMAS born ca. 1777, NY, was listed in the 1850 census of Fairfield Twp., Lenawee Co., Mich. in a Baker household. Note: There was a THOMAS in the 1800 census index of Cayuga Co., NY.

HENDRYX, CORNELIUS R. (probably son of JEREMIAH S., following) born ca. 1824, NY, and wife, JERUSHA, born ca. 1827, Mich., were listed in the 1850 census of Franklin Twp., Lenawee Co., Mich. with ALICE, age 3, b. Mich., in their household (next door to JEREMIAH).

HENDRYX, JEREMIAH S., son of JOHN (following), born ca. 1801, probably in Madison Co., NY, and wife, ELEANOR, born ca. 1804, NY, was listed in the 1850 census of Franklin Twp., Lenawee Co., Mich. with WILLIAM, age 12, b. Mich., in the household, next door to CORNELIUS R. (preceding). Jeremiah retired to Tecumseh, Mich. where he resided in 1888. Also note HARRIET & HENRIETTA, following. Ref: P&BA-Len pg. 669-70.

HENDRYX, HARRIET, age 18, born NY, was listed in the 1850 census of Madison Twp., Lenawee Co., Mich. in a Cadman household.

HENDRYX, HENRIETTA, age 21, born NY, was listed next door to CORNELIUS & JEREMIAH S., in the 1850 census of Franklin Twp., Lenawee Co., Mich. in the household of Henry J. and Esther (born 1822, NY) Slater. Was Esther a Hendryx?

HENDRYX, JOHN born in Rhode Island, moved to Madison Co., NY where he married DOLLY (SMITH) born Conn. In 1810, they removed to Steuben Co., NY, and he served in the War of 1812. He was killed in Steuben Co. in a Mill accident at age 45. Known children: JEREMIAH S. (preceding); Daughter (went to Ohio); #5. THOMAS (following). Dolly married again to James Griffith who d. in 1838; and she afterwards went to Ohio where she married third to ? Loveland. Ref: P&BA-Len pg. 669-70.

HENDRYX, THOMAS, son of JOHN (preceding), born June 1807, probably in Madison Co., NY, moved to Steuben Co., NY with parents. He moved to Coshocton, NY, and married 22 Oct. 1828, Auburn, NY to HARRIET (BISHOP) born 1812, Utica, NY. They lived in Florida, before moving to Franklin Twp., Lenawee Co., Mich. in 1864. Children: 1. J. DWIGHT; 2. CHARLOTTE A.; 3. MARY; 4. CHARLES W.; 5. HATTIE A.; 6. DELL; 7. EDSON T. Ref: P&BA-Len pg. 669-70.

HENION, ABRAHAM A. born ca. 1806 and wife, MARY "POLLY" (WALWORTH), born ca. 1812, were natives of Seneca Co., NY, and they moved briefly to Wayne Co., Mich., but returned to (Wayne Co.?) NY. About 1843, they removed to Rome Twp., Lenawee Co., Mich. She died in Morenci, Mich. in 1855, and he died in Dover Twp. in 1864. Children: 1. JOHN; 2. PETER D. b. ca. 1834; 3. DUDLEY C. (probably he who m. Mary M. Clark, dau. of Edward, also see); 4. ANNA S. b. 22 Jan. 1840, Palmyra, NY (m. Albert White, also see); 5. JULIA b. ca. 1842; 6. MARY J. b. ca. 1847, Mich.; 7. MILLARD; 8. FREDERICK. Ref: P&BA-Len pg. 639-40. (Note: In the 1850 census, son, John, was not listed, nor was Dudley C., perhaps, Peter D. is actually Dudley?

HENNIKER, WILLIAM of "New England" was a pioneer settler to Batavia, NY. Known daughter, MEHITABLE (m. Thomas Lee, also see). Ref: P&BA-Len pg. 1098-1100.

HENRY, F. M. (See Justus Love)

Pioneer Families of Southeastern Michigan

HENRY, ISAAC, age 1, born Mich., was listed in the 1850 census of Woodstock Twp., Lenawee Co., Mich. in the household of Isaac and Mary Smith, possibly his grandparents.

HENRY, JOEL, age 8, born Ohio, was listed in the 1850 census of Hudson Twp., Lenawee Co., Mich. in a Dean household.

HENRY, JOHN born ca. 1806, and wife, JANE, born ca. 1803, both in Ireland, were listed in the 1850 census of Tecumseh Twp., Lenawee Co., Mich. with HUGH, age 21, b. Penn.; SARAH, age 17; SAMUEL, age 15, both b. NJ; and JOHN, age 12; ANN, age 10; MATILDA, age 8, all b. Mich., in their household.

HENRY, JOHN born ca. 1815, and wife, HARRIET, born ca. 1817, both in England, were listed in the 1850 census of Franklin Twp., Lenawee Co., Mich. with BRASILLA (female), age 6, b. Mich., in their household.

HENRY, JOHN, son of ROSWELL (following) was born 4 Feb. 1833, Monroe Co., NY. He married in Ransom Twp., Hillsdale Co., Mich. on 21 Jan. 1853 to SAVILLA E. (PALMER), daughter of Fenner (also see). He died in August 1866 in Hudson, Lenawee Co., Mich. Five children (one deceased, name not stated): 1. MARY E. (m. Charles East, Macon Twp.); 2. CHARLES R. (m. Flora Parsheel, AuSable, Mich.); 3. JULIA (m. George L. Cornville, Tawas City, Mich.); 4. ADA (m. Prof. Willard Phillips, Manchester, Mich.). Ref: P&BA-Len pg. 736-7.

HENRY, MARY (See Robert Kerr)

HENRY, ROSWELL was a great-nephew of Patrick Henry. He married ANN (BLOOMER) and they remained in New York. Known son, JOHN (preceding). Ref: P&BA-Len pg. 736-7.

HENRY, SAMUEL S. born ca. 1820, Ohio, married Mrs. MARGARET (HENDERSHOTT) COLLER, widow of Thomas. They were listed in the 1850 census of Tecumseh Twp., Lenawee Co., Mich. with ALMEDA?, age 4, b. Mich., in their household.

HERENDEEN, C. K. was listed in the 1840 census index of Medina Twp., Lenawee Co., Mich. (spelled "Herrindian.")

HERENDEEN, CALEB was listed in the 1840 census index of Plymouth Twp., Wayne Co., Mich. (spelled "Herindeen.")

HERENDEEN, GAMALIEL was listed in the 1840 census index of Rome Twp., Lenawee Co., Mich. (spelled "Herindien." Note: There is an ELEAZER "HERINDEEN" listed in the 1800 census index of Chenango Co., NY.

HERENDEEN, THOMAS moved probably from Steuben Co., NY to Washtenaw Co., Mich. in 1832, and later moved to Newaygo Co., Mich. Known daughter, ALMEDA b. ca. 1814, Steuben Co., NY (m. Lyman Gilmore, also see, and came first to York, Washtenaw Co., Mich.; and then Macon Twp., Lenawee Co.)

HERETT, ELIZABETH (See George Laur)

HERKERT, PETER had known daughter, ELIZABETH, born in Virginia (m. James Robertson, also see, before 1835). Ref: P&BA-Len pg. 667-8.

HERRICK, JAMES H. (See Cyrenus Sanford)

HERRICK, PETER born ca 1806, and wife, MAGDALENE, born ca. 1814, both in Germany, were listed in the 1850 census of Madison Twp., Lenawee Co., Mich. with CATHARINE, age 15; HENRY, age 12; JOHN, age 9; MARY, age 6, all b. Germany, and HARVEY, age 2, b. Mich., in their household.

HERRICK, PHEBE (See William Ladd)

HERRINGTON also see HARRINGTON
HERRINGTON, ABE (See James Smith)

HERRIOT see HARRIOT

HERRON, FRED (See Levi L. Stockwell)
HERRON, WILLIAM W. (See John Forbes)

HERVEY also see HARVEY

HERVEY, HERMON, son of OBED, Jr. (following), was born 22 Sept. 1783, Dutchess Co., NY; and married HANNAH (TYLER), daughter of David, born 24 Mar. 1784. Hermon died 29 Dec. 1843, probably in Durham, Greene Co., NY; and she died 21 Apr. 1862. Known son, RUSSELL (following). Ref: P&BA-Len pg. 450-1.

HERVEY, OBED, Jr.. son of OBED, Sr. (following), was born 21 Feb. 1752. He married ABIGAIL (BELL), and were residing in Dutchess Co., NY in 1783; and moved to Durham, Greene Co., NY. He died 26 Oct. 1838, and she died 11 Aug. 1817, Durham, NY. Known son, HERMON (preceding). Ref: P&BA-Len pg. 450-1.

HERVEY, OBED, Sr. born 1722, married MERCY (SYKES) born 1731. They probably lived in Dutchess Co., NY, and moved to Durham, Greene Co., NY where he died 11 Jan. 1808, and she died Feb. 1814. Known son, OBED, Jr. (preceding). Ref: P&BA-Len pg. 450-1.

HERVEY, RUSSELL, son of HERMON (preceding), born 6 Feb. 1807, Durham, NY, married first to ? (NOYES), daughter of Amos & Miriam (Barney) Noyes, and they moved to Adrian, Lenawee Co., Mich. before 1840 (listed in census index as "Harvey.") She died 29 June 1849. Russell married again to LOVISA (READ), daughter of William (also see). Known son, WILLIAM H. (following). Ref: P&BA-Len pg. 450-1.

HERVEY, WILLIAM H., son of RUSSELL (preceding), born 23 Dec. 1853, Adrian Twp., Lenawee Co., Mich., married there to ELLA (MARSH), daughter of John (also see). Children: 1. LEILA b. 1 Mar. 1881; 2. BERTHA A. b. 23 Nov. 1882. Ref: P&BA-Len pg. 450-1.

HEWITT, ALMERA (See Isaac Hamton)
HEWITT, ANNIE (See John Churchill)
HEWITT, CELINA, age 12, born Ohio, was listed in the 1850 census of Dover Twp., Lenawee Co., Mich. in the Philip Brown household.

HEWITT, CHARLES (probably son of HENRY, following) born ca. 1802, NY, was listed in the 1840 census index of Tecumseh Twp., Lenawee Co., Mich., and was listed in the 1850 census with (second wife?) MARY, age 34, b. Mass.; ELISA, age 27; HENRY, age 22, both b. NY; and CHARLES, age 7; RICHARD, age 5; MARY, age 3, all b. Mich.; and HENRY (following), in their household.

HEWITT, HENRY born ca. 1763, Conn., was listed in the 1850 census of Tecumseh Twp., Lenawee Co., Mich. in the household of CHARLES (preceding).

HEWITT, JOSEPH born ca. 1820, Penn., and wife, MARGARET, born ca. 1821, Ohio, were listed in the 1850 census of Woodstock Twp., Lenawee Co., Mich. with SARAH, age 2, b. Mich., in their household.

HEWITT, M. L. was listed in the 1840 census index of Dover Twp., Lenawee Co., Mich. Note MERRITT, following.

HEWITT, MERRITT born ca. 1808, NY, and wife, ALICE, born ca. 1815, Del?, were listed in the 1850 census of Woodstock Twp., Lenawee Co., Mich. with ADDISON, age 13, b. NY; RUSSELL, age 11; MARY, age 9 (may be she who m. Abram Harris, son of Garrett F., also see); GEORGE, age 6; WILLIAM, age 4, all b. Mich., in their household.

HEWITT, REBECCA born ca. 1812, NY, was head of household in the 1850 census of Medina Twp., Lenawee Co., Mich. with NANCY M., age 16; MARY J., age 15; PALINA A., age 10, all b. NY; and GEORGE, age 5, b. Ohio, in her household. Also note CELINA, preceding.

HEWLETT also see HULETT

HEWLETT, MARTHA born ca. 1810, NY, was listed in the 1850 census of Dover Twp., Lenawee Co., Mich. with LEWIS, age 19; JULIA, age 17; BETSEY A., age 15; MARY, age 12, all b. NY; and DALLAS, age 5, b. Mich., in her household.

HEWLETT, PARLEY was listed in the 1840 census index of Hudson Twp., Lenawee Co., Mich.

HIBBARD, G. B. (See John W. Winne)

HIBBARD, SALLIE (See Enoch Morrell)

HICKMAN, D. W. (See Sheldon Wyman)

HICKOX, ALBERT K. born ca. 1797, Conn., and wife, SARAH A., born ca. 1802, NY, were listed in the 1840 census index of Blissfield Twp., Lenawee Co., Mich.; and in the 1850 census (written "Heacox") with SARAH, age 15; ELIZABETH, age 10; GEORGE, age 6, all b. Mich., in their household.

HICKOX, ALONZO was listed in the 1840 census index of Blissfield Twp., Lenawee Co., Mich.

HICKOX, AMELIA was a native of Avon Springs, NY (See Frank W. Clay).

HICKOX, DAVID, age 12, born Ohio, was listed in the 1850 census of Seneca Twp., Lenawee Co., Mich.

HICKOX, WELLS G. born ca. 1819, Mass., and wife, ELIZABETH, born ca. 1818, NY, were listed in the 1850 census of Rome Twp., Lenawee Co., Mich. with JANE, age 9; LEORY (LEROY?), age 6; CHESTER J., age 3, all born Mich.; and (sister?) CAROLINE, age 17, born NY, in their household.

HICKS also see HIX

HICKS, BROADSTREET S. born ca. 1800, and wife, ANN, born ca. 1805, both in NY, were listed in the 1850 census of Tecumseh Twp., Lenawee Co., Mich. with FANNY, age 19, b. NY; and Adelia Page, age 18; Augusta Page, age 16; Catharine Page, age 14; Charles Page, age 4; Leander Page, age 2, all b. Mich., in their household.

HICKS, DANIEL was listed in the 1840 census index of Madison Twp., Lenawee Co., Mich. Note MARY, following.

HICKS, HARRIET E., possibly daughter of JOSEPH (following), born Nassau, Rensselaer Co., NY, married Reuben Knapp (also see). Ref: P&BA-Len pg. 1004-6.

Note: In the 1850 census, JOHN & HUBBARD lived adjacent to Reuben Knapp.

HICKS, HORATIO G., son of PELEG (following), born 8 Apr. 1817, Ontario Co., NY, removed in 1836 to Fairfield Twp., Lenawee Co., Mich., and in 1849 to Madison Twp. He married 14 Dec. 1845 to SUSAN M. (HOLMES), daughter of Conrad (also see), and they were listed in 1850 census of Fairfield Twp. One child, MATILDA E. (d. age 14 mos.) Ref: P&BA-Len pg. 527-8.

HICKS, HUBBARD, probably son of JOSEPH (following), born ca. 1806, NY, and wife, CAROLINE, born ca. 1812, Mass., were listed in the 1850 census of Rome Twp., Lenawee Co., Mich. (next door to JOHN) with CAROLINE, age 12; BETSEY, age 10, both b. NY; and PERMELIA, age 8; RUTH E., age 6, both b. Mich., in their household. See ROSWELL, following.

HICKS, JACOB born ca. 1826, and wife, HARRIETT, born ca. 1830, both in NY, were listed in the 1850 census of Tecumseh Twp., Lenawee Co., Mich.

HICKS, JOHN, son of JOSEPH (following), born 22 Mar. 1808, Rensselaer Co., NY, after the death of his father, made his home with uncle, MORDICAI HICKS. John married on 25 Oct. 1833 to JANE (WINEGAR), daughter of Ulric (also see). They moved to Rome Twp., Lenawee Co., Mich., and were listed in the 1850 census with ROSWELL H. (following); JOSEPH, age 14; both b. NY; and POMEROY, age 6, b. Mich., in their household. Ruth Hunter, age 63, b. Conn., also in the household, may be RUTH (HUBBARD) HICKS, mother of JOHN, who may have married again to a Hunter?

HICKS, JOHN F. (See William H. Osborne)

HICKS, JOSEPH born Rensselaer Co., NY, and married there to RUTH (HUBBARD), born ca. 1776 (1786?), Conn. Joseph died as a young man. Known son, JOHN (preceding); & probably HUBBARD (preceding, possibly ROSWELL HUBBARD?); and probably daughter, HARRIET E. (preceding). Note Ruth in the household of JOHN, preceding. Ref: P&BA-Len pg. 1121-2.

HICKS, MARY born ca. 1819, Conn., was listed in the 1850 census of Adrian Twp., Lenawee Co., Mich. with JANE E., age 11; HARRIET A., age 7, both b. Mich.; and DANIEL C, age 4/12, b. NY, all in the household of Peter Morey. Note DANIEL, preceding.

HICKS, PELEG and wife, POLLY (PITTS), were natives of Mass., who moved to Ontario Co., NY after their marriage. Children: 1. ANGELINE; 2. CATHERINE; 3. HORATIO G. (preceding); 4. POLLY P. Ref: P&BA-Len pg. 527-8.

HICKS, ROSWELL and wife, CAROLINE, of Rome Twp., Lenawee Co., Mich. had known daughter, EMILY b. 22 Sept. 1844 (m. William Hood on 7 Man. 1863). Note HUBBARD, preceding, with wife, CAROLINE, possibly same family, as daughter RUTH E. may be EMILY, as age is correct.

HICKS, ROSWELL H., son of JOHN (preceding), born 28 Nov. 1834, Rensselaer Co., NY, came to Rome Twp., Lenawee Co., Mich. with parents. He married 20 Dec. 1868 to CHARLOTTE (MARKS), daughter of Hollen (also see), who died leaving children: 1. MYRON; 2. NELLIE. Roswell married again to SARAH (SMITH), born Dover, England. Son: 3. ARTHUR P. Sarah died 8 Nov. 1879. Roswell married third to SARAH (THOMPSON), daughter of George (also see), who had first married

Pioneer Families of Southeastern Michigan

Gilbert M. Pettys (also see), and second to Marshall Blanchard. Ref: P&BA-Len pg. 1121-2.

HIGBEE also see HIGBY

HIGBEE, GAD C. and wife, EMILY, of Palmyra, Wayne Co., NY, had known daughter, NEUBELIA b. 29 Jan. 1826, Palmyra, NY (m. William D. Archer, also see). Ref: P&BA-Len pg. 542-3. Note HIRAM M. HIGBY, following.

HIGBY also see HIGBEE

HIGBY, EMILY born ca. 1825, Penn., was listed in the 1850 census of Medina Twp., Lenawee Co., Mich. in the household of Alvin D. & Lydia J. Rice.

HIGBY, HIRAM M. born 8 June 1820, and wife, POLLY (HARRIS), born ca. 1825, both in NY, lived first in Wayne Co., NY. About 1844, they removed to Madison Twp., Lenawee Co., Mich. where they remained. Known son, MERRITT H. (following). Ref: P&BA-Len pg. 1100.

HIGBY, MERRITT H., son of HIRAM M. (preceding), born 23 Jan. 1844, Wayne Co., NY, moved to Madison Twp., Lenawee Co., Mich. with parents. He married SARAH H. (DAVIS), daughter of Isaac (also see), and settled in Adrian. Known daughter, EMILY E. Ref: P&BA-Len pg. 1100.

HIGGINS, ISAAC and wife, NANCY (ARTHUR), settled first in Tioga Co., NY; then in 1836 moved to Cook Co., Ill. He died in 1853, and she afterwards came to Fairfield Twp., Lenawee Co. Mich., where she died in Oct. 1876. Known daughter, SALLY b. 25 Jan. 1827, Tioga Co., NY (m. Orlando H. Alger, also see). Ref: P&BA-Len pg. 1087-8.

HIGGINS, JULIUS born ca. 1806, and wife, FLORA, born ca. 1808, both in NY, were listed in the 1850 census of Rollin Twp., Lenawee Co., Mich. with ALVA, age 14; JERUSHA, age 12; HELEN, age 10, all b. Ohio, in their household.

HIGGINS, M. L. (See Richard H. Osborn)

HIGGS, SARAH (See William Fisher)

HILE, NICHOLAS VALENTINE, son of PETER (following), born 21 July 1840, Rockingham, VA, removed to Ogden Twp., Lenawee Co., Mich. at age 16. He married in 1865 to CAROLINE (ROBERTSON), daughter of James (also see), and settled in Ogden Twp. Children: 1. JAMES R.; 2. GEORGE P.; 3. ALPHEUS J.; 4. JESSE MAUD. Ref: P&BA-Len pg. 1151-2.

HILE, PETER born in Germany, came to Rockingham Co., VA at age 21. He married there to LUCY A. (PENSE), daughter of Valentine (also see). He died 17 Dec. 1887 and she died 30 June 1881, Ogden Twp., Lenawee Co., Mich. Known son, NICHOLAS VALENTINE (preceding). Known daughter, MARGARET E. b. 10 Jan. 1839, Rockingham Co., VA (m. David B. Heckert, also see). Ref: P&BA-Len pg. 1108-9 & 1151-2. Note: LUCY A. who married John G. Heckert (also see) in Ogden Twp. probably relates to this family.

HILL, ALVIN born ca. 1806, VT, and wife, EMILY, born ca. 1816, New Hampshire, were listed in the 1840 census index of Palmyra Twp., Lenawee Co., Mich. (adjacent to HIRAM, following); and in the 1850 census with AUGUSTA, age 11; LIONEL B., age 8; DEBORAH, age 1/12, all b. Mich., in their household. Note JONATHAN, following.

HILL, ASA born ca. 1797, and wife, REBECCA, born ca. 1800, both in Mass., were listed in the 1840 census index of Adrian Twp., Lenawee Co., Mich.; and in the 1850 census with FRANCIS, age 23; MARY, age 17; CORDELIA, age 15, all b. NY, in their household. Note CLARK (following), listed next door in census.

HILL, CLARK (probably son of ASA, preceding) born ca. 1824, and wife, CHARLOTTE, born ca. 1821, both in NY, were listed in the 1850 census of Adrian Twp., Lenawee Co., Mich. with CHARLES, age 2, b. Mich. (prob. he who m. Margaret E. Lewis, dau. of Halsey, also see), in their household.

HILL, EBBINS S. born ca. 1802, and wife, CAROLINE E., born ca. 1801, both in NY, were listed in the 1850 census of Palmyra Twp., Lenawee Co., Mich. with ROSELLA?, age 21; WILLIAM, age 16; ROBERT, age 11; MELISSA F. b. 18 Mar. 1842, Cattaraugus Co., NY (m. Peter DeGraff, also see). Ref: P&BA-Len pg. 763.

HILL, ELIZABETH (See John Fisher)

HILL, HIRAM born ca. 1807, Rhode Island, and wife, JULIA, born ca. 1817, Penn., were listed in the 1840 census index of Palmyra Twp., Lenawee Co., Mich. (adjacent to ALVIN, preceding); and in the 1850 census with CORDELIA, age 8; REUBEN D., age 5 (prob. he who m. Eunice Bitely, dau. of John, also see); JULIA A., age 4; ELIAS, age 2, all b. Mich., in their household.

HILL, HORACE born ca. 1807, and wife, LUCY, born ca. 1812, both in NY, were listed in the 1850 census of Fairfield Twp., Lenawee Co., Mich. with Philo Henderson, age 12, b. Mich., in their household.

HILL, JAMES WILLISON (son of an Englishman who was a pioneer to Wood Co., Ohio) married in 1846 in NY to MARTHA (LEWIS), daughter of Ephraim, and they removed to Adams Twp., Lucas Co., Ohio. He died there 14 July 1858, and she was still living there in 1888. Known daughter, ADELMA (m. Isaac B. Kellogg, also see). Ref: P&BA-Len pg. 1176-7.

HILL, JOHN born ca. 1818, and wife, CAROLINE, born ca. 1819, both in NY, were listed in the 1850 census of Woodstock Twp., Lenawee Co., Mich. with ANGELIA, age 8, b. NY; and MARYETTA, age 5, b. Mich., in their household.

HILL, JONATHAN born ca. 1784, and wife, SALLY, born ca. 1785, both b. Mass., were listed in the 1840 census index of Rollin Twp., Lenawee Co., Mich.; and in the 1850 census with JOSEPH C., age 28, b. VT; and Mary A. Sloan, age 14, b. Mich., in their household. Note ALVIN (preceding), & MARY (following).

HILL, MELISSA, age 17, born VT, was listed in the 1850 census of Blissfield Twp., Lenawee Co. Mich. in a Hall household.

HILL, ROLLIN R. born ca. 1800, and wife, SUSAN M. (CASSON) born ca. 1809, both in Conn., moved first to Wayne Co., Mich. in 1832; and in 1837 to Medina Twp., Lenawee Co., Mich. He died in Morenci, Mich. on 4 July 1883, age 83; and she died in 1872, age 63. In the 1850 census of Medina Twp., they listed HARVEY E., age 20, b. NY; and EMILY S., age 17; ROSALIE M. b. 14 Aug. 1836, Wayne Co., Mich. (m. Charles B. Wilson, also see); HARRIET E., age 13; RODERICK H., age 11;

CHARLES R., age 9; GERTRUDE S., age 7; LOUISA R., age 5, all b. Mich., in their household. Ref: P&BA-Len pg. 568-9.

HILL, RUTH (See Miner Hilliard)

HILL, SABRINA (See William Camburn)

HILL, SAMPSON (See Erastus Knight)

HILL, SYLVESTER PERRY born ca. 1800, Conn., and wife, CAROLINE, born ca. 1808, VT, were listed in the 1850 census of Adrian Twp., Lenawee Co., Mich. with RILEY H., age 15; LUTHER, age 12, both b. Conn.; and CHARLOTTE, age 10; SYLVESTER, age 7, both b. NY; and HANNAH E., age 1, b. Mich., in their household.

HILL, THOMAS born ca. 1804, NY, and wife, AMANDA, born ca. 1816, both in NY, were listed in the 1850 census of Adrian Twp., Lenawee Co., Mich. with MARY, age 13; STEPHEN, age 10; ALBERT, age 8; ERWIN, age 5; MARANDA, age 2, all b. NY, in their household.

HILL, THOMAS born ca. 1799, and wife, MARY, born ca. 1809, both in England, were listed in the 1850 census of Palmyra Twp., Lenawee Co., Mich. with RICHARD, age 4, b. Mich.; and William Esper, age 12; Betsey Esper, age 8, both b. England, in their household.

HILLER, ISAAC Rev., son of JOHN (following), born 21 July 1779, Herkimer Co., NY, moved to Monroe Co., NY with his parents. He married PAMELIA (PHELPS), daughter of Silas (also see), and about 1832 removed to Michigan via the Erie Canal. They settled first in West Bloomfield Twp., Oakland Co., Mich.; and about 1840, purchased in Macon Twp., Lenawee Co., Mich. (Note: There were 2 "J" and a "D" in the 1840 census index of West Bloomfield Twp., Oakland Co.; none in Lenawee Co. in 1840 or 1850) He died in 1855 in Macon Twp.; and she died March 1865, Hudson. Known son, THOMAS J. (following). Ref: P&BA-Len pg. 1111-2.

HILLER, JOHN born Germany, and wife ? (FRANK), settled first in Herkimer Co., NY, and later in Monroe Co., NY. He joined a son in Pontiac, Oakland Co., Mich. a few years before his death. (Note: There was a "Mrs HILLER" listed in Pontiac, Oakland Co. Mich. in the 1840 census index). Known son, Rev. ISAAC (preceding). Ref: P&BA-Len pg. 1111-2.

HILLER, THOMAS J., son of Rev. ISAAC (preceding), born 28 Nov. 1830, Monroe Co., Mich., moved with his parents to Macon Twp., Lenawee Co., Mich. He married 1 Sept. 1859 to CLARA (NICHOLS), daughter of Samuel (also see). They eventually settled in Hudson village, Lenawee Co. Children: 1. ALEXANDER H.; 2. CHARLES C. P.; 3. FRANCIS L. L. Ref: P&BA-Len pg. 1111-2.

HILLIARD, MINER was a Capt. in the Revolutionary War (probably he spelled "Minor Hilyard," Rev. Pension Appl. #S22302, Conn. & VT service). Miner and wife, ABIGAIL, settled in Danby, Rutland Co., VT. Known daughter, MATILDA b. 1795, Danby (m. John Miller, also see, 1818, Londonderry, NH). Miner may have married again, as it was said his wife, was RUTH (HILL), a cousin of Ethan Allen of Rev. fame. Ref: P&BA-Len pg. 655-6.

HILYARD see HILLIARD

HINCKLEY also see HINKLEY

HINCKLEY, BENJAMIN and wife, LYDIA, moved from NY to Mich. in 1845; and eventually lived in Johnstown, Mich. Known daughter, JERUSHA T. b. 1 June 1831, Batavia, Genesee Co., NY (m. Lyman W. Baker, also see, in Rome Twp., Lenawee Co., Mich.) Ref: P&BA-Len pg. 541-2.

HINES, ANN (See John Onsted)

HINES, FREDUS, age 14, born NY, was listed in the 1850 census of Tecumseh Twp., Lenawee Co., Mich. in the household of Caleb Brewster.

HINES, GEORGE and wife, SOPHIA (MAINE), were natives of New Jersey, who came to Cambridge Twp., Lenawee Co., Mich. where he died at age 32. She died age 67. Ten children (names not stated, except): SUSAN E. (m. Henry C. Christman, also see). Ref: P&BA-Len pg. 201. Note: Sophia probably married again to Amos M. Gates, as in the 1850 census of Rollin Twp., Lenawee Co., Mich., he is listed with wife, Sophia, age 46, b. NJ, and in the household are HINES children: JANE, age 16, b. NJ, and SUSAN, age 14, b. NY. BENJAMIN, age 18, born NJ, listed in the 1850 census of Rome Twp., Lenawee Co., Mich., is probably another son. Note FREDUS (preceding) & LOUISA (following).

HINES, LOUISA, age 23, born NY?, was listed in the 1850 census of Cambridge Twp., Lenawee Co., Mich.

HINES, MEEKER (See Charles F. Smith)

HINKLEY also see HINCKLEY

HINKLEY, DAVID born ca. 1828, NY, was listed in the 1850 census of Hudson Twp., Lenawee Co., Mich. in a John & Lucina Belcher household.

HINKLEY, JAMES was listed in the 1840 census of Rollin Twp., Lenawee Co., Mich.

HINKLEY, SAMUEL born 20 July 1830, Barre, Worcester Co., Mass., married first on 1 Feb. 1827, South Hadley, Mass. to SARAH (DeWITT). After the birth of 2 children, they moved to Seneca Co., NY. In 1834, they moved to what is now Fairfield Twp. Sarah died there 2 Sept. 1876. Children: 1. SARAH S. (d. 8 Aug. 1852, Fairfield Twp., not in their household in 1850 census); 2. SOPHIA J. b. ca. 1830, Mass. (d. 20 May 1864, Adrian); 3. SAMUEL J. b. ca. 1833, NY; 4. FRANCIS B. b. ca. 1836, Mich.; 5. FANNY M. b. ca. 1838; 6. (CHARLES) DWIGHT b. ca. 1841; 7. JOHN W. b. ca. 1843. Samuel married again at Weston, Mich. on 6 Oct. 1879 to MARY L. (RENO) born 22 Sept. 1847, Wayne Co., NY. Children: 8. MARY L.; 9. CLARA E.; 10. IDA B. Ref: P&BA-Len pg. 487-8.

HINKLEY, WALTER born ca. 1821, NY, was listed in the 1850 census of Fairfield Twp., Lenawee Co., Mich.

HINSDALE, CHARLES M. (See Vaughn)

HINSDALE, ELISHA and wife, ELIZABETH (DOLPH), came from Summit Co., Ohio to Madison Twp., Lenawee Co., Mich. in 1853. He died in 1855, and she was still living in 1888. Known children: 1. Son (name not stated); 2. ALICE b. 9 Aug. 1851, Summit Co., Ohio (m. Thomas Randolph, also see). Ref: P&BA-Len pg. 397-8.

HITCH, HUBBARD of Rome Twp., Lenawee Co., Mich. married CAROLINE ?; and she married second to Abraham Wheeler (also see). Note: See HUBBARD HICKS, probably same man.

Pioneer Families of Southeastern Michigan

HITCHCOCK, JAMES born ca. 1795, Mass., and wife, HANNAH, born ca. 1800, NY, were listed in the 1840 census (as "Hitchcox") of Adrian Twp., Lenawee Co., Mich.; and as "Hitchcock" in the 1850 census with JAMES H., age 22, b. NY; CATHARINE, age 22, b. NY; WILLIAM, age 8, b. Mich.; and Alphine Welch, age 15, b. NY, in their household.

HITCHCOCK, SAMUEL born ca. 1826, NY, and wife, JANE born ca. 1827, Mich., were listed in the 1850 census of Adrian Twp., Lenawee Co., Mich. with ELLA A., age 2, b. Mich., in their household.

HITCHCOX may be HITCHCOCK; also see HICKOX

HITCHCOX, SUSAN (See Chauncey Root)

HITCHCOX, WILLIAM born ca. 1825, Canada, was listed in the 1850 census of Madison Twp., Lenawee Co., Mich.

HITCHINGS, JOSEPH came from England and settled in Milan Twp., Monroe Co., Mich. He died in 1857, age 68. His wife, MARY A. (ROGERS) died in Macon Twp., Lenawee Co., Mich. at age 52. Known daughter, BETSEY b. 16 Apr. 1828, England (m/1 William Doriell; m/2 William Pilbeam, see both). Ref: P&BA-Len pg. 1145.

HITCHINGS, MARY (See William King of Rollin Twp., Lenawee Co., Mich.).

HIX also see HICKS

HIX, EPHRAIM born ca. 1799, and wife, PHEBE, born ca. 1799, both in Mass., were listed in the 1840 census index of Ogden Twp., Lenawee Co., Mich.; and in the 1850 census with BENJAMIN, age 30, b. NY, and Eliza C. Colvin, age 4, b. Mich., in their household.

HOAG - In the 1840 census index of Lenawee Co., Mich., the following family was listed as follows: Adrian Twp.: AMOS; BEMAN (BEEMAN?); ISAAC J.; Raisin Twp.: BURTIS; ISRAEL; JACOB; JESSEY; JONATHAN; Rollin Twp.: NATHANIEL P.; Madison Twp.: PRICE (BRICE?); Seneca Twp.: MARVIN (MARTIN?); STEPHEN; Tecumseh Twp.: HAZAEL; JAMES B.; JOHN; JOSEPH; WILLIAM A. Please note these men following.

HOAG, ABNER I. born ca. 1792, and wife, LUCINDA (BARRAGER), born ca. 1787, both in NY, moved to Raisin Twp., Lenawee Co., Mich. in 1844. Six children (names not stated, except): MARIA b. 17 Dec. 1821 (m. Stephen Gallaway, also see, Raisin Twp., Lenawee Co.) In the 1850 census they listed Alfred Aldridge, age 10, b. Mich., in their household. Ref: P&BA-Len pg. 220-1.

HOAG, ALFRED T. (See James B. Hood)

HOAG, AMANUEL (EMANUEL?) born ca. 1823, NY, was listed in the 1850 census of Madison Twp., Lenawee Co., Mich. in the Nash household.

HOAG, AMOS born ca. 1805, Vermont, and wife, EMELINE, born ca. 1808, NJ, were listed in the 1850 census of Madison Twp., Lenawee Co., Mich. with ADDISON, age 11; CORNELIA J., age 10; EDWIN A., age 4; and listed last in the household were DORCAS, age 21, & ELIZABETH, age 17, both b. NY. Note: There was a LYDIA A., age 24, b. VT, listed in the 1850 census of Madison Twp., In an institution who may relate to this family. Note BEEMAN, following.

HOAG, ANN born 1 Sept. 1803, Saratoga Co., NY, married Seth Holmes (also see) in Erie Co., NY. Ref: P&BA-Len pg. 547-8. Note: In the 1800 census index, there was a JEDIDIAH in Saratoga Co., NY.

HOAG, BEEMAN born ca. 1777, NY, wife, DESIRE, born ca. 1781, Rhode Island, were listed in the 1850 census of Adrian Twp., Lenawee Co., Mich. with MICHAEL (MICAH?), age 28, b. NY (and his wife, SARAH, age 19, b. Maine, married within the year) in their household. Note AMOS & ISAAC J.

HOAG, BRICE W. (probably PRICE in 1840 census index) born 1809, and wife, SAPHRONA, born ca. 1816, both in NY, were listed in the 1850 census of Madison Twp., Lenawee Co., Mich. Note AMOS; BEEMAN; & ISAAC J.

HOAG, BURTIS listed in the 1840 census index of Raisin Twp., Lenawee Co., Mich., was not listed in 1850.

HOAG, CAROLINE, age 14, born Mich., was listed in the 1850 census of Madison Twp., Lenawee Co., Mich. in the household of Benjamin & Ann Crane.

HOAG, DAVID S., age 9, born Mich., was listed in the 1850 census of Adrian Twp., Lenawee Co., Mich. in the household of Betsey Baker, age 58, possibly his grandmother. Note this same name in household of STEPHEN, following.

HOAG, DON C. married FANNY L. (BACON), daughter of Charles C., also see. Ref: P&BA-Len pg. 576-7.

HOAG, ELIZA (See George Conger)

HOAG, H. A. (See Samuel Hopkins, son of Levi)

HOAG, HAZAEL was listed in the 1840 census index of Tecumseh Twp., Lenawee Co., Mich.; but was not listed in 1850. Note ISABELLA, following.

HOAG, INA V. (See Henry Ragless)

HOAG, ISAAC J. born ca. 1792, New Jersey, and wife, ANN, born ca. 1806, Maine, were listed in the 1850 census of Fairfield Twp., Lenawee Co., Mich. with STEPHEN H., age 14, b. NY; and ADONIRAM, age 9; ISAAC R., age 7; MARY, age 4, all b. Mich. Note BEEMAN, preceding.

HOAG, ISABELLA born ca. 1789, New Hampshire, was listed as head of household in the 1850 census of Raisin Twp., Lenawee Co., Mich. with MILTON, age 23, b. NY, in her household. Immediately adjacent were JONATHAN (age 25, following); and JOSEPH (following); also note HAZAEL, preceding.

HOAG, ISRAEL born ca. 1796, NY, and wife, SUSANNAH, born ca. 1793, Mass., listed in the 1840 census index of Raisin Twp.; were listed in the 1850 census of Palmyra Twp., with no family.

HOAG, JACOB listed in the 1840 census index of Raisin Twp., Lenawee Co., Mich., not listed in 1850.

HOAG, JAMES B. born ca. 1805, NY, and wife, EMELINE, born ca. 1807, Mass., were listed in the 1850 census of Tecumseh Twp., Lenawee Co., Mich. with no family.

HOAG, JESSE born ca. 1813, and wife, ABIGAIL, born ca. 1816, both in NY, were listed in the 1850 census of Raisin Twp., Lenawee Co., Mich. with WILLIAM H., age 15, b. Mich., in their household.

HOAG, JOHN born ca. 1804, and wife, SARAH, born ca. 1802, both in NY, were listed in the 1850 census of Raisin Twp., Lenawee Co., Mich. with BYRON, age 17; HELEN A., age 14; GEORGE R., age 12; FRANCEL H., age 10, all b. NY, in their household.

HOAG, JOHN, born ca. 1806, NY was listed in the 1850 census of Madison Twp., Lenawee Co., Mich. with EDSON, age 8; and JESSE, age 7. both b. Mich., in his household.

HOAG, JONATHAN born ca. 1794, and wife, DEBORAH, born ca. 1795, both in NY, were listed in the 1840 census index of Raisin Twp., Lenawee Co., Mich.; and in the 1850 census of Palmyra Twp., with ANNA, age 32; ABNER, age 18, both b. NY, in their household.

HOAG, JONATHAN born ca. 1825, and wife SALINDA, born ca. 1825, both in NY, were listed in the 1850 census of Raisin Twp., Lenawee Co., Mich. (immediately adjacent to ISABELLA; and JOSEPH, both preceding) with GEORGE, age 2; SARAH A., age 1/12, both b. Mich., in their household.

HOAG, JOSEPH born ca. 1805, and wife, LAURA, born ca. 1805, both b. NY, were listed in the 1850 census of Raisin Twp., Lenawee Co., Mich. (immediately adjacent to ISABELLA & JONATHAN, both preceding) with EDWARD, age 23; AMY, age 21; JONATHAN, age 19; SARAH, age 16; REUBEN, age 13; JAMES, age 10; LYDIA A., age 7, all shown b. NY.

HOAG, LEVI H. born ca. 1821, and wife ANNA F., born ca. 1819, both in NY, were listed in the 1850 census of Palmyra Twp., Lenawee Co., Mich. They listed Loren McCracken, age 45, b. VT, and dittoed after him were children Sally, age 3; Loring, age 10, assumed to McCracken.

HOAG, LYDIA B. (See Thomas Wilson)

HOAG, MARTIN (MARVIN in 1840 index) born ca. 1813, and wife, ADELINE E., born ca. 1818, both in NY, were listed in the 1850 census of Seneca Twp., Lenawee Co., Mich. with BYRAM G., age 14; PHILA A., age 12, both b. Mich., in their household.

HOAG, MARY born ca. 1791, NY, was head of household in the 1850 census of Raisin Twp., Lenawee Co., Mich. and is immediately adjacent to STEPHEN (age 24, following).

HOAG, MICHAEL born ca. 1815, and wife, SARAH M., born ca. 1817, both in NY, were listed in the 1850 census of Medina Twp., Lenawee Co., Mich. with WILLIAM N., age 8; IRA, age 11, both b. NY; and ELLEN M., age 4; BENJAMIN D., age 2, both b. Mich., in their household.

HOAG, NATHANIEL P. was listed in the 1840 census index of Rollin Twp., Lenawee Co., Mich.

HOAG, PRICE (See BRICE W.)

HOAG, SARAH of Colonial Nantucket, Mass. (See John Worth).

HOAG, SARAH born ca. 1800, Mass., is listed in the 1850 census of Raisin Twp., Lenawee Co., Mich. in the household of Benjamin S. & Emily H. (age 26, b. NY) Steer.

HOAG, SARAH, age 18, both NY, was listed in the 1850 census of Franklin Twp., Lenawee Co., Mich. in the household of Joseph and Sally Smith.

HOAG, SARAH J., age 14, and EMMA A., age 11, both b. Mich., were listed in the 1850 census of Raisin Twp., Lenawee Co., Mich. in the household of Nathan Chase.

HOAG, STEPHEN born ca. 1814, and wife, EUNICE C., born ca. 1821, both in NY, were listed in the 1850 census of Fairfield Twp., Lenawee Co., Mich. with DAVID S., age 10 (See preceding); JANE B., age 10; SARAH, age 7; MARY, age 5; EUGENE, age 1, all b. Mich., in their household.

HOAG, STEPHEN born ca. 1826, and wife, HANNAH, born ca. 1825, both in NY, were listed in the 1850 census of Raisin Twp., Lenawee Co., Mich. (next to MARY, preceding), with ELLEN M., age 3, b. Mich., in their household.

HOAG, STEPHEN P. born ca. 1822, NY, and wife, LYDIA J., born ca. 1831, Canada, were listed in the 1850 census of Raisin Twp., Lenawee Co., Mich.

HOAG, WILLIAM born ca. 1820, NY, and wife, JANE, born ca 1825, Mich., were listed in the 1850 census of Ogden Twp., Lenawee Co., Mich.

HOAG, WILLIAM A. (H?) born ca. 1787, NY, was probably he listed in the 1840 census index of Tecumseh Twp., Lenawee Co., Mich.; and in 1850 was listed with ELLEN, age 26, b. NY; CHARLOTTE, age 6; CHARLES, age 11/12, all b. Mich., all in an Inn.

HOAGLAND, CORNELIUS (note JOHN, following) born ca. 1816, and wife, CHARLOTTE, born ca. 1818, both in NY, were listed in the 1850 census of Ridgeway Twp., Lenawee Co., Mich. with AUGUSTA, age 8; WILLIAM H., age 6; SARAH M., age 5; JULIA A., age 7/12, all b. NY, in their household.

HOAGLAND, DELLA (spelled "Hogland," see John B. Clement).

HOAGLAND, HENRY, son of JOHN (following), born 1800, NJ, moved to Romulus, Seneca Co., NY with his parents. He married there in 1824 to MARY (VAN TYLE), daughter of Thomas (also see). They removed to Ridgeway Twp., Lenawee Co., Mich. in 1832; and she died in 1839. In the 1840 census index, Henry was listed in Macon Twp.; and in the 1850 census in Ridgeway Twp. listed children: 1. WILMINA b. 13 Jan. 1828, Romulus, NY (m. David B. Osterhout, also see); 2. CYRUS, age 21; 3. CORNELIUS, age 19; 4. SARAH E. b. 2 July 1832, Romulus, NY (m. Lester Osgood, also see); 5. THOMAS V. (following). Henry married second to AMANDA (GODDARD), daughter of Lyman (also see). Children: 6. LUCINDA, age 9; 7. LYMAN E., age 8; 8. (ANGELINE) ANGIE b. 7 Aug. 1845 (m. Samuel Kniffen, also see).; 9. ELIZABETH, age 3; 10. CHARLES H., age 1. Henry died ca. 1851/2. Ref: P&BA-Len pg. 374-5; 377-8; 1127-8.

HOAGLAND, JOHN born New Jersey, moved to Romulus, Seneca Co., NY where he remained. Known son, HENRY (preceding). Also note CORNELIUS, preceding, & JOHN V., following, possibly other sons.

HOAGLAND, JOHN V. (note JOHN, preceding) born ca. 1805, NJ, and wife, ANNA (DOREMUS), born ca. 1817, NJ, were called "natives of Seneca Co., NY." They removed to Macon Twp., Lenawee Co., Mich. where they are listed in the 1850 census with JOHN, age 19; MARY, age 17; HELEN, age 14; HENRY V., age 7, all born NY; and EMMA, age 5; ELIZA b. 8 Sept. 1847, Macon Twp. (m. Edmund R. Smith, also see); CHARLES E., age 1, b. Mich., in their household.

HOAGLAND, THOMAS V., son of HENRY (preceding), born 7 Mar. 1838, Ridgeway Twp., Lenawee Co., Mich., served in the Civil War. He married on 6 Nov. 1866 to HARRIET E. (SMITH), daughter of George W. (also see), born 1849, Ridgeway Twp. Children: 1. LAMOUNT C.; 2. LETTAH M.; 3. Child deceased. Ref: P&BA-Len pg. 1127-8.

Pioneer Families of Southeastern Michigan

HOAR, EUNICE (See William Read)

HODGE, EDWARD, son of THOMAS (following), born in Grafton, NH, married BETSEY (PITTS), daughter of Levi (also see), born Onondaga Co., NY. They settled first in Seneca Co., NY; and in 1836, moved to Dover Twp., Lenawee Co., Mich., and in 1846 to Fairfield Twp. They resided with daughter, Lucy, when he died 13 Feb. 1862, and she died 31 Dec. 1869. Children: 1. NANCY J. (m. E. A. Spooner, Brown Co., KS); 2. ADELPHI K. (m. Luther L. Todd; d. Atchison, KS on 22 Nov. 1882); 3. LUCY E. b. 21 Jan 1836, Seneca Co., NY (m. Daniel Cole Tunison, also see). Ref: P&BA-Len pg. 514-5.

HODGE, THOMAS was a Revolutionary soldeir, and he married LUCY (WEBBER). Thirteen children; only name stated: EDWARD (preceding). Ref: P&BA-Len pg. 514-5.

HODGE, WARREN W. was listed in the 1840 census index of Blissfield Twp., Lenawee Co., Mich.

HODGES, JAMES (See Josephus White)

HODGES, NATHANIEL born ca. 1788, NY, and wife, MINERVA, born ca. 1789, VT, were listed in the 1850 census of Rollin Twp., Lenawee Co., Mich. with DARIUS, age 26; GEORGE, age 21; ANN, age 18, all b. NY; and MALISSA, age 10, b. Mich., in their household. Also see NATHANIEL, Jr. (following). Note: There was a NATHANIEL & NATHAN listed in the 1840 census index of Van Buren Twp., Wayne Co., Mich.

HODGES, NATHANIEL, Jr., probably son of NATHANIEL, preceding, born ca. 1824, and wife, ELIZA, born ca. 1826, both in NY, were listed in the 1850 census of Rollin Twp., Lenawee Co., Mich. with OPHELIA A., age 3, b. Mich., in their household.

HODGES, RODMAN and wife, NANCY (POOL), moved from Wyoming Co., NY to Kent Co. Mich. in 1859. Known daughter, child #6., MARY J. b. 20 Feb. 1833, Wyoming Co., NY (m. Roswell Bennett, also see). Ref: P&BA-Len pg. 1072.

HOEY also see HOY

HOEY, BRIDGET born ca. 1795, Ireland (See James Campbell).

HOGABOAM, JACOB born Dutchess Co., NY was and early settler of Saratoga Co., NY; and then Harford, NY (Cortland Co.?). He married MARIAN (SPRAGUE), daughter of Rev. David (also see). She died in 1810 leaving 10 children; only one name stated: JOHN C. (following). Jacob married again and had 11 more children, no names stated. Ref: P&BA-Len pg. 1105-6.

HOGABOAM, JOHN C., son of JACOB (preceding), born 17 Mar. 1807, Harford, NY, married on 14 Sept. 1826 to BETSEY (BROUNELL), daughter of John (also see) of Osnabruck, Stormont, Canada. They settled first in Cornwall, Ontario, Canada. In 1836, they moved to Monroe, Mich.; and later to Hudson, Lenawee Co., Mich. They afterwards lived for 21 years in Hillsdale Co.., Mich., but returned to Hudson village. Children: 1. RUTH C. (m. P. H. Stroud, Hudson Twp.); 2. JAMES IRA (to Chicago, Ill.); 3. HARRIET L. Ref: P&BA-Len pg. 1105-6.

HOGAN, MICHAEL and wife, CATHARINE (GRIFFIN), were born in Co. Clare, Ireland, where they remained. She died in 1872, and he died in 1873. There were 2 sons & 7 daughters (names not all stated), "most of whom came to the United States." Children mentioned: KATE (to St. Louis, MO); BRIDGET (Medina Twp., Lenawee Co., Mich.); JOHN (Adams Twp., Hillsdale Co., Mich.); PATRICK (following). Note: Michael had a brother, PATRICK, who lived in Cattaraugus Co., NY. Ref: P&BA-Len pg. 907-8.

HOGAN, PATRICK, son of MICHAEL (preceding), born 18 May 1824, Co. Kerry, Ireland, sailed to the US from Galway in 1849. After visiting friends and relatives in Albany and Buffalo, NY, he went to Cattaraugus Co., NY. He married there on 9 April 1853 to ELLEN (REYNOLDS) born 1824, whose parents were natives of Co. Clare, Ireland, and moved in 1854 to Medina Twp., Lenawee Co., Mich. Four children, those mentioned: 1. BRIDGET (m. Michael Maloney, Defiance, Ohio); 2. JOHN (m. Katie Kelly, daughter of John W., had children Laura & Jenny); 3. KATIE. Ellen died 30 July 1862, age 38. Patrick married second to ANN (BRANAGAN) in 1863. Ref: P&BA-Len pg. 907-8.

HOGARTH, JANE (See Abram DeMott)

HOGARTH, JOHN and wife, JANE, were natives of Ireland who came to America in 1790, located in Seneca Co., NY where they remained. Known daughter, MARY (m. Thomas Osborne in 1802.). Also note JANE, preceding, also from Seneca Co., NY. Ref: P&BA-Len pg. 421-2.

HOGLAND see HOAGLAND

HOGUE, SAMUEL (See Isaac C. Gunn)

HOLBIN also see HULBON

HOLBIN, CHRISTIAN born ca. 1780, and wife, CATHARINE, born ca. 1782, both in Penn., were listed in the 1850 census of Medina Twp., Lenawee Co., Mich. next door to SOLOMON (following).

HOLBIN, SOLOMON, probably son of CHRISTIAN (preceding), born ca. 1821, Penn., and wife, ELIZABETH, born ca. 1824, NY, were listed in the 1850 census of Medina Twp., Lenawee Co., Mich. with KATA A., age 4; JOSEPH, age 3, both b. NY; and LEVI, age 1, b. Ohio; and Perry Sergeant, age 20, b. NY, in their household (next door to CHRISTIAN).

HOLCOMB, BENJAMIN came to Michigan "during its early settlement," and had known daughter, CHARLOTTE A. (m. Dr. Leonidas Jones, also see). Ref: P&BA-Len pg. 402-3.

HOLCOMB, CHANCY and wife, ELMIRA (RICHARDS), lived in Wyoming Co., NY as late as 1888; and had a known daughter, ELIZA H. b. 3 Sept. 1833, Varysburg, NY (m. Willard F. Day, also see; Eliza had come to Somerset Twp., Hillsdale Co., Mich. with her cousin, William Richards.)

HOLCOMB, CHARLES born ca. 1811, Conn., and wife, ELISA, born ca. 1871, NY, were listed in the 1850 census of Tecumseh Twp., Lenawee Co., Mich. with HENRIETTA, age 8, b. NY; and WILLIAM, age 5; GEORGE, age 2, both b. Mich., in their household.

HOLCOMB, JOHN H. born in England settled in New Jersey. Known daughter, REBECCA (m. 1806 to Samuel Tingley², also see). Ref: P&BA-Len pg. 863-4.

HOLCOMB, NOAH was listed in the 1840 census index of Macon Twp., Lenawee Co., Mich.

HOLCOMB, OSCAR of Bloomville, Seneca Co., Ohio (See Hiram S. Whiting).

HOLDEN, BELLE (See John T. Mead)

HOLDEN, JOSIAH born ca. 1776, NY, may have been he listed in the 1840 census index of Dundee Twp., Monroe Co., Mich. In the 1850 census of Ridgeway Twp., Lenawee Co., Mich. he was listed in the household of John Osterhout (also see) and wife, Sarah.

HOLDEN, SAMUEL moved to Lenawee Co., Mich. from NY; and his wife (name not stated) died in Blissfield, Mich. Known daughter, ARLETTA b. NY (m. Isaac N. Pilbeam, also see). Ref: P&BA-Len pg. 337.

HOLDRIDGE, ELEAZER S., son of FELIX (following), born 14 Sept. 1814, Onondaga Co., NY, married MEHITABLE (STONE), daughter of Isaiah (also see) of Royalton, Niagara Co., NY. They removed to Raisin Twp., Lenawee Co., Mich. in 1837. Children: 1. WARREN J. (following); 2. HORACE P. (following); 3. ELIZA E. b. 14 Dec. 1842 (m. Harmon Camburn, Adrian); 4. THOMAS J. b. 13 Aug. 1844 (to Anthony, KS); 5. HANNAH E. b. 2 May 1846 (m. Amos Graves); 6. SPENCER b. 2 Feb. 1849 (d. 1849); 7. MARY M. b. 4 Aug. 1850 (m. G. Olin Green, Adrian); 8. ELEAZER S, b, 11 Sept. 1854 (Adrian). Ref: P&BA-Len pg. 239-40.

HOLDRIDGE, FELIX born ca. 1781, NY, and wife, DEBORAH (SLOCUM), moved from Onondaga Co., NY to Royalton, Niagara Co., NY ca. 1820. They moved to Raisin Twp., Lenawee Co., Mich. in 1837 with known son, ELEAZER S. (preceding); known daughter, ELIZABETH b. 13 Aug. 1803, Onondaga Co., NY (m/1 Uriel Spencer of Maumee, Ohio, who d. Raisin Twp.; m/2 Lewis Horton of Royalton, NY where she d. 1872). Deborah died in 1839, lost in the woods. Apparently Felix married again, as in the 1850 census of Raisin Twp. had wife, COMFORT, age 64, b. NH. They listed Caroline M. Chandler, age 7, b. Mich.; and William Edmundson, age 37; Polly Edmundson, age 31 (possibly a daughter?), both b. NY, in the household. Felix died in 1855. Ref: P&BA-Len pg. 239-40

HOLDRIDGE, GERSHOM born ca. 1782, and wife, JOANNA, born ca. 1780, both in NY, were listed in the 1840 census index of Madison Twp., Lenawee Co., Mich.; and in the 1850 census witn MYRON, age 37; LYDIA M., age 22; MARIA, age 18, all b. NY, in their household.

HOLDRIDGE, HORACE, son of ELEAZER S. (preceding), born 28 Aug. 1840, Raisin Twp., Lenawee Co., Mich., married there to ADALINE (HOLLOWAY), daughter of Edwin (also see). Children: 1. ELLEN R. b. 5 Sept. 1863, Raisin Twp. (m. Archibald R. Boyd, also see); 2. CLARENCE E. Ref: P&BA-Len pg. 416-9.

HOLDRIDGE, WARREN J., son of ELEAZER S. (preceding), born 1 Aug. 1838, Raisin Twp., Lenawee Co., Mich., married there to MARY I. (BOSS) born 4 Nov. 1842, Blackman Twp. (Jackson Co., Mich.?) Seven children, only 4 surviving listed: 1. FRANK H. (to Finney Co., KS); 2. BERT (m. Bertha Kranz, Kearney Co., KS); 3. VIOLA M.; 4. WARREN B. Ref: P&BA-Len pg. 670-1.

HOLLAND, GEORGE born ca. 1806, Penn. and wife, SARAH, born ca. 1818, NY, were listed in the 1850 census of Woodstock Twp., Lenawee Co., Mich. with no family.

HOLLAND, HATTIE (See Philip Wareham³)

HOLLAND, JOHN born ca. 1809, Penn., and wife, MARIA?, born ca. 1817, NY, were listed in the 1850 census of Cambridge Twp., Lenawee Co., Mich. with THOMAS, age 14; PETER, age 12; ABIGAIL, age 4, all b. Mich., and Abigail Harris, age 64, b. NY, possibly mother-in law?, in their household.

HOLLEN, LUCY (See Joseph Patterson)

HOLLISTER, AMAZI born England, and wife, MOLLIE, born Holland, were parents of SOPHIA b. ca. 1816, Vermont (m. Lorentus S. Calkins, also see, in NY). Ref: P&BA-Len pg. 1171-2.

HOLLOWAY, BENJAMIN moved from St. Lawrence Co., NY to Seneca Co., NY by 1812; and remained there till 1834, then moved to Peru Twp., Huron Co., Ohio, where he remained. Known son, IRA (following). Ref: P&BA-Len pg. 1139-40.

HOLLOWAY, BUTLER, son of WILLIAM (following), was born 14 Feb. 1814, Conway, Mass., and moved in 1833 with father to Raisin Twp., Lenawee Co., Mich. He married on 2 Apr. 1846 to ANN (RICHARD), daughter of Archibald (also see), born 1817, Ireland. Children: 1. ELLEN Z. (d. 22 Oct. 1875, age 26); 2. GEORGE (following); 3. Daughter (d. infancy). Ref: P&BA-Len pg. 509-10.

HOLLOWAY, EDWARD was listed in the 1840 census index of Fairfield Twp., Lenawee Co., Mich.; and may be EDWIN (following).

HOLLOWAY, EDWIN, son of WILLIAM (following), born ca. 1811, Mass., married in Lockport, Niagara Co., NY to MARY A. (SEBER) born ca. 1814, NY, and they removed to Raisin Twp., Lenawee Co., Mich. in 1832. He died in the Civil War, but she was still living in 1888, age 74. Nine children (names not stated, except Adaline), from the 1850 census of Fairfield Twp.: 1. WILLIAM M., age 13; 2. ADALINE b. 16 Mar. 1840 (m. Horace Holdridge, also see); 3. NATHANIEL, age 7; 4. JOHN, age 5; 5. PAULINA, age 2. Ref: P&BA-Len pg. 416-9.

HOLLOWAY, GEORGE, son of BUTLER (preceding), was born 19 Apr. 1852, Lockport, Niagara Co., NY, and moved with parents to Raisin Twp., Lenawee Co., Mich. He married ELIZABETH (STRETCH), daughter of Jesse (also see). Son, KENNETH. Ref: P&BA-Len pg. 509-10 & portrait of farm.

HOLLOWAY, HORACE, son of IRA (following), born ca. 1850, Peru, Huron Co., Ohio, served in the Regular Army, enlisting age 16, on 26 Mar. 1866. He served for 3 years in Co. H., 22nd Reg. Inf. in Dakotas & Wyoming. He returned first to Ohio, then to Ogden Twp., Lenawee Co., Mich. He married 12 July 1876 to MARIE (MALONEY), daughter of Edward (also see). Children: 1. BERTHA; 2. BESSIE; 3. IRVIN; 4. BLANCHE. Ref: P&BA-Len pg. 1139-40.

HOLLOWAY, IRA, son of BENJAMIN (preceding), born 15 Sept. 1812, Covert, Seneca Co., NY, moved to Peru, Huron Co., Ohio with his parents. He married on 15 Oct. 1837 to ACHSAH (BOUGHTON), daughter of Guy

Pioneer Families of Southeastern Michigan

C. (also see). They settled first in Norwich Twp., Huron Co., Ohio, and later purchased parents' farm in Peru, where they remained until 1882. They moved to Ogden Twp., Lenawee Co., Mich. where he died 3 Sept. 1887. Children: 1. LOUISA (m. Adams, lived Buffalo Co., Nebr.); 2. EMELINE (m. McFarland, lived Ia.); 3. CAROLINE (m. Gribben, lived Appanoose Co., Nebr.); 4. JAMES (Fairfield Twp., Lenawee Co.); 5. CHESTER (Buffalo Co., Nebr.); 6. ALMENA (m. Tilson, lived Eaton Co., Mich.); 7. HORACE (preceding); 8. CAL C. (Buffalo Co., Nebr.); 9. HATTIE (m. Hambrook, lived Palmyra Twp., Lenawee Co.); 10. ELMER E. (San Luis Obispo, CA). Ref: P&BA-Len pg. 1139-40.

HOLLOWAY, NELLIE (See James Knox)

HOLLOWAY, SILAS, son of Dr. WILLIAM (following), born ca. 1812, Mass., and wife, SARAH, born ca. 1818, VT, were listed in the 1840 census index of Raisin Twp., Lenawee Co., Mich.; and in the 1850 census of Dover Twp. with HARRIET, age 9; WILLIAM, age 7; MARY, age 4, all b. Mich., and Ephraim Converse, age 19, b. Mass., in their household.

HOLLOWAY, WILLIAM Dr. born 1781, Mass., moved in 1816 to York, Livingston Co., NY. In 1833, he moved to Raisin Twp., Lenawee Co., Mich. He was married 3 times, and had 5 children by first marriage, and 4 by second, all names not stated. In the 1850 census of Raisin Twp., he had wife, PAULINA, born ca. 1792, VT, in the household. Known sons probably from first marriage: WILLIAM (following); 2. SILAS (preceding); 3. BUTLER (preceding); 4. EDWIN (preceding). Ref: P&BA-Len pg. 509-10.

HOLLOWAY, WILLIAM, son of Dr. WILLIAM, born ca. 1810, Mass., was listed in the 1850 census of Raisin Twp., Lenawee Co., Mich. in the household of BUTLER (preceding), with ABIGAIL, age 35, b. Mass., possibly his wife.

HOLMES, ABRAM (ABIRAM) born ca. 1798, NY, and wife, BETSEY, born ca. 1800, VT, were listed in the 1840 census index of Raisin Twp., Lenawee Co., Mich.; and in the 1850 census of Tecumseh Twp. with JULIUS, age 27; JULIA, age 27, both b. NY; and Elizabeth Nichols, age 84, b. Mass., and Rev. Erastus Nichols, age 52, b. Mass., Margaret Nichols, age 50, b. NY, and Charlotte J Sholes, age 1, b. Mich., in their household.

HOLMES, BENJAMIN born 1786, NY, and wife, LUCY, born ca. 1793, both in NY, were listed in the 1840 census index of Dover Twp., Lenawee Co., Mich.; and in the 1850 census with WILLIAM, age 13, b. Mich., in their household. Note: They were 2 doors from Ira Waterman, whose mother was FRANCES (HOLMES) b. near Stonington, Conn., and married in Chenango Co., NY.

HOLMES, BENJAMIN born 1797, NY, son of BENJAMIN T. (a Revolutionary soldier, born 20 July 1760, Mass.), married in Mass. to MARY C. (?), and moved first to NY (before 1824); and to Medina Twp., Lenawee Co., Mich. in 1836. (Listed in 1850 census as "Homes"). He died in Mar. 1881, and she died 3 Aug. 1875. Children: 1. ALBINA S.; 2. ARTHUR M. b. ca. 1824, NY (SOPHIA, age 23, b. England, also in the household in 1850 census, may be wife of Arthur?); 3. S.(SARAH) HORTENSA b. ca. 1827, NY (m. John T. Colegrove, also see); 4. JAMES L. b. ca. 1830, NY. Note: Ref: P&BA-Len pg. 204.

HOLMES, BETSEY (See Sylvanus Kinney)

HOLMES, CHARLES ISAAC, son of CONRAD (following), born 12 June 1850, Dover Twp., Lenawee Co., Mich., married on 10 Apr. 1873 to IDA (WILCOX), daughter of Edwin C. (also see), born 21 July 1856, Hudson Twp. Children: 1. WILLIE E.; 2. ARTHUR M.; 3. FREDDIE E. Ref: P&BA-Len pg. 212-3.

HOLMES, CONRAD born ca. 1794, NY, and wife, SARAH (MURRAY), born Ireland, settled first in Monroe Co., NY. They removed to Madison Twp., Lenawee Co., Mich. in 1834, and he died in 1838, age 44; and in the 1840 census index of Madison Twp., she was listed head of household. She died in 1870, age 74. Children: 1. SUSAN M. b. 15 Jan. 1825 (m. Horatio F. Hicks, also see); 2. JOHN M. (may be he, age 22, b. NY, in a Gifford household in 1850 census of Medina Twp.?); 3. MARGARET M. b. ca. 1832, NY; 4. NANCY A.; 5. MARY A.; 6. WILLIAM J. (may be he, age 16, b. NY, in 1850 census of Madison Twp.); 7. SYLVESTER F.; 8. ISAAC W. Ref: P&BA-Len pg. 527-8. Note: It is probably this Sarah, age 54, b. Ireland, listed as wife of Joseph A. Saudey?, age 56, b. NY, with MARGARET HOLMES, age 18, in their household.

HOLMES, CONRAD, son of ISAAC (following), born 25 Mar. 1814, Clarkson, Monroe Co., NY, moved with parents to Pittsfield, Washtenaw Co., Mich., where he married in 1838 to JULIA (DIX), daughter of William Dix (also see). They moved to Dover Twp., Lenawee Co., Mich. in 1841; and she died 28 Oct. 1885, aged 70y/7m/5d. Children: 1. WILLIAM J. b. ca. 1839 (d. 1863, age 24, Dover Twp.); 2. CHARLES ISAAC (preceding). Ref: P&BA-Len pg. 212-3.

HOLMES, ELIZABETH (See John Bryant)
HOLMES, FRANCES (See Ira Waterman)
HOLMES, HANNAH (See John Bryant)
HOLMES, HENRY, age 18, born NY, was listed in the 1850 census of Madison Twp., Lenawee Co., Mich. in a Brown household. Note MARENA, following.

HOLMES, ISAAC born Dutchess Co., NY, and wife, MARY (BROWN), born Ireland, settled first in Clarkston, Monroe Co., NY. In 1834, they moved to Washtenaw Co., Mich.; then to Matamoras, Ohio, Ingham Co., Mich., and last to Dover Twp., Lenawee Co. to live with son, CONRAD (preceding). She died 20 Mar. 1863, and he died 15 Apr. 1877. Nine children, only Conrad was mentioned. Ref: P&BA-Len pg. 212-3.

HOLMES, JAMES W. was listed in the 1840 census index of Blissfield Twp., Lenawee Co., Mich. Note WILLIAM, following.

HOLMES, JANE of Londonderry, NH (See William Moore[3]).

HOLMES, JEFFERSON born ca. 1805, NY, and wife, ABIGAIL, born ca. 1813, Mass., were listed in the 1850 census of Ogden Twp., Lenawee Co., Mich. with LUCINDA, age 3; JOHN, age 1, both b. Mich.; and Mary Sharp, age 10; Ellen Sharp, age 7, both b. Mich., in their household. Note MARY, following.

HOLMES, JEREMIAH born ca. 1807, Mass., was listed in the 1840 census index of Franklin Twp. (also note MANLY, following); and in the 1850 census with WILLIAM, age 13; ALVILLA?, age 12; GEORGE, age 10; SARAH, age 8; MARY, age 3, all b. Mich., in his household.

HOLMES, JOHN M. and wife, MERCY (HOYT), resided in Saratoga Springs, NY in 1793; and later removed to Wales, Erie Co., NY. Known daughter, BALSORA b. 17

Feb. 1793, Saratoga Springs (m. Malachi Sanford, also see). Ref: P&BA-Len pg. 956-7. Note OLIVER & SETH, both following.

HOLMES, MANLY born ca. 1810, NY, and wife, CLARISSA, born ca. 1808, Rhode Island, were listed in the 1840 census of Franklin Twp., Lenawee Co., Mich.; and in the 1850 census of Cambridge Twp. with ALVIRA, age 15; JOHN, age 12, both b. NY; and CHARLES, age 4; HENRY, age 1, both b. Mich., in their household. Note JEREMIAH, preceding.

HOLMES, MARENA, age 43, b. (?), was head of household in the 1850 census of Madison Twp., Lenawee Co., Mich. with GEORGE, age 16; DANIEL, age 6, both b. NY, in her household. Next door in an Amanda Winney (age 22, b. NY) household were JOSEPH S., age 13; WILLIAM R., age 8, both b. NY. Also note HENRY, preceding.

HOLMES, MARY, age 68, born NY, was listed in the 1850 census of Ogden Twp., Lenawee Co., Mich. in an Elizabeth Ross household. Also note JEFFERSON, preceding.

HOLMES, OLIVER of Wales, Erie Co., NY (See Charles W. Pelham, and note JOHN M., preceding).

HOLMES, RANDALL R. born ca. 1821, and wife, MARY A., born ca. 1826, both in NY, were listed in the 1850 census of Rome Twp., Lenawee Co., Mich. with NATHANIEL F., age 4, b. NY; and WILLIAM B., age 2. b. Mich., in their household.

HOLMES, SALMON H. and wife (name not stated) moved from Conn. to Jackson Co., Mich. Known daughter, NELLIE D. b. 30 Jan. 1846, Liberty Twp., Jackson Co. (m. Charles A. Smith, also see). Ref: P&BA-Len pg. 1056-7.

HOLMES, SETH born 7 Mar. 1801, Saratoga Co., NY, married ANNA (HOAG) born 1 Sept. 1803, Saratoga Co. in Erie Co., NY where they had moved with their parents. He died there 17 Aug. 1885, and she died 25 Mar. 1874. Nine children, only name mentioned, JOSEPHINE b. 30 Jan. 1835, Erie Co., NY (m. Alvin Joslin, also see, of Woodstock Twp., Lenawee Co., Mich.). Ref: P&BA-Len pg. 547-8. Note JOHN M., preceding.

HOLMES, VINA (See Philip Wareham[3])

HOLMES, WILLIAM was listed in the 1840 census index of Blissfield Twp., Lenawee co., Mich. Note following, possibly same man? Also see JAMES W., preceding.

HOLMES, WILLIAM born ca. 1817, and wife, MARY A., born ca. 1820, both in NY, were listed in the 1850 census of Riga Twp., Lenawee Co., Mich. with no family.

HOLT, ALVA born ca. 1803, NH, and wife, MARY, born ca. 1804, Mass., were listed in the 1840 census index of Seneca Twp., Lenawee Co., Mich.; and in the 1850 census with JANET, age 14; HENRY C., age 3, both b. Mich., in their household.

HOLT, ANNA, age 8, born Mich., was listed in the 1850 census of Adrian Twp., Lenawee Co., Mich. in a Mandeville household. Note TRUMAN, following.

HOLT, CHANDLER (See Erastus Back)

HOLT, FIFIELD born ca. 1809, NH, and wife, FANNY, born ca. 1809, Ireland, were listed in the 1840 census index of Medina Twp., Lenawee Co., Mich.; and in the 1850 census with no family.

HOLT, PHILO (See Erastus Back)

HOLT, SAPHRONA age 42, born NY, with HELEN, age 2/12, b. Mich., was listed in the 1850 census of Madison Twp., Lenawee Co., Mich. in the "poor house." Note TRUMAN, following.

HOLT, STEPHEN, age 13, b. Mich., was listed in the 1850 cdensus of Adrian Twp., Lenawee Co., Mich. in a Sanders household. Note TRUMAN, following.

HOLT, TRUMAN was listed in the 1840 census index of Adrian Twp., Lenawee Co., Mich.; not listed in 1850. Note ANNA; SAPHRONA; & STEPHEN, all preceding.

HONSINGER, HARVEY (See Levi Eddy)

HOOD, A. married PHILURA (WHEELER), daughter of James (also see). Ref: P&BA-Len pg. 471-2.

HOOD, ANDREW, son of WILLIAM (following), born 20 Apr. 1836, married 16 Oct. 1860 to MELISSA (HALSTED), daughter of Edward (also see) of Rome Twp., Lenawee Co., Mich., and she died 6 Feb. 1861. He married second to HARRIET (BASCOM), daughter of George (also see). Son, GEORGE L. b. 2 Sept. 1866. Ref: P&BA-Len pg. 188-9.

HOOD, ANDREW J., son of JOHN & NANCY (BEERS), following, and wife, MARY S. (KNIGHT), daughter of William (also see), first came to Adrian Twp., Lenawee Co., Mich. in 1846, but returned to NY, where they remained until 1851, then returned to Adrian Twp. Children: 1. ELLA H. (m. Rev. Lyman E. David, Brooklyn, NY); 2. Dr. CHARLES J.; 3. Dr. WILLIAM H. (Battle Mtn., Nev.); 4. HERBERT N.; 5. BERTIE L.; 6. ARTHUR J. Ref: P&BA-Len pg. 455-6.

HOOD, CALVIN born ca. 1832, Penn., in listed in the 1850 census of Adrian Twp., Lenawee Co., Mich. in the household of Abraham & Lucinda Knapp (she b. 1828, Penn. sister?).

HOOD, DORCAS (See Oramon Tuttle, Jr.)

HOOD, JAMES married in Seneca Co., NY to CATHERINE (McNELLY), and in the 1830s moved to Novi Twp., Oakland Co., Mich.; and later to Livingston Co., Mich. (Note: There was a James "Houed" in the 1840 census index of Wayne Co., Mich.?) Catherine died in 1842, and he moved to Hillsdale Co., Mich. where he died in 1867. Known children: KATE A. b. 27 Oct. 1835, Novi Twp. (lived with Blackwood family after death of mother, and m. 5 Feb. 1856, Plymouth, Wayne Co. Mich. to Isaac C. Mills, also see, Macon Twp., Lenawee Co., Mich.) Ref: P&BA-Len pg. 1053-4.   HOOD, JAMES B., son of ROBERT M. (following), born 25 Sept. 1825, Seneca Co., NY, came first to Wayne Co., Mich.; and in 1844 moved to Rome Twp., Lenawee Co., Mich. He married 8 Oct. 1846 to LOURICA (KNOWLES), daughter of Hezekiah Knowles, Sr. (also see). In the 1850 census of Rome Twp., they were next door to MOSES G. (following). In 1861, they moved to Adrian Twp., and in 1874 to Madison Twp. Children: 1. IRVING A. b. ca. 1848 (m. Mary A. Van Doren, Kansas); 2. ROBERT ADOLPHUS b. ca. 1850 (m. Lucretia A. Todd, Adrian); 3. MARGARET A. (m. Alfred T. Hoag, Seneca Falls, NY); 4. CHARLES O. (m. Emma Wickham, Madison Twp.); 5. JOSEPHINE (d. age 4); 6. CORA A. (m. Augustus A. Ilseman, Madison Twp.). Ref: P&BA-Len pg. 762-3.

HOOD, JOHN, Jr., son of JOHN, Sr. (possibly he following), born ca. 1799, Seneca Co., NY, went at age 22 to Erie Co.,

Pioneer Families of Southeastern Michigan

Penn. He married there to OLIVE (HALL), daughter of Harvey (also see), born ca. 1803, Conn. In 1833, they moved from Penn. to Rome Twp., Lenawee Co., Mich.; and later to Adrian Twp. He died in Hudson, Mich. in Apr. 1878; and she lived in 1888 with daughter, MARY A. b. 28 May 1825, Penn. (m. Charles G. Bird, also see). In the 1850 census of Rome Twp., listed in John's household: HARRY, age 21, b. Penn.; CAROLINE, age 12, b. Penn. (may be she m. John O. Maynard, son of John, also see); SARAH J., age 10, b. Penn.? (who was in Bird household in 1850); WILLIAM b. 3 Aug. 1839, Adrian; HENRY, age 8, b. Mich.; JOHN, age 5, b. Mich. Probably also LUCINDA, born ca. 1828, Penn. who m. Abraham Knapp; and listed in the Knapp household in 1850, CALVIN, age 18, born Penn.

HOOD, JOHN, (Sr.?) born 10 June 1762, Sunbury, Northumberland Co., Penn., was a Revolutionary soldier, whom with 3 brothers moved to Seneca Co., NY. He married LUCINDA (MOODY), born ca. 1773, Mass. He died in Romulus, Seneca Co., NY, and Lucinda afterwards moved to Rome Twp., Lenawee Co., Mich. where she died in 1862, over age 90. In the 1850 census, she was in household of known son, WILLIAM, following. Known daughter, JANE A. b. ca. 1815 (m/1 Seth Atwood; m/2 Isaac Raymond, see both). Ref: P&BA-Len pg. 188 & 1068. Note: JOHN, Jr., preceding, and MOSES G. & ROBERT M., both following, are probably other sons. In the 1850 census, JANE (HOOD) RAYMOND is listed next door to MOSES G.

HOOD, JULIUS born Virginia, where he was reared and married, resided in Preston Co., W. Va., but moved to Ohio when it was opened to settlement. He became ill and died there as a young man. Known daughter, RUTH (m. Abram Wotring, born 1810, also see). Ref: P&BA-Len pg. 455-6.

HOOD, MOSES G., probably son of JOHN, Sr. (preceding), was born 6 Nov. 1807, probably Seneca Co., NY. He married ADELIA A. (KNOWLES) born 1804/11, Conn. They moved to Rome Twp., Lenawee Co., Mich. by 1840; and in the 1850 census were listed next door to JANE, daughter of JOHN, Sr. Known children (last 3 dates from 1850 census): 1. MIRIAM b. 24 Nov. 1840 (m. Levi Hawley); 2. HOMER b. ca. 1843; 3. PHILINDA b. ca. 1846; 4. MILTON b. ca. 1848. Ref: P&BA-Len pg. 194.

HOOD, ROBERT M., possibly son of JOHN, Sr. (preceding), and wife, LYDIA (LAUTENSCHLAGER), were born in Penn., and after their marriage moved to Varick, Seneca Co., NY, where they remained. Children: 1. JAMES B. (preceding); 2. SUSAN (note SUSAN A., following); 3. CHARLES; 4. MARGARET. Ref: P&BA-Len pg. 762-3.

HOOD, SUSAN A. b. 1827, NY, married James T. Finch, also see, of Rome Twp., Lenawee Co., Mich.

HOOD, WILLIAM, son of JOHN, Sr. (preceding), born 27 Dec. 1805, Romulus, Seneca Co., NY, married on 1 Dec. 1831, Romulus, to LOUISA (BARTLETT), daughter of Thomas (also see). They moved to Rome Twp., Lenawee Co., Mich. in 1835. Children: 1. HANNAH B. b. 8 Nov. 1832 (m. E. W. Beers, Adrian Twp.); 2. MARY b. 14 July 1834 (m. Stephen Beers, lived Adrian then Nebraska); 3. ANDREW (preceding); 4. CAROLINE b. 27 Mar. 1838, Mich. (d. 6 Jan. 1851); 5. LEWIS b. 21 July 1840 (lived Ithaca, Mich.); 6. NANCY b. 29 Apr. 1842 (m. Franklin Jerrells, son of David, also see); 7. HARRIET A. b. 22 Aug. 1848 (d. Sept. 1868); 8. EMMA K. b. 15 Aug. 1852 (m. Oscar Smith, Adrian); 9. WILLIAM H. b. 19 Jan. 1856 (Rome Twp.). Ref: P&BA-Len pg. 188.

HOOD, WILLIAM, son of JOHN, (Jr., preceding), born 3 Aug. 1839, Adrian Twp., Lenawee Co., Mich., married 7 Jan. 1863 to EMILY (HICKS), daugher of Roswell (also see). Children: 1. HENRY P. b. 22 May 1868; 2. CARRIE E. b. 27 May 1873. Ref: P&BA-Len pg. 190-1.

HOOD, WILLIAM H. (possibly son of WILLIAM, preceding, of Rome Twp.) married Elnora P. Bates, daughter of Caleb (also see). Ref: P&BA-Len pg. 551-2.

HOOD, ZORAIDA (HENDERSON) Mrs. was the daughter of Dr. R. H. Henderson of Washtenaw Co., Mich. She married second to John Fisher^2 (also see). Note: There was an ANDRUS HOOD listed in the 1840 census index of Lodi Twp., Washtenaw Co., Mich., listed adjacent to a Betsey Henderson.

HOOKER, JEANNETTE (note HOOPER, following)

HOOPER, ELIZABETH, born ca. 1771, England, was listed in the 1850 census of Franklin Twp., Lenawee Co., Mich. in the household of John & Joanna Blythe (b. ca. 1814, England).

HOOPER, JEANNETTE (See John P. Silvers, Clinton Twp., Lenawee Co., Mich.; name given as both Hooker and Hooper).

HOOPER, PONTIUS was listed in the 1840 census index of Clinton, Lenawee Co., Mich.

HOOPER, SAMUEL was listed in the 1840 census index of Clinton, Lenawee Co., Mich.

HOOVER, SUSAN was born in Penn., and married by 1830 in Niagara Co., NY to Henry Stahler (also see).

HOPKINS, BETSEY A., age 11, and HOWARD, age 8, both b. NY, were listed in the 1850 census of Rome Twp., Lenawee Co., Mich. in the household of Jeremiah & Matilda Ferguson. Note DAVID, following.

HOPKINS, BRONSON born ca. 1810, NY, and wife, MAHALA D., born ca. 1814, NH, were listed in the 1840 census index of Adrian Twp., Lenawee Co., Mich., and in the 1850 census of Madison Twp. with ELLEN J., age 15, b. NY; and LAURA, age 6, b. Mich.; and Philip Tolford, age 28. born NH, in their household.

HOPKINS, CHARLES W. (note JOSEPH, following) born ca. 1822, and wife, MARIA, born ca. 1828, both in England, listed James R. Ingall, age 30, b. England, in their household.

HOPKINS, DAVID was listed in the 1840 census index of Rome Twp., Lenawee Co., Mich. Note BETSEY, preceding.

HOPKINS, IRA of Cayuga Co., NY had known daughter, FANNIE (m. John N. Cary, also see), and 7 other children (names not stated). Ref: P&BA-Len pg. 191.

HOPKINS, JOSEPH and wife, ANN (CHURCH), lived in Berkshire, England, where they remained. Known daughter, MARY ANN (m. 22 Aug. 1836 to George A. Ingall, also see). Ref: P&BA-Len pg. 539-40. Note CHARLES W., preceding.

HOPKINS, LEVI, son of Rev. SAMUEL (following), born ca. 1750, Great Barrington, Mass., married ELIZABETH (HAUTZ) of Hagerstown, MD. About 1795, they moved to Preston Co., VA (now W. Va.). Known son, SAMUEL (following). Ref: P&BA-Len pg. 912-3.

HOPKINS, LOONAM?, age 63, born NY, was listed in the 1850 census of Madison Twp., Lenawee Co., Mich. in the household of Sylvester and Eliza Kenyon.

HOPKINS, MERCY of Rhode Island (See Daniel Colwell[1]).

HOPKINS, NATHANIEL born ca. 1808, NY, and wife, HANNAH C., born ca. 1812, Conn., were listed in the 1850 census of Hudson Twp., Lenawee Co., Mich. with HELEN H., age 16; NATHANIEL A., age 11; EDWARD B., age 8, all b. NY, in their household. In a neighboring Hawser household were ANDREW S., age 19; MARY A., age 15, both b. Conn., who may relate to this family

HOPKINS, SAMUEL Rev. was a minister during Colonial times. (His father was a cousin to the elderly SAMUEL who signed the Declaration of Independence). Known son, LEVI (preceding). Ref: P&BA-Len pg. 912-3.

HOPKINS, SAMUEL, son of LEVI (preceding), born 26 June 1818, Preston Co., W. Va., married on 8 July 1838 to SUSANNAH (LOAR), daughter of George (also see). In 1855, after the birth of 8 children, they moved to Ogden Twp., Lenawee Co., Mich. Children: 1. MARY L. (m. W. R. Fisher); 2. DAVID H. (to Bear Lake, Manistee Co., Mich.); 3. MARGARET A. E. (m. Henry F. Dawson, Ogden Sta., Mich.); 4. GEORGE W. (Bear Lake, Mich.); 5. LOVINIA E.; 6. VIRGINIA C. (m. Charles Blake, Ogden Twp.); 7. MARTHA E. (m. John Collons, Bear Lake, Mich.); 8. MISSOURI S. (m. Enos T. Huey, Ogden Twp.); 9. WILLIAM (Bear Lake, Mich.); 10. ROSALINDA J. (m. H. A. Hoag, Tecumseh Twp.); 11. J. WESLEY MILTON (Arkansas). Ref: P&BA-Len pg. 912-3.

HOPKINS, SARAH (See Daniel Cole)

HOPKINS, SOPHIA (See Matthias Hall)

HORNBECK - this family was among the Dutch families of Ulster Co., NY who migrated along the "Old Mine Rd." from Kingston, NY to Sussex Co., NJ; and the following family no doubt is a descendant. There are many records for this surname in the Registers of the Dutch Church of Kingston, NY, 1660-1809, by R. R. Hoes. The History of Sussex & Warren Cos., NJ, by Snell, states that a BENJAMIN was an early settler of Montague, NJ. In the Revolutionary Census of NJ, by Stryker-Rodda, listed in 1778-1780 in Montague were ABRAHAM; BENJAMIN; & JACOB. In 1793, these same men were listed in the militia of Montague.

HORNBECK, BENJAMIN, son of JAMES, born 21 Dec. 1808, Sussex Co., NJ (sketch said "Milford," and that is in Hunterdon Co., NJ); and he moved with his parents to Phelps, Ontario Co., NY. He married on 14 Feb. 1833 to PHOEBE (REED), daughter of Robert, born ca. 1818, NY. They removed to Morenci, Mich. in 1834 (Note: There was a KEY? listed in the 1840 census index of Medina Twp., Lenawee Co.) Phoebe died in Medina Twp. 25 Oct. 1869, age 55. In the 1850 census of Medina Twp. they listed the children through #6, all b. Mich. Children: 1. JAMES D. b. ca. 1836 (m. Libbie Wilcox; children: Frank, Clara, Freddie, Maud, lived Dakotas); 2. ELIZABETH b. ca. 1838 (m. Sylvester Packer; d. 27 Mar. 1886); 3. JUDSON D. b. ca. 1841 (m. Annie Colegrove; served Civil War; children: Dewitt, Rosa, Bert, Bertha; lived Saline Co., KS); 4. ADEN b. ca. 1843 (m. Maria Beckwith, children: Lewis, Rollin, Bertha); 5. BENJAMIN C. b. ca. 1845; 6. LEWIS C. b. ca. 1847 (to Kalamazoo, Mich.); 7. ANNA (m. C. W. Mallory; lived Fulton Co., Ohio); 8. EMMA (m. Melford Baker, Morenci, Mich.); 9. JENNIE. Ref: P&BA-Len pg. 563-4.

HORNBECK, CORNELIUS D., son of JAMES (following), b. 29 Oct. 1811, Phelps, NY, moved to Medina Twp., Lenawee Co., Mich. in 1836 (not listed in 1840). He and wife, ISABEL, born ca. 1827, NY, were listed in the 1850 census of Medina Twp. with HARRIET F., age 6, b. NY, in their household.

HORNBECK, JAMES born New Jersey, served in the War of 1812, probably in NY. He married in Milford?, Sussex Co., NJ to ELIZABETH (DeWITT), daughter of Capt. Cornelius (also see). They removed to Phelps, Ontario Co., NY. Known sons: BENJAMIN (preceding); CORNELIUS D. (preceding). Ref: P&BA-Len pg. 563-4.

HORNBY, JOHN J. (See Eliab Park)

HORNBY, WILLIAM born ca. 1814, and wife, JANE, born ca. 1814, both in England, were listed in the 1850 census of Raisin Twp., Lenawee Co., Mich. with RICHARD, age 10, b. England; and ELIZABETH, age 7; JOHN (note JOHN J., preceding), age 3, both b. Mich., in their household.

HORTON, ARASWOOD? born ca. 1810, NY, was head of household in the 1850 census of Woodstock Twp., Lenawee Co., Mich. with OLIVE, age 23, b. NY; and JANNET, age 16; JOSIAH, age 14; ELIZABETH, age 7, both b. Mich., and the family of William Allen, in his household.

HORTON, DAVID born ca. 1799, NY, and wife, BETSEY M., born ca. 1809, Rhode Island, were listed in the 1840 census index of Adrian Twp., Lenawee Co., Mich.; and in the 1850 census with CAROLINE, age 11, CHARLES, age 7; WILLIAM, age 2, all b. Mich., in their household. ELEANOR, age 32, born NY, was listed last, perhaps a sister? Also in their household was Thomas M. Cooley, age 26; wife, Mary E., age 21, both b. NY, and Eugene, age 6/12, b. Mich.

HORTON, DAVID M. born ca. 1817, VT, and wife JANE, born ca. 1827, NY, were listed in the 1850 census of Woodstock Twp., Lenawee Co., Mich. with CHARLES, age 7; SARAH, age 4; URILINDA? (male), age 1, all b. Mich., in their household.

HORTON, ELIZA A. born 1 Nov. 1811, Ulster Co., NY married in Cayuga Co., NY to William Stockwell, also see.

HORTON, ELIZABETH (See John Burnett)

HORTON, EVERETT born ca. 1812, and wife, MARY, born ca. 1815, both in NY, were listed in the 1850 census of Woodstock Twp., Lenawee Co., Mich. with GILBERT, age 13; FRANCIS, age 12; ROBERT, age 10; WILLIAM, age 8; JAMES, age 4, all b. NY; and EVERETT, age 1, b. Mich., in their household.

HORTON, FREDERICK V., son of RICHARD S. (following), born 14 Feb. 1826, Orange Co., NY, came to Lenawee Co., Mich. in 1831, and lived in Raisin Twp.; and in Tecumseh Twp., then moved to LaGrange Co., Ind. He married in Eaton Rapids, Mich. on 14 May 1850 to CORNELIA S. (LONG) born ca. 1825, NY (listed in the 1850 census of Raisin Twp.). They returned to Clinton Twp., Lenawee Co., Mich., where they resided in 1888. Children: 1. FREDERICK A. (m. Hattie I. Long, Eaton Co., Mich.); 2. HENRY L. Ref: P&BA-Len pg. 311-2.

HORTON, GEORGE B., son of SAMUEL (following), born 17 Apr. 1845, Lafayette, Ohio, came to Fairfield Twp.,

Lenawee Co., Mich. with his parents ca. 1853. He married on 3 Jan. 1878 to MENTHA AMANDA (BRADISH), daughter of Norman F. (also see). Children: 1. ALICE L. b. 27 Sept. 1878; 2. NORMAN D. b. 18 July 1881; 3. SAMUEL W. b. 3 May 1885. Ref: P&BA-Len pg. 990-1.

HORTON, GILBERT, probably son of RICHARD S. (following), born ca. 1819, and wife, CONTENT, born ca. 1825, both in NY, were listed in the 1850 census of Raisin Twp., Lenawee Co., Mich. with FRANCIS G., age 7; CORNELIA J., age 5; LEWIS C., age 2, all b. Mich., in their household. Listed 2 doors from RICHARD S.

HORTON, JAMES (See Garrett F. Harris)

HORTON, LEWIS of Royalton, NY (See Felix Holdridge).

HORTON, MARY, age 52, born Mass., was listed in the 1850 census of Franklin Twp., Lenawee Co., Mich. in a Daniel Allen household.

HORTON, OSMER was listed in the 1840 census index of Raisin Twp., Lenawee Co., Mich. adjacent to RICHARD S. (following).

HORTON, RICHARD S. born 1790, Orange Co., NY, married on 24 Nov. 1814, Presbyterian Church, Goshen, NY to KEZIAH (VALENTINE), daughter of Ananias (also see) born 3 Nov. 1794. Two daughters and three sons were born in Orange Co.,NY, and they moved about 1831 to Raisin Twp., Lenawee Co., Mich. Richard S. died in Jan. 1863, age 73, and she died in 1867, age 71. One child, age 6 mos. (name not stated) died in Orange Co., NY 19 Sept. 1816. Had probably son, GILBERT (preceding); known son, FREDERICK V. (preceding). In Richard's household in the 1850 census of Raisin Twp.: HANNAH, age 16; CATHARINE, age 14; JOHN J., age 12, all b. Mich. Also note OSMER, preceding.

HORTON, SAMUEL born in England, and wife, LUCINA A. (PERKINS), born Herkimer Co., NY, moved first to Medina Co., Ohio; returned to Orleans Co., NY; then moved to Niagara Co. NY. In 1853, they moved to Fairfield Twp., Lenawee Co., Mich. where he died 25 Apr. 1872. Lucina was living in Morenci, Mich. in 1888. Children: ALICE M. b. 26 Mar. 1842 (m. Casper Rorick, Seneca Twp.); GEORGE B. (preceding); HARRIET A. b. 16 Oct. 1853, Fairfield Twp. (m. Dr. H. S. Jewett, Dayton, Ohio). Ref: P&BA-Len pg. 990-1.

HOSMER, ALONZO born 9 Feb. 1792, Haddam, Conn., and wife, ASENATH, born Rutland, VT, settled in Parkman, Geauga Co., Ohio. Known daughter, SARAH M. b. 22 May 1830, Parkman, Ohio (m. William Hayden, also see). Ref: P&BA-Len pg. 548-9.

HOSTETTLER, BARBARA born Bavaria, Germany (See Christopher Shaler).

HOTCHKISS, JOHN (note Rev LAUREN, following) born ca. 1807, NY, and wife, ANN E., born ca. 1815, both in NY, were listed in the 1850 census of Hudson Twp., Lenawee Co., Mich. with JOHN C., age 12; MARVIN, age 5, both b. Mich., and Lydia A. Liscomb, age 11, b. Mich., in their household. Note: John may be listed as "J" in the 1840 census index of Medina Twp.

HOTCHKISS, LAUREN Rev. born ca. 1787, and wife, LUCY, born ca. 1789, both in Conn., were listed in the 1850 census of Hudson Twp., Lenawee Co., Mich. JOHN, preceding, was 2 doors away. Lauren may be listed as "L" in the 1840 census index of Medina Twp.

HOTCHKISS, MAMRE (See John Knapp)

HOTCHKISS, ROSEMOND, age 16, born NY, was listed in the 1850 census of Madison Twp., Lenawee Co., Mich. in the household of Nancy Babcock.

HOTCHKISS, SARAH born ca. 1796, NY, was listed in the 1850 census of Medina Twp., Lenawee Co., Mich. in the household of son, OLIVER, age 22, b. NY.

HOUGABOOM see HOGABOAM

HOUGH also see HUFF

HOUGH, AMOS born ca. 1790, Conn., was listed in the 1850 census of Rome Twp., Lenawee Co., Mich. in household of PHILANDER (following).

HOUGH, D. M., married ARLETTA (HAYWARD), daughter of Henry$_4$ (also see) of Seneca Twp., Lenawee Co., Mich., later went to Eaton Co., Mich. Children: 1. HELEN N.; 2. CLIFFORD R.

HOUGH, ELEAZER L. born ca. 1810, and wife, AMY, born ca. 1811, both in NY, were listed in the 1850 census of Rome Twp., Lenawee Co., Mich. with SARAH A., age 16; NICHOLAS V., age 15; WILLIAM, age 12; HENRY, age 10; HIRAM, age 6, all b. NY; and HENRIETTA, age 2, b. Mich., in their household.

HOUGH, MORGAN, age 14, born NY, was listed in the 1850 census of Rollin Twp., Lenawee Co., Mich. in household of Edwin C. & Lucretia Cole.

HOUGH, OLMSTEAD born ca. 1798, and wife, MARY, born ca. 1805, were listed in the 1840 census index of Tecumseh Twp., Lenawee Co., Mich.; and in the 1850 census with LUCIUS, age 17; JULIA, age 14; MARY, age 1, all b. Mich., in their household.

HOUGH, PHILANDER born ca. 1811, and wife, ALICE, born ca. 1811, both in NY, were listed in the 1850 census of Rome Twp., Lenawee Co., Mich. with WILLIAM, age 11, b. Mich.; and AMOS (preceding) in their household. Note: He was listed in the 1840 census index as HUFF.

HOUGHTALIN, BENJAMIN F. and wife, GERTRUDE (HARDER), were natives of NY "of German descent." They resided in Livonia, Livingston Co., NY in 1828; and in 1848 moved to Somerset, Hillsdale Co., Mich. Known son, NICHOLAS P. (following). Ref: History of Jackson Co., Mich., pg. 943.

HOUGHTALIN, NICHOLAS P., son of BENJAMIN F. (preceding), born 14 Apr. 1828, Livingston Co., NY, moved in 1852 to Liberty Twp., Jackson Co., Mich. He married on 18 Mar. 1852 to NANCY A. (CRAWFORD). Children: 1. ESTHER S.; 2. ROSE M. (prob. she who m. Wilbur W. Town, also see). Nancy died 22 Apr. 1854; and Nicholas married again on 16 Sept. 1860 to SARAH C. (BABCOCK) who died 20 Aug. 1864. He married on 16 Mar. 1869 to Mrs. SABRA TOWN, probably widow of Calvin (also see). Children: 3. CORA B.; 4. GERTRUDE. Ref: History of Jackson Co., Mich., pg. 943.

HOUGHTALING, PETER of Henrietta, Monroe Co., NY had known daughter, PHOEBE (m. Solomon Jeffords, also see).

HOUGHTBY, JOHN born ca. 1794, Lincolnshire, England, married there to ELIZABETH (GODFREY) born 1794. In 1844, with their 9 children, a son-in-law, and 4 grandchildren, they came to the US, and settled first in Lucas Co., Ohio (now Fulton Co.) In 1849, they removed to Ogden Twp., Lenawee Co., Mich. There were 12 children (names not stated), but 3 died young in England. Known daughter, HARRIET (m. William Ash, also see); known son, WILLIAM (following). In the 1850 census of Ogden Twp., John listed in the household: JOHN, age 18; MARY, age 16; HENRY, age 12, all b. England. Elizabeth died a few years after settling in Ogden Twp., and John married twice more (wives' names not stated). Ref: P&BA-Len pg. 1186-7. Note: GEORGE, age 19, born England, listed in the 1850 census of Raisin Twp., Lenawee Co., Mich., probably belongs to this family.

HOUGHTBY, WILLIAM, son of JOHN (preceding), born 2 Jan. 1822, Lincolnshire, England, came to the US with his parents. He married in 1849 to MELINDA (RITCHEY), daughter of Joseph (also see) in Ogden Twp., Lenawee Co., Mich. where they settled. Children: 1. AMANDA A. b. 1850 (m. Daniel D. Baluss, also see); 2. HATTIE (m. Luther Harsh, Ogden Twp.); 3. HENRY; 4. JOHN; 5. LIBBIE (m. M. H. Rubey, Randolph Co., Ind.); 6. ESTHER; 7. ALBERT. Ref: P&BA-Len pg. 1186-7.

HOUGHTON, CHARLOTTE born ca. 1824, NY, came from Orleans Co., NY to Lenawee Co., NY with her parents (names not stated, born Vermont & New Jersey). She married first to John Treat (age 45, b. Conn.) with whom she was listed in the 1850 census of Adrian Twp., Lenawee Co., Mich. She married again to Peter Onsted (also see).

HOUGHTON, EZRA was listed in the 1840 census index of Raisin Twp., Lenawee Co., Mich.

HOUGHTON, FERRIS born ca. 1820, place not known, and wife, MARGARET, born ca. 1830, NY, were listed in the 1850 census of Adrian Twp., Lenawee Co., Mich. with EVELINE, age 3, b. Mich., in their household.

HOUGHTON, HARVEY born ca. 1814, Penn., and wife, MARY G., born ca. 1817, NY, were listed in the 1840 census index of Woodstock Twp., Lenawee Co., Mich.; and in the 1850 census of Rollin Twp., with WILLIAM, age 14, b. NY; and SARAH J., age 12; SOPHIA E., age 9; ALZORA C., age 3; HOLLIS J., age 6/12, all b. Mich., in their household.

HOUGHTON, JOTHAM born ca. 1802, and wife, CATHARINE, born ca. 1807, both in NY, were listed in the 1850 census of Adrian Twp., Lenawee Co., Mich. with JOHN M., age 18; SUSAN A., age 16; ASENATH, age 14; FRANCES M., age 12; EMILY J., age 9; PERRY, age 6, all shown b. NY, in their household.

HOUGHTON, LOUISA (See Caleb Thurber)

HOUGHTON, LUCAS (spelled "Hoten") was listed in the 1840 census index of Adrian Twp., Lenawee Co., Mich.

HOUGHTON, LUTHER (See Ezra Sanford)

HOUGHTON, NOAH born ca. 1790, New Hampshire, and wife, SARAH, born ca. 1804, England, were listed in the 1840 census index of Woodstock Twp., Lenawee Co., Mich., and in the 1850 census with HENRY, age 7; WESLEY, age 4, both b. Mich., in their household.

HOUGHTON, PLUTARCH born ca. 1789, and wife, SARAH, born ca. 1790, both in NY, were listed in the 1850 census of Woodstock Twp., Lenawee Co., Mich. with ELIZABETH, age 14, b. Mich.

HOUSE also see HAUSE
HOUSE, MORRIS B. (See MORRIS B. HAUSE)
HOUSE, R. B. Dr. (See Dr. Leonidas M. Jones; & James Boyd, Jr.).

HOUSEN, JULIA A. (See Godfrey Stock)

HOUSS, NAOMI (See John Burr)

HOUSTON, NANCY (See Harrison Fitts)

HOWARD, ALMON and wife, REBECCA born ca. 1800, NY, moved from NY before 1840 to Dover Twp., Lenawee Co., Mich.; and in the 1850 census of Dover Twp., Rebecca, age 50, was listed head of household with all following (except Betsey) in her household: GEORGE S., age 32; LEVI D., age 24; RICHARD E., age 22; POLLY, age 19, all b. NY; BETSEY b. 16 May 1832, NY (m. Edward Roberts, also see); MARTHA D. b. 10 June 1834, b. NY (m. Edward Roberts, as 2nd wife); and DANIEL D., age 13; ALMOND, age 12; DARIUS M., age 8, all b. Mich. Ref: P&BA-Len pg. 614-5. Note: FRANCES, following, listed next door may be a daughter-in-law of this family?

HOWARD, ANSEL born New England, moved by 1800 to Oneida Co., NY; and was a pioneer to Madison Co., NY. He died in Madison Co., and with wife, name not stated, had known daughter, CLARISSA b. New York Mills, Oneida Co., NY (m. George Patterson who d. 1849, Madison Co., NY, also see). Ref: P&BA-Len pg. 697-8.

HOWARD, BENJAMIN was listed in the 1840 census index of Cambridge Twp., Lenawee Co., Mich.

HOWARD, DIANA (See Leonard Carlton)

HOWARD, FRANCES born ca. 1824, born Conn., was listed head of household in the 1850 census of Dover Twp., Lenawee Co., Mich. (next door to REBECCA, wife of ALMON, preceding) with CHARLES S., age 1, b. Mich., in her household.

HOWARD, FRANCIS A. born ca. 1804, NY, and wife, ELIZABETH "BETSEY" (CARPENTER) born ca. 1810, NJ, came to Rome Twp., Lenawee Co., Mich. in 1837, probably from Yates Co., NY. He died in Rome Twp. on 29 May 1884; and she was still living there in 1888. Children: 1. LORETTA L b. 15 Aug. 1833, Starkey, Yates Co., NY (m/1 John F. Sammons, son of Sampson, also see, & he d. 19 May 1879, Rome Twp.; m/2 Augustus F. Daniels, also see); those following are from Francis' household in 1850 census of Rome Twp.: 2. ALBERT, age 14, b. NY; and 3. LEWIS, age 11; 4. BENJAMIN, age 6; 5. HORACE, age 3, all b. Mich. Note: LOVISA who m. Ira Trim in 1852 probably also related to this family, as Ira (age 28, b. NY) was alone next door in the 1850 census. Note JUSTIS, following.

HOWARD, JOEL born ca. 1814, NH, and wife, MARY, born ca. 1824, VT, were listed in the 1850 census of Blissfield Twp., Lenawee Co., Mich. with CHARLES, age 7;

Pioneer Families of Southeastern Michigan

DeWIT, age 6; ELIZA, age 4/12, all b. Mich., in their household.

HOWARD, JOSEPH born NY, married NANCY (SMITH) born Scipio, NY; and he was killed in the War of 1812 leaving her with 4 children, only son, MARVIN (following) was mentioned. Nancy married again in Herkimer Co., NY to ? West. Ref: P&BA-Len pg. 1096-7.

HOWARD, JUSTIS was listed in the 1840 census index of Rome Twp., Lenawee Co., Mich., adjacent to FRANCIS A., preceding.

HOWARD, MARVIN, son of JOSEPH (preceding), born 12 Feb. 1809, Herkimer Co., NY, was raised by Asa Smith after the death of his father. In January 1833, he moved to Manchester, Washtenaw Co., Mich.; and married there in 1835 to LAVINA (REED) of Manchester, born Niagara Co., NY. They moved to Cambridge Twp., Lenawee Co., Mich. (after 1850?), and finally to Tecumseh Twp. Lavina died in 1871. Children: 1. ALBERT R. (d. age 2-1/2); 2. ORLANDO P. (m. Eliza Weadhead, he d. 1870, leaving son, Albert O.). Ref: P&BA-Len pg. 1096-7.

HOWARD, MATTIE C. (See James B. Wells)

HOWARD, PATTIE b. ca. 1800, Livingston Co., NY (See Calvin Lewis).

HOWARD, ROWEYN, age 17, born NY, was listed in the 1850 census of Woodstock Twp., Lenawee Co., Mich. in the Ewing household.

HOWARD, SEABRING born ca. 1806, NY, and wife, ELLEN, born ca. 1808, Maryland, were listed in the 1850 census of Adrian Twp., Lenawee Co., Mich. with JOHN, age 18; ORRIN, age 15; REBECCA, age 12, all b. MD; and EMOGENE, age 2, b. Mich., in their household.

HOWARD, WILLIAM, age 20, born Ohio, was listed in the 1850 census of Adrian Twp., Lenawee Co., Mich. in a hotel.

HOWARD, WILLIAM O., born ca. 1812, NY, and wife, ALICE, born ca. 1812, VT, were listed in the 1850 census of Adrian Twp., Lenawee Co., Mich. with BYRON S., age 12, b. VT; and ALBERT W., age 10. b. NY, in their household.

HOWD, ANTHONY, son of SAMUEL (following), born 6 July 1768, married on 11 Mar. 1797 to MARTHA (HARRINGTON) born 12 Mar. 1777, and they lived in Cazenovia, Madison Co., NY by 1816. He died 16 June 1841, and she died 2 Dec. 1857. Children: 1. HANNAH b. 9 June 1798; 2. LAURA b. 21 July 1800; 3. ELSNA b. 30 Sept. 1802 (d. 29 Dec. 1841); 4. HARRIET b. 11 Feb. 1805 (d. 13 Oct. 1885); 5. SAMUEL B. b. 17 Sept. 1807 (d. 25 Sept. 1881); 6. AMY b. 14 Mar. 1810 (d. 22 June 1883); 7. JOHN W. b. 8 May 1813 (d. 6 May 1886); 8. HARVEY B. (following); 9. ELI S. (following). Ref: P&BA-Len pg. 1190-1.

HOWD, ELI S., son of ANTHONY (preceding), born 22 Nov. 1818, married on 4 Feb. 1844 to PHEBE A. (RENYAN). She died 1 Aug. 1875, and he was still living in 1888. Children: 1. CHARLES; 2. ORIN A.; 3. DELOS; 4. HARVEY J.; 5. JENNIE M. Ref: P&BA-Len pg 1190-1.

HOWD, HARVEY B., son of ANTHONY (preceding), born 11 June 1816, Cazenovia, NY, moved to Rollin Twp., Lenawee Co., Mich. in 1842. He married there on 19 Feb. 1844 to ELIZABETH "BETSEY" E. (PITCHER), daughter of Henry (also see). He died 28 Mar. 1875, age 59. Children: 1. AMELIA b. ca. 1845; 2. HENRY W. b. 8 May 1848, Rollin Twp.; 3. HELEN I. (m. Homer Tingley, son of John H.[3], also see); 4. HARVEY. Ref: P&BA-Len pg. 597-8 & 1190-1.

HOWD, SAMUEL born 1 Dec. 1712, and wife, AMY (BALDIN) born 12 Oct. 1724, married on 14 Feb. 1754. Children: 1. AMY b. 2 Dec. 1754; 2. ABIGAIL b. 3 July 1757; 3. SAMUEL b. 26 Apr. 1759; 4. ALTHERA b. 6 Feb. 1763; 5. HANNAH b. 24 Oct. 1764; 6. ANTHONY preceding). Ref: P&BA-Len pg. 1190-1.

HOWE also see HOWES

HOWE, ALBERT was listed in the 1840 census index of Clinton, Lenawee Co., Mich.

HOWE, ANNA (See Levi Fowler; Anna was sister of SUSAN, following).

HOWE, CHARLES born ca. 1795, NY, was listed in the 1850 census of Hudson Twp., Lenawee Co., Mich. in a Bovee household.

HOWE, EDWIN born ca. 1823, and wife, ALVIRA, born ca. 1823, both in Mass., were listed in the 1850 census of Palmyra Twp., Lenawee Co., Mich. with no family

HOWE, HOLLIS born ca. 1799, Mass., was listed in the 1840 census index of Hudson Twp., Lenawee Co., Mich.; and in the 1850 census with wife, JULIA, born ca. 1804, Conn., with Charlotte L. Curtis, age 16, b. NY; Asahel Fenton, age 9, b. Mich.; Elvira Fisk, age 19, b. NY, in their household.

HOWE, J. G. was listed in the 1840 census index of Hudson Twp., Lenawee Co., Mich.

HOWE, JOSEPH was listed in the 1840 census index of Macon Twp., Lenawee Co., Mich.

HOWE, LUTHER (See Isaac A. Bartlett)

HOWE, MARY born ca. 1785, Mass., was listed in the household of Porter L. Howland in the 1850 census of Hudson Twp., Lenawee Co., Mich.

HOWE, SUSAN (See Horace Fowler; Susan was sister of ANNA, prreceding).

HOWELL, ANDREW[5], son of JOSEPH[4] (following), born 5 May 1803, Seneca Co., NY, came to Macon Twp., Lenawee Co., Mich. with his parents. He married in June 1859 to MARY ADELIA BEECHER (TOWER), daughter of Rev. Philo (also see) of Rochester, NY. They settled in Adrian where he was a Judge. Children: 1. ROBERT BEECHER; 2. CHARLES ARTHUR. Ref: P&BA-Len pg. 1036-7.

HOWELL, ANSON (ALANSON?) born 13 Apr. 1786, Suffolk Co., NY, at age 20 went to Ontario Co., NY. He married there to CHARLOTTE (ROCKWOOD) whose parents were from VT. They removed to Adrian Twp., Lenawee Co., Mich. in 1827. She apparently died before 1850; and he died 8 Oct. 1873. Known daughter, ALPHA A. (m. Eliab Park, also see). In the 1850 census of Adrian Twp., he was listed Alanson, age 63; and also in his household was Maria Odell (also see), age 39, b. NY with children, who may be another daughter?

HOWELL, CHARLES[1] from Wales settled in New Jersey in 1735; and had known son, DAVID[2] of Bound Brook, NJ who had known son, JOSEPH[3] (following). Ref: P&BA-Len pg. 1036-7.

HOWELL, EDWIN born ca. 1832, Ohio, was listed in the 1850 census of Madison Twp., Lenawee Co., Mich.

HOWELL, ETTIE MAY (See Anthony Poucher)

HOWELL, GEORGE[5] Dr., son of JOSEPH[4] (following), born 4 Nov. 1836, Macon Twp., Lenawee Co., Mich., married 7 Jan. 1864 to AMELIA (REMINGTON) born 8 Feb. 1844. They lived first in Macon Twp., and moved in Sept. 1866 to Tecumseh, Mich. Children: 1. EDITH; 2. VEVA; 3. GERTRUDE. Ref: P&BA-Len pg. 1168-9.

HOWELL, JARED A. born ca. 1821, and wife, AMELIA, born ca. 1829, both in NY, were listed in the 1850 census of Rome Twp., Lenawee Co., Mich. with daughter, ALTHI? A., age 2, b. Mich., in their household.

HOWELL, JOHN born ca. 1801, and wife, SHADY (CURTIS), born ca. 1804, place not legible, were listed in the 1840 census index of Cambridge Twp., Lenawee Co., Mich.; and in the 1850 census with MARIAH, age 24; ALVAH, age 9, in their household. He died 4 Oct. 1851, age 50y/5m; and she died 25 July 1878, and they are buried in the Mills Cemetery, Franklin Twp., Lenawee Co., Mich. Note: Probably Shady is related to Julia, wife of William Pentecost, also see, as they named a daughter, Shady, and the two couples are buried together in the Mills Cemetery.

HOWELL, JOSEPH[3], son of DAVID[2] (See CHARLES[1], preceding), married CATHERINE (SEABRING) on 7 Dec. 1788; and about 1800 they removed to Seneca Co., NY and settled between Ovid & Lodi. Known son, JOSEPH[4] (following). Ref: P&BA-Len pg. 1036-7.

HOWELL, JOSEPH[4], son of JOSEPH[3] (preceding), born 5 May 1803, Seneca Co., NY, married on 5 Nov. 1826 to LUTETIA (VAN DUYN), daughter of Dennis (also see). About 1831, they removed to Macon Twp., Lenawee Co., Mich. She died 30 Apr. 1876, age 73; and he was living in 1888 in Macon Twp. with a daughter. Six sons and 2 daughters, all names not stated. Known children (first 7 in household in 1850 census): 1. ANDREW b. 18 Dec. 1827, Seneca Co., NY; 2. CHARLES b. ca. 1830; 3. EDWIN b. ca. 1834, Mich.; 4. GEORGE b. 4 Nov. 1836, Macon Twp.; 5. ELLEN b. ca. 1839; 6. DANIEL b. ca. 1842; 7. ANN b. ca. 1845; 8. (Son b. after 1850?). Ref: P&BA-Len pg. 1036-7 & 1168-9.

HOWELL, MARY A. (See David Alexander)

HOWES also see HOWE

HOWES, AMOS, son of EZRA (following), born ca. 1819, and wife, CAROLINE, born ca. 1827, both in NY, were listed in the 1850 census of Adrian Twp., Lenawee Co., Mich. with DELORA, age 2; JULIA, age 1/12, both b. Mich., in their household. Also in the household were parents, following, and brother, ISAAC, and the Terrys.

HOWES, EZRA born ca. 1787, and wife, SALLY, born ca. 1790, both in Mass., were listed (as HOWE) in the 1840 census index of Adrian Twp., Lenawee Co., Mich.; and in the 1850 census were listed in the household of son, AMOS, preceding. Son, ISAAC, b. ca. 1826, NY and daughter, THANKFUL b. ca. 1818 (and husband, Noah Terry, also see) were listed in household.

HOWES, HENRY (See Benjamin Laur)

HOWES, SAMUEL (listed as HOWE) was listed in the 1840 census index of Adrian Twp., Lenawee Co., Mich. adjacent to EZRA, preceding.

HOWLAND, BENJAMIN born ca. 1811, NY was listed in the 1850 census of Cambridge Twp., Lenawee Co., Mich. MARIA, age 21, b. NY, may be a second wife, as she was too young to be mother of all the following in the household: JOHN, age 18; MARGARET, age 14; LOVISA, age 12, all b. Ohio; SOPHRONIA, age 10; THOMAS, age 8; FRANKLIN, age 3; ADELBERT, age 3; BENJAMIN, age 3/12, all b. Mich.

HOWLAND, CHARLES born ca. 1830, NY, was listed in the 1850 census of Adrian Twp., Lenawee Co., Mich. as a "student" in the household of Dr. David Kelley. Note JONATHAN & THOMAS J., following.

HOWLAND, CHESTER born ca. 1805, NY, was head of household in the 1850 census of Hudson Twp., Lenawee Co., Mich. with SAPHRONA, age 25; CLARK G., age 18, both b. NY; DeWIT C., age 15; and AMANDA D., age 4; ACHSAH S., age 1, all b. Mich., in their household.

HOWLAND, JABEZ was a farmer of Tompkins Co., NY, and he died 19 Dec. 1834, age 52y/11mos, and is buried in the Ithaca Cemetery, with a wife, MAHITABLE who died 21 Apr. 1822, age 37. He apparently married again as a wife, ELIZABETH, born ca. 1786, Rhode Island, moved with children to Tecumseh Twp., Lenawee Co., Mich. (not listed in 1840 census index). She was head of household in the 1850 census of Tecumseh Twp. with LUTHER, age 26; PHILLIP (following); MAHITABLE, age 24, all b. NY, in her household. Ref: History of Jackson Co., Mich. pg. 799-800; and NYG&BR Records of Tompkins Co. Cemeteries. Note: Other Howland families listed in the 1850 census of Ithaca, Tompkins Co., NY had Mass. origins.

HOWLAND, JONATHAN born ca. 1789, Adams, Mass., married first to MARY born ca. 1786, Worcester, Rhode Island; and they resided in Manchester, Ontario Co., NY until 1846 when they moved to Adrian Twp., Lenawee Co., Mich. Known daughter, ALMEDA b. 6 Dec. 1812 (m. Norton Baker, also see); son, JONATHAN Jr. b. ca. 1833, NY (m. Emeline A. Snedeker, daughter of James J., also see). Jonathan Sr. married second (before 1850) to ELIZABETH b. ca. 1793, R.I., as she was listed in the household in 1850 census of Adrian Twp. Also in the household was Lucy A. Powers, age 17, b. NY. Also note CHARLES (preceding) & THOMAS J., & MELINDA, both following. Jonathan died in 1871. Ref: P&BA-Len pg. 957-8.

HOWLAND, KATE (See Cornelius Gilson)

HOWLAND, MELINDA born ca. 1820, Ontario Co., NY, married Welcome Teachout (also see). Note JONATHAN, preceding & THOMAS J., following.

HOWLAND, PHILIP, son of JABEZ (preceding), born 11 Aug. 1824, Tompkins Co., NY, moved with the family to Tecumseh Twp., Lenawee Co., Mich., and married there on 17 Oct. 1858 to CATHERINE (VEST), daughter of Eli (also see) of Tecumseh. In 1877, they moved to Norvell, Jackson Co., Mich.; and in 1879 to Columbia Twp. Children: 1. AVORICE E.; 2. JABEZ; 3. MARY BELL; 4. GRACE; 5. PHILLIP; 6. HILLARD; 7. BENJAMIN ALONZO. Ref: P&BA-Len pg. 799-800.

HOWLAND, PORTER L, born ca. 1813, Mass., was listed in the 1840 census index of Hudson Twp., Lenawee Co., Mich.; and in the 1850 census listed in his household GEORGE H., age 9; SARAH E., age 6; SAMUEL P., age 4; EMARANDA, age 3/12, all b. Mich. Mary Howe, age 65, b. Mass., was also listed.

HOWLAND, THOMAS J. was listed in the 1840 census index of Adrian Twp., Lenawee Co., Mich., not listed in 1850. (Possibly a daughter?) MARY E., a "native of Mass.,"

Pioneer Families of Southeastern Michigan

was said to have come to Adrian Twp. with her parents (names not stated) who returned to Manchester, Ontario Co., NY, where they remained. Mary E. married Addison P. Halladay, also see. Ref: P&BA-Len pg. 456-7.

HOWLEY, MICHAEL and wife, MARY (MARTIN), of Co. Sligo, Ireland, had known daughter, ANN b. 25 Dec. 1839 (came to the US in 1851, and m. Patrick Donnelly, also see). Ref: P&BA-Len pg. 1045-6.

HOXIE see HOXSIE

HOXSIE, ALEXANDER born ca. 1802, Mass., and wife, JANE, born ca. 1801, NY, were listed in the 1840 census index of Adrian Twp., Lenawee Co., Mich.; and in the 1850 census with ORVILL O., age 9; BETSEY J., age 1, both b. Mich., in their household.

HOXSIE, CONTENT born 7 Nov. 1771, Cape Cod, Mass., married John W. Kelley (also see). Ref: P&B-Len pg. 1216-7.

HOXSIE, EZRA, son of JOHN (following), born ca. 1817, NY, came to Palmyra Twp., Lenawee Co., Mich. from NY, and married there to SUSAN (KELLEY), daughter of Libni (also see). She died at Holloway, Mich. on 30 Oct. 1885, age 64. He retired to Mapleton, Cayuga Co., NY in 1886. Children: 1. ALBERT b. ca. 1845; 2. ELLEN b. ca. 1847; MARY (called ELIZABETH? in sketch) b. ca. 1848 (deceased by 1888); 4. GEORGE L. (following); 5. VERNON. Ref: P&BA-Len pg. 219-20. (Listed next door to EZRA in census).

HOXSIE, GEORGE L., son of EZRA (preceding), born 26 May 1855, Palmyra Twp., Lenawee Co., Mich., married on 31 Aug. 1882 to ALMA (BARRETT) born Blissfield, Mich. Son, GLENN (d. age 10 mos.) Ref: P&BA-Len pg. 219-20.

HOXSIE, HORACE, probably son of JOHN, born ca. 1814, NY, and wie, MARY, born ca. 1814, Maine, were listed in the 1850 census of Palmyra Twp., Lenawee Co., Mich. (2 doors from EZRA) with THERESA, age 4; HORACE, age 2; ZACHARIAH T., age 4/12, all b. Mich., in their household.

HOXSIE, JOHN, son of JOSEPH (following), born ca. 1780/3, Dutchess Co., NY, married on 4 Nov. 1804, Saratoga Co., NY to PHEBE (SLADE), daughter of Buffen (also see). In 1833, they removed to Palmyra Twp., Lenawee Co., Mich.; where she died 8 Aug. 1842, age 56. In the 1850 census of Palmyra Twp., John was head of household, age 70, b. NY, with son, Orvin and family in the household, and was listed between Leonard and Ezra. He died 24 Jan. 1873, age about 90, Raisin Twp., at home of daughter, Jane Malinda. Children: LEONARD (following); HORACE; & EZRA (both preceding); ORVIN? (following); and LYDIA (m. Libni Kelley, also see); BETSEY (m. Edson Walker, also see); JANE MALINDA b. Mar. 1827 (m. Benjamin Kelley, also see). Ref: P&BA-Len pg. 619-20; 761-2; 1216-7.

HOXSIE, JOSEPH married in Mass. to ELIZABETH (BENSON) and they removed to Dutchess Co., NY, where she died, and he afterwards moved to Saratoga Co., NY. Known son, JOHN (preceding). Ref: P&BA-Len pg. 1216-7.

HOXSIE, JULIUS and wife, ANNIE, of Macedon, Wayne Co., NY were parents of MARIE S. (m/1 Smith; m/2 Francis A. Dewey, Cambridge Twp., Lenawee Co., Mich., also see). Ref: P&BA-Len pg. 877-8.

HOXSIE, LEONARD, probably son of JOHN (preceding), born ca. 1813, and wife, MARY, born ca. 1815, both in NY, were listed in the 1850 census of Palmyra Twp., Lenawee Co., Mich. with CAROLINE, age 12; ADELINE, age 10; ALONZO, age 8; JANE, age 6; CHARLES, age 4; CATHARINE, age 2, all b. Mich., in their household (2 doors from JOHN).

HOXSIE, ORVIN?, son of JOHN (preceding), born ca. 1822, and wife, MARY, born ca. 1825, both in NY, were listed in the 1850 census of Palmyra Twp., Lenawee Co., Mich. (in household of JOHN) with HOMER, age 2; ZACHARIAH T., age 1/12, both b. Mich., in the household.

HOXSIE, ZORA was reared as a foster child by Benjamin & JANE MALINDA (HOXSIE) Kelley (also see).

HOXTER, HEZEKIAH W., son of WILLIAM (following) born 24 Jan. 1832, Varick, Seneca Co., NY, came to Rome Twp., Lenawee Co., Mich. with parents. He married 14 Mar. 1854 to LOIS B. (SUTTON), daughter of Pharis (also see). Daughter, ELLA M. (m. Edwin P. Gambee, son of John, also see). Ref: P&BA-Len pg. 471.

HOXTER, WILLIAM born 12 Jan. 1808, Seneca Co., NY, married JANNETT (KNOWLES), probably daughter of Hezekiah Sr. (also see), born 13 Apr. 1813, Haddam, Conn. They remained in Varick, Seneca Co., NY till May 1836, then removed to Rome Twp., Lenawee Co., Mich. (where they were listed in the 1840 census index and 1850 census); and later moved to Adrian Twp. Seven children (a son died infancy, unnamed): 1. HEZEKIAH W. (preceding); 2. SUSAN b. ca. 1833 (m. John H. Todd); 3. HEMAN b. ca. 1835; 4. WILLIAM JR. b. ca. 1839 (deceased by 1888); 5. ELIZABETH b. ca. 1842 (m. Bertram Skeels, Rome Twp.); 6. JOSEPHINE (b. after 1850). Ref: P&BA-Len pg. 471.

HOY also see HOEY
HOY, MARGARET (See John Monahan^2)

HOYT, BURGESS purchased in Jackson Co., Mich. in 1836.

HOYT, BURTIS married MELINDA (WOOD), see _?_ Wood, and died in Jackson Co., Mich.

HOYT, CHARLES Dr. born ca. 1814, and wife, EMILY, born ca 1820, were listed in the 1850 census of Adrian Twp., Lenawee Co., Mich. with CHARLES, age 8/12, b. Mich., in their household.

HOYT, CHARLES A. (See Smith Briggs)

HOYT, EBENEZER born ca. 1804, and wife, MARIA, born ca. 1815, both in NY, were listed in the 1850 census of Seneca Twp., Lenawee Co., Mich. with HERMAN, age 17; CORTEZ, age 13; JOHN, age 11; DAVID, age 10; JAMES, age 7; SARAH, age 4, all b. NY, in their household.

HOYT, JONATHAN L., son of LOUIS (following) born 27 June 1802, Onondaga Co., NY, came to Jackson Co., Mich. with his father. He married on 20 Oct. 1842 to SAMANTHA L. (CLARK), daughter of Chester (also see). He was listed in Sandstone Twp., Jackson Co. in 1840 census index. Children: 1. THEODORA M. b. 14 Apr. 1843; 2. LUCIEN C. b. 20 Sept. 1844; 3. NELLIE A. b. 12 Feb. 1846; 4. ANNA L. b. 6 Sept. 1848; 5. EMMA W. b. 24 Aug. 1850; 6. LILLIE B. b. 20 Oct. 1854. Samantha died 23 Mar. 1881. Ref: History of Jackson Co., Mich., pg. 766.

HOYT, JOHN L. (See Alonzo James)
HOYT, KEELER and wife, CHARITY (BALSLEY) of Oneida Co., NY were parents of NELSON (following). They moved to Waterloo Twp., Jackson Co., Mich. in 1853, and he died there in Mar. 1861. Ref: History of Jackson Co., Mich., pg. 1145.
HOYT, LEVI and wife, MARGARET (SPRAGUE) had known daughter, ELIZABETH b. 20 Feb. 1834, Hector, Monroe Co., NY (m/1 Smith; m/2 NELSON HOYT, also see, Jackson Co., Mich.).
HOYT, LOUIS (Lewis) born 3 Dec. 1786, Conn., married ELIZABETH (HOYT) born Aug. 1788, Conn. They removed to Onondaga Co., NY by 1802; and she died in NY in 1819. He afterwards moved with son, JONATHAN L. (preceding) to Jackson Co., Mich. where he died in 1842 (listed in Jackson Twp. in 1840 census index). Ref: History of Jackson Co., Mich., pg. 766.
HOYT, MOSES R. born ca. 1811, and wife, APPHIA?, born ca. 1810, both in NY, were listed in the 1850 census of Dover Twp., Lenawee Co., Mich. with JONATHAN, age 4, b. Mich., in the household.
HOYT, NELSON, son of KEELER (preceding), born 16 Jan. 1820, Oneida Co., NY, married in 1846 to BETSEY (BARBER) born Sept. 1831, Oneida Co., NY. They moved to Jackson Co., Mich. in 1853. Seven children: Deceased before 1881, were WILLIAM; CATHERINE; & SETH; and surviving were: ALBINE L.; PETER B.; CHARLES K.; HENRY H. Betsey died in 1863; and he married second to Mrs. ELIZABETH (HOYT) SMITH, daughter of LEVI (preceding). Ref: History of Jackson Co., Mich. pg. 1145.
HOYT, SAMUEL born ca. 1769, Guilford, Conn., married MARY (BARTLETT), daughter of Samuel of Vermont. About 1812, they removed to Sheshequin, Bradford Co., Penn. He died there 21 Dec. 1842, age 73y/6mo.; and she died 9 Aug. 1849, age 70y/5mo. Children: 1. CHLOTILDA (m. 3 July 1814 to Obediah Gore Spalding, also see); 2. HANNAH M. (m. Samuel Marshall); 3. STATIRA b. 9 mar. 1807 (m. Amos P. Spalding); 4. SAMUEL B. (m/1 Flora Ames; m/2 Matilda Angle); 5. GILES M. b. 20 Mar. 1810 (m. Almira Green). Ref: Pioneer & Patriot Families of Bradford Co., Penn., by C. F. Heverly, 1913; & PB&A-Len pg. 1178-80.

HUBBARD, ALLEN was listed in the 1840 census index of Rome Twp., Lenawee Co., Mich. (spelled Hubard).
HUBBARD, CYRENE (See John Hurlbut)
HUBBARD, DANIEL born ca. 1798, and wife, LOISA, born ca. 1806, both b. NY, were listed in the 1840 census index of Franklin Twp., Lenawee Co., Mich.; and in the 1850 census with CORDELIA, age 20; NOAH, age 16, both b. NY; and AMANDA, age 12; JOHN, age 10; NORMAN, age 8; EDGAR, age 5; ELLEN, age 2, all b. Mich., in their household. Note GILES & SAMUEL A., following.
HUBBARD. GEORGE W. born ca. 1813, NY, was listed in the 1840 census index of Blissfield Twp., Lenawee Co., Mich., and in the 1850 census with LORRIS W. (female), age 17, b. Mich., in his household.
HUBBARD, GILES born ca. 1794, Conn., and wife, SARAH, born ca. 1798, NY, were listed in the 1840 census index of Franklin Twp., Lenawee Co., Mich.; and in the 1850 census with JAMES, age 20; AMOS, age 14; WILLIAM, age 11, all b. Mich., in their household. (In 1840 listed adjacent to DANIEL & SAMUEL A.)
HUBBARD, ISAAC P. was listed in the 1840 census index of Ogden Twp., Lenawee Co., Mich.
HUBBARD, KATE married ? Johnson who was born in Conn. and moved to Herkimer Co., NY. In 1817, they moved to Huron Co., Ohio. (See William J. Johnson). Ref: P&BA-Len pg. 803-4.
HUBBARD, LEWIS born ca. 1811, and wife, LUCY B., born ca. 1820, both in Mass., were listed in the 1850 census of Adrian Twp., Lenawee Co., Mich. in a Rice household.
HUBBARD, MARIA Mrs. was the daughter of Zibra Corbett (also see).
HUBBARD, RUSSELL (may be he called ROSWELL in 1840 census index of Woodstock Twp., Lenawee Co., Mich.) was born ca. 1791, Conn., and was listed in the 1850 census of Woodstock Twp. with GEORGE, age 9, b. Mich., in his household.
HUBBARD, RUTH (See Joseph Hicks)
HUBBARD, SAMUEL A. born ca. 1799, Conn., and wife, SUSAN, born ca. 1800, NY, were listed in the 1840 census index of Franklin Twp., Lenawee Co., Mich.; and in the 1850 census with RUTH, age 22; SAMUEL, age 21; ARISTARCHUS?, age 19; MARTHA, age 16, all b. NY; and ALONSO, age 11, b. Mich., in their household. Note DANIEL & GILES, both preceding.
HUBBARD, SARAH (See Clark Ames)
HUBBARD, SARAH born ca. 1796, Mass., was listed in the 1850 census of Madison Twp., Lenawee Co., Mich. with SANFORD, age 29, b. Mass. (a handicapped person), both in the household of Newell and Cornelia S. Mitchell (age 21, b. Mass., perhaps a daughter of Sarah?)

HUDNUTT, NATHANIEL had known daughter, ELIZABETH (m. before 1832 to Rev. William G. Wisner, also see). Ref: P&BA-Len pg. 1118-9.
HUDSON, FANNIE (See Eben Sparhawk)

HUEY, ENOS T. (See Samuel Hopkins, son of Levi)

HUFF also see HOUGH
HUFF, ISAAC B. was listed in the 1840 census index of Macon Twp., Lenawee Co., Mich.
HUFF, PETER and wife, NELLIE, had known daughter, SOPHIA (m/1 to Burroughs and had 4 children; m/2 John P. Silvers, also see). Ref: P&BA-Len pg. 233-4. Note: There was a PETER listed in Cass Co., Mich. in the 1840 census index.
HUFF, SAMUEL W. (or GANUEL W.) was listed in the 1840 census index of Adrian Twp., Lenawee Co., Mich.
HUFF, SARAH (See Lewis Miller)

HUGHES, RACHE (See William Smith)

HULBON also see HOLBIN
HULBON, GIDEON married CATHARINE A. (GEORGE), daughter of Abraham (also see). Children: HELENA; & ERVIN. They probably lived in Medina Twp., Lenawee Co., Mich., as after 1865, Catharine married there to John A. Baer.

HULETT also see HEWLETT
HULETT, SYLVANUS born 1801, Conn., and wife, RUTH, born ca. 1802, NY, were listed in the 1850 census of

Rollin Twp., Lenawee Co., Mich. with LUCY, age 10, b. Ohio, in their household.

HULL, BENJAMIN had known daughter, LYDIA born 11 Dec. 1819, Herkimer Co., NY (m. Hiram A. Curtiss, also see, in 1842 in Paris, Oneida Co., NY, and moved to Ridgeway Twp., Lenawee Co., Mich.). Benjamin went to Wisconsin late in life, where he died. Ref: P&BA-Len pg. 976-7.

HULL, BENJAMIN born ca. 1830, NY, was listed in the 1850 census of Medina Twp., Lenawee Co., Mich.

HULL, DANIEL E. born Hampden, Mass., married there to ELIZA E. (CAMPBELL). They moved to Cincinnati, Ohio; and after 3 years to Dayton, Ohio. In 1867, they removed to Adrian, Lenawee Co., Mich. where they remained. Son, Dr. HARRY D. b. Westfield, Hampden Co., Mass., was a Physician in Adrian. Ref: P&BA-Len pg. 487.

HULL, GERHSAM (See Joseph C. Newell)

HULL, GUERNSEY was listed in the 1840 census index of Tecumseh Twp., Lenawee Co., Mich.

HULL, LARANSA (See Asa Morrell)

HULL, MARY ANN (See David Alexander)

HULL, SARAH (See Harvey Hall)

HUME, ALONZO F. born ca. 1812, NY, and wife, ELIZABETH, born ca. 1820, England, were listed in the 1850 census of Medina Twp., Lenawee Co., Mich. with GEORGE, age 8; JANE, age 6; EDWIN, age 4; CHARLES, age 2; AUGUSTUS, age 6/12, all b. Mich., in their household.

HUME, GEORGE born ca. 1827, NY, was listed in the 1850 census of Medina Twp., Lenawee Co., Mich.

HUME, MOSES and wife, SALLY, natives of Berkshire Co., Mass., settled first in Monroe Co., NY. About 1854, they moved to Lenawee Co., Mich. He died in Hudson Village on 15 June 1864, and she died 7 Nov. 1868, while visiting, son, Dr. STEPHEN, in NY, but is buried in Hudson. Son, RODERICK R. (following). There were 6 sons and 2 daughters, names not stated, except those stated above. Ref: P&BA-Len pg. 924-5. Also note ALONZO F. & GEORGE, both preceding.

HUME, RODERICK R., son of MOSES (preceding), married in 1846 in Monroe Co., NY to ANN P. (PAYNE), daughter of Stephen (also see). They moved to Medina Twp., Lenawee Co., Mich. Children: 1. Dr. CHARLES R. b. 21 Oct. 1847 (m. Nettie Ross, Caldwell, KS, children: Ross & Ray); 2. FRANK L. b. 14 Oct. 1849 (m. Mary Fulton, Caldwell, KS, children: James & Francis); 3. ANNA CAROLINE b. 21 July 1852 (d. before 1888); 4. SARAH THANKFUL b. 14 Apr. 1856 (m. Otis B. Fitch, also see); 5. MARY P. b. 27 Jan. 1860 (d. before 1888); 6. WILL E. b. 2 Sept. 1862; 7. ALICE M. b. 8 Jan. 1866. Ref: P&BA-Len pg. 924-5.

HUMPHREY, AARON came to America and settled in Hallowell, Maine, where he married SHOAL (LIBBY). They moved to Beloit, Wisc. where he died at age 92. Known son, REUBEN (following). Ref: P&BA-Len pg. 941-2.

HUMPHREY, ALICE, age 12, born Mich., was listed in the 1850 census of Medina Twp., Lenawee Co., Mich.

HUMPHREY, ALLEN, age 15, born Mich., was listed in the 1850 census of Fairfield Twp., Lenawee Co., Mich. in a Russell household.

HUMPHREY, CHARLES, son of JOHN (following), born 31 Oct. 1834, Canandaigua, NY, moved with his parents to Hillsdale Co., NY. After attending Hillsdale College, he went to Missouri to teach in 1858, and returned to Adrian Twp., Lenawee Co., Mich. in 1861. He married CAROLINE (RIEHL), daughter of Nicholas (also see). Children: 1. JOHN C.; 2. CAROLINE A. Ref: P&BA-Len pg. 470-1.

HUMPHREY, CHAUNCEY born ca. 1816, and wife, HARRIET, born ca. 1819, NY, were listed in the 1850 census of Medina Twp., Lenawee Co., Mich. with JAMES, age 2, b. Mich., in their household.

HUMPHREY, ELIZABETH (See Benjamin F. Tabor)

HUMPHREY, H. G. (See Samuel Nichols)

HUMPHREY, JOHN born 21 Mar. 1798, Hopewell, Hunterdon Co., NJ, went at age 17 to Geneva, Ontario Co., NY; and married in 1825 to JANE (HALL), daughter of Moses (also see). They remained in Canandaigua, NY for 10 years, and then in 1838 moved to Wheaton Twp., Hillsdale Co., Mich. He died there 16 Oct. 1870. Known sons: Gen. WILLIAM (following); CHARLES (preceding). Ref: P&BA-Len pg. 470-1. Note SILAS, following. There was a JOHN listed in the 1800 census of Ontario Co., NY; related to above?

HUMPHREY, PETER born ca. 1795, NY, was listed in the 1840 census index of Woodstock Twp., Lenawee Co., Mich.; and in the 1850 census of Rollin Twp., with (second wife?) ALMIRA, age 29, b. Mass.; and LUKE W., age 26; SAMUEL, age 19, all b. NY; and SARAH J., age 7; ALBERT, age 3; EMMA, age 1, all b. Mich., in the household.

HUMPHREY, R. P. (See William Corbin)

HUMPHREY, REUBEN, son of AARON (preceding), born 1808, probably in Hallowell, ME, married ADAH ANN (BUTLER), daughter of Silas (also see) of Lanesboro, Mass.; and she died there at age 78. Known daughter, MINERVA S. b. 22 Apr. 1829, Lanesboro (m. there to Stephen M. Mead^8, also see). Ref: P&BA-Len pg. 941-2.

HUMPHREY, SAMUEL born ca. 1787, NY, and wife, CYNTHIA, born ca. 1794, VT, were listed in the 1850 census of Medina Twp., Lenawee Co., Mich. with SAMUEL, age 19 (may be he listed again, age 20, in another household in Medina Twp.); ANDREW, age 17; MARY J., age 16; WALLACE, age 13, all b. NY, in their household.

HUMPHREY, SILAS was listed in the 1840 census index of Fayette Twp., Hillsdale Co., Mich. Note JOHN, preceding.

HUMPHREY, WILLIAM Gen., son of JOHN (preceding), born 12 June 1828, Canandaigua, NY, moved to Hillsdale Co., Mich. with his parents. He served in the Civil War in 2d Mich. Cav., becoming a Brigadier General. He married MARY E. (SINCLAIR), daughter of Daniel D. (also see) on 9 Oct. 1867, Adrian, Lenawee Co., Mich. He served as Auditor General of the State of Mich., living in Lansing, where daughter, KATE, was born 31 Dec. 1872; and served as Supt. of Jackson State Prison. They resided in Adrian in 1888. Ref: P&BA-Len pg. 341-2.

HUNT, ABNER born ca. 1793, and wife, LYDIA, born ca. 1795, both in NY, were listed in the 1840 census index of Seneca Twp., Lenawee Co., Mich.; and in the 1850 census of Hudson Twp. with ERASTUS, age 25; ABNER, age 23; MARTHA J., age 17; CLARK, age 18; THOMAS, age 12, all b. NY; and ELIBIUS? (female), age 8 (b. NY?); HENRYETTE, age 6, born Mich., in their household.

HUNT, ABRAHAM V. born ca. 1797, and wife, MARGARET, born ca. 1801, both in NY, were listed in the 1840 census index of Macon Twp., Lenawee Co., Mich.; and in the 1850 census with WILLIAM H., age 13; ABRAHAM D., age 11, both b. Mich., in their household. Next door was JAMES, age 29, born NJ, probably related? Note GARRET V., following.

HUNT, CHARLES W. born ca. 1808, NY, and wife, JULIA M., born ca. 1811, NJ, were probably they listed in the 1840 census index of Adrian Twp., Lenawee Co., Mich.; and in the 1850 census of Madison Twp., Lenawee Co., Mich. with NATHAN, age 12; FRANCES, age 7; ANN M., age 2, all b. Mich.; and Ann Wright, age 18, b. NY, in their household.

HUNT, CORNELIUS born ca. 1794, and wife, MARIA, born ca. 1797, born in NY, were listed in the 1840 census index of Madison Twp., Lenawee Co., Mich.; and in the 1850 census with CATHARINE, age 26; EDWARD W., age 21 (possibly he who went with a group of young men to California in 1852, remained there and was killed in an accident 20 yrs later, see Marvin A. Packard); WALTER C., age 20; CORNELIUS, age 16, all b. NY, in their household.

HUNT, EBENEZER (See David Gander)

HUNT, GARRET V. was listed in the 1840 census index of Macon Twp., Lenawee Co., Mich. Also see ABRAHAM V., preceding.

HUNT, GEORGE (See Norton Baker)

HUNT, GEORGE W., age 20, b. Penn; SUSANNAH, age 22, b. Penn.; and SARAH, age 14, b. Mich., apparently siblings, were listed in the 1850 census of Adrian Twp., Lenawee Co., Mich. in a Burges household. Note JOSEPH, following.

HUNT, HUGH L. born ca. 1821, place not known, and wife, KEZIAH, born ca. 1822, NJ, were listed in the 1850 census of Rollin Twp., Lenawee Co., Mich. with OSCAR, age 5; EUGENE, age 2, both b. NY, in their household.

HUNT, JACOB born ca. 1805, VT, and wife, HARRIET, born ca. 1810, NY, were listed in the 1850 census of Cambridge Twp., Lenawee Co., Mich. with ABRAHAM, age 18, b. NY; and MAR--(female), age 15; ALONSO, age 13; DEXTER, age 9; IRA, age 3, all b. Mich., in their household. Note: In the 1840 census index there was a JACOB in Jackson Co. and another in Macomb Co.

HUNT, JACOB W. born ca. 1815, and wife, MARY, born ca. 1820, both in NY, were listed in the 1850 census of Madison Twp., Lenawee Co., Mich. with EMILY E., age 4; WILLIAM E., age 2, both b. Mich., and Erastus Hawkins (also see) and wife, Polly, in their household.

HUNT, JOHN L., age 8, born Mich., was listed in the 1850 census of Adrian Twp., Lenawee Co., Mich. in the Anson Howell (also see) household.

HUNT, JOHN S., age 25, born Penn., was listed in the 1850 census of Madison Twp., Lenawee Co., Mich.

HUNT, JOSEPH was listed in the 1840 census index of Adrian Twp., Lenawee Co., Mich. Note GEORGE W., preceding.

HUNT, JOSEPH M. born Long Island, NY, married in Seneca Co., NY to ANZOLETTE (LaTOURRETTE), daughter of Abraham (also see). He died in Seneca Co., NY on 21 Mar. 1865. Known daughter, SARAH L. (m. Arthur C. Green, Raisin Twp., Lenawee Co., Mich.). Anzolette married again to George V. Osgood (also see). Ref: P&BA-Len pg. 581-2.

HUNT, WILLIAM C., age 33, born NY, was listed in the 1850 census of Adrian Twp., Lenawee Co., Mich. in a Murray household.

HUNTER, ANDREW J. born ca. 1820, and wife, ABIAL (WIMPLE), born ca. 1822, both in NY, were listed in the 1850 census of Franklin Twp., Lenawee Co., Mich. with LLEWELLYN, age 8; ELIZABETH, age 6; AMY? (or ANNIE who m. Edwin LeRoy Mills, also see), age 4; MILLARD, age 1, all b. Mich., in their household. Ref: P&BA-Len pg. 1060-3. Note: THOMAS, following, was a few doors away.

HUNTER, RACHEL born ca. 1804, NY, was listed in the 1850 census of Franklin Twp., Lenawee Co., Mich. in the household of James and Lydia Alexander (also see).

HUNTER, THOMAS born ca. 1791, Maryland, and wife, ELIZABETH, born ca. 1793, NJ, were listed in the 1840 census index of Franklin Twp., Lenawee Co., Mich.; and in the 1850 census with DAVID, age 25; EMILY, age 18, both b. NY, in their household. Also note ANDREW J., preceding, listed nearby in the census.

HUNTINGTON, ALBERT C., son of JONATHAN (who d. ca. 1842, VT), was born 3 Jan. 1834, Middlebury, VT. He married there to SARAH E. (STEARNS), daughter of Ansel D. (also see), and remained until 1864, when they moved to Illinois. About 1886, they settled in Clinton village, Lenawee Co., Mich. Children: 1. CARRIE; 2. SADIE; 3. LAURA (deceased by 1888). Ref: P&BA-Len pg. 1089.

HUNTINGTON, GORDON (JURDON?), age 33, born Conn., was listed in the 1850 census of Tecumseh Twp., Lenawee Co., Mich. in an Inn.

HUNTINGTON, MARSHALL born ca. 1805, Canada, and wife, ANN, born ca. 1809, NY, were listed in the 1850 census of Adrian Twp., Lenawee Co., Mich. with HIRAM S., age 17, b. Canada; and WILLIAM J., age 8, born Mich., in their household.

HUNTINGTON, NATHANIEL was listed in the 1840 census index of Franklin Twp., Lenawee Co., Mich.

HURLBURT also see HURLBUT

HURLBURT, HENRY was born Albany, NY, and wife, ELMIRA (JENNINGS), was born Norwalk, Conn.; and he went to Norwalk, Ohio in 1818, and the family joined him in 1819. He died there in 1851, and she died in 1885. Five sons and two daughters, only mentioned HENRY L. (following). Ref: P&BA-Len pg. 416.

HURLBURT, HENRY L., son of HENRY (preceding), born 2 Feb. 1818, Norwalk, Conn., moved to Norwalk, Ohio with his parents. He married there to NANCY (CARTER), daughter of William (also see), and she died 6 May 1848. Children: 1. CHARLES L. (m. Julia Fuller, Adrian); 2. MARY E. (d. age 20, Erie Co., O.); 3.

Pioneer Families of Southeastern Michigan

WILLIAM H. (drowned 24 June 1867). Henry L. married again on 21 Oct. 1849 to MATILDA (GURLEY), daughter of Thomas (also see). In Dec. 1867, they moved to Fairfield Twp., Lenawee Co., Mich. Children: 4. FREDERICK T. (m. Ada Vaughn, Fairfield Twp.); 5. GEORGE E. (m. Alice Coah, Toledo, O.). Ref: P&BA-Len pg. 416.

HURLBURT, MARCIA (See John P. Silvers)

HURLBUT also see HURLBURT

HURLBUT, FRANCIS born ca. 1803, NY, and wife, JANE, born ca. 1805, both in NY, were listed in the 1840 census index of Adrian Twp., Lenawee Co., Mich.; and in the 1850 census (as "Hulbert") with Martha Turner, age 21; Sally Turner (or Hurlbut?), age 24, both b. NY; Francis Goddard, age 8; James Goddard, age 6; Seter (Peter?) Goddard, age 4, all b. NY, in their household.

HURLBUT, JOHN born 1799, Palmyra, Wayne Co., NY, married ELIZABETH (POST) born Long Island, and they remained in Palmyra. Nine children of whom 4 sons and 2 daughters lived to maturity, only #3. JOHN (following); and SILAS (who also came to Adrian Twp., Lenawee Co., Mich.) were memtioned.

HURLBUT, JOHN, son of JOHN (preceding), born 2 Mar. 1832, Wayne Co., NY, moved to Yates, Orleans Co., NY. He married there to CYRENE (HUBBARD) born 1837, Orleans Co. They removed to Adrian, Lenawee Co., Mich. in 1857, she died leaving children: 1. WILLIS N. b. Dec. 1864; 2. JOHN T. b. Dec. 1872. John married again to Mrs. CHARLOTTE (SELLECK) KNAPP, widow of Hiram. Ref: P&BA-Len pg. 633.

HURLESS, ISAAC and wife, MARY (SNYDER), of Harrison Co., Ohio, moved to Wood Co., Ohio., where she died in Mar. 1865. Known daughter, L. MARY (m. John Loe, also see). Ref: P&BA-Len pg. 396-7.

HUSTED, CATHARINE (See Squire Wedge)
HUSTED, LYDIA (See William Rusk)

HUTCHENS also see HUTCHINS

HUTCHENS, ANNA born ca. 1794, NY, was probably the "A" listed in the 1840 census index of Hudson Twp., Lenawee Co., Mich.; and was listed head of household in the 1850 census with CAROLINE, age 24; WARREN A., age 18, both b. NY, in her household. Note HORACE & SABIN S., following.

HUTCHENS, AVERY born ca. 1814, and wife, PHEBE (RICE, probably dau. of Joseph^2, also see), born ca. 1814, both in NY, (possibly listed as A. L. in 1840 census index of Medina Twp.) were listed in the 1850 census of Medina Twp., Lenawee Co., Mich. with HARRIET, age 7; ADALINE, age 6; GILBERT, age 3; SELICK, age 1, all b. Mich., and Nelson Rice, probably brother of Phebe, in their household.

HUTCHENS, DELINDA born ca. 1810, VT, with children, GEORGE, age 8; MARY, age 2, both b. Mich., were listed in the 1850 census of Rollin Twp., Lenawee Co., Mich. in the household of Alvin Allen, age 35, b. VT.

HUTCHENS, HORACE born ca. 1819, and wife, ELIZA, born ca. 1823, both in NY, were listed in the 1850 census of Hudson Twp., Lenawee Co., Mich. with MARY E., age 7; SABIN D., age 4; LYMAN L., age 7/12, all b. Mich., in their household. Note ANNA, preceding & SABIN S., following.

HUTCHENS, JOHN was listed in the 1840 census index of Madison Twp., Lenawee Co., Mich. Note JUDITH, following.

HUTCHENS, JUDITH born ca. 1820, NY, and children, MARY, age 6; AMELIA, age 4; ELLA, age 1, all b. Mich., were listed in the 1850 census of Madison Twp., Lenawee Co., Mich. in the household of Joseph & Sarah Merrick (parents of Judith??)

HUTCHENS also see HUTCHINS

HUTCHENS, LEVEN was listed in the 1840 census index of Hudson Twp., Lenawee Co., Mich.

HUTCHENS, PHINEAS C. born ca. 1819, NY, and wife, JERUSHA S., born ca. 1820, Mass., were listed in the 1850 census of Madison Twp., Lenawee Co., Mich. with FRANCES M., age 4; FLORENCE H., age 2; ARTHUR, age 1/12, all b. Mich., in their household.

HUTCHENS, SABIN S. born ca. 1823, and wife, HULDAH, born ca. 1827, both in NY, were listed in the 1850 census of Hudson Twp., Lenawee Co., Mich. with Caroline Smith, age 12, b. Mich., in the household. Note ANNA & HORACE, both preceding.

HUTCHENS, WILLIAM, age 5, b. NY, was listed in the 1850 census of Rome Twp., Lenawee Co., Mich. in a Swartout household.

HUTCHINS also see HUTCHENS
HUTCHINS, CHRISTOPHER (See Edwin A. Baker)
HUTCHINS, CLARISSA (See Philip W. Aldrich)
HUTCHINS, GEORGE born ca. 1804, England, and wife, ISABELLA, born ca. 1822 Ireland, were listed in the 1840 census index of Adrian Twp., Lenawee Co., Mich.; and in the 1850 census with ROBERT M., age 9; ELIZA A., age 6; MARY J., age 4; SAMUEL A., age 1, all b. Mich., in their household.

HUTCHINS, GEORGE P., born ca. 1820, and wife, AMANDA M., born ca. 1822, NY, were listed in the 1850 census of Adrian Twp., Lenawee Co., Mich. with GEORGE H., age 7 (note G. H., following); MARY M., age 3, both b. NY, and MARGARET C., age 1, b. Mich., in their household.

HUTCHINS, G. H. (See David Pearson)

HUTCHINSON, CHESTER and wife, RACHEL (CHILDS) born ca. 1810, NY, moved from Genesee Co., NY to Madison Twp., Lenawee Co., Mich. in 1831. He died in 1844, and she died in 1886, Dover Twp. She was listed head of household in the 1850 census of Madison Twp. with CYNTHIA, age 22; JOHN, age 21; DANIEL, age 22, all b. NY, Abram June, age 34, b. NY; and Huldah Chittenden, age 10, b. Mich., in her household. Known daughter, LUCINDA (m. Jesse H. Warren, also see). MARY, age 24, b. NY, was listed in the census next door to Rachel. Ref: P&BA-Len pg. 264-5.

HUTCHINSON, E. W. (See Wanton Green Smith)
HUTCHINSON, GEORGE was listed in the 1840 census index of Macon Twp., Lenawee Co., Mich.
HUTCHINSON, HARRY was listed in the 1840 census index of Madison Twp., Lenawee Co., Mich. adjacent to CHESTER & JOHN, also see.

HUTCHINSON, JOHN was listed in the 1840 census index of Madison Twp., Lenawee Co., Mich. adjacent to HARRY & CHESTER, preceding.

HUTCHISON, female (See Andrew McClenahan)

HUTE, MARY, of Hesse-Darmstadt, Germany (See Valentine Wenzel[1]).

HYDE, ALBERT born ca. 1821, and wife, CAROLINE, born ca. 1815, both in NY, were listed in the 1850 census of Franklin Twp., Lenawee Co., Mich. with FRANCES, age 4; ELLBRIDGE, age 3, both b. Mich.; and Joseph Kingston, age 9, b. Mich. (stepchild?), in their household. Note MORRIS, following.

HYDE, CHANCELLOR of Litchfield, Conn., and wife, POLLY (BIRDSEY), lived in Brockport (Monroe Co.), NY in 1834. They also lived for a time in Seneca Co., NY (perhaps he listed in the 1800 census index of Tioga Co., NY). They died in NY. Known daughter, ELIZABETH b. 31 Dec. 1815, Seneca Co., NY (m. Daniel D. Sinclair, also see). Ref: P&BA-Len pg. 500-1.

HYDE, MORRIS born ca. 1807, NY, and wife, HARRIET, born ca. 1809, Mass., were listed in the 1840 census index of Franklin Twp., Lenawee Co., Mich.; and in the 1850 census of Tecumseh Twp. with STEPHEN, age 18 (may be he listed again in Raisin Twp., age 19, b. NY, in Lovett household); CAROLINE, age 16; CLARISSA, age 14, all b. NY; and ALBERT, age 11; MYRON, age 9; HENRIETTA, age 4; ALTHIA, age 1, all b. Mich., in their household. Note ALBERT, preceding.

- I -

ICKLER, CONRAD, son of J. CONRAD (following), born 20 Nov. 1860, Riga Twp., Lenawee Co., Mich., married on 28 Apr. 1885 to ELLA (DINGS), daughter of John (also see). No children were listed. Ref: P&BA-Len pg. 266-7.

ICKLER, J. CONRAD, and wife, BARBARA (SMITH), were born in Hesse-Cassel, German, and came to the US, and settled in Vermillion, Ohio in 1851. They moved before 1860 to Riga Twp., Lenawee Co., Mich., and he died 8 Sept. 1881. Children: 1. ADAM; 2. JOHN; 3. DAVID; 4. HENRY; 5. CONRAD (preceding); and a deceased son, name not stated. Ref: P&BA-Len pg. 266-7.

IFFLAND, JUSTUS born 2 Sept. 1822, Germany, served there in the Army. He married in Feb. 1849 to ANNA (LOHR) who was born 16 Feb. 1822. About 1851, they came to America with their first child, and settled first in Lorain Co., Ohio. In 1868, they moved to Riga Twp., Lenawee Co., Mich. He died 3 Nov. 1833, and she was still living there in 1888. Children: 1. CATHERINE C. (m. William Mitchell, Ida, Monroe Co., Mich.); 2. GEORGE (Ogden Twp.); 3. MAGGIE (m. Henry Rohrback, Riga Twp.); 4. JOHN (Riga Twp.); 5. PETER W.; 6. Dr. CHARLES (Ida, Monroe Co., Mich.) Ref: P&BA-Len pg. 588-9.

ILGER, JACOB & wife, CATHERINE, were natives of Penn. who moved to Ashland, Ohio. Known daughter, SUSAN b. Penn. (m. Rev. John Crabbs, also see). Ref: P&BA-Len pg. 1211.

ILSEMAN, AUGUSTUS (See James B. Hood)

IMHOF, ELIZABETH (See Henry Finger[1])

INGALL also see INGALLS

INGALL, CHARLES born 16 Dec. 1774, London, England, and wife, SOPHIA (KITTELBUTER), born 4 Jan. 1779, Deptford, Kent Co., England, married 17 Feb. 1798, and lived in Middlesex Co., England, near London, where they remained. Eleven children, only name stated: #10. GEORGE A. (following). Ref: P&BA-Len pg. 539-40. Note JAMES R., following.

INGALL, GEORGE A., son of CHARLES (preceding), born 22 May 1815, Westratron, Middlesex Co., England, married there on 22 Aug. 1836 to MARY ANN (HOPKINS), daughter of Joseph (also see). They came to New York City in 1836, and remained for 10 years, during which time their first 5 children were born. In 1846, they removed to Medina Twp., Lenawee Co., Mich. She died 13 May 1875. Children: 1. JOSEPH b. 28 Sept. 1837 (m. Julia A. Luck, St. John, Mich.); 2. SOPHIA b. 1 Jan. 1840 (d. 24 Aug. 1840); 3. GEORGE A. b. 10 July 1841 (d. 13 Feb. 1843); 4. MARTHA H. b. 6 June 1843 (d. 24 Mar. 1844); 5. ISABELLA A. b. 11 Feb. 1846 (d. 13 Dec. 1846); 6. MARIA b. 13 May 1850 (d. 13 Mar. 1853); 7. CHARLES B. b. 13 Mar. 1853 (m. Sarah C. Graham on 17 Oct. 1875, children: Samuel, Maude, Edith); 8. FREDERICK J. b. 7 Sept. 1856 (m. Martha E. Diewey 12 Mar. 1879, children: Ralph G., Harlow, Ethel). Ref: P&BA-Len pg. 539-40.

INGALL, JAMES R. (possibly son of CHARLES, preceding) born ca. 1820, England, was listed in the 1850 census of Medina Twp., Lenawee Co., Mich. in a Hopkins household.

INGALLS also see INGALL

INGALLS, ABIGAIL born ca. 1767, NY, was listed in the 1850 census of Fairfield Twp., Lenawee Co., Mich. in the household of William and Olive Tubbs (she b. 1805, NY, possibly daughter of Abigail?)

INGALLS, HATTIE (See George W. Stephenson)

INGALLS, IRA born ca. 1798, NY, and wife, BETSEY, born ca. 1798, Conn., were listed in the 1840 census index of Adrian Twp., Lenawee Co., Mich. adjacent to RANDALL W., (following); and are listed in the 1850 census.

INGALLS, RANDALL W., probably son of IRA (preceding), born ca. 1811, and wife, ASENATH, born ca. 1817, both in NY, were listed in the 1840 census index of Adrian Twp. (under "R. W."); and were listed in the 1850 census with FRANCES, age 13; ELIZABETH, age 9; WILLIAM, age 1, all b. Mich., in their household.

INGERSOLL, A. M. born ca. 1820, and wife, ELLEN, born ca. 1822, both in NY, were listed in the 1850 census of Medina Twp., Lenawee Co., Mich. with ALICE, age 11/12, b. Mich.; and MARY, age 20, b. NY, probably sister, and Cathrine Fisher, age 13; Anna Fisher, age 7, both b. NY, in their household. Note LEWIS, following.

INGERSOLL, AARON[2], son of WILLIAM[1] (who came from England and settled in Mass.), was born in Mass.[3] and married there to LYDIA. Known son, STEPHEN[3] (following). Ref: P&BA-Len pg. 740-3.

INGERSOLL, CAROLINE (See Marshall Watkins)

Pioneer Families of Southeastern Michigan

INGERSOLL, CHARLES born ca. 1811, Conn, and wife, MARY, born ca. 1814, NJ, were listed in the 1840 census index (as "Ingelsol') of Adrian Twp., Lenawee Co., Mich.; and in the 1850 census with HANNAH E., age 12; JAMES M., age 10; SARAH, age 5; MARY F., age 10/12, all b. Mich., in their household.

INGERSOLL, DAVID was listed in the 1840 census index of Tecumseh Twp., Lenawee Co., Mich.

INGERSOLL, ISAAC was listed in the 1840 census index of Allen Twp., Hillsdale Co., Mich. Note STEPHEN[3], following.

INGERSOLL, JONATHAN E.[4], son of STEPHEN[3] (following), born 20 May 1820, Victor, Ontario Co., NY, and removed in 1842 to Ransom Twp., Hillsdale Co., Mich., and his parents followed in 1843. He married 31 Dec. 1844 to MARIA (HAMMOND), daughter of John (also see), and remained in Ramson Twp. till 1856; then moved to Palmyra Twp., Lenawee Co., Mich. Children: 1. EDGAR J. b. 17 May 1846; 2. LYDIA A. b. 30 July 1847 (m. Harrison Crommer); 3. CYRUS B. b. 13 Dec. 1848 (to Jefferson, Hillsdale Co.); 4. PHEBE P. b. 3 Jan. 1850 (m. Christopher C. Crommer); 5. EDNA M. b. 21 Feb. 1852 (m. Charles Miller, Raisin Twp., Lenawee Co.); 6. ESTHER F. b. 1 Jan. 1856 (m. Frederick W. Nichols); 7. JOHN S. b. 13 Oct. 1858; 8. HEBER D. b. 15 Sept. 1863 (Colorado); 9. THOMAS H. b. 22 Dec. 1865. Ref: P&BA-Len pg. 740-3 & portraits of Jonathan & Maria.

INGERSOLL, LEVI was listed in the 1840 census index of Rome Twp., Lenawee Co., Mich. Note MARY, following.

INGERSOLL, LEWIS was listed in the 1840 census index of Medina Twp., Lenawee Co., Mich. Note A. M., preceding.

INGERSOLL, MARY born ca. 1822, Conn., was listed in the 1850 census of Rome Twp., Lenawee Co., Mich. with (sister?) SARAH, age 26, b. Conn., a mentally handicapped person, in her household. Note LEVI, preceding.

INGERSOLL, REUBEN S. born ca. 1811, and wife, OLIVIA L., born ca. 1812, both in Mass., were listed in the 1850 census of Palmyra Twp., Lenawee Co., Mich. with LOUISA, age 17; EXENA?, age 14; RALPH, age 12; LYDIA, age 10 (m. William Bowerman, also see, in 1861), all born Ohio; and SETH C., age 5; CATHARINE, age 1, both b. Mich., in their household. Ref: P&BA-Len pg. 965-6. Note STEPHEN[3] (following).

INGERSOLL, SAMUEL was listed in the 1840 census index of Raisin Twp., Lenawee Co., Mich.

INGERSOLL, STEPHEN[3], son of AARON[2] (preceding), married in Mass. to JOAN (ROOT), daughter of Isaac (also see); and they removed from Lynn, Mass. to Ontario Co., NY. They remained there until 1843, then joined son, #8. JONATHAN E. (preceding), in Ransom, Hillsdale Co., Mich. He died in 1858, and she died 20 Apr. 1853, Hillsdale Co. Nine children (only name above stated). Ref: P&BA-Len pg. 740-3. Note REUBEN S., preceding.

INGOLD, JACOB (See Jacob Kurtz)

INGRAHAM, BENJAMIN born Conn., and wife, HANNAH M. (WHITE), daughter of William of Conn., were a pioneers to Ottawa Co., Ohio. They may have also resided in Trumbull Co., Ohio. Known daughter, MARY M. (m. before 1831 to Jonathan Smith, also see). Ref: P&BA-Len pg. 723-4.

INGURSON, MARTHA (See James Haviland)

IRELAND, DAVID (See Henry Pontius)
IRELAND, DEBORAH (See Hiram Lefferts)
IRELAND, LEWIS (See Henry Pontius)
IRELAND, MARY P. (See Gabriel Todd)

IRONSIDE, ALEXANDER had daughter, HELEN (See Joseph Atkinson Thompson).

ISLEY, THOMAS C., son of WILLIAM (following), born 15 Nov. 1825, Ramsey, Huntingdonshire, England, married there to ANN (DeCAMP), daughter of John (also see). On 11 Oct, 1852, with their first child, they sailed from Liverpool to New York City. They settled first in Cleveland, Ohio, and then about 1860 to Olmstead Twp., Cuyahoga Co., Ohio. In 1866, they moved to Palmyra Twp., Lenawee Co., Mich. where they remained. Eleven children of whom twins died in Cleveland and 2 died in Lenawee Co., names not stated. Surviving children: 1. CHARLES; 2. WILLIAM; 3. GEORGE (m. Cora M. Weter, daughter of Thomas S., also see); 4. BELLE (m. Malvin Bowen); 5. EDWARD (m. Mary A. Coffin, see Eliza Coffin); 6. THOMAS; 7. FRED. Ref: P&BA-Len pg. 746-7.

ISLEY, WILLIAM and wife ?, were natives of England, and she died there. About 1853, William came to the US to join son, Thomas C. He spent his last years with his oldest daughter in Evansville, Ind. Six children lived to maturity. 1. ANN (m. William Bedford, Evansville, Ind.); 2. JOHN (LaGrange Co., Ind.); 3. THOMAS C. (preceding); 4. MARY (remained in England); 5. MARTHA (m. Matthew Wilson, Cleveland, O.); 6. SARAH (m. William Bedford, d. Evansville, Ind.) Ref: P&BA-Len pg. 746-7.

IVES, ATWATER born ca. 1792, NY, and wife, ELISA, born ca. 1808, VT, were listed in the 1840 census index of Tecumseh Twp., Lenawee Co., Mich.; and in the 1850 census with Electa A. McLouth, age 11, b. Mich.; and Loren Bowers, age 21, b. NY, in their household.

IVES, DARIUS C. born ca. 1820, and wife, REBECCA, born ca. 1823, both b. NY, were listed (as "D. C.") in the 1840 census index of Seneca Twp., Lenawee Co., Mich.; and in the 1850 census of Medina Twp. with RANCY? A., age 9; CYRUS J., age 7; DANIEL, age 5, all b. Mich., in their household.

IVES, ELISA, age 59, born Canada, was listed in the 1850 census of Franklin Twp., Lenawee Co., Mich. in household of Franklin and Sarah Brown.

IVES, CYRUS B. born ca. 1817, NY, and wife, NANCY A., born ca. 1817, NJ, were listed in the 1840 census index of Seneca Twp., Lenawee Co., Mich. (as "G. B."?); and in the 1850 census with George Rideler?, age 6, b. NY, in their household.

IVES, SALLY (See Levi Fowler)

IVES, THELUS born ca. 1789, Conn., and wife, AMARILLA, born ca. 1793, VT, were listed in the 1840 census index of Adrian Twp., Lenawee Co., Mich., and in the 1850 census with HENRY, age 34?, born NY, in their household.

IVESON, JAMES born ca. 1817, England, and wife, MARY, born ca. 1818, NY, were listed in the 1850 census of Madison Twp., Lenawee Co., Mich. with EMILY, age 8; NANCY A., age 5, both b. Mich., in their household.

IVESON, JOHN[1] born ca. 1791, and wife, ANNA (BEARDWOOD), born ca. 1791, were born and married in England. They came to the US by 1816 and settled first in Queens Co., Long Island. About 1838, they removed to Woodstock Twp., Lenawee Co., Mich. Known children: 1. THOMAS (following); 2. JOHN (following); 3. BENJAMIN b. ca. 1830, NY; 4. ELIZABETH b. ca. 1832, NY (in household in 1850 census). Ref: P&BA-Len pg. 1084-5.

IVESON, JOHN[2], son of JOHN[1] (preceding), born 1 Dec. 1822, Long Island, came to Lenawee Co., Mich. with his parents, and married 27 Dec. 1845 to MIRANDA (CHANDLER), daughter of David (also see). They settled in Macon Twp., Lenawee Co., Mich., and moved after 1850 to Ridgeway Twp. Children: 1. MARY J. (d. age 13 mos); 2. ANGELINE b. ca. 1846 (m. Oliver Darlington, Wheeler, Gratiot Co., Mich.); 3. WILLIAM b. ca. 1848 (m. Priscilla Tompkins, Blissfield Twp.); 4. LIBBIE (m. Herman Atwell, Ridgeway Twp.). Ref: P&BA-Len pg. 1084-5.

IVESON, THOMAS[2], son of JOHN[1] (preceding), born ca. 1816, NY, and wife, RHODA, born ca. 1823, Ohio. were listed in the 1850 census of Woodstock Twp., Lenawee Co., Mich. with JOEL, age 4; DARIUS, age 2 (probably he m. Harriet M. Pearson, daughter of David, also see, went to Nebraska). ANN, born after 1850, probably is another daughter, and married Fletcher Pearson, son of David, also see.

- J -

JACKSON, ANDREW married MARY A. (ANDREWS) who was born after 1855, daughter of William J. (also see), Ridgeway Twp., Lenawee Co., Mich.; and afterwards went to Wilmington, Will Co., Ill. Children: 1. WILLIAM S.; 2. CHARLES; 3. Infant (name not stated). Ref: P&BA-Len pg. 277-8. Note JACOB, following, with son, ANDREW.

JACKSON, CATHERINE (See Egbert Wheaton)

JACKSON, DARIUS C. born ca. 1813 was listed in the 1840 census index of Adrian Twp., Lenawee Co., Mich.; and in the 1850 census of Woodstock Twp. with wife, MARY, born ca. 1829, both born in NY, ADDISON, age 9; WILLIAM, age 7; HARRIET, age 5; ALBERT, age 3, all b. Mich., in their household.

JACKSON, ISAAC (See Isaac A. Bartlett)

JACKSON, J. J. born ca. 1817, VT, and wife, ALVIRA, born ca. 1816, NY, were listed in the 1850 census of Woodstock Twp., Lenawee Co., Mich. with ALPHA, age 14?; HENRY, age 12; MINERVA, age 10; ARABILA?, age 4; EMILISSA, age 2, all b. Mich., in their household.

JACKSON, JACOB born ca. 1786, Monroe Co., NY, apparently moved to Victor, Ontario Co., NY by 1813. They moved to Madison Twp., Lenawee Co., Mich. ca. 1830/1; and he is listed in the 1840 census index of Madison Twp., and in the 1850 census, age 64. Known sons: WILLIAM W. (following); ANDREW b. ca. 1833, NY (in household in 1850). Ref: P&BA-Len pg. 788-9. Also note MARY, wife of Harvey Hart (also see), born before 1800, Monroe Co., NY and died Victor, Ontario Co., NY.

JACKSON, JAMES born ca. 1816, and wife, CATHERINE, born ca. 1818, both in NY, were listed in the 1850 census of Macon Twp., Lenawee Co., Mich. with DELIA, age 10; ALFRED, age 8; ELBRIDGE, age 6; CATHERINE, age 4; ELIZABETH, age 1, all b. Mich., in their household. Note LYDIA, following.

JACKSON, JANE ADELIA (See Willis Thompson Lawrence)

JACKSON, JESSE born ca. 1816, NY, and wife, BRIDGET, born ca. 1818, Ireland, were listed in the 1850 census of Dover Twp., Lenawee Co., Mich. with James Abbott, age 24, b. NY, in their household.

JACKSON, LYDIA, age 59, born NY, was listed in the 1850 census of Macon Twp., Lenawee Co., Mich. in the household of Ira & Elisa (age 39, b. NY) Steward, next door to JAMES, preceding.

JACKSON, MARY (See Abner Hall; Col. Samuel McMath; & Harvey Hart).

JACKSON, OBID was listed in the 1840 census index of Macon Twp., Lenawee Co., Mich.

JACKSON, PETER born ca. 1805, NJ, and wife, ELIZA, born ca. 1817, NY, were listed in the 1850 census of Seneca Twp., Lenawee Co., Mich. with DAVID M., age 12; MARILLA, age 10; GEORGE W., age 6, all b. NY; DELPHIA, age 2, born Mich., in their household. Note: May be he listed in the 1840 census index of Wheaton Twp., Hillsdale Co., Mich., adjacent to an ANSON.

JACKSON, OBID was listed in the 1840 census index of Macon Twp., Lenawee Co., Mich. Note SAMUEL & SETH, following.

JACKSON, ROB R. was listed in the 1840 census index of Clinton Twp., Lenawee Co., Mich.

JACKSON, SAMUEL was listed in the 1840 census index of Macon Twp., Lenawee Co., Mich. Note OBID & SETH.

JACKSON, SETH was listed in the 1840 census index of Macon Twp., Lenawee Co., Mich. Note OBID & SAMUEL.

JACKSON, VOLNEY born ca. 1800, and wife, HANNAH, born ca. 1812, both in NY, were listed in the 1850 census of Hudson Twp., Lenawee Co., Mich. with MARIAH A., age 17; ALBERT T., age 15; HARRISON W., age 13; SARAH E., age 10, all b. NY; MARY, age 2, b. Mich., in their household.

JACKSON, WALLACE born ca. 1815 was listed in the 1850 census of Woodstock Twp., Lenawee Co., Mich. with AMANDA, age 20, b. NY (wife?); and JACOB, age 12; RUTH, age 11; DRUSILLA, age 9; ALVIRA, age 5; WILLIAM, age 10/12, all b. Mich.; and WILLIAM, age 25 (brother?), b. NY, in his household.

JACKSON, WALTER W. born ca. 1810, and wife, CATHARINE P., born ca. 1816, both in NY, were listed in the 1850 census of Seneca Twp., Lenawee Co., Mich. with JOHN, age 12, b. Mich., in their household. Note: May have been he listed in the 1840 census index of Green Oak Twp., Livingston Co., Mich.

JACKSON, WARREN, age 22, born NY, was listed in the 1850 census of Adrian Twp., Lenawee Co., Mich. in a Boarding House.

JACKSON, WILLIAM born ca. 1792, NJ, may be he listed in the 1840 census index of Raisin Twp., Lenawee Co., Mich.; and in the 1850 census of Madison Twp., in the "Poor House," mentally incompetent.

Pioneer Families of Southeastern Michigan

JACKSON, WILLIAM W., son of JACOB (preceding), born 3 Oct. 1813, Victor, Ontario Co., NY, moved with his father to Madison Twp., Lenawee Co., Mich.; and by 1840 moved to Adams Twp., Hillsdale Co., Mich. He married AMANDA (GILSON), daughter of Simon (also see). They later went to Monroe Co., Wisc. where he was founder of the town of Jacksonville. Known daughter, MARY S. (m. Llewellyn Hart, also see, Addison, Mich., Nov. 1882.) Ref: P&BA-Len pg. 788-9.

JACOB, JOHN and wife, MARTHA (LAPP), remained in Germany, but known sons: PETER (following); JOHN (Ogden Twp., Lenawee Co., Mich.); & CHRISTOPHER (Ogden Twp., Lenawee Co., Mich.), all came to the US. Ref: P&BA-Len pg. 744-5.

JACOB, PETER, son of JOHN (preceding), born 4 Jan. 1837, Germany, came to the US in 1855 to join a brother. He lived first in Quebec, Canada, before moving to Erie Co., Ohio. He married in Dec. 1860 to MARGARET (REAS) of Erie Co.; and they removed to Ogden Twp., Lenawee Co., Mich. Seven children (2 died infancy, names not stated): 1. MARY A.; 2. MARGARET A.; 3. LOUISA F.; 4. GEORGE LEWIS; 5. JOHN BENJAMIN. Ref: P&BA-Len pg. 744-5.

JACOBS, EDWARD (See Valentine Wenzel^2)
JACOBS, HENRY (See Aaron J. Palmer)
JACOBS, IRA born ca. 1801, Mass., and wife, ALMIRA, born ca. 1803, NY, were listed in the 1850 census of Palmyra Twp., Lenawee Co., Mich. with GEORGE, age 20; PHILO, age 16; EMELINE, age 13, all b. NY; and CHARLES H., age 10; FRANCIS M., age 7; EUGENE A., age 5, all b. Ohio; and CAROLINE, age 2, b. Mich., as well as Elizabeth Butler, age 24, b. NY, with children, David, age 3, b. Mich., & Letta, age 2, b. Ohio, in their household.
JACOBS, JOHN (See Edwin J. Wilcox)

JAGER, CATHERINE (See Joseph Patterson)

JAMES, ALONZO and wife, MINERVA (TITUS), of Orleans Co., NY, had children: 1. FIDELIA (m. John L. Hoyt, Hudson Twp., Lenawee Co., Mich.); 2. NORMAN B. (m/1 Mary Moshire; m/2 May Titus, Hudson Twp.); 3. SARAH E. (m. Stephen Connor; she d. Aug. 1885, Big Rapids, Mich.); 4. WILLIAM D. (following); 5. OSCAR S. (m. Dora Baker, Dakota Terr.). Ref: P&BA-Len pg. 1010.

JAMES, ASA of NY had known daughter, HALLIE (m. Albert H. Bassett, son of Nathan H., also see).

JAMES, SAMUEL born ca. 1791, and wife ANNA, born ca. 1797, both born England, were listed in the 1850 census of Tecumseh Twp., Lenawee Co., Mich. with JOSEPH, age 22; SARAH, age 20; ALFRED, age 19; CAROLINE, age 18; MARY, age 17, all b. England, in their household.

JAMES, WILLIAM D., son of ALONZO (preceding), born 2 Feb. 1836, NY, came to Hudson Twp., Lenawee Co., Mich. in 1853. He married on 3 Apr. 1859 to HARRIET D. (PERKINS), daughter of Stephen (also see). They settled in Medina Twp., Lenawee Co., Mich. Children: 1. FREDERICK P. (DDS in Sleepy Eye, Minn.); 2. MINERVA L. (m. Charles Sutton, Medina Twp.); 3. WILLIAM D.; 4. FRANK S. Ref: P&BA-Len pg. 1010.

JEFFERY, JAMES, son of HUNT, born 27 Feb. 1777, Sandgate, Kent, England, married in 1796 to REBECCA (SANDFORD), daughter of Mark (also see) of Folkstone, England. James died 7 Dec. 1839, and she died in 1843. Known son, JAMES K. (following). Ref: P&BA-Len pg. 1004-6 & 1157-8.

JEFFERY, JAMES K., son of JAMES (preceding), born 28 Jan. 1803, Sandgate, Kent, England, married on 8 Mar. 1826 to HARRIET (MARSH), daughter of Edward (also see). After the birth of 3 children, they sailed on 8 May 1830 for New York City. In the Spring of 1831, they moved to Oneida Co., NY, and in 1836 moved to Rome Twp., Lenawee Co., Mich. Children: 1. HARRIET H. b. ca. 1827 (m. Cornelius Knapp, also see); 2. MARGARET b. ca. 1828 (m. Daniel O'Dell, Stockton, CA); 3. REBECCA; 4. ELIZA M. b. ca. 1830 (m. William Willitts, son of John, also see); 5. NANCY b. ca. 1832, NY (m. Jared Rider, Ingham Co., Mich.); 6. ELEANOR b. ca. 1834 (m. John Hart; Stockton, CA); 7. EDWARD J. b. ca. 1835 (to Portland, OR); 8. SUSANNA b. ca. 1841 (m. George W. Darling, Lenawee Co.). Ref: P&BA-Len pg. 1004-6 & 1157-8.

JEFFERY, THOMAS born ca. 1814, England, and wife, PRISCILLA, born ca. 1822, NY, were listed in the 1850 census of Adrian Twp., Lenawee Co., Mich.

JEFFORDS, DAVID was listed in the 1840 census index of Palmyra Twp., Lenawee Co., Mich. There was also a David "Jefferds" in Franklin Twp., Lenawee Co. in 1840 census index.

JEFFORDS, SOLOMON married in Henrietta, NY to PHOEBE (HOUGHTALING), daughter of Peter. They moved from Monroe Co., NY to Washtenaw Co., Mich. She died 8 Apr. 1873, Leslie, Ingham Co., Mich., but is buried with her son in Dexter, Washtenaw Co., Mich. Children: 1. Col. HARRISON H. b. 21 Aug. 1834 (d. 3 July 1863, Civil War). 2. CARRIE C. (m. F. Werner); 3. HELEN M. (m. H. C. Cooper, Adrian, Lenawee Co., Mich.); 4. ETTA (m. Edwin M. Lawn; Chicago, Ill.); 5. ROSE N. (m. J. F. Steck, Kingman, KS); 6. IDA M. (d. infancy). Ref: P&BA-Len pg. 263-4.

JENKINS, EDWARD of Ontario, Canada, died there in 1870, age 68; and his wife, ELIZA (EMBURY), a descendant of Philip Embury, died there 5 Feb. 1852. Nine children, 1 died infancy, only named mentioned: JOHN F. (following). Ref: P&BA-Len pg. 404-5.

JENKINS, JOHN F. Dr., son of EDWARD (preceding), born 10 Sept. 1836, Napanee, Lennox, Ontario, Canada, married there to SUSAN (McQUEEN), daughter of Col. James (who served in WAr of 1812, Canada, and died age 85). They settled ca. 1870 in Tecumseh, Lenawee Co., Mich. after a brief stay in Detroit. Children: 1. EDA BELL b. May 1878 (d. age 13); 2. AUGUSTA (d. 10 Aug. 1875, age 2); 3. MABEL; 4. MILTON; 5. FLORENCE. Ref: P&BA-Len pg. 404-5.

JENKINS, KATIE A. (See Stephen C. Lombard)
JENKINS, SARAH (See Uriyon Mackey)
JENKINS, WILLIAM (See John Cheney^2)

JENNINGS, ABIGAIL of Flint, Mich. (See Orrin Safford, Sr.)
JENNINGS, CHANDLER? born ca. 1826, and wife, MARGARET, born ca. 1828, both in NY, were listed in the 1850 census of Woodstock Twp., Lenawee Co.,

Mich. with MARY, age 4; MEHITABLE, age 2, both b. Mich., in their household.

JENNINGS, DANIEL born Otsego Co., NY, and wife, POLLY (CLARK), born Colerain, Franklin Co., Mass., settled first in Cortland Co., NY. They moved to Wayne Co., NY where she died 25 July 1861; and he died 6 Oct. 1868. Twelve children, only name stated: #2. MARY A. b. 25 Jan. 1814 (m. Calvin Bradish, also see, Madison Twp., Lenawee Co., Mich.). Ref: P&BA-Len pg. 395.

JENNINGS, ELMIRA (See Henry Hurlburt)

JENNINGS, FRANKLIN was listed in the 1840 census index of Franklin Twp., Lenawee Co., Mich.

JENNINGS, HENRY born 1777, and wife, MERIBAH (DEXTER), born 16 Aug. 1770, both in New Bedford, Mass., moved before 1800 to Saratoga Co., NY; and later to what is now Penfield, Monroe Co., NY. He died there, age 39, and she died, age 93. Seven children, only name stated: #6. LEVI (following). Ref: P&BA-Len pg. 533-4.

JENNINGS, HIRAM born ca. 1802, and wife, MARY A., born ca. 1818, both in NY, were listed in the 1850 census of Ogden Twp., Lenawee Co., Mich. with GEORGE P., age 12; MARY, age 8, both b. NY, in their household.

JENNINGS, JOHN born ca. 1818, and wife, MARY, born ca. 1816, both in Ireland, were listed in the 1850 census of Hudson Twp., Lenawee Co., Mich. with MICHAEL, age 8; MARTIN, age 6; MARY J., age 4, all b. Mich., in their household.

JENNINGS, JOSEPH W. born ca. 1811 was listed in the 1840 census index of Woodstock Twp., Lenawee Co., Mich.; and in the 1850 census with HARRIET, age 16; ELISA, age 13?; SALOMA, age 10, all b. Mich., in his household.

JENNINGS, LEVI, son of HENRY (preceding), born 2 apr. 1808, Milton, Saratoga Co., NY, married 22 Jan. 1829 to ANN (CROUT) born 25 Feb. 1811, Ontario Co., NY (census said b. NJ?). They came to Rollin Twp., Lenawee Co., Mich. in 1834. Children: 1. PHEBE ANN b. 17 Aug. 1831 (m. Charles Langdon, Rollin Twp.); 2. CLARISSA b. 25 Apr. 1835 (m. Orson Crandall, also see); 3. MARY ELIZABETH b. 16 Aug. 1837 (m. George Peters, she d. 3 Sept. 1880); 4. HENRY L. b. 14 Aug. 1839 (m. Jane Whitney, Litchfield, Mich.); 5. JULIA b. 1 Sept. 1842 (m. Arnold Bennett, Bushnell, Mich.); 6. SARAH L. b. 11 Oct. 1845 (m. Joseph Marks, Rollin Twp.); 7. HARRIET DEFLORA b. 19 Dec. 1849 (m. David Wooster, Wayne Co., Mich.). Ann died 17 Apr. 1852, and Levi married again on 22 Mar. 1859 to Mrs. CATHERINE ANN (DITMARS) BELCHER, daughter of William B., and widow of Andrew (see both). Children: 8. IDA JANE (m. William M. Clark, Rollin Twp.); 9. FRANK I. (m. Bertha Wood). Ref: P&BA-Len pg. 533-4.

JENNINGS, ZERA born Mass. and wife, POLLY (WHALEY), born NY, both died in NY. Known daughter, HANNAH b. 6 Aug. 1821, NY (m. Edward P. Allis, Hudson Twp., Lenawee Co., Mich., also see). Ref: P&BA-Len pg. 329-30. Note: In the 1850 census of Rome Twp., Lenawee Co., Mich., Hannah was listed in the household of William and Marsha Rider.

JERRELLS, DAVID, son of EBENEZER, born 18 July 1806, Trumbull, Fairfield Co., Conn., moved with parents to Perinton, Monroe Co., NY. In 1831, he moved to Michigan, and eventually to Adrian, Lenawee Co., Mich. and lived with brother-in-law, Samuel Keyes. He went to NY for a brief time, but returned in 1832. He married in Rome Twp., Lenawee Co., Mich. to ALICE (LUTHER), daughter of William (also see), the first marriage in the township. Children: 1. MARY E. b. ca. 1836; 2. PHEBE J. b. ca. 1838; 3. FRANKLIN L. b. ca. 1841 (m. Nancy Hood, dau. of John, also see); 4. HARVEY E.; 5. GEORGE E.; 6. ALICE A. (m. Bowman E. Seger, also see); 7. CHARLES H. Ref: P&BA-Len pg. 983-4.

JERRELLS, EBENEZER was a native of Trumbull, Fairfield Co., Conn., and he married there in 1804 to NANCY (ROWELL) born 1786. They moved to Perinton, Monroe Co., NY about 1814. He died there in 1821, and she died in 1865. Eight children (names not all stated), those known: DAVID (preceding); LUCINDA b. 4 Aug. 1818, Monroe Co., NY (m/1 Almarin K. Armstrong; m/2 Theodorick Luther, see both); Daughter (m. Samuel Keyes, Adrian Twp.). Ref: P&BA-Len pg. 587-8.

JEWELL, HENRY (See Albern Raymond)

JEWELL, ISAAC born ca. 1795, and wife, ABIGAIL, born ca. 1802, both in New Hampshire, were listed in the 1850 census of Medina Twp., Lenawee Co., Mich. with ANDREW, age 19; MARY, age 17; ELBRIDGE, age 16; ALBERT, age 8, all b. NH, in their household.

JEWELL, JOHN M. and wife, CELESTA (CRAWFORD), moved from Onondaga Co., NY to Ohio ca. 1848. She died there at age 45; and he moved to Michigan during the Civil War, and died at age 69. Known daughter, LOUISA E. b. 10 Feb. 1837, Onondaga Co., NY (m. Henry W. Burke, also see, Hillsdale Co., Mich.). Ref: P&BA-Len pg. 813-4.

JEWELL, JULIA (See Dr. S. C. Ayers)

JEWELL, STEPHEN born ca. 1773, and wife, JANE, born ca. 1772, both in NY, were listed in the 1850 census of Cambridge Twp., Lenawee Co., Mich. in the household of John B. Drake and wife, Clarissa (age 36, b. NY), possibly daughter of Stephen? Note: The 1800 census index listed a STEPHEN in Saratoga Co., NY.

JEWETT, DANIEL born ca. 1808, New Hampshire, and wife, ELIZABETH, born ca. 1820, NY, were listed in the 1850 census of Madison Twp., Lenawee Co., Mich. with ADELINE, age 9; MALVINA, age 5, both b. Mich., in their household.

JEWETT, ERI, son of JONATHAN (who was a pioneer to NY, and died at age 82 or 90? on 11 June 1872, Sangerfield, NY), married HARRIET (WINCHELL), daughter of William F. (also see) in Sangerfield, Oneida Co., NY; and moved to Austinburg, Ohio about 1855, and 1868 to Constantine, St. Joseph Co., Mich. In 1871, he removed to Vistula, Ind., where he later died. Known son, Dr. WILLIAM E. (following). Ref: P&BA-Len pg. 800-1 & 1079-80.

JEWETT, H. S. Dr. (See Samuel Perkins)

JEWETT, WILLIAM E. Dr., son of ERI (preceding), born 8 Dec. 1842, Sangerfield, Oneida Co., NY, moved to Ohio with his parents. He served in Co. K., 87th Ohio Inf. during the Civil War. After the war, he became a Doctor, and set up practice in Constantine, Mich. He married in May 1868 to CLARA A. (ROOT), daughter of Henry E. (also see) of Constantine. About 1872, they moved to Adrian, Lenawee Co., Mich. Children: 1.

Pioneer Families of Southeastern Michigan

HENRY R. b. 24 Oct. 1870; 2. WILLIAM E. b. 11 June 1872. Ref: P&BA-Len pg. 800-1 & 1079-80.

JOHNSON, AARON born ca. 1812, and wife, ELSA, born ca. 1817, both in NY, were listed in the 1850 census of Dover Twp., Lenawee Co., Mich. with LORINDA, age 10, born Mich., in their household. Note ESTHER, following. It is probably he listed as "Jonson" in the 1840 census index of Dover Twp., adjacent to SOSEP (JOSEPH?).

JOHNSON, ABIGAIL (See Jesse Disbrow)

JOHNSON, ALEXANDER born ca. 1807, Scotland, was listed in the 1850 census of Franklin Twp., Lenawee Co., Mich. with MARY, age 30, born Scotland, and Patrick Hendershott (also see) with wife, Margaret, age 22, b. Scotland (possibly daughter?), in the household.

JOHNSON, ALFRED (See John G. Mason)

JOHNSON, ANNA Mrs. born ca. 1795, NY, was listed in the 1850 census of Dover Twp., Lenawee Co., Mich. in the household of LUKE, age 35, b. NY; and also in the household were FANNY, age 20; JACOB C., age 25; MELISSA, age 20, all b. NY; and Emily J. Hayden, age 8, b. Mich. Also note AARON, preceding, & ESTHER, JOSEPH, LEANDER, PARRIS, all following.

JOHNSON, BARTHOLMEW born ca. 1782, Rhode Island, and wife, SOPHIA, born ca. 1783, New Hampshire, were listed in the 1840 census index of Clinton Twp., Lenawee Co., Mich.; and in the 1850 census of Tecumseh Twp. with DEWIT C., age 25, b. NY, in their household.

JOHNSON, BENJAMIN, age 18, b. NY, was listed in the 1850 census of Tecumseh Twp., Lenawee Co., Mich. in the household of Milton & Isabella Smith.

JOHNSON, C. B. Mrs. was daughter of Chester Buck (also see). Note CHESTER B., following?

JOHNSON, C. W. (See Edward F. Muir)

JOHNSON, CHESTER B., age 24, born NY, was listed in the 1850 census of Madison Twp., Lenawee Co., Mich. in the household of Joseph R. Bennett.

JOHNSON, CYNTHIA, age 18, born NY, was listed in the 1850 census of Rome Twp., Lenawee Co., Mich. in the household of Joseph & Amy Rockwood.

JOHNSON, DANIEL born 27 Mar. 1770, Waterford, New London, Conn., married RUTH (GRIFFING) born 17 Oct. 1766, Lynn, Conn. They moved to Berlin, Erie Co., Ohio, and he died there 19 Apr. 1836, and she died 21 Feb. 1839. Known son, JOHN (following). Ref: P&BA-Len pg. 585-7.

JOHNSON, DANIEL L. born ca. 1796, and wife, ELIZABETH, born ca. 1797, both in NY, were listed in the 1850 census of Adrian Twp., Lenawee Co., Mich. with Johnson Havens, age 1, b. Mich., possibly a grandson, in their household.

JOHNSON, DAVID M. born Monroe Co., NY, and wife, JANE M. (WHEELER) born Monroe Co., Mich., lived first in Monroe Co., Mich., but moved to Fairfield Twp., Lenawee Co., Mich. Later they moved to Branch Co., Mich. Children: 1. HELEN M. b. 28 Feb. 1848, Monroe Co., Mich. (m. Samuel Bryant, also see); 2. WILLIS J. (d. Apr. 1879, age 27, Reading, Hillsdale Co., Mich.); 3 WARREN G. (Nebraska); 4. FLORA A. (m. Leslie Squires, Reading, Hillsdale Co., Mich.); 5. MERTIE B. (m. Nelson Buchanan, Reading, Mich.); 6. CURTIS P. (m. Orpha Rugg); 7. STELLA. Ref: P&BA-Len pg. 766-7.

JOHNSON, E. H. was listed in the 1840 census index of Medina Twp., Lenawee Co., Mich.

JOHNSON, ELI and wife, SARAH (PARK), of Livingston Co., NY, and possibly Cleveland, Ohio had known daughter, MARY A. (m. William Bresie, also see, on 20 Mar. 1839).

JOHNSON, ELIJAH was listed in the 1840 census index of Madison Twp., Lenawee Co., Mich.

JOHNSON, ELLEN (See Andrew Belcher)

JOHNSON, ELISHA, age 30, born NY, was listed in the 1850 census of Rollin Twp., Lenawee Co., Mich.

JOHNSON, ESTHER Mrs. born ca. 1792, NY, was listed in the 1850 census of Dover Twp., Lenawee Co., Mich. in the household of WILLIAM, age 34, b. NY, with REBECCA, age 34; ISAAC, age 24, both b. NY, in the household. Also note AARON; JOSEPH, LEANDER & PARRIS.

JOHNSON, FITCH was listed in the 1840 census index of Raisin Twp., Lenawee Co., Mich.

JOHNSON, HIRAM born NY, listed in the 1840 census index of Woodstock Twp., Lenawee Co., Mich., married Mrs. MARY (OSBORN) TURRELL, widow of Stephen (also see). They were listed in the 1850 census of Woodstock Twp., but ages appear to be incorrect. They are shown as both age 24, born NY; however in their household, all b. Mich., were SARAH, age 17; NOBLE, age 12; and known daughter, AUGUSTA D. b. ca. 1846 (m. Prof. George Barnes, Howell, Livingston Co., Mich.). Note: Mary was married first to George W. Clark (also see), and second to Stephen Turrell. Hiram Johnson was her third husband. Ref: P&BA-Len pg. 1132-3.

JOHNSON, HOLLIS born ca. 1801, NY, and wife, HANNAH, born ca. 1808, Conn., were listed in the 1840 census index of Dover Twp., Lenawee Co., Mich.; and in the 1850 census with HOLLIS, age 17; MASON D., age 15; CORDELIA, age 13; FLORILLA, age 9; FERDINAND, age 6, all b. Mich., in their household.

JOHNSON, JAMES K. born ca. 1820, NJ, and wife, ELIZA A., born ca. 1819, NY, were listed in the 1850 census of Madison Twp., Lenawee Co., Mich. with no family. There was a JAMES in the 1840 census index of Macon Twp.

JOHNSON, JANE, age 21, born NY, was listed in the 1850 census of Tecumseh Twp., Lenawee Co., Mich. in an Inn.

JOHNSON, JEDEDIAH F. was listed in the 1840 census index of Woodstock Twp., Lenawee Co., Mich.

JOHNSON, JOEL J. born ca. 1816, and wife, MARTHA, born ca. 1827, both in NY, were listed in the 1850 census of Fairfield Twp., Lenawee Co., Mich. with WARREN S., age 1, b. Mich., in their household.

JOHNSON, JOHN, son of DANIEL (preceding), born 1798, Waterford, Conn., married ABIGAIL (SKINNER) born 15 Jan. 1802, Windsor, Hartford Co., Conn. In 1826, after the birth of 2 children, they moved to Berlin, Erie Co., Ohio. About 1835, they removed to Rome Twp., Lenawee Co., Mich.; and in 1862 to Lansing, Mich. He died 9 Mar. 1865 while visiting in Hudson, Mich. She died 2 Jan. 1867 in Clayton, Mich. Children: 1. JASPER G. b. ca. 1825, Conn. (North Adams, Hillsdale Co., Mich.); 2. RUTH b. ca. 1829, Ohio (m. Caleb W. Stephens, Rome Twp., Lenawee Co.); 3. ANN (m. David T. Rowley, Hudson, Lenawee Co.); 4. MABEL b. ca. 1831, Ohio (m. Aaron Bennett, Clayton, Mich.); 5. MELISSA b. ca. 1834, Ohio (m. Emmons H. Marks,

Quincy, Branch Co., Mich.); 6. MARY b. ca. 1837, Mich. (d. age 24, Rome Twp.); 7. JOHN (following); 8. ELVIRA b. ca. 1844 (m. Aaron Jones; she d. Dec. 1884, Leslie, Mich.). Ref: P&BA-Len pg. 585-7.

JOHNSON, JOHN born ca. 1804, and wife, CHARLOTTE, born ca. 1819, both in NY, were listed in the 1850 census of Macon Twp., Lenawee Co., Mich. with ANDREW, age 7; GEORGE, age 5, both b. NY; and PETER, age 3; MARGARET, age 1, both b. Mich., in their household.

JOHNSON, JOHN, son of JOHN (of Rome Twp., preceding), born 1 Jan. 1842, Rome Twp., married on 21 Jan. 1868 in Hudson, Mich. to IDA A (BREWER) born in Attica, Wyoming Co., NY. She died in Tekonsha, Mich. on 5 Jan. 1885. They had lived variously in Fulton Co., Ohio; Detroit, Mich.; and Tekonsha. He married again on 18 Jan. 1887 in Burbank, Wayne Co., Ohio to ALICE V. (HEMLER), daughter of James C. (also see). They settled in Clayton, Lenawee Co., Mich. Son, JOHN C. b. 26 Oct. 1887. Ref: P&BA-Len pg. 585-7.

JOHNSON, JOHN (See Orville Woodworth)

JOHNSON, JOHN G.?, age 23, born England, was listed in the 1850 census of Adrian Twp., Lenawee Co., Mich. in the Webb household.

JOHNSON, JOHN S., son of ZEPHANIAH (following), born ca. 1834, NY, came to Medina Twp., Lenawee Co., Mich. with his parents. He married JANE ANN (LOCKMAN), daughter of Capt. James in Medina Twp., but they married in Tompkinsville, NY, and settled in Medina Twp., Lenawee Co. She died 8 June 1861. Daughter, 1. CARRIE b. 22 May 1857 (d. 2 May 1861). John S. married again to EMMA JANE (BRADISH), daughter of William (also see) of Medina Twp. Children: 2. McLELLAND (d. infancy); 3. R. M. (d. age 2-1/2); 4. ALBINA; 5. NELLIE; 6. LENA; 7. LETTIE. Ref: P&BA-Len pg. 1008-9.

JOHNSON, JOSEPH was listed in the 1840 census index of Dover Twp., Lenawee Co., Mich. written as "SOSEP JONSON," adjacent to AARON, preceding. Also see ESTHER.

JOHNSON, JOSEPH M. born ca. 1820, England, and wife, HARRIET, born ca. 1823, NY, were listed in the 1850 census of Hudson Twp., Lenawee Co., Mich. with STEPHEN S., age 4, b. Mich., in their household (2 doors from WILLIAM H., also see).

JOHNSON, KATIE (HUBBARD) Mrs. was the wife of _?_ (name not stated) who was born in Conn. and had moved to Herkimer Co., NY. In 1817, they moved to Huron Co., Ohio and lived in Bronson Twp., Newark Twp., and finally Sherman Twp., where they died. Known son, WILLIAM J. (following). Ref: P&BA-Len pg. 803-4.

JOHNSON, LAVINIA, age 79, born Mass., was listed in the 1850 census of Rome Twp., Lenawee Co., Mich. in the household of John M. Coe and wife, Maria (age 44, b. Mass., possibly daughter of Lavinia?).

JOHNSON, LEANDER, age 23, born NY, was listed in the 1850 census of Dover Twp., Lenawee Co., Mich. in the Cleveland household. Note ESTHER, preceding.

JOHNSON, LEVI (See William Paul)

JOHNSON, LUCETTA born in Ohio, daughter of a family from Conn., were pioneer settlers near Cleveland. She married Francis Brown (also see) before 1807 near Streetsboro, Ohio. Ref: P&BA-Len pg. 989-90.

JOHNSON, LUCINDA married in Vermont to Richard Kilbury[2] (also see).

JOHNSON, MARY (See John Scott)

JOHNSON, MARY born Co. Fermanagh, Ireland married Philip Wareham[2] (also see) before 1807, Cumberland Co., Penn. Ref: P&BA-Len pg. 939-40.

JOHNSON, MELINDA, age 20, born NY, was listed in the 1850 census of Medina Twp., Lenawee Co., Mich. in a Gardner household.

JOHNSON, MIMA?, age 20, born NY, was listed in the 1850 census of Medina Twp., Lenawee Co., Mich. in a Scott household.

JOHNSON, NICHOLAS and wife, LUCY (MOORE), had known daughter, EMELINE (m. Aziah Ash, also see). He died in Allegany Co., NY and she died in Steuben Co., NY.

JOHNSON, P. was listed in the 1840 census index of Adrian Twp., Lenawee Co., Mich.

JOHNSON, PARRIS? born ca. 1822, and wife, SARAH, born ca. 1829, both in NY, were listed in the 1850 census of Dover Twp., Lenawee Co., Mich. with ELLEN, age 2, b. Mich., in their household (a few doors from ESTHER, preceding).

JOHNSON, ROBERT, age 14, born NY, was listed in the 1850 census of Tecumseh Twp., Lenawee Co., Mich. in an Inn.

JOHNSON, SANLANDER was listed in the 1840 census index of Medina Twp., Lenawee Co., Mich.

JOHNSON, SARDIS born ca. 1811, and wife, POLLY, born ca. 1820, both in NY, were listed in the 1850 census of Madison Twp., Lenawee Co., Mich. with LUTHER, age 10; LEVI, age 9; MARY J., age 6; LUCIUS, age 4; ALFRED, age 1, all b. Mich., in their household.

JOHNSON, SUSAN born Co. Fermanagh, Ireland (See Peter Hanlon).

JOHNSON, THEODORE was listed in the 1840 census index of Medina Twp., Lenawee Co., Mich.

JOHNSON, THOMAS born ca. 1799, Ireland, came to the US at age 21. He married NANCY (DONELSON), born ca. 1799, Ireland; and about 1835 they settled in Rome Twp., Lenawee Co., Mich. He died 26 Feb. 1883, and she died 5 June 1885. Five children (those following in 1850 census of Rome Twp.): JOHN, age 27, b. VT; THOMAS JR., age 24, b. NY; ANN E b. 24 Aug. 1828, Genesee Co., NY (m. Manson Carpenter, also see). Ref: P&BA-Len pg. 612-3.

JOHNSON, WILL (See John W. Ormsby)

JOHNSON, WILLIAM born ca. 1800, Lancaster, England, and he married in Seneca Falls, Cayuga Co., NY to Mrs. MARY (MURPHY) TEEPLE, daughter of Isaac, and widow of Peter (see both). They moved to Fulton Co., Ohio; and then in 1836 to Ogden Twp., Lenawee Co., Mich. He died 1 Mar. 1878, and she died 14 May 1862. In the 1850 census of Ogden Twp., they listed PHEBE A., age 14; WILLIAM M. (following), age 13; MARTHA, age 8 (m. Alfred Young), all b. Mich. Also in the household was Elizabeth Teeple, age 34, b. NY, daughter of Peter & Mary. Ref: P&BA-Len pg. 917-31.

JOHNSON, WILLIAM H. born ca. 1818, England, was listed in the 1850 census of Hudson Twp., Lenawee Co., Mich. with (wife?) ELIZA J., age 18, born Mich., and Elizabeth E. Daniels, age 21, b. England, and Jabez J. Daniels, age 19, b. Mich., in his household. Note JOSEPH M., preceding.

Pioneer Families of Southeastern Michigan

JOHNSON, WILLIAM J., son of ? & KATIE (HUBBARD), preceding, was born 20 Apr. 1819, Bronson Twp., Huron Co., Ohio, and married there to LUCINDA (CASE) born 14 May 1830, Richland Co., Ohio. They lived in LaGrange Co., Ind., but returned to Huron Co., Ohio until 1858 when they removed to Ogden Twp., Lenawee Co., Mich. He died 1 July 1874, and she was residing in Fairfield Twp. in 1888. Children: 1. AMOS S.; 2. SAVILLA; 3. LESTER; 4. FRAZEY; 5. STERRY A. b. 25 Apr. 1859, Ogden Twp. (m. Dora A. Carney, daughter of James, also see). Ref: P&BA-Len pg. 803-4.

JOHNSON, WILLIAM M., son of WILLIAM (preceding), was born 27 Jan. 1839, Ogden Twp., Lenawee Co., Mich., and married in Dec. 1860 to ANN (GALLIGAN) who died in 1870 leaving son: 1. EUGENE (m. Caroline Stock; went to Anaheim, CA). William M. married again to SARAH (YOUNG), a native of Penn., who died in 1880 leaving son: 2. ARBIE. William M. married third on 10 Jan. 1882 to LIBBIE (STOCK), daughter of Godfrey (also see), and sister of Caroline who married Eugene. Children: 3. ESTHER MAY; 4. EVA JULIA. Ref: P&BA-Len pg. 927-31.

JOHNSON, WILLIAM W. born ca. 1806, and wife, ESTHER, born ca. 1807, both in New Hampshire, were listed in the 1850 census of Medina Twp., Lenawee Co., Mich. with OLIVER, age 20. b. VT; and ANN J., age 10, b. Mich., in their household.

JOHNSON, ZACHARIAH born ca. 1817, and wife, MARY, born ca. 1821, both in Penn., were listed in the 1850 census of Cambridge Twp., Lenawee Co., Mich. with WILLIAM, age 10; SAMUEL, age 9; ROBERT, age 7, all b. Penn.; and ELIZABETH, age 6; ZACHARIAH, age 4; MARY, age 4; MORES (MORRIS?), age 2, all b. Mich., in their household.

JOHNSON, ZEPHANIAH K. born 18 Oct. 1801, Yates Co., NY, married possibly in Seneca Co., NY to CATY (SCHUYLER) born 11 Aug. 1802, Roxbury, Morris Co., NJ. They moved in 1844 to Medina Twp., Lenawee Co., Mich. Known children from 1850 census of Medina Twp.: JOHN S. (preceding); GEORGE J. b. ca. 1840; RICHARD b. ca. 1844. In other households were HYEL, age 21, MINA, age 20, who MAY relate to this family. Ref: P&BA-Len pg. 1008-9.

JOHNSTON, JOHN H. born ca. 1797, Virginia, and wife, PHOEBE, born ca. 1801, NY, were listed in the 1850 census of Tecumseh Twp., Lenawee Co., Mich. with SARAH, age 18, b. NY, in their household.

JOHNSTON, ROBERT, son of WILLIAM (following), born in New York City, lived in Dutchess Co., NY, and moved to Cayuga & Wayne Cos., NY. He moved to Michigan in 1859, and died at age 88, and his wife, name not stated, died at age 71. Known daughters: ELIZABETH O. b. 25 Sept. 1820 (m. Walter Robinson, also see); & CHARLOTTE D. b. 15 Oct. 1833, Cayuga Co., NY (m. Walter Robinson, as 2nd wife). Ref: P&BA-Len pg. 432-3.

JOHNSTON, WILLIAM, son of a Scottish immigrant, came to New York City. He served in the American Revolution, and settled in Dutchess Co., NY where he died. Known son, ROBERT (preceding). Ref: P&BA-Len pg. 432-3.

JONES, AARON (See John Johnson, son of Daniel; and note ABNER, following).

JONES, AARON born ca. 1814, NY, and wife, SAMANTHA, born ca. 1822, NY, were listed in the 1840 census index of Dover Twp., Lenawee Co., Mich.; and in the 1850 census with PRUDENCE C., age 9; JAMES M., age 5; EMILY b. 25 July 1846, Dover Twp. (m. Arthur C. Manchester, also see, 4 Nov. 1866, Medina Twp.), all b. Mich. Ref: P&BA-Len pg. 1128-9.

JONES, ABNER born ca. 1788, NJ, and wife, DEANA, born ca. 1798, NY, were listed in the 1840 census index of Adrian Twp., Lenawee Co., Mich.; and in the 1850 census with SYLVESTER, age 29; ALVIN, age 23; AARON, age 21, all b. NY; and ELIZABETH, age 13; JOHN J., age 11, both b. Mich., in their household.

JONES, ABRAHAM H. born ca. 1827, NY, and wife, AMANDA, born ca. 1822, NY, were listed in the 1850 census of Tecumseh Twp., Lenawee Co., Mich. with Elisa Halstead, age 25, b, NY, and James Hillock, age 18, b. Mich., in their household.

JONES, ALVA was listed in the 1840 census index of Seneca Twp., Lenawee Co., Mich.

JONES, AMOS born ca. 1784, New Hampshire, and wife, CLARISSA, born ca. 1794, Conn., were listed in the 1840 census index of Adrian Twp., Lenawee Co., Mich.; and in the 1850 census of Seneca Twp., Lenawee Co., Mich. with JAMES J., age 24, b. Penn., in their household.

JONES, ARBA and family came to Lenawee Co., Mich. in 1837 from Martinsburg, Lewis Co., NY (not listed 1840 census index).

JONES, BELA B. Dr. born ca. 1786, NY, and wife, FATIMA W., born ca. 1803, Mass., were listed in the 1850 census of Hudson Twp., Lenawee Co., Mich. with WILLIAM A., age 24, b. Mass.; CATHARINE P., age 22, b. NY (possibly wife of William A.?); HENRY W., age 19, b. Mass.; CHARLES, age 18, b. Mass. Note ELIPHAS B., following, listed next door in census.

JONES, BENJAMIN born ca. 1810, Newfoundland, and wife, ESTHER, born ca. 1814, NY, were listed in the 1850 census of Tecumseh Twp., Lenawee Co., Mich. with SAMUEL, age 13; NATHANIEL, age 12; SARAH, age 9, all b. NY; and BENJAMIN, age 4; RACHEL, age 2/12, both b. Mich., in their household.

JONES, BENJAMIN H., age 26, born NY, was listed in the 1850 census of Fairfield Twp., Lenawee Co., Mich. in a Livesay household.

JONES, CHARLES R., age 40, born NY, was listed in the 1850 census of Blissfield Twp., Lenawee Co., Mich. in a Hubbard household.

JONES, DANIEL, born Conn., married there to LUCRETIA (YOUNG), and they removed to NY by 1810. They sketch says that he spent the Winter of 1816 in the "barracks at Buffalo?" In 1817, they removed to Cleveland, Ohio, where they remained. Known daughter, LUCRETIA b. 28 May 1808, Conn. (m. Enoch Sperry, also see). Ref: P&BA-Len pg. 1204-6.

JONES, DAVID of Tecumseh, Lenawee Co., Mich. had known daughter, ESTELLA b. 1858, Tecumseh (m. George W. Smith, also see). Ref: P&BA-Len pg. 828-31.

JONES, ELIPHALET born ca. 1808, Mass., and wife, LYDIA, born ca. 1810, Conn., were listed in the 1840 census index of Raisin Twp., Lenawee Co., Mich.; and in the 1850 census with ELISHA, age 17, b. NY; and JOSEPH, age 9; FRANCIS, age 7; SARAH, age 6; LYDIA M., age 1, all b. Mich., in their household.

JONES, ELIPHAS B., age 36, born Mass., was listed in the 1850 census of Hudson Twp., Lenawee Co., Mich. In household next door to Dr. BELA, preceding.

JONES, ELIZABETH, age 47, born NY, was head of household in the 1850 census of Adrian Twp., Lenawee Co., Mich. with MARY E., age 15, b. Mich., in her household.

JONES, ELIZABETH born Wales (See George Price).

JONES, ELLA (See Newman J. Ganun)

JONES, FIDELIA, age 25, born NY, was listed as head of household in the 1850 census of Blissfield Twp., Lenawee Co., Mich. with PYNIA? E., age 10; LYDIA J., age 7; WILLIAM R., age 1, all b. Mich., in her household.

JONES, GEORGE, age 24, born NY, was listed in the 1850 census of Adrian Twp., Lenawee Co., Mich.

JONES, GEORGE married ANN (CALKINS), daughter of Lorentus (also see), and lived Palmyra Twp., Lenawee Co., Mich. Note SILAS, following.

JONES, GEORGE W. born ca. 1801, NJ, and wife, DENCY, born ca. 1806, NY, were listed in the 1840 census index of Tecumseh Twp., and in the 1850 census with SARAH, age 18, b. NY; and JANE, age 15; MARIA, age 8; CHARLES, age 3, all b. Mich., in their household.

JONES, HENRY B. born ca. 1821, and wife, ABIGAIL, born ca. 1825, both in NY, were listed in the 1850 census of Adrian Twp., Lenawee Co., Mich. with LOUISA, age 2, b. Mich., all in the household of Isaac Dean.

JONES, JAMES J., son of ? & ELSIE (GARDNER), born 16 July 1834, Litchfield, Herkimer Co., NY, was grandson of RICHARD who was said to have come from Montgomery Co., NY to Herkimer Co. James J. married there in 1856 to ABBIE (TREADWAY), daughter of Christopher (also see). In 1867, they moved to Adrian Twp., Lenawee Co., Mich., and in 1869 to Riga Twp. Children: 1. HERVEY; 2. MARK; 3. SUSIE E. Ref: P&BA-Len pg. 995-6.

JONES, J. W. was listed in the 1840 census index of Medina Twp., Lenawee Co., Mich.

JONES, JOHN, son of ROBERT (following), born Rowan Co., NC, married there to ELEANOR M. (AUSTIN), daughter of Samuel (also see). They moved to Clermont Co., Ohio, and then to Anderson Twp., Hamilton Co., Ohio, where he died in 1859. Eleanor moved to Kenton Co., KY in 1870, where she died 6 Sept. 1882. Known daughter, NORA b. Anderson Twp., Hamilton Co., O. (m. Joseph Atkinson Thompson, also see). Ref: P&BA-Len pg. 270-1.

JONES, JOHN born ca. 1792, England, and wife, RACHEL, born ca. 1802, VT, were listed in the 1850 census of Franklin Twp., Lenawee Co., Mich. with ELEANOR, age 13; JOHN, age 9, both b. Ohio, in their household.

JONES, JOHN F. born ca. 1819, and wife, ANN E., born ca. 1820, both in NY, were listed in the 1850 census of Madison Twp., Lenawee Co., Mich. with Catherine Roberts, age 22, b. NY, in their household.

JONES, JOHN F. (See George L. Crane; and note SAMUEL, following.)

JONES, LEONIDAS M. Dr. born Painesville, Ohio in 1831, was son of ? (name not stated) who served in the War of 1812 and settled at an early date in Hillsdale Co., Mich. and died at age 80. His mother, LOIS, died in Brooklyn, Jackson Co., Mich. at age 84. Leonidas married CHARLOTTE A. (HOLCOMB), daughter of Benjamin, and they settled first in Hillsdale Co. They moved to Texas for a time, but returned to Brooklyn, Mich. Children: 1. ELLA (m. Dr. R. B. House; d. 1882); 2. SUSAN C. (d. age 21); 3. OLIVER QUINCY (following). Ref: P&BA-Len pg. 402-3.

JONES, MARY married Nathaniel W. Woolsey (also see) before 1808, Seneca, Ontario Co., NY. Ref: P&BA-Len pg. 841-2.

JONES, MARY (See David Sprague)

JONES, MARY E. (See John Forbes)

JONES, MOSES born ca. 1810, and wife, SARAH, born ca. 1811, both in NY, were listed in the 1840 census index of Franklin Twp., Lenawee Co., Mich.; and in the 1850 census of Tecumseh Twp. with JOHN, age 16; WILLIAM, age 14; MARY ANN, age 12, all b. NY, in their household.

JONES, OLIVER QUINCY Dr., son of Dr. LEONIDAS M. (preceding), born 24 apr. 1851, Camden, Hillsdale Co., Mich.; married on 19 Feb. 1874 to DELIA (SANFORD), daughter of Abram (also see) of Jackson Co., Mich. They settled in Adrian, Lenawee Co., Mich. Son, LEONIDAS M. b. 1875. Ref: P&BA-Len pg. 402-3.

JONES, PRUDENCE (See Moses D. Bennett)

JONES, SAMUEL and wife, LYDIA, of Adrian, Lenawee Co., Mich. were parents of known children: ABBIE J. b. 6 Sept. 1827, DeRuyter, Madison Co., NY (m. Dr. Nelson H. Kimball, also see); and JOHN F. (note preceding). Ref: P&BA-Len pg. 693-4.

JONES, SAMUEL JR. Rev. born ca. 1816, and wife, ANN, born ca. 1824, both in NY, were listed in the 1850 census of Hudson Twp., Lenawee Co., Mich. with EDWIN T. H., age 11/12, b. Mich., in their household.

JONES, SEYMOUR, age 23, born NY, wa listed in the 1850 census of Tecumseh Twp., Lenawee Co., Mich. in an Inn.

JONES, SILAS born ca. 1806, Mass., and wife, MARY E., born ca. 1806, NY, were listed in the 1840 census index of Palmyra Twp., Lenawee Co., Mich.; and in the 1850 census with MARTHA, age 18; GEORGE (note preceding), age 15, both b. NY; and CHARLES, age 13; HENRY, age 7; ELVIN, age 3; ELIZA, age 2, all b. Mich., in their household.

JONES, THOMAS born 15 Nov. 1776, and wife, LUCY (GUNN), born 25 Dec. 1776, both in NY, lived in Onondaga Co., NY by 1829, and later in Seneca Falls, NY. He died 17 Mar. 1860. Lucy died in Mar. 1864, Albany, NY, living with daughter, LAURA b. 8 May 1829, Onondaga Co., NY (m. Smith Briggs, also see, moved to Jackson Co., Mich.). There were 10 children, but only Laura was mentioned. Ref: P&BA-Len pg. 1173-4.

JONES, WALTER of Raisin Twp., was father of JOSIE who married George H. Rawson.

JONES, WILLIAM H. born ca. 1808, ?, and wife, ANN A., born ca. 1813, Penn., were listed in the 1850 census of Seneca Twp., Lenawee Co., Mich. with ELIZABETH J., age 15; JOHN W., age 14; WILLIAM H., age 11; WALTER T., age 10; HESTER A., age 8; PHILO A., age 1, all b. Ohio, in their household. Note AMOS, preceding.

JORDAN, ANN (See Richard Pickering)

JORDAN, EDWARD J. born ca. 1817, England, and wife, LAURA A., born ca. 1819, NY, were listed in the 1850 census of Ogden Twp., Lenawee Co., Mich. with

Pioneer Families of Southeastern Michigan

ELIZABETH A., age 9; WILLIAM E., age 7, both b. NY, in their household.

JORDAN, GEORGE W. (See SAMUEL, following) born ca. 1819, VT, and wife, POLLY, born ca. 1818, NY, were listed in the 1850 census of Madison Twp., Lenawee Co., Mich. with MARGARET, age 9; WILLIAM, age 7; CHARLES, age 6; SYBIL, age 4; MARY, age 2, all b. Mich., in their household.

JORDAN, JAMES born ca. 1817, England, may be he listed in the 1840 census index of Adrian Twp., Lenawee Co., Mich.; and was listed in the 1850 census with FREDERICK, age 6, b. Mich., in the household.

JORDAN, JAMES was listed in the 1840 census index of Franklin Twp., Lenawee Co., Mich. May be he following who was listed in the 1850 census of Tecumseh Twp.

JORDAN, JAMES born ca. 1807, and wife, ELISA, born ca. 1814, both in England, were listed in the 1850 census of Tecumseh Twp., Lenawee Co., Mich. with MARY, age 12; WILLIAM, age 9; JAMES, age 7; SUSANNAH, age 4; HARRIET, age 2; WILLSON, age 2/12, all b. Mich., in their household.

JORDAN, JOSEPH S., probably son of SAMUEL, born ca. 1817, VT, was listed in the 1840 census index of Madison Twp., Lenawee Co. Mich.; and in the 1850 census with (second wife?; sister?), BETSEY, age 20, b. NY; and PERMELIA, age 12, b. NY, in his household (next door to SAMUEL).

JORDAN, JOSIAH born ca. 1789, VT, and wife, CATHARINE, born ca. 1811, Canada, were listed in the 1850 census of Madison Twp., Lenawee Co., Mich. with GEORGE, age 16; JOHN, age 12; JOANNA, age 9; AMANDA, age 6; JAMES, age 4; MARY, age 1, all b. Canada, in their household.

JORDAN, SAMUEL born ca. 1787, Mass., and apparently lived in VT, and possibly NY, before moved to Madison Twp., Lenawee Co., Mich. By a first wife had known son, JUDSON b. ca. 1829, VT (in household in 1850 census); and probably JOSEPH S. (preceding); GEORGE W. (preceding). Samuel married again in 1850 to Mrs. AMANDA (WILBER) RICHARDSON, daughter of William, and widow of Elias (see both); and they afterwards went to Sturgis, Mich. Ref: P&BA-Len pg. 875-6.

JORDON see JORDAN

JOSELYN also see JOSLIN

JOSELYN, JULIA, age 34, born NY, was listed in the 1850 census of Tecumseh Twp., Lenawee Co., Mich. with Thomas Van Deuser, age 4, b. Mich., in her household.

JOSELYN, SUSAN married first to a Chapman, and married second on 23 Sept. 1847 to Russell Lewis (also see) in Canton, Wayne Co., Mich., and lived in Superior Twp., Washtenaw Co., Mich. Note: There was a Carlos "Joslin" in Superior Twp., Washtenaw Co., Mich. in the 1840 census index.

JOSLIN also see JOSELYN

JOSLIN, ALVIN, son of WILLARD (following), born 1 Feb. 1821, Erie Co., NY, came to Woodstock Twp., Lenawee Co., Mich. with his parents. He married on 5 Feb. 1858 to JOSEPHINE (HOLMES), daughter of Seth (also see) of Erie Co., NY. He died 29 June 1884, and she was still living on the farm in Woodstock Twp. in 1888. Children: 1. SETH W. b. 21 Nov. 1858 (m. Gertie O. Wright, dau. of William, also see, had dau, Nina G. b. 12 Jan. 1887); 2. CHARLES C. b. 13 Apr. 1862 (m. Mary Turner, dau. of Joseph, b. 25 Apr. 1865); 3. SARAH A. b. 4 Nov. 1864 (m. Eugene Turk, Jackson Co., Mich.); 4. THEODORE M. b. 21 Dec. 1869; 5. EBEN H. b. 19 Nov. 1873; 6. PAULINE b. 8 Oct. 1886 (d. infancy); 7. ALVIN JR. b. 30 June 1884. Ref: P&BA-Len pg. 547-8.

JOSLIN, JOHN was listed in the 1840 census index of Adrian Twp., Lenawee Co., Mich. JONATHAN following?

JOSLIN, JONATHAN born ca. 1795, and wife, BETSEY, born ca. 1798, both in NY, were listed in the 1850 census of Medina Twp., Lenawee Co., Mich. with MILLER, age 26; MARGARET, age 22, both b. NY, and Henrietta Bannister, age 28, b. NY, with her children, Betsey J., age 5; Martha M., age 2, both b. Ill., possibly a daughter, and grandchildren, in their household.

JOSLIN, MARGARET, age 23, born NY, was listed in the 1850 census of Hudson Twp., Lenawee Co., Mich. in a Parmlee household.

JOSLIN, PELEG and wife, CYNTHIA (MOORE), were natives of Oneida Co., NY, and they moved in 1815 to Clarkson, Monroe Co., NY. She died there, but he moved later to Erie Co., Penn. where he died at "an advanced age." Six sons and 3 daughters, names not stated, except #5. EMILY b. 8 Dec. 1809, Sangerfield, Oneida Co., NY (m. William Whelan, also see, Monroe Co., NY). Ref: P&BA-Len pg. 458-9.

JOSLIN, WILLARD born 29 Apr. 1793, married SARAH (WOODWORTH) born June 1795. They moved from Erie Co., NY to Woodstock Twp., Lenawee Co., Mich. in 1834. He died there on 18 Sept. 1842, and she died 22 Apr. 1853. In the 1850 census of Woodstock Twp., Sarah ("Sally") was age 55, born VT, and was in the household of known son, ALVIN (preceding); and also listed were SARAH, age 13, b. Mich.; and Calista Crosby, age 27, b. NY, possibly a daughter, and her children, Charles, age 4, b. Mich.; William, age 2, Agnes, age 7/12, both b. Ill. Ref: P&BA-Len pg. 547-8.

JOYCE, MARY (See Edwin Pickford)

JUDSON, CLARENCE E., son of LUCIUS V. (following), born 4 Feb. 1850, Raisin Twp., Lenawee Co., Mich., lived in Lenawee Junction about 1870, and 1872 in Sandusky, Ohio; and 1875 in White Pigeon, Mich. He married in 1875 to HARRIET E. (CALKINS), daughter of Lorentus (also see) of Palmyra Twp. They settled in Lenawee Junction, Mich. Children: 1. GLENN M. b. 20 Jan. 1879; 2. LINN C. b. 15 July 1887. Ref: P&BA-Len pg. 751-2.

JUDSON, JOHN born ca. 1807, Mass., was listed in the 1850 census of Tecumseh Twp., Lenawee Co., Mich. with no family.

JUDSON, L. V. of Raisin Twp., married EMILY MATILDA (MILLER), daughter of Van R. (also see), born ca. 1846. Had daughter, ALICE H. No proof whether this is LUCIUS V., following? Note LUCIUS, following, who married Ida Pontius, also had daughter, ALICE H.?

JUDSON, LUCIUS was listed in the 1840 census index of Raisin Twp., Lenawee Co., Mich., probably an older man than LUCIUS V. Note FANNA in household of LUCIUS V., following.

JUDSON, LUCIUS V. born ca. 1826, and wife, MARY (HORTON), born ca. 1828, both in NY, were listed in the 1850 census of Raisin Twp., Lenawee Co., Mich. with their only son, CLARENCE E., b. 4 Feb. 1850; and (mother?) FANNA, age 43, b. NY; LEWIS C., age 6, b. Mich., in their household. Ref: P&BA-Len pg. 751-2.

JUDSON, LUCIUS possibly born after 1850, married IDA A. (PONTIUS), daughter of David (also see) of Dover Twp., Lenawee Co., Mich. Known daughter, ALICE H. Ref: P&BA-Len pg. 687.

JUDSON, WILLIAM (See Ira D. Waterman)

- K -

KAHOWE, BELLE (See Chancy Rowlson)

KAISER, LYDIA (See Daniel Gambee)

KAMP also see CAMP
KAMP, E. R. (See Wilber West)

KANE also see CAIN/CANE
KANE, HENRY W. (also known as WILSON H., following)
KANE, IDA A. (See Charles W. Greenleaf)
KANE, MARY (See Peter M. Wheaton)
KANE, WILSON H. born NY, married BETSEY (WILSEY), daughter of Jeremiah² (also see), born Ohio. They settled in Woodstock Twp., Lenawee Co., Mich. Known daughter, NELLIE b. Oct. 1865 (m. Joseph B. Robinson, also see). Ref: P&BA-Len pg. 1142-5.

KARCHER, CHRISTOPHER from Baden, Germany, came to the US in 1869 to lived with son, MICHAEL (following), in Macon Twp., Lenawee Co., Mich. where he died Feb. 1877, age 78. His wife, name not stated, died in Germany. Ref: P&BA-Len pg. 462-5.

KARCHER, MICHAEL, son of CHRISTOPHER (preceding), born 23 Jan. 1823, Spillbach, Baden, Germany, came alone to New York City. He married there on 8 July 1852 to ANNA E. (DINGLE), born 26 Mar. 1826, Bavaria, Germany (who had come alone to the US in 1850). They settled in Macon Twp., Lenawee Co., Mich. in 1861. Children: 1. EDWARD (d. age 9m/24d); 2. LESETTE (d. age 3 mos); 3. EMMA (m. Frederick Miller, son of John G., also see); 4. HENRY (m. Annie G. Harold); 5. THEODORA (Addison, Mich.); 6. MICHAEL (deceased by 1888). Ref: P&BA-Len pg. 462-5.

KAUMEIER, MARGARET (See John L. Matthes)

KAYNER, CHARLES, son of GEORGE (following), born 27 Aug. 1834, Niagara Co., NY, came to Raisin Twp., Lenawee Co., Mich. with his mother. He married PHEBE (HAVILAND) who died 21 July 1880. Children: 1. CHESTER (Raisin Twp.); 2. IDA J. (m. George L. Waite, also see); 3. EDWIN (Medina Twp.); 4. BERTHA M. Charles married again to Mrs. ANN (BRITTAIN) KENT, daughter of A. W. (also see). Children: 5. JESSE; 6. NELLIE. Ref: P&BA-Len pg. 225. Note Wing Haviland, with daughter, Phebe.

KAYNER, GEORGE Dr. of Niagara Co., NY married DORCAS (BOWMAN) born ca. 1813, NY. He died there in 1839. Children: 1. CHARLES (preceding); 2. ELIZABETH b. ca. 1835, NY (m. Haviland). Dorcas married again to Jeremiah Westgate (also see) and they moved to Raisin Twp., Lenawee Co., Mich. They were listed in the 1850 census of Raisin Twp., with CHARLES & ELIZABETH also in the household. Ref: P&BA-Len pg. 225.

KEALEY, EDMOND was listed in the 1840 census index of Rollin Twp., Lenawee Co., Mich., adjacent to THOMAS, following.

KEALEY, EDWARD born ca. 1765, Ireland, was listed in the 1850 census of Hudson Twp., Lenawee Co., Mich. with HUGH, age 30; ELLEN, age 25; ELIZABETH, age 22; JOHN, age 20, all b. Ireland, in his household. Note ELIZA & MARY, following.

KEALEY, ELIZA, age 23, born Ireland, was listed in the 1850 census of Adrian Twp., Lenawee Co., Mich. (may be same as ELIZABETH, in household of EDWARD, preceding).

KEALEY, MARY, age 18, born Ireland, was listed in the 1850 census of Adrian Twp., Lenawee Co., Mich., possibly related to EDWARD, preceding.

KEALEY, THOMAS was listed in the 1840 census index of Rollin Twp., Lenawee Co., Mich. adjacent to EDMOND, preceding. He was probably husband of HENRIETTA, age 36, born New Jersey, listed as head of household in the 1850 census of Rollin Twp., Lenawee Co., Mich. with SARAH, age 15, b. NJ; and LEONARD, age 10; STEPHEN, age 6; THOMAS H., age 1, born Mich., in her household, and also JOSEPH, following, and wife. Note JOHN, following, possibly also related.

KEALEY, JOHN, age 13, born NY, was listed in the 1850 census of Rollin Twp., Lenawee Co., Mich. in a Marvin household.

KEALEY, JOSEPH born ca. 1815, NY, was listed in the 1850 census of Rollin Twp., Lenawee Co., Mich. in the household of HENRIETTA (See Thomas, preceding), with wife?, EUNICE, age 23, b. NY.

KEDZIE, WILLIAM (See Robert Burnett, Sr.)

KEEBER, CHARLES (See Henry Nichols)

KEEFER, FREDERICK and wife, CATHERINE (PEIFER), were natives of Northumberland Co., Penn. She died in 1848 in Elk Co., Penn.; and he went to Mt. Pleasant, Iowa and died in 1880 at home of a son, JOSHUA. There were 9 sons and 2 daughters, only mentioned were preceding, and daughter, SARAH b. 31 Dec. 1811, Penn. (m. Isaac Farst, also see, Seneca Co., NY). Ref: P&BA-Len pg. 997-8.

KEELER, A. R. Rev. (See David Pearson)
KEELER, JANE probably born VT, married 1 Dec. 1803 to Seth Fenton² (also see). Ref: P&BA-Len pg. 711-2.
KEELER, REBECCA of Rutland Co., VT, married ? Harrison and had known daughter, Rebecca Harrison (also see) who was born 8 Apr. 1792. Ref: P&BA-Len pg. 1114-7.
KEELER, SARAH born ca. 1788, Mass., was listed head of household in the 1850 census of Adrian Twp., Lenawee Co., Mich,
with JANE, age 24; ISAAC, age 22; ELIZABETH, age 20, all b. NY, in her household (aboarding house).

Pioneer Families of Southeastern Michigan

KEELER, SARAH of Erie Co., NY m. Albert M. Baker (also see) in Aug. 1837.

KEELEY see KEALEY

KEENE, SAMUEL B. born New Hampshire, and wife, COMFORT (WHITE), born Homer, Corland Co., NY, apparently went to Baldwinsville, Onondaga Co., NY after 1810. Known daughter, SARAH E. b. ca. 1810, Homer, NY (m/1 Hiram Goodale in Baldwinsville, NY; m/2 Joseph Tenant, see both). Note: Simeon Keeney was an early settler of Fabius, Onondaga Co., NY.

KEENEY also see KEENE

KEENEY, JOHN W. (Dr.?), son of JOSEPH (following), born ca. 1811, and wife, ERENAH?, born ca. 1817, both in Conn., were listed in the 1850 census of Franklin Twp., Lenawee Co., Mich. with WILLIE, age 2; JOSEPH, age 3/12, both b. Mich., in their household.

KEENEY, JONATHAN B. settled in Franklin Twp., Lenawee Co., Mich. by the 1840 census index; and is probably "BISHOP," son of JOSEPH (following).

KEENEY, JOSEPH and wife, MARY (BISHOP), moved about 1814 from Lyme, New London Co., Conn. to LeRoy, Genesee Co., NY where they remained, and she died at age 93-1/2. Children: 1. ALLEN; 2. BETSEY (m. Parsons, LeRoy, NY); 3. MARY b. 8 June 1808, Conn. (m. Philo C. Mills, also see); 4. JOHN W. (preceding); 5. NANCY (m. Cadman, note Dr. John Cadman with wife, Hannah N.); 6. BISHOP (to Lenawee Co., note JONATHAN B., preceding); 7. EZRA (d. young); 8. NICHOLAS; 9. Dr. JOSEPH (Lebanon, Ill.); 10. EMMA L. b. 6 Oct. 1824, LeRoy, NY (came to Adrian with her sister; m. Alonzo Foster Bixby, also see). Ref: P&BA-Len pg. 1021-2.

KEEP, SAMUEL and wife, FLAVIA, of Long Meadow, Mass., were parents of 8 children, and only mentioned were Rev. JOHN (founder of Oberlin College, Ohio); and EXPERIENCE (m. Lemuel Boies, also see, in 1813).

KEHOE, PATRICK, son of PHILIP (who d. in Ireland), born Wexfordshire, Ireland, married there to ANN (MARAH), daughter of M. P. After the birth of 9 children, of whom 2 died in Ireland, Patrick came alone to Howard Co., MD. In 1850, he sent for son, PHILIP (following); and in 1851 for the rest of the family. They joined Philip in Clinton Twp., Lenawee Co., Mich. in 1856. Ref: P&BA-Len pg. 297-8.

KEHOE, PHILIP, son of PATRICK (preceding), born 4 May 1833, Co. Wexford, Ireland, came to the US to join his father in 1850. He married first in Virginia to MARY (MALONE), daughter of Henry (who d. in Ireland, and Mary had come to the US at age 20 with an uncle who was a Catholic Priest). She died in Clinton Twp., Lenawee Co., Mich. in 1861, age 28. Children: 1. ELIZABETH A.; 2. MARY. Philip married again to MARY (McGOVERN), probably daughter of Andrew (also see) who had come to Macon Twp. in 1840. Children: 3. AGNES A.; 4. CATHERINE; 5. FRANCES M.; 6. MARTHA T.; 7. ANDREW W.; 8. PATRICK L.; 9. MARGARET C.; 10. ELLEN. Ref: P&BA-Len pg. 1092-3.

KEITH, A. P. married PHEBE ROSILLA (ALDRICH), daughter of Silas (also see) born 19 Aug. 1847. They settled in Adrian Twp., Lenawee Co., Mich. Known daughter, LINA. Ref: P&BA-Len pg. 1092-3.

KEITH, OZEN (See Philip S. DePuy)

KELLEM, ELIZABETH (See William Patee)

KELLEY also see KELLY

KELLEY, ALLEN (See George Price)

KELLEY, BENJAMIN, son of LIBNI (following), born 7 Sept. 1823, Sidney, Kennebec Co., ME, came to Michigan with his parents. He married on 23 May 1847 to JANE MALINDA (HOXSIE), daughter of John (also see). They had no children, but raised 4 foster children: Louisa Milligan; Zora Hoxsie; Madison Graves (See William Graves); and FANNY G. KELLEY (relationship not given). In the 1850 census, RUFUS, age 23, b. NY, probably a brother, was in their household. In 1888, they were living in Holloway Station, Raisin Twp. Ref: P&BA-Len pg. 761-2.

KELLEY, CLARA (See William Henry Brooks)

KELLEY, DANIEL born ca. 1817, Mass., and wife, SALLY, born ca. 1821, NY, were listed in the 1850 census of Rome Twp., Lenawee Co., Mich. with DANIEL P., age 5; GEORGE W., age 3, both b. Mich., in their household.

KELLEY, DAVID Dr. born ca. 1817, and wife, ELIZABETH, born ca. 1818, both in NY, were listed in the 1850 census of Adrian Twp., Lenawee Co., Mich. with JOHN A., age 12; ANNA ELIZA, age 10, both b. NY, and Charles Howland, age 20, b. NY, and Roxa Hugg, age 14, b. Ohio, in their household. Note NANCY, following.

KELLEY, EVA (See Morgan M. Florance)

KELLEY, IRA, son of JOHN (following), born ca. 1818, probably in Seneca Co., NY, married there to ELIZABETH (BRAMBLE), daughter of Clement (also see). They moved to Lenawee Co., Mich. in 1863, and he died in 1883, age 65. In 1888, she was residing with daughter, PHEBE J. (m. Charles W. Selleck, also see). Ref: P&BA-Len pg. 491-2.

KELLEY, JOHN married CHARITY (COVERT) probably in Seneca Co., NY, and it is probably he listed in the 1800 census index of Tioga Co., NY (later Seneca Co.) He served in the War of 1812. Known son, IRA (preceding). Ref: P&BA-Len pg. 491-2.

KELLEY, JOHN W. born 23 Nov. 1768, Cape Cod, Mass., was son of WAYNE who was born and died in Mass., and grandson of JOHN, a Quaker who had come to Mass. from Ireland. John W. married in Mass. to CONTENT (HOXSIE) born 7 Nov. 1771, also of Quaker lineage. They moved about 1800 to Kennebec, Maine. There were 10 children, 1 dying in infancy, but only mentioned were LIBNI (following) whom they joined in Raisin Twp., Lenawee Co., Mich. in 1839 "at an advanced age;" and ZENO (following); also note WAYNE "WING" (following). John W. died 14 Aug. 1841, and she died 3 Feb. 1850. Ref: P&BA-Len pg. 1216-7.

KELLEY, LIBNI, son of JOHN W. (preceding), born 27 Jan. 1799, Cape Cod, Mass., moved to Kennebec, ME with his parents. He married first to DEBORAH (ESTES), daughter of Benjamin, also of Quaker lineage. They moved to Wheatland, Monroe Co., Mich. in 1836, and she died in 1839, age 36. Known children: 1. BENJAMIN (preceding); 2. RUFUS b. ca. 1827, NY (in Benjamin's household in 1850 census); following were in household of Libni in 1850 census: 3. MARY, age 21; 4. JOHN W., age 17; 5. SARAH E., age 13, all b. NY. (Also note SUSAN, born ca. 1821, m. Ezra Hoxsie, also see). Libni married again on 6 May 1840 to LYDIA (HOXSIE), daughter of John (also see), born ca. 1811, NY. Known children (in household in 1850): 6. EDWIN, age 9 (m. Eda Potter; Ellis Co., KS); 7. ALLEN H., age 6 (m. Elizabeth Price); 8. BETSEY M., age 4 (m. Garrison Moore, Battle Creek, Mich.)

KELLEY, MARIAH, age 42, born Rhode Island, was listed in the 1850 census of Adrian Twp., Lenawee Co., Mich. with children: SALOME, age 19; MARIAH A., age 17, both b. Ohio; HARRIET, age 10; JOHN A., age 4, both b. Indiana, all in the household of Andrew Baker who was also b. Rhode Island. ELIZABETH, age 7, born Ind., in the household of Eleazer Baker, probably relates to this family.

KELLEY, MICHAEL, age 18, born NY, was listed in the 1850 census of Adrian Twp., Lenawee Co., Mich. in a Pawlding household.

KELLEY, NANCY, age 69, born NY, was listed in the 1850 census of Rome Twp., Lenawee Co., Mich. in a Hugg household. Note DAVID, preceding.

KELLEY, NELSON of Columbia Twp., Jackson Co., Mich., married MARGARET (BROOKS), daughter of Merchant (also see).

KELLEY, PATRICK born ca. 1800, and wife, MARY, born ca. 1798, both born Ireland, were listed in the 1850 census of Adrian Twp., Lenawee Co., Mich. with JOHN, age 12, b. NY; and PETER, age 9, b. Mich., in their household.

KELLEY, PERCEY (See William Henry Brooks)

KELLEY, PHILIP, age 21, born NY, was listed in the 1850 census of Rollin Twp., Lenawee Co., Mich. May be he who married HANNAH A. (CARPENTER), daughter of Josiah (also see) of Woodstock Twp.

KELLEY, SARAH born 2 July 1792 (See James D. Follett).

KELLEY, SUSAN (Note LIBNI, preceding)

KELLEY, THOMAS born ca. 1825, and wife, CATHARINE, born ca. 1826, both in Ireland, were listed in the 1850 census of Adrian Twp., Lenawee Co., Mich. with JULIA, age 1, b. Mich., in their household.

KELLEY, WAYNE "WING," probably son of JOHN W. (preceding), and wife, ANNE (VARNER), were both natives of Maine, and Quakers. They moved to Tecumseh Twp., Lenawee Co., Mich. in 1839, and then moved to Raisin Twp. In the 1850 census of Raisin Twp., he was called "Wing," age 45, and wife, Anna, age 42, with entire family shown born Maine. He died 19 Feb. 1854, and she died 1 Dec. 1886. In the household in 1850 were: 1. WILLIAM L., age 22; 2. MARY A. b. 26 Mar. 1831, Sidney, ME (m. William R. Wilson, also see); 3. ELIZABETH B., age 17; 4. LOUISA H., age 15. Ref: P&BA-Len pg. 313. In 1850, they were next door to LIBNI, preceding.

KELLEY, ZENO, son of JOHN W. (preceding), is probably he written as "TENO" in the 1840 census index of Raisin Twp., Lenawee Co., Mich. adjacent to LIBNI & WAYNE, preceding. He was listed in the 1850 census of Tecumseh Twp., age 39, born Maine, with wife, MARY ANN, age 33, born Mass.; SARAH, age 17,; HARRIET, age 15, both b. Maine; and HELEN, age 6, b. Mich., in their household. John Shepard, age 28, b. Mass.; and George Norton, age 16, b. Mich., were also listed. Zeno was said to have gone later to Oakland, Calif.

KELLOGG, ANN J. born Ireland, married in Monroe Co., Mich. before 1838 to John Albain (also see). Note LEVI H., following.

KELLOGG, CARRIE D. was daughter of Rev. ?, and she married on 10 Apr. 1866 to Leslie T. Goff (also see) of Blissfield Twp., Lenawee Co., Mich.

KELLOGG, EBENEZER W. born ca. 1815, Mass., and wife, ADELINE, born ca. 1818, NY, were listed in the 1850 census of Cambridge Twp., Lenawee Co., Mich. with MARY?, age 7; FRANCES, age 3, both b. Mich., in their household.

KELLOGG, HARVEY, son of JOSEPH (following), born Canaan, Litchfield Co., Conn., married there in 1836 to BETSEY (KELLOGG), and moved in 1838 to Adams Twp., Lucas Co., Ohio. There were 5 children, but only following mentioned: JOSEPH G. (Lucas Co., O.); ISAAC B. (following). Ref: P&BA-Len pg. 1176-7.

KELLOGG, ISAAC B., son of HARVEY, born 26 July 1847, Lucas Co., Ohio, married there on 28 Feb. 1872 to ADELMA (HILL), daughter of James Willson Hill, also see. They remained there until 1875, then moved to Riga Twp., Lenawee Co., Mich. Children: 1. EUGENE (d. age 4 mos); 2. HOWARD D.; 3. BESSIE; 4. WALDO B.; 5. CHARLES (d. age 1); 6. HAZEL DELL. Ref: P&BA-Len pg. 1176-7.

KELLOGG, JOSEPH and wife MARTHA (BEEBE), were natives of Canaan, Litchfield Co., Conn., where they remained. Known son, HARVEY (preceding). Ref: P&BA-Len pg. 1176-7.

KELLOGG, LEWIS B. of Clyde, Wayne Co., NY married EMMA C. (LIVERMORE), daughter of James (also see). He died 3 Dec. 1875. Known daughter, MARY L. b. 23 Apr. 1871. Emma C. married again to Calvin H. Crane, also see. Ref: P&BA-Len pg. 966-7.

KELLOGG, LEVI H. was listed in the 1840 census index of Monroe Twp., Monroe Co. Mich. Note ANNE J., preceding.

KELLOGG, MARY B. (See James Welch)

KELLS, ABRAHM married ZUBA (THORNTON), daughter of a Revolutionary soldier (name not stated) in Columbia Co., NY. Known son, PHILLIP H. (following). Ref: P&BA-Len pg. 424-5.

KELLS, PHILLIP H., son of ABRAHAM (preceding), born 4 Apr. 1813, Columbia Co., NY, married probably in New Albany, Ind. to CHARLOTTE (SHELDON), daughter of John (also see), native of Livingston Co., NY. They resided for a time in New Albany, and then moved to Adrian, Lenawee Co., Mich. Children (1 deceased by 1888, name not stated, those surviving): 1. ABRAHAM; 2. JACOB M.; 3. PHILLIP; 4. MARIA; 5. CATHARINE (m. A. C. Clark, Petoskey, Mich.). Ref: P&BA-Len pg. 424-5.

KELLY also see KELLEY

KELLY, CLINTON, age 21, born NY, was listed in the 1850 census of Tecumseh Twp., Lenawee Co., Mich.

KELLY, DANIEL was a native of Ireland who came to America and fought in the Revolutionary War. He died in Livingston Co., NY at age 97. Known daughter, MARY (m. Aaron Norcross, also see).

Pioneer Families of Southeastern Michigan

KELLY, DANIEL born ca. 1802, and wife, MARY, born ca. 1809, both in NY, were listed in the 1840 census index of Tecumseh Twp., Lenawee Co., Mich.; and in the 1850 census with JEFFERSON, age 17, b. NY; and WASHINGTON, age 15; DANIEL, age 13; MARY, age 3, all b. Mich., in their household. Note CLINTON, preceding; JOHN; LAFAYETTE, following.

KELLY, ED (See Patrick Donnelly)

KELLY, ELLEN (See Obediah Gore Spalding)

KELLY, JAMES, age 15, born Ireland, was listed in the 1850 census of Tecumseh Twp., Lenawee Co., Mich. Note JOHN, following.

KELLY, JOHN born ca. 1786, Ireland, and may be he listed in the 1840 census index of Hudson Twp., Lenawee Co., Mich.; and was listed alone in the 1850 census of Tecumseh Twp.

KELLY, JOHN, age 18, born Mich., was listed in the 1850 census of Tecumseh Twp., Lenawee Co., Mich.

KELLY, JOHN W. of Medina Twp., Lenawee Co., Mich. had known daughter, KATIE (m. John Hogan, son of Patrick, also see).

KELLY, LAFAYETTE, age 18, born Mich., was listed in the 1850 census of Tecumseh Twp., Lenawee Co., Mich.

KELLY, MARY M. born Seneca Co., NY (m. Ansel P. Coddington, also see). Ref: P&BA-Len pg. 1012-5 Note JOHN KELLEY, preceding.

KELLY, ORSON born ca. 1827, and wife, POLLY, born ca. 1828, both in NY, were listed in the 1850 census of Woodstock Twp., Lenawee Co., Mich. with MARVIN?, age 4, b. Mich., in their household.

KELLY, PHILLIP, age 50, born NY, was listed in the 1850 census of Medina Twp., Lenawee Co., Mich. in a Baker household.

KELLY, SALOMA, age 19, born Ohio, was listed in the 1850 census of Madison Twp., Lenawee Co., Mich. May be same as SALOME KELLEY, in household of MARIAH KELLEY, preceding.

KELSEY, JOHN (See George M. Lewis)

KEMBERLING, HENRY (See Roswell Bennett)

KEMP, DANIEL born ca. 1802, and wife, ORPHA, born ca. 1803, both in New Hampshire, were probably they listed in the 1840 census index of Adrian Twp., Lenawee Co., Mich.; and were listed in the 1850 census of Seneca Twp., Lenawee Co., Mich. with HANNAH, age 19, b. VT; and BYRON E., age 17; VICTORIA A., age 9; JOSEPHINE, age 5, all b. Mich., in their household.

KEMP, ELIAS J. born ca. 1803, Canada, and wife, MARY, born ca. 1807, NY, came to Franklin Twp., Lenawee Co., Mich. in 1835. In the 1850 census they listed: 1. SYLVESTER (following); 2. MILTON, age 22; 3. JOHN, age 20; 4. ALBERT, age 18; 5. JEHIEL, age 16, all b. NY; and 6. SUSANNAH, age 14; 7. ORVILLA, age 12; 8. MARIA, age 10; 9. MARY, age 5; 10. ELLEN, age 2, all b. Mich. Ref: P&BA-Len pg. 265-6. Note: In the 1840 census index of Franklin Twp., Elias was adjacent to LEWIS, following.

KEMP, LEWIS, porbably son of OLIVER (following), born ca. 1804, and wife, TABBY, born ca. 1809, both in Mass., were listed in the 1840 census index of Franklin Twp., Lenawee Co., Mich.; and in the 1850 census of Adrian Twp., Lenawee Co., Mich. with OLIVER, age 79, b. Mass.; and James McKay, age 22, b. Mich.; and wife, Mary W., age 19, b. VT, in their household.

KEMP, OLIVER, age 79, born Mass., was listed in the 1850 census of Adrian Twp., Lenawee Co., Mich. in the household of LEWIS, preceding.

KEMP, SYLVESTER, son of ELIAS J. (preceding), born 25 Jan. 1825, NY, married first to ELIZABETH (MORFELT) who died after a few years; and he married again on 14 Dec. 1867 to Mrs. JULIA (MORSMAN) DeLAPP, daughter of Herman, and widow of Richard (see both). They lived in Franklin Twp., Lenawee Co., Mich. The sketch said he died 17 May 1857, which is obviously incorrect, possibly 1875? Children: 1. CHARLES (m. Josephine M. Butrick, Franklin Twp.); 2. DELIA (m. Charles Pentecost, see Jesse, of Napoleon, Jackson Co., Mich.); 3. MINNIE. Ref: P&BA-Len pg. 265-6.

KENADY see KENNEDY

KENDALL, AMOS Dr. born ca. 1821, and wife, MARY (McCRILLIS), born ca. 1824, both in NY, moved first to Fulton Co., Ohio, and then to Michigan by 1842, Ohio by 1844, and to Medina Twp., Lenawee Co., Mich. by 1846. At an elderly age, they moved to Fayette, Ohio where he died on 16 Nov. 1884. There were 2 daughters and 4 sons, names not stated, following from 1850 census of Medina Twp.: 1. ANDREW J., age 8, b. Mich.; 2. MARTIN B., age 8, b. Mich.; 3. ADELIA L., age 6, b. Ohio (m. McKinzey Seeley, also see); 4. ELLEN F., age 4, b. Mich. Ref: P&BA-Len pg. 864.

KENDALL, GEORGE married ANN E. (FLETCHER), daughter of Alfred, born 14 June 1836; and he died in Fulton Co., Ohio. Children: 1. CARRIE L. (m. Edgar A. Sanford, Fairfield Twp., Lenawee Co., Mich.); 2. MARVIN D. (m. Nettie Mizner; was in US Cavalry). Ann E. married again in 1866 to Cyrenus Sanford (also see) in Morenci, Lenawee Co., Mich. Ref: P&BA-Len pg. 804-5.

KENDALL, JANE (See Obediah Gore Spalding)

KENDRICK, CHARLES H., son of WILLIAM (following), born 13 Dec. 1827, Schlotheim, Germany, came to the US with his father and lived first in Macomb Co., Mich. He worked there, and briefly in Canada, before 1846. He was listed in the 1850 census of Blissfield Twp., Lenawee Co., Mich. in the Colyer household; and he married there on 9 Oct. 1851 to MARIA (AUSTIN), daughter of Isaac S. (also see). There were 6 children, and CHARLES W. & MARY M. were deceased before 1888; surviving were: ETTA (m. Ruel Payne, Blissfield Twp.); EMMA; CICERO (m. Irene Beach); JENNIE. Ref: P&BA-Len pg. 933-4.

KENDRICK, WILLIAM and wife, DORETHA, were natives of Germany, and she died there; and he afterwards in 1843 came to the US and settled in Macomb Co., Mich. He moved last to Newport, Monroe Co., Mich. Children: 1. HENRIETTA (m. Charles Haghan, Waverly, Iowa); 2. FREDERICK D. (Detroit, Mich.); 3. CHARLES H. (preceding). Ref: P&BA-Len pg. 933-4.

KENNEDY, ASA, age 24, born Mass., was listed in the 1850 census of Seneca Twp., Lenawee Co., Mich.

KENNEDY, BENJAMIN F., probably son of FREDERICK A. (following), born ca. 1823, NY, and wife, ANGELINE, born ca. 1825, Conn., were listed in the 1850 census of Ridgeway Twp., Lenawee Co., Mich. with ALFRED, age 4; HENRY, age 3, both b. Mich., in their household (next door to FREDERICK A.)

KENNEDY, FREDERICK A. born ca. 1786, and wife, MARGARET, born ca. 1784, both in England, were listed in the 1840 census index of Macon Twp., Lenawee Co., Mich.; and were listed in the 1850 census of Ridgeway Twp. (spelled "Kenady") adjacent to JAMES, following, and BENJAMIN F., preceding.

KENNEDY, GEORGE born ca. 1788, NY, and wife, EUNICE, born ca. 1789, Conn., were listed in the 1850 census of Madison Twp., Lenawee Co., Mich. with CAROLINE, age 22, born NY, in their household.

KENNEDY, JAMES, probably son of FREDERICK A. (preceding), born ca. 1818, England, and wifE, ELIZABETH, born ca. 1822, NY, were listed in the 1850 census of Ridgeway Twp., Lenawee Co., Mich. with ALBERT, age 7; JEFFERSON, age 3, both b. Mich., in their household.

KENNEDY, JAMES married NANCY (BOWERMAN), daughter of Moses, Jr. (also see), born ca. 1842, probably in Raisin Twp., Lenawee Co., Mich.

KENNEDY, JOHN was listed in the 1840 census index of Tecumseh Twp., Lenawee Co., Mich. It may be he listed in the 1850 census of Adrian Twp., age 37, born England, with wife, MARGARET, age 31, born Scotland, and Margaret Andrews, age 62, born Scotland (mother-in-law?), in their household.

KENNEDY, MARGARET (See Peter Campbell)

KENT, ANN (BRITTAIN) Mrs. was the daughter of A. W. Brittain and married first to ? Kent; and second to Charles Kayner (also see).

KENT, AUGUSTUS (See Samuel Day)

KENT, BURTON^5, son of RICHARD^4 (following), born 24 July 1814, Londonderry, New Hampshire, came to Adrian Twp., Lenawee Co., Mich. with parents. He married on 4 Dec. 1844 to CAROLINE A. (PALMER), daughter of Thomas (also see), and settled in Adrian Twp. Children: 1. AUGUSTUS PALMER b. 19 May 1847, Adrian (to Elkhart, Ind.); 2. ELEANOR E. b. 9 Nov. 1852 (m. Augustus E. Curtis, Saginaw, Mich.) Ref: P&BA-Len pg. 654-5.

KENT, MARINER^3, son of RICHARD^2 (following), born 14 Aug. 1757, Mass., moved in 1798 to Londonderry, NH, where he married SARAH ?. He died 7 Dec. 1842/3, and she died the same year. Known son: RICHARD^4 (following). Ref: P&BA-Len pg. 297-9.

KENT, RICHARD^2, son of RICHARD^1 (from England), born 1710, married in 1734 to HANNAH (NORTON) of Boston, Mass. He died in 1794 in Newburyport, Mass., and she died 1790. Known son, MARINER^3 (preceding). Ref: P&BA-Len pg. 297-9.

KENT, RICHARD^4, son of MARINER^3 (preceding), born 30 Oct. 1786, Newburyport, Mass., married in Londonderry, NH to LOIS (ELA), daughter of David (also see). They moved to Adrian Twp., Lenawee Co., Mich. in 1835. He died Aug. 1867, and she died 7 Jan. 1876. Five sons and one daughter; those known: BURTON^5 (preceding); RICHARD, JR. (following); LEWIS b. ca. 1828, NH. Another son, name not stated, went to Cincinnati, Ohio. Ref: P&BA-Len pg. 297-9 & 654-5.

KENT, RICHARD, JR^5, son of RICHARD^4 (preceding), born 3 Aug. 1825, Londonderry, Rockingham Co., NH, moved to Adrian Twp., Lenawee Co., Mich. with parents. He married 24 Feb. 1859 to ELLEN M. (REYNOLDS), daughter of Stephen (also see) and settled in Adrian Twp. Children: 1. LUCY M. b. 5 July 1861; 2. LOUISE S. b. 2 Jan. 1864. Ref: P&BA-Len pg. 297-9.

KENT, WILLIAM was listed in the 1840 census index of Franklin Twp., Lenawee Co., Mich.

KENYON, SYLVESTER born 4 Dec. 1808, Hinesburg, VT, married on 11 May 1834 in Williston, VT to ELIZA (GOODRICH), daughter of George (also see). They moved in 1834 to Hudson Twp., Lenawee Co., Mich., and were listed there in the 1840 census index and 1850 census. He died there 29 Mar. 1879, and she died 24 Dec. 1879. Children: 1. SARAH A. b. ca. 1838 (m. G. G. Williams, Vanderbilt, Otsego Co. Mich.); 2. LOUISE M. b. 15 Feb. 1840 (m. John Velie Munger, also see); 3. MARTIN H. b. ca. 1842 (to Pittsford, Hillsdale Co., Mich.) Ref: P&BA-Len pg. 816-7.

KENYON, SYLVESTER born ca. 1822, and wife, ELIZA, born ca. 1820, both in NY, were listed in the 1850 census of Madison Twp., Lenawee Co., Mich. with ELLEN M., age 2, b. Mich., in their household.

KERR, MATHEW H., son of ROBERT (following), born 18 Nov. 1830, Co. Antrim, Ireland, came to the US in 1850, and settled by 1851 in Lenawee Co., Mich. He married on 14 Mar. 1852 to SUSAN (LANG), daughter of John (also see); and lived first in Palmyra Twp., then in Dover Twp. Children: 1. WILLIAM J. (m. Tillie VanSyckle, Hillsdale Co., Mich.); 2. JOHN R. (m. Emeline Clemensen, Dover Twp.); 3. DAVID (m. Addie Furman, Dover Twp.); 4. GEORGE (to Jack Fish Bay, Canada); 5. MATHEW; 6. MARY E. Ref: P&BA-Len pg. 221-2.

KERR, ROBERT and wife, MARY (HENRY), lived out their lives in Co. Antrim, Ireland. Children: 1. JOHN (came to US); 2. MATHEW H. (preceding); 3. DAVID; 4. WILLIAM J.; 5. NANCY; 6. MARY. Ref: P&BA-Len pg. 221-2.

KESLER, also see KESSLER

KESLER, ADAM born ca. 1791, and wife, CATHERINE, born ca. 1801, both in Penn., were listed in the 1850 census of Rollin Twp., Lenawee Co., Mich. with SARAH, age 19; MARY, age 15, both b. NY; and GEORGE, age 11; DAVID, age 9, both b. Ohio, in their household.

KESLER, JOHN married LOUISA (BEACH), daughter of Roswell (also see). John died prior to 1888, as Louisa married again on 12 Jan. 1888 to Abraham Lerch (also see). Ref: P&BA-Len pg. 1032-3.

KESSLER also see KESLER

KESSLER, BETSEY (See Alexander Forbes)

KETCHAM, GEORGE W. was listed in the 1840 census index of Tecumseh Twp., Lenawee Co., Mich. Note HELEN, following.

KETCHAM, HELEN, age 6, born Mich., was listed in the 1850 census of Tecumseh Twp., Lenawee Co., Mich. in the

Pioneer Families of Southeastern Michigan

household of George Williamson, age 28, and wife, Phebe, age 34, b. NY, and may be a stepchild of the household. JACOB, following, was in the same household.

KETCHAM, ISAAC had known daughter, MARIA b. 18 Mar. 1817, NY (m. Horace Brewer, 4 Nov. 1841, Tecumseh Twp., Lenawee Co., Mich.) Ref: P&BA-Len pg. 313-4. Note: Could this be an error, and Maria possibly daughter of JACOB?

KETCHAM, ISAAC H., possibly son of JACOB (following), born ca. 1806, and wife, GERTRUDE, born ca. 1808, both in NY, were listed in the 1840 census index of Tecumseh Twp., Lenawee Co., Mich. (adjacent to JACOB, following); and in the 1850 census with CHARLES, age 20, b. NY; and CATHARINE, age 15; CAROLINE, age 12; GEORGE, age 7, all b. Mich., in their household.

KETCHAM, JACOB born ca. 1780, NY, was listed in the 1840 census index of Tecumseh Twp., Lenawee Co., Mich. adjacent to ISAAC H. (preceding). It is probably he called "Jacob Kitcham" who was father of NELLA b. ca. 1810 (m. Joseph W. Gray, also see). Also probably sons, ISAAC H.; & GEORGE W. (both preceding). In the 1850 census of Tecumseh Twp., Jacob was listed in the household of Charles and Phebe (age 34, b. NY) Williamson, who also had HELEN KETCHAM, age 6, b. Mich., listed as a child of this household. Ref: P&BA-Len pg. 448-9

KETCHUM also see KETCHAM

KETCHUM, CHARLES born ca. 1827, and wife, CORNELIA, born ca. 1830, Ohio, were listed in the 1850 census of Riga Twp., Lenawee Co., Mich. with LORETTA, age 1, b. Mich., all in a Knight household.

KETCHUM, DANIEL[1] born Winsted, Conn., married ELEANOR (BARHYDT), daughter of Jerome (also see) born in Schenectady, NY; and they remained in Schenectady. Known son, DANIEL[2] (following). Ref: P&BA-Len pg. 359-60.

KETCHUM, DANIEL[2], son of DANIEL[1] (preceding), born 19 Oct. 1828, Schenectady, NY, married there on 5 Mar. 1853 to MARTHA E. (RICHARDS), daughter of Ellis (also see). They moved to Adrian, Lenawee Co., Mich. in 1855. Four children (names not stated) died young; those surviving: 1. Mrs. W. H. Crane; 2. FANNIE C. Ref: P&BA-Len pg. 359-60.

KETCHUM, MILLICENT (See Eliab Munger)

KETTLE, LEAH (See Daniel Van Auken)

KEUSCH, MARTIN[1] and wife, MAGDALENA (CHRIST), were born in Alsace, Germany, and married there. They came first to Detroit, Mich., and then moved to Freedom Twp., Washtenaw Co., Mich. Late in life, they moved to Clinton Twp., Lenawee Co., Mich. to live with their son, MARTIN (following). She died in 1869, age 72; and he died in 1873, age 77, Chelsea, Washtenaw Co., Mich. Ref: P&BA-Len pg. 651-2.

KEUSCH, MARTIN[2], son of MARTIN[1] (preceding), born 18 Feb. 1835, Germany, moved to Michigan with his parents. He married BRIDGET (MORRISROE), probably daughter of Thomas M. (also see), who was born in Ireland. They lived first in Adrian Twp., Lenawee Co., Mich., and then in Freedom Twp., Washtenaw Co., Mich. About 1866, they moved to Clinton Twp., Lenawee Co. Children: 1. EMELINE; 2. JOHN; 3. MARY ANN (deceased by 1888); 4. PHILIP M. Ref: P&BA-Len pg. 651-2.

KEYES also see KIES

KEYES, EMILY, age 19, born NY, was listed in the 1850 census of Cambridge Twp., Lenawee Co., Mich. in the household of John and Emily Hart.

KEYES, ERASTUS was listed in the 1840 census index of Medina Twp., Lenawee Co., Mich. Note LOUISA, following.

KEYES, GEORGE, age 20, born NY, was listed in the 1850 census of Madison Twp., Lenawee Co., Mich. in a Jermain? household.

KEYES, JAMES born 28 Nov. 1789, Newburyport, Mass., married ABIGAIL (DAVIS), born 13 Feb. 1789, New Hampshire. They lived first in Townsend, Mass., and about 1817 moved to Wayne Co., NY. He died 22 Jan. 1819, Lyons, NY. The family moved to Blissfield Twp., Lenawee Co., Mich. where she died 26 Dec. 1854. Known daughter, SARAH B. b. 12 Feb. 1813, Townsend, Mass. (m. Edwin D. Crane, also see). HARRIET, age 13, b. Penn., was listed in the 1850 census of Blissfield Twp. in the household of Edwin & Sarah Crane. Ref: P&BA-Len pg. 1204-6.

KEYES, JOSEPH born ca. 1793, Mass., and wife, POLLY, born ca. 1796, NY, were listed in the 1850 census of Woodstock Twp., Lenawee Co., Mich. with PARMENUS? (female), age 32; LORAINUS, age 25; LUCAS, age 22; DAVIS (DARIUS?), age 19; ELIJAH, age 15, all b. NY, in their household.

KEYES, LOUISA, age 19, born NY, was listed head of household in the 1850 census of Medina Twp., Lenawee Co., Mich. with ADALINE A., age 10; ELIZABETH E., age 3, both b. Mich., in her household. Note ERASTUS, preceding.

KEYES, SAMUEL was listed in the 1840 census index of Adrian Twp., Lenawee Co., Mich. It's probably he who married a daughter of David Jerrells (also see) and moved to Adrian Twp. by 1832. Ref: P&BA-Len pg. 983-4.

KEYSER, HENRY born ca. 1789, NY, and wife, SALLY (CONNER), born ca. 1793, NY, came to Tecumseh Twp., Lenawee Co., Mich. in 1830. He died at age 84, and she died at age 80. In the 1850 census of Tecumseh Twp., they listed HORATIO, age 26; CALVIN, age 22; WILLIAM, age 19; RUFUS (following), in their household. HENRY H. (following) was a few doors away. Ref: P&BA-Len pg. 419-20.

KEYSER, HENRY H., probably son of HENRY (preceding), born ca. 1820, NY, and wife, MARY, born ca. 1825, NY, were listed in the 1850 census of Tecumseh Twp., Lenawee Co., Mich. a few doors from HENRY.

KEYSER, JOHN, age 31, born NY; and (sister?) SARAH A., age 25, born NY, were listed in the 1850 census of Tecumseh Twp., Lenawee Co., Mich. in the household of Asa & Margaret Whitehead, both b. NJ.

KEYSER, PETER born ca. 1803, NJ, and wife, ANN, born ca. 1803, Penn., were listed in the 1850 census of Tecumseh Twp., Lenawee Co., Mich. with JAMES, age 16; PATRICK, age 14; GEORGE, age 10; ELISA, age 7; CHARLES, age 4, all b. Mich., in their household.

KEYSER, RUFUS, son of HENRY (preceding), born ca. 1826, NY, came to Tecumseh Twp., Lenawee Co., Mich. with his parents. He married first to CHARITY (UPDIKE), probably daughter of James (also see) born ca. 1829, NY (and they were listed in his father's household in 1850 census of Tecumseh Twp.) Charity died after the birth of twins: WESLEY B. (following) & MATILDA (d. age 6 mos). Henry married again to her sister, ESTHER (UPDIKE), and had 2 children, of whom one died (name not stated). Surviving son, MILBURN. After 22 years of marriage, Esther died; and Henry married again to ELIZABETH (SHAFER). He died in 1878, age 52. Ref: P&BA-Len pg. 419-20.

KEYSER, WESLEY B., son of RUFUS (preceding), born 8 Feb. 1851, Tecumseh Twp., Lenawee Co., Mich., married EMMA (WELCH), daughter of William (also see) in Franklin Twp. In 1883, they moved to Clinton Twp., Lenawee Co., Mich. Children: 1. LEORA E.; 2. LEON K.; 3. ETHEL MAY; and a deceased child (name not stated). Ref: P&BA-Len pg. 419-20.

KIDDER, HIRAM came to Raisin Twp., Lenawee Co., Mich. in 1833, in company of Charles Ames; and was listed in the 1840 census index of Hudson Twp., Lenawee Co., Mich. In the 1850 census of Hudson Twp., the following was the only family of this surname in Lenawee Co. SARAH C., age 29, born NY, was head of household, with CELISTA, age 24; ADDISON, age 23; MARIAH, age 18, all b. NY; and NATHAN, age 17; JULIA, age 12; EPHRAIM, age 15; MARY, age 6, all b. Mich.; and Julia Finney, age 26, and Byron A. Finney, age 2, b. Mich., in her household.

KIES, ALPHEUS (written "Keyes" in 1850 census), son of JOSEPH P. (following), born ca. 1788, and wife, ELIZABETH (LAZELL), daughter of Calvin (also see), born ca. 1791, both in Conn., (Sketch said she was b. Ashfield, NH?) moved to Cayuga Co., NY; and in 1829 to Clinton Twp., Lenawee Co., Mich., where they were listed in the 1840 census index; and in the 1850 census of Tecumseh Twp. Known son, JOSEPH S. (following). Note DANFORTH, JULIUS, & HARRIET, following. Also note DWIGHT, in household of JOSEPH S.

KIES (KEYES), DANFORTH born ca. 1816, Conn., and wife, MARY ANN, born ca. 1819, Mass., were listed in the 1850 census of Tecumseh Twp., Lenawee Co., Mich. with CYNTHIA, age 9; CHARLES, age 6; ARTHUR, age 3, all b. Mich., in their household.

KIES (KEYES), HARRIET, age 19, was listed in the 1850 census of Tecumseh Twp., Lenawee Co., Mich. in the household of Warren & Henrietta Wood. Note ALPHEUS, preceding.

KIES, JOSEPH P. served in the French & Indian War, and had one brother killed, and another die of Small pox during the conflict. He served under Gen. Montgomery and was at the siege of Quebec. Known son, ALPHEUS (preceding). Note: In the Revolutionary War Pension Applications there was a Joseph Kies, with wife, Mary, who served with the Green Mountain Boys in New Hampshire, Appl. #W20352.

KIES JOSEPH S., son of ALPHEUS (preceding), born 13 July 1820, Cayuga Co., NY, came to Clinton Twp., Lenawee Co., Mich. with his parents. He married on 28 Sept. 1846 in Clinton to FRANCES ELIZABETH (PARKS), daughter of James (also see); and they were listed in the 1850 census of Tecumseh Twp., Lenawee Co., Mich. with first 2 children in their household: 1. JAMES, age 3 (d. 1863); 2. MARY IDA, age 1, (m. Dr. Samuel Chandler), both b. Mich.; 3. GEORGE A. (Elkhart, Ind.); 4. KATE b. 20 Dec. 1854 (m. Charles Fred Field, also see); 5. WILLIE J. (Elkhart, Ind.); Ref: P&BA-Len pg. 227-8. DWIGHT, age 22, b. NY, also in the household may be a brother?

KIES (KEYES), JULIUS born ca. 1813, and wife, URSULA, born ca. 1817, both in Conn., were listed in the 1840 census index of Franklin Twp., Lenawee Co., Mich.; and in the 1850 census with GEORGE, age 12, b. Conn.; and JANE, age 9; SOPHIA, age 8; DAVID, age 6/12, all b. Mich., in their household.

KILBORN, LUTHER C. and wife, CHLOE P. (THAYER), were natives of Vermont who settled in Concord Twp., Jackson Co., Mich. by 1845. About 1859, they moved to Pittsford Twp., Hillsdale Co., Mich. Known daughter, ELLEN C. b. Concord, Mich. (m. James B. Thorn, also see). Ref: P&BA-Len pg. 905-7.

KILBURN, ELIJAH, son of ELIJAH, born 4 Apr. 1813, Great Barrington, Mass., moved to Bloomfield Penn. where he married VANILLIA (BATES) who was born Maysville, NY. She died 26 May 1854. In 1882, he moved to Centerville, Penn., where he died 6 Nov. 1887. Known daughter, ADDIE R. (m. John McClelland Burnett, also see, in Deerfield, Lenawee Co., Mich. Ref: P&BA-Len pg. 642. Note: There was an ELIJAH & DAVID listed in the 1840 census index of Branch Co., Mich.

KILBURY, ELLIOT R., son of RICHARD^2 (following), born 6 Sept. 1827, Vermont, moved with his parents to Ohio. He came to Cambridge Twp., Lenawee Co., Mich. ca. 1850 in the company of Capt. Case (See Aaron Case). He married 10 Feb. 1851 to CATHARINE E. (SHEELER), daughter of George (also see) of Cambridge Twp. There were 6 children, and 3 died infancy (names not stated), those surviving: 1. GEORGE R.; 2. VIOLA J. (m. Harvey Griffin); 3. PERRIE SENIA (d. age 18 yrs). Ref: P&BA-Len pg. 935-6.

KILBURY, RICHARD^1 came from Scotland to America, and eventually settled near Cleveland, Ohio where he died. He married (name not stated) and had known son, RICHARD^2 (following). Ref: P&BA-Len pg. 935-6.

KILBURY, RICHARD^2, son of RICHARD^1 (preceding) moved from Ohio to Vermont where he married LUCINDA (JOHNSON), and later returned to Ohio, possibly near Windsor, Ashtabula Co. They and 3 children (names not stated) died of Cholera, leaving son, ELLIOT R. (preceding). Ref: P&BA-Len pg. 935-6.

KIMBALL also see KIMBLE

KIMBALL, ALVON was listed in the 1840 census index of Rome Twp., Lenawee Co., Mich. In the 1850 census of Rome Twp., CHARITY M., age 31. b. NY, was head of household with ALVON, age 8; WILLIAM H., age 7; CAROLINE M., age 4 (m. Daniel Webster Teachout, also see), all b. Mich., in her household. Note: In the sketch, the father of Caroline M. was said to be "AVERY," however, it appears it was Alvon. Ref: P&BA-Len pg. 847-8.

KIMBALL, DARIUS, son of a Revolutionary soldier (name not stated), born 1768, Mass. (or NH?), married there to CATHERINE (BROWN), daughter of Samuel (also see). The name was altered from "Campbell" in Colonial times when the family came from Scotland. The family lived near Boston, and later moved to Cheshire Co., NH. They moved to Susquehanna Co., Penn., and later to Livingston Co., NY. In 1846, they moved to Franklin Twp., Lenawee Co., Mich. to join son, James. In the 1850 census of Franklin Twp., they were listed in that household, he age 81, b. NH?; she age 81, b. Mass. He died in 1864, age 95, and she died in 1868, over 100, and they are buried in the Mills Cemetery, Franklin Twp. There were 4 sons and 3 daughters. Those known: JAMES (following); LEANDER (following); SAMUEL (following). Also note EZRA, following. Ref: P&BA-Len pg. 779-90.

KIMBALL, DAVID (note DARIUS, preceding) born ca. 1801, NH, and wife, NANCY, born ca. 1798, NY, were listed in the 1850 census of Madison Twp., Lenawee Co., Mich. with HENRY, age 19; ELIZABETH O., age 17, both b. NY; and ADELINE B., age 9, b. Mich., in their household. Note: There was a DAVID in the 1840 census index of Monroe Twp., Monroe Co., Mich.

KIMBALL, EZRA had a son, WINIFRED S., who died 23 Jan. 1831, age 7 mos., 7 days, who was buried in the Mills Cemetery, Franklin Twp., Lenawee Co., Mich., adjacent to DARIUS, preceding.

KIMBALL, JAMES, son of DARIUS (preceding), born 4 Jan. 1806, Stoddard, Cheshire Co., NH, married first to M. ELIZA (CASE) of Livingston Co., NY. They moved to Franklin Twp., Lenawee Co., Mich. in 1844, and she died 1 Oct. 1849, age 32 (or 34), with no children. He married after 1850 to SARAH (GREYTRAX, also see) in Genesee Co., Mich. He died in 1903, and she died in 1900, and all are buried in Mills Cemetery, Franklin Twp. Children: 1. EUGENE; 2. HATTIE (m. Andrew Wilson); 3. JAMES; 4. SIDNEY. Ref: P&BA-Len pg. 779-80.

KIMBALL, JOHN born ca. 1795, and wife, ELISA, born ca. 1810, both in Mass., were listed in the 1850 census of Franklin Twp., Lenawee Co., Mich. with PHILANDER, age 19; FRANCIS, age 17; SARAH, age 15; HENRY, age 13; LEVI, age 10; ALONZO, age 8, all b. NY; and LAVERNE? (male), age 5; THEODORE, age 2, both b. Mich., in their household.

KIMBALL, LEANDER, son of DARIUS (preceding), born ca. 1809, NH, and wife, JANE, born ca. 1810, NY, were listed in the 1850 census of Franklin Twp., Lenawee Co., Mich. with JOHN, age 8, b. NY; and MORRIS, age 7; ESTHER, age 5; WILLIAM, age 2, all b. Mich., in their household.

KIMBALL, NANCY (See Moses Wakefield)

KIMBALL, NELSON Dr., son of JARVIS (who d. 1822, NY), was born 22 Sept. 1820, Martinsburg, Lewis Co., NY. He was adopted into the Arba Jones family of Martinsburg, and came to Seneca Twp., Lenawee Co., Mich. in 1837 with them. He married 14 May 1850 to ABBY (JONES), daughter of Samuel (also see), and they were listed in the 1850 census of Madison Twp., Lenawee Co., Mich., with her parents, in the household of James and Rachel Underwood. No children mentioned. Next door was WILLIAM E., following.

KIMBALL, SAMUEL born ca. 1810, died 1898, and is buried in the Mills Cemetery, Franklin Twp., Lenawee Co., Mich., adjacent to DARIUS (preceding). Buried with Samuel is MEHITABLE (1812-1879) relationship not known.

KIMBALL, SAMUEL B. born ca. 1816, and wife, ALICE K. T., born ca. 1816, both in New Hampshire, were listed in the 1850 census of Madison Twp., Lenawee Co., Mich. with GEORGE D., age 10, b. NH, in their household.

KIMBALL, WILLIAM E. born ca. 1809, and wife, SARAH E., born ca. 1820, both in NH, were listed in the 1850 census of Madison Twp., Lenawee Co., Mich. with CHARLES W., age 13, in their household (next door to Dr. NELSON, preceding).

KIMBLE also see **KIMBALL**

KIMBLE, ADALIZA (written as "Kimbly"), age 21, born VT, was listed in the 1850 census of Adrian Twp., Lenawee Co., Mich. in a Burton household.

KIMBLE, CHARLES born ca. 1822, and wife, ELIZABETH, born ca. 1825, both in NY, were listed in the 1850 census of Adrian Twp., Lenawee Co., Mich. with DUANE, age 7; PHILANA, age 5/12, both b. Mich., in their household.

KIMBLE, JOHN H. born ca. 1800, VT, and wife, MARIETTA, born ca. 1812, NY, were listed in the 1850 census of Adrian Twp., Lenawee Co., Mich. with EMILY B., age 20, born VT, and ALPHEUS, age 1, b. Mich.; and Ruth A. Nelson, age 16; Seymour Nelson, age 14, both b. NY, in their household.

KIMIS, MELISSA A. (See Benjamin Reasoner)

KINER, CONRAD born ca. 1811, and wife, ELIZABETH (STUMBAUGH), born ca. 1815, both in Penn., lived in Penn., Ohio, & Illinois before 1848 when they moved to Seneca Twp., Lenawee Co., Mich. Children: 1. EPHRAIM b. ca. 1835; 2. WILLIAM b. ca. 1838, both b. Penn.; 3. MARGARET b. ca. 1840, Ohio; 4. SUSAN b. ca. 1842, Ill.; 5. SARAH J. b. 3 Sept. 1847, Columbus, O. (m. Elias Brower, also see); 6. HARRIET b. ca. 1848, Ohio. Ref: P&BA-Len pg. 1009-10.

KING, AMOS, age 28, born England, was listed in the 1850 census of Palmyra Twp., Lenawee Co., Mich. in a Baker household.

KING, ABIGAIL, age 3, born Mich., was listed in the 1850 census of Adrian Twp., Lenawee Co., Mich. in the household of Dr. Thomas F. Dodge and wife, Lucinda (age 23, b. NY), and Abigail may be a stepdaughter?

KING, ANN born 1810, Ohio (See Roswell Beach).

KING, ASAPH had known daughter, SAMANTHA b. 15 Aug. 1791 (m. ca. 1808, Covert Seneca Co., NY to Lewis Porter, also see).

KING, CHARLES born ca. 1811, NJ, and wife, SARAH, born ca. 1815, NY, were listed in the 1850 census of Macon Twp., Lenawee Co., Mich. with CATHERINE C., age 11; ABRAHAM R., age 9; JAMES K., age 8; CHARLOTTE A., age 1, all b. Mich., in their household.

KING, DANIEL born ca. 1815, and wife, MARY, born ca. 1820, both in England, were listed in the 1850 census of Madison Twp., Lenawee Co., Mich. with THOMAS, age 1, born England; and EDWARD, following in their household.

KING, DAVID C. and wife, REBECCA (REYNOLDS), of Litchfield, Conn., were parents of SUSAN A. (m. Frederick W. Wickwire, also see). David C. served in the War of 1812, and died soon after; and Rebecca died in 1821.

KING, EDWARD, age 48, born England, was listed in the 1850 census of Madison Twp., Lenawee Co., Mich. in the household of DANIEL, preceding. Also in the household were EDWARD, age 14; ELIJAH, age 10; THOMAS, age 7, all b. England, exact relationship not known.

KING, ELIJAH born ca. 1820, and wife, HARRIET, born ca. 1821, both born England, were listed in the 1850 census of Adrian Twp., Lenawee Co., Mich. with no children.

KING, HARRIET Mrs. was the daughter of Thomas Galloway (also see) of Palmyra, NY who m/1 to King; and m/2 Samuel E. Hart.

KING, HENRY N. Capt., son of RUFUS S. (following), born 26 Mar. 1839, Bridgewater, Washtenaw Co., Mich., raised a Company during the Civil War, and was attached to Co. F., 47th Ohio Inf., where he eventually became a Captain. He married 4 Apr. 1864 to FRANCES E. (BOLLES), daughter of Frederick E. (also see) of Chelsea, Mich. They settled in Adrian, Lenawee Co., Mich. Children: 1. FREDIE E.; 2. HARRY R.; 3. FLORENCE C. Ref: P&BA-Len pg. 592-3.

KING, JAMES W. was listed in the 1840 census index of Clinton Twp., Lenawee Co., Mich.

KING, JASON (See Justus Cooley)

KING, MARY A. (See Henry Owen)

KING, MARY P., age 40, born Maine, was listed in the 1850 census of Madison Twp., Lenawee Co., Mich. in a Stebbins household.

KING, PETER and wife, CHRISTINA (ARCHIBALD), were natives of Scotland, where he died in 1836, and she died in 1853. Known son, WILLIAM F. (following). Ref: P&BA-Len pg. 364-5.

KING, ROXANA, age 47, born NY, was listed head of household in the 1850 census of Franklin Twp., Lenawee Co., Mich., with ROBERT, age 19, b. NY, in her household.

KING, RUFUS S. born Augusta, Oneida Co., NY, married in Monroe Co., NY in 1830 to MARY E. (NICHOLS), daughter of Solomon. They removed to Adrian Twp., Lenawee Co., Mich., but returned to NY; and later moved to Bridgewater, Washtenaw Co., Mich. where Rufus was living in 1888. Five sons & five daughters, names not stated, except #2. HENRY N. (preceding). Ref: P&BA-Len pg. 592-3. Note: In the 1840 census index there was a RUFUS listed in Eaton Twp., Eaton Co., Mich.

KING, SAMUEL, son of MATTHEW & MARGARET of Norfolk, England, married there to ELIZABETH (REED) and they remained there. Known children (all following came to the US): JAMES (settled first in NY, then Hudson Twp., Lenawee Co., Mich., and last in Jefferson Twp., Hillsdale Co.); SARAH (m. Stephen Thurston, Osseo, Mich.); SAMUEL (following). Ref: P&BA-Len pg. 987-8.

KING, SAMUEL, son of SAMUEL (preceding), born 19 Dec. 1819, Norfolk, England, came to the US about 1852. He married 23 Aug. 1865, Hudson Twp., Lenawee Co., Mich. to Mrs. LUCENA (VAN AKIN) BELCHER, daughter of Hiram, and widow of John (see both), and settled in Hudson Twp. Children: 1. SAMUEL; 2. MARY; 3. MARGARET. Ref: P&BA-Len pg. 987-8.

KING, SUSAN born ca. 1793, Conn. (See Charles Spafford).

KING, SYLVESTER born NJ, married SARAH (COLE) born ca. 1806, Dutchess Co., NY, and settled in Dutchess Co. She died in 1885, age 79; and he was still living in 1888, age 88. Two sons and four daughters, names not stated, except #1. LOUISA b. 12 Dec. 1824 (m. John C. Porter, also see). Ref: P&BA-Len pg. 552-3.

KING, THADDEUS of Conn. was a Capt. in the Revolutionary War, and he married ALICE (GRANGER) and settled in Suffield, Conn. Known daughter, ALICE (m. John Ladd, also see). Ref: P&BA-Len pg. 519-20.

KING, WILLIAM born 1813, Ayrshire, Scotland, came first to NY, and then about 1840 to Niles, Mich. (possibly he listed in the 1840 census index of Cass Co., Mich.) He later (after 1850?) moved to Rollin Twp., Lenawee Co., Mich. He married on 1 Apr. 1858 to Mrs ANN (BEATTIE) SLOAN, daughter of James, and widow of Robert (see both). He died in Rollin Twp. in 1884. Children: 1. ROBERT B. b. 10 Apr. 1861 (d. age 3yr/3mo); 2. WILLIAM W. b. 10 Oct. 1864 (m. Mary Hitchings, Rollin Twp.). Ref: P&BA-Len pg. 977.

KING, WILLIAM F., son of PETER (preceding), born 11 Sept. 1832, Stirling, Scotland, came to the US and settled in 1856 in Adrian, Lenawee Co., Mich. He married in Adrian on 4 June 1860 to SARAH M. (PEGLER), daughter of George (also see). She was born in London, Ontario Canada, 21 Oct. 1834. Children: 1. S. HELEN; 2. WILLIAM F.; 3. CHARLES E.; 4. JESSIE I. Ref: P&BA-Len pg. 364-5.

KING, W. R. (See John R. Gurnee)

KINNEY, ALBERT (spelled "KINNY") was listed in the 1840 census index of Rome Twp., Lenawee Co., Mich.

KINNEY, AMOS A., son of ELIAS (following), born 28 Apr. 1812, Johnsonburg, Sussex Co., NJ, moved to Canandaigua, Ontario Co., NY with his parents. He married on 17 June 1834 to MARY ANN (HAYWARD) of Farmington, NY. In 1835, they moved to Seneca Twp., Lenawee Co., Mich. She died 15 Sept. 1846. Children: (1 & 2 died infancy, names not stated); 3. HENRY E. (d. age 3 yr.); 4. GEORGE W. b. ca. 1839 (m. Louise Ashley; d. St. Charles Co., MO, leaving children: Charles, Amos, Bert, May). Amos A. married again in 1849 to LUCINDA M. (STUCK), daughter of Benjamin (also see). Children: 5. MARGARET C. b. ca. 1850 (m. Coleman Young, Medina Twp.); 6. MYRON (d. child); 7. FRANK A. (m. Elva Coonrad, Medina Twp.); 8. MARY LAVINA (d. infancy); 9. JOHN A. Ref: P&BA-Len pg. 512-3.

KINNEY, BISHOP born ca. 1815, NY, and wife, AMELIA, born ca. 1820, Mass., were listed in the 1850 census of Cambridge Twp., Lenawee Co., Mich. with HELEN, age 8; NANCY, age 6; ZALMON, age 4, all b. Mich., in their household.

KINNEY, ELEANOR (SWIFT) married Abram Hamilton (also see).

KINNEY, ELIAS, son of RICHARD (following), born ca. 1788, Hardwick, Sussex Co., NJ, married there to MARGARET (ANDERSON), daughter of Benjamin (also see), born 12 Aug. 1788 (Penn. according to census.) Elias served in the War of 1812. In 1824, they

Pioneer Families of Southeastern Michigan

removed to Canandaigua, Ontario Co., NY; and in 1836 to Seneca Twp., Lenawee Co., Mich. She died 21 Apr. 1858, age 70; and he died 3 Sept. 1859, age 71. Children: 1. AMOS A. (preceding); 2. JAMES S. (following); 3. MARY ANN (d. young); 4. SAMUEL K. (following); 5. RICHARD H. (following); 6. SALLY ANN (d. young); 7. WILLIAM S. (following); 8. ELIZABETH M.; 9. JOHN OXFORD. Ref: P&BA-Len pg. 512-3.

KINNEY, GEORGE W., age 11, born Mich., was listed in the 1850 census of Madison Twp., Lenawee Co., Mich. in the Young household. Note: This may be son of AMOS A., preceding, listed again.

KINNEY, J. D. (See Wanton Green Smith)

KINNEY, JAMES S., son of ELIAS (preceding), born ca. 1818, NJ, and wife, ARVILLA, born ca. 1819, NY, were listed in the 1850 census of Seneca Twp., Lenawee Co., Mich. with FRANCES A., age 1, b. Mich., in their household.

KINNEY, JOEL born Conn., married BETSEY (HOLMES) born VT, and they settled in Livingston Co., NY, where she died in 1811. Known sons: SYLVANUS (following). Joel may have married again, and had son, NELSON (following). Ref: P&BA-Len pg. 223-4.

KINNEY, JOHN S., son of THOMAS (following), born 14 Nov. 1827, Alford, Mass., was reared in Allegany Co., NY. He married in 1847 to CLARISSA (BRESIE). The moved in 1861 to Cleveland, Ohio; and lived variously in Ohio, and Tecumseh Twp., Lenawee Co., Mich., and finally in Tecumseh Twp. Children: 1. WILLIAM L. (killed in Ohio in hunting accident); 2. ALMA F. (m. George H. Tansley); 3. WALTER S. Ref: P&BA-Len pg. 386.

KINNEY, JOSHUA born ca. 1817, and wife, MARY, born ca. 1821, both in NY, were listed in the 1850 census of Medina Twp., Lenawee Co., Mich. with ALONZO, age 4, b. Mich., in their household.

KINNEY, NELSON (note JOEL, preceding) born ca. 1814, and wife, MARGARET, born ca. 1816, both in NY, were listed in the 1850 census of Cambridge Twp., Lenawee Co., Mich. (next door to SYLVANUS, following) with FREDUS, age 7; FRANKLIN, age 4; FRANCES, age 4; FLAVIUS, age 1; LAWRENCE, age 1, all b. Mich., in their household.

KINNEY, PETER B. was listed in the 1840 census index of Adrian Twp., Lenawee Co., Mich.

KINNEY, RHODA born New Hampshire, married by 1818 to Thomas Clark (also see) and resided in Homer, Cortland Co., NY. Ref: P&BA-Len pg. 1148-9.

KINNEY, RICHARD died in Hardwick, Sussex Co., NJ. His estate was recorded 7 Apr. 1825 and notes that his widow, ELIZABETH, had since married Gabriel Ogden, Esq. Heirs were sons, RICHARD; ELEAZER; JAMES (possibly he who went to New York City); ELIAS (probably he preceding); & SAMUEL.

KINNEY, RICHARD H., son of ELIAS (preceding), born 3 Dec. 1820, Sussex Co., NJ, moved with parents to NY and Seneca Twp., Lenawee Co., Mich. He married in May 1845 to WEALTHY ANN (BUCK), daughter of Chester (also see), and in the 1850 census of Seneca Twp., were listed in household of Elias, with the first 2 children. Children: 1. SARAH b. ca. 1848 (m. William Hart, Pittsburg, Pa.); 2. (ELIAS) ODELL b. ca. 1848 (m. Mary Ella Driver, Kansas City, MO, children Willie & Luella); 3. IDA (Pittsburg, Pa.); 4. IRA (m. Hattie Lyon, Medina Twp.); 5. CLARENCE. After the death of Wealthy Ann, Richard married again on 15 June 1869 to MARY (WAGONER), daughter of Israel (also see). Ref: P&BA-Len pg. 532-3.

KINNEY, SAMUEL K., son of ELIAS (preceding), born ca. 1818, came to Seneca Twp., Lenawee Co., Mich. with brother, AMOS. He married 29 Nov. 1846 to MARY (SECOR), daughter of Benjamin (also see). Daughter, HANNAH ELIZABETH b. ca. 1849 (m. Benjamin F. Graves, also see). Ref: P&BA-Len pg. 502-3 & 1090-1.

KINNEY, SYLVANUS, son of JOEL (preceding), born 20 June 1809, Livingston Co., NY, married HANNAH (CRANE) and moved to Cambridge Twp., Lenawee Co., Mich. by 1836. Hannah died in 1849. Known children: 1. JOHN CLEVELAND b. ca. 1836; 2. WILLIAM C. b. ca. 1837 (to Chicago, Ill.); 3. JOEL F. b. ca. 1841 (to Cincinnati, O.); 4. JOSHUA P. b. ca. 1843 (Polk Co., MO); 5. JULIUS b. ca. 1845 (d. Franklin Co., Tenn., age 21); 6. S. HARVEY b. ca. 1847 (Kansas City, MO). Sylvanus married again by 1850 census to SARAH (CRAIN) born Mass., but she died after 2-1/2 yrs with no children; and he married again to ABIGAIL (BRIGGS), a native of Mass., who died 1 Aug. 1867, Adrian. Children: 7. VERNON (to Milwaukee Co., Wisc.); 8. DEWITT (N. Springfield, MO); 9. CLARA E. Sylvanus married last to Mrs. ABBIE (FOOTE) MOORE, daughter of Milton (also see), and widow of Alonzo. Ref: P&BA-Len pg. 223-4.

KINNEY, THOMAS and wife, LUCRETIA (DODGE), were natives of Mass. who resided first in Berkshire Co., Mass., and then moved to Allegany Co., NY, where they remained. There were 3 sons and 1 daughter, names not stated except: JOHN S. (preceding), and only he and the daughter were living in 1888. Ref: P&BA-Len pg. 386.

KINNEY, WILLIAM S., son of ELIAS (preceding), born ca. 1825, and wife, MARY M. born ca. 1824, both in NY, were listed in the 1850 census of Seneca Twp., Lenawee Co., Mich. with GEORGE C., age 6/12, both b. Mich., in their household.

KINSMAN, ADNAH and wife, ASENATH (CHADLER/CHANDLER?), moved from Vermont to Chautauqua Co., NY. There were 4 sons and 4 daughters, only mentioned EMILY M. b. 4 Mar. 1836, VT (m. Robert P. Boody, also see, on 19 Dec. 1858, possibly Fulton Co., O.) Ref: P&BA-Len pg. 1007-8.

KIRBY, SARAH (See Benjamin Estes)

KIRKPATRICK, LYDIA (See Jacob Bedell)
KIRKPATRICK, OSCAR (See Jacob Bedell)

KIRTLAND, LUCY (See Joseph Hart)

KISHBAUGH see KISHPAUGH

KISHPAUGH, JONAS born ca. 1796, and wife RACHEL (ONSTED), born ca. 1806, both in NJ, married in Sussex Co., NJ, and after the birth of 6 children, moved in 1849 to Adrian Twp., Lenawee Co., Mich.; and by the 1850 census to Tecumseh Twp. He died in Feb. 1873, age 77, and she died in 1869. Known children (from 1850 census): 1. JOHN, age 24; 2. GEORGE, age 20; 3. PETER (following); 4. CHARITY, age 15; 5. JANE, age 13, all b. NJ. Ref: P&BA-Len pg. 324-5. Note Peter Onsted.

KISHPAUGH, PETER, son of JONAS (preceding), born 3 June 1833, Sussex Co., NJ, came to Michigan with his parents, and married in Dundee, Mich. to ANN E. (LAMBERT), daughter of Ansel (also see). Children: 1. JOHN L. (m. Carrie Brown, dau. of Solomon, also see; Manchester, Washtenaw Co., Mich.); 2. Dr. GEORGE W.; 3. SARAH (m. W. H. Dorr, Franklin Twp., Lenawee Co.); 4. MARY E.; 5. ANSEL J.; 6. ALBERT F.; 7. Daughter d. age 9. Ref: P&BA-Len pg. 324-5.

KITCHAM see KETCHAM

KITCHEN, MARY (See William Hendershott)

KITTELBUTER, SOPHIA born England (See Charles Ingall).

KLIBLINGER, MARY (See George W. Clark)

KLINE, ELIZABETH (See George Rohrback)
KLINE, WILLIAM (See Dr. William Brown)

KNAPP, female married in Westchester Co., NY to William Derbyshire, who was said to have been a Revolutionary soldier (also see).

KNAPP, ABRAM born ca. 1785, NY, married ELIZABETH (DRAKE) born New Jersey. They moved to Rome Twp., Lenawee Co., Mich. in 1834 with their nine children (names not stated). She died 9 Oct. 1843, and he died at age 81. He was listed in the 1850 census of Rome Twp. with SARAH, age 45, b. NY; HIRAM, age 23, b. NY; JAMES, age 16, b. Mich., in his household. Known son, JOHN L. (following); also probably ABRAHAM, JR. (following). Ref: P&BA-Len pg. 611-2. Sarah J. Hervey, age 7, b. Mich., in the household in 1850 census may be a stepchild or grandchild.

KNAPP, ABRAHAM, JR., probably son of ABRAM (preceding), born ca. 1823, NY, and wife, LUCINDA, born ca. 1827, Penn., were listed in the 1850 census of Adrian Twp., Lenawee Co., Mich. with Calvin Hood, age 18, born Penn. (brother-inlaw?), in their household.

KNAPP, ALBERT, age 23, born NY, was listed in the 1850 census of Hudson Twp., Lenawee Co., Mich.

KNAPP, AMOS born ca. 1810, and wife LYDIA, born ca. 1816, were listed in the 1850 census of Dover Twp., Lenawee Co., Mich. with PERCILA, age 18; MELINDA, age 16; EUGENE, age 13; CALVIN, age 11; CAROLINE, age 9, all b. NY; and RACHEL, age 7; DELIA, age 5; GEORGE, age 3; CHARLES, age 8/12, all b. Mich., in their household. BENAJAH (following) listed next door, probably another son.

KNAPP, AMOS S. born ca. 1812, and wife, SARAH, born ca. 1816, VT, were listed in the 1850 census of Adrian Twp., Lenawee Co., Mich. with JANE H., age 13; JULIA A., age 7; SARAH E., age 2/12, all b. Mich., in his household. Note: This is probably "A. S." listed in the 1840 census index of Medina Twp. Note JOHN, following.

KNAPP, BENAJAH born ca. 1825, and wife, LUCY, born ca. 1830, both in NY, were listed in the 1850 census of Dover Twp., Lenawee Co., Mich. next door to AMOS, preceding.

KNAPP, BETSEY (See Howland Marks)
KNAPP, CHARLES born ca 1817, and wife, CYNTHIA, born ca. 1823, both in NY, were listed in the 1850 census of Rome Twp., Lenawee Co., Mich. with MARY J., age 8; JACOB, age 6; CAROLINE, age 1, all b. Mich., in their household.

KNAPP, CORNELIUS, son of REUBEN (following), was born 12 June 1824, Rensselaer Co., NY, and came to Rome Twp., Lenawee Co., Mich. in 1835 with his parents. He married 27 July 1848 to HARRIET E. (JEFFERY), daughter of James K. (also see), and settled in Rome Twp. Children: 1. Son (d. age 3 mos); 2. REBECCA b. 21 Dec. 1848 (m. Henry H. Ferguson, she d. 3 Mar. 1887, leaving a son). Ref: P&BA-Len pg. 1004-6.

KNAPP, EBENEZER born ca. 1799, and wife, HANNAH, born ca. 1802, both in NY, were listed in the 1840 census index of Franklin Twp., Lenawee Co., Mich.; and in the 1850 census with BRONSON, age 20, b. NY; and CHAUNCEY, age 15; HARRIET, age 11, both b. Mich., in their household.

KNAPP, HARTWRIGHT born ca. 1803, and wife, GINCY, born ca. 1804, both in NY, were listed in the 1850 census of Medina Twp., Lenawee Co., Mich. with HENRY, age 18, b. NY; and ALBERT, age 6, b. Mich., in their household.

KNAPP, HENRY Dr. born ca. 1816, and wife, MARIA, born ca. 1817, both in NY, were listed in the 1850 census of Madison Twp., Lenawee Co., Mich. with RICHARD, age 10; MARY H., age 8; MARIA E., age 7; DEXTER W., age 5; ANN E., age 3, all b. Mich., in their household.

KNAPP, HIRAM, son of ABRAM (preceding) is probably be he who married CHARLOTTE (SELLECK), daughter of Ebenezer L. (also see) and probably resided in Adrian, Lenawee Co., Mich. He died and Charlotte married again in 1873 to John Hurlbut of Adrian. Ref: P&BA-Len pg. 633.

KNAPP, ITHAMER had known daugher, SUSANNA b. ca. 1806, Canada (m. Trueman Shelden, also see). Ref: P&BA-Len pg. 993.

KNAPP, JAMES was listed in the 1840 census of Rome Twp., Lenawee Co., Mich. adjacent to ABRAM, preceding.

KNAPP, JAMES, age 25, and wife?, LYDIA, age 25, both born NY, were listed in the 1850 census of Tecumseh Twp., Lenawee Co., Mich. in a Currier household.

KNAPP, JOHN born ca. 1786, NY, and wife, MAMRE (HOTCHKISS) born ca. 1786, Conn., lived in Cayuga Co., NY and moved about 1835 to Medina Twp., Lenawee Co., Mich. where he was said to have erected the first building (Note: In the 1840 census index the only one of this surname in Medina Twp. was AMOS S., preceding, and there was no JOHN in Lenawee Co.) In the 1850 census, they were listed in Fairfield Twp., with JOHN D., age 24, b. NY, in their household. Apparently they later moved back to Medina Twp. Known daughter, ABIGAIL b. ca. 1817 (m. John D. Sutton, also see). John died 25 July 1877, age 94, and she died at age 92. Ref: P&BA-Len pg. 696-7. Also note JOSEPH H. (following).

KNAPP, JOHN L., son of ABRAM (preceding), born ca. 1825, married 2 Apr. 1851 in Adrian Twp., Lenawee Co., Mich. to MATILDA (SELLECK), daughter of Ebenezer L. (also see). They settled in Rome Twp. Children: 1. ELIZABETH b. 18 Mar. 1851 (m. Charles Brittain); 2. WILLIAM P. b. 2 Mar. 1857; 3. CARRIE J. b. 9 Jan. 1863 (m. James Barrow, Blissfield Twp.); 4. FRANK A. b. 30 Dec. 1864. Ref: P&BA-Len pg. 611-2.

KNAPP, JONATHAN of Cherry Valley, Otsego Co., NY, served in the Revolutionary War, and moved to

Pioneer Families of Southeastern Michigan

Rensselaer Co., NY where he died. Known sons: ISAAC (served in War of 1812); REUBEN (following). Ref: P&BA-Len pg. 1004-6. Note: There was a JONATHAN with NY service in Rev. War Pension Applications, with widow, MARY, Appl. #W15921.

KNAPP, JOSEPH B. was listed in the 1840 census index of Adrian Twp., Lenawee Co., Mich.

KNAPP, JOSEPH H., possibly son of JOHN (preceding), born ca. 1817, and wife, EMMARETTE, born ca. 1822, both in NY, were listed in the 1850 census of Medina Twp., Lenawee Co., Mich. with ALBERT, age 13; EMILY, age 11, both b. NY; and ALONZO E., age 3, b. Mich., in their household.

KNAPP, MARTIN, age 21, born NY, was listed in the 1850 census of Woodstock Twp., Lenawee Co., Mich. with MARIETTA, age 11?, b. Mass., in the household. Note SAMUEL S., following.

KNAPP, REUBEN, son of JONATHAN (preceding), born 1799, Cherry Valley, Otsego Co., NY, moved with parents to Nassau, Rensselaer Co., NY. He married 22 Oct. 1822 to POLLY (MARKS), daughter of Joseph (also see), and about 1823 moved to Perintown, Monroe Co., NY, and in 1827 to Wayne Co., NY. In 1835, they removed to Rome Twp., Lenawee Co., Mich. Polly died 24 Dec. 1847, leaving 6 children (names not stated). Known children: CORNELIUS (preceding); and following in household in 1850 census: JOSEPH, age 21; CYRUS, age 19, both b. NY. Reuben married again on 31 Oct. 1848 to HARRIET E. (HICKS), a native of Nassau, NY, who died 12 Aug. 1849. He married again on 24 May 1850 to MARIAH E. (GURLEY) and she was in the household in 1850 listed as ELLEN M., age 35, b. VT. They had 2 sons, not named in sketch. Ref: P&BA-Len pg. 1004-6.

KNAPP, RHODA born Rochester, NY, came with parents to Lenawee Co., Mich. (m. Samuel Brown, also see).

KNAPP, SAMUEL, age 21, born NY, was listed in the 1850 census of Fairfield Twp., Lenawee Co., Mich.

KNAPP, SAMUEL F. was listed in the 1840 census index of Woodstock Twp., Lenawee Co., Mich.

KNAPP, SAMUEL P. born ca. 1810, and wife, FANNA M., born ca. 1819, both in NY, were listed in the 1850 census of Rome Twp., Lenawee Co., Mich. with MILES A., age 11, b. NY; SAMUEL W., age 8, b. Penn., and FANNA M., age 3, b. Mich., in their household.

KNAPP, SARAH (See Ebenezer Mead)

KNAPP, SYLVESTER born ca. 1797, Mass., and wife, LUCINDA, born ca. 1792, Conn., were listed in the 1840 census index of Rome Twp., Lenawee Co., Mich., and in 1850 with ELIZA, age 28, b. NY, in their household. Also note CHARLES, preceding.

KNAPP, WALLACE born ca. 1821, and wife, LAVINA, born ca. 1826, both in NY, were listed in the 1850 census of Woodstock Twp., Lenawee Co., Mich. with JOHN, age 6; EDGAR, age 4; JOEL, age 1, all b. Mich., in their household.

KNAPP, WILLIAM born ca. 1822, and wife, LUCY, born ca. 1826, both in NY, were listed in the 1850 census of Woodstock Twp., Lenawee Co., Mich. with SARAH, age 3; AMELIA, age 8/12, both b. Mich., in their household.

KNEELAND, ABNER and wife, LUCINDA (FLANDERS), came to Raisin Twp., Lenawee Co., Mich. from Paper Mill Village, NH, and had known daughter, LUCINDA (m. Aziah Ash, also see). They returned to New Hampshire.

KNEELAND, THOMAS T. born ca. 1807, NY, and wife, SARAH, born ca. 1820, Conn., were listed in the 1840 census index (spelled "Neeland") of Tecumseh Twp., Lenawee Co., Mich.; and in the 1850 census with SAMUEL, age 12; HENRY, age 1, both b. Mich., in their household.

KNICKERBOCKER, MARY (See Michael Pulver)

KNIFFEN, BENJAMIN of Westchester Co., NY had known son, JAMES (m. Sarah Underhill, daughter of James, also see, and moved to Scipio, Cayuga Co., NY after 1800).

KNIFFEN, ISAAC L. born ca. 1814, VT, and wife, ELIZABETH (FOWLE), born ca. 1821, NY, were both reared in Seneca Co., NY. In 1840, they moved to Macon Twp., Lenawee Co., Mich, and in 1841 to Ridgeway Twp. He died 5 Sept. 1881, age 66, and she was still living in 1888. Known children: 1. CAROLINE b. 13 Sept. 1839, Seneca Co., NY (m. Lyman E. Hause, also see); 2. LANA A. b. ca. 1841; 3. CHARLES b. ca. 1843, Mich.; 4. SAMUEL (following). Ref: P&BA-Len pg. 377-8 & 475-6.

KNIFFEN, SAMUEL, son of ISAAC L. (preceding), born 6 Mar. 1849, Ridgeway Twp., Lenawee Co., Mich., married there on 13 Feb. 1877 to ANGIE (HOAGLAND), daughter of Henry (also see). Known children: 1. BLANCHE; 2. Infant (name not stated in sketch). Ref: P&BA-Len pg. 377-8.

KNIFFEN, SYLVANUS of Westchester Co., NY had known daughter, MARY Z. (See Lewis Ganun).

KNIFFEN, WILLIAM of Ridgeway Twp., Lenawee Co., Mich. (See Frederick E. Morrell).

KNIFFIN see KNIFFEN

KNIGHT, BENJAMIN born ca. 1787, Rhode Island, and wife, CYNTHIA, born ca. 1789, VT, were listed in the 1840 census index of Franklin Twp., Lenawee Co., Mich. and in the 1850 census with no family in their household. In 1840 he was listed adjacent to ELI, following.

KNIGHT, BETSEY (See Maj. Daniel P. Bigelow)

KNIGHT, CAROLINE born ca. 1817, NY, was head of household in the 1850 census of Franklin Twp., Lenawee Co., Mich. with HARRIET, age 7; PHILINIA, age 5; JANE, age 3; MELLVINA, age 1, all b. Mich., in her household. Note MERLIN, following.

KNIGHT, EDWARD was a "pioneer to Lenawee Co., Mich." Known daughter, EVA (m. Carroll A. Knowles, son of Edwin A., also see). There was an EDWARD in Avon Twp., Oakland Co., Mich. in the 1840 census index. Ref: P&BA-Len pg. 426-9.

KNIGHT, ELI born ca. 1808, and wife, PARMELIA, born ca. 1809, both in NY, were listed in the 1840 census index of Franklin Twp., Lenawee Co., Mich. with FLORENCE, age 13; MARY, age 10; CHARLOTTE, age 8; DEXTER, age 7, all b. Mich., in their household. Note: In the 1840 census index he was adjacent to BENJAMIN, preceding.

KNIGHT, ENOCH born ca. 1806, England, and wife, ELIZA, borh ca. 1802, NY, were listed in the 1850 census of Rome Twp., Lenawee Co., Mich. with MARCUS, age 18; EDWARD, age 16; ALBERT, age 14; FRANCES, age

12; LUCY A., age 10; ELIZA, age 7; JAMES, age 5, all b. NY, in their household.

KNIGHT, ERASTUS, son of JOSHUA (following), born Mass., married first to POLLY (LITTLE), and she died in Mass. in 1809. Known son, WILLIAM (following). Erastus married again to LUCY (SMITH) of Blandford, Mass., and she died in Chesterfield, Mass. at age 45. He married THEODORA (CUSHMAN) of Groton, and she died in Chesterfield, Mass. He married last to ? (HILL), daughter of Sampson, and she died in 1877. Ref: P&BA-Len pg. 433-4.

KNIGHT, FRED A. (See Winslow Bates)

KNIGHT, IRA born ca. 1827, NY, was listed in the 1850 census of Riga Twp., Lenawee Co., Mich. in the household of WILLIAM G. (following), with CAROLINE, age 25, b. NY, relationship not known.

KNIGHT, JOHN R. born ca. 1816, NY, and wife, JANE, born ca. 1816, Ohio, were listed in the 1850 census of Riga Twp., Lenawee Co., Mich. with HIRAM, age 12, b. Ohio; and WILLIAM, age 9, b. Mich., in their household (listed next door to WILLIAM G., following). Also note ROSWELL, following, as there was a "JNO" listed adjacent in the 1840 census index of Blissfield Twp.

KNIGHT, JOSHUA born Conn., son of a man from England, served in the Revolutionary War. He married ? (WRIGHT), daughter of Ephraim, and they settled in Chesterfield, Mass., where they both died, she in 1825. Known son, ERASTUS (preceding). Ref: P&BA-Len pg. 433-4.

KNIGHT, MARY E., age 7, born Mich., was listed in the 1850 census of Palmyra Twp., Lenawee Co., Mich. in household of Hiram & Jane McRoberts.

KNIGHT, MERLIN was listed in the 1840 census index of Franklin Twp., Lenawee Co., Mich. Note CAROLINE, preceding.

KNIGHT, MYRON born ca. 1821, and wife, CAROLINE, born ca. 1825, Mich., were listed in the 1850 census of Riga Twp., Lenawee Co., Mich. with HOLLIS P., age 8, b. Mich., all in household of WILLIAM G. (following). Note ROSWELL, following.

KNIGHT, ORSON born ca. 1816, and wife, MARY, born ca. 1822, were listed in the 1850 census of Franklin Twp., Lenawee Co., Mich. with GEORGE, age 6, b. Mich., in their household.

KNIGHT, ROSWELL born ca. 1792, Conn., and wife, AMANDA, born ca. 1803, NY, were listed in the 1840 census index of Blissfield Twp., Lenawee Co., Mich.; and in the 1850 census of Riga Twp. with ANDREW J., age 20, b. NY; and MARTIN V., age 13; ARMINA?, age 12; LEWIS C., age 7; SERAPH C., age 4, all b. Mich., and Ira Bacon, age 23, and wife, Adelia, age 17, both b. NY; Charles Ketchum, age 23, and wife, Cornelia, age 20, and Loretta, age 1, both b. Ohio, in their household. Note IRA; JOHN R., MYRON; & WILLIAM G.

KNIGHT, STEPHEN born ca. 1815, Maine, and wife, ELIZA A., born ca. 1825, NY, were listed in the 1850 census of Adrian Twp., Lenawee Co., Mich. with OCILLA?, age 9; GRANVILLE, age 7, both b. Mich., in their household.

KNIGHT, WILLIAM, son of ERASTUS (preceding), born 17 Jan. 1807, Northampton, Mass., went to New Jersey ca. 1829, and then returned to Mass. In 1834, he removed to Rome Twp., Lenawee Co., Mich., then to Adrian Twp. (where he was listed in 1840 census). He married 25 Dec. 1834 to ANNA S. (SMEAD), daughter of Rufus (also see) of Tecumseh Twp. Children: 1. MARY SOPHIA b. ca. 1837 (m. A. J. Hood, Adrian Twp.); 2. MYRA A. b. 11 Dec. 1840 (m. J. S. Lane; she d. 12 Feb. 1874); 3. WILLIAM H. b. ca. 1843; 4. JULIA E. b. ca. 1845 (m. Alfred Edwards, Adrian Twp.); 5. MARGARET H. b. 30 Dec. 1847 (d. 13 May 1865); 6. CHARLES ABNER b. 8 Sept. 1849 (d. 3 Dec. 1872, Lincoln, Nebr.); 7. HERBERT C. b. 30 May 1852. Ref: P&BA-Len pg. 433-4.

KNIGHT, WILLIAM G., age 30, born NY, was listed in the 1850 census of Riga Twp., Lenawee Co., Mich., as an "Innkeeper," and in his household were MYRON (following) and family; and IRA (preceding). Note: JOHN R., preceding, was next door.

KNOWLES, ABRAM A. born ca. 1822, and wife, MARTHA A., born ca. 1832, both in NY, were listed in the 1850 census of Rollin Twp., Lenawee Co., Mich. married within the year.

KNOWLES, ADELIA (See Moses G. Hood; and note HEZEKIAH, following).

KNOWLES, ALBERT W., son of HEZEKIAH[2] (following), married on 6 Apr. 1880 in Rome Twp., Lenawee Co., Mich. to JESSE E. (SMITH), daughter of David Jr. (also see). Child: 1. EDITH MAY b. 12 May 1884. Ref: P&BA-Len pg. 955-6.

KNOWLES, BRAINARD C., son of JONATHAN (following), born ca. 1829, New Hampshire, married ORRA C. (BAKER), daughter of Lyman (also see) of Rome Twp., Lenawee Co., Mich., and they were listed in the 1850 census of Rome Twp., married within the year.

KNOWLES, BENJAMIN born ca. 1797, Rhode Island and wife, ELISA, born ca. 1814, VT, were listed in the 1840 census index of Clinton Twp., Lenawee Co., Mich., and in the 1850 census of Tecumseh Twp. with SARAH, age 10; GEORGE, age 9; CHARLES, age 7, all b. Mich., in their household.

KNOWLES, C. R. (See David Smith, Jr.; probably CASSIUS R., son of JONATHAN, following.)

KNOWLES, CASSIUS M., son of EDWIN A. (following), born 11 Oct. 1863, married JESSIE E. (HARDER), daughter of Jacob A. (also see). They moved to McIntosh Co., Dakota. Daughter, SABRINA b. 20 Aug. 1885. Ref: P&BA-Len pg. 529-30.

KNOWLES, DAVIS D., son of JONATHAN (following), born ca. 1814, New Hampshire, was listed as head of household in the 1850 census of Adrian Twp., with JONATHAN (following) & family in his household.

KNOWLES, EDWIN A., son of JONATHAN, born 25 Aug. 1833, Wayne Co., NY, came to Adrian Twp., Lenawee Co., Mich. with his parents. He married 20 Apr. 1854 to ELIZABETH A. (GALLOWAY), daughter of John (also see) of Monroe Co., Mich. They settled in Adrian Twp. Children: 1. CULLAN E. b. 4 Sept. 1856 (m. Emma Cook, Adrian Twp.); 2. CARROLL A. b. 5 Apr. 1858 (m. Eva Knight, dau. of Edward, also see); 3. CASSIUS M. (preceding). Ref: P&BA-Len pg. 425-6 & 529-30.

KNOWLES, HENRY A. born ca. 1811, Rhode Island, and wife, MARY C., born ca. 1816, NY, were listed in the 1840 census of Woodstock Twp., Lenawee Co., Mich.; and in the 1850 census of Raisin Twp. with SHEFFIELD, age 16; ELIZA, age 14, both b. NY; and ABRAHAM H., age 7; LUCY L., age 3, both b. Mich., in their household. Note BENJAMIN, preceding.

Pioneer Families of Southeastern Michigan

KNOWLES, HEZEKIAH[1] born 1786, Haddam, Conn., married in 1807 to ANNA (SMITH), born 1789, daughter of Henry & Susan of Haddam, and they moved in 1817 to Varick, Seneca Co., NY. In 1837, they moved to Adrian Twp., and then to Rome Twp., where he died 22 Mar. 1846. She died in 1870, Adrian. There were seven daughters (names not stated) and one son, HEZEKIAH[2] (following). Known daughters: LOURICA b. 11 July 1828, Romulus, Seneca Co., NY (m. James B. Hood, also see); and possibly JANNETT b. 13 Apr. 1817, Haddam, Conn. (m. William Hoxter, also see); and note ADELIA (preceding, who m. Moses G. Hood). In the 1850 census of Rome Twp., Anna, age 61, was in the household of Hezekiah[2]. Ref: P&BA-Len pg. 471.

KNOWLES, HEZEKIAH[2], son of HEZEKIAH[1] (preceding), born 23 Aug. 1808, Haddam, Middlesex Co., Conn.; lived at Varick, Seneca Co., NY. He married 12 Nov. 1833 to ELIZABETH (VREELAND), daughter of Michael & Elizabeth of Fayette, Seneca Co., NY. They moved to Warsaw, Adrian Twp., Lenawee Co., Mich. in 1837. He moved by 1840 to Rome Twp., and she died 20 Dec. 1840 leaving children: 1. ELIZABETH ANNA (probably she written "Sally A.," age 16, 1850 census; m. Dr. Perkins, Hudson, Mich.); 2. OLIVER W. (d. 22 Aug. 1839, age 1 yr.) Hezekiah married again 10 Oct. 1844 to MARGARET (SHUMAKER), daughter of Abraham & Maria; and she died 20 Jan. 1849 leaving children: 3. LORISSA A.; 4. MARY A. b. ca. 1849 (d. 1851). Hezekiah married last to Mrs. ELIZABETH (SOOP) GARDNER, daughter of Abram & Maria, born Albany, NY on 3 Sept. 1816. She died 5 Nov. 1874, Rome Twp. Son: 5. ALBERT W. (preceding). Ref: P&BA-Len pg. 955-6.

KNOWLES, JONATHAN, son of JONATHAN & SALLY, born 15 Apr. 1791, Middletown, NH, married ELIZABETH "BETSEY" (DAVIS) born 25 Jan. 1792, NH. They lived for a time in Vermont, and then moved to Wayne Co., NY. In 1847, they removed to Adrian Twp., Lenawee Co., Mich., and in 1850 were listed in household of son, 1. DAVIS D. (preceding); 2. CALISTA A. b. ca. 1836, VT (m. Almon Galloway, also see); 3. BRAINARD C. (preceding); 4. EDWIN A. (preceding); 5. CASSIUS R. b. ca. 1835, Wayne Co., NY (See C. R., preceding). Jonathan died 6 Aug. 1851, and she died 27 Feb. 1851, Adrian Twp. Ref: P&BA-Len pg. 426-9.

KNOWLES, PATRICK was listed in the 1840 census index of Macon Twp., Lenawee Co., Mich.

KNOX, HARRIET (See Thomas Tunison)

KNOX, JAMES[1] and wife, AGNES (BRAIDS) of Headington (or Haddington), Scotland, were parents of 8 children, only name stated was JAMES (following). Ref: P&BA-Len pg. 588.

KNOX, JAMES[2], son of JAMES[1] (preceding), was born 12 Aug. 1817, Headington, Scotland, and came to the US in 1845 and settled in Fairfield Twp., Lenawee co., Mich. He married in the Spring of 1847 to DEBORAH (BOYER), daughter of Thomas (also see). She died in 1849, age 24, following childbirth, and her child also died. He married again to her sister, EMELINE (BOYER), born 1831, NY. She died 22 Jan. 1875, Fairfield Twp. Children (all b. after 1850): 1. JAMES (m. Nettie Holloway, Seneca Twp.); 2. LOUISA (m. John Salsbury, widowed by 1888); 3. WILLIAM H. (following); 4. DEBORAH; 5. FLORENCE; 6. ARCHIE; 7. THOMAS. Ref: P&BA-Len pg. 588 & 855-6.

KNOX, WILLIAM H.[3], son of JAMES[2] (preceding), born 22 Nov. 1857, Fairfield Twp., Lenawee Co., Mich., married on 21 June 1882 to IDA (SPENCER), daughter of George W. (also see) born Camden, Oneida Co., NY. They were living in Hudson Twp. in 1888. They had twins (sketch said a son & daughter?), LEON & LEO. Ref: P&BA-Len pg. 588.

KOONEY also see KUNEY
KOONEY, IDA (See Eli E. Munn)

KOONS, JACOB (See John Ladd)
KOONS, SALLY (See John Ladd)

KORN, JACOB (See Samuel Nichols)

KRANZ, BERTHA (See Warren J. Holdridge)

KRENSENG, THEODORA (See John Beland[1])

KRERGER, MAGDALENA (See John Miller)

KRIGER, ANN (See Norman Torrey)

KRUPP, MARGARET (See Henry Smitt)

KUBLER, URSULA (See George Walter)

KUDER, JOSHUA born ca. 1812, Penn., and wife, REBECCA (GAMBLE), born ca. 1817, NY, both came with their parents to Groveland, Livingston Co., NY at an early date and married there. They removed to Clinton, Lenawee Co., Mich. in 1837. They were listed in the 1850 census of Tecumseh Twp. (spelled "Couder") with DAVID, age 7; GEORGE, age 6; MATILDA b. 13 Nov. 1845 (m. James R. Liddel, also see); JOHN, age 2; JOSHUA, age 1/12, all b. Mich. He died in 1884, and she was still living in 1888. Ref: P&BA-Len pg. 801-2.

KUNEY also see KOONEY
KUNEY, CHRISTIAN, son of HENRY (following), born 5 June 1816, Fayette, Seneca Co., NY, married there on 29 Nov. 1835 to MARY A. (GAMBER), daughter of John (also see). They remained there until 1863, then moved to Madison Twp., Lenawee Co., Mich. Children: ABRAHAM (d. age 4 yrs); LOUISA (d. age 19 yrs) and surviving in 1888 were JOHN A. (m. Sarah A. Plate, Seneca Co., NY); PERRY (m. Amelia Bryant, Dover Twp.); JAMES (m. Martha Turner, Madison Twp.); ELLEN (m. William Nothnagle, Seneca Co., NY); LUTHER (m. Alvida Mann, Madison Twp.); HARLAND (m. Lucy Wood, Deerfield Twp.); SEYMOUR m. Ruth Erilla/Aurilla Bates, dau. of Winslow, also see); ELTON; LEROY. Ref: P&BA-Len pg. 420-1.

KUNEY, HENRY and wife, SUSAN (BROWN), were natives of Penn. who moved to Seneca Co., NY before 1816. He died there in June 1863, and she died in 1832. Children: 1. SAMUEL; 2. CATHERINE; 3. MARGARET; 4. JACOB; 5. HENRY; 6. JOSEPH; 7. CHRISTIAN (preceding); 8. ABRAM; 9. SUSAN; 10. LEVI; 11. MARTIN. Ref: P&BA-Len pg. 420-1.

KUNEY, REUBEN married SUSANNA (GAMBEE), daughter of Jacob (also see), born 25 Apr. 1825, Seneca Cco., NY. Reuben died 12 Apr. 1854, Fayette, Seneca Co., NY, leaving children: 1. LORENZO; 2. MINERVA R.; 3. Child (name not stated); all deceased by 1888. Susanna married again to Jacob Reed (also see). Ref: P&BA-Len pg. 845-6.

KURTZ, JACOB born 18 Dec. 1814, and wife, FREDERICA (SWADERRER), born 4 May 1819, both in Wurtemburg, Germany, lived in Oedernhardt, Wurtemburg until 1847, then immigrated to the US. They went first from New York City to Albany, then to Detroit, Mich.; and afterwards settled in Riga Twp., Lenawee Co., Mich. She died there 7 Oct. 1878; and in 1886, he went to live with daughter, Jennie. Children: 1. MATHEW b. 18 Jan. 1840; 2. FREDERICK b. 9 Mar. 1842 (to Mattoon, Ill.); 3. CHARLES G. b. 3 Nov. 1843 (d. 6 May 1882, Deerfield Twp.); 4. JOHN L. b. 16 June, d. 16 July 1843); 5. LUDWIG b. 27 July 1846 (d. 21 Oct. 1847); 6. WILLIAM H. (following); 7. LOUISA b. 28 Aug. 1851 (m. Jacob Ingold, Blissfield Twp.); 8. JOHN D. b. 28 July 1853 (d. 12 Feb. 1876); 9. PAULINA b. 21 May 1855 (m. John Wagenlander; she d. Riga Twp., 15 June 1877); 10. CARRIE b. 10 Jan. 1858 (d. 10 Nov. 1883); 11. HELEN b. 3 Apr. 1860 (d. 3 Nov. 1862); 12. JENNIE b. 11 Apr. 1863 (m. Henry R. Snyder). Ref: P&BA-Len pg. 1161-2.

KURTZ, WILLIAM H., son of JACOB (preceding), born 11 Apr. 1849, Riga Twp., Lenawee Co., Mich., married on 4 Feb. 1875 to MARY (CROUSE), daughter of Casper (also see). They settled in Blissfield Twp. Daughter, ELLA M. b. Birmingham, Erie Co., Ohio. Ref: P&BA-Len pg. 1161-2.

KYLE, JANE (See James Boyd, Jr.; and note resemblance to family of ROBERT, following).

KYLE, ROBERT and wife, NANCY (GREGG), came from Co. Antrim, Ireland to Livingston Co., NY ca. 1849. They moved to Macon Twp., Lenawee Co., Mich. in 1857. He died at age 80, and she died in 1883, at age 82. Known daughters: NANCY b. 3 Aug. 1833, Co. Antrim (m. Henry McCarbery, also see); ESTHER b. ca. 1837 (m. James T. Boyce, also see). Ref: P&BA-Len pg. 704-5. Note JANE, preceding.

- L -

LACOCK also see LAYCOCK & LEACOCK

LACOCK, DAVID from Tompkins Co., NY, purchased land in Jackson Co., Mich. in 1835, and was listed in Leoni Twp., Jackson Co. in the 1840 census index adjacent HENRY (following); JOHN; JUNIUS; MARTIN S.; & RACHEL.

LACOCK, HENRY purchased land in Napoleon, Jackson Co., Mich. in 1836. He had wife, SUSAN, and they had a known daughter, ELIZABETH b. 11 Sept. 1840. They moved from Jackson Co. to Lenawee Co., Mich. Apparently he died prior to 1850, as in the 1850 census of Tecumseh Twp., Lenawee Co., Mich., ELIZABETH, age 10, b. Mich., was listed in the household of Asa Gilmore who had wife, Susan, age 40, who was probably the widow of Henry.

LACY, ALICE born Wisconsin (See Aaron Norcross^2).

LADD, EZEKIEL^1 was born 16 Sept. 1654, Haverhill, Mass., and was descended from the family who came on the "John & Mary" from England in 1633. He married MARY (FOLSOM) of Exeter, New Hampshire, and after the birth of the children following, they moved to Stratham, NH and no further records was found. Children: 1. LYDIA b. 18 Feb 1688; 2. MARY b. 17 Jan. 1690; 3. Child (d. May 1693); 4. NATHANIEL^2 (following). Ref: P&BA-Len pg. 519-20.

LADD, EZEKIEL^3, son of NATHANIEL^2 (following), was said to have served in Gen. Waldo's Regt., Capt. Charles Morris' Co., whom attempted in 1747 the subjection of Canada, and was poisoned by the French and Indians. He was married (wife's name not given), and had known son, WILLIAM^4 (following). Ref: P&BA-Len pg. 519-20.

LADD, IRA and wife, ANN (BINGHAM) came probably from Niagara Co., NY to Adrian Twp., Lenawee Co., Mich. ca. 1854. She died there in 1859. Known son, MARVIN A. (following). Ref: P&BA-Len pg. 731-2.

LADD, JOHN^5, son of WILLIAM^4 (following), born 17 Jan. 1774, Mass., married ALICE (KING), daughter of Thaddeus (also see); and apparently went to New York state. Children: 1. EZEKIEL b. 10 Oct. 1799 (m. Katie Lester); 2. HANNAH b. 18 Dec. 1800 (m. Silas Wilber); 3. LYDIA b. 30 July 1802 (d. young); 4. LYDIA (2nd) b. June 1803 (d. young); 5. JOHN^6 (following); 6. ALICE b. 2 Nov. 1808; 7. WILLIAM K. b. 15 Nov. 1818 (m. Mary Buchanan). After Alice's death, John married again (wife's name not stated) and had children: 8. ELIZABETH b. 5 June 1813 (d. young); 9. ALONZO b. 23 Jul 1818 (m/1 Sally Koons; m/2 Sarah Morse); 10. HARRIET b. 17 Sept. 1820 (m. Jacob Koons). Ref: P&BA-Len pg. 519-20.

LADD, JOHN^6, son of JOHN^5 (preceding), born NY, married REBECCA (DISBROW), daughter of Jesse (also see). They settled in Schenectady, NY, where they remained. Known son, LAFAYETTE (following). Ref: P&BA-Len pg. 519-20.

LADD, JOHN, son of JOHN (who was a pioneer to what is now Schuyler Co., NY, served War of 1812; and died Schuyler Co.), was born in Mass., and moved with his father to Schuyler Co., NY. He moved to Herkimer Co., NY, but by 1816 moved to Victor, Ontario Co., NY. His wife was ELIZABETH "BETSEY" (OLNEY), born Rhode Island; and both died in Victor, NY. Children: 1. ELVIRA b. 18 Oct. 1814, Herkimer Co., NY (m. John Hart, also see); 2. ELIAS R. (d. age 3 mos); 3. MAHALA b. ca. 1818 (m. Alanson Woolsey, also see).; 4. CASSANDARA; 5. WILLIAM; 6. HIRAM; 7. CALISTA; 8. ADALINE E.; 9. SMITH; 10. JENNETTE (m. Stephen W. Curtis, Sept. 1857, Hudson Twp., Lenawee Co., Mich.) Ref: P&BA-Len pg. 696-7; 844-5; 1037-8.

LADD, LAFAYETTE^7, son of JOHN^6 (preceding), born 19 Jan. 1840, Braman's Corners, Schenectady Co., NY, moved to Adrian, Lenawee Co., Mich. by 1864. By first wife (name not stated) had children: 1. IDA MAY; 2. JAMES H. He married again on 12 Apr. 1868 to LUCINDA B. (HAWLEY), daughter of William (also see). Children: 3. FRED b. 11 Jan. 1870; 4. LOUISE b. 16 Nov. 1873; 5. JOHN W. b. 7 Apr. 1877. Ref: P&BA-Len pg. 519-20.

Pioneer Families of Southeastern Michigan

LADD, MARVIN A., son of IRA (preceding), born 4 Oct. 1853, Newfane, Niagara Co., NY, came to Adrian Twp., Lenawee Co., Mich. with his parents. He went first to Wyandotte, Mich., and in 1874 settled in Springville, Cambridge Twp., Lenawee Co. He married 27 Nov. 1877 to DELIA (LAMB) born 15 Mar. 1860, Woodstock Twp. Known son, IRA G. Ref: P&BA-Len pg. 731-2.

LADD, NATHANIEL[2], son of EZEKIEL[1] (preceding), is said to have been the father of EZEKIEL[3] (preceding). Ref: P&BA-Len pg. 519-20.

LADD, WILLIAM[4], son of EZEKIEL[3] (preceding), was a seafaring man, and acted as a pilot for General DeGrasse during a battle of the Revolutionary War. He married ELIZABETH (VINING) and lived in Abington, Mass. Children: 1. THOMAS (m. Jennie Conkhite); 2. WILLIAM (m. Norche Hannon); 3. BETSEY (m. Abner Goodspeed); 4. SALLY (m. Joseph Heatherton); 5. MEHITABLE (m. Stephen Curtis); 6. JOHN[5] (preceding); 7. HANNAH (m. Robert Estes); 8. LEMUEL (m. Phebe Herrick); 9. POLLY (m. Jacob Markel); 10 SUSAN (m. Henry Wiltse); 11. LEVI (m. Eliza Parlor). Ref: P&BA-Len pg. 519-20.

LAGORE, JOHN born ca. 1774, NY was son of a man (name not stated) who had come from France, fought in the Revolution, married in NY, and whose wife had died in Canada. John married first to LUCRETIA (DARBY) of Washington Co., NY; and she died in NY. Eight children, names not stated except MOSES & WILLIAM (both following) and probably, LAFAYETTE (following); and others settled in NY and Ohio. John married again to Mrs. ELIZABETH (COFFIN) WARNER, born ca. 1785, NY, who had came first to Lenawee Co., Mich. in 1845. They lived in Sandusky, Ohio but had returned to Fairfield Twp., Lenawee Co., Mich. by the 1850 census. He died in 1860, age 86. Ref: P&BA-Len pg. 834-5.

LAGORE, LAFAYETTE A., (probably son of JOHN, preceding), born ca. 1825, NY, and wife, CHARLOTTE M., born ca. 1827, Mass., were listed in the 1850 census of Hudson Twp., Lenawee Co., Mich., married within the year, in the household of Silas Eaton, perhaps in-laws?

LAGORE, MOSES, son of JOHN (preceding), born ca. 1814, and wife JANE, born ca. 1813, both in NY, were listed in the 1850 census of Fairfield Twp., Lenawee Co., Mich. with CLARISSA, age 14, b. NY; and ELIZA A., age 12; MARY J., age 10, both b. Mich., in their household (next door to JOHN).

LAGORE, WILLIAM, son of JOHN (preceding), born 5 Mar. 1817, Fort Edward, Washington Co., NY, moved first to Sandusky, Ohio. He married first to LUCINDA (GILBERT) in 1840, and she died in Ohio at age 32, leaving a son: 1. RUDOLPHUS (who served in the Civil War, lived Adrian). William remained in Ohio until 1862, then moved to Adrian Twp., Lenawee Co., Mich. He married again to MARY J. (PENOYER), daughter of John (also see). Children: 2. AMANDA E. (m. H. Selleck, Adrian); 3. MARY E. (m. Charles Earle); 4. MARION (twin of Mary E., d. infancy); 5. WILLIAM S. (Adrian Twp.); 6. CHARLES F. (m. Lena Muck, Adrian Twp.). Ref: P&BA-Len pg. 834-5.

LAING, ABRAM was listed in the 1840 census index of Raisin Twp., Lenawee Co., Mich.

LAING, BENJAMIN I., son of SMITH (following), born ca. 1834, Raisin Twp., Lenawee Co., Mich., is probably he who married MARY J. (CONE) and lived in Palmyra Twp. in 1888. Known daughter, ALICE M., b. 6 Aug. 1852, Raisin Twp. (m. Charles A. Slayton, also see). Ref: P&BA-Len pg. 516-7.

LAING, SMITH born ca. 1794, and wife, ABBA, born ca. 1794, both born New Jersey were listed in the 1850 census of Raisin Twp., Lenawee Co., Mich. with JOSEPH S., age 25, b. NY; and BENJAMIN, age 16 (preceding); WEBSTER A., age 14, both b. Mich., and Mercy Earl, age 80, born NJ, possibly mother of Abba, in their household. Note: In Monmouth Co. 1790 Freeholders List, by E. D. Anderson & E. T. Morris, 1985, there was a JACOB listed in Shrewsbury; and in New Jersey in 1793, by Norton, ABRAHAM; ISAAC; & JOSEPH are listed in Middlesex Co. Militia.

LAKE, FLORY M. (See Justus Fowler[2])

LAKE, LUCRETIA Mrs. married Israel Wagoner (also see).

LAMB, CURTIS was listd in the 1840 census index of Palmyra Twp., Lenawee Co., Mich.

LAMB, DELIA born 15 Mar. 1860, Woodstock Twp., Lenawee Co., Mich. married Marvin A. Ladd (also see). Note ORSAMUS, following.

LAMB, ERASTUS was listed in the 1840 census index of Macon Twp., Lenawee Co., Mich.

LAMB, F. B. (See Dr. Henry Wyman; also note FRANKLIN in household of ORSAMUS, following.)

LAMB, GEORGE R., probably son of ROSWELL (following), born ca. 1823, and wife, MATILDA, born ca. 1827, both in NY, were listed in the 1850 census of Rollin Twp., Lenawee Co., Mich. (next door to ROSWELL) with NITSON (NELSON?), age 2, b. Mich., in their household.

LAMB, IDA (See Peter V. Smith)

LAMB, JAMES (See Lewis Sanford)

LAMB, NATHAN (or NAHUM) born ca. 1793, Mass., was probably he listed as "Nahum: in the 1840 census index of Woodstock Twp., Lenawee Co., Mich., and NATHAN in the 1850 census with (second?) wife, ADELINE, born ca. 1812; and WILLARD, age 12; WILLIAM, age 10; ELLBRIDGE, age 3, all b. Mich., in their household. Next door was ORSAMUS, following.

LAMB, ORSAMUS, possibly son of NATHAN (preceding), born ca. 1819, and wife, CAROLINE, born ca. 1824, both in NY, were listed in the 1840 census of Woodstock (adjacent to "NAHUM"); and in the 1850 census with CHARLES, age 7; FRANKLIN, age 4; PHOEBE, age 1, all b. Mich. Also note DELIA, preceding.

LAMB, ROSWELL born ca. 1795, Mass., and wife, NANCY (MILLS) born Berkshire Co., Mass., moved to Genesee Co., NY where known daughter, POLLY, was born 16 Aug. 1821 (m. John H. Tingley, also see, in 1837). Nancy died 22 Apr. 1838, probably in Rollin Twp., Lenawee Co., Mich., as Roswell was listed there in the 1840 census index. Known children: GEORGE R. (preceding); MILLS, age 21, b. NY (listed in the 1850 census of Adrian Twp.); WILLIAM, age 20, b. NY (was in Tingley household in 1850); and in Roswell's household were LYMAN, age 18, b. NY; and LOUISA, age 16, b. Mich. Roswell had a wife, LOVINA, age 45, b. NY, in the 1850 census of Rollin Twp.; and probably she was mother of ROSWELL S.(SYLVESTUS), age 4, b. Mich. Roswell lived with "Sylvestus" in 1888, age 93. Ref: P&BA-Len pg. 728-9.

LAMBERSON, CONRAD born ca. 1787, NJ, and wife, LYDIA, born 1791, NY, lived in Camillus, Onondaga Co., NY where she died in 1823. He moved to Ridgeway Twp., Lenawee Co., Mich. where he was listed in the 1850 census as "Coonrod" with no family in his household. Known daughter, MARY b. 28 Dec. 1802, Camillus, NY (m. Justus Lowe, also see). Ref: P&BA-Len pg. 383-4. Note: in French's *Gazeteer of NY State,* NICHOLAS LAMBERSON is among the early settlers of Camillus, NY. This surname was spelled "Lambertson" in Middlesex & Monmouth Cos, NJ. There was a NICHOLAS in Kalamazoo Co., Mich. in the 1840 census index.

LAMBERT, ANSEL C. and wife, SARAH (DILLINGHAM), came to Palmyra Twp., Lenawee Co., Mich. in 1833 from NY and were listed there in the 1840 census index. They moved before 1850 to Dundee Twp., Monroe Co., Mich. He died in Dundee village on 5 Oct. 1882, age 73. She was still living in 1888, age 74. Known daughter, ANN E. b. 18 Sept. 1840 (m. Peter Kishpaugh, also see). Ref: P&BA-Len pg. 324-5.

LAMBIE, JOHN C. born July 1848, Oneida Co., NY was the son of JOHN and ? (RICHMOND) who had come from Scotland. John C. moved to Adrian, Lenawee Co., Mich in 1874. Ref: P&BA-Len pg. 1149-50.

LAMOREAUX, CLANCY was listed in the 1840 census index of Rome Twp., Lenawee Co., Mich.

LAMOREAUX, EDWIN born ca. 1822, NY, married CHARLOTTE (LUTHER), daughter of Theodorick (also see), and they were listed in the 1850 census of Rome Twp., Lenawee Co., Mich. with CLARISSA M., age 4, b. Mich., in their household. A daughter, ?, born after 1850 may be who married Cicero J. Pickford, son of Edwin (also see).

LAMOREAUX, WILLIAM was listed in the 1840 census index of Rome Twp., Lenawee Co., Mich.

LAMPHERE, LYDIA (See Andrew Stephenson)

LAMPHERE, STACY born ca. 1788, VT, was listed in the 1850 census of Woodstock Twp., Lenawee Co., Mich. with CHARLES, age 10; FRANCIS (either "ditto" after Charles or age 11?), both b. Mich., in his household.

LAMUNYAN, ANN M. (See Albert Maples)

LANCASTER, DENNIS came from North Ireland at age 11, and lived first in Canada, then moved to Lockport, Niagara Co., NY, where he worked for 14 years on the Erie Canal. In Dec. 1831, he moved to Bridgewater, Washtenaw Co., Mich. He married there on 9 June 1833 to HARRIET (FREDERICK) and it was the first marriage in that township. He died there 2 Dec. 1868, and she was still living in 1888, age 75, in Clinton, Lenawee Co., Mich. There were 3 sons and 3 daughters, names not stated, except: F. D. (following). Ref: P&BA-Len pg. 662-3.

LANCASTER, F. D., son of DENNIS (preceding), born 2 Apr. 1834, Bridgewater, Mich., moved to Clinton, Lenawee Co., Mich. He married in May 1857 in Clinton Twp. to MARY E. (ROWLAND) born 6 Sept. 1839, Lenawee Co. Three children, names not stated, except surviving in 1888: JENNIE B. (m. C. S. Burroughs, had son Frank). Ref: P&BA-Len pg. 662-3.

LANCE, MARY (See George Garling²)

LANDGRAFF, FRED married a daughter of Arnold Smeltzer (also see).

LANDON, BINGHAM born ca. 1820, and wife, ESTHER, born ca. 1822, both in NY, were listed in the 1850 census of Rollin Twp., Lenawee Co., Mich. Next door was Samuel Langdon, so this family MAY be Langdon?

LANDON, ELECTA, age 22, born NY, was listed in the 1850 census of Madison Twp., Lenawee Co., Mich.

LANDON, JOHN born Conn., and wife (name not stated), moved to Erie Co., NY where she died at age 70. Known son, SILAS (following). Ref: P&BA-Len pg. 367-8.

LANDON, JOHN, son of SILAS (following), was born in Delaware Co., NY on 29 Nov. 1811, and married in NY to LUCRETIA (HANDY), daughter of Michael (also see). In 1834, they moved to Rollin Twp., Lenawee Co., Mich. Children: 1. SILAS b. 3 Aug. 1833 (to Clayton, Mich.); 2. WEALTHY (1st) b. 13 Apr. 1835 (d. 23 Sept. 1835); 3. WEALTHY (2nd) b. 20 Apr. 1837 (m. Gilbert Griffin, prob. son of Daniel R., also see, lived Ohio); 4. CORNELIA b. 2 Mar. 1842 (m. H. Crandall; d. 29 Apr. 1876, Round Lake, Mich.); 5. LEWIS b. 30 July 1847 (to Addison, Mich.) Lucretia died 27 Jan. 1874. John married again to Mrs. JANE (GRANDY) CRANE, widow of Amos R., and daughter of Edmund (see both). Ref: P&BA-Len pg. 367-8.

LANDON, SILAS, son of JOHN, born Conn., was reared in Erie Co., NY. He married NANCY (BEADLE), daughter of Abraham (also see) who died in 1873, age 70 (whom seems too young to be mother of JOHN, preceding), in Rollin Twp., Lenawee Co., Mich. Ref: P&BA-Len pg. 367-8.

LANE, ANNA (See John H. Wilson)

LANE, BERIAH H. born ca. 1801, Enfield, Hampshire, Mass., married there to PHEBE (PARKMAN), and in 1834 he came alone to Hudson Twp., Lenawee Co., Mich. He returned to Mass., and moved his family as far as Elyria, Ohio where they remained for a short time, before moving on to Hudson Twp. Phebe died ca. 1842 leaving children: 1. ANNA MARIA b. ca. 1829, Mass.; 2. NATHANIEL (following); 3. EDWARD P. (d. age 2). Beriah married again to JULIA M. (ANDERSON) born ca. 1809, NY, and she was in the household in the 1850 census; and following children: 4. EDWARD T., age 8; 5. LOUISA A., age 6; 6. EVERETT J., age 4; 7. THERESA E., age 3 (m. C. W. Rose). Also in the household was MARTHA, age 62, b. NY.

LANE, ELIZABETH, daughter of MATHIAS, born New Jersey, married Phineas Davis (also see). Mathias was a Revolutionary soldier, and it may be he in the Reading,

Pioneer Families of Southeastern Michigan

Hunterdon Co., NJ militia in 1793, and with Rev. Pension Appl. #S23297, NJ.

LANE, GEORGE, son of JACOB (following), born 27 Mar. 1827, Blissfield Twp., Lenawee Co., Mich. He married 20 Jan. 1850 to SARAH A. (ELSEY), daughter of William (also see), born Staten Island, NY. They may have lived for a time in Ohio, but returned to Blissfield, Lenawee Co., Mich. Children: 1. CHARLES (to Gentry Co., MO); 2. LEONA (m. J. L. Hazard, Florida); 3. WILLIAM (Gentry Co., MO); 4. GEORGE (note George H., following); 5. MARY (m. William R. Edgar, Lima, O.); 6. CLARA (m. Charles E. Bird, Blissfield); 7. BRADFORD; 8. ANNA BELLE; 9. JOHN; 10. JENNIE. Ref: P&BA-Len pg. 202-3.

LANE, GEORGE H. (See Lyman W. Baker)

LANE, GEORGE M., age 35, b. NY, was listed in the 1850 census of Blissfield Twp., Lenawee Co., Mich.

LANE, J. S. (See William Knight)

LANE, JACOB born New Jersey, came to Monroe Co., Mich. ca. 1825, and married in 1826 to LOUISA (GILES), daughter of General Giles (also see), and moved to Blissfield Twp., Lenawee Co., Mich. Louisa died in 1836, and Jacob afterwards moved to Philadelphia, Detroit, and finally Monroe Co., Mich. where he was killed in 1847 by railroad cars while working. Children: 1. GEORGE (preceding); 2. JOHN (d. 1833); 3. WILLIAM (to Quincy, Ill.); 4. CHARLES (killed in Civil War, 1864); 5. Daughter d. infancy. Ref: P&BA-Len pg. 202-3.

LANE, JACOB L. born ca. 1807, and wife, SYLVIA, born ca. 1814, both in NY, were listed in the 1850 census of Woodstock Twp., Lenawee Co., Mich. with THOMAS, age 21; SARAH, age 19; EMILY, age 12; PETER, age 10; ALBERT, age 7; CORNELIA, age 3, all b. NY, in their household.

LANE, JAMES T. (See Edmund Hall)

LANE, JASON born ca. 1776, and wife, BETSEY, born ca. 1779, both in Conn, were listed in the 1840 census of Fairfield Twp., Lenawee Co., Mich.; and in the 1850 census in household of probably son, LYMAN (following); adjacent to probably son, LUCIUS L. (following). In 1840, they were listed adjacent to URI, following.

LANE, JOHN (See Ezra Sanford)

LANE, LUCIUS L., probably son of JASON (preceding), born ca. 1806, and wife, HANNAH, born ca. 1812, both in NY, were listed in the 1850 census of Fairfield Twp., Lenawee Co., Mich. with ELECTA A., age 17, born Ohio; and GEORGE W., age 7; RODNEY, age 3; HARRIET, age 1, all b. Mich., in their household.

LANE, LYMAN, probably son of JASON (preceding), born ca. 1803, Conn., and wife NANCY, born ca. 1806, Virginia, were listed in the 1850 census of Fairfield Twp., Lenawee Co., Mich. with RODERICK, age 14; MARY E., age 13, both b. Ohio; EMELINE, age 5; ALICE?, age 3; CAROLINE, age 1, all b. Mich., (and JASON & BETSEY, preceding) in their household.

LANE, NATHANIEL was a native of Enfield, Hampshire Co., Mass. He married MARTHA, born ca. 1788, and they moved in 1834 to Hudson Twp., Lenawee Co., Mich. He had known son, BERIAH H. (preceding), and in the 1850 census Martha was in Beriah's household, though she seems young to be mother of Beriah?

LANE, NATHANIEL, son of BERIAH H. (preceding), was born 1 July 1830, Enfield, Mass., and moved with his parents to Lenawee Co., Mich. As an adult, he went to Newark, Ohio about 1848, and lived variously in Urbana & Dayton, Ohio; St. Louis MO; and Chicago, Ill. He married in May 1858 to MARTHA (FULLER), daughter of Lewis (also see) of Calhoun Co., Mich. They settled in Hudson Twp., Lenawee Co., Mich. Children: 1. ANNE; 2. GRACIE MAY. Ref: P&BA-Len pg. 1098-1100.

LANE, URI was listed in the 1840 census index of Fairfield Twp., Lenawee Co., Mich. adjacent to JASON, preceding.

LANG, JOHN and wife, MARY (LISCOE), natives of Co. Fermangh, Ireland came to the US in 1849, and settled in Canada, where they died. Known daughter, SUSAN b. 25 Mar. 1826, Ireland (m. Mathew H. Kerr, also see). Ref: P&BA-Len pg. 221-2.

LANGDON, BINGHAM see LANDON, BINGHAM

LANGDON, CHARLES born ca. 1826, NY, was listed in the 1850 census of Rollin Twp., Lenawee Co., Mich. with ROSETTA, age 22, b. NY in his household. Charles was said to have married PHOEBE (JENNINGS), daughter of Levi (also see), so she may have been a second wife? (In the 1850 census, Phoebe was listed two doors away in the household of her father).

LANGDON, CAROLINE, age 25, born NY, was listed in the 1850 census of Franklin Twp., Lenawee Co., Mich. in the household of William & Julia Ann Simonson (2 doors from HENRY, following).

LANGDON, EMELINE (See Robert Smith)

LANGDON, HENRY W. born ca. 1808, and wife, CAROLINE, born ca. 1815, both b. NY, were listed in the 1840 census index of Franklin Twp., Lenawee Co., Mich.; and in the 1850 census with REUBEN, age 5; ETHALIDA?, age 3; ARETHA?, age 11/12, all b. Mich., in their household.

LANGDON, MYRON K. born ca. 1806, NY, was listed in the 1850 census of Franklin Twp., Lenawee Co., Mich.

LANGDON, PAMELIA (See David Sharer)

LANGDON, SAMUEL was listed in the 1840 census index of Rome Twp., Lenawee Co., Mich.; and it is probably he, age 37, with wife, LUCINDA, age 32, both b. NY, listed in the 1850 census of Rollin Twp. with MARY, age 8; GERHARDUS, age 6, both b. Mich., in their household. Note: Next door was Bingham Landon.

LANNING, CORNELIUS and wife CHARITY (YOUNG), of Sussex Co. New Jersey, remained there, and he died in 1825, and she died in 1835. There were 3 sons and 6 daughters, names not stated, except JOSEPH (following); & JAMES (following). Ref: P&BA-Len pg. 797-8.

LANNING, JAMES, son of CORNELIUS (preceding), born 5 Oct. 1810, Huntington, NJ, went at age 19 to Seneca Co., NY, and married there to MARGARET (BODINE), daughter of Peter (also see). They moved in 1832 to Raisin Twp., Lenawee Co., Mich. She died 25 Feb. 1840, leaving children: 1. GEORGE b. 6 Aug. 1831, NY; 2. RACHEL ANN b. 18 Feb. 1833, NY (m. William Allen); 3. MARY E. b. 30 Mar. 1837, Mich. (m. William Mattis, prob. son of Garret, also see, Franklin, Lenawee Co.); 4. PETER B. b. 20 Feb. 1840 (d. 5 June 1840). James married again on 31 May 1847 to MARIA (DALLEY), daughter of Julius (also see). Children: 5. MARTHA H. b. 3 Mar.

1848 (m. Chauncey Vedder, 12 Mar. 1868, Franklin, Mich.); 6. JOSEPH b. 20 Feb. 1853 (m. Ida Shurtz, 12 Nov. 1871). Ref: P&BA-Len pg. 797-8 with portrait.

LANNING, JOSEPH, son of CORNELIUS (preceding), born ca. 1808, and wife, ELIZABETH, born ca. 1813, both in NJ, were listed in the 1850 census of Raisin Twp., Lenawee Co., Mich. (next door to JAMES, preceding) with SAMUEL, age 13; ABRAHAM W., age 9, both b. NJ; and MARY J., age 5; HANNAH, age 2, SARAH, age 1/12, all b. Mich., in their household. Also in their household were John Mattis (also see) with wife, ANGELINE, age 18, b. NJ, who is probably daughter of Joseph.

LAPHAM, EDMUND, son of JACOB (following) born 6 Feb. 1815, Dutchess Co., NY moved to Rome Twp., Lenawee Co., Mich. with his parents. In 1849, he went to California, but later returned to Rome Twp. He married 3 June 1861 to ALVIRA (WAGGONER), daughter of Nicholas (also see). Children: 1. WALTER b. 24 Nov. 1864 (m. Jennette Ryder); 2. FLORA b. 2 Mar. 1866 (m. Llewellyn Raymond); 3. ADELL b. 10 Feb. 1869 (m. George Onsted); 4. ROSANNA b. 12 Jan. 1872; 5. ALFARATA I. b. 24 Apr. 1878; 6. BESSIE L. b. 25 Aug. 1881. Ref: P&BA-Len pg. 1212-3.

LAPHAM, ELLA (See Winslow Bates)

LAPHAM, JACOB, son of REUBEN (following), born 27 Nov. 1792, Dutchess Co., NY, married there on 27 Dec. 1813 to MARY (CASE), daughter of Ephraim (also see). They brought 3 sons and an adopted daughter (names not stated) to Rome Twp., Lenawee Co., Mich. in 1836. He died 7 Jan. 1876, and she died 27 Apr. 1886. Known son, EDMUND (preceding). Ref: P&BA-Len pg. 1212-3. Also note NATHANIEL; & JAMES R., following.

LAPHAM, JAMES R. born ca. 1812, NY, and wife, MARIA, born ca. 1809, VT, were listed in the 1850 census of Rollin Twp., Lenawee Co., Mich. with JANE, age 13; EMILY A., age 11; ANN M., age 8, all b. Mich., in their household.

LAPHAM, JONATHAN J. born ca. 1817, and wife, ELIZABETH, born ca. 1821, both in NY, were listsed in the 1850 census of Adrian Twp., Lenawee Co., Mich. with EMMA L., age 2/12, b. Mich., in their household.

LAPHAM, NATHANIEL born ca. 1819, and wife, AMANDA, born ca. 1825, both in NY, were listed in the 1850 census of Rome Twp., Lenawee Co., Mich. with AMZI, age 4; MARY E., age 1, both b. Mich., in their household.

LAPHAM, NELSON of Wayne Co., NY married LOSINA (PARKER), daughter of Joshua (also see), and died in Wayne Co. Losina married again to William D. Archer, and third to Samuel White (see both). Ref: P&BA-Len pg. 784-5.

LAPHAM, REUBEN and wife, BETSEY (FINCH), were natives of Dutchess Co., NY. He went to Columbia Co., NY after 1800, where he died at age 78. Known son, JACOB (preceding). Ref: P&BA-Len pg. 1212-3.

LAPHAN, CHARLOTTE C. (See John Hancock)

LAPP, MARTHA (See John Jacob)

LARABEE, FREDERICK born ca. 1825, NY, was listed in the 1850 census of Madison Twp., Lenawe Co., Mich.

LARABEE, HENRY born ca. 1804, and wife, HANNAH, born ca. 1812, both in NY, were listed in the 1850 census of Seneca Twp., Lenawee Co., Mich. with GEORGE, age 17, b. Ohio; and MARIA, age 3, b. Mich., in their household.

LARABEE, HORATIO B. born ca. 1828, and wife, MARY, born ca. 1832, married within the year, were listed in the 1850 census of Rome Twp., Lenawee Co., Mich. next door to ROSWELL (following).

LARABEE, JOHN was listed in the 1840 census index of Raisin, Monroe Co., Mich.

LARABEE, NETTIE (See Charles F. Smith)

LARABEE, ROSWELL, probably son of SAMUEL (following), born ca. 1796, VT, was listed in the 1840 census index of Rome Twp., Lenawee Co., Mich., and in the 1850 census with AUSTIN, age 20, b. NY, and PRISCILLA, age 13, b. Mich., and SAMUEL (following) in his household. HORATIO (preceding), was probably another son, listed next door.

LARABEE, SAMUEL born ca. 1773, Vermont, was listed in the 1840 census index of Rome Twp., Lenawee Co., Mich. adjacent to ROSWELL (preceding), and was listed in the 1850 census in his household.

LARD, DEBORAH (BUTTERFIELD) Mrs. (See Justice Andrews).

LARUE, FANSING (See Don A. Read)

LARZELERE, CHARLES was listed in the 1840 census index of Tecumseh Twp., Lenawee Co., Mich.

LARZELERE, DANIEL born ca. 1804, and wife, ELIZA, born ca. 1812, both in NY, were listed in the 1850 census of Madison Twp., Lenawee Co., Mich. with CLEMINA, age 18, b. NY; and JANE E., age 10; GEORGE, age 8; DWIGHT, age 1, all b. Mich., in their household. Note: There was a "D. D." listed in the 1840 census index of Augusta Twp., Washtenaw Co., Mich.

LARZELERE, HENRY born ca. 1812, and wife, ELIZABETH, born ca. 1820, both in NY, were listed in the 1850 census of Tecumseh Twp., Lenawee Co., Mich. with no children (spelled "Lasalere.")

LARZELERE, HIRAM was a boatman on the Erie Canal; and also lived in Seneca Falls, NY. He married ? (PITCHER) and they and their children came to Michigan in 1832. It is probably he listed in the 1840 census index of Franklin Twp., Lenawee Co., Mich. They moved to Manchester, Washtenaw Co., Mich. where his wife died; and he married again to her sister, MARY A. (PITCHER). They had 4 children, and only name stated was youngest, SUSAN b. 15 Jan. 1848, Manchester Twp. (m. Charles Burleson, also see). Ref: P&BA-Len pg. 815-6.

LARZELERE, SUSAN born ca. 1783, NJ, was listed in the 1850 census of Tecumseh Twp., Lenawee Co., Mich. in the household of Cornelia Aburnettia?, age 45, also b. NJ. Note CHARLES, preceding; and WILLIAM, following

LARZELERE, WILLIAM was listed in the 1840 census index of Clinton Twp., Lenawee Co., Mich.

LASALERE see LARZELERE

Pioneer Families of Southeastern Michigan

LATHAM, BENJAMIN married ELIZABETH (CARY), daughter of John M. (also see) and moved to Moville, Iowa.

LATHAM, EDWARD B. Dr. born ca. 1807, and wife, ABBY, born ca. 1814, both in NY, were listed in the 1850 census of Cambridge Twp., Lenawee Co., Mich with HANNAH, age 16; LUCINDA, age 15; EDWARD, age 14; LYDIA, age 13; ALICIA?, age 11; HARRIET, age 8; JULIA, age 6; MARK, age 4, all b. NY; and OCTAVIA, age 2, b. Mich., in their household.

LATHAM, ELIZA (See Charles A. Chaloner)

LATHAM, ROBERT born ca. 1791, Mass., and wife, JANE, born ca. 1800, NY, were listed in the 1850 census of Dover Twp., Lenawee Co., Mich. with SALLY, age 20; EPHRAIM, age 16; JAMES, age 18, all b. NY; and ALZINA, age 13; LAFAYETTE, age 11; EDWIN, age 9, all b. Mich., in their household. Note: It may be he written as "Lathrop" in the 1840 census index of Dover Twp.

LATHROP, ANDREW J. born ca. 1826, NY, and wife, ELIZA, born ca. 1832, Ohio, married within the year, were listed in the 1850 census of Blissfield Twp., Lenawee Co., Mich.

LATHROP, LUCIAN D. Col. of Lucas Co., Ohio had known daughter, MARY A. (m. William Wilson, also see).

LATOURRETTE, ABRAHAM was born in New Jersey, and his wife, PHEBE (BODINE), was born in Penn., and they married in Seneca Co., NY (Note Peter Bodine). He died there at age 80, and she died age 88. Five sons and five daughters, only name stated, #9. ANZOLETTE b. 16 June 1833, Lodi, Seneca Co., NY (m/1 Joseph M. Hunt; m/2 George V. Osgood, see both). Ref: P&BA-Len pg. 581-2. Note: This surname appears in New Jersey in 1793, by Norton, in the militia of Hunterdon Co., NJ.

LATOURRETTE, ORANGE was listed in the 1840 census index of Macon Twp., Lenawee Co., Mich.

LAUR also see LOAR; LOHR & LOUR

LAUR, BENJAMIN, son of GEORGE (following), born 17 May 1827, Elgin Co., Ontario, Canada, came to the US first in 1846, but returned to Canada. In 1848, he came to the US and travelled in Illinois. He married in Adrian, Lenawee Co., Mich. on 28 Feb. 1849 to LYDIA P. (SCOTT), daughter of George (also see). They went to Elgin Co., Canada for 4 years, then returned to Cambridge Twp., Lenawee Co., Mich. Children: 1. MARY E. (m. Henry Howes, Fairfield Twp.); 2. EMMELLITTA (m. Thomas Smith, Jackson Co., Mich.); 3. ELIZA JANE (m. William Lindsey, Oceana Co., Mich.); 4. DELPHINE A. (m. Martin Lee, Cambridge Twp.); 5. KATE (m. Elston Fullmer, Antrim Co., Mich.) Ref: P&BA-Len pg. 962-3.

LAUR, GEORGE, son of JOHN (following), born 1797, lived out his life in Elgin Co., Canada. He served in the War of 1812 as a Sgt. in the English Army. He married first to ELIZABETH (HERRETT), and she died in 1828 leaving 7 children, only names stated were JOHN (of Elgin Co., Canada); and BENJAMIN (preceding). George married again to JANE (MARSH). He died in 1860, age 63. Ref: P&BA-Len pg. 962-3.

LAUR, JOHN immigrated from Germany to Pennsylvania before the American Revolution, and later moved to Welland Co., Canada, where he and his wife (name not stated) remained. Known son, GEORGE (preceding). Ref: P&BA-Len pg. 962-3.

LAUTENSCHLAGER, LYDIA (See Robert M. Hood)

LAW, HENRY (See Benjamin Reasoner)

LAWN, EDWIN M. (See Solomon Jeffords)

LAWRENCE, A. J. (See William H. H. Van Akin)

LAWRENCE, ALBERT D., son of CALVIN (following), born 17 Dec. 1845, Seneca Co., NY, came to Tecumseh Twp., Lenawee Co., Mich. with his parents. He served in Co. B; 9th Mich. Cav. during the Civil War. He married 2 Mar. 1871 to FLORENCE (SANFORD), daughter of Henry (also see) of Kalamazoo, Mich. Ref: P&BA-Len pg. 763-4.

LAWRENCE, AUGUSTA (See John M. Payne)

LAWRENCE, CALVIN born 15 Apr. 1814, Mass., married on 15 June 1840 to E. P. (WEEKS), daughter of John (also see). They lived first in Syracuse, NY; and in 1848 removed to Tecumseh Twp., Lenawee Co., Mich. In the 1850 census of Tecumseh her named appears to be "Alaphee" She died 8 Aug. 1865, and he died in 1884. Children: 1. EDMOND; 2. EDGAR (twin of Edmond, both d. infancy); 3. CHARLES A. b. ca. 1840 ; 4. ALMIRA b. ca. 1841 (deceased by 1888); 5. ALBERT D. (preceding). Ref: P&BA-Len pg. 763-4.

LAWRENCE, CHARLES born ca. 1810, Mass., and wife HARRIET, born ca. 1818, NY, were listed in the 1840 census index of Dover Twp., Lenawee Co., Mich., and in the 1850 census with JANE, age 12; EMILY, age 10; RUSSEL, age 8; SARAH, age 6; GEORGE, age 4, all b. Mich., in their household.

LAWRENCE, EFFIE B. (See George W. Moore)

LAWRENCE, ELIZABETH born ca. 1796, England, was listed in the 1850 census of Ridgeway Twp., Lenawee Co., Mich. head of household with RICHARD, age 27; WILLIAM, age 25; THOMAS, age 24, all b. England, in her household.

LAWRENCE, MARTHA (See Martin Fuller)

LAWRENCE, WILLIAM born 8 Dec. 1789, lived in Ontario Co., NY where he married in 1808 to SELA (THOMPSON) of West Bloomfield. He served in the War of 1812. About 1864, they moved to Rochester, NY, where he died 20 Mar. 1864. She came to Michigan and resided with known son, WILLIS THOMPSON (following); and she died 24 Feb. 1871. Ref: P&BA-Len pg. 917-8. Note: WILLIAM was said to have been descended from a JOHN who came from England and settled in Monmouth Co., NJ in Colonial times. From Old Times in Old Monmouth, by Salter & Beekman, 1980: "The first Lawrences who came to America were two brothers, JOHN, age 17, and WILLIAM, age 12, and also, MARY, age 9, who embarked on the barque "Planter, Apr. 2nd 1635; her passengers chiefly from St. Albans, Hertfordshire, England. Another brother named THOMAS came over in 1655, about 20 years later. The greater portion of the Lawrences in America are descended from William."

LAWRENCE, WILLIS THOMPSON, son of WILLIAM (preceding), born 12 Oct. 1819, West Bloomfield, Ontario Co., NY, married on 11 Oct. 1841 to JANE ADELIA (JACKSON) of Bradford Co., Penn., who died 14 May 1846. He married again on 25 May 1847 to MARIAN (WADSWORTH), daughter of Joseph (also see) in Rochester, NY. They lived in Oswego, NY in 1854, and moved to Adrian, Lenawee Co., Mich. in 1863. Children: 1. MARIA SELA b. 15 May 1848, Rochester, NY (m. Dwight Avery Whitney, son of Wm. Augustus, also see; Detroit, Mich.); 2. ERIN HICKOK b. 31 Dec. 1849 (d. 12 Oct. 1850). Ref: P&BA-Len pg. 187 & 917-8.

LAWTON, JOSHUA W., son of JOSEPH & MARY (DENNISON) of New England, married MATILDA (AYERS) and afterwards moved to Oneida Co., NY. They later moved to Albion, Dane Co., Wisc., where they died at an advanced age. Known daughter, HENRIETTA A. (m. Frederick C. Morrell, also see). Ref: P&BA-Len pg. 497-8.

LAYCOCK also see LACOCK & LEACOX

LAYCOCK, A. B. born ca. 1809, and wife, HULDAH, born ca. 1808, both in NY, were listed in the 1850 census of Fairfield Twp., Lenawee Co., Mich. with NOAH P., age 5, b. Mich., and Stephen D. Brockway, age 14, b. NY, and Almira Reynolds, age 12, b. Mich., in their household.

LAYCOCK, JONATHAN born ca. 1788, and wife, MARTHILLE, born ca. 1809, both in NJ, were listed in the 1840 census index of Seneca Twp., Lenawee Co., Mich.; and in the 1850 census with ALEXANDER A., age 19, b. NJ; RUTH, age 16; HATTY? A., age 13, both b. NY; and JOHN, age 9, born Mich., in their household. HANNAH, age 26, born NJ (m. Seth B. Sayers) probably another daughter, as they're listed nearby in census. Note: In New Jersey in 1793, by Norton, there was an ELISHA listed in the militia of Alexandria, Hunterdon Co., NJ.

LAYMAN, HATTIE (See Isaac Farst)

LAYTON, WILLIAM V. R. M. (See James Whitney)

LAZELL, CALVIN and wife, ELIZABETH, moved from New Hampshire to Sempronius, Cayuga Co., NY. Known daughter, ELIZABETH b. 16 Oct. 1790, Ashfield, NH (m. Alpheus Kies, also see). Ref: P&BA-Len pg. 337-8.

LEACH, ALVIN born ca. 1810, Ohio, and wife, EUNICE, born ca. 1820, VT, were listed in the 1850 census of Blissfield Twp., Lenawee Co., Mich. with ELIZA A., age 10; AMELIA M., age 6; HEPSY M., age 4; JAMES W., age 4/12, all b. Mich., in their household. Note ELIZABETH, following.

LEACH, BEEBER? born ca. 1803, VT, and wife, BETSEY E., born ca. 1809, Ohio, were listed in the 1850 census of Blissfield Twp., Lenawee Co., Mich. with ABIGAIL, age 22; REBECCA, age 18; ELIZABETH, age 16, all b. Ohio; and HOMER, age 11, b. Mich., in their household. Note ELIZABETH, following.

LEACH, ELIZABETH was listed in the 1840 census of Blissfield Twp., Lenawee Co., Mich. adjacent to WILLIAM, following.

LEACH, GEORGE C., age 16, born Ohio, was listed in the 1850 census of Raisin Twp., Lenawee Co., Mich. in a Wells household.

LEACH, TIMOTHY lived near Monmouth Co., NJ where he died in 1800, and the family afterwards moved to Ontario Co, NY. Known daughter, PATIENCE b. 19 Feb. 1789, NJ (m. Barzillai Clark, also see, Ontario Co., NY; and in the 1850 census of Adrian, Lenawee Co., Mich., she, age 61, was living in home of son, John R. Clark.) Ref: P&BA-Len pg. 774-5.

LEACH, WILLIAM born ca. 1815, and wife, EMILY born ca. 1820, both in NY, were probably they listed in the 1840 census index of Blissfield Twp., Lenawee Co., Mich. (as "Leech"); and in the 1850 census with ISAAC, age 5; FRANCIS, age 2, both b. Mich., in their household.

LEACOCK also see LACOCK, LAYCOCK & LEACOX

LEACOX, EMMA (See John Bryant)

LEARNARD, JAMES (See Albern Raymond)

LEASE, FRANK was the adopted son of Asa Phetteplace (also see).

LEASE, JULIUS was listed in the 1840 census index of Branch Co., Mich.

LEAVENS, ALICE (See Noah Green, Sr.)

LEE, CARRIE E. (See Robert L. Rogers)
LEE, CLAMANIA (See George Goodrich)
LEE, ELIZABETH (See Benjamin Beevers)
LEE, JAY born ca. 1817, Ohio, and wife, MARSHA, born ca. 1822, NY, were listed in the 1850 census of Madison Twp., Lenawee Co., Mich. with ARABELLA, age 4; ISABELLA, age 4, born Mich., and DANIEL, age 2, b. NY, in their household. Note JONAS, & NORMAN, following.

LEE, JOHN born ca. 1824, and wife?, HANNAH, born ca. 1812, both in NY, were listed in the 1850 census of Cambridge Twp., Lenawee Co., Mich. with Sarah Burgess, age 10, b. NY, perhaps a stepchild, in their household. Note MARY, following.

LEE, JONAS born ca. 1818, and wife, SARAH, born ca. 1819, both in Ohio, were listed in the 1840 census index of Ogden Twp., Lenawee Co., Mich.; and in the 1850 census of Palmyra Twp. with ELECTA, age 12; NORMAN, age 9; JAY H., age 7; CHARLES N., age 2, all b. Mich., in their household. Note JAY, preceding, & NORMAN, following, possibly brothers.

LEE, JOSEPH of Derbyshire, England was the son of ? & MARY (PIERPOINT); and he married (wife's name not stated) and remained in England. There were 2 sons and 5 daughters, names not stated, except JOSEPH P. (following). Note: Joseph's mother, MARY, after the death of his father, went to New Jersey and died there in 1840. Ref: P&BA-Len pg. 521-2.

LEE, JOSEPH P., son of JOSEPH (preceding), born 1 Feb. 1793, Derbyshire, England, came alone to New Jersey, and lived for a time in Philadelphia, Penn. He married DOROTHEA B. (TAYLOR) born ca. 1798, NJ, and lived in Columbia, New Jersey until 1836 when they moved to Raisin Twp., Lenawee Co., Mich. He died 3 July 1879, and she died 20 Nov. 1876. Known children, all born NJ, were listed in their household in the 1850 census of Raisin Twp.: 1. ANNA, age 22; 2. JOSEPH P. JR., age 21; 3. MARY E. b. 1 Oct. 1834, Burlington Co., NJ (m. John Handley, b. Ireland, 25 Mar. 1870); 4. JOEL, age 16. Ref: P&BA-Len pg. 521-2.

LEE, LOVINA, age 19, born NY, was listed in the 1850 census of Adrian Twp., Lenawee Co., Mich.

LEE, MARION (male), age 5, born Ohio, was listed in the 1850 census of Rollin Twp., Lenawee Co., Mich. in the household of Levi Bennett. See PHEBE, following.

LEE, MARTIN (See Benjamin Laur)

LEE, MARY born ca. 1803, NJ, was head of household in the 1850 census of Cambridge Twp., Lenawee Co., Mich. with PETER, age 27, b. NJ; GARRETT, age 16; DON?, age 14, both b. NY; and MARGARET, age 12; REUBEN, age 10; EDWIN C., age 7; MARY, age 5, all b. Mich., in her household. Note JOHN, preceding.

LEE, NORMAN, age 21, born NY, was listed in the 1850 census of Madison Twp., Lenawee Co., Mich.

LEE, PAULINE (See Joseph Sparling)

LEE, PHEBE, age 42, born NY, was listed in the 1850 census of Rollin Twp., Lenawee Co., Mich. with IRA, age 19, b. NY (listed head of household); REBECCA, age 14, b. Mich., in the household. MARION (preceding) was a few doors away and probably of this family. MARY M., age 6, b. Mich., in the household of Eli & Elizabeth Marvin in the 1850 census of Rollin Twp. may relate to this family.

LEE, ROBERT born Yorkshire, England, died there 19 Dec. 1865, age 82; and his wife, ELIZABETH (SMITH), was still living there in 1888, age 97, with son, GEORGE. There were 5 daughters and 5 sons, but only named were the preceding, and THOMAS (following). Ref: P&BA-Len pg. 807-8.

LEE, THOMAS, son of ROBERT (preceding), born 5 Mar. 1828, Yorkshire, England, came first to Tecumseh, Lenawee Co., Mich., but by the 1850 census was listed, age 21, in Ridgeway Twp. He married 3 Mar. 1854 to ELLEN (EAST), daughter of James (also see). Ten children, but only the following surviving in 1888 were mentioned: 1. ALBERT N. (m. Maggie Gregg, Milan, Monroe Co., Mich.); 2. MINNIE (m. Samuel Boyed, Macon Twp.); 3. ARTHUR. Ref: P&BA-Len pg. 807-8.

LEE, THOMAS married MEHITABLE (HENNIKER), daughter of William (also see) who was a pioneer settler of Batavia, NY; and they moved to Greece, Monroe Co, NY. Known daughter, CHLOE (m. Lewis Fuller, also see, and moved to Calhoun Co., Mich. in 1835). Ref: P&BA-Len pg. 1098-1100.

LEE, WILLIAM was listed in the 1840 census index of Adrian Twp., Lenawee Co., Mich. Note PHEBE, preceding.

LEET, ELIZABETH (See Israel Allen)

LeFEVER, ANDREW married HANNAH (DUBOIS) on 8 Jan. 1808, Ulster Co., NY. He died 18 Jan. 1818, and she died 30 Apr. 1826. Known son, CORNELIUS DUBOIS b. 25 Sept. 1808; JOHANNES A. (following); known daughters: GERTRUDE b. 23 Sept. 1812 (Record of New Paltz Reformed Church); ELIZABETH b. 10 Dec. 1815 (Record in New Hurley Ref. Church). Ref: P&BA-Len pg. 1046-9.

LeFEVER, JOHANNES A., son of ANDREW (preceding), born 2 Oct. 1810, Ulster Co., NY, made his home with his grandparents after the death of his parents. He married there on 5 July 1864 to Mrs. SARAH J. (BEVIER) DRAKE, daughter of Jeremiah, and widow of William (see both). They moved to Palmyra Twp., Lenawee Co., Mich., and he died in 1886, age 75. Children: 1. JOHN; 2. JENNIE (twin of John; d. age 11); 3. ANDREW. Ref: P&BA-Len pg. 1046-9 with portraits of he and wife.

LEFFERTS, EDWARD born ca. 1816, and wife, MARY, born ca. 1825, NY, were listed in the 1850 census of Madison Twp., Lenawee Co., Mich. (as "Leffert").

LEFFERTS, HIRAM born ca. 1810, and wife, DEBORAH (IRELAND), born ca. 1809, both in NY, were listed in the 1850 census of Rome Twp., Lenawee Co., Mich. with ELIZABETH b. ca. 1834, New Rochelle, Westchester Co., NY (m/1 to Ransom Cerrow; m/2 John Forbes, see both); GEORGE, age 15; WALTER, age 13; EMMA, age 12; CATHARINE, age 10, all b. NY; and ERVIN M., age 1, b. Mich., in their household. Ref: P&BA-Len pg. 344-5.

LEHR, BENJAMIN (See Andrew Nufer)
LEHR, FRANK (See Andrew Nufer)

LEMBARGER, HARRIET (PLANK) Mrs. was the widow of ? Lembarger who died in the Civil War (and was the daughter of Robert Plank, also see). Daughter, EVA (m. John T. Byce). Harriet married again to White Cleveland (also see). Ref: P&BA-Len pg. 378-9.

LENDAHL, J. O. (See Samuel Cook)

LEONARD, BENJAMIN born ca. 1786, Mass., and wife, JANE, born ca. 1795, Conn., were listed in the 1850 census of Tecumseh Twp., Lenawee Co., Mich. in the household of James S. Clark and wife, Catherine (age 27, b. Mass.), possibly in-laws?

LEONARD, BRIDGET, age 25, born Ireland, was listed in the 1850 census of Adrian Twp., Lenawee Co., Mich.

LEONARD, CATHERINE (See Alford Crane)

LEONARD, FREMONT and wife, ADDIE L. (LOVE), daughter of D. W. (also see) had children: DELIA E.; BERTHA L.; HIRAM W.

LEONARD, JAMES born ca. 1810, NH, and wife, ELIZABETH, born ca. 1810, England, were listed in the 1840 census index of Cambridge Twp., Lenawee Co., Mich.; and in the 1850 census of Franklin Twp. with MALINDA, age 16?/10?; JAMES, age 5; FRANCIS, age 2; DEWITT, age 8/12, all b. Mich., in their household.

LEONARD, LESTER born ca. 1816, and wife, CYNTHIA, born ca. 1824, both in NY, were listed in the 1850 census of Dover Twp., Lenawee Co., Mich. with SILAS, age 6; ANSON, age 5; LUCINDA, age 2, all b. Mich., and Jane Hare, age 21, b. NY, in their household.

LEONARDSON, JAMES moved as a young man from Montgomery Co., NY to Lucas Co., Ohio to join his parents (names not stated) who had moved to Lucas Co. at an earlier date. He married in Whiteford Twp., Lucas Co. to HANNAH (DEAN), and it was the first marriage in that township. They later returned to NY, but about 1843 moved back to Lucas Co., Ohio; then to

Bridgewater, Williams Co., Ohio; and in 1852 to Richfield Twp., Lucas Co. where they remained. Known sons: HEZEKIAH; LEVI; & JOHN (m. Lovina B. Ford, daughter of George F., also see). All 3 sons served in the Civil War. Known daughter, NANCY b. 17 June 1834, Lucas Co., O. (m. Levi B. Ford, also see). Ref: P&BA-Len pg. 1136-8.

LEPPER, CATHARINE (See William Bedell of Ashtabula Co. O.)

LERCH, ABRAHAM, son of SAMUEL (following), born 15 Jan. 1819, Northampton Co., Penn., moved to Seneca Co., NY with his parents. He married 28 Dec. 1841, Fayette, NY to MARY C. (SINGER) born 28 Nov. 1820. They remained in Seneca Co., NY until 1864, then moved to Dover Twp., Lenawee Co., Mich. About 1884, they moved to Clayton village where she died 8 Jan. 1887. Children (all b. NY): 1. JESSE (to Naperville, Ill.); 2. GEORGE (served Co. D., 148th NY Inf., died in prison during Civil War); 3. SAMUEL (d. age 12, NY); 4. SARAH (m. Lee Schaffer, Seneca Twp., Lenawee Co.); 5. LINNUS (Detroit, Mich.) Abraham married again on 12 Jan. 1888 to Mrs. LOUISA (BEACH) KESLER, daughter of Roswell (also see), and widow of John. Ref: P&BA-Len pg. 1032-3.

LERCH, FRANK married FRANCES A. (YOUNG), daughter of John (also see). She died in Waukegan, Ill. They had son, LUCIAN G. who was adopted by her sister, E. Matilda and husband, James Harvey Terwilliger (also see). Ref: P&BA-Len pg. 868-9.

LERCH, SAMUEL and wife, REGINA (BEYL), moved about 1823 from Penn. to Seneca Co., NY. There were 12 children, names not stated, except eldest, ABRAHAM (preceding). Ref: P&BA-Len pg. 1032-3.

LeSAGE, NELLIE (See Eli E. Munn)

LESTER, DAVID lived out his life on eastern Long Island, NY. It may be he listed in the 1800 census index of Albany Co., NY and went afterwards to Long Island. His wife, ? (TALMADGE), died on Long Island at age 93. Known son, JOHN (following). Ref: P&BA-Len pg. 559-60.

LESTER, GULAELMA married Ambrose Greene (who was b. 9 Apr. 1746, Suffolk Co., Long Island, also see). Ref: P&BA-Len pg. 948-50.

LESTER, JOHN, son of DAVID (preceding), born on Long Island, married there to EUNICE (GEORGE) who was born in Albany Co., NY. They later removed to Gorham, Ontario Co., NY. Four sons and two daughters, only name mentioned #5. LEWIS G. (following). Ref: P&BA-Len pg. 559-60.

LESTER, KATIE (See John Ladd)

LESTER, LEWIS G., son of JOHN (preceding), born 6 July 1827, Ontario Co., NY, moved first to Sturgis, Mich. He moved to Tecumseh Twp., Lenawee Co., Mich. and married there in 1859 to HARRIET (SCOFIELD), daughter of Enos (also see). Children: 1. CLEMENT b. 18 Mar. 1860 (m. Frances M. Matteson; St. Louis, Mich.); 2. SPENCER b. 7 Oct. 1866. Ref: P&BA-Len pg. 559-60.

LESTER, WESLEY (See John Thackray)

LEWIS, ABIAL born 1796, Otsego Co., NY, moved to Wayne Co., NY, where he married ILEY (BELCHER) born ca. 1804, Wayne Co., NY. In 1849, they moved to Monroe Co., Mich. where "his brother already lived." Iley died 11 July 1864, and she was said to have died in Riga Twp., Lenawee Co., Mich., but is buried in Sylvania, Lucas Co., Ohio. They were listed in the 1850 census of Whiteford Twp., Monroe Co., Mich. Children: 1. ADDINA (ADELINA A.) b. ca. 1824; 2. CHARLES B. CA. 1833; 3. THOMAS JASPER (following); 4. OSCAR b. ca. 1844; 5. JULIA ANN b. ca. 1845; (ABIAL) ADELBERT b. 13 Nov. 1846 (m. Margaret Finger, daughter of Jacob^2, also see, Lucas Co., O.) Abial Sr. married again to MARY A. who died 21 Dec. 1886, age 76y/2m/16d. Abial died in Monroe Co., Mich. 14 Feb. 1878. Ref: P&BA-Len pg. 396. Note: In the 1830 census of Monroe Co., Mich. Territory, there was a JOHN listed. In the 1840 census index, there were CHARLES (following), JOHN, & LEVI (following) listed in Monroe Co., Mich., one possibly brother of Abial mentioned above.

LEWIS, ADOLPHUS came to Adrian, Lenawee Co., Mich. in 1873, and died there. Known daughter, MARY b. 8 Feb. 1860, Otsego Co., NY (m. William H. Wood, also see). Ref: P&BA-Len pg. 1146-7.

LEWIS, ALANSON born ca. 1824, and wife, HENRIETTA A., born ca. 1822, both in NY, were listed in the 1850 census of Macon Twp., Lenawee Co., Mich. with BELOIT N.?, age 4, b. Mich., in their household.

LEWIS, BENJAMIN H. born ca. 1797, Mass. was listed in the 1840 census index of Palmyra Twp., Lenawee Co., Mich. It appears to be his wife, ADELINE M., who died in Sept. 1849, age 44, Palmyra Twp. In the 1850 census of Palmyra, he listed ANTOINETTE, age 16, b. Mass.; and LUCIUS J., age 13; EDWARD H., age 8; CELIA E., age 4, all b. Mich., in his household.

LEWIS, CALVIN^7, son of TIMOTHY^6 (following), born 1793, VT, moved at age 14 from Burlington, VT to Livingston Co., NY. He served in the War of 1812. He married PATTIE (HOWARD) who was born and reared in Livingston Co., NY. She died ca. 1837\40; and he moved in 1854 to Cambridge Twp., Lenawee Co., Mich. About 1866, he moved to Pentwater, Mich., where he died 9 Mar. 1868. Seven children (names not stated). Those known from 1860 census of Cambridge Twp. In Calvin's household were CHRISTINE, age 31, b. NY; CALVIN, age 29 (listed next door); NEWTON, age 27 (with wife, ELLEN, age 29, both b. NY); DELOSS (following). Known daughter, ELLEN b. 10 Mar. 1836, Wyoming Co., NY (m. William B. White, also see). Ref: P&BA-Len pg. 786-7.

LEWIS, CHARLES born ca. 1797, NY, and wife, LUCY, born ca. 1800, Mass.?, were listed in the 1840 census index of Whiteford Twp., Monroe Co., Mich.; and in the 1850 census with LUCY, age 14; L--SA, age 6, both b. Mich., in their household. Listed next door was CHARLES F., age 31, b. NY, with wife, name illegible, and child, LUCY A., age 2/12. Note ABIAL, preceding, and LEVI, following.

LEWIS, CHARLES M., son of RUSSELL (following), born 6 May 1841, Superior Twp., Washtenaw Co., Mich., married on 2 Nov. 1864 in Canton, Wayne Co., Mich. to MARY E. (MOTT), daughter of Adam (also see). In 1866, they settled in Hudson Twp., Lenawee Co., Mich.

Pioneer Families of Southeastern Michigan

Children: 1. OTIS BURTON; 2. CHARLES LEONARD; 3. GRACE ELOISE. Ref: P&BA-Len pg. 1080-1.

LEWIS, CHARLES P. was listed in the 1840 census index of Macon Twp., Lenawee Co., Mich. adjacent to DANIEL & NICHOLAS, following.

LEWIS, DANIEL Dr. of New York City (See Lemuel C. P. Vaughan).

LEWIS, DANIEL T. (G?) born ca. 1802, and wife, CANDACE, born ca. 1807, both b. NY, were listed in the 1840 census inddex of Macon Twp., Lenawee Co., Mich.; and in the 1850 census with ABIGAIL, age 19, b. NY; and ALFRED, age 16; ALONSO, age 13; LYMAN, age 11; EDWARD, age 7; ANSON, age 3; LOUISA, age 9/12, all b. Mich., in their household. In 1840 were adjacent to CHARLES P.; & NICHOLAS.

LEWIS, DELOSS^8, probably son of CALVIN^7 (preceding), born ca. 1824, and wife, MARY, born ca. 1831, both in NY, were listed in the 1860 census of Cambridge Twp., Lenawee Co., Mich. with BURTON, age 8; EVA, age 4, in their household.

LEWIS, EPHRAIM had known daughter, MARTHA (m. in 1846 in NY to James Willison Hill, also see, and moved to Lucas Co., Ohio). P&BA-Len pg. 1176-7.

LEWIS, ELISHA born ca. 1794, NY, and wife, DEBORAH, born ca. 1807, Mass., were listed in the 1850 census of Macon Twp., Lenawee Co., Mich. with BENJAMIN, age 23; EUNICE, age 18, both b. NY; and JUDSON, age 17; MATTHEW, age 14; ELISA, age 11; LUCY, age 8; FREEMAN, age 4; FRANKLIN, age 2, all b. Ohio, in their household.

LEWIS, FRED married HELEN D. (MANCHESTER) daughter of Arthur C. (also see). Had son, ARTHUR. Ref: P&BA-Len pg. 1128-9.

LEWIS, GEORGE (See Lewis Sanford)

LEWIS, GEORGE E. (Note GEORGE M., following)

LEWIS, GEORGE M.^{8}, son of JOHN^7 (following), born 28 Aug. 1825, Whitestown, Oneida Co., NY, moved to Brooklyn, Jackson Co., Mich. about 1843, and about 1845 to Addison, Lenawee Co., Mich. He married 26 Nov. 1846 to ELIZABETH B. (TOWER), daughter of Joseph P. (also see). In the 1850 census they were listed in Woodstock Twp. Children: 1. IMOGENE b. 21 Oct. 1847 (m. George Bowen); 2. CASPORETTA b. 26 May 1850 (m/1 J. M. Wyand; m/2 John Kelsey); 3. BERTHA L. b. 26 Nov. 1851 (m. Eugene Woodward); 4. JOHN b. 20 Feb. 1854 (d. 27 Aug. 1854); 5. BYRON b. 3 Feb. 1856 (d. age 14 days); 6. FRANKIE R. b. 4 July 1858 (m. GEORGE E. LEWIS); 7. ALICE b. 1 Jan. 1860 (d. 15 Aug. 1860); 8. CHARLES b. 15 Oct. 1861 (d. same month); 9. GEORGE M. (twin of Charles, d. same); 10. JOHN F. b. 1 Aug. 1865. Ref: P&BA-Len pg. 1126-7.

LEWIS, HALSEY, son of MARTIN (following), born 9 May 1811, Tompkins Co., NY, came with another family to Adrian, Lenawee Co., Mich. He lived in Monroe Co., Mich. in 1825. He married MARY E. (SHURTS), daughter of George L. (also see) of Adrian, and they settled there. Children: 1. GEORGE H. b. 20 June 1849; 2. MARGARET E. b. 9 Oct. 1850 (m. Charles Hill, prob. son of Clark, also see); 3. WINFIELD S. b. 17 May 1852 (d. June 1886, leaving 4 ch.); 4. MARTIN b. 15 Aug. 1854 (d. 3 July 1859); 5. MARY J. b. 2 June 1855 (m. William Snook, Raisin Twp.); 6. EMMA J. b. 22 Sept. 1857; 7. CHARLES J. b. 17 June 1859; 8. WILLIAM E. b. 1 Aug. 1861; 9. EVA A. b. 13 Nov. 1863 (m. John Handgen, Dover Twp.) Ref: P&BA-Len pg. 1068-9. Note ABIAL (preceding).

LEWIS, JAMES, son of SYLVESTER^3 (REUBEN^2; JAMES^1) was born 13 June 1843, Valparaiso, Ind. (His parents, Sylvester & Anna L.(Smith) Lewis had moved from Ashtabula Co., Ohio to Williams Co., O., and then to Valparaiso, Ind., where she died in 1846. Sylvester went to California in the Gold Rush, and 20 years later returned as far as Westmoreland, KS where he died. James never saw him again). After the death of his mother, James was sent back to live with maternal relatives in Ohio, and remained there until about 1861 when he moved with relatives to Cheboygan, Mich. He enlisted in the 3rd Mich. Cav. during the Civil War, and served 2 years. He was discharged seriously ill from Typhoid, and went first to Grant Co., Wisc. near his brother and sister. He married there on 10 Mar. 1866 to Mrs. ADELIA (RUSSELL) MERRILL, a young widow, daughter of William and Emma (Cook). She died in Jan. 1867, following the birth of son, 1. LESTER WILLIAM b. Dec. 1866. James returned to Cheboygan, Mich. and married there on 4 July 1869 to SARAH E. (BLACKMAR), daughter of John W. (also see). They lived first at Mullet Lake, Mich., but moved to Kaufman Co., Texas by 1876. They returned to Mich. in the 1880s, and eventually settled in Addison, Lenawee Co., Mich. He died 20 June 1918, Saline, Mich.; and she died 28 Dec. 1922, Clayton, Lenawee Co., and they are buried in Dover Cemetery, Lenawee Co. Children: 2. OWEN THEODORE b. 1870 (d. 6 Jan. 1872); 3. ANNA BETSEY b. 9 Jan. 1872; 4. REUBEN WESLEY b. 3 Feb. 1876, Kaufman Co., TX; 5. WILLIAM ALVIN b. 10 Dec. 1878, TX (m. Carrie A. Ormsby, dau. of John W., also see); 6. MABEL LYDIA b. 12 Aug. 1884, Mich.; 7. GRACE ESTELLE b. 2 Mar. 1890, Addison, Lenawee Co., Mich. Ref: Lewis Family Records.

LEWIS, JOHN^2, son of WILLIAM^1 (who was b. England 1610; m. Amy Weld, d. 3 Dec. 1671, Roxbury, Mass.), born 1 Nov. 1635, Roxbury, Mass., m/1 MARGARET (WHITCOMB), resided Dorchester, Mass., and had among his children, BARACHIAH^3 born 31 July 1663 of Lancaster, Mass. BARACHIAH^3 may have had 2 wives, HANNAH (DWIGHT) MANNING & JUDITH (surname not known), and had among his children ISAAC^4 born 17 Nov. 1701; married Apr. 1734 to MARY (WHITING), dau. of Nathaniel & Joanna (Ellis); and died 5 Jan. 1749, Dedham, Mass. They had among their children JOHN^5 (following). Ref: Pioneer Lewis Families, by M. L. Cook.

LEWIS, JOHN^5, son of ISAAC^4 (See preceding in JOHN^2), born 15 Dec. 1735, Dedham, Mass. married DEBORAH (FISHER) on 21 Sept. 1758, probably lived Walpole, Mass. Children: JOHN^6 (following); MARY; DAVID; DEBORAH; SARAH; JOSEPH; OLIVER.

LEWIS, JOHN^6, son of JOHN^5 (preceding), born 18 Aug. 1759, Dedham, Mass., married first to ANNA (PRATT). He served in the Revolutionary War. They settled first in Rensselaer Co., NY, then moved to Whitestown, Oneida Co., NY where she died. Children: JOHN^7 (following); DEBORAH (m. Oliver Roberts); POLLY (m. Jonas White); ABIGAIL (unmarried); BETSEY (m. Simon Rogers); ANNA (m. Samuel Andrews). He married again to Mrs. ? (SWEETING) DANBY; and died in Whitestown, NY. Ref: P&BA-Len pg. 1124-5.

LEWIS, JOHN[7], son of JOHN[6] (preceding), born 10 Feb. 1783, married RIZPAH (SMITH) born 21 Nov. 1786. They resided in Whitestown, Oneida Co., NY. They had a large family but only mentioned GEORGE M.[8] (preceding). Ref: P&BA-Len pg. 1125-6.

LEWIS, JOHN born ca. 1795, place not legible, possibly Spain?, may be he listed in Adrian in the 1840 census index. His wife, MARGARET, was born Maryland in 1800, and they were listed as "Mulatto." In the 1850 census of Madison Twp. they listed the following: 1. JOHN b. ca. 1828, Penn. (or Livingston Co., NY?); 2. GEORGE b. ca. 1832, NY; 3. WILLIAM b. ca. 1838, Mich.; 4. SARAH b. ca. 1844, Mich.; 5. CHARLES H. b. ca. 1847. Ref: P&BA-Len pg. 299-300.

LEWIS, JOHN born 27 Aug. 1794, married on 19 Apr. 1814 to PHEBE (CASE), born 29 Aug. 1797, daughter of Stephen (b. 1 May 1770, Mass.) They lived in Newfane, Niagara Co., NY, and moved to Liberty Twp., Jackson Co., Mich. by 1844. He died there 10 Mar. 1867; and she was still living in 1881. Children: 1. JACOB b. 11 Dec. 1815 (d. 10 May 1852); 2. RACHEL M. b. 8 Feb. 1818; 3. JOHN Q. b. 29 Jan. 1820 (d. 21 Apr. 1844); 4. CORNELIA b. 23 Mar. 1822; 5. SARAH E. b. 20 Apr. 1824 (d. 27 Oct. 1850); 6. ANN C. b. 6 July 1826 (d. 14 Feb. 1853); 7. STEPHEN b. 29 Nov. 1828 (d. 7 Oct. 1865); 8. ADELINE b. 8 Feb. 1831 (d. 8 May 1854); 9. ANGELINE (twin of Adeline; d. Aug. 1832); 10. PHILETUS b. 5 July 1833 (m. Arvilla M. Root; daus: Edith & Clara); 11. EMERY A. b. 21 Jan. 1836; 12 MARGARET C. b. 18 May 1839 (d. 17 Oct. 1878); 13. ROBERT B. b. 17 Sept. 1841. Ref: History of Jackson Co., Mich., 1881, pg. 946.

LEWIS, JOHN born ca. 1800, and wife, SUSAN, born ca. 1816, both in NY, were listed in the 1850 census of Cambridge Twp., Lenawee Co., Mich. with GEORGE, age 15; SUNDERLAND, age 13; WILLIAM, age 11; LAURA, age 10; JOHN, age 4, all b. NY, and Patrick Henry, age 1, b. Mich., in their household.

LEWIS, LEVI born ca. 1811, and wife, ERSA?, born ca. 1811, both in NY, were listed in the 1840 census index of Monroe Co., Mich.; and in the 1850 census of Whiteford Twp., Monroe Co. with ANNIE, age 15; JAMES, age 11, both b. Mich., in their household. They were listed a few pages from ABIAL (preceding). Also see CHARLES.

LEWIS, MARTIN was listed in the 1820 census index of Mentz, Cayuga Co., NY, and is probably the father of HALSEY (preceding). Ref: P&BA-Len pg. 1068-9. Martin may have been deceased by 1830, as he was not listed in that census, however, there was a JOHN listed in Mentz in 1830.

LEWIS, NICHOLAS born ca. 1807, and wife POLLY, born ca. 1804, both b. Mass., were listed in the 1840 census index of Macon Twp., Lenawee Co., Mich.; and in the 1850 census with WARREN, age 19, b. NY; and BETSEY, age 13; LAURA, age 10; LOUISA, age 7; THEODORE, age 5, all b. Mich., in their household. In 1840 were listed adjacent to CHARLES P.; & DANIEL, preceding.

LEWIS, RACHEL (See Elus M. Shelby of St. Joseph Co., Mich.)

LEWIS, RICHARD M., age 40, born NY, was listed in the 1850 census of Madison Twp., Lenawee Co., Mich.

LEWIS, RUSSELL, son of SAMUEL (following), born ca. 1805, Cayuga Co., NY, was living in 1820 in Ossian (then Allegany, now Livingston Co., NY). He lived also in Gaines, Orleans Co., NY, and moved from there in 1828 to Superior Twp., Washtenaw Co., Mich. He married first to EMILY (FREEMAN) who died in June 1846 leaving 6 children. Those known listed in the 1850 census were ANDREW, age 16; ALMIRA, age 13; CHARLES M. (preceding); JANE, age 4, all b. Mich. Russell married again on 23 Sept. 1847 to Mrs. SUSAN (JOSELYN) CHAPMAN in Wayne Co., Mich. They had 2 children, names not stated. In their household in 1850, they listed Seliah Chapman, age 13, b. Mich., probably child of Susan.

LEWIS, SALLIE (See Samuel Colbath)

LEWIS, SAMUEL probably from Mass., was in Cayuga Co., NY before 1805. His known children: 1. FILA; 2. NANCY; 3. POLLY; 4. LLOYD; 5. CHARITY b. ca. 1791\2, Mass. (m. James Foster; lived Eaton Co., Mich.; she d. 17 Mar. 1858); 6. SAMUEL b. ca. 1794/5 (m. Asenath Sill, lived Ossian, NY 1820, Gaines, Orleans Co., NY 1830); 7. SALLY b. ca. 1796 (m/1 Dudley Thompson; m/2 Charles Carpenter; d. 22 Feb. 1879, Ypsilanti, Mich.); 8. RUSSELL (preceding); 9. ELIZA b. ca. 1806/10 (m/1 Chester Curtis; m/2 John Cody, 24 Mar. 1842, Washtenaw Co., Mich.; she d. 10 Dec. 1879, Battle Creek, Mich.)

LEWIS, SARAH of E. Kent, England (See Samuel Curtis)

LEWIS, SUSAN born 10 Apr. 1815, Francestown, NH (See Ezra Ames).

LEWIS, THOMAS JASPER, son of ABIAL (preceding), born 7 Oct. 1837, Butler, Wayne Co., NY, married SARAH M. (LOE), daughter of John (also see), a native of West Wheeling, Ohio. Children: 1. JOHN G.; 2. ARDIE. Ref: P&BA-Len pg. 396-7.

LEWIS, TIMOTHY[6], son of TIMOTHY[5] & SARAH of Harwich, Mass., born 24 May 1764, descends from GEORGE[1] of Barnstable, Mass., as follows: GEORGE[1] (son of GEORGE of Brenchley, Kent Co., England) born 1600, Brenchley, came to America and married SARAH (JENKINS), and eventually settled Barnstable Co., Mass. where he died in 1663. A son, EDWARD[2] married HANNAH (COBB) and they had a son, JOHN[3] born 1 Jan. 1666, married ELIZABETH (HUCKINS). Their son, JOHN[4] married MARY (HOPKINS) and had a son, TIMOTHY[5] born 25 Jul 1727, Harwich, Mass. who married SARAH, and were the parents named above. TIMOTHY[6] served in the Revolutionary War. He married THANKFUL "MOLLY" (BRADLEY), and they lived in Vermont, NY, Michigan, Wisconsin, and finally in Belvidere, Boone Co., Ill. where he died at age 94. There were 8 children, only known are CALVIN[7] (preceding); and ISAAC (of Pentwater, Mich.). Ref: P&BA-Len pg. 786-7 & Pioneer Lewis Families, by M. L. Cook, Evanston, Ind.

LEWIS, W. (See James L. Brown)

LIBBY, SHOAL (See Aaron Humphrey)

LIDDEL, ANN born 10 Dec. 1824, Schenectady Co., NY, lived Columbia Twp., Jackson Co., Mich. (See James Templer).

LIDDEL, JAMES R., son of ROBERT (following), born ca. 1835, Saline, Washtenaw Co., Mich., moved to Macon Twp., Lenawee Co. with his parents. He married MATILDA (KUDER), daughter of Joshua on 27 Nov.

Pioneer Families of Southeastern Michigan

1867. Children: 1. FRANK R.; 2. EDITH; 3. JENNIE; 4. SUMNER; 5. PEARL. Ref: P&BA-Len pg. 801-2.

LIDDEL, ROBERT, son of THOMAS (following), born ca. 1800, Schenectady Co., NY, married JANET (ADAIR), daughter of Alexander (also see). They apparently lived also in Montgomery Co., NY. In 1835, with wife and 2 children, he removed first to Washtenaw Co., Mich., and by 1840 to Macon Twp., Lenawee Co., Mich. She died 24 Dec. 1865, age 65. Children (in household in 1850 census of Macon Twp.): 1. THOMAS A. (following); 2. JANE A. b. ca. 1834 (m. Solomon Brown, also see); 3. JAMES R. (preceding); 4. JOHN b. ca. 1838. Robert married again to Mrs. SUSAN MILLER, and moved to Clinton, Mich., where he died 1 May 1879, age 79. Ref: P&BA-Len pg. 745-6.

LIDDEL, THOMAS possibly from Scotland, married JANET (ROBISON) and settled in Schenectady Co., NY. He died there age 80, and she died at age 100. Known son, ROBERT (preceding). Ref: P&BA-Len pg. 745-6.

LIDDEL, THOMAS A., son of ROBERT (preceding), born 28 July 1832, Florida, Montgomery Co., NY, moved with his parents to Macon Twp., Lenawee Co., Mich. He married on 5 Mar. 1856 to MARY E. (RICHART), daughter of Robert (also see), and settled in Macon Twp. Children: 1. MARILLA R.; 2. MARY E. (m. Charles Wilkins, Macon Twp.); 3. IVY (m. David Sloan). Ref: P&BA-Len pg. 745-6.

LIDDELL/LIDDLE see LIDDEL

LIFORT, WILLIAM (See John A. Baer)

LIGDEN, JAMES married in England to ELIZABETH (CURTIS), daughter of Samuel (also see). He apparently died in England, and Elizabeth came to the US in 1853 with her brother. Eight children, names not stated, were living in Rome Twp., Lenawee Co., Mich. in 1888. Elizabeth married again in Rome Twp. to Abraham Bateman (also see) as his second wife. Ref: P&BA-Len pg. 747-8.

LIGHTFALL, ELIZABETH (See A. W. Ellis)

LILLEY, LUCIUS, son of ZENAS (following), born 21 Feb. 1823, Homer, Cortland Co., NY, moved about 1840 to Akron, Ohio and then Cleveland. He married 18 July 1848 to SARAH (McEACHRON) born 5 Feb. 1829, Nova Scotia, who had come to Cleveland with her parents. They lived in Adrian, Lenawee Co., Mich. by 1854, and in 1855 in Tecumseh, Lenawee Co., where they remained. Children: 1. J. RAYNOR b. 3 Sept. 1854, Adrian (m. Jeanine Daniels, Buffalo, NY); 2. JULIA G. b. 3 Sept. 1856, Tecumseh (m. Lester P. Tribou). Ref: P&BA-Len pg. 822.

LILLEY, ZENAS born Mass., moved before 1823 to Homer, Corland Co., NY. He later moved to Wayne Co., NY where he remained. Known son, LUCIUS (preceding). Ref: P&BA-Len pg. 822.

LINCOLN, BENJAMIN and wife, ELIZABETH (WHITE), of Mass. had known daughter, CHARITY b. 7 Aug. 1782, Bristol or Taunton (m. George Crane, also see). Ref: P&BA-Len pg. 370-2.

LINCOLN, EDWARD and wife, RACHEL (PACKARD), were natives of Vermont, where they married. In 1844, they removed to Madison Twp., Lenawee Co., Mich., and he died in 1845. In 1888, she was living in Watseka, Iroquois Co., Ill., apparently gone from Lenawee Co. before 1850. Known daughter, ELIZABETH b. 16 Mar. 1845, Madison Twp. (m. Charles L. Miller, also see); probably a son, EDSON b. ca. 1832, VT (listed in 1850 census of Blissfield Twp.) Ref: P&BA-Len pg. 716-7.

LINCOLN, GEORGE S., born ca. 1812, and wife, SARAH, born ca. 1825, both in NY, were listed in the 1850 census of Madison Twp., Lenawee Co., Mich. with WILLARD, age 7; LUCIUS, age 3; ELIZA, age 1, all b. Mich., in their household. Note WILLARD, following.

LINCOLN, POLLY, age 74, born Conn., note in household of WILLARD (following).

LINCOLN, RICHARD and wife, MATILDA, of Napoleon, Jackson Co., Mich. had known daughter, CLARA b. 22 Apr. 1849, Napoleon (m. Alanson B. Treat, also see, in 1871). Ref: P&BA-Len pg. 1167-8.

LINCOLN, WILLARD born ca. 1803, and wife, ARTHESIA?, born ca. 1812, both in NY, were listed in the 1840 census index of Rome Twp., Lenawee Co., Mich., and in the 1850 census with SYLVINCENT, age 18; MALVINA, age 15, both b. NY; and MARY J., age 12; THADDEUS, age 7; EMORY, age 2; JULIA, age 1, all b. Mich.; and POLLY (mother?), age 74, born Conn., in their household

LINDERMAN, MICHAEL born Germany, and wife, CATHARINE (BARCH), born Penn., moved to Richland Co., Ohio where they remained. There were 4 daughters and 3 sons, and only one mentioned #6. BARBARA b. 4 Mar. 1848, Richland Co., Ohio (m. Albert D. Osborn, also see). Ref: P&BA-Len pg. 860-1.

LINDSEY, WILLIAM (See Benjamin Laur)

LINN, ADAM born ca. 1811, was listed in Ridgeway Twp., Lenawee Co., Mich. in 1840 census index; and in the 1850 census as with (wife?) POLLY, age 25, born NY, REBECCA, age 15, b. NY; and DANIEL, age 13; SARAH, age 9; ELI, age 1, all b. Mich., in his household.

LINN, DELILAH who married Russell Wells (also see) "was a sister of JOHN" (JR?) and probably daughter of JOHN (following).

LINN, JOHN was listed in the 1840 census index of Ridgeway Twp., Lenawee Co., Mich. It is probably he, age 69, born NJ, listed in the 1850 census of Ridgeway Twp., with MARY, age 38; CHESTER A., age 27; JOHN JR., age 25; GEORGE, age 23; SIMON H., age 20, all b. NY, and Edgar Wells, age 10, b. Mich., in his household, and next door is SAMUEL, following; and see DELILAH, preceding.

LINN, SAMUEL, probably son of JOHN (preceding), born ca. 1808, Penn., and wife, ABIGAIL (ARCHIE), moved from NY to Ridgeway Twp., Lenawee Co., Mich. in 1838. He died in 1866, and she was still living there in 1888, age 82, in home of son, John. Children from 1850 census of Ridgeway Twp.: 1. MARTHA, age 17; 2. LETITIA, born 7 Mar. 1837, Ithaca, NY (m. Joseph E. Exelby (also see); 3. ESTHER, age 10, b. Mich.; 4. JAMES, age 8; 5. NANCY, age 4; JOHN, age 1/12. Ref: P&BA-Len pg. 461-2.

LINSLEY, SARAH (See Hiram D. Dewey)

LINTON, ELLEN & NANCY (See William Gregg)

LISCOE, MARY (See John Lang)

LISTER, ELIZABETH (See William Taylor)

LITE, PETER and wife, CHRISTINE, were natives of Bavaria, Germany, who settled in Erie Co., Ohio. Known daughter, ANNA MARIA (m. Jacob Mitchell, also see). Ref: P&BA-Len pg. 1141-2.

LITTLE, POLLY (See Erastus Knight)

LIVERMORE, JAMES born 25 Aug. 1815, and wife, HARRIET, (RILEY), born 26 Sept. 1813, both in Sangerfield, Oneida Co., NY. Apparently in Madison Co., NY ca. 1842. He died Sangerfield on 12 Sept. 1854, and she died in Hamilton, Oneida Co. on 20 Apr. 1853. Known daughter, EMMA C. b. 23 Aug. 1842, Madison, Madison Co., NY (m. Calvin H. Crane, also see). Ref: P&BA-Len pg. 966-7.

LIVESAY, CHARLES born ca. 1798, and wife, HANNAH, born ca. 1806, both in NY, were listed (as "Liverstry") in the 1840 census index of Fairfield Twp., Lenawee Co., Mich.; and in the 1850 census with ALLETTA, age 19; PHEBE, age 17, both b. NY; and REBECCA, age 13; JAMES, age 10; CHARLES, age 6, all b. Mich., in their household.

LIVESAY, GEORGE born ca. 1800, and wife, ILLEY?, age 43, both born NY, were listed in the 1840 census index of Madison Twp., Lenawee Co., Mich. (adjacent to JUDAH); and in the 1850 census with MYRON, age 20, b. NY (probably he m. Emma Sparhawk, dau. of Eben, also see); and CHARLES, age 17; HANNAH, age 16; ANNA, age 23; JOHN, age 10; GERSHOM, age 7; AUGUSTA, age 1, all b. Mich., in their household.

LIVESAY, JAMES born 7 Nov 1811, Horseheads (then Tioga, now Chemung Co.), NY, married ORPHA ARMENIA (SALSBURY) born ca. 1812, NY. They moved first to Fulton Co., Ohio, and then in 1836 to Fairfield Twp., Lenawee Co., Mich. He died there in 1885, and she died 6 Dec. 1860. Known children: 1. ELLEN M. b. 23 Nov. 1842 (m. John Colvin, also see); 2. MARY L. b. 29 May 1844 (m. Stillman W. Bennett, also see); 3. GEORGE b. ca. 1848. Ref: P&BA-Len pg. 193 & 535-6.

LIVESAY, JONATHAN born ca. 1809, and wife, RHODA, born ca. 1820, both in NY, were listed in the 1850 census of Fairfield Twp., Lenawee Co., Mich. with RICHARD M., age 11; PERLINA, age 8; ALMIRA, age 5, all b. Mich., in their household.

LIVESAY, JUDAH born ca. 1808, and wife, CAROLINE, born ca. 1809, both in NY, were listed in the 1840 census index of Madison Twp., Lenawee Co., Mich., adjacent to GEORGE, preceding; and in the 1850 census with JOHN H., age 18; HANNAH, age 16; ELIZA, age 14, all b. NY; and REBECCA, age 12; GEORGE, age 10; ELIZABETH, age 7; SARAH, age 5, all b. Mich., in their household.

LOAR also see LAUR; LOHR & LOUR

LOAR, GEORGE, son of JACOB, born in Alleghany Co., Maryland, married there to MARGARET (RHINEHART), daughter of George (also see), and remained in Maryland. Known daughter, SUSANNAH b. 22 Apr. 1819 (m. Samuel Hopkins, also see). Ref: P&BA-Len pg. 912-3.

LOBDELL, ELIZABETH (See John Caton)
LOBDELL, GEORGE W. (See George S. Stranahan)

LOCKE, ELIZAABETH born Yorkshire, England (See William Thackray)

LOCKLAND, ANN (See William Pocklington)

LOCKMAN, JAMES Capt. was a native of Staten Island, NY. He had known daughter, JANE ANN (m. John S. Johnson, Tompkinsville, NY). Ref: P&BA-Len pg. 1008-9.

LOCKWOOD, CHARLES born ca. 1794, NY, was listed in the 1850 census of Madison Twp., Lenawee Co., Mich. in a Perkins household.
LOCKWOOD, CHARLOTTE (See George Byrton)
LOCKWOOD, GEORGE, son of JEREMIAH^3 (following), born 4 Sept. 1842, Herkimer Co., NY, moved with his parents to Rollin Twp., Lenawee Co., Mich. He served in Co. D, 11th Mich. Cav. during the Civil War. He married on 21 Sept. 1865 to LIZZIE (ROLF) born 17 Dec. 1848 near Chicago. She died 19 July 1883. There were 6 children, and named were only those surviving in 1888: 1. CAROLINE b. 5 Oct. 1866; 2. ELIZA b. 2 Sept. 1871; 3. GEORGE H. JR. b. 2 July 1879; 4. MINNIE b. 15 Jan. 1881. George married second on 30 Sept. 1885 to STELLA (WORDEN), daughter of Dudley (also see). Ref: P&BA-Len pg. 1035-6.
LOCKWOOD, GILBERT of Orange Co., NY married ANN (PENNEY), daughter of William of Orange Co., NY. Known children: 1. DANIEL (came to Lenawee Co., Mich. in 1834); 2. RUTH A. (m. Joshua Waring, also see); 3. WILLIAM (came to Franklin Twp., Lenawee Co. ca. 1834). Ref: P&BA-Len pg. 630-2.
LOCKWOOD, HENRY born ca. 1790, Conn., was listed in the 1850 census of Madison Twp., Lenawee Co., Mich. in the household of Seneca C. and Eliza Bruce.
LOCKWOOD, JEREMIAH^3, son of JEREMIAH^2 (son of JEREMIAH^1, a Revolutionary soldier), born 1807 Herkimer Co., NY, married there to CAROLINE (HALL). They remained there until 1852, then moved to Rollin Twp., Lenawee Co., Mich. He died 19 Apr. 1876. There were 4 sons and 3 daughters, and only named was GEORGE H. (preceding). Ref: P&BA-Len pg. 1035-6.
LOCKWOOD, SAMUEL S. born ca. 1770, NY, was listed in the 1840 census index of Woodstock Twp., Lenawee Co., Mich.; and in the 1850 census was listed in household of son, SAMUEL S. b. 1811, NY. Also in the household were (wife of Samuel S., Jr.?) REBECCA, age 20, b. NY; and JOHN, age 14; SARAH, age 11; ELLEN, age 3; MARY, age 1, all b. Mich.

LOE, JOHN, son of ROBERT (who died in Wood Co., Ohio), was born in Philadelphia, and moved with his father to West Wheeling, Ohio. He married there to L. MARY (HURLESS), daughter of Isaac (also see). Known

Pioneer Families of Southeastern Michigan

daughter, SARAH M. (m. Thomas J. Lewis, also see). Ref: P&BA-Len pg. 396-7.

LOEBSTER, THOMAS (See William Taylor)

LOHR also see LAUR; LOAR & LOUR
LOHR, ANNA (See Justus Iffland)
LOHR, DELIA (See Theodore Abbott)

LOMBARD, ALMEDA, age 44, born NY, was listed in the 1850 census of Rollin Twp., Lenawee Co., Mich. with children, ALBERT, age 17, b. NY; MARY L., age 2, b. Mich., all in the household of Alvirus Webster.

LOMBARD, L. C. was called the "foster father" of Elizabeth Adele McCurran (See Anthony McCurran). Also note LEWIS, following.

LOMBARD, LEWIS born 1798, New Hampshire, was son of a Revolutionary soldier, and his grandfather was a Major in the Revolution. He moved at age 12 with his parents to New York. He married PHILURA (CHEESBROUGH) who was a native of Chenango Co., NY, and they lived in Ontario Co., NY until 1859. They moved to Rollin Twp., Lenawee Co., Mich. where he died 6 months later at at age 61. There were 3 children, and those following were surviving in 1888: 1. STEPHEN C. (following); 2. EDWARD R. (Eaton Co., Mich.) Ref: P&BA-Len pg. 1016-7.

LOMBARD, STEPHEN C., son of LEWIS (preceding), born 25 Nov. 1829, Ontario Co., NY, married on 27 Oct. 1858 to MARY A. (RICHARDSON), daughter of Silas (also see). They moved to Rollin Twp., Lenawee Co., Mich. Children: 1. CHARLES b. 5 Dec. 1859 (d. 11 Nov. 1863); 2. HARRY b. 18 Apr. 1862 (m. Katie A. Jenkins, Rollin Twp.); 3. ALBERT G. b. 24 Sept. 1864 (m. Florence Rogers, dau. of John C., also see); 4. EDWARD A. b. 14 Oct. 1866; 5. E. GRACE b. 19 Jan. 1869. Ref: P&BA-Len pg. 1016-7 & portrait of farm.

LONG, APPOLOS and wife, SARAH (GREEN), were natives of Mass. who moved to Caledonia, Livingston Co., NY; and then to Geneseee Co., but returned to Livingston Co. where he died in 1845, age 55. Sarah and her children moved to Raisin Twp., Lenawee Co., Mich., and later to Eaton Rapids, Mich. where she died at the home of a son in 1863, age 70. Eleven children, but only mentioned #2. CORNELIA S. b. 30 Mar. 1825, Alabama, Genesee Co., NY (m. F. V. Horton, also see). Note: HATTIE I. of Eaton Co. Mich. m. F. V. Horton, probably also of this family. Ref: P&BA-Len pg. 311-2.

LONG, DENNIS and wife, MARGARET, moved from New York City to Chicago, Ill. ca. 1839. They lived in Kane Co., Ill, and late in lived in DuPage Co. He died in St. Charles, Ill. in 1862. She died in 1857. Three children, only mentioned the youngest, MICHAEL (following). Ref: P&BA-Len pg. 791-2.

LONG, JOHN was listed in the 1840 census index of Tecumseh Twp., Lenawee Co., Mich.

LONG, MICHAEL P., son of DENNIS (preceding), was born 12 Aug. 1835, New York City, and move with his parents ot Chicago, Ill. He moved to Cedar Springs, Mich. in 1861, and enlisted in Co. E., 3rd Mich. Inf. He was mustered out a Capt. & Brevet Major. After the war, he settled in Adrian, Lenawee Co., Mich. where he married in 1866 to LIZZIE C. (COLE), daughter of William F. (also see). Ref: P&BA-Len pg. 791-2.

LONG, MORRIS born Dublin, Ireland, married there (wife's name not stated). They moved first to Montreal, Canada, and then to Malone, NY. In 1855, they moved to Lenawee Co., Mich. He died in 1857, age 61, and she was still living in 1888, age 89. Known children: 1. JOHN; MARY b. 2 July 1827, Dublin (m. in Perinton, Monroe Co., NY to Eli E. Munn, also see). Ref: P&BA-Len pg. 1057-8.

LONG, PATRICK born ca. 1808, NJ, and wife, LYDIA, born ca. 1824, NY, were listed in the 1850 census of Cambridge Twp., Lenawee Co., Mich. with MARY, age 9, b. NY; and LAFAYETTE, age 7; AMOS, age 5; EDGAR, age 3; ELISA, age 1, all b. Mich., in their household.

LONGCORE, BETSEY had parents who were natives of New Jersey, and went first to Seneca Co., NY; and the moved to Franklin Twp., Lenawee Co., Mich. with Betsey and her husband, James Osborn (also see). Ref: P&BA-Len pg. 261-2.

LONKHOR see LONGCORE

LOOK, THOMAS was a whaler in New Bedford, Mass. and had known daughter, THANKFUL b. 1800, Martha's Vineyard (m. Walter Harris, also see). Ref: P&BA-Len pg. 196.

LOOMIS, ALMIRA (See John Cleveland)
LOOMIS, DANIEL born ca. 1811, and wife JANE, born ca. 1811, both in Mass., were listed in the 1850 census of Adrian Twp., Lenawee Co., Mich. with WILLIAM, age 16, b. NY; and Maria Chapman, age 15, b. NY, in their household.

LOOMIS, HIRAM born ca. 1808, VT, and wife, CLARISSA, born ca. 1811, NY, were listed in the 1850 census of Adrian Twp., Lenawee Co., Mich. with HENRY, age 9; ALICE, age 5, both b. Mich., in their household. Note: It is probably he listed as "Hyman" in the 1840 census index of Adrian Twp.

LOOMIS, POLLY (See Rev. Stephen Curtis)
LOOMIS, SERENO born 24 Apr. 1821, Ashtabula Co., Ohio, and wife, ANN A. (NOBLE) born 11 July 1828, VT (from where she had moved at age 7), were living in Windsor, Ashtabula Co. in 1888. Children: 1. ELLA J. b. 9 May 1853 (m. Alba J. Case, also see); 2. ELWIN; 3. ALICE; 4. ALLISON; 5. HARRIET. Ref: P&BA-Len pg. 911-2.

LOOMIS, WILLIAM was listed in Clinton Twp., Lenawee Co., Mich. in the 1840 census index.

LORD, HIRAM born ca. 1814, and wife, LOVIS? (LOIS?), born ca. 1814, both in NY, were listed in the 1840 census index of Dover Twp., Lenawee Co., Mich.; and in the 1850 census with ALLEN, age 9; JEROME, age 7; CHARLES, age 6; GEORGE, age 4; MARY, age 2; MARTHA, age 4/12, all b. Mich., in their household.

LORD, JAMES born ca. 1817, and wife, ORPHA, born ca. 1826, both in NY, were listed in the 1850 census of Seneca Twp., Lenawee Co., Mich. with ELLEN, age 8; EMILY, age 5; FRANKLIN, age 1, all b. Mich., in their household.

LORD W. A. (See Dr. Alexander W. Seger)

LOSS, SARAH A. born 10 Nov. 1807 (m. Hiram Parsons, also see, Woodstock Twp., Lenawee Co., Mich.) She was daughter of a family who moved from Oneida Co., NY to Michigan in 1853, and settled in Calhoun Co., Mich., where her father died almost 96, and her mother died age 96. Ref: P&BA-Len pg. 698-9.

LOUDEN, JEFFERSON, son of WILLIAM, born Oct. 1831, Adrian Twp., Lenawee Co., Mich., married 22 Mar. 1871 to HANNAH U. (BOOHER), daughter of Jacob (also see) of Cambridge Twp. They settled in Cambridge Twp. Children: 1. NELLIE; 2. MARY A.; 3. CLARENCE. Ref: P&BA-Len pg. 993-4.

LOUDEN, WILLIAM born in NY married ELIZABETH (VADER) born Mass., and in 1829, after the birth of 4 children, moved to Adrian Twp., Lenawee Co., Mich. (where they were listed in the 1840 census index). They returned to NY where they both died. Known son, JEFFERSON b. 8 Oct. 1831. Note: In the 1850 census of Rome Twp., Lenawee Co., Mich., there was a JEFFERSON, age 15, b. NY, listed in household of Warren & Almira Gilbert; and in the 1850 census of Raisin Twp. there was a JAMES, age 12, b. Mich., in the household of Thomas Lovett; and THOMAS, age 16, b. NY, in the household of Thomas Chandler.

LOUR also see LAUR; LOAR; LOHR
LOUR, HOWARD E. (See David B. Heckert)

LOWDEN see LOUDEN

LOVE, AUSTIN was the son of WILLIAM, born ca. 1802, NY (book says Barry Co., NY, but there is none). William was said to be the son of Scottish parents who had settled in Barry Co. Also it should be noted that there was a William listed in the 1800 census index of Chenango Co., NY. Austin married CLARA A. (BRADLEY) born ca. 1810, NY, and they settled first in Monroe Co. (NY?), then moved to Franklin Twp., Lenawee Co., Mich. by the 1840 census. He died there in 1872; and she died 10 June 1874, age 66. Children from 1850 census of Franklin Twp.: 1. HORACE, age 20; 2. JULIA ANN, age 17, both b. NY; and 3. DANIEL W. (following); 4. ARMENIA, age 11; 5. FRANCES, age 10; 6. EDITH, age 7; 7. SIDNEY, age 5; 8. HARRIET, age 4/12, last 6 b. Mich. Ref: P&BA-Len pg. 252-3.

LOVE, DANIEL W., son of AUSTIN, born 22 Oct. 1836, NY, married 22 Sept. 1858 to DELIA A. (FISHER), daughter of Pliny (also see), Franklin Twp., Lenawee Co., Mich. She died there 1 Nov. 1866. Known daughter, ADDIE L. (m. Fremont Leonard, also see). He married again on 22 Dec. 1868 to Mrs. MARY E. (SMITH) EDWARDS, daughter of Robert (also see), and widow of Charles. Ref: P&BA-Len pg. 252-3.

LOVEJOY, ELECTA (See John Smith)
LOVEJOY, HENRY born ca. 1817, Maine, and wife, SARAH E., born ca. 1823, NY, were listed in the 1850 census of Raisin Twp., Lenawee Co., Mich. with MARIAM J., age 5, b. Mich., in their household. Note MARTHA, following.

LOVEJOY, JAMES L. born ca. 1820, Maine, was head of household in the 1850 census of Raisin Twp., Lenawee Co., Mich. ELIZA A., born ca 1830, NY, may be his wife; and he had in his household the family shown following with MARTHA.

LOVEJOY, LOVISA, age 19, born Maine, was listed in the 1850 census of Woodstock Twp., Lenawee Co., Mich. in the household of William & Sarah Grant (also born Maine). Note MARTHA, following.

LOVEJOY, MARTHA, age 58, born Mass., was listed in the 1850 census of Raisin Twp., Lenawee Co., Mich., and was in household of JAMES L. (preceding), and she is probably also mother of

HENRY, LOVISA, & possibly Sarah Grant (age 28, b. Maine). With her in the household were OLIVER, age 25; and LOYAL, age 13, both b. Maine.

LOVELAND, DOLLY (SMITH) Mrs. had married first to John Hendryx (also see), and second to James Griffith. She married last to Loveland.

LOVELAND, WINTHROP born ca. 1818, Maine, and wife, LAURA, born ca. 1825, NY, were listed in the 1850 census of Ogden Twp., Lenawee Co., Mich. with HARRIET, age 3, b. Mich., in their household.

LOVELL, JONATHAN and wife, CHARILA (SELLECK), died at fairly young ages, and had known daughter, ORAL b. 13 July 1824, Seneca Co., NY (m. James M. Richardson, also see, in Ontario Co., NY.) After the death of her parents, Oral had lived with an "elder sister," name not stated. Ref: P&BA-Len pg. 808-9.

LOVETT, ANN, age 31, born Penn., was listed head of household in the 1850 census of Tecumseh Twp., Lenawee Co., Mich. with FRANCES, age 6, b. Mich., in her household.

LOVETT, EUGENE (See William H. Mather)
LOVETT, JOHN was listed in the 1840 census index of Raisin Twp., Lenawee Co., Mich. It is probably his wife, ELIZABETH, born ca. 1801, NJ, listed as head of household in the 1850 census of Raisin Twp. with CATHARINE, age 22, b. Penn; and JOHN, age 16; CORNELIA, age 7, both b. Mich., and Lydia Williams, age 78 b. NJ, possibly mother of Elizabeth, in her household. She was adjacent to THOMAS (following), and also note WILLIAM (following).

LOVETT, THOMAS, probably son of JOHN (preceding), born ca. 1825, Penn., and wife, CATHARINE, born ca. 1828, NY, were lised in the 1850 census of Raisin Twp., Lenawee Co., Mich. with LAMOTTE, age 1, b. Mich., in their household.

LOVETT, WILLIAM, probably son of JOHN (preceding), born ca. 1823, Penn., and wife, MINERVA, born ca. 1823, NY, were listed in the 1850 census of Raisin Twp., Lenawee Co., Mich. with WILLIAM C., age 3, b. Mich., in their household.

LOW, STEPHEN and wife, REBECCA (THORNE), were natives of New England who married in NY. By 1820, they moved to Erie Co., Ohio where they remained. Children: 1. PHEBE; 2. ANN; 3. JANE b. 4 Sept. 1820, Erie Co., O. (m. Ira D. Waterman, also see); 4. DAVID b. ca. 1829, Ohio (listed in the 1850 census of Madison Twp., Lenawee Co., Mich.); 5. DANIEL; 6. DEBORAH. Ref: P&BA-Len pg. 802.

Pioneer Families of Southeastern Michigan

LOWE, ABRAHAM born 2 Nov. 1777, NJ, moved to Big Flats, Chemung Co., NY (then Tioga Co.) before 1800. He married on 18 Apr. 1802 in NY to MARY (ATWOOD) born 13 Dec. 1779, near Montreal, Canada. About 1822, they moved to Genesee Co., NY (an area now Orleans Co.), and he died in May 1834. Mary afterwards came to Fairfield Twp., Lenawee Co., Mich. where she was listed in the 1850 census, age 70, b. NY?; and died at the home of son, ISAIAH (following) on 5 Sept. 1865. There were 5 children, but only he was mentioned. Ref: P&BA-Len pg. 881-2.

LOWE, ALLIE born NJ, married John Tenbrook (also see) and moved to Chemung Co., NY before 1804. Ref: P&BA-Len pg. 1213.

LOWE, CONRAD L., son of JUSTUS (following), born 25 June 1838, Raisin Twp., Lenawee Co., Mich., married on 29 Oct. 1858, Ypsilanti, Mich. to EMMA (SMITH), daughter of Charles (also see). Children: 1. JESSIE (m. William Birdsell); 2. CHARLES C. Ref: P&BA-Len pg. 291-2.

LOWE, DANIEL and wife, JANE, moved from New Jersey to Kinderhook, Columbia Co., NY, and then Onondaga Co. He apparently died there, as Jane came to Tecumseh Twp., Lenawee Co., Mich. in 1833 with grandson, JUSTUS (following). Known son, JOHN (following). Also note GEORGE W. (following).

LOWE, GEORGE W. was listed in the 1840 census index of Tecumseh Twp., Lenawee Co., Mich. Note DANIEL, preceding. Also see WILLIAM, following.

LOWE, HENRY C. (See William H. Osborne)

LOWE, ISAIAH, son of ABRAHAM (preceding), born 15 July 1811, Big Flats, Chemung Co., NY, moved to Adrian, Lenawee Co., Mich. in 1832. He lived in Fairfield Twp. by 1840, and last in Jasper, Mich. In the sketch he lists no family, but in the 1850 census of Fairfield Twp. he had in his household ELEANOR, age 38, b. NY; and LYDIA A., age 18; JERUSHA b. 13 Apr. 1834, Adrian Twp. (m. Henry S. White, also see); ABRAHAM, age 14; CAROLINE M. ("CARRIE") b. 20 Dec. 1846, Fairfield Twp. (m. John C. Mabee, also see). Ref: P&BA-Len pg. 570; 859; & 881-2.

LOWE, JOHN, son of DANIEL (preceding), born 1790, NJ, moved with his parents to New York. He married MARY (SKUTT), born ca. 1799, NY, in Onondaga Co., NY. In 1827, they removed to Raisin Twp., Lenawee Co., Mich., and in 1836 to Napoleon, Jackson Co., Mich.; and after 1840 to Barry Co., Mich. where he died in 1858 in the home of a son. She died 1838 in Brooklyn, Washtenaw Co., Mich. Ten children, but only name mentioned: JUSTUS (following). Ref: P&BA-Len pg. 383-4.

LOWE, JOHN, possibly son of WILLIAM (following), born ca. 1825, and wife, RACHEL, born ca. 1830, both in NY, were listed in the 1850 census of Medina Twp., Lenawee Co., Mich. with ISABELLA, age 10/12, b. Mich., in their household.

LOWE, JONATHAN and wife, JANE, were natives of Ulster Co., NY and had known daughter, LAVINA (m. Amos Opdyke, also see, in Fayette, Seneca Co., NY). Ref: P&BA-Len pg. 1075-6.

LOWE, JUSTUS, son of JOHN (preceding), born 10 Nov. 1815, Onondaga Co., NY, came to Tecumseh Twp., Lenawee Co., Mich. with his grandmother in 1833. He was listed in Macon Twp. in the 1840 census index. He married MARY (LAMBERSON), daughter of Conrad (also see) in Ridgeway Twp. and was listed there in the 1850 census. Children: (A son & daughter died infancy, names not stated) 1. CONRAD L. (preceding); 2. JOHN W. b. 11 Nov. 1842 (d. 21 Aug. 1867, Trinidad, West Indies); 3. ADELIA (MARY) b. 11 Oct. 1844 (m. James L. McIntyre, Raisin Twp.); 4. JAY J. b. 23 Apr. 1847; 5. MABELLE b. 12 Aug. 1850 (m. Edward DePuy, Saline, Washtenaw Co., Mich.); 6. ELEANOR C. b. 2 Nov. 1853 (m. F. M. Henry, Lowville, Lewis Co., NY); 7. LOGIER L. b. 7 Apr. 1856; 8. AMIABLE b. 23 Dec. 1857; 9. ELDRIDGE L. b. 10 Sept. 1860. Ref: P&BA-Len pg. 383-4.

LOWE, WILLIAM born ca. 1801, and wife, LYDIA, born ca. 1799, were listed in the 1850 census of Medina Twp., Lenawee Co., Mich. with WILLIAM C., age 23; PHEBE E., age 19, both b. NY; and JACKSON T., age 16; GEORGE W., age 14; NATHAN C., age 12, all b. Mich., in their household. They were 2 doors from JOHN, age 25, (preceding). Note: This may be GEORGE W. listed in Tecumseh Twp. in 1840 census index? Note that he has a son by that name.

LOWRY, MARTHA (See Israel Biddle)

LOYSTER, ABRAM[1] was an early settler to Cayuga Co., NY. Known son, PETER[2] (following). Ref: P&BA-Len pg. 704-5. Note: In the 1800 census index of Cayuga Co., NY there is a "Jerhoikim Loister," probably Joachim Loyster.

LOYSTER, ABRAM[3], son of PETER[2] (following), born 7 Apr. 1831, Niles, Cayuga Co., NY, married there on 1 Oct. 1857 to LUCY (SMITH), daughter of Nathaniel (also see). In 1858, they moved to Wheatland, Hillsdale Co., Mich., and in 1862 to Pittsford Twp. In 1864, they removed to Hudson Twp., Lenawee Co. Children: 1. HERBERT; 2. MARY L.; 3. MARTHA A.; 4. G. (GEORGE?) HARVEY. Ref: P&BA-Len pg. 704-5.

LOYSTER, PETER[2], son of ABRAM[1] (preceding), born ca. 1800, Cayuga Co., NY, married there to ANGELINE (VAN AUKEN) born ca. 1802, Cayuga Co. They first settled just over into Onondaga Co., NY, but returned to Niles, NY. He died in 1840, and she died in 1844, age 42. Large family, but only mentioned #4. ABRAM[3] (preceding). Ref: P&BA-Len pg. 704-5.

LOZIER, SARAH (See Charles W. Phillips)

LUCAS, ANNA (See John W. Tolford)

LUCAS, GEORGE married in Ovid, Seneca Co., NY, on 9 Dec. 1827 to BETSEY (SANDERS), daughter of Loudwick (also see). They may have moved to Troy, Bradford Co., Penn. Known son, ISAIAH b. ca. 1828, Seneca Co., NY (to Woodstock Twp., Lenawee Co., Mich.). Betsey married again on 4 Mar. 1830 to Jeremiah Wilsey[2] (also see) of Troy, Penn. Ref: P&BA-Len pg. 752-3.

LUCAS, HENRY born ca. 1824, and wife, MARTHA, born ca. 1827, both in NY, were listed in the 1850 census (spelled "Lucus") of Medina Twp., Lenawee Co., Mich. with FRANCES A., age 2, b. Mich., and William Richardson, age 25, b. NY, in their household. Note NANCY, following.

LUCAS, HIRAM born ca. 1808, and wife, ANN, born ca. 1808, both in NY, were listed in the 1850 census of Madison Twp., Lenawee Co., Mich. with FRANCES A., age 12, born Mich., in their household. It is probably they written "Hiram Luchus" in the 1840 census index of Adrian Twp., Lenawee Co.

LUCAS, NANCY, age 63, born NY, was listed in the 1850 census of Medina Twp., Lenawee Co., Mich. in the household of Alonzo L. and Nancy A. (age 29, b. NY) Downer, and she may be mother of Nancy A. Note HENRY, preceding; & WILLIAM, following.

LUCAS, WILLIAM may be he listed as "William Lucius" in the 1840 census index of Medina Twp., Lenawee Co., Mich. Note NANCY, preceding.

LUCAS, REUBEN born ca. 1808, and wife, MELINDA born ca. 1807, were listed in the 1850 census of Hudson Twp., Lenawee Co., Mich. with NANCY E., age 18; WILLIAM B., age 16; MADISON, age 14, all b. NY; and JAMES H., age 12; GOVENOR, age 10; JOHN R., age 8; MARY M., age 5, all b. Mich.

LUCE, C. W., son of HENRY T. (following), born 21 Aug. 1846 near Manchester, Washtenaw Co., Mich., married KATE E. (EnEARL), daughter of James (also see) of Raisin Twp., Lenawee Co., Mich. They lived first in Napoleon, Jackson Co., Mich., and then moved in 1879 to Franklin Twp., Lenawee Co. Children: 1. IRVING C.; 2. ALMA J.; 3. HENRY D.; 4. JAMES L.; 5. HOWARD. Ref: P&BA-Len pg. 246-7.

LUCE, HENRY T. born 6 Jan. 1811, Penn., married in Clermont (Columbia Co.?), NY to LUCIA O. (FISHER) who was born and reared in New Hampshire. They were early settlers to Manchester, Washtenaw Co., Mich.; but in the 1840 census index were listed in Albion, Calhoun Co., Mich. In 1858, they moved to Napoleon, Jackson Co., MIch., where he died 25 June 1886, and she was residing in 1888, age 74. There were 3 sons & 3 daughters, and mentioned was youngest, C. W. (preceding). Ref: P&BA-Len pg. 246-7.

LUCE, SAMUEL H. born ca. 1812, and wife, ELIZA (PEEBLES), born ca. 1811, both in NY, were married in Onondaga Co., NY and moved to Rome Twp., Lenawee Co., Mich. in 1837. She died in 1882, and he died 1 May 1886. They were listed in the 1850 census of Rome Twp. and Eliza was called "Loisa," age 39, b. NY, and also listed were MARY M., age 13, b. NY; SARAH I. b. ca. 1841, Mich. (m. John Van Vleet, also see) 3. DWIGHT b. ca. 1844; 4. EMMA A. b. ca. 1847. Ref: P&BA-Len pg. 262-3.

LUCK, JULIA A. (See George A. Ingall)

LUCK, WILLIAM born ca. 1797, NY, and wife, JEMIMA (PARTRIDGE) born ca. 1800, England, lived first in Hudson, Palmyra, and Buffalo, NY, then about 1846 moved to St. Clair, MIch. He died in 1875, and she died in 1881. Five sons and 5 daughters, and eight lived to maturity, only one listed was WILLIAM W. (following). Ref: P&BA-Len pg. 717-8. Note: There was a WILLIAM listed in the 1800 census index of Albany Co., NY.

LUCK, WILLIAM W., son of WILLIAM (preceding), born 17 July 1819, Auburn, NY, came to Michigan with his parents. In 1854, he lived in Monroe Co., Mich. The name of his first wife was not stated, but he married again on 23 Aug. 1856, Hudson, NY, to MARY G. (BENSON). They lived first in Cleveland, Ohio, and then about 1864 settled in Adrian, Lenawee Co., Mich. Five children, of whom 2 died infancy, and 2 daughters, names not stated, died as young women. A surviving daughter married E. D. Williams, Chicago, Ill. Ref: P&BA-Len pg. 717-8.

LUCKHAM, SUSAN (See Daniel Eccles)

LUKE, ELIJAH born ca. 1786, and wife, ABAGAIL?, born ca. 1792, both in NJ, apparently lived about 1815 in Penn., and by 1822 in Ohio. They were listed in the 1850 census of Ogden Twp., Lenawee Co., Mich. adjacent to JOHN C. & NOAH B. (both following), and with WILLIAM, age 28; HENRY, age 23; MARY A., age 21; ELIJAH, age 19; ABIGAIL A., age 14, all b. Ohio, in their household.

LUKE, JOHN C., probably son of ELIJAH (preceding), born ca. 1815, and wife, PHEBE, born ca. 1813, both in Penn., were listed in the 1850 census of Ogden Twp., Lenawee Co., Mich. (next door to ELIJAH) with MARTHA J., age 5; MARY E., age 4, both b. Ohio; and HENRY, age 3, b. Mich., in their household. Known daughter, LOETTA (b. after 1850), m. Erastus Brockway, Jr., also see). Ref: P&BA-Len pg. 757-8.

LUKE, NOAH B., probably son of ELIJAH (preceding), born ca. 1815, and wife, MARY, born ca. 1819, both in Penn., were listed in the 1850 census of Ogden Twp., Lenawee Co., Mich. with JANE, age 9; ADDISON, age 7; WILLIAM, age 5, all b. Ohio, in their household (next door to JOHN C.)

LUPTON, GIDEON born ca. 1795, and wife, SUSANNAH, born ca. 1801, both in Virginia, were listed in the 1840 census index of Woodstock Twp.; and in the 1850 census with BENJAMIN, age 12, b. Mich., in their household and next door, WILLIAM C. (following).

LUPTON, THOMAS and wife, MARY (COOPER), born Yorkshire, England, came to the US in the 1820s and settled first in Detroit, Mich. They moved to Macon Twp., Lenawee Co., Mich. before 1840; and moved later to Ridgeway Twp. He died in 1885, and she died in 1862. In the 1850 census, he was age 44, and she was age 46, and they listed ELLEN, born ca. 1830, England (m. Charles F. Smith, also see); MARY A. b. ca. 1835, Mich.; CHRISTIANA b. ca. 1837; ELIZABETH b. ca. 1840; RACHEL L. b. 3 June 1843, Ridgeway Twp. (m. James Patterson, also see). Ref: P&BA-Len pg. 366-7 & 793-4.

LUPTON, WILLIAM C., probably son of GIDEON (preceding), born ca 1830, and wife, EMILY, born ca. 1823, both in Ohio, were listed in the 1850 census of Woodstock Twp., Lenawee Co., Mich. next door to GIDEON.

LUSK, ADELINE (See Henry Waite)

LUSK, EMELINE b. 28 Dec. 1814, Ontario Co., NY (m. Marcus Bennett, also see, Niagara Co., NY).

LUTHER, ALDEN born ca. 1822, and wife, CYNTHIA, born ca. 1824, both in NY, were listed in the 1850 census of Woodstock Twp., Lenawee Co., Mich. with LORENZO, age 2; EMMA?, age 3/12, both b. Mich., in their household.

LUTHER, BENJAMIN F., son of WILLIAM (following), born ca. 1818, NY, and wife, MARIA, born ca. 1826, Conn., were listed in the 1850 census of Rome Twp., Lenawee Co., Mich. with MARTIN, age 9; EUNICE, age 7;

Pioneer Families of Southeastern Michigan

EMELINE, age 5; ALLEN, age 2, all b. Mich., and his mother, EUNICE, age 74, born VT, in their household.

LUTHER, JOHN born ca. 1822, NY, was listed in the 1850 census of Hudson Twp., Lenawee Co., Mich. with a child, EUGENE, age 1, b. Mich., both in the Hamilton household.

LUTHER, RACHEL (See Moses Negus)

LUTHER, THEODORICK, son of WILLIAM (following), born 23 Mar. 1799, South Hero, VT, married on 29 Apr. 1821 in Clinton Co., NY to AMELIA (HALL), daughter of Nathaniel (also see). In 1831, they moved to Superior Twp., Washtenaw Co., Mich.; and in 1834 joined his father in Rome Twp., Lenawee Co., Mich. Amelia died 24 Jan. 1875, Rome Twp. Children (first 5 b. Chazy, Clinton Co., NY): 1. MARIA b. 20 Feb. 1822 (m. William Codding, also see); 2. GEORGE W. A. b. 20 Sept. 1823 (lived next door in 1850 with wife, Mary); 3. CHARLOTTE b. 11 Nov. 1825 (m. Edwin Lamoreaux, Rome Twp.); 4. EUNICE b. 3 Nov. 1828 (d. 27 Sept. 1837); 5. AMELIA b. 7 Apr. 1830 (m. Seth S. Walker, also see); 6. MARY b. 11 May 1832, Superior Twp, Washtenaw Co. (m. Lyman Chafee; she d. 10 July 1860, Rome Twp.); 7. ALVIRA b. 11 May 1838, Rome Twp. (m. Ransom Cerrow, also see); 8. DIANA T. b. 16 June 1842 (m. P. H. Dowling, Rome Twp.) Theodorick married again to Mrs. LUCINDA (JERRELLS) ARMSTRONG, daughter of Ebenezer, and widow of Almarin K. (see both). Ref: P&BA-Len pg. 587-8.

LUTHER, WILLIAM born 28 Sept. 1774, Bristol Co., Rhode Island, and moved as a child to New Hampshire. He afterwards went to Vermont, where he married in 1798 to EUNICE (ALLEN), daughter of Col. Ebenezer (also see). They lived first in South Hero, VT, and about 1800 moved to Plattsburgh, Clinton Co., NY. In 1832, they removed to Rome Twp., Lenawee Co., Mich. He died there 2 Oct. 1841, and she died 24 Jan. 1852 (in 1850 she was living in household of Benjamin F.) Known daughters: BATHSHEBA b. 26 Dec. 1800, VT (m. Daniel McRobert, also see); ALICE (m. David Jerrells, also see. Known sons: THEODORICK (preceding); BENJAMIN F. (preceding). Ref: P&BA-Len pg. 587-8; 884-5 & 983-4. Note: Also in the 1850 census of Raisin Twp., EUNICE, age 33, b. NY, in a Luke VanOrman household may relate to this family. There is an AMELIA, age 20, NY, in the 1850 census of Adrian in a Cummings household.

LYBARKER, HENRY born Penn., and wife, NANCY (WRIGHT), born Detroit, Mich., settled first in Erie Co., Penn., and then moved to Green Creek Twp., Sandusky Co., Ohi. They later moved to Isabella Co., Mich., where he died. Nancy died in Springfield, Erie Co., Penn. at the home of a daughter. There were 7 sons and 4 daughters, names not stated, except #8. MARY b. 12 Apr. 1828, Springfield, Penn. (m. Lyman H. Aldrich, also see). Ref: P&BA-Len pg. 1039-40.

LYKE, SAMUEL born NY, and wife, SARAH (TEED), born Nova Scotia, settled in Delaware Co., NY, and then some years later in Tompkins Co., NY where he died in Nov. 1873, and she died in 1862. There were 4 sons and 7 daughters, names not stated, except JANE b. 29 Sept. 1815, Delaware Co., NY (m. Charles C. Russell, also see). Ref: P&BA-Len pg. 852-3.

LYMAN, OTIS born ca. 1805, VT, and wife, SARAH, born ca. 1805, Mass., were listed in the 1840 census index of Cambridge Twp., Lenawee Co., Mich.; and in the 1850 census with SARAH, age 18; EMILY, age 17, both b. NY; and JOSEPHINE, age 14; SILAS, age 12; WARREN, age 10; GRANVILLE, age 8; FRANCES, age 6; THEODORE, age 8/12, all b. Mich., in their household.

LYMAN, POLLY (See Leonard Case)

LYMAN, RUSSELL born ca. 1801, Mass., and wife, EUNICE, born ca. 1804, VT, were listed in the 1840 census index of Adrian Twp., Lenawee Co., Mich.; and in the 1850 census with ELIZA J., age 13; HENRY, age 5, both b. Mich.; and Amelia Winter, age 71, b. Conn., and Marsha Winter, age 31, b. Penn.; and Zuba Follett, age 44, b. VT, in their household.

LYON, BAXTER born ca. 1797, Conn., and wife, MARY, born ca. 1798, VT, were listed in the 1850 census of Medina Twp., Lenawee Co., Mich. with GEORGE, age 10, b. Mich., in their household. It was probably Baxter listed as "DEXTER" in the 1840 census index of Madison Twp., Lenawee Co.

LYON, DANIEL R. born ca. 1816, NJ, and wife, LOVINA M., born ca. 1816, Mass., were listed in the 1850 census of Madison Twp., Lenawee Co., Mich. with MARTHA A., age 10, b. NY; DENNIS R., age 6, b. Mich.; and Lucy J. Roberts, age 28, b. Mass., in their household.

LYON, HATTIE (See Richard H. Kinney)

LYON, LYMAN J. born ca. 1818, and CAROLINE A., born ca. 1826, both in NY, were listed in the 1850 census of Hudson Twp., Lenawee Co., Mich. with FRANKLIN D., age 5; LEANDER? D., age 2; CAROLINE A., age 2/12; and listed last, MARY E., age 7, b. NY, in their household.

LYONS, DELLA (See William Derbyshire)

LYONS, ELIZABETH (See Samuel Phillips)

LYONS, LYMAN A. born ca. 1824, NY, and wife, MARY A., born ca. 1828, VT, were listed in the 1850 census of Seneca Twp., Lenawee Co., Mich. with HELEN A., age 3; GEORGE W., age 1, both b. Mich.; and listed last (sister?) HANNAH C., age 12, b. NY, in their household.

- M -

MABEE, BENJAMIN C. born ca. 1816, NY, and wife, SARAH, born ca. 1818, England, were listed in the 1850 census of Fairfield Twp., Lenawee Co., Mich. with ALPHONSO, age 11, b. NY, in their household. (Spelled "Maybee" in census).

MABEE, JAMES from Niagara Co., NY died on a ship enroute to California in 1852. Afterwards, his wife and children moved from NY to Jackson Co., Mich.; and in 1860/1 moved to Fairfield Twp., Lenawee Co., Mich. Known son, JOHN C. (following). Ref: P&BA-Len pg. 570.

MABEE, JOHN C., son of JAMES (preceding), born 10 Mar. 1842, Royalton, Niagara Co., NY, moved to Fairfield Twp., Lenawee Co., Mich. with his mother. He served in Co. I, 18th Mich. Inf. during the Civil War 1862-5. He married on 30 Dec. 1867 to CARRIE M. (LOWE), daughter of Isaiah (also see). Children: 1. JAMES L.; 2. BERTIE (d. as a child); 3. CHARLES R. Ref: P&BA-Len pg. 570.

MACEY also see MACKEY
MACEY, ANNA (See John Worth Family)
MACEY, LYDIA, age 70, born Mass., was listed in the 1850 census of Raisin Twp., Lenawee Co., Mich. in the household of Dyer H. & Eliza (age 27, b. Mass.) Mudge, possibly she was mother of Eliza?

MACHAM, A. D., son of JOHN (following), born 25 Apr. 1853, Grey Co., Ontario, Canada, moved with parents to Deerfield Twp., Lenawee Co., Mich. He married on 17 Jan. 1877 to JENNIE (RECTOR), daughter of John (also see). Children: 1. BERTHA; 2. BLANCHE. Ref: P&BA-Len pg. 893-4.

MACHAM, JOHN born Ireland, moved to Scotland, and the to Canada with his parents. He moved to Deerfield Twp., Lenawee Co., Mich. in 1867. There were 7 sons and 3 daughters, and only one named was A. D. (preceding). Ref: P&BA-Len pg. 893-4.

MACK, ASENATH (See Rev. Paul Shepherd)
MACK, RUEL born ca. 1815, NH, and wife, LYDIA, born ca. 1815, Mass., were listed in the 1850 census of Adrian Twp., Lenawee Co., Mich. with HARRIET A., age 5, b. Mich., in their household.

MACKEY also see MACEY
MACKEY, ELIAS probably of Delaware Co., NY married ELIZA A. (SIMMONS), daughter of Noble (also see). They moved first to Rome Twp., Lenawee Co., Mich., and later to Adrian Twp., where he died. She was living in 1888, age 70, with granddaughter, Ella (Tiffany) Uloth. Daughter, ELIZA J. (m/1 Erastus Tiffany, also see, Roxbury, Delaware Co., NY; & m/2 to ?_ after 1859, Raisin Twp.). Ref: P&BA-Len pg. 783-4.

MACKEY, URIYON of Stamford, Delaware Co., NY was born ca. 1783, and married first to JANE who died in 1811. They had known daughter, MARY (m. Alanson Bangs, also see, on 15 Dec. 1824). They came to Michigan in 1858, and settled in Raisin Twp., Lenawee Co., where he died in 1873, age 90. Ref: P&BA-Len pg. 909-10.

MACOMBER see McCAMBER; McCUMBER & McOMBER

MACOMBER, MARTHA (See William Gallaway)

MAGEE also known as McGEE
MAGEE, JOHN of Ireland, and wife, ANNABELLA (SALTON), were both of Scottish ancestry. Daughter, FANNIE b. 1780, Co. Antrim, Ireland (m. James Moreland[2], also see). Ref: P&BA-Len pg. 363-4.

MAIN also see MAINE & MAYNE
MAIN, A. D. was listed in the 1840 census index of Seneca Twp., Lenawee Co., Mich. and may be ANSEL A. MAINE born ca. 1810, NY, who was listed in the 1850 census of Seneca Twp. with no family. Then in the 1850 census of Medina Twp. there is an ANSEL A. MANE, listed as age 38, b. NY, and had HARVEY, age 12; SEYMOUR, age 8; HANNAH, age 6, all b. Mich., in his household, who may be the same man?.

MAIN, JOHN born ca. 1805, and wife, FRANCES (CARD), probably daughter of William (also see) born 32 Sept. 1804, both in England, settled in Franklin Twp., Lenawee Co., Mich. by 1840. In the 1850 census, they were listed with Mary Ann Card, age 17, b. NY, and John P. Pawson, age 6, b. Mich., in their household. He died 22 June 1900, and she died 31 Mar. 1902, and they are buried in the Mills Cem., Franklin Twp.

MAIN, JOSEPH A. born ca. 1808, and wife, EMILY, born ca. 1818, both in NY, were listed in the 1850 census of Dover Twp., Lenawee Co., Mich. with GEORGE R., age 15, b. NY; and HENRY C., age 12; MARY A., age 10; JANET H., age 8; FRANKLIN P., age 4. ARZEL? (Ansel?) A., age 2, all b. Mich., in their household. Note: It is probably he listed as J. A. Mane in the 1840 census index of Dover Twp.

MAINE also see MAIN
MAINE, CATHERINE (See William Sheeler)
MAINE, SOPHIA (See George Hines)

MALLARD, FRANCES (RICHARDSON) Mrs. (See George Conger)

MALLERY also see MALLORY
MALLERY, ANGELINE E. (See Silas Beal) Note ALANSON MALLORY, following.

MALLORY, ALANSON (See ZALMON, following) born ca. 1817, Mass., and wife, ANGELINE E., born ca. 1824, both in NY, were listed in the 1850 census of Macon Twp., Lenawee Co., Mich. with AUGUSTUS, age 1, b. Mich., in their household. Note: It may have been this Angeline who married Silas Beal (also see) in 1858?

MALLORY, C. W. (See Benjamin Hornbeck)
MALLORY, GEORGE born ca. 1827, NY, was listed in the 1850 census of Rollin Twp., Lenawee Co., Mich. as a "student" in the household of Dr. Daniel Tims.

MALLORY, JOHN G., probably son of ZALMON (following), born ca. 1812, and wife, LYDIA, born ca. 1812, both in Mass., were listed in the 1850 census of Cambridge Twp., Lenawee Co., Mich. with ADELL, age 12, b. NY; and EDWARD, age 6?, b. Mich., in their household (next door to ZALMON).

MALLORY, ZALMON Dr. born ca. 1784, Mass., and wife, ANNA, born ca. 1780, Conn., were listed in the 1840 census index of Franklin Twp., Lenawee Co., Mich.;

Pioneer Families of Southeastern Michigan

and in the 1850 census of Cambridge Twp., next door to JOHN G. Also note ALANSON, preceding. Also see GEORGE.

MALONE, MARY, daughter of HENRY (See Philip Kehoe).

MALONEY, CLINTON, probably son of JOHN (following), born ca. 1822, and wife, ELECTA, born ca. 1821, both in NY, were listed in the 1850 census of Palmyra Twp., Lenawee Co., Mich. with LUCY, age 9; ELECTA, age 3, both b. Mich., in their household.

MALONEY, EDWIN, probably son of JOHN (following), born ca. 1819, and wife, SARAH. born ca. 1920, both in NY, were listed in the 1850 census of Palmyra Twp., Lenawee Co., Mich. with MARY, age 9, b. Mich., and William W. Bates, age 3, b. Mich., in the household. This is probably the family called "EDWARD" & SARAH, who were parents of "MARIE" who married on 12 July 1876 to Horace Holloway, Ogden Twp. Ref: P&BA-Len pg. 1139-40.

MALONEY, JAMES was listed in the 1840 census index of Adrian Twp., Lenawee Co., Mich. See JOHN, following. Also there was CALVIN, age 7, b. Mich., listed in the 1850 census of Palmyra Twp., Lenawee Co., Mich. in the household of Elijah & MARY (MALONEY) Earles, who relates to this family.

MALONEY, JOHN and wife, POLLY (DUSENBURY) born ca. 1786, NY, moved from Monroe Co., NY to Adrian Twp., Lenawee Co., Mich. in 1834, and he died there in 1837. There were 7 children, names not stated. In the 1850 census of Palmyra Twp., POLLY is listed head of household with only CHANCY, age 22, b. NY, in her household. She is a few doors from JOHN, CLINTON, EDWIN, & MARY b. ca. 1818, NY (m. Elijah Earles, also see). Ref: P&BA-Len pg. 557-8.

MALONEY, JOHN, son of JOHN (preceding), born ca. 1812, and wife, CLARISSA, born ca. 1822, both in NY, were listed in the 1850 census of Palmyra Twp., Lenawee Co., Mich. with MARTHA, age 10; CHARLES, age 7; JULIUS, age 6; LUCY I., age 4; CHANCY, age 8/12, all b. Mich., in their household.

MALONEY, MICHAEL (See Patrick Hogan)
MALONEY, THOMAS (See Walden Wing)

MALTBY, DELINDA (See Miles Baker)

MANCHESTER, ARTHUR C., son of JAMES D. (following), born 1 Dec. 1845, Madison, Madison Co., NY, moved with his parents to Seneca Twp., Lenawee Co., Mich. He married on 4 Nov. 1866 in Medina Twp. to EMILY (JONES), daughter of Aaron (also see). Children: 1. HELEN D. (m. Fred Lewis, also see); 2. FRANK; 3. JULIA. Ref: P&BA-Len pg. 1128-8.

MANCHESTER, ELIAS born Dutchess Co., NY, married PATIENCE (BOIES), and they were early settlers to Washington Co., NY where they are listed in the 1800 census index. He died at the home of children in Scipio, Cayuga Co., NY; and she died in Oscela, Penn. at the home of a daughter, and both are buried in Scipio, NY. Known daughter, PHEBE b. Jackson, Washington Co., NY (m. Edward Murray, also see). Ref: P&BA-Len pg. 536-7.

MANCHESTER, ELIAS C. was listed in the 1840 census index of Battle Creek, Calhoun Co., Mich.

MANCHESTER, JAMES D. born 14 May 1806, and wife, DEBORAH (CHURCH) born 4 Oct. 1810, Madison Co., NY, moved about 1836 to Seneca Twp., Lenawee Co., Mich., but returned to NY probably before 1840, where they remained until 1866. They returned to Seneca Twp. where he died 27 Feb. 1879, and she died 18 Sept. 1886. Children: 1. JULIA C. (m. P. F. Richmond, Madison Twp.); 2. ARTHUR C. (preceding). Ref: P&BA-Len pg. 1128-9.

MANHEART, CAROLINE (See George G. Niedhammer)

MANN, ALVILDA (See Christian Kuney)

MANN, CLARISSA, age 18, born NY, was listed in the 1850 census of Madison Twp., Lenawee Co., Mich. in the household of Silas A. Scofield.

MANN, DANIEL born ca. 1812, New Hampshire, and wife, ANNA, born ca. 1817, NY, were listed in the 1850 census of Rome Twp., Lenawee Co., Mich. with LORETTA, age 8; CHARLES, age 6; DANIEL W., age 3; GEORGE W., age 1, all b. Mich., in their household.

MANN, GILBERT B. born ca. 1805, Mass., married after 1844 to Mrs. AMANDA (COMPTON) PACKARD, widow of Ira (also see) in Madison Twp., Lenawee Co., Mich. and they were listed in the 1850 census with her children in the household. Note: LYDIA, following.

MANN, LOIS (See Dr. John D. Tripp)

MANN, LOUIS born ca. 1827, NY, was listed in the 1850 census of Tecumseh Twp., Lenawee Co., Mich. as a "student" in the household of Dr. Increase S. Hamilton.

MANN, LYDIA born ca. 1768, Mass., was listed in the 1850 census of Madison Twp., Lenawee Co., Mich. in the household of William Foster and wife, Phebe (age 58, b. NY). Also note GILBERT B., preceding.

MANN, MARY (STOWERS) Mrs. was daughter of John Stowers (also see). Ref: P&BA-Le pg. 384-5.

MANN, THOMAS born ca. 1786, Rhode Island, apparently lived in NY, and moved to Medina Twp., Lenawee Co., Mich. after 1840. He was listed in the 1850 census of Medina Twp. with ELIZA, age 31; THOMAS, age 28; ADIA?, age 26; OLIVE, age 24; LOUIS, age 21; CHAUNCEY, age 19; ZELPHIA, age 16, all b. NY, in his household.

MANN, WILLIS G. (See Vaughn)

MANNING, BENJAMIN, age 18, born NY, was listed in the 1850 census of Tecumseh Twp., Lenawee Co., Mich. in a Blossom household.

MANNING, JANE (See Moses Tobias)
MANNING, ROCKWELL born ca. 1794, Conn., and wife, MARGARET, born ca. 1809, NY, were listed in the 1850 census of Adrian Twp., Lenawee Co., Mich. with FRANCES B., age 16; ELIZABETH, age 8, both b. Mich., in their household.

MANNIX, ELIZABETH (See Michael Flynn)

MANWARING, HENRY, son of ISAAC (following), born 8 Aug. 1834, Waterford, Conn., was placed with relatives at age 9 following the death of his father. About 1856, he moved with George Beebe to Fulton Co., Ohio; and also lived Waterville, Ohio, and Springfield, Lucas Co., Ohio. He married on 30 Aug. 1857, Springfield, to MARIA (BEMIS), daughter of Abel (also see). In 1858, they removed to Ottawa Lake, Monroe Co., Mich. He served in Co., K., 18th Mich. Inf. during Civil War. They lived for a time in Adrian, Lenawee Co., but moved about 1866 to Riga Twp. Children: 1. LAURA b. 3 Apr. 1860 (d. age 6 mos); 2. EMMA b. 11 Jan. 1868. Ref: P&BA-Len pg. 922-4.

MANWARING, ISAAC and wife, EUNICE (BEEBE), daughter of Paul (also see) were natives of Waterford, Conn. He died ca. 1841 leaving 7 children, names not stated, except HENRY (preceding). She died in New London, Conn. in 1852. Ref: P&BA-Len pg. 922-4.

MAPES, DAVID WILSON, son of ISAIAH (who served in War of 1812), born ca. 1812, and wife, NANCY, born ca. 1820, both in NY, were listed in the 1840 census index of Franklin Twp., Lenawee Co., Mich.; and in the 1850 census with WILLIAM, age 11; DAVID, age 9; EZRA, age 8; ADELINE, age 6; LYDIA b. 14 Apr. 1846 (m. Nathan A. Bailey, also see); CONSIDER, age 3; HORACE, age 4/12, all b. Mich. Nancy died at age 33; and he later went to Manistee, Mich. where he died on 14 Apr. 1879, age 69. Three of the sons served in the Civil War, and 2 were wounded and 1 killed (names not stated). Ref: P&BA-Len pg. 1019-20. In the 1840 census index, David was adjacent to SARAH (following).

MAPES, EDMUND, born ca. 1816, NY, was listed in the 1850 census of Adrian Twp., Lenawee Co., Mich.

MAPES, ELIZABETH, age 51, born NY, was listed in the 1850 census of Adrian Twp., Lenawee Co., Mich. in the household of Franklin Titus and wife, Sarah J. Note: Was she originally Elizabeth Titus who was listed in the 1840 census index of Adrian Twp. as head of household?

MAPES, ELLA (See James L. Brown)

MAPES, GENESS? (male), age 32, was listed in the 1850 census of Adrian Twp., Lenawee Co., Mich. in the Bennett household.

MAPES, HENRY was listed in the 1840 census index of Madison Twp., Lenawee Co., Mich. Note ELIZABETH, preceding.

MAPES, ISAAC born ca. 1810, and wife, NANCY, born ca. 1818, both in NY, were listed in the 1850 census of Hudson Twp., Lenawee Co., Mich. with MELISSA, age 13; SAMUEL, age 11; WILLIAM, age 9; GEORGE, age 3; HARRIET, age 1, all b. Mich., in their household.

MAPES, MARY G. (See James L. Brown)

MAPES, S. R. born ca. 1821, NY, and wife, SAMANTHA, born ca. 1819, VT, were listed in the 1850 census of Adrian Twp., Lenawee Co., Mich. with Minerva Woodward, age 10, b. Mich.; and Lucy Woodward, age 21, b. VT, in their household.

MAPES, SARAH was listed head of household in the 1840 census index of Franklin Twp., Lenawee Co., Mich. adjacent to DAVID W. (preceding).

MAPES, WILSON (See DAVID WILSON MAPES, preceding)

MAPLES, ALBERT born ca. 1818, NY, and wife ANN M. (LAMUNYAN), were natives of NY who settled first in Saline, Washtenaw Co., Mich., and then in 1844 to Macon Twp., Lenawee Co. where she died in 1848, age 28, leaving daughter, AUGUSTA born ca. 1844 (census said b. NY?) Augusta was raised by the Isaac Pennington family and she was in their household in the 1850 census of Macon Twp. ANDREW, age 10, b. NY, in the household of John Pennington in 1850 may also relate to this family. Albert was probably the "A.," age 32, listed in the 1850 census of Tecumseh Twp., Lenawee Co. in an Adams household. He married again to MARGARET (ANSELUS) also born NY, and they resided in Macon Twp. in 1888. Ref: P&BA-Len pg. 513-4.

MARAH, ANN was daughter of M. P. (See Patrick Kehoe).

MARBLE, CHARLES born Mass., and wife, name not stated, moved to Canandaigua, Ontario Co., NY before 1820. About 1843, they moved to Oakland Co., Mich. His wife died in Coldwater, Mich. at the home of a daughter, ? (m. Uri Blodgett). Another daughter, PHEBE, b. ca. 1795, Mass. (m. Samuel Brightman, also see). Ref: P&BA-Len pg. 1120-1.

MARKEL, JACOB (See William Ladd)

MARK, CATHERINE, age 63, born England, was listed in the 1850 census of Woodstock Twp., Lenawee Co., Mich. in the household of Jane Newbury.

MARK, JAMES born ca. 1798, and wife, REBECCA, born ca. 1805, both in Ireland, were listed in the 1840 census index of Tecumseh Twp., Lenawee Co., Mich. with SAMUEL, age 22; WILLIAM, age 19, all b. Ireland; and JAMES, age 17; JOSEPH, age 6, both b. Mich., in their household. THOMAS, age 14, b. Mich., in another household probably relates to this family.

MARKS, CALEB, probably son of JOSEPH (following), age 38, born NY, was listed in the 1850 census of Rome Twp., Lenawee Co., Mich. in the Reuben Knapp household.

MARKS, CAROLINE born near Cleveland, Ohio married Aaron J. Palmer (also see). Ref: P&BA-Len pg. 596-7.

MARKS, CORNELIUS, son of JEREMIAH (following), born 6 Apr. 1804, and wife, FANNA, born ca. 1811, both in NY, were listed in the 1850 census of Rome Twp., Lenawee Co., Mich. with GEORGE, age 21, b. NY; and MYRON, age 14; JEREMIAH, age 8 (served Civil War in DeGoyler's Battery); SARAH, age 12; JANE E., age 10; CALINDA, age 6; REBECCA, age 3; JOSEPH, age 6/12, all b. Mich., in their household.

MARKS, EMMONS H., possibly son of HOWLAND (following). Also see John Johnson, son of Daniel).

MARKS, HOWLAND, son of JEREMIAH (following), born 11 Apr. 1800, and wife, ELIZABETH "BETSEY" (KNAPP), born ca. 1798, both b. NY, lived in Nassau, Rensselaer Co., NY, and in 1830 in Galen, Wayne Co., NY. About 1846, they removed to Adrian, Lenawee Co., Mich. There were 6 sons and 3 daughters (names not stated). In the 1850 census of Rome Twp., Lenawee Co. they listed JOHN S. (following); EMONS, age 23 (note EMMONS H., preceding); EDWARD, age 17; CHARLOTTE, age 14 (m. Roswell H. Hicks, also see); ADDISON, age 13; JEREMIAH, age 9, all b. NY. Howland died 17 Oct. 1873, age 73, and Elizabeth died 7 Apr. 1878, age 80. Ref: P&BA-Len pg. 1121-2 & 1209-10.

MARKS, JEREMIAH, son of JOSEPH (following), born 29 Nov. 1775, married probably in Rensselaer Co., NY to ELIZABETH (SOULS) born 4 Dec. 1775. Children: 1.

Pioneer Families of Southeastern Michigan

MALINDA b. 11 Mar. 1796; 2. JOSEPH (following); 3. HOWLAND (preceding); 4. HANNAH b. 6 Apr. 1802; 5. CORNELIUS (preceding); 6. SALLY MARIAH b. 18 June 1806; 7. DEBORAH b. 22 Mar. 1808; 8. JUDITH b. 5 Apr. 1810; 9. MALVINA b. 3 May 1812; 10. MARTIN b. 10 June 1814; 11. DELIA b. 30 Dec. 1824. Ref: P&BA-Len pg. 1209-10.

MARKS, JOHN S., son of HOWLAND (preceding), born 3 July 1824, Nassau, Rensselaer Co., NY, moved to Adrian, Lenawee Co., Mich. with his parents. He married in Jackson, Mich. on 14 apr. 1858 to JULIA A. (STOCKWELL), daughter of Curtis (also see). No children were listed in sketch. Ref: P&BA-Len pg. 1209-10. Note: Mentioned was an uncle, John Wilber of Rome Twp.

MARKS, JOSEPH born 28 Jan. 1748, married on 11 Mar. 1771 to HANNAH (WITLESY) born 14 Feb. 1750. Children: 1. HANNAH b. 27 Sept. 1772; 2. JEREMIAH (preceding); 3. MARY b. 25 Nov. 1781; 4. BENONI b. 7 Sept. 1782; 5. SARAH b. 9 Sept. 1787; 6. POLLY b. 25 Oct. 1790. Ref: P&BA-Len pg. 1209-10.

MARKS, JOSEPH, son of JEREMIAH (preceding), born 28 Apr. 1798, Rensselaer Co., NY, is probably he who married SARAH (STEINHART) in Rensselaer Co., NY. They had a known daughter, POLLY (m. Reuben Knapp, also see). CALEB, born ca. 1812, NY, is probably a son, and he resided in 1850 with Reuben Knapp. Ref: P&BA-Len pg. 1004-6.

MARKS, JOSEPH (See Levi Jennings)

MARKS, NEHEMIAH born Conn. married in South Cleveland, Ohio to CLARISSA (PARMENTER) born VT. They both died in Cuyahoga Co., Ohio at age 82. Daughter, ROSETTA (m/1 Charles Chamberlian, and m/2 Addison P. Halladay, see both). Ref: P&BA-Len pg. 456-7.

MARLATT see MARLOTT

MARLOTT, BENJAMIN born ca. 1801, and wife, ANNA, born ca. 1805, both b. NY, were listed in the 1850 census of Adrian Twp., Lenawee Co., Mich. with ESTHER, age 16; ANGELINE, age 11, both b. Mich., in their household.

MARLOTT, DANIEL born ca. 1811, and wife, BETSEY, born ca. 1815, both in NY, were listed in the 1850 census of Rome Twp., Lenawee Co., Mich. with MARGARET, age 17; MARY, age 15; FRANCES, age 10; SARAH J., age 6; MARTHA, age 4, all b. Mich., in their household. Note: There was a DANIEL MARLATT in the 1840 census index of Superior Twp., Washtenaw Co., Mich.

MARLOTT, DANIEL born ca. 1825, and wife, MARY, born ca. 1820, both in NY, were listed in the 1850 census of Cambridge Twp., Lenawee Co., Mich.

MARLOTT, ELIAS born ca. 1827, NY, was listed in the 1850 census of Ogden Twp., Lenawee Co., Mich. in the household of William Paul (whose wife was MARIA, following).

MARLOTT, ENOCH born ca. 1813, and wife, HANNAH, born ca. 1818, both in NY, were listed in the 1850 census of Dover Twp., Lenawee Co., Mich. with WELLINGTON, age 10; ROSAMOND A., age 8; GEORGE W., age 6; MARY E. E., age 2, all b. Mich., in their household.

MARLOTT, HENRY born ca. 1822, and wife, JANE, born ca. 1828, were listed in the 1850 census of Rollin Twp., Lenawee Co., Mich. with CLARZINA, age 6/12, b. Mich., and James B. Stone, age 6, b. Mich., in their household. Note JOHN, following.

MARLOTT, JOHN moved from Ridgeway, Orleans Co., NY to Rollin Twp., Lenawee Co., Mich. by 1840. Known daughter, CHARITY b. 10 Mar. 1823, Yates, Orleans Co., NY (m. Nicholas Amos Page, also see). Also note HENRY (preceding). This JOHN may also be the father of SOPHIA, born Seneca Co., NY ca. 1824 (m. John Cain, also see). Ref: P&BA-Len pg. 333-4.

MARLOTT, L. married Zachary T. Tingley, son of John H.[3] (also see).

MARLOTT, MARIA born 18 Sept. 1820 near Buffalo, NY married William Paul (also see). Ref: P&BA-Len pg. 776-7. Note ELIAS, preceding.

MARLOTT, MICHALL b. ca. 1813, and wife, LUCY, born ca. 1825, were listed in the 1850 census of Cambridge Twp., Lenawee Co., Mich. with ELLEN, age 7; GEORGE, age 2, both b. Mich., in their household.

MARLOTT, PETER married VIOLA (WELCH), daughter of James (also see); and had children: JAMES E.; ALTA O.; MIRAH; and infant's name not stated.

MARSH, ABE A. born ca. 1812, Mass., and wife, PRUDENCE, born ca. 1815, Conn., were listed in the 1850 census of Tecumseh Twp., Lenawee Co., Mich. with NEWTON, age 14, b. Conn., in their household.

MARSH, CAROLINE born ca. 1817, NY, was listed in the 1850 census of Seneca Twp., Lenawee Co., Mich. in the Andrew Stevenson household and "dittoed" following her were HENRIETTA, age 9; ADALADE, age 4, both b. Mich., not certain if they are Marsh or Stevenson children.

MARSH, EDWARD and wife, MARY, of Dover, England, were parents of HARRIET (m. James K. Jeffery, also see). Ref: P&BA-Len pg. 1004-6.

MARSH, EDWARD, age 10 or 20, born NY, was listed in the 1850 census of Fairfield Twp., Lenawee Co., Mich. in a Compton household.

MARSH, ELIAS born ca. 1813, NY, and wife, ARVILLA, born ca. 1817, NJ, were listed in the 1850 census of Cambridge Twp., Lenawee Co., Mich. with LAURA, age 13; MALVINA, age 10, both b. NY; and MARY, age 6; GEORGE, age 5; SILVIA, age 4, all b. Mich., in their household.

MARSH, GEORGE born ca. 1816, and wife, ALMIRA, born ca. 1816, both in NY, were listed in the 1850 census of Tecumseh Twp., Lenawee Co., Mich. with SUSAN, age 14; SAMUEL, age 13; GEORGE, age 11; HENRY, age 9, all b. NY; and DANIEL, age 2, b. Mich., in their household.

MARSH, GEORGE W. born ca. 1810, and wife, POLLY, born ca. 1815, both in NY, were listed in the 1850 census of Rome Twp., Lenawee Co., Mich. with MARY, age 12, b. NY; and NORMAN, age 10; MARGARET, age 7; ALVA, age 3, all b. Mich., in their household.

MARSH, JANE of Elgin Co., Ontario, Canada (See George Laur).

MARSH, JOHN and wife, MARY, were parents of ELLA (m. William H. Hervey, also see, Adrian Twp., Lenawee Co., Mich.). Ref: P&BA-Len pg. 450-1.

MARSH, JOSEPH (See Matthew B. McConnel)

MARSH, LEWIS born ca. 1797, France, and wife, ROSETTA, born ca. 1818, NY, were listed in the 1850 census of Riga

Twp., Lenawee Co., Mich. with MARY E., age 14, b. NY; and ROSELLA, age 10; ELIZA, age 5; SARAH, age 3, all b. Mich., in their household.

MARSH, MATTHEW born ca. 1790, England, was listed in the 1850 census of Ridgeway Twp., Lenawee Co., Mich. in the household of David and Elizabeth Harrison (both also b. England).

MARSH, MARY (See David Upton)

MARSH, MERCY (AMINGTON) Mrs., born 1810, NY, had married first to Daniel Chittenden (also see) and in 1836 moved to Madison Twp., Lenawee Co., Mich. She apparently married again after this death to ? Marsh, as she was listed in the 1850 census of Dover Twp., head of household as MARSH, with children CYNTHIA A., age 4; MARIAN, age 1, both b. Mich. Also in her household were Chittenden children.

MARSH, MOSES born Vermont, and wife, SARAH (BUTTERFIELD), born 14 Oct. 1833, St. Lawrence Co., NY, were early settlers to Jefferson Co., NY. She died there in February 1834. He afterwards went to St. Lawrence Co., NY, but returned to Hounsfield, Jefferson Co. where he remained. Known daughter, SUSAN (m. 8 Nov. 1847 to Joseph C. Newell, also see). Ref: P&BA-Len pg. 358-9.

MARSH, STEPHEN born ca. 1810, and wife, LOVINA, born ca. 1807, both in NY, were listed in the 1850 census of Hudson Twp., Lenawee Co., Mich.

MARSHALL, ADAMS, age 20, born NY, was listed in the 1850 census of Macon Twp., Lenawee Co., Mich. in the Ganoung household. Note BETSEY, following.

MARSHALL, BETSEY was listed head of household in the 1840 census index of Macon Twp., Lenawee Co., Mich. Note ADAMS, preceding.

MARSHALL, CATHARINE M. (See David Ramsdell)

MARSHALL, CHARLES M. born 10 May 1806, Conn., married on 14 Oct. 1833 to HARRIET (OSBORN). Children: 1. Infant died; 2. JANE b. 4 Aug. 1834 (m. Theodore Nash). Harriet died and Charles married again on 19 May 1840 to MARY (PRUDEN) daughter of Daniel (also see) of Morris Twp., New Jersey. They were living in Adrian Twp., Lenawee Co., Mich. in the 1850 census. Charles died 5 Sept. 1880 in Adrian Twp., Lenawee Co., Mich. Children: 3. FREDERICK D. b. 4 June 1841 (served Civil War; went to Chicago, Ill.); 4. MARY ELIZABETH b. 15 May 1843 (m. Jefferson Schoonover, a Civil War Vet, and moved to Texas); 5. CAROLINE A. b. 10 Mar. 1845 (d. 24 June 1859); 6. JOSEPHINE P. b. 18 Feb. 1847, Lenawee Co. (m. Henry G. Wilder, also see); 7. CHARLES H. b. 1 Aug. 1850 (d. 12 Dec. 1858). Ref: P&BA-Len pg. 305-6.

MARSHALL, GEORGE W. born ca. 1823, NY, and wife, JULIA, born ca. 1821, Conn., were listed in the 1850 census of Woodstock Twp., Lenawee Co., Mich. with CHARLES, age 6; GEORGE, age 4; RUFUS, age 1, all b. NY, in their household.

MARSHALL, GRACE A. E. (See James B. Wells)

MARSHALL, JOHN A. born ca. 1813, and wife, ALVIRA, born ca. 1816, both in NY, were listed in the 1850 census of Madison Twp., Lenawee Co., Mich. with EDWIN, age 16, b. NY; and JEROME, age 12; MARY A., age 7, both b. Mich., in their household.

MARSHALL, ROBERT G. born ca. 1809/11, Ontario Co., NY married LUCY N. (RICE). About 1848, they removed to Ogden Twp., Lenawee Co., Mich., where they were living in 1850. They moved for a time to Metamora, Ohio, but returned to Ogden Twp. He enlisted in Oct. 1861 in Co. F., 67th Ohio Inf., and was killed in 1863. His wife died in Ogden Twp. in 1882. Children: 1. CATHARINE A. b. ca. 1842, NY (m. J. H. Garnsey, Metamora, Ohio); 2. WILLIAM H. (following); 3. ELIZA b. ca. 1846, NY (m. E. E. Dow, Toledo, Ohio); 4. ELEANOR b. Ogden Twp. (m. Thomas Mills); 5. JAMES A. (Ogden Twp.) Ref: P&BA-Len pg. 710-1.

MARSHALL, SAMUEL (See Samuel Hoyt)

MARSHALL, SILAS, son of WILLIAM O. (following), born 3 Jan. 1838, Geauga Co., Ohio moved with his parents to Michigan, and married in June 1853 in Hillsdale Co., Mich. to PHEBE J. (HAVENS), daughter of Peter (also see). They settled in Seneca Twp., Lenawee Co., Mich. in 1855. Children: 1. ELLA B. (m. Marion Hart, also see); 2. EMMA E. Ref: P&BA-Len pg. 1088-9.

MARSHALL, THOMAS born ca. 1819, and wife, MARY, born ca. 1815, both in NY, were listed in the 1850 census of Tecumseh Twp., Lenawee Co., Mich. with WILLIAM, age 5; GARRETT, age 2, both b. Mich., in their household.

MARSHALL, THOMAS C. born ca. 1821, NY, and wife, EMILY, born ca. 1829, place not legible, were listed in the 1850 census of Woodstock Twp., Lenawee Co., Mich. with EUNICE?, age 9/12, b. Mich., all in a Taylor household.

MARSHALL, WILLIAM H., son of ROBERT G. (preceding), born 8 Feb. 1844, Seneca, Ontario Co., NY, came to Ogden Twp., Lenawee Co., Mich. with his parents. He enlisted on 7 Aug. 1862 in Co. C., 18th Mich. Inf. and served till 1865. He married in 1869 to JULIA E. (CROCKETT), daughter of Nathaniel (also see), and she died 2 Jan. 1879. He married again to ADDIE E. (HARRINGTON), daughter of James. Children: 1. BLANCHIE; 2. MAUDE EDNA; 3. WILLIAM H. Ref; P&BA-Len pg. 710-1.

MARSHALL, WILLIAM O. born New Hampshire, married (wife's name not stated) and moved to Ohio where she died. He married again to POLLY (RYDER) born Mass. They lived in Chardon, Geauga Co., Ohio, and last in Wisconsin where he died in 1860. Polly died in Pewamo, Mich. ca. 1870. Children: 1. BETSEY; 2. GEORGE; 3. SETH; 4. NATHAN; 5. SILAS (preceding). Ref: P&BA-Len pg. 1088-9.

MARTIN, EXPERIENCE (See Joseph Baker)

MARTIN, HARRIET, age 7, born NY, was listed in the 1850 census of Dover Twp., Lenawee Co., Mich. in a Morse household.

MARTIN, IDA (See John Beland)

MARTIN, JAMES and wife, MARGARETTA (HAMMEL), had known daughter, ANNA b. Butler Co., Penn. (m. John T. Underwood, see Edwin). Ref: P&BA-Len pg. 413-4.

MARTIN, JAMES born ca. 1814, England, and wife, MARY, born ca. 1805, NY, were listed in the 1850 census of Dover Twp., Lenawee Co., Mich. with HIRAM E., age 16, b. NY, and perhaps stepchildren, Silas Elliott, age 14; Adeline Elliott, age 11; Fidelia Elliott, age 7, all b. Mich., in their household.

MARTIN, JOHN born ca. 1810, England, may be he listed in the 1840 census index of Dover Twp., Lenawee Co.,

Mich. In the 1850 census of Dover Twp., he listed LOIZA, age 21, b. NY, in the household.

MARTIN, JOHN C. was listed in the 1840 census index of Macon Twp., Lenawee Co., Mich. Also see THADDEUS, following.

MARTIN, KUNIGUNDA (See Frederick J. Schreyer)

MARTIN, LEMUEL born ca. 1801, Mass., and wife, MARY, born ca. 1810, NY, were listed in the 1850 census of Adrian Twp., Lenawee Co., Mich.

MARTIN, LEVI was listed in the 1840 census index of Raisin Twp., Lenawee Co., Mich. adjacent to STEPHEN, following.

MARTIN, MARY of Co. Sligo, Ireland (See Michael Howley).

MARTIN, MICHAEL J., son of STEPHEN P. E. (following), born 23 Mar. 1829, Middlesex Co., NJ, moved with his parents to Lodi, Seneca Co., NY, and then to Macon Twp., Lenawee Co., Mich. He married on 22 Oct. 1856, Macon Twp., to JANE A. (MILLER), daughter of Lewis V. (also see). She died 28 Oct. 1881, Macon Twp. Children: 1. IDA B. (m. Frederick Beland, probably son of John², also see); 2. J. DEWITT (to Mooreville, Washtenaw Co., Mich.); 3. S. SOPHIA; 4. HARRY T. Ref: P&BA-Len pg. 970-1.

MARTIN, PETER was born, reared, and married in Germany, and he brought his family to Alleghany Co., MD, an area now in Garrett Co., where he remained. Known daughter, MARIA b. Germany (m. ? Wilt, Preston Co., W. Va., see Michael Wilt¹). Ref: P&BA-Len pg. 1092.

MARTIN, PETER was listed in the 1840 census index of Adrian Twp., Lenawee Co., Mich.

MARTIN, STEPHEN P. E., son of MICHAEL, was born in Middlesex Co., NJ, and married possibly in Woodbridge Twp. before 1829 to ABIGAIL (CLARKSON) born ca. 1802. After the birth of the first 2 children, they moved to Lodi, Seneca Co., NY; and then about 1832 to Macon Twp., Lenawee Co., Mich., and by 1840 to Raisin Twp. He died in 1846, age about 54. Apparently the family returned to Macon Twp., as in the 1850 census of Macon Twp. Abigail was listed head of household with MICHAEL (preceding); MARY, age 18; HARRIET, age 12, last 2 born Mich., in her household. She died 2 Apr. 1887, age 93? (doesn't agree with 1850 census showing age 48, b. NJ). Ref: P&BA-Len pg. 970-1. Note: There was a LOUIS, age 13, b. Mich., in an Osborn household in 1850 who may relate to this family. Note LEVI, preceding.

MARTIN, THADDEUS born ca. 1789, NY, and wife, LUCY, born ca. 1789, Mass. were listed in the 1850 census of Macon Twp., Lenawee Co., Mich. with MARSHAL, age 18; & CAROLINE, age 16, both b. Mich., in their household. Note: It is probably he listed as "Sadius" in the 1840 census index of Macon Twp. Note JOHN C., preceding.

MASON, E. R. married MARY ANN (WELCH), daughter of James (also see). Had known children: ARVILLA; JAY; CHARLES. They lived in Fairfield Twp., Lenawee Co., Mich. Note: May be son of ERASTUS B., following.

MASON, ELIZABETH (See Edward Clark)

MASON, ERASTUS B. born ca. 1801, and wife, MARY, born ca. 1805, both in Mass., were listed in the 1850 census of Fairfield Twp., Lenawee Co., Mich. with SALLY, age 22, b. NY; and ANOZINA?, age 16; E---- R. (male), age 13 (may be "E. R.," preceding); MARTHA S., age 11; JOHN E., age 8, all b.Mich., in their household. Note JOHN, following.

MASON, GARDNER P., son of JOHN (following), born 3 Aug. 1808, Bristol, Ontario Co., NY, married there to OLIVE P. (WEST), daughter of Nathan (also see). They moved by 1840 to Ogden Twp., Lenawee Co., Mich. and by 1850 to Fairfield Twp. They moved to Ogden Twp. ca. 1854-5, and he died there 15 Oct. 1865. Son, JOHN G. (following). Ref: P&BA-Len pg. 198-9.

MASON, HEPZIBAH born ca. 1773, Conn., was listed in the 1850 census of Adrian Twp., Lenawee Co., Mich. in the household of William and Maria Moore (also see).

MASON, IRA was listed in the 1840 census index of Blissfield Twp., Lenawee Co., Mich. Note SAPHRONA, following.

MASON, JOHN born 1767, Swansea, Mass., and wife, SALLY, born 1771, Dighton, Mass., lived first in Mass. where he was a seafarer. About 1801, they moved to Ontario Co., NY where he died at Bristol in 1836. She died 11 July 1860. There were 7 children, names not stated, except #6. GARDNER P. (preceding). Ref: P&BA-Len pg. 198-9. Also note ERASTUS B. (preceding); & MARTHA (following).

MASON, JOHN born ca. 1818, Mass., and wife, ALMIRA, born ca. 1824, NY, were listed in the 1850 census of Fairfield Twp., Lenawee Co., Mich. with NATHAN A., age 1, b. Mich., in their household.

MASON, JOHN E. (See Sheldon Wyman)

MASON, JOHN G., son of GARDNER P. (preceding), born 1835, near Richmond, Ontario Co., NY, married on 3 Feb. 1856 in Ogden Twp., Lenawee Co., Mich. to AMANDA D. (CARTER), daughter of Norman B. (also see). They resided first in Ogden Twp, and later moved to Adrian. Children: 1. GLENDORA b. 20 Aug. 1857 (m. Alfred Johnson); 2. STELLA D. b. 28 Sept. 1859 (m. George L. Bennett, son of Gershom B., also see). Ref: P&BA-Len pg. 198-9.

MASON, L. Q. (See Zebina White)

MASON, LETITIA, age 20, born NY, was listed in the 1850 census of Franklin Twp., Lenawee Co., Mich. in a Bradley household. Note THOMAS L., following.

MASON, MARTHA born 26 June 1810, probably in Ontario Co., NY, married Stephenson Dennison (also see). Ref: P&BA-Len pg. 493-4. Note JOHN, preceding.

MASON, MARY J., age 15, born NY, was listed in the 1850 census of Madison Twp., Lenawee Co., Mich. in a Millard household.

MASON, REUBEN born 12 Sept. 1773, and wife, MARY (PLATT), born 22 Apr. 1779, Lanesboro, Mass., had known daughter, LUCY b. 29 Nov. 1798, Lanesboro (m. Seymour Mead¹, also see). Ref: P&BA-Len pg. 941-2.

MASON, S. T., age 14, b. Mich., was listed in the 1850 census of Franklin Twp., Lenawee Co., Mich. in a Campburn household. Note THOAS L., following.

MASON, SAPHRONA born ca. 1814, NY, was listed head of household in the 1850 census of Riga Twp., Lenawee Co., Mich., with PAULINA, age 18; LUCIUS, age 16; OSCAR, age 15; THEODORE, age 12, all b. NY; and SAPHRONA, age 10; JOSEPHINE, age 8; MARIA, age 4, all b. Mich., in her household. Note IRA, preceding.

MASON, SENECA born ca. 1799, Mass., and wife, BETSEY, born ca. 1805, NY, were listed in the 1850 census of Riga Twp., Lenawee Co., Mich. with ARMENIA, age 17;

LEVI S., age 13; HARVEY, age 8, all b. NY; and ADALAIDE, age 4, b. Mich., in their household.

MASON, THOMAS L. born ca. 1802, Mass., and wife, SARAH, born ca. 1803, NY, were listed in the 1840 census index of Franklin Twp., Lenawee Co., Mich.; and in the 1850 census with LUTHER, age 19; FRANKLIN, age 18; LEWIS, age 15; FANNY, age 13; SARAH, age 13, all b. NY; and GEORGE, age 11; LOUISA, age 10; EVALINA, age 6; ORANGE?, age 5, all b. Mich., in their household. Also note LETITIA, & S. T., preceding.

MASON, W. S. G. born Seneca Co., NY, and wife, MARY A. (MAY), born in Townsend, Sandusky Co., Ohio, removed to Fairfield Twp., Lenawee Co., Mich. ca. 1858. About 1878, they moved to Fulton Co., Ohio where they were living in 1888. Two sons & three daughters, names not stated, except #3. ALICE b. 25 July 1851, Townsend, Ohio (m. George W. Woodworth, 9 Dec. 1879, Lansing, Mich.) Ref: P&BA-Len pg. 622-5.

MASTEN, ABRAHAM was listed in the 1840 census index of Milan Twp., Monroe Co., Mich. Note JACOB, following.

MASTEN, JACOB and wife, SUSAN (HANLON), were settlers to Milan Twp., Monroe Co., Mich. and had known daughter, ADELINE b. 9 July 1855, Milan Twp. (m. Thomas J. Pilbeam, also see). Ref: P&BA-Len pg. 690.

MASTERS, WILLIAM of Monroe Co., Mich. was father of MARY E. (m. Lysander Ormsby, also see).

MATHER, DAVID S., son of JOSEPH (following), born 14 Dec. 1795, Fairfield Co., Conn., married ELIZABETH (FANCHER) born Warwick, Orange Co., NY, daughter of S. (See Sylvanus). They settled first in Darien, Conn. In 1845, they removed to Three Rivers, St. Joseph Co., Mich., where he died 26 Sept. 1845; and she died 6 June 1883. There were 6 children, and only named were the following living in 1888: WILLIAM H. (following); HANNAH M. (m. P. P. Bates, Constantine, Mich.). Ref: P&BA-Len pg. 495.

MATHER, EDWARD born ca. 1826, and wife, JANE, born ca. 1827, both in England, were listed in the 1850 census of Medina Twp., Lenawee Co., Mich. with ALVIRA J., age 6/12, b. Mich., in their household.

MATHER, FRANK Mrs. (See Ebenezer Fisk[2])

MATHER, JOSEPH born in Conn., was a Colonel in the Revolutionary War. He married ? (SCOTT) of Danbury, Conn. Known son, DAVID S. (preceding). Ref: P&BA-Len pg. 495.

MATHER, PETER J. born ca. 1808, NY, and wife, ANGELINE, born ca. 1811, Conn., were listed in the 1850 census of Tecumseh Twp., Lenawee Co., Mich. with MYNUSE? (male), age 16; LOUISA, age 14, both b. NY; and WILLIAM, age 9; ROSALDO, age 6; FRANCES, age 3, all b. Mich., in their household.

MATHER, SIDNEY born ca. 1820, VT, and wife, LUCRETIA, born ca. 1822, NY, were listed in the 1850 census of Fairfield Twp., Lenawee Co., Mich. with EMILY, age 7, b. NY; and ALMANZER, age 6; LUCRETIA, age 4/12, both b. Mich., in their household.

MATHER, WILLIAM H., son of DAVID S. (preceding), born 17 May 1822, Darien, Conn., came to Michigan with his parents. He married on 26 Mar. 1846, Clinton Co., Mich. to CLARINDA F. (BREWSTER), daughter of Clinton (also see). They resided in Tecumseh Twp. for many years, but in 1880 retired to Tecumseh village. Of their 5 children, 3 died young (names not stated), and surviving were: 1. HARRIET N. (m. Rufus Raymond, Mason, Mich.); 2. ANN (m. Eugene Lovett, Tecumseh Twp.); 3. CHARLES B. (d. age 22 years). Ref: P&BA-Len pg. 495.

MATTHES, C. FREDERICK, son of JOHN L. (following), born 20 July 1854, Monroe Co., Mich., married in Adrian, Lenawee Co. on 18 Sept. 1880 to CARRIE (SCHWARTZ), daughter of Henry & Barbara (Mennel). Children: 1. CLARA; 2. ARTHUR; 3. HERMANN; 4. EDWIN; 5. HAROLD. Ref: P&BA-Len pg. 467.

MATTHES, GODFREY and wife, MARGARET (MEYER), were natives of Bavaria, Germany, where they remained. He died in 1826, and she died in 1843. Known son, JOHN L. (following). Ref: P&BA-Len pg. 943-4.

MATTHES, JOHN L., son of GODFREY (preceding), born 12 Oct. 1824, Bavaria, Germany, came to the US at age 23. He married in 1847 in Monroe Co., Mich. to MARGARET (KAUMEIER) also born in Germany. In 1865, they moved to Adrian, Lenawee Co. Children: 1. JOHN L.; 2. JOHN GODFREY; 3. MARGARET C.; 4. C. FREDERICK (preceding); 5. CATHARINE; 6. MARY; 7. WILLIAM; 8. EMILY; 9. HERMAN; 10. LOUISA; 11. AUGUST. Ref: P&BA-Len pg. 467 & 943-4.

MATTESON also see MATTISON

MATTESON, FRANCES M. (See Lewis G. Lester)

MATTESON, PELEG was listed in the 1840 census index of Palmyra Twp., Lenawee Co., Mich.

MATTHEWS, HENRY born ca. 1819, NY, was listed in the 1850 census of Franklin Twp., Lenawee Co., Mich. in the household of Luther Rexford. Listed also was LUCINDA, age 35, relationship not known. It is probably this Henry who came from Seneca Co., NY and married NANCY (SLATER), daughter of Joseph (also see). Henry died 3 Dec. 1876, Franklin Twp. Children: 1. EMMA D. (m. B. J. Slater, Tecumseh Twp.); 2. FLORENCE (m. M. J. Cumming, Jackson Co., Mich.); 3. ABBIE L. Ref: P&BA-Len pg. 772-3. Note: Nancy married again to Jesse Pentecost (also see).

MATTHEWS, HESTER (See William Waldron)

MATTHEWS, WILSON born ca. 1824, and wife, MARTHA (FLEMING?), born ca. 1825, both in NY, were listed in the 1850 census of Tecumseh Twp., Lenawee Co., Mich., with MARY, age 1, b. Mich.; and Martha A. Parker, age 9, b. Ind. in their household. Note: Wife, Martha may be the daughter of James Fleming (also see), as Martha A. Parker in their household was the daughter of William K. & Jane (Fleming) Parker, and granddaughter of James Fleming.

MATTIS, GARRETT born ca. 1799, and wife, CATHARINE, born ca. 1806, both in NJ, were listed in the 1840 census index of Macon Twp., Lenawee Co., Mich., and in the 1850 census with MARTHA, age 20; WILLIAM, age 19 (m. Mary E. Lanning, dau. of James, also see); ELIZABETH, age 17; RICHARD, age 15, all b. NJ; and

Pioneer Families of Southeastern Michigan

SARAH, age 11; CHARLES, age 9; ISAIAH, age 7; ANN, age 5; MARGARET, age 1, all b. Mich., in their household. Known daughter, MARIA, age 14, b. NJ (m. James L. Brown, also see), was in the household of John & Joannah Usborn, and Joannah was age 25, b. NJ, possibly another daughter. Garrett died at age 75, and Catharine at age 82, in Franklin Twp. Ref: P&BA-Len pg. 1208-9. Note JOHN, following.

MATTIS, JOHN, possibly son of GARRETT (preceding), born ca. 1828, and wife, ANGELINE (LANNING?), born ca. 1832, both in NJ, were listed in the 1850 census of Raisin Twp., Lenawee Co., Mich. in the household of Joseph Lanning (also see).

MATTISON also see MATTESON

MATTISON, NORMAN (See Stephen Conger)

MATTOON, female (See Nathan Goodale)

MAUK, J. W. Prof. (See Bishop H. Ames)

MAURER, BARBARA (See George Gussenbauer)

MAWDSLEY, JOHN, son of WILLIAM & ELIZABETH (ANDERSON), wa born 31 Oct. 1841, Manchester, England, and his parents were of Scottish descent. He came to the US in 1864, living variously in New York City, New Orleans, LA, & Chicago, Ill. before settling in Adrian, Lenawee Co., Mich. ca. 1870. He married in Jan. 1872 in Adrian to MARY C. (ANTHONY) of Mendon, NY, and she died 8 May 1874 leaving daughters: ESTHER E.; & MARGARET. John married again to ALICE (NICHOLSON) of Hillsdale Co., Mich., born 5 Mar. 1845. (Her parents moved to Adrian by 1888). Ref: P&BA-Len pg. 479-80.

MAXSON, JESSE, son of JOSEPH (following), born Stephentown, Rensselaer Co., NY, went in 1834 to Pittsford Twp., Hillsdale Co., Mich. where he purchased land, then returned to New York until 1836. He married MARIETTA (DAYTON) born Rensselaer Co., who died in 1844 in Pittsford Twp., Hillsdale Co. There were 4 children, but only named were those living in 1888: MARIETTA MATILDA (m. Beach, resided Livingston Co., Mich.); MARVIN M.; MANLEY M. (following). Ref: P&BA-Len pg. 1155-6.

MAXSON, JOSEPH was the descendant of a Colonial family who settled first in Conn. in 1638. JOHN^1 born 24 Mar. 1638 and wife, MARY (MOSHER) were among the families who settled near Hopkinton, Rhode Island in 1661. The exact descent was not given. Joseph moved from Rensselaer Co., NY to Centreville, Allegany Co., NY where he remained. Known son, JESSE (preceding). Ref: P&BA-Len pg. 1155-6.

MAXSON, MARVIN M., son of JESSE (preceding), born 20 Oct. 1831, Centreville, Allegany Co., NY, moved with his parents to Pittsford Twp., Hillsdale Co., Mich. He married in Apr. 1865 to DELIA (CHIPMAN), daughter of Elan (also see). They moved to Hudson, Lenawee Co. Son, GUY. Ref: P&BA-Len pg. 1155-6 & portrait.

MAXWELL, ISRAEL BAKER^4, son of JOHN^3 (following), born 3 Feb. 1803, Sussex Co., NJ, married MARY A. (ONSTED), daughter of John (also see). After the birth of 3 children, they moved to Milo, Yates Co., NY. In 1835, they removed to Cambridge Twp., Lenawee Co., Mich. He went in the Gold Rush to California and died there (he was listed in the 1850 census of Cambridge Twp.) She died 5 Mar. 1865, living with son, Peter. Children: 1. NANCY (m. Amon Pratt; d. Aug. 1871); 2. ESTHER born ca. 1826, NJ (m. Henry Powell, also see); 3. EUNICE b. ca. 1832, NJ (m. Lewis Swarthout; d. Aug. 1858); 4. JOHN O. (following); 5. JACOB B. b. ca. 1838, Mich. (m. Catherine Aten); 6. PETER b. ca. 1842 (m. H. Van Alstine). Ref: P&BA-Len pg. 971-2.

MAXWELL, JOHN^1 was the son of a man who came from Scotland with a brother and settled first in Rhode Island and then on Long Island. John^1 moved from Long Island to Westfield, NJ in 1665. He had children: WILLIAM; JOHN^2; DAVID; ESTHER. JOHN^2 served in the Continental Army from Virginia during the Revolution and was killed. He had known sons NATHANIEL (who also d. in the Revolution); and JOHN^3 (following). Ref: P&BA-Len pg. 971-2.

MAXWELL, JOHN^3, son of JOHN^2 (note JOHN^1, preceding), married on 6 Nov. 1785 to EUNICE (OSBORNE) of Morris Co., NJ. About 1800, they moved to Sparta, Sussex Co., NJ. Children: 1. JACOB BRITTON (m/1 T. Russell; m/2 Mary Little); 2. ELIZABETH (m/1 Van Buskirk; m/2 Montoguil); 3. JOHN OSBORN (m/1 Betsey Corey; m/2 Mrs. ? (Little) McPeek); 4. ESTHER (d. child); 5. ISRAEL BAKER (preceding). Ref: P&BA-Len pg. 971-2.

MAXWELL, JOHN O.^{5}, son of ISRAEL BAKER (preceding), born 25 Dec. 1834, Milo, Yates Co., NY, came to Lenawee Co., Mich. with his parents. He married on 24 Apr. 1858, Cambridge Twp., to CHARLOTTE (ONSTED), daughter of Peter (also see). Daughter, HELEN E. (m. George E. Bennett, also see). Ref: P&BA-Len pg. 971-2.

MAY, MARY A. (See W. S. G. Mason)

MAYBEE see MABEE

MAYBIN, MARY (See Charles Blanchard)

MAYNARD, DAVID T. born 29 July 1808, Seneca Co., NY married there in 1833 to ELIZABETH (WHITING), daughter of Alanson (also see). They removed to Huron Co., Ohio where he died 29 Dec. 1886, and she died 12 Jan. 1863. Six children, names not stated, except #3. ANNA E. b. 13 Dec. 1838, Ripley, Ohio (m/1 Charles C. Bacon; m/2 Dr. Francis Grandy, see both). Ref: P&BA-Len pg. 576-7.

MAYNARD, HAYDEN W., son of JOHN (following), born 20 July 1833, Adrian Twp., Lenawee Co., Mich., married on 9 Mar. 1859 to LUCY L. (ABBOTT) of Rome Twp. They lived in Minnesota until 1863, then returned to Dover Twp., Lenawee Co., Mich. Son, ASA N. (m. Iza Sharell, Dover Twp.) Ref: P&BA-Len pg. 764-5.

MAYNARD, JOHN born 29 July 1796, Conn., and wife, CHARLOTTE (MERCHANT) born 12 Oct. 1801, New Hampshire, lived first in Binghampton, NY. In 1833, they removed to Adrian Twp., Lenawe Co., Mich.; and he died 21 Aug. 1840, and she died 24 Jan. 1879. Nine children (2 died infancy, names not stated): 1. SAMANTHA b. ca. 1828, NY (m. Asa Smith, also see); 2.

SUSAN (m. Erastus Hart; to Wisconsin); 3. MARY M. b. ca. 1830, NY (m. Silas Thompson; d. May 1858, Adrian Twp.); 4. JOHN O. b. ca. 1832 (m. Caroline Hood, dau. of John Hood, Jr., also see); 5. HAYDEN W. (preceding); 6. ALBERT Q. b. ca. 1837, Mich. (m. Marietta Willey); 7. MORTON A. b. ca. 1840 (m. Dora Brashears). Ref: P&BA-Len pg. 764-5.

MAYNARD, TRUMAN T. born ca. 1822, Mass., and wife, RUTH, born ca. 1824, NY, were listed in the 1850 census of Madison Twp., Lenawee Co., Mich. with CHARLES, age 9, b. NY; and HANNAH, age 4; MELISSA, age 2, both b. Mich., in their household.

MAYNARD, WILLIAM D. born ca. 1818, Mass., and wife, SARAH, born ca. 1821, Conn., were listed in the 1850 census of Seneca Twp., Lenawee Co., Mich. with no family.

MAYNE also see MAIN/MAINE

MAYNE, JAMES born 7 Oct. 1818, married MARY (BROOK) born 1 Jan. 1823. He died in May 1904, and she died 11 Mar. 1896, and they are buried in the Mills Cemetery, Franklin Twp., Lenawee Co., Mich. Also note JOHN MAIN.

MAYO D married LUCRETIA (VAN VLECK); and after his death, Lucretia married Erastus Park (also see) possibly in Niagara Co., NY.

McADAM, ANDREW born ca. 1815, Ireland, was listed in the 1850 census of Adrian Twp., Lenawee Co., Mich. in a McKey household. Note MICHAEL, following.

McADAM, MICHAEL born 23 Apr. 1816, Co. Fermanagh, Ireland, came to the US with his brother (name not stated, note ANDREW, preceding) and settled first in Adrian, Lenawee Co., Mich. He married on 12 Apr. 1847 to ESTHER (BAKER), daughter of Thomas (also see), and settled in Ogden Twp. where they were listed in the 1850 census. Seven children, names not stated except the eldest, SARAH M. b. 25 Mar. 1848 (m. Ruel A. Freeman, son of William, also see). Ref: P&BA-Len pg. 668-9.

McARTY see McCARTY

McBRIDE, MARGARET (See Evan Hendershott)

McCABE, ELIZABETH (See John W. Tolford)

McCALMONT, MARGARET (See Andrew McClenahan)

McCAM, MARY (See John Exelby)

McCAMBER also see MACOMBER; McCUMBER; McOMBER

McCAMBER, MARIE (See Henry F. Daly)

McCARBERY, CHARLES and wife, ELIZABETH (COUPPLE), were born and married in Co. Antrim, Ireland. He died there in 1848, age 55. Soon after this death, she immigrated to Groveland, Livingston Co., NY. In 1854, she removed to Tecumseh Twp., Lenawee Co., Mich. Five children, only known are following. She died Oct. 1872, Macon Twp., age 80, at home of known son, JAMES; also known #3. HENRY (following). Ref: P&BA-Len pg. 732-3.

McCARBERY, HENRY, son of CHARLES (preceding), born ca. 1834, Co. Antrim, Ireland, came to Livingston Co., NY with his mother. He married there on 31 Oct. 1854 to NANCY (KYLE), daughter of Robert (also see) of Mt. Morris, NY. They settled in Macon Twp., Lenawee Co., Mich. by 1861. Children: 1. LIZZIE (m. Masa Vandeventer); 2. CHARLES H. (to Detroit, Mich.); 3. NANCY (m. Lavern Osterhout, son of David B., also see, Ridgeway Twp.); 4. BERT; 5. WILLIAM. Ref: P&BA-Len pg. 732-3.

McCARTY, ANN, age 18, born Ireland, was listed in the 1850 census of Adrian Twp., Lenawee Co., Mich.

McCARTY, H. NELSON, probably son of WILLIAM (following), born ca. 1819, and wife, REGINA (UNGANST), born ca. 1826, were natives of Penn., who came to Hudson, Lenawee Co., Mich. where known daughter, RACHEL was born 26 Feb. 1850 (m. William C. Moran, also see). Ref: P&BA-Len pg. 1082-4. Note: In the 1850 census of Hudson Twp, they were listed as Nelson McArty, age 31, and Rebecca, age 24, with Rachel, age 4/12, in the household, next door to William

McCARTY, SAMUEL, age 13, born Mich., was listed in the 1850 census of Adrian Twp., Lenawee Co., Mich. in a Perkins household.

McCARTY, WILLIAM born ca. 1793, and wife, MARY, born ca. 1791, both in Penn., were listed in the 1850 census of Hudson Twp., Lenawee Co., Mich. with LAWRENCE, age 35; (and possibly grandchildren?) WILLIAM, age 11; SARAH E., age 9, all b. Penn.; and ELIZABETH A., age 4, b. Ohio, in their household. NELSON was listed next door.

McCLEOD, JOHN married a daughter (name not stated) of Arnold Smeltzer (also see).

McCLENAHAN, ANDREW was the son of a man who had come from Ireland to Erie Co., Penn. Andrew married there to ? (HUTCHINSON), and they moved to Lewisburg, Penn. in the Susquehanna Valley. His wife died leaving a daughter JANE (m. John P. Sipley, Cass Co., Mich.). Andrew married again to MARGARET (McCALMONT) of Centre Co., Penn. About 1862, they removed to Seneca Co., Ohio, and she died at Tiffin. He afterwards removed to Adrian Twp., Lenawee Co., Mich., where he died in 1877, age 42. Children: JOHN b. Union Co., Penn.; ELEANOR; EMELINE; MAGGIE; and an adopted son, Andrew Ranck. Ref: P&BA-Len pg. 790-1.

McCLURE, ? and wife, FANNIE (CANBURR) from London, Ontario, Canada, moved to Gratiot Co., Mich., where she died. He moved to Branch Co., Mich. where he died at age 63. They had known daughter, CYNTHIA b. 6 July 1854, London, Canada (m. George W. Allen, Jr., also see). Ref: P&BA-Len pg. 230.

McCOLLUM, E---AM? (male), born ca. 1825, Penn., was listed in the 1850 census of Cambridge Twp., Lenawee Co., Mich.

McCOLLUM, JACOB was listed in the 1840 census index of Hudson Twp., Lenawee Co., Mich.

Pioneer Families of Southeastern Michigan

McCOLLUM, JOHN born ca. 1820, and wife, SALLY, born ca. 1825, both in NY, were listed in the 1850 census of Cambridge Twp., Lenawee Co., Mich. with CHARLES, age 5; EMILY, age 4; MARY, age 3; JAMES, age 11/12, all b. Mich., and Sally Lawson, age 63, possibly mother of Sally?, in their household.

McCOLLUM, JOSEPH born ca. 1807, NY, and wife, FANNY, born ca. 1824, Penn., were listed in the 1850 census of Tecumseh Twp., Lenawee Co., Mich. with HUGH, age 3; MARY, age 1, both b. Mich., in their household.

McCOLLUM, MARY M. born ca. 1824, NY, was listed in the 1850 census of Tecumseh Twp., Lenawee Co., Mich. in a Dearborn household.

McCOLLUM, MOSES and wife, ? (BURKE), were natives of NJ and parents of PETER (following). It may be this Moses listed in Bernards, Somerset Co., NJ in 1778-1780; and in the Militia in Bernards in 1793. Ref: P&BA-Len pg. 1195-6. Note: There was a MOSES listed in the 1840 census index of Lodi Twp., Washtenaw Co., Mich.

McCOLLUM, PETER, son of MOSES (preceding), born ca. 1782, and wife, MARY (NESBIT), born ca. 1786, both in NJ, were married in LeRoy, Genesee Co., NY. In 1828, they removed to Tecumseh Twp., Lenawee Co., Mich. He died there at age 78, and she died 15 years later at age 86 in Franklin, Mich. Ten children, names not stated. The following were in their household in the 1850 census (note places of birth): 1. MARGARET, age 32, b. NY; 2. JOHN, age 25, b. Mich.; 3. GEORGE, age 19, b. NY; 4. MARY, age 23, b. Mich.; 5. HARRIET b. 12 Oct. 1829, Tecumseh Twp. (m. Matthew B. McConnel, also see); and probably a grandchild, CHARLES, age 3, b. Mich. Ref: P&BA-IEN PG. 1195-6. Also note JOSEPH; & MARY M. (preceding).

McCOLLUM, ROBERT C. (See James B. Wells)

McCOLLUM, SAMUEL was listed in the 1840 census index of Franklin Twp., Lenawee Co., Mich.

McCOMB, WILLIAM, possibly son of WILLIAM A. (following), born ca. 1823, Scotland, and wife, ELIZABETH, born ca. 1824, Penn., were listed in the 1850 census of Ogden Twp., Lenawee Co., Mich. with REUBEN, age 1, b. Mich., in their household (next door to WILLIAM A.). They may also be parents of WILLIAM probably born after 1850 who m. ALICE BELLE (WOTRING), daughter of Capt. Jehu F. (also see). Ref: P&BA-Len pg. 1107-8.

McCOMB, WILLIAM A. born ca. 1795, and wife, MARY (GLASGOW), born ca. 1804, both in Ireland, may have been in Scotland in 1823. They came to the US and apparently lived first in NY, and then moved before 1840 to Ogden Twp., Lenawee Co., Mich. In the 1850 census of Ogden Twp. they listed THOMAS, age 14, ELIZABETH, age 13, both b. NY; and GEORGE, age 11; ROSEANN, age 8; MARY E., age 6 (m. James Carney, also see), all b. Mich., in their household. Ref: P&BA-Len pg. 803-4. Note WILLIAM, preceding.

McCONNEL also see McCONNELL

McCONNEL, AMSEY L., son of MATTHEW (following), was a native of Orleans Co., NY, and he married CATHARINE (BEERS), daughter of Henry (also see). In 1833, they removed to Adrian Twp., Lenawee Co., Mich. probably from Elmira, NY; and he died in 1836 at age 45. There were 8 children, and 7 grew to maturity (names not stated). Known sons, MATTHEW B. (following); and THOMAS (following). In the 1850 census of Adrian Twp., Catharine, age 56, was living in the household of Thomas. Ref: P&BA-Len pg. 1195-6.

McCONNEL, MATTHEW and wife, LUDLAM (not certain if this is given name or surname), were early settlers near Elmira, NY, and it is probably they listed in the 1800 census index of Tioga Co. (Elmira is in present day Chemung Co.) They were parents of a large family, and only named was AMSEY L. (preceding). Matthew was said to have married again, wife's name not given. Ref: P&BA-Len pg. 1195-6.

McCONNEL, MATTHEW B., son of AMSEY L. (preceding), born ca. 1814, NY, came to Adrian Twp., Lenawee Co., Mich. with his parents. He married in 1838 to HANNAH (SOOP) born ca. 1819, NY, and settled in Adrian Twp. Children: 1. MARIA b. ca. 1841 (m. Henry Brazee (also see); 2. DAVID b. ca. 1845 (served 7th Mich. Cav., Civil War); 3. MADISON b. ca. 1847 (prob. he who served 11th Mich. Cav., Civil War, lived Wayne Co., Mich.); 4. MATTHEW (called twin of Madison, but only Madison, age 3, was listed in 1850 census, said to have served in 11th Mich. Cav., Civil War?); 5. RACHEL (d. young); 6. HATTIE (m. Eugene Westfall, Wayne Co., Mich.); 7. DORA (m. Joseph Marsh, Springville, Mich.) Hannah died in Feb. 1862. Matthew B. married again to her sister, Mrs. ? (SOOP) MOODY, widow of W. R. Moody, and she died 2 months later. He married again on 6 Jan. 1864 to HARRIET (McCOLLUM), daughter of Peter (also see). Children: 8. SUSAN J. b. 14 Mar. 1865 (m. Nathan W. Simons, Adrian Twp.); 9. JOSEPH b. 12 Jan. 1867 (d. 10 Jan. 1873); 10. EUGENE K. b. 24 June 1869. Ref: P&BA-Len pg. 1195-6.

McCONNEL, THOMAS, son of AMSEY L., born ca. 1825, NY, and wife, ELIZA, born ca. 1828, Mich., were listed in the 1850 census of Adrian Twp., Lenawee Co., Mich. with mother, CATHARINE, age 56, in the household.

McCONNELL also see McCONNEL

McCONNELL, DAVID and wife, ELIZABETH (FARR) born ca. 1776, both born in County Antrim, Ireland, came to the US in 1831/3. He died near Toledo, Ohio in 1838, and Eliza moved to Lenawee Co., Mich. and lived with children till her death. She was buried in Fairfield Twp. Known daughter, ELIZA b. 26 June 1814, Ireland (m. James Green, also see). Ref: P&BA-Len pg. 459. Known sons, HUGH (following); and DAVID (following) with whom Elizabeth was living in 1850 census of Raisin Twp.

McCONNELL, DAVID, son of DAVID (preceding), born ca. 1798, Ireland, was listed head of household in the 1850 census of Raisin Twp., Lenawee Co., Mich. with mother, ELIZABETH, age 74, born Ireland, and some children ELIZABETH, age 8; MARTHA, age 5, both b. Mich., in his household. SARAH B., age 14, born Mich., a few doors away in the household of Robert and Sarah Boyd, both born Ireland, probably relates to this family.

McCONNELL, FANNIE (See Richard Pelham)

McCONNELL, HUGH, probably son of DAVID (preceding), was born ca. 1821, Co. Antrim, Ireland. He came to Canada with his parents, and then to Toledo, Ohio; and afterwards to Fairfield Twp., Lenawee Co., Mich. He married MARGARET JANE (COLVIN), daughter of

William (also see) and settled in Fairfield Twp. by 1849. Children: ARTHUR; EVA; & ARTHUR J. were deceased before 1888; and surviving were ELIZA J. b. ca. 1849 (m. F. L Williams, lived Ker City, FL); SUSANNA (m. John Shoemaker, Fairfield Twp.); LEO H. (following); EDWARD C. (to Montana). Ref: P&BA-Len pg. 958-9.

McCONNELL, JOHN born ca. 1808, and wife, ELIZABETH, born ca. 1810, both in Ireland, were listed in the 1840 census index of Tecumseh Twp., Lenawee Co., Mich., and in the 1850 census with MARY, age 15; JANE, age 12; EMMA, age 8; ELLEN, age 6; CHARLES, age 5; WILLIAM, age 1, all b. Mich., in their household.

McCONNELL, JOHN born ca. 1828, NY, was listed in the 1850 census of Rome Twp., Lenawee Co., Mich. in the Theodore Abbott household.

McCONNELL, LEO H., son of HUGH (preceding), born 22 Jan. 1859, Fairfield Twp., Lenawee Co., Mich., married on 16 Nov. 1822 to CLARA E. (MORLEY) who was born 10 Jan. 1861, Chicago, Ill. They settled in Raisin Twp. Children: 1. NINA C.; 2. NORMAN C.; 3. EDWARD H. Ref: P&BA-Len pg. 958-9.

McCONNELL, MARY born ca. 1821, NY, was listed in the 1850 census of Rome Twp., Lenawee Co., Mich. in the household of James Fleming.

McCORMICK, LEMUEL, son of WILLIAM (following), born 21 Mar. 1832, Butler Co., Penn., moved with parents to Riga Twp., Lenawee Co., Mich. He married on 1 July 1877 to SARAH (HAMILTON), daughter of John (also see). Son, GEORGE b. 10 Nov. 1878. Ref: P&BA-Len pg. 327-8.

McCORMICK, WILLIAM born Washington Co., Penn., married MARGARET (GRAY), daughter of James (also see) and settled in Butler Co., Penn. About 1854, they moved to Riga Twp., Lenawee Co., Mich., where he died on 20 Oct. 1855. Margaret died there in 1881, age 71. Children: 1. LEMUEL (preceding); 2. MANUEL b. 21 Mar. 1834, Penn.; 3. WILLIAM O.; 4. JAMES; 5. MARY E.; 6. MARGARET J.; 7. PETERSON; 8. HENRY C.; 9. CHRISTIANA (m. Thomas O. Turner, also see, on 6 May 1876); 10. GEORGE W. Ref: P&BA-Len pg. 327-8; 376; 951-2.

McCOWAN, JOHN married IDA (JAMES), daughter of Bishop H. (also see). Children: HENRY B.; MAUD; WILLIAM A.; BELLE; JOHN C.

McCRACKEN, SARAH (See Solomon Brown)

McCRILLIS, JAMES born ca. 1800, and wife, BETSEY, born ca. 1804, both in NY, were listed in the 1850 census of Medina Twp., Lenawee Co., Mich. with JAMES, age 17; EDWARD, age 14, both b. NY; and AMELIA A., age 11; WILLIAM, age 7, both b. Mich., in their household. Note MARY, following.

McCRILLIS, MARY (See Dr. Amos Kendall)

McCULLEY, HUGH born ca. 1797, and wife, MARY, born ca. 1805, both in Ireland, were listed in the 1840 census index of Tecumseh Twp., Lenawee Co., Mich.; and in the 1850 census of Raisin Twp., with SAMUEL, age 25; JOHN, age 23, both b. Ireland; and MATILDA, age 21, b. NY (m. Franklin Bates, 11 Apr. 1852, Raisin Twp.); MARY, age 17; JAMES, age 15, both b. NY; and ELIZABETH, age 14; ANN, age 11, both b. Mich., in their household.

McCUMBER also see MACOMBER; McCAMBER; McOMBER.

McCUMBER, JOSEPH born ca. 1795, and wife, ELIZA, born ca. 1807, both in NY, were listed in the 1850 census of Medina Twp., Lenawee Co., Mich. with CHARILLA, age 23; SARAH, age 21; HARMON, age 14; DAVID, age 6, all b. NY, in their household. Also note PHILIP & RICHARD, following; and SARAH, age 22, b. NY, in another household may also relate to this family.

McCUMBER, PHILIP, probably son of JOSEPH (preceding), born ca. 1821, and wife, CATHARINE, born ca. 1822, both in NY, were listed in the 1850 census of Medina Twp., Lenawee Co., Mich. with CELINDA, age 4, b. Mich., in their household (2 doors from JOSEPH & next door to RICHARD, following).

McCUMBER, RICHARD, probably son of JOSEPH (preceding), born ca. 1831, NY, was listed in the 1850 census of Medina Twp., Lenawee Co., Mich. next door to PHILIP (preceding) in a Richmond household.

McCURRAN, ANTHONY and wife, ANNA (GILLIS), had 4 children, and but only mentioned daughters: ELIZABETH ADELE b. 20 Aug. 1850 (reared by L. C. Lombard; m. Samuel D. Tingley, also see); and MARY ANNA (m. Col. John R. Thompson). Ref: P&BA-Len pg. 876-7.

McDERMOTT, MARY J. was called an "orphan girl of Lenawee Co." in the sketch of Charles Brown of Medina Twp.

McDOWELL, WILLIAM H., son of CHARLES J. (born Broome Co., NY), was born 26 Apr. 1838, Cohocton, Steuben Co., NY, and served in Co. F, 35th NY Inf, in the Civil War, 1861-3. After the War, he moved to Palmyra Twp., Lenawee Co., Mich. He married 9 Aug. 1867 to CATHARINE W. (MOORE), born Cohocton, NY, and they settled in Palmyra Twp. Son, FRED C. Ref: P&BA-Len pg. 289-90.

McDOWELL, HANNAH married Israel Stevens (also see). Her Great-grandfather, JOHN, was the first Presbyterian Minister to preach in Newfane, Mass. Ref: P&BA-Len pg. 661-2.

McEACHRON, SARAH born 5 Feb. 1829, Nova Scotia, moved with parents to Cleveland, Ohio in 1835. She married Lucius Lilley (also see). Ref: P&BA-Len pg. 822.

McFALL, CORNELIUS and wife, CATHERINE (DENISON), of Monroe Co., Mich., had known daughter, MARIA b. 23 Nov. 1841, Monroe Co., Mich. (m. John Dubois, also see). Ref: P&BA-Len pg. 314-5. Note: There was a man by this name in the 1840 census index of Sumpter Twp., Wayne Co., Mich.

McFARLAND, DAVID was a native of Bowdoinham, ME, and his wife, MARTHA (SWEET), was a native of Wales, ME, and they had a known daughter, JENNIE (m. Edwin Eaton, MD, also see, Wales, ME).

Pioneer Families of Southeastern Michigan

McFARLAND, EMELINE Mrs. was the daughter of Ira Holloway (also see).

McFARLAND, MARGARET, age 22, born Penn., was listed in the 1850 census of Tecumseh Twp., Lenawee Co., Mich. in a Rose household.

McFARLAND, T. M. (See James Farrar)

McFARLIN, ANDREW born ca. 1805, was listed in the 1840 census index of Medina Twp., Lenawee Co., Mich.; and in the 1850 census with wife, ELLEN, born ca. 1824, both in Ireland, and MARY A., age 6/12, b. Mich., in their household (next door to MICHAEL, following).

McFARLIN, MICHAEL born ca. 1807, and wife, ALICE, born ca. 1810, both in Ireland, were listed in the 1840 census index of Medina Twp., Lenawee Co., Mich. with LAWRENCE, age 15, b. Ireland; and MARY, age 11; ANNA, age 9; PATRICK, age 7; ANDREW, age 5; MICHAEL, age 3, all b. Mich., and Jane Conroy, age 7, b. Mich., in their household.

McGEE also see MAGEE

McGEE, JOHN W. (See Dr. Lewis H. Bedell)

McGOVERN, ANDREW born ca. 1808, and wife, ANN, born ca. 1815, both in Ireland, were said to have settled in Macon Twp., Lenawee Co., Mich. ca. 1840. They were listed in the 1850 census with MARY, age 15, b. NY (probably she who m. Philip Kehoe, also see); and THOMAS, age 14; BERNARD, age 11; AGNES A., age 9; MARGARET, age 7; CATHARINE, age 5; ELIZABETH, age 2, all b. Mich., in their household.

McCOWEN, ANIS (See James Patterson Sr.)

McGRAW, R. B. (See Charles Raynor)

McILWAIN, SARAH (See Solomon Brown)

McINTOSH, NELLIE (See John B. Clement)

McINTYRE, AGNES (See Joseph Blaine)

McINTYRE, JAMES born ca. 1794, Canada, and wife, MARY, born ca. 1811, NY, were listed in the 1850 census of Adrian Twp., Lenawee Co., Mich. with ALONZO, age 14, b. Canada; and JAMES JR., age 12; PRISCILLA, age 8, both b. Mich., in their household.

McINTYRE, JAMES L. (See Justus Lowe; and note JAMES JR. in household of JAMES, preceding?)

McKAY, SADIE (See Silas Aldrich)

McKEE, ? was the daughter of a couple who had come from Scotland to Montgomery Co., NY in "the early days of its settlement." Her parents and a sister were killed by indians, and she, age 9, was taken prisoner and held by the indians for 9 months. She was rescued and as an adult married Alexander Adair (also see) and they remained in Montgomery Co. She died in middle age. Ref: P&BA-Len pg. 745-6.

McKEY, ANTHONY was listed in the 1840 census index of Blissfield Twp., Lenawee Co., Mich. He was not listed in 1850, but there is a HARRIET S., age 26, born Mass., listed as head of household with WALLACE A., age 19; WALTER S., age 14; EDWARD W., age 3, all b. Mich., and Bishop W. Tucker, age 40, with wife, Elizabeth J., age 22, both b. NY, married within the year, in her household.

McKEY, GEORGE born ca. 1809, and wife, MARY, born ca. 1813, both in Ireland, were listed in the 1850 census of Adrian Twp., Lenawee Co., Mich. with SARAH J., age 9, b. Ohio; and ELIZA, age 6; SAMUEL, age 6, (twins?) both b. Mich., in their household.

McKELVEY, JANE (See Truman Gilbert)

McKENZIE, ARCHIBALD F., born ca. 1820, Scotland, and wife, ELIZA, born ca. 1819, England, were listed in the 1850 census of Adrian Twp., Lenawee Co., Mich. with FANNY L., age 7, b. Canada; ARCHIBALD W., age 6; BARBARY, age 2, both b. NY; and William Simons, age 12, b. Canada, in their household.

McKENZIE, CHARLES M. born ca. 1801, and wife, ANN H., born ca. 1803, both in VT, were listed in the 1840 census index of Woodstock Twp., Lenawee Co., Mich.; and in the 1850 census of Adrian Twp. with CHARLES H., age 24; RICHARD H., age 21; LAURA A., age 19, all b. VT; and JOSEPH C., age 16; SAMUEL C., age 12; FRANCES A., age 8; ELLEN E., age 4, all b. Mich., in their household.

McKENZIE, GEORGE T. born ca. 1810, VT, and wife, ANGELINE, born ca. 1812, NY, were listed in the 1840 census index of Dover Twp., Lenawee Co., Mich.; and in the 1850 census with SAIRY? J., age 14; OSCAR, age 12; EDWIN, age 4; MARY A., age 2, all b. Mich., in their household.

McKENZIE, RICHARD (See John Forbes; Note RICHARD H. in household of CHARLES M., preceding).

McKENZIE, SARAH (See Robert Monier)

McKIBBY, POLLY (See Daniel Westfall)

McKINNEY, CYNTHIA born ca. 1807, Penn., married Amos Franklin (also see) and moved to Seneca Twp., Lenawee Co., Mich. Ref: P&BA-Len pg. 997.

McKINNEY, JOHN born ca. 1821, Ireland, and wife, JANE, born ca. 1831, NY, were listed in the 1850 census of Tecumseh Twp., Lenawee Co., Mich. with no family. ROSA, probably born after 1850, may be a daughter (m. Adelbert Workman Mills, Tecumseh Twp.)

McKINNEY, PATRICK born ca. 1810, and wife, MARY, born ca. 1810, both in Ireland, were listed in the 1850 census of Medina Twp., Lenawee Co., Mich. with JOHN, age 15; THOMAS, age 13; CATHERINE, age 8; JANE, age 4, all b. Mich., in their household.

McKINSTRY, ELIZABETH (See Joseph Slater)

McKNIGHT, ALFRED born in Scotland came to the US and settled in Cleveland, Ohio. His wife, MARY, was born in Ireland. He died a young man, but his wife still resided in Cleveland in 1888. There were 2 sons and 2 daughters, names not stated, except, ALFRED A. b. 14 Apr. 1844, Cleveland (adopted by Tobias Miller, also see). Ref: P&BA-Len pg. 1162-5.

McKNIGHT, ELIZA (See Edward Roberts)

McKNIGHT, JOHN born ca. 1823, and wife, MARY, born ca. 1822, both in Ireland, were listed in the 1850 census of Madison Twp., Lenawee Co., Mich. with THOMAS, age 5, b. Ireland; and JOHN, age 2, b. NY; and MARY, age 1, b. Mich., in their household.

McKNIGHT, R. A. (See John W. Tolford)

McKNIGHT, ROBERT born ca. 1826, and wife, MARY A., born ca. 1823, both in Ireland, were listed in the 1850 census of Madison Twp., Lenawee Co., Mich. with no family.

McKNIGHT, WILLIAM H. (See John Phillips)

McLEOD see McCLEOD

McLOTH see McLOUTH

McLOUTH, ELECTA A. born ca. 1839, Mich., was listed in the 1850 census of Tecumseh Twp., Lenawee Co., Mich. in the household of Atwater & Elisa Ives.

McLOUTH, JOHN from Berkshire Co., Mass. settled in Manchester, Ontario Co., NY in 1795. Ref: Gazeteer of NY State, by French, 1860.

McLOUTH, JOHN born ca. 1813, Wayne Co., NY, moved to Michigan before 1837. His wife, MARY, was born ca. 1814, England, and they were listed in the 1850 census of Rollin Twp., Lenawee Co., Mich. with THOMAS, age 9; JANE E., age 6; OLIVER C. (following), all b. Mich., in their household. They afterwards settled in Somerset Twp., Hillsdale Co., Mich. Note OLIVER C., following.

McLOUTH, LEWIS born ca. 1817, and wife, MARY L., born ca. 1820, both in NY, were listed in the 1840 census index of Fairfield Twp., Lenawee Co., Mich.; and in the 1850 census with MARIA A., age 12, b. NY; and JULIUS, age 10; HENRY E., age 8; ORRIN B., age 6; ALICE A. b. ca. 1849 (m. Charles D. Hall, also see), all b. Mich., in their household. They afterwrds moved to Adrian. Ref: P&BA-Len pg. 243-4.

McLOUTH, NEWTON born ca. 1832, Mich., was listed in the 1850 census of Dover Twp., Lenawee Co., Mich. Note WILLIAM W., following.

McLOUTH, NOWELL born ca. 1841, Mich., was listed in the 1850 census of Adrian Twp., Lenawee Co., Mich. in the Pegg? household.

McLOUTH, OLIVER C. was listed in the 1840 census index of Somerset Twp., Hillsdale Co., Mich. Note JOHN, preceding, who was not listed in the 1840 census index, possibly son?

McLOUTH, OLIVER C., son of JOHN, born 20 Jan. 1847, Rollin Twp., Lenawee Co., Mich., married in Oct. 1872 to MARY C. (BEAL), daughter of William (also see) and settled in Rollin Twp. Children: 1. DEWITT b. 24 Nov. 1875; 2. FLORENCE b. 6 Dec. 1884. Ref: P&BA-Len pg. 1141.

McLOUTH, PETER born ca. 1819, NY, married FIDELIA A. (SHAW), daughter of Brackley, Sr. (also see). They settled in Dover Twp., Lenawee Co., Mich. by 1850. He died there 28 Dec. 1863. Children were born after 1850 census: 1. CHARLES N. (m. Ida Wallace, Chicago, Ill.); 2. EDWARD (m. Abbie Abbott, Dakota). Fidelia married again to William J. Wilber, also see, Dover Twp. Ref: P&BA-Len pg. 875-6. Note WILLIAM W., following.

McLOUTH, WILLIAM W. born ca. 1793, and wife, BETSEY, born ca. 1798, both in Mass., came to Michigan by 1834, and were listed in the 1840 census index of Dover Twp., Lenawee Co.; and in the 1850 census with ALVA, age 25; JANE, age 20; ORVILLE, age 18; CYRUS, age 16, all b. NY; and ANGELINE, age 15 (See Charles M. Tobias); LAURENCE, age 12, both b. Mich., in their household. Also note JOHN; PETER; & NEWTON (preceding).

McMATH, FLEMING, son of Col. SAMUEL (following), born 14 Jan. 1808, Seneca Co., NY, came to Michigan in 1826 with his father. He married 24 Apr. 1829 in Seneca Co., NY to ELIZA (PRUDEN), daughter of Moses (also seel, and they returned to Washtenaw Co., Mich.; and then in 1835 moved to Dover Twp., Lenawee Co. Eliza died there 3 Dec. 1887, age 78. Children: 1. FRANCIS b. ca. 1830 (m. Mary E. Waite); 2. ROXANNA b. 13 June 1831, Ypsilanti, Mich. (m. James H. Shepherd, also see); 3. (MARY) ELIZABETH b. ca. 1833 (m. S. D. Vaughn; she d. 26 Jan. 1857, Dover Twp.); 4. ELIZA b. ca. 1835 (m. Charles I. Shaw); 5. LAURA A. b. ca. 1838 (m. S. D. Vaughn, as 2nd wife); 6. FLEMING b. ca. 1846 (m. Julia Deming); 7. ESTHER (m. Charles W. Gilbert, see Warren Gilbert). Ref: P&BA-Len pg. 409-10.

McMATH, SAMUEL Col. was a native of Penn., and married there to MARY (JACKSON). He served in the War of 1812 where he obtained his rank. They moved to Seneca Co., NY. In 1826, he came ahead to Washtenaw Co., Mich., and he died there in 1827. His wife, MARY, and family afterwards came to Washtenaw Co. There were 7 children, but only FLEMING (preceding) was mentioned. Ref: P&BA-Len pg. 409-10. Note: In the 1840 census index of Washtenaw Co., Mich., there was an A. listed in Ypsilanti Twp.; and J. B. & SAMUEL in Superior Twp. probably additional sons of SAMUEL.

McMILLAN, ALEXANDER born ca. 1817, and wife, ELIZABETH, born ca. 1823, both in NY, were listed in the 1850 census of Blissfield Twp., Lenawee Co., Mich. with no family.

McMILLAN, JAMES, probably son of JOHN (following), born ca. 1817, and wife, JANET, born ca. 1820, both in NY, were listed in the 1850 census of Blissfield Twp., Lenawee Co., Mich. with WILLIAM, age 3, b. Mich., in their household (next door to JOHN, following).

McMILLAN, JOHN born ca. 1785, NJ, and wife, JANE, born ca. 1790, NY, were listed in the 1840 census index of Blissfield Twp., Lenawee Co., Mich.; and in the 1850 census with WILLIAM, age 27; GEORGE, age 22; PETER, age 19; HARRIET, age 16, all b. NY, in the household and JAMES (preceding) listed next door.

McMILLAN, SUSIE (See James H. Shepherd)

McMURTY, MARGARET (See Henry Beers)

McNAIR, STEWART S. born ca. 1813, Ohio, was listed in the 1850 census of Blissfield Twp., Lenawee Co., Mich. Note WILLIAM P., following.

McNAIR, WILBUR (See Levi L. Stockwell)

McNAIR, WILLIAM born ca. 1800, Penn., and wife, ELIZABETH, born ca. 1809, NY, were listed in the 1840 census index of Raisin Twp., Lenawee Co., Mich.; and in the 1850 census with ELIZA, age 16; JAMES, age 14;

Pioneer Families of Southeastern Michigan

DAVID, age 10; SARAH, age 8; AGNES, age 6, all b. Mich., in their household.

McNAIR, WILLIAM P. born ca. 1793, Penn., and wife, REBECCA, born ca. 1797, VT, were listed in the 1840 census index of Madison Twp., Lenawee Co., Mich.; and in the 1850 census with EATON, age 27; HENRY, age 25; JAMES, age 21, b. NY; and JOHN, age 14, b. Ohio; and FRANCES, age 10, b. Mich., in their household. WILLIAM M., age 18, b. NY, in another household probably relates to this family.

McNAUGHTON, CHRISTIE (See Duncan Sinclair)

McNEIL, RACHEL (See Conrad Dewey)

McNELLY, CATHERINE (See James Hood)

McOMBER also see MACOMBER; McCAMBER; McCUMBER

McOMBER, MARIA born ca. 1823, NY, married in June 1846, possibly in Ontario Co., NY to Erasmus Darwin Allen and moved to Medina Twp., Lenawee Co., Mich. In the 1850 census of Medina Twp., SARAH, age 14, b. NY, was listed in the household of Erasmus and Maria. Ref: P&BA-Len pg. 1064-6.

McPHERSON, JAMES B. Gen. (See John Russell)

McQUARIE, NEAL (See Ephraim Hall)

McQUEEN, JAMES Col. of Ontario, Canada was father of SUSAN who married Dr. John F. Jenkins (also see).

McROBERT, DANIEL, son of WILLIAM (following), born 27 Oct. 1798, Springfield, VT, moved with his parents to Champlain, Clinton Co., NY about 1801. He married 21 Jan. 1821 to BATHSHEBA (LUTHER), daughter of William (also see). About 1833, they removed to Rome Twp., Lenawee Co., Mich. He serves as a Capt. in the Militia during the Toledo War. He died 1 Dec. 1877. There were 4 children, and those known from the 1850 census of Rome Twp. 1. LYCURGUS b. ca. 1825, NY; 2. MARY J. b. ca. 1833, NY; and youngest child, 3. LUTHER (following). Ref: P&BA-Len pg. 884-5.

McROBERT, LUTHER, son of DANIEL (preceding), born 31 Dec. 1836, Rome Twp., Lenawee Co., Mich., married there on 19 Feb. 1860 to MARTHA (PARKER), daughter of William K. (also see), and settled in Rome Twp. Children: 1. MARY JANE b. 4 Dec. 1863 (m. Willis Granger); 2. GEORGE P. b. 27 Feb. 1872. Ref: P&BA-Len pg. 884-5.

McROBERT, WILLIAM came from Scotland, and settled at an early date in Rutland Co., VT. He removed about 1801 to Clinton Co., NY. He died at age 80, and his wife (name not stated), who was born in Conn., had preceded him. Known son, DANIEL (preceding). Ref: P&BA-Len pg. 884-5.

MEACH also see MEECH

MEACH, AARON was listed in the 1840 census index of Medina Twp., Lenawee Co., Mich.

MEACH, LORENZO D. born ca. 1824, and wife, CLARA, born ca. 1824, both in NY, were listed in the 1850 census of Madison Twp., Lenawee Co., Mich. with CYNTHIA J., age 3, b. Mich. in their household.

MEACH, PETER born ca. 1796, Mass., and wife, CATHARINE, born ca. 1800, NY, were listed in the 1840 census index of Madison Twp., Lenawee Co., Mich.; and in the 1850 census of Rollin Twp. with JOHN W., age 25; LYDIA, age 15, both b. NY; and MINERVA, age 10; ANGELINE, age 6, both b. Mich., in their household.

MEACHAM, FLORA (See Joseph Sparling)

MEACHAM, SILAS born ca. 1812, and wife, SALLY, born ca. 1818, both in NY, were listed in the 1850 census of Medina Twp., Lenawee Co., Mich. with LAURA, age 9, b. NY, in their household.

MEAD, ALEXANDER D. born ca. 1818, and wife, LUCY, born ca. 1828, both in NY, were listed in the 1850 census of Tecumseh Twp., Lenawee Co., Mich. with LUCY, age 1, b. Mich., in their household.

MEAD, DARIUS born ca. 1797, and wife, MINERVA B., born ca. 1801, both in Mass., were listed in the 1840 census index of Blissfield Twp., Lenawee Co., Mich.; and in the 1850 census were listed in the household of known daughter, MINERVA b. ca. 1824, Mass. (m. Joel Carpenter, also see, in 1844). Ref: P&BA-Len pg. 1202-3. DANIEL S., born 1833, Mass., may relate to this family, and in the 1850 census of Blissfield Twp. was in household of Marvin S. Stone and wife, Helen M. (b. 1829, Mass., possibly another daughter of Darius?)

MEAD, JEMIMA (See Horace Read)

MEAD, JOHN born ca. 1792, and wife, ANNA (TENBROOK), born ca. 1796, both in NY, lived in Tioga Co., NY, and moved to Fairfield Twp., Lenawee Co., Mich. in 1836. Children (#4-7 were in the household in 1850 census, all b. NY): 1. ELIZABETH; 2. ALLIE; 3. PETER (note following); 4. EZRA b. ca. 1826; 5. JOHN T. (following); 6. GARRET b. ca. 1830; 7. LEWIS b. ca. 1834 (probably LEWIS P. who m. Mary A. Hagaman, dau. of Ira J., and later went to Jasper, Iowa, as family was a neighbor in 1850 census). Ref: P&BA-Len pg. 1140-1.

MEAD, JOHN T., son of JOHN (preceding), born 22 Oct. 1827, Tioga Co., NY, and moved to Fairfield Twp., Lenawee Co., Mich. with parents. He married on 22 Apr. 1852 to ELIZABETH H. (BENNETT), daughter of Davis D. (also see). They lived in Ohio till 1861, they moved back to Fairfield Twp. Children: 1. FRANCIS E. (d. age 2); 2. CARRIE E. (m. Francis "Frank" Quick, son of Cornelius, also see); 3. CHARLES S. (m. Belle Holden, moved to Kansas). Ref: P&BA-Len pg. 1140-1.

MEAD, LEROY, son of SQUIRE & NANCY, born 4 Jan. 1831, North Salem, Westchester Co., NY, came to Michigan and served from Michigan in the Civil War. He married 19 Feb. 1867 in Macon Twp., Lenawee Co., Mich. to JOSEPHINE (CLARKSON), daughter of Daniel (also see). Children: 1. NETTIE L. (d. age 14); 2. MARY E.; 3. BLANCHE; 4. CAMILLA D. Ref: P&BA-Len pg. 469-70.

MEAD, PETER (note JOHN, preceding) born ca. 1823, and wife, ANGELINE, born ca. 1827, both in NY, were listed in the 1850 census of Seneca Twp., Lenawee Co., Mich. with HARRIET, age 2, b. Mich., in their household.

MEAD, SEYMOUR[7], son of STEPHEN[6] (following), born 11 Nov. 1789, Lanesboro, Mass., married there to LUCY (MASON), daughter of Reuben (also see). They remained in Lanesboro until 1847, then moved to Willoughby, Ohio; and in 1851 to Blissfield Twp.,

Lenawee Co., Mich. He died there 16 Mar. 1869, and she died 1 May 1875. Children: 1. D. R. (d. Blissfield Twp.); 2. MARY (m. D. S. Harrington, Bangor, Mich.); 3. STEPHEN M. (following); 4. S. LAFAYETTE (lived Dedham & Nanctucket, Mass. till 1865, then moved to Blissfield Twp. where he d. 24 Aug. 1869); 5. GEORGE A. b. 16 Oct. 1826, Lanesboro, Mass (moved with sister to Willoughby, Ohio in 1840; and to Blissfield Twp., Lenawee Co. in 1851 where he d. 6 Dec. 1875). Ref: P&BA-Len pg. 941-2.

MEAD, STEPHEN^5, son of CALEB^4 (See WILLIAM^1, following), born 2 Mar. 1741, married ELIZABETH (HOLLEY), and resided in the area "known as Horseneck," which lies on the line between Conn. and NY (probably Westchester Co.). About 1766, they moved to Lanesboro, Mass. Known son, STEPHEN^6 (following). Ref: P&BA-Len pg. 941-2.

MEAD, STEPHEN^6, son of STEPHEN^5 (preceding), born ca. 1766, Horseneck, NY, moved with his parents to Lanesboro, Mass. He married there (wife's name not stated), and remained there and died in 1863, age 97. Known son, SEYMOUR^7 (preceding). Ref: P&BA-Len pg. 941-2.

MEAD, STEPHEN M.^{8}, son of SEYMOUR^7 (preceding), born 18 Sept. 1822, Lanesboro, Mass., married there on 5 Oct. 1842 to HARRIET (GARLICK), daughter of Eli (also see). They lived in Pittsfield, Mass. where she died 20 Sept. 1846 leaving son, 1. DWIGHT S. (lived Blissfield Twp., Lenawee Co.). Stephen M. married again on 30 May 1848 in Lanesboro to MINERVA S. (HUMPHREY), daughter of Reuben (also see). Child: 2. CARRIE S. b. 21 Mar. 1849 (d. 16 Dec. 1877, Cleveland, Ohio; buried in Blissfield Twp., Lenawee Co., Mich.). Ref: P&BA-Len pg. 941-2.

MEAD, WALTER born ca. 1826, NY, was listed in the 1850 census index of Madison Twp., Lenawee Co., Mich.

MEAD, WILLIAM^1 born 1641, Stamford, Conn., and wife (name not mentioned) were parents of 8 sons and 1 daughter, and only mentioned was son, EBENEZER^2 born 1663 who married SARAH (KNAPP). Their son, EBENEZER^3, born 25 Oct. 1692, married HANNAH (BROWN); and their son, CALEB^4, married HANNAH (BUNNELL). They had known son, STEPHEN^5 (preceding). Ref: P&BA-Len pg. 941-2.

MEECH also see MEACH

MEECH, JOHN and wife, SALLY (BOARDMAN), were natives of Conn. who settled in Cayuga Co., NY. Known daughter, POLLY, married there to Constant Rowley (also see).

MEECH, EUNICE born ca. 1795, Conn., married Squire Sayres (also see). Note JOHN, preceding, as Sayres were also in Cayuga Co., NY for a time.

MEEKER, ELIZABETH (See Ananias Valentine)

MELLEN, DANIEL born England, came to New Hampshire, and had a known daughter, SENA (m. Daniel Farrar). Ref: P&BA-Len pg. 259-60.

MENNEL, BARBARA (See Henry Schwartz)

MERCHANT, CHARLES G. born ca. 1817, NY, and wife, MELISSA, born ca. 1819, VT, were listed in the 1840 census index of Adrian Twp., Lenawee Co., Mich.; and in the 1850 census of Hudson Twp. with HELEN, age 11; MARIA, age 9; WALLACE, age 8; NATHALIA, age 7; PHEBE, age 6; ANN, age 5; WELCOME, age 3; LUCY, age 1, all b. Mich., in their household.

MERCHANT, CHARLES M. was listed in the 1840 census index of Adrian Twp., Lenawee Co., Mich. He was not listed in 1850 census of Adrian Twp., however, there were the following listed in 2 other households: MARCUS, age 26. b. NY; ANN, age 25, b. NY, possibly related.

MERCHANT, CHARLOTTE born 12 Oct. 1801, New Hampshire (See John Maynard).

MERCHANT, MARIA of Broome Co., NY (See Benjamin Bird & William Moore).

MERING, LEVI (See Isaac C. Gunn)

MERRICK also see MIRRICK

MERRICK, GEORGE W., probably son of RUFUS, born ca 1824, NY, and probably wife, LOVISA, age 19, b. NY, were listed in the 1850 census of Adrian Twp., Lenawee Co., Mich., next door to Rufus, with no family.

MERRICK, GEORGE W., probably son of JOSEPH (following), born ca. 1808, Mass., married LUCINDA (GRAVES), daughter of Stephen Wells (also see); and they were listed in the 1840 census index of Adrian Twp., Lenawee Co., Mich. adjacent to RUFUS & JOSEPH, following. In the 1850 census of Madison Twp. Lucinda was listed as NANCY L., age 37, b. Conn.; and in the household were LANDIALA? Lucinda? (female), age 13; HARLAN?, age 11; BENSON, age 8, all b. Mich.; and Ann Halsted, age 21, b. NY.

MERRICK, JOSEPH born ca. 1773, Mass., and wife, SARAH, born ca. 1781, NH, were listed in the 1840 census index of Adrian Twp., Lenawee Co., Mich.; and in the 1850 census with (daughter?) Judith Hutchins, age 30, b. NY and children Mary Hutchins, age 6; Amelia Hutchins, age 4; Ellen Hutchins, age 1, all b. Mich., in their household. Probably sons, GEORGE W. (preceding); & JOSEPH Jr. (following). Also note RUFUS, who was listed adjacent in the 1840 census index.

MERRICK, JOSEPH, Jr., probably son of JOSEPH (preceding), born ca. 1805, Mass., and wife, ELIZABETH, born ca. 1817, NY, were listed in the 1850 census of Madison Twp., Lenawee Co., Mich. with MARY, age 9; CYNTHIA, age 8; HERBERT J., age 4; FREMONT, age 2; ELIZABETH, age 1, all b. Mich., in their household.

MERRICK, RUFUS born ca. 1800, VT, was listed in the 1840 census index of Adrian Twp., Lenawee Co., Mich. adjacent to JOSEPH & GEORGE W., preceding. In the 1850 census of Adrian Twp., he listed wife, ARTIMISIA, age 40, b. Conn.; and they listed RUFUS P., age 7; SARAH E., age 5, both b. Mich., in their household. Probably a son, GEORGE W. (preceding), was listed next door, though Artemisia seems too young to be his mother?

MERRILL, NAOMI (See W. H. Worden)

MERSEREAU, CORNELIUS, son of DANIEL (following), born ca. 1803, probably in Tioga Co., NY, moved to Lucas Co., Ohio where he married SARAH (PHILLIPS). They returned to Owego, Tioga Co., NY. In 1847, they

Pioneer Families of Southeastern Michigan

returned to Sylvania, Ohio, and she died there; and in 1888, he was living in Lucas Co., Ohio with a son (name not stated). Known daughter, CELESTIA b. 10 Mar. 1843, Owego, NY (m. John H. Van Pelt, also see). Ref: P&BA-Len pg. 281-3.

MERSEREAU, DANIEL was born in Penn., but resided in Tioga Co., NY by the 1800 census. His wife's name was not stated. They died in NY. Known son, CORNELIUS (preceding). Ref: P&BA-Len pg. 281-3. Note: They may relate to CORNELIUS who was listed in the 1800 census index of Richmond Co., NY.

METCALF, JOHN of Middleham, Yorkshire, England, was a direct descendant of the old family of Metcalfe Towers, Wensleydale, England. John and wife, name not stated, remained in England. They had a known daughter, MARY, b. 14 Sept. 1793, Middleham (m. John Robinson, also see). Ref: P&BA-Len pg. 1198-1200.

METCALF, JOSIAH, son of WILLIAM (following), born 7 Feb. 1837, Ashland Co., Ohio, moved to Seneca Twp., Lenawee Co., Mich. with his parents. He married on 29 Mar. 1859, Osseo, Hillsdale Co., Mich. to MARY H. (SEELEY), daughter of James (also see), and settled in Seneca Twp. Children: 1. LOZELLA C.; 2. ROSA (m. Walter Plummer; Chesterfield, O.); 3. LILLY; 4. OTHA; 5. STELLA; 6. OLE. Ref: P&BA-Len pg. 1097.

METCALF, VACHEL (note WILLIAM, following) born ca. 1824, Ohio, and wife, MARY, born ca. 1827, Penn., were listed in the 1850 census of Seneca Twp., Lenawee Co., Mich. with SARAH E., age 1, b. Ohio, in their household.

METCALF, WILLIAM born Washington Co., Penn., married there to MARY (NEWELL) of Ashland Co., Ohio; and the settled in Ashland Co. They remained there until 1852, then moved to Seneca Twp., Lenawee Co., Mich. He died in 1869. There were 5 sons and 2 daughters, and only one named was JOSIAH (preceding). Ref: P&BA-Len pg. 1097. Also see VACHEL, preceding.

METTLER, DANIEL of Penn. was the father of MARGARET who married George L. Shurts (also see). Ref: P&BA-Len pg. 1068-9.

MEYER, MARGARET (See Godfrey Matthes)
MEYER, NELLIE (See Welcome V. Fisk)

MICHAEL, JOSEPH (See Andrew Nufer)

MICKLEY, CHARLES E., son of DANIEL (following), born 26 Aug. 1818, Northumberland Co., Penn., moved with his mother & brother to Buffalo, and then in 1833 to Fairfield Twp., Lenawee Co., Mich. He married on 12 Feb. 1837 to ADELINE J. (HAYWARD), probably daughter of Theodore (also see), and settled in Fairfield Twp. Children: 1. ELIZA M. b. 1 July 1838 (m. L. P. Russell); 2. MARY J. b. 10 Dec. 1842 (lived Adrian). Ref: P&BA-Len pg. 1122-3.

MICKLEY, DANIEL born Penn. of German descent, married in 1799 in Northumberland Co. to TAMAR ELIZABETH (EVANS) born 5 Dec. 1779, Philadelphia, of Welch ancestry and Quaker faith. He died in Northumberland Co. There were 7 children, names not stated, except DANIEL (following); & CHARLES E. (preceding). Tamar moved with her sons to Buffalo, and later to Fairfield Twp., Lenawee Co., Mich. where she died 23 May 1865 in the home of Charles. Ref: P&BA-Len pg. 1122-3.

MICKLEY, DANIEL, son of DANIEL (preceding), born ca. 1810, Penn., and wife, SYBIL, born ca. 1815, VT, were listed in the 1840 census index (spelled "Meekley") of Fairfield Twp., Lenawee Co., Mich.; and in the 1850 census of Madison Twp. with GEORGE, age 16; HENRY, age 11; SAMUEL, age 9; SYBIL, age 7; ESTHER, age 5, all b. Mich., in their household.

MIKESELL, J. N. (See Philip Wareham[3])

MILES, CASSIUS (See Philip W. Aldrich)
MILES, FRANKLIN H. born ca. 1817, and wife, RUBA, born ca. 1823, both in NY, were listed in the 1850 census of Madison Twp., Lenawee Co., Mich. with SARAH, age 6, b. NY, in their household.

MILES, GEORGE was in Jackson Co., Mich. in 1838.

MILES, IRA L., son of NAHUM (following) born VT, settled before 1836 in Adrian Twp., Lenawee Co., Mich., but by 1840 lived in Rives Twp., Jackson Co., Mich. His wife, name not stated, was born in Germany. He died at age 68 in Jackson Co. Known daughter, EMILY M. b. 27 May 1836, Adrian Twp. (m. Benjamin P. Emery, also see, as his second wife). Ref: P&BA-Len pg. 411-2.

MILES, IVES H. born ca. 1803, and wife, SARAH, born ca. 1808, both in NY, were listed in the 1840 census index of Tecumseh Twp., Lenawee Co., Mich., and in the 1850 census with MARY, age 8, b. NY?; CHARLES, age 3; SAMINDA?/LAMINDA?, age 10/12, both b. Mich.; and LAMINDA?, age 40, b. NY, in their household.

MILES, JEROME born ca. 1827, NY, was listed in the 1850 census of Seneca Twp., Lenawee Co., Mich. in a Neff household, 2 doors from WILLIAM J. (following).

MILES, NAHUM was a "pioneer to Jackson Co., Mich." where he died at age 68. He was listed in Rives Twp., in the 1840 census index. Known son, IRA L. (preceding). Ref: P&BA-Len pg. 411-2. MILES, WILLIAM (note NAHUM, preceding) born in VT was listed in the 1840 census index of Dover Twp., Lenawee Co., Mich. where he died at age 45. In the 1850 census of Dover Twp., HATTIE, age 44, b. NY, was listed head of household with BELINDA, age 17, b. Penn.; CATHARINE b. 12 Sept. 1834, Mich. (m. Benjamin P. Emery, also see); STEPHEN, age 13; JOHN, age 11, both b. Mich., in her household. ALVIRA, age 19, b. Penn., listed in another household in the 1850 census of Dover Twp. probably relates to this family. Ref: P&BA-Len pg. 411-2.

MILES, WILLIAM J. born ca. 1812, NY, may be he listed in the 1840 census index of Palmyra Twp., Lenawee Co., Mich. He is listed in the 1850 census of Seneca Twp., Lenawee Co., Mich. with wife, LUCY J., age 24, born Ohio, and LEWIS, age 7, b. Mich., in his household.

MILLER, ABRAM of Orleans Co., NY married LORETTA (WOOD), daughter of ?, and sister of Wilson (also see). Ref: P&BA-Len pg. 719-20.

MILLER, ALBERT married in 1859 to ALVINA (SWICK), daughter of John E. (also see). Albert was killed in a boiler explosion in Saline, Washtenaw Co., Mich. in 1871. Children: 1. CASSIUS M. C.; 2. EMMA A.; 3. CHARLES S. Alvina married again to Daniel Wiggins (also see). Ref: P&BA-Len pg. 963-4.

MILLER, ALBERT N., age 21, born NY, was listed in the 1850 census of Madison Twp., Lenawee Co., Mich.

MILLER, ALFRED A., adopted son of TOBIAS (following), born 14 Apr. 1844, Cleveland, Ohio, was the son of Alfred McKnight. He enlisted in Co. H., 15th Mich. Inf. during the Civil War. He married on 2 Apr. 1873 to HARRIET E. (FITCH), daughter of James (also see), and settled in Blissfield Twp., Lenawee Co., Mich. Children: 1. ALFRED D.; 2. GRACE E.; 3. CLIFFORD J.; 4. GALEN M.; Daughter (d. 5 Oct. 1883). Ref: P&BA-Len pg. 1162-5 with portrait.

MILLER, AMOS and wife, CATHARINE (BARTLETT), moved from Moravia, Cayuga Co., NY to Bridgewater, Washtenaw Co., Mich. in 1837 and were listed there in the 1840 census index. Known son, Capt. CHARLES R. (following). Ref: P&BA-Len pg. 1003-4.

MILLER, ANDREW born ca. 1816, and wife, CATHERINE, born ca. 1819, both in Germany, were listed in the 1850 census of Madison Twp., Lenawee Co., Mich. with CHRISTINA, age 12?; JACOB, age 10; ANDREW, age 8, all b. Germany; CATHERINE, age 5, b. Penn.; and LEWIS, age 1, b. Mich., in their household.

MILLER, ANNA (See William H. Schooley)

MILLER, AUGUSTA, age 26, born NY, was listed in the 1850 census of Tecumseh Twp., Lenawee Co., Mich.

MILLER, BARBARY (See George Garling)

MILLER, BENSON was listed in the 1840 census index of Macon Twp., Lenawee Co., Mich. adjacent to DAVID O., following.

MILLER, BERNHARDT came from near Westphalia, Germany to near Rochester, NY in 1849. His wife had died in Germany in 1845. Daughter, CATHERINE, b. 3 May 1831, Westphalia (came to US with father; m. John P. Schwab, also see). Ref: P&BA-Len pg. 545-6.

MILLER, CATHARINE (See George Vandyne)

MILLER, CATHERINE (See Harvey I. Baldwin)

MILLER, CHARLES born ca. 1810, and wife, MARIA, born ca. 1816, both in NY, were listed in the 1840 census index of Blissfield Twp., Lenawee Co., Mich.; and in the 1850 census with MARTHA, age 8; ADELIA, age 7; MARY A., age 4, all b. Mich., in their household.

MILLER, CHARLES J., son of JOHN (b. Baden, Germany), born 18 June 1844, Baden, Germany, came to Erie Co., Ohio with his parents. He served in Co. D, 16th Ohio Cav. during the Civil War. After the war, he moved to Blissfield Twp., Lenawee Co., Mich. He married on 29 Aug. 1867 to ELIZABETH (LINCOLN), daughter of Edward (also see). Children: 1. NETTIE; 2. WALTER. Ref: P&BA-Len pg. 716-7.

MILLER, CHARLES R. Capt., son of AMOS (preceding), born 7 June 1834, Moravia, Cayuga Co., NY, came to Michigan with his parents, obtained a Law Degree and went first to St. Joseph, Missouri. He returned to Michigan by 1862 and enlisted in the 18th Mich. Inf. where he became a Captain. He married in Ann Arbor, Mich. to MARY L. (BECKER) born ca. 1838, NY, and they settled in Adrian, Lenawee Co., Mich. Children: 1. MARY A.; 2. JESSIE (female). Ref: P&BA-Len pg. 1003-4.

MILLER, CHARLES S. born ca. 1816, and wife, ELEANOR, born ca. 1816, both in NY, were listed in the 1840 census index of Fairfield Twp., Lenawee Co., Mich.; and in the 1850 census with MARY, age 8; ELMINA, age 7; DARIUS, age 1/12, all b. Mich., in their household.

MILLER, CHARLES W., son of VAN R. (following), born 4 June 1845, Raisin Twp., Lenawee Co., Mich., married EDNA M. (INGERSOLL), daughter of Jonathan E. (also see). Children: 1. ALBERT E. b. 5 Oct. 1871; 2. ELMER G. b. 9 Mar. 1873; 3. ERNEST L. b. 17 June 1880; 4. Daughter b. 4 Mar. 1888, name not stated. Ref: P&BA-Len pg. 655-6.

MILLER, DANIEL was listed in the 1840 census index of Clinton Twp., Lenawee Co., Mich.

MILLER, DAVID O. born ca. 1779, and wife, SUSANNAH, born ca. 1768, both in Conn., were listed in the 1840 census index of Macon Twp., Lenawee Co., Mich.; and in the 1850 census were next door to ISAIAH (following).

MILLER, DeLASKIE Dr. was a resident of Lapeer, Mich. in 1843, and had a practice with Dr. Nathaniel Buel Eldredge (also see).

MILLER, ELEANOR married Flower Osterhout (also see), probably in Seneca Co., NY, and came to Macon Twp. where he died in 1844, and she died a young woman, leaving a daughter, Sarah A. Osterhout, who was raised by Eleanor's mother. In the 1850 census of Macon Twp., Sarah Osterhout, age 13, was listed in the household of JEHIEL (following), though he and his wife are too young to be her grandparents.

MILLER, ELISHA R. born ca. 1819, and wife, CHARITY, born ca. 1829, both in NY, were listed in the 1850 census of Franklin Twp., Lenawee Co., Mich. with SARA?, age 9/12, b. Mich., in their household.

MILLER, ELIZABETH (See John P. Tunison; & see Andrew Poucher).

MILLER, EMILY (See Harvey I. Baldwin)

MILLER, FREDERICK (Note both GEORGE; & JOHN G., following)

MILLER, GEORGE and wife, DOROTHEA (ENGLEHART), were natives of Bavaria, and sailed to Quebec, Canada in 1847; and then to Trumbull Co., Ohio. They later came to Macon Twp., Lenawee Co., Mich. where he died at age 84, and she died at age 80. Son, JOHN G. (following); and there were 5 daughters, but only 4 mentioned: Mrs. David Eastlick; Mrs. John Bachman; Mrs. John Hahn; Mrs. FRED MILLER. Ref: P&BA-Len pg. 939-40.

MILLER, GEORGE, age 10, born Mich., was listed in the 1850 census of Dover Twp., Lenawee Co., Mich. in the Albert Wilcox household.

MILLER, GEORGE H. (See Charles G. Stowers)

MILLER, GEORGE H. born ca. 1816, NY, and wife MARY ANN, born ca. 1815, Mass., were listed in the 1850 census of Cambridge Twp., Lenawee Co., Mich with BENJAMIN, age 9; GERTRUDE, age 3; ELLWIN, age 1, all b. Mich., in their household.

MILLER, GEORGE R. born ca. 1814, and wife, AMELIA, born ca. 1828, both in NY, were listed in the 1850 census of Dover Twp., Lenawee Co., Mich., adjacent to ORRIN, following.

MILLER, GEORGE W. born ca. 1823, and wife, MARY A., born ca. 1824, both in NY, were listed in the 1850 census of Ridgeway Twp., Lenawee Co., Mich. with ANNA, age 4; LUCY J., age 2; MORGAN, age 6/12, all b. Mich. in their household.

MILLER, HATTIE (See Solomon M. Newton)

MILLER, HENRY S. of Seneca Co., NY (See Aaron Phillips).

Pioneer Families of Southeastern Michigan

MILLER, ISAAC born ca. 1768, and wife, ANNA, born ca. 1776, both in NY, were listed in the 1840 census index of Macon Twp., Lenawee Co., Mich.; and in the 1850 census were listed in the household of son, JAMES M. (following).

MILLER, ISAAC born ca. 1798, and wife, MARY, born ca. 1801, VT, were listed in the 1840 census index of Cambridge Twp., Lenawee Co., Mich.; and in the 1850 census with Henry Wilcox, age 35, b. NY, in their household.

MILLER, ISAAC D., probably son of DAVID O. (preceding), born ca. 1801, NY, and wife, REBECCA, born ca. 1801, NJ, were listed in the 1840 census index of Macon Twp., Lenawee Co., Mich.; and in the 1850 census with GILBERT R., age 21; MONMOUTH, age 18; WARREN, age 17, all b. NY; and CAROLINE, age 13; JAMES, age 9, both b. Mich., in their household, next door to DAVID O.

MILLER, ISAIAH and wife, name not stated (note NANCY, following), were of German descent and "natives of Pennsyvania" who had moved to Lodi, Seneca Co., NY. They moved to Macon Twp., Lenawee Co., Mich. in 1833, where he died. They had known daughter, CERENA (m. Simeon Davidson, also see, in 1829, Seneca Co., NY). Also note MINOR & JEHIEL, as these given names appear in the family of Cerena).

MILLER, ISAIAH C., son of JONAH (following), born 24 July 1810, Hartford, Conn., moved with his parents to Wayne Co., NY. In May of 1833, he removed to Rollin Twp., Lenawee Co., Mich. He married on 13 Sept. 1833, Rollin Twp., to DEBORAH F. (PRATT), daughter of Joseph (also see). They were listed in the 1840 census index as "Asah C." There were 7 children (known 6 listed in the 1850 census of Rollin Twp.): 1. ADELIA S. b. ca. 1837 (m. E. H. Cogswell, Hudson Twp.); 2. WILLIAM H. b. ca. 1839; 3. MARY J. b. ca. 1842 (m. Henry Adams); 4. RACHEL B. CA. 1843 (m. Thomas Scott); 5. ABIGAIL A. b. ca. 1845; 6. LYDIA b. ca. 1849 (m. Van Doren). Ref: P&BA-Len pg. 722-3.

MILLER, JAMES was listed in the 1840 census index of Adrian Twp., Lenawee Co., Mich.; and another was listed in the 1840 census index of Franklin Twp., Lenawee Co.

MILLER, JAMES M., son of ISAAC (of Macon Twp., preceding), born ca. 1820, NY, married MARY A. (CADMUS), daughter of Abraham (also see). In the 1850 census of Macon Twp., Lenawee Co., Mich. they listed ELLERT? (male), age 12; ELIZABETH, age 2, both b. Mich., and father, ISAAC, & mother, ANNA, preceding, in their household. Mary A. died in Clinton Co., Mich. in 1886.

MILLER, J. R. (See George W. Clark)

MILLER, JEHIEL (possibly son of OLIVER, following) born ca. 1810, and wife, CATHARINE, born ca. 1810, both in NY, were listed in the 1840 census index of Macon Twp., Lenawee Co., Mich.; and in the 1850 census with EDWARD, age 8; A--(female), age 5; WINFIELD, age 2, all b. Mich. Also in the household were LOUIS (See LEWIS, following), age 42, & TUNIS, age 11, b. Mich.; and Sarah Osterhout, age 13 (See ELEANOR, preceding). JOHN A.; and OLIVER, were listed next door.

MILLER, JEPTHA born ca. 1802, NJ, and wife, ELISA, born ca. 1807, Penn., were listed in the 1850 census of Tecumseh Twp., Lenawee Co., Mich. with FRANCES, age 2 b. Mich., in their household.

MILLER, JOHN born 1783, Londonderry, NH, was a descendant of a North Ireland family who settled ca. 1714 in Londonderry. John served in the War of 1812. He married in 1818 to MATILDA (HILLIARD), daughter of Miner Hilliard (also see). After the war, they moved to Plattsburg, Clinton Co., NY, and also lived near Albany, NY. They moved by 1850 to Raisin Twp., Lenawee Co., Mich. He died 7 Apr. 1857, age 75, and she died 24 Aug. 1878. Known son, VAN R. (following); and in the 1850 census in their household were CHARLES C., age 14; EMILY E., age 12, both b. NY. Ref: P&BA-Len pg. 655-6.

MILLER, JOHN born ca. 1810, NY, and wife, ESTHER, born ca. 1815, Mass., were listed in the 1850 census of Medina Twp., Lenawee Co., Mich. with no family. May be he listed in the 1840 census index of Adrian Twp.

MILLER, JOHN born ca. 1808, and wife, NANCY, born ca. 1808, both in NY, were listed in the 1840 census index of Tecumseh Twp., Lenawee Co., Mich.; and in the 1850 census with JULIA, age 17; LAFAYETTE, age 13; EMMA, age 10; FRANK, age 6; JOHN, age 4, all b. Mich., in their household.

MILLER, JOHN born Baden, Germany, married there to MAGDALENA (KRERGER); and in 1847 they immigrated to Margaretta Twp., Erie Co., Ohio. He died there in 1852. She was still living in 1888 in Blissfield Twp., Lenawee Co. Mich. with son, Charles. Children: 1. NICHOLAS; 2. CHRISTOPHER (Blissfield Twp.); 3. MAGDELENA (m. William Langewell, Blissfield Twp.); 4. CHARLES J. (preceding). Ref: P&BA-Len pg. 716-7.

MILLER, JOHN married BARBARA (TAGSOLD), daughter of John (also see). He died by 1871. Known son, WILLIAM. Barbara married again on 10 Sept. 1871, Riga Twp., Lenawee Co., Mich. to August Glaser (also see). Ref: P&BA-Len pg. 959-60.

MILLER, JOHN A. born 7 Mar. 1784, NY, married on 20 Feb. 1816 to ELEANOR (SUTPHEN/SUTFIN), born 3 July 1786, Seneca Co., NY. She died 18 June 1839. Known daughter, ELEANOR ANN b. 28 Dec. 1828, Lodi, Seneca Co., NY (m. James K. Wheeler, also see). John A. married again to MARIA (BREESE), and settled in Macon Twp., Lenawee Co., Mich. It appears to be they listed in the 1850 census of Macon Twp., he age 66, and HELEN M., age 46; and "ELLEN A." (ELEANOR), age 22, all b. NY. He died 5 Nov. 1852. Ref: P&BA-Len pg. 848-9. Note: In the 1850 census, OLIVER (following); and JEHIEL (preceding) are listed next door.

MILLER, JOHN G., son of GEORGE (preceding), born 29 Nov. 1824, Bavaria, Germany, came to the US in 1847 with his parents. He went to Mercer Co., Penn., but after 2-1/2 years returned to Ohio. He married in Trumbull Co., Ohio to CAROLINE (DENIGER) who was also born Bavaria and had come to the US with the Miller family. They moved to Macon Twp., Lenawee Co., Mich. ca. 1854. Children: Those deceased by 1888 were MAGGIE (who had married); KATIE (who had married); CHRISTIE; & MARY. Surviving were FREDERICK (m. Emma Karcher, dau. of Michael, also see, Macon Twp.); CARRIE (m. Henry Smith, Muskegon, Mich.); EDWARD (m. Maggie Quinn,

Clare, Mich.); LEONARD (Macon Twp.) Ref: P&BA-Len pg. 939-40.

MILLER, JONAH, born in Conn., moved about 1817 to Wayne Co., NY. He married SARAH (CURTIS) who died in Wayne Co., NY at age 50. Jonah moved first to Michigan, and then to Fulton Co., Ohio where he died at age 76. Ten children, but only named was ISAIAH C. (preceding). Ref: P&BA-Len pg. 722-3.

MILLER, LATHRAM of Chelsea, Mich. (See Levi C. Richmond).

MILLER, LEWIS V. and wife, SARAH (HUFF), moved in 1832 from Seneca Co., NY to Hillsdale Co., Mich., and Sarah died in Jonesville in 1849. Children: 1. DAN B.; 2. JANE A. (m. Michael J. Martin, also see); 3. TUNIS H. b. ca. 1839, Mich.; 4. SARAH L. b. 8 Nov. 1847, Hillsdale Co., Mich. (m. Henry H. Osgood, also see). It is probably this Lewis written as "Louis," age 42, b. NY, with Tunis, age 11, both in the household of JEHIEL, preceding. Lewis married again to Mrs. ELIZABETH (SCHOFIELD) VANDUZEN, and they resided near Ridgeway, Lenawee Co., Mich. In 1888, Lewis was living at age 81, with a son in Macon Twp. Ref: P&BA-Len pg. 240-1.

MILLER, MINOR born ca. 1816, and wife, ELIZABETH, born ca. 1816, both in NY, were listed in the 1840 census index of Macon Twp., Lenawee Co., Mich.; and in the 1850 census of Ridgeway Twp., with GEORGE, age 17; LEWIS, age 15, both b. NY; and RILEY, age 13; SARAH J., age 8; MARY A., age 7; DAVID, age 3; RANSON, age 6/12, all b. Mich., in their household. Note DAVID O.; JEHIEL, preceding; & OLIVER, following, as they were adjacent in the 1840 census index of Macon Twp.

MILLER, NANCY born ca. 1801 (possibly in Penn., place not legible in census), was listed head of household in the 1840 census index of Tecumseh Twp., Lenawee Co., Mich.; and in the 1850 census of Macon Twp. with FRANCIS, age 25; ISABELLA, age 22; JEPHTHA, age 20, also possibly b. Penn., in her household. Note JEPHTHA (preceding).

MILLER, OLIVER born ca. 1777, New Jersey, was listed in the 1840 census index of Macon Twp., Lenawee Co., Mich., and also in the 1850 census adjacent to JEHIEL; & JOHN A. (preceding).

MILLER, OLIVER born ca. 1801, NY, and wife, ELIZA, born ca. 1804, Conn., were listed in the 1840 census index of Macon Twp., Lenawee Co., Mich.; and in the 1850 census of Ridgeway Twp. with AUGUSTUS, age 27; DAN, age 22, both b. NY; and VOLNEY, age 10; MILTON, age 8, both b. Mich., Jacob Arner, age 30, b. Penn. with wife, Ellen, age 20, b. NY (married within the year); and Mary A. Tingley, age 13, b. Mich., in their household.

MILLER, ORRIN born ca. 1810, and wife, SARAH B., born ca. 1814, both in NY, were listed in the 1850 census of Ridgeway Twp., Lenawee Co., Mich. with SARAH, age 17; AMOS, age 11; CHARLES H., age 8, all b. NY, in their household (next door to GEORGE R., preceding).

MILLER, PETER born ca. 1790, and wife, LYDIA, born ca. 1783, both in NY, were listed in the 1840 census of Macon Twp., Lenawee Co., Mich.; and in the 1850 census with PETER W., age 30; LYDIA, age 25, both b. NY, in their household.

MILLER, PETER born ca. 1794, Penn., was listed in the 1840 census index of Tecumseh Twp., Lenawee Co., Mich.; and in the 1850 census with WILLIAM, age 19, b. NY; and HENRY, age 17; CHARLES, age 8, both b. Mich., in his household.

MILLER, PETER of Rockingham Co., VA was the father of MARGARET (m. Valentine Pense, also see, and remained in Rockingham Co.) Ref: P&BA-Len pg. 1151-2.

MILLER, RELIEF born 20 Feb. 1775, Marlboro, Mass., married William Weatherby (also see). Ref: P&BA-Len pg. 1020-1.

MILLER, RICHARD (See James Green)

MILLER, ROBERT T. born ca. 1810, and wife, SOPHIA, born ca. 1812, both in Penn., were listed in the 1850 census of Fairfield Twp., Lenawee Co., Mich. with WILLIAM, age 17; and CHARLES, age 8, both b. Penn., in their household. Note CHARLES S. in Fairfield Twp., preceding.

MILLER, SAMUEL was listed in the 1840 census index of Woodstock Twp., Lenawee Co., Mich.

MILLER, STEPHEN born ca. 1804, and wife, MARTHA, born ca. 1805, both in NY, were listed in the 1840 census index of Macon Twp., Lenawee Co., Mich.; and in the 1850 census with SOPHIA, age 18, b. NY; and LUTHER, age 13; ADELIA, age 9; LEWIS C., age 7; STEPHEN, age 5; JAMES P., age 2, all b. Mich., in their household.

MILLER, SUSAN Mrs. married second to Robert Liddel (also see) after 1865, probably in Macon Twp., Lenawee Co., Mich.

MILLER, SUSANNA (See John Stumbaugh)

MILLER, TILDA (See Charles F. Smith)

MILLER, TOBIAS moved ca. 1853 from Westfield, Medina Co., Ohio to Cambridge Twp., Lenawee Co., Mich.; and then to Palmyrra Twp. In Ohio, he had adopted ALFRED A. (preceding), who was Alfred A. McKnight, son of Alfred, also see. Ref: P&BA-Len pg. 1162-5.

MILLER, VAN R. (VANINSALER in census, possibly VAN RENSSELAER?), son of JOHN (preceding), born 29 Aug. 1819, Plattsburg, NY, went to Norwich, Oxford Co., Canada ca. 1838. He married there on 28 Nov. 1842 to PHEBE (WEST), daughter of Benjamin (also see). In 1844, they moved to Raisin Twp., Lenawee Co. She died 7 Sept. 1886, age 62-1/2. Children: 1. JOHN H. b. ca. 1843, Canada (d. 15 Dec. 1863 of Smallpox during service in the Civil War); 2. CHARLES W. (preceding); 3. EMILY M. (MATILDA in census, age 4; m. L. V. Judson, Raisin Twp.); 4. HIRAM L. b. ca. 1848 (d. Measles, Feb. 1864, Lexington, KY while serving in Civil War); 5. MARY. Ref: P&BA-Len pg. 655-6.

MILLER, WILLIAM of Maryland went to Dutchess Co., NY and was father of MARGARET (m. Enis Scofield, also see).

MILLER, WILLIAM, age 11, born Mich., was listed in the 1850 census of Tecumseh Twp., Lenawee Co., Mich.

MILLER, ZEBA born ca. 1826, and wife, ANN, born ca. 1827, both in NY, were listed in the 1850 census of Fairfield Twp., Lenawee Co., Mich. with GEORGE, age 4; ANDREW, age 3, both b. Mich., in their household.

MILLETT, ALEXANDER born ca. 1820, and wife, HANNAH, born ca. 1823, both in NY, were listed in the 1850 census of Madison Twp., Lenawee Co., Mich. with THERON, age 6; JONATHAN, age 4; EDMUND, age 2, all b. Mich., in their household. Note MARTIN, following.

Pioneer Families of Southeastern Michigan

MILLETT, CALEB G. born ca. 1810, and wife, ALMA, born ca. 1813, both in NY, were listed in the 1850 census of Fairfield Twp., Lenawee Co., Mich. with REBECCA, age 14; LEE, age 12; MARY J., age 9; ALONZO? (male), age 7, all b. Mich., in their household.

MILLETT, JULIA A. of Fairfield Twp., Lenawee Co., Mich. married ca. 1834 to Archibald Brower (also see) in Seneca Twp. The only Millett listed in Lenawee Co. in the 1840 census index was MARTIN, following.

MILLETT, MARTIN was listed in the 1840 census index of Madison Twp., Lenawee Co., Mich.

MILLIGAN, JOHN born ca. 1814, England, and wife, SARAH A., born ca. 1820, Penn., were listed in the 1850 census of Palmyra Twp., Lenawee Co., Mich. with MARY J., age 8; FRANCES O., age 6; SARAH, age 4; JOSEPHINE, age 11/12, all b. Mich., in their household.

MILLIGAN, LOUISA was the foster child of Benjamin Kelley (also see).

MILLIKEN, EDWARD A. born near Peterboro, New Hampshire, married SUSAN E. (TOWNE) born near Keene, NH. They moved to Orleans Co., NY where she died in 1842. He returned to New Hampshire where he apparently married again, wife's name not stated, and then moved ca. 1851 to Hudson Twp., Lenawee Co., Mich. He moved later to the town of Medina. Known son, EDWARD A. (following), and at least 2 more children. Ref: P&BA-Len pg. 899-900. Note: Edward A. (Sr.) had a brother, "N. J.," in Canandaigua, NY; and a 1/2 brother, name not stated, who came to Lenawee Co.

MILLIKEN, EDWARD A., son of EDWARD A. (preceding), born 14 Dec. 1840, Cheshire Co, NH, moved to New York, and then Lenawee Co., Mich. with his parents. He went to Canandaigua, NY where he worked in the print shop of his uncle, N. J. MILLIKEN. He enlisted in Co. G, 18th NY Inf. during the Civil War. After being mustered out, he reenlisted in Co. H, 4th NY Heavy Artl. Afterwards he lived in NY; Elkhart, Ind.; & Canada. He returned to Lenawee Co., Mich. where he married in Jan. 1872, Adrian, to NELLIE M. (DROWN), daughter of Apollos (also see). They lived for a time in Tonawanda, NY, but returned to Adrian. No children were listed. Ref: P&BA-Len pg. 899-900.

MILLIMAN, ROLLIN M. and wife, HANNAH, of Wayne Co., NY were parents of 9 children, and only one mentioned was NETTIE CAROLINE b. ca. 1813, NY (m. James E. Round, also see). Ref: P&BA-Len pg. 887-8.

MILLS, ABEL born ca. 1800, and wife, ANN, born ca. 1794, both in England, were listed in the 1850 census of Adrian Twp., Lenawee Co., Mich. with EDWARD, age 29; SARAH A., age 17, both b. England in their household.

MILLS, ADELBERT WORKMAN, son of PHILO C. (following), born 20 July 1843, Franklin Twp., Lenawee Co., Mich., served in Co. G, 11th Mich. Cav. during the Civil War. He married on 10 Oct. 1876 to ROSA (McKINNEY), possibly daughter of John (also see) of Tecumseh. Known children: 1. MARY ALICE b. 22 Nov. 1877; 2. MABEL DIXON b. 29 July 1882; 3. TRUMAN RAYMOND b. 19 Feb. 1887. Ref: P&BA-Len pg. 1060-3.

MILLS, ALONZO S., son of RANCELIER (following), born ca. 1850, Franklin Twp., Lenawee Co., Mich., married ALICE J. (ELLIS) and settled in Franklin Twp. Known children (twins), INA & RENA. Ref: P&BA-Len pg. 1086-7.

MILLS, CASSIUS M. (See Michael Hendershott) Also note CASSIUS M. MILLER, son of ALBERT.

MILLS, CHARLES born ca. 1824, and wife, JANE, born ca. 1831, both in NY, were listed in the 1850 census of Seneca Twp., Lenawee Co., Mich. with CHARLES H., age 2, b. Mich., in their household.

MILLS, CHARLOTTE came from Wayne Co., NY in 1840 with her husband Samuel Baker (also see). Ref: P&BA-Len pg. 927. Also note PHEBE J., following.

MILLS, EBENEZER G., son of PHILO (following), born ca. 1808, NY, and his wife, ANN (BREERS), born ca. 1812, England, came to Franklin Twp., Lenawee Co., Mich. in 1832. He died 2 Apr. 1887, age 78; and she died 25 Jan. 1905, age 93, and are buried in the Mills Cemetery, Franklin Twp. Known children from 1850 census: 1. NANCY, age 17; 2. PHILO, age 15; 3. ELIZABETH B., age 13 (m. T. M. Camburn, also see; d. 5 Apr. 1875); 4. HENRIETTA, age 11; 5. RANSON, age 7; 6. JANE/JENNIE, age 4 (m. T. M. Camburn as 2nd wife); 7. EDWARD J., age 3 (d. 8 Dec. 1871, age 24y/7mo, buried in Mills Cem. with a GAR marker); 8. EMMA, age 2/12. Ref: P&BA-Len pg. 297-300.

MILLS, EDWIN LEROY, son of PHILO C. (following), born 16 Nov. 1846, Franklin Twp., Lenawee Co., Mich., married in Jan. 1873 to ANNIE (HUNTER), daughter of Andrew J. (also see). Known children: 1. HUGH HUNTER b. 10 Feb. 1872; 2. HARRIE LEROY b. 8 Jan. 1877; 3. HERBERT WADE b. 27 Jan. 1887. Ref: P&BA-Len pg. 1060-3.

MILLS, GABRIEL born ca. 1793, in Monmouth Co., NJ (now Ocean Co.), married in 1827 to HANNAH (COLLINS), born ca. 1807, NJ, both of Quaker lineage. They resided first in Barnegat, NJ and then in 1834, after the birth of 3 children, they removed to Macon Twp., Lenawee Co., Mich. He died on 1 Feb. 1851, age 58. She was still living in 1888 at age 82 in Lenawee Co. There were 8 children, all names not stated, ages from 1850 census of Macon Twp.: JOHN, age 19; ISAAC C. (following), both b. NJ; GRANVILLE (following); ANNA J., age 11; JAMES C., age 2, last 3 b. Mich. Ref: P&BA-Len pg. 473-4 & 1053-4. Note: In 1790 in Monmouth Co., NJ, there was a JAMES in Dover Twp.; and WILLIAM in Shrewsbury Twp.

MILLS, GERTRUDE (See Gershom B. Bennett)

MILLS, GRANVILLE, son of GABRIEL (preceding), born 27 FEb. 1835, Macon Twp., Lenawee Co., Mich., married in Clinton Twp., Lenawee Co., Mich. on 29 Jan. 1863 to MARIA (FERGUSON), daughter of John (also see) and settled in Macon Twp. They adopted a son, GABRIEL (also named Mills). Ref: P&BA-Len pg. 473-4.

MILLS, HULDA A. born ca. 1814, NY, was listed head of household in the 1850 census of Adrian Twp., Lenawee Co., Mich. with JANE, age 17; JOHN N., age 14, both born Ohio, in her household.

MILLS, ISAAC C., son of GABRIEL (preceding), born 31 July 1832, NJ, came to Macon Twp., Lenawee Co., Mich. with his parents. He married on 5 Feb. 1856 to KATE A. (HOOD), daughter of James (also see) of Plymouth, Wayne Co., Mich., and settled in Macon Twp.

Children: 1. PERRIS E. (d. age 25); 2. JAMES H. (d. age 16); 3. FRANK (to Texas); 4. ROBERT B.; 5. CARL; 6. GABRIELLE. Ref: P&BA-Len pg. 1053-4.

MILLS, JAMES born ca. 1814, and wife, SARAH, born ca. 1812, both in England, were listed in the 1850 census of Madison Twp., Lenawee Co., Mich. with JOSEPH, age 17, b. Canada; and LOUISA, age 8; ALVIRA, age 6; EMILY, age 4; ALFRED, age 3; CHARLOTTE, age 1, all b. Mich., in their household.

MILLS, JOHN born ca. 1786, and wife, CHARLOTTE, born ca. 1786, both in England, were listed in the 1850 census of Adrian Twp., Lenawee Co., Mich. with CHARLOTTE, age 22, b. England, in their household. Note JOHN & WILLIAM, following.

MILLS, JOHN, age 25, born England, was listed in the 1850 census of Adrian Twp., Lenawee Co., Mich. in a hotel. Note WILLIAM, following, both called "hatter" by trade. Also note JOHN, preceding.

MILLS, JOHN F. born ca. 1807, NY, was listed in the 1850 census of Franklin Twp., Lenawee Co., Mich. in household of Caroline Knight.

MILLS, JOSIAH born ca. 1800, NH, and wife, NANCY, born ca. 1805, NY, were listed in the 1850 census of Rollin Twp., Lenawee Co., Mich. with JASON, age 22; SARAH, age 17; MARY, age 14, all b. NY, in their household.

MILLS, MICAH of Warwick, Orange Co., NY, had a will dated 31 Mar. 1810; probated 20 June 1810. Mentioned is wife, JULIANA; Son, MICAH, JR. (minor); and daughters: ANNA; RUTH; DEBORAH; CATHERINE; CHARITY b. ca. 1790 (m. Benjamin Bradner, also see); MARIA; ELIZABETH; CLARY; JULIANA. Exec.: Wife & Nathaniel Wheeler & James Wheeler. Witnesses: John Wheeler; Jeffrey Wisner; Sarah Wheeler. Ref: Early Wills of Orange Co., NY, OCGS. & P&BA-Len pg. 1114-8.

MILLS, NANCY (See Roswell Lamb)

MILLS, PHEBE J. born ca. 1823, Wayne Co., NY (m. Ambrose Camp, also see). Ref: P&BA-Len pg. 114-8. See CHARLOTTE, preceding.

MILLS, PHILO Maj., son of Rev. SAMUEL (following), born 1775, Conn., settled in Mt. Morris, Livingston Co., NY. He married MARY (GREEN), daughter of Ebenezer (also see) of the Mohawk Valley of NY. According to Tombstone Inscriptions in Lenawee Co., Mich., by the NW Ohio Genealogical Society, Philo donated the land for the Mills Cemetery located on the north side of highway M-50, just 2.4 miles from Springville, Mich., and there was supposedly a burial there as early as 1810(?). Philo died 27 Aug. 1847, age 65 (72?), and his wife's stone was apparently now illegible. Children: 1. SAMUEL J.; 2. NANCY J. (m. ? Turner); 3. JOHN P. b. ca. 1808, NY (unmarried listed next door to Philo C. in 1850 census in Long household); 4. EBENEZER G. (preceding); 5. MARY A. (m. ? Workman); 6. PHILO C. (following); 7. SARAH A. b. ca. 1815 (m. Erastus Rundell, also see); 8. HARRIET N. b. ca. 1815 (m. Isaac H. Hampton, also see); 9. GEORGE H.; 10. JANE MATILDA (d. 3 Mar. 1845, age 26); 11. HENRIETTA M. (d. 18 Jan. 1847, age 26); 12. ALMIRA N. (m. D. B. Greene, Ypsilanti, Mich.); 13. EDWIN J. (to Ypsilanti, Mich.). Ref: P&BA-Len pg. 1060-3.

MILLS, PHILO C., son of PHILO Maj. (preceding), born 16 Aug. 1810, Mt. Morris, Livingston Co., NY, came to Franklin Twp., Lenawee Co., Mich. with his parents. He returned to NY where he married on 10 Sept. 1834 to MARY (KEENEY), daughter of Joseph (also see) of LeRoy, Genesee Co., NY. They settled in Franklin Twp. where they remained until 1873, then moved to Tecumseh; and in 1882 to Adrian. She died 23 Feb. 1887. Children: 1. HATTIE (d. age 9); 2. MARY E. b. 11 Aug. 1835 (m. Daniel C. Blair, also see); 3. HELEN L. b. 11 Aug. 1837 (m. David A. Dodge, also see); 4. FRANCES M. b. 11 Mar. 1840 (m. Henry M. Pomeroy, also see); 5. ADELBERT WORKMAN (preceding); 6. EDWIN LEROY (preceding). Ref: P&BA-Len pg. 1060-3.

MILLS, RALPH born ca. 1804, and wife, CHARITY, born ca. 1807, both in New Jersey, were listed in the 1850 census of Macon Twp., Lenawee Co., Mich. with ANGELINE, age 21; ABNER, age 18, both b. NJ; and JAMES, age 14; JOHN, age 13; MATILDA, age 11; MARIA, age 9, all b. Mich., and John Birdsall, age 27, b. NY, with wife, MARY, age 19, b. NJ, probably daughter of Ralph, married within the year, in their household.

MILLS, RANCELIER (RENSSELAER?) born 13 July 1805, Niles, Cayuga Co., NY, married there to ELIZABETH (DUYREE), and after the birth of 3? children, moved in 1837 to Franklin Twp., Lenawee Co., Mich. Elizabeth died before 1846. A son, "LANSEN," was said to have gone to Dallas, Texas, perhaps one of following who were listed in the household in the 1850 census of Franklin Twp.

1. MARIA, age 18; 2. JONATHAN, age 17; 3. FREDUS?, age 15; 4. GEORGE, age 13 (to Huron, Dakota), all b. NY; and 5. WILLIAM, age 12, b. Mich. Rancelier married again to Mrs. SALLIE A. (WRIGHT) BOOTH, daughter of Elijah (also see), and widow of Belden of Clinton Twp. Children: 6. WRIGHT E. b. ca. 1846 (in 1850 was in household of grandfather, Elijah Wright); 7. RANCELIER B. b. ca. 1848 (m. Maggie Brooks, dau. of David); 8. ALONSO, age 5/12 (preceding). There were 3 deceased children, MARY J.; CHARLES W.; & IDA, dates of birth not given. Ref: P&BA-Len pg. 1086-7.

MILLS, SAMUEL Rev. was a native of Conn., who moved at an early date to Livingston Co., NY. Children: 1. ALEXANDER (lived Belfast & Olean, NY, and then Cleveland, O.); 2. Capt. LEWIS (of Mt. Morris, NY); 3. Gen. WILLIAM (d. Mt. Morris, NY); 4. Maj. PHILO (preceding); 5. SALLY (m. ? Whitney, d. Fishkill, NY). Ref: P&BA-Len pg. 1060-3.

MILLS, THOMAS (See Robert G. Marshall)

MILLS, WILLIAM born ca. 1823, and wife, ANN, born ca. 1823, both in England, were listed in the 1850 census of Adrian Twp., Lenawee Co., Mich. with FANNY, age 2; GEORGE, age 1/12, both b. Mich., in their household. Note JOHN, preceding.

MILLS, WRIGHT E., son of RANCELIER (preceding), born ca. 1846, Franklin Twp., Lenawee Co., Mich., married CLARA (ENGLISH), and later moved to Allegan Co., Mich. Children: 1. WILLEY; 2. EDWARD. Ref: P&BA-Len pg. 1086-7.

MILLSON, JOHN born Yorkshire, England, married in Detroit, Mich. to Mrs. ANN (GUIETT) PIERCE, a widow, born Leicestshire, England. They settled in Bridgewater, Washtenaw Co., Mich., where she died at age 52, and he died at age 77. Known daughter, MARY

Pioneer Families of Southeastern Michigan

(m. Samuel Underwood, also see). Ref: P&BA-Len pg. 329.

MINER, ANDERSON died in 1878, age 83, Liberty Twp., Jackson Co. Mich. His wife, name not stated, moved to Montcalm Co., Mich. Known daughter, OLIVE R. (m. Justus Fowler², also see).

MIRRICK also see MERRICK

MIRRICK, GEORGE W. and wife, ELSIE, lived Rose, Wayne Co., NY. They moved to Adrian, Lenawee Co., Mich. where he died 31 July 1887, and she was residing in 1888. Known daughter, JENNIE B. b. 14 Apr. 1838 (m. Calvin H. Crane, also see. 11 Apr. 1866, Rose, NY). Ref: P&BA-Len pg. 966-7.

MISER, MARY E. (See Stephen Conger)

MITCHEL see MITCHELL

MITCHELL, ALICE (BAER) Mrs. was the daughter of John A. Baer (also see).

MITCHELL, ALONZO, son of WILLIAM (following), born 28 Mar. 1807, Cummington, Hampshire Co., Mass., married there on 16 Aug. 1831 to LYANDA (SHAW) born Worthington, Mass. They moved to Palmyra Twp., Lenawee Co., Mich. by 1840. There were no children named in the sketch, however in the 1850 census of Palmyra they listed HENRY, age 10; CLARISSA, age 11, both b. Mich., in their household. Ref: P&BA-Len pg. 284-6.

MITCHELL, ANNA (See Edward Underwood)

MITCHELL, CHARLES, son of DAVID (following), born 24 Aug. 1814, Delaware Co., NY, moved to Michigan in 1836. He married on 24 Mar. 1839 to ANN D. (DENNIS), daughter of Elias (also see). They settled first in Calhoun Co., Mich.; and in 1843 moved to Barry Co., Mich. In 1845, they removed to Madison Twp., Lenawee Co., Mich. Children: 1. BETSEY A. b. 8 July 1840, Marengo, Calhoun Co. (m. Norman J. Strong, also see); 2. JEANNETTE b. ca. 1844 (m. C. D. West, Madison Twp.); 3. DAVID D. born ca. 1847 (to Worcester, Mass.); 4. CHARLES E. Note: In the 1850 census of Madison Twp., they listed ZACHARIAH T., age 4/12, in the household, not mentioned in sketch. Ref: P&BA-Len pg. 920.

MITCHELL, DAVID and wife, SARAH (DIBBLE), of Delaware Co., NY, had nine children, names not stated, except CHARLES (preceding). Ref: P&BA-Len pg. 920.

MITCHELL, FRANZ JOSEPH born in Rhenish Prussis, of French ancestry, immigrated to Milwaukee, Wis. in 1845, and to Peoria, Ill. about the time of the Civil War. He died in 1866, age 66; and his wife, name not stated, was still living in Peoria in 1888, age 88. Children: 1. ANNA MARIA (m. Charles Fox); 2. JACOB (following); 3. KATE (m. Prof. William Walter, Milwaukee); 4. MARY (m. Henry Moenighoff, Peoria); 5. LEONARD (Monroe, Mich.); 6. ELIZA (m. William Faber, Peoria); 7. ANDREW (Monroe, Mich.) Ref: P&BA-Len pg. 1141-2.

MITCHELL, J. W. (See Jacob Cole Tunison)

MITCHELL, JACOB, son of FRANZ JOSEPH (preceding), born 20 Nov. 1836, Rhenish Prussia. He came to Milwaukee, Wis. with his parents. He married in Oct. 1856 to ANNA MARIA (LITE), daughter of Peter (also see). He owned paper mills in Milwaukee; Appleton, Ill., etc. In 1862, he had a paper mill in Monroe, Mich., and in 1871 in Tecumseh, Lenawee Co. Children: 1. CHARLES (Monroe, Mich.); 2. ALBERT (Adrian, Mich.); 3. LEONARD; 4. HENRY; 5. JACOB; 6. ELLA; 7. CLARA. Ref: P&BA-Len pg. 1141-2.

MITCHELL, JAMES born ca. 1821, England, and wife, MARY P., born ca. 1832, NY, were listed in the 1850 census of Raisin Twp., Lenawee Co., Mich. with SUSANNA, age 1, b. Mich., all in the household of Stephen H. Aldridge.

MITCHELL, JOSEPH from Nantucket Island was an early pioneer to Madison Co., NY. It may be he listed in the 1800 census index of Dutchess Co., NY, as son, WILLIAM (following), was born in Dutchess Co. He moved from Madison Co., NY to Victory, Cayuga Co. where he died in 1852. Known daughter, ANNA (m. Edward Underwood, also see). Ref: P&BA-Len pg. 537-8 & 579-80.

MITCHELL, LUTHER born ca. 1816, and wife, AUGERONA?, born ca. 1815, both in NY, were listed in the 1850 census of Medina Twp., Lenawee Co., Mich. with LUTHER E., age 4; MARY, age 2, both b. Mich., and Eli D. Fisk, age 26, b. NY, in their household.

MITCHELL, MARTHA K. born 1 Feb. 1816, Mass. (See Charles M. Baldwin).

MITCHELL, NEWELL born ca. 1821, and wife, CORNELIA S., born ca. 1829, both in Mass., were listed in the 1850 census of Madison Twp., Lenawee Co., Mich. with LORA C., age 2; IRA N., age 1, both b. Mass.; and Sarah Hubbard, age 54, and Sanford Hubbard, age 29, both b. Mass., in their household.

MITCHELL, PYRON?, JR. born ca. 1823, Mass., and wife, MARY C., born ca. 1823, NH, were listed in the 1850 census of Medina Twp., Lenawee Co., Mich. with OLIVE, age 72?, b. Mass., in their household.

MITCHELL, ROBERT born ca. 1810, and wife, JANE, born ca. 1814, came from Ireland about 1848, and settled in Raisin Twp., Lenawee Co., Mich. They were listed in the 1850 census of Raisin Twp. with MARGARET b. 16 Oct. 1844, Ireland (m. John Rainey, also see); WILLIAM J., age 2, both b. Ireland. Also in their household was mother?, MARGARET, age 70, b. Ireland, and brother?, JOHN, age 44, b. Ireland; and Lucius Neal, age 11, b. Mich. Ref: P&BA-Len pg. 608-9. STEPHEN, following, was listed next door in census.

MITCHELL, STEPHEN born ca. 1808, and wife, MARY, born ca. 1812, both in Ireland, were listed in the 1850 census of Raisin Twp., Lenawee Co., Mich. next door to ROBERT, preceding.

'MITCHELL, TIMOTHY born ca. 1791, Conn., and wife, JERUSHA, born ca. 1806, NY, were listed in the 1840 census index of Raisin Twp., Lenawee Co., Mich.; and in the 1850 census with NARTHA, age 15; MARY, age 13; HELEN, age 7, all b. NY; and John Calkins, age 71, b. NY, and Deborah Calkins, age 69, b. Conn., possibly in-laws, in their household.

MITCHELL, TYLER born ca. 1787, and wife, DEBORAH, born ca. 1786, both in NY, were listed in the 1840 census index of Medina Twp., Lenawee Co., Mich.; and in the 1850 census with JOHN, age 27, b. NY; and Sally Comer, age 24, & Nelson Comer, age 26, both b. NY, in their household.

MITCHELL, WILLIAM born 10 Dec. 1782, Cummington, Hampshire Co., Mass., was son of a man who had moved from Bridgewater to Cummington. William was one of 12 children, names not stated. He married CLARISSA (BISBEE) born 6 June 1788, Plainfield, Mass. They moved to Palmyra Twp., Lenawee Co., Mich. in 1833. He died 17 July 1856, and she died 17 June 1856. There were 7 sons and 5 daughters, and only mentioned was #2. ALONZO (preceding). In the 1850 census of Palmyra Twp., ARTHUR, age 20, b. Mass., was in the household. Ref: P&BA-Len pg. 284-6.

MITCHELL, WILLIAM, son of JOSEPH (preceding), born Dutchess Co., NY, married probably in Madison Co., NY to MELLE (CLAPP), daughter of Henry (also see). Known daughter, MARIA b. 22 Dec. 1822, Madison Co., NY (m. Wanton Green Smith, also see, in Wayne Co., NY). Ref: P&BA-Len pg. 579-80.

MITCHELL, WILLIAM of Ida, Monroe Co., Mich. (See Justus Iffland).

MIZNER, NETTIE (See George Kendall)

MOBAS, GEORGE (See L. T. Rathbun)

MOENIGHOFF, HENRY (See Franz Joseph Mitchell)

MONAHAN, JOHN^2, son of JOHN^1 (who remained in Ireland), was born ca. 1790, Co. Louth, Ireland, and married there by 1827 to MARGARET (HOY) born ca. 1800, Drogheda. He came ahead to the US in 1837, and the family joined him in New York state, and then moved in 1840 to Medina Twp., Lenawee Co., Mich. where she died in Apr. 1859. He died 31 Dec. 1875 in Toledo, Ohio at the home of a daughter, Mrs. John Coleman. Children, all born Ireland: 1. JOHN^3 (following); 2. MARY b. ca. 1833; 3. BRIDGET b. ca. 1834. Ref: P&BA-Len pg. 1109-10.

MONAHAN, JOHN^3, son of JOHN^2 (preceding), born 1827, Co. Louth, Ireland, came to Medina Twp., Lenawee Co., Mich. with his parents. In 1856, he went by ship to California, but returned to Lenawee Co. He married ELIZA (HALEY), daughter of William (also see), and settled in Medina Twp. She died 3 Mar. 1878. Children: 1. JOHN W.^{4} (following); 2. MARY; 3. LOUISA; 4. EVA. John^2 married again on 11 Nov. 1878 to MARY (O'NEIL), daughter of Daniel (also see). Children: 5. DANIEL; 6. BLANCHE; 7. CHARLOTTE; 8. MABEL C. Ref: P&BA-Len pg. 1109-10.

MONAHAN, JOHN born ca. 1810, and wife, MARGARET, born ca. 1818, both in Ireland, were listed in the 1850 census of Tecumseh Twp., Lenawee Co., Mich. with no family.

MONAHAN, JOHN W.^{4}, son of JOHN^3 (preceding), born Medina Twp., Lenawee Co., Mich., married DEBORAH (O'NEIL), daughter of Daniel (also see) and settled in Medina Twp. Children: 1. DANIEL; 2. DON; 3. JOHN J. Ref: P&BA-Len pg. 1109-10.

MONIER, ROBERT born in Steuben Co., NY, and wife, SARAH (McKENZIE) born in Newark, NJ, came to Rollin Twp., Lenawee Co., Mich. at an advanced age and died there. Known daughter, MEHITABLE b. 27 July 1843, Steuben Co., NY (m. John H. Hawkins, also see). Ref: P&BA-Len pg. 730-1.

MONROE, MARY (See James Henry Thorn)

MONROE, PHEBE (See Lawton Slade)

MONTAGUE, ? born 1 Oct. 1808, Union Co., Penn., married CHRISTINA (SCOUT), a native of Northumberland Co., Penn., and granddaughter of William Scout, a Revolutionary officer. Montague died a young man leaving his wife with 4 children. Christina moved (after 1850?) to Raisin Twp., Lenawee Co., Mich. and was living there in 1888, age 78, with her children. Children: 1. JOHN (m. Amanda Efland, Danville, Penn.); 2. WILLIAM (following); 3. JAMES (m. Alice Payne, Tecumseh Twp.); 4. ELIZABETH (m. Daniel H. Chase, son of Levi H., also see, Tecumseh, Mich.) Ref: P&BA-Len pg. 190.

MONTAGUE, WILLIAM, son of ? (preceding), came to Raisin Twp., Lenawee Co., Mich. with his mother. He married 22 Dec. 1869 to LYDIA L. (SOUTHWORTH), born 3 Oct. 1851, Raisin Twp., and they settled in Raisin Twp. Children: 1. PAUL A. b. 6 May 1872; 2. J. HERBERT b. 12 Nov. 1877. Ref: P&BA-Len pg. 190.

MONTGOMERY, AUGUSTUS born ca. 1807, and wife, ESTHER, born ca. 1809, both in NY, came from Yates Co., NY to Macon Twp., Lenawee Co., Mich. in 1833, and by 1850 to Ridgeway Twp. Son, HENRY, b. ca. 1834, Mich. Morgan J. Florance (also see) came with them from NY and was in their household in the 1850 census of Ridgeway Twp. Harriet Brooks, age 14, b. Mich., was also in their household.

MONTGOMERY, LILLIE (See Marvin A. Packard)

MONTGOMERY, SUSAN born ca. 1834, and FRANCES, born ca. 1837, both in Mich., were listed in the 1850 census of Madison Twp., Lenawee Co., Mich. in the household of Elisha G. & Eveline Budlong.

MONTGOMERY, THOMAS H. born ca. 1815, and wife, ELIZA A., born ca. 1824, both in NY, were listed in the 1850 census of Rome Twp., Lenawee Co., Mich. with no family.

MOODY, LUCINDA (See John Hood)

MOODY, MARTHA (See William Richart)

MOODY, SAMUEL born ca. 1825, NY, was listed in the 1850 census of Madison Twp., Lenawee Co., Mich. in the household of Timothy Baker.

MOODY, W. R. married ? (SOOP) and died before 1864, as his widow married Matthew B. McConnel (also see) as his 2nd wife.

MOON, ? married James Vaughn (also see) before 1815 in Washington Co., NY. Ref: P&BA-Len pg. 1002-3.

MOON, ALICE born ca. 1810, NY, was probably mother of LUCY b. 27 May 1832, Niagara Co., NY (m. Ezra Ames, also see). Alice was listed in the household of Ezra & Lucy Ames in the 1850 census of Hudson Twp., Lenawee Co., Mich. MARIAN M., age 23, b. NY, in a Wilcox household in the 1850 census of Hudson Twp. may also relate to Alice.

MOON, CATHARINE born ca. 1793, NY, was listed in the 1850 census of Palmyra Twp., Lenawee Co., Mich. in the household of Joel & Hannah (age 23, b. NY) Bellamy, possibly mother of Hannah?

MOON, JOHN and wife, RUTH, had known daughter, PHEBE (m. Philip Roberts, also see, 26 Nov. 1794,

Pioneer Families of Southeastern Michigan

Stephentown, Rensselaer Co., NY). Ref: P&BA-Len pg. 1092-3.

MOON, LUDWIG of Avon, Lorain Co., Ohio had known daughter, AUGUSTA (m. Madison Reynolds, also see). Ref: P&BA-Len pg. 425-6.

MOORE, ADDIE (See Anthony Poucher)

MOORE, ALONZO born ca. 1810, NY, and wife, ABBIE (FOOTE), daughter of Milton (also see), born Conn., were listed in the 1850 census of Rome Twp., Lenawee Co., Mich. with ABBA M., age 14; DELIA M., age 10; ANALIZA, age 8; SUSAN A., age 6; WILLIAM A., age 4; HENRY H., age 2, all b. Mich., in their household. After the death of Alonzo, Abbie married Sylvanus Kinney (also see).

MOORE, ANN born Orange Co., VT married on 4 Dec. 1852 to Neley Bancroft (also see) as his second wife.

MOORE, CALISTA, age 20, born NY, was listed in the 1850 census of Adrian Twp., Lenawee Co., Mich. in the Hoxie residence.

MOORE, CATHERINE W. (See William H. McDowell)

MOORE, CHARLES was listed in the 1840 census index of Clinton Twp., Lenawee Co., Mich.

MOORE, CYNTHIA (See Peleg Joslyn)

MOORE, DIANA born Staffordshire, England (See Charles A. Chaloner).

MOORE, DOUGALD, son of JOHN (following), born 1815, Argyleshire, Scotland, married in Middlesex Co., Ontario, Canada, to JANET (HENDERSON) born 1819, Inverness, Scotland. They resided first in Middlesex Co., and later moved to Strathroy where she died in 1878. He was residing with a daughter in Adelaide, Middlesex Co. in 1888. Nine children, only name stated was #8. JOHN H. MD b. 4 Oct. 1859, settled in Ogden Center, Lenawee Co., Mich. in 1886. Ref: P&BA-Len pg. 705-6.

MOORE, GARRISON (See Libni Kelley)

MOORE, GEORGE W.^{5}, son of NATHANIEL^4 (following), born 3 Apr. 1814, Peterboro, New Hampshire, went to Medina Twp., Lenawee Co., Mich. in 1834 and purchased land then returned to New Hampshire. In 1836, he again went to Medina Twp., but returned to New Hampshire in 1837, and married there on 29 Aug. to CAROLINE (MORRISON) born 20 June 1813, Peterboro. They returned to Medina Twp., where she died on 17 Mar. 1849, leaving children: 1. WILLIAM C. b. ca. 1842 (served Co. K, 1st Mich. Inf., and Capt. in Co. I, 18th Mich. Inf., Civil War; he d. in Mar. 1866, Indian Territory); 2. NATHANIEL M. (d. age 7); 3. CHANNING b. ca. 1844, not mentioned in sketch, but listed in household in 1850 census); 4. EMILY C. b. ca. 1846 (m. George F. Phelps, Ionia, Mich. In 1850, George W.^{5} went to California, but returned to Medina Twp., NY to HARRIET P. (BIGELOW), daughter of Maj. Daniel P. (also see). Children: 5. HATTIE L. Harriet P. died 15 Apr. 1880, Medina Twp. George W.^{5} married on 6 Apr. 1882, Clarkson, Monroe co., NY to Mrs. ALTHEA (BLODGETT) BORDWELL, daughter of John, and widow of Joseph (see both). Ref: P&BA-Len pg. 1000-2. Note: In the 1850 census, George W. had also in his household John G. Smith, also see, and wife, Sarah M. who was age 34, b. NH, probably sister of George W.?

MOORE, H. E. married George I. Harder (also see) of Fairville, Wayne Co., NY.

MOORE, HENRY born Long Island, NY, and wife, RACHEL (STEWART), born NY, had known daughter, SAMANTHA b. 1 Dec. 1812, Cayuga Co., NY (m. William Queal, also see). Ref: P&BA-Len pg. 721-2.

MOORE, HENRY, age 88, born England, was listed in the 1850 census of Madison Twp., Lenawee Co., Mich. in the household of William and Mary Flowers, also b. England.

MOORE, HENRY, age 6, born Penn., was listed in the 1850 census of Blissfield Twp., Lenawee Co., Mich. in the household of Calvin Hagaman.

MOORE, JOHN^1 was born in Argyleshire, Scotland in 1648, and was killed at the Massacre of Glencoe on 13 Mar. 1692. He left a son, JOHN^2, born 13 Mar. 1692 in Glencoe, who went as an infant to Londonderry, Ireland. He crossed the Atlantic in 1720 and settled in Londonderry, New Hampshire, and married there to JANET (COCHRAN). They had 4 sons and 3 daughters, and only one mentioned was WILLIAM^3 (following). Ref: P&BA-Len pg. 1000-2.

MOORE, JOHN was born in Argyleshire, Scotland, and married there. They lived for a time in Southampton, England where one child died. In 1833, the family moved to Middlesex Co., Ontario, Canada. Known children: WILLIAM; NEIL; DOUGLAD (preceding); JOHN; JANET. Ref: P&BA-Len pg. 705-6.

MOORE, JOHN born ca. 1839, and wife, ANN, born ca. 1814, both in England, were listed in the 1840 census index of Franklin Twp., Lenawee Co., Mich. with ROBERT, age 12, b. NY; and MARY, age 11,; HESTER, age 9; SARAH, age 7; WILLIAM, age 5; EMELINE, age 3; MARTHA, age 1, all b. Mich., in their household. Note ROBERT, following.

MOORE, LEVI was listed in the 1840 census index of Palmyra Twp., Lenawee Co., Mich.

MOORE, LUCY (See Nicholas Johnson)

MOORE, LYDIA (See Jonathan Austin)

MOORE, MARY (See Aaron Farst)

MOORE, NATHANIEL^4, son of WILLIAM^3 (following), born 28 Mar. 1770, Peterboro, NH, married there on 14 Mar. 1800 to SARAH (FERGUSON), daughter of Henry (also see). She died 10 Apr. 1850, age 74; and he died 27 Oct. 1853, age 83. Children: 1. HENRY; 2. WILLIAM; 3. JOHN; 4. NATHANIEL (New Hampshire); 5. JAMES; 6. JANE; 7. SARAH (may be she, Sarah M., age 34, b. NH, wife of John G. Smith, in household of GEORGE W.^{5} in the 1850 census of Medina Twp., Lenawee Co., Mich.); 8. GEORGE W.^{5} (preceding); 9. MARTHA F.; 10. THOMAS F.^{5} (following). Ref: P&BA-Len pg. 915-6; 1000-2.

MOORE, RICHARD (See Peter Onsted)

MOORE, RICHARD C. born ca. 1820, and wife, HELEN, born ca. 1830, both in NY, were listed in the 1850 census of Tecumseh Twp., Lenawee Co., Mich. with JAMES, age 3, b. Mich., in their household.

MOORE, ROBERT born ca. 1810, England, and wife, ELIZABETH, born ca. 1813, Penn., were listed in the 1840 census index of Cambridge Twp., Lenawee Co., Mich.; and in the 1850 census with JOHN, age 15, b. Ohio; and HENRY, age 13; MARY, age 11; AS--(male), age 7; KESIAH, age 5; and another, HENRY, age 1, all b. Mich., in their household. Note JOHN born England, preceding.

MOORE, THOMAS S.^{5}, son of NATHANIEL^4 (preceding), born 2 Oct. 1819, Peterboro, NH, went at age 18 to Erie Co., NY. In 1839, he went to Lenawee Co., Mich. but returned to New York. He married on 28 May 1840 in Byron, Genesee Co., NY to RACHEL D. (TODD), daughter of James B. (also see). They moved about 1850 to Medina Twp., Lenawee Co., Mich., and later to Madison Twp. Of their 6 children, 3 died infancy, names not stated. Children: 1. JAMES M. b. ca. 1845 (m. Delophene Smith, dau. of Asa, also see; moved to Jackson, Mich.); 2. HATTIE N. (m. Warren N. Beal, Madison Twp.); 3. SAMUEL A. (d. 14 Jan. 1878, age 18.) Ref: P&BA-Len pg. 857-8 & 915-6.

MOORE, WILLIAM married in 1830 in Broome Co., NY to Mrs. MARIA (MERCHANT) BIRD, widow of Benjamin (also see). In 1831, they moved to Adrian Twp., Lenawee Co., Mich. In the 1850 census of Adrian Twp, he was age 52, and Maria was age 52, both b. NY, and in their household was WILLIAM R., age 17, b. Mich.; AVIRAL? I., age 9, b. Mich., and Harriet Bird, age 33, b. NY, and Hepzibah Mason, age 77, born Conn. Maria died 10 Mar. 1874; and in 1881 he moved into Adrian where he was still living in 1888, age about 91. Ref: P&BA-Len pg. 1172-3.

MOORE, WILLIAM C. born 4 Mar. 1810, Bradford, VT, married LUCINDA W. (WELLS) born 30 Apr. 1814, Marshfield, Washington Co. (NY?). About 1844, they moved to Washtenaw Co., Mich., and in 1852 to Union, Branch Co., Mich. He died in Union on 12 Apr. 1873. Known children: WILLIAM H. (Served 9th Mich. Cav., Civil War); DAVID W. (served 4th Battery, Civil War); HARRIET M. b. 11 Sept. 1835, Bradford, VT (m. Cornelius Bancroft, also see). Ref: P&BA-Len pg. 738-9.

MOORE, WILLIAM G. born ca. 1811, and wife, LUCY, born ca. 1813, both in NY, were listed in the 1850 census of Dover Twp., Lenawee Co., Mich. with AMELIA, age 5; ADELIA, age 4, both b. NY, in their household.

MOOREHOUSE also see MOREHOUSE
MOOREHOUSE, BETSEY (See Ira Seymour)
MOOREHOUSE, MARY J. (See James Patrick)

MORAN, MICHAEL born 1813, Staplestown Parish, Co. Kildare, Ireland, came to the US at age 19. He located first in NY, but then traveled extensively, and married in Toledo, Ohio to LUCY (ANDREWS). They settled near Hudson, Lenawee Co., Mich. He died 9 May 1881, age 68; and she was still residing there in 1888, age 60. Children: 1. WILLIAM C. (following); and the following who all resided in Warsaw, Ind.: 2. MATTHEW C.; 3. JULIA E. (m. B. F. Richardson); 4. MARY F.; 5. ADDISON B. Ref: P&BA-Len pg. 1082-4.

MORAN, WILLIAM C., son of MICHAEL (preceding), born 23 Nov. 1848, near Hudson, Lenawee Co., Mich., married on 18 Mar. 1874 to RACHEL (McCARTY), daughter of H. Nelson (also see). Children: 1. GERTIE C.; 2. BERTHA E.; 3. CHARLES FREDERICK; 4. JEROME N.; 5. WILLIAM M.; 6. BENJAMIN R. Ref: P&BA-Len pg. 1082-4 & portrait.

MOREHOUSE also see MOOREHOUSE
MOREHOUSE, AARON and wife, LUCINDA (THUMB), moved from Orleans Co., NY to Calhoun Co., Mich. in 1869. She died there at age 47, and he came to Lenawee Co., Mich. where he died at age 71. Children: 1. CHARLES W. (d. Civil War); 2. ALICE (m. J. W. Page, also see); 3. HELEN b. 6 July 1835 (m. Walden Wing, also see). Ref: P&BA-Len pg. 946-7.

MORELAND, DAVID, age 11, born Penn., was listed in the 1850 census of Woodstock Twp., Lenawee Co., Mich. in the household of Hiram & Lydia Smith.

MORELAND, JAMES^1 of Ireland married ANN (SCOTT) and had known son, JAMES^2 who married first in 1788 to MARGARET (CURRY). Margaret died after the birth of 6 children, names not stated, and he married again in 1804 to FANNIE (MAGEE), daughter of John (also see). James^2 died in 1828, and she died in 1842. There were 2 daughters and 4 sons, and only name mentioned was JAMES^3 (following). Ref: P&BA-Len pg. 363-4. Note JOHN & WILLIAM, following, possibly additional sons of JAMES^2.

MORELAND, JAMES^3, son of JAMES^2 (See JAMES^1, preceding), born 14 Feb. 1816, Co. Down, Ireland, came to the US in 1841, and in 1843 settled in Hillsdale Co., Mich. In 1844, he removed to Adrian, Lenawee Co., Mich. He married 30 May 1849 to ANN (STEPHENSON), daughter of William (also see). In the 1850 census, they were listed in Madison Twp., Lenawee Co., Mich. She died in 1871 in Hudson, Mich. Children: 1. FANNIE JANE b. 21 Apr. 1850, Adrian; 2. ROBERT S. b. 8 Feb. 1854; 3. JAMES H. b. 19 Feb. 1857; 4. WILLIAM T. b. 7 July 1864 (lived Hudson). James^3 married again to Mrs. ELIZABETH (STRONG) YUND, daughter of Robert (also see), of Moscow, Hillsdale Co. Ref: P&BA-Len pg. 363-4.

MORELAND, JOHN born ca. 1816, Ireland, and wife, SARAH, born ca. 1824, England, were listed in the 1850 census of Madison Twp., Lenawee Co., Mich. with SAMUEL, age 2, b. Mich., in their household. Note JAMES^1, preceding.

MORELAND, WILLIAM was listed in the 1840 census index of Moscow, Hillsdale Co., Mich. Note that JAMES^3, preceding, had connections to Moscow, Hillsdale Co.

MORFELT, ELIZABETH (See Sylvester Kemp)

MORGAN, A. E. (See Aaron Palmer)
MORGAN, CHARLES born ca. 1790, Penn., came from Genesee Co., NY, and it may be he listed in the 1840 census index of Pittsfield Twp., Washtenaw Co., Mich. He moved to Macon Twp., Lenawee Co., Mich. by the 1850 census. Known childen: SAMUEL (following, adjacent in 1850 census); CALISTA b. Genesee Co., NY (m. Henry P. Downs, also see, Macon Twp.); ELIZABETH b. ca. 1825, NY (m. John Camburn, also see). In Charles' household in 1850 were MARGARET, age 18; CHARLES, age 17, both b. NY. Charles had married again before 1850 to Mrs. SOPHRONIA (WAKELY) WARD, born ca. 1798, VT. Also in their household in 1850 were Mary A. Ward, age 13; Martha A. Ward, age 12, both b. Mich., probably children of Sophronia by her second husband, Jacob Ward (her first husband ws Reuben Downs, also see).

MORGAN, H. C. of Palmyra, Wayne Co., NY (See William Schermerhorn).

MORGAN, JOHN K. born ca. 1809, and wife, MARY, born ca. 1822, probably in NY (not legible), were listed in the 1850 census of Seneca Twp., Lenawee Co., Mich. with

Pioneer Families of Southeastern Michigan

(sister?) CORNELIA, age 21, b. NY; and MARCUS, age 9, b. NY; and MILLY, age 5; ERASMUS, age 1, both b. Mich.; Sarah Powell, age 9; Henry Powell, age 7; Laura Powell, age 6, all b. Mich., in their household.

MORGAN, SAMUEL, probably son of CHARLES (preceding), born ca. 1819, NY, and wife, SARAH, born ca. 1819, NJ, were listed in the 1850 census of Macon Twp., Lenawee Co., Mich. with EMMETT, age 6; SPENCER, age 4; WILLIAM, age 2, all b. Mich., in their household (next door to CHARLES).

MORIARTY, JAMES and wife, MARY (CONNOR), both born Co. Kerry, Ireland, remained there where he died in 1855, and she died in 1864, age 60. There were 4 sons, one of whom was deceased, and 3 went to Michigan. Only known were MICHAEL; & JOHN (following). Ref: P&BA-Len pg. 1027-8.

MORIARTY, JOHN, son of JAMES (preceding), born 24 June 1830, Trallee, Co. Kerry, Ireland, sailed on 9 June 1851 to New York. He went first to Cayuga Co., NY to join brother, MICHAEL. He married there on 1 Nov. 1854 to CATHERINE (STACK), daughter of Maurice (also see). They moved to Medina Twp., Lenawee Co., Mich. Children: 1. JAMES; 2. MARY (deceased before 1888); 3. MICHAEL; 4. FLORENCE (lived Ypsilanti, Mich.); 5. THOMAS (1st, d. child); 6. ELLEN; 7. THOMAS, 2D (may be he who m. Anna Breen, sketch said "John," but there is no son, John); 8. CATHERINE (1st, d. child); 9. CATHERINE 2d. Ref: P&BA-Len pg. 1027-8.

MORLEY, ROBERT born in England, married SERENA (SPARROWS), and she died in Chicago, Ill. He afterwards came to Fairfield Twp., Lenawee Co., Mich. in 1881, where died that year. Known daughter, CLARA E. b. 10 Mar. 1861, Chicago (m. Leo H. McConnell, also see). Ref: P&BA-Len pg. 958-9.

MORRELL, ASA, son of ENOCH (following), born in Maine, married LARANSA (HULL) born in NY. They settled in Verona, Oneida Co., NY, where he died in 1874, age 72; and she died in 1872, age 70. Known son, FREDERICK C. (following). Ref: P&BA-Len pg. 497-8.

MORRELL, ENOCH and wife, SALLIE (HUBBARD), were both born in Maine. They removed to Verona, Oneida Co., NY where they remained, and he died at age 56. Known son, ASA (preceding). Ref: P&BA-Len pg. 497-8.

MORRELL, FREDERICK C., son of ASA (preceding), born 27 June 1836, Verona, Oneida Co., NY, married on 23 Mar. 1862 to HENRIETTA A. (LAWTON), daughter of Joshua W. (also see). In 1870, they settled in Macon Twp., Lenawee Co., Mich. Children: 1. LILLY L.; 2. MINNIE L.; 3. EDITH M. (m. William Kniffen; d. 4 mos after marriage). Ref: P&BA-Len pg. 497-8.

MORRIS, ADELILA (See Jefferson Dunn; & Nelson Smith)

MORRIS, CAROLINE was listed head of household in the 1840 census index of Adrian Twp., Lenawee Co., Mich.

MORRIS, CHARLES G. born ca. 1814, Ohio, and wife, REBECCA, born ca. 1820, Penn., were listed in the 1850 census of Woodstock Twp., Lenawee Co., Mich. with FRANKLIN, age 8, b. Mich., in their household.

MORRIS, CORNELIUS V. H. Dr. born ca. 1810, and wife, CAROLINE, born ca. 1820, both in NY, were listed in the 1850 census of Ridgeway Twp., Lenawee Co., Mich. with ELIZA, age 8/12, b. Mich., in their household.

MORRIS, JAMES W. born ca. 1816, and wife, DELIGHT, born ca. 1817, both in NY, were probably they listed as "J. W." in the 1840 census index of Seneca Twp., Lenawee Co., Mich.; and in the 1850 census with JAMES O., age 14; EMERY W., age 12; SILAS W., age 10 (following); SABRA H., age 4, all b. Mich., in their household. Note: In the 1840 census index were adjacent to ROBERT, following.

MORRIS, MARIA (See Joshua Turner)

MORRIS, PATRICK born ca. 1827, Ireland, was listed in the 1850 census of Tecumseh Twp., Lenawee Co., Mich. with MARY, age 28; ANN, age 21; WILLIAM, age 12, all b. Ireland, in the household of John Kelley.

MORRIS, ROBERT born ca. 1807, and wife, CAROLINE, born ca. 1812, both in NY, were listed in the 1840 census index of Seneca Twp., Lenawee Co., Mich.; and in the 1850 census with EZRA C., age 17; GEORGE A., age 15; DAVID L., age 13; MYRON W., age 10; AMANDA, age 9; LAURA?, age 2, all b. Mich., in their household. Note JAMES W., preceding.

MORRIS, SILAS W., son of JAMES W. (preceding), born ca. 1840, Seneca Twp., Lenawee Co., Mich., married BETSEY (HAYWARD), daughter of Micajah (also see) and probably settled in Seneca Twp. Children: 1. ROSWELL JAMES; 2. HELEN; 3. ALTA D.; 4. WILFORD C.; 5. CLIFFORD M.; 6. CLARA; 7. ADA P.

MORRIS, THOMAS M. born ca. 1785, Penn., was probably he listed in the 1840 census index of Rollin Twp., Lenawee Co., Mich.; and in the 1850 census in the household of Beal Sloan (also see) and wife, MARY T., age 35, b. Penn., obviously daughter of Thomas M.

MORRIS, URIAH and wife, SARAH, of Vermont, were parents of known daughter, SARAH b. 1778, VT (m. John Stowers, also see). Ref: P&BA-Len pg. 384-5.

MORRISON, CAROLINE born 20 June 1813, Peterboro, NH, married George W. Moore (also see). Ref: P&BA-Len pg. 1000-2.

MORRISON, CLARENCE (See George Price)

MORRISON, DANIEL was listed in the 1840 census index of Hudson Twp., Lenawee Co., Mich.

MORRISON, DAVID, son of JOHN (probably from Columbia Co., NY who was a pioneer to Princeton, Schenectady Co.), born Schenectady Co., NY, married there to CYNTHIA (DODGE). Known daughter, MARIA b. 30 Aug. 1816, Duanesburg, NY (m. Jonathan Hare, also see). Ref: P&BA-Len pg. 729-30.

MORRISON, ORRIN, son of DAVID (who died in Mass.), was a native of Colerain, Franklin Co., Mass., but went as a child to Oneida Co., NY. (Note: There was a Roderick Morrison in Oneida Co. in the 1800 census index). Orrin married there to LAURA (BARRETT), daughter of Gaius (also see), born Conn. He died 25 Mar. 1862, and she died 1863, Oneida Co. Known daughters: H. LOUISA b. 23 June 1830, Vernon, Oneida Co., NY (m. Lewis Westfall, also see); EMILY b. 6 Aug. 1844, Oneida Co. (m. S. J. Bartholomew, also see). Ref: P&BA-Len pg. 286-7.

MORRISON, OWEN (called "Orrin" in another sketch, see preceding).

MORRISON, SARAH (See Charles L. Palmer)

MORRISROE, THOMAS M. born ca. 1810, and wife, CATHARINE, born ca. 1820, both in Ireland, were listed in the 1850 census of Tecumseh Twp., Lenawee Co., Mich. with BRIDGET, age 10; MARY, age 8, both b. Ireland; and MICHAEL, age 4, b. Canada; and ANNA, age 1, b. Mich., in their household. Note: The preceding was written as "MORRIS" in the census, however, based on the following, believe they are "Morrisroe." MORRISROE, BRIDGET came with parents (names not stated) from Ireland to Canada; and later to Palmyra Twp., Lenawee Co., Mich. and then Clinton Twp. He died in 1861, and the mother was living in 1888, age 71, in Clinton Twp. Bridget married Martin Kuesch² (also see). Ref: P&BA-Len pg. 651-2. Note: In 1850, Clinton Twp. was apparently included in the census of Tecumseh Twp., as there was none for Clinton Twp.

MORSE, BENJAMIN was among the early settlers of to Kendall, Orleans Co., NY in 1815; and BARTLETT was the first child born there in 1816. Ref: Gazeteer of NY State, by French.

MORSE, CHARLES C., son of LEMUEL (following), born ca. 1815, NY, moved with parents when quite young to Bellevue, Ohio. He married there to SARAH C. (FOLLETT), daughter of James D. (also see). In 1844, they removed to Medina Twp., Lenawee Co., Mich. Children's ages from 1850 census of Medina Twp. 1. ALICE C., age 10, b. Ohio (m. W. D. Stalker, also see); 2. ADELAIDE B., age 8, b. Ohio (m. J. M. Consaul, also see); 3. LEMUEL JAMES, age 5, b. Mich.; 4. NERINA E., age 3 (m. ? Goldsborough, Hudson Twp, also see.); 5. CHARLES F. b, 16 Dec. 1848 (m. Lydia Ayers, dau. of John, also see); 6. CARROLL C.; 7. HETTIE S. Note: WALTER W. listed next door in 1850 census, possibly brother of CHARLES C. John Christopher had come to Medina Twp. from Ohio with Charles C. and was listed in the household in 1850. Charles C. died 22 Aug. 1886, age 71; and Sarah C. died 26 Dec. 1887, age 77. Ref: P&BA-Len pg. 898-9 & 1006.

MORSE, CHARLES F. born ca. 1805, and wife, HARRIET, born ca. 1816, both in NY, were listed in the 1850 census of Fairfield Twp., Lenawee Co., Mich. with Ann Ellison, age 14, b. Mich., in their household. Next door to LORENZO, following.

MORSE, ENOS was among the early settlers mostly from Mass. who settled ca. 1807 in Riga, Monroe Co., NY. Ref: Gazeteer of NY State, by French. Note LYDIA, following.

MORSE, FIELDING, age 30, and JACKSON, age 18, both b. NY, were listed in the 1850 census of Fairfield Twp., Lenawee Co., Mich. Note PHILIP, following.

MORSE, HIRAM born ca. 1799, and wife, JANE, born ca. 1797, both in NY, were listed in the 1850 census of Fairfield Twp., Lenawee Co., Mich. with JAMES, age 17; STEPHEN, age 14, both b. NY, in their household. Note PHILIP, following.

MORSE, IRAD? born ca. 1801, NY, and wife, FLORILLA, born ca. 1806, VT, were listed in the 1850 census of Dover Twp., Lenawee Co., Mich. with Harriet Martin, age 7, b. NY, in their household.

MORSE, JAMES, born ca. 1838, born Mich., was listed in the 1850 census of Adrian Twp., Lenawee Co., Mich. in "jail." (Note: Only ROBERT & SYDNEY were listed in Lenawee Co. in 1840; note this name in household of Robert).

MORSE, LEMUEL born 25 Feb. 1779, Mass., was an early settler to Ontario Co., NY. He moved his family from there to near Bellevue, Huron Co., Ohio. Known son, CHARLES C. (preceding); and probably WALTER W. (following). Ref: P&BA-Len pg. 898-9.

MORSE, LEMUEL JAMES, son of CHARLES C. (preceding), born 30 July 1844, Medina Twp., Lenawee Co., Mich., married in May 1875 to SARAH (COGSWELL), daughter of Henry (also see) and settled in Medina Twp. Known daughter, JENNIE H. Ref: P&BA-Len pg. 898-9.

MORSE, LOGRITTA, age 17, born NY, was listed in the 1850 census of Adrian Twp., Lenawee Co., Mich. in a Dodge household, possibly same listed in household of PHILIP, following.

MORSE, LORENZO born ca. 1816, and wife, SYLVIA, born ca. 1828, both in NY, were listed in the 1850 census of Fairfield Twp., Lenawee Co., Mich. with ALONZO, age 7/12, b. Mich., in their household (next door to CHARLES F., preceding).

MORSE, LYDIA was a native of Mass. and daughter of one of the first settlers of Monroe Co., NY (note ENOS, preceding). She married first before 1822 to John Canniff (also see) in Orleans Co., NY. After his death, she lived in Orleans & Monroe Co., NY with her sisters until 1839; then came to Pittsford, Monroe Co., Mich. to live with son, Stephen Canniff, until she married again to John Bird (also see). She afterwards lived in Clayton, Mich. MORSE, NEHEMIAH born ca. 1801, and wife, LYDIA, born ca. 1816, both in NY, were listed in the 1850 census of Tecumseh Twp., Lenawee Co., Mich. with ELIZABETH, age 14; JEROME, age 12, both b. NY; and ALMIRA, age 10; JOSEPHINE, age 4, both b. Mich.; and Reuben Bennett, age 69, b. NY, in their household.

MORSE, PHILIP born ca. 1800, and wife, ABIGAIL, born ca. 1806, both in NY, were listed in the 1850 census of Fairfield Twp., Lenawee Co., Mich. with JEFFERSON, age 20; LOGRATA?, age 17, both b. NY; and SARAH M., age 14; LAFAYETTE, age 8, both b. Mich., in their household. Note HIRAM, preceding.

MORSE, ROBERT B. born ca. 1799, Penn., and wife, DIDAMA, born ca. 1806, VT, were listed in the 1840 census index of Adrian Twp., Lenawee Co., Mich.; and in the 1850 census of Madison Twp. with JAMES, age 12, b. NY; and JULIAETTE, age 10; MARGARET J., age 8; WILLIAM M., age 4, all b. Mich., in their household. In 1840, they were listed adjacent to SYDNEY.

MORSE, SARAH (See John Ladd)

MORSE, SYDNEY was listed in the 1840 census index of Adrian Twp., Lenawee Co., Mich. adjacent to ROBERT, preceding.

MORSE, WALTER W., probably son of LEMUEL (preceding), born ca. 1809, NY, was listed in the 1850 census of Medina Twp., Lenawee Co., Mich. with LUCY E., age 17; EDWIN R., age 14; ELLEN, age 6, all b. Ohio, in his household. They were listed next door to CHARLES C., preceding.

MORSE, WILLIAM B., age 23, b. NY, was listed in the 1850 census of Adrian Twp., Lenawee Co., Mich.

MORSMAN, HERMAN and wife, MARY A. (ZIBBLE), came to Tecumseh Twp., Lenawee Co., Mich. (after 1850?),

Pioneer Families of Southeastern Michigan

and shortly afterwards to Ridgeway Twp. They moved last to Jonesville, Hillsdale Co., Mich. where they were living in 1888, both age 82. Their known daughter, #2. JULIA b. 27 Apr. 1831 (m/1 Richard DeLapp; m/2 Sylvester Kemp, see both). Ref: P&BA-Len pg. 265-6.

MORTON, ASA was was listed in the 1840 census index of Franklin Twp., Lenawee Co., Mich. adjacent to ALEXANDER B., following.

MORTON, ALEXANDER B. was listed in the 1840 census index of Franklin Twp., Lenawee Co., Mich. adjacent to ASA, preceding.

MORTON, CHARLES A. born ca. 1822, Penn., and wife, SOPHIA, born ca. 1822, NH, were listed in the 1850 census of Cambridge Twp., Lenawee Co., Mich. with ARTHUR, age 3, b. Mich., in their household.

MORTON, JOHN[1] born 1777, VT, married EUNICE (ALDRICH) born ca. 1780, NY (sketch called them "natives of Mass.," but census had Eunice b. NY). Eunice's parents had moved from Canada to NY where they remained. John & Eunice moved in 1802 to Oswego Co., NY; and in 1832 to Cambridge Twp., Lenawee Co., Mich. He died at age 67; and she died at age 79. She was head of household in the 1850 census of Cambridge Twp., with Lemuel Smith, age 33, and wife, Philena, age 33 (daughter?), both b. NY, and Charles Smith, age 9; Henrietta Smith, age 4, both b. Mich., in her household. There were 7 children, and only names stated were: JOHN[2]; & the youngest, MILES P. (both following). Ref: P&BA-Len pg. 231-2.

MORTON, JOHN[2], son of JOHN[1] (preceding), born 29 Nov. 1802, Oswego Co., NY, married on 28 July 1824 to POLLY C. (DAVIS), daughter of Asa (also see). He operated the first sawmill in Adrian Twp.; and afterwards purchased all of his father's homestead in Cambridge Twp. They had no children except adopted daughter, Mrs. HESTER Fitch. In the 1850 census of Cambridge Twp., they listed GEORGE, age 8, b. Mich., relationship not known, in their household. Ref: P&BA-Len pg. 231-2.

MORTON, LYDIA born Co. Antrim, Ireland (See William Stephenson).

MORTON, MILES P., son of JOHN[1] (preceding), born ca. 1821, NY, married HANNAH born ca. 1827, NY, and they were listed next door to Eunice in the 1850 census of Cambridge Twp., Lenawee Co., Mich. Hannah died in 1868; and he married again on 23 Oct. 1870 to LOIS (VAN VLEET), daughter of Peter P. (also see). Miles P. died 24 Jan. 1884, Cambridge Twp. No children were listed. Ref: P&BA-Len pg. 580-1.

MOSHER also see MOSHIER & MOSIER
MOSHER, ABIGAIL (See Simeon Smith)
MOSHER, CALVIN was listed in the 1840 census index of Fairfield Twp., Lenawee Co., Mich. adjacent to GEORGE.
MOSHER, ESTHER (See Charles Haviland)
MOSHER, FANNY (See Daniel Derbyshire)
MOSHER, G. G. Dr. (See Frederick G. Beagle; and also note GEORGE in household of SHUBAL, following).
MOSHER, GEORGE was listed in the 1840 census index of Fairfield Twp., Lenawee Co., Mich. adjacent to CALVIN.

MOSHER, JOHN born ca. 1800, NJ, and wife, SARAH, born ca. 1790, NY, were listed in the 1850 census of Blissfield Twp., Lenawee Co., Mich. with EDWARD, age 30, b. NJ, in their household.

MOSHER, MARCHUS was listed in the 1840 census index of Rome Twp., Lenawee Co., Mich.

MOSHER, MERCY (See Richard Woolsey)

MOSHER, SHUBAL born ca. 1800, and wife, HANNAH, born ca. 1805, both in NY, were listed in the 1840 census index of Tecumseh Twp., Lenawee Co., Mich.; and in the 1850 census with ISAAC, age 17, b. NY; and GEORGE, age 12, b. Mich., in their household.

MOSHER, THOMAS born ca. 1807, and wife, LUCY, born ca. 1810, both in NY, were listed in the 1840 census index of Madison Twp., Lenawee Co., Mich.; and in the 1850 census with ISAAC, age 14; SARAH, age 10, both b. Mich., in their household.

MOSHIER also see MOSHER
MOSHIER, JABEZ? born ca. 1818, and wife, CORDELIA, born ca. 1824, both in NY, were listed in the 1850 census of Woodstock Twp., Lenawee Co., Mich. with CHARLES, age 2, b. Mich.; and (brothers?) JOHN, age 23; LOUIS, age 21, both b. NY; Elizabeth Nichols, age 19, b. NY, in their household.
MOSHIER, MARY (See Alonzo James)
MOSHIER, THOMAS H. born ca. 1816, and wife, HARRIET, born ca. 1818, both in NY, were listed in the 1850 census of Cambridge Twp., Lenawee Co., Mich. with RACHEL, age 7, b. Mich., and Franklin Crane, age 24, b. NY, in their household.

MOSIER also see MOSHER & MOSHIER
MOSIER, PHILIP born ca. 1819, NY, and wife, MARY J., born ca. 1822, Canada, were listed in the 1850 census of Rome Twp., Lenawee Co., Mich. with GEORGE T., age 4; MARY A., age 9/12, both b. Mich., in their household.
MOSIER, STEPHEN born ca. 1825, and ELIZABETH, born ca. 1828,
both in NY, were listed in the 1850 census of Adrian Twp., Lenawee Co., Mich. in the household of Lewis Davis.

MOTT, ADAM, son of THOMAS (following), born near New Bedford, Mass., moved with parents to Columbia Co., NY. He married there to BETSEY (PATRICK). In 1829, they moved to Canton, Wayne Co., Mich. where she died on 4 Nov. 1860. There were 4 children, and only name stated was MARY E. (m. Charles M. Lewis, also see). Adam married again to ISABELLA (ROBINSON) FRANCISCA and had one child, name not stated. He died Mar. 1886. Ref: P&BA-Len pg. 1080-1.

MOTT, BERNARD H. born ca. 1820, and wife, JULIA, born ca. 1822, both in NY, were listed in the 1850 census of Tecumseh Twp., Lenawee Co., Mich. with EUGENE, age 2, b. NY, all in the household of William C. Weir.

MOTT, THOMAS, a Quaker, moved from New Bedford, Mass. to Columbia Co., NY. Known son, ADAM (preceding). Ref: P&BA-Len pg. 1080-1.

MOULTON, ARBA N. Dr., son of NATHANIEL (following), born 2 July 1793, Greene Co., NY, married there 16 Feb. 1816, to PATIENCE (VIRGIL) born 8 Jan. 1800, Greene Co. Apparently moved to Union, Broome Co., NY by 1820. About 1835, they moved to Cambridge Twp.,

Lenawee Co., Mich. where they were listed in the 1840 census index. They apparently moved away prior to 1850 census. He died in South Haven, Mich. on 8 June 1869. Known daughter, ELVIRA b. 1 Oct. 1820, Union, NY (m. Capt. Charles H. Dewey, also see, 30 Mar. 1843, Cambridge Twp.). Ref: P&BA-Len pg. 1101-2.

MOULTON, GEORGE born ca. 1810, NY, and wife, SARAH, born ca. 1805, Mass., were listed in the 1850 census of Adrian Twp., Lenawee Co., Mich. with PHILO, age 15; LUCY A., age 13; GEORGE D., age 9; SARAH J., age 7; EMELINE E., age 4, all b. NY, in their household.

MOULTON, NATHANIEL born in Mass., married ELIZABETH (GRANT) born Scotland and resided in Greene Co., NY in 1793. They had known son, Dr. ARBA N. (preceding).

MOYER, HANNAH (See Don A. Read)

MUCK, LENA (See William Lagore)

MUDGET also see MUDGETT
MUDGET, DAVID born ca. 1796, NH, and wife, CLARISSA, born ca. 1797, VT, were listed in the 1840 census index of Tecumseh Twp., Lenawee Co., Mich. (adjacent to TRUMAN); and in the 1850 census with STEPHEN, age 25, b. NY, in their household.

MUDGET, TRUMAN born ca. 1794, VT, and wife, CHARLOTTE, born ca. 1793, Canada, were listed in the 1840 census index of Tecumseh Twp., Lenawee Co., Mich. (adjacent to DAVID); and in the 1850 census with ROXA, age 25; LEWIS, age 24; MARY, age 20, all b. NY; and SCHUYLER, age 17, b. Mich., in their household.

MUDGETT also see MUDGET
MUDGETT, EDWIN S. (See Frederick W. Wickwire)
MUDGETT, LEVI was listed in the 1840 census index of Franklin Twp., Lenawee Co., Mich.; and is not listed in 1850. Note SARAH, following.

MUDGETT, SARAH born ca. 1814, NY, was listed in the 1850 census of Franklin Twp., Lenawee Co., Mich. with EMILY, age 8; CHARLES, age 6; MARY, age 4, all b. Ill., all in the household of Richard Edwards. PHILURA, age 13, b. Mich., in another household may relate to this family. Note LEVI, preceding.

MUIR, EDWARD F. born 30 Mar. 1828, Jefferson Co., NY, is probably he listed as FRANKLIN, age 22, b. NY, in the 1850 census of Tecumseh Twp., Lenawee Co., Mich. He married in Clinton to LUCY (COREY), daughter of Levi (also see). Five children, of whom 2 died young, names not stated: 1. ARTHUR W. (m. Etta Stanfield; children, Frank & Blanche); 2. CARRIE (m. C. W. Johnson, lived Detroit); 3. MINA L. Ref: P&BA-Len pg. 368-9.

MULL, HENRY (See Hiram S. Whiting)

MULLER, AMELIA (See Nicholas Riehl)

MULLINEX, SAMUEL & wife, SUSAN, of Erie Co., Ohio had known daughter, SARAH J. (m. Dennis O. Grimes, also see). Ref: P&BA-Len pg. 524-5.

MULZER, MICHAEL, born 11 June 1826, was the youngest son of the five children of JOHN G. & ELIZABETH (RUPPRECHT) of Bavaria, Germany. He came to the US in 1848 and settled in Adrian, Lenawee Co., Mich. He married in 1849 to MARGARET (FINZEL), also born Bavaria, who had come as child with her parents to the US. Children: 1. M. GEORGE (to Seattle, WA); 2. JOHN G.; 3. ROSA; 4. CAROLINE (d. age 23); 5. CHRISTINE A. (m. D. Campse); 6. MARY; 7. F. CONRAD; 8. FREDERICK; 9. MAGGIE; 10. LOUISA; 11. WILLIAM (d. 1879). Ref: P&BA-Len pg. 499-500.

MUNGER, BENJAMIN born ca. 1810, NY, and wife, SARAH A., born ca. 1811, Mass., were listed in the 1850 census of Rome Twp., Lenawee Co., Mich. with MARY, age 10; ELON G., age 9, both b. Ohio, in their household. Note EPHRAIM, following.

MUNGER, ELIAB, son of EPHRAIM (following), born 12 Dec. 1784, Conn., married there on 1 Nov. 1804 to MILLICENT (KETCHUM), born 13 Jan. 1786. They moved ca. 1820 to Huron Twp., Erie Co., Ohio. He died there at age 52, and she died at age 54. Ten children, only name mentioned was JAMES F. (following). Ref: P&BA-Len pg. 589-90.

MUNGER, EPHRAIM was a native of Conn., where his first wife (name not stated) died. He married again, and she died in Erie Co., Ohio at age 65. Ten children, only name mentioned was ELIAB (preceding). Ref: P&BA-Len pg. 589-90.

MUNGER, JAMES F., son of ELIAB (preceding), born 7 Nov. 1820, Erie Co., Ohio married there to CAROLINE (SWEET), daughter of William (also see). They lived in Milan Twp., Erie Co., Ohio until 1882, then moved to Rome Twp., Lenawee Co., Mich. Children: 1. FRANK S. b. 15 Dec. 1857 (lived Huron Twp., Erie Co., O.); 2. WILLIAM b. 10 Aug. 1860 (d. Sept. 3, 1860); 3. JABIN R. b. 17 Apr. 1862 (lived Rome Twp.); 4. CLARK W. b. 16 Feb. 1865. Ref: P&BA-Len pg. 589-90.

MUNGER, JOHN born 26 May 1796, Saratoga Co., NY, married there to MARIA (VELIE) born 25 May 1804, Stillwater, NY. They later moved to Erie Co., Penn., and then in 1835 to Pittsford Twp., Hillsdale Co., Mich. In 1855, they removed to Amboy Twp., Lee Co., Ill. where he died in 1857, and she died in 1875. Known son, JOHN VELIE (following). Ref: P&BA-Len pg. 816-7.

MUNGER, JOHN VELIE, son of JOHN (preceding), born 17 July 1829, Stillwater, Saratoga Co., NY, came to Michigan with parents. He married on 21 Apr. 1855 to EMILY (ALLEN), daughter of Robert (also see), and they settled in Hudson, Lenawee Co., Mich. She died 25 Apr. 1881. Known daughter, EDITH (m. Lewis Graham, Wheatland Twp., Hillsdale Co. Mich.) John married again to LOUISE M. (KENYON), daughter of Sylvester (also see) of Hudson Twp. In 1888, they moved to Hudson Twp. from the village of Hudson. Ref: P&BA-Len pg. 816-7.

MUNGER, LEVI born ca. 1816, NY, and wife, HENRIETTA, borhn ca. 1830, NJ, were listed in the 1850 census of Franklin Twp., Lenawee Co., Mich.

MUNGER, SALLY (See Henry Chandler)

MUNN, ELI E., son of HORACE (following), born 26 Sept. 1820, Ontario, Wayne Co., NY, married on 27 Mar. 1844

Pioneer Families of Southeastern Michigan

in Perinton, Monroe Co., NY to MARY (LONG), daughter of Morris (also see). In 1853, they lived in Gratiot Co., Mich.; and later moved to Dover Twp., Lenawee Co., Mich. They went to Pennsylvania, but returned to Deerfield Twp., Lenawee Co., Mich., and lived last in Adrian Twp. Children: 1. SARAH S. (m. W. White; Elkhart, Ind.); 2. HORACE (m. Mary Bemendiffer, Morenci, Mich.); 3. SCHUYLER J. (m. Nellie LeSage, Clayton, Ill.); 4. CHARLES H. (m. Ida Kooney, Toledo, O.); 5. ADDIE DELLA (m. Ira Wilcox, Rome Twp.); 6. BYRON E. Ref: P&BA-Len pg. 1057-8 & portrait of home.

MUNN, HORACE, son of ISRAEL, was born in Mass., and moved with his parents to Ontario Co., NY. He married at Skaneateles, NY to ROWENA (GARDNER), daughter of John (also see). They lived in Wayne Co., NY, and Monroe Co., NY where he died at age 45. Rowena was still living in 1888, age 93, in Ionia, Mich. Known son, ELI E. (preceding). Ref: P&BA-Len pg. 1057-8.

MUNN, OLIVER born ca. 1775, NY, was listed in the 1850 census of Adrian Twp., Lenawee Co., Mich. in the household of Warren and Malinda Chaffee (also see).

MURPHY, ISAAC was the father of MARY b. ca. 1795, NJ (m. Peter Teeple, also see, by 1812, Seneca Co., NY. Appears to be she who married again to William Johnson, also see).

MURPHY, JOHN born ca. 1800, and wife, MARY, born ca. 1805, both in Ireland, were listed in the 1840 census index of Palmyra Twp., Lenawee Co., Mich.; and in the 1850 census with TIMOTHY, age 21, b. NY; and MARGARET, age 18; ELLEN, age 17; JOHN, age 16; WILLIAM, age 13; JOSEPH, age 9; JAMES, age 6; DOROTHY, age 3, all b. Mich., in their household.

MURPHY, JOHN born ca. 1811, and wife, MARY (SAMPLE), born ca. 1820, Ireland, married at Carnlea, Co. Antrim, Ireland. They came to the US (1880?) to join son, THOMAS (following), in Macon Twp., Lenawee Co., Mich., where they were still living in 1888. Known daughter, ESTHER b. 31 Aug. 1859, Ireland, came to the US in 1880 (m. John V. Goheen, also see). Ref: P&BA-Len pg. 510-1 & 643-4.

MURPHY, SALLIE (See Thomas Wright)

MURPHY, THOMAS, son of JOHN (preceding), came to the US in 1868, and settled first in Tecumseh, Lenawee Co., Mich.; and in 1877 in Macon Twp. He married 3 Apr. 1878 to JENNIE (ANDERSON), daughter of William (also see). Childen: 1. JAMES A.; 2. LIZZIE M.; 3. ANNA F. Ref: P&BA-Len pg. 510-1.

MURRAY, ALONZO born ca. 1806, and wife, MARY, born ca. 1809, both in VT, were listed in the 1840 census index of Tecumseh Twp., Lenawee Co., Mich.; and in the 1850 census with JEROME, age 23, b. VT; ABIGAIL "ABBIE" b. 14 Sept. 1838, VT (census said b. Mich.?; m. William C. Fisher, also see); & Sarah Cox, age 21, b. Penn., in their household. Ref: P&BA-Len pg. 359.

MURRAY, EDWARD, son of JAMES (following), born near Arlington, Bennington Co., VT, married PHEBE (MANCHESTER), daughter of Elias (also see) and settled in Arlington. In 1832, they removed to Cayuga Co., NY where they remained. Known daughter, DELIA b. 7 Dec. 1819, Arlington, VT (m. Bishop H. Ames, also see). Ref: P&BA-Len pg. 536-7.

MURRAY, FILA (BAKER) Mrs., daughter of Appolos (also see), was also called Fila (Balcom) Murray?

MURRAY, JAMES born in either Ireland or Scotland, came to the US probably before 1800. He married DELIA (PRESTON) and settled near Arlington, Bennington Co., VT. Known son, EDWARD (preceding). Ref: P&BA-Len pg. 536-7.

MURRAY, JAMES born ca. 1810, Penn., and wife, PERMELIA, born ca. 1816, VT, were listed in the 1850 census of Adrian Twp., Lenawee Co., Mich. with JAMES, age 10; SEYMOUR, age 8, both b. Mich.; Susan Stedman, age 40; and Jane M. Stedman, age 17, both b. NY, in their household.

MURRAY, SARAH (See Conrad Holmes)

MURRAY, WILLIAM (See Patrick Donnelly)

MURTEY, CORNELIUS and wife, MARY (CAHILL), came to the US from Ireland in 1851 and settled first in Sandusky, Ohio. About 1866, they moved to Dover Twp., Lenawee Co., Mich. Ten children, but only name mentioned was #6. ROSE b. Aug. 1848, Co. Meath, Ireland (m. Peter Campbell, also see, Medina Twp.). Ref: P&BA-Len pg. 904-5.

MYERS, CHARLES (See Christopher Beagle)

MYERS, DANIEL R. was listed in the 1840 census index of Cambridge Twp., Lenawee Co., Mich. He was not listed in 1850, however the following may be his family. MYERS, HIDL--? (male) born ca. 1820, NY, was listed head of household in the 1850 census of Cambridge Twp. with (Mother?) DEBORAH, age 48; MORTIMER, age 22; DANIEL, age 18; HARRISON, age 16; MELVINA, age 15, all b. NY; and GEORGE, age 13, b. Mich., in his household.

MYERS, EDGAR born ca. 1824, NY, and wife, ELIZABETH, born ca. 1825, Ohio, were listed in the 1850 census of Adrian Twp., Lenawee Co., Mich. with no family.

MYERS, EPHRAIM, son of PETER, born in Quebec, Canada, moved with his parents to Cobleskill, Schoharie Co., NY and married there to MARIA (SAGENDORF). They moved to Otsego Co., NY where he died. Known daughter, REBECCA b. 31 July 1824, Otsego Co., NY (m. Nathaniel Carpenter Bennett, also see). Ref: P&BA-Len pg. 503-4.

MYERS, GARDNER born ca. 1808, and wife, ESTHER, born ca. 1806, were listed (as "Geordan Mires") in the 1840 census index of Rome Twp., Lenawee Co., Mich.; and in the 1850 census with MARGARET, age 20; ELIZABETH, age 19; DAVID, age 17; NATHAN, age 16, all b. NY; and ELECTA, age 14; GARDNER J., age 11; WILLIAM H., age 9; SABRA A., age 7; JOHN R., age 6; NANCY, age 2, all b. Mich., in their household. Note NATHAN, following, probably brother, listed adjacent in 1840 census index.

MYERS, J. W. was listed in the 1840 census index of Dover Twp., Lenawee Co., Mich.

MYERS, LUELLA (See James K. Wheeler)

MYERS, NATHAN born ca. 1814, and wife, ELECTA (COLE), born ca. 1812, both in NY, moved by 1837 from Oneida Co., NY to Rome Twp., Lenawee Co., Mich. In 1840, they were listed in the census adjacent to GARDNER, preceding. In the 1850 census of Rome

Twp., they listed HARRIET, age 17; HENRY, age 15, both b. NY; and ELIZA, age 13; MAHALA, age 11 (m. Robert Curtis, also see); LANGFORD, age 9; MERCY, age 7; DANTHFORD, age 5; FERDINAND, age 3, all b. Mich., in their household. Ref: P&BA-Len pg. 835-6.

MYERS, PHEBE A. (See Ezeriah Stowell)

MYERS, SUSANNA born ca. 1789, NY, was listed head of household in the 1850 census of Adrian Twp., Lenawee Co., Mich. with Parcena Skeif?, age 40, b. NY and Alice Skeif, age 3; Eugene Skeif, age 1, both b. NY, in her household.

- N -

NASH, BARBARA born ca. 1772, Conn., was listed in the 1850 census of Madison Twp., Lenawee Co., Mich. in the household of Harvey & Maria Todd (also see), as Maria born ca. 1803, Conn., may be daughter of Barbara. Note NATHAN, father of SAMUEL (following).

NASH, CHARLES was listed in the 1840 census index of Adrian Twp., Lenawee Co., Mich. adjacent to SAMUEL, following.

NASH, CHARLOTTE, age 29, born NY, was listed in the 1850 census of Madison Twp., Lenawee Co., Mich. in a Harrison household.

NASH, LEWIS was listed in the 1840 census index of Palmyra Twp., Lenawee Co., Mich.

NASH, MARVIN born ca. 1803, and wife, ABIGAIL, born ca. 1810, both in NY, were listed in the 1850 census of Madison Twp., Lenawee Co., Mich. with SARAH M., age 16; JOHN W., age 14, both b. NY; and HANNAH, age 9, b. Mich., in their household. Note: This may be same as "Myron" following.

NASH, MYRON was listed in the 1840 census index of Madison Twp., Lenawee Co., Mich.

NASH, SAMUEL, son of NATHAN (who came to Adrian and died at home of Samuel), born 10 Apr. 1805, Norwich, Conn., married on 6 Mar. 1828 to SARAH M. (BECKER) born 1809, NY. They apparently lived for a time near Hamilton, Ontario, Canada before moving to Lenawee Co., Mich. It was probably they listed in the 1840 census index of Adrian Twp., Lenawee Co., Mich. (adjacent to CHARLES, preceding); and they were listed in the 1850 census of Medina Twp. with the first 8 children in their household. She died 22 June 1863, Madison Twp.; and he died 16 Oct. 1875 in Palmyra Twp. Children: 1. SAMUEL b. ca. 1829, Canada (lived Palmyra Twp.); 2. NATHAN b. ca. 1832, Canada (lived Adrian); 3. NANCY b. 10 Oct. 1834. near Hamilton, Canada (m. Samuel M. Hamilton, also see); 4. HARVEY T. b. ca. 1836, NY (lived Adrian); 5. GERARDUS J. b. ca. 1838, Mich. (lived Palmyra Twp.); 6. HENRY H. b. ca. 1840 (to Saline Co., KS); 7. SARAH LOUISA b. ca. 1845 (m. John A. Townsend, also see); 8. ESTHER b. 20 July 1849, Madison Twp. (m. David E. Palmer, also see); 9. FRANCES E. (m. Franklin S. Phillips, Ogden Twp.) Ref: P&BA-Len pg. 398-9 & 506-7. Note BARBARA & CHARLES, both preceding.

NASH, THEODORE was listed as age 17, place of birth not known, in 1850 census of Adrian Twp., Lenawee Co., Mich. in a Theodore Billings household. It may be he who married JANE (MARSHALL), daughter of Charles M. (also see).

NASH, THOMAS born ca. 1796, Conn., and wife, ELIZA, born ca. 1810, NY, were listed in the 1850 census of Dover Twp., Lenawee Co., Mich. with MARIAH, age 10; OSCAR, age 8, both b. NY, in their household.

NASH, THOMAS was listed in the 1840 census index of Rome Twp., Lenawee Co., Mich.

NECTELL, WILLIAM (See William Gregg)

NEEDHAMMER see NEEDHEIMER; NEIDHAMMER

NEEDHEIMER also see NEEDHAMMER; NEIDHAMMER
NEEDHEIMER, CATHERINE (See Valentine Wenzel)

NEGUS also see NYGUS

NEGUS, CHARLES, son of MOSES (following), born ca. 1819, Mass., came first to Lenawee Co., Mich. in 1840/1, but returned to New York. In 1843, he returned to Michigan, but married in Ontario Co., NY in Oct. 1843 to ELECTA A. (BROCKELBANK), daughter of ? (See Brockelbank), born ca. 1821, NY. They settled in Seneca Twp., Lenawee Co., Mich. where they were listed in the 1850 census with no family Children (b. after 1850): 1. CHARLES W. (m. Eliza Whaley; had children, Maude & Bertha); 2. EMMA (m. George L. Ackley, also see); 3. EDDIE D. (deceased prior to 1888). Ref: P&BA-Len pg. 573-4 & portrait.

NEGUS, ISAAC, probably son of MOSES, was listed as age 28, b. Mass., but age seems incorrect, head of household with MARY J., age 37, b. VT, and LOVICA J., age 13, b. NY, in his household.

NEGUS, MOSES born ca. 1790, Rhode Island, and wife, LYDIA (DAWS), born ca. 1793, Mass., settled first in Peru, Berkshire Co., Mass., and remained there for 30 or 40 years before moving in 1846 to Seneca Twp., Lenawee Co., Mich. Known son, CHARLES (preceding). However, it should be noted that their place of birth and that of their children in the household in the 1850 census of Seneca Twp. were all given as New York: MARY, age 25; HARVEY, age 21; WHITFIELD, age 18; JOHN, age 12. Ref: P&BA-Len pg. 573-4. Also note ISAAC (preceding); MOSES & WARREN (following).

NEGUS, MOSES, possibly son of MOSES (preceding), married RACHEL (LUTHER). They had known daughter, CLARA I. b. 3 Sept. 1860, Seneca Twp., Lenawee Co., Mich. (m. Benjamin C. Franklin, also see). Ref: P&BA-Len pg. 997.

NEGUS, WARREN born ca. 1818, and wife, MABLE, born ca. 1821, both in NY, were listed in the 1850 census of Medina Twp., Lenawee Co., Mich. with JANE E., age 9, b. Mich., in their household.

NEINBORN, MARGARET (See Philip Faelbeck)

NELLIS, HENRY born ca. 1780, and wife, MARY, born ca. 1787, NY, were listed in the 1840 census index of Fairfield Twp., Lenawee Co., Mich. (adjacent to JACOB); and in the 1850 census with JACOB, age 40; WILLIAM, age 19, both b. NY, and Mary S. Berry, age 18, b. NY, in their household.

NELSON, DIANA born ca. 1783, NY, was listed in the 1850 census of Adrian Twp., Lenawee Co., Mich. in the

Pioneer Families of Southeastern Michigan

household of John A. Rice and wife, Catherine (age 41, b. NY).

NELSON, FRANCIS born ca. 1808, and wife, DEBORAH, born ca. 1813, both in NY, were listed in the 1840 census index of Madison Twp., Lenawee Co., Mich., and in the 1850 census of Medina Twp., with WILLIAM, age 12; WILBER, age 11; THEODORE, age 9; SYBIL A., age 7; MARY E., age 4, all b. Mich., in their household.

NELSON, HENRY born ca. 1832, Mich., was listed in the 1850 census of Adrian Twp., Lenawee Co., Mich. Note THOMAS, JR., following.

NELSON, JOHN, age 8, born Mich., was listed in the 1850 census of Madison Twp., Lenawee Co., Mich. in the household of Rev. Isaac & Elizabeth Crabb, perhaps grandparents? Note JOHN, following, possibly same person.

NELSON, JOHN married JUDITH P. (HAYWARD), daughter of Micajah (also see) probably in the 1860s. Children: JANETTE; LOUISE; JOHN M.; BENJAMIN. Ref: P&BA-Len pg. 913-4.

NELSON, MARTHA was listed head of household in the 1840 census index of Adrian Twp., Lenawee Co., Mich.

NELSON, RUTH A. born ca. 1834, and SEYMOUR, born ca. 1836, both in NY, probably siblings, were listed in the 1850 census of Adrian Twp., Lenawee Co., Mich. in the household of John H. Kimble and wife Marietta (age 38, b. NY). Possibly stepchildren?

NELSON, THOMAS, Jr. was listed in the 1830 census of Lenawee Co., Michigan Territory. He listed males: 1 10-15; 2 15-20; 1 40-50; females; 2 und 5; 2 5-10; 1 10-15; 1 30-40. Note DIANA & MARTHA & HENRY, preceding.

NELSON, WILLIAM born ca. 1808, NY, and wife, JANE, born ca. 1809, Maine, were listed in the 1840 census index of Fairfield Twp., Lenawee Co., Mich.; and in the 1850 census with LYMAN, age 11?; WILLIAM, age 11; EDWIN, age 7; GEORGE, age 3, all b. Mich., in their household.

NESBIT, MARY (See Peter McCollum)

NESS, HENRIETTA (See Ralph N. DeGreene)

NETTLETON, CLARISSA (See Austin Wilcox)

NEWCOMB, ANDREW Capt. came from England to Mass. in Colonial Times and married GRACE, and resided in Boston by 1663. He was the direct ancestor of BETHUEL (following). Mentioned was a published Genealogy of the Newcomb Family, by John B. Newcomb of Elgin, Ill.

NEWCOMB, ARMINA born ca. 1820, NY, was listed in the 1850 census of Rome Twp., Lenawee Co., Mich. in the household of Elijah Allis.

NEWCOMB, BETHUEL born 11 Feb. 1810, VT, was the 7th generation from Capt. ANDREW (preceding). He married on 5 June 1838, Stanstead, Canada to HANNAH (ROBINSON), daughter of John (also see). They later moved to Prairie du Sac, Wisc. She died 22 Mar. 1870, West Point, Wisc.; and he was still living in 1888 with a son in Lodi, Wisc. Children: 1. LAURA (d. infancy); 2. MARY J. (m. John W. Allen, also see, on 15 Mar. 1860, Rollin Twp., Lenawee Co., Mich.); 3. LAURA ANN (m. George Robbins, Omaha, NE); 4. JOHN I. (m. Della Chrisler, Lodi, Wisc.) Ref: P&BA-Len pg. 1198-1200. Also note JUSTUS G., following.

NEWCOMB, JANE E. (See John S. Clark)

NEWCOMB, JUSTUS G. born ca. 1791, VT, and wife, ARTIMITTA?, borh ca. 1807, NY, were listed in the 1840 census index of Rollin Twp., Lenawee Co., Mich.; and in the 1850 census with HEBIRT, age 6; MANDANE, age 4; CYNTHIA, age 3, all b. Mich. (grandchildren?), in their household. Next door was WARREN, following; and Note Dr. R. R. C. (following), possibly sons.

NEWCOMB, R. R. C. Dr. born ca. 1822, VT, was listed in the 1850 census of Palmyra Twp., Lenawee Co., Mich.

NEWCOMB, WARREN, probably son of JUSTUS G. (preceding), born ca. 1823, and wife, ELIZABETH, born ca. 1821, both in NY, were listed in the 1850 census of Rollin Twp., Lenawee Co., Mich. (next door to JUSTUS G.) with JOSEPH, age 1, b. Mich., and Helen Potter, age 5, both b. Mich., in their household.

NEWELL, JAMES was listed in the 1840 census index of Adrian Twp., Lenawee Co., Mich.; and in the 1850 census as "J. J.," age 35, with wife, JOANNA, age 32, both b. Mass., and MARY, age 9; FRANCES, age 4; NORMAN, age 2, all b. Mich., in their household.

NEWELL, JOSEPH C., son of LOWRY (following), born 14 July 1823, Edinburg, Saratoga Co., NY, moved with his parents to Jefferson Co., NY. He married there on 8 Nov. 1847 to SUSAN (MARSH), daughter of MOSES (also see). In 1854, they moved to Somerfield, Monroe Co., Mich.; and in 1861 to Deerfield, Lenawee Co. Children: 1. EDWIN (m. Mary Carpenter, Deerfield Twp.); 2. MARY (m. Gersham Hull, Howell Co., MO). Ref: P&BA-Len pg. 358-9.

NEWELL, LEROY born ca. 1818, and wife, LUCINDA, born ca. 1827, both in NY, were listed in the 1850 census of Riga Twp., Lenawee Co., Mich. with CALISTA, age 8, b. NY; and HARRIET, age 6; ALBERT, age 5; DELBERT, age 3; ALONZO, age 1, all b. Mich., in their household.

NEWELL, LOWRY and wife, HANNAH (CHAPMAN), were natives of Saratoga Co., NY, who moved ca. 1846 to Jefferson Co., NY and lived at Pamelia & Alexandria. She died in Alexandria. Eleven of their twelve children lived to maturity, and only name mentioned was JOSEPH C. (preceding). Ref: P&BA-Len pg. 358-9.

NEWELL, MARY born Ashland Co., Ohio married William Metcalf (also see) by 1837.

NEWELL, WILLIAM B. born ca. 1806, Mass., and wife, NANCY, born ca. 1812, both in NY, were listed in the 1840 census index of Rome Twp., Lenawee Co., Mich.; and in the 1850 census with HARRIET L., age 14; TYLER H., age 13; CHARLOTTE E., age 8; W. BURNEY, age 6; EDWARD P., age 3, all b. Mich., in their household.

NEWITT, JOHN and wife, BELINDA (BURDICK) of Madison Co., NY had known daughter, MARIA b. 29 Dec. 1834, Madison Co. (m/1 Charles Wood; m/2 William Derbyshire (see both). Ref: P&BA-Len pg. 642-3.

NEWMAN, J. R. (See Calvin Town)

NEWTON, DAVID T. born ca. 1827, and PHEBE, born ca. 1833, both in NY, were listed in the 1850 census of Adrian Twp., Lenawee Co., Mich.

NEWTON, EZRA was listed in the 1840 census index of Blissfield Twp., Lenawee Co., Mich. ESTHER, daughter of "E. NEWTON of Blissfield," age 21, born Mich. (m. Joel Carpenter, also see). In the 1850 census, Esther was listed in the 1850 census of Blissfield Twp. in the household of Sewall S. Goff, and wife, Lucy (age 31, b. Mich.), and Lucy may be another daughter of Ezra? Ref: P&BA-Len pg. 1202-3.

NEWTON, GEORGE, age 19, born Mass., was listed in the 1850 census of Blissfield Twp., Lenawee Co., Mich. in a Barrett household.

NEWTON, JEREMIAH T., son of JOHN (following), born 10 Mar. 1819, Truxton, Cortland Co., NY, moved in 1830 to Wayne Co., Ohio with his parents; and to Spencer, Medina Co., Ohio in 1839. He married there on 17 Sept. 1843 to CLARISSA (BENFER), daughter of George (also see). In 1853, they settled in Sullivan Twp., Ashland Co., Ohio; and in 1864 in Ogden Twp., Lenawee Co., Mich. He died 23 July 1884. Children: 1. JAMES (lived Ohio); 2. GEORGE FRANKLIN (d. age 20); 3. SOLOMON M. (following). Ref: P&BA-Len pg. 771-2.

NEWTON, JOHN Dr. born 14 Jan. 1772, VT, married first to ? He married second to HANNAH (HADLEY) born 6 Feb. 1775, and had 3 daughters and 1 son (names not stated). Hannah died and he married again in 1810 to REBECCA (RADWAY) born 26 May 1783, VT. In 1815, they moved to Truxton, Cortland Co., NY; and on 2 May 1830 to Milton Twp., Wayne Co., Ohio. In 1839, they moved to Medina Co., Ohio where he died on 11 May 1848, age 76. She came to Ogden Twp., Lenawee Co., Mich. where she died on 23 Nov. 1878. Six sons and one daughter, and only one mentioned was JEREMIAH T. (preceding). Ref: P&BA-Len pg. 771-2.

NEWTON, REUBEN C. Dr. born ca. 1820, and wife, LORETTA, born ca. 1824, both in NY, were listed in the 1850 census of Franklin Twp., Lenawee Co., Mich. with ELLEN, age 9; HENRY, age 7; THEODORE, age 4; FRANK, age 7/12, all b. Mich., in their household.

NEWTON, SOLOMON M., son of JEREMIAH T. (preceding), born 9 Nov. 1855, Sullivan Twp., Ashland Co., Ohio, moved with his parents to Ogden Twp., Lenawee Co., Mich. in 1864. He married there on 9 Nov. 1878 to AUGUSTA M. (HENDEE) born 14 May 1857, Spencer, Medina Co., Ohio. She died 11 Jan. 1885, Ogden Twp., leaving son, ELLIS A. b. 7 July 1884, Amboy, Fulton Co., O. Solomon M. married again on 24 Dec. 1887 to HATTIE (MILLER) born in Amboy, Fulton Co., Ohio 14 Apr. 1868. They resided in Ogden Twp. Ref: P&BA-Len pg. 771-2.

NEYGUS see NEGUS

NIBLACK, JOHN and wife, HANNAH (HARRISON), married in Sparta, Livingston Co., NY, and moved in 1833 to Saline, Washtenaw Co., Mich. (where they were listed in the 1840 census index). She died there in 1859; and he moved to Tecumseh Twp., Lenawee Co., Mich. where he died in 1862, age 70. There were 10 children, and only known are ARVILLA (m. ? Davis); and #10. CHARLOTTE b. 16 Aug. 1826 (m. E. W. Goheen, also see). Ref: P&BA-Len pg. 287-8.

NIBLACK, SAMUEL JR. was listed in the 1840 census index of Macon Twp., Lenawee Co., Mich. It is probably he in the 1850 census of Tecumseh Twp. (written Samuel "Niblic"), age 44; with wife, NANCY, age 32, both both NY, and in their household DELOS, age 9; WELLS, age 2, both b. Mich.

NICHOLAS, JOHN of Clinton Twp., Lenawee Co., Mich. was mentioned in the sketch of George Burton.

NICHOLAS, THANKFUL (See Joshua Beaman)

NICHOLS, BENJAMIN born ca. 1810, NJ, and wife, CATHARINE, born ca. 1803, NY, were listed in the 1850 census of Cambridge Twp., Lenawee Co., Mich. with EDWIN, age 22; CHARLOTTE, age 19; DANIEL, age 20; SAMUEL, age 16, all b. NY, in their household. Note: It may be he listed as Benjamin "Nickles" in Dover Twp. in the 1840 census index.

NICHOLS, BETSEY (See Ambrose Fenton)

NICHOLS, DANIEL B. (See Jonathan Hare; and note JAMES, following.

NICHOLS, DAVID, age 20, born NY, was listed in the 1850 census of Hudson Twp., Lenawee Co., Mich. in a Cady household.

NICHOLS, ELIZABETH, age 19, born NY, was listed in the 1850 census of Woodstock Twp., Lenawee Co., Mich. in a Moshier household.

NICHOLS, ENOCH born ca. 1824, and wife, SARAH, born ca. 1831, both in NY, were listed in the 1850 census of Medina Twp., Lenawee Co., Mich.

NICHOLS, ERASTUS N. Rev. born ca. 1798, Mass., and wife, MARGARET, born ca. 1800, NY, were listed in the 1840 census index of Tecumseh Twp., Lenawee Co., Mich.; and in the 1850 census with ELIZABETH, age 84, born Mass., probably his mother, all listed in the household of Abiram O. Holmes.

NICHOLS, FREDERICK W. (See Jonathan Ingersoll)

NICHOLS, GEORGE (See Lagrange H. Dewey)

NICHOLS, HENRY, son of RUSSELL (following), born ca. 1811, NY, moved to Washtenaw Co., Mich. in 1840, and after 3 months moved to Lenawee Co., Mich. He purchased in both Lenawee and Ingham Cos, Mich., but settled in Dover Twp., Lenawee Co. in 1843. He married first on 7 Apr. 1842 to REBECCA (WILSON) and had children: 1. ORRIN (d. age 6); 2. EDWIN born after 1850 census? (m. Harriet Deming; Palmyra Twp.) In the 1850 census of Dover Twp., Henry had no children in the household. Rebecca died in 1851; and he married again on 22 Feb. 1852 to CAROLINE M. (ROBB), daughter of Gardner (also see). Children: 3. ESTELLE (m. Charles Dutcher; Palmyra Twp.); 4. WILLIAM H. (m. Frances Bodine); 5. IDA P. (m. Charles Keeber, Palmyra Twp.); 6. JOHN. Ref: P&BA-Len pg. 232-3.

NICHOLS, JAMES born ca. 1826, and wife, MARGARET, born ca. 1827, both in NY, were listed in the 1850 census of Seneca Twp., Lenawee Co., Mich. with SALLY, age 3, b. Mich., and (brother?) DANIEL, age 20, b. NY, in their household. Note DANIEL B., preceding.

NICHOLS, LEVI and wife, REBECCA (WATROUS), had known daughter, REBECCA A. b. 19 Mar. 1817, Plattsburg, Clinton Co., NY (m/1 Thomas C. Smith; m/2 Albert Humphrey Bump, see both, in Medina Twp., Lenawee Co., Mich.) Ref: P&BA-Len pg. 940-1.

NICHOLS, MARTHA (See Franklin F. Palmer)

NICHOLS, NASON was listed in the 1840 census index of Blissfield Twp., Lenawee Co., Mich.

Pioneer Families of Southeastern Michigan

NICHOLS, OLIVE (See Garrett F. Harris)

NICHOLS, RUSSELL born Vermont, married MARGARET (FRAVER) born Otsego Co., NY, and settled in western NY. In 1836, they moved to Oakland Co., Mich. where they remained. Children: 1. PALMER; 2. MARY; 3. HENRY (preceding); 4. NANCY; 5. ELIZA; 6. WILLIAM. Ref: P&BA-Len pg. 232-3.

NICHOLS, SAMUEL, son of THOMAS (following), was born 1789, Antrim, Hillsboro Co., NH, and moved first with his mother to Black River Country and then to Bloomfield, Ontario Co., NY. He married there, but his wife, name not stated, died; and he moved in 1831 to London Twp., Monroe Co., Mich. He married again on 18 Nov. 1831 to EVELINA (SEYMOUR), daughter of Ira (also see). They had known daughters: CLARA b. 20 May 1834, London, Mich. (m. Thomas J. Hiller, also see); ALICE E. (m. Jacob Korn; Kansas); CORNELIA S. (m. H. G. Humphrey; Lansing, Mich.). Ref: P&BA-Len pg. 1111-2. Note: In the 1840 census index of London Twp., Monroe Co., Mich. listed were SAMUEL & SAMUEL 2d.

NICHOLS, SAMUEL born ca. 1823, England, and wife, ELLEN, born ca. 1827, NY, were listed in the 1850 census of Adrian Twp., Lenawee Co., Mich. with ALICE, age 4; WARNER, age 1, both b. Mich.; Helen Francisco, age 82, b. VT; Helen Ferguson, age 9; Amei Ferguson, age 7, both b. Mich., in their household.

NICHOLS, SARAH, age 16, born Penn., was listed in the 1850 census of Palmyra Twp., Lenawee Co., Mich. in a Webster household.

NICHOLS, SOLOMON of Monroe Co., NY had known daughter, MARY E. (m. Rufus S. King, also see, 1830). Ref: P&BA-Len pg. 592-3. Note: There was a SOLOMON in the 1840 census index of East Portage (now Waterloo?), Jackson Co., Mich.

NICHOLS, THOMAS probably born in Scotland settled in Antrim, Hillsboro Co., NH. He married HANNAH (CLARKE); and died in Antrim. Hannah moved the family to the "Black River Country" (Jefferson Co., NY?) and then to Bloomfield, Ontario Co., NY. Known son, SAMUEL (preceding). Ref: P&BA-Len pg. 1111-2.

NICHOLLS also see NICHOLS

NICHOLLS, ADA born 2 June 1861, Lenawee Co., Mich. (See Jabez Briggs, Woodstock Twp.)

NICHOLSON, ALICE (See John Mawdsley)

NICHOLSON, EMMA (See William Henry Brooks)

NICHOLSON, HANNAH, age 14, born Canada, was listed in the 1850 census of Ogden Twp., Lenawee Co., Mich. in the Alonzo Brown household (all b. Canada). Note JAMES^2 (following).

NICHOLSON, JAMES^1 born in Yorkshire, England moved to Ramsey, Ontario Canada about 1825 and remained there. Known son, JAMES?^{2} (following). Ref: P&BA-Len pg. 557-8.

NICHOLSON, JAMES^2, son of JAMES^1 (preceding), though it is not certain from the sketch if his given name was James, was born in England, and moved from Canada to Beaver Creek, VT. He married there to NANCY (CHURCHILL), daughter of John (also see). They later moved to Montreal where they remained. Six children, of whom 5 grew to maturity, names not stated, except JAMES^3 (following). Ref: P&BA-Len pg. 557-8. Note HANNAH, preceding.

NICHOLSON, JAMES^3, son of JAMES^2 (preceding), came to Lenawee Co., Mich. first as a very young man. He reurned to Canada, lived afterwards variously in Kankakee, Ill, then back to Canada. He married on 14 Dec. 1851 to REBECCA (EARLE), daughter of Elijah (also see) of Palmyra Twp., Lenawee Co., Mich. They settled in Riga Twp. Children: 1. WILLIAM (Ogden Twp.); 2. MELISSA (m. Charles Mason, Riga Twp.) Ref: P&BA-Len pg. 557-8.

NICHOLSON, MARY born ca. 1820, Ireland, was listed head of household in the 1850 census of Tecumseh Twp., Lenawee Co., Mich. with AUGUSTA, age 5, b. Mich., in her household.

NICKERSON, IRA S., son of LEWIS (following), born 25 Feb. 1826, Wayne Co., NY, moved with parents to Madison Twp., Lenawee Co., Mich. He married on 5 Oct. 1856 in Pittsford Twp., Hillsdale Co., Mich. to SARAH E. (WATSON), daughter of E. T. (also see). Known daughter, IDA B. (m. Robert Savage, also see). Ref: P&BA-Len pg. 422-3.

NICKERSON, LEWIS born in Mass., married BETTY (BLOOD) born in NY, and they settled first near Ticonderoga, NY; and moved later to Junius, Wayne Co., NY. In 1830, they moved to Madison Twp., Lenawee Co., Mich. He died in 1836, and she died in 1846. In the 1830 census of Lenawee Co., Mich. Territory, he listed males: 1 und 5; 2 10-15; 2 30-40; female: 1 30-40. Children: 1. SULLIVAN A. (Hillsdale Co., Mich.); 2. MELVIN T. (following); 3. IRA S. (preceding). Ref: P&BA-Len pg. 422-3.

NICKERSON, MELVIN T., son of LEWIS (preceding), born 19 Mar. 1819, Junius, Wayne Co., NY, moved with his parents to Madison Twp., Lenawee Co., Mich. He married there on 6 June 1844 to AMANDA C. (BRADISH), daughter of Calvin^1 (also see), and settled there. Children: 1. name not stated (d. infancy); 2. THERESA E. (deceased before 1888); 3. FRANCES A. (called "Amanda," age 4/12 in 1850 census; deceased before 1888); 4. NORMAN F. b. ca. 1847; 5. HELEN A.; 6. NETTIE E. Ref: P&BA-Len pg. 1031-2.

NIEDHAMMER also see NEEDHEIMER

NIEDHAMMER, GEORGE G., son of LEWIS (following), born 10 May 1810, Wurtemburg, Germany, came alone to the US at age 16, sailing from Holland to Baltimore, MD, and then to Harrisburg, Penn. According to the sketch, he returned to Baltimore where he married CAROLINE (MANHEART) and they moved about 1836 to Adrian Twp., Lenawee Co., Mich. Supposedly, Caroline died 4 years after their marriage leaving only daughters: 1. BARBARA b. ca. 1837, Mich. (1850 census of Adrian Twp., lived in household of Walter & Elizabeth Robinson); 2. CAROLINE born ca. 1838 (deceased before 1888). However, in the 1850 census of Madison Twp., Lenawee Co. he listed wife, ELIZA, born ca. 1810, NY. with AMANDA, age 20; JOHN, age 17; LAFAYETTE, age 17, all b. NY; and CAROLINE, age 12; GEORGE, age 5; FANNY, age 4; MARY, age 2; CHARLES, age 2/12, all b. Mich., in their household. The sketch also says that he married in 1858 in Adrian to Mrs. CAROLINE (BRIGGS) and then lists their children as the last 4 listed above WHO WERE IN THE HOUSEHOLD IN 1850? Possibly they married in 1844?, and wife was called "Eliza?" Possibly the children shown born NY in the household were actually stepchildren? Ref: P&BA-Len pg. 633-4.

NIEDHAMMER, LEWIS and wife, BARBARA, were natives of Wurtemburg, Germany who came to the US in 1828 to join known son, George G. in Harrisburg, Penn. Lewis died in Harrisburg, but she later came to Blissfield Twp., Lenawee Co., Mich. to join George, where she died ca. 1848. Six children, names not stated, except #5. GEORGE G. (preceding). Ref: P&BA-Len pg. 633-4.

NILES, ELISHA, probably son of SAMUEL (following), born ca. 1813, and wife, MARY, born ca. 1823, both born NY, were listed in the 1850 census of Madison Twp., Lenawee Co., Mich. with SARAH, age 1, b. Mich., in their household.

NILES, JOHN was listed in the 1840 census index of Madison Twp., Lenawee Co., Mich. Note SAMUEL, following.

NILES, JOHN W. (See Frederick W. Wickwire)

NILES, LEVI, probably son of SAMUEL (following), born ca. 1804, Canada, is listed in the 1840 census index of Raisin Twp., Lenawee Co., Mich.; and in the 1850 census of Madison Twp. with wife, MARANDA, age 35, born NY and DEWIT, age 16; ELECTA, age 12, both b. NY; and PHILANDA, age 8; MELINDA, age 8; LUCY, age 6; OSCAR, age 3, ELTHERI (ALATHEAR?), age 2, all b. Mich., in their household.

NILES, RIAL, son of SAMUEL (following), born 10 Apr. 1822, Ontario, Ontario Co. (then Onondaga Co.), NY, came with his family to Lenawee Co., Mich. in 1838. She married MARY H. (PHETTEPLACE), daughter of Asa (also see) and settled in Madison Twp. (The sketch gives their date of marriage as 25 Mar. 1856, but they were married by the 1850 census). In the census they listed in their household his mother, ALATHEAR (written ELTHERI), age 70, b. VT; probably sister, SALLY, age 26, b. NY; George P. Fuller, age 7, b. Mich. They moved to Adrian in 1856; and in 1871 went to Baxter Springs, Kansas, but returned to Adrian by 1874. In 1877, they settled in Madison Twp. Children: 1. ELSIE (d. Kansas, age 21); 2. CLARA. Ref: P&BA-Len pg. 736.

NILES, SAMUEL married ALATHEAR (WOODWORTH) born ca. 1780/4 in VT. Note that they may have lived in Canada in 1804. They were in Ontario Co., NY in 1822, and he died in 1824, leaving her with 9 children (names not stated). She came to Madison Twp., Lenawee Co., Mich. in 1838; and was living in the 1850 census in the household of known son, #8. RIAL (preceding), and listed also in the household was SALLY, age 26, b. NY, possibly her daughter? Also see JOHN; LEVI; & ELISHA (all preceding). CATHERINE, born ca. 1826, NY, wife of John Phetteplace (also see), may be another daughter, as they named a son, Rial.

NILES, WATY (See Clark Rogers)

NINES, CHRISTIAN of Preston Co., VA. was the father of MARIA who married Solomon Heckert (also see). Ref: P&BA-Len pg. 1180.

NIVERSON, WILLIAM (See Joseph Thackray)

NOBLE, ANN A. (See Sereno Loomis)

NOBLE, EMMA (See Zibra Corbett)

NOBLE, HENRY, age 7, born Mich., was listed in the 1850 census of Ogden Twp., Lenawee Co., Mich. in the household of William A. & Elizabeth Chappell.

NOBLES, ABEL born ca. 1804, and wife, MARY, born ca. 1804, were listed in the 1840 census index of Raisin Twp., Lenawee Co., Mich.; and in the 1850 census of Macon Twp. with JAMES M., age 19; GEORGE A. A., age 16; ALMYRA C., age 14, all b. NY; and REBECCA, age 13; ENOS, age 10; DANIEL, age 6; MARY A., age 4, all b. Mich., in their household.

NOBLES, EDMOND was listed in the 1840 census index of Madison Twp., Lenawee Co., Mich.

NORCROSS, AARON[2], son of JOHN[1] (following), married MARY (KELLY), daughter of Daniel (also see) and settled in Grover, Livingston Co., NY. In 1832, they moved to Sulphur Springs, Monroe Co., Mich.; and before 1840 to Tecumseh Twp., Lenawee Co., Mich., where he died at age 66. She died in Monroe Co., Mich. There were 6 children, all born Livingston Co., NY and only named was #4. AARON[3] (following). In the 1850 census of Tecumseh Twp., ELIZABETH, age 48, who was listed head of household, and MARY ANN, age 36, both b. NY, in her household, were probably sisters, and possibly daughters of Aaron[2]. Ref: P&BA-Len pg. 264. Note JOHN of Tecumseh Twp., following.

NORCROSS, AARON[3], son of AARON[2] (preceding), born 23 Apr. 1812, Livingston Co., NY, came to Michigan with his parents. He married HELEN (ALLEN), daughter of Ethan (also see) born ca. 1824/6, VT, and were listed in the 1850 census of Tecumseh Twp., Lenawee Co., Mich. She died 22 July 1876, age 50. Children: 1. EUGENE (called Aaron in census, age 4; m. Alice Lacy; Franklin Twp.); 2. FRANKLIN "FRANK" b. ca. 1849 (m. Lettie Bradley, Franklin Twp. In addition to these children, they listed Lemuel Allen, age 13, b. Mich., in their household.

NORCROSS, JOHN was a native of New Jersey, and served in the Revolutionary War. He and wife, MARY (SOLOMON), removed to Penn.; and then to Geneseo, Livingston Co., NY, where he died at age 77. Known son, AARON[1] (preceding). Ref: P&BA-Len pg. 264.

NORCROSS, JOHN, probably son of AARON[2], born ca. 1808, and wife, SARAH, born ca. 1814, both in NY, were listed in the 1840 census index of Tecumseh Twp., Lenawee Co., Mich.; and in the 1850 census with MARY, age 9; NANCY, age 7; HARRIET, age 4; SARAH, age 2; EMMA, age 1, all b. Mich., in their household.

NORTH, ALVA born ca. 1806, Conn., and wife, ORISSA E., born ca. 1818, NY, were listed in the 1850 census of Blissfield Twp., Lenawee Co., Mich. with GUY, age 14, born NY, in their household.

NORTH, AMOS was listed in the 1840 census index of Madison Twp., Lenawee Co., Mich.

NORTHRUP, DANIEL and wife, SARAH, had known daughter, EUNICE b. 10 Mar. 1781, Saratoga Co., NY (m. Asa Osborn, also see). Ref: P&BA-Len pg. 551-2.

Pioneer Families of Southeastern Michigan

NORTHRUP, PHEBE, age 30, born NY, and ELIZABETH, age 6, born Mich., were listed in the 1850 census of Fairfield Twp., Lenawee Co., Mich. in a Carpenter household.

NORTHRUP, STEPHEN born ca. 1783, Conn., and wife, PHEBE, born ca. 1796, NY, were listed in the 1840 census index of Fairfield Twp., Lenawee Co., Mich.; and in the 1850 census with CHARLOTTE, age 19, born NY, in their household. Also note PHEBE, preceding. EUNICE, age 19, b. NY, listed in the 1850 census of Fairfield Twp. in another household may also relate to this family.

NORTON, ABIGAIL, age 64, born Conn., was listed in the 1850 census of Tecumseh Twp., Lenawee Co., Mich. in the household of Benjamin and Elisa Knowles (also see).

NORTON, ANN, age 63, born Mass., was listed in the 1850 census of Palmyra Twp., Lenawee Co. Mich. in a Pomeroy household.

NORTON, CALEB came to America from France about the time of the French & Indian War, and possibly settled in Conn. He was killed in that War in 1763. Known son, SEBA (following). Ref: P&BA-Len pg. 551-2.

NORTON, DANIEL was listed in the 1840 census index of Cambridge Twp., Lenawee Co., Mich.

NORTON, ELIZA (See Greytrax)

NORTON, EZRA born ca. 1799, Conn., and wife, HANNAH, born ca. 1799, Maine, were listed in the 1850 census of Blissfield Twp., Lenawee Co., Mich. with MARTHA A., age 14; WILLIAM, age 12, both b. Mich., in their household.

NORTON, G. W. was listed in the 1840 census index of Dover Twp., Lenawee Co., Mich.

NORTON, GEORGE, age 16, born Mich., was listed in the 1850 census of Tecumseh Twp., Lenawee Co., Mich. in a Zeno Kelly household.

NORTON, HANNAH (See Richard Kent[2])

NORTON, JAMES R. and wife, CHLOE (SAVAGE), were natives of Vermont who moved to Ohio ca. 1835. He died there at age 83, and she died 6 years later at age 84. Known daughter, CHARLOTTE b. 24 Oct. 1818, Rutland Co, VT (m. Chancy Rowlson, also see). Ref: P&BA-Len pg. 625-6.

NORTON, NORE was listed in the 1840 census index of Adrian Twp., Lenawee Co., Mich. Note SARAH, following.

NORTON, RILEY, age 24, born NY, was listed in the 1850 census of Madison Twp., Lenawee Co., Mich. in the Ebenezer Bird household.

NORTON, SARAH, age 59, born NY, was listed head of household in the 1850 census of Adrian Twp., Lenawee Co., Mich. with MARIAN, age 15, born Mich., in her household. Note NORE (preceding); and WILLIAM (following).

NORTON, SEBA, son of CALEB (preceding), was a Revolutionary soldier. It may be he in the Revolutionary Pension Applications with Conn. service, with widow, MARGARET, #W19927. Seba died in Ontario Co., NY, age 82; and his wife died at age 88. Known daughter, MARGARET b. ca. 1782, NY (m. Stephen Powell, also see). Ref: P&BA-Len pg. 551-2.

NORTON, WARREN born ca. 1813, NY, and wife, MARY, born ca. 1817, Mass., was listed in the 1850 census of Rome Twp., Lenawee Co., Mich. with ORRIN, age 9; ALICE, age 3, both b. Mich., in their household.

NORTON, WILLIAM was listed in the 1840 census index of Adrian Twp., Lenawee Co., Mich. Note SARAH, preceding. NORTON, WILLIAM was listed in the 1840 census index of Rome Twp., Lenawee Co., Mich. Note WARREN, preceding.

NOTHNAGLE, WILLIAM (See Christina Kuney)

NOYES, AMOS and wife, MIRIAM (BARNEY), probably of Greene Co., NY, were parents of ? (given name not stated), first wife of Russell Hervey (also see). Note: In the 1800 census index, there was an AMOS B. in Oneida Co., NY.

NOYES, RUTH E., age 21, born Ohio, was listed in the 1850 census of Palmyra Twp., Lenawee Co., Mich. in a Green household.

NUFER, ANDREW, son of PETER (following), born 13 Sept. 1828, Bavaria, Germany, came to Monroe, Mich. with his parents. As an adult, he went to Long Island and Brooklyn, NY. He married in Adrian, Lenawee Co., Mich. in 1853 to MAGDALENA (ROSE) formerly of Monroe Co., Mich. In 1859, they settled in Adrian. Children: 1. LOUISA; 2. LENORA 1st (d. child); 3. GEORGE A.; 4. LENORA 2d (m. Joseph Michael); 5. CLARA (m. Frank Lehr); 6. MARY (m. Benjamin Lehr); 7. JOHN F.; 8. AGADA ISABELLE. Ref: P&BA-Len pg. 629-30.

NUFER, PETER and wife, SUSANNAH (ROSE), came to America from Bavaria in 1833. They moved via Buffalo, NY, and Toledo, Ohio, finally settling in Monroe, Mich. in 1836. He died at the home of children, age 69, and she died age 83. Twelve children, only ones mentioned #8. ANDREW (preceding); and LEONARD. Ref: P&BA-Len pg. 629-30.

NYE, ELLEN (See Benjamin Reasoner)
NYE, ISABELLA (See Warren Gilbert)

NYGUS also see NEGUS

NYGUS, JOHN married CARRIE (ROUND), daughter of James E. (also see), had known children: RUTH & ORRIN. (Note John Negus, son of Moses, preceding?)

NYLAND, ANTHONY of Holland remained there, however, a son (name not stated) and daughter, ANGELINA came to Cleveland, Ohio in 1853. Angelina married George Heesen (also see), son of Rudolph. Note resemblance to FREDERICK, following, perhaps same man?

NYLAND, FREDERICK and wife, JANNA T. (VAARWERK), lived in Holland. She died there before 1854, but he was still living in 1888. Known son, JOHN H. (following). Ref: P&BA-Len pg. 394-5.

NYLAND, JOHN H., son of FREDERICK (preceding), came to America in 1854, and settled in Cleveland, Ohio. He married there in April 1858 to HANDRENA (HEESEN), daughter of Rudolph (also see), who had come from Holland with her family at age 10. Children: 1. NELLIE; 2. JENNIE A. (Orange City, Iowa); 3. FRANK; 4. ANGELINE; 5. JOHN R. Ref: P&BA-Len pg. 394-5.

- O -

O'CONNER, CORNELIUS born ca. 1818, and wife, LUCINDA, born ca. 1816, both in Ireland, were listed in the 1850 census of Palmyra Twp., Lenawee Co., Mich. with CORNELIUS, age 4; WILLIAM, age 2, both b. Mich., in their household.

O'CONNER, MICHALIKE was listed in the 1840 census index of Adrian Twp., Lenawee Co., Mich.

O'CONNOR, MARGARET (See Daniel O'Neil)

ODELL, AUGUSTINE M. born ca. 1799, and wife, LYDIA, born ca. 1798, both in NY, settled in Iosco Twp., Livingston Co., Mich. before 1838. They were listed in the 1850 census of Iosco Twp. with GEORGE, age 28; JAMES, age 23; SARAH, age 21; AUGUSTINE, age 19; JACOB, age 17; MARY, age 15, all b. NY; and LEMUEL, age 12; REUBEN, age 8, both b. Mich., in their household. CHARLES, following, was listed a few doors away. Note SILAS, following.

ODELL, CHARLES, probably son of AUGUSTINE M. (preceding), born ca. 1823, and wife, MARIETT, born ca. 1829, both in NY, were listed in the 1850 census of Iosco Twp., Livingston Co., Mich. with ADALADE, age 1, b. Mich., and Jonathan Lamb, age 50, b. VT, in their household.

ODELL, DANIEL born ca. 1818, NY, and wife, MARGARET (JEFFERY), daughter of James K. (also see), born ca. 1828, England, were listed in the 1850 census of Rome Twp., Lenawee Co., Mich. with no family in the household. They later went to Stockton, California.

ODELL, JESSE B., son of SILAS (following), born 9 Mar. 1824, Orange Co., NY, moved to Pennsylvania, and married in Tioga Co. on 3 July 1845 to POLLY A. (ROBERTS), daughter of Zenus (also see). About 1856, after the birth of 3 children, they moved to Fairfield Twp., Lenawee Co., Mich. Children: 1. SARAH E. (m. James Carpenter; he d. 1872, Fairfield Twp.); 2. HANNAH L. (m. George C. Brown, Fairfield Twp.); 3. CORNELIA (m. ? Pentecost; she d. 221 June 1887). Ref: P&BA-Len pg. 601.

ODELL, JOHN C. born ca. 1812, Orange Co., NY, married MARY A. (GERINGER) born ca. 1810, Maryland (whose family had moved to NY). They moved by 1836 to Fairfield Twp., Lenawee Co., Mich.; apparently were in Ohio ca. 1845, but were listed in Fairfield Twp. in the 1850 census with the following children in their household, all but #6 born Mich.: 1. HARRIET, age 14; 2. GILBERT, age 12; 3. THOMAS, age 10; 4. MARTIN (following); 5. ELIZABETH, age 6; 6. MARTHA A., age 5, b. Ohio; 7. SARAH J., age 3; 8. MARIA?, age 2/12. Ref: P&BA-Len pg. 422.

ODELL, JONATHAN born ca. 1818, and wife, RACHEL, born ca. 1822, both in NY, were listed in the 1850 census of Brighton Twp., Livingston Co., Mich. with HENRY, age 8; JOHN, age 6, both b. NY, in their household. Note SILAS, following.

ODELL, MARIA (Mrs.) was born ca. 1811, NY, and was listed in the 1850 census of Adrian Twp., Lenawee Co., Mich. with MARY, age 19, b. Mich.; and GEORGE, age 11; CHARLOTTE, age 9, both b. Iowa Territory, all listed in the household of Alanson Howell, also see. JAMES, age 14, b. Mich., listed in the 1850 census of Adrian Twp. in the household of Richard & Deborah Harkness may relate to this family.

ODELL, MARTIN, son of JOHN C. (preceding), born 4 Dec. 1842, Fairfield Twp., Lenawee Co., Mich., married in Madison Twp. on 28 Mar. 1867 to MARY (HALE), daughter of Israel (also see) and settled in Fairfield Twp. Children: 1. ELMER S.; 2. LEROY M.; 3. BURTON H.; 4. MARY E.; 5. JOHN C. (d. infancy). Ref: P&BA-Len pg. 422.

ODELL, OLIVE married Marcus Bennett (also see) in Niagara Co., NY in 1836.

ODELL, SILAS and wife, MARY (COMFORT), were natives of Orange Co., NY who moved first to Bradford Co., Penn.; then Chemung Co., NY, and later to Livingston Co., Mich. He died in 1867, and she afterwards moved to Fairfield Twp., Lenawee Co., Mich. where she died in 1875. Of 13 children, 6 daughters and 3 sons lived to maturity (only known following): 1. JESSE B. (preceding); 2. SILAS J. b. 14 Dec. 1828, Chemung Co., NY (to Fairfield Twp. in 1853). Ref: P&BA-Len pg. 601.

ODLE see ODELL

OGDEN, BENJAMIN born ca. 1790, and wife, JULIA A., born ca. 1806, both in NY, were listed in the 1850 census of Blissfield Twp., Lenawee Co., Mich. with BENJAMIN, age 14; HENRY, age 12; CHARLES, age 10; GILBERT, age 7; EPHRAIM, age 5, all b. NY, in their household.

OGDEN, MARY born Sussex Co., NJ married Jacob Gunn (also see). Ref: P&BA-Len pg. 945-6.

OHOUT, ELIZABETH (See Jacob Bedell)

OLCOTT, TIMOTHY and wife, HANNAH (CHANDLER), of Windsor, VT, had known daughter, HANNAH (m. Joshua Beaman, also see).

OLDS, AMANDA (See Israel Hale)

OLDS, CHARLES born ca. 1823, possibly son of STEPHEN P. (following), and wife, ORPHA, born ca. 1825, both in NY, were listed in the 1850 census of Macon Twp., Lenawee Co., Mich. with SARAH J., age 6; JAMES H., age 4, both b. Ohio; and ELSA, age 3; CHARLES, age 10/12, both b. Mich., in their household.

OLDS, HARLEY J., son of JAMES (following), born 1816, Painesville, Ashtabula Co., Ohio, came to Jonesville, Mich. with his parents. He married there to DIANTHA (BOWMAN) born 31 July 1817, Claremont, NH. Known daughter, ELLEN C. b. Fayette, Hillsdale Co., Mich. (m. Charles B. Stowell, also see). Ref: P&BA-Len pg. 1072-3.

OLDS, HIRAM born ca. 1810, NY, and wife, MARY J., born ca. 1818, VT, were listed in the 1850 census of Adrian Twp., Lenawee Co., Mich. with FRANKLIN, age 7, b. NY; and ALFRED, age 5; EMILY, age 3, both b. Mich., in their household.

OLDS, JAMES of Mass. was a pioneeer to Painesville, Ashtabula Co., Ohio. In 1830, they removed to Jonesville, Hillsdale Co., Mich. Known son, HARLEY J. (preceding). Ref: P&BA-Len pg. 1072-3. Note: In the History of Ashtabula Co., Ohio, "In 1807, EZEKIEL & THOMAS OLDS settled in the (Conneaut) Township."

OLDS, STEPHEN P. born ca. 1784, Conn., and wife, MARY, born ca. 1798, NJ, were listed in the 1850 census of Macon Twp., Lenawee Co., Mich. with LEVERETT, age

Pioneer Families of Southeastern Michigan

29; WILLIAM, age 18, both b. NY, in their household. Also see CHARLES, preceding.

OLIVER, A. O. Mrs. was the daughter of Simeon Sheldon (also see).

OLIVER, BRIDGET, age 82, born NY, was listed in the 1850 census of Enfield, Tompkins Co., NY with DIANA, age 9, both in the household of Nathan & Betsey Georgia. Note SIMON, following.

OLIVER, GEORGE L., son of SIMON (following), born 9 Apr. 1832, Tompkins Co., NY, moved with his parents to Rome Twp., Lenawee Co., Mich. He married in Adrian to MARY (WYRILL) born 5 Dec. 1833, Yorkshire, England who had come to Tecumseh with her father. The sketch stated that children ANNA, NANCY M., GEORGE W., and an unnamed infant were deceased prior to 1888, and surviving were OLIVE E. b. 19 Nov. 1865; CORA B. b. 14 Jan. 1868; ERNEST H. b. 7 Jan. 1870. Ref: P&BA-Len pg. 309-10.

OLIVER, JAMES wife, MARTHA (HAWKINS) were natives of England who went first to Rochester, NY, and then in 1857 to Franklin Twp., Lenawee Co., NY. Known daughter, ANNA N. (m. Henry C. Owen, also see).

OLIVER, JAMES born ca. 1797, NY, and wife, ELIZABETH, born ca. 1807, Penn., were listed in the 1850 census of Tecumseh Twp., Lenawee Co., Mich. with ALMIRA, age 2, b. Mich., in their household. Note SIMON, following.

OLIVER, SIMON born ca. 1806, Tompkins Co., NY, moved to Albany where he married MARY (WRIGHT) born ca. 1810, NY. In 1844, they removed to Rome Twp., Lenawee Co., Mich.; and about 1848 to Tecumseh Twp. There were 13 children, and only one mentioned was GEORGE L. (preceding). In the 1850 census, in addition to the preceding, they listed ELIZABETH, age 16; WILLIAM, age 15; EDWARD, age 13; HENRY, age 12; DIANNA, age 10; JAMES, age 8; MARY, age 7, all b. NY; and SIMON, age 6; OLIVE, age 2; JULIA, age 12, both b. Mich. in their household. Note BRIDGET; & JAMES, both preceding.

OLNEY, ELIZABETH "BETSEY" born Rhode Island, lived Herkimer Co., NY married John Ladd (also see) and lived Victor, Ontario Co. NY.

OLNEY, ISAAC born ca. 1827, NY, was listed in the 1850 census of Medina Twp., Lenawee Co., Mich. with mother?, POLLY, age 66, b. Mass., in his household.

O'NEIL, DANIEL and wife, MARGARET (O'CONNOR), were natives of Co. Kerry, Ireland, who came to Cayuga Co., NY by 1848. In 1850, they moved to Medina Twp., Lenawee Co., Mich. He died 23 Oct. 1877, and she was still living in 1888. There were 2 sons and 5 daughters, only names mentioned were MARY (m. John Monahan[3], also see, as 2nd wife; DEBORAH (m. John W. Monahan[4], also see). Ref: P&BA-Len pg. 1109-10.

ONSTEAD see ONSTED

ONSTED - From <u>History of Sussex & Warren Cos. NJ</u>, by J. P. Snell, 1881. MICHAEL ONSTED from Germany settled in "Germany Flats," Andover, Sussex Co., NJ "long before 1800," and died there in 1820. Mentioned were sons GEORGE & MICHAEL, JR. (d. ca. 1815. JOHN, a son of MICHAEL, settled in Andover village in 1827 and remained there. The preceding is probably the ancestry of the following, exact descent not known.

ONSTED, ADELIA born ca. 1831, NJ, was listed in the 1850 census of Raisin Twp., Lenawee Co., Mich. in the Joseph Gray household. Note JOHN, following.

ONSTED, BENJAMIN, probably son of JOHN (following), born ca. 1821, NJ, and wife, CLARISSA, born ca. 1822, NY, were listed in the 1850 census of Cambridge Twp., Lenawee Co., Mich. with CHRISTIANNA, age 7; CAROLINE, age 5; ANNETTA, age 2, all b. Mich., in their household.

ONSTED, GEORGE born ca. 1813, NJ (See JOHN, following).

ONSTED, GEORGE (See Edmund Lapham)

ONSTED, JANE born 9 Mar. 1810, Sussex Co., NJ (See George Sheeler; also note JOHN, following.)

ONSTED, JOHN and wife, ANN (HINES) born ca. 1782, were natives of Sussex Co., NJ who moved to Cambridge Twp., Lenawee Co., Mich. in 1836. There were 13 children, names not stated, except #3. PETER (following); & ADENIA b. 4 Dec. 1824, Sussex Co., NJ (m. Augustus Bedell, also see). In the 1850 census, Ann was listed in household of probably son, WILLIAM (following); and in the household were GEORGE, age 37; CATHARINE, age 20, both b. NJ. Also probably their children: ADELIA; BENJAMIN; JANE (all preceding); and MARY A. (following). Ref: P&BA-Len pg. 753-4.

ONSTED, LEWIS, son of PETER (following), born ca. 1847, Cambridge Twp., Lenawee Co., Mich., married on 19 Mar. 1869 to EDNA (POWELL), daughter of Henry (also see), and settled in Cambridge Twp. Children: 1. MABEL (d. age 8 mos); 2. PETER H. Ref: P&BA-Len pg. 1100-1.

ONSTED, MARY A. born ca. 1803, Sussex Co., NJ, married Israel Baker Maxwell (also see). Ref: P&BA-Len pg. 971-2. Note JOHN, preceding.

ONSTED, PETER, son of JOHN (preceding), born 10 Mar. 1808, Sparta, Sussex Co., NJ, married on 21 Mar. 1829 (1828?) to ELIZABETH (CONKLIN), daughter of Isaac (also see) of Sparta. About 1830, they removed to Yates Co., NY; and in 1836 to Cambridge Twp., Lenawee Co., Mich. Children (ages from 1850 census of Cambridge Twp.): 1. ANN, age 22, b. NJ (m. William Pulver, Hillsdale Co.); 2. MARY, age 18, b. NY (m. Richard Moore, St. Johns, Mich.); 3. JOHN, age 16, b. NY (d. age 18); 4. LAFAYETTE, age 14, b. Mich. (to Iowa); 5. CHARLOTTE b. 7 Jan. 1839 (m. John O. Maxwell[5], also see); 6. GEORGE H., age 10 (d. Civil War, New Madrid, Miss.); 7. SARAH, age 8 (m. Edwin Taylor, Cambridge Twp.); 8. DELILAH, age 6 (m. Isaac Russell); 9. LEWIS, age 3 (preceding); 10. MELISSA E., age 1 (m. Andrew Riley, son of Philemon, also see). Elizabeth died in 1852. Peter married again to MARTHA (ALDRICH), daughter of William (also see); and she died 26 Nov. 1870, leaving 8 children (names not stated). Peter married third to Mrs. CHARLOTTE (HOUGHTON) TREAT, widow of John, and in 1871, they moved to the city of Adrian. He died there in 1883, age 71. Ref: P&BA-Len pg. 971-2; 1100-1.

ONSTED, RACHEL (See Jonas Kishpaugh)

ONSTED, WILLIAM, probably son of JOHN (preceding), born ca. 1816, NJ, was listed in the 1850 census of Cambridge Twp., Lenawee Co., Mich. with ANN (probably his mother), age 68; ALFRED, age 3, b. Mich.;

GEORGE, age 37; CATHARINE, age 20, both b. NJ, in his household.

OPDYKE also see UPDIKE

OPDYKE, AMOS³, son of LUTHER² (preceding), born 9 June 1819, Hunterdon Co., NJ, moved with his parents to Seneca Co., NY. He married there to LAVINA (LOWE), daughter of Jonathan (also see). In 1853, they moved from Seneca Co., NY to Hudson Twp., Lenawee Co., Mich. They lived last in Hudson village. Children: 1. GEORGE; 2. JANE; 3. CHARLES; 4. FRANCES; 5. DELLA MAY. Ref: P&BA-Len pg. 1075-6.

OPDYKE, LUTHER¹ of "near Everittstown," Hunterdon Co., NJ, was the father of LUTHER² (following). In The Division of Estates of Hunterdon Co., NJ, it is probably the estate of Luther¹ of Alexandria Twp., deceased, that mentions the dower of wife, MARY, said to be located "along the Quakertown to Everittstown Rd." (dated 1838). Ref: P&BA-Len pg. 1075-6.

OPDYKE, LUTHER², son of LUTHER¹ (preceding), moved from Hunterdon Co., NJ to Fayette, Seneca Co., NY in 1831. His wife, name not stated, died there, and he later moved to Waterloo, NY where he died. Known son, AMOS³ (preceding). Ref: P&BA-Len pg. 1075-6.

ORAM, ARTHUR of Adrian, Lenawee Co., Mich. was a cousin to GEORGE H. (following). Ref: P&BA-Len pg. 645-6.

ORAM, GEORGE born 3 Feb. 1812, England, married MARY (PARSONS), daughter of John (also see) of Brighton, England. They came to the US in 1853, and settled in Adrian, Lenawee Co., Mich. He died 7 May 1863, and she died 12 Oct. 1877. Children: 1. ELIZABETH b. 9 Jan. 1840 (m. ? Wood; she d. 1875, Adrian Twp., leaving 4 children); 2. JULIA b. 8 Mar. 1842 (m. W. Wickham, also see); 3. GEORGE H. (following). Ref: P&BA-Len pg. 645-6.

ORAM, GEORGE H., son of GEORGE (preceding), born 21 Sept. 1851, England, came to Adrian, Lenawee Co., Mich. with his parents. He married in June 1878 to JOSEPHINE (DALY), daughter of Henry F. (also see), and settled in Adrian. Children: 1. LIBBIE (d. infancy); 2. MARY L. b. 17 Feb. 1880; 3. ETHEL b. 16 Jan. 1882; 4. GEORGE HARRY b. 19 May 1885. Ref: P&BA-Len pg. 645-6.

ORAM, LUCINDA married in Canada to James Blair (also see).

ORMSBY, AMOS and brother, EPHRAIM & NATHANIEL, came from England to Colonial America. One settled in New Hampshire; one went to an unknown location; and NATHANIEL settled in Norwich, Conn. Note SAMUEL (following). Ref: P&BA-Len pg. 306-7.

ORMSBY, C. N. was listed in the 1830 census of Lenawee Co., Michigan Territory, with males: 2 20-30; and female: 1 30-40 in the household. There is a C. N. "Omsby" in the 1840 census index of Washtenaw Co., Mich.

ORMSBY, JOHN W. born 15 Mar. 1831, Conn., married JULIA (FINN), daughter of John (also see) of Rollin Twp., Lenawee Co., Mich. By 1880, they lived in Rome Twp., Lenawee Co., Mich. He died 4 Aug. 1888, and she died 8 May 1917. She is buried in Dover Cemetery, Lenawee Co. Children: 1. LUCY M. b. ca. 1867 (m. Thomas Pulling; d. 1905); 2. MARY ELIZABETH "ELLA" b. ca. 1870 (m/1 William H. Sharrar; m/2 William Tuttle); 3. HENRY B. b. ca. 1874 (m. Allie Clark); 4. CARRIE AMANDA b. 6 Mar. 1833 (m/1 William A. Lewis; m/2 Will Johnson; she d. 1961, buried Dover Cem.) Ref: Lewis Family Records.

ORMSBY, LYSANDER, son of SAMUEL (following), born 5 July 1815, Westhampton, Hampshire Co., Mass., came first to Blissfield Twp., Lenawee Co., Mich. in April 1837. Before 1840, he moved to Somerfield Twp., Monroe Co., Mich. He married there on 27 FEb. 1840 to OLIVE C. (BURNHAM), daughter of Calvin (also see). In 1852, they moved to Deerfield, Lenawee Co., Mich. Children: 1. ELIZA C. (d. age 24); 2. EDWIN S. (to Emmetsburg, IA); 3. ALVIN C. (New York City); 4. HATTIE A. (d. age 6); 5. CHARLES G. BLIVEN (Emmetsburg, IA); 6. ETTA B. (m. William Federman; d. Mar. 1884, Deerfield). Olive C. died 28 July 1884; and Lysander married again to MARY E. (MASTERS), daughter of William of Monroe Co., Mich. Ref: P&BA-Len pg. 306-7.

ORMSBY, MARIA (See Lorenzo Tabor, and note Mrs. SUSAN, following).

ORMSBY, NATHANIEL came from England, and settled in Norwich, Conn. in Colonial times. He married ELIZABETH (PERKINS); and in 1776, they moved to Huntington, Hampshire Co., Mass. He served from there in the Revolution, and died in Albany during the War. Known son, SAMUEL (following). Elizabeth married again to a Deacon Miller and remained in Mass. Ref: P&BA-Len pg. 306-7.

ORMSBY, SAMUEL, son of NATHANIEL (preceding), born ca. 1775, Norwich, Conn., moved with his parents to Huntington, Mass. He married RACHEL (DAY) born 1 Apr. 1785, Chester, Mass. He died in Chester on 15 Oct. 1830. Twelve children, of whom 11 grew to maturity, and only known are #7. LYSANDER (preceding); and E. D. (who also came to Michigan). Ref: P&BA-Len pg. 306-7.

ORMSBY, SUSAN born ca. 1783, Vermont, was listed in the 1850 census of Adrian Twp., Lenawee Co., Mich. in the household of Lorenzo Tabor. Also listed was CHRISTIANA, age 39, born VT. MARIA, age 34, born VT (m. Lorenzo Tabor on 13 May 1839, Springfield, VT) is also probably her daughter.

ORR, HUDSON (See William M. Corbett)

ORSBORN see OSBORN - Note: In the 1840 census index of Lenawee Co., Mich., were the following, all written as "Orsborn or Orsburn," and in 1850 were in the census written "Osborn." ABRAM; SAMUEL; JESSE in Woodstock Twp.; GEORGE in Madison Twp.; CALVIN in Rome Twp.; CHLOE in Raisin Twp.; JAMES in Adrian Twp.; JOHN & WILLIAM H. in Macon Twp.

OSBORN also see OSBORNE

OSBORN, ABRAM was listed as "Orsborn" in the 1840 census index of Woodstock Twp., Lenawee Co., Mich. as a "pensioner, 85y." Adjacent to him were SAMUEL; & JESSE (both following).

OSBORN, ALBERT D., son of RICHARD H. (following), born 25 June 1847, Medina Twp., Lenawee Co., Mich., married BARBARA (LINDERMAN), daughter of

Pioneer Families of Southeastern Michigan

Michael (also see). Children: 1. EUSEBIUS (d. 17 mos); 2. ELWIN D.; 3. EDITH I.; 4. LURA E. Ref: P&BA-Len pg. 860-1.

OSBORN, ALVIN, probably son of JESSE (following), born ca. 1819, and wife, ANGELIQUE, born ca. 1819, both in NY, were listed in the 1850 census of Woodstock Twp., Lenawee Co., Mich. (next door to JESSE) with FRANCINE, age 8; NATHANIEL, age 6, both b. Mich., in their household.

OSBORN, ASA, son of JOEL (following), born 20 Dec. 1775, Berkshire Co., Mass., married on 26 Feb. 1807 in Saratoga Co., NY to EUNICE (NORTHRUP). He served in the War of 1812. They settled in Batavia, Genesee Co., NY; and then moved to Montgomery Co., NY. In 1836, they moved to Fairfield Twp., Lenawee Co., Mich. in the area later ceded to Ohio, first as Lucas Co., then as Royalton, Fulton Co., Ohio. He died there in 1845, and she was still living in 1888. Known children: 1. TRUMAN (d. 1844, Steuben Co., Ind.); 2. Daughter (m. Rev. A. Foster 19 Apr. 1844; Minnesota); 3. VAN RENSSELAER J. (following). Ref: P&BA-Len pg. 713-4.

OSBORN, BENJAMIN D.^{3}, son of WILLIAM^2 (following), born ca. 1816, NY, married first about 1841 in Dutchess Co., NY to MARY (BAKER). They moved possibly to Genesee Co., NY; and moved from there to Hillsdale Co., Mich.; and about 1844 to Medina Twp., Lenawee Co., Mich. There were 12 children, and those known were in the household in the 1850 census: 1. JOHN b. ca. 1843 (m. Martha Consaules, Medina Twp.); 2. HORACE G. b. ca. 1845 (d. Civil War); 3. GEORGE b. ca. 1848; 4. ZACHARIAH T. b. ca. 1850. Mary died, and Benjamin D. married again on 5 Mar. 1873 to Mrs. MARY L. (WILLIAMS) EDWARDS, daughter of Thomas (also see). Ref: P&BA-Len pg. 1077-8.

OSBORN, CHARLES H. born ca. 1821, NY, and wife, JEMIMA, born ca. 1831, Ohio, were listed in the 1850 census of Woodstock Twp., Lenawee Co., Mich. with IRA, age 1, b. Mich., in the household.

OSBORN, CHLOE was listed head of household in the 1840 census index of Raisin Twp., Lenawee Co., Mich.

OSBORN, DAVID N. born ca. 1807, Penn., and wife, MARY, born ca. 1815, NJ, were listed in the 1840 census index of Tecumseh Twp., Lenawee Co., Mich.; and in the 1850 census with CAROLINE, age 16; DAVID, age 14, both b. NY; and WILLIAM, age 12, b. Mich., in their household.

OSBORN, ERASMUS born ca. 1829, NY (See RICHARD of Woodstock Twp., following).

OSBORN, GEORGE, age not known, born NY, and wife, MARIA, born ca. 1807, Mass., were listed in the 1840 census index of Madison Twp. as "Orsborn." In the 1850 census they listed JOHN W., age 19, b. NY; and HARRIET A., age 17; EDWIN J., age 15; CORNELIUS R., age 10; CHARLES H., age 5, all b. Mich., in their household.

OSBORN, HARRIET (See Charles M. Marshall)

OSBORN, HIRAM was listed in the 1840 census index of Hudson Twp., Lenawee Co., Mich. In the 1850 census, there was a younger man, HIRAM T., age 20, born NY, listed with SARAH J., age 22, and EMA? (female), age 15, both b. NY, in the household.

OSBORN, JAMES born ca. 1830, Mass., and wife, MARGARET, born ca. 1832, NY, were listed in the 1850 census of Tecumseh Twp., Lenawee Co., Mich. with no family in their household.

OSBORN, JAMES born ca. 1810, NY, and wife, ABBY, born ca. 1814, NJ, were probably they listed as "Orsborn" in the 1840 census index of Adrian Twp., Lenawee Co., Mich.; and were listed in the 1850 census with ANGELINE, age 15; JOHN C., age 13; MARY, age 11; EMERY, age 10; ELIZABETH, age 8; JANE, age 4; JAMES L., age 2?/12, all b. Mich., in their household.

OSBORN, JESSE born ca. 1784, and wife, RACHEL, born ca. 1794, both in NY, were listed in the 1840 census index of Woodstock Twp., Lenawee Co., Mich. adjacent to ABRAM (preceding). In the 1850 census of Woodstock Twp., they listed WILLIAM, age 16; Rosana McClure, age 17, both b. Mich., in the household. Next door in the census was ALVIN (preceding).

OSBORN, JOEL and wife, THEDA (TIEDEN), were natives of Berkshire Co., Massachusetts, and parents of ASA (preceding) born 20 Dec. 1775. Ref: P&BA-Len pg. 713-4.

OSBORN, JOHN born ca. 1790, New Hampshire, and wife, ELIZABETH, born ca. 1800, NJ, were listed in the 1850 census of Macon Twp., Lenawee Co., Mich. with WILLIAM, age 31; MALCOM?, age 31; OLIVER, age 21; ELIZABETH A., age 17, all b. NY, in their household.

OSBORN, JOHN "of a Conn. family" served in the War of 1812; and afterwards settled in Perinton, Monroe Co., NY. In 1840, he settled in the village of Hudson, Lenawee Co., Mich. His wife, Mrs. MERCY ANN EATON, was born in Duanesburg, then Albany Co., now Schenectady Co., NY. They lived in Pittsford, Hillsdale Co. He died 28 Apr. 1867. Children: 1. ELIZA ANN (d. age 6 yrs); 2. JOHN M. (following); 3. DELORA O. b. 9 Mar. 1821 (m. William Baker, also see). Ref: P&BA-Len pg. 180-1; 931-2; 1180-5.

OSBORN, JOHN M., son of JOHN (preceding), born 9 Mar. 1819, Perinton, Monroe Co., NY, moved with his parents to the village of Hudson, Lenawee Co., Mich. He married first in 1851 to ELIZABETH (DANIELS) of Wayne Co., Mich., and she died in 1866. He married again on 5 Apr. 1870 to Mrs. HARRIET A. (WHITE) ROBINSON, daughter of Rev. William (also see) of Jacksonville, Tompkins Co., NY. No children were listed. Ref: P&BA-Len pg. 1180-5 with portrait.

OSBORN, JOHN V? born ca. 1808, and wife, MARY, born ca. 1810, both in Mass., were listed in the 1850 census of Tecumseh Twp., Lenawee Co., Mich. with SUSANNAH, age 22; JOHN, age 18; CAROLINE, age 16; ABIGAIL, age 13; BENJAMIN, age 10, all b. Mass.; and GEORGE, age 7; LEWIS, age 4; LUCRETIA, age 2, all b. Mich.; and Emma Whiting, age 56, born Mass., in their household.

OSBORN, MARY (See George W. Clark; Stephen Turrell; & Hiram Johnson of Woodstock Twp.)

OSBORN, PETER born ca. 1821, NY, was listed in the 1850 census of Tecumseh Twp., Lenawee Co., Mich. in an Inn.

OSBORN, RICHARD born ca. 1785, Mass., and wife, LYDDA? (SYBBA?), born ca. 1793, NY, were listed in the 1840 census of Woodstock Twp., Lenawee Co., Mich. with RICHARD, age 30; MILTON, age 27; JOSEPH, age 23; HOMER, age 21; EUNICE, age 18, all b. NY; and LYDDA/SYBBA?, age 14; JULIA, age 10, both b. Mich., and listed last was ERASMUS, age 21, b. NY, possibly not a son of this household?

OSBORN, RICHARD H.[1] was born Long Island, and served in the American Revolution. He was the grandson of WILLIAM FRITZ OSBORN of Glasgow, Scotland. Richard H. was the father of WILLIAM[2] (following). Ref: P&BA-Len pg. 1077-8.

OSBORN, RICHARD H.[3], son of WILLIAM[2] (following), born 10 Feb. 1819, Dutchess Co., NY, moved to Hillsdale Co., Mich. in 1836 with his parents. When of age, he moved to Medina Twp., Lenawee Co., Mich. where he married on 15 Nov. 1843 to PERMELIA (GALLUP), daughter of Ezekiel (also see). She died 15 July 1884. Children: 1. RICHARD A. b. ca. 1845 (m. Hattie E. Roberts); 2. ALBERT D. (preceding); 3. GERTRUDE (m. F. F. Wright, Wright Twp., Hillsdale Co.); 4. EMMA (m. M. W. Higgins, Wright Twp., Hillsdale Co.); 5. LYDIA (d. age 18). Ref: P&BA-Len pg. 530-1.

OSBORN, SAMUEL born ca. 1802, and wife, ELIZABETH, born ca. 1803, were listed in the 1840 census index (as "Orsborn") of Woodstock Twp., Lenawee Co., Mich. adjacent to ABRAM (preceding); and in the 1850 census with JOHN, age 18; SUSAN, age 16; BULA? (male), age 15, all b. NY; and RACHEL, age 13; GEORGE, age 7, both b. Mich., in their household.

OSBORN, SUSAN, age 22, born Mass., was listed in the 1850 census of Madison Twp., Lenawee Co., Mich. in a Waite household.

OSBORN, VAN RENSSELAER J., son of ASA (preceding), born 2 Apr. 1816, Montgomery Co., NY, moved to Michigan with his parents. He married on 24 Sept. 1840 in Adrian Twp., Lenawee Co., Mich. to URSULA A. (WARNER), daughter of John (also see). They moved into the city of Adrian in 1865. Children: 1. JONATHAN B. b. 18 July 1842 (served Civil War); 2. DEXSEY A. b. 20 Aug. 1844 (m. J. H. Baylor; E. Portland, Ore.); 3. THEDA b. 1847 (d. 1858); 4. JULIA A. b. 14 Nov. 1852 (m. C. M. Weaver; d. 25 June 1885, Hillsdale, Mich.); 5. CHARLES W. b. 20 Aug. 1855 (d. July 1875); 6. MARY (d. infancy). Ref: P&BA-Len pg. 713-4.

OSBORN, WILLIAM[2], son of RICHARD H.[1] (preceding), born 1791, married CATHARINE (DAVIS), born 1797, both in Dutchess Co., NY, later moved to Orange Co., NY. In 1836, they moved to Morenci, Lenawee Co., Mich.; then settled in Waldron, Mich. where they remained. Eleven children, those mentioned were RICHARD H.[3]; and BENJAMIN D.[3] (both preceding). Ref: P&BA-Len pg. 530-1; 1076-7.

OSBORNE also see OSBORN

OSBORNE, FRANKLIN, son of JAMES (following), was born 16 Aug. 1820, Ovid, Seneca Co., NY, and married there on 1 Jan. 1845 to ALICE D. (GROVE), daughter of William (also see), and moved to Franklin Twp., Lenawee Co., Mich. He was injured in a train accident in Ashtabula Co., Ohio in 1876 while enroute to visit in New York, and died as a result on 6 Feb. 1881. There were 5 children, and those known were listed in the household in the 1850 census of Franklin Twp.: 1. WALTER b. ca. 1846; 2. WILLIAM b. ca. 1848. Ref: P&BA-Len pg. 261-2.

OSBORNE, JAMES born Colerain, Mass., moved to NY where he married in Seneca Co., NY before 1816 to BETSEY (LONGCORE). They moved to Franklin Twp., Lenawee Co., Mich. (possibly after 1850). His parents, names not stated, also moved to Franklin Twp. where they died after 10 years at an advanced age. Known sons: RICHARD (following); FRANKLIN (preceding). Ref: P&BA-Len pg. 261-2.

OSBORNE, JOHN H. born ca. 1819, and wife, LORAIN, born ca. 1820, both in NY, were listed in the 1850 census of Macon Twp., Lenawee Co., Mich. with REBECCA, age 10; HENRY, age 8, both b. NY; and GIDEON P., age 2, b. Mich., in their household.

OSBORNE, JOSEPH W., son of WILLIAM H. (following), born 29 June 1849, Macon Twp., Lenawee Co., Mich., married on 8 Feb. 1871 to HELEN (HAND), daughter of Edward (also see). Children: 1. ANNA M.; 2. HATTIE J. Ref: P&BA-Len pg. 1025-6.

OSBORNE, POLLY (See Abraham Bedell)

OSBORNE, RICHARD, son of JAMES (preceding), born 18 June 1816, Ovid, Seneca Co., NY, married in Dec. 1842 to CHARLOTTE (TILLYAR), daughter of William (also see). They moved first to Findlay, Hancock Co., Ohio; and then in 1863 moved to Tecumseh Twp., Lenawee Co., Mich. He was killed in the Ashtabula Co., Ohio train disaster. Charlotte married again to Edwin Cook (also see). Ref: P&BA-Len pg. 352-3.

OSBORNE, THOMAS was born 1784, Mass., and as an adult moved to Ovid, Seneca Co., NY. He married in 1802 to MARY (HOGARTH), daughter of John (also see) born 1783, Ireland. They moved to Macon Twp., Lenawee Co., Mich. in 1830; and Mary died in Franklin Twp. in 1850. Known son, WILLIAM H. (following). Ref: P&BA-Len pg. 421-2.

OSBORNE, WILLIAM H., son of THOMAS (preceding), born 29 Oct. 1814, Ovid, Seneca Co., NY, married there on 26 Apr. 1836 to ANN HEX (WOODWARD), daughter of John (also see). They moved to Macon Twp., Lenawee Co., Mich. where Ann died on 24 Dec. 1840, leaving a daughter, 1. MARY ELIZABETH b. 16 Sept. 1839, Ovid (m. John F. Hicks, Tecumseh Twp.) William H. married again before 1843 to MARY JANE (FOOTE), daughter of David (also see). In 1883, they moved into Tecumseh, Mich. Children: 2. ANN HEX b. 19 Apr. 1843 (m. John Hagerman; Colorado Spring, CO); 3. SOPHIA M. b. 10 Apr. 1845 (m. George L. Graves; Milwaukee, WI); 4. THOMAS b. 22 Feb. 1847; 5. REBECCA J. (twin of Joseph) b. 29 June 1849 (m. Henry C. Lowe; Detroit Mich.); 6. JOSEPH W. (preceding); 7. IRVING S. b. 21 June 1851 (Tecumseh Twp.); 8. WILLIAM H. b. 16 Oct. 1853 (to Milwaukee, WI). Ref: P&BA-Len pg. 421-2; 1025-6.

OSGOOD, CALVIN born ca. 1787, Mass., and wife, LUCY, born ca. 1798, NY, were listed in the 1850 census of Rome Twp., Lenawee Co., Mich. with LOVICA, age 25; GERSHOM, age 23; GARDNER, age 16, all b. NY; and ALBERT, age 6, b. Mich., in their household.

OSGOOD, CORNELIUS born 1813, Seneca Co., NY, came to Canandaigua, Seneca Twp., Lenawee Co., Mich. in 1834. It may be he listed as "C." in the 1840 census index of Medina Twp. He married in Macon Twp. to PHOEBE A. (TAYER) born ca. 1820, NY. Cornelius engaged in mining, and was killed in a mine shaft accident in Caribou, Boulder Co, Colorada in August 1868. In the 1850 census of Madison Twp., Lenawee Co., Mich., he was apparently away as Phoebe was listed head of household, with only son 1. (HENRY) HARRISON b. 23 Oct. 1840, in her household; other children

Pioneer Families of Southeastern Michigan

mentioned in sketch: 2. PERRY; 3. TUNIS C.; 4. ELIZA JANE. In 1888, Phoebe was living in Adrian. Ref: P&BA-Len pg. 240-1.

OSGOOD, D. was listed in the 1840 census index of Macon Twp., Lenawee Co., Mich.

OSGOOD, GEORGE V., son of JOHN (following), born 1 Jan. 1833, Lodi, Seneca Co., NY, came with his mother to Macon Twp., Lenawee Co., Mich. in 1845. He married on 15 Apr. 1857 to MARY E. (BIRD), daughter of Burtis (also see). They moved to Clinton Co., Ill, where she died on 7 Oct. 1864. Children: 1. MURTIE B. (d. age 10); 2. CLARA (d. age 2 mos); 3. JOHN S. (m. May Fitzmyer, Grand Haven, Mich.) George V. married again on 11 Mar. 1868 to Mrs. ANZOLETTE (LaTOURRETTE) HUNT, daughter of Abraham, and widow of Joseph M. (see both). They settled in Macon Twp. Children: 4. JOSEPH M. (d. age 1 mo); 5. PHEBE; 6. EVELINE. Ref: P&BA-Len pg. 581-2.

OSGOOD, HENRY, son of CORNELIUS (preceding), born 23 Oct. 1840, Seneca Twp., Lenawee Co., Mich., married on 23 Nov. 1868 to SARAH L. (MILLER), daughter of Lewis (also see). Sarah's mother had died when she was 18 months old, and she was returned to Seneca Co., NY where she lived with an aunt, Mrs. T. C. OSGOOD, and where she had remained until age 18. Children: 1. MANSON P.; 2. W. HARRY C. Ref: P&BA-Len pg. 240-1.

OSGOOD, HUBBARD of Conn. was the father of WILLIAM (following); and there were other sons, names not stated, who were Baptist Ministers. He remained in Conn. where he died age 104. Ref: P&BA-Len pg. 1040-1.

OSGOOD, JOEL born ca. 1806, and wife, ANNA, born ca. 1810, both in NY, were listed in the 1850 census of Fairfield Twp., Lenawee Co., Mich. with LYMAN, age 16; BENNETT, age 12; PERRY, age 9; JOEL, age 4, all b. Ohio, in their household.

OSGOOD, JOHN, son of WILLIAM (following), born 1800, Seneca Co., NY, married there to MARTHA (VAN VLEET), daughter of George (also see). He died there at age 41; and about 1845, Martha moved with 6 children to Macon Twp., Lenawee Co., Mich. Known children: 1. LESTER (following); 2. GEORGE V. (preceding); 3. MARY M. (twin of George; m. Richard Clarkson, also see); 4. JAMES b. ca. 1837; 5. ELIZABETH b. ca. 1842. WILLIAM, age 20, b. NY, in the 1850 census of Tecumseh Twp. may be another son. Ref: P&BA-Len pg. 240-1 & 467-8.

OSGOOD, JOSIAH, son of WILLIAM, born 11 Apr. 1817, Lodi, Seneca Co., NY, married 10 Sept. 1844 to MARY C. (FOSTER), daughter of John R. (also see) and settled in Medina Twp. Children: 1. OMER D. b. ca. 1848 (m. Harriet Stites; children: Frederick E.; Edith May; Burt F.; Anna; lived Morenci, Mich.); 2. ELLEN A. (m. N. V. Coomer, also see); 3. ELMER W. (m. Ada Frantz, Britton, Mich.); 4. WILLIAM R. (Britton, Mich.); 5. DARWIN H. Ref: P&BA-Len pg. 1040-1.

OSGOOD, LESTER, son of JOHN (preceding), born 26 Apr. 1829, Lodi, Seneca Co., NY, moved with his mother to Macon Twp., Lenawee Co., Mich. He married there 21 Oct. 1863 to SARAH E. (HOAGLAND), daughter of Henry (also see) and settled there. Children: 1. MARY M.; 2. JENNIE H. Ref: P&BA-Len pg. 405-6.

OSGOOD, WILLIAM, son of Hubbard (preceding), born 3 Oct. 1770, Conn., moved to Ovid, Seneca Co., NY where he married MAGDALENA (COVERT) born 12 June 1779, NJ. They lived in Lodi, Seneca Co., NY; and he died there in 1823, age 45, and she died in 1853, age 76. Fifteen children, names not stated, except JOHN (preceding); & youngest, JOSIAH (preceding). Ref: P&BA-Len pg. 1040-1. Also note CORNELIUS, preceding.

OSTERHOUT, DAVID B., son of JOHN (following), born 9 Jan. 1826, Lodi, Seneca Co., NY, moved to Michigan with his parents. He married on 1 Jan. 1850(1?) in Ridgeway Twp., Lenawee Co., Mich. to WILMINA (HOAGLAND), daughter of Henry (also see). He served in the Mexican War. He died 9 Feb. 1879, and his wife was still residing on their farm in 1888. Children: 1. HENRY B. (d. 5 Apr. 1858, age 3y/5m); 2. LAVERN (m. Nancy McCarbery, dau. of Henry, also see); 3. MARY E. (m. Stephen V. Dibble; she d. 26 July 1882); 4. CLARA (d. 8 Sept. 1880, age 18); 5. GRANT H. Ref: P&BA-Len pg. 374-5.

OSTERHOUT, FLOWER and wife, ELEANOR (MILLER), moved from Seneca Co., NY to Macon Twp., Lenawee Co., Mich. He died in 1844, a young man, and she may have also died before 1850. Known daughter, SARAH A., born ca. 1837, NY, was listed in the 1850 census of Macon Twp. in the household of Jehiel Miller (also see). Sarah A. married in 1855 in Hillsdale Co., Mich. to John Britton, Jr. (also see) and settled in Britton, Lenawee Co., Mich. Ref: P&BA-Len pg. 902-3. COVET (COVERT?), age 16, b. NY, listed in the 1850 census of Macon Twp. in a household next door to Stephen Miller, may be another child of Flower?

OSTERHOUT, JOHN born ca. 1786, NY, and wife, SARAH "SALLY" (BAILEY), born ca. 1796, Penn., moved from Seneca Co., NY to Michigan in 1842. They were listed in the 1850 census of Ridgeway Twp., Lenawee Co., Mich. Known children: MARY (m. John Dubois, also see) and the following were in the household in 1850: DAVID B. (preceding); BARTON, age 21; JAMES, age 17, all b. NY. Also in the household was Joseph Holden, age 74, b. NY, relationship not known. Ref: P&BA-Len pg. 314-5; 374-5. Also note FLOWER, preceding.

OSTERHOUT, L. B. was listed in the 1840 census index of Fayette Twp., Hillsdale Co., Mich.

OSTERHOUT, ROSANNA born ca. 1840, NY, was listed in the 1850 census of Adrian Twp., Lenawee Co., Mich. in the household of John & Almira Vandegriffe. Note FLOWER, preceding.

OUDEKIRK, PAMELIA (See Cornelius Vail)

OWEN also called OWENS

OWEN, AMAZIAH? born ca. 1800, and wife, CATHARINE, born ca. 1808, both in NY, were listed in the 1850 census of Rollin Twp., Lenawee Co., Mich. with ANANIAS?, age 20; ELIZABETH, age 17; LOUISA, age 16; WESLEY, age 13; MARY M., age 10, all b. NY; and WILLIAM H., age 6; GILFORD L., age 3, both b. Mich., in their household.

OWEN, CALVIN born ca. 1794, and wife, REBECCA, born ca. 1790, both in NY, were listed in the 1840 census index of

Palmyra Twp., Lenawee Co., Mich.; and in the 1850 census of Rome Twp. with JAMES, age 32, born VT, in the household. ELIZABETH A., age 16, b. NY, listed in a Bailey household in the 1850 census of Rome Twp., may relate to this family.

OWEN, CATHARINE E. born ca. 1829, NY, with CHARLES W., age 4/12, b. Mich., were listed in the 1850 census of Adrian Twp., Lenawee Co., Mich. in the household of Benjamin G. & Lavonia Green.

OWEN, CHARLES born ca. 1802, and wife, ELIZABETH "BETSEY," born ca. 1808, both in NY, lived in Wolcott, Wayne Co., NY in 1829. They were in the 1850 census of Rome Twp., Lenawee Co., Mich. Children: HANNAH ELIZABETH b. 4 Dec. 1829, Wolcott, NY (m. Hiram C. Colbath, also see). In Charles' household in 1850 were: CHARLES W., age 18; SALLY A., age 16; WILLIAM, age 14, all b. NY; and THOMAS, age 11; DAVID, age 8; SOLOMON, age 3, all b. MIch. Ref: P&BA-Len pg. 862-3.

OWEN, DERICK W. was listed in the 1840 census index of Clinton, Lenawee Co., Mich. adjacent to HENRY (following).

OWEN, EPHRAIM was listed in the 1840 census index of Cambridge Twp., Lenawee Co., Mich. He was not listed in 1850 census of Cambridge Twp., however, there is a NANCY C., age 42, b. NY, listed in the household of Willard Smith.

OWEN, HENRY born ca. 1827, NY, was listed in the 1850 census of Riga Twp., Lenawee Co., Mich.

OWEN, HENRY born 17 May 1804, Herkimer Co., NY, came to Clinton Twp., Lenawee Co., Mich. at a young age, and married there in July 1836 to MARY A. (KING) born 12 July 1807, Suffield or Hartford, Conn. He died there 1 Aug. 1880; and she died 17 Aug. 1881. Known children: 1. ELIZABETH M. b. 23 May 1837 (m. Bridgeman J. Wells, also see); 2. HENRY C. (following). Ref: P&BA-Len pg. 256-8.

OWEN, HENRY C., son of HENRY (preceding), born 10 Nov. 1846, Clinton, Lenawee Co., Mich., married on 13 Aug. 1883 to ANNA N. (OLIVER), daughter of James (also see). Children: 1. GRACE M.; 2. DWIGHT H. Ref: P&BA-Len pg. 496.

OWEN, WILLIAM was listed in the 1840 census index of Blissfield Twp., Lenawee Co., Mich.

OWEN, WOODLAND born ca. 1820, and wife, JANE, born ca. 1822, both in England, were listed in the 1850 census of Adrian Twp., Lenawee Co., Mich. with FRANK, age 4, b. Mich., and Sarah Illenden, age 67, born England, in the household.

OWENS see OWEN

- P -

PACKARD, ELISHA born ca. 1810, Mass., was probably he listed as "Elishel" in the 1840 census index of Franklin Twp., Lenawee Co., Mich,; and in the 1850 census with (second?) wife, SARAH, age 28, b. NY; and HENRY, age 15; PHOEBE, age 13; ADELADE, age 13; ELLEN, age 5, all b. Mich., in their household.

PACKARD, IRA born ca. 1799, and wife, AMANDA (COMPTON) born ca. 1806, VT, were both reared and married in Wayne Co., NY. About 1838, they removed to Madison Twp., Lenawee Co., Mich. He died 24 Feb. 1844, age 45. Mentioned were the following chilren: MARVIN A. (following); JOSEPH b. ca. 1833 (went to Butler Co., IA); IRA JR. b. ca. 1838 (served in Co. B, 18th Mich. Inf., Civil War, taken prisoner, was released by died as result of treatment); JANE A. b. ca. 1836; JAMES b. ca. 1840 (went to Minneapolis, Minn.) Three daughters were deceased by 1888, possibly including Jane. Amanda married second to Gilbert B. Mann (also see). She died in 1877, age 72, Madison Twp. Ref: P&BA-Len pg. 890-1. Also note RUSSELL B. & LUCRETIA, following.

PACKARD, JOHN F. was listed in the 1840 census index of Fairfield Twp., Lenawee Co., Mich. Though he was not listed in 1850, there was the following family: MARIA, age 46, born VT, head of household, with CASSIUS, age 19, b. NY; and EMELINE, age 10; ADELINE, age 7, both b. Mich., in her household. Note: Nancy, age 18, b. NY who married Ebenezer Thompson may be a Packard & relate to this family, as EMELINE was listed again in their household in the 1850 census of Palmyra Twp.

PACKARD, LUCRETIA born ca. 1830, NY, married in Seneca Twp., Lenawee Co., Mich. to Augustus B. Wiley (also see). Ref: P&BA-Len pg. 1091-2.

PACKARD, MARVIN A., son of IRA (preceding), born ca. 1831, NY, moved with his parents to Madison Twp., Lenawee Co., Mich. In 1852, went by ship with a group of young men to California. In the party was his brother, JOSEPH, and 4 Cutshaw boys; Edward Hunt, son of Cornelius (also see); James Phetteplace; & Jonas Thayer. He returned by ship, coming via New York City, and was back in Lenawee Co., Mich. in 1853. He married on 25 May 1853 to ELSIE (PHETTEPLACE), daughter of Asa (also see). They moved briefly to Johnson Co., Nebr., but returned to Lenawee Co. He attempted to move the family to Pikes Peak, Col., but returned. They settled finally in Seneca Twp., Lenawee Co. Children: 1. FRANK (m. Lillie Montgomery; had children, George & Ira, lived Fairfield Twp.); 2. NETTIE. Ref: P&BA-Len pg. 890-1.

PACKARD, NATHANIEL and wife, MARY (PATTIN), moved from NY to Fulton Co., Ohio. Known daughter, AMANDA b. Fulton Co. (m. Isaiah W. Robertson, also see, 17 Mar. 1867, Ogden Twp., Lenawee Co., Mich.). Ref: P&BA-Len pg. 870-1.

PACKARD, RACHEL (See Edward Lincoln)

PACKARD, RUSSELL B. born ca. 1812, and wife, LYDIA W., born ca. 1819, both in NY, were listed in the 1840 census index of Madison Twp., Lenawee Co., Mich. (adjacent to IRA, preceding); and in the 1850 census with CLARK R., age 14; LYDIA D., age 6; CLARINDA, age 4; ADA A., age 2, all b. Mich., in their household.

PACKER, AMOS B. born ca. 1815, and wife, ELIZABETH, born ca. 1819, both in Penn., were listed in the 1850 census of Medina Twp., Lenawee Co., Mich. with DAVID, age 12, b. Penn.; and NARY A., age 10; ISAAC M., age 8; JAMES K., age 6; SARAH J., age 4, all b. Ohio; and SAPHRONA, age 2, born Mich., in their household. Note ELI, following.

PACKER, ELI born Penn., and wife, ANN (THOMAS) born Philadelphia, Penn., married probably in Berks Co., Penn. and remained there until 1840, then moved to Goshen Twp., Fulton Co., Ohio. They later moved to Isabella Co., Mich. where they remained. Known son, ISAAC D. (following). Ref: P&BA-Len pg. 671-2.

Pioneer Families of Southeastern Michigan

PACKER, ISAAC D., son of ELI (preceding), born 2 Apr. 1819, Berks Co., Penn., married in Howard Twp., Center Co., Penn. to LAVINIA (CARSKADDON), daughter of James (also see). They moved to Medina Twp., Lenawee Co., Mich. in 1851; and about 1863 to Seneca Twp.; and 1865 to Morenci, Mich.; 1867 to Seneca Twp., then back to Morenci in 1873. Children: 1. MARTHA A.; 2. LUCY A.; 3. MARGARET J.; 4. SUSAN H.; 5. ELLEN M.; 6. CHARLES H.; 7. MINERVA L. (m. John C. Crabbs, son of Rev. John, also see); 8. HARVEY C.; 9. MINILLA E.; 10. IDA L.; 11. ISAAC D.; 12. MYRTIE B. (prob. she who m. Ernest Scofield, son of Silas A., also see). Ref: P&BA-Len pg. 671-2.

PACKER, SYLVESTER (See Benjamin Hornbeck)

PADDOCK, ELIZABETH (See Philetus Finch)

PADDOCK, LEWIS born ca. 1822, and wife, LOUISA, born ca. 1830, both in NY, were listed in the 1850 census of Medina Twp., Lenawee Co., Mich. with JONATHAN, age 7, born NY, in the household.

PADDOCK, NATHAN born ca. 1790, and wife, MARY, born ca. 1795, both born NY, came probably from Scipio, Cayuga Co., NY to Palmyra Twp., Lenawee Co., Mich. before 1840. They moved to Blissfield Twp. where they are listed in the 1850 census. Nathan died there in 1866, and she died 27 Mar. 1875. Known daughter, ELIZABETH b. ca. 1819, Scipio, NY (m. Ira J. Hagaman, also see); and in Nathan's household in the census: GEORGE, age 21; ADELINE, age 17; MARTHA, age 15; NANCY, age 14, all b. NY. Ref: P&BA-Len pg. 1044-5.

PAGE, ADELIA, age 18; AUGUSTA, age 16; CATHARINE, age 14; CHARLES, age 4; LEANDER, age 2, all born Mich., were listed in the 1850 census of Tecumseh Twp., Lenawee Co., Mich. in the household of Broadstreet S. Hicks and wife, Ann, age 45, b. NY, and are possibly stepchildren Note CURTISS, following.

PAGE, CURTISS was listed in the 1840 census index of Tecumseh Twp., Lenawee Co., Mich. Note ADELIA, preceding.

PAGE, DOBSON, son of JEREMIAH (following), born 1780, New London, Conn., moved about 1797 with his parents to Columbus, Chenango Co., NY. He married there in 1814 to EVELINA S. (HALL), daughter of Prince Bryant (also see). They moved first to New York City where they operated a boat on the Hudson River. About 1823, they removed to western NY, and then on 7 June 1834 went to Lenawee Co., Mich. They settled in Rollin Twp., where he died in 1847. Known sons: NICHOLAS AMOS (following); 2. JOHN OLSON. In the 1850 census, Evelina was listed alone, next door to Gilbert Sackett and wife, Hannah (born ca. 1826, NY, possibly a daughter?) who had in their household WALLACE, age 8; HENRY C., age 4, possibly grandchildren of Dobson.

PAGE, GEORGE born ca. 1812, was listed in the 1840 census index of Fairfield Twp., Lenawee Co., Mich., adjacent to WILLIAM D. In the 1850 census, he and wife, SARAH, born ca. 1825, both in NY, listed MARCUS M., age 1 b. Mich.; and Lucy Silsby, age 18, b. NY, in their household.

PAGE, HENRY (See Alfred Belcher; also note HENRY C. mentioned above in DOBSON.)

PAGE, J. W. (See Aaron Morehouse)

PAGE, JAMES born ca. 1812, and wife, HULDAH, born ca. 1816, both in NY, were listed in the 1850 census of Tecumseh Twp., Lenawee Co., Mich. with HARRIET, age 11, b. Ohio; and ANN, age 3; JANE, age 9/12, both b. Mich., and Daniel Ensign, age 63, b. Conn., in their household.

PAGE, JAMES married ELLEN N. and died in 1866 leaving daughters: LULU (m. Charles H. Foster; & JENNIE. Ellen N. married again on 22 Oct. 1879 to David M. Blair (also see). Ref: P&BA-Len pg. 849-50.

PAGE, JEFFERSON was listed in the 1840 census index of Blissfield Twp., Lenawee Co., Mich. Note MARGARET, following.

PAGE, JEREMIAH came from England about 1765 and settled in New London, Conn. He married ? (AMES), said to be a descendant of the Mayflower family. They moved to Columbus, Chenango Co., NY about 1797. Known son, DOBSON (preceding). Ref: P&BA-Len pg. 1200-1.

PAGE, MARGARET, age 12, born Mich., was listed in the 1850 census of Blissfield Twp., Lenawee Co., Mich. in a Bliss household. Note JEFFERSON, preceding.

PAGE, NICHOLAS AMOS, son of DOBSON (preceding), born 23 June 1817, New York City, moved in 1834 with his parents to Rollin Twp., Lenawee Co., Mich. He married on 4 July 1841 to CHARITY (MARLATT), daughter of John (also see), and settled in Rollin Twp. She died 7 May 1882. Children: 1. MELISSA A. b. 5 Mar. 1842 (m. David H. Allen, son of Joseph S., also see); 2. GEORGE S. b. 6 Aug. 1844 (m. 15 Nov. 1882 to Anna J. Coppins, b. 15 Nov. 1853); 3. ORIEN C. b. 15 Jan. 1847 (d. 5 Aug. 1847); 4. FRANK A. b. 28 July 1854 (m. 12 Dec. 1877 to Ida Roys, son, Carter I. b. 30 Nov. 1882, Wheatland, Hillsdale Co.); 5. EVA b. 15 Feb. 1857 (m. George S. Roys, also see); 6. HARRISON W. b. 24 Nov. 1858 (d. 25 Dec. 1871); 7. STEPHEN A. b. 13 Sept. 1860 (m. 5 Dec. 1883, Lottie Raymond, dau. of Selah H., also see); 8. JOHN T. b. 13 Nov. 1862 (d. 25 Aug. 1864). Ref: P&BA-Len pg. 1200-1.

PAGE, WILLIAM D. born ca. 1809, and wife, FANNY, born ca. 1814, both in NY, were listed in the 1840 census index of Fairfield Twp., Lenawee Co., Mich. (adjacent to GEORGE, preceding); and in the 1850 census with CHARLES M., age 18; MARY A., age 15; JAMES M., age 13; WILLIAM A., age 11; MARSHALL E., age 8; LYMAN L., age 6; SUSAN E., age 4; HENRY D., age 2, all b. Mich., in their household.

PAINE see PAYNE This name was spelled both ways in the census, and it is not certain which was the correct spelling.

PALMER, AARON born Mass., married JANE (TERWILLEYER, probably Terwilliger?), born Ulster Co., NY. He served in the War of 1812, and supposedly received Bounty Land for his service. They settled in Greene Co., NY; and she died in Hunter, NY in 1853. Known children: 1. HARRIET E. (m. A. E. Morgan, Poughkeepsie, NY); 2. AARON J. (following). Ref: P&BA-Len pg. 596-7. Note: There was an AARON in the 1840 census index of Washtenaw Co., Mich.

PALMER, AARON J., son of AARON (preceding), born 7 Oct. 1830, near Hunter NY, went to Bedford, Ohio. He married in Ohio to CAROLINE (MARKS) who was born near Cleveland. In 1859, they moved to Parma, Jackson Co., Mich.; and later to Tecumseh, Lenawee Co., Mich. Children: 1. FRANCES W. (m. Henry Jacobs); 2. AARON (deceased by 1888); 3. ORLANDO; 4. CAROLINE. Ref: P&BA-Len pg. 596-7.

PALMER, ABE? B. born ca. 1812, and wife, ELIZABETH, born ca. 1820, VT, were listed in the 1850 census of Madison Twp., Lenawee Co., Mich.

PALMER, ADDISON born ca. 1815, and wife, LOVINA, born ca. 1825, both in NY, were listed in the 1850 census of Rollin Twp., Lenawee Co., Mich. with BYRON, age 5/12; and Phebe J. Talbot, age 8; David Talbot, age 7; Margaret Talbot, age 4, all b. Mich., in their household.

PALMER, ALBERT A. born ca. 1826, and wife, PHILANCY, born ca. 1826, both in NY, were listed in the 1850 census of Hudson Twp., Lenawee Co., Mich. with PHIDELIA, age 10/12, b. Mich., in their household. Note ALONZO, following.

PALMER, ALONZO born ca. 1816, was listed head of household in the 1850 cxensus of Dover Twp., Lenawee Co., Mich. with EPHRAIM, age 32; STILLWELL, age 22; and probably mother, POLLY, age 60, all born NY, in the household. Note JOSEPH, following.

PALMER, ALONZO born ca. 1828, NY, was listed in the 1850 census of Hudson Twp., Lenawee Co., Mich. a few doors from ALBERT A., preceding.

PALMER, BENJAMIN born ca. 1797, Rhode Island, and wife, STATIRA, born ca. 1807, NY, were listed in the 1840 census index of Adrian Twp., Lenawee Co., Mich.; and in the 1850 census with CALISTA, age 16; THERISHA, age 6; FRANK, age 5; HOMER, age 2, all b. Mich., in their household. Note WILLIAM, following.

PALMER, CHARITY married first to ? Stearns; and married again in Rome Twp., Lenawee Co., Mich. in 1860 to Andrew Taylor (also see). Ref: P&BA-Len pg. 563.

PALMER, CHARLES L. and wife, SARAH (MORRISON), lived in Wayne Co., NY where she died in 1850. Charles later moved to Kansas where he was still living in 1888. Known son, DAVID E. (following). Ref: P&BA-Len pg. 563. Note FENNER, following.

PALMER, DAVID E., son of CHARLES L. (preceding), born 23 Feb. 1847, Walworth, Wayne Co., NY, after the death of his mother in 1850, went to lived with B. Taber in Virginia. He remained for 7 years, then returned to Wayne Co., NY. In 1866, he moved to Raisin Twp., Lenawee Co., Mich. He married on 5 Feb. 1879 to ESTHER (NASH), daughter of Samuel (also see). In 1882, they moved to Madison Twp. Children: 1. CHARLES D. b. 15 June 1880; 2. HARRISON N. (d. infancy). Ref: P&BA-Len pg. 563.

PALMER, E. C. (See Thomas Williams)

PALMER, ELIZABETH, age 22, born NY, was listed in the 1850 census of Rome Twp., Lenawee Co., Mich. in a Todd household.

PALMER, FENNER born 5 Dec. 1799, Granville, Washington Co., NY, moved in 1824 to Wayne Co., NY. He married there to JULIA ANN (GODDARD), a native of Vermont. In 1832, they moved to Ridgeway Twp., Lenawee Co., Mich. to join his brother, JOHN (following) and both were listed in the 1840 census index of Macon Twp. About 1846, they moved to Ransom, Hillsdale Co., Mich.; and later returned to Macon Twp. He died in Hudson, Mich. on 10 July 1886; and she was still living in 1888. Children: 1. FRANKLIN F. (following); 2. SEVILLA E. (m. John Henry, also see); 3. CHARLES G. (lived Ranson, Hillsdale Co.); 4. MARY C. (m. E. W. Rose; Grand Crossing, Ill.); 5. JOHN B. (Hudson, Mich.); 6. GEORGE RODNEY (Manchester, Washtenaw Co.); 7. OLIVER (Petersburg, Monroe Co., Mich.); 8. BENJAMIN (St. Johns, Mich.) Ref: P&BA-Len pg. 653-4.

PALMER, FENNER born ca. 1820, and wife, PHEBE, born ca. 1821, both in NY, were listed in the 1850 census of Ridgeway Twp., Lenawee Co., Mich. with ANN b. 4 Aug. 1841 (m. George Exelby, also see); LEONODUS, age 7; ENOS, age 4; ALBERT, age 2, all b. Mich., and Elon Eddy, age 56, born NY, in their household.. Note: Probably nephew of FENNER, preceding, note JOHN (following).

PALMER, FRANKLIN F., son of FENNER (preceding), born 1 Apr. 1830, Walworth, Wayne Co., NY, came to Ridgeway Twp., Lenawee Co., Mich. with his parents. He married in July 1851 to MARY J. (HANNIBAL) born Oswego Co., NY. They lived first in Hudson, then moved to Jackson Co., Mich. They returned to Hudson later. Children: 1. DURVIN D. (m. Martha Nichols); 2. MAUD ALZINA (m. James Colville; Rockford, Ill.); 3. EVA D. Ref: P&BA-Len pg. 653-4.

PALMER, GILBERT born ca. 1800, and wife, ANN, born ca. 1790, both in NY, were listed in the 1840 census index of Dover Twp., Lenawee Co., Mich.; and in the 1850 census with WILLIAM W. (following) listed next door.

PALMER, HENRY born ca. 1789, and wife, LYDIA, born ca. 1795, VT, were listed in the 1850 census of Ridgeway Twp., Lenawee Co., Mich. with CATHERINE, age 24; HARVEY, age 20, both b. NY; and LOUISA, age 16, b. Mich. Note: There was a HENRY in the 1840 census index of Raisin Twp., Lenawee Co., Mich.

PALMER, JOHN came to Ridgeway Twp., Lenawee Co., Mich. in 1831, and was listed with brother, FENNER, in the 1840 census of Macon Twp. He had come ahead and purchased land for both he and his brother; and later settled in what is now Ridgeway Twp. In the 1850 census of Ridgeway Twp., he was age 61, born NY, and wife, NANCY, was age 57, born VT, and DECATOR, age 17; HARVY, age 14, both b. Mich., were in the household; and JOHN C. (following) was listed next door. Also note the younger FENNER, preceding.

PALMER, JOHN and wife, RUTH B., were natives of Masonville, Delaware Co., NY. Known daughter, CAROLINE A. (m. Burton Kent, also see, on 4 Dec. 1844, Adrian, Lenawee Co., Mich.) Ref: P&BA-Len pg. 654-5.

PALMER, JOHN born ca. 1824, and wife, MARTHA, born ca. 1825, both in NY, were listed in the 1850 census of Dover Twp., Lenawee Co., Mich. with no family in the household.

PALMER, JOHN C., probably son of JOHN (preceding), born ca. 1818, and wife, NANCY, born ca. 1826, were listed in the 1850 census of Ridgeway Twp., Lenawee Co., Mich. (next door to JOHN) with MARTHA E., age 9; SARAH, age 2; JOHN H., age 1, all b. Mich., in their household.

PALMER, JOSEPH was listed in the 1840 census index of Dover Twp., Lenawee Co., Mich. Note ALONZO, preceding.

PALMER, LORENZO born ca. 1803, Conn., and wife, RUTH, born ca. 1803, NY, were listed in the 1850 census of Hudson Twp., Lenawee Co., Mich. with WILLIAM, age

Pioneer Families of Southeastern Michigan

14; EMMA, age 12; RUTH, age 10; OSCAR, age 8, all b. NY; and HELEN M., age 2, b. Mich., in their household.

PALMER, LOUIS E. (See James M. Scarritt)

PALMER, LUCY Mrs. born ca. 1817, NY, listed in the 1850 census of Ridgeway Twp., Lenawee Co., Mich. with children EMILY, age 11; JEROME, age 9; LAVINA, age 6, all born Ohio, were listed in the Lyman Daly household 2 doors from HENRY (preceding).

PALMER, MARCUS? (MAVUS/MARIUS?) C. born ca. 1805, New Hampshire and wife, HANNAH, born ca. 1817, Canada, were listed in the 1850 census of Rome Twp., Lenawee Co., Mich. with HORACE, age 7; IRA, age 2, both b. Mich., in their household. It may be they listed as "M. C." in the 1840 census index of Dover Twp.?

PALMER, MARVIN E. born ca. 1812, and wife, PHEBE L., born ca. 1822, both in NY, were listed in the 1850 census of Dover Twp., Lenawee Co., Mich. with CHARLES W., age 14; SARAH M., age 6, both b. NY, in their household. Also listed was Lydia Beals, age 58, b. Mass., probably wife of Caleb (also see). and possibly mother of Phebe L.?

PALMER, RANDALL, age 30, born VT; and HENRY, age 24; STEPHEN, age 22, both b. NY, were listed together in a Boarding house in the 1850 census of Adrian Twp., Lenawee Co., Mich. Note SOPHIA, following.

PALMER, ROSE (See Charles Perry)

PALMER, SILAS born ca. 1813, and wife, ADELIA, born ca. 1818, both in NY, were listed in the 1840 census index in Hudson Twp., Lenawee Co., Mich.; and in the 1850 census with JUDSON, age 10; ELLEN, age 8; AMELIA, age 6; SARAH, age 2, all b. Mich.; and Daniel Salsbury, age 57, b. NY, in their household.

PALMER, SOPHIA born ca. 1790, VT, was listed in the 1850 census of Madison Twp., Lenawee Co., Mich. in the household of Charles and Emily Cotton. Note RANDALL, preceding.

PALMER, STILLWELL (See Eliathah Stockwell; also note STILLWELL in household of ALONZO, preceding.)

PALMER, THOMAS B. JR. born ca. 1815, and JAY E., age 20, both b. NY, were listed in the 1850 census of Rome Twp., Lenawee Co., Mich. in the household of Charity Kimble.

PALMER, WILLIAM W., probably son of GILBERT (preceding), born ca. 1823, and wife, LYDIA M., born ca. 1823, both in NY, were listed in the 1850 census of Dover Twp., Lenawee Co., Mich. with IDA, age 1, b. Mich., in their household (next door to GILBERT).

PALMER, WILLIAM born ca. 1809, Rhode Island, was listed in the 1850 census of Adrian Twp., Lenawee Co., Mich. with MATILDA, age 28, born Rhode Island; NELSON, age 18; NOAH A., age 16; LUCY A., age 14; MATILDA, age 12; DELILA A., age 5, all born NY, in his household. Note BENJAMIN, preceding.

PALMETER, CLARISSA (See Nehemiah Marks)

PARK also see PARKS

PARK, ABIJAH born ca. 1793, and wife, RHODA, born ca. 1795, both in VT, were listed in the 1850 census of Hudson Twp., Lenawee Co., Mich. with SUSAN, age 17; HENRY, age 14, both b. VT, in their household. Also see THOMAS K; & ISAAC W., both following, probably additional sons; and EMMA M., age 18, b. VT, in household of Thomas, probably another daughter. Also see CHARLES, following.

PARK, AMOS^5, son of HEZEKIAH^4 (son of ROBERT^3, THOMAS^2, ROBERT^1 who came to America in 1630), was an Army surgeon. It may be he listed in the 1800 census index of Tioga Co., NY. He died in NY at age 85. Known son, ERASTUS^6 (following). Ref: P&BA-Len pg. 403-4.

PARK, CHARLES born ca. 1828, VT, was listed in the 1850 census of Madison Twp., Lenawee Co., Mich., in a Hathaway household.

PARK, ELIAB, son of ERASTUS (following), born 22 Mar. 1817, Niagara Co., NY, lived in Wisconsin briefly, but came to Adrian Twp., Lenawee Co., Mich. in 1847. He married in 1849 to ALPHA A. (HOWELL), daughter of Anson (also see). She died in Adrian at age 59. Children: 1. LUCRETIA (m. John J. Hornby); 2. ELLA (m. Charles C. Potter, as 2nd wife; Dundee, Mich.); 3. FRANCIS; 4. MARY (to California). Ref: P&BA-Len pg. 403-4.

PARK, ERASTUS^6, son of AMOS^5 (preceding), born ca. 1780, NY, married Mrs. LUCRETIA (VAN VLECK) MAYO, born ca. 1790, NY, widow of D. Mayo. In 1836, they removed to Adrian Twp., Lenawee Co., Mich. She died there in 1869; and he went to Walworth, Wayne Co., NY, where he died at age 82. Eight children, of whom 6 were surviving in 1888, names not stated, except ELIAB (preceding). In Erastus' household in the 1850 census of Adrian Twp. were JANE, age 24; ABRAHAM, age 22; CATHARINE, age 19; AMOS, age 18, all b. NY. Ref: P&BA-Len pg. 403-4. Note VANRANSILAR, following.

PARK, ISAAC W., probably son of ABIJAH (preceding), born ca. 1824, and wife, MARIAN L., born ca. 1826, both in VT, were listed in the 1850 census of Hudson Twp., Lenawee Co., Mich. with ALMIRA M., age 3; HENRIETTA, age 6/12, both b. Mich., in their household.

PARK, JONATHAN S. born ca. 1803, Conn., and wife, EMILY, born ca. 1819, NY, were listed in the 1850 census of Madison Twp., Lenawee Co., Mich. with Franklin Coleman, age 14, b. NY, in their household

PARK, JOSEPH born ca. 1815, NY, was listed in the 1850 census of Palmyra Twp., Lenawee Co., Mich. with wife?, MARY, born ca. 1825, NY; (brother?) ELIAS, age 31; and ANN, age 24, both b. NY, in his household.

PARK, PAUL S. was listed in the 1840 census index of Adrian Twp., Lenawee Co., Mich.

PARK, SARAH (See Eli Johnson of Livingston Co., NY).

PARK, THOMAS K., probably son of ABIJAH (preceding), born ca. 1816, and wife, SABRINA, born ca. 1818, both in VT, were listed in the 1850 census of Hudson Twp., Lenawee Co., Mich. (2 doors from ABIJAH), with ROSETTA V., age 10; WILLIAM S., age 7, both b. VT; and MONROE C., age 4; RHODA E., age 6/12, all b. Mich.; and (sister?), EMMA M., age 18, b. VT, in their household.

PARK, VANRANSILAR (Van Rensselaer?) born ca. 1824, NY, was listed in the 1850 census of Madison Twp., Lenawee Co., Mich. in a Munson household.

PARKER, ALVIN born ca. 1825, and wife, ELIZA A., born ca. 1823, both in NY, were listed in the 1850 census of Palmyra Twp., Lenawee Co., Mich. with ALLEN, age 1,

b. Mich., in the household. Note PASCHAL, who was next door in the census, possibly brother?

PARKER, CALEB born Conn. went as a young man to Erie Co., NY. He married there to CAROLINE (STEWARD). He died in 1857, age 68; and she died in 1859, age 59. There were 10 children, and only mentioned were: Son (went to Grand Rapids, Mich.); L. A. (lived Erie Co., NY); CINTHY E. (Erie Co., NY); ALBERT C. (served Co. B, 3rd Mich. Inf., Civil War); Dr. GOULD (Surgeon with 11th Kansas Inf., settled Spring Hill, KS; d. Oct. 1872); HARRISON (Buffalo, NY); WARREN J. (following). Ref: P&BA-Len pg. 889-90.

PARKER, DAYTON MD, son of MORGAN (following), born 17 Jan. 1846, Dundee Twp., Monroe Co., Mich., served in Co. K, 6th Mich. Heavy Artl, Civil War. He married 18 Nov. 1869 to EMILY C. (HANCOCK), daughter of John (also see). He became a Physician and practiced first in 1873 in Ogden Centre, Mich.; and in 1879 moved to Blissfield, Lenawee Co. His wife died 10 Jan. 1873, Ann Arbor, Mich. He married again on 16 Mar. 1874 to IDA E. (COGGSWELL), daughter of R. S. (also see). Children: 1. BERTHA E.; 2. BURTON D.; 3. BRACE MORGAN; 4. ALMA E.; 5. BEATRICE. Ref: P&BA-Len pg. 599-600.

PARKER, FIDELIA, age 21, born NY, was listed in the 1850 census of Madison Twp., Lenawee Co., Mich. in a Payne household.

PARKER, GEORGE born ca. 1807, and wife, AMERILLA, born ca. 1820, both in NY, were listed in the 1850 census of Blissfield Twp., Lenawee Co., Mich. with GEORGE E., age 14, b. NY; JULIA M., age 9, b. Ohio, in their household. Possibly they are parents of MARY E. (b. after 1850; m. Lewis F. Pearson, son of David, also see).

PARKER, HIRAM born ca. 1803, and wife, RUTH, born ca. 1812, were probably they listed in the 1840 census index of Ogden Twp., Lenawee Co., Mich.; and in the 1850 census listed SAMUEL, age 19; ANN, age 17; ALMIDA, age 15; MELISSA 11, all b. NY; and MARK, age 9; SALLY M., age 7; MELISSA, age 6/12, all b. Mich., in their household.

PARKER, IRA was the father of SOPHIA b. ca. 1821, NY (m. in Blissfield Twp. on 9 Dec. 1840 to Seymour Barrett, also see). Ref: P&BA-Len pg. 584-5.

PARKER, JACOB W., age 4, born Mich., was listed in the 1850 census of Raisin Twp., Lenawee Co., Mich. in the household of John & Dina Colvin.

PARKER, JAMES H. born ca. 1803, was listed in the 1840 census index of Rome Twp. as "J. H."; and in the 1850 census with wife, BETSEY, born ca. 1806, both in NY, and MARY J., age 24, b. NY, and William Secor, age 10; John Secor, age 8, both b. Mich., in their household.

PARKER, JASON, age 16, born Mich., was listed in the 1850 census of Fairfield Twp., Lenawee Co., Mich. in a Brown household.

PARKER, JOSHUA and wife, SUSANNA (RAWSON), were natives of Mass. who moved after their marriage to Delaware Co., NY; and later to Wayne Co., NY. He died at age 55, and she died age 66. Eleven children, and only named was LOSINA (m/1 Nelson Lapham; m/2 William D. Archer of Wayne Co.; m/3 Samuel White, also see). Ref: P&BA-Len pg. 784-5.

PARKER, JOSHUA born Hollingsworth, VT, and wife (name not stated) moved by 1819 to Oneida Co., NY. They remained there until about 1825, then moved to Dundee, Monroe Co., Mich. where they remained. In the 1830 census of Monroe Co., Mich. Territory, he counted males: 1 10-15; 1 50-60; females: 1 10-15; 1 15-20; 1 30-40. Known son, MORGAN (following). Ref: P&BA-Len pg. 599-600.

PARKER, MORGAN, son of JOSHUA (preceding), born 1 Jan. 1820, Oneida Co., NY, came to Monroe Co., Mich. with his parents. He married ROSETTA C. (BRENINGSTALL), daughter of Abraham (also see). He served in Co. F, 1st Mich. Engrs & Mechanics, Civil War, and died 4 Apr. 1862, Louisville, KY of Typhoid; and buried in Dundee, Mich. Rosetta died 15 Sept. 1881, age 57. Children: 1. BURTON (Monroe, Mich.); 2. DAYTON (preceding); 3. DWIGHT (Petersburg, Monroe Co.); 4. ELLEN (m. G. R. Brown, Petersburg, Mich.); 5. FRANCES (m. Perry Closser). Ref: P&BA-Len pg. 599-600.

PARKER, PASCHAL born ca. 1830, NY, was listed in the 1850 census of Palmyra Twp., Lenawee Co., Mich. next door to ALVIN, preceding, in a Thompson household.

PARKER, RHODA born ca. 1824, NY, was listed head of household in the 1850 census of Hudson Twp., Lenawee Co., Mich. with EMILY E., age 3; JULIUS A., age 1, both b. Mich., in her household.

PARKER, ROBERT born ca. 1814, Ireland, and wife, MAARGARET, born ca. 1820, NY, were listed in the 1850 census of Madison Twp., Lenawee Co., Mich. with ANN J., age 5; LOUISA, age 3; WILLIAM, age 1, all b. Mich., and Saloma Kelly, age 19, b. Ohio, in their household.

PARKER, SOPHIE (See Frederick W. Samsen)

PARKER, WARREN J., son of CALEB (preceding), born 18 Dec. 1844, Erie Co., NY, served in Co. H, 100th NY Inf., Civil War. He married in Erie Co. on 20 Dec. 1865 to ADELL E. (STOWELL), daughter of Ezeriah (also see). About 1867, they moved to Tecumseh, Lenawee Co., Mich.; went briefly to Jackson Co., Mich.; then moved to Woodstock Twp. Lenawee Co. in 1868. Children: 1. ALVIN A. b. 30 Oct. 1866, Erie Co., NY (d. 19 Sept. 1884); 2. JAMES H. b. 10 Oct. 1868, Jackson Co., Mich.; 3. FERNANDO C. b. 4 Apr. 1874; 4. EARL E. b. 18 Sept. 1876; 5. ALVY C. b. 5 Feb. 1885. Ref: P&BA-Len pg. 889-90.

PARKER, WILLARD was listed in the 1840 census index of Rollin Twp., Lenawee Co., Mich.

PARKER, WILLIAM was listed in the 1840 census index of Palmyra Twp., Lenawee Co., Mich. Note ALVIN & PASCHAL, preceding.

PARKER, WILLIAM of Rhode Island had known daughter, ELIZA C. (m. Allen Burr, also see).

PARKER, WILLIAM K. married JANE (FLEMING), daughter of James (also see) possibly in Seneca Co., NY. They lived in LaPorte Co., Ind. by 1841. Known daughter, MARTHA b. 2 Feb. 1841, Laporte Co. (came to Rome Twp., Lenawee Co., Mich. with her grandparents, James & Martha Fleming; m. Luther McRobert, also see). Note: In the 1850 census of Tecumseh Twp., Lenawee Co., MARTHA, age 9, b. Ind., was listed in the household of Wilson & Martha Matthews. Ref: P&BA-Len pg. 884-5.

PARKHURST, JAMES A. married ELIZA A. (WILSEY), daughter of Jeremiah[2] (also see) in Woodstock Twp., Lenawee Co. He served in the Civil War. They settled

Pioneer Families of Southeastern Michigan

in Madison Twp., Lenawee Co. where they remained. Ref: P&BA-Len pg. 875-6.

PARKS also see PARK

PARKS, EBENEZER born ca. 1790, Conn. was listed in the 1850 census of Blissfield Twp., Lenawee Co., Mich. with CAROLINE, age 21; AARON, age 17; MARGARET, age 13; JOHN, age 11, all b. Ohio; and WESLEY, age 1/12, b. Mich., in his household.

PARKS, HARVEY, age 19, born 1831, NY, was listed in the 1850 census of Franklin Twp., Lenawee Co., Mich. in a Wheaton household.

PARKS, JAMES born Salisbury, Conn., and wife, LUCRETIA, born Middletown, Conn., moved to Meadville, Penn. In 1830, they removed to Clinton Twp., Lenawee Co., Mich.; and were listed there in the 1840 census index. He died in 1859, and she died 9 Nov. 1883. Known daughter, FRANCES E. b. 19 Oct. 1823, Meadville, Penn. (m. Joseph S. Kies, also see). Ref: P&BA-Len pg. 337-8.

PARKS, MARGARET (See Hiram Rockwell)

PARLOR, ELIZA (See William Ladd)

PARMELE also see PARMLEE

PARMELE, D. C. born ca. 1808, and wife, ALLEPHEE, born ca. 1809, were listed in the 1850 census of Macon Twp., Lenawee Co., Mich. with ARSELE? (female), age 15, b. NY; and HARMON, age 12; CYNTHIA, age 10; EMILY, age 7; MELISSA M., age 2, all b. Mich., in their household. Note: There was DENNIS in the 1840 census index of Howard Twp., Cass Co., Mich.

PARMENTER, HARRIET (See Isaac Brown)

PARMLEE also see PARMELE

PARMLEE, EVERETT P. of Vermont was father of MARIE (m. Henry N. Skeels, also see).

PARMLEE, THOMAS C. born ca. 1804, and wife, CHLOE, born ca. 1807, both in NY, were listed in 1850 census of Palmyra Twp., Lenawee Co., Mich. with ERASTUS, age 22; PHE--? (female), age 20; MARTHA A., age 18, all b. NY; OLIVER A., age 15, b. Ohio; and WASHINGTON, age 12; THOMAS, age 5; REUBEN, age 3, all b. Mich., in their household.

PARSHEEL, FLORA (See John Henry)

PARSONS, BETSEY Mrs. of Leroy, Genesee Co., NY was the daughter of Joseph Keeney (also see).

PARSONS, CHARLES W. born ca. 1823, VT, and wife, OLIVE, born ca. 1830, Ohio, were listed in the 1850 census of Madison Twp., Lenawee Co., Mich. with FRANCES, age 4; CHARLES, age 2; FRED, age 3/12, all b. Mich.; and GEORGE C., age 26, b. VT, probably brother; and Cornelia Allen, age 11; C. E. (male) Allen, age 16; Julia Ames, age 18, all b. Ohio, in their household. Note VIRTUE, following.

PARSONS, HIRAM, son of TIMOTHY (following), born 26 Dec. 1803, Greene Co., NY, married on 24 Sept. 1828 to SARAH A. (LOSS) born 10 Nov. 1807. They lived in a number of NY states, and then on 23 May 1842, moved to Saline, Washtenaw Co., Mich. They later moved to Franklin Twp., Lenawee Co.; and then Woodstock Twp. where he died on 7 Oct. 1850. Sarah afterwards moved to Brooklyn, Jackson Co.; but later lived with a daughter in Adrian, where she died 2 Mar. 1884. They were listed in the 1850 census of Woodstock Twp. with children: 1. LOSS (written "Helos," following); 2. ALBERT, age 16; ELI, age 14; SARAH, age 10, all b. NY; and EDNA, age 6/12, b. Mich., in their household. Ref: P&BA-Len pg. 698-9.

PARSONS, JOHN of Brighton, England was the father of MARY b. 26 Aug. 1816 (m. George Oram, also see). Ref: P&BA-Len pg. 645-6.

PARSONS, LOSS (Helos), son of HIRAM (preceding), born 12 June 1832, Verona, Oneida Co., NY, moved with parents to Michigan. He married on 6 Apr. 1858, probably in Woodstock Twp., Lenawee Co. to HELEN M. (HOLLISTER) born 2 Nov 1835, Genesee Co., NY. She died there at age 34, leaving children: 1. NELLIE E. b. 4 Jan. 1861 (m. Benjamin Tayer, Adrian); 2. FRANK L. b. 10 July 1863; 3. MAY b. 6 Dec. 1865 (d. Aug. 1868); 4. EDWIN A. b. 13 Nov. 1868. Loss married again to ANGIE (TEMPLAR), daughter of James (also see). Children: 5. CARL b. 30 June 1870; 6. LaVERN b. 11 Oct. 1872; 7. SARAH A. b. 22 Mar. 1878; 8. ETHEL b. 27 May 1880. Ref: P&BA-Len pg. 698-9. Ref: P&BA-Len pg. 698-9. Note: Mentioned in the sketch in "Uncle George Taylor."

PARSONS, OLIVE (See Alvin D. Rice)

PARSONS, SAMUEL born ca. 1814; and wife, REBECCA, born ca. 1825, both in England, were listed in the 1850 census of Cambridge Twp., Lenawee Co., Mich. with MARY ANN, age 3; RICHARD, age 1, both b. Mich., in their household.

PARSONS, TIMOTHY may be he listed in the 1800 census index of Suffolk Co., NY. He married HULDAH (PARSONS) and they lived in Greene Co., NY by 1803. He died ca. 1815, NY. Known son, HIRAM (preceding). Ref: P&BA-Len pg. 698-9.

PARSON, VIRTUE? F. (female), age 14, born NY, was listed in the 1850 census of Madison Twp., Lenawee Co., Mich. in a Turner household. Note CHARLES, preceding.

PARSONS, WILLIAM born ca. 1824, and wife, MARIA, born ca. 1827, both in NY, were listed in the 1850 census of Madison Twp., Lenawee Co., Mich., with EMMA? M., age 3; WEALTHY A., age 1, both b. Mich., in their household.

PARTRIDGE, ADAM W. (spelled "Patrage") was listed in the 1840 census index of Raisin Twp., Lenawee Co., Mich.

PARTRIDGE, DANIEL born ca. 1818, and wife, DELILAH, born ca. 1828, both in NY, were listed in the 1850 census of Seneca Twp., Lenawee Co., Mich. with SARAH E., age 2, b. Mich., in their household.

PARTRIDGE, IRA J. born ca. 1814, and wife, MARIA, born ca. 1818, both in NY, were listed in the 1840 census index of Seneca Twp., Lenawee Co., Mich.; and in the 1850 census with ELLEN A., age 11, b. NY; and L--(male), age 10; EBENEZER, age 8; JOHN, age 6; ALIDA J., ?/12, all b. Mich., in their household.

PARTRIDGE, JEMIMA born ca. 1800 England (See William Luck).

PARTRIDGE, LEONARD was listed in the 1840 census index of Fairfield Twp., Lenawee Co., Mich.

PARTRIDGE, LUCRETIA (See Harvey Rowlson)

PARTRIDGE, WILLIAM H. born ca. 1817, and wife, CLARISSA A., born ca. 1823, both in NY, were listed in the 1850 census of Madison Twp., Lenawee Co., Mich. with ELIZA, age 15; CHARLES H., age 3, both b. Mich., in their household.

PATEE also see PATTEE

PATEE, WILLIAM born in Delaware Co., Ohio, married ELIZABETH (KELLEM) born in Knox Co., Ohio; and settled first in Knox Co. They moved to Defiance Co., Ohio, and then to Steuben Co., Ind., where he died. Children: 1. SAMUEL (d. infancy); 2. ELIZABETH (d. age 33); 3. POLLY; 4. GEORGE; 5. SARAH; 6. SUSAN b. 20 Aug. 1844, Defiance Co., O. (m. Edwin Cross, also see); 7. PHEBE; 8. WILLIAM. Ref: P&BA-Len pg. 1024-5.

PATRICK, BETSEY (See Adam Mott)

PATRICK, JAMES and wife, AMANDA (DRAKE), lived in Palmyra, Wayne Co., NY, and moved to Orleans Co., NY where he died a young man (by 1826). It may be she listed in the 1850 census of Rollin Twp., Lenawee Co., Mich. as Amanda Smith, age 51, b. VT, in the household of known son, JAMES (following). Ref: P&BA-Len pg. 850-1.

PATRICK, JAMES, son of JAMES (preceding), born 12 Nov. 1818, Palmyra, Wayne Co., NY, went at age 8 to live with a Samuel Beals from whom he learned the Cooper's trade. He married on 5 June 1841 to MARY J. (MOOREHOUSE) born ca. 1820, NY, and soon afterwards moved to Rollin Twp., Lenawee Co., Mich. Children: 1. VIORNA A. b. 4 Mar. 1842, Rollin Twp. (m. Perry N. Rowley, also see); 2. WILLIS W. b. 19 Sept. 1855 (d. 3 Feb. 1862). Ref: P&BA-Len pg. 850-1.

PATTEE, ELBRA (See Earl Whitmore)

PATTERSON, BINGHAM born ca. 1788, and wife, EDA, born ca. 1787, both in NY, were listed in the 1840 census index of Raisin Twp., Lenawee Co., Mich.; and in the 1850 census with PHILANDER, age 23; BENJAMIN F., age 21, and Polly Heich, age 21, all b. NY, in their household. Note CALEB, & ELVA, following, who were listed adjacent in the 1840 census index.

PATTERSON, CALEB was listed in the 1840 census index of Raisin Twp., Lenawee Co., Mich. adjacent to BINGHAM (preceding), and ELVA (following).

PATTERSON, ELVA was listed in the 1840 census index of Raisin Twp., Lenawee Co., Mich. adjacent to BINGHAM & CALEB, both preceding.

PATTERSON, GEORGE married CLARISSA (HOWARD), daughter of Ansel (also see); and he died in Madison Co., NY in August 1849. Clarissa moved to Michigan in her late years. Known daughter, LUCINDA b. 11 Nov. 1831, Madison, NY (m. Daniel Root, also see). Ref: P&BA-Len pg. 697-8.

PATTERSON, JAMES, son of ALEXANDER, born ca. 1800, Ireland, married there to ANIS (McGOWEN). In 1852, they came to America, and settled first in Baltimore, MD. They moved in 1855 to Macon Twp., Lenawee Co., Mich. He died in 1879, age 79; and she died Mar. 1885, age 86. Seven children, and only the 2 eldest survived in 1888, names not stated, except JAMES (following). Ref: P&BA-Len pg. 793-4.

PATTERSON, JAMES, son of JAMES (preceding), born 1831, Co. Antrim, Ireland, came in 1847 at age 16 to Baltimore, MD. He married there to CATHERINE (DUNHAM) born Ireland, who died in Baltimore, leaving daughter, 1. MAGGIE J. James served in the Civil War. He married again to RACHEL (LUPTON), daughter of Thomas (also see) of Ridgeway Twp., Lenawee Co., Mich. They lived first in LaGrange Co., Ind., but returned to Ridgeway Twp. about 1871. Children: 2. MARY M. (m. William Scheder; this may be MELVINA who m. Wm. Schreder, son of Israel H.); 3. IRVIN; 4. ROBERT; 5. JEMIMA; 6. CLARENCE. Ref: P&BA-Len pg. 793-4.

PATTERSON, JAMES born ca. 1814, and wife, LOUISA, born ca. 1815, both in NY, were listed in the 1840 census index of Cambridge Twp., Lenawee Co., Mich.; and in the 1850 census with WILLIAM, age 13; PHILLIP, age 10; LOUISA, age 6; THOMAS, age 4, all b. Mich., in their household.

PATTERSON, JOHN born 15 Dec. 1810, Ireland, came to the US at age 17 "with an older brother." He worked first in Lockport, NY for about 2 years, and then about 1831, he moved to Adrian, Lenawee Co., Mich. He later moved to Hillsdale Co., but returned to Adrian. He married on 10 Jan. 1841 to JANE (FARRAH), daughter of Thomas (also see) of Raisin Twp. Child: MARY E. (m. Lindley R. Harkness, also see). Ref: P&BA-Len pg. 388-9.

PATTERSON, JOHN born ca. 1820, and wife, ELIZABETH, born ca. 1824, both in Ireland, were listed in the 1850 census of Ogden Twp., Lenawee Co., Mich. with DAVID, age 9; JANE, age 6; WILLIAM J., age 4, all b. Ireland, and ROBERT, age 1, born Mich., in their household.

PATTERSON, JOSEPH born 27 July 1793, Ireland, moved at age 19 to the US and settled first in Orange Co., NY. He married there to CATHERINE (JAGER) born 2 Feb. 1804, NY. They moved to Wayne co., NY; and then about 1848 moved to Woodstock Twp., Lenawee Co., Mich. He died 18 Apr. 1871, age 78. Children: 1. BENJAMIN; 2. WILLIAM L.; 3. CATHERINE (m. Theron Andrews, Hillsdale Co., Mich.); 4. MARIA b. ca. 1829; 5. ROBERT C. b. ca. 1831 (m. Mehala White, Hillsdale Co., Mich.); 6. JOHN J. b. 24 Jan. 1834, Orange Co., NY (m. Eliza A. Ellsworth, dau. of Alexander, also see); 7. JOSEPH b. ca. 1842 (m. Lucy Hollen); 8. MARY L. b. ca. 1847 (m. Charles Ellsworth, son of Alexander, also see). Ref: P&BA-Len pg. 715-6.

PATTERSON, JOSEPH H. born ca. 1801, Ireland, and wife, LUCINTHA, born ca. 1817, NY, were listed in the 1840 census index of Raisin Twp., Lenawee Co., Mich.; and in the 1850 census with ROBERT, age 12; JAMES, age 10; MARY, age 8; ELIZA, age 7; JEMIMA, age 5; SARAH L., age 3; JOHN, age 1, all b. Mich., in their household.

PATTERSON, MELVINA (Note JAMES, preceding; and Israel H. Schreder).

PATTERSON, MICHAEL A. Dr. born ca. 1804, Penn., and wife, FRANCES, born ca. 1815, Mass., were listed in the 1840 census index of Tecumseh Twp., Lenawee Co., Mich.; and in the 1850 census with HARRIET, age 16; STEWART, age 13; AUGUSTA, age 11; WILIAM, age 7; JAMES, age 5, all b. Mich., in their household.

Pioneer Families of Southeastern Michigan

PATTERSON, ROENA, age 35, born Ohio; and JANET, age 4, born Mich., were listed in the 1850 census of Fairfield Twp., Lenawee Co., Mich. in a Baker household.

PATTERSON, SAMUEL born ca. 1800, Ireland, and wife, MARGARET, born ca. 1815, Scotland, were listed in the 1840 census index of Raisin Twp., Lenawee Co., Mich.; and in the 1850 census with THOMAS, age 13, b. NY; and JANE, age 11; CATHARINE, age 8; AMBROSE, age 6, all b. Mich., in their household.

PATTEN also see PATTIN & PATTON

PATTEN, GEORGE settled in Commerce Twp., Oakland Co., Mich. by 1840. He was father of JEANNETTE (m. 21 Apr. 1839 to Nathaniel Buel Eldredge, also see). Ref: P&BA-Len pg. 937-8.

PATTEN, EVERT born ca. 1808, and wife, ELIZABETH, born ca. 1808, both in NY, were listed in the 1850 census of Palmyra Twp., Lenawee Co., Mich. with WILLIAM, age 10; MARY A., age 18; DAVID, age 16; SPENCER, age 14; JULIA, age 12, all b. NY, in their household.

PATTIN, MARY (See Nathaniel Packard)

PATTON, MARY ANN (See John S. Wells; also note MARY A. PATTEN, in household of GEORGE (preceding).

PAUL, CATHERINE (See Abel Hall)

PAUL, WILLIAM, born in Ontario Co., NY, married MARIA (MARLOTT) born 18 Sept. 1820 near Buffalo, NY. They removed to Ogden Twp., Lenawee Co., Mich. by 1841. He died there 3 Dec. 1848; and Maria was head of household in the 1850 census of Ogden Twp. In addition to the children following, Elias Marlott, age 23, b. NY, was in her household. Children: 1. LYDIA D. b. 18 Oct. 1841 (m. Peter Wyman, also see); 2. SETH b. ca. 1844; 3. JANE b. ca. 1847 (m. Levi Johnson). Ref: P&BA-Len pg. 776-7.

PAWSEN also see PAWSON
PAWSEN, EFFIE L. (See Edwin Cook)

PAWSON, JAMES R. born 1843, died 1918, and buried with him in the Mills Cemetery, Franklin Twp., is MARY A. 1843-1899. This may actually be JOHN R. noted below with the family of JOHN (following).

PAWSON, JOHN born ca. 1806, and wife, CHARLOTTE, born ca. 1814, both b. England, were listed in the 1840 census index of Cambridge Twp., Lenawee Co., Mich.; and in the 1850 census of Franklin Twp. with known children: 1. WILLIAM, age 14; 2. CAROLINE, age 12; CHARLES, age 10; MARTHA A., age 8; CHRISTOPHER, age 2, in their household; and JOHN R., age 6, b. Mich., in the household of John Main, may also relate to this family. Charlotte died 8 Sept. 1854, age 39y/6mo, and is buried with John in the Mills Cemetery, Franklin Twp. John was said to have married again and had 7 children, names not stated. In the Mills Cemetery, there is an ANN "Mother" with dates 1827-1907; and adjacent CHARLOTTE 1835-1902; and BLANFORD 1867-1925, not identified. John died 19 Feb. 1881, aged 75y/1m/17d.

PAWSON, THOMAS born ca. 1797, and wife MARY, born ca. 1814, both in England, were listed in the 1840 census index of Cambridge Twp., Lenawee Co., Mich.; and in the 1850 census of Franklin Twp. with ELIZABETH, age 9; MELISSA, age 7; REBECCA, age 5; THOMAS, age 2, all b. Mich., in their household.

PAYNE, ABRAM W. born ca. 1773, and wife, MARY, born ca. 1773, both in NY, were listed in the 1840 census of Franklin Twp., Lenawee Co., Mich.; and in the 1850 census in the household of REED (following).

PAYNE, ALICE (See Montague)

PAYNE, BENJAMIN T. born ca. 1813, VT, and wife, OCTAVIA born ca. 1811, NY, were listed in the 1840 census index of Madison Twp.; Lenawee Co., Mich.; and in the 1850 census with WILLIAM, age 15; ERASMUS, age 11; HELEN, age 10; SUSAN, age 7, all b. Mich., in their household.

PAYNE, CELIA (See Alfred Belcher)

PAYNE, DAVID was a neighbor of Henry F. Townsend, Dover Twp., Lenawee Co., Mich. in 1835.

PAYNE, DANIEL born ca. 1802, Conn., and wife, ELIZA, born ca. 1818, NY, were listed in the 1850 census of Rome Twp., Lenawee Co., Mich. with ROMANDA, age 14; LEANDER, age 12; DANIEL, age 10, all b. Mich.; and DELEVAN, age 7, b. NY; and WELSEY, age 6; LUCIA, age 3; RUFUS, age 8/12, all b. Mich., in their household.

PAYNE, ERASMUS W. born ca. 1810, and wife, CASIAH?, born ca. 1815, were listed in the 1850 census of Madison Twp., Lenawee Co., Mich.

PAYNE, GEORGE was listed in the 1840 census index of Hudson Twp., Lenawee Co., Mich.

PAYNE, GEORGE F. born ca. 1819, and wife, CAROLINE, born ca. 1824, both in England, were listed in the 1850 census of Madison Twp., Lenawee Co., Mich. with WILLIAM, age 2; ROBERT, age 1, both b. Mich., in their household.

PAYNE, HANNAH born ca. 1800, VT, and probably daughter, AURILLA, age 17, born NY, were listed in the 1850 census of Madison Twp., Lenawee Co., Mich. in the household of Jay and Marsha Lee. Note JOHN, & WILSON, both following.

PAYNE, IRA was listed in the 1840 census index of Clinton Twp., Lenawee Co., Mich. Note RILEY, following.

PAYNE, JAMES born ca. 1804, Mass., was listed in the 1850 census of Madison Twp., Lenawee Co., Mich. with ELECTA A., age 17, b. Ohio; MARY J., age 11, b. Canada; JAMES H., age 10, b Ohio; CHARLES D., age 7, b. Ohio; and Fidelia Parker, age 21, b. NY, in the household.

PAYNE, JOHN was listed in the 1840 census index of Madison Twp., Lenawee Co., Mich., adjacent to WILSON, following. Note HANNAH, preceding.

PAYNE JOHN born Greenbush, Rensselaer Co., NY, married there to JANE (VAN BUREN); and he died 28 Aug. 1838. Jane moved to Dover Twp., Lenawee Co., Mich. in 1862, and died 9 Oct. 1872. Children: 1. HARMON VAN BUREN; 2. NATHANIEL; 3. JAMES H.; 4. JOHN M. (following); 5. CATHARINE S.; 6. CHAUNCEY S. Ref: P&BA-Len pg. 292.

PAYNE, JOHN born ca. 1813, and wife, MELINDA, born ca. 1815, both in NY, were listed in the 1850 census of Blissfield Twp., Lenawee Co., Mich. with LAURA, age 5; VELETTA, age 3, both b. Mich., in their household.

PAYNE, JOHN M., son of JOHN (preceding), born 3 Aug. 1829, Schodack, NY, married in East Schodack on 6 Apr. 1850 to CLARISSA (WINTERS), daughter of James (also see). They moved to Dover Twp., Lenawee Co., Mich.

in 1858. Children: 1. SPENCER (m. Ellen Dutcher, Dover Twp.); 2. JOHN M. (m. Augusta Lawrence; Chicago, Ill.); 3. IDA (m. William Sanborn; Toledo, O.) Ref: P&BA-Len pg. 292.

PAYNE, LEMUEL was listed in the 1840 census index of Macon Twp., Lenawee Co., Mich.

PAYNE, OLIVE (See Levi Hawley)

PAYNE, REED, probably son of ABRAM W. (preceding). born ca. 1810, NY, and wife, CATHARINE, age 33, born VT, were listed in the 1850 census of Franklin Twp., Lenawee Co., Mich. with LOUISA, age 8; ADELINE, age 6; CLARK, age 5, all b. Mich., and ABRAM W. (preceding) & wife, MARY, listed in the household.

PAYNE, REUEL born ca. 1804, NY, was listed in the 1840 census index of Blissfield Twp., Lenawee Co., Mich.; and in the 1850 census with (second wife?) THANKFUL, age 21, b. NY; and CLARISSA, age 14; ELIZA, age 13; BYRON, age 10; GEORGE, age 9; AMBROSE, age 5; ANNA, age 6; SARAH, age 3; LAURA, age 1/12, all b. Mich., in his household. RUEL, possibly born after 1850, married Etta Kendrick, dau. of Charles H. (also see), Blissfield Twp., probably is of this family.

PAYNE, RILEY, age 12, b. Mich. (spelled "Pain") was listed in the 1850 census of Hudson Twp., Lenawee Co., Mich. in a Perry household. Note IRA, preceding.

PAYNE, STEPHEN born ca. 1791, Mass., and wife, RUTH (SMITH), born ca. 1796, Conn., moved before 1823 to Genesee Co., NY; and about 1830 to Monroe Co., NY. She died in 1844, age 48; and he died 7 Feb. 1880, age 89, in NY, at home of known son, LEWIS. There were 2 sons & 3 daughters, and only mentioned were preceding, and daughter #3. ANN P. b. 10 Feb. 1823, Bergen, Genesee Co., NY (m. Roderick R. Hume, also see). Ref: P&BA-Len pg. 924-5.

PAYNE, THANKFUL b. Rhode Island (See Daniel Colwell[2] of Seneca Castle, Ontario Co., NY).

PAYNE, WILSON was listed in the 1840 census index of Madison Twp., Lenawee Co., Mich. adjacent to JOHN, preceding. Note HANNAH, preceding.

PEARSON also see PEIRSON/PIERSON

PEARSON, DAVID, son of FRANCIS (following), born 18 Mar. 1812, Yorkshire, England, married there to JANE (PICKERING), daughter of Richard (also see). In 1837, they came to the US and settled first in Livingston Co., NY. In 1839, they removed to Woodstock Twp., Lenawee Co., Mich. He died there 8 Mar. 1872. Children: 1. FRANCIS "FRANK" R. (following); 2. HANNAH P. b. 12 Sept. 1840 (m. G. H. Hutchins); 3. ANN ELIZABETH b. 12 Aug. 1843 (m. Charles Hacket; Napoleon, Mich.); 4. CHARLES WESLEY b. 11 May 1846 (m. Eva Richardson); 5. ALFRED R. b. 13 June 1848 (m. Eola Salsbury; Nebraska); 6. HARRIET M. b. 28 June 1850 (m. Darius Iveson, son of Thomas, also see; Nebraska); 7. FLETCHER b. 28 Nov. 1853 (m. Ann Iveson, dau. of Thomas, also see); 8. EMMA J. b. 31 Dec. 1855 (m. Rev. A. R. Keeler; Kent Co., Mich.); 9. LEWIS F. b. 18 June 1859 (m. Mary E. Parker, dau. of George; Woodstock Twp.). Ref: P&BA-Len pg. 689-90.

PEARSON, FRANCIS born ca. 1764, and wife, ELIZABETH, born ca. 1780, both in Yorkshire, England, came to the US in 1839 to join son, David. They resided in Woodstock Twp., Lenawee Co., Mich. where he died in 1840, age 76. She was living in Woodstock Twp. in the 1850 census, age 70; and died there at age 99. Known sons, DAVID (preceding); FRANCIS b. ca. 1821, England.

PEARSON, FRANK R., son of DAVID (preceding), born 24 Apr. 1838, Livingston Co., NY, moved to Woodstock Twp., Lenawee Co., Mich. with his parents. He married on 28 Jan. 1862 to ADELAIDE (SANFORD), daughter of Lewis (also see) and settled in Woodstock Twp. Children: 1. LEWIS D. b. 9 Nov. 1864; 2. DELBERT F. b. 20 Jan. 1869; 3. EUGENE W. b. 24 Aug. 1873. Ref: P&BA-Len pg. 683-4.

PEARSON, HENRY (See Winslow Bates)

PEASE, AMANDA born ca. 1827, NY, was listed in the 1850 census of Blissfield Twp., Lenawee Co., Mich. in household of Seymour & Sophia Barrett. Note OLIVER C., following.

PEASE, HENRY born ca. 1802, VT, and wife, MARY, born ca. 1812, NY, were listed in the 1850 census of Tecumseh Twp., Lenawee Co., Mich. with JAMES, age 14, b. NY; and MARY, age 13, b. Mich., in their household.

PEASE, HENRY C., probably son of OLIVER (following), born ca. 1810, Mass., and wife LOVINA, born ca. 1818, NY, were listed in the 1840 census index of Blissfield Twp., Lenawee Co., Mich.; and in the 1850 census with REBECCA, age 9; ZIBA, age 8; HENRY, age 6; OLIVER, age 4; HAMPTON, age 2, all b. Mich., in their household. Note: They were listed next door to OLIVER.

PEASE, JOHN was listed in the 1840 census index of Adrian Twp., Lenawee Co., Mich.

PEASE, LYMAN (spelled "Peas") was listed in the 1830 census of Lenawee Co., Michigan Territory, with males: 1 und 5; 1 10-15; 1 30-40; females: 1 und 5; 1 20-30.

PEASE, OLIVER born ca. 1778, Mass., and wife, ESTHER, born ca. 1792, Conn., were listed in the 1840 census index of Blissfield Twp., Lenawee Co., Mich.; and in the 1850 census with JANE, age 24, b. Mass., in the household; and HENRY C. (preceding) listed next door; & OLIVER C. (following) who was adjacent in 1840.

PEASE, OLIVER C., probably son of OLIVER, born ca. 1803, Mass., was listed in the 1840 census index of Blissfield Twp., Lenawee Co., Mich.; and in the 1850 census with SARAH, age 20; SETH, age 18; RICHARD, age 15, all b. NY; and JOHN, age 11; RUTH, age 10, both b. Mich., in the household.

PEASE, THIRZA born 3 Oct. 1822, Chittenden Co., VT, married David Carpenter (also see) in Toledo, Ohio.

PECK, COMFORT was listed in the 1840 census index of Madison Twp. Lenawee Co., Mich.

PECK, ELKANAH JR. was listed in the 1840 census index of Macon Twp., Lenawee Co., Mich. adjacent to PHINEAS P.; PHILIP P.; & JAMES, all following.

PECK, IRA and wife, POLLY (PORTER), of Seneca, Ontario Co., NY, were parents of B. JENNIE b. 24 Mar. 1833, Seneca, NY (m. Alonzo Marshall Carson, also see). Ref: P&BA-Len pg. 832-4.

PECK, JAMES born ca. 1811, Conn., and wife, SARAH, born ca. 1815, NY, were listed in the 1850 census of Ridgeway Twp., Lenawee Co., Mich. with MALISSA, age 16; MARY J., age 14, both b. Ohio, in their household. Note: May be he listed in the 1840 census index of

Pioneer Families of Southeastern Michigan

Macon Twp. adjacent to ELKANAH JR.; PHINEAS P.; PHILIP P.

PECK, JEN was listed in the 1840 census index of Adrian Twp., Lenawee Co., Mich.

PECK, JOSEPH W. born ca. 1818, VT, and wife, MARY E., born ca. 1819, Canada, were listed in the 1850 census of Adrian Twp., Lenawee Co., Mich. with HORACE W., age 10; FRANCES E., age 6; MYRON A., age 4, all b. NY, in their household.

PECK, MARY (See Jacob Appleby)

PECK, NORMAN born ca. 1800, NY, and wife, MARY, born ca. 1798, NJ, were listed in the 1850 census of Franklin Twp., Lenawee Co., Mich. with WILLIAM, age 15; CANDIS (CANDACE?), age 13; WARREN, age 10, all b. Mich., in their household.

PECK, PHILIP P. was listed in the 1840 census index of Macon Twp., Lenawee Co., Mich. adjacent to PHINEAS P., following.

PECK, PHINEAS P. born ca. 1825, Mass., was listed in the 1840 census index of Macon Twp., Lenawee Co., Mich.; and in the 1850 census of Adrian Twp. with wife, SUSAN F., born ca. 1814, England, and OSCAR E., age 2/12, b. Mich.; and Mary J. Gilbert, age 19, b. England; Adelaide Bond, age 9; Martha A. Bond, age 5, both b. Ohio, in their household. In 1840, he was listed adjacent to ELKANAH JR.; JAMES; PHILIP P.

PECK, WILLIAM H. born ca. 1814, Conn., and wife, LAURA, born ca. 1816, NY, were listed in the 1850 census of Woodstock Twp., Lenawee Co., Mich. with SARAH, age 5, b. NY, in their household.

PEEBLES, BRUEN E., son of JOHN B. (following), born 16 Dec. 1840, Rome Twp., Lenawee Co., Mich., went as an adult to Reading, Hillsdale Co., Mich.; then to Fairfield Twp., Lenawee Co. He married 3 Dec. 1869, Ogden Twp., to EMMA E. (WORDEN), daughter of W. H. (also see). They settled in Madison Twp. Children: 1. BESSIE E.; 2. MABLE; 3. MAUDE A. Ref: P&BA-Len pg. 637.

PEEBLES, ELIZA (See Samuel H. Luce)

PEEBLES, JOHN B. born in NY, and wife, LYDIA (BIDWELL), born Mass., moved from NY to Lorain Co., Ohio; and then about 1834 to Rome Twp., Lenawee Co., Mich. They moved by 1850 to Ogden Twp., and moved "late in life" to Adrian, where he died 16 Oct. 1886, age 83; and she died 15 Nov 1886, age 82. In the 1850 census of Ogden Twp., he was listed as "BEEBEE," JOHN B. born ca. 1803, Mass., and wife, LYDIA, born ca. 1805, NY, with WILLIAM, age 22; MARIA, age 19; LOUISA, age 18; LEPHA, age 14, all b. NY; and WALLACE, age 13, b. Ohio; BRUEN E. (preceding); RACHEL, age 7; JOHN, age 5; HENRY, age 3; OSCAR, age ?/12, all b. Mich., in their household. Ref: P&BA-Len pg. 637. Note: The sketch gave "Barry Co., NY" as the place of birth, but there is none.

PEGLER, GEORGE was listed in the 1840 census index of Monroe, Monroe Co., Mich.; and a GEORGE M. PEGLAR in Lasalle, Monroe Co., Mich. SARAH M. born 21 Oct. 1834, London, Ontario, Canada, may be daughter of George, as she came to Monroe Co., Mich. with her parents; and then they moved to New Brunswick, NJ. They returned to Monroe, Mich. in 1849, and both parents died there. Sarah married William F. King (also see). Ref: P&BA-Len pg. 364-5.

PEIFER, CATHERINE (See Frederick Keefer)

PEIRSON also see PEARSON & PIERSON

PEIRSON, EDWIN D.[7], son of WILLIAM[6] (following), born 10 Dec. 1819, Richmond, Berkshire Co., Mass., went to St. Louis, Mo. and Springfield & Bloomfield, Ill. ca. 1838. He returned to Richmond where he married on 7 Apr. 1847 to CLEMENZA EUNICE (WELLS), daughter of Daniel P. (also see). They were living in Hudson Twp., Lenawee Co., Mich. in the 1850 census with no children in the household. About 1854 they lived in the village of Hudson, but returned to the township in 1858. They retired to Hudson village where he died 16 Dec. 1885. Children: 1. CHARLES DWIGHT (d. infancy); 2. IDA E. (m. Charles Fitts, Blissfield Twp.); 3. EUGENE DOUGLAS[8] (following); 4. EVA CLEMENZA. Ref: P&BA-Len pg. 675-6 & portrait.

PEIRSON, EUGENE DOUGLAS[8], son of EDWIN D.[7] (preceding), born 30 July 1856, Hudson, Lenawee Co., Mich., married ELECTA J. (WARNER), daughter of Sheldon (also see). Children: 1. WARNER DWIGHT b. 28 Jan. 1882; 2. HARRY EUGENE b. 4 Apr. 1886 (d. 27 Aug. 1886); 3. ROBERT HENRY b. 2 Oct. 1887. Ref: P&BA-Len pg. 858-9.

PEIRSON, LEVI R.[6], son of WILLIAM[6] (following), born 29 Mar. 1827, Richmond, Mass., came to Hudson Twp., Lenawee Co., Mich. ca. 1849. He married 27 Nov. 1857 to Mrs. HARRIET (ALLEN) DOTY, daughter of Nathan (also see). Ref: P&BA-Len pg. 709-10 & portrait.

PEIRSON, NATHAN[4], son of THEOPHILUS[3], born 9 Aug. 1722, probably Long Island, NY, had the following ancestry. THEOPHILUS[3], was son of HENRY[2], son of MATTHEW[1]. Matthew[1] had come from England probably to Long Island in 1637. Nathan[4] moved about 1772 to Berkshire Co., Mass. where he died 5 Feb. 1810. Known son, ZACHARIAH[5] (following). Ref: P&BA-Len pg. 675-6.

PEIRSON, WILLIAM[6], son of ZACHARIAH[5] (See NATHAN[4], preceding), born 2 May 1793, Richmond, Mass., married NANCY (RICHARDS). He died 17 Aapr. 1862. Nancy died while enroute to Utah with brother, Willard Richards. Eight children, seven grew to maturity, names not stated, except EDWIN D. (preceding); & LEVI R. (preceding). Ref: P&BA-Len pg. 675-6; 709-10.

PELHAM also see PELLAM

PELHAM, ABRAHAM, age 18, born NY, was listed in the 1850 census of Tecumseh Twp., Lenawee Co., Mich. Note: There was an ABRAM & AVERY listed in the 1840 census index of Washtenaw Co., Mich.

PELHAM, CHARLES W., son of RICHARD C. (following), born 13 Mar. 1842, Woodstock Twp., Lenawee Co., Mich., married MARY MATILDA (LAPHAM). There were 9 children, but only mentioned META (m. Oliver Holmes; Wales, Erie Co., NY). Ref: P&BA-Len pg. 691.

PELHAM, ELLEN, age 10, born Mich., was listed in the 1850 census of Tecumseh Twp., Lenawee Co., Mich.

PELHAM, HENRY died as a young man in Greene Co., NY; and his wife, MARGARET (GRAY), died at age 84 in

Ulster Co., NY. Known son, RICHARD C. (following). Ref: P&BA-Len pg. 691.

PELHAM, RICHARD C., son of HENRY (preceding), born 8 Aug. 1810, Greene Co., NY, married in 1831 in Delaware Co., NY to ABIGAIL (EVERY/AVERY). In 1835, they removed to Woodstock Twp., Lenawee Co., Mich. Children: 1. HANNAH S. b. ca. 1832 (m. James Peterson; Jackson Co., Mich.); 2. HENRY b. 20 Feb. 1834 (m. Helen Bolton; Dakota); 3. LORETTA b. 18 Apr. 1836 (m. James R. Terpeney); 4. HARMON I. Q. b. 18 July 1838 (m. Fannie McConnell); 5. CHARLES W. (preceding); 6. EDSON b. ca. 1850. Ref: P&BA-Len pg. 691.

PELLAM, JANE (See Moses Quimby)

PENCE see PENSE

PENNEY, ANN, daughter of WILLIAM, of Orange Co., NY, married Gilbert Lockwood (also see). Note: In early Orange Co., NY Wills, a William Penny witnessed the will of Peter Young of Deerpark, Orange Co. in 1804.

PENNINGTON, ANN M. born ca. 1842, Mich., was listed in the 1850 census of Macon Twp., Lenawee Co., Mich. in the household of James Wheeler, Jr.

PENNINGTON, ISAAC, probably son of JOHN (following), born ca. 1823, NY, and wife, MARY, born ca. 1829, NJ, were listed in the 1850 census of Macon Twp., Lenawee Co., Mich. They reared Augusta Maples, daughter of Albert (also see) who was listed in their household in 1850.

PENNINGTON, ISRAEL, probably son of JOHN (following), born ca. 1808, and wife, HANNAH, born ca. 1810, both in NY, were listed in the 1850 census of Macon Twp., Lenawee Co., Mich. with DAVIS, age 5; BARRON H., age 3, both b. Mich.; and possibly stepchildren, Hamilton Davis, age 15; Franklin Davis, age 9, both b. Mich., in their household.

PENNINGTON, JOHN born ca. 1779, and wife, HANNAH, born ca. 1789, both born NJ, are probably they who moved to Raisin Twp., Lenawee Co., Mich. as early as 1831. In the 1850 census of Macon Twp., they were listed next door to ISRAEL (preceding). Also note JOHN; JOSEPH; & ISAAC. Note: There was an ISRAEL listed in the militia of Stafford, Monmouth Co., NJ in 1793.

PENNINGTON, JOHN, JR., probably son of JOHN (preceding), born ca. 1813, and wife, MARY A., born ca. 1821, both in NY, were listed in the 1840 census index of Macon Twp., Lenawee Co., Mich., adjacent to John; and in the 1850 census with SARAH E., age 5; MARY J., age 4; ALLETTA, age 2; ELIZABETH, age 1/12, all b. Mich., and Andrew Maples, age 10, b. NY, in their household.

PENNINGTON, JOHN M. married ELLA S. (CLARKSON), daughter of Richard, also see, and resided in Macon Twp.

PENNINGTON, JOSEPH, probably son of JOHN (preceding), born ca. 1821, and wife, AMANDA, born ca. 1821, both in NY, were listed in the 1850 census of Macon Twp., Lenawee Co., Mich. with HANNAH, age 6; ISRAEL, age 2; WESLEY, age 4/12, all b. Mich., in their household.

PENNINGTON, MARY (See Rev. Herman C. Smith)

PENNOCK, IRA born ca. 1810, VT, and wife, MARY ANN, born ca. 1817, NY, were listed in the 1840 census index of Tecumseh Twp., Lenawee Co., Mich.; and in the 1850 census with MARTIN, age 10; CORNELIA, age 13; ALONSO, age 7; LABAN, age 5; FRANCES, age 2, all b. Mich., in their household.

PENNOCK, GEORGE W. born ca. 1809, VT, was listed in the 1840 census index of Tecumseh Twp., Lenawee Co., Mich. adjacent to IRA, preceding; and in the 1850 census with (second wife?) HEPSIBAH, age 27, born NY; and MARY, age 17; ELIZABETH, age 15, both b. Canada; and GEORGE, age 6; WILLIAM, age 4; CHARLES, age 1, all b. Mich., in their household.

PENNOCK, JAMES B. born ca. 1803, and wife, RHODA, born ca. 1802, both in NY, were listed in the 1850 census of Woodstock Twp., Lenawee Co., Mich. with MARY, age 9; IRA, age 8, both b. Mich., in their household. Note: It is probably he listed as "Pennick" in the 1840 census index of Adrian Twp., Lenawee Co., adjacent to THOMAS, following.

PENNOCK, LEONARD born ca. 1823, NY, and wife, AMANDA, born ca. 1825, Canada, were listed in the 1850 census of Woodstock Twp., Lenawee Co., Mich. with GARDENINE? (female), age 4; GEORGE, age 2, both b. Mich., in their household.

PENNOCK, THOMAS accompanied Charles Ames in 1833 from Geneva, NY to Raisin Twp., Lenawee Co., Mich. It may be he listed as Thomas J. "Penick" in the 1840 census index of Adrian Twp., Lenawee Co., Mich., adjacent to JAMES, preceding.

PENOYER, GEORGE, possibly son of JOHN (following), born ca. 1810, and wife, HANNAH, born ca. 1817, both in NY, were listed in the 1850 census of Fairfield Twp., Lenawee Co., Mich. with JOSEPH S., age 16, b. NY; and HARRIET E., age 14; GEORGE D., age 13; JOHN C., age 12; WILLIAM H., age 10, all b. Mich., in their household.

PENOYER, JAMES, age 16, born NY, was listed in the 1850 census of Fairfield Twp., Lenawee Co., in the household of James Livesay. Note GEORGE, preceding.

PENOYER, JOHN and wife, ELIZABETH (WILKINSON), natives of Conn., moved to Ontario Co., NY before 1822. She died there at age 67, and he died at age 54. Thirteen children, names not stated, except MARY J. b. 3 Feb. 1822, Ontario Co., NY (m. William Lagore, also see). Also note GEORGE, preceding. Ref: P&BA-Len pg. 834-5.

PENSE, GEORGE served in the War of 1812, and moved from either Penn. or Virginia to Rockingham Co., Va. Known son, VALENTINE (following). Ref: P&BA-Len pg. 1151-2.

PENSE, VALENTINE, son of GEORGE (preceding), moved with his parents to Rockingham Co., VA. He married there to MARGARET (MILLER), daughter of Peter, and settled 8 miles from Harrisburg, where they remained. Known daughter, LUCY A. (m. Peter Hile, also see, before 1840). Ref: P&BA-Len pg. 1151-2.

PENTECOST, JESSE was born 23 June 1817, Somersetshire, England, and his parents (names not stated) remained in England where his mother died at age 97. Jesse

Pioneer Families of Southeastern Michigan

married there to ELIZABETH (SHEPHERD) born 10 Feb. 1820, England, and they came to the US in 1848 and settled in Franklin Twp., Lenawee Co., Mich. Elizabeth died 15 June 1882, age 62, and is buried in Mills Cemetery, Franklin Twp. In the 1850 census, they listed the first children #1 & 3 who were born in England: 1. MARY A. b. 7 Aug. 1841 (d. 4 July 1853); 2. WILLIAM S. b. 4 Oct. 1842 (d. 28 Sept. 1849); 3. JOSEPH b. 1845 (d. 1907; unmarried in 1888); 4. JOHN S. (1855-1926; had wife, Lillian E. 1855-1943, both bur. Mills Cem.); 5. SARAH E.; 6. CHARLES S. b. 1859 (d. 1900; poss. he who m. Delia Kemp, dau. of Sylvester, also see); 7. CARRIE E. Jesse married again on 25 Nov. 1884 to Mrs. NANCY (SLATER) MATTHEWS, daughter of Joseph, and widow of Henry (see both). Ref: P&BA-Len pg. 772-3. JOSEPH, following, is probably a brother.

PENTECOST, JOSEPH born ca. 1815, England, and wife, MARGARET, born ca. 1815, Penn., were listed in the 1840 census index of Franklin Twp., Lenawee Co., Mich.; and in the 1850 census (next door to JESSE, preceding), with MARGARET, age 16; WILLIAM, age 10; MORRIS, age 5, all b. Mich., in their household.

PENTECOST, WILLIAM born ca. 1801, England, and wife, JULIA, born ca. 1807, NY, were listed in the 1850 census of Franklin Twp., Lenawee Co., Mich. with WARREN, age 6; MARY, age 4; PHILIS (PHYLLIS?), age 3; SHADY, age 1, all b. Mich. Note: Julia may be a Curtis; as she named a daughter, Shady, probably after Shady (Curtis) Howell. William & Julia, and John & Shady Howell, are buried adjacent in the Mills Cemetery, Franklin Twp.

PERKINS, ABRAHAM T. born ca. 1803, and wife, HARRIET, born ca. 1805, both b. NY, were listed in the 1840 census index of Adrian Twp., Lenawee Co., Mich.; and in the 1850 census with CATHERINE E., age 23; ALAMANDER, age 19; LEWIS, age 17, all b. NY; and SAMUEL H., age 13, b. Mich.; and Emily Terpenning, age 13, b. Mich., in their household.

PERKINS, CHRISTOPHER was listed in the 1800 census index of Saratoga Co., NY; and may have moved to Ira, Cayuga Co., NY. Also, it may be he listed in the 1840 census index of Rome Twp., Lenawee Co., Mich. He had wife, HANNAH, and it may be she, age 84, listed in the household of MARTIN B. (following). Known son, MOSES (following); known daughter, ESTHER b. 8 July 1799, Saratoga Co., NY (m. Eliathah Stockwell, also see, in Ira, NY). In the 1840 census index, adjacent to Christopher were ELMRION (AMERIEN); HIRAM; WILLIAM, all following.

PERKINS, Dr. (See Hezekiah Knowles, Jr.)

PERKINS, EDWARD C. born ca. 1817, and wife, NANCY, born ca. 1825, both in New Hampshire, were listed in the 1850 census of Medina Twp., Lenawee Co., Mich.

PERKINS, ELMIRON born ca. 1814, and wife, ELIZA, born ca. 1811, both in NY, were listed in the 1840 census index (as "Amerien") of Rome Twp., Lenawee Co., Mich., adjacent to CHRISTOPHER (preceding); and in the 1850 census with OLIVER N., age 9; REUBEN, age 7; JUDSON H., age 3, all b. Mich., in their household.

PERKINS, EUGENE (See John H. Todd)

PERKINS, GEORGIA born 5 Dec. 1863, Kalamazoo Co., Mich., married in Lenawee Co. to William W. Crabbs (also see).

PERKINS, HIRAM born ca. 1805, and wife, CATHARINE, born ca. 1819, are probably they listed in the 1840 census index of Rome Twp., adjacent to CHRISTOPHER (preceding); and in the 1850 census of Rollin Twp. with MARY, age 14; SAMANTHA, age 12; CHESTER, age 7, all b. Mich., in their household.

PERKINS, JABEZ, age 28, born NY, was listed in the 1850 census of Cambridge Twp., Lenawee Co., Mich. in a Buttefield household.

PERKINS, JOHN T. born ca. 1811 was listed in the 1840 census index of Dover Twp., Lenawee Co., Mich. adjacent to STEPHEN (following); and in the 1850 census with wife, MARY M., born ca. 1821, NY; and HELEN M., age 6; AMELIA, age 4; EMMA, age 2/12, all b. Mich., in their household. John T. died and Mary M. married again to John Forbes (also see).

PERKINS, JOSEPH, age 16, born NY; and ANTHONY, age 13; SUSAN A., age 10; JOHN, age 7, all b. Mich., probably siblings, were listed in the 1850 census of Rollin Twp., Lenawee Co., Mich. possibly stepchildren in the household of Joel Wilson (age 37, b. VT) and wife, Phebe, age 40, b. NJ.

PERKINS, LUCINA (See Samuel Horton)

PERKINS, LYMAN P. born ca. 1819, and wife, MARY S. (probably SHAW, daughter of Brackley, also see), born ca. 1824, both in NY, were listed in the 1850 census of Madison Twp., Lenawee Co., Mich. with ALMIRA E., age 3; EDGAR S., age 1, both b. Mich., in their household.

PERKINS, MARTIN B. born ca. 1811, NY, was head of household in the 1850 census of Hudson Twp., Lenawee Co., Mich. with HANNAH, age 84 (note CHRISTOPHER, preceding); and JOHN, age 7, b. NY; GALUSHA, age 4; MOSES, age 2, both b. Mich., in his household.

PERKINS, MOSES, son of CHRISTOPHER (preceding), born 1797, probably in Saratoga Co., NY; and wife, ELIZA, born ca. 1799, NY, probably lived in Ira, Cayuga Co., NY. By 1840, they were listed in the census index in Madison Twp., Lenawee Co., Mich.; and in the 1850 census listed ALMEDA, age 21; ELIZA A., age 17; WARREN B., age 12, all b. NY; and MARY A., age 13; MOSES N., age 11; ELEANOR C., age 8, all b. Mich., in their household. Next door were PALMER; & STEPHEN P., both following.

PERKINS, MYRON born ca. 1828, NY, was listed in the 1850 census of Adrian Twp., Lenawee Co., Mich. in a hotel.

PERKINS, NELSON, son of STEPHEN (following), born 1 Apr. 1827, Cayuga Co., NY, and wife, MARY A., born ca. 1830, NY, were listed in the 1850 census of Dover Twp., Lenawee Co., Mich. with WILLIAM, age 2, b. Mich., in their household.

PERKINS, NEWMAN born ca. 1784, NY, and wife, BETSEY, born ca. 1786, Rhode Island, were listed in the 1850 census of Dover Twp., Lenawee Co., Mich. with BARBER T., age 28; WILLIAM T., age 21, both b. NY, in their household. It may be this Newman who married Mrs. HARRIET JEWELL, widow of Henry, as her 4th husband (also see Albern Raymond & James Learnard).

PERKINS, NEWMAN born ca. 1819, and wife, OLIVE, born ca. 1817, both in NY, were listed in the 1850 census of Hudson Twp., Lenawee Co., Mich. with MARION (male), age 7, b. NY; and ALMOND, age 3; MARY J., age 2, both b. Mich., and Richard Card, age 8/12, born Mich., in their household.

PERKINS, NOAH, probably son of WILLIAM, born ca. 1823, and wife, ELLEN, born ca. 1826, both in NY, were listed in the 1850 census of Adrian Twp., Lenawee Co., Mich. (next door to WILLIAM) with EDGAR, age 4; NOAH, age 7/12, both b. Mich., in their household.

PERKINS, PALMER, probably son of MOSES (preceding), born ca. 1822, and wife ALIDA C., born ca. 1825, both in NY, were listed in the 1850 census of Madison Twp., Lenawee Co., Mich., next door to MOSES.

PERKINS, PHEBE (See Moses Cook; and James Converse).

PERKINS, PHILENA (See Azariah Bickford)

PERKINS, S. P. (See LYMAN P.; sketch said "S.P." married Mary Shaw, daughter of Brackley, Jr.; this was probably Lyman P.)

PERKINS, SAMUEL C., son of STEPHEN (following), born 5 Feb. 1823, and wife, MARGARET, born ca. 1825, both in NY, were listed in the 1850 census of Hudson Twp., Lenawee Co., Mich. with ALVIRA, age 7; MELISSA, age 5; MINERVA, age 4, all b. Mich., in their household.

PERKINS, STEPHEN (note CHRISTOPHER, preceding) born 26 June 1797, and wife, FREELOVE (TERPENNING), born ca. 1801, both in NY, married there 23 Dec. 1819. They moved from Cayuga Co., NY to Michigan in 1831, and settled in Dover Twp., Lenawee Co., Mich. before 1840 (where the were listed adjacent to JOHN T. in the census). They were listed in the 1850 census of Madison Twp. He died in 1874 in Hudson Twp., and she was still living there in 1888. Children: 1. JOHN b. 4 Nov. 1820; 2. SAMUEL C. (preceding); 3. MOSES b. 2 Feb. 1825; 4. NELSON (preceding); 5. FRANKLIN b. 8 June 1829; 6. LEWIS F. b. 7 May 1831; 7. SUSAN b. 20 Aug. 1835; 8. CYNTHIA M. b. 4 Oct. 1837; 9. HARRIET D. b. 17 Nov. 1839 (m. William D. James, also see); 10. STEPHEN HARRISON b. 24 Mar. 1842. Ref: P&BA-Len pg. 1010.

PERKINS, STEPHEN P., probably son of MOSES (preceding), born ca. 1825, and wife MARTHA J., born ca. 1827, both in NY, were listed in the 1850 census of Madison Twp., Lenawee Co., Mich. next door to Moses; and listed again in the 1850 census of Dover Twp. in a Marvin Cleveland household (in-laws?)

PERKINS, WILLARD Dr. (See Norton Baker)

PERKINS, WILLIAM born ca. 1780, and wife SUSAN, born ca. 1782, both in NY, were listed in the 1840 census index of Rome Twp., Lenawee Co., Mich. adjacent to CHRISTOPHER, also see; and there was also a WILLIAM JR. They were listed in the 1850 census ages 70 & 68, respectively.

PERKINS, WILLIAM born ca. 1789, New Hampshire, and wife, FELINDA?, born ca. 1794, VT, were listed in the 1850 census of Adrian Twp., Lenawee Co., Mich., next door to NOAH (preceding).

PERKINS, WILLIAM born ca. 1810, and wife, JANE, born ca. 1813, both in NY, were listed in the 1850 census of Adrian Twp., Lenawee Co., Mich. with JANE, age 4, b. Mich.; and Samuel B. McCarty, age 13, b. Mich., in their household.

PERRY, ABEL born ca. 1784, Onondaga Co., NY, married there to LUCINDA (AINSWORTH) born VT. She died there in April 1838; and he moved his family by 1840 to Medina Twp., Lenawee Co., Mich. He died there in 1849, age 65. All children were born Onondaga Co., except George W. who was born Steuben Co., NY. 1. AMOS (d. Mar. 1887); 2. SALLY; 3. (SARAH) MARIE b. Lysander, NY (m. Hiram N. Fellows, also see); 4. CHARLES (following); 5. MARY ANN; 6. IRA b. ca. 1828 (following); 7. HENRY b. ca. 1830; 8. JONAS (d. infancy); 9. ABEL b. ca. 1833; 10. GEORGE W. (following); 11. EDGAR ALONZO (following). Ref: P&BA-Len pg. 620-1. Note: There is a JOSHUA in the 1800 census index of Onondaga Co., NY.

PERRY, CHARLES, son of ABEL (preceding), born 25 Apr. 1822, near Lysander, NY, went to Gorham Twp., Lucas Co., (now Fulton Co.), Ohio where he married on 19 May 1844 to PHILA (FARWELL), daughter of Hiram (also see). They removed to Medina Twp., Lenawee Co., Mich.; but also had property in Wright Twp., Hillsdale Co. (In the 1850 census of Medina Twp., she was called "Polly," age 24). Children: 1. HIRAM b. ca. 1845 (d. age 5); 2. ESTHER b. ca. 1847 (d. same day as Hiram, age 3); 3. CHARLES MORTIMER (m. Rose Palmer; children: Inez & Ray; Wright Twp.; Hillsdale Co.); 4. ABEL L. (m. Ida E. Garling; children, Clarence & Lee; Wright Twp., Hillsdale Co.); 5. HENRY L. (m. Etta Blanchard); 6. DAVID (twin of Henry, d. age 15 mos). Ref: P&BA-Len pg. 620-1.

PERRY, EDGAR ALONZO, son of ABEL (preceding), born 18 Feb. 1836, Onondaga Co., NY, moved to Medina Twp., Lenawee Co., Mich. with his father. In 1852, he went with a group of 21 persons overland to California. Some others in the party were Lawrence Cottrell; Harvey Snow; William Thorp; & Jesse Thorp. Edgar remained there until 1863, then returned to Medina Twp. where he married on 14 Aug. 1866 to LUCY I. (COOLEY), daughter of Justus (also see). Children: 1. ELMER A. (Dover Twp.); 2. AMOS J.; 3. SIDNEY A.; 4. NELLIE I. Ref: P&BA-Len pg. 620-1.

PERRY, ELIAS was listed in the 1840 census index of Cambridge Twp., Lenawee Co., Mich.

PERRY, GEORGE W., probably son of ABEL (preceding), born ca. 1815, and wife, RUBY A., born ca. 1820, both in NY, were listed in the 1850 census of Medina Twp., Lenawee Co., Mich. with CHARLES C., age 7; EDWIN P., age 5, both b. Mich., in their household.

PERRY, GIDEON D. born ca. 1812, and wife, MARGARET, born ca. 1817, both in NY, were listed in the 1850 census of Franklin Twp., Lenawee Co., Mich. with MARY, age 5; THOMAS, age 3; MARGARET, age 1/12, all b. Mich., in their household.

PERRY, IRA, son of ABEL (preceding), born ca. 1828, was listed in the 1850 census of Medina Twp., Lenawee Co., Mich. with HENRY shown as head of household. Also in the household, listed following Ira, was MARTHA, age 20, b. NY, and listed last was a child, JANE A., age 3, born Mich. This may be their child? Note that proof is needed.

PERRY, JOHN born ca. 1820, and wife, BETSEY, born ca. 1826, both in England, were listed in the 1850 census of Raisin Twp., Lenawee Co., Mich. with WILLIAM, age 5, b. Ohio; and CHARLES, age 3; MARY, age 1; FRANCES, age 1/12, all b. Mich., in their household.

PERRY, ORRIN born ca. 1809, and HENRIETTA, born ca. 1809, both in NY, were listed in the 1850 census of Hudson Twp., Lenawee Co., Mich. with Riley Pain, age 12, b. Mich. in the household.

Pioneer Families of Southeastern Michigan

PERRY, ROSWELL and wife, DOLLY (FOSTER), both born Genesee Co., NY, lived there and in Saratoga Springs, NY. They moved to "western NY," where he died in 1844, age 74. She later moved to Seneca Twp., Lenawee Co., Mich. were she died in 1855, age 76, at the home of known daughter, #3. MARGARET b. 5 Mar. 1829, Genesee Co., NY (m. Aaron R. Tufts, also see). Ref: P&BA-Len pg. 565-6. Note: Genesee Co., NY was formed in 1802 from Ontario Co.; and in the 1800 census index of Ontario Co., there is a ROUSE (Roswell?); and also a MOSE(S).

PERRY, SUSAN, age 20, born Mich., was listed in the 1850 census of Madison Twp., Lenawee Co., Mich. in a Palmer household. Note WARREN, following.

PERRY, TRUMAN D. was listed in the 1840 census index of Macon Twp., Lenawee Co., Mich.

PERRY, WARREN was listed in the 1830 census of Lenawee Co., Michigan Territory with males: 2 20-30 & 1 30-40; female: 1 20-30 in the household. It may be he in the 1840 census index of Dundee Twp., Monroe Co., Mich.

PERRY, WILLIAM Capt. and wife, MIRIAM (BARNARD) of "Holley, Orleans Co., NY," were parents of MARY M. b. 28 July 1805, Canada (m. 7 Jan. 1825, Ontario Co., NY to Horace W. Comstock, also see). Ref: P&BA-Len pg. 648-9.

PERRY, WILLIAM born ca. 1798, was listed in the 1850 census of Cambridge Twp., Lenawee Co., Mich. with JAMES, age 19; WILLIAM, age 16; ELISA, age 13; ANSON, age 11, all b. NY; and CHANCEY, age 9; JASPER, age 4, both b. Mich., in his household.
Note ELIAS, preceding.

PETERS, GEORGE (See Levi Jennings)

PETERSON, F. (See Garrett F. Harris)
PETERSON, JAMES (See Richard Pelham)

PETTY, CATHARINE ANN (See William V. Ditmars)

PETTYS, GILBERT M. married SARAH (THOMPSON), daughter of George (also see). He served in Co. A, 101st Ohio Inf, Civil War, and died as a result of illness during the War. Children: 1. EMMA b. 10 July 1860 (m. Frank Poucher); 2. CLEMIE R. (m. F. M. Harlow, Jackson Co., Mich.) Sarah married again to Marshall Blanchard; and third to Roswell H. Hicks (also see) in Rome Twp., Lenawee Co., Mich. Ref: P&BA-Len pg. 1121-2.

PHELPS, ELIAS born ca. 1817, and wife, CLARINDA, born ca. 1820, both in NY, were listed in the 1840 census index of Hudson Twp., Lenawee Co., Mich.; and in the 1850 census with BURTON, age 10; ELIAS D., age 6; JANETTE, age 9/12, all b. Mich., in their household.
PHELPS, FRANCES (See James E. Rounds)
PHELPS, GEORGE F. (See George W. Moore)
PHELPS, HENRY was listed in the 1840 census indes of Rome Twp., Lenawee Co., Mich.
PHELPS, NATHAN born ca. 1820, and wife, MARY J., born ca. 1827, both in NY, were listed in the 1850 census of Dover Twp., Lenawee Co., Mich. with MARGARET J., age 7/12, b. Mich., in their household. Note ORLIN, following.

PHELPS, ORLIN married in Cayuga Co., NY to LYDIA L. (BRACKLEY), daughter of Brackley Sr. (also see) probably born ca. 1816. They moved to Dover Twp., Lenawee Co., Mich. in 1834; and were listed there in the 1840 census index. Not listed in 1850 census, children, if any, not given. She died in Toledo, Ohio.

PHELPS, PHILO P. and wife, EMELINE (DEWEY), moved from Ontario Co., NY to Rome Twp., Lenawee Co., Mich. in 1846. They apparently moved by 1850 to Osceola Co., Mich. where he died in 1888. age 67. She died 3 Sept. 1866 (sketch said in NY?) Known daughter, ARISTEEN b. 13 Sept. 1844, Ontario Co., NY (m. Ralph B. Baker, also see, Rome Twp.) Ref: P&BA-Len pg. 541-2.

PHELPS, SILAS, born Conn., enlisted at age 16, in the Revolutionary War; was captured and held several months as a prisoner, released and later contracted Smallpox. His father, name not stated, a surgeon in the Merchant Marine, treated him, but caught the disease and died. Silas reenlisted in the War. He was a pioneer to Phelps, Ontario Co., NY. (Note: The sketch said it was named for Silas, but French's Gazeteer of New York State, says that it was named for Oliver Phelps, an original proprietor.) After the war, he returned to Phelps where he died almost 100 yrs old. Known daughter, PAMELIA born 8 Apr. 1804, Phelps, NY (m. Rev. Isaac Hiller, also see, in Monroe Co., NY, moved to Macon Twp., Lenawee Co., Mich.) Ref: P&BA-Len pg. 1111-2. Note: There is a SILAS, Conn. service, listed in Rev. War Pension Appl. with widow, MARY, Appl. #W26883; and BLWt.284-60-5. There was a SILAS listed in the 1800 cenus index of Oneida Co., NY. Note the following, who may be the same man.

PHELPS, SILAS was a Revolutionary soldier, and was father of ORA called a "native of Monroe Co., NY" (m. before 1818 in Walworth, Wayne Co., NY to Russell Warner, also see, lived Manchester, Ontario Co., NY; then after he d. 1828, m. John Thompson.) Ref: P&BA-Len pg. 932-3. Note SILAS, preceding.

PHETTEPLACE, ASA born ca. 1790, and wife, HANNAH (WATERS), born ca. 1794, both in Warren Co., NY, lived first in Buffalo, NY. In 1833, they moved from Niagara Co., NY to Madison Twp., Lenawee Co., Mich. There were 6 children, names not stated.
Known daughter, MARY H. b. 28 Aug. 1824, Niagara Co., NY (m. Rial Niles, also see). In the 1850 census of Madison Twp., Asa listed JAMES, age 24 (prob. he who went to Calif. in 1852 with Marvin Packard, and returned in 1853); ELSA, age 18, both b. NY; and FRANCIS, age 14, b. Mich. (This may be adopted son, Frank Lease, who served 9th Mich. Cav., Civil War). JOHN (following) is probably also a son. Ref: P&BA-Len pg. 736; 890-1. Note: There was a JOHN listed in the 1800 census index of Washington Co., NY.
PHETTEPLACE, ESECK was listed in the 1840 census index of Branch Co., Mich.
PHETTEPLACE, JOHN, probably son of ASA (preceding), born ca. 1820, and wife, CATHARINE, age 24, both b. NY, were listed in the 1850 census of Ogden Twp., Lenawee Co., Mich. with RIAL, age 1, b. Mich., in their household. Note: Was Catharine also a Niles? See Samuel Niles.

PHILIPS see PHILLIPS

PHILLIPS, AARON born 6 Aug. 1791, and wife, LAVINA (BURROUGHS), born 19 Aug. 1797, both in Hunterdon Co., NJ, lived there first, then moved before 1819 to Seneca Co., NY. She died there 8 May 1836, age 38, and he moved the family to Michigan in 1837. He stopped first in Wayne Co., Mich. till the Spring of 1838, then went to Madison Twp., Lenawee Co.; and in the Fall to Dover Twp. Children: 1. TITUS (d. 14 Apr. 1877, Wisc.); 2. AARON M. (following); 3. PHEBE (d. 7 Nov. 1822, Seneca Co., NY); 4. PHEBE M. (m. Gilbert Gage); 5. SUSANNA A. b. ca. 1829, NY (m. Henry S. Miller, Seneca Co., NY after 1850); 6. MARTHA (d. 30 Oct. 1833, age 4). In the 1850 census of Dover Twp., Aaron listed wife, ELECTA, age 50, born NY, and only SUSANNA was still in the household. He died 16 Mar. 1877, age 86. Ref: P&BA-Len pg. 1187-8.

PHILLIPS, AARON M., son of AARON (preceding), both 15 May 1819, Seneca Co., NY, came to Michigan with his father. He married on 1 Nov. 1840, Adrian Twp., Lenawee Co. to CATHERINE E. "Esther" (STOCKWELL), daughter of Eliathah (also see) and settled in Dover Twp. Children: 1. AARON P. b. ca. 1842 (m. Eleanor A. Raymond; d. 2 Feb. 1869, age 27, Dover Twp.); 2. CELESTIA A. (d. 25 July 1846, age 2); 3. CHARLES W. (following); 4. HELEN (d. 12 Feb. 1864, age 12); 5. GEORGE C. Ref: P&BA-Len pg. 1187-8.

PHILLIPS, ALANSON born ca. 1805, Mass., and wife, ELIZA W. (WALKER), born ca. 1810, NY, lived first in Ontario Co., NY, then about 1835 moved to Madison Twp., Lenawee Co., Mich. In 1837, they moved to Fairfield Twp. He died there 7 Apr. 1879, and she died 14 Aug. 1885. Known children (from 1850 census of Fairfield Twp.): 1. GEORGE, age 19; 2. ELIZABETH C. b. 5 Feb. 1834, Ontario Co., NY (m. Ira Goodsell, also see); 3. MARY, age 14; 4. HENRY, age 8, last 2 b. Mich. Ref: P&BA-Len pg. 968-9.

PHILLIPS, ALLEN born ca. 1795, and wife, LYDIA, born ca. 1797, were listed in the 1840 census index of Dover Twp., Lenawee Co., Mich.; and in the 1850 census with WILLIAM, age 32; ER (male), age 23; SALLY M., age 17; LUCINDA J., age 14, all b. NY, in their household.

PHILLIPS, ANN ELIZA, age 38, born NY, was listed in the 1850 census of Adrian Twp., Lenawee Co., Mich. in the Addison J. Comstock household.

PHILLIPS, CHARITY (See John R. Foster)

PHILLIPS, CHARLES W., son of AARON M. (preceding), born ca. 1847, Dover Twp., Lenawee Co., Mich., married SARAH (LOZIER). Children: ELMER A.; ETHEL C.; ROBB V.; LENA M.; SEWARD W. Ref: P&BA-Len pg. 1187-8.

PHILLIPS, ELIZABETH, age 18, born England, was listed in the 1850 census of Hudson Twp., Lenawee Co., Mich. Note JANE & TAMAR, following.

PHILLIPS, FRANKLIN S. (See Samuel Nash)

PHILLIPS, HELEN, age 60, born Ireland, was listed in the 1850 census of Cambridge Twp., Lenawee Co., Mich. in an Agard household.

PHILLIPS, HENRY born ca. 1820, and wife, MARY, born ca. 1826, both in NY, were listed in the 1850 census of Adrian Twp., Lenawee Co., Mich. with MELISSA, age 5, b. Ohio, in their household.

PHILLIPS, J. E. (See Archibald M. Sickly)

PHILLIPS, JANE, age 18, born England, was listed in the 1850 census of Adrian Twp., Lenawee Co., Mich. Note ELIZABETH; & TAMAR.

PHILLIPS, JEREMIAH S. born ca. 1830, NY, was listed in the 1850 census of Raisin Twp., Lenawee Co., Mich. with ELIZABETH, age 29, b. NY, in his household. It may be he listed again alone in another household in the 1850 census of Raisin Twp.

PHILLIPS, JOEL born ca. 1815, Mass., and wife, AROSETTA, born ca. 1819, NY, were listed in the 1840 census index of Dover Twp., Lenawee Co., Mich.; and in the 1850 census with WILLIAM H., age 11, b. Mich., in their household.

PHILLIPS, JOHN born ca. 1826, Ohio, was listed in the 1850 census of Raisin Twp., Lenawee Co., Mich.

PHILLIPS, JOHN, son of SAMUEL (following), born 26 June 1802, Bennington, VT, moved to Monroe Co., NY with his parents. He married there to PAMELIA (WOOD), daughter of Levi (also see). She died near Canandaigua, NY leaving children: 1. ELIZABETH (m. William McKnight; Bloomington, Ind.); 2. LAURA (m. David I. Daniels; Wacousta, Mich.); 3. ZELORA (Chicago, Ill.); 4. MARY (m. George Goodnow, Hudson, Mich.); 5. DORR (Osseo, Mich.); 6. JENNIE (m. Almon Pratt; Webster, NY); 7. RAY (Hazen, Prairie Co., Ark.). In 1866, John moved from NY to Hillsdale Co., Mich.; and in 1877 to Hudson, Lenawee Co. He married again on 29 Aug. 1866 to Mrs. ELIZA (SMITH) CLARK, daughter of John (also see); and widow of Seymour. Ref: P&BA-Len pg. 699-700.

PHILLIPS, MARY (See Daniel Bryant)

PHILLIPS, NICHOLAS had known daughter, JANE A. b. ca. 1813, NY (m. Surrajah Wines, also see, before 1833, possibly in Wayne Co., NY). Ref: P&BA-Len pg. 846-7. Note: There were 2 NICHOLAS in the 1800 census index of NY in Onondaga & Dutchess Cos.

PHILLIPS, SAMUEL born Bennington, VT, married there to ELIZABETH (LYONS) born VT. In 1811, they moved to North Penfield, near Webster, Monroe Co., NY. He died there at age 84. Nine children, 7 lived to maturity, names not stated, except #4. JOHN (preceding). Ref: P&BA-Len pg. 699-700.

PHILLIPS, SARAH (See Cornelius Mersereau)

PHILLIPS, TAMAR, age 16, born England, was listed in the 1850 census of Adrian Twp., Lenawee Co., Mich. Note ELIZABETH & JANE, preceding.

PHILLIPS, WILLARD (See John Henry)

PICKARD, JANE (See Reuben Sayers[1])

PICKERING, RICHARD and wife, ANN (JORDAN), lived out their lives in Yorkshire, England, where he died at age 76; and she died at age 72. Children: 1. MARY; 2. HARRIET; 3. JANE b. 25 Mar. 1815 (m. David Pearson, also see); 4. HANNAH; 5. ROBERT. Ref: P&BA-Len pg. 689-90.

PICKFORD, EDWIN, son of JOHN & MARY (JOYCE), born 2 Mar. 1828, Somersetshire, England, married there to CECELIA (POPE), daughter of James (also see). In 1852, they came to the US, landing in New York City, then going to Rollin Twp., Lenawee Co., Mich. to join his brother (name not stated). They settled in Rome Twp. Children: 1. JAMES E. b. 2 Nov. 1851; 2. CICERO J. b. 2

Pioneer Families of Southeastern Michigan

May 1854 (m. ? Lamoreaux, Rome Twp.); 3. HARRIET B. b. 5 Sept. 1860 (m. Jesse Chase who served Civil War & d. 1874); 4. AUSTIN b. 8 Nov. 1865; 5. LESLIE J. b. 24 Sept. 1869. Ref: P&BA-Len pg. 692-3.

PIERCE, ABEL A. born ca. 1820, and wife, ELIZABETH M., born ca. 1832, both in NY, were listed in the 1850 census of Blissfield Twp., Lenawee Co., Mich. with ALEXAS C. (male), age 8/12, b. Mich., in their household. Note DANIEL, following.

PIERCE, ABNER GORHAM, son of ABNER (who remained in Mass.), born Cambridge, Mass., married LAURA (PRIEST) born Nottingham, Mass. About 1850, they moved to Palmyra, Wayne Co., NY; and in 1858 to Farmington, Ontario Co., NY. They were in Cambridge, Mass. for 6 months ca. 1861, but returned to Palmyra, NY till about 1866 when they moved to Chicago, Ill. In 1868, they settled in Hudson, Lenawee Co., Mich. He died 25 Mar. 1886, and she died May 1887, Hudson. Children: 1. HARRIET (m. Calvin Rice; to Chicago, Ill.); 2. CHARLES (d. age 19, Farmington, NY); 3. ORRIN (following); 4. LAURA (d. age 12, Farmington, NY). Ref: P&BA-Len pg. 646-7.

PIERCE, ALLEN married MEHITABLE (WILLIAMS) possibly in Cayuga Co., NY; and they moved to near Buffalo, NY where he died of Cholera. She returned to Cayuga Co., NY where known daughter, ABIGAIL was born in 1832 (m. Jonathan Rowley, son of Constant, also see). Mehitable moved to Lenawee Co., NY where she married again to Constant Rowley (also see) as his 3rd wife. Ref: P&BA-Len pg. 665-6.

PIERCE, ANN (GUIETT) Mrs. (See John Millson)

PIERCE, ASAPH born ca. 1823, and wife, FANNY P., born ca. 1822, both in New Hampshire, were listed in the 1850 census of Hudson Twp., Lenawee Co., Mich. Note LUKE A., following.

PIERCE, DANIEL, born VT, moved after 1810 to New York, possibly Steuben Co. Known daughter, LOUISA b. ca. 1810, VT (m. Isaac S. Austin, Steuben Co., NY). Daniel came to Blissfield Twp., Lenawee Co., Mich. late in life and lived with his children. Ref: P&BA-Len pg. 933-4. Also note MASON; MELVIN B.; MORRIS, following, and ABEL A., preceding.

PIERCE, DANIEL, age 8; and JOHN, age 4, both b. Mich., were listed in the 1850 census of Fairfield Twp., Lenawee Co., Mich. in an Arnold household. Note JOHN of Fairfield Twp., following.

PIERCE, DAVID S. born ca. 1776, VT, and wife, BETSEY, born ca. 1794, NY, were listed in the 1850 census of Seneca Twp., Lenawee Co., Mich. in the household of Thomas B. & Betsey A. (age 27, b. NY) Williams. Betsey A. may be their daughter?

PIERCE, EDWIN, age 18, born NY, was listed in the 1850 census of Fairfield Twp., Lenawee Co., Mich. in a Barto household. Note JOHN, following.

PIERCE, HORACE was listed in the 1840 census index of Palmyra Twp., Lenawee Co., Mich.

PIERCE, JOHN born ca. 1769, and wife, DEBORAH, born ca. 1777, both in NY, were listed in the 1850 census of Fairfield Twp., Lenawee Co., Mich. with the following in their household in this order, relationship not known: HANNAH, age 42; EDWARD, age 40, both b. NY; and MARY, age 15; WILLIAM, age 13; JERVIS, age 9, all b. Mich. Note JOHN, following.

PIERCE, JOHN born ca. 1798, NY, and wife, MARIETTA (REYNOLDS) born ca. 1800/3, Conn., lived first in Otsego Co., NY; then moved to Orleans Co. before 1834. In 1846, they removed to Fairfield Twp., Lenawee Co., Mich. She died in Apr. 1853, age 50, while visiting in NY. He died Jan. 1857 resulting from a fall on the way to visit a son in Clyde, Ohio. There were 5 sons and 3 daughters, names not stated, except #7. NORMAN B. (BIRD N.) following; & JEFFERSON b. ca. 1835, NY (in the household in 1850). Ref: P&BA-Len pg. 492-3. Note JOHN, & NEWELL S., following.

PIERCE, JOHN called an "early settler of Madison Twp., Lenawee Co., Mich." was the father of SUSAN born ca. 1826 (m. 1850 to Robert M. Bailey, also see; however, in the 1850 census, he listed a wife, Cornelia?). John went to Ohio where he died at an advanced age. Ref: P&BA-Len pg. 1168.

PIERCE, LUKE A. born ca. 1804, and wife, MARGARET, born ca. 1812, both born New Hampshire, were listed in the 1840 census index of Franklin Twp., Lenawee Co., Mich.; and in the 1850 census with NANCY, age 17; SARAH, age 11, both b. Mich., in their household. Note ASAPH, preceding.

PIERCE, MARTHA, age 23, born New York, was listed in the 1850 census of Madison Twp., Lenawee Co., Mich. in a Graham household; and it may be she listed again, age 22, in the 1850 census of Adrian Twp., in a Barrick household.

PIERCE, MASON was listed in the 1840 census index of Blissfield Twp., Lenawee Co., Mich.

PIERCE, MELVIN B. was listed in the 1840 census index of Blissfield Twp., Lenawee Co., Mich. There was a MELVIN, age 8, born Mich., listed in the 1850 census of Blissfield Twp. in a Blazedell household.

PIERCE, MORRIS, probably son of DANIEL, born ca. 1807, VT, and wife, MARY A., born ca. 1811, NY, were listed in the 1850 census of Blissfield Twp., Lenawee Co., Mich. with JONATHAN, age 11; GUY C., age 10; SARAH E., age 8; MARTHA I, age 7, all b. NY; and ALICE E., age 5, b. Mich., in their household.

PIERCE, NEWELL S., possibly son of JOHN (preceding), born ca. 1814, and wife, EMMA, born ca. 1820, both in NY, were listed in the 1850 census of Fairfield Twp., Lenawee Co., Mich. with AMANDA, age 15; HIRAM, age 10, both b. NY, in their household.

PIERCE, NORMAN B. (BIRD N.), son of JOHN (preceding), born 2 Mar. 1834, Orleans Co., NY, moved to Fairfield Twp., Lenawee Co., Mich. with his parents. At age 18, he returned to NY where he married on 18 Jan. 1854 to SARAH E. (REMINGTON), daughter of Ira H. (also see). In 1856, they went to Columbia Co., Wisc. but in 1859 returned to Fairfield Twp., Lenawee Co. Son: FRANK L. (m. Lora Heminway, Weston, Mich. Ref: P&BA-Len pg. 492-3.

PIERCE, ORRIN R., son of ABNER GORHAM (preceding), born 16 Sept. 1849, Cambridge, Mass., moved to first to NY, then to Hudson, Lenawee Co., Mich. with his parents. He married in 1875 in Hudson to MARY (WILLIAMSON), daughter of Henry (also see). Known children: 1. LAURA; 2. GRACE. Ref: P&BA-Len pg. 646-7.

PIERCE, WILLIAM F. born ca. 1802, and wife, LAMIRA?, born ca. 1807, both in NY, were listed in the 1840 census index of Ogden Twp., Lenawee Co., Mich.; and in the

1850 census with JOSEPH M., age 18, b. NY; and ELIZA J., age 16/11?; HANNAH, age 11; MYRON, age 8; LYDIA, age 3, all b. Mich., in their household.

PIERPOINT, MARY (See Joseph Lee)

PIERSON also see PEARSON/PEIRSON

PIERSON, HENRY born 16 May 1762, New Jersey, moved to Ontario Co., NY where his wife (name not stated) died in 1830. He died there at age 84. Known daughter, ELIZABETH b. NJ (m. Jeshurun Emery, also see, Ontario Co., NY). Ref: P&BA-Len pg. 411-2.

PIERSON, JOHN born ca. 1797, NJ, and wife, ELIZA, born ca. 1815, Conn., were listed in the 1850 census of Adrian Twp., Lenawee Co., Mich. with PHEBE A., age 26; RHODA, age 20, both b. NY; and JENETTE, age 10; JOHN S., age 5; ELIZABETH, age 1; and Ann E. DeLong, age 4, all b. Mich., in their household.

PIERSON, JOHN L. born ca. 1795, NJ, and wife, FRANCES, born ca. 1794, NY, were listed in the 1850 census of Fairfield Twp., Lenawee Co., Mich. with LEWIS, age 20, b. NY, in their household.

PIKE, RUTH (See Andrew Fitts)

PILBEAM, ELIZABETH born England married William J. Andrews (also see) in 1855, Ridgeway Twp., Lenawee Co., Mich. It is probably she listed in the 1850 census of Tecumseh Twp., age 17, born England, in a Daniel & Mary Ann (b. 1810, England) Warring household. Ref: P&BA-Len pg. 277-8. Note JOSEPH, following.

PILBEAM, GEORGE born ca. 1818, England, and wife, CATHARINE, born ca. 1827, NY, were listed in the 1850 census of Ridgeway Twp., Lenawee Co., Mich. with MARY E., age 5, b. NY, in their household.

PILBEAM, ISAAC N., son of JOSEPH (following), born 3 Feb. 1846, Ridgeway Twp., Lenawee Co., Mich., served in the Civil War. He married ARLETTA (HOLDEN), daughter of Samuel (also see) in Clinton Co., Mich. in 1867. Children: 1. CHESTER; 2. LAVINIA; 3. GERTRUDE; 4. IRENE; 5. SYLVA. Ref: P&BA-Len pg. 337.

PILBEAM, JOSEPH born ca. 1810, Kent Co., England, came to the US at age 18. He came first to Tecumseh and lived with a Lambertson family. He was listed in the 1840 census index of Macon Twp., Lenawee Co., Mich. He married first to SARAH (BOLTON) and had 6 children, names not stated, but listed in his household in 1850 census of Ridgeway twp. were GEORGE W., age 16; JOHN T., age 14; EDWARD, age 11, all b. Mich. Sarah died before 1846, and he married again to Mrs. MARY A. (FRAMPTON) BODKIN, probably widow of Thomas (also see), born ca. 1812, England, who had come alone to the US. Joseph & Mary A. had 5 children, names not stated, first 3 were in household in 1850 census: ISAAC N. (preceding); MARY E., age 3; CAROLINE, age 6/12; ADELAIDE J. (m/1 Michael Underwood; m/2 William Underwood; see both). Ref: P&BA-Len pg. 337; 401-2.

PILBEAM, THOMAS J., son of WILLIAM (following), born 25 Aug. 1844, Ridgeway Twp., Lenawee Co., Mich., married there to ADELAIDE (HALL), born Tecumseh Twp.; and had 3 children: 1. MARY EDITH b. 12 Mar. 1873; 2. IDA L. b. 1 Jan. 1876; 3. one d. infancy. Adelaide died in 1876 in Dundee Twp. He married again to ADELINE (MASTEN), daughter of Jacob (also see) of Milan Twp., Monroe Co., Mich. Children: 4. WILLIAM J.; 5. JESSIE L.; 6. MYRTIE E.; 7. SHIRLEY; 8. MINERVA. Ref: P&BA-Len pg. 690.

PILBEAM, WILLIAM born 14 May 1812, Kent Co., England, came to the US at age 20. He settled first in Ridgeway Twp., Lenawee Co., Mich. He married in Dec. 1842 to HANNAH (HAUSE), daughter of Sanford (also see) and settled in Ridgeway Twp. He also owned property in Macon Twp. There were 16 children, names not stated, but in their household in the 1850 census of Ridgeway Twp. were: THOMAS J. (preceding); JAMES, age 4; EDWARD, age 2; EDGAR, age 2, all b. Mich. Hannah died in 1866. William married again to Mrs. BETSEY (HITCHINGS) DORIELL, daughter of Joseph, and widow of William (see both). William and Betsey had 4 children, names not stated, except MINNIE. Ref: P&BA-Len pg. 1145.

PINER, ELIZABETH (See John Underwood)

PITCHER, ABBIE E. probably born after 1850 (See James M. Richardson). Note ANDREW, following.

PITCHER, ANDREW, son of HENRY (following), born ca. 1830, and wife, POLLY A., born ca. 1827, both in NY, were listed in the 1850 census of Rome Twp., Lenawee Co., Mich. with MARY P., age 5/12, b. Mich., in their household. Ref: P&BA-Len pg. 808-9.

PITCHER, HENRY born ca. 1787, and wife, MARIA (SCOTT), born 1788, Johnstown, NY, married there in 1812; and he served in the War of 1812. In 1835, they moved to Ohio, and settled near Painesville in 1836. He died 7 Dec. 1837 leaving his wife, with eight children: 1. SALLY; 2. WILLIAM b. ca. 1816; 3. CATHERINE; 4. BETSEY E. b. 26 Jan. 1821, Arcadia, Wayne Co., NY (m. Harvey B. Howd, also see); 5. JOHN b. ca. 1825; 6. RHODA; 7. ANDREW (preceding); 8. ABRAM b. ca. 1833, Ohio. In 1838, Maria and her children moved to Rome Twp., Lenawee Co., Mich. where WILLIAM was listed as head of household in the 1840 census index; and in the 1850 census with Maria, age 60; John, age 25; Abraham, age 13, in his household.

PITCHER, MARY A. was the second wife of Hiram Larzeler (also see) and her sister, name not stated, was his first wife. They lived first in Franklin Twp., Lenawee Co., Mich. then moved to Manchester, Washtenaw Co., Mich. Note: In the 1840 census index of Washtenaw Co., Mich. there was a HARRISON PITCHER in Lodi, and J. P. in Salem Twp.

PITTS, LEVI and wife, HANNAH (WILBUR), had known daughter, BETSEY b. Onondaga Co., NY (m. Edward Hodge, also see). Ref: P&BA-Len pg. 514-5.

PITTS, LYDIA, age 17, born NY, was listed in the 1850 census of Fairfield Twp., Lenawee Co., Mich. in the Asaph Porter household.

PITTS, POLLY born Mass. (See Peleg Hicks).

PLANK, EVE was listed in Dundee Twp., Monroe Co., Mich. in the 1840 census index.

PLANK, JAMES was listed in the 1840 census index of Dundee Twp., Monroe Co., Mich.

Pioneer Families of Southeastern Michigan

PLANK, ROBERT and wife, PHEBE, settled in Dundee, Monroe Co., Mich. by 1840. They moved to Franklin Twp., Lenawee Co., Mich. Known daughter, HARRIET (m/1 ? Lembarger who d. Civil War; m/2 White Cleveland, see both). Ref: P&BA-Len pg. 378-9.

PLATE, SARAH A. (See Christian Kuney)

PLATT, ABEL born ca. 1793, and wife, SOPHIA, born ca. 1796, both in New Hampshire, were listed in the 1840 census index of Medina Twp., Lenawee Co., Mich.; and in the 1850 census with ELIZABETH, age 18; GEORGE, age 16, both b. NY; COLUMBUS, age 12, b. Mich., in their household.

PLATT, HENRY S. was an early resident to Ondondaga Co., NY were he died at age 69. Known daughter, MARIA S. b. ca. 1799, NY (m/1 in 1816 to John Combs; m/2 Joseph Rhodes, see both). Ref: P&BA-Len pg. 960-1.

PLATT, MARY (See Reuben Mason)

PLATT, OBEDIAH married Mrs. HANNAH (BONFOEY) TREAT, widow of Hosea Treat of Holland Patent, NY, as her second husband. Obediah was apparently deceased before 1850, as in the 1850 census of Adrian Twp., Lenawee Co., Mich., Hannah was listed in the household of her son, Butler Treat (also see). Ref: P&BA-Len pg. 1167-8.

PLETCHER, ANDREW born ca. 1811, and wife, POLLY (GARDNER), born ca. 1809, both in Penn., moved from Centre Co., Penn. to Seneca Twp., Lenawee Co., Mich. about 1847. There were 2 sons & 2 daughters, names not stated, but in the 1850 census of Seneca Twp. they listed OLIVER S., age 15; CLARINDA b. 15 Oct. 1837 (m. Royal A. Youngs, also see); SARAH R. b. 25 Dec. 1844/6 (m. Robert Power, also see), all b. Penn., in their household. Ref: P&BA-Len pg. 627-8; 781.

PLUES, MOSES came from England as a young man and married in NY to LAURA (GIFFORD). They settled in Macon Twp., Lenawee Co., Mich. before 1840; and afterwards in Ridgeway Twp. Daughter, CHARLOTTE b. 22 Feb. 1840, Ridgeway Twp. (m. Joseph Thackray, also see). Ref: P&BA-Len pg. 481-2. Moses was not listed in the 1850 census of Ridgeway Twp., however there was a STEPHEN, age 7; and EDWIN, age 9, both b. Mich., listed in other households.

PLUMB, SETH G. moved from Middletown, Conn. to Monroe Co., NY after the birth of known daughter, MARY E. b. 18 Apr. 1835, Middletown (m. James W. Bradner, also see). Seth and family (names not stated) moved to Clinton Twp., Lenawee Co., Mich. about 1861. Ref: P&BA-Len pg. 1114-8.

PLUMB, SYLVIA (See Scarritt family)

PLUMLEY, ELIZABETH (See Benjamin Converse)

PLUMMER, WALTER (See Joseph Metcalf)

POCKLINGTON, CHARLES born ca. 1817, England, was listed in the 1850 census of Raisin Twp., Lenawee Co., Mich. in an Eaton household. See MARY & CHRISTOPHER, both following.

POCKLINGTON, CHARLES A., son of JOHN (following), born 28 Mar. 1853, Ridgeway Twp., Lenawee Co., Mich., married on 7 Feb. 1878 to SARAH J. (TRAVIS), daughter of Jerome E. (also see). Son, GUY G. b. 7 Jan. 1879. Ref: P&BA-Len pg. 385-6.

POCKLINGTON, CHRISTOPHER born ca. 1819, England, and wife, RACHEL, born ca. 1819, NY, were listed in the 1850 census of Raisin Twp., Lenawee Co., Mich. with MARY E., age 9; GEORGE C., age 3, both born Mich., in their household, and were next door to JOHN (following); and 2 doors from MARY, following.

POCKLINGTON, EMMA born 1846, Yorkshire, England, married Lyman E. Hause (also see). Ref: P&BA-Len pg. 475-6.

POCKLINGTON, GEORGE born ca. 1820, and wife, SARAH, born ca. 1825, both in England, were listed in the 1850 census of Tecumseh Twp., Lenawee Co., Mich. with JULIA, age 2, born Mich., in their household.

POCKLINGTON, JOHN born ca. 1824, England, first settled in Raisin Twp., then moved to Ridgeway Twp. He married JULIA A. (ALLEN) born ca. 1824, NY, who had came to Ridgeway Twp. with her parents (names not stated) who died there. There were 7 children, names not stated. They were listed in the 1850 census of Raisin Twp., Lenawee Co., Mich. with ELIZA, age 10/12 in their household. MARY, age 11, born England, was also in their household, see MARY (following). Known son, #3. CHARLES A. (preceding). Ref: P&BA-Len pg. 385-6. Note: In the 1850 census they were next door to CHRISTOPHER (preceding) & 2 doors from MARY (following).

POCKLINGTON, MARY Mrs., age 60, born England, was listed in the 1850 census of Raisin Twp., Lenawee Co., Mich. with (grandson?) SMITH, age 5, born England, in her household. She may be mother of CHARLES; CHRISTOPHER; GEORGE; JOHN, all preceding; and WILLIAM, following. Note: In the household of Shubel Vincent, and wife, Jane A. of Ridgeway Twp. was WILLIAM, age 14, b. England. GEORGE, age 12, born England was listed in the household of Israel Schreder, Raisin Twp.; CAROLINE, age 11, born England was listed in household of Christopher Barrett in Raisin Twp.; and MARY, age 11, born England, was listed in the household of JOHN in Raisin Twp.

POCKLINGTON, WILLIAM and wife, ANN (LOCKLAND) were natives of Yorkshire, England, who came to the US and settled eventually in Ridgeway Twp., Lenawee Co., Mich. where they still resided in 1888. They were parents of ELIZA born 24 Jan. 1837 (1847?), England (m. John H. Zeluff, also see). Ref: P&BA-Len pg. 378-9. However, it appears that this is WILLIAM, age 37, with a wife, JANE, age 36, both born England, listed in the 1850 census of Ridgeway Twp., Lenawee Co. Listed in the household were MARY A., age 10; JOHN, age 8; EMELINE, age 6; ELIZA, age 3; WILLIAM H., age 3/12, all shown b. England.

POLHEMUS, CORNELIUS moved from New Jersey to Cayuga Co., NY. It may be he listed in the militia of Amwell, Hunterdon Co., NJ in 1793. He married REBECCA (STEVENSON), born NJ, who died in 1864, age 80. They moved from Cayuga Co., NY to Freedom Twp., Washtenaw Co., Mich. in 1832. He died in 1860, age 81. Nine children, names not stated, except #5. SARAH b. 6 June 1814, Sussex Co., NJ (m/1 Adam Van

Tuyle; and m/2 Rev. William P. Wastell, see both). Ref: P&BA-Len pg. 445-50. Note: In the 1840 census index of Washtenaw Co., Mich. in addition to Cornelius (written "C."), were EDWARD, Freedom Twp.; & JACOB A. with no Twp. listed; and a LEWIS in Calhoun Co., Mich.

POLLARD, MARY born Conn. (See Russell Skeels)

POLLARD, ROBERT born ca. 1815, England was listed in the 1850 census of Blissfield Twp., Lenawee Co., Mich. MARY, age 7, born Mich., listed in the household of Abel Pierce, 2 doors away, may relate.

POMEROY, HENRY B. born ca. 1810, and wife, ELIZA, born ca. 1810, both in Mass., were listed in the 1840 census index of Palmyra Twp., Lenawee Co., Mich.; and in the 1850 census and listed no family.

POMEROY, HENRY M. married 4 Nov. 1871 to FRANCES M. (MILLS), daughter of Philo C. (also see) of Adrian, Lenawee Co., Mich. Children: 1. FLOSSIE HELEN b. 8 Feb. 1875; 2. MARGERY LINCOLN b. 12 Oct. 1881. Ref: P&BA-Len pg. 1060-3. Note HENRY in household of QUARTERS W., following.

POMEROY, GEORGE E., probably son of SETH (following), born ca. 1808 Mass., and wife, HANNAH, born ca. 1816, NY, were listed in the 1850 census of Tecumseh Twp., Lenawee Co., Mich. with MARY, age 14; MILTON, age 12; HENRY, age 7; GEORGE, age 2, all b. Mich.; SETH & HANNAH (following); and listed last M. S. (male), age 7, born NY, apparently not a child of this family, in their household.

POMEROY, JOSIAH, age 25. born NY, was listed in the 1850 census of Tecumseh Twp., Lenawee Co., Mich. in a Blowers household.

POMEROY, NORMAN, age 22, born NY, was listed in the 1850 census of Tecumseh Twp., Lenawee Co., Mich. in an Inn.

POMEROY, QUARTERS W. born ca. 1806, Mass., and wife, CLARISSA, born ca. 1811, NY, were listed in the 1850 census of Palmyra Twp., Lenawee Co., Mich. with GEORGE M., age 22; HENRY, age 17 (Note HENRY M., preceding); QUARTERS, age 12; CLARINDA H., age 10; LEWIS, age 7, all b. NY, and Ann Norton, age 63, born Mass., in their household.

POMEROY, SETH born ca. 1776, and wife, HANNAH, born ca. 1781, both in Mass., were listed in the 1850 census of Tecumseh Twp., Lenawee Co., Mich. in the household of GEORGE E. (preceding).

POMEROY, SILAS born ca. 1787, and wife, AMELIA, born ca. 1790, both in Conn., were listed in the 1840 census index of Tecumseh Twp., Lenawee Co., Mich.; and in the 1850 census with MARY, age 19, b. NY, in their household. ELISA, age 32, b. NY, was listed in the Hoag household next door.

POND, ELIHU (See Stephen Allen)

POND, SAMUEL born ca. 1817, Mass., and wife, EMMDER?, born ca. 1818, Canada, were listed in the 1850 census of Adrian Twp., Lenawee Co., Mich. with ESDOUGLAS, age 2, b. Mass.; and EMMA, age 2/12; and Elizabeth Mahertir, age 8, both b. Mich., in their household.

PONTIUS, CATHERINE married George Farst (also see) in Northumberland Co., Penn. before 1811, and moved to Fayette, Seneca Co., NY. Ref: P&BA-Len pg. 997-9.

PONTIUS, DAVID, son of HENRY (following), born 11 Apr. 1830, Fayette, Seneca Co., NY, married there on 13 Feb. 1851 to CORDELIA (BRYANT), daughter of Daniel (also see). They later moved to Dover Twp., Lenawee Co., Mich.; and settled in Clayton in the Spring of 1886. Children: 1. ALICE C. (m. Robert B. Sutton, also see); 2. IDA A. (m. Lucius Judson, also see). Ref: P&BA-Len pg. 687.

PONTIUS, HENRY and wife, MARY (SMITH), were natives of Northumberland Co., Penn. who moved to Seneca Co., NY. About 1854, they removed to Dover Twp., Lenawee Co., Mich. He died 23 Oct. 1869 while visiting a daughter in Grand Haven, Mich.; and she died 18 Oct. 1877/8 in Dover Twp. Children: 1. ANN (m. David Ireland who d. Sept. 1866, Barry Co., Mich.); 2. ELIZA (m. Lewis Ireland; she d. Sept. 1882, Allegan Co., Mich.; 3. SARAH b. 2 Dec. 1825, Fayette, NY (m. John Gambee, also see); 4. WILLIAM (m. Rosanna Goodman; he d. 22 Feb. 1850); 5. DAVID (preceding); 6. CAROLINE (m. Henry Spoon); 7. MARGARET (m. William B. Downe, Coldwater, Mich.); 8. MARY C. b. 11 Nov. 1837, Seneca Co., NY (m. George W. Baley, also see); 9. EMMA (m. Charles Gambee). Ref: P&BA-Len pg. 687; 726-7; 1089-90.

POOL, ALANSON born ca. 1813, and wife, MARY, born ca. 1819, both in NY, were listed in the 1850 census of Blissfield Twp., Lenawee Co., Mich. with HEMAN A., age 6; LOUISA A., age 3; HERBERT A., age 7/12, all b. Mich., in their household, next door to OLIVE (See AVERY, following).

POOL, AVERY was listed in the 1840 census index of Blissfield Twp., Lenawee Co., Mich. In the 1850 census, OLIVE, age 53, born NY, was listed head of household with EZRA, age 20; JANE S., age 13, both b. NY, in her household. Next door to her was ALANSON (preceding); and CHARLES (following) was 2 doors away.

POOL, CHARLES born ca. 1828, NY, and CORNELIA A., born ca. 1833, Ohio, were listed in the 1850 census of Blissfield Twp., Lenawee Co., Mich. 2 doors from OLIVE (See AVERY, preceding).

POOL, HARRISON born ca. 1814, and wife, MELINDA, born ca. 1820, both in NY, were listed in the 1850 census of Hudson Twp., Lenawee Co., Mich. with CHESTER, age 10; ROSETTA, age 8, both b. NY; and JUDSON, age 3, born Mich., in their household.

POOL, LYDIA born 20 Apr. 1791. Abington, Plymouth Co., Mass. married Brackley Shaw, Sr. (also see). Note POLLY, following, possibly sister.

POOL, NANCY of Wyoming Co., NY (See Rodman Hodges)

POOL, POLLY born ca. 1787, Mass., was listed in the 1850 census of Dover Twp., Lenawee Co., Mich. in household of Brackley and LYDIA (POOL) Shaw. Posibly her sister.

POOL, VOLENTINE born ca. 1835, Virginia, was listed in the 1850 census of Medina Twp., Lenawee Co., Mich. in the household of Daniel Pratt, and wife, Elizabeth (age 33, born Virginia).

Pioneer Families of Southeastern Michigan

POOLEY, EDWARD of Marion, Wayne Co., NY had known daughter, MARY b. 17 July 1824 (m. Thomas Shepherd Weter, also see).

POOLEY, NATHAN born ca. 1823, England, and wife, MARY JANE, born ca. 1825, NJ, were listed in the 1850 census of Franklin Twp., Lenawee Co., Mich. with WILLIAM, age 5; EMMA, age 4; MARY/MAY, age 5/12, all b. Mich., in their household.

POPE, ALMOND, age 23, born NY, was listed in the 1850 census of Palmyra Twp., Lenawee Co., Mich.

POPE, ARNOLD, son of GERSHAM (following), born 5 Mar. 1778, Burlington, Otsego Co., NY, married there to HANNAH (THOMPSON), daughter of Elihu (also see). Arnold served in the War of 1812. They settled on a farm in Hamilton, Madison Co., NY. She died there 4 July 1865; and he died 21 Dec. 1868. Seven children, names not stated, except #2. HORATIO G. (following). Ref: P&BA-Len pg. 578-9. Note ALMOND, preceding.

POPE, ARNOLD, son of HORATIO G. (following), born 23 May 1837, Hamilton, Madison Co., NY, removed to Palmyra Twp., Lenawee Co., Mich. in 1856. He married there 19 July 1862 to ELIZA C. (STREET), daughter of Robert (also see). Four children, names not stated, except, RALPH T. b. 20 June 1867 (m. Flora Bancroft, dau. of James, also see). Ref: P&BA-Len pg. 578-9.

POPE, EZRA, age 38, born NY, was listed in the 1850 census of Madison Twp., Lenawee Co., Mich. with ABBA, age 60, born NY, "dittoed" after him, both in the household of John & Laurinda Bird (also see).

POPE, GEORGE, age 25, born NY, was listed in the 1850 census of Franklin Twp., Lenawee Co., Mich.

POPE, GERSHAM born Bennington, VT, removed before 1778 to Burlington, Otsego Co., NY. Known son, ARNOLD (preceding). Ref: P&BA-Len pg. 578-9. Note: In the 1800 census index of Otsego Co., NY listed with GERSHAM were (2) BENJAMIN; EDWARD; GATES; ICHABOD; JEDEDIAH; JOB; JOHN; LEWIS; (2) SETH; SQUIRE; TIMOTHY.

POPE, HORATIO G., son of ARNOLD (preceding), born 2 Feb. 1806, Burlington, Otsego Co., NY, moved with his parents to Hamiton, Madison Co., NY where he married on 23 Jan. 1831 to DIANA (THAYER), daughter of Hosea (also see). In 1856 they removed to Palmyra Twp., Lenawee Co., Mich. Children: 1. HOSEA T. b. 13 Jan. 1835 (d. 14 Jan. 1872, Palmyra Twp.); 2. ARNOLD (preceding); 3. LUCY H. (adopted) b. 17 Feb. 1848 (m. Charles B. Conklin; Quincy, Ill.). Ref: P&BA-Len pg. 578-9.

POPE, JAMES and wife, ? (BELDING), of Somersetshire, England remained in England where he died age 52, and she died age 46. They were parents of CECELIA (m. Edwin Pickford, also see). Ref: P&BA-Len pg. 692-3.

PORTER, ALEXANDER born ca. 1814, Canada, and wife, ELIZABETH, born ca. 1818, VT, were listed in the 1850 census of Franklin Twp., Lenawee Co., Mich. with EMMA, age 12; LAVIRA, age 11, both b. Canada; and IRA, age 3; CLARK, age 7/12, both b. Mich., in their household.

PORTER, ALLEN born 24 Aug. 1795, Franklin Co., Mass., moved with parents about 1806 to Ontario Co., NY. He served in the War of 1812, and afterwards moved to Albion, Orleans Co., NY, where he died at age 89. Known daughter, SARAH (m. Sheldon Warner, also see).

PORTER, ALVIN, age 18, born NY, was listed in the 1850 census of Madison Twp., Lenawee Co., Mich. in a Crabb household.

PORTER, AMANDA J. born 18 Jan. 1828, near Westfield, Chautauqua Co., NY, came to Lenawee Co., Mich. with her parents. She married John Ayers (also see) in 1852, Fairfield Twp. Ref: P&BA-Len pg. 1045.

PORTER, AMELIA (See Abda Dolph)

PORTER, ASAHEL was listed in the 1840 census index of Palmyra Twp., Lenawee Co., Mich.

PORTER, ASAPH K., son of LEWIS (following), born 26 Mar. 1812, Covert, Seneca Co., NY, married RACHEL (GLAZIER), daughter of Walker (also see) in Covert. He prospected first for land in Seneca Co., Ohio, but sold it, as he and "brother-in-law," Hartwell Russell moved to Fairfield Twp., Lenawee Co., Mich. in 1833. They were listed in the 1850 census of Fairfield Twp. Children: 1. EDWIN b. ca. 1838 (deceased by 1888); 2. WALKER b. ca. 1840 (prob. he is WALKER G. who m. Susan Tenbrook, dau. of John, also see); 3. JAMES T. b. ca. 1842; 4. SARAH CORNELIA b. ca. 1844 (deceased by 1888); 5. LEWIS b. ca. 1846; 6. EMMA (deceased by 1888); 7. JANE (m. M. L. Foster, Woodbridge, Mich.); 8. ROSALIA (m. E. C. Chandler; Steubenville, Ohio); 9. EZRA H. Ref: P&BA-Len pg. 702-3.

PORTER, DARIUS born ca. 1839, Mich., was listed in the 1850 census of Raisin Twp., Lenawee Co., Mich. in the household of Zophar Smith.

PORTER, DAVID born ca. 1813, VT, and wife, NARCISSA, born ca. 1819, NY, were listed in the 1850 census of Adrian Twp., Lenawee Co., Mich. with JANE, age 16; ANNA, age 14, both b. NY; and NOAH, age 12; SETH, age 10; IDA, age 8; ELIZA, age 5; EMMA, age 2, all b. Mich., in their household.

PORTER, EDWIN C., son of ASAPH (preceding), born 24 FEb. 1837, Fairfield Twp., Lenawee Co., Mich., married there on 27 Mar. 1860 to MARY C. (SACKETT), daughter of Oramel A. (also see). Children: 1. HERBERT W. (m. Florence Quick, daughter of Cornelius, also see); 2. CORA. Ref: P&BA-Len pg. 685.

PORTER, ELLEN (See George Sheeler)

PORTER, GEORGE, age 19?, born NY, was listed in the 1850 census of Hudson Twp., Lenawee Co., Mich.

PORTER, JOHN C., son of LEWIS P. (following), born 24 June 1822, Seneca Co., NY, married there to LOUISA (KING), daughter of Sylvester (also see) and removed to Seneca Twp., Lenawee Co., Mich. Children: 1. FRANCES H. (d. before 1888); 2. SYLVESTER K. (m. Melissa Rorick); 3. MARY S. (m. Mark C. Rorick, also see); 4. HATTIE (m. Leroy W. Rorick, also see). Ref: P&BA-Len pg. 552-3.

PORTER, LEWIS P. born 24 May 1786, Conn., was son of a Revolutionary soldier who had moved at an early date to Tompkins Co., NY. Lewis P. married in 1808 to SAMANTHA (KING), daughter of Asaph (also see). They lived first in the Catskills, then followed his parents to Tompkins Co., NY, then settled in Covert, Seneca Co., NY where she died 21 Mar. 1817. Six children, names not stated, except #3. ASAPH K. (preceding); and probably MARY C. b. ca. 1813 (m. Hartwell Russell, also see). Lewis P. married again to THIRZA (COLE). He died in NY in 1862, age 76; and she died in 1867, age 77. They had 3 sons and 3 daughters, names not stated, except JOHN C. (preceding). Ref: P&BA-Len pg. 552-3.

PORTER, MARTHA ELLEN born 7 Aug. 1837 near Frostburg, MD, married in Preston Co., W. Va. to John Peter Heckert (also see). Ref: P&BA-Len pg. 1180.

PORTER, NOAH born ca. 1801, and wife, AMANDA, born ca. 1809, both in NY, were listed in the 1850 census of Madison Twp., Lenawee Co., Mich. with NOAH, age 14; SUSAN A., age 13; ROBY, age 10; ROSEMAN, age 9; MARINA, age 5, all b. Mich. in the household. AMANDA, age 12, born Mich., listed 2 doors away in the household of Calvin Bradish may relate to this family. Note WILLIAM R., following.

PORTER, P. B. (See George I. Harder)

PORTER, PHILO and wife, ELIZABETH, of Batavia, Branch Co., Mich. were parents of MARTHA E. born 20 June 1843 (m. Willard Stearns[2], also see). Ref: P&BA-Len pg. 615-6.

PORTER, POLLY (See Ira Peck)

PORTER, SEYMOUR S., age 25, born NY, was listed in the 1850 census of Madison Twp., Lenawee Co., Mich.

PORTER, WILLIAM (See Clark Ames)

PORTER, WILLIAM R. born ca. 1799, and wife, MARINA?, born ca. 1806, both in NY, were listed in the 1840 census index of Madison Twp., Lenawee Co., Mich.; and in the 1850 census with CULLEN R., age 25, b. NY; HALSEY D., age 11, b Mich., in the household. Note NOAH, preceding.

PORTER, WILLIAM R. probably born after 1850 (See Frederick H. Corwin).

POST, CHARLES S., age 13; CLARISSA A., age 11; JANE A., age 7, all b. NY, probably siblings, and probably stepchildren, were listed in the household of William Adams, age 62, b. NJ, and wife, LODUSKY, age 45, b. Conn., (married within the year). POST, ELIZABETH (See John Hurlbut[1])

POST, JANE, age 81, born Virginia, was listed in the 1850 census of Tecumseh Twp., Lenawee Co., Mich. in a Beard household.

POST, JOHN born ca. 1812, and wife, CHRISTINA, born ca. 1828, both in Germany, were listed in the 1850 census of Madison Twp., Lenawee Co., Mich. with GEORGE, age 3; CATHARINE, age 1, both b. Mich., in their household.

POST, NANCY (See Calvin Bradish)

POST, RACHEL (See Addison P. Halladay)

POTTER, ANDREW, age 19, born NY, was listed in the 1850 census of Palmyra Twp., Lenawee Co., Mich.

POTTER, CATHARINE, age 55, born Canada, was listed in the 1850 census of Rollin Twp., Lenawee Co., Mich. with no family in her household. It may be she listed head of household in the 1840 census index of Woodstock Twp.

POTTER, CHARLES C. (See Eliab Park)

POTTER, CHARLES E., age 10, born Mich., was listed in the 1850 census of Rollin Twp., Lenawee Co., Mich. in a Bonney household, 2 doors from HELEN, preceding. It is probably he who married AGNES MATILDA (ROBINSON), daughter of Richard (also see) of Rome Twp.

POTTER, CLARK born ca. 1819, and wife, JANE, born ca. 1825, both in NY, were listed in the 1850 census of Madison Twp., Lenawee Co., Mich. with ELIZA, age 11, b. NY; and WILSON, age 6; GORDON, age 1, both b. Mich., and Henry Brooks, age 17, b. NY, in their household.

POTTER, DAVID was listed in the 1840 census index of Madison Twp., Lenawee Co., Mich.

POTTER, EDA (See Libni Kelley)

POTTER, EVA (See Micajah Hayward)

POTTER, FEAR (See Fernando C. Beaman)

POTTER, HELEN, age 5, born Mich., was listed in the 1850 census of Rollin Twp., Lenawee Co., Mich. in a the household of Warren & Elizabeth Newcomb, perhaps a stepchild? Note CHARLES E., preceding.

POTTER, JAMES, age 40, born NY, was listed in the 1840 census index of Rome Twp., Lenawee Co., Mich.; and in the 1850 census with no family in his household.

POTTER, JEREMIAH was listed in the 1840 census index of Hudson Twp., Lenawee Co., Mich. Note OLIVER & PHILIP, following.

POTTER, JOHN born ca. 1819, NY, married in Raisin Twp., Lenawee Co., Mich. to MARY (COLVIN), daughter of of William (also see). They settled in Tecumseh Twp., Lenawee Co., Mich.; and in the 1850 census listed STEPHEN, age 6; CAROLINE, age 3, both b. Mich.; and Mary's mother, Letitia Colvin, and her daughter, Caroline, and a child, Elisa, age 6, in their household.

POTTER, MARY of Erie Co., NY (See Lemeuel C. P. Vaughn)

POTTER, MATILDA, age 12, born Mich., was listed in the 1850 census of Dover Twp., Lenawee Co., Mich. in a Merrifield household.

POTTER, MOWRY S. and wife, MINERVA, were parents of PAULINE b. Herkimer Co., NY (m. John Crockett, also see, 12 Mar. 1855, Ogden Twp., Lenawee Co., Mich.) Ref: P&BA-Len pg. 672-5.

POTTER, PHILIP, age 25, born Penn., was listed in the 1850 census of Hudson Twp., Lenawee Co., Mich. in a Olcutt household. Note JEREMIAH, preceding.

POTTER, OLIVER, age 17, born Mich., was listed in the 1850 census of Hudson Twp., Lenawee Co., Mich. in a Purchase household. Note JEREMIAH, preceding.

POTTER, STEPHEN was listed in the 1840 census index of Raisin Twp., Lenawee Co., Mich.

POTTER, WILLIAM was listed in the 1840 census index of Tecumseh Twp., Lenawee Co., Mich.

POUCHER, ABRAHAM of Seneca Co., NY was the father of FRANCES P. (b. ca. 1850?) who married Edward P. Fisk, son of Ebenezer (also see).

POUCHER, ANDREW born ca. 1788, and wife, ELIZABETH "BETSEY" (MILLER), born ca. 1785, were natives of Columbia Co., NY. They moved to Adrian Twp., Lenawee Co., Mich. about 1846, and in later years moved to Morenic where he died. In the 1850 census of Adrian Twp., they listed son, ANTHONY (following); and HIRAM, age 14, b. NY, in their household. Ref: P&BA-Len pg. 735-6.

POUCHER, ANTHONY was listed in the 1840 census index of Washtenaw Co., Mich.

POUCHER, ANTHONY, son of ANDREW (preceding), moved with his parents to Lenawee Co., Mich. in 1844, and married there on 15 Nov. 1849 to MARGARET (CLAPPER), daughter of John W. (also see). They were

Pioneer Families of Southeastern Michigan

living in Andrew's household in the 1850 census of Adrian Twp. They moved to Madison Twp. Children: 1. GEORGE S.; 2. IRVIN M. (m. Addie Moore; Ionia, Mich.); 3. ELMER R. (m. Ettie May Howell, Madison Twp.). Ref: P&BA-Len pg. 735-6.

POUCHER, FRANK (See Gilbert M. Pettys)

POUCHER, MARIAH born ca. 1792, NY (See PHILIP, following).

POUCHER, MARTIN born ca. 1821, and wife, MATILDA A., born ca. 1825, both in NY, were listed in the 1850 census of Rome Twp., Lenawee Co., Mich. with AARON, age 5; LEISA, age 1, both b. Mich., in their household.

POUCHER, PHILIP born ca. 1799, and wife, HANNAH, born ca. 1803, both in NY, may have been they listed in Freedom Twp., Washtenaw Co., Mich. in the 1840 census index. They were listed in the 1850 census of Medina Twp., Lenawee Co., with ALBERT J., age 29; and ELIZABETH, age 20 (possibly wife of Albert J.?), and MARIAH, age 58, born NY; Ruel Rounds, age 10, b. NY, in their household.

POULEY, ROBERT F. (See Martin P. Stockwell)

POWELL, DAVID was listed in the 1840 census index of Medina Twp., Lenawee Co., Mich. Note orphaned children listed with STEPHEN (following).

POWELL, HENRY born ca. 1820, NY, married in Cambridge Twp., Lenawee Co., Mich. to ESTHER (MAXWELL), daughter of Israel Baker (also see). Known daughters: PHEBE b. ca. 1845, Mich. (m. _?_ Smith); 2. EMILY b. ca. 1849; 3. EDNA (m. Lewis Onsted, also see). Ref: P&BA-Len pg. 1100-1.

POWELL, ISAAC N, probably son of STEPHEN (following), born ca. 1810, NY, and wife, MARY, born ca. 1819, NJ, were listed in the 1840 census index of Seneca Twp., Lenawee Co., Mich.; and in the 1850 census with ALEXANDER, age 10; DAVID, age 5; NANCY, age 4; MARTHA, age 2, all b. Mich., in their household.

POWELL, JOHN, possibly son of STEPHEN (following), born ca. 1818, and wife, MARIA, born ca. 1821, both in NY, were listed in the 1850 census of Seneca Twp., Lenawee Co., Mich. with ALBERT, age 4; SYLVANUS, age 2, both b. Mich., in their household.

POWELL, JOSEPH born ca. 1777, New Jersey, and wife, BETSEY, born ca. 1790, NY, were listed in the 1850 census of Tecumseh Twp., Lenawee Co., Mich. with Stephen Bidwell, age 22, b. NY, in their household. Note THOMAS, following.

POWELL, ROBERT Rev. (See Benjamin B. Fisk)

POWELL, STEPHEN born ca. 1782, VT (census said Mass.?), moved to Orleans Co., NY. He married MARGARET (NORTON), daughter of Seba (also see). In 1823, they moved to Genesee Co.; and in 1824 to Steuben Co., NY. By 1840, they removed to Seneca Twp., Lenawee Co., Mich., where he died at age 89. Known daugher, MALINTHA b. 9 Dec. 1824, Steuben Co., NY (m. Caleb Bates, also see). In the 1850 census they listed ALVIRA, age 9, b. Mich., probably a granddaughter, in their household, and next door in the household of John & Mary Morgan, were SARAH, age 9 (may be she listed again in the 1850 census of Madison Twp. in a Graham household); HENRY, age 7; LAURA, age 6, obviously related to this family. Ref: P&BA-Len pg. 551-2. Also note DAVID; ISAAC & JOHN, all preceding; & STEPHEN W., following.

POWELL, STEPHEN W., possibly son of STEPHEN (preceding), born ca. 1813, and wife, RHODA, born ca. 1811, both in NY, were listed in the 1850 census of Seneca Twp., Lenawee Co., Mich. with ARTHUR, age 11; NANCY, age 9; LUCY S., age 6; STEPHEN W., age 5; ALICE S., age 3, all b. Mich., in their household.

POWELL, THOMAS born ca. 1811, and wife, CLARINDA, born ca. 1818, both in NY, were listed in the 1850 census of Tecumseh Twp., Lenawee Co., Mich. with SYDNEY, age 16 (he was listed again in a Smith household); CYNTHIA, age 15; BETSEY, age 10; JILLIN? (female), age 9; JOSEPHINE, age 6; LYSANDER, age 4; ALMYRA, age 1, all b. Mich., in their household. Note JOSEPH, preceding.

POWER also see POWERS

POWER, ARTHUR and wife, MARY (DILLINGHAM), moved from Ontario Co., NY to Oakland Co., Mich. before 1844. Known daughter, DEBORAH b. 19 Nov. 1820 (m. Calvin Crane, also see, in Mich. on 7 Feb. 1844). Ref: P&BA-Len pg. 370-2.

POWER, HARVEY H. Dr. born ca. 1826, NY, was listed in the 1850 census of Hudson Twp., Lenawee Co., Mich.

POWER, ROBERT, son of THOMAS (following), born 18 Mar. 1846, Monroe Co., Mich., enlisted in Feb. 1865 in the 11th Mich. Inf., Civil War. He married in Adrian, Lenawee Co., Mich. on 23 Mar. 1871 to SARAH (PLETCHER), daughter of Andrew (also see). Known daughters: 1. EDITH; 2. LOTTIE. Ref: P&BA-Len pg. 627-8.

POWER, THOMAS and wife, ELIZABETH (SEAMAN), were born in NY; and moved to Palmyra Twp., Lenawee Co., Mich. in 1835. Apparently moved to Monroe Co., Mich. by 1846. They returned to Palmyra Twp. where he died in 1870, and she was still living in 1888, age 74. Eight children, only name mentioned was ROBERT (preceding). Ref: P&BA-Len pg. 627-8.

POWERS also see POWER

POWERS, ANTONETTE, age 22, born Germany, was listed in the 1850 census of Adrian Twp., Lenawee Co., Mich. in a Winans household.

POWERS, C. H. born ca. 1828, and wife, SARAH, born ca. 1831, both in Mich., were listed in the 1850 census of Woodstock Twp., Lenawee Co., Mich. with SARAH J., age 1, b. Mich. in their household.

POWERS, ISAAC was listed in the 1830 census of Lenawee Co., Michigan Territory, with males: 1 und 5; 2 10-15; 1 20-30; females: 2 und 5; 1 5-10; 1 15-20. He was listed in the 1840 census index of Woodstock Twp., Lenawee Co. It is probably he in the 1850 census of Woodstock Twp., born ca. 1812, Ohio, with (second?) wife, ALVIRA, born ca. 1820, NY, with WILLIAM, age 14; HENRY, age 12; ISAAC, age 10; CHARLES, age 8; JANE, age 6, all b. Mich., in their household. Note ISAAC, following.

POWERS, ISAAC, age 60, born VT, with wife, HANNAH, age 44, born Conn., were listed in the 1840 census index of Cambridge Twp., Lenawee Co., Mich.; and in the 1850 census with HARRIET, age 16; ELEANOR, age 14; SOPHIA, age 11; MARY, age 9, all b. Mich., in their household.

POWERS, JERRY was listed in the 1840 census index of Rome Twp., Lenawee Co., Mich. Note WILLIAM, following.
POWERS, JOHN was listed in the 1840 census index of Medina Twp., Lenawee Co., Mich. Not listed in 1850; however, there was a SUSAN, age 11, b. Mich. in a Staples household; and LUCY A., age 8, b. Mich. in an Osborn household who may relate to John?
POWERS, JOHN, age 21, born Mich.(?), was listed in the 1850 census of Madison Twp., Lenawee Co., Mich.
POWERS, LUCY A., age 17, born NY, was listed in the 1850 census of Adrian Twp., Lenawee Co., Mich. in a Howland household.
POWERS, MARY E. Mrs. was the daughter of Zibra Corbett (also see).
POWERS, REUBEN, age 39, born Alla?, was listed in the 1850 census of Woodstock Twp., Lenawee Co., Mich.
POWERS, WHITCOMB, age 17, born Mich., was listed in the 1850 census of Adrian Twp., Lenawee Co., Mich. in the Stebbins household.
POWERS, WILLIAM born ca. 1812, and wife, BETSEY ANN, born ca. 1819, both in NY, were listed in the 1840 census index of Cambridge Twp., Lenawee Co., Mich.; and in the 1850 census with LEONARD, age 55, b. VT, in their household. Note ISAAC, preceding.
POWERS, WILLIAM born ca. 1823, and wife, MARY J., born ca. 1827, both in NY, were listed in the 1850 census of Rome Twp., Lenawee Co., Mich. with LORENZO, age 1, b. Mich., in their household. Note JERRY, preceding.
POWERS, WILLIAM R. was listed in the 1840 census index of Adrian Twp., Lenawee Co., Mich.

PRATT, ALMON (See John Phillips)
PRATT, AMELIA (See Robert Burnett, Sr.)
PRATT, AMON was listed in the 1840 census index of Cambridge Twp., Lenawee Co., Mich. In the 1850 census, SALLY, age 52, born NY, is head of household with MARIA, age 22; JANETTE, age 15, both b. NY; and WILLIAM, age 12; AMON, age 10 (prob. he who m. Nancy Maxwell, dau. of Israel, also see), both b. Mich., in her household.
PRATT, ASA born ca. 1810, and wife, MARIA, born ca. 1820, both in NY, were listed in the 1850 census of Palmyra Twp., Lenawee Co., Mich. with MALDEN (female), age 7; CORNELIA, age 5; FRANKLIN, age 4; EDGAR, age 2, all b. Mich., in their household. Note HIRAM, following, listed next door in census.
PRATT, ASHLEY born ca. 1810, and wife, MARY, born ca. 1814, both in NY, were listed in the 1850 census of Blissfield Twp., Lenawee Co., Mich. with ANSEL, age 12, b. Ohio; and ALBERT, age 10; BETSEY M., age 8; ARTHUR, age 4/12, all b. Mich., in their household. Note: It may be he listed in the 1840 census index of Whiteford Twp., Monroe Co., Mich.
PRATT, CHARLES born ca. 1788, Mass., and wife, BETSEY, born ca. 1784, Conn., were listed in the 1840 census index of Adrian Twp., Lenawee Co., Mich.; and in the 1850 census with CLARISSA A. b. 1818, NY (prob. she who m. Josiah Carpenter, also see); THOMAS E., age 29; STEPHEN S., age 24, all b. NY; CHARLES D., age 13, b. Mich., in their household. Note JOSEPH, following.
PRATT, D. was listed in the 1840 census index of Hudson Twp., Lenawee Co., Mich. It may be his family: PRATT, PHILENA Mrs. born ca. 1792, NY, was listed head of household in the 1850 census of Hudson Twp., Lenawee Co., Mich. with JAMES B., age 25, b. NY (and wife, DOLLY R., age 19, b. Conn., married within the year); ELIZABETH A., age 18; MARY D., age 15, both b. NY, in her household.
PRATT, DANIEL born ca. 1808, NY, was listed in the 1840 census index of Medina Twp., Lenawee Co., Mich.; and in 1850 with wife, ELIZABETH, born ca. 1817, VA; and FRANKLIN, age 21, b. NY; Woodward Williams, age 20, b. Ohio; Mary Williams, age 18, b. NY; and Volentine Pool, age 15, b. VA (stepchild?), in their household. Note WILLIAM T., following, listed 3 doors away in census.
PRATT, DANIEL D. born ca. 1817, and wife, MARY E., born ca. 1826, both in NY, were listed in the 1850 census of Dover Twp., Lenawee Co., Mich. with MARIAN, age 2, b. Mich., in their household.
PRATT, HARVEY born ca. 1819, NY, and wife, CHLOE, born ca. 1826, VT, were listed in the 1850 census of Blissfield Twp., Lenawee Co., Mich. with ALTON F., age 3; ALBERT, age 2; SEYMOUR, age 1/12, all b. Mich., in their household. Note JARED, & REUBEN following.
PRATT, HIRAM born ca. 1804, and wife, SOPHIA, born ca. 1818, were listed in the 1850 census of Palmyra Twp., Lenawee Co., Mich. with STEPHEN, age 19, b. NY; and JULIA, age 6, b. Mich. in their household. Note ASA, preceding, next door in 1850 census.
PRATT, JARED born ca. 1792, Conn., and wife, BETSEY, born ca. 1792, NY, were listed in the 1840 census index of Blissfield Twp., Lenawee Co., Mich.; and in the 1850 census were in the household of DAVID C., age 35, b. NY; and also listed was MARY A., age 33, b. NY, in the household. Note ASHLEY, & HARVEY, both preceding; and REUBEN, following..
PRATT, JESSE born ca. 1789, and wife, MARY A., born ca. 1810, both in Conn., moved to Newcastle, Penn.; and then to Ohio, before moving to Seneca Twp., Lenawee Co., Mich. by 1850. In the 1850 census they listed HENRY, age 18, b. Conn.; and MARY D., age 9, b. Penn. (m. George W. Carter, Hudson Twp., also see); CASSIUS?, age 7; DIANA, age 7, all b. Penn.; and I---TA (female), age 1, b. Ohio, in their household. Ref: P&BA-Len pg. 812-3. Note ZENAS, following.
PRATT, JOSEPH and wife, REBECCA (WILBUR), settled near Adrian, Lenawee Co., Mich. in 1827. He died there at age 50, apparently by 1840, as she was listed head of household in the 1840 census index. Rebecca died there at age 80. Known daughters, DEBORAH F. (m. Isaiah C. Miller, also see, 13 Sept. 1833); MARY b. ca. 1806, NY (m. George Scott, also see). Ref: P&BA-Len pg. 722-3; 962-3. CHARLES (preceding) listed adjacent in 1840.
PRATT, LUCY born 11 July 1778, Belchertown, Mass., married Ephtaim Converse (also see).
PRATT, REUBEN born ca. 1780, Mass., and wife, EXPERIENCE, born ca. 1800, NY. were listed in the 1840 census index of Blissfield Twp., Lenawee Co., Mich. (adjacent to JARED, preceding); and in the 1850 census with CHARLES N., age 27; MARY A., age 18; HELEN I., age 16; JOHN E., age 13, all b. NY, in their household. Note: There was a REUBEN in the 1800 census index of Washington Co., NY.
PRATT, WILLIAM T. born ca. 1812, and wife, RHENA E., born ca. 1817, both in NY, were listed in the 1840 census index of Medina Twp. (adjacent to DANIEL,

Pioneer Families of Southeastern Michigan

preceding); and in the 1850 census with GILLIS A., age 2; GILBERT W., age 2/12, both b. Mich., in their household.

PRATT, ZENAS A. born ca. 1815, Conn., and wife, DELILAH, born ca. 1820, Mass., were listed in the 1850 census of Hudson Twp., Lenawee Co., Mich. with CURTIS Z., age 12; CORDELIA L., age 10, both b. Ohio, in their household. Note JESSE, preceding.

PREBBLE, FRANK of Lynn, Mass. (See Witham)

PRENTIS, HENRY E. (See Garrett Vrooman)

PRESTON, DELIA (See James Murray)

PRESTON, HANNAH, age 60, born Ireland, was listed in the household of George McKey and wife, Mary (age 37, b. Ireland, perhaps daughter of Hannah?) in the 1850 census of Adrian Twp., Lenawee Co., Mich.

PRESTON, JANE born Ireland (See Thomas Boyd).

PRESTON, JOHN born ca 1775, Conn., and wife, EUNICE, born ca. 1774, Mass., were listed in the 1840 census index of Blissfield Twp., Lenawee Co., Mich.; and in the 1850 census with SAMUEL (following) and JOHN, JR. (following) both listed next door.

PRESTON, JOHN JR., son of JOHN (preceding), born ca. 1809, VT, and wife, JANE E., born ca. 1816, NY, were listed in the 1840 census index of Blissfield Twp., Lenawee Co., Mich.; and in the 1850 census with CECILIA, age 18; SYLVIA, age 16; JARED, age 14; CYNTHIA, age 11; LYDIA, age 8; SARAH, age 5, all b. Mich., in their household.

PRESTON, LUCIUS was listed in the 1840 census index of Macon Twp., Lenawee Co., Mich.

PRESTON, MARY born 1831, Co. Antrim, Ireland (See Robert Boyd).

PRESTON, SAMUEL, son of JOHN (preceding), born ca. 1817, VT, and wife, LUCRETIA, born ca. 1820, NY, were listed in the 1840 census index of Blissfield Twp., Lenawee Co., Mich.; and in the 1850 census with CATHERINE, age 10; MARIA, age 8; NELSON, age 6; DANIEL J., age 5; ALLEN E., age 3; GEORGE F., age 1, all b. Mich., in their household.

PRESTON, THOMAS born ca. 1827, Ireland, and wife, ELIZA, born ca. 1830, NY, were listed in the 1850 census of Palmyra Twp., Lenawee Co., Mich. with SAMUEL, age 11/12, b. Mich., in their household.

PRICE, CHARLES born ca. 1823, and wife, ELECTA S., born ca. 1827, both in NY, were listed in the 1850 census of Hudson Twp., Lenawee Co., Mich. with DEMETERIUS, age 3; CHASTNIS (CHARLES?), age 1, both b. Mich., in their household.

PRICE, CHARLES (See Aaron B. Sutfin)

PRICE, DANIEL born ca. 1806, NJ, and wife, REBECCA, born ca. 1800, Maryland, resided in Rome Twp., Lenawee Co., Mich. by 1838. In the 1850 census of Rome Twp., they listed DAVID, age 18; MARY A., age 16; LOUISA, age 14, all b. NY; and HENRIETTA, age 10; PERMELIA, age 9, both b. Mich., in their household.

PRICE, DAVID born ca. 1771, NY, is probably he written "Daniel" in the 1840 census index of Seneca Twp., Lenawee Co., Mich.; and in 1850 he listed MARIA, age 44, born NY, in his household. Also note EDWARD, listed adjacent in 1840.

PRICE, EBENEZER G., son of GEORGE (following), born 10 Feb. 1855, Ridgeway Twp., Lenawee Co., Mich., married on 21 Mar. 1878 to EMMA (DUBOIS), daughter of John (also see). Known children: 1. LYDIA b. 17 Jan. 1881; 2. GEORGE W. b. 7 Jan. 1883. Ref: P&BA-Len pg. 304-5.

PRICE, EDWARD, possibly son of DAVID, born ca. 1814, and wife, ELIZABETH, born ca. 1816, both in NY, were listed in the 1840 census index of Seneca Twp., Lenawee Co., Mich.; and in the 1850 census of Adrian Twp., with JOHN M., age 10; THEODORE, age 9; EMMA C., age 6; ADELINE, age 4, all b. Mich., in their household.

PRICE, ELIZABETH (See Libni Kelly)

PRICE, GEORGE, son of THOMAS (following), born 25 July 1820, Radnorshire, Wales, married there to ELIZABETH (JONES) and moved in 1851 to Ridgeway Twp., Lenawee Co., Mich. Elizabeth died in 1852 in Tecumseh. Children: 1. ELIZABETH (m. Allen Kelley, Raisin Twp.); 2. MARY (m. Clarence Morrison); 3. LYDIA; 4. ASENATH. George married again in 1853 to Mrs. MARY HALL (called MARY WALKER in sketch of Ebenezer G.) Son: 5. EBENEZER G. b. 10 Feb. 1855. Ref: P&BA-Len pg. 439.

PRICE, GEORGE, age 12, and MARY ANN, age 8, both born Ohio, were listed in the 1850 census of Woodstock Twp., Lenawee Co., Mich. in a Foster household.

PRICE, JOHN born ca. 1828, NY, was listed in the 1850 census of Medina Twp., Lenawee Co., Mich.

PRICE, LEWIS, age 14, and MARGARET, age 12, both b. Mich., were listed in the 1850 census of Fairfield Twp., Lenawee Co., Mich. in the household of Levi and Elizabeth Russell (probably stepchildren.)

PRICE, PHINEAS born ca. 1807, and wife, HANNAH, born ca. 1809, both in NY, were listed in the 1840 census index of Madison Twp., Lenawee Co., Mich.; and in the 1850 census with GEORGE W., age 18, b. NY; and ALBERT E., age 16; CHARLES A., age 14; SUZETTE R., age 13; MARY J., age 5; OSCAR J., age 5, all b. Mich., in their household.

PRICE, THOMAS of Radnorshire, Wales was father of GEORGE (preceding); and a son, THOMAS who was said to have returned to America with George who had been visiting in Wales. Thomas (Sr.) remained in Wales.

PRICHARD also see PRITCHARD

PRICHARD, BENJAMIN F. was listed in the 1840 census index of Woodstock Twp., Lenawee Co., Mich.

PRICHARD, JOSEPH B. born ca. 1817, and wife, PARMELIA, born ca. 1820 both in Conn., were listed in the 1850 census of Tecumseh Twp., Lenawee Co., Mich. with Edward Dayton, age 12, b. Mich., in their household.

PRIEST, LAURA (See Abner Gorham Pierce)

PRINDLE, ELIZABETH (See Clement Bramble)

PRINGLE, ELIZABETH also called ELIZABETH PRINDLE, see preceding.

PRITCHARD also see PRICHARD
PRITCHARD, CARRIE HELEN (See Rosingrave M. Eccles, MD)

PRUDEN, DANIEL and wife, ELIZABETH born ca. 1778, Morris Twp., Morris Co., NJ, moved to Adrian Twp., Lenawee Co., Mich. before 1840. In the 1840 census index of Adrian Twp., Elizabeth was listed head of household; and in the 1850 census of Madison Twp., listed MARGARET, age 29, b. NJ; and JOANNA, age 28; DANIEL C., age 26, both b. NY, in her household. Known daughter, MARY born 1807, NJ (m. Charles M. Marshall, also see); known son, MOSES C. (following). Ref: P&BA-Len pg. 305-6.

PRUDEN, MOSES C. (or L.), son of DANIEL (preceding), born ca. 1805, NJ, and wife, JANE B., born ca. 1812, NY, were listed in the 1840 census index of Adrian Twp., Lenawee Co., Mich. (adjacent to ELIZABETH, see DANIEL); and in the 1850 census of Adrian Twp. with JOSEPHINE, age 14, v. NY; and ELIZABETH, age 11; EMILY, age 9; EUGENE, age 4, all b. Mich.; and John Briggs, age 7, b. NY, in their household.

PULLEN, CYNTHIA (See Joseph P. Tower)

PULLING, THOMAS (See John W. Ormsby)

PULVER, BENJAMIN born ca. 1817, and wife, SALLY A., born ca. 1827, both in NY, were listed in the 1850 census of Rome Twp., Lenawee Co., Mich. with ROENA M., age 8; JAY E., age 6; MARY E., age 1, all b. Mich., in their household.

PULVER, HENRY, son of MICHAEL (following), born 8 May 1825, Dutchess Co., NY, came to Cambridge Twp., Lenawee Co., Mich. in 1847. He was living in the Greenleaf household in the 1850 census; and married 13 Jan. 1851 to HARRIET (GREENLEAF), daughter of John (also see). She died in August 1864; and he married again on 22 July 1865 to ELIZABETH (STEPHENSON), daughter of John (also see). In 1886, they moved to Onsted, Mich. No children were mentioned. Ref: P&BA-Len pg. 691-2.

PULVER, MICHAEL born ca. 1798, NY, and wife, MARY (KNICKERBOCKER) born ca. 1793, Columbia Co., NY, lived in Dutchess, Wayne, & Onondaga Cos., NY. They were listed in the 1840 census index of Cambridge Twp., Lenawee Co., Mich. In 1868, they removed to Grand Traverse, Mich. He died in 1872. Eight sons and 1 daughter, names not mentioned, but known son, HENRY (preceding); and listed in the household in the 1850 census of Cambridge Twp. were ENOS, age 21; CALVIN, age 19. Also see BENJAMIN, preceding; and MILTON & WILLIAM, following. Ref: P&BA-Len pg. 691-2.

PULVER, MICHAEL W. was listed in the 1840 census index of Rome Twp., Lenawee Co., Mich.

PULVER, MILTON, possibly son of MICHAEL (preceding), born ca. 1819, NY, and wife, SARAH, born ca. 1820, NJ, were listed in the 1850 census of Cambridge Twp., Lenawee Co., Mich. with ALMENIA, age 5; ANN MARY, age 1, both b. Mich., in their household.

PULVER, WILLIAM was listed in the 1840 census index of Rome Twp., Lenawee Co., Mich. It may be he who married ANN (ONSTED), daughter of Peter of Cambridge Twp., Lenawee Co., Mich. They moved to Hillsdale Co., Mich.

PURCHASE also see PURCHIS

PURCHASE, PHILIP born ca. 1773, and wife, REBECCA, born ca. 1786, both in NY, were listed in the 1840 census index of Cambridge Twp., Lenawee Co., Mich.; and in the 1850 census with ROBERT, age 39; PHILANDER (following) and family in their household.

PURCHASE, PHILANDER, son of PHILIP, born ca. 1827, NY, and wife, CAROLINE, born ca. 1831, Ohio, were listed in the 1850 census of Cambridge Twp., Lenawee Co., Mich. with PHILIP, age 1/12, born Mich., all in the household of PHILIP.

PURCHASE, WILLIAM born ca. 1801, and wife, LUCRETIA, born ca. 1810, both in NY, were listed in the 1850 census of Hudson Twp., Lenawee Co., Mich. with SALOMA, age 18, b. Mich., in their household.

PURCHIS also see PURCHASE

PURCHIS J. (See Ralph P. Baker)

PUTNAM, BENJAMIN born ca. 1821, NY, and wife, MINERVA, born ca. 1824, Canada, were listed in the 1850 census of Adrian Twp., Lenawee Co., Mich. with GERTRUDE, age 3, b. Mich., in their household.

PUTNAM, JOSIAH J., son of SILAS (following), born 20 Dec. 1828, Chesterfield, VT, moved to Madison Twp., Lenawee Co., Mich. with his parents. He married CATHERINE (TENBROOK), daughter of Garret (also see). Son: ELMER E. Ref: P&BA-Len pg. 211.

PUTNAM, SILAS married in 1823, in VT to MARTHA (JORDAN) born ca. 1802, VT. They moved in 1831 to Madison Twp., Lenawee Co., Mich., and he died in 1849. Four sons and 5 daughters lived to maturity. Martha was listed head of household in the 1850 census of Madison Twp. with SILAS, age 24; JOSIAH J. (preceding), both b. VT; and MARY, age 18; HENRIETTA, age 16; SUSANNAH, age 15; JOANNA, age 11; OSCAR, age 8, all b. Mich., in her household.

-Q-

QUEAL, JOHN born in Ireland came to Oneida Co., NY where his wife (name not stated) died. He married again to HANNAH (CAMPBELL) in Rome, NY, and they settled in Utica, NY. He died there, and his wife survived him many years dying at age 80. There were 2 sons and 7 daughters, names not stated, except WILLIAM (following); and Rev. ROBERT (Decatur, Mich.). Ref: P&BA-Len pg. 721-2.

QUEAL, WILLIAM, son of JOHN (preceding), born 9 Oct. 1812, Utica, NY; studied for the Ministry and first served in Mottville, Onondaga Co., NY. He married on 14 Jan. 1835 in Aurelius, Cayuga Co., NY to SAMANTHA (MOORE), daughter of Henry (also see). In 1836, they went to Chicago and he founded the First Universalist Church. They returned to Bristol, Ontario Co., NY. About 1848, he became ill and resided for a year in Indiana; and then moved to Cambridge Twp., Lenawee Co., Mich. where they are listed in the 1850 census. Due to illness, he gave up the ministry. Children: 1. ELLEN G. b. ca. 1839; 2. MARY ALICE b. ca. 1841. Ref: P&BA-Len pg. 721-2.

QUICK, ALBERT born ca. 1827, and wife, MARY, born ca. 1828, both in NY, married within the year, were listed

Pioneer Families of Southeastern Michigan

in the 1850 census of Tecumseh Twp., Lenawee Co., Mich.

QUICK, CORNELIUS, son of PETER (following), born 30 Sept. 1822, Hunterdon Co., NJ, moved with his mother to Fairfield Twp., Lenawee Co., Mich. in 1838. He married there on 8 May 1849 to SAMANTHA P. (COLE), probably daughter of Ezra (also see). There were 8 children, and 4 grew to maturity: 1. FRANCIS "FRANK" (m. Carrie Mead; children: Mabel & Francis H.); 2. MYRON H. (m. Nina F. Reed, daughter of James Burt, also see); 3. FLORENCE E. (m. Herbert W. Porter, son of Edwin C., Weston, Mich.); 4. EDITH S. Samantha P. died 3 Jan. 1870; and Cornelius married again to NANCY (BENNETT), daughter of Davis D. (also see). Ref: P&BA-Len pg. 617-8.

QUICK, DAVID born ca. 1811, Penn., and wife, LUCY, born ca. 1812, NY, were listed in the 1840 census index of Fairfield Twp., Lenawee Co., Mich. adjacent to MARY (see PETER, following); and in the 1850 census with HARVEY, age 11; PHEBE, age 9; EMILY, age 2, all b. Mich., in their household, next door to CORNELIUS, preceding.

QUICK, JOSEPH was listed in the 1840 census index of Adrian Twp., Lenawee Co., Mich.

QUICK, LEWIS and wife, MARIA (CLAPP), of Saratoga Co., NY went to Chemung Co., NY. Two sons (names not stated) and one daughter, ELIZABETH b. 6 May 1823 (m. Daniel Fisk, also see). Lewis died July 1881, age 78; and his wife died 1884, age 83. Ref: P&BA-Len pg. 1041-2.

QUICK, MARY, age 19, born NY, was listed in the 1850 census of Tecumseh Twp., Lenawee Co., Mich. in the household of Elijah Wright, age 58, and wife, Mary, age 53. Note ALBERT, preceding. QUICK, PETER and wife, MARY (EVERITT) moved from Hunterdon Co., NJ to Seneca Co., NY and died there in 1824. About 1838, Mary moved with her 2 children to Lenawee Co., Mich. She died in 1876. Children: 1. CORNELIUS (preceding); 2. MARY A. Ref: P&BA-Len pg. 617-8. Note: in Hunterdon Co., NJ Division of Estates is GARRET of Hillsborough Twp. who had heirs: JOACHIN; JAMES; GARRET SNEDERKER; & JOSEPH HAGERMAN QUICK. Mentioned in the estate is PETER SR. who had adjoining property (Recorded in 1822).

QUIMBY, MOSES and wife, JANE (PELLAM) of Northcastle, Westchester Co., NY had known daughter ELIZABETH b. 17 Feb. 1731 (m. Richardson Sutton, also see). Ref: Westchester Patriarchsm by N. Davis, 1988.

QUINN, MAGGIE (See John G. MIller)
QUINN, SUE M. (See Lester H. Salsbury)

- R -

RADWAY, REBECCA b. 26 May 1783, VT (See John Newton).

RAGLESS, HENRY[1] and wife, SARAH, came from Sussexshire, England to Fairfield Twp., Lenawee Co., Mich. They had 5 children born in England, and only mentioned HENRY (following) who had come ahead to Fairfield Twp., and with whom they made their home. Ref: P&BA-Len pg. 523-4.

RAGLESS, HENRY[2], son of HENRY[1] (preceding), born 25 Sept. 1832, Sussexshire, England, came to the US ca. 1850, and about 1853 to Fairfield Twp., Lenawee Co., Mich. He married there on 1 May 1857 to LUCRETIA M. (CARPENTER), daughter of Benjamin (also see). Children: 1. SARAH E. (d. 1876, age 17); 2. THOMAS H. (m. Mary M. Smith; Fairfield Twp.); 3. JAMES B. (m. Ina V. Hoag); 4. ROBERT J. (m. Florence D. Ashbill); 5. BYRON; 6. LETTIE J.; 7. LUCY L.; 8. WILLIAM S.; 9. GEORGE. Ref: P&BA-Len pg. 523-4.

RAILSBACK, LYDIA (See Samuel Austin)

RAINEY also see RANEY
RAINEY, JOHN, son of ROBERT & MARGARET (DUNBAR) who both remained in Ireland, was born 10 Jan. 1840 in Co. Antrim, Ireland. He came to the US in 1860 and first settled in Washtenaw Co., Mich.; and by 1871 in Raisin Twp., Lenawee Co., Mich. He married on 28 Nov. 1868 to MARGARET (MITCHELL), daughter of Robert (also see). Children: 1. JANE b. 3 May 1870; 2. WILLIAM P. b. 8 Oct. 1871; 3. ANNA b. 25 May 1876; 4. ELLA b. 8 Dec. 1878; 5. MAUD b. 20 Feb. 1884. Ref: P&BA-Len pg. 608-9.

RAINEY, THOMAS born ca. 1818, and wife, BRIDGET, born ca. 1816, both in Ireland, were listed in the 1850 census of Hudson Twp., Lenawee Co., Mich. with MARY A., age 4; PETER F., age 4; CATHERINE, age 10/12, all b. Mich., in their household.

RAMSDELL, DAVID L. born ca. 1819, and wife, CATHARINE M. (MARSHALL), born ca. 1821, were "natives of Macedon, Wayne Co., NY." In 1847, they moved to Madison Twp., Lenawee Co., Mich. He died 2 Dec. 1873; and she died 6 May 1872. Children: 1. ELIZABETH M. b. ca. 1845; 2. JOHN D. (following); 3. JENNIE b. 18 Nov. 1854 (m. Isaac Waterman, son of Ira, also see; she d. 21 Oct. 1887). Ref: P&BA-Len pg. 805-6.

RAMSDELL, GIDEON born 30 Jan. 1780, Cummington, Mass., married HANNAH (SMITH), daughter of Jeremiah (also see). About 1800, they moved to Perinton, Monroe Co., NY. He died there in 1860. Known daughter: #7. LEAH b. 27 Apr. 1815, Perinton, NY (m. George L. Crane, also see).

RAMSDELL, JOHN D., son of DAVID L. (preceding), born 15 July 1847, Macedon, Wayne Co., NY, moved with his parents to Madison Twp., Lenawee Co., Mich. He married on 6 July 1872 to MARGARET (WATERMAN), daughter of Ira D. (also see) in Dover Twp. He died 10 May 1882. No children were listed. Ref: P&BA-Len pg. 805-6.

RAMSDELL, NATHAN born ca. 1811, and wife, MARY A., born ca. 1813, both in NY, were listed in the 1850 census of Dover Twp., Lenawee Co., Mich. with GEORGE, age 17; LYDIA, age 15; RACHEL, age 13; IRA, age 11; MARTHA, age 8; CHARLES, age 6; and another MARTHA, age 3; and Phebe Emory, age 25, all b. NY, in their household.

RAMSDELL, RUTH born Mass. (See Sylvanus Estes).
RAMSDELL, SYLVIA A. (See Jacob Wales)
RAMSDELL, THOMAS D. born ca. 1807, and wife, MARTHA H., born ca. 1809, both in NY, were listed in the 1850 census of Madison Twp., Lenawee Co., Mich. with

ELIZA A., age 19; MARGARET M., age 17; WILLIAM D., age 13, all b. NY, in their household.

RANCK, ANDREW (See Andrew McClenahan)

RANDALL, A. H. was listed in the 1840 census index of Hudson Twp., Lenawee Co., Mich.

RANDALL, ALEXANDER was listed in the 1840 census index of Palmyra Twp., Lenawee Co., Mich. Note ANN E., following.

RANDALL, ANANAIS?, age 6, born Mich., was listed in the 1850 census of Madison Twp., Lenawee Co., Mich. in a Baker household.

RANDALL, ANN E., age 5, born Mich., was listed in the 1850 census of Palmyra Twp., Lenawee Co., Mich. in the household of Betsey Wilcox.

RANDALL, CHESTER born ca. 1820, NY, and wife, AMANDA M., born ca. 1826, Mich., were listed in the 1850 census of Blissfield Twp., Lenawee Co., Mich. with MOSES B., age 4/12 b. Mich., and probably brother, FRANCIS, age 21, b. NY, in their household.

RANDALL, ENOCH was listed in the 1840 census index of Blissfield Twp., Lenawee Co., Mich. Note ISAAC & JAMES, following.

RANDALL, GEORGE M., age 13; EMORY, age 11; LOUISA, age 9, probably siblings, all b. Mich., were listed in the 1850 census of Madison Twp., Lenawee Co., Mich. in the household of Levi & Louisa Webster, possibly grandparents.

RANDALL, HENRY born ca. 1819, and wife, VIOLETTA, born ca. 1825, both in NY, were listed in the 1850 census of Cambridge Twp., Lenawee Co., Mich. with FRANCES, age 7; VIENNA, age 4, both b. Illinois; and JOSEPH, age 1; HARVEY, age 1/12, both b. Mich., in their household.

RANDALL, ISAAC born ca 1786, Maine, was listed in the 1840 census index of Blissfield Twp., Lenawee Co., Mich.; and in the 1850 census of Raisin Twp., Lenawee Co., Mich. with wife, ELECTA, age 68, born Mass., and Electa F. Hawks, age 12, b. Mich., in their household.

RANDALL, JAMES was listed in the 1840 census index of Blissfield Twp., Lenawee Co., Mich. as "pensioner, 45y,." adjacent to ISAAC & ENOCH, preceding.

RANDALL, JOHN born ca. 1821, and wife, EUNICE, born ca. 1824, borh in NY, were listed in the 1850 census of Adrian Twp., Lenawee Co., Mich. with LYMAN, age 6; ORRILLA, age 3; STEPHEN, age 1, all b. Mich., in their household.

RANDALL, RUSSELL & wife, PHEBE, probably of Washtenaw Co., Mich. had known daughter, CALPERNA (m. William F. Babcock, also see, of Norvell, Jackson Co., Mich.) Ref: History of Jackson Co., Mich., pg. 993.

RANDALL, SARAH (See Noble Simmons)

RANDALL, WILLIAM born ca. 1812, NY, and wife, MARIA, b. ca. 1812, Mass., were listed in the 1850 census of Blissfield Twp., Lenawee Co., Mich. with children listed in this order (perhaps more than one family): CHESTER, age 9; ELIZABETH, age 11; MURRAY, age 7; LOUISA, age 11, all b. Mich., in their household.

RANDALL, WILLIAM E. born ca. 1805, and wife, LAURA, born ca. 1815, both in Conn., were listed in the 1840 census index of Tecumseh Twp., Lenawee Co., Mich.; and in the 1850 census with RICHARD, age 9, b. Mich.; and Abraham Pelham, age 18, b. NY, in their household.

RANDLE see RANDALL

RANDOLPH, ABEL born ca. 1809, Canada, and wife, FANNY, born ca. 1817, NY, were listed in the 1840 census index of Seneca Twp., Lenawee Co., Mich.; and in the 1850 census of Medina Twp. Lenawee Co., Mich. with HIRAM, age 13; CHARLES J., age 8; EMILY T., age 7; IRENA?, age 4; MILICENT A., age 2, all b. Mich., in their household. Note JOSIAH, following.

RANDOLPH, CORNELIUS S. born 14 Nov. 1811, Warren Co., NY, and came to Seneca Twp., Lenawee Co., Mich. where he married 10 June 1838 to MARGARET C. (BARBER) born 23 Dec. 1808, Catlin, Chemung Co., NY. They resided in Seneca Twp. in the 1850 census; and afterwards in Madison & Palmyra Twps. In 1882, they moved to Gratiot Co. Mich. where he was living in 1888. Children (first 5 in the household in 1850): 1. SILAS b. ca. 1839 (prob. he who m. Rachel Sparhawk, dau. of Eben, also see; to Gratiot Co., Mich.); 2. THOMAS (following); 3. MARTHA b. ca. 1843; 4. JAMES b. ca. 1845; 5. CORNELIUS b. ca. 1847; 6. HENRY. Ref: P&BA-Len pg. 397-8. Note: Cornelius' father, name not stated, was said to have come to Lenawee Co. in "middle life," and died there. Note JOSIAH, following.

RANDOLPH, DAVID born ca. 1790, and wife, HELEN, born ca. 1791, both in NY, were listed in the 1840 census index of Clinton Twp., Lenawee Co., Mich.; and in the 1850 census of Madison Twp., with (grandchildren?) LOVINA, age 12; ANN M., age 9, both b. Mich., in their household.

RANDOLPH, HENRY born ca. 1802, VT, and wife, ALMIRA, born ca. 1803, NY, were listed in the 1840 census index of Madison Twp., Lenawee Co., Mich.; and in the 1850 census with SMITH, age 21; (brother?) MERIT J., age 32; AZUBA, age 24; ANGOLETTE, age 19, all b. NY; and ALMIRA, age 14; ALVIRA, age 14; ALNORA, age 10; MIRANDA, age 7, all b. Mich., in their household.

RANDOLPH, HENRY, age 11, born Mich., was listed in the 1850 census of Fairfield Twp., Lenawee Co., Mich. in a Stout household.

RANDOLPH, JOSIAH born ca. 1776, and wife, ESTHER, born ca. 1778, were listed in the 1840 census index of Seneca Twp., Lenawee Co., Mich. adjacent to ABEL (preceding); and in the 1850 census with JOSIAH (following) listed next door.

RANDOLPH, JOSIAH, probably son of JOSIAH (preceding), born ca. 1815, and wife, ALICE, born ca. 1821, were listed in the 1850 census of Seneca Twp., Lenawee Co., Mich. with JOHN, age 11; ESTHER, age 8; ANNA, age 6; MARTHA, age 3; MARGARET, age 4/12, all b. Mich., in their household.

RANDOLPH, NANCY (See Jeremiah Bennett)

RANDOLPH, THOMAS, son of CORNELIUS S., born 16 Mar. 1841, Seneca Twp., Lenawee Co., Mich., married on 26 Dec. 1867, Madison Twp., to ALICE (HINSDALE), daughter of Elisha (also see). Children: 1. LeELLA; 2. CARRIE. Ref: P&BA-Len pg. 397-8.

RANDOLPH, WILLIAM G. born ca. 1820, and wife, HENRIETTA, born ca. 1823, both in NY, were listed in the 1850 census of Seneca Twp., Lenawee Co., Mich.

Pioneer Families of Southeastern Michigan

with ELIZA, age 10; FRANKLIN, age 7, both b. Mich., in their household.

RANEY see RAINEY

RANNEY, LUCRETIA born Buckland, Mass. (See Darius Cross).

RANNEY, MARY born Mass. (See Augustus F. Daniels).

RANSOM, AZUBAH (See George Wood)

RAPPLEYE, SAMUEL born ca. 1811, NY, and wife, SARAH A., born ca. 1811, Conn., were listed in the 1850 census of Macon Twp., Lenawee Co., Mich. with OSCAR A., age 17; ERASTUS, age 15; HANNIBAL, age 13; LAFAYETTE, age 11, all b. NY; and BUEL, age 9, b. Mich., in their household. Note WILLIAM, following, as there were Swick families also in Macon Twp., and a Rachel Swick, age 11, in the household next door to Samuel

RAPPLEYE, WILLIAM and wife, BARBARA (SWICK), native of New Jersey, moved to Seneca Co. NY. Known daughter, LYDIA b. 18 Feb. 1817, Covert, NY (m. Aaron H. Cole, also see). Ref: P&BA-Len pg. 228.

RATHBONE also see RATHBUN

RATHBONE, MARY ANN (See Ariel Cornwell)

RATHBUN, DANIEL was listed in the 1840 census index of Fairfield Twp., Lenawee Co., Mich. There was a Daniel "Rathburn" age 40, b. NY, listed in the 1850 census of Adrian Twp. "in Jail." No proof it is the same man.

RATHBUN, DANIEL born ca. 1806, NY, and wife, HANNAH, born ca. 1806, NJ, were listed in the 1850 census of Adrian Twp., Lenawee Co., Mich. with CATHARINE L., age 16; CAROLINE M., age 13; DANIEL S., age 11; SARAH A., age 8; ISAAC H., age 5; ELIZABETH, age 5; JANE M., age 3, all b. NY, in their household.

RATHBUN, ISAAC (spelled "Rathun") was listed in the 1840 census index of Ogden Twp., Lenawee Co., Mich. Note SARAH, following.

RATHBUN, JAMES R. born ca. 1819, and wife, LAURA, born ca. 1825, both in NY, were listed in the 1850 census of Medina Twp., Lenawee Co., Mich. with MARY M., age 7; WILLIAM P., age 5; ISAIAH P?, age 4; LUCY M., age 1, all b. Mich., and SEGUNT?, age 25, b. NY, in their household.

RATHBUN, LEWIS T., son of RUFUS H. (following), born 1 May 1836, Palmyra Twp., Lenawee Co., Mich., married on 13 Dec. 1855 to CAROLINE E. (WHITE), daughter of Josephus (also see). They resided in Fairfield Twp. Children: 1. CLARA D. (m. Artemus Swick, also see); 2. MELVEN (d. age 6); 3. ALTA D. (m. George Mobas). Ref: P&BA-Len pg. 802-3.

RATHBUN, LUCY (spelled "Rathbone"), age 62, b. Conn., was listed in the 1850 census of Madison Twp., Lenawee Co., Mich. in a Hall household.

RATHBUN, RACHEL born ca. 1804/8, Yorkshire, England (See Abraham Bateman).

RATHBUN, RUFUS H. born ca. 1815, and wife, ELEANOR (ROBBINS), born ca. 1818, both in NY, married in Ontario Co., NY, and moved soon afterwards in 1836 to Palmyra Twp., Lenawee Co., Mich. They moved to Madison Twp., then for about 6 weeks in Williams Co., Ohio; and by 1840 in Hillsdale Co. From there they moved to Ogden Twp., and by 1850 were listed in Fairfield Twp. with first 4 children in their household. She died 4 Dec. 1883, and in 1888 lived with eldest son, 1. LEWIS T. (preceding); 2. EMILY b. ca. 1840; 3. ELIZA J. b. ca. 1841 (m. Peter Gussenbauer); 4. REUBEN b. ca. 1843; 5. ARLETTA. Ref: P&BA-Len pg. 802-3.

RATHBUN, SARAH, age 40, born NY, was listed in the 1850 census of Ogden Twp., Lenawee Co., Mich. in a Webster? household. Note ISAAC (preceding).

RATHBURN, RACHEL (See James Wirt)

RAWSON, HENRY H., son of THEODORE (following), born 9 May 1817, Ontario Co., NY, prospected for land in Michigan in 1839. He married probably in NY on 30 Oct. 1844 to MARY J. (CORNELIUS), daughter of William (also see). In 1846, they removed to Rollin Twp., Lenawee Co., Mich. Seven children, of whom 3 died young, those named in sketch: 1. WILLIAM C. b. ca. 1847 (d. young, after 1850 census); 2. ALONZO P. b. 4 May 1848 (m. Harriet Tuttle, dau. of John, also see; Hillsdale Co.); 3. GEORGE H. b. 19 May 1857 (m Josie Jones, dau. of Walter, also see; Hillsdale Co.); 4. MARTIN L. b. 8 Nov. 1859 (m. Sadie Hadley of Hillsdale Co.; lived Rollin Twp., Lenawee Co.); 5. EDWARD M. b. 11 Mar. 1864 (m. Celia Cole, dau. of Amos R., also see). Ref: P&BA-Len pg. 684-5.

RAWSON, SARAH born England (See John Ashley).

RAWSON, SILAS was a Revolutionary soldier from Mass.; and was a direct descendant of EDWARD of colonial times. Known son, THEODORE (following); known daughter, ANNA b. ca. 1782, NY? (m. Levi Stevens, also see). Ref: P&BA-Len pg. 649-50. Note: There was a SILAS in the Rev. Pension Applications, with Mass. service, Appl. #S14241, possibly this man.

RAWSON, SUSANNA (See Joshua Parker)

RAWSON, THEODORE, son of SILAS (preceding), born Mass., lived in Ontario Co., NY where he married on 2 Feb. 1813 to ELIZABETH (BUSSEY). They came to Michigan where she died at age 72; and he died in Rollin Twp., Lenawee Co. at age 84 in household of Gershom B. Bennett. Ten children, only names stated were HENRY H. (preceding); and MARIA b. 26 Apr. 1822 (m. Gershom B. Bennett, also see). Ref: P&BA-Len pg. 649-50.

RAYMER, MARY (See Bradbury S. Clay)

RAYMOND, ALBERN H. born ca. 1816, Steuben Co., NY, and wife, HARRIET L. (TUTTLE), moved to Rollin Twp., Lenawee Co., Mich. in 1837; and died there age 42 (ca. 1858). Known children (from 1850 census): 1. CLARINDA M. b. ca. 1836 (m. Charles K. Densmore, Jackson Co., Mich.); 2. SELAH H. (following); 3. TRIPHENA H. b. ca. 1845. Ref: P&BA-Len pg. 650-1.

RAYMOND, ALONZO, probably son of NATHANIEL (following), born ca. 1826, NY, and wife, DELIA B., born ca. 1830, Mich., were listed in the 1850 census of Adrian Twp., Lenawee Co., Mich. (next door to NATHANIEL).

RAYMOND, ALVAH born ca. 1797, and wife, PHEBE, born ca. 1804, both in NY, were listed in the 1850 census of Raisin Twp., Lenawee Co., mich. with DANIEL R., age 19; SARAH A., age 15, both b. Mich., in their household.

RAYMOND, ALVAH born ca. 1821, and wife, MARY, born ca. 1821, both in NY, were listed in the 1850 census of Woodstock Twp., Lenawee Co., Mich. with ALVIRA, age 6; RUFUS, age 2, both b. Mich., in their household. Note RUFUS, following.

RAYMOND, ALVIRA born ca. 1814, NY, sister of ALBERN H. (preceding), married on 12 Jan. 1837, probably in Steuben Co., NY to Walden Wing (also see). Ref: P&BA-Len pg. 946-7.

RAYMOND, ALZADA, age 7, and EUDORA, age 4, both born Mich., probably sisters, were listed in the 1850 census of Adrian Twp., Lenawee Co., Mich. in the household of Joseph & Eunice Rickey (perhaps grandparents?)

RAYMOND, CLARK married SOPHIA (ATWOOD), daughter of Seth (also see). It may be he written as "Charles, age 18," in the 1850 census of Rome Twp., Lenawee Co., Mich. See ISAAC (following).

RAYMOND, DANIEL was listed in the 1840 census index of Raisin Twp., Lenawee Co., Mich.

RAYMOND, FREELOVE (See John Whelan)

RAYMOND, HIRAM born ca. 1819, was listed as head of household in the 1850 census of Raisin Twp., Lenawee Co., Mich. with probably mother, LUCY, age 56, born Mass., and siblings ELIJAH, age 29; AMANDA, age 26; HANNAH, age 25; CAROLINE b. 20 Apr. 1829, Steuben Co., NY (m. William E. Doty, also see); DANIEL B., age 16, b. Mich., in his household. Note DANIEL, preceding.

RAYMOND, ISAAC by first marriage had children, CHARLES (or CLARK?), born ca. 1832; SAMUEL b. ca. 1837. He married second to Mrs. JANE A. (HOOD) ATWOOD, daughter of John, and widow of Seth (see both). They had daughter, MARY b. ca. 1846 (m. ? Bacome). In the 1850 census of Rome Twp., Jane A. was listed as head of household with the Raymond children listed above, and her Atwood children in the household. Isaac was said to have died in California in 1880. Ref: P&BA-Len pg. 1068. Note: CLARK RAYMOND, preceding, who married Sophia Atwood, so CHARLES listed in the household may actually have actually been CLARK?

RAYMOND, JOHN was listed in the 1840 census index of Adrian Twp., Lenawee Co., Mich.; and it may be he in the 1850 census of Seneca Twp., Lenawee Co., Mich., age 45, with ELIZA S., age 30, both born NY, and ELEANOR A., age 6 (prob. she who m. Aaron P. Phillips, son of Aaron M., also see); WILLIAM A., age 4, both b. Mich., in the household.

RAYMOND, LLEWELYN born probably in 1860s (See Edmund Lapham).

RAYMOND, LUCY born ca. 1794, Mass. (See HIRAM, preceding).

RAYMOND, NATHANIEL born ca. 1802, and wife, SUSAN, born ca. 1805, both in NY, were listed in the 1850 census of Adrian Twp., Lenawee Co., Mich. with GEORGE W., age 26; WILLIAM H., age 22; MARY M., age 19, all born NY; and JANE E., age 16; CHARLES S., age 14; BRADFORD A., age 5, all b. Mich., in the household. ALONZO H. (preceding), was listed next door.

RAYMOND, ORICA (See George W. Spencer)

RAYMOND, PAUL born ca. 1817, Mass., and wife, HARRIET, born ca. 1824, NY, were listed in the 1850 census of Madison Twp., Lenawee Co., Mich. with ERVIN, age 5; LOUISA, age 3; HELEN M., age 3/12, all b. Mich.; and Sarah Smith, age 70, born Mass., in their household.

RAYMOND, PERMELIA married John I. Rector (also see). Ref: P&BA-Len pg. 1123-4.

RAYMOND, RUFUS born ca. 1786, NY, married RUHAMA (AULLS) in Steuben Co., NY. They moved to Raisin Twp., Lenawee Co., Mich. in 1834; and she died in 1845. There were 13 children, names not stated, excepet eldest, LUCRETIA b. 24 Apr. 1811, Wheeler, Steuben Co., NY (m. Edmund Hall, also see). In Rufus' household in the 1850 census were ELIZABETH, age 38; ROSWELL, age 25; HIRAM, age 18, all b. NY. Rufus apparently married again before 1850, as he listed wife, LAURA A. born ca. 1792, Conn. in the household. Ref: P&BA-Len pg. 1043-4. Also note ALVAH; DANIEL; & HIRAM, preceding.

RAYMOND, SELAH H., son of ALBERN H. (preceding), born 31 Aug. 1840, Rollin Twp., Lenawee Co., Mich., married on 8 Mar. 1861 to MARTHA A. (PAWSON) of Franklin Twp., born 21 Apr. 1842. Children: 1. IDA S. b. 11 Apr. 1862 (d. 2 Sept. 1862); 2. LOTTIE M. b. 3 Feb. 1864 (m. Stephen A. Page, son of Nicholas, also see); 3. ALBERN H. b. 25 Nov. 1865. Ref: P&BA-Len pg. 650-1.

RAYNOR, CHARLES and wife, EMMA J. (HALSEY), were natives of Long Island, NY. Children: 1. CHARLES H. (following); 2. LYDIA (m. R. B. McGraw, New York City). Ref: P&BA-Len pg. 516-7.

RAYNOR, CHARLES H., son of CHARLES (preceding), born 12 Jan. 1841, New York City, married in Adrian, Lenawee Co., Mich. on 4 Oct. 1870 to CLARA P. (WEBSTER), daughter of John (also see). Children: 1. CLARENCE W. b. Sept. 1875; 2. EMMA W. b. May 1877. Ref: P&BA-Len pg. 516-7.

READ also see REED

READ, ELIZABETH born England (See Joseph Smith).

READ, DON A., son of HORACE (following), born ca. 1805, VT, moved with his parents to Livingston Co., NY where he married HANNAH (MOYER). About 1830, they removed to Clinton Twp., Lenawee Co., Mich.; and she died there in 1833 leaving 3 children: 1. HENRY (followiong); 2. MARIA; 3. JANE b. ca. 1832. Don married again to FANSING? (LARUE) born ca. 1810, NJ. They were listed in Cambridge Twp. in the 1840 census index (adjacent to FITCH REED, following); and in the 1850 census in addition to Henry & Jane, preceding, listed THOMAS, age 8, b. Mich.; and father, HORACE (written "Horatio"), age 69, b. Mass., said to be blind. Ref: P&BA-Len pg. 882-2. Note: FITCH was listed adjacent in 1840.

READ, HENRY, son of DON A. (preceding), born 22 Oct. 1827, Mt. Morris, NY, moved to Cambridge Twp., Lenawee Co., Mich. with his parents. He married on 2 Dec. 1853, Rome Twp., to ALICE W. (CHAMPENOIS), daughter of William A. (also see) and settled in Cambridge Twp. Children: 1. CHARLES H.; 2. LENA; 3. FRANCES. Ref: P&BA-Len pg. 882-3.

READ, HORACE born ca. 1781, Mass., lived before 1805 in Vermont. He married JEMIMA (MEAD) and probably moved to Livingston Co., NY. She died in 1844 in NY. He moved to Cambridge Twp., Lenawee Co., Mich. "late in life," and was living in household of son, DON

Pioneer Families of Southeastern Michigan

A. (preceding), in the 1850 census. Ref: P&BA-Len pg. 882-3. Also note STEPHEN H., following.

READ, STEPHEN H. born ca. 1809, VT, and wife, LIVERA, born ca. 1822, NJ, were listed in the 1850 census of Cambridge Twp., Lenawee Co., Mich. with JANE, age 10; MARY, age 9; LIVERA, AGE 7 (may be she who m. Albert D. Briggs, son of Jabez, also see); CHARLES, age 5, all b. Mich., and LAMIRA?, age 18, b. NY, in their household.

READER see REEDER

REAS, GEORGE and his wife (name not stated) were born and married in Germany; and she died there. Known daughter, MARGARET b. 13 Nov. 1841, Germany (m. Peter Jacob, also see, Erie Co., Ohio). George married again to JULIA (SCHULTZ), and in 1850 they came to the US and settled first in Erie Co., Ohio. They moved to Fulton Co., Ohio where he was living in 1888. Ref: P&BA-Len pg. 744-5.

REASONER, BENJAMIN, son of JACOB (following), born 15 Oct. 1807, Dutchess Co., NY, moved with his parents probably to Schoharie Co., NY. He married 11 July 1830 to MARTHA (ROUND), daughter of Samuel (also see). They may have lived in Niagara Co., NY for a time, then moved before 1839 to Ohio. They moved to Medina Twp., Lenawee Co., Mich. by the 1850 census. There were 10 children (exact order not known): 1. GUELMA (deceased before 1888); 2. LETTIE (d. age 4); and the following were in the household in 1850: 3. ZILPHA MARIE b. ca. 1835, NY (m. Jerry Rice, also see); 4. MARTHA b. ca. 1836, b. NY (m. Samuel Craig, also see); 5. JACOB b. ca. 1839, Ohio (deceased by 1888); 6. BENJAMIN b. ca. 1841, Ohio (to Otsego Co., Mich.); 7. JAMES H. b. ca. 1844, Ohio (m. Melissa A. Kimis, children: George B.; James H., Ruel D.); 8. FRANCIS b. ca. 1846, Ohio; 9. MARY (MINERVA) b. ca. 1848, Ohio (m. William Walker, Medina Twp.); 10. CHLOE (m. Henry Law, VT). Ref: P&BA-Len pg. 1017-8.

REASONER, JACOB born Dutchess Co., NY, served in the War of 1812. He married HANNAH (ACKER) of Schoharie Co., NY; and she died there ca. 1843. He came to Medina Twp., Lenawee Co., Mich. to live with his children. There were 6 sons and 8 daughters, names not stated, except BRADLEY B. (to Mills Co., Iowa); and #7. BENJAMIN (preceding). Ref: P&BA-Len pg. 1017-8.

REASONER, PETER born ca. 1822, and wife, CATHARINE, born ca. 1828, both in NY, were listed in the 1850 census of Madison Twp., Lenawee Co., Mich., married within the year, in the household of Thomas and Eleanor Robbins (in-laws?)

RECTOR, JOHN I. born ca. 1810, NY, had moved as a youth to Tecumseh Twp., Lenawee Co., Mich., and married there to PERMELIA (RAYMOND). They moved to Delta (York Twp., Fulton Co.), Ohio. Known daughters: LUCY A. b. 14 Dec. 1845 (m. Richard B. Gillespie[3], also see); & JENNIE b. 28 June 1853 (m. A. D. Macham, also see). In 1858, they moved to Raisin Twp., Lenawee Co., and then to Tecumseh Twp., where he died 30 Dec. 1887, age 77; and she was still residing in 1888, age 73. Ref: P&BA-Len pg. 893-4; 1123-4.

RECTOR, WILLIAM born ca. 1825, NY, was listed in the 1850 census of Madison Twp., Lenawee Co., Mich. in the household of Samuel & Sally A. Smith.

REDFIELD, ASIL of Adrian, Lenawee Co., Mich. was father of MARY E. b. 29 Aug. 1844, Albany, NY (m. Charles H. Adam, also see).

REDFIELD, BERIAH, probably son of EDMUND (following), born ca. 1794, and wife, SARAH, BORN CA. 1792, both in Mass., were listed in the 1850 census of Cambridge Twp., Lenawee Co., Mich., next door to HENRY M., age 30, b. Mass (with wife, MARY, age 24, b. NY, no family); and with EMILY, age 16, b. NY, in their household.

REDFIELD, BETSEY, age 57, born NH, was listed in the 1850 census of Madison Twp., Lenawee Co., Mich. with JANE S., age 24, b. NH, both in the household of William E. Kimball and wife, Sarah E. (age 30, also b. NH).

REDFIELD, EDMUND born ca. 1773, Conn., was listed in the 1850 census of Cambridge Twp., Lenawee Co., Mich. in the household of probably daughter, CONTENT (b. 1812, NY), and her husband, Leander Austin, next door to BERIAH (preceding).

REDFIELD, WILLIAM F. born ca. 1823, and wife, MARTHA, born ca. 1828, both in NY, were listed in the 1850 census of Woodstock Twp., Lenawee Co., Mich. (spelled "Readfield"), with CORNELIA, age 9/12, b. Mich., in their household.

REED. C. E. (See James B. Wells)

REED, D. B. was listed in the 1830 census of Lenawee Co., Michigan Territory, with males: 1 und 5; 1 20-30; 1 40-50; and females: 1 5-10; 1 30-40 in his household.

REED, DANIEL born ca. 1808, Mass., and wife, MARY, born ca. 1809, NY, were listed in the 1850 census of Seneca Twp., Lenawee Co., Mich. with David Hecox, age 12, b. Ohio; and Jane A. Bill, age 3, born Indiana, in their household.

REED, DAVID, age 23, born Mich., was listed in the 1850 census of Tecumseh Twp., Lenawee Co., Mich. in a Bigelow household.

REED, EDWARD (See David Gander)

REED, ELIZABETH born Norfolk, England (See Samuel King).

REED, FITCH, possibly son of WHEELER (following), born ca. 1812, NY, and wife, ANN, born ca. 1816, England, were listed in the 1840 census index of Cambridge Twp., Lenawee Co., Mich., and in the 1850 census with ELIZABETH, age 9; ELLEN, age 7; MARSHA, age 5; MARSHALL, age 1; MARY, age 1, all b. Mich., in their household.

REED, GEORGE born ca. 1823, and wife, ELIZABETH, born ca. 1826, both in NY, were listed in the 1850 census of Rome Twp., Lenawee Co., Mich. with FAYETTE, age 3; DUDLEY, age 2, both b. Mich., in their household.

REED, GERSHOM was listed in the 1830 census of Lenawee Co., Michigan Territory with males: 1 10-15; 2 15-20 1 40-50; and females: 2 10-15; 1 30-40 in his household.

REED, H. (See Egbert Wheaton)

REED, HENRY S. born ca. 1806, and wife, LUCY, born ca. 1810, both in NY, were listed in the 1850 census of Woodstock Twp., Lenawee Co., Mich. with HENRY, age 17; EMELINE, age 15; SARAH, age 13; CRAMER, age 11; CHARLES, age 9; HULDAH, age 7; LUCY, age 5;

CAROLINE, age 3; MARYETTE, age 1, all b. NY, in their household.

REED, JACOB born 2 Aug. 1800, Cumberland Co., Penn., of German descent, married in Fayette, Seneca Co., NY to CATHERINE (SMITH) who was born 27 Apr. 1801, Turbor, Northumberland Co., Penn. They remained in Fayette, NY where he died 17 Nov. 1869, and she died 14 Dec. 1876. Children: 1. JOHN; 2. JACOB (following); 3. CHARLES (d. 8 Mar. 1863, Fayette, NY); 4. WILLIAM; 5. FRANKLIN (d. age 12); 6. ELIZABETH; 7. HANNAH (d. infancy); 8. ENOCH (Madison Twp., Lenawee Co.); 9. ANNA S. (d. 27 July 1886, Seneca Co., NY); 10. EDWARD (Madison Twp., Lenawee Co.) Ref: P&BA-Len pg. 845-6.

REED, JACOB, son of JACOB (preceding), born 30 Sept. 1825, Seneca Co., NY, lived in NY and briefly in Ohio before moving to Dover Twp., Lenawee Co., Mich. in 1860. He returned to Seneca Co., NY where he married on 7 Nov. 1861 to Mrs. SUSANNA (GAMBEE) KUNEY, daughter of Jacob, and widow of Reuben (see both). They settled in Dover Twp. Children: 1. FRANKLIN; 2. MARY C. Ref: P&BA-Len pg. 845-6.

REED, JAMES BURT, grandson of JOSEPH (following), born 28 Mar. 1840, Seneca Co., Ohio, married on 25 Feb. 1863 to LUCY (GOODSELL), daughter of Franklin (also see). They settled first in Fairfield Twp., Lenawee Co., Mich.; and in 1881 moved to Ogden Twp. Children: 1. NINA G. (m. Myron H. Quick, son of Cornelius, also see); 2. CHARLES A.; 3. ERVIN E.; 4. NETTIE I. Ref: P&BA-Len pg. 574-5.

REED, JEMIMA (See Jacob Rudesill)

REED, JOHN, age 18, born Mich., was listed in the 1850 census of Ridgeway Twp., Lenawee Co., Mich. in a Wiggins household.

REED, JOSEPH from NY was a pioneer settler of Seneca Co., Ohio and "Reedstown" was named for him. He came to Michigan and died at the home of a daughter, name not stated. His SON (name not stated) was born in NY, married CYNTHIA (THOMPSON), and was the father of JAMES BURT (preceding). They lived in Seneca Co., Ohio and about 1842 moved to Fulton Co., Ohio; and he died in 1850 while visiting in Seneca Co. Cynthia married again and moved to Fairfield Twp., Lenawee Co., Mich. Ref: P&BA-Len pg. 574-5. Note NATHAN, following.

REED, LUCY J., age 16, born NY, was listed in the 1850 census of Ridgeway Twp., Lenawee Co., Mich. in a Wilson household.

REED, MARSHALL, son of WHEELER (following), born 21 Aug. 1833, Richmond, NY, moved to Rome Twp., Lenawee Co., Mich. He married 22 Nov. 1855 to JULIA (BARRUS), daughter of William (also see), and settled in Cambridge Twp. Children: 1. FREDERICK P. (m. Elsie Russell, Cambridge Twp.); 2. ALICE C. (m. J. B. Daniels, Rome Twp.); 3. BYRON L. (m. C. Maude Willits, Wilmington, NC). Ref: P&BA-Len pg. 1191-2.

REED, MARY ANN, age 31, was listed in the 1850 census of Tecumseh Twp., Lenawee Co., Mich. in a Comstock household.

REED, N. H. was listed in the 1840 census index of Adrian Twp., Lenawee Co., Mich.

REED, NATHAN born ca. 1825; and ELIZA, born ca. 1822, both in Ohio, married within the year, were listed in the 1850 census of Dover Twp., Lenawee Co., Mich. in the Cleveland household. Eliza may be a daughter of that household. Note JOSEPH, preceding.

REED, PHILIP, son of JACOB, born 1756, Saybrook, Conn., went at age 16 to Vermont. He served in the Revolution under General Stark of Bennington; and married there to MARGARET (FITCH), daughter of William (also see). About 1795, they removed to Ontario Co., NY; and she died in Richmond, NY in 1833. There were 6 children, names not stated, except the youngest, WHEELER (following). Ref: P&BA-Len pg. 1191-2. Also note WILLIAM, following.

REED, ROBERT of Ontario Co., NY was father of PHEBE (m. Benjamin Hornbeck, also see, on 14 Feb. 1833.) Ref: P&BA-Len pg. 563-4. There was a man by this name listed in Macon Twp., Lenawee Co., Mich. in the 1840 census index.

REED, REUBEN born ca. 1805, and wife, CATHARINE, born ca. 1824, both in NY, were listed in the 1850 census of Tecumseh Twp., Lenawee Co., Mich. with FRANCES, age 1; JAMES M., age 1, born in Mich., in their household.

REED, SAMUEL was listed in the 1840 census index of Seneca Twp., Lenawee Co., Mich.

REED, SAMUEL B. born ca. 1830, and wife, RHODA, born ca. 1828, both in NY, were listed in the 1850 census of Cambridge Twp., Lenawee Co., Mich.

REED, THOMAS was listed in the 1830 census of Lenawee Co., Michigan Territory, with males: 1 und 5; 1 5-10; 1 10-15; 1 15-20; 1. 20-30; 1 40-50; and females: 1 und 5; 1 10-15; 1 40-50 in the household.

REED, WHEELER, son of PHILIP (preceding), born ca. 1788, VT, moved with his parents to Ontario Co., NY. He married there to MARGARET (RISDON) who died leaving 3 children (names not stated). He married again to her sister, HANNAH (RISDON), with whom he had 13 children (names not stated). "Several of his children moved to Michigan." Those known: ALMIRA M. b. 29 Sept. 1825 (m. Warren Gilbert, also see); & #11. MARSHALL (preceding). Wheeler died in 1868, and she died in 1878, age 80, Ontario Co., NY. Ref: P&BA-Len pg. 694-5; 1191-2. Also note FITCH, preceding.

REED, WILLIAM born ca. 1820, NY, was listed in the 1850 census of Cambridge Twp., Lenawee Co., Mich. with PHILANDER, age 18, born NY, in his household.

REED, WILLIAM born 1787, Rockingham, Windham Co., VT, married on 29 Apr. 1819 to EUNICE (HOAR) born ca. 1797, Nova Scotia. They lived in New Brunswick, Canada till 1837, then moved to Rome Twp., Lenawee Co., Mich. He died 25 Mar. 1870, age 82, and she died 21 Feb. 1875, age 79, at the home of her grandson, William H. Hervey (also see). They were listed in the 1840 census index of Dover Twp.; and in the 1850 census with LOVISA b. 10 Nov. 1828, Albert Co., New Brunswick, Canada (m. Russell Hervey, also see); WILLIAM, age 19, and ELVIN, age 16, both b. New Brunswick, in their household. Ref: P&BA-Len pg. 450-1. Note PHILIP (preceding).

REEDER, FRANK probably born after 1850 (See Levi L. Stockwell; and note PETER, following).

REEDER, PETER born ca. 1802, Penn., and wife, JANE, born ca. 1806, NY, were listed in the 1850 census of Medina twp., Lenawee Co., Mich. with HENRY, age 21;

MAARGARET J., age 18; SARAH, age 15; MARY, age 14; ELIZABETH, age 12; HARRIET, age 8; CAROLINE, age 5; JOHN, age 3; CATHARINE, age 1, all b. NY, in their household. Note FRANK, preceding.

REMINGTON, ? Mrs., age 42, born Conn., was listed in the 1850 census of Adrian Twp., Lenawee Co., Mich. with CLARISSA, age 5, b. Mich., in a hotel.

REMINGTON, AMELIA (See George Howell)

REMINGTON, ANN M., age 8, born Mich., was listed in the 1850 census of Macon Twp., Lenawee Co., Mich. in the household of James Jr. and Sarah Wheeler, perhaps grandparents. Note JAMES L., following.

REMINGTON, FRANCIS, age 18, born Conn., was listed in the 1850 census of Adrian Twp., Lenawee Co., Mich. in a Woodbury household. Note Mrs. ?, preceding.

REMINGTON, IRA H. born NY, and wife, SARAH R. (CALKINS) born Nova Scotia, lived in Monroe Co., NY and possibly in Orleans Co. About 1856, they removed to Columbia Co., Wisc., and in 1860 to Jackson Co., Mich. Children: 1. SARAH ELIZA b. 12 Jan. 1835, Monroe Co., NY (m. Norman B. Pierce, also see); 2. HELEN C.; 3. LEONARD C.; 4. M. VINA; 5. CLARA M.; 6. CHARLEY R.; 7. ARHUR E. Ref: P&BA-Len pg. 492-3.

REMINGTON, JAMES L. was listed in the 1840 census index of Macon Twp., Lenawee Co., Mich. Note ANN M., preceding.

RENO, MARY L. (See Samuel Hinkley)

RENYAN, PHEBE A. (See Eli S. Howd)

REXFORD, ? Mrs. of Woodstock Twp. was the daughter of Daniel Bates (also see).

REXFORD, ELMER probably born after 1850 (See James M. Richardson; and note LUTHER, following).

REXFORD, HENRY born ca. 1829, and wife, MARY ANN, born ca. 1832, both in NY, were listed in the 1850 census of Tecumseh Twp., Lenawee Co., Mich.

REXFORD, LUTHER born ca. 1818, Conn., and wife, ELISA, born ca. 1822, NY, were listed in the 1850 census of Franklin Twp., Lenawee Co., Mich. with WILLIAM, age 7; SUSAN, age 5; HARRIET, age 3, all b. Mich., in their household.

REYNOLDS, ALMIRA, age 12, born Mich., was listed in the 1850 census of Fairfield Twp., Lenawee Co., Mich. in a Laycock household.

REYNOLDS, B. F. (See Alvinza Whelan)

REYNOLDS, DAVID was listed in the 1840 census index of Fairfield Twp., Lenawee Co., Mich. Also see PETER, following.

REYNOLDS, ELLA A. (See Philip S. DePuy)

REYNOLDS, ELLEN born ca. 1824 was the daughter of parents who had come from Co. Clare, Ireland to Cattaraugus Co., NY. Ellen married Patrick Hogan (also see). Ref: P&BA-Len pg. 907-8.

REYNOLDS, HIRAM born ca. 1810, and wife, MARY, born ca. 1805, both in NY, were listed in the 1840 census index of Franklin Twp., Lenawee Co., Mich. (adjacent to SIDNEY, following); and in the 1850 census with SARAH, age 15; BENJAMIN, age 13; HIRAM, age 10; CLARINDA, age 8; DELIA, age 5; MARY, age 2, all b. Mich., in their household. Note RODMAN, following.

REYNOLDS, IRA (See Jeremiah Wilsey²)

REYNOLDS, ISAIAH (See Sheldon Wyman)

REYNOLDS, JAMES born ca. 1814, and wife, MARY, born ca. 1816, both in NY, were listed in the 1850 census of Raisin Twp., Lenawee Co., Mich. with CHARLES, age 9; ROSETTA, age 7; LYDIA A., age 4, all b. Mich., in their household. It may be they listed as JAMES C. in the 1840 census index of Palmyra Twp.

REYNOLDS, JAMES H. Dr., son of MADISON (following), born 14 May 1845, South Amherst, Lorain Co., Ohio, moved with his parents to Monroe Co., Mich. He served in the Civil War. He married on 21 Oct. 1869 to MARGARETTA (STEELE), daughter of Solomon (also see) of Palmyra Twp., Lenawee Co., Mich. In 1883, they moved to Adrian, Mich. Children: 1. BERTHA L.; 2. FLORENCE A. Ref: P&BA-Len pg. 425-6.

REYNOLDS, JARED and wife, JANE (WORDEN), of Westchester Co., NY were parents of JANE A. (m. Nathan Gunn, also see). Ref: P&BA-Len pg. 321-2.

REYNOLDS, JEHIEL M. born ca. 1813, and wife, LOVINA M., born ca. 1812, both in NY, were listed in the 1850 census of Madison Twp., Lenawee Co., Mich. with HERBERT, age 13; SARAH, age 6, both b. NY; and MARY, age 3, b. Penn., in their household.

REYNOLDS, JOSEPH B., son of SAMUEL (following), born ca. 1818, was listed in the 1850 census of Adrian Twp., Lenawee Co., Mich. with WILLIAM P. (following) and family, and mother, ABIGAIL, in his household.

REYNOLDS, LEONARD, son of SAMUEL (following), born in Aug. 1800, Greene Co., NY, married there to BETSEY (HALSTED) born Aug. 1804, Greene Co. They moved to Rome Twp., Lenawee Co., Mich. by 1839. He died there 27 Mar. 1882; and she died 3 Oct. 1880. Children: 1. REUBEN (following); 2. NORMAN b. ca. 1825 (m. Sabra ? b. ca. 1832, NY); 3. MARY ANN; 4. EMILY; 5. JOHN b. ca. 1833; 6. WESLEY b. ca. 1836; 7. MELISSA b. ca. 1839, Mich.; 8. ABIJAH b. ca. 1841; 9. JEROME b. ca. 1843; 10. LUCINDA b. ca. 1845; 11. ELIZABETH JANE b. ca. 1848. Ref: P&BA-Len pg. 1085-6.

REYNOLDS, MADISON born "near Lake Champlain, NY," married in Lorain Co., Ohio to AUGUSTA (MOON), daughter of Ludwig (also see) of Avon, Lorain Co. Madison died there, and she remained until 1850, then moved to Somerfield, Monroe Co., Mich. She died there in 1886. Four children, names not stated except #3. JAMES H. (preceding). Ref: P&BA-Len pg. 425-6.

REYNOLDS, MARIETTA (See John Pierce)

REYNOLDS, MARGARET Mrs. born ca. 1822, Ireland, was listed in the 1850 census of Madison Twp., Lenawee Co., Mich. with MARY E., age 4; LAURA, age 1/12, both b. Mich., in their household.

REYNOLDS, MOSES born ca. 1807, and wife, EMELINE, born ca. 1813, both in NY, were listed in the 1850 census of Rome Twp., Lenawee Co., Mich. with ANDREW J., age 18; MYRON? O., age 14; MARTIN V., age 12, all b. NY, in their household. Note SAMUEL (following).

REYNOLDS, PETER was listed in the 1840 census index of Fairfield Twp., Lenawee Co., Mich. Note DAVID, preceding.

REYNOLDS, REUBEN, son of LEONARD (preceding), born ca. 1823, and wife, AURILLA, born ca. 1829, both in NY, were listed in the 1850 census of Rome Twp., Lenawee

Co., Mich. with MARIONA? E., age 2; MARY, age 1, both b. Mich., in their household.

REYNOLDS, RODMAN born ca. 1796, and wife, GESENIAH?, born ca. 1804, both in NY, were listed in the 1840 census index of Franklin Twp., Lenawee Co., Mich.; and in the 1850 census with MILAN? (female), age 15; CHARLES, age 13; CALISTA, age 10; SARAH, age 6, all b. Mich., in their household.

REYNOLDS, ROSWELL born ca. 1793, and wife, DIANTHA, born ca. 1797, both in VT, were listed in the 1850 census of Adrian Twp., Lenawee Co., Mich. with PHILEMON, age 20, b. VT (with wife, MARY, age 17, married within the year); & RUSSELL, age 11, b. Ohio, in their household.

REYNOLDS, SAMUEL born Greene Co., NY, married there to ABIGAIL (BELDING) born ca. 1780, Conn. He served in the War of 1812. They moved to Yates Co., NY and then to Allegany Co. Late in life, they moved to Adrian Twp., Lenawee Co., Mich. to live with son, William, where he died at age 76 (before 1850), and she died at age 75. Known children: LEONARD (preceding); WILLIAM P. (following); JOSEPH B. (preceding). Also note MOSES, preceding. Ref: P&BA-Len pg. 1085-6.

REYNOLDS, SIDNEY was listed in the 1840 census index of Franklin Twp., Lenawee Co., Mich. adjacent to HIRAM, preceding. Also note RODMAN, preceding.

REYNOLDS, STEPHEN, son of Gen. DANIEL (of Revolutionary fame), of Derry, NH, married SALLY (ELA), daughter of Samuel (also see). She died in Sept. 1861. Ref: P&BA-Len pg. 297-9.

REYNOLDS, WESLEY, son of LEONARD (preceding), born ca. 1836, NY, married in Rome Twp., Lenawee Co., Mich. on 20 Nov. 1860 to CLARISSA (THOMAS), daughter of Charles L. (also see). They went first to Ionia, Mich., but returned to Rome Twp. Children: 1. LUELLA b. 30 Oct. 1862; 2. CHARLES L. b. 21 May 1865. Ref: P&BA-Len pg. 1085-6.

REYNOLDS, WILLIAM born ca. 1817, England, and wife, HANNAH, born ca. 1820, NY, were listed in the 1850 census of Medina Twp., Lenawee Co., Mich. with WILLIAM H., age 8, b. NY; and SIMEON A., age 4; MARY L., age 4, both b. Mich., in their household.

REYNOLDS, WILLIAM P., son of SAMUEL (preceding), born ca. 1816, and wife, MELISSA, born ca. 1825, both in NY, wee listed in the 1850 census of Adrian Twp., Lenawee Co., Mich. with ABIGAIL, age 9; MELISSA, age 6, both b. NY; and GEORGE, age 6/12, b. Mich., all in the household of JOSEPH B.

RHINEHART also see RINEHART

RHINEHART, JOHN, age 21, born NY, was listed in the 1850 census of Medina Twp., Lenawee Co., Mich.

RHINEMILLER, HENRY, son of JOHN (following), born 5 Jan. 1837, Huron Twp., Erie Co., Ohio, married there on 17 Aug. 1869 to ANNA C. (SMITT), daughter of Henry (also see). They went first to Green Bay, Mich.; and then about 1873 to Ogden Twp., Lenawee Co. Children: 1. NELLIE MAORA; 2. MARTHA VIOLA; 3. Infant d. unnamed. Ref: P&BA-Len pg. 714-5.

RHINEMILLER, JOHN born Breitenbach, Ker-Rothenburg, Hessen, Germany, married there in 1827 to ANNA (BRUNDOW). In 1833, they immigrated to Lorain Co., Ohio. In 1834, they settled in Huron Twp., Erie Co., Ohio, where he died 9 June 1878, and she died in Jan. 1879. Children (order of birth not known): WILLIAM; ELIZA; CHRISTINA; HENRY (preceding); JOHN; JOSEPH; and 2 deceased before 1888, MARTHA; & TINA. Ref: P&BA-Len pg. 714-5.

RHODES, DANIEL born ca. 1790, Rhode Island, and wife, ABIGAIL, born ca. 1792, Mass., were residents of Rollin Twp., Lenawee Co., Mich. in 1834 (as Dr. Leonard Hall, also see, resided with them that year). In the 1850 census of Rollin Twp., they listed GEORGE, age 23; MARY E., age 18, both b. Mass., in their household. Note Rev. WILLIAM, following.

RHODES, JOSEPH born ca. 1799, NY, married in Onondaga Co., NY to Mrs. MARIA S. (PLATT) COMBS, daughter of Henry S., and widow of John (see both). They removed to Adrian Twp., Lenawee Co., Mich. in 1838. In the 1850 census of Adrian Twp., they listed HANNAH, age 27; MARGARET, age 17, both b. NY, in their household. Ref: P&BA-Len pg. 960-1.

RHODES, JOSEPHINE born ca. 1838, Mich., was listed in the 1850 census of Raisin Twp., Lenawee Co., Mich. in the household of Gershom Aldridge, age 59, b. Mass.; and Mariam, age 64, b. Rhode Island. Note DANIEL, preceding.

RHODES, WILLIAM Rev. born ca. 1816, and wife, GULIELMA?, born ca. 1816, both in Mass., were listed in the 1850 census of Rollin Twp., Lenawee Co., Mich. with SARAH J., age 13, b. Mich.; and ETHALINE, age 8, b. Mass.; and CLARENZA A., age 6, b. Mich., in their household. Note DANIEL, preceding.

RICE, ADAM was an early settler to Seneca Co., NY. Known son, SAMUEL L. (following). Also see LUCY, following, who resided in 1850 census near Samuel L. Ref: P&BA-Len pg. 662

RICE, ALVIN D.^{3}, son of JOSEPH^2 (following), born 21 May 1825, Madison Co., NY, prospected for land in Medina Twp., Lenawee Co., Mich. in 1842. He returned to NY, and came back with his parents in 1845. He married on 3 July 1848 to LYDIA JANE (DROWN), daughter of Appolos (also see). After 23 years, they moved from Medina Twp. to Rome Twp. Seven children, 3 died infancy (names not stated): 1. LUCY M. b. 10 Aug. 1852 (m. Charles D. Sickles); 2. DELOS E. b. 17 Jan. 1855 (m. Amey Everett; Aurora, Ill.); 3. IRVIN A. b. 13 Aug. 1857 (m. Olive Parsons; Chicago, Ill.); 4. OSCAR N. b. 2 Nov. 1866 (Rome Twp.) Ref: P&BA-Len pg. 598-9.

RICE, AMOS born ca. 1797, and wife, BETSEY, born ca. 1796, both in NY, were listed in the 1850 census of Tecumseh Twp., Lenawee Co., Mich. with ARTEMAS, age 19; ELIZABETH, age 22, both b. NY, in their household. Also see NORMAN, following.

RICE, AMOS born ca. 1810, and wife, ELIZABETH, born ca. 1807, both in NY, were listed in the 1850 census of Seneca Twp., Lenawee Co., Mich. with ROXANA, age 17, b. NY; WILLIAM, age 15, b. Penn.; and NORTON, age 8, b. Mich., in their household.

RICE, ARNOLD was listed in the 1840 census index of Franklin Twp., Lenawee Co., Mich.

RICE, CALVIN of Chicago, Ill. (See Abner Gorham Pierce).

RICE, EDWARD H. was listed in the 1840 census index of Adrian Twp., Lenawee Co., Mich. adjacent to ORRIN, following.

Pioneer Families of Southeastern Michigan

RICE, FRANCES J. (See John T. Colegrove)

RICE, FREEMAN and wife, LUCRETIA (VAN VOORHEES), were natives of Wayne Co., NY who removed to Hudson Twp., Lenawee Co., Mich. in 1855. He died there at age 60; and she died at age 53. Children: 1. ALMERON (to San Diego, CA); 2. ANSEL A. (to Washington Terr.); 3. ALICE E. b. 13 June 1859 (m. Elvin D. Cole, also see). Ref: P&BA-Len pg. 610-11. Note NATHAN, preceding.

RICE, GEORGE T. Maj., son of NATHAN (following), born 16 Dec. 1826, Macedon, Wayne Co., NY, married MINERVA J. (RIPLEY), daughter of John (also see). (Note: Date of marriage given as 27 June 1847, however, in the 1850 census of Rollin Twp., Lenawee Co., Mich., George was living with his brother, William H., with no wife). They moved to Marietta, Ohio in 1852, and he served in Co. B, 31st Ohio Inf., during Civil War. They were living in NY in 1865, and in 1866 moved to Rollin Twp., Lenawee Co. Children: 1. JULIA E. b. Macedon, NY (d. age 7 mos); 2. CLARA b. Marietta, Ohio (d. age 8 mos); 3. HARRIET E. b. Marietta, Ohio (d. age 7, Rollin Twp.). Ref: P&BA-Len pg. 663-4.

RICE, HORACE^3, son of JOSEPH^2 (following), born ca. 1806, NY, and wife, ELIZABETH, born ca. 1812, Ohio, were listed in the 1840 census index of Dover Twp.; and in the 1850 census of Medina Twp. with ELIZA, age 13; CHARLOTTE, age 11; SIDNEY, age 8; HORACE F., age 4, all b. Mich.; and Sterling Chatfield, age 16; Henry Chatfield, age 14, both b. Ohio, possibly stepchildren.

RICE, JACOB, age 23, born NY, was listed in the 1850 census of Hudson Twp., Lenawee Co., Mich. in a Davis household.

RICE, JANE (See Demmon Cowen)

RICE, JERRY married ZILPHA MARIE (REASONER), daughter of Benjamin (also see) of Medina Twp., Lenawee Co., Mich. Children: 1. BRADLEY D.; 2. VIOLA ADELIA; 3. CHARLOTTE G.; 4. JERRY E. Ref: P&BA-Len pg. 1017-8.

RICE, JOHN born ca. 1814, NY, and wife, MINERVA R., born ca. 1813, Mass., were probably they listed in the 1840 census index of Hudson Twp., Lenawee Co., Mich.; and in the 1850 census with CHARLES, age 13, b. Mich.; and George Douglas, age 22; Henry Douglas, age 20, both b. Mass., in their household.

RICE, JOHN born ca. 1821, and wife, MARY, born ca. 1823, both in NY, were listed in the 1850 census of Dover Twp., Lenawee Co., Mich. with ANN, age 3; GILBERT, age 2, both b. Mich., in their household.

RICE, JOHN A. born ca. 1807, and wife, CATHARINE, born ca. 1809, both in NY, were listed in the 1850 census of Adrian Twp., Lenawee Co., Mich. with ANNA L., age 7, b. Ind., in their household.

RICE, JOSEPH^1 was son of a man who had come from England to Mass. in Colonial times. Joseph had a twin brother, BENJAMIN, and when one of them was drafted in the Revolution, they agreed to serve alternately, as they both had families. They also had two younger brothers who were kidnapped as children by Indians and raised by them. These two brothers were not seen again until they were adults, and they returned to their Indian lifestyle. Known son, JOSEPH^2 (following). Ref: P&BA-Len pg. 598-9.

RICE, JOSEPH^2, son of JOSEPH^1 (preceding), born 6 May 1780, Conway, Mass., married there in 1802 to MARY (BUSHNELL), daughter of John (Note: The sketch calls her Mary Bushnell, but called her father John "Burnett," which raises a question). They removed to Madison Co., NY. They remained there until 1845, then moved to Medina Twp., Lenawee Co., Mich. He died 5 May 1864; and she died in the Winter of 1860, both in Medina Twp. In the 1850 census of Medina Twp., JOSEPH^2, age 70, was living in the household of son, Alvin D.; and Mary, age 68, was living in the household of daughter, Eliza Irish. Ten children, order of birth not known. 1. DENON; 2. CAROLINE; 3. HORACE (preceding); 4. PHEBE (prob. she b. ca. 1814, m. Avery Hutchens, also see, as NELSON resided with them in 1850 census); 5. JOSEPH^3 (following); 6. JOHN; 7. NELSON b. ca. 1823, NY; 8. ALVIN D. (preceding); 9. MARY; 10. ELIZA b. 1817, NY (m. Thomas Irish; Medina Twp.) Ref: P&BA-Len pg. 598-9. RICE, JOSEPH^3, son of JOSEPH^2 (preceding), born ca. 1811, NY, and wife, ELIZA, born ca. 1818, Conn., were listed in the 1850 census of Medina Twp., Lenawee Co., Mich. with SOPHIA, age 12; ANSON, age 8; HARMOND, age 2, all b. Mich.; and Amanda Whitman, age 27, b. Ohio, in their household.

RICE, JOSEPH born ca. 1816, NY, and wife, SARAH, born ca. 1821, Mass., were listed in the 1850 census of Rollin Twp., Lenawee Co., Mich. with ELLEN M., age 3; WILLIAM T., age 2, both b. Mich., in their household (next door to WILLIAM, following).

RICE, LUCY N. born ca. 1815, NY, married Robert G. Marshall, also see. She may be related to ADAM (preceding), as she resided in the 1850 census of Ogden Twp., Lenawee Co., Mich. near SAMUEL L. (following).

RICE, M. L. (See Oramel Sackett)

RICE, MARY J. (See John H. Tingley^3)

RICE, MOSES born ca. 1800, Mass., and wife, MARY, born ca. 1809, NY, were listed in the 1850 census of Medina Twp., Lenawee Co., Mich. with ADELIA, age 20; EMERSON, age 17; MARTHA, age 16; MARIAH, age 10; MARY, age 8, all b. NY; and ORCELIA, age 6; JANE, age 4; FLORILLA, age 7/12, all b. Mich., in their household.

RICE, NATHAN born 1785, and wife, DORCAS (TIBBETS), were natives of Rhode Island. They removed to Macedon, Wayne Co., NY; and Dorcas died there in 1844. There were 9 children, names not stated, except those surviving in 1888: 1. WILLIAM H. (following); 2. JUDSON; 3. GEORGE T. (preceding). Nathan married again to Mrs. SILINDA SCOVEL, widow of Russell. She was born 4 July 1805, Pompey, Onondaga Co., NY. They were listed in the 1850 census of Rollin Twp., Lenawee Co., Mich. with Lura A. Adams (also see) and family in their household. Ref: P&BA-Len pg. 663-4. Note FREEMAN, preceding.

RICE, NORMAN born ca. 1822, and wife, SARAH, born ca. 1823, both in NY, were listed in the 1850 census of Tecumseh Twp., Lenawee Co., Mich. with HENRY, age 6; SALINA, age 2, both b. Mich., in their household.

RICE, OLIVER born ca. 1790, VT, was listed in the 1850 census of Hudson Twp., Lenawee Co., Mich. in the household of Martin V. & Cynthia J. Crumb.

RICE, ORRIN born ca. 1800, and wife, SARAH, born ca. 1812, both in NY, were listed in the 1840 census index of Adrian Twp., Lenawee Co., Mich. (adjacent to EDWARD H.); and in the 1850 census of Seneca Twp.

with JULIET, age 15; RUFUS, age 11; SILAS, age 8, all shown born NY?

RICE, PHEBE, age 68, born New Jersey, was listed in the 1850 census of Macon Twp., Lenawee Co., Mich. in the household of Jesse B. and Sarah Collar.

RICE, PHILIP born in Wayne Co., NY, was grandson of a man who had come from England to Canada. Philip married on 9 Jan. 1853 to MARY (SMITH), daughter of Robert (also see). They moved to Medina Twp., Lenawee Co., Mich. Known daughter, FRANCES b. 4 July 1859 (m. Benjamin Colegrove, also see, 20 Jan. 1878).

RICE, RACHEL born ca. 1794, NY, was reared and married in Jefferson Co., NY to Jacob Cheever (also see). Ref: P&BA-Len pg. 982-3.

RICE, SAMUEL L., son of ADAM (preceding), born ca. 1810, Seneca Co., NY, married in Jan. 1834 to MARGARET (SEBRING), daughter of Cornelius (also see). In 1835, they removed to Ogden Twp., Lenawee Co., Mich. He died 17 July 1884, and she was still living there in 1888. Known children (from 1850 census): 1. JANET b. ca. 1844; 2. HANNAH E. b. ca. 1846 (m. Willard Crockett, also see); 3. JOSEPHINE b. ca. 1849. Ref: P&BA-Len pg. 662.

RICE, WILLIAM born ca. 1801, and wife, AMANDA, born ca. 1811, both in Rhode Island, were listed in the 1850 census of Medina Twp., Lenawee Co., Mich. with ALBERT, age 6/12, b. Mich., in their household.

RICE, WILLIAM born ca. 1810, and wife, ESTHER, born ca. 1811, both in NY, were listed in the 1850 census of Rollin Twp., Lenawee Co., Mich. (next door to JOSEPH, preceding).

RICE, WILLIAM H., son of NATHAN (preceding), born ca. 1815, and wife, CAROLINE, born ca. 1815, both in NY, were listed in the 1850 census of Rollin Twp., Lenawee Co., Mich. with HARRIET, age 7, b. Mich., and brother, GEORGE, age 24 (probably Maj. George T., preceding), in their household (2 doors from NATHAN).

RICHARD also see RICHARDS

RICHARD, ARCHIBALD born ca. 1781, Ireland, came from Co. Antrim to Raisin Twp., Lenawee Co., Mich. in 1833. Known son, JOHN (following); known daughters: ANN b. 13 May 1818, Co. Antrim (m. Butler Holloway, also see); NANCY b. ca. 1823, Ireland (m. James Boyd, Jr., also see); ELLEN b. ca. 1826, Ireland (in household in the 1850 census of Raisin Twp.). JANE born ca. 1816, Ireland, in the household of Robert Boyd in 1850, probably also of this family. Ref: P&BA-Len pg. 526-7.

RICHARD, JOHN, son of ARCHIBALD (preceding), born ca. 1809, and wife, ELIZABETH, born ca. 1804, both in Ireland, were listed adjacent to Archibald in the 1840 census index of Raisin Twp., Lenawee Co., Mich.; and in the 1850 census with ALEXANDER, age 17, b. NY, in their household.

RICHARDS also see RICHARD

RICHARDS, ELLIS and wife, EMELINE, were natives of Ashland, Mass. who apparently moved to Schenectady, NY. Daughter, MARTHA E. b. 30 Mar. 1834, Northboro, Mass. (m. Daniel Ketchum^2, also see, 5 Mar. 1853, Schenectady, NY). Ref: P&BA-Len pg. 359-60.

RICHARDS, ELMIRA (See Chancy Holcomb)

RICHARDS, HALLAM born ca. 1808, VT, and wife, CATHARINE, born ca. 1812, NY, were listed in the 1850 census of Adrian Twp., Lenawee Co., Mich. with EMILY, age 19; SUSAN, age 12, both b. Mich.; and CATHARINE M., age 7, b. NY, in their household.

RICHARDS, JAMES J., age 15, born Mich., was listed in the 1850 census of Palmyra Twp., Lenawee Co., Mich. in a Warner household.

RICHARDS, JOSIAH was listed in the 1840 census index of Adrian Twp., Lenawee Co., Mich.

RICHARDS, NANCY (See William Pierson^6)

RICHARDS, WILLIAM from Wyoming Co., NY settled in Somerset Twp., Hillsdale Co., Mich. He was a cousin to Eliza H. Holcomb, who came with them, and married Willard F. Day (also see).

RICHARDS, WILLIAM born ca. 1810, Ireland, and wife, MARY, born ca. 1825, NY, were listed in the 1850 census of Tecumseh Twp., Lenawee Co., Mich. with brother?, HUGH, age 26, b. Ireland, in their household.

RICHARDSON, B. F. (See Michael Moran)

RICHARDSON, DAVID born ca. 1786, Penn., was listed in the 1850 census of Hudson Twp., Lenawee Co., Mich., next door to WILLIAM (following).

RICHARDSON, ELIAS married AMANDA (WILBER), daughter of William (also see), and he died before 1850 in Victor, Ontario Co., NY. Amanda moved to Dover Twp., Lenawee Co., Mich., and in the 1850 census was listed, age 41, b. NY, with MARY, age 16; JEREMIAH, age 6, both b. NY, in the household of her sister, Abishaq? and husband, Gilbert Gage. Amanda married Samuel Jordan between the time the census was taken in July 1850 in Dover Twp., and September 1850 in Madison Twp. where she was listed again. They later moved to Strugis, Mich. Ref: P&BA-Len pg. 875-6.

RICHARDSON, EVA (See David Pearson)

RICHARDSON, FRANCIS MALLARD (See George Conger)

RICHARDSON, GEORGE was listed in the 1840 census index of Palmyra Twp., Lenawee Co., Mich.

RICHARDSON, JAMES^2, son of JAMES^1 (who d. in Cayuga Co., NY), born ca. 1791, a "native of Cayuga Co., NY," married in Aurelius, NY to LYDIA (ELLSWORTH). They resided in Junius, Seneca Co., NY in 1825. There were 5 sons and 3 daughters, names not stated, except following. They remained in NY until they were quite elderly, they came to Franklin Twp., Lenawee Co., Mich. to live with known son, JAMES M.^{3} (following). Ref: P&BA-Len pg. 808-9.

RICHARDSON, JAMES M.^{3}, son of JAMES^2 (preceding), born 26 Mar. 1825, Junius, Seneca Co., NY, went to California in 1849. He remained there until 1852, then returned to NY. He married on 2 Nov. 1852 to ORAL (LOVELL), daughter of Jonathan (also see) in Gorham, Ontario Co., NY. In 1853, they removed to Cambridge Twp., Lenawee Co., Mich.; and in 1862 to Franklin Twp. Children: CHARLES M. & FRANCIS B. (both d. young with Scarlet Fever); and surviving were: MARY (m. Alvin Coleman, son of Henry, Franklin Twp.); DAVID A. (m. Abbie E. Pitcher); LIVA A.; ALICE J. (m. Elmer E. Rexford); EDWIN J.; ALBERT J. Ref: P&BA-Len pg. 808-9.

RICHARDSON, JOHN born ca. 1802, NY, moved to Ohio where he married LUCY (WRIGHT), daughter of Peter, born ca. 1822, NY. They moved to Ogden Twp., Lenawee Co., Mich., where he died in Feb. 1887, and she was still living in 1888. In the 1850 census of Ogden

Twp., they listed PETER, age 7; MARY F., age 1, both b. Mich.; and known daughter, RACHEL b. Lorain Co., Ohio (m. Martin Luther Robertson, also see). Ref: P&BA-Len pg. 1203-4. Note MARY F., following.

RICHARDSON, JONATHAN born ca. 1799, Delaware, and wife, PHEBE, born ca. 1800, Virginia, was listed in the 1850 census of Adrian Twp., Lenawee Co., Mich. with REBECCA, age 22; JONATHAN, age 20; HARRIET J., age 13, all b. Ohio, in their household.

RICHARDSON, JOSEPH born ca. 1800, England, was listed in the 1850 census of Tecumseh Twp., Lenawee Co., Mich. with REBECCA, age 23, b. England, both in the Spears household.

RICHARDSON, LUSANAH (See Obadiah Hamilton)

RICHARDSON, MARY, age 12, born NJ, was listed in the 1850 census of Madison Twp., Lenawee Co., Mich. in a Walker household.

RICHARDSON, MARY (See Levi Corey)

RICHARDSON, MARY F. born Lorain Co., Ohio, married in 1855 to George P. Robertson, also see, of Ogden Twp., Lenawee Co., Mich. Note: She may be sister of JOHN (preceding)?

RICHARDSON, SAMUEL was listed in the 1840 census index of Tecumseh Twp., Lenawee Co., Mich.

RICHARDSON, SILAS and wife, HANNAH (SNEDEKER), lived in Ontario Co., NY, where she died at age 49, and he was still living in 1888. A son, name not stated, served in the Civil War, and afterwards lived in Virginia, where he died in 1872; a known daughter MARY A. b. 20 Mar. 1835 (m. Stephen C. Lombard, also see). Ref: P&BA-Len pg. 1016-7.

RICHARDSON, STEPHEN P. (See Joshua P. Thurber)

RICHARDSON, WILLIAM, probably son of DAVID (preceding), born ca. 1822, Penn., and wife, SALLY A., born ca. 1832, NY, were listed in the 1850 census of Hudson Twp., Lenawee Co., Mich. with GEORGE H., age 2, b. Mich., in their household (next door to DAVID).

RICHARDSON, WILLIAM born ca. 1825, NY, was listed in the 1850 census of Medina Twp., Lenawee Co., Mich. in a Chase household (and probably he listed again in a Lucas household).

RICHART, ROBERT, son of WILLIAM (following), born ca. 1796, Montour Co., Penn., married MARY J. (BIDDLE), daughter of Israel (also see). They lived in Northumberland Co., Penn.; then in 1846 moved to Macon Twp., Lenawee Co., Mich. He died 21 May 1875, and she died 21 Oct. 1877, over age 75. In the 1850 census of Macon Twp., they listed the following in their household. 1. ISAAC b. ca. 1823; 2. WALTER b. ca. 1825; 3. MARY A. b. ca. 1829 (m. Thomas A. Liddel, also see); 4. WILLIAM b. ca. 1832. Ref: P&BA-Len pg. 745-6. In the 1850 census of Tecumseh Twp., is BIDDLE, age 25, b. NY, probably of this family, and probably also born Penn. Ref: P&BA-Len pg. 745-6.

RICHART, WILLIAM and wife, MARTHA (MOODY), of Montour Co., Penn. were parents of ROBERT (preceding). They supposedly remained in Montour Co. Ref: P&BA-Len pg. 745-6.

RICHMOND, ALONZO or ALVIN? born ca. 1814, and wife, SABRINA, born ca. 1820, both in NY, were listed in the 1850 census of Medina Twp., Lenawee Co., Mich. with MARY E., age 6; MONTFORD A., age 3, both b. Mich., in their household.

RICHMOND, ANDREW born ca. 1802, and wife, ELIZABETH, born ca. 1800, both in Ireland, were listed in the 1840 census index of Tecumseh Twp., Lenawee Co., Mich.; and in the 1850 census with JOHN, age 26; MATILDA, age 25, both b. Ireland; and ELISA ANN, age 18; ANDREW, age 16; WILLIAM, age 12; JAMES, age 9; ROBERT, age 7, all b. Mich., in their household.

RICHMOND, DAVID born ca. 1812, and wife, SALLY, born ca. 1810, both in NY, were listed in the 1850 census of Woodstock Twp., Lenawee Co., Mich. with WARREN?, age 18, HARRIET, age 10, both b. NY, in their household.

RICHMOND, LEVI C. born 11 Dec. 1809, Herkimer co., NY, moved when of age to Pontiac, Mich.; and 1 year later to Bridgewater, Washtenaw Co., Mich. (where he was listed in the 1840 census index). He married 2 Mar. 1837 to SARAH (WARNER), daughter of Samuel (also see). They later moved to Clinton Twp., Lenawee Co., Mich. where he died on 7 Jan. 1887, age 77; and she was still living there in 1888. Children: 1. MASON (m. Della Crawford, Jackson Co., Mich.); 2. JEROME (m. Ophelia Brocaw, Jackson Co., Mich.); 3. SAMUEL W. (to Arizona); 4. ELIZABETH (m. Lathram Miller; Chelsea, Mich.); 5. SARAH b. 7 Feb. 1852, Clinton Twp. (m. James Halladay, Jr., also see); 6. CHARLES (m. Ida Tompkins; Oregon); 7. WILLIAM (unmarried in 1888). Ref: P&BA-Len pg. 244 & 373.

RICHMOND, OTIS and wife, HARRIET (VAN BRUNT), from NY were early settlers of Manchester, Washtenaw Co., Mich. (probably he written "Otice" in the 1840 census index). Harriet was born in Lodi, Livingston Co. (Seneca Co.?), NY, and they married there. He died 23 Nov. 1867, and she died 23 Mar. 1873. Known daughter, JANE b. 29 June 1840, Manchester, Mich. (m. Arnold T. Graves, also see). Ref: P&BA-Len pg. 531-2. Note: Listed adjacent in the 1840 census index was LINCON; and also in Washtenaw Co. were "M;" BENJAMIN; & LEVI.

RICHMOND, P. F. (See James D. Manchester)

RICHMOND, WILLIAM H. born ca. 1804, and wife, ELCSY, born ca. 1807, both in Mass., were listed in the 1840 census index of Rollin Twp., Lenawee Co., Mich.; and in the 1850 census with DOLPHUS, age 17, b. NY; OSCAR F., age 15, b. Ohio; and JOHN, age 10, b. Mich., in their household.

RIDER also see RYDER

RIDER, ELIZABETH born ca. 1773, Ireland, was listed head of household in the 1850 census of Madison Twp., Lenawee Co., Mich. with Eliza Eccles, age 20; Mary A. Eccles, age 18, both b. Ireland; & Charles Eccles, age 16, b. NY, in her household.

RIDER, JOSEPH T. born ca. 1820, NY, and wife, JANE, born ca. 1826, Canada, were listed in the 1850 census of Franklin Twp., Lenawee Co., Mich. with no family in the household.

RIDER, JOSHUA born ca. 1790, Rhode Island, and wife, ABIGAIL, born ca. 1795, NY, were listed in the 1850 census of Rome Twp., Lenawee Co., Mich., next door to WILLIAM (following), and with JARED, age 18 (prob. he who m. Nancy Jeffery, dau. of James K., also see;

went to Ingham Co., Mich.); HANNAH, age 16; LAFAYETTE, age 12, all b. NY, in their household.

RIDER, WILLIAM, probably son of JOSHUA (preceding), born ca. 1817, and wife, MARSHA, born ca. 1816, both in NY, were listed in the 1850 census of Rome Twp., Lenawee Co., Mich. with CHARLES H., age 10; PERRY J., age 4, both b. Mich., in their household.

RIEHL, NICHOLAS and wife, AMELIA (MULLER), were natives of France, who moved to St. Louis, Missouri. Nicholas died in Carondelet, MO, but his wife came to Adrian, Lenawee Co., Mich. to live with known daughter, CAROLINE b. St. Louis (m. Charles Humphrey, also see). Ref: P&BA-Len pg. 470-1.

RILEY, DAVID A. born ca. 1812, and wife, CATHARINE, born ca. 1822, both in Ireland, were listed in the 1850 census of Tecumseh Twp., Lenawee Co., Mich. with WILLIAM, age 13; JOHN, age 5; DAVID, age 3, all b. Mich., in their household. Note: It may be this DAVID in the 1840 census index of Jackson, Jackson Co., Mich.

RILEY, ELIAS, age 30, born NY, was listed in the 1850 census of Blissfield Twp., Lenawee Co., Mich. in a Hall household.

RILEY, HARRIET (See James Livermore of Oneida Co., NY).

RILEY, PHILEMON born ca. 1818, and wife, MARIA, born ca. 1819, both in NY, were listed in the 1850 census of Cambridge Twp., Lenawee Co., Mich. with SARAH, age 8; LOVINA, age 6; ANDREW, age 2 (m. Melissa E. Onsted, dau. of Peter, also see).

RINEHART also see RHINEHART

RINEHART, CATHERINE married Frederick Wotring (also see); and note THOMAS[2] (following), possibly her father?

RINEHART, GEORGE, probably son of THOMAS[1] (following), born Allegany Co., MD. George had known daughter, MARGARET (m. George Loar, also see, before 1819, Allegany Co., MD). Ref: P&BA-Len pg. 912-3.

RINEHART, JACOB S., son of THOMAS[2] (following), born 21 Nov. 1831, Preston Co., W. Va., married there on 9 Apr. 1857 to DELILAH (WERNER), daughter of Casper (also see). In 1864, they removed to Ogden Twp., Lenawee Co., Mich. Children: 1. WILLIAM H. (d. age 8); 2. ALICE; 3. SAVILLA ANNIE; 4. THOMAS EDWARD; 5. ANDREW JOHNSON; 6. LEO PENCE; 7. EMMA LOUISE; 8. GEORGE LEWIS. Ref: P&BA-Len pg. 540-1.

RINEHART, THOMAS[1] was a Revolutionary soldier. (Note: It may be he with Maryland service, Rev. Pension Appl. #S5986.) He may have come from Germany to Virginia. He was a pioneer to Preston Co., W. Va. when it was part of Randolph Co., VA. Known son, THOMAS[2] (following). Also note GEORGE (preceding). Ref: P&BA-Len pg. 540-1.

RINEHART, THOMAS[2], son of THOMAS[1] (preceding), born in Preston Co., W. Va., moved to Allegheny Co., MD, where he married ANNA (BOHEN). They settled in Preston Co., where they remained until they joined their children in Ogden Twp., Lenawee Co., Mich. in 1864. Ten children, names not stated, except JACOB S. (preceding); and SUSANNA b. 11 Apr. 1824, Preston Co. (m. Nicholas Wotring, also see). Also note CATHERINE, preceding. Ref: P&BA-Len pg. 540-1; 734-5.

RIPLEY, JOHN and wife, ELIZABETH (ELLIOTT), lived in Schoharie Co., NY; and also in Macedon, Wayne Co., NY where he died at age 77, and she died at age 88. Children: 1. ANN S.; 2. MINERVA J. b. 2 Sept. 1824, Summit, Schoharie Co. (m. Maj. George T. Rice, also see); 3. RUTH A.; 4. PHILETUS; 5. THERON P. Ref: P&BA-Len pg. 663-4.

RIPLEY, MADISON born ca. 1828, NY, was listed in the 1850 census of Rollin Twp., Lenawee Co., Mich. in a Whitmore household.

RIPLEY, WHITMAN born ca. 1802, VT, and wife, THANKFUL, born ca. 1804, NY, were listed in the 1840 census index of Rome Twp., Lenawee Co., Mich.; and in the 1850 census with MARY A., age 17, b. NY; and LORIN H., age 12; ANTONETTE, age 9, both b. Mich., in their household.

RIPLEY, WILLIAM, age 25, born Conn., was listed in the 1850 census of Adrian Twp., Lenawee Co., Mich. in a hotel.

RISDON, HANNAH (See Wheeler Reed)
RISDON, MARGARET (See Wheeler Reed)

RISE, LIZZIE (See Charles W. Greeleaf)

RITCHEY, JOSEPH and wife, REBECCA (YOUNG) of Cambria Co., Penn., were parents of MELINDA (m. William Houghtby in 1849, Ogden Twp., Lenawee Co., Mich.). Ref: P&BA-Len pg. 1186-7.

RITER, MARY (See Augustus F. Daniels)

ROACH, FRANCES born 1818, Cumberland, England, and her family came first to Canada, and afterwards to Cortland Co., NY. They later moved to Ohio, and then about 1855 to Seneca Twp., Lenawee Co., Mich. Frances married in Canada to Jonathan G. Bell (also see). Ref: P&BA-Len pg. 976.

ROBB, BETSEY (See James F. Santee)

ROBB, DAVID born ca. 1797, NH, and wife, POLLY M., born ca. 1802, NY, were called "neighbors" of Henry F. Townsend in Dover Twp., Lenawee Co., Mich. in 1835, and are listed in the 1840 census index of Dover Twp. (adjacent to GARDNER, following); and in the 1850 census with MARVIN W., age 26; LEMAN D., age 23; WILLIAM T., age 20; MINERVA M., age 18, all b. NY; and Margaret Straneham, age 7, b. Mich., in their household.

ROBB, GARDNER born ca. 1800, NH, married CATHERINE (TERWILLIGER), probably daughter of James[3] (also see), and settled in Ontario, Wayne Co., NY. In 1832, they removed to Dover Twp., Lenawee Co., Mich., where they were listed adjacent to DAVID in the 1840 census index. They later moved to Clayton, where he died 12 May 1879, and she was living in 1888. Children (ages from 1850 census of Dover Twp.): 1. MARY S. ("SALLY," age 20 in census); 2. CAROLINE M. b. 11 Aug. 1830, Ontario, NY (m. Henry Nichols, also see); 3. JAMES W.; 4. CATHERINE A. (called "AMANDA," age 15 in census); 5. POLLY A., age 14, b. Mich.; 6. JULIA G. (written JOHN J., age 11, in census?); 7. JANE. Ref:

Pioneer Families of Southeastern Michigan

P&BA-Len pg. 232-3. Note: In the 1850 census of Hudson Twp., daughter, AMANDA C. was listed again in household of James Harvey Terwilliger, probably brother of Catherine.

ROBBINS, AMANDA, age 12, born Ohio, was listed in the 1850 census of Palmyra Twp., Lenawee Co., Mich. (spelled "Robin") in the Foote household.

ROBBINS, ELEANOR born 1818, NY, married in Ontario Co., NY ca. 1836 to Rufus H. Rathbun (also see), and moved to Lenawee Co., Mich. Ref: P&BA-Len pg. 802-3. Note THOMAS, following.

ROBBINS, GEORGE (See Bethuel Newcomb)

ROBBINS, JOHN (spelled "Robins") born ca. 1822, VT, and wife, JANE A., born ca. 1830, NY, were listed in the 1850 census of Rollin Twp., Lenawee Co., Mich.

ROBBINS, LUCINDA born 31 May 1806, Shaftsbury, VT, married Joseph S. Allen (also see). Ref: P&BA-Len pg. 1198-1200.

ROBBINS, MINERVA, age 14, born NY, was listed in the 1850 census of Raisin Twp., Lenawee Co., Mich. in a Place household.

ROBBINS, RICHARD B. Col. born 27 Apr. 1832, NJ, left home at age 16 and went alone to Ohio. He moved to Palmyra Twp., Lenawee Co., Mich. in 1854; served in the Civil War where he obtained his rank. No marriage mentioned. Ref: P&BA-Len pg. 400-1.

ROBBINS, THOMAS born ca. 1791, and wife, ELEANOR, born ca. 1794, both in NY, were listed in the 1840 census index of Madison Twp., Lenawee Co., Mich.; and in the 1850 census with WILLIAM, age 24; TUNIS, age 19, both b. NY; and Peter Reasoner, age 28, and wife, Catharine, age 22, b. NY (daughter of THOMAS?), & George W. Reasoner, age 1/12, in their household. Note ELEANOR, preceding.

ROBERTS, ABEL C., age 20, born NY, was listed in the 1850 census of Madison Twp., Lenawee Co., Mich., a "student" in the household of Dr. Cadman.

ROBERTS, CATHARINE, age 22, born NY, was listed in the 1850 census of Madison Twp., Lenawee Co., Mich. in a Jones household.

ROBERTS, CHESTER J. born ca. 1805, and wife, EMILY, born ca. 1815, both in NY, were listed in the 1850 census of Madison Twp., Lenawee Co., Mich. with IRA?/IVES?, age 10; WINFIELD, age 8; GAINES, age 7; W---(male), age 5; WAYNE, age 3 (note following); EMILY, age 1, all b. Mich., in their household. Note: There was a "C. J." listed in the 1840 census index of Browns Twp., Wayne Co., Mich.

ROBERTS, CLARINDA born 1808, NY (See Richard B. Gillespie[3]).

ROBERTS, DAVID and wife, LYDIA, moved from VT to Quebec, Canada after 1789. Known daughter, LYDIA b. 3 May 1789, Vermont (m. David Smith, Sr., also see, on 6 Nov. 1807, Quebec). Ref: P&BA-Len pg. 994-5.

ROBERTS, EDWARD, son of JOHN (following), born 1831, England, came to the US with his parents in 1838. He married first to BETSEY (HOWARD), daughter of Almon (also see). She died 11 Mar. 1864, Dover Twp. Children: 1. ALMON (m. Eliza McKnight, Dover Twp.); 2. BETSEY (m. Willard Bristol, Seneca Twp.) Edward married again to MARTHA (HOWARD), sister of Betsey. She died 16 June 1875, Dover Twp. Children: 3. PETER; 4. MARTHA; 5. EARL. Ref: P&BA-Len pg. 614-5.

ROBERTS, ENOCH was listed in the 1840 census index of Clinton Twp., Lenawee Co., Mich.

ROBERTS, ESTHER Mrs. was the daughter of Jeremiah Brown (also see).

ROBERTS, HATTIE E. (See Richard H. Osborn; also note HARRIET in household of WILLIAM, following.)

ROBERTS, HIRAM M. born ca. 1810, NY, and wife, JANE, born ca. 1820, Mich., were listed in the 1850 census of Palmyra Twp., Lenawee Co., Mich. with WILLIAM, age 3; ELINA, age 2, both b. Mich; and Mary E. Knight, age 7, b. Mich.; and Margaret A. Close, age 20, b. Mich., in their household.

ROBERTS, JOHN born ca. 1797, and wife, MARTHA (WILLIAMS), born ca. 1793, both in Wales, came to the US in 1838. They settled in Dover Twp., Lenawee Co., Mich. by 1840. They were listed in the 1850 census with all of the following born England: 1. PETER b. ca. 1827; 2. JOHN b. ca. 1828; 3. WILLIAM b. ca. 1830; 4. EDWARD (preceding); 5. LAURY b. ca. 1842. Ref: P&BA-Len pg. 614-5.

ROBERTS, LUCY I., age 28, born Mass., was listed in the 1850 census of Madison Twp., Lenawee Co., Mich. in the household of Daniel R. Lyon and wife, Lovina (age 34, b. Mass.) sister?

ROBERTS, MARTHA, age 22, and AMELIA, age 16, both b. Mich., were listed in the 1850 census of Franklin Twp., Lenawee Co., Mich. in a Wimple household.

ROBERTS, MARY (See Rufus Adams)

ROBERTS, MARY Mrs. of Riga Twp., Lenawee Co., Mich. was daughter of Nathan Vickery (also see).

ROBERTS, METILRIA (MATILDA?) born ca. 1808, NY, was listed head of household in the 1850 census of Dover Twp., Lenawee Co., Mich. with PHILIP, age 24; STEPHEN, age 23; ABEL, age 20; IRA, age 18; LUCINDA, age 16; MARY, age 12; PHEBE, age 11; DANIEL, age 10; JONATHAN, age 9, all b. NY; and WILLIAM, age 8; ELIZA, age 6; CHLOE, age 2, all b. Mich., in their household.

ROBERTS, MYRON H. born ca. 1821, and wife, POLLY A., born ca. 1825, both in NY, were listed in the 1850 census of Adrian Twp., Lenawee Co., Mich. with LUTHER, age 4, b. Mich., in their household.

ROBERTS, PHILIP born 4 Mar. 1768, Putnam Co., NY, moved with his parents ca. 1777 to Chatham, Columbia Co., NY. He married in Stephentown, Rensselaer Co., NY on 26 Nov. 1794 to PHEBE (MOON), and they settled first in Columbia Co., NY. They moved to Rome Twp., Lenawee Co., Mich. where he died 1 Nov. 1855. Known daughters: LUCY A. b. ca. 1821 (m. Silas Aldrich, also see); CHARITY b. 2 Jan. 1816 (m. Silas Aldrich, as second wife). Ref: P&BA-Len pg. 1092-3.

ROBERTS, WAYNE (See Thomas S. Weter; and note WAYNE in household of CHESTER J., preceding.)

ROBERTS, WILLIAM born ca. 1815, and wife, CAROLINE, born ca. 1823, both in NY, were listed in the 1850 census of Medina Twp., Lenawee Co., Mich. with ELLEN L., age 8, b. NY; and HARRIET, age 4, b. Mich. (note HATTIE E., preceding), in their household.

ROBERTS, ZENUS and wife, ELIZABETH (DANIELS), were natives of Mass., who died in Tioga Co., Penn. They had 4 sons and 4 daughters, names not stated, except

#7. POLLY A. b. 7 Mar. 1821, Berkshire co., Mass. (m. Jesse B. Odell, also see). Ref: P&BA-Len pg. 601.

ROBERTSON, AGNES was listed in the 1840 census index of Tecumseh Twp., Lenawee Co., Mich. Note JOHN C. adjacent in the 1840 census.

ROBERTSON, ALPHEUS J., son of JAMES (following), born 28 Jan. 1837, Preston Co., W. Va., moved to Ohio, then Ogden Twp., Lenawee Co., Mich. with his parents. He married there on 6 May 1866 to JULIA (WILCOX), daughter of A. P. (also see). Children: 1. EUGENE HERBERT; 2. ALONZO EDSON. Ref: P&BA-Len pg. 591-2.

ROBERTSON, ASHBEL born ca. 1801, and wife, NANCY, born ca. 1814, both in New Jersey, were listed in the 1840 census index of Macon Twp., Lenawee Co., Mich.; and in the 1850 census with CORNELIA, age 15; PHOEBE, age 15; EDWIN, age 12; SELINDA?, age 10; SOPHIA, age 9; MARY, age 4; JOHN C., age 2, all b. Mich., in their household.

ROBERTSON, CALVIN moved from New York City to Steuben Co., NY at an early date. Known daughter, SALLY b. ca. 1794, New York City (m. Jonathan Gray, also see). Ref: P&BA-Len pg. 950-1.

ROBERTSON, CALVIN born ca. 1818, NY, and wife, FRANCES, born ca. 1827, England, were listed in the 1850 census of Tecumseh Twp., Lenawee Co., Mich. with brother?, SAMUEL R., age 34, b. NY; and Maria Ferguson, age 8, born England, possibly a stepchild, in their household.

ROBERTSON, GEORGE P., son of JAMES (following), born 15 Mar. 1835, Preston Co., W. Va., moved with his parents to Ohio then to Ogden Twp., Lenawee Co., Mich. He married there in June 1855 to MARY F. (RICHARDSON), born Ohio. They farmed in Ogden Twp., but also had a home in Blissfield, Mich. Children: 1. PERLEY E. (m. William E. Scribner MD, also see); 2. ALICE; 3. CORA; 4. LESTER B. Ref: P&BA-Len pg. 667-8; 730.

ROBERTSON, ISAIAH W., son of JAMES (following), born 11 Apr. 1842, Preston Co., W. VA., moved with his parents to Ohio, and

Ogden Twp., Lenawee Co., Mich. He served in Co. B, 18th Mich. Inf., Civil War. He married on 17 Mar. 1867 to AMANDA (PACKARD), daughter of Nathaniel (also see). Son, JOSEPH NATHANIEL b. 13 Dec. 1867. Ref: P&BA-Len pg. 870-1.

ROBERTSON, JAMES, son of GEORGE P., born Berkley Co., VA, married there to ELIZABETH (HERKERT), daughter of Peter (also see). They lived first in Preston Co., W. Va., then moved about 1844 to Wayne Co., Ohio; and then Medina Co., Ohio. In 1854, they settled in Ogden Twp., Lenawee Co., Mich. About 1881, they moved to Anthony, Florida. Known children: 1. GEORGE P. (preceding); 2. ALPHEUS J. (preceding); 3. MARTIN LUTHER (following); 4. SARAH b. 3 May 1851, Medina Co., O. (m. George W. Wilt, also see); 5. CAROLINE b. Medina Co., O. (m. Nicholas Valentine Hile). Ref: P&BA-Len pg. 591-2; 667-8; 730; 870-1; 1092; 1151-2; 1203-4.

ROBERTSON, JOHN C. was listed in the 1840 census index of Tecumseh Twp., Lenawee Co., Mich. adjacent to AGNES, preceding.

ROBERTSON, MARTIN LUTHER, son of JAMES (preceding), born 15 Mar. 1840, Preston Co., W. Va., moved with parents to Ohio and Ogden Twp., Lenawee Co., Mich. He married RACHEL (RICHARDSON), daughter of John (also see). Children: 1. GEORGE MANFRED; 2. JOHN HIRAM. Ref: P&BA-Len pg. 1203-4.

ROBERTSON, NATHAN C. was listed in the 1840 census index of Franklin Twp., Lenawee Co., Mich.

ROBERTSON, PHOEBE (See Robert Wilson)

ROBERTSON, SAMUEL R. (See CALVIN, preceding).

ROBINSON, BARTLETT born 25 Jan. 1776, Mass., married ? (name not stated) born 25 Sept. 1781. They moved to Palmyra, NY where he died 25 Jan. 1851, and she died 18 Sept. 1853. Known son, WALTER (following). Ref: P&BA-Len pg. 432-3.

ROBINSON, CHARLES, age 10; JOHN H., age 8; NANCY, age 5; CAROLINE, age 1, all born Mich., probably siblings, were listed in the 1850 census of Hudson twp., Lenawee Co., Mich., possibly stepchildren in the household of William H. Cogswell, and wife, Margaret, age 34, b. NJ.

ROBINSON, ELIZABETH "BETSEY" (See Nehemiah Hand)

ROBINSON, GAIN Dr. born Mass., and wife, CHLOE (BRADISH) born 1 Apr. 1775, Hardwick, Mass., removed to Palmyra, Wayne Co., NY. He died there in 1828, age 63; and Chloe afterwards went to Northampton, Mass. where she died at the home of a daughter at age 93. There were 10 children, names not stated, except: ABIGAIL B. (m. Alexander Tiffany, also see, on 3 Sept. 1823); #7. ROLLIN (following). Ref: P&BA-Len pg. 1103-4.

ROBINSON, H. P. (See Rev. Paul Shepherd)

ROBINSON, HARRIET (See Norman C. Baker)

ROBINSON, HARRIET A. (WHITE) - See Rev. William White; and John M. Osborn.

ROBINSON, ISABELLA married first to ? Francisca; and married again after 1860 to Adam Mott (also see) in Canton, Wayne Co., Mich.

ROBINSON, JAMES born ca. 1810, and wife, MARY, born ca. 1810, both in NY, were listed in the 1850 census of Tecumseh Twp., Lenawee Co., Mich. with NELSON, age 20; LAVINA, age 13; LOUISA, age 10, all b. NY; and SARAH ANN, age 9, b. Ohio, in their household.

ROBINSON, JOHN born 13 Aug. 1787, London, England, married MARY (METCALF), daughter of John (also see). They moved to Quebec, Canada, and had known daughter, HANNAH b. 28 June 1818, Quebec (m. Bethuel Newcomb, also see, at Stanstead, Canada). Ref: P&BA-Len pg. 1198-1200.

ROBINSON, JOSEPH born ca. 1816, NY, and wife, NANCY, born ca. 1817, Penn., were listed in the 1850 census of Hudson Twp., Lenawee Co., Mich. with ELIZABETH, age 10, b. Penn.; and MARY E., age 6; AUGUSTUS, age 4; JOSEPH R., age 6/12, all b. Mich., in their household.

ROBINSON, JOSHUA born ca. 1819, and wife, ELIZABETH, born ca. 1823, both in NY, were listed in the 1850 census of Franklin Twp., Lenawee Co., Mich. with THERETSA?, age 6, b. NY; FRANCES, age 5; HUDSON, age 2, both b. Mich., in their household.

ROBINSON, LUCIUS G., age 22, born NY, was listed in the 1850 census of Palmyra Twp., Lenawee Co., Mich. in a Pomeroy household.

Pioneer Families of Southeastern Michigan

ROBINSON, PHILIP was listed in the 1840 census index of Macon Twp., Lenawee Co., Mich.

ROBINSON, RICHARD born ca. 1810, Yorkshire, England, came to the US in 1834, and settled first in Ogden, NY. In 1835, he removed to Springville, Mich.; and shortly afterwards to Rome Twp., Lenawee Co., Mich. He married SUSANNA (SMITH), daughter of Joseph (also see). He died 30 May 1869; and she was living in Rome Twp. in 1888. Children: 1. AGNES MATILDA b. 1 May 1841 (m. Charles E. Potter; she d. 10 July 1885, Rollin Twp.); 2. WILLIAM H. b. 17 Oct. 1842 (m. Caroline Baker, Rollin Twp.); 3. RICHARD A. JR. b. 9 July 1844 (served 11th Mich. Cav.; d. 21 Jan. 1865, Civil War); 4. SUSANNAH E. b. 25 Dec. 1850 (d. 8 Aug. 1852); 5. JOSEPH B. (m. Nellie Kane, daughter of Wilson H., also see, Woodstock Twp.); 6. DORA B. b. 5 Aug. 1860. Ref: P&BA-Len pg. 1142-5.

ROBINSON, ROLLIN, son of Dr. GAIN (preceding), born 3 June 1810, Wayne Co., NY, came in 1832 to Palmyra Twp., Lenawee Co., Mich. to purchase land, but did not remain. He married on 12 Feb. 1835 to CELESTIA ANN (CORBETT), daughter of Ziba (also see) in Palmyra Twp. They returned to NY until 1843, then moved to Adrian, Lenawee Co. About 1848, they went to Buffalo, NY, and returned about 1854. Celestia died 17 May 1885, Palmyra Twp. Known daughter, MARGARET (d. age 5, Adrian). Ref: P&BA-Len pg. 1103-4.

ROBINSON, SAMUEL born ca. 1820, NY, and wife, HARRIET, born ca. 1825, Mich., were listed in the 1850 census of Tecumseh Twp., Lenawee Co., Mich. with CHARLES, age 1, b. Mich., all in the household of Asahel Taylor.

ROBINSON, SAPHRONIA (See George W. Spencer)

ROBINSON, WALTER, son of BARTLETT (preceding), born 17 Dec. 1818, Wayne Co., NY, married there to ELIZABETH O. (JOHNSTON), daughter of Robert (also see). Elizabeth died 30 July 1856, Adrian, Lenawee Co., Mich. Children: (4 died infancy, names not stated) 1. ANN B. b. 20 May 1851 (m. Javilla Chaffee); 2. WALTER B. b. 2 Dec. 1853 (Geneva, NY); 3. EBER J. b. 4 May 1856 (m. Adella Chaffee). Walter Sr. married again to CHARLOTTE D. (JOHNSTON), sister of Elizabeth. Children: 4. CHARLOTTE E. b. 6 Apr. 1858; 5. LUCIUS O. b. 18 May 1860; 6. WILLIAM L. b. 12 Mar. 1862 (to Calif.); 7. META K. b. 28 May 1864; 8. MABEL b. 23 June 1866 (d. 22 Aug. 1886); 9. HATTIE L. b. 2 Aug. 1868; 10. LESTER F. b. 16 Sept. 1870; 11. CLARA L. b. 22 Aug. 1872; 12. LUTHER B. b. 2 Feb. 1875; 13. CULLEN M. b. 9 Nov. 1877. Ref: P&BA-Len pg. 432-3.

ROBISON, JANET (See Thomas Liddel)
ROBISON, LUVINIA (See James Cummins)

ROCKAFELLER, TEAL probably from Columbia Co., NY came to Riga Twp., Lenawee Co., Mich. Known daughter, ELIZABETH b. Columbia Co., NY (m. John Dings, also see). Ref: P&BA-Len pg. 266-7.

ROCKWELL, HIRAM and wife, MARGARET (PARKS), lived in Chautauqua Co., NY ca. 1830. They moved to Michigan and he died in Farmington, Mich.; and she was living in Minnesota in 1888. Seven children, names not stated, except: MARY A. b. ca. 1832, Chautauqua Co., NY (m. Alfred Belcher, also see, ca. 1850, Rollin Twp., Lenawee Co., Mich.) Ref: P&BA-Len pg. 969-70.

ROCKWELL, JABEZ moved from Danbury, Conn. to Milford, Pike Co., Penn. He had known daughter, DIANTHA b. ca. 1792, Danbury (m. Cyrus Stearns, also see).

ROCKWELL, NATHANIEL born ca. 1800, NY, was listed in the 1850 census of Cambridge Twp., Lenawee Co., Mich., with probably wife?, IRENA, age 28, b. NY; MAHALA, age 13; JEROME?, AGE 11; jane, AGE 10; MALISSA, age 9; MARGARETTE, age 7; LYDIA, age 4, all b. NY; and MATTHEW, age 1, b. Mich., in their household.

ROCKWELL, SETH was listed in the 1840 census index of Franklin Twp., Lenawee Co., Mich.

ROCKWOOD, CHARLOTTE (See Anson Howell)
ROCKWOOD, JOSEPH born ca. 1794, Mass., and wife, AMY, born ca. 1800, NY, were listed in the 1850 census of Rome Twp., Lenawee Co., Mich. with WILLIAM H., age 19, b. NY; and Cynthia A. Johnson, age 18, b. NY, in their household.

RODGERS see ROGERS

RODNEY, LAMIRA Mrs. was the daughter of Obediah Gore Spalding (also see).

ROE also see ROWE

ROE, ALVIRA, age 18, born Mich., was listed in the 1850 census of Madison Twp., Lenawee Co., Mich. in a Cadman household.

ROE, ELISHA born ca. 1795, NY, was listed in the 1850 census of Palmyra Twp., Lenawee Co., Mich. with no family in his household.

ROE, JAMES, age 34, born NY, was listed in the 1850 census of Hudson Twp., Lenawee Co., Mich. in a Purchase household.

ROE, NATHAN born ca. 1768, died 5 Dec. 1840, age 72; and his wife, ELIZABETH, born ca. 1771, died 11 Aug. 1847, age 76. They are buried in the cemetery "at the corner of Sterns Rd. and Lewis Ave., about 2 miles from the Ohio line" (which is on the border of Monroe & Lenawee Cos., Mich. There is a NATHAN, SR. & NATHAN, JR. listed in the 1840 census index of Erie Twp., Monroe Co., Mich., and listed adjacent were ANTOIN; I. P.; JEAN B.; JOSEPH; & MARY. In the cemetery records, it was written "Rowe," but the census was "Roe."

ROE, SILVIA, age 20, born NY, was listed in the 1850 census of Blissfield Twp., Lenawee Co., Mich. in a Watson household.

ROGERS, ALBERT born ca. 1809, Conn., and wife, HELEN, born ca. 1805, Ireland, were listed in the 1840 census index of Tecumseh Twp., Lenawee Co., Mich.; and in the 1850 census of Madison Twp. with JEREMIAH, age 12; SARAH, age 7, both b. Mich., in their household. Note WILLIAM in Tecumseh Twp., following.

ROGERS, ANGELINE (See James Whitney)
ROGERS, ANSEL born ca. 1812, Mass., was listed in the 1850 census of Rollin Twp., Lenawee Co., Mich. with SILAS, age 17; NATHAN, age 14; DANIEL T., age 9; ALONZO, age 6; SARAH L., age 10/12, all b. Mich., and Mary E. Brown, age 19, b. Mich., in his household.

ROGERS, BENJAMIN born ca. 1804, Mass., and wife, ELIZA, born ca. 1818, NH, were listed in the 1840 census index of Medina Twp., Lenawee Co., Mich. (adjacent to CALVIN S., & JAMES, both following); and in the 1850 census with BENJAMIN F., age 20; BETSEY H., age 18; ELLEN M., age 16; JOHN M., age 13, all b. Mass.; and LUCY, age 12; ABNER, age 10; AMORET, age 8; JULIA E., age 6; EMMA, age 3, all b. Mich., in their household.

ROGERS, CALVIN S. born ca. 1814, Mass., and wife, HARRIET, born ca. 1820, Canada, were listed in the 1840 census index of Medina Twp., Lenawee Co., Mich. adjacent to BENJAMIN, preceding, & JAMES, following; and in the 1850 census with CALVIN A., age 9; WILLIAM F., age 7; GEORGE W., age 5, all b. Mich.; and HARRIET M., age 2, b. Ohio, in their household.

ROGERS, CAREY born ca. 1805, and wife, RHODA, born ca. 1809, both in NY, were listed in the 1840 census index of Adrian Twp., Lenawee Co., Mich.; and in the 1850 census with SYLVESTER, age 21, b. NY; and ARVILLA, age 18; JOSEPH H., age 11; CYNTHIA, age 8, all b. Mich., in their household.

ROGERS, CLARK was born NY and it may be he listed in the 1800 census index of Rensselaer Co., NY. He had a wife, REBECCA (BABCOCK) who was mother of son, IRA (following); and by 1816, had a wife, WATY (NILES) who was mother of son, WILLIAM L. (following); & probably JOHN (to Elkhart, Ind.). There were 8 children, but only mentioned were preceding. Clark lived in Onondaga and Cayuga Cos., NY, and was said to have died in NY. Ref: P&BA-Len pg. 595-6. Note: There was a CLARK listed in the 1840 census index of Pittsfield Twp., Washtenaw Co., Mich.; also note JACOB, following.

ROGERS, COMFORT born ca. 1810, and wife, ANN, born ca. 1810, both in NY, were listed in the 1850 census of Palmyra Twp., Lenawee Co., Mich. with JOHN K., age 12, b. Ohio; and ALBRO C., age 9; BYRON, age 6; JULIA, age 3; COMFORT, age 1, all b. Mich., in their household.

ROGERS, DWIGHT born ca. 1818, Mass., and wife, BETSEY, born ca. 1821, NY, were listed in the 1850 census of Palmyra Twp., Lenawee Co., Mich. with JESSE? A., age 4; MILLARD F., age 1, both b. Mich., in their household.

ROGERS, ERMINA born ca. 1828, NY, was listed in the 1850 census of Fairfield Twp., Lenawee Co., Mich. in an Andrews household.

ROGERS, HANNAH (See Lewis Cole)

ROGERS, HANNAH Mrs. (See Oramon Tuttle, Jr.)

ROGERS, IRA, son of CLARK (preceding), born ca. 1800/4, Onondaga Co., NY, married first to NANCY (TOMER). They resided in Pultney, Steuben Co., NY by 1831; and in 1837 moved to Cambridge Twp., Lenawee Co., Mich. Nancy died in 1847, age 39, leaving children: 1. REBECCA; 2. ROBERT L. (following); 3. ADELSA (this may be "NANCY," age 15, in household in 1850 census); 4. WILLIAM C. b. ca. 1835 (twin of Nancy?); 5. JOHN A. b. ca. 1838, Mich. (served Co. K, 12th Tenn. Artly, killed 14 June 1864); 6. WESLEY b. ca. 1840; 7. EMILY b. ca. 1845; 8. JOEL b. ca. 1847. Ira married again by 1850 to Nancy's sister, Mrs. CLARISSA (TOMER) RUSS, born ca. 1801, NJ, widow of Nathaniel (also see). She died 14 July 1866. He married last to Mrs. DELILAH (GULLICK) HATHAWAY, and they moved to Rome Twp. in 1869. He died 23 Oct. 1886, and Delilah survived him. Ref: P&BA-Len pg. 1177-8.

ROGERS, J. E. was listed in the 1840 census index of Adrian Twp., Lenawee Co., Mich. Note JABEZ, following.

ROGERS, JABEZ born ca. 1805, NJ, and wife, SARAH, born ca. 1840, Penn., were listed in the 1850 census of Adrian Twp., Lenawee Co., Mich. with no family in the household.

ROGERS, JACOB born NY, and wife, SUSANNA (BROWN), born Mass., married in NY, and moved to Elk Creek Twp., Erie Co., Penn. He died there 19 Mar. 1856, age 69, and she died 19 Feb. 1876, age 83. Children: 1. NATHAN C. (m. Sylvia Davis, Albion, Erie Co., Penn.); 2. LUCY (d. infancy); 3. IRA (deceased by 1888); 4. REUBEN (m. Polly Spaulding, Venago Co., Penn.); 5. SUSAN b. 1 Sept. 1833, Erie Co., Penn. (m. ROBERT L., following). Ref: P&BA-Len pg. 1177-8. Note: JACOB possibly another son of CLARK? (preceding).

ROGERS, JAMES born in Ashfield, Mass., married 1837 in Mass. to LUCY (COTRELL) born Worthington, Mass., and they afterwards moved to Medina Twp., Lenawee Co., Mich. In the 1840 census index they were adjacent to BENJAMIN & CALVIN S., both preceding. They moved to Williams Co., Ohio where he died in 1846; and she was still living in 1888, age 68. Known daughter, LUCY (m. Oren E. Green, also see, 1859). Ref: P&BA-Len pg. 914-5.

ROGERS, JAMES H., son of JAMES L. (following), born 20 Dec. 1825, Saratoga Co., NY, moved with his parents to Woodstock Twp., Lenawee Co., Mich. He married on 2 Apr. 1865 to MARIETTA (WILSON), daughter of John (also see). Children: 1. KATE N. b. 14 Nov. 1866 (d. age 17); 2. JOHN W. b. 12 Oct. 1868; 3. EUGENE C. b. 30 Sept. 1871. Ref: P&BA-Len pg. 677-8.

ROGERS, JAMES L., son of JOHN (following), born 1790, Saratoga Co., NY, married on 25 Jan. 1818 to CHARILLA (CURTIS). They moved to St. Joseph, Mich. in 1845; and then to Woodstock Twp., Lenawee Co., Mich. (after 1850?). He died 7 Feb. 1882, age 92; and she died Mar. 1887, age 90. Large family, names not stated, except JOHN C. (following); JAMES H. (preceding). Ref: P&BA-Len pg. 647-8; 677-8.

ROGERS, JEMIMA married in 1838 to Andrew Taylor (also see), Rome Twp., Lenawee Co., Mich. Ref: P&BA-Len pg. 943.

ROGERS, JOHN, son of WILLIAM, lived out his life in Saratoga Co., NY, where he died at age 76. His wife, name not stated, who was older, had died previously at age 80. Eight daughters and 4 sons, names not stated, except JAMES L. b. 1790 (preceding). Ref: P&BA-Len pg. 647-8; 677-8.

ROGERS, JOHN C., son of JAMES L. (preceding), born 4 June 1833, Saratoga Co., NY, moved with his parents to Mich. He married on 22 Sept. 1859, Woodstock Twp., Lenawee Co., Mich. to FRANCES (FARNSWORTH), daughter of Charles (also see). Children: 1. NETTIE M. b. 22 July 1862 (m. Chester Binns, also see); 2. FLORENCE E. b. 28 Aug. 1864 (m. Albert Lombard, son of Stephen C., also see); 3. JOHN ARTHUR b. 4 July 1853 (d. 5 Aug. 1884). Ref: P&BA-Len pg. 647-8.

ROGERS, JOSEPH Dr. born ca. 1823, Mass., was listed in the 1850 census of Seneca Twp., Lenawee Co., Mich.

ROGERS, JOSEPHINE O. (See Charles C. Wakefield)

Pioneer Families of Southeastern Michigan

ROGERS, LUCINDA, age 20, born NY, was listed in the 1850 census of Madison Twp., Lenawee Co., Mich. in a Clark household.

ROGERS, MARTIN C. Dr. born ca. 1809, and wife, POLLY, born ca. 1807, both in Vermont, were listed in the 1850 census of Hudson Twp., Lenawee Co., Mich. with LUCY, age 15; FIDELIA, age 12; ELIZABETH, age 9, all b. VT; NANCY, age 7, b. Ohio; and ELIZA, age 5; ALMA J., age 1, both b. Mich., in their household.

ROGERS, MARY was born Waterford, Conn. and married Paul Beebe (also see). Mary was a lineal descendant of John Rogers who was burned at the stake in England during religious persecution. Her ancestors came to New England early in the 17th century. Ref: P&BA-Len pg. 922-4.

ROGERS, MARY A. (See Joseph Hitchings)

ROGERS, OBADIAH born ca. 1792, and wife, LYDIA, born ca. 1795, both in Mass., were listed in the 1840 census index of Raisin Twp., Lenawee Co., Mich.; and in the 1850 census with AZUBAH C., age 29; JOHN F., age 21; SAMUEL R., age 19, all b. Mass.; and OBADIAH, JR., age 16; LYDIA, age 13, both b. Mich., in their household.

ROGERS, RODA (RHODA?) was listed in the 1840 census index of Blissfield Twp., Lenawee Co., Mich.

ROGERS, ROBERT L., son of IRA (preceding), born 3 Feb. 1831 Pultney, Steuben Co., NY, came to Cambridge Twp., Lenawee Co., Mich. with his parents in 1837. He married on 28 Sept. 1853, Erie Co., Penn., to SUSAN (ROGERS), daughter of JACOB (preceding). They lived in Marshall Co., Iowa in 1856 & 1857. They returned to Cambridge Twp., Lenawee Co. Children: 1. MARY F. (m. Joseph H. Smith, also see); 2. J. IRA (m. Carrie E. Lee; had twins, Lelia Fay & Leda May); 3. BURT E. (m. Cora Van Sickles, Cambridge Twp.); 4. WINNIE I. (m. Herberts S. Werring, Tecumseh Twp.); 5 CECIL E. Ref: P&BA-Len pg. 1177-8.

ROGERS, SAMUEL was listed in the 1840 census index of Palmyra Twp., Lenawee Co., Mich.

ROGERS, THOMAS was listed in the 1840 census index of Blissfield Twp., Lenawee Co., Mich.

ROGERS, WILLIAM came from Ireland to Saratoga Co., NY in Colonial times and remained there. Known son, JOHN (preceding). Ref: P&BA-Len pg. 677-8.

ROGERS, WILLIAM born ca. 1799, and wife, MARINDA, born ca. 1812, both in NY, were listed in the 1850 census of Madison Twp., Lenawee Co., Mich. with LEVI M., age 16; SARAH J., age 15; WILLIAM H., age 13; NATHAN M., age 10; CHARLES E., age 8; ALONZO M., age 6, all b. NY; and MARY E., age 4, b. Mich., in their household.

ROGERS, WILLIAM born ca. 1824, NY, and wife, MARY ANN, born ca. 1827, NY, were listed in the 1850 census of Tecumseh Twp., Lenawee Co., Mich. with PHOEBE (mother?), age 53, born Conn., in their household. Also note ALBERT, preceding.

ROGERS, WILLIAM L., son of CLARK (preceding), born 2 May 1816, Cayuga Co., NY, moved to Rome Twp., Lenawee Co., Mich. in 1839. He married in 1840 to SUSAN (SCOTT), daughter of Cornelius (also see), and settled in Adrian Twp. She died there in 1871. Children: 1. JEANNETTE b. ca. 1841 (d. 1864); 2. LAURETTE b. ca. 1843 (m. John Anderson; Ohio); 3. CLARK b. ca. 1846; 4. LOUIS C. b. ca. 1848 (to NY state); 5. PEARLEY E. b. ca. 1849 (m. W. Chambers); 6. HATTIE (m. Charles Chambers); 7. NILES; 8. BELL (m. John Hawley). William L. married again to SALLIE (DICKSON), daughter of Isaac (also see); and she died in Adrian Twp. in 1881, age about 50. Ref: P&BA-Len pg. 595-6.

ROHRBACK, GEORGE, son of HENRY & MARTHA (both remained in Germany), was born 25 Oct. 1823, Germany, and came to the US in 1853, settling first in Texas. He married ELIZABETH (KLINE), also born Germany. About 1854, they removed to Ohio; and in 1860 to Ogden Twp., Lenawee Co., Mich. He served in Co. F., 67th Ohio Inf, during Civil War, and suffered a crippled arm from wounds received. Children: 1. LABERES; 2. GEORGE; 3. ANNIE; 4. MARTHA. Ref: P&BA-Len pg. 1185-6.

ROHRBACK, HENRY (See Justus Iffland)

ROLAND, JANE E. (See Albert G. Burton)

ROLF, LIZZIE (See George H. Lockwood)

ROLLIN, ? (See Merchant Brooks)

ROOD, ELINDA was listed in the 1840 census index of Adrian Twp., Lenawee Co., Mich.; and it is probably she listed as "ELEDICY," age 59, born VT, head of household in the 1850 cnesus with MARY E., age 19, b. NY, in her household.

ROOD, LANSING born ca. 1807, and wife, RUBY?, born ca. 1812, both in NY, were listed in the 1850 census of Madison Twp., Lenawee Co., Mich. with ALMOND, age 14; RICHMOND, age 12; RALPH, age 10; ASHER, age 7, all b. NY; and ALBERT, age 1, b. Mich., in their household.

ROOD, ORANGE M. born ca. 1814, NY, and wife, LOVICA (HART), daughter of Joseph (also see), were listed in the 1840 census index of Adrian Twp., Lenawee Co., Mich.; and in the 1850 census of Madison Twp. with JANE H., age 12, b. Mich.; and MARY E., age 18, b. NY, and Samuel E. Hart (also see), age 28, b. NY, in their household.

ROOKER, THEODOCIA (See Osmyn Salsbury)

ROOSA was also known as ROSE

ROOSA, CALEB born ca. 1811, NY, and wife, SALLY M., born ca. 1816, VT, were listed in the 1850 census of Medina Twp., Lenawee Co., Mich. with JOHN J., age 16; MARY A., age 13, both b. NY; and DELIA, age 11; SOLOMON, age 8, both b. Ohio. SIMON, following, was next door in the census.

ROOSA, JOSHUA (written "Rosa") born ca. 1808, and wife, ELLEN, born ca. 1805, both in NY, were listed in the 1850 census of Medina Twp., Lenawee Co., Mich. with JACOB, age 18; ISAAC, age 17; ELIZA A., age 16; MARGARET, age 15; HIRAM, age 13; MOSES, age 11, all b. NY; and JOSHUA, age 3, b. Mich., in their household.

ROOSA, SIMON born ca. 1830, and wife, MARY, born ca. 1830, both in NY, were listed in the 1850 census of Medina Twp., Lenawee Co., Mich. with MARY J., age 1, b .Mich., in their household. Note: MARY J. may be she who m. Edmund G. Farnsworth, also see, though also note MARY A., in household of CALEB.

ROOT, ANSON was listed in the 1840 census index of Somerset Twp., Hillsdale Co., Mich.

ROOT, CHAUNCEY N. born ca. 1800, and wife, SUSAN (HITCHCOX), born ca. 1802, both in NY, moved to Jackson Co., Mich. in 1840. They were listed in the 1850 census of Madison Twp., Lenawee Co., with JULIA, age 28; NEWELL, age 24; MARY JANE b. 18 Sept. 1830, Orleans Co., NY (m. William H. Fowler, also see); SUSAN, age 12; DAVID, age 11, all b. NY; and SOPHIA, age 5, b. Mich., in their household. Chauncey died in Jackson Co.; and Susan died near Adrian in 1877. Ref: P&BA-Len pg. 1106-7.

ROOT, CLARENCE E. (See Oliver S. Colwell)

ROOT, DANIEL, son of JUSTUS (following), born 23 Nov. 1828, Eaton, Madison Co., NY, married there on 26 Mar. 1854 to LUCINDA (PATTERSON), daughter of George (also see). In 1863, they moved to Rollin Twp., Lenawee Co., Mich. Children: 1. WARREN G. (m. E. Georgina Williams); 2. ARTHUR H. (to Dakota); 3. BURDETTE M. Ref: P&BA-Len pg. 697-8.

ROOT, HENRY born ca. 1824, NY, and wife, ELLEN, born ca. 1825, Ireland, were listed in the 1850 census of Medina Twp., Lenawee Co., Mich. with LIBIUS? H., age 1, b. Mich., in their household.

ROOT, HENRY E. and wife, LUCINDA, settled in Constantine, St. Joseph Co., Mich. by 1840. Known daughter, CLARA A. (m. Dr. William E. Jewett, also see, in Constantine). Ref: P&BA-Len pg. 800-1.

ROOT, ISAAC was a Revolutionary soldier and lived in Stockbridge, Mass. He married MARY, and had known daughter, JOAN b. 23 Jan. 1780 (m. Stephen Ingersoll, also see, and went first to Ontario Co., NY, then Ransom, Hillsdale Co., Mich.) Ref: P&BA-Len pg. 740-3.

ROOT, JUSTUS, son of SOLOMON (who d. Conn.), was born in Grafton, Conn. At age 8, he went to live with a brother in Madison Co., NY. He married there to SARAH (GRISWOLD), daughter of William (also see). Sarah died in Eaton, Madison Co., NY in 1862; and he died in 1868. Eight children, names not stated, except DANIEL (preceding). Ref: P&BA-Len pg. 697-8.

ROOT, P. PHILANTHROPOS (spelled "Roots") was listed in the 1840 census index of Tecumseh Twp., Lenawee Co., Mich.

ROOT, RANSOM born ca. 1817, NY, was listed in the 1850 census of Blissfield Twp., Lenawee Co., Mich. in the George Hubbard household.

ROOT, SARAH A. born ca. 1823, Penn., was listed alone in the 1850 census of Medina Twp., Lenawee Co., Mich.

ROOT, SIMEON^1 moved from Vermont to NY, and it may be he listed in the 1800 census index of Oneida Co., NY. He died near Syracuse, NY. Known son, SIMEON^2 (following). Ref: P&BA-Len pg. 553-4.

ROOT, SIMEON^2, son of SIMEON^1 (preceding), born ca. 1786, VT, married probably in NY to MERIBAH (GEORGE) born 1792, VT. In 1816, they removed to Huron Co., Ohio. About 1851, they moved to Rome Twp., Lenawee Co., Mich. He died in 1870, age 84; and she died in 1868, age 76. Known daughter, MINERVA b. 21 Sept. 1826, Sandusky, Ohio (m. Warren Gilbert, also see). Ref: P&BA-Len pg. 553-4.

ROOT, SOPHRONIA (See Esben Burch)

RORICK, ESTELL born ca. 1809, Mass.?, and wife, HANNAH, born ca. 1819, NY, settled by 1838 in Seneca Co., NY. In the 1840 census index they were adjacent to WILLIAM (following); and were in the 1850 census of Dover Twp. with the first 4 children in his household: 1. CASPER b. ca. 1838 (m. Alice M. Horton, dau. of Samuel, also see); 2. DEBORAH A. b. ca. 1840; 3. LOVINA b. ca. 1841; 4. MELISSA A. b. ca. 1846 (m. Sylvester K. Porter, son of John C., also see); 5. LEROY W. (following).

RORICK, G. (male), age 19, born NY, was listed in the 1850 census of Adrian Twp., Lenawee Co., Mich. in a boarding house.

RORICK, JACOB N. see Jacob N. Borick

RORICK, LEROY W., son of ESTELL (preceding), married HATTIE (PORTER), daughter of John C. (also see). Children: 1. NELLIE; 2. CASPER. Ref: P&BA-Len pg. 552-3.

RORICK, LEWIS M. (See Rev. John Crabbs)

RORICK, MARK C. of Seneca Twp., Lenawee Co., Mich. married MARY S. (PORTER), daughter of John C. (also see). Children: 1. JOHN B.; 2. MYRTLE; 3. MAUDE. Ref: P&BA-Len pg. 552-3.

RORICK WILLIAM was listed in the 1840 census index of Seneca Twp., Lenawee Co., Mich. adjacent to ESTELL.

ROSA, JOSHUA see ROOSA, JOSHUA

ROSE, AURILLA C. (See Chancy Rowlson)

ROSE, C. W. (See Beriah H. Lane)

ROSE, DANIEL W. born ca. 1819, and wife, CATHARINE, born ca. 1815, both in NY, were listed in the 1850 census of Cambridge Twp., Lenawee Co., Mich. with VIENNA?, age 17; JULIANNA, age 15; DANIEL, age 7, all b. NY; and RODOLPHA, age 4; CATHARINE, age 2, both b. Mich., in their household.

ROSE, E. W. (See Fenner Palmer)

ROSE, LUCINDA, age 12, born Mich., was listed in the 1850 census of Adrian Twp., Lenawee Co., Mich. in a Sheldon household.

ROSE, MARY (See James Wheeler)

ROSE, MOSES born ca. 1820, and wife, MINA?, born ca. 1822, both in Penn., were listed in the 1850 census of Medina Twp., Lenawee Co., Mich. with WATERMAN, age 7; MILFORD, age 5, both b. Penn.; and ALVIRA, age 1, b. Mich., in their household.

ROSE, PHILIP and wife, CATHERINE, of Monroe Co., Mich. and Adrian, Lenawee Co. had known daughter, MAGDALENA (m. Andrew Nufer, also see, in 1853). Ref: P&BA-Len pg. 629-30.

ROSE, ROSWELL, age 35, born Ohio, was listed in the 1850 census of Hudson Twp., Lenawee Co., Mich. in a Wilcox household.

ROSE, SAMUEL B. born ca. 1814, NH, and wife, MARCY, born ca. 1817, NY, were listed in the 1850 census of Tecumseh Twp., Lenawee Co., Mich. with EDGAR, age 7; EDWIN, age 7; EMMA, age 3, all b. Mich., in their household.

ROSE, SARAH, age 20, born NY, was listed in the 1850 census of Hudson Twp., Lenawee Co., Mich. in a Brownell household.

ROSE, SUSANNAH b. Bavaria (See Peter Nufer).

ROSE, WILLIAM born ca. 1810, and wife, MARY, born ca. 1812, both in Canada, were listed in the 1850 census of

Pioneer Families of Southeastern Michigan

Madison Twp., Lenawee Co., Mich. with MARTHA, age 12; LOUISA, age 10; RUTH, age 7; EDWIN, age 5, all b. NY, in their household.

ROSS, ABRAM born ca. 1805, VT, and wife, SALLY A., born ca. 1817, Mass., were listed in the 1840 census index of Hudson Twp., Lenawee Co., Mich.; and in the 1850 census of Madison Twp. with SARAH R., age 16; OZIAS, E., age 5, both b. Mich., in their household.

ROSS, ALMEDA (See Welcome V. Fisk)

ROSS, ELIZABETH Mrs. born ca. 1806, NY, was listed head of household in the 1850 census of Ogden Twp., Lenawee Co., Mich. with WILLIAM, age 18, b. NY; and SARAH, age 9; CHARLES, age 7; ELLEN, age 4, all b. Mich., in her household. Note SAMUEL, following.

ROSS, MARTHA (See John B. Clement)

ROSS, MILTON born ca. 1836, Mich., was listed in the 1850 census of Tecumseh Twp., Lenawee Co., Mich. in a Sattherwaite household. (Also see Joseph W. Gray.)

ROSS, NETTIE (See Roderick R. Hume)

ROSS, SAMUEL was listed in the 1840 census index of Blissfield Twp., Lenawee Co., Mich. Note ELIZABETH, preceding.

ROSS, WILBER born ca. 1801, and wife, RACHEL, born ca. 1807, both in NY, were listed in the 1840 census index of Raisin Twp., Lenawee Co., Mich.; and in the 1850 census with REBECCA B., AGE 20; MARGARETTE, age 17; WILLIAM, age 14, all b. NY; and ALBERT, age 4, b. Mich., in their household.

ROTHDOW, WILLIAM (See John P. Schwab)

ROTNOUR, GEORGE of Lenox, Madison Co., NY had known daughter, MALANY (m. Walter White, also see, in 1823). Ref: History of Jackson Co., Mich., pg. 819.

ROUND, JAMES E., son of SAMUEL S. (following), born ca. 1812, Rutland Co., VT, moved about 1832 to Lenawee Co., Mich. He married in 1833 to NETTIE CAROLINE (MILLIMAN), daughter of Rollin M. (also see) of Wayne Co., NY, and they settled in Medina Twp., Lenawee Co. Children: 1. WILLIAM (m. Frances Phelps; Quincy, Mich. Note: In the 1850 census, eldest child was called NATHAN, age 15, not mentioned in sketch, is this same as William?); 2. RUEL b. ca. 1838 (may be he listed again in the 1850 census as age 10? in the household of Philip Poucher?); 3. FRANCIS (d. young); 4. JAMES (d. young); 5. LYDIA (d. young); 6. HELEN b. ca. 1843 (m. Jonas Sprague, son of Samuel, also see); 7. MARTHA b. ca. 1848 (m. Benjamin Brink; Quincy, Mich.); (following all born after 1850) 8. MORGAN (following); 9. CARRIE (m. John Nygus, also see); 10. ELMIRA (m. George Ferris); 11. HATTIE (m. Seymour Esteline; W. Unity, O.) Ref: P&BA-Len pg. 887-8.

ROUND, MORGAN, son of JAMES E. (preceding), married first to SADIE (TRUMBULL), and had daughter, MYRTLE. They separated and he married again to ALZINA (ESTELINE) and had daughter, LOUISA. Ref: P&BA-Len pg. 887-8.

ROUND, RUEL A., probably son of SAMUEL S. (following), born ca. 1821, and wife, MARY A., born ca. 1826, both in NY, were listed in the 1850 census of Medina Twp., Lenawee Co., Mich. with RUEL A., age 1, b. Mich., in their household.

ROUND, SAMUEL S. born ca. 1791, and wife, ZILPHA (EDDY), were natives of Rutland Co., VT who lived in Clarendon Springs. They moved to Niagara Co., NY where she died. He moved to Madison Twp., Lenawee Co., Mich. before 1840. There were 3 sons & 3 daughters, names not stated, except JAMES E. (preceding); and MARTHA b. ca. 1813 (m. Benjamin Reasoner, also see); and probably RUEL A. (preceding); and OZIEL, age 16, b. NY who was listed in Samuel's household in the 1850 census of Madison Twp. Samuel lists a wife, CHARLOTTE, age 58, born VT, in the 1850 census. Ref: P&BA-Len pg. 887-8; 1017-8.

ROUP, CHRISTIAN (See Edward Goheen)

ROWE also see ROE

ROWE, WILLIAM H. born ca. 1806, Mass., and wife, MARY G., born ca. 1813, NY, were listed in the 1840 census index of Adrian Twp., Lenawee Co., Mich.; and in the 1850 census with ABI E., age 18; CHARLOTTE L., age 16; LUCY A., age 15; SARAH M., age 10; MAHALA E., age 8; DWIGHT W., age 5, all b. Mich., in their household.

ROWELL, HOMER B. born ca. 1811, Conn., and wife, ELIZABETH, born ca. 1821, NY, were listed in the 1850 census of Adrian Twp., Lenawee Co., Mich. with no family in their household.

ROWELL, NANCY born 1786, Trumbull, Conn. (See Ebenezer Jerrells).

ROWLAND, CHARLES born ca. 1806, Penn. was listed in the 1850 census of Tecumseh Twp., Lenawee Co., Mich. and listed with him (probably an error, and probably should have been a wife) was another CHARLES, age 41, b. VT. In the household were GEORGE, age 15; ELIZABETH, age 13; MARY, age 12 (note MARY b. 1839, following); ALBERT, age 7, all b. Mich. in the household. Note: There was a CHARLES in the 1840 census index of York Twp., Washtenaw Co., Mich.

ROWLAND, CLARISSA, age 20, born NY, was listed in the 1850 census of Madison Twp., Lenawee Co., Mich. in a Bassett household. Note: May be same as daughter of JOHN C., following.

ROWLAND, CLINTON, age 19, born Mich.?, was listed in the 1850 census of Tecumseh Twp., Lenawee Co., Mich. in a Clark household.

ROWLAND, DAVID born ca. 1798, Conn., and wife, MARY, born ca. 1801, NY, were listed in the 1850 census of Ridgeway Twp., Lenawee Co., Mich. with JOSEPH, age 20; ELIZABETH, age 17; DANIEL, age 14; JANE, age 12; GEORGE, age 10, all b. NY; and JOHN, age 8, b. Ohio; and STEPHEN, age 6, b. Mich., in their household.

ROWLAND, JOHN C. born ca. 1795, NY, and wife, OLIVE, born ca. 1798, Canada, were listed in the 1850 census of Palmyra Twp., Lenawee Co., Mich. with CLARISSA, age 18 (note preceding); NORTON, age 23 (listed again in Madison Twp. in Treat household); JANE, age 17, all b. Canada; and PERRY, age 14; MARY, age 1, both b. NY, in their household.

ROWLAND, MARY born ca. 1779, Penn., was listed in the 1850 census of Tecumseh Twp., Lenawee Co., Mich. in the household of probably son, WILLIAM B. (following). Note CHARLES, preceding.

ROWLAND, MARY born 6 Sept. 1839, Lenawee Co., Mich., married F. D. Lancaster, also see, and lived in Clinton, Mich. Ref: P&BA-Len pg. 662-3.

ROWLAND, WILLIAM B. (note MARY, preceding) born ca. 1819, and wife, REBECCA, born ca. 1822, both in NY, were listed in the 1850 census of Tecumseh Twp., Lenawee Co., Mich. with PHOEBE, age 10; CAROLINE, age 8; WILLIAM EDWARD, age 5; MARY, age 3; LAFAYETTE, age 1, all b. Mich.; and mother, MARY (preceding), in their household.

ROWLEY, CALEB S. born ca. 1794, NY, and wife, SOPHIA, born ca. 1804, NY were listed in the 1850 census of Hudson Twp., Lenawee Co., Mich. with EMELINE, age 20; WARREN, age 18, both b. NY; and PERRY N. (following); ORSON B., age 9; MARY, age 5, all b. Mich., in their household. Note: Is Caleb another son of JONATHAN (See CONSTANT, following).

ROWLEY, CONSTANT, son of JONATHAN, was born Conn. and went with his father at age 7 to Brutus, Cayuga Co., NY, where they were pioneer settlers. He served in the War of 1812. He married first to POLLY (MEECH), daughter of Joseph (also see), and she died in Cayuga Co. in 1829. Known son, JONATHAN (following). Constant moved to Hudson Twp., Lenawee Co., Mich. by 1835. He married again to Mrs. EMELINE (SMITH) FREEMAN who died in Hudson Twp.; and married last to Mrs. MEHITABLE (WILLIAMS) PIERCE, widow of Allen (also see). They removed about 1849 to near Lansing, Mich., where he died. She returned afterwards to Hudson Twp., where she died. Ref: P&BA-Len pg. 665-6.

ROWLEY, DAVID T. born ca. 1827, NY, married ANN (JOHNSON), born ca. 1828, NY, and there were listed in the 1850 census of Dover Twp., Lenawee Co., Mich. (See John Johnson, son of Daniel). Ref: P&BA-Len pg. 585-7.

ROWLEY, F. S. was listed in the 1840 census index of Hudson Twp., Lenawee Co., Mich. adjacent to "C." (CONSTANT?).

ROWLEY, JONATHAN, son of CONSTANT (preceding), born 21 May 1822, Brutus, Cayuga Co., NY, came at age 13 to Michigan with his father. He married ABIGAIL (PIERCE), daughter of Allen (also see), and they were listed in the 1850 census of Hudson Twp., Lenawee Co., Mich. with her as LYDIA A., age 18, born NY. Children (born after 1850): 1. CLARA (m. John Thompson; Clayton, Mich.); 2. ADELBERT (m. Addie Curtis); 3. ALFRED. Ref: P&BA-Len pg. 665-6.

ROWLEY, NANCY J. born 1824, Onondaga Co., NY (m. Joseph R. Bennett, also see, in 1840, at Hudson, Lenawee Co., Mich.). Ref: P&BA-Len pg. 981-2.

ROWLEY, PERRY N., son of CALEB S. (preceding), born ca. 1839, NY, married VIORNA A. (PATRICK), daughter of James (also see). Perry N. was killed in the Civil War., leaving a son, WILLIS P. (m. Elizabeth W. Seelye, had known son, Perry J. b. ca. 1888).

ROWLSON, CHAUNCEY, son of HARVEY (following), born 6 Feb. 1808, Wayne Co., NY, at age 8 went to Vermont to live with an uncle. In 1838, he removed to Woodstock Twp., Lenawee Co., Mich. He married on 28 Apr. 1842 in Ohio to CHARLOTTE L. (NORTON), daughter of James (also see); and settled in Woodstock Twp. He died there on 30 June 1883, and she was still living there in 1888. Children: 1. SARAH b. ca. 1843 (m. Jackson Carpenter, also see); 2. MARTHA (d. age 2/12); 3. HARRIET "HATTIE" L. b. 5 Feb. 1845 (m. Miles Bennett, Jackson Co., Mich.); 4. HARVEY b. 10 Apr. 1848 (m. Belle Kahowe, Woodstock Twp.); 5. FRED b. 10 Oct. 1860 (m. Aurilla C. Rose, Woodstock Twp.) Ref: P&BA-Len pg. 625-6 & portraits of Chauncey & Charlotte.

ROWLSON, HARVEY and wife, LUCRETIA (PARTRIDGE), were born in Conn. They moved to Wayne Co., NY where he died. Lucretia came to Woodstock Twp., Lenawee Co., Mich. to live with CHAUNCEY (preceding), and it is probably she, age 65, born Conn., listed as "LAURACETTA," in his household in the 1850 census. She died in 1864, over age 82. Four children, names not stated, except preceding. Ref: P&BA-Len pg. 625-6.

ROWLSON, HARVEY B. came to Woodstock Twp., Lenawee Co., Mich. from Vermont, and was a relative of Chauncey, probably a cousin. Ref: P&BA-Len pg. 625-6.

ROY also see ROYS

ROY, ELIZABETH S., age 60, born NY, was listed in the 1850 census of Franklin Twp., Lenawee Co., Mich., head of household, with HENRY, age 12, b. NY, in her household.

ROY, MARY ANN (See Phineas Bartlett)

ROYCE see ROYS

ROYS also see ROY

ROYS, GEORGE S. born 13 Feb. 1851 married on 27 Nov. 1878 to EVA (PAGE), daughter of Nicholas Amos (also see) in Rollin Twp., Lenawee Co., Mich. Known son, HERVEY N. b. 16 Nov. 1879. Note the GEORGE S. in household of JOSEPH S., following, possibly same man? Birthdate preceding may be an error?

ROYS, JOSEPH S. born ca. 1809, Conn. (spelled "Royce," in census), and wife, MARILLA, born ca. 1821, NY, were listed in the 1850 census of Madison Twp., Lenawee Co., Mich. with GEORGE S., age 5; HOWARD M., age 2, both b. Ohio; and WILLIAM H., age 1/12, b. Mich., in their household. Also possibly of this family was IDA b. 27 Oct. 1855 (m. Frank A. Page, son of Nicholas Amos, also see).

ROYSTON, ALBERT & WILLIAM (See George W. Rudesill).

RUBEY, M. H. (See John Houghtby)

RUDESILL, GEORGE was son of ? (See JOHN, following) and moved at an early date from Penn. to Medina Co., Ohio. George had a known son, JACOB (following). Ref: P&BA-Len pg. 618-9.

RUDESILL, GEORGE W., son of JACOB (following), born 21 Aug. 1829, Medina Co., Ohio, married there on 18 Jan. 1855 to ANN J. (HANCHETT), daughter of Watson (also see). They resided first in Ohio, but about 1862 moved to Ridgeway Twp., Lenawee Co., Mich.; and in 1866 moved to Woodstock Twp. Children: 1. BETSEY J. b. 25 May 1857 (m. Charles Sanders); 2. SYLVA M. b. 8 July 1861 (m. William Royston); 3. BURT b. 5 Aug. 1865; 4. ELLA b. 18 Feb. 1868 (m. Albert Royston; Eaton Co., Mich.); 5. HATTIE b. 31 Oct. 1870; 6. NETTIE b. 27 Mar. 1874; 7. MILTON b. 4 Oct. 1879; 8. MABEL b. 11 Oct. 1883. Ref: P&BA-Len pg. 618-9.

RUDESILL, JACOB, son of GEORGE (preceding), born 11 Nov. 1808, Westmoreland Co., Penn., married JEMIMA (REED) probably in Medina Co., Ohio. He died there at age 82; and she died at age 76. Known son, GEORGE W. (preceding). Ref: P&BA-Len pg. 618-9.

RUDESILL, JOHN and his brother, ? (name not stated, perhaps also GEORGE?), came from Germany and settled in Westmoreland Co., Penn. This unnamed brother was the father of GEORGE (preceding). Ref: P&BA-Len pg. 618-9.

RUDOLPH, JOHN, son of PETER (who was a pioneer to near Aurora, Preston Co., W. VA.), married there to ANNA M. (HECKERT). He died there; but Anna M. afterwards came to Ogden Twp., Lenawee Co., Mich. to live with known daughter, ANN SALOME b. 2 Aug. 1830, Preston Co. (m. George Frederick Harsh, also see). Ref: P&BA-Len pg. 1023-4.

RUGG, ORPHA (See David M. Johnson)

RULOFF, HENRY (See John Forbes)

RUNDELL, ALVIRA born ca. 1827, NY, came with her parents to Franklin Twp., Lenawee Co., Mich. "when quite young." She married Robert Cairns (also see) in 1852. Ref: P&BA-Len pg. 806-7. In the 1850 census, she was listed, age 23, in the household of William, Jr. & Ursual Bradley, 4 doors from ERASTUS, following.

RUNDELL, ERASTUS born ca. 1816, and wife, SARAH A. (MILLS), daughter of Maj. Philo (also see), born ca. 1815, both in NY, settled in Franklin Twp., Lenawee Co., Mich. She died 4 Oct. 1859, age 46, buried in the Mills Cemetery, Franklin Twp. In the 1850 census of Franklin Twp., they listed EUSEBIA, age 6, b. Mich., in their household.

RUNDELL, WILLIAM born ca. 1825, and wife, SARAH, born ca. 1827, were listed in the 1850 census of Cambridge Twp., Lenawee Co., Mich. with EMMA, age 1, b. Mich., in their household.

RUNYAN, WILLIAM was a native of Penn. who moved to Ohio (possbily Lucas Co.) He had known daughter, HANNAH (m. Cornelius Van Fleet, also see, ca. 1840). Ref: P&BA-Lenpg. 1147.

RUPPRECHT, ELIZABETH (See Michael Mulzer)

RUSK, WILLIAM was a native of Ireland, and he married LYDIA (HUSTED) born New York. Known daughter, JULIANA (m. Nathan Vickery, also see). Ref: P&BA-Len pg. 369-70.

RUSS, CHRISTOPHER born ca. 1823, and wife, OLIVIA, born ca. 1827, both in NY, were listed in the 1850 census of Cambridge Twp., Lenawee Co., Mich. with Marietta Stone, age 82, in their household.

RUSS, DANIEL was listed in the 1840 census index of Rollin Twp., Lenawee Co., Mich.

RUSS, HENRY born ca. 1801, and wife, ELIZA, born ca. 1811, both in NY, were listed in the 1850 census of Seneca Twp., Lenawee Co., Mich. with JOHN N., age 16; MARY A., age 14; DANIEL, age 9; ISAAC P., age 7; NATHAN A., age 5; GEORGE S., age 1, all b. NY, in their household.

RUSS, JOEL born ca. 1826, and wife, MARY, born ca. 1826, both in NY, were listed in the 1850 census of Cambridge Twp., Lenawee Co., Mich. with Caroline Bibbins, age 21, b. NY, in their household. (Listed about 3 doors from SILAS H., following).

RUSS, NATHAN from Livingston Co., NY was listed in the 1840 census index of Jackson Twp., Jackson Co., Mich. Note OLIVER, following.

RUSS, NATHANIEL was born in New Hampshire, and wife, CLARISSA (TOMER) was born 17 Mar. 1801, New Jersey. They came from Steuben Co., NY to Cambridge Twp., Lenawee Co., Mich. in 1837; and he died in 1839. Clarissa was listed head of household in the 1840 census index. There were 9 children, names not stated, except DIANA F. b. 23 Sept. 1819, Pultney, Steuben Co., NY (m/1 Solomon G. Crego; m/2 Henry N. Skeels, see both). Also note CHRISTOPHER; JOEL (both preceding); & SILAS H. (following). Clarissa married second to Ira Rogers (also see) and she died 14 July 1866, Cambridge, Lenawee Co. Ref: P&BA-Len pg. 241-2.

RUSS, OLIVER Dr. was probably he listed in the 1840 census index of Jackson Twp., Jackson Co., Mich.; and he is a brother of NATHANIEL, preceding.

RUSS, SILAS H. born ca. 1819, NY, and wife, SOPHIA, born ca. 1819, Mass., were listed in the 1850 census of Cambridge Twp., Lenawee Co., Mich. with CLARISSA A. b. 19 Feb. 1845 (m. William H. Wiggins, as 2nd wife, also see); LAFAYETTE, age 3; IRVING, age 1, all b. Mich., in their household. Note NATHANIEL, preceding.

RUSSELL, ?, son of JOHN (following), born 30 Aug. 1803, Ontario Co., NY, was bound out at age 10 to a farmer in Steubem Co., NY, where he remained until 1824. He married ELIZABETH (BEACH) born Ontario Co., NY, and they moved to York Twp., Sandusky Co., Ohio. She died there in 1852, and he moved in 1863 to Fremont, Ohio. He died in Clyde, Ohio in Apr. 1874. Eight children, names not stated, except #3. SPENCER (following). Ref: P&BA-Len pg. 660-2. Note ASA, following.

RUSSELL, ABIJAH born ca. 1792, New Jersey, and wife, NAOMI, born ca. 1794, NY, were listed in the 1840 census index of Macon Twp., Lenawee Co., Mich. (adjacent to ASA, following); and in the 1850 census of Ridgeway Twp. with EMELINE, age 17, b. Mich., and Rhoda Graves, age 10, b. Mich., in their household; and WILLIAM D. (following) listed next door. NAOMI, age 15, b. Mich., in the household of WILLIAM D., probably of this family.

RUSSELL, ALANSON born ca. 1828, and wife, CATHARINE, born ca. 1821, both in NY, were listed in the 1850 census of Macon Twp., Lenawee Co., Mich. with ALBERT, age 2; ELISA A., age 7/12, both b. Mich., in their household.

RUSSELL, ANDREW A., son of SAMUEL (following), born 24 Apr. 1824, Seneca Co., NY, came to Fairfield Twp.,

Lenawee Co., Mich. with his parents. He married first to CLARINDA (EDWARDS), AND she died after 8 months. He married again to MARGARET (SALSBURY) and she died in 1869. He married third to JENNIE (BARNES) born 19 Aug. 1839, Seneca Twp. Daughter, ANNIE L. Ref: P&BA-Len pg. 380-3.

RUSSELL, ASA born ca. 1800, and wife, LYDIA, born ca. 1802, both in Conn., came from New Hampshire to Macon Twp., Lenawee Co., Mich. in 1834. Known daughter, ELIZABETH b. 15 Aug. 1824, Plainfield, NH (m. Richard Cadmus, also see). In the 1850 census of Ridgeway Twp., Lenawee Co., Mich. Asa listed CAROLINE, age 24; EDWARD, age 21 (may be Edward L. who m. Hulda M. Bangs, dau. of Alanson, also see), both b. NH; and ASAHEL, age 17, b. Ohio; HELEN, age 12, b. Mich., in the household. Asa died in Raisin Twp.; but Lydia was living in Macon Twp. in 1888 with son, Asa(hel). Ref: P&BA-Len pg. 331-3.

RUSSELL, CHARLES C., son of SAMUEL (following), born 14 June 1820, Seneca Co., NY, married there on 9 Mar. 1839 to JANE (LYKE), daughter of Samuel (also see). It may be he listed in the 1840 census index of Fairfield Twp., Lenawee Co., Mich. Adopted son, GEORGE S. Ref: P&BA-Len pg. 852-3.

RUSSELL, DANIEL born ca. 1814, and wife, EMILY J., born ca. 1826, both in NY, were listed in the 1850 census of Hudson Twp., Lenawee Co., Mich. with ALFRED, age 4, b. Mich., in their household. Note SAMUEL H. of Hudson Twp., following.

RUSSELL, E. (See Hanry A. Angell)

RUSSELL, ELSIE (See Marshall Reed)

RUSSELL, FRANCES born ca. 1780, VT, probably mother of SAMUEL H. (following), was listed in his household in the 1850 census of Hudson Twp., Lenawee Co., Mich. Also note DANIEL, preceding; and JOSEPH, following.

RUSSELL, HARTWELL, son of SAMUEL (following), born ca. 1813, and wife, MARY C. (PORTER), daughter of Lewis (also see), both b. NY, settled in Fairfield Twp., Lenawee Co., Mich. by 1834, and were listed in the 1850 census of Fairfield Twp., near his "brother-in-law, Asaph Porter," with SAMANTHA, age 16; ALBERT H., age 14; LEWIS, age 11; ERVIN, age 9, all b. Mich.; and his father, SAMUEL (following), in their household.

RUSSELL, JESSE born ca. 1797, and wife, CATHARINE, born ca. 1802, both in New Jersey, were listed in the 1840 census of Cambridge Twp., Lenawee Co., Mich.; and in the 1850 census with LYDIA, age 18; JACOB, age 14, both b. NY; and ISAAC, age 8 (may be he who m. Delilah Onsted, dau. of Peter, also see, Cambridge Twp.), b. Mich., in their household.

RUSSELL, JOHN moved from New England to Ontario Co., NY during its early settlement, and it is probably he listed there in the 1800 census index; and he died there in 1813. His wife's name was not stated, however, she married 2 more times, and her last husband was Isaac Slocum, the brother of Frances Slocum (who was the girl kidnapped in the Wyoming Valley of Penn. by Indians and not found until she was an adult). Also, it said that a grandson was Gen. James B. McPherson of Civil War fame. She was living in Clyde, Ohio in 1888, over the age of 100. Known son, ? (preceding).

RUSSELL, JOHN born ca. 1806, and wife, ESTHER, born ca. 1814, both in NY, were listed in the 1850 census of Fairfield Twp., Lenawee Co., Mich. with SPENCER A., age 17; LYDIA M., age 15; FRANKLIN I., age 12, all b. NY; and MARY A., age 9; REUBEN B., age 7; LORENZO I., age 3; POLLY A., age 4/12, all b. Mich., in their household.

RUSSELL, JOHN born ca. 1825, and wife, LUCY, born ca. 1830, both in NY, were listed in the 1850 census of Madison Twp., Lenawee Co., Mich.

RUSSELL, JOSEPH was listed in the 1840 census index of Hudson Twp., Lenawee Co., Mich. Note FRANCES; & DANIEL, both preceding; and SAMUEL H., following.

RUSSELL, JOSEPH born ca. 1822, Ohio, and wife, ALVIRA, born ca. 1830, Conn. were listed in the 1850 census of Medina Twp., Lenawee Co., Mich. with ALVIRA J., age 1, b. Mich., and Hannah Wilson, age 19, b. Conn., in their household. Note: Perhaps Hannah Wilson, and Alvira are both daughters of Philo Wilson (also see) who was listed next door in the census.

RUSSELL, L. P. (See Charles E. Mickley)

RUSSELL, LEVI, probably son of SAMUEL (following), born ca. 1812, and wife, ELIZABETH "BETSEY" (BROSS) born ca. 1807, both in NY, were listed in the 1840 census index of Fairfield Twp., Lenawee Co., Mich. (adjacent to SAMUEL); and in the 1850 census with ANNA H., age 10; SARAH ADELIA b. 27 June 1844 (m. Jerome Camp, also see), both b. Mich., and Lewis Price, age 14; Margaret Price, age 12, both b. Mich., in their household.

RUSSELL, LOIZA of Monroe Co., Mich. (See David Zeluff).

RUSSELL, LYDIA A. of Jackson Co., Mich. (See Henry J. Crego).

RUSSELL, MARY born Ireland (See William Haley).

RUSSELL, MARY E. of Jackson Co.. Mich. (See Henry Hawley).

RUSSELL, RILEY H. born ca. 1822, and wife, SARAH?, born ca. 1823, both in NY, were listed in the 1850 census of Fairfield Twp., Lenawee Co., Mich. with MARY I., age 6; AN---(male), age 4; ALICE, age 3; MILDEN? (male), age 1, all b. Mich., in their household.

RUSSELL, SAMUEL born ca. 1790, and wife, BETSEY (SPRAGUE), were natives of Dutchess Co., NY, who removed to Seneca Co., NY. In 1836, they came to Fairfield Twp., Lenawee Co., Mich. She died there in 1846, and he died in 1879. There were 3 daughters and 7 sons; 9 children lived to maturity, and in 1888, all were in Mich. but a son in Toledo, Ohio, those known following. In the 1850 census, Samuel was living in the household of HARTWELL (preceding); CHARLES C. (preceding); #6. ANDREW A. (preceding). Also note RILEY H. (preceding). Ref: P&BA-Len pg. 380-3; 852-3.

RUSSELL, SAMUEL H. born ca. 1822, NY, and wife, MELISSA G., born ca. 1825, both in NY, were listed in the 1850 census of Hudson Twp., Lenawee Co., Mich. with FRANCES A., age 3/12; and probably mother, FRANCES, age 70, b. VT, in their household. Note JOSEPH, preceding.

RUSSELL, SPENCER Capt., son of ? (preceding), born 17 Apr. 1836, Clyde, Sandusky Co., Ohio, served in Co. A, 72d Ohio Inf., Civil War., and resigned in Sept. 1863 with rank of Capt. He married HANNAH (SANFORD), daughter of Elias (also see) in Ohio on 15 Sept. 1864. They lived in Sandusky until 1868, they moved to Hudson Twp., Lenawee Co., Mich. Children:

Pioneer Families of Southeastern Michigan

1. JAMES McPHERSON; 2. LUCILE; 3. SPENCER. Ref: P&BA-Len pg. 660-2.

RUSSELL, THOMAS born ca. 1793, and wife, ELIZABETH, born ca 1790, both in England, were listed in the 1850 census of Rollin Twp., Lenawee Co., Mich. with ELIZA, age 22; HENRY, age 20, both b. England; ELIZABETH, age 18; REUBEN, age 16; TILDING, age 15; GOODWILL, age 12, all b. NY, in their household.

RUSSELL, WILLIAM was listed in the 1840 census index of Franklin Twp., Lenawee Co., Mich.

RUSSELL, WILLIAM D., son of ABIJAH, born ca. 1820, and wife, BETSEY J., born ca. 1828, both in NY, were listed in the 1850 census of Ridgeway Twp., Lenawee Co., Mich. with NAOMI, age 15; DAVID, age 1, both b. Mich., in their household.

RUTH, JOHN born Co. Carlow, Ireland, came to Sacketts Harbor, Jefferson Co., NY. He was a brother of MARY of Co. Carlow who married Andrew Welch (also see). Ref: P&BA-Len pg. 775-6.

RYAN, ? was was the father of ALICE (m. Allen Skinner, also see, 1826 probably in Lockport, NY); and CATHERINE b. ca. 1796, VT (m. Thaddeus Clark, also see, NY and moved to Clinton Twp., Lenawee Co., Mich. in 1831). Ref: P&BA-Len pg. 900-1.

RYDER also see RIDER
RYDER, J. (See Henry W. Burke)
RYDER, JENNETTE (See Edmund Lapham)
RYDER, POLLY (See William O. Marshall)

RYND, JOSEPH (See Elliott Gray)

- S -

SACKETT, FANNA born ca. 1780, Mass., was listed in the 1850 census of Raisin Twp., Lenawee Co., Mich. in the household of son, MORRISON (following).

SACKETT, GILBERT born ca. 1826, and wife, HANNAH, born ca 1826, both in NY, were listed in the 1850 census of Rollin Twp., Lenawee Co., Mich. with Wallace Page, age 6; Henry C. Page, age 4, both b. Mich., possibly stepchildren.

SACKETT, JUSTUS born ca. 1819, NY, was listed in the 1850 census of Raisin Twp., Lenawee Co., Mich. in the household of Ann Craft.

SACKETT, MORRISON born ca. 1815, and wife, MARY, born ca. 1813, both in NY, were listed in the 1840 census index of Raisin Twp., Lenawee Co., Mich.; and in the 1850 census with FRANCES, age 5, born Mich.; and mother, FANNA (preceding), in their household.

SACKETT, ORAMEL A. born 20 Jan. 1807, and wife, CORNELIA (WILLEY), of Dutchess Co., NY, moved before 1840 to Blissfield Twp., Lenawee Co., Mich. She died there in 1848; and he died 11 Sept. 1879. Known children: DANIEL (d. age 2); MARY C. b. 26 Sept. 1838 (m. Edwin C. Porter, also see); ELIZA b. ca. 1840 (m. M. L. Rice, Washtenaw Co., Mich.). Ref: P&BA-Len pg. 685.. Note: In the 1850 census, listed in his household was (second wife?) SUSAN, age 28, b. NY; and only ELIZA was listed in the household.

SAFFORD, ORRIN Sr. from Woodstock, VT, moved to Flint, Genesee Co., Mich. as a young man and is listed there in the 1840 census index. By his first wife (name not stated) he had son, 1. CHARLES (lived Calif. in 1888). He married again to ABIGAIL (JENNINGS). Children: 2. JENNIE E. b. 9 Jan. 1851, Flint (m. Dr. John L. Tuttle, also see); 3. ORRIN P. (m. Eleanor C. Tuttle, daughter of John L. Sr. (also see). Orrin Sr. was still living in 1888, age 92, in Flint, Mich. Ref: P&BA-Len pg. 373-4.

SAGENDORF, MARIA (See Ephraim Myers)

SAGER also see SEAGER & SEGER
SAGER, RICHARD born ca. 1814, NJ, and wife, SALLY, born ca. 1816, NY, were listed in the 1850 census of Rome Twp., Lenawee Co., Mich. with MARIA, age 14, b. NY; JEROME, age 11, b. Ohio; and WARREN, age 10; MARYETT, age 4; LOUISA, age 3 (m. George Sheeler, also see).

ST. JOHN, CHARLES born ca. 1823, NY, and wife, ANN, born ca. 1824, Mich., were listed in the 1850 census of Woodstock Twp., Lenawee Co., Mich. with JULIA, age 7/12, b. Mich., in their household.

ST. JOHN, CHARLOTTE (See David Curtis)

ST. JOHN, DARIUS born ca. 1820, Conn., and wife, CURENCE?, born ca. 1822, NY, were listed in the 1850 census of Tecumseh Twp., Lenawee Co., Mich. with REUBEN, age 9; WILLIAM, age 5, both b. Mich., in their household.

ST. JOHN, DAVID was listed in the 1840 census index of Monroe Twp., Monroe Co., Mich.

ST. JOHN, EZRA was listed in the 1840 census index of Clinton Twp., Lenawee Co., Mich. It may be he who purchased in Jackson Co., Mich. in 1836.

ST. JOHN, FROST was listed in the 1840 census index of Tecumseh Twp., Lenawee Co., Mich.

ST. JOHN, JACOB was purchasing land in Jackson Co., Mich. in 1836.

ST. JOHN, JAMES of Wayne Co., Mich. was purchasing land in Jackson Co., Mich. in 1835. May be he listed in Columbia Twp., Jackson Co. Mich. in 1840 census index.

ST. JOHN, JASON born ca. 1806, Conn. is probably he listed in the 1840 census index of Columbia Twp., Jackson Co., Mich. (as "Lason," adjacent to JAMES; & TINA); and in the 1850 census of Tecumseh Twp., Lenawee Co., Mich. with wife, LUCY ANN, age 28, born NY, and FLORENCE, age 4; IRVIN, age 2, both b. Mich., in their household.

ST. JOHN, MARY E., age 18; and ESTHER A., age 16, probably sisters, were listed in the 1850 census of Madison Twp., Lenawee Co., Mich. in the household of Samuel & Sally A. Smith.

ST. JOHN, SAMUEL of Jackson Co., Mich. (See Reuben Downs).

ST. JOHN, TRIPHENA (See John Briggs)

SALSBURY, CUMMINS was listed in the 1840 census of Hudson Twp., Lenawee Co., Mich.

SALSBURY, D. C. and wife, MARGARET (FORCE), possibly daughter of Solomon (also see), came to "southern Michigan" about 1840. He died in 1847, and she is listed head of household, age 26, born NY, in the 1850 census of Fairfield Twp., Lenawee Co., Mich. with 2 daughters following: CLARISSA M. b. ca. 1846, Mich. (m. James H. Green, also see); FRANCES E. b. ca. 1847. Margaret died in 1867. Ref: P&BA-Len pg. 457. Note: D. C. may be DAVID (following).

SALSBURY, DANIEL was lsted in the 1840 census index of Seneca Twp., Lenawee Co., Mich.; and it probably he listed as "Saulsbury" in the 1850 census, age 65, with wife, ELIZABETH, age 62, both born Vermont.

SALSBURY, DANIEL born 1792, Conn., may be he listed in the 1850 census of Hudson Twp., Lenawee Co., Mich. in the Palmer household; and again in the "poor house" in Madison Twp.

SALSBURY, DAVID was listed in the 1840 census of Dover Twp., Lenawee Co., Mich. adjacent to OSMYN, following. Also note D. C. (preceding).

SALSBURY, EOLA (See David Pearson)

SALSBURY, JAMES W. born ca. 1826, NY, was listed head of household in the 1850 census of Hudson Twp. Lenawee Co., Mich. with a Beebe family in the household. Note DANIEL, preceding.

SALSBURY, JOHN (See James Knox²)

SALSBURY, JONATHAN born ca. 1808, VT, and wife, ANN, born ca. 1824, NY, were listed in the 1850 census of Medina Twp., Lenawee Co., Mich. with son, IRA, age 3, b. Mich., in their household. Note: JONATHAN, following, may be another son born after 1850; also see DANIEL of Seneca Twp., preceding.

SALSBURY, JONATHAN married OLIVE ANN (HAYWARD)³, daughter of Micajah (also see) who was born after 1850, Seneca Twp., Lenawee Co., Mich. Note JONATHAN, preceding.

SALSBURY, LESTER H., son of OSMYN (following). born ca. 1840, Mich., served in Co. B, 4th Mich. Inf., Civil War. He married on 29 Sept. 1881 to SUE M. (QUINN) of Wilmington, Clinton Co., Ohio, and they settled in Adrian, Lenawee Co., Mich. No children listed. Ref: P&BA-Len pg. 1050-1.

SALSBURY, LEVI was listed in the 1840 census index of Medina Twp., Lenawee Co., Mich. It may be who was born in Scotland, one of 12 brothers who eventually settled in Orleans Co., NY. He was father of OSMYN (following). Though not listed in the 1850 census, there is SARAH, age 66, born NY, possibly his wife, listed head of household with SARAH, age 30, b. NY, in her household. Next door is MOSES, age 38, b. NY (following). Also note LEVI, following.

SALSBURY, LEVI, possibly son of LEVI (preceding), born ca. 1824, and wife, CORDELIA, born ca. 1826, both in NY, were listed in the 1850 census of Medina Twp., Lenawee Co., Mich. with FRANCES, age 2, born Mich., in their household

SALSBURY, MARGARET (See Andrew A. Russell)

SALSBURY, MARY, age 16, born Mich., is listed in the 1859 census of Hudson Twp., Lenawee Co., Mich. in a Baker household. Note DANIEL of Hudson Twp., preceding.

SALSBURY, MOSES, possibly son of LEVI (preceding), born ca. 1812, and probably wife, CAROLINE L., age 34, both born NY; and AMANDA M., age 13; ALBERT W., age 11; MARY M., age 8 (prob. she who m. Henry J. Wirt, also see), all b. NY; and FRANCES A., age 6; ALVA B., age 4; SARAH C., age 3; FLORENCE I., age 1, all b. Mich., in their household, listed next door to SARAH (preceding, see LEVI).

SALSBURY, MOSES born ca. 1806, Penn., and wife, SALLY, born ca. 1806, NY, were listed in the 1840 census index of Rome Twp., Lenawee Co., Mich.; and in the 1850 census with ELIAS, age 14; DEXTER, age 13; AARON, age 10; GILES, age 8, all b. Mich., in their household.

SALSBURY, OSMYN, son of LEVI (preceding), born 30 Apr. 1804, Orleans Co., NY, came to Adrian, Lenawee Co., Mich. in 1826. He married there in 1830 to THEODOCIA (ROOKER) born 30 Apr. 1809, Whitehall, NY. They moved to Dover Twp. by 1840; and in the 1850 census listed LOVERNA, age 18; LYDIA, age 15; LEVI O., age 11; LESTER H. (preceding); SARAH C., age 2, all b. Mich., in their household. Theodocia died in 1872; and Osmyn afterwards moved to Ann Arbor, Mich. where he died 5 June 1879. Ref: P&BA-Len pg. 1050-1.

SALSBURY, PHILIP and wife, CLARISSA (CURTIS) of Warsaw (then Genesee, now Wyoming Co.), NY were parents of ORPHA ARMENIA (or AMELIA?) born 13 Dec. 1811 (m. James Livesay, also see). Ref: P&BA-Len pg. 535-6.

SALSBURY, PHILIP F. born ca. 1822, and wife, MARY J., born ca. 1828, both in NY, were listed in the 1850 census of Fairfield Twp., Lenawee Co., Mich. Note: He is listed in the census next door to Solomon Force, and note D. C. (preceding).

SALTON, ANNABELLA of Ireland (See John Magee).

SAMMONS, SAMPSON born ca. 1790, NY, was an early settler of Adrian where operated a hotel. In the 1850 census of Adrian Twp., Lenawee Co., Mich. he listed with MARY, age 33, born NY, in his household. Known son, JOHN L. (m. Loretta L. Howard, dau. of Francis A., also see; he d. 19 May 1879, Rome Twp.; Loretta married again to Augustus F. Daniels, also see) Ref: P&BA-Len pg. 362-3.

SAMPLE, MARY (See John Murphy)

SAMPSON also see SAMSEN & SAMSON

SAMPSON, CORNELIUS born ca. 1826, NY, was listed in the 1850 census of Woodstock Twp., Lenawee Co., Mich. with probably mother, SARAH, age 67, born NY, in their household. It was probably she listed head of household in the 1840 census index of Woodstock Twp.

SAMSEN also see SAMSON

SAMSEN, FREDERICK W., son of HENRY H. (following), born 31 Mar. 1855, Toledo, Ohio, came to Adrian, Lenawee Co., Mich. in 1873; and to Blissfield in 1874. He married in 1876 to SOPHIE (PARKER) born 4 Sept. 1855, Bryan, Ohio. Children: 1. LAWRENCE B. b. 3 Sept. 1878; 2. RALPH G. b. 16 July 1880. Ref: P&BA-Len pg. 634-5.

SAMSEN, HENRY H., son of LEWIS (following), born ca. 1811, Germany, came to the US with his parents to Toledo, Ohio. He remained there until 1881, then moved to Denver, Colo. Children: 1. HENRY (Denver, CO); 2. FREDERICK W. (preceding); 3. LOUISA (m. Bitter? (Denver, CO); 4. JOHN (Pueblo, CO); 5. FREDERICK W. (preceding); 6. LEWIS; 7. EDDIE. Ref: PB&A-Len pg. 634-5.

SAMSEN, LEWIS and wife (name not stated), came from Germany to the US in 1825, and settled near Toledo, O.

He died in Jan. 1877 in Toledo, and his wife had preceded him. Children: 1. HENRY H. (preceding); 2. JOHN (Wood Co., O.); 3. WILLIAM (d. Toledo, O.); 4. LEWIS (Toledo, O.); 5. ELIZA (m. Henry Schepler, Wood Co., O.); 6. MARY (m. Fred Schultz). Ref: P&BA-Len pg. 634-5.

SAMSON also see SAMPSON & SAMSEN

SAMSON, WILLIAM HOLLAND married MINNIE E. (BIXBY), daughter of Alonzo Foster (also see), born 16 Oct. 1858. Had a known son, RUSSELL ALONZO. Ref: P&BA-Len pg. 1021-2.

SANBORN, DANIEL was listed in the 1840 census index of Seneca Twp., Lenawee Co., Mich.

SANBORN, WILLIAM (See John M. Payne)

SANDERS, CHARLES (See George W. Rudesill)
SANDERS, EMMA (See Warren Gilbert)
SANDERS, GEORGE was listed in the 1840 census index of Raisin Twp., Lenawee Co., Mich.
SANDERS, JACOB born ca. 1789, Penn., married there to LYDIA (EGBERT), daughter of James (also see). They moved first to NY, then in 1838 to Adrian Twp., Lenawee Co., Mich. They were listed in the 1850 census with Stephen Holt, age 13, born Mich., in their household. Known daughter, ALMIRA b. ca. 1825, NY (m. Stephen Bugbee, also see). Jacob died 9 Jan. 1860. Lydia married again, name not stated, but he only lived 6 months. She died 30 Aug. 1864. Ref: P&BA-Len pg. 974-5.
SANDERS, LOUDWICK and wife, MARY, moved from Middle Smithfield, Penn. to Ovid, Seneca Co., NY after 1805. She died there in 1840, age 52. He afterwards (after 1850?) went to Woodstock Twp., where he died 29 Aug. 1859, age 83. Known daughter, BETSEY b. 22 Dec. 1805, Middle Smithfield (m/1 George Lucas; m/2 Jeremiah Wilsey, see both). Ref: P&BA-Len pg. 752-3.
SANDERS, WILLIAM was listed in the 1840 census index of Rome Twp., Lenawee Co., Mich.

SANDERSON, ALBERT (See Joseph Atkinson Thompson)
SANDERSON, DEACON was a blacksmith during the Revolutionary War; and afterwards moved to Barre, NY. Known daughter, CYNTHIA (m. Daniel Colwell, also see). Ref: P&BA-Len pg. 820-2.
SANDERSON, GEORGE born ca. 1800, and wife, ELIZABETH, born ca. 1803, both in England, were listed in the 1850 census of Adrian Twp., Lenawee Co., Mich.
SANDERSON, JOHN was listed in the 1840 census index of Macon Twp., Lenawee Co., Mich.

SANDFORD, MARK of Folkstone, Kent, England, had known daughter, REBECCA b. 1777 (m. James Jeffery, also see, of Sandgate, England). Ref: P&BA-Len pg. 1004-6.

SANDS, JAMES, born 1662, and wife, SARAH (CORNELL), of Sands Point, Long Island, NY, were parents of MARY (m. Joseph Sutton, also see).

SANFORD, ABRAHAM was listed in the 1840 census index of Liberty Twp., Jackson Co., Mich. Adjacent were DANIEL; & W. G.
SANFORD, ABRAM, only son of JOHN (following), born 10 Sept. 1822, Mt. Morris, (then Genesee Co., now Livingston Co.), NY, and moved to Saline, Washtenaw Co., Mich. with his father. He married there on 10 Mar. 1841 to MARANDA (STRANAHAN), daughter of George S. (also see). In the 1850 census of Woodstock Twp., Lenawee Co., Mich. they were listed next door to JOHN. After a brief sojourn in California, they returned to Brooklyn, Jackson Co., where they made their home. Children who were surviving in 1881: 1. CORDELIA b. 5 Apr. 1852, Jackson Co. (m. Dr. Oliver Quincy Jones, also see); 2. SARAH E. (m. John L. DeLamater). Ref: P&BA-Len pg. 402-3 & History of Jackson Co., Mich., pg. 812.
SANFORD, ASAHEL born ca. 1794, and wife, ABBY, born ca. 1800, Conn., may be he listed in the 1840 census index of Saline, Washtenaw Co., Mich., adjacent to an EZRA; and was listed in the 1850 census of Tecumseh Twp., Lenawee Co., Mich. in the household of probably daughter, ABBY ANN b. ca. 1820, NY and husband, John B. Curry.
SANFORD, CARRIE (See Charles C. Bradish)
SANFORD, CHLOE (See Charles C. Bradish)
SANFORD, CYRENUS, son of ISAAC (following), born 19 Mar. 1815, married in Cayuga Co., NY on 24 Mar. 1839 to LOUISA (GARDNER). In 1841, they moved from Cayuga Co. to Huron Co., Ohio, and she died there in 1844, leaving children: 1. LYDIA M. (m. Albert C. Daniels, Fulton Co., O.); 2. FRANCES A. (m. Schuyler Bradley); 3. LOUISA B. (m. James H. Herrick); 4. JAMES M. (m. Carrie Wilson, Fairfield Twp., Lenawee Co.). Cyrenus married again in Huron Co., Ohio to JULIA A. (DEMMING); and they moved to Fairfield Twp. in 1851 where she died in 1865 (no children). He married third in 1866 at Morenci, Mich. to Mrs. ANN E. (FLETCHER) KENDALL, daughter of Alfred, and widow of George (see both). Children: 5. CORA L. (m. Oscar J. Mead, Fulton Co., O.); 6. FLORENCE I. Ref: P&BA-Lenpg. 804-5.
SANFORD, E. N., son of MALACHI (following), born ca. 1830, NY, and wife, MARGARET, born ca. 1825, Penn., were listed in the 1850 census of Woodstock Twp., Lenawee Co., Mich. with ALICE, age 2; JAMES, age 1, both b. Mich., in their household.
SANFORD, EDGAR A. (See George Kendall)
SANFORD, EDITH (See Garrett F. Harris)
SANFORD, ELIAS, son of ZACHARIAH (following), born 1818, Conn., went to Genesee Co. NY with his father. He married ADELINE (STEVENS), daughter of Israel (also see) and settled in Sandusky Co., Ohio. He died there at age 24 (ca. 1842); and his wife was still living in Clyde, Sandusky Co., Ohio in 1888. Known daughter, HANNAH b. Sandusky (m. Capt. Spencer Russell, also see). Ref: P&BA-Len pg. 661-2.
SANFORD, ELIJAH was listed in the 1840 census index of Saline, Washtenaw Co., Mich. adjacent to ASAHEL & EZRA, also see.
SANFORD, EPHRAIM was a Revolutionary patriot in Penn., and a Baptist Minister. His wife was ? (VAN CAMPEN); and they moved first to Vermont; and afterwards to Steuben Co., NY. He had 2 known sons:

EZRA (following); JOHN (following). History of Livingston Co., Mich., pg. 442-3.

SANFORD, EZEKIEL born ca. 1766, New Lebanon, Conn., married SUSANNAH (BADGER) born ca. 1778, Conn. They went to Ontario Co., NY ca. 1799, and Erie Co., NY before 1820. He died there in 1828, age 62. Susannah was listed head of household in the 1840 census index of Woodstock Twp., Lenawee Co., Mich. (adjacent to another EZEKIEL; EZRA; MALACHI; & JOSEPH, all following). She died in 1844, age 66. There were 6 sons and 2 daughters. Known son, MALACHI, and the others listed in 1840 are probably all their sons. Youngest son, LEWIS (following). Ref: P&BA-Len pg. 1129-30.

SANFORD, EZEKIEL W., probably son of EZEKIEL (preceding), born ca. 1804, and wife, EMILY, born ca. 1808, both born NY, were listed in the 1850 census of Woodstock Twp., Lenawee Co., Mich. (2 doors from MALACHI) with GEORGE, age 19; MARIA, age 16?, both b. NY; and HORACE?, age 13; MORTIMER, age 7; LAURA, age 3, all b. Mich., in their household.

SANFORD, EZRA, son of EPHRAIM (preceding), and wife, SARAH, came to Cohoctah, Livingston Co., Mich. from Steuben Co., NY on 9 July 1835. He died in Cohoctah Twp. on 2 Jan. 1844, and she died ca. 1855. In the 1850 census of Cohoctah Twp. (then called Tuscola), Livingston Co., Mich., she was age 69, born NY, head of household, with only Samuel & James in the household. Children: 1. ESTHER (m/1 Ziba Stone; m/2 Daniel Barlow); 2. HANNAH (m. Michael Thatcher, also see); 3. JOHN H. (to Wright, Ottawa Co., Mich.); 4. Dr. EZRA; 5. JAMES b. ca. 1825, NY; 6. DAVID (to Flushing, Genesee Co., Mich.); 7. EPHRAIM H. (Wabaunsee, KS); 8. SAMUEL b. ca. 1829, NY (killed in Kansas, 1859); 9. EMILY (m. William Stroud, Cohoctah); 10. ELIZABETH (m/1 Luther Houghton; m/2 John Lane). History of Livingston Co., Mich., pg. 442-3; 445.

SANFORD, EZRA, probably son of EZEKIEL (preceding), born ca. 1811, NY, was listed in the 1850 census of Woodstock Twp., Lenawee Co., Mich. with WENDELL? (female), age 14; ANDREW, age 11; PHOEBE, age 10; ALA--(male), age 7; BETSEY, age 3 or 5, all b. Mich., in his household.

SANFORD, EZRA born ca. 1793, VT, and wife, SARAH, born ca. 1797, Penn., were listed in the 1850 census of Franklin Twp., Lenawee Co., Mich. with no family in their household. Note LUTHER N., following. Also EZRA may be he listed in the 1840 census index of Saline, Washtenaw Co., Mich. adjacent to ASAHEL (preceding).

SANFORD, HENRY and wife, LAURA (WELLS), were early settlers to Raisin Twp., Lenawee Co., Mich. They went to Jackson Co., Mich., and it may be he listed as "H. P." in Springport, Jackson Co., Mich. in the 1840 census index. They also lived in Kalamazoo Co., Mich. Known daughter, FLORENCE b. 17 Sept. 1853, Jackson Co., Mich. (m. Albert D. Lawrence, also see). Ref: P&BA-Len pg. 763-4.

SANFORD, ISAAC and wife, RACHEL (WILBUR), were reared and married in Dutchess Co., NY; and they settled in Cayuga Co., NY. Children's names not mentioned except #5. CYRENUS (preceding). Ref: P&BA-Len pg. 804-5.

SANFORD, ISBURN born ca. 1817, and wife, AMANDA, born ca. 1820, both in NY, moved first to about 4 miles south of Norwalk, Huron Co., Ohio. About 1849, they removed to Fairfield Twp., Lenawee Co., Mich. Children: 1. MARY J. b. 1 May 1838, Ohio (census said NY?; m. Charles W. Dunn, also see); 2. MARTHA E. (d. infancy); 3. EDGAR A. (lived Fairfield Twp.) Ref: P&BA-Len pg. 922. Note CYRENUS & ISAAC, preceding.

SANFORD, JAMES, probably son of JOHN (following), born ca. 1814, and wife, MARY, born ca. 1812, both in NY, were listed in the 1850 census of Livingston Co., Mich. with CHILSON, age 12; JOHN, age 11; MARY, age 8; WILLIAM, age 4, all b. Mich.; and mother, MARY, age 64, b. Penn., in their household.

SANFORD, JOHN, son of EPHRAIM (preceding), with wife, MARY, born ca. 1783 (sketch said b. NY, census said b. Penn.), came first to Mich. in 1832, possibly first to Salem, Washtenaw Co., Mich., then to Oakland Co., and to Cohoctah by 1834. He died there in Nov. 1845; and she died at age 92. In the 1850 census, she was listed in the household of daughter, JANE b. 1808, NY (m. Anthony Clark, Cohochtah); and it is probably Mary listed again in the household of JAMES (preceding). Known daughter, PHEBE b. ca. 1811, NY (m. William Bennett, Hamburg, Livingston Co., Mich.). Ref: History of Livingston Co., Mich., pg. 442-3. Note: In the 1840 census index, also listed in Tuscola, Livingston Co. with JAMES was EARLE.

SANFORD, JOHN, probably son of EZEKIEL (preceding), born ca. 1800, NY, and wife, CLARINDA, born ca. 1797, NJ, were listed in the 1850 census of Woodstock Twp., Lenawee Co., Mich., next door to son, ABRAHAM (preceding).

SANFORD, JOSEPH, probably son of EZEKIEL (preceding), born ca. 1810, and wife, HULDAY, born ca. 1815, both in NY, were listed in the 1850 census of Woodstock Twp., Lenawee Co., Mich. with HIRAM, age 16; SUSANNAH, age 14, both b. NY; and MARY, age 12; MERCY, age 10; CYNTHIA, age 8; ESTHER, age 6; SYLVESTER, age 4, all b. Mich., in their household.

SANFORD, LEWIS, son of EZEKIEL (preceding), born 14 Apr. 1820, Wales, Erie Co., NY, left there at age 16 and went to Michigan. He married DELILAH (WHEATON), daughter of Egbert (also see) of Raisin Twp., Lenawee Co.; and settled in Woodstock Twp. In the 1850 census they were listed next door to EZRA (preceding). Children: 1. ADELAIDE A. b. 28 June 1844 (m. Frank R. Pearson, also see); 2. LEWIS b. 15 Oct. 1847 (d. 12 Aug. 1850); 3. HORACE b. 31 Mar. 1850 (d. 22 Sept. 1850); 4. ADELINE D. b. 15 Sept. 1851 (m. George Lewis); 5. CHARLES WESLEY b. 27 Sept. 1853 (m. Agnes Bakewell of Ingham Co., Mich.); 6. ELSIE b. 28 May 1855 (m. Charles D. Binns); 7. ELLA D. b. 31 Oct. 1859 (m. James Lamb); 8. LEROY b. 1 July 1866 (d. 25 Mar. 1870); 9. IDA M. b. 26 Oct. 1868 (d. 3 Nov. 1885). Ref: P&BA-Len pg. 1129-30.

SANFORD, LUTHER N. born ca. 1803, Conn., and wife, CATHARINE, born ca. 1797, NY, were listed in the 1850 census of Franklin Twp., Lenawee Co., Mich. with ESTHER ANN, age 17, b. NY; and ELLMORE, age 15; WESLEY, age 13; DORITA?, age 10, all b. Mich., in their household. Note: It may be he listed in the 1840 census

Pioneer Families of Southeastern Michigan

index of Milan, Monroe Co., Mich. Also note ZACHARIAH, following.

SANFORD, MALACHI, son of EZEKIEL (preceding), born 31 Dec. 1799, Phelps, Ontario Co., NY, married in Wales, Erie Co., NY to Mrs. BALSORA (HOLMES) SCOTT, daughter of John M. (also see), and widow of Jared of Wales, NY. They removed to Woodstock Twp., Lenawee Co., Mich. in 1837. He died on 3 Mar. 1870; and she was still living there in 1888. Four children, names not stated, and those known are: E. N. (preceding); & LORETTA b. 9 Sept. 1826, Wales, NY (m. Peter W. Wheaton, also see). Ref: P&BA-Len pg. 956-7.

SANFORD, SARAH (See William Harriott)

SANFORD, SUSAN (See Isaac Benedict)

SANFORD, ZACHARIAH born Saybrook, Conn., moved first to Genesee Co., NY; and then to Townsend Twp., Sandusky Co., Ohio where he died in 1862. Known son, ELIAS (preceding). Also note LUTHER N. (preceding).

SANGER, BENJAMIN and wife, BETSEY (WOODWARD), natives of Conn., had moved in their youth to Canandaigua, Ontario Co., NY and married there. He served in the War of 1812. She died in 1827/8, age 42, in NY. He came to Seneca Twp., Lenawee Co., Mich. in July 1833, and died there in Feb. 1849, age 66. There were 9 children, names not stated, except SARAH JANE b. ca. 1817, NY (m. Stephen Hayward, also see); & PHILA b. 3 Sept. 1822 (m. Micajah Hayward); and probably sons, JONATHAN & HENRY P. (following). Ref: P&BA-Len pg. 913-4; 998-9.

SANGER, CHLOE (See John B. Brockelbank)

SANGER, HENRY P., probably son of BENJAMIN (preceding), born ca. 1821, and wife, LYDIA, born ca. 1823, both in NY, were listed in the 1850 census of Seneca Twp., Lenawee Co., Mich. with PAMELIA M., age 10/12, b. Mich., in their household.

SANGER, JONATHAN, probably son of BENJAMIN, born ca. 1818, NY, and wife, JANE, born ca. 1823, Scotland, were listed in the 1850 census of Seneca Twp., Lenawee Co., Mich. with JOSEPHINE, age 4; MARGARET, age 3; ELNORA, age 2; RICHARD, age 10/12; BENJAMIN, age 10/12, all b. Mich., in their household.

SANTEE, GEORGE born Lancaster Co., Penn. married CALISTA (PARENT), daughter of Benjamin and Betsey (Robb), of Lorain Co., Ohio. They settled in Amherst Twp., Lorain Co., Ohio, and later in Royalton, Fulton Co. Known son, JAMES G. (following). Ref: P&BA-Len pg. 198.

SANTEE, JAMES G., son of GEORGE (preceding), had a known daughter, ABBIE J. (m. Adam H. Uloth, also see). Ref: P&BA-Len pg. 198.

SATHERWAITE, JOSEPH born ca. 1822, NJ, and wife, ELIZABETH M., born ca. 1825, Penn., were listed in the 1850 census of Raisin Twp., Lenawee Co., Mich. with ANN E., age 7/12, b. Mich., and brother?, WILLIAM, age 26, b. NJ; and Jonathan J. Comfort, age 20, b. Penn., in their household. Note SAMUEL, following.

SATHERWAITE, REUBEN and wife, RACHEL, were "pioneers to Raisin Twp., Lenawee Co., Mich." In the 1830 census of Lenawee Co., Territory of Mich., they were listed both ages 20-30 with no family. Known daughter, MARY E. b. 27 June 1835 (m. Nehemiah H. Sutton, also see).

SATHERWAITE, SAMUEL born ca. 1790, and wife, ELIZABETH, born ca. 1794, both in New Jersey, were listed in the 1840 census index of Tecumseh Twp., Lenawee Co., Mich.; and in the 1850 census with WILLIAM, age 25; SAMUEL, age 23; ELIZABETH, age 21, all b. NJ, in their household.

SAULSBURY see SALSBURY

SAUNDERS also see SANDERS

SAUNDERS, SOPHIA (See David Gander)

SAVAGE, AARON born ca. 1802, and wife, CAROLINE, born ca. 1809, both in NY, were listed in the 1840 census index of Medina Twp., Lenawee Co., Mich. (adjacent to JUSTUS); and in the 1850 census with SARAH, age 18; CHARLES, age 16; JOHN R., age 10, all b. NY; and JULIET, age 9; GEORGE, age 7, both b. Mich., in their household.

SAVAGE, ASAHEL was born 1783, Mass., and was listed in the 1850 census of Fairfield Twp., Lenawee Co., Mich., with ISAAC O., age 16, b. NY, both in the household of son, PHILANDER (following). Note: ISAAC O. was said to have operated a sawmill in Lenawee Co., In 1865.

SAVAGE, CHESTER born ca. 1798, and wife, AURELIA, born ca. 1797, both in NY, were listed in the 1850 census of Seneca Twp., Lenawee Co., Mich. with EUNICE, age 23; CHESTER, age 18, both b. NY; and VILETTA, age 15; JAMES, age 12, both b. Mich., in their household.

SAVAGE, CHLOE born VT (See James R. Norton).

SAVAGE, E. G. (See John Gurnee)

SAVAGE, EBER M. was listed in the 1840 census index of Clinton Twp., Lenawee Co., Mich.

SAVAGE, JOHN F. born ca. 1822, and wife, JULIA A., born ca. 1821, both in NY, were listed in the 1850 census of Dover Twp., Lenawee Co., Mich. with HARRIET A., age 8?; and FRANCIS E., age 3, both b. Mich., in their household.

SAVAGE, JUSTUS was listed in the 1840 census index of Medina Twp., Lenawee Co., Mich. adjacent to AARON (preceding).

SAVAGE, PHILANDER, probably son of ASAHEL (preceding), born ca. 1817, and wife, LOVINA (ABBOTT), daughter of Daniel C. (also see), born ca. 1825, both in NY, were listed in the 1850 census of Fairfield Twp., Lenawee Co., Mich. with MARY, age 5, b. Mich.; and also ASAHEL (preceding), in their household.

SAVAGE, ROBERT married IDA V. (NICKERSON), daughter of Ira S. (also see) of Madison Twp., Lenawee Co., Mich. Son, FRED N. b. 24 Aug. 1885. Ref: P&BA-Len pg. 422-3.

SAVAGE, THOMAS (See Peleg C. Haviland)

SAVIER, LEMUEL Gen. (See Perley Bills)

SAWYER, ARMENIA (See William White)

SAWYER, JOSEPH of Poland, Maine was father of MARY (m. Stephen Yeaton).

SAWYER, MERCY (See Isaiah Stone)

SAYERS also see SAYRES

SAYERS, REUBEN[1] born 21 Jan. 1814, Sussex Co., England, married there on 14 Nov. 1833 to JANE (PICKARD) born 9 Mar. 1817. In 1849, with 4 children, they came to the US and settled in Madison Twp., Lenawee Co., Mich. They were listed in the 1850 census of Madison Twp. with REUBEN[2] (following); HENRY, age 9; AMOS, age 7; JAMES, age 4, all b. England; and ELIZA, age 1/12, born Mich., in their household. Reuben died 4 July 1853. Ref: P&BA-Len pg. 1054-5.

SAYERS, REUBEN[2], son of REUBEN[1] (preceding), born 10 Oct. 1834, near London, England, came to Lenawee Co., Mich. with his parents. He married ADELINA A. (SNEDEKER), daughter of James (also see), and settled in Adrian Twp. Children: 1. EDGAR B. b. 27 Feb. 1861 (m. Lucy Hill). They also adopted Mattie E. Chapman b. 8 May 1876. Ref: P&BA-Len pg. 1054-5.

SAYERS also see SAYRES

SAYRES, EDGAR or AGER born ca. 1809, NY, and wife, LUCY, born ca. 1811, VT, were listed in the 1840 census index of Adrian Twp., Lenawee Co., Mich.; and in the 1850 census with HELEN, age 15; ADALINE, age 11; WILLIAM, age 9; EDGAR, age 7; EMILY, age 5; LUCY, age 7/12 (may be this child listed again in DeGraff household in the 1850 census of Palmyra Twp.)

SAYRES, ERVIN EUGENE born ca. 1848, Mich., was adopted at age 10 months by SETH B. (following). Ervin was the son of a sister (name not stated) of Seth's wife, Hannah (Laycock). He married JULIA (BATES) and settled in Rome Twp., Lenawee Co., Mich. Two known children: 1. ARTHUR; 2. HALSEY. Ref: P&BA-Len pg. 1188-90.

SAYRES, SAMUEL, son of SQUIRE (following), died in 1848 in Kalamazoo, Mich. leaving 2 children: JULIA & EDMUND. These children were reared by SETH B. Ref: P&BA-Len pg. 1188-90.

SAYRES, SETH B., son of SQUIRE (following), born 21 Aug. 1817, Saratoga Co., NY, removed to Seneca Twp., Lenawee Co., Mich. He married there on 12 Feb. 1840 to HANNAH (LAYCOCK), probably daughter of Jonathan (also see). She died 18 Aug. 1865 in Seneca Twp. In the 1850 census, they had only adopted son, ERVIN EUGENE (preceding) in their household. Seth married again on 22 Oct. 1866 to Mrs. ELIZA (FOOT) WHITE, widow of Warren (also see); and she died 20 Aug. 1880. Seth married Mrs. CATHERINE (BAGERLY) SLOAN, daughter of Tyson & Sarah (Bell), and widow of Robert. Ref: P&BA-Len pg. 1188-90.

SAYRES, SQUIRE was a native of New Jersey, and his wife, EUNICE (MEECH), was a native of Conn. He was a Lt. in the Amsterdam Volunteers during the War of 1812. After the war, the family moved to Galway, Saratoga Co., NY; and about 1823 to Auburn, NY. They then moved to Genesee Co., NY; and later to Seneca Twp., Lenawee Co., Mich. to join son, SETH B. (preceding). There were 7 sons and 3 daughters, and 9 lived to maturity, names not stated, except preceding and SAMUEL (preceding); and probably HENRY b. ca. 1827, NY (with wife, Rebecca, age 21, b. Mich., was listed in 1850 census next door to Seth B.) Ref: P&BA-Len pg. 1188-90.

SCANLAN, BRIDGET (See Michael Davitt)

SCARRITT, JAMES[3], son of JAMES[2] (See JEREMIAH[1], following), married in Conn. to SYLVIA (PLUMB) and remained there until about 1806, then removed to Smyrna, Chenango Co., NY where he lived out his life. Known son, JAMES[4] (following). Ref: P&BA-Len 701-2.

SCARRITT, JAMES[4], son of JAMES[3] (preceding), born 1 Jan. 1799, Conn., moved with his parents to Smyrna, Chenango Co., NY where he married POLLY (WOOLDRIDGE), daughter of John (also see) and remained there. Five children, names not stated, except JAMES M.[5] (following). Ref: P&BA-Len pg. 701-2.

SCARRIT, JAMES M.[5], son of JAMES[4] (preceding), born 1 Sept. 1834, Smyrna, NY, married on 31 July 1854 at Shelburne, NY to CLARISSA ALMEDA (TACKABERRY), daughter of Middleton (also see). They lived several places in NY, before moving to Hudson, Lenawee Co., Mich. Children: 1. CLARA A. (m. Louis E. Palmer; Rochester, Mich.); 2. MATTIE M. (m. Charles Steuerwald). Ref: P&BA-Len pg. 701-2.

SCARRIT, JEREMIAH[1] came from Leicestershire, England to Conn. in Colonial times. Among his large family, names not stated, was JAMES[2] born in New Haven Co., Conn. who served in the American Revolution. He had a known son, JAMES[3] (preceding). Ref: P&BA-Len pg. 701-2.

SCHAFFER, JAMES (See Dr. Alexander W. Seger)

SCHEDER, WILLIAM probably SCHREDER (son of ISRAEL H., also see).

SCHEPLER, HENRY (See Lewis Samsen)

SCHERMERHORN, WILLIAM was a descendant of the "Knickerbocker Families," who with his wife, HELEN, lived in Claverack, Columbia Co., NY in 1835; but afterwards moved to Palmyra, Wayne Co., NY, where he died. Known son, WILLIAM TenBROECK (following). Helen married again to H. C. Morgan. Ref: P&BA-Len pg. 872-3.

SCHERMERHORN, WILLIAM TenBROECK, son of WILLIAM (preceding), born 18 Mar. 1835, Claverack, Columbia Co., NY, married in 1857 at Lyons, Wayne Co., NY to JENNIE (TERRY), daughter of Capt. Horace (also see). They later moved to Hudson, Lenawee Co., Mich. where he died on 15 Dec. 1884. There were 12 children, but only 10 named in sketch. 1. WILLIAM T. JR. (d. 18 Apr. 1887); 2. EMMA W. (m. Frank Barnes of Colorado); 3. NELLIE C.; 4. JAMES; 5. MARY B.; 6. BYRON R.; 7. CHARLIE T.; 8. FREDERICK N.; 9. VILETTE T.; 10. HARRY V. C. Ref: P&BA-Len pg. 872-3.

SCHISLER, ELIZA (See Jonathan Hartman)

SCHMIDT, MICHAEL born 9 Nov. 1828, Wurtemburg, Germany, came to the US in 1852; and settled first in Amherst, Lorain Co., Ohio. He married there on 30 Dec. 1854 to ROSANNA (BUHL) born 13 Mar. 1837, Wurtemburg. After 2-1/2 years, they moved to Sandusky Co., Ohio; and in 1863, settled in Madison Twp., Lenawee Co., Mich. There were 8 children, exact order of birth not known, but first 3 listed were said to be deceased by 1888: ELIZABETH R.; JOHN F.; MARX

Pioneer Families of Southeastern Michigan

J.; and surviving were GEORGE A.; JACOB M.; FRED W.; HENRY C.; EDWARD A. Ref: P&BA-Len pg. 570-1.

SCHNEIRLA, CHRISTIAN, son of JACOB (following), born 22 May 1840, Wurtemburg, Germany, came to the US about 1853 with his aunt, Mrs. Shoemaker, and lived first in Ann Arbor, Washtenaw Co., Mich. In 1861, he went to California, afterwards visited Germany, then returned to Mich. where he settled in Clinton Twp., Lenawee Co. He married in 1868 in Washtenaw Co. to REGINA (WALTER) who had come to the US in 1861 from Wurtemburg with her parents. Children: 1. ANNA; 2. JACOB; 3. CHRISTIAN; 4. PAULINE; 5. EDDIE; 6. REGINA; 7. CHARLES; 8. WILLIAM; 9. CLARA; 10. WALTER; 11. CLARENCE; 12. EMMA. Ref: P&BA-Len pg. 213-4.

SCHNEIRLA, JACOB and wife, BARBARA (FRY), of Wurtemburg, Germany were parents of 4 sons and 2 daughters, only mentioned was CHRISTIAN (preceding). Jacob died there in 1846, and his wife married again and remained there. Ref: P&BA-Len pg. 213-4.

SCHOFIELD also see SCOFIELD
SCHOFIELD, ELIZABETH married first to ? Van Dusen; and second to Lewis V. Miller (also see).
SCHOFIELD, WILLIAM (See Samuel Bryan)

SCHOMP, EVA probably born after 1860 (See Edwin Smith).
SCHOMP, GEORGE B. (See William W. Wyman; and note GEORGE H. in MAHLON, household, probably same).
SCHOMP, MAHLON born ca. 1806, and wife, MARIAH, born ca. 1814, both in NY, were listed in the 1850 census of Fairfield Twp., Lenawee Co., Mich. with GEORGE H., age 16; CORNELIA A., age 14, both b. NY; and MARGARET, age 11; CAROLINE, age 4, both b. Mich., in their household. Note: It appears to be MAHLON in the 1840 census index of Lyons Twp., Oakland Co., Mich.

SCHOOLEY, WILLIAM H. and wife, ANNA (MILLER), from Romulus, Seneca Co., NY had known daughter, PAULINA (m. John Young, also see, born 1796).

SCHREDER, ELIJAH R. born ca. 1791, and wife, SUSAN, born ca. 1798, both in NY, were listed in the 1840 census index of Macon Twp., Lenawee Co., Mich. (adjacent to JOHN F., following); and in the 1850 census of Ridgeway Twp. with GEORGE, age 16, b. Penn.; and ESTHER, age 12; CHARLES, age 8, both b. Mich., in their household.

SCHREDER, ISRAEL H., son of JOHN F. (following), born 5 Dec. 1819, Moreland, Montgomery Co., Penn., moved to Ridgeway Twp., Lenawee Co., Mich. with his parents. He married there to ANSAH (FLORENCE) who died after 2 years of marriage. He married again on 4 July 1841 to MARGARET (GILLESPIE), daughter of Richard B. (also see); and there were no children in the household in the 1850 census of Raisin Twp., Lenawee Co., so apparently most born after 1850. Children: 1. ELIZA M. (d. infancy); 2. MARY C. (m. Casper Cook, Milan, Monroe Co., Mich.); 3. JOHN F. 2ND (following); 4. ANN (m. Dwight A. Goodrich; Mendon, St. Joseph Co., Mich.); 5. WILLIS G. (m. Melvina Patterson; Clinton Twp.); 6. EMMA J. (m. Lewis M. Waldron). Ref: P&BA-Len pg. 228-9.

SCHREDER, JOHN F. was born ca. 1789, Orange Co., NY, and went to Penn. as a young man. He married there to SUSAN (WAMBOLD); and after the birth of 4 children, they moved by 1840 census to Macon Twp., Lenawee Co., Mich. (listed adjancent to ELIJAH R., preceding); and moved to Ridgeway Twp. before 1850. He died 26 Nov. 1882, almost 95; and she died 24 May 1842, Ridgeway Twp. He was listed in the 1850 census of Ridgeway Twp. with CATHARINE, age 28, b. Penn.; CRISCELDA, age 12; HELEN, age 1, both b. Mich., in his household. Known son, ISRAEL H. (preceding). Ref: P&BA-Len pg. 227-8.

SCHREDER, JOHN F. 2ND, son of ISRAEL H. (preceding), born 15 Feb. 1852, Raisin Twp., Lenawee Co., Mich., and married on 15 Dec. 1875 in Tecumseh to JENNIE M. (STEVENSON), daughter of William (also see). They settled in Clinton Twp. Children: 1. LOVICA C.; 2. LOVINA J.; 3. CHARLES F.; 4. LYDIA M.; 5. MAGGIE M.; BLANCHE R. Ref: P&BA-Len pg. 641-2.

SCHREYER, FREDERICK J. and wife, KUNINGUNDA (MARTIN), of Bavaria, came to New York City ca. 1841. They moved to Macon Twp., Lenawee Co., Mich. in 1862, to join their children. He died 9 Oct. 1871, and she died in Apr. 1879, over age 80, at home of known daughter, MARGARET b. 24 Mar. 1833, Bavaria (m. John Beckley, also see).

SCHRIBER, JOHN W. born Catskill, NY, married ELLEN (SEAMANS), daughter of Daniel (also see). They remained in NY (possibly New York City) until about 1857, then moved to Sturgis, Mich.; and afterwards to Detroit, Mich. He returned to New York City in 1861, but returned to Mich. where he lived in Jackson and Detroit, ca. 1870, and Petersburg, Mich. till 1873. He also resided in Blissfield and Metamora, Mich.; and Detroit in 1888. There were 8 children, but only mentioned #5. WILLIAM E. (following). Ref: P&BA-Len pg. 730.

SCHRIBER, WILLIAM E. MD, son of JOHN W. (preceding), born 28 June 1859, Detroit, Mich., married on 29 July 1883 to PEARLIE (ROBERTSON), daughter of George P. (also see). Children: 1. HARRY; 2. LYNN. Ref: P&BA-Len pg. 730.

SCHULL, JOHN D. (See Peter R. Adams)

SCHULTZ, JUDITH (See Casper Werner)

SCHUYLER, CATY (See Zephaniah Johnson)

SCHWAB, CATHERINE (See Casper Crouse)
SCHWAB, CHRISTIAN born ca. 1822, Germany, was listed in the 1850 census of Raisin Twp., Lenawee Co., Mich. in a Judson household.
SCHWAB, JOHN P., son of JOHN (following), born 26 June 1830, Baden, Germany, came to the US at age 18, and lived first in Rochester, NY. He married there in Apr. 1853 to CATHERINE (MILLER), daughter of Bernhardt (also see); and they moved to Ridgeway Twp., Lenawee Co., Mich. Catherine died 26 Aug. 1878. Children: 1. HENRY B. (d. 16 Mar. 1868); 2. MARY (m. William

Rothdow, Monroe Co., Mich.); 3. HELEN; 4. THERESA (m. Walter Hackett; Monroe Co., Mich.); 5. MATILDA; 6. FRANCES; 7. ROSA; 8. JOHN P.; 9. CELIA; 10. HERMAN; 11. IDA. Ref: P&BA-Len pg. 545-6 & portrait of farm.

SCHWAB, JOSEPH and wife, MARY ANN (WITT), remained in Baden, Germany, where he died ca. 1844. Known son, JOHN P. (preceding). Ref: P&BA-Len pg. 545-6.

SCHWARTZ, HENRY and wife, BARBARA (MENNEL) were natives of Germany who came to Adrian, Lenawee Co., Mich. Known daughter, CARRIE (m. C. Frederick Mathes, also see).

SCOFIELD also see SCHOFIELD

SCOFIELD, CHARITY (See Dennis Wakefield; and also note SILAS A., following).

SCOFIELD, EDWIN was listed in the 1840 census index of Tecumseh Twp., Lenawee Co., Mich., adjacent to ELIAS (following).

SCOFIELD, ELIAS born ca. 1798, and wife, REBECCA, born ca. 1807, were listed in the 1840 census index of Tecumseh Twp., Lenawee Co. Mich. (adjacent to EDWIN); and in the 1850 census with HARRIET, age 22; VICTORINE?, age 9; CYRUS, age 7, listed in their household. Note LAURA, following.

SCOFIELD, ENOS, son of RUFUS (following), born ca. 1800, Dutchess Co., NY, moved to Steuben Co., NY. He married there to MARGARET (MILLER), daughter of William of Maryland, born ca. 1804/6. In 1837, they moved to Raisin Twp., Lenawee Co., Mich.; and in 1848 moved to Tecumseh Twp. He died there age 56; and she died in Mar. 1886, age 83. In the 1850 census they listed known daughter, HARRIET b. 11 May 1836, Steuben Co., NY (m. Lewis G. Lester, also see). Ref: P&BA-Len pg. 559-60.

SCOFIELD, LAURA born ca. 1833, Mich., was listed in the 1850 census of Tecumseh Twp., Lenawee Co., Mich. in a Doty household.

SCOFIELD, POLLY A. born ca. 1828, NY, was listed in the 1850 census of Adrian Twp., Lenawee Co., Mich. in the household of SILAS A. (following), probably her brother.

SCOFIELD, RUFUS was a native of Sharon, Penn. who married RHODA (GRIFFITH) in Dutchess Co., NY. They moved to Steuben Co., NY where they remained. Known son, ENOS (preceding). Ref: P&BA-Len pg. 559-60.

SCOFIELD, SILAS A. born 5 Oct. 1826, Lysander, Onondaga Co., NY, lived various places in NY until age 20, then went to Gorham Twp., Fulton Co., Ohio "where he had relatives residing." The next spring he settled in Adrian Twp., Lenawee Co., Mich.; and remained there until 1851 when he moved to Morenci. He married in Morenci on 1 Jan. 1850 to EMILY A. (WAKEFIELD), daughter of Hiram (also see). In the 1850 census of Madison Twp., they were listed with sister?, POLLY A., age 22, b. NY, in their household. All children born after 1850: 1. ANDREW (d. aged 8 yrs); 2. JOSEPHINE (d. age 19); 3. VERNON (d. age 16); 4. SARAH C. (m. F. E. Cawley, Morenci); 5. ERNEST W. (m. Myrtie V. Packer, dau. of Isaac D., also see); 6. BLANCHE. Ref: P&BA-Len pg. 733-4.

SCOTT, CLARK born ca. 1813, and wife, MARY, born ca. 1825, both in NY, were listed in the 1850 census of Riga Twp., Lenawee Co., Mich. with JOHN, age 3; WILLIAM, age 1, both b. Mich., in their household.

SCOTT, CORNELIUS born ca 1792, and wife, SALLIE (DICKSON), were natives of NY, and early settlers to Rome Twp., Lenawee Co., Mich. (there in 1840 census index). She died before 1850. They had 8 children, names not stated, except SUSAN b. ca. 1818, NY (m. William L. Rogers, also see); & probably MATILDA, b. ca. 1833, who was in his household in the 1850 census. Also listed in his household in the 1850 census were ELIZA A., age 33, b. NY (possibly second wife?); and SHELDON, age 10, b. Mich.; EDWARD, age 8, b. Ohio; and MARY, age 6; CALANTHA, age 5; ABIGAIL, age 1, all b. Mich.

SCOTT, EDWIN, age 24, born NY, was listed in the 1850 census of Madison Twp., Lenawee Co., Mich. in a Mudge household.

SCOTT, ELVIRA born ca. 1825, NY, was listed in the 1850 census of Ridgeway Twp., Lenawee Co., Mich. in a Taylor household.

SCOTT, ELIZABETH, age 17, born Mich., was listed in the 1850 census of Ridgeway Twp., Lenawee Co., Mich. in a Stowell household.

SCOTT, GEORGE, son of THOMAS (who remained in England), born 12 Mar. 1803, England, came first to New York City in 1824, and lived first in Henrietta, NY. He married in 1825 to MARY (PRATT), daughter of Joseph (also see), and they moved to near Adrian, Lenawee Co., Mich. It is probably they listed in the 1840 census index of Adrian Twp. She died in 1874. Children: 1. LYDIA P. b. 8 Jan. 1827, Farmington, Wayne Co., NY (m. Benjamin Laur, also see); 2. REBECCA b. ca. 1829, Mich. (m. Aleck Brown, Monroe Twp., Monroe Co., Mich.); 3. DEBORAH W. b. Ca. 1832; 4. MELISSA A. b. ca. 1837 (m. Benjamin Bevelhammer); 5. MARY b. ca. 1842; 6. JAMES K. b. ca. 1845 (twin of George, killed age 16 in accident); 7. GEORGE M. b. ca. 1845; 8. THOMAS H. b. ca. 1847 (m. Abbie Miller). Ref: P&BA-Len pg. 962-3; 1211-2.

SCOTT, GEORGE D., son of GEORGE (preceding), born ca. 1845, Mich., married D. (WIMPLE), daughter of John (also see). He died 15 Aug. 1880, leaving children: 1. JOHN F.; 2. LENA MAY. His wife married again in 1882 to Frank Chaffee (also see). Ref: P&BA-Len pg. 1211-2.

SCOTT, GEORGE S. born ca. 1812, Ireland, and his wife, ROXA L., born ca. 1814, NY, were listed in the 1840 census index of Palmyra Twp., Lenawee Co., Mich.; and in the 1850 census with BENJAMIN F., age 9; MILTON L., age 7; LUCILE, age 5; GEORGE W., age 3, all b. Mich., in their household.

SCOTT, HENRY, age 19, born NJ, was listed in the 1850 census of Hudson Twp., Lenawee Co., Mich. in a Cressey household.

SCOTT, JARED of Wales, Erie Co., NY, married BALSORA (HOLMES), daugher of John M. (also see). He died there; and Balsora married again to Malachi Sanford (also see).

SCOTT, JOB born ca. 1813, and wife, DIANTHA, born ca. 1815, both in VT, were listed in the 1850 census of Adrian Twp., Lenawee Co., Mich. with ROYAL M., age 13; SAMANTHA, age 12, both b. VT; and FRANCIS M.,

Pioneer Families of Southeastern Michigan

age 8; WELTHA, age 6; ROSILLA A., age 4; RANSOM, age 8/12, all b. Ohio, in their household.

SCOTT, JOHN born 11 June 1826, Yorkshire, England, married there on 11 Nov. 1846 to EMILY (TAYLOR), daughter of Thomas B. (also see). About 1849, they came to the US and settled first in Ridgeway Twp., Lenawee Co., Mich. They were listed in the 1850 census with MARY M., age 1, b. England in their household. Known son, LUKE T. b. 25 May 1852, Ridgeway Twp. After retiring, John & Emily moved into Adrian. Ref: P&BA-Len pg. 395-6.

SCOTT, JOSEPH W. born ca. 1798, and wife, SUSAN, born ca. 1797, both in Conn., were listed in the 1850 census with WILLIAM, age 25; FRANK J., age 22, both born in SC (South Carolina?), in their household.

SCOTT, LEMUEL was a native of Warren Co., VT who moved to Wayne Co., NY. Known daughter, BETSEY H. born ca. 1806, VT (m. Calvin D. Skinner, also see) in 1826 in Wayne Co., NY). After the death of Lemuel, Betsey H. had made her home with the Russell Fletcher family in Wayne Co. Ref: P&BA-Len pg. 1112-4.

SCOTT, LEONARD born ca. 1818, Penn., and wife, LAURA, born ca. 1826?, NY, were listed in the 1850 census of Palmyra Twp., Lenawee Co., Mich. with ALFRED, age 6; MARY M., age 4, both b. Penn.; and EDLIZABETH, age 1, b. Mich., in their household.

SCOTT, LUTHER born ca. 1810, and probably wife, MARY, born ca. 1814, both in NY, were listed in the 1850 census of Medina Twp., Lenawee Co., Mich. with no family. He married second to BETSEY (TABOR) and had an only child, WINFIELD (following). Ref: P&BA-Len pg. 697.

SCOTT, MARIA (See Henry Pitcher)

SCOTT, PATRICK born ca. 1822, Ireland, and wife, MARY, born ca. 1824, England, were listed in the 1850 census of Ogden Twp., Lenawee Co., Mich. with JAMES, age 8, b. Mich., in their household.

SCOTT, RUFUS born ca. 1798, and wife, ELISA, born ca. 1802, both in Conn., were listed in the 1850 census of Woodstock Twp., Lenawee Co., Mich. with BETSEY, age 25; WALTER, age 21, both b. Conn., in their household.

SCOTT, WILLIAM B. born ca. 1817, Nova Scotia, and wife, CATTARINA, born ca. 1820, NY, were listed in the 1850 census of Tecumseh Twp., Lenawee Co., Mich. with WALTER, age 5; ANGELINE, age 3; EDWARD, age 1, all b. Mich., in their household.

SCOTT, WINFIELD, son of LUTHER (preceding), born 6 Sept. 1867, Medina Twp., Lenawee Co., Mich., married on 15 June 1886 to MARY (HARTMAN), daughter of Jonathan (also see). Known daughter, DELTHY. Ref: P&BA-Len pg. 697.

SCOUT, WILLIAM and wife, MARY (STINE), moved from Penn. to Raisin Twp., Lenawee Co., Mich. in 1856. Only child mentioned, 3rd daughter, MARIA b. Columbia Co., Penn. (m. Samuel Bryan, also see).

SCOVILL, ANN (See John Cain)

SCOVILL, RANSADAN?, age 50, born NY, noted as "deaf & dumb" was listed in the 1850 census of Palmyra Twp., Lenawee Co., Mich. in the household of Charles and Jane Gray.

SCOVILL, STEPHEN, age 43, born Conn., noted as "deaf & dumb" was listed in the 1850 census of Palmyra Twp., Lenawee Co., Mich. in the household of Richard Carter.

SEAGER also see SAGER & SEGER

SEAGER, CORNELIUS D. born Phelps, NY, moved at an early day with his parents to Crawford Co., Penn., to an area about 3 miles from the Ashtabula Co., Ohio line. He married there to MARY (TURNER), daughter of Carmi (also see). After a few years, they moved to Pierpont, Ashtabula Co.; and later to Richmond Twp. About 1846, they removed to Sylvania Twp., Lucas Co., Ohio. Known son, PHILO C. (following). Ref: P&BA-Len pg. 369-70.

SEAGER, PHILO C., son of CORNELIUS D. (preceding), born 8 Apr. 1836, Pierpont, Ashtabula Co., Ohio, served in the Civil War in Co. K, 3rd Ohio Cav., which became attached to the Army of the Cumberland. He married in 1866 to ANNA J. (VICKERY), daughter of Nathan (also see). About 1872, they removed to Malvern Mills, Iowa; but returned to Riga Twp., Lenawee Co., Mich. in 1873. Children: 1. WILLIAM E.; 2. CHARLES D. Ref: P&BA-Len pg. 369-71.

SEAMANS, DANIEL born in Wales, came first to Providence, RI. He moved from there to Petersburg, Monroe Co., Mich. Known daughter, ELLEN b. Providence, RI (m. William E. Schriber, MD, also see). Ref: P&BA-Len pg. 730.

SEBRING, ANDREW, son of RICHARD (following), born ca. 1795, and wife, HARRIET, born ca. 1810, both in NY, were listed in the 1840 census index of Ogden Twp., Lenawee Co., Mich.; and in the 1850 census with ELIZABETH, age 27; GARDNER, age 23; MYRON, age 20; JOSEPH, age 18; JEROME, age 15, all b. NY; and DAVID, age 13; NORMAN, age 9; MARY, age 6, all b. Mich., in their household.

SEBRING, CORNELIUS and wife, ELIZABETH, died before 1835 in NY, and a daughter (name not stated) moved to Michigan in 1835 bringing a sister, MARGARET b. 18 June 1819, Lyons, Wayne Co., NY with her. Margaret married Samuel L. Rice (also see). Note: In 1793, in the militia of Somerset Co., NJ were CORNELIUS; & FULKERT. In the 1800 census index of Cayuga Co., NY were CORNELIUS; FULKERT; RULOFF (note following); THOMAS.

SEBRING, JACOB, probably son of RICHARD (following), born ca. 1802, and wife, HANAH, born ca. 1805, both in NY, were listed in the 1850 census of Ogden Twp., Lenawee Co., Mich. with JACKSON, age 17; ELIZABETH, age 8, both b. NY, in their household.

SEBRING, JANE born NJ (See James Brooks).

SEBRING, PERRY, probably son of RICHARD (following), born ca. 1809, and wife, DORCAS, born ca. 1822, both in NY, were listed in the 1850 census of Ogden Twp., Lenawee Co., Mich. with JULIA A., age 7; VOLNEY, age 5; SALLY, age 3; POLLY, age 1, all b. Mich., in their household (listed between RICHARD & ANDREW in the census).

SEBRING, RICHARD, born ca. 1769, NJ, and wife, ELIZABETH, born ca. 1778, Penn., were listed in the 1840 census index of Ogden Twp., Lenawee Co., Mich., adjacent to ANDREW; and in the 1850 census next door to ANDREW; and close to JACOB (preceding).

SEBRING, RULOFF born ca. 1776, NJ, was listed in the 1850 census of Ridgeway Twp., Lenawee Co., Mich. in the household of Nathan Ellis, age 56, and wife, Phebe, age 55, both b. NY, possibly father-in-law? Note: It may be he listed in the 1800 census index of Cayuga Co., NY.

SECOR, BENJAMIN born Rockland Co., NY, and wife, SARAH, born Orange Co., NY, lived in Orange Co. when she died at age 50. He moved his family to Seneca Twp., Lenawee Co., Mich. in 1843, and died in 1848. There were 6 sons and 6 daughters, names not stated, except MARY b. 19 Mar. 1824, New York City (m. Samuel K. Kinney, also see). In the 1850 census of Seneca Twp. listed as head of household was THOMAS, age 21, b. NY, with probably siblings, ELIZABETH, age 19; GEORGE, age 18; SAMUEL, age 14; DAVID, age 11?; JANE, age 9; and Joseph Smith, age 38, with wife, Hannah, age 28, b. NY (possibly another daughter of Benjamin?) and Smith children, Sarah J., age 3; Willis, age 12, relationship not known. Note WILLIAM & JOHN following.

SECOR, WILLIAM, age 10; & JOHN, age 8, both b. Mich., were listed in the 1850 census of Rome Twp., Lenawee Co., Mich. in the household of James H. & Betsey Parker, perhaps additional children of BENJAMIN (preceding).

SEEKELL, WILLIAM (See William Cairns)

SEELEY, ELIZABETH W. (See Perry W. Rowley)

SEELEY, JAMES and wife, SARAH A. (HARPER), of Seneca Co., NY, moved to Dover Twp., Lenawee Co., Mich. in 1854, and later to Seneca Twp. They resided in Morenci in 1888. Children: WILLIAM E.; MARY H. b. 26 Sept. 1841, Seneca Co., NY (m. Josiah Metcalf, 29 Mar. 1858, Osseo, Hillsdale Co., Mich.); ELLEN M.; ISAAC (deceased by 1888); HAMLIN. Ref: P&BA-Len pg. 1097.

SEELEY, JONATHAN served in the Revolutionary War. He married FREELOVE S. (BROMLEY). They had moved to Seneca Twp., Lenawee Co., Mich. in 1839, and Jonathan died that year. There were 4 sons and 5 daughters, names not stated, except McKINZEY (following). As noted in the pension record, following, Freelove had married again to Ether Barnes (also see). Ref: P&BA-Len pg. 864. In the Revolutionary War pension Applications is Jonathan "Seelye," VT sevice, Green Mountain Boys, Mrs. Freelove Barnes, former Widow, #W29614; BLWt.30704-160-55.

SEELEY, McKINZEY, son of JONATHAN (preceding), born 26 Sept. 1835, Franklin Co., NY, came to Lenawee Co., Mich. with his parents. He married on 22 Dec. 1862, Adrian, to ADELIA L. (KENDALL), daughter of Dr. Amos (also see). They lived first in Medina Twp., and retired to Morenci in 1887. Children: 1. MARY E.; 2. LILLIAN (m. Millard George); 3. JENNIE M.; 4. Infant not named. Ref: P&BA-Len pg. 864.

SEGAR also see SEGER & SEAGER
SEGAR, JEROME (See Harrison Fitts)

SEGER also see SEAGER & SEGAR

SEGER, AARON, son of ELIJAH (a Revolutionary soldier), was born 26 Apr. 1794, Chittenden, Rutland Co., VT, and married there on 1 Jan. 1822 to REBECCA (HARRISON) born 8 Apr. 1792. She died 10 July 1876, Rutland Co., VT. Known son, Dr. ALEXANDER W. (following). Ref: P&BA-Len pg. 1114-7. Note NATHAN, following.

SEGER, ALEXANDER Dr., son of AARON (preceding), born 15 Oct. 1822, Chittenden, VT, after obtaining his education, moved to Dover Twp., Lenawee Co., Mich. in 1847. He married there on 30 Sept. 1847 to PHILURA M. (STOCKWELL), daughter of Curtice W. (also see). They were listed in the 1850 census of Rome Twp., Lenawee Co., Mich. Children: 1. ELLEN J. b. 20 July 1848 (m. W. A. Lord, St. Joseph, MO); 2. LUCY T. b. 26 June 1850 (d. 17 Sept. 1851); 3. VIOLA M. b. 20 apr. 1853 (m. James Schaffer, Adrian); 4. IDA ADELL b. 30 Mar. 1856 (d. 28 July 1856); 5. AARON W. b. 5 May 1858 (d. infancy). Philura died 20 Jan. 1859. Dr. Seger married again on 11 Oct. 1859 to OLIVE L. (EGGLESTON), daughter of James (also see). Children: 6. FRANK G. b. 9 Jan. 1861 (d. 30 Aug. 1886); 7. FRED R. b. 3 Feb. 1863; 8. MATTIE R. b. 19 Dec. 1867 (m. Charles R. Burr, Adrian). Ref: P&BA-Len pg. 1114-7.

SEGER, BOWMAN E. (See David Jerrels)

SEGER, GEORGE born ca. 1814, and wife, CHARLOTTE, born ca. 1810, both in VT, were listed in the 1850 census of Adrian Twp., Lenawee Co., Mich. with Lucy A. Godard, age 22, b. NY, in their household.

SEGER, NATHAN born ca. 1812, VT, and wife, ABIGAIL, born ca. 1815, Mass., were listed in the 1850 census of Rome Twp., Lenawee Co., Mich. with EVELINE, age 14; CAROLINE, age 12; LUCY J., age 10; ADALINE, age 8; WILLIAM H., age 7, all b. NY; and NANCY, age 5, b. Mich., in their household.

SELLECK, EBENEZER L., son of PETER (following), born 19 Sept. 1796, Stafford, Conn., moved to Oneida Co., NY with his parents and married there on 3 Apr. 1822 to NANCY (WETMORE), daughter of Elisha (also see). They moved to Adrian Twp., Lenawee Co., Mich. in 1836, and he died there in Feb. 1881. Children: 1. MORRIS (following); 3. NANCY MATILDA b. 12 Sept. 1826, Oneida Co. NY (m. John L Knapp, also see); 3. JAMES b. ca. 1829 (d. before 1888); 4. RUTH b. ca. 1832 (d. before 1888); 5. MARY LOUISA b. ca. 1834; 6. CHARLOTTE b. ca. 1838 (m/1 Hiram Knapp; m/2 John Hurlbut, see both); 7. HARRIET IRENE b. 28 Oct. 1840 (m. George N. Torrey, also see); 8. CHARLES WETMORE (following); 9. HOMER ELISHA b. ca. 1847; 10. CYNTHIA E. (d. before 1888). Ref: P&BA-Len pg. 491-2; 1094-5.

SELLECK CHARLES (See Jonathan Lovell)

SELLECK, CHARLES W., son of EBENEZER L. (preceding), born 9 Mar. 1843, Adrian Twp., Lenawee Co., Mich., married on 23 Jan. 1867 to PHOEBE J. (KELLEY), daughter of Ira (also see). Children: 1. CLARA I. b. 20 Sept. 1869; 2. LOTTA E. b. 27 Mar. 1872; 3. ELBERT L. b. 7 Feb. 1875. Ref: P&BA-Len pg. 491-2.

SELLECK, H. (See William Lagore)

SELLECK, HOLBERT, age 20, born NY, was listed in the 1850 census of Medina Twp., Lenawee Co., Mich. in a Sloan houssehold (spelled "Selic.")

Pioneer Families of Southeastern Michigan

SELLECK, MORRIS, son of EBENEZER L. (preceding), born ca. 1825, Oneida Co., NY, moved with his parents to Adrian Twp., Lenawee Co., Mich. He married there in 1849 to OLIVE ARABELLA (SHAW), daughter of Nathan (also see). They settled in Hudson Twp., Lenawee Co., Mich. Adopted son, JAMES B. Ref: P&BA-Len pg. 1094-5.

SELLECK, PETER was a Revolutionary soldier who moved from Conn. to Paris Twp., Oneida Co., NY. He died there in 1838. Known son, EBENEZER L. (preceding). Ref: P&BA-Len pg. 1094-5. Note: Probably this PETER listed in Rev. War Pension Appl., Conn. service, #S15226.

SERVICE, DAVID born ca. 1810, Ireland, and wife, MARGARET (GAMBLE), born ca. 1811, Penn., were reared and married in Groveland Twp., Livingston Co.. NY; and in 1834 came to Clinton Twp., Lenawee Co., Mich. They were listed in the 1840 census index of Tecumseh Twp., Lenawee Co., Mich.; and in the 1850 census with REBECCA, age 17, b. NY; and THOMAS, age 15; ELIZABETH, age 13; JANE, age 11; DAVID, age 9; ROBERT, age 7; MARGARET, age 5; ANN, age 1/12 (m. Gragg), all b. Mich., in their household. Daughter, MARY b. 20 Aug. 1852 (m. Peter B. Sutfin, also see). David died 20 June 1867, age 59; and in 1888, Margaret, age 75, was residing in Clinton Twp. with her daughter, Mrs. Ann Gragg. Ref: P&BA- Len pg. 260-1.

SERVICE, JAMES born ca. 1784, Lanarkshire, Scotland, married there in 1806 to JANNETT (SCOTT). They came to the US in 1816, and first settled on a farm near Philadelphia, Penn. They moved to Susquehanna Co., Penn., where they remained about 7 years, then in 1825 moved to Canandaigua, Ontario Co., NY. In 1840, they moved to Fairfield Twp., Lenawee Co., Mich. She died befoe 1850, as James was listed with no family in the 1850 census. There were 9 children, names not stated, except WILLIAM (following). Also note JOHN; and WALTER (in John's household in 1850); and next door in the 1850 census was Isabella, age 35, b. Scotland, wife of Robert G. Thurber, also see, possibly a daughter of James?

SERVICE, JOHN, probably son of JAMES (preceding), born ca. 1814, Scotland, and wife, MARY, born ca. 1813, NY, were listed in the 1850 census of Fairfield Twp., Lenawee Co., Mich. with SARAH G., age 13; JOHN, age 11, both b. NY; and EDWARD, age 9; ROBERT, age 6; WILLIAM, age 4; CATHERINE, age 2, all b. Mich., and probably brother, WALTER, age 27, b. Penn., in their household.

SERVICE, WILLIAM, son of JAMES (preceding), born 23 Feb. 1807, Lanarkshire, Scotland, married on 9 July 1830, Canandaigua, NY to ANN (BULREES). They came to Mich. in 1836, and settled in Madison Twp., Lenawee Co. Children: 1. MARIAN b. 6 June 1831 (m. Eli Sparhawk, Madison Twp.); 2. WILLIAM b. 17 Apr. 1833 (d. 24 Aug. 1873); 3. CLARISSA G. 1st b. 30 July 1835 (d. 5 Apr. 1836); 4. CLARISSA G. 2nd b. 25 Apr. 1837 (d. 18 Oct. 1838); 5. JAMES B. b. 25 Mar. 1840; 6. ANN ELIZA b. 29 May 1842 (m. Charles Gaumer, Madison Twp.); 7. CLARISSA G. 3RD b. 16 Aug. 1844 (d. 8 June 1848); 8. ALEXANDER b. 27 Apr. 1847 (d. 28 Feb. 1878). Ann died 17 Feb. 1869, Madison Twp. Ref: P&BA-Len pg. 445-6.

SEVEY, MARY (See Daniel Boody)

SEYMOUR, HARRIET (See Albert G. Burton)

SEYMOUR, HORACE and wife, MARY (STANDISH), were natives of Hadley, Mass., and she was a descendant of Miles Standish. They both died in Hadley. There were 2 sons and 4 daughters, names not stated, except LOVICA C. b. 6 Jan. 1814, Hadley (m. Edwin Cook, also see). Ref: P&BA-Len pg. 352-3.

SEYMOUR, IRA and wife, BETSEY (MOREHOUSE), of Victor, Ontario Cco., NY, moved in 1826 to Webster Twp., Washtenaw Co., Mich. She died there in 1845; and he died in 1861, Lansing, Mich. Known daughter, EVELINA b. 1801 (m. Samuel Nichols, also see, on 18 Nov. 1831).

SEYMOUR, SARAH (See James W. Brown)

SHALER, CHARLES, son of CHRISTOPHER (following), born 12 July 1835, Bavaria, came to the US with his parents. He married 12 Nov. 1865 in Milan, Monroe Co., Mich. to ROSA (HANLON), daughter of Peter (also see). They settled in Macon Twp., Lenawee Co. Children: 1. MINNIE F. b. 4 Aug. 1868; 2. CLARA A. b. 5 Aug. 1871. Ref: P&BA-Len pg. 541.

SHALER, CHRISTOPHER married in Bavaria to BARBARA (HOSTETTER), and after the birth of 4 children, immigrated to the US. They settled first in Brookfield Twp., Trumbull Co., Ohio; but after a few years moved to Macon Twp., Lenawee Co., Mich. He died 8 Nov. 1865, age 58; and she died 31 July 1886, age 82. Only mentioned eldest son, CHARLES (preceding). Ref: P&BA-Len pg. 541.

SHARER, DAVID born ca. 1807, Maryland, married PAMELIA (LANGDON) of Wayne Co., NY, born ca. 1809. They moved to Michigan in 1835. She died in Rome Twp. Lenawee Co., Mich. on 18 May 1881. Known daughter, LUCY b. 30 Mar. 1834, NY (m. Dr. Henry Combs, also see).

SHARER, WILLIAM born ca. 1812, and wife, LUCINDA, born ca. 1813, both in NY, were listed in the 1840 census index of Rome Twp., Lenawee Co., Mich.; and in the 1850 census with GEORGE, age 16; HENRIETT, age 13; SELLECK, age 11; LYDIA A., age 9; MARY E., age 5, all shown b. NY?, and HENRY, age 3, b. Mich., in their household.

SHARRAR also see SHARER

SHARRAR, WILLIAM H. (See John W. Ormsby)

SHAW, ANDERSON born ca. 1815, VT, and wife, EMILY, born ca. 1821, Canada, were listed in the 1850 census of Tecumseh Twp., Lenawee Co. Mich. with JOSEPH, age 2; ALICE, age 5/12, both b. Mich.; and MARY, age 16, b. Ohio, possibly sister of Anderson?

SHAW, BRACKLEY born in April 1790, and wife, LYDIA (POOL), born 20 Apr. 1791, were both natives of Abington, Plymouth Co., Mass. He was a Lt. in the War of 1812, and after the war settled in Plainfield, Mass. In 1825, they removed to Ira, Cayuga Co., NY; and in 1835 to Dover Twp., Lenawee Co., Mich. He died 2 May 1869; and she died 23 May 1881. Children: 1. LYDIA L. (m. Orlin Phelps, also see); 2. BRACKLEY (following); 3. HARRIET A. (m. Russell Skeels); 4. Rev. HORATIO W. b. ca. 1823, Mass. (to Binghamton, NY); 5. FIDELIA A. (m/1 Peter McLouth; m/2 W. J. Wilber, see both); 6. MARY M. b. ca. 1831, NY (m. Lyman P. Perkins, also see); 7. CHARLES I. born ca. 1834, NY (prob. he who m. Eliza McMath, dau. of Fleming, also see; lived Iowa; then Louisiana); 8. BETSEY ANN (d. infancy). Ref: P&BA-Len pg. 237-9. Note: Polly Pool, age 63, also b. Mass., was in their household in 1850.

SHAW, BRACKLEY, son of BRACKLEY (preceding), born 21 May 1818, Plainfield, Mass., moved with his parents to NY and Dover Twp., Lenawee Co., Mich. He married ELVIRA M. (GRAVES), daughter of S. Wells (also see). Children: 1. BYRON L. b. ca. 1843 (m. Olive Stockwell, Adrian); 2. Rev. HORATIO W. born ca. 1847 (m. Susie B. Shaw). Brother, HORATIO W., age 27, was in his household in 1850. Ref: P&BA-Len pg. 237-9.

SHAW, CHARLES S. born ca. 1804, and wife, SABRINA G., born ca. 1802, both in VT, were listed in the 1850 census of Hudson Twp., Lenawee Co., Mich. with CHARLES H., age 18; JOHN M., age 15, both b. VT; and Hiram Coville, age 23, with wife, MARY H. (probably daughter of Charles), age 19, b. VT, and child, Harriet E., b. Mich. in their household.

SHAW, CHARLES W. born ca. 1788, Rhode Island, and wife, SARAH, born ca. 1794, NY, were listed in the 1840 census index of Dover Twp., Lenawee Co., Mich. (nearby to BRACKLEY, preceding); and in the 1850 census with ANDREW J., age 18, b. NY, in their household.

SHAW, DELIA, age 13, born Mich., was listed in the 1850 census of Madison Twp., Lenawee Co., Mich. in an Ingalls household.

SHAW, EMILY A., age 7; ADELINE J., age 3, both b. Mich., were listed in the 1850 census of Madison Twp., Lenawee Co., Mich. in a Bellows household. Note DELIA, preceding.

SHAW, HENRY was listed in the 1840 census index of Fairfield Twp., Lenawee Co., Mich. Not listed in 1850, however, there was a HENRY, age 17, b. NY, listed in the 1850 census of Adrian Twp., "in jail."

SHAW, JOHN born ca. 1821, and wife, SAMANTHA J., born ca. 1830, both in NY, wer elisted in the 1850 census of Adrian Twp., Lenawee Co., Mich. with HERTFORD, age 6; HARTTISAM (female), age 3; HARTULA (female), age 1/12, all b. Mich., in their household.

SHAW, NATHAN, son of THOMAS (who d. in Chautauqua Co., NY), born near Saratoga Springs, NY, married ESTHER (CONKLIN) who was born Poughkeepsie, NY. They remained in Saratoga Springs until 1835, then moved to Castile, NY. In 1839, they removed to Hanover Twp., Jackson Co., Mich. She died there 15 Sept. 1877; and he moved into the village of Hanover where he died 22 Feb. 1884. Known daughter, OLIVE ARABELLA b. 29 Aug. 1834, Saratoga Springs (m. Morris Selleck, also see). Ref: P&BA-Len pg. 1094-5.

SHAW, STEPHEN born ca. 1799, Mass., and wife, DOROTHY (DAWS?), born ca. 1806, both in Mass., were listed in the 1840 census index of Medina Twp., Lenawee Co., Mich.; and in the 1850 census with LYDIA D., age 8; HESTER?, age 3, both b. Mich., and POLLY DAWS, age 75, b. Mass., in their household.

SHAY, ANSON Rev. and wife, HANNAH, of Canandaigua, NY, were parents of ESTHER (m. Daniel Smith before 1816).

SHAY, EDWARD born ca. 1812, Ireland, and wife, ISABEL, born ca. 1812, VT, were listed in the 1850 census of Ogden Twp., Lenawee Co., Mich. with EMILY, age 12; THOMAS, age 12; MARY, age 10; EDWARD, age 8, all b. Ohio, in their household.

SHAY, WILLIAM born ca. 1811, and wife, ELIZABETH, born ca. 1817, both in Ireland, were listed in the 1850 census of Franklin Twp., Lenawee Co., Mich. with MARY, age 3; ELIZABETH, age 1, both b. Mich., in their household.

SHEELER, GEORGE, son of WILLIAM^2 (following), born 9 May 1805, Newton, Sussex Co., NJ, married ca. 1828 to JANE (ONSTED), born 9 Mar. 1810, Sussex Co., NJ. About 1836, they removed to Cambridge Twp., Lenawee Co., Mich. She died 2 June 1885. Children: 1. CATHARINE (m. Elliot R. Kilbury; 2. JOHN b. ca. 1833 (m. Susan Winnie, Jackson Co., Mich.); 3. ANN L. b. 25 Sept. 1834 (m. Charles W. Greenleaf, also see); 4. RHODA b. ca. 1838; 5. SARAH b. ca. 1840 (m. Israel Edwards); 6. WILLIAM b. ca. 1842; 7. ISRAEL b. ca. 1844 (m. Louisa Sager, dau. of Richard, also see); 8. LEMUEL b. ca. 1849 (m. Jennie Bingham); 9. FRANKLIN P. (m. Ellen Porter, children: George; Hettie); 10. EMARILLA. Ref: P&BA-Len, pg. 1028-9.

SHEELER, WILLIAM^2, son of WILLIAM^1 & MARGARET (HEM), born Newton, Sussex Co., NJ, married CATHERINE (MAINE). He died in middle life in Sussex Co. leaving 6 sons and 6 daughters, names not stated, except GEORGE (preceding). Ref: P&BA-Len pg. 1028-9.

SHEFFIELD, CHARLES W., son of WILLIAM (following), born 18 Dec. 1824, Oneida Co., NY, came alone at age 11 to Monroe, Mich.; and then to Adrian, Lenawee Co. where he made his home with an uncle for 5 or 6 years. He enlisted in the Mexican War on 9 Feb. 1848. In the 1850 census of Adrian Twp., he was listed age 25, in the household of James L. Austin, age 60, and wife, Hannah, age 57, both b. RI. He married on 5 May 1853 to MARY E. (SKINNER), daughter of Calvin D. (also see). Children: 1. LEONORA H. (to Shawneetown, Ill.); 2. WILLIAM C. (d. age 2); 3. WARD B.; 4. CLARA W. (to Ill.); 5. MARY A.; 6. VIOLA B. (m. C. C. Fisher); 7. LAURA F. Ref: P&BA-Len pg. 1113-4.

SHEFFIELD, WILLIAM, son of WILLIAM, was a native of Rhode Island, and he married MARY (CARPENTER) of Long Island, NY, and they settled in Utica, NY where they remained. Known son, CHARLES W. (preceding). Ref: P&BA-Len pg. 1113-4.

SHELBY, ELUS M. was son of ? & OLIVE ANN (COCHRAN), and he came to Michigan with his mother and step-father, Samuel Cook (also see). He married RACHEL (LEWIS) and settled in Fawn River Twp., St. Joseph Co., MIch. Ref: P&BA-Len pg. 352-3.

SHELDEN also see SHELDON

SHELDEN, GIDEON born ca. 1806, and wife, HARRIET, born ca. 1807, Canada, were listed in the 1840 census of Ogden Twp., Lenawee Co., Mich. (adjacent to TRUEMAN); and in the 1850 census with LEVI, age 18,

Pioneer Families of Southeastern Michigan

b. Canada; and NATHAN, age 11; OLIVE, age 1, both b. Mich., in their household.

SHELDEN, HARVEY, son of TRUEMAN (following), born 17 Mar. 1832, Leeds Co., Ontario, Canada, came to Ogden Twp., Lenawee Co., Mich. at age 6 with his parents. In 1854, he went to California for 4 years. He returned to Ogden Twp. where he married on 14 Apr. 1860 to MARY ANN (CROCKETT), daughter of Nathaniel (also see). Children: 1. MINNIE (m. Albert Brown); 2. PERLEY H. Ref: P&BA-IEN PG. 993.

SHELDEN, SAMUEL born ca. 1802, Canada, and wife, LOUISA J., born ca. 1822, NY, were listed in the 1850 census of Ogden Twp., Lenawee Co., Mich. with FRANCES? A., age 1, b. Mich., in their household.

SHELDEN, THOMAS, probably son of TRUEMAN (following), age 28, and wife, NANCY, age 27, both b. Canada, were listed in the 1850 census of Ogden Twp., Lenawee Co., Mich. next door to TRUEMAN.

SHELDEN, TRUEMAN born ca. 1797, Ontario, Canada, son of a man believed to have come from VT, married there to SUSANNA (KNAPP), daughter of Ithamar (also see), and settled in Leeds. About 1838, they removed to Ogden Twp., Lenawee Co., Mich., and are listed there in 1840 near GIDEON (preceding). Known children: THOMAS (preceding); & probably TRUEMAN (following); and the following who were in the household in 1850 census: HARVEY (preceding); RUTH, age 12; STEPHEN, age 10; WILLIAM, age 8. Susanna died and Trueman was said to have married again, and about 1868 went to Plattsburg, MO, where he died in 1882. Ref: P&BA-Len pg. 993.

SHELDEN, TRUEMAN, possibly son of TRUEMAN (preceding), born ca. 1830, and wife, RHODA, born ca. 1830, both in Canada, were listed in the 1850 census of Ogden Twp., Lenawee Co., Mich.

SHELDON also see SHELDEN, preceding.
SHELDON, ELISHA born ca. 1795, and wife, POLLY, born ca. 1809, both in NY, were listed in the 1850 census of Adrian Twp., Lenawee Co., Mich. with Lucinda Post, age 12, b. Mich., in their household.

SHELDON, HORACE J. born ca. 1812, and wife, MARY, born ca. 1820, both in NY, were listed in the 1850 census of Blissfield Twp., Lenawee Co. Mich. with LOUISET?, age 8; OSCAR, age 5; HORACE, age 3, all b. Mich., in their household.

SHELDON, JOHN (See Maria Brazee)
SHELDON, LORENZO born ca. 1810, and wife, AMARILLA, born ca. 1810, both in Mass., were listed in the 1840 census index of Rollin Twp., Lenawee Co., Mich.; and in the 1850 census with SYLVIA, age 17, b. Mass.; and WARREN, age 12; IRA, age 10; CHARLES A., age 8, all b. Mich., in their household.

SHELDON, SETH P., son of SIMEON (following), born 20 Nov. 1838, Rupert, VT, served in Co. C, 14th VT Inf., in the Army of the Potomac during the Civil War. After the war, he moved to Wyoming Co., NY where he married on 30 Jan. 1867 to ELLA (STARK), daughter of John J. (also see). They remained there until about 1883, then moved to Clinton Twp., Lenawee Co., Mich. Children: 1. HELEN L.; 2. FRED S.; 3. LOUIS S. Ref: P&BA-Len pg. 446-7.

SHELDON, SIMEON, born Conn., went as a young man to Vermont. He married in Rupert, Bennington Co., VT to LOIS (EASTMAN) who was born there. They remained until late in life, then went to live with children in Gibson City, Ill., where he died in Nov. 1885, age 78. Lois died at the home of her known daughter, Mrs. A. O. Oliver, in Rock Falls, Ill., age 80. Known son, SETH P. (preceding). Ref: P&BA-Len pg. 446-7.

SHELDON, WILLIAM M. born ca. 1810, NY, was listed in the 1840 census index of Adrian Twp., Lenawee Co., Mich.; and in the 1850 census of Madison Twp. in a Bachus household.

SHEPARD also see SHEPHERD & SHEPPARD
SHEPARD, RUTH (See Spalding family)

SHEPHERD also see SHEPARD & SHEPPARD
SHEPHERD, BETHIAH (See Daniel Goodrich)
SHEPHERD, EDWIN J., son of JAMES H. (following), born 10 Aug. 1859, Dover Twp., Lenawee Co., Mich., married in June 1885 to LENA R. (ANGELL), daughter of David (also see) of Adrian. Known son, JAMES J. b. 9 June 1886. Ref: P&BA-Len pg. 616-7.

SHEPHERD, ELIZABETH (See Jesse Pentecost)
SHEPHERD, JAMES H., son of Rev. PAUL (following), born 13 Dec. 1829, Angelica, Allegany Co., NY, moved to Dover Twp., Lenawee Co., Mich. with his parents. He married on 7 Apr. 1852 to ROXANNA (McMATH), daughter of Fleming (also see). Children: 1. FRANK (m. Susie McMillan, Cheboygan, Mich.); 2. ELIZA (d. infancy); 3. EDWIN J. (preceding); 4. IDA J. (m. John M. Abbott, son of Theodore, also see); 5. WILLIAM F. (m. Eva Bovee, Dover Twp.); 6. OTIS H. Ref: P&BA-Len pg. 410-11.

SHEPHERD, PAUL Rev. born 1804 near Penn Yan, Yates Co., NY, married there in 1826 to ASENATH (MACK). After about 2 years, they moved to Genesee Co., NY. He studied medicine first, and then went into the Ministry at Oberlin, Ohio. About 1835, they came to Allegan Co., Mich.; and later to Dover Twp., Lenawee Co. They went to Kansas for a time, then returned to Dover Twp. by 1859 and died there in 1864. Children: 1. JANE E. (m. Samuel Benham; d. Kansas 1858); 2. JAMES H. (preceding); 3. MARTHA (m. Rev. J. P. Robinson; 4. SANDERS R. (lived Leavenworth, KS); 5. ASENATH (d. infancy); 6. WILLIAM M. (went to St. Joseph, MO; note William M. Sheppard, following). Ref: P&BA-Len pg 410-11.

SHEPPARD also see SHEPARD; SHEPHERD
SHEPPARD, WILLIAM M. married THEODOSIA (GILBERT), daughter of Warren (also see), and had known son, WARREN G. Note WILLIAM M. in household of Rev. Paul Shepherd, preceding.

SHERMAN, KELLY of Berkshire Co., Mass. had known daughter LYDIA born ca. 1792 (m. Caleb Beals, also see, in Adams Co., Mass.).

SHERMAN, MARY A. (See William Ellis)

SHETLER, CHRISTINA born Wurtemburg, Germany married in Ohio in 1857 to August Glaser (also see).

SHETLY, SUSAN (See Samuel Dersham)

SHILEY, ELIZABETH (See Jacob Acker)

SHIPMAN, ELIZABETH (See Caleb Hendershott)

SHIPMAN, STEPHEN and wife, MARY, of Warsaw, NY were parents of ELLEN M. b. 29 Oct. 1841, Wyoming Co., NY (m. William H. Wiggins (also see).

SHIPPY, DEBORAH (See Mathias Crater)

SHIRK, LYDIA (See Daniel Gambee)

SHIRTS see SHURTS

SHOEMAKER also see SHUMAKER
SHOEMAKER, JOHN (See Hugh McConnel)
SHOEMAKER, SUSAN (See Moses Bennett)

SHUFFLEBOTHAM, GEORGE born ca. 1791, England (probably Manchester), was listed in the 1850 census of Tecumseh Twp., Lenawee Co., Mich. with FREDUS, age 20; MARY, age 14, both b. England, and Mrs. CAROLINE (SHUFFLEBOTHAM) FERGUSON, probably his daughter (widow of John; m/2 David Hatch, see both) and Emma Ferguson, age 10, both b. England in his household. JAMES, age 28, b. England, listed in the 1850 census of Madison Twp. probably relates to this family; and FRANCES, age 24, b. England who m. Calvin Robertson MAY also relate, as Caroline's daughter, Maria, was in their neighboring household in the 1850 census.

SHULTIS, CHRISTIAN and BARBARA (WAGNER) of Baden, Germany lived and died in their native country. There were 4 sons and 1 daughter, names not stated, except SIMON (following), who was the only to come to the US.

SHULTIS, SIMON, son of CHRISTIAN (preceding), born 21 Oct. 1826, Baden, Germany, served in the German army for about 6 years. In 1854, he immigrated to the US arriving first in New York City. He moved to Detroit, MIch.; and then to Lenawee Co., Mich. He married on 6 Mar. 1859 to CATHERINE M. (BOOHER), daughter of Jacob (also see), and they settled in Cambridge Twp. Children: 1. WILLIAM J. (m. Dora Taylor; Springville, Mich.); 2. SIMON J.; 3. CHARLES. Ref: P&BA-Len pg. 1150-1.

SHUMAKER also see SHOEMAKER
SHUMAKER, ABRAHAM and wife, MARIA, were parents of MARGARET who married Hezekiah Knowles, Jr. (also see) on 10 Oct. 1844.

SHUMWAY, ABIGAIL was listed in the 1840 census index of Madison Twp., Lenawee Co., Mich.
SHUMWAY, CHARLES, age 28, born NY, a "student," was listed in the household of Dr. Increase S. Hamilton in the 1850 census of Tecumseh Twp.
SHUMWAY, HARRIET, age 24, b. Mass., was listed in the 1850 census of Cambridge Twp., Lenawee Co., Mich. in the household of Willard Smith.
SHUMWAY, LYDIA Mrs., age 48, born Mass., was head of household in the 1850 census of Fairfield Twp., Lenawee Co., Mich., with LYDIA J., age 2, b. Mich. in her household. CLARISSA, age 16, b. Mich., was listed in the household of Josiah and Lydia Alvord (also see), possibly their granddaughter. Mrs. LYDIA married after 1850 to William Freeman (also see).
SHUMWAY, NANCY, age 26, born NY, was listed in the 1850 census of Palmyra Twp., Lenawee Co., Mich. with MARY, age 4; LEVI, age 3, both b. Mich., all in the household of Polly Davis, age 56, b. Conn., perhaps mother of Nancy?

SHURTS also see SHURTZ (also spelled "Shirts" in census).
SHURTS, CORNELIA born ca. 1837, Mich., was listed in the 1850 census of Fairfield Twp., Lenawee Co., Mich. in the household of Horace and Susan Hicks (perhaps sister?).
SHURTS, FRANCIS E., age 2, born Mich., was listed in the 1850 census of Adrian Twp., Lenawee Co., Mich. with GEORGE B., following, both in the household of William Kies.
SHURTS, GEORGE B. born ca. 1847, Mich., may be he listed both in the 1850 census of Fairfield Twp., Lenawee Co., Mich. in the household of William & Catherine Wilber; and listed again in the 1850 census of Adrian Twp. in the household of William Kies, with FRANCIS E. (preceding) also listed.
SHURTS, GEORGE L., son of JACOB (following), born Penn., married MARGARET (METTLER), daughter of Daniel. They resided first in Seneca Co., NY, and then in 1833 moved to Adrian Twp., Lenawee Co., Mich. She died at age 39, and he died in 1848. Known daughter, MARY E. b. 4 Nov. 1828, Seneca Co., NY (m. Halsey Lewis, also see). JAMES (following), is probably a son, and LUCINDA E., age 15, b. Mich., in his household; and HANNAH M., age 11, b. Mich., in the Halsey Lewis household are probably additional daughters. CORNELIA; FRANCIS E.; GEORGE B., all preceding, were possibly children of this household. Note: Susan, age 24, b. NY, wife of Horace G. Hicks; and Catharine, age 25, wife of William J. Wilber, may also be daughters, as they had these Shurts children in their households??
SHURTS, JAMES, probably son of GEORGE L., born ca. 1824, Penn., was listed in the 1850 census of Adrian Twp., Lenawee Co., Mich. with BETSEY, age 24, born NY, and ROZILLA, age 5; REUBEN H., age 1, both b. Mich., in their household. As noted above, LUCINDA, age 15, was also in his household.

SHURTZ, IDA (See James Lanning)

SICKLES, CHARLES D. (See Alvin D. Rice[3])
SICKLES, JOHN was apparently father of JOHN JR. (following); and ADEL (m. Benjamin F. Teachout, son of George W.[3] (also see).
SICKLES, JOHN Jr., probably son of JOHN (preceding), married ELLEN A. (TEACHOUT) daughter of George W.[3] (also see); and had known daughter, JENNIE F.

SICKLY, ARCHIBALD, son of WILLIAM (following), born 7 Dec. 1829, Morris Co., NJ, went to New York City in 1850, but returned to New Jersey. He visited his parents in Woodstock Twp., Lenawee Co., Mich. and decided to settle there. He married 31 May 1856 to SARAH M. (CLARK), daughter of George W. (also see). Children: 1. NEVADA M. b. 4 Apr. 1857 (m. J. E. Phillips, Ionia, Mich.); 2. JOHN W. b. 29 Nov. 1858 (d. 15

Pioneer Families of Southeastern Michigan

Feb. 1861); 3. MARY E. b. 22 Feb. 1862 (m. M. F. Turrell, Springville, Mich.); 4. CHARLOTTE E. b. 17 Aug. 1864 (d. 17 Mar. 1865); 5. FRED L. b. 16 June 1866 (lived Somerset, Mich.); 6. CATHERINE M. b. 27 Nov. 1867; 7. BESSIE W. b. 22 Sept. 1869; 8. ERNEST b. 15 Apr. 1872; 9. ARCHIBALD M. b. 20 Sept. 1873 (d. 24 Apr. 1876); 10. THEO b. 23 June 1875. Ref: P&BA-Len pg. 1132-3.

SICKLY, WILLIAM born 1801, married SARAH A. (SUTFIN), born 1808, both near Hackettstown, NJ. (William's grandfather had come from Holland in Colonial times and served in the American Revolution.) They lived in Morris Co., NJ until about 1833, then removed to Livingston Co., NY where they remained until about 1850. They moved to Woodstock Twp., Lenawee Co., Mich., where he died at age 66; and she died 5 June 1887, Somerset, Mich., age 79. Children: 1. JOHN W. (E. Groveland, Livingston Co., NY); 2. ARCHIBALD (preceding); 3. MARY J. (m. Turrell, lived Somerset, Mich.); 4. SARAH A. (m. Chapman; lived Chico, CA); 5. MARTIN B. (Macon Twp.); 6. LOUISA MARIA (m. Babcock; lived Leslie, Ingham Co., Mich.); 7. LYDIA W. (m. Lamb; Blissfield, Mich.); 8. JAMES AUGUSTUS (Somerset, Mich.) Ref: P&BA-Len pg. 1132-3.

SIGGONS, SARAH (See George Smell)

SILL, ASENATHA (See Samuel Lewis)

SILLIMAN, HULDAH (See Joseph Bangs)

SILVERS, BENJAMIN was a native of Sussex Co., NJ who removed about 1806 to Fayette, Seneca Co., NY. He was killed in the winter of 1818 in an accident with a team of horses. His wife, JOHANNA, died in Tyre, NY in 1829. Known son, JOHN P. (following). Ref: P&BA-Len pg. 233-4. Note: There was a LEVI listed in both Hopewell & Amwell, Hunterdon Co., NJ in 1778-1780; and in 1793, there was BENJAMIN & JAMES listed in the Militia of Hopewell; and a JOB who was "exempt" in Hunterdon Co.

SILVERS, JOHN P., son of BENJAMIN (preceding), born 14 Apr. 1803, Sussex Co., NJ, moved to Seneca Co., NY with his parents, and married in Mar. 1823, Seneca Falls, to JEANETTE (HOOPER or HOOKER). After the birth of 6 children, they moved in the Spring of 1833 to Clinton Twp., Lenawee Co., Mich. Jeanette died in 1839 leaving 8 children, names not stated. Known children: CAROLINE b. 31 Mar. 1826, Seneca Falls, NY (m. George Sisson, also see); LYDIA b. 6 Dec. 1830, Seneca Falls, NY (m. Jacob B. Smith, also see); and youngest son, WILLIAM P. (following). John P. married again to MARCIA (HURLBURT) and had 7 children (names not stated); however listed in their household in the 1850 census were: EDWARD, age 9; CHARLES, age 5; FRANKLIN, age 3. Marcia died in Clinton in 1856. John P. married third to Mrs. SOPHIA (HUFF) BURROUGHS, daughter of Peter (also see). John P. died in 1882. Ref: P&BA-Len pg. 233-4; 851-2.

SILVERS, WILLIAM P., son of JOHN P. (preceding), born 3 Nov. 1832, Seneca Falls, NY, moved to Clinton Twp., Lenawee Co., Mich. with his parents, and married there to CHARLOTTE C. (VANDEMARK), daughter of Orson (also see). Children: 1. MARCIA J. (d. age 6 on 27 Jan. 1864); 2. ALTIE E. (m. W. D. Van Tuyle; Clinton); 3. WILLIAM O.; 4. CHARLES L. Ref: P&BA-Len pg. 233-4.

SILVERSIDE, ANNA (See John Wiggins)

SIMMONS also note SIMONS

SIMMONS, CORNELIUS was listed in the 1840 census index of Tecumseh Twp., Lenawee Co., Mich.

SIMMONS, NOBLE and wife, SARAH (RANDALL), of Roxbury, Delaware Co., NY had known daughter, ELIZA A. b. ca. 1818 (m. Elias Mackey, also see).

SIMMONS, SILAS born ca. 1793, Conn., was listed in the 1840 census index of Madison Twp., Lenawee Co., Mich.; and in the 1850 census with no family in his household.

SIMONS also note SIMONDS & SIMMONS

SIMONS, MATTHEW W. (See Matthew B. McConnel)

SIMONS, SARAH, age 20, born NY, was listed in the 1850 census of Ogden Twp., Lenawee Co., Mich. in the Andrew Sebring household.

SIMONS, STEPHEN born ca. 1824, and wife, ANN, born ca. 1823, both in England, were listed in the 1850 census of Madison Twp., Lenawee Co., Mich. with ROBERT, age 8; DAVID, age 6; ELIZABETH, age 4; JOSEPH, age 2, all b. England, in their household.

SIMONS, WILLIAM, age 12, born Canada, was listed in the 1850 census of Adrian Twp., Lenawee Co., Mich. in a McKenzie household.

SIMONDS also see SIMONS

SIMONDS, ABNER W. born ca. 1820, and wife, MARY, born ca. 1825, both in NY, were listed in the 1850 census of Franklin Twp., Lenawee Co., Mich. with CHARLES, age 5, b. NY, in their household.

SIMONDS, ALFRED S born ca. 1810, and wife, WELTHY, born ca. 1812, both in NY, were listed in the 1850 census of Macon Twp., Lenawee Co., Mich. with ADOLPHUS E., age 15; MARY J., age 12, both b. NY, in their household.

SIMONDS, JAMES N. born ca. 1824, NY, was head of household with mother?, DEBORAH, age 57, b. NY; and ORPHA, age 22; ORISA C., age 20; SARAH M., age 18, all b. NY, in his household.

SIMONDS, WILLIAM B. born ca. 1799, and wife, JANE, born ca. 1802, both in NY, were listed in the 1850 census of Franklin Twp., Lenawee Co., Mich. with ESTHER, age 20; RUTH, age 18; BYRON, age 16; MARGARET, age 14; CHARLOTTE, age 11; MARY, age 10, all b. NY; and ALLEN, age 5, b. Mich., in their household.

SINCLAIR, DANIEL D., son of DUNCAN (following), born 16 Apr. 1805, Broadalbin, NY, after the death of his father, moved with his mother to Livingston Co., NY. About 1830, he removed to Adrian, Lenawee Co., Mich. He married on 2 Oct. 1834 in Brockport, NY to ELIZABETH "BETSEY" (HYDE), daughter of Chancellor (also see), and settled in Adrian. Children: 1. HENRY b. ca. 1840; 2. EDWARD W. b. ca. 1842 (to St. Louis, MO); 3. ; 3. MARY ELIZABETH b. ca. 1845 (m. Gen. William Humphrey, also see); 4. HARRIET M. b. ca. 1846 (m. Thomas S. Applegate, also see); 5. DANIEL C. b. ca. 1849 (to Troy, KS) Ref: P&BA-Len pg. 500-2.

SINCLAIR, DUNCAN, son of HUGH, born 15 Mar. 1772, Scotland, married there in 1798 to CHRISTIE

(McNAUGHTON) and they came to the US and settled in Montgomery Co., NY. He served in the War of 1812; and died at Broadalbin at age 54. Christie removed with her children to Hillsdale Co., Mich., where she died in 1849. There were 10 children, and only mentioned DANIEL D. (preceding). Ref: P&BA-Len pg. 500-2. Note: In the 1840 census index of Moscow Twp., Hillsdale Co., Mich. were DUNCAN; HUGH; & JOHN.

SINCLAIR, ELLA (See Edward Clark)

SINCLAIR, JAMES born ca. 1830, and wife, MARY, born ca. 1832, NY, were listed in the 1850 census of Rollin Twp., Lenawee Co., Mich. in the household of Julius Higgins; and Mary may be daughter of Julius?

SINCLAIR, POLLY (MARY?) born ca. 1805, NY, was head of household in the 1850 census of Rollin Twp., Lenawee Co., Mich. with ASA, age 17, b. NY; and POLLY, age 15; BENJAMIN, age 13; SALLY, age 10; REBECCA, age 8; GEORGE, age 5, all b. Mich., in her household.

SINCLAIR, WILLIAM, age 28, born NY, was listed in the 1850 census of Adrian Twp., Lenawee Co., Mich. in the household of Cornelius A. Stout.

SINGER, MARY (See Abraham Lerch)

SINGER, SAMUEL C. born ca. 1792, and wife, MARY, born ca. 1786, both in Penn., were listed in the 1850 census of Rollin Twp., Lenawee Co., Mich. with no family in their household.

SISSON, COOK, born ca. 1801, Rhode Island, was descendant of a family who had come from England in Colonial times; and his father, name not stated, had moved from RI to Genesee Co., NY, and later to Indiana settling near the Wabash River. Cook married in Genesee Co., NY to LOVISA (CARLTON), daughter of Jacob, born ca. 1802, NY. He went ahead in 1829 to Tecumseh Twp., Lenawee Co., Mich.; and in 1832 moved the family from NY. She died in Feb. 1886, age 85; and he died 2 months later at age 87. Children: 1. GEORGE (following); 2. LLEWELLYN b. ca. 1824 (lived Deerfield Twp.; Note: in the 1850 census was written as "Luellen," female); 3. LEWIS (d. age 2, Buffalo, NY). Ref: P&BA-Len pg. 811-2.

SISSON, ELLERY born ca. 1816, NY, married in NY to MARY (BRYAN), daughter of Gideon (also see), were listed in the 1840 census index of Raisin Twp., Lenawee Co., Mich.; and in the 1850 census of Tecumseh Twp. with CHARLES, age 10; SUSAN, age 9; JOHN, age 7; ALMIRA, age 1, all b. Mich. Mary was said to have died a young woman, leaving a family of children.

SISSON, GEORGE, son of COOK (preceding), born 2 Sept. 1822, Genesee Co., NY, moved to Lenawee Co., Mich. with his parents. He married on 3 Sept. 1844 to CAROLINE E. (SILVERS), daughter of John P. (also see). Children: 1. GEORGE B. b. ca. 1845; 2. JENETTE (in 1850 census, called "ALLIS" ALICE?, age 7/12; Jenette m. E. K. Bliss); 3. BENJAMIN; 4. LYDIA (m. Charles Fitch; Norwalk, O.); 5. JOHN. Ref: P&BA-Len pg. 812-3.

SISSON, GEORGE with a wife, FRANCES (TAYLOR), were called parents of JULIA A. (m. Albert Waring, also see).

SISSON, ISAAC born ca. 1824, and wife, EMILY, born ca. 1832, both in NY, were listed in the 1850 census of Tecumseh Twp., Lenawee Co., Mich. in the household of Alpheus Stearns, also see, and wife, SUSAN (SISSON), age 33, b. NY. Isaac may be brother of Susan? Note: As Susan married Alpheus Stearns in Raisin Twp., note THOMAS, following.

SISSON, THOMAS was listed in the 1840 census index of Raisin Twp., Lenawee Co., Mich. Note ISAAC, preceding.

SISSON, WILLIAM (See George W. Bliven)

SIZER, ADELIA (See Henry A. Angell)
SIZER, ALICE E. (See Abram Wing)
SIZER, AMANDAS married Elizabeth M. Collins.
SIZER, ANSON of Huron Co., Ohio had known daughter, MARY M. (m. George Anson Baker, also see).
SIZER, CLARISSA (See John Abbott)

SKEELS, DIMMIS (See Ambrose Green^3)
SKEELS, HENRY N., son of RUSSELL (following), born 27 Nov. 1822, VT, married in 1846 to MARIE (PARMLEE), daughter of Everett P. Marie died 19 Nov. 1861 in Brandon, VT. Children: 1. ELLA M. (d. 1850); 2. EVELYN (d. 1865); 3. child d. infancy. Henry N. moved to Lenawee Co., Mich. in 1862, and eventually settled in Adrian Twp. He married again to Mrs. DIANA F. (RUSS) CREGO, daughter of Nathaniel, and widow of Solomon G. (see both). Ref: P&BA-Len pg. 241-2.

SKEELS, RUSSELL born 6 Aug. 1782, Woodbury, Conn., descendant of a Colonial family, married first to MARY (POLLARD) of Conn., and about 1802 removed to Rutland Co., VT. They had 6 children, names not stated. After Mary's death, he married again in VT to MARY (FULTON), daughter of William (also see), and there were 8 children, names not stated, except HENRY N. (preceding); and SAMUEL (of Hampton, NY). Also note RUSSELL, & WILLIAM N., following. Ref: P&BA-Len pg. 241-2.

SKEELS, RUSSELL, possibly son of RUSSELL (preceding), born ca. 1811, VT, and wife, HARRIET, born ca. 1820, Mass., were listed in the 1840 census index of Rome Twp., Lenawee Co., Mich. (adjacent to WILLIAM N.); and in the 1850 census with BERTRAND, age 9 (probably he called "Bertram," who m. Elizabeth Hoxter, dau. of William, also see); SOPHIA, age 3, both b. Mich., in their household.

SKEELS, WILLIAM N. was listed in the 1840 census index of Rome Twp., Lenawee Co., Mich., adjacent to RUSSELL, preceding.

SKINNER, BETSEY, age 56, born VT, was listed in the 1850 census of Adrian Twp., Lenawee Co., Mich. in the household of Robert & Laura Bradley (Laura b. 1821, VT, perhaps daughter of Betsey?)

SKINNER, CALVIN D., son of SOLOMON, born 1801, was an early settler of Wayne Co., NY. He married at age 25 to BETSEY H. (SCOTT), daughter of Lemuel (also see). They moved to Michigan first in 1831, but returned to NY for a few years, then returned to Adrian Twp., Lenawee Co. They were listed in the 1850 census of Adrian Twp.; but about 1850 he was said to have started for California, but died enroute in Salt Lake City at age 49. Children (all in household in 1850): 1. MARY E. b. 25 May 1829 (m. Charles W. Sheffield, also see); 2. CHARLES b. ca. 1834, Mich.; 3. PERLEY b. ca. 1837, Mich.; 4. BETSEY A. b. ca. 1842, NY; 5. FRANKLIN b. ca. 1845, Mich.; 6. CALVIN b. ca. 1849, Mich.

Pioneer Families of Southeastern Michigan

SKINNER, JOHN born ca. 1796, VT, and wife, PHOEBE, born ca. 1804, NY, were listed in the 1850 census of Macon Twp., Lenawee Co., Mich. with MINERVA, age 24, b. NY; NELSON L., age 10; CHARLES V., age 6, both b. Ohio, in their household. POLLY, age 16, born Ohio, in the 1850 census of Seneca Twp. in a Baker household, may relate to this family.

SKUTT, MARY (See John Lowe)

SLACK, BAKER and wife, POLLY, of Rhode Island, had known daughter, CONTENT b. 1779, Swansea, NH (m. Uriah Carpenter, also see).

SLADE, BENJAMIN born ca. 1782, Mass., and wife, MARGARET, born ca. 1783, NY, were listed in the 1840 census index of Palmyra Twp., Lenawee Co., Mich.; and in the 1850 census with William Graves, age 27, with wife, Lucinda, age 26, both b. NY, and Madison M. Graves, age 1, b. Mich., in their household.

SLADE, LAWTON (Layton?) born ca. 1793, and wife, PHEBE (MONROE), born ca. 1792, both b. NY, were listed in the 1840 census index of Raisin Twp., Lenawee Co., Mich.; and in the 1850 census in the household of Jeremiah Westgate, Jr. and wife, Phebe R. (age 29, b. NY, possibly daughter of Lawton?)

SLATER, ABIAL born ca. 1789, VT, and wife, MARY, born ca. 1792, NY, were listed in the 1850 census of Fairfield Twp., Lenawee Co., Mich. with JOHN, age 23; JANE, age 21; LOUIS A. (LOUISA?, female), age 20; WILLIAM, age 9, all b. NY, in their household.

SLATER, B. J. (See Henry Matthews)

SLATER, BENJAMIN born ca. 1800, and wife, MARY, born ca. 1800, both in NJ, were listed in the 1850 census of Adrian Twp., Lenawee Co., Mich. with JOSEPH, age 24; HENRY, age 20; ELIZABETH, age 18, all b. NY; and JACOB, age 16; SELIMA, age 14; GEORGE, age 11; MATILDA, age 8, all b. Mich., in their household. Note: Probably he listed as "Slaten" in the 1840 census index of Adrian Twp. Note WILLIAM, following.

SLATER, DAVID, age 26, born NY, was listed in the 1850 census of Raisin Twp., Lenawee Co., Mich. in the Gideon Bryan household; it is probably he who married CLARISSA (BRYAN), daughter of Gideon (also see), and lived in Franklin Twp., though sketch called him David "Slayton."

SLATER, HENRY born ca. 1801, NJ, was listed in the 1850 census of Franklin Twp., Lenawee Co., Mich. with ESTHER, age 29, b. NY; and MARY ANN, age 15; JAMES, age 11; LAVINA, age ?, all b. Mich., in his household.

SLATER, JOHN born ca. 1800, New Jersey, was listed in the 1850 census of Franklin Twp., Lenawee Co., Mich. in the household of JOSEPH (following), probably brother.

SLATER, JOSEPH born ca. 1805, NJ, and wife, ELIZABETH (McKINSTRY), born ca. 1802, VT, lived in Ovid, Seneca Co., NY until 1829, then after the birth of 2 children, moved to Franklin Twp., Lenawee Co., Mich. In the 1850 census of Franklin Twp., they listed JOHN, age 21, b. NY; and CATHERINE, age 15; NANCY, age 14 (m/1 Henry Matthews; m/2 Jesse Pentecost, see both); HIRAM, age 12; MARY, age 9; LUCY, age 4, all b. Mich., in their household.

SLATER, THOMAS S. born ca. 1804, NJ, and wife, LOUISA, born ca. 1801, NY, were listed in the 1850 census of Franklin Twp., Lenawee Co., Mich. with LOUIS, age 19, b. NY; and CANDIS, age 16; SARAH, age 14; ORVIS, age 12; ELIZABETH, age 9, all b. Ohio, in their household.

SLATER, WILLIAM born ca. 1823, NJ, and wife, MERCY, born ca. 1829, NY, were listed in the 1850 census of Adrian Twp., Lenawee Co., Mich. with WALTER, age 1, b. Mich., in their household. Note BENJAMIN, preceding.

SLAYTON, AUGUSTUS W., son of JAIRUS P. (following), born 9 Dec. 1843, Steuben Co., NY, came to Tecumseh Twp., Lenawee Co., Mich. with his parents. He enlisted in Co. E, 18th Mich. Inf. during the Civil War. He married on 22 Sept. 1870 to CYNTHIA (GOODWIN), daughter of Seth (also see) of Detroit. Children: 1. EARL G. b. 19 May 1877; 2. ETHEL B. b. 12 Sept. 1884. Ref: P&BA-Len pg. 549-50.

SLAYTON, CHARLES A., son of JAIRUS P. (following), born 14 Oct. 1848, Penn Yann, Yates Co., NY, moved to Michigan with his parents. He married in Oct. 1879 to ALICE M. (LAING), daughter of Benjamin I. (also see). Children: 1. WILLIAM E. b. ca. 1884; 2. PERCY F. b. ca. 1888. Ref: P&BA-Len pg. 516-7.

SLAYTON, DAVID see DAVID SLATER.

SLAYTON, JAIRUS P., son of REUBEN (following), born 1 Mar. 1819, Yates Co., NY, married in Jan. 1843 to MARY A. (FOWLER), daughter of A. (also see) of Steuben Co., NY. After a few years, they removed to Tecumseh Twp., Lenawee Co., Mich. Children: 1. AUGUSTUS W. (preceding); 2. CHARLES A. (preceding); 3. MARY F. (m. Joseph Waring). Ref: P&BA-Len pg. 431-2.

SLAYTON, REUBEN and wife, ESTHER (WATKINS), were natives of Mass., who moved to Yates Co., NY at an early date. He died there in 1845, age 71; and she died about 1855. Of 12 children, 7 grew to maturity, names not stated. Known son, JAIRUS P. (preceding). Ref: P&BA-Len pg. 431-2.

SLOAN, BEAL born ca. 1802, VT, and wife, MARY T., born ca. 1815, Penn., were listed in the 1840 census index of Rollin Twp., Lenawee Co., Mich. with EPHRAIM, age 12; MORRIS T., age 10; ELIZA A., age 7; HARRIET, age 1, all b. Mich., in their household. Thomas Morris, age 65, b. Penn., in their household, probably father of Mary T. Also, MARY, age 16, b. Mich., in the household of Jonathan Hill in the 1850 census of Rollin Twp., may relate to this family.

SLOAN, EPHRAIM born ca. 1806, VT, and wife, CHARITY G., born ca. 1814, Mass., were listed in the 1850 census of Rollin Twp., Lenawee Co., Mich. with WILLIAM J., age 7; ELLEN, age 2, both b. Mich., in their household.

SLOAN, ROBERT born ca. 1815, NY, married in 1838 to CATHERINE (BAGERLY), daughter of Tyson (also see) born ca. 1820, NY. They were listed in the 1850 census of Medina Twp., Lenawee Co., Mich. Children: 1. MARY ANN b. ca. 1843, Mich. (m Jacob N. Borick, also see, Seneca Twp., Lenawee Co., Mich.; note that this may be "Rorick?"); 2. (WILLIAM) SPENCER b. ca. 1845, Mich. (m. Allie Bemandiefer, son: Robert). Robert died, and Catherine married again to Seth B. Sayres (also see) of Seneca Twp. Ref: P&BA-Len pg. 1188-90.

SLOAN, ROBERT came to the US from Scotland; and ANN (BEATTIE) came from Scotland to Livingston Co., NY to join him, and married there on 9 Oct. 1855. They moved to Hillsdale Co., Mich., and he died there in June 1857. Known daughter, KATIE b. 1 Jan. 1857 (m. William W. King). Ann married again, after the death of Robert, to William King (also see) who was born 1813.

SLOAN, JOHN (See WILLIAM, following)

SLOAN, WILLIAM born ca. 1821, and wife, MARY E., born ca. 1823, both in NY, were listed in the 1850 census of Medina Twp., Lenawee Co., Mich. with ROBERT S., age 4; WINFIELD S., age 3; ISAAC W., age 1, all b. Mich., and Mary Smith, age 16, b. NY, and probably brother, JOHN, age 36, b. NY, in their household.

SLY, MARY of Orange Co., NY (See Benjamin Bradner).

SLY, CHARLES born ca. 1810, and wife, SARAH, born ca. 1818, both in NY, were listed in the 1850 census of Rome Twp., Lenawee Co., Mich. with LOISA, age 18, b. NY; and GEORGE, age 1, b. Mich.; Mary A. Beers, age 11, b. Mich., in their household.

SLYTTER, LIZZIE (See James K. Wheeler)

SMALL, MARTHA of Ireland (See William Stephenson).

SMALLEY, FRANCIS, possibly son of JAMES (following), born ca. 1815, New Jersey, and wife, POLLY, born ca. 1813, NY, were listed in the 1840 census index of Adrian Twp. (adjacent to JAMES); and in the 1850 census of Ogden Twp., with FREEMAN, age 19, b. NY (may be listed again in household of JOHN, following); and WILLIAM, age 17; GEORGE, age 14; LUCY, age 12; IRA, age 9; HULDAH, age 7; BLOOMER, age 6; MARY, age 4; ANN, age 1, all b. Mich., in their household.

SMALLEY, JAMES was a native of New Jersey, who settled in Adrian Twp., Lenawee Co., Mich. in 1835; and may have lived later in Palmyra Twp. Known daughter, PERMELIA b. ca. 1820, NJ (m. John Bitely³, also see). Ref: P&BA-Len pg. 991-2. Also note JOHN, following, & FRANCIS, preceding.

SMALLEY, JOHN, possibly son of JAMES (preceding), born ca. 1824, NJ, and wife, MARY A., born ca. 1828, NY, were listed in the 1850 census of Seneca Twp., Lenawee Co., Mich. with SARAH J., age 7/12, b. Mich.; and FREEMAN, age 18, probably same as he in family of FRANCIS (preceding).

SMART, ROSETER born ca. 1816, and wife, CLARISSA S., born ca. 1816, both in NY, were listed in the 1850 census of Madison Twp., Lenawee Co., Mich. with ANSON R., age 9 (probably Dr. A. R. who m. Ione C. Hall, dau. of Dr. Leonard G., also see; to Toledo, O.); AGNES G., age 3; WILLARD N., age 10/12, all b. Mich., in their household.

SMEAD, RUFUS born ca. 1757, Montague or Sherburne, Franklin Co., Mass., married ANNA (HAWKS) born 1774/5, Sherburne. They apparently moved to Warren Co., NY by 1810, but may have returned to Mass. They removed to Adrian, Lenawee Co., Mich. in 1834. He died age 87 (or 83); and she died age 94, Adrian. Large family, names not stated, except those following: MOSES H. b. ca. 1808, Mass. (head of household in 1850, with only mother in his household); RUFUS, JR. (following); ANNA b. 14 Sept. 1810, Bolton, NY (m. William Knight, also see); LAVINA b. ca. 1812, Mass. (m. John A. Hawks, also see); ELIZABETH b. Jan. 1817 (m. Ebenezer Fisk, also see). Ref: <u>Index of Pioneers from Mass. to the West</u>, C. A. Flagg, 1980; & PB&A-Len pg. 255-6; 334; 433-4.

SMEAD, RUFUS JR., son of RUFUS (preceding), born ca. 1814, Mass., and wife, JANE F., born ca. 1820, VT, were listed in the 1850 census of Adrian Twp., Lenawee Co., Mich. with MALINDA, age 11; JOHN D., age 5 (m. Helen M. Crane, dau. of Edwin D., also see); GEORGE A., age 2; SELINDA, age 5/12, all b. Mich., in their household.

SMELL, GEORGE and wife, SARAH (SIGGONS), were natives of Virginia and parents of MARY b. 18 Sept. 1843, Taylor Co., W. Va. (m. Samuel G. Wotring, also see). Ref: P&BA-Len pg. 720-1.

SMELTZER, ARNOLD born 29 Dec. 1805, Co. Limerick, Ireland, went first on 15 May 1831 to Quebec, Canada; and then to Seneca Co., NY. In 1837, he removed to Lenawee Co., Mich. and lived in Ridgeway, Macon, and Raisin Twps. In the 1850 census of Macon Twp., he listed wife, MARIA, age 30, born NY, and in their household were: 1. MICHAEL (following); 2. ELIZABETH, age 2; MARY, age 1/12. The sketch mentioned daughters, Mrs. John McLeod of Detroit; Mrs. Fred Landgraff of Adrian, and another, name not stated. Arnold died 29 Dec. 1871, Raisin Twp. Ref: P&BA-Len pg. 1059-60.

SMELTZER, MICHAEL, son of ARNOLD (preceding), born ca. 1843, Macon Twp., Lenawee Co., Mich., moved with his parents in 1864 to Raisin Twp. He married on 14 Mar. 1872 to MARY JOSEPHINE (BANGS), daughter of John (also see), and settled in Raisin Twp. Children: 1. LUELLA b. 10 Apr. 1872 (d. 27 July 1881); 2. BERTHA FLORINE b. 6 Mar. 1875. Ref: P&BA-Len pg. 1059-60.

SMITH - In the 1840 census index of Lenawee Co., Mich. were the following: <u>Adrian Twp.</u>: ABNER; ASEL; BENJAMIN; CARLTON; CLEMENT; DANIEL; DAVID; EDWARD; ELY; HENRY; HENRY B.; HORATIO M.; SAMUEL; (2) WILLIAM. <u>Blissfield Twp.</u>: LUTHER; MINOR; ZEBINA. <u>Cambridge Twp.</u>: HARLOW C.; HENRY; (2) JOHN; JOSEPH; NORMAN; WILLIAM. <u>Clinton Twp.</u>: EDWIN; JACOB; JOHN; WILSON. <u>Dover Twp.</u>: NELSON; PHILIP; W. I.; WOOSTER. <u>Fairfield Twp.</u>: AMERICUS; CHARLES; LEVI; ROWLAND D.; THOMAS P. <u>Franklin Twp.</u>: GEORGE; GEORGE F.; ROBERT; WILLIAM F. <u>Hudson Twp.</u>: DEXTER; FRANK. <u>Macon Twp.</u>: JAMES. <u>Ogden Twp.</u>: BENJAMIN G. <u>Raisin Twp.</u>: ZEBULON. <u>Rome Twp.</u>: DAVID JR.; L. R. <u>Seneca Twp.</u>: JOHN; P. <u>Tecumseh Twp.</u>: DAVID; DAVIS; ELISHA C.; HENRY; MOSES; URIAH P. <u>Woodstock Twp.</u>: ALONZO S.; FREEMAN; ISAAC.

SMITH, ABRAHAM and wife, SOPHIA, of Penn., had known daughter, MARY born before 1809 (m. Peter Baer on 6 Feb. 1825, possibly in Berks Co., Penn.) Ref: P&BA-Len pg. 841-2.

SMITH, ALONZO, possibly son of ISAAC (following), born ca. 1814, and wife, LAVINA, born ca. 1813, both in NY, were listed in the 1840 census index of Woodstock Twp., Lenawee Co., Mich. (adjacent to ISAAC); and in

Pioneer Families of Southeastern Michigan

the 1850 census with MARY, age 11; GEORGE, age 8; CYNTHIA, age 5; HARRIET, age 2/12, all b. Mich., in their household.

SMITH, AMA born ca. 1800, Rhode Island (See Davis Youngs).

SMITH, AMANDA (See James Patrick)

SMITH, AMELIA is possibly related to SIMEON, following; also see Davis Youngs.

SMITH, AMERICUS born ca. 1801, and wife, MARTHA (BEAL), born ca. 1808, both in NY, came by 1835 to Fairfield Twp., Lenawee Co., Mich.; and afterwards to Rollin Twp. In the 1850 census of Rollin Twp., they listed ELMINA b. 29 Aug. 1835 (m. Dr. William B. Town, See Dr. Nathan); EMELINE, age 9; WILLIAM P., age 4, all b. Mich. Ref: P&BA-Len pg. 874-5.

SMITH, ASA born ca. 1816, NY, married in Lenawee Co., Mich. to SAMANTHA (MAYNARD), daughter of John (also see); and they were listed in the 1850 census of Adrian Twp. with DELAPHENE, age 5 (prob. she who m. James M. Moore, son of Thomas S., also see); ADELBERT, age 2, both b. Mich., in their household.

SMITH, AUSTIN, born Conn., removed to Trumbull Co., Ohio by 1825. He had been a seaman and lighthouse keeper at Port Clinton, Ohio. He retired to near Elmore, Ottawa Co., Ohio where he died in 1868. Known son, JONATHAN (following). Ref: P&BA-Len pg. 723-4.

SMITH, AZARIEL and wife, MARY (ANDREWS), moved from Danbury, Conn. to Somerset Twp., Hillsdale Co., Mich. in 1839. Known children: 1. GEORGE A. (Addison, Lenawee Co., Mich.); 2. JULIA A.; 3. william; 4. HENRY; 5. F. HART; 6. LEGRAND J. (Addison, Mich.); 7. CHARLES A. (following). Ref: P&BA-Len pg. 1056-7.

SMITH, BARBARA (See J. Conrad Ickler)

SMITH, CALVIN born ca. 1795, and wife, LUCINDA, born ca. 1798, both in Mass., were listed in the 1850 census of Medina Twp., Lenawee Co., Mich. with EUGENE, age 11; EMMA J., age 8; CHRISTIAN, age 5/12, probably grandchildren, in their household.

SMITH, CATHERINE born 27 Apr. 1801, Turbot, Northumberland Co., Penn. (m. Jacob Reed, also see, in Fayette, Seneca Co., NY).

SMITH, CHARLES born 1804, England, and wife, AMA, born ca. 1807, NY, were listed in the 1850 census of Fairfield Twp., Lenawee Co., Mich. with MARY A., age 11; ALONZO, age 9, both b. Mich., and Richard Caswell, age 19, b. NY, in their household.

SMITH, CHARLES, age 26, born England, was listed in the 1850 census of Ridgeway Twp., Lenawee Co., Mich. in a Vincent household.

SMITH, CHARLES A., son of AZARIEL (preceding), born 20 Feb. 1842, Hillsdale Co., Mich., married on 2 July 1867 to NELLIE D. (HOLMES), daughter of Salmon H. (also see) of Jackson Co., Mich. They settled in Addison, Lenawee Co., Mich., but also had property in Woodstock Twp. Children: 1. SHIRLEY H. b. 7 May 1870; 2. BRUCE b. 9 Sept. 1873; 3. CHARLES B. b. 31 May 1876; 4. ZOE N. b. 4 Nov. 1877. Ref: P&BA-Len pg. 1056-7.

SMITH, CHARLES F., son of JOHN (following), born 1821, Yorkshire, England, came to the US in 1843 and settled in Ridgeway Twp., Lenawee Co., Mich. He married there to ELLEN (LUPTON), daughter of Thomas (also see). Of eleven children, 5 were deceased by 1888, names not stated. Those surviving: 1. MARY b. ca. 1849 (m. Meeker Hines, Ridgeway Twp.); 2. ALBERT (m. Tilda Miller, Ridgeway Twp.); 3. HORACE (m. Nettie Larabee, Ridgeway Twp.); 4. DARIUS; 5. LENA; 6. CHARLES. Ref: P&BA-Len pg. 366-7.

SMITH, CHARLES H. born ca. 1807, and wife, MARY (CLAYTON), born ca. 1810, came from England to the US in 1842, and settled in Ridgeway Twp., Lenawee Co., Mich. He died in 1872; and she died in 1874. Four daughters and one son, names not stated, except eldest, EMMA b. 26 Feb. 1839, near Leeds, England (m. Conrad L. Lowe, also see); and also in the household in the 1850 census were, JANE A., age 6; CHARLES, age 4; MARY, age 2, all b. Mich. Ref: P&BA-Len pg. 291-2.

SMITH, DANIEL born in Dutchess Co., NY (probably by 1790), married ESTHER (SHAY), daughter of Rev. Anson (also see) before 1816, probably in Ontario or Genesee Co., NY. In 1831, they removed to Plymouth, Wayne Co., Mich.; and in 1835 to Williams Co., Ohio. Known daughter, CELESTIA ALVIRA b. 2 Sept. 1816, Genesee Co., NY (m. John Hancock Carleton, also see). Ref: P&BA-Len pg. 838-40.

SMITH, DANIEL born Sudbury, VT, and wife, SARAH, born Troy, NY, lived in Sudbury, then removed to Royalton, Niagara Co., NY. He died there in 1871; and she died in 1886, age 93. Known daughter, MARY A. b. Sudbury, Rutland Co. VT (m. Ephraim Hall, also see, Niagara Co., NY, moved to Deerfield, Lenawee Co., Mich.). Ref: P&BA-Len pg. 254.

SMITH, DAVID, son of EZEKIEL (following), born 8 Feb. 1786 (census said Mass.), was a "native of Conn." He moved with his father to Vermont, and then to Canada. He married on 6 Nov. 1807, Quebec, Canada to LYDIA (ROBERTS), daughter of David (also see). During the War of 1812, they fled Canada, and lived near Constable, St. Lawrence Co., NY. They moved to near Manchester, Ontario Co., NY; and then in 1833 to Adrian Twp., Lenawee Co., Mich. He died at the home of a son in Rome Twp., age 95. She died 14 May 1875, age 86. Known son, DAVID, Jr. (following); known daughter, EMILY b. ca. 1820, NY (m. Dellence "Delancy" Barrus, also see, 1836 in Rome Twp.); and probably ALBERT (who was 2 doors away in the 1850 census of Adrian Twp., with wife, CALANTHA, age 21, b. NY); & PEMBROKE, age 17, b. NY, who was in the household in 1850. Ref: P&BA-Len pg. 853-4. Also note HARVEY; & ELISHA C., both following. DAVIS; HENRY; MOSES; & URIAH P. were all listed adjacent in the 1840 census index.

SMITH, DAVID (Jr.), son of DAVID (preceding), born 30 Oct. 1812, St. Lawrence Co., NY, came to Lenawee Co., Mich. in 1832, a year before his father. He married EMELINE (HAWLEY), daughter of Levi (also see) of Rome Twp. Children: 1. HERCELIA b. 28 Oct. 1838 (m. Miran Every, Rome Twp.); 2. HARRIET S. b. ca. 1840; 3. WILLIAM H. b. ca. 1844 (served Civil War; m. Elizabeth Wood, Adrian); 4. EMILY b. ca. 1847 (m. Philip M. Bates, also see); 5. FLORENCE A. b. 20 Nov. 1849 (m. C. R. Knowles, Hudson, Mich. - Note: In the 1850 census, she may be listed as "Jane," age 6/12, no Florence in household); 6. THADDEUS (deceased by 1888); 7. JENNIE E. b. 23 Jan. 1857 (m. Albert W. Knowles). Ref: P&BA-Len pg. 853-4.

SMITH, DAVID, age 25, born NY, was listed in the 1850 census of Adrian Twp., Lenawee Co., Mich. in an Abner Jones household.

SMITH, DAVIS born ca. 1808, and wife, LAURA R., born ca. 1813, both in NY, were probably they listed in the 1840 census index of Tecumseh Twp., Lenawee Co., Mich. adjacent to DAVID (preceding). In the 1850 census of Medina Twp., they listed EMELINE, age 15; OLIVE, age 10, both b. Mich., in their household.

SMITH, DOLLY, born in Conn., married in Madison Co., NY to John Hendryx (also see). She married second to James Griffith; and last to ? Loveland. Ref: P&BA-Lenpg. 669-70.

SMITH, E. J. (See William H. H. Van Akin)

SMITH, EDMUND R., son of JAMES (following), born 16 Apr. 1842, Ridgeway Twp., Lenawee Co., Mich., married on 23 Feb. 1870 to ELIZA (HOAGLAND), daughter of John V. (also see). Children: 1. ARTHUR b. 12 June 1872; 2. ANNA b. 25 June 1876.

SMITH, EDWARD J., age 24, born NY, was listed in the 1850 census of Rome Twp., Lenawee Co., Mich. in a Sharer household.

SMITH, EDWIN, son of SIMEON (following), born 13 Oct. 1832, Tioga Co., NY, came from Ohio in 1853 with his mother to Fairfield Twp., Lenawee Co., Mich. He went to California for a time, but returned to Fairfield Twp. where he married on 1 Jan. 1860 to ELIZA (GREEN), daughter of James (also see). She died in Fairfield Twp. on 19 Aug. 1871. Children: 1. GEORGE E. (m. Eva Schomp, Fairfield Twp.); 2. FRANCENIA (m. Seth Seward, Fulton Co., O.) Edwin married again in Huron Co., Ohio to ANNA (CATLIN) who died 21 Dec. 1877. He married third in Williams Co., Ohio on 24 May 1886 to FANNY (FISER), daughter of Michael (also see), and they were residing in Fairfield Twp. in 1888. Ref: P&BA-Len pg. 430-1.

SMITH, ELEANOR (DePUY) was daughter of Philip DePuy (also see).

SMITH, ELISHA CARR born ca. 1815, VT, and wife, MARY, born ca. 1816, NY, were listed in the 1840 census index of Tecumseh Twp., Lenawee Co., Mich. adjacent to DAVID (preceding); and in the 1850 census of Adrian Twp. with EDWIN T., age 13, b. Mich., in their household.

SMITH, ELIZABETH (See John Bryant)

SMITH, ELIZABETH of Yorkshire, England (See Robert Lee).

SMITH, EMELINE married first to ? Freeman; and second to Constant Rowley (also see).

SMITH, EMMA G. (See Lemuel C. P. Vaughn)

SMITH, EZEKIEL possibly of Mass., moved from Conn. to Vermont at an early date. His first wife, MARY (FLINT), drowned there in the Lamoille River. He married again to MARY (BULLEN) and moved to Lower Canada by 1798. The War of 1812 forced him to move from Canada to near Constable, St. Lawrence Co., NY. He later moved to Ontario Co., NY where he died. Known son, DAVID (preceding). Also note EZEKIEL, following.

SMITH, EZEKIEL born ca. 1779, Mass., was listed in the 1850 census of Fairfield Twp., Lenawee Co., Mich. in the household of John Baker and wife, Polly (age 49, b. Canada, probably dau. of Ezekiel). Note EZEKIEL, preceding.

SMITH, EZRA (See Zebina White)

SMITH, F. A. married ELEANORA (WENZEL), daughter of Valentine[2] (also see).

SMITH, FRANK B. (See Charles B. Wilson)

SMITH, FRANKLIN of Adrian (See Charles G. Stowers).

SMITH, FRANKLIN R., son of MOSES (following), born ca. 1831, and wife, SARAH ANN, born ca. 1825, both in NY, were listed in the 1850 census of Hudson Twp., Lenawee Co., Mich. with VIOLETTA, age 5; ORVILLE, age 3; JULIAN, age 2, all b. Mich., in their household.

SMITH, GEORGE, age 50, born England was head of household in the 1850 census of Ridgeway Twp., Lenawee Co., Mich. with SOLOMON, age 48, born England, in the household.

SMITH, GEORGE F. of Dover Twp., Lenawee Co., Mich. (See David Gander).

SMITH, GEORGE W., son of JAMES (following), born 29 Mar. 1840, Ridgeway Twp., Lenawee Co., Mich., married first in 1863 to LIBBIE (DUBOIS), daughter of John (also see); and she died in 1881. Children: 1. MINNIE (d. age 18); 2. ADDIE (deceased by 1888); 3. CYRUS; 4. LAVERN. George W. married again to ESTELLA (JONES), daughter of David (also see) of Tecumseh. Child: 5. WINNIE. Ref: P&BA-Len pg. 828-31.

SMITH, HARVEY born ca. 1811, Canada, and wife, SARAH B., born ca. 1819, NY, were listed in the 1850 census of Adrian Twp., Lenawee Co., Mich. with LUCIEN G., age 10/12, b. Mich., in their household. Note DAVID (preceding).

SMITH, HENRY and wife, SUSAN, of Haddam, Conn., had known daughter, ANNA b. 1790, Haddam (m. Hezekiah Knowles, Sr., also see). Ref: P&BA-Len pg. 762-3.

SMITH, HENRY born 1791, Conn., went to Cayuga Co., NY where he married ANNA M. (BOYER), born there in 1793. They moved to Erie Co., NY where they remained for 25 years; then moved to Michigan. They were listed in the 1850 census of Tecumseh Twp., Lenawee Co., Mich. with only son, JACOB B. (following) and wife in their household.

SMITH, HENRY born ca. 1820, and wife, JANE, born ca. 1830, both in NY, were listed in the 1850 census of Tecumseh Twp., Lenawee Co., Mich. with ELLEN, age 4; CHARLES, age 3, both b. Mich., in their household.

SMITH, HENRY (See John G. Miller)

SMITH, HENRY R. born ca. 1815, and wife, JULIA A., born ca. 1812, both in NY, were listed in the 1850 census of Fairfield Twp., Lenawee Co., Mich. with MARY A., age 16, b. NY; and SARAH, age 11; LUCINDA, age 10; WILLIAM, age 8; GEORGE, age 6, all b. Mich., in their household. Note: May be he listed "Henry B." in the 1840 census index of Adrian Twp.?)

SMITH, HERMAN C. Rev. born ca. 1823, married MARY (PENNINGTON), born ca. 1826, both in NY; and they were listed in the 1850 census of Macon Twp., Lenawee Co., Mich. Children: ALMIRA "MIRA" b. ca. 1849 (m. Elwin M. Camburn, also see); & ISAAC b. after 1850. Rev. Smith went to Minnesota for his health, and died there on 15 Mar. 1855. She returned to Macon Twp., and lived with her son, Isaac, in 1888. Ref: P&BA-Len pg. 1010-11.

SMITH, HERVEY of Northampton, Mass. had known daughter, EUNICE J. (m. Henry H. Wilcox, also see, on 28 Oct. 1845). Ref: P&BA-Len pg. 485-6.

Pioneer Families of Southeastern Michigan

SMITH, HIRAM born ca. 1820, and wife, LYDIA, born ca. 1826, both in New Jersey, were listed in the 1850 census of Woodstock Twp., Lenawee Co., Mich. with ELIZABETH, age 58, b. NJ, probably mother of Hiram, and David Moreland, age 11, b. Penn., in their household. Note: There was a FREEMAN listed in the 1840 census index of Woodstock Twp.

SMITH, ISAAC born ca. 1787, and wife, MARY, born ca. 1790, both in Conn., apparently were in Paris, Oneida Co., NY in 1815. They moved to Lenawee Co. in 1835, and were listed in the 1840 census index of Woodstock Twp. Known children: MARY ANN b. 24 Sept. 1815, Paris, NY (m. Francis A. Dewey, also see); and the following were in the household in the 1850 census of Woodstock Twp.: JOSEPH, age 24, b. NY (with apparently wife, CATHARINE, age 20, b. Ohio); HARRIET b. 26 July 1827, Paris, NY (m. Francis A. Dewey, as 3rd wife); WILLIAM, age 16, b. NY; EMILY, age 13, b. Mich.; and Isaac Henry, age 1, b. Mich. (possibly a grandchild). Ref: P&BA-Len pg. 877-8. Note ALONZO, preceding.

SMITH, J. F. of Franklin Twp., Lenawee Co., Mich. (See Edwin Cook).

SMITH, J. HUGO born 3 Dec. 1820, Breslan, Germany, served in the German military 1840-3. In 1849, he came to the US, and lived variously in Penn., Louisiana, and Ohio. In 1865, he moved to Raisin Twp., Lenawee Co., Mich., and married there on 13 Feb. 1868 to MARGARET (TRABEN), daughter of George (also see). Children: 1. LENA; 2. PAUL; 3. GEORGE; 4. FRED; 5. KITTIE MAY. Ref: P&BA-Len pg. 560-1.

SMITH, JACOB born ca. 1800, and wife, ELIZABETH, born ca. 1801, both in Penn., were listed in the 1850 census of Medina Twp., Lenawee Co., Mich. with JOHN S., age 17, b. NJ; MARIAH, age 15, b. NY, in their household. MARY, age 16, b. NY, in the Sloan household next door may relate to this family.

SMITH, JACOB B., son of HENRY (preceding), born 6 Dec. 1820, Newstead, Erie Co., NY, came to Michigan with his parents. He married on 22 Feb. 1848 to LYDIA (SILVERS), daughter of John P. (also see). They settled in Clinton Twp., Lenawee Co., Mich. Children: 1. PORTER C. (m. Grace Fisk, dau. of Welcome, also see; had children, Eva B.; Leander V.; Willie P.); 2. BELLE (deceased by 1888); 3. CARRIE (m. Dow Draper, Clinton, Mich.) Ref: P&BA-Len pg. 851-2.

SMITH, JAMES, age 19, born NY, was listed in the 1850 census of Adrian Twp., Lenawee Co., Mich. in a Burges household.

SMITH, JAMES and wife, JENNIE, of Carnlea, Co. Antrim, Ireland, remained there; and had known daughter, LETITIA b. 10 July 1791 (m. William Colvin, also see). Ref: P&BA-Len pg. 687-8.

SMITH, JAMES born ca. 1800, and wife, CLARISSA, born ca. 1803, both in NY, were listed in the 1850 census of Rome Twp., Lenawee Co., Mich. with AMOS, age 20; BARNET, age 18; CUYLER, age 15; MARTHA, age 13; WILSON, age 11; GEORGE, age 9; CHARITY, age 8 (listed last in household); ALDICE, age 6, all b. NY; and JEROME, age 6/12, b. Mich., in their household.

SMITH, JAMES born 9 May 1802, Yorkshire, England, came to the US in 1830, and lived 3 years near Troy, NY. In 1833, he moved to Ridgeway Twp., Lenawee Co., Mich. He married in Tecumseh to AMELIA (WHALLEY) born ca. 1820 near Dublin, Ireland, who had come to the US at age 18 with a sister. They settled in Ridgeway Twp. Amelia was still living in 1888, age 73. Children: 1. HANNAH b. ca. 1838, Mich. (m. Abe Herrington, Macon Twp.); 2. GEORGE W. (preceding); 3. EDMUND R. (preceding); 4. SOLOMON b. ca. 1846; 5. HARRIET E. b. ca. 1846 (m. Thomas V. Hoagland, also see); 6. SOPHIA M. b. ca. 1849 (m. William P. Emons, see Jacob); 7. GILBERT (m. Mary Brown, Ridgeway Twp.); 8. ALBERT (m. "Tib" Auten, Milan Twp., Monroe Co., Mich.). Ref: P&BA-Len pg. 386-7.

SMITH, JAMES of Franklin Center, Lenawee Co., Mich. (See Robert Boyd).

SMITH, JAMES H. born ca. 1820, and wife, EMELINE, born ca. 1823, both in NY, were listed in the 1850 census of Ridgeway Twp., Lenawee Co., Mich. with PHEBE J., age 8; SULAVAN (SULLIVAN?), age 6, both b. NY; and GEORGE W., age 4; SARAH M., age 2, both b. Mich., in their household.

SMITH, JANE born 1767, Mass. (See Nathan Ball).

SMITH, JEHIEL born ca. 1822, NY, and wife, AURILLA, age 16, born Ohio, married within the year, were listed in the 1850 census of Fairfield Twp., Lenawee Co., Mich. in the household of Henry & Rachel Clink, possibly parents of Aurilla.

SMITH, JEREMIAH and wife, RACHEL, were parents of HANNAH b. 11 Nov. 1783, North Adams, Mass. (m. Gideon Ramsdell, also see).

SMITH, JOB A. born ca. 1816, NJ, and wife, HANNAH, born ca. 1811, NY, were listed in the 1840 census index of Woodstock Twp.; and in the 1850 census of Rome Twp. with EMELINE, age 10; FRANKIN, age 7; GEORGE, age 3, all b. Mich., in their household. SMITH, JOHN, son of SAMUEL (following), born in Killingworth, Conn., moved with his parents in 1810 to LeRoy, Genesee Co., NY. He married first to ELECTA (LOVEJOY) who died. He married again to RHODA (WOODARD) and had known daughter, ELIZA A. b. ca. 1821, LeRoy, NY (m/1 Seymour Clark; m/2 John Phillips, see both). Ref: P&BA-Len pg. 699-700.

SMITH, JOHN and wife, ALICE (FLOCKTON), were born and married in Yorkshire, England. He died there at age 57, and she came to Ridgeway Twp., Lenawee Co., Mich. to live with son, CHARLES F. (preceding), and died at age 77. Ref: P&BA-Len pg. 366-7.

SMITH, JOHN born ca. 1806, and wife, JANE, born ca. 1808, both in England, were listed in the 1850 census of Franklin Twp., Lenawee Co., Mich. with GEORGE, age 20; MARY, age 18; SARAH, age 5, all b. Mich.; snd JOHN, age 9; JOSEPH, age 7, both b. England; and REBECCA, age 4; SUSANNA, age 2; FRANCES, age 6/12, all b. Mich., in their household.

SMITH, JOHN born ca. 1799, NY, and wife, PHEBE, born ca. 1808, Penn., were listed in the 1850 census of Hudson Twp., Lenawee Co., Mich. with JAMES, age 13, b. NY; and MARY, age 11; JOHN, age 8; CHARLOTTE, age 6; SARAH, age 4; PHEBE, age 3; EMMA, age 1, all b. Mich., in their household.

SMITH, JOHN of Tecumseh Twp., Lenawee Co., Mich. (See John H. Wilson).

SMITH, JOHN, probably son of JOSEPH (following), born ca. 1815, and wife, ALLIS (ALICE?), age 29, both born England, with MARGARET, age 4; ELIZABETH, age 3, both b. England, all in the household of JOSEPH in the 1850 census of Cambridge Twp., Lenawee Co., Mich.

Note: If the place of birth of the children is correct, then John came to the US later than his father.

SMITH, JOHN, probably son of SILAS P. (following), born ca. 1817, and wife, JANE, born ca. 1820, both in NY, were listed in the 1850 census of Fairfield Twp., Lenawee Co., Mich. (next door to SILAS P.) with RHODA, age 16; SILAS, age 8; MATILDA, age 5; JOHN, age 2, all b. NY, in their household.

SMITH, JOHN D. (See Hiram S. Whiting)

SMITH, JOHN G. born ca. 1812, and wife, SARAH M., born ca. 1816, both in New Hampshire, were listed in the 1850 census of Medina Twp., Lenawee Co., Mich. with JAMES M., age 13; SARAH, age 12; ELLEN E., age 8, all b. NY, all in the household of George W. Moore (also see), also b. NH.

SMITH, JOHN J. born ca. 1792, and wife, HANNAH, born ca. 1801, both in NY, were probably they listed in the 1840 census index of Cambridge Twp., Lenawee Co., Mich.; and in the 1850 census with BETSEY, age 19; NATHAN, age 16, both b. NY; and MARGARET, age 13; MARIAH, age 11; ELLWOOD, age 8, all b. Mich., in their household. Also note NORMAN, following.

SMITH, JONATHAN, son of AUSTIN (preceding), born Conn., moved with his parents to Trumbull Co., Ohio. He married MARY M. (INGRAHAM), daughter of Benjamin (also see); and about 1836, moved to Ottawa Co., Ohio near Elmore. They later moved to Harris Twp., Ottawa Co. where they were living in 1888. Known daughter, ESTHER MARIA b. 13 Dec. 1831, Farmington Twp., Trumbull Co., O. (m. Cornelius Gilson, also see). Ref: P&BA-Len pg. 723-4.

SMITH, JOSEPH born Smithfield, England, married ? born Paris, France; and before 1776, they came to America, and settled first in Berkshire Co., Mass. About 1783, they moved to Ontario Co., NY, and were pioneers to the area now encompassed by Farmington and Victor, NY. Joseph died in 1815. Known son, WANTON (following). Ref: P&BA-Len pg. 579-80.

SMITH, JOSEPH born ca. 1786, and wife, ELIZABETH (READ), born ca. 1786, both born near East Kent, Dover, England, came to the US and settled in Cambridge Twp., Lenawee Co., Mich. There were 3 sons and 6 daughters, all names not stated. Known children: SUSANNA b. 25 July 1817, England (m. Richard Robinson, also see); and the following in Joseph's household in the 1850 census: SARAH, age 35; RHODA M. b. 13 Feb. 1829, England (m. John A. Bennett, also see); JOHN, age 35 (and family, preceding). Joseph died 20 Apr. 1861, age 75; and she died 22 Sept. 1865, almost 80. Ref: P&BA-Len pg. 758-9; 1142-5.

SMITH, JOSEPH born ca. 1817, and wife, SALLY, born ca. 1822, both in NY, were listed in the 1850 census of Franklin Twp., Lenawee Co., Mich. with THEODORE, age 9; FLETCHER?, age 7; WILLIAM, age 4; ALVAH, age 1, and Sarah Hoag, age 18, b. NY, in their household.

SMITH, JOSEPH H. of Tecumseh, Lenawee Co., Mich. married MARY F. (ROGERS), daughter of Robert L. (also see) and had known children: WILLIAM LAVERNE; 2. LENA F. Ref: P&BA-Len pg. 1177-8.

SMITH, LOWENA (See William Hawley)

SMITH, LUCRETIA married Elmer Cole (also see). In the sketch, it states that her "Grandfather" Sled was a Revolutionary soldier who died in Conn. Ref: P&BA-Len pg. 594-5.

SMITH, LUCY (See Erastus Knight)

SMITH, MARGARET (See K. N. Brown)

SMITH, MARGARET C. (See Albert G. Burton)

SMITH, MARIA J. (See SARAH J., following)

SMITH, MARY born Penn. (See Henry Pontius)

SMITH, MARY of Preston Co., W. Va. married Abraham Wotring, also see, and remained in Preston Co.

SMITH, MARY M. (See Henry Ragless)

SMITH, MOSES born ca. 1788, Conn., and wife, VIOLETTA, born ca. 1788, Mass., lived in NY, and Columbia Co., Penn., but moved to Tecumseh Twp., Lenawee Co., Mich. by 1840. They were listed in the 1850 census next door to probably sons, OSCAR (following); and FRANKLIN R. (preceding). Known daughter, LAURA (m. Samuel Bryan, also see). Ref: P&BA-Len pg. 296-7.

SMITH, NANCY (See Albert J. Bartholomew)

SMITH, NANCY of Hillsboro Co., NH (See George Daniels).

SMITH, NANCY of Herkimer Co., NY, married first to Joseph Howard (also see) before 1809, and married again to a West. An ASA SMITH raised her son, Marvin Howard. Ref: P&BA-Len pg. 1096-7.

SMITH, NATHANIEL[1] born Mass., married ANNIE (FORD) born England, and they were original settlers to Amsterdam, Montgomery Co., NY. Nathaniel[1] died in Ira, Cayuga Co., NY at the home of known son, NATHANIEL[2] (following). Ref: P&BA-Len pg. 1120-1.

SMITH, NATHANIEL[2], son of NATHANIEL[1] (preceding), born by 1797, Amsterdam, NY, was a pioneer to Ira, Cayuga Co., NY. He married there to MARY (VOORHEES), daughter of John I. (also see). They remained in Ira, NY for 60 years, but moved to Hudson, Lenawee Co., Mich. about 1867, and he died at home of daughter, Lucy, age about 90 years. His wife died in 1868. Known children: LUCY (m. Abram Loyster[3], also see); & PETER V. (following). Ref: P&BA-Len pg. 704-5; 1120-1.

SMITH, NELSON born ca. 1804, VT, and wife, RACHEL, born ca. 1804, NY, were listed in the 1840 census index of Dover Twp., Lenawee Co., Mich.; and in the 1850 census with JOHN, age 23; MARY, age 19; LYDIA, age 16, all b. NY; and GEORGE, age 14; IRI, age 11; and Nelson Deforrest, age 11/12, all b. Mich., in their household.

SMITH, NELSON born ca. 1815, and wife, DELIA, born ca. 1805, were listed in the 1850 census of Fairfield Twp., Lenawee Co., Mich. He married Mrs. ADELIA (MORRIS) DUNN, widow of Jefferson (also see). The following were in the household: MARY E., age 8, b. NY (possibly dau. by first marriage); and WELLINGTON C., age 5; FANNY S., age 4, both b. Mich.; and Charles M. Dunn, age 16; Robert J. Dunn, age 12, both b. Mich.; and Nancy Pearce, age 17, b. NY.

SMITH, NORMAN born ca. 1800, and wife, ABIGAIL, born ca. 1810, both in NY, were listed in the 1840 census index of Cambridge Twp., Lenawee Co., Mich.; and in the 1850 census of Woodstock Twp. with ISAAC, age 18, b. NY; JAMES, age 16; LOIS, age 15; MARY, age 13; all b. Mich. Also note JOHN H. (preceding).

SMITH, OSCAR, probably son of MOSES (preceding), born ca. 1819, NY, and wife, SARAH, borh ca. 1830, Mich., were listed in the 1850 census of Tecumseh Twp., Lenawee Co., Mich. with no family in the household.

Pioneer Families of Southeastern Michigan

SMITH, OSCAR possibly born after 1850 (See William Hood).

SMITH, PETER V.³, son of NATHANIEL² (preceding), born 14 June 1822, Ira, Cayuga Co., NY, came to Hudson Twp., Lenawee Co., Mich. with his parents. He married on 27 Oct. 1850 to LUCIA (BRIGHTMAN), daughter of Samuel (also see). Children: 1. GEORGE HARVEY b. 24 June 1852 (m. Ida Lamb; had son, Floyd L.); 2. WILLIS b. 22 Nov. 1857 (m. Anna C. Teeling, had dau., Mabel L.; Marshalltown, IA). Ref: P&BA-Len pg. 1120-1.

SMITH, PHILIP S. born ca. 1796, NY, and wife, POLLY, born ca. 1797, Conn., were listed in the 1840 census index of Dover Twp., Lenawee Co., Mich.; and in the 1850 census with BENJAMIN, age 20, b. NY; and CORDELIA, age 10, b. Mich.; Ellery Foote, age 28, with wife, Lydia A., age 22, both b. NY, and Maryette Foote, age 8/12, b. Mich., in their household. Lydia A. may be daughter of Philip?

SMITH, ROBERT and wife, CATHARINE (SPEED), were parents of MARY born Columbia Co., NY (m. Philip Rice, also see, on 9 Jan. 1853). Ref: P&BA-Len pg. 952-3.

SMITH, ROBERT born ca. 1801, Yorkshire, England, married there and came to Lenawee Co., Mich. by 1840. His wife, name not stated, died. Known children (in household in the 1850 census): HARRIET, age 24; ANGELINE, age 18; JOHN, age 17, all b. England; and MARTHA, age 14, b. Mich. (not certain which wife is her mother) He married again to EMELINE (LANGDON), born 1802, NY, by 1840 in Franklin Twp. Known daughters, MARY E. b. ca. 1840 (m/1 Charles Edwards; m/2 D. W. Love, also see); and SARAH, born ca. 1842. Myron K. Langdon, age 44, b. NY, probably brother of Emeline, was also in their household. Ref: P&BA-Len pg. 252-3.

SMITH, ROBERT born ca. 1810, and wife, ANN, born ca. 1813, both in England, were listed in the 1850 census of Ridgeway Twp., Lenawee Co., Mich. with GEORGE, age 9; ANN, age 7, all b. England; and ROBERT, age 5; JOHN, age 3; WILLIAM, age 2; CHARLES, age 1, all b. Mich., in their household.

SMITH, RUTH (See Stephen Payne)

SMITH, SAMUEL and wife, SARAH (BUELL), were natives of Conn., who moved from Killingworth, Conn. to LeRoy, Genesee Co., NY about 1810. He died there. Known son, JOHN (preceding). Ref: P&BA-Len pg. 699-700.

SMITH, SANFORD and wife, PRISCILLA (WHIPPO), of Cambridge, Washington Co., NY, had known daughter, LUCY b. 13 Jan. 1793 (m. Thomas Comstock, also see). Ref: P&BA-Len pg. 413-4.

SMITH, SARAH (See Roswell H. Hicks)

SMITH, SARAH J. or MARIA J. (See Philp S. DePuy).

SMITH, SILAS P. born ca. 1783, Conn., and wife, RHODA, born ca. 1785, NY, were listed in the 1850 census of Fairfield Twp., Lenawee Co., Mich. with MATILDA, age 18, b. NY, in their household. They were next door to probably son, JOHN (preceding).

SMITH, SIMEON and wife, ABIGAIL (MOSHER), both born NY, settled in Tioga Co., NY. They later moved to Huron Co., Ohio, where he died after 7 years. They family then moved to Fairfield Twp., Lenawee Co., Mich. where she lived out her life. There were 6 daughters and 4 sons, names not stated. Those known, twins, EDWIN (preceding); and EDWARD (lived Lyons, Fulton Co., Ohio). Ref: P&BA-Len pg. 430-1. Also note AMELIA (m. William E. Green, see James), as Edwin married Eliza Green.

SMITH, SUSANNAH born ca. 1810, England, came to the US in 1831, and her parents settled in Jackson Co., Mich. Her father died there age 65, and her mother died age 90. Susannah married Edward Curtis, also see. Ref: P&BA-Len pg. 835-6.

SMITH, THOMAS born ca. 1817, and wife, MARY, borh ca. 1824, both in England, were listed in the 1850 census of Rome Twp., Lenawee Co., Mich. with WILLIAM, age 6; ANNA, age 4; CHARLES H., age 1, all b. Mich., in their household.

SMITH, THOMAS C. married probably in Clinton Co., NY to REBECCA A. (NICHOLS), daughter of Levi (also see), who was born 19 Mar. 1817, Plattsburg, NY. He died in NY in 1860; and Rebecca came to Medina Twp., Lenawee Co., Mich. in 1862 with her 3 sons. Children: 1. CORNELIA (m. Haff; Clinton Co., NY); 2. HARVEY T. (Mt. Pleasant, Isabella Co., Mich.); 3. EUGENE (Medina Twp.); 4. LEVI N. (Mt. Pleasant, Mich.) Ref: P&BA-Len pg. 940-1. Rebecca married again on 13 Aug. 1872 to Albert Humphrey Bump (also see).

SMITH, URIAH P. born ca. 1802, and wife, MARIA, born ca. 1804, were listed in the 1840 census index of Tecumseh Twp., Lenawee Co., Mich.; and in the 1850 census with REBECCA, age 21, b. NY; and Mary Helm, age 20, b. Mich., in their household.

SMITH, W. F. (See Oren E. Green)

SMITH, W. W. (See Leslie T. Goff)

SMITH, WANTON, son of JOSEPH (preceding), born ca. 1776, Berkshire, Mass., moved with his parents ca. 1783 to Ontario Co., NY. He married near Canandaigua, NY to LUCY (EDDY), daughter of Caleb G. (also see). Of seven children, only 4 lived to maturity; and those mentioned were : 1. PHILANDER (d. age 9); 2. WANTON G. (following); 3. GEORGE (d. Farmington, NY, age 30). Ref: P&BA-Len pg. 579-80.

SMITH, WANTON G., son of WANTON (preceding), born 26 Jan. 1822, Farmington, Ontario Co., NY, married there on 11 Oct. 1849 to MARIA (MITCHELL), daughter of William (also see). About 1860, they removed to Palmyra Twp., Lenawee Co., Mich. Children: 1. MITCHELL C. (Calmar, Iowa); 2. FRANCES A. (m. E. W. Hutchison; Oceana Co., Mich.); 3. HENRY C. (Adrian, Mich.); 4. CLARENCE G. (twin of Clara; to Oxford, IA); 5. CLARA E. (m. J. D. Kinney, Adrian); 6. LOUIS G. Ref: P&BA-Len pg. 579-80.

SMITH, WILLIAM Deacon of Jackson Co., Mich. (See Benjamin B. Fisk).

SMITH, WILLIAM born Ohio, and wife, RACHEL (HUGHES), born Penn., lived in Fulton Co., Ohio. He died in 1852 on a boat in the Erie Canal on which he was Captain. She was living in Fairfield Twp., Lenawee Co., Mich. in 1888. Children: 1. MARGARET A.; 2. OBEDIAH; 3. CARRIE b. 23 July 1847, Fulton Co., Ohio (m. Martin DeLand, also see); 4. WILLIAM H.; 5. MELISSA. Ref: P&BA-Ln pg. 694.

SMITH, WILLIAM F. born ca. 1808, and wife, LYDIA, born ca. 1814, both in NY, were listed in the 1850 census of Fairfield Twp., Lenawee Co., Mich. with DANIEL, age 19, b. NY; and LORENZO, age 13; ALLEN, age 11; LUCIEN, age 7; EUGENE, age 4, all b. Mich., in their household.

SMITH, WILLIAM H. (See William Wood; also note this given name in household of WILLIAM, preceding, & WILLIAM R., following).

SMITH, WILLIAM P. (See Nathaniel Buel Eldridge)

SMITH, WILLIAM R. born ca. 1809, and wife, LYDIA, born ca. 1816, both in NY, were listed in the 1850 census of Dover Twp., Lenawee Co., Mich. with ELIZABETH, age 12; MARTHA A., age 10; WILLIAM H., age 8; MARY A., age 6; DAVID B., age 3; LLEWELLYN E., age 1, all b. Mich., in their household.

SMITH, WOOSTER born ca. 1800, Conn., and wife, HARRIET, born ca. 1805, NY, were listed in the 1840 census index of Dover Twp., Lenawee Co., Mich.; and in the 1850 census with WILLIAM S., age 19; CHARLES H., age 17; GEORGE G., age 14, all b. NY; and JOHN W., age 10; HARRIET R., age 8; SUSAN M., age 4; ELIZA A., age 1, all b. Mich., in their household.

SMITT, HENRY born Brunswick, Germany, married MARGARET (KRUPP) born Hessen, Germany, and they immigrated to Vermillion Twp., Erie Co., Ohio. He died 20 July 1853; and she was still living in 1888 in Huron Twp., Erie Co. Known daughter, ANNA C. b. 9 Feb. 1851, Vermillion (m. Henry Rhinemiller, also see). Ref: P&BA-Len pg. 714-5.

SNEDEKER, DWIGHT, son of JAMES J. (following), born 17 Nov. 1845, Adrian Twp., Lenawee Co., Mich., married there to ADELAIDE (BOGERT), daughter of Peter (also see). Children: 1. MAUD E. b. 24 June 1871; 2. FLORENCE M. b. 17 Aug. 1874. Ref: P&BA-Len pg. 372-3.

SNEDEKER, HANNAH of Ontario Co., NY (See Silas Richardson).

SNEDEKER, JAMES J. born 29 June 1802, Monmouth Co., NJ, came to Adrian Twp., Lenawee Co., Mich. in 1829. He married there on 14 Feb. 1837 to PHEBE (VAN AKEN), daughter of Benjamin (also see). He died 10 Feb. 1874, Adrian Twp. Children: 1. EMELINE A. b. 20 Feb. 1838 (m. Jonathan Howland); 2. ADELINE A. b. 5 Oct. 1839 (m. Reuben Sayers, also see); 3. DWIGHT (preceding); 4. DUANE (twin of DWIGHT; d. 4 Mar. 1869). Ref: P&BA-Len pg. 372-3.

SNEDEKER, MAGGIE G. (See George A. Stimson)

SNEDICOR see SNEDEKER

SNOOK, WILLIAM (See Halsey Lewis)

SNOW, EBENEZER born ca. 1807, Mass., and wife, ELVIRA, born ca. 1815, NY, were listed in the 1850 census of Adrian Twp., Lenawee Co., Mich. with JEROME T., age 15; LIBENUS, age 13; SEVERUS, age 13, all b. NY; and John Andrews, age 74, b. VT, in their household.

SNOW, FIELDER S. born ca. 1814, and wife, CAROLINE, born ca. 1815, both in Conn., were listed in the 1840 census index of Clinton Twp., Lenawee Co., Mich.; and in the 1850 census of Tecumseh Twp. with ARTHUR, age 7; ALICE, age 5; and Lucy Bigelow, age 16, all b. Mich., in their household.

SNOW, HARVEY went from Lenawee Co., Mich. overland to California in 1852 (See Edgar Alonzo Perry).

SNYDER, DORA (See Alfred Belcher)

SNYDER, HENRY R. (See Jacob Kurtz)

SNYDER, JACOB born ca. 1815, Penn., and wife, ABIGAIL, born ca. 1816, NY, were listed in the 1850 census of Macon Twp., Lenawee Co., Mich. with HANNAH, age 6; JOHN, age 3, both b. Mich., in their household. Note: In 1888, JEANETT (COLVIN), daughter of William (also see), born 15 June 1817, was called "widow of Jacob Snyder of Macon Twp." Ref: P&BA-Len pg. 687-9.

SNYDER, JANE (See Josiah Hawley)

SNYDER, JOSEPH, age 14, born NY, was listed in the 1850 census of Tecumseh Twp., Lenawee Co., Mich. in the household of Solomon and Harriet Mangus.

SNYDER, MARGARET (See Jacob Booher)

SNYDER, MARY (See Isaac Hurless)

SOLOMON, MARY (See John Norcross)

SONES, DANIEL born ca. 1813, Penn., and wife, ANNIS, born ca. 1825, Canada, were listed in the 1850 census of Macon Twp., Lenawee Co., Mich. with JOHN, age 4 (prob. he who m. Almeda Ellis, dau. of Abner W., also see); PHOEBE, age 1; and Rachel Swick, age 11, all b. Mich., in their household.

SONES, FRANCES (See Adam Van Tuyle)

SONES, HENRY was listed in the 1840 census index of Macon Twp., Lenawee Co., Mich. adjacent to PETER, following.

SONES, PETER born ca. 1786, and wife, POLLY, born ca. 1789, both in Penn., were listed in the 1840 census index of Macon Twp., Lenawee Co., Mich. (adjacent to HENRY, preceding); and in the 1850 census about 5 doors from DANIEL (preceding), with JOHN, age 26; ANNA, age 24; PETER, age 23; CHRISTIANN, age 21, all b. Penn., in their household.

SOOP, ABRAM and wife, MARIA, moved from Albany, NY to Michigan in 1832. They had known daughter, ELIZABETH b. 3 Sept. 1816, Albany (m/1 David Gardner; m/2 Hezekiah Knowles, also see). Possibly another daughter, MARIA, born Mohawk Valley of NY (m. William Wing, also see).

SORBY, JOHN, son of RICHARD (following), born 28 June 1849, Yorkshire, England, came to the US in 1870. He married MARY (DeGREENE), daughter of Richard (also see); and they returned to England. About 1872, they came to Rollin Twp., Lenawee Co., Mich. Children: 1. JOHN b. 25 May 1873; 2. child d. infancy; 3. EDGAR A. b. 29 Jan. 1876; 4. FLORENCE M. b. 23 Aug. 188q; 5. EARNASTEEN b. 28 May 1885; 6. JOSEPHINE E. b. 7 Sept. 1886. Ref: P&BA-Len pg. 1058-9.

SORBY, RICHARD had come from England to southern Michigan when it was wilderness, but returned to England. He married MARGARET (DeGREENE) who died in 1877, age 65, in England. There were 7 children, and only mentioned JOHN (preceding), who was the only one to come to the US. Ref: P&BA-Len pg. 1058-9.

SOULS, ELIZABETH (See Jeremiah Marks)

SOUTHARD, NEAL born ca. 1821, and wife, MARY, born ca. 1826, both in NY, were listed in the 1850 census of Rome Twp., Lenawee Co., Mich. with no family. However, FRED D., probably born after 1860, may be a son of this family. (See Henry W. Burke).

Pioneer Families of Southeastern Michigan

SOUTHWORTH, ALBERT, son of JOSEPH JR. (following), born 15 Jan. 1817, Edmeston, Otsego Co., NY, married on 12 Sept. 1848 to ANTOINETTE (SOUTHWORTH), daughter of HARVEY (following). Children: 1. MARIE ANTOINETTE b. 11 Aug. 1849 (d. 1850); 2. LYDIA L. b. 3 Oct. 1851 (m. William Montague, also see); 3. LUNETTA C. b. 11 Dec. 1854; 4. ALBERT J. b. 20 Dec. 1856 (d. age 2); 5. HERBERT W. b. 22 Feb. 1859; 6. KATE L. b. 4 May 1862; 7. ARTHUR W. b. 19 Dec. 1863; 8. ALEXANDER P. b. 4 Apr. 1869. Ref: P&BA-Len pg. 189-90.

SOUTHWORTH, ANDREW A. born ca. 1822, Penn., and wife, ELIZABETH, born ca. 1825, NY, were listed in the 1850 census of Dover Twp., Lenawee Co., Mich. with DELORA, age 4; HARRIET, age 3; CHARLES A., age 2; LEVI, age 3/12, all b. Mich., in their household. Note HARVEY, following.

SOUTHWORTH, ESLI?, age 24, born NY, was listed in the 1850 census of Adrian Twp., Lenawee Co., Mich. an employee in a hotel.

SOUTHWORTH, HARVEY, and wife, ELSIE, moved from Erie Co., Penn. to Pittsford Twp., Hillsdale Co., Mich. by 1840; and were parents of ANTOINETTE b. 24 Dec. 1831, Erie Co., Penn. (m. ALBERT, preceding). Ref: P&BA-Len pg. 189-90.

SOUTHWORTH, JOSEPH and wife, LYDIA, of Mansfield, Tolland Co., Conn., were parents of JOSEPH JR. (following); and they died in Edmeston, Otsego Co., NY. Ref: P&BA-Len pg. 189-90.

SOUTHWORTH, JOSEPH JR., son of JOSEPH (preceding), born 30 Jan. 1788, Mansfield, Tolland Co., Conn., married HANNAH WHITE (See Low White) on 18 Oct. 1810; and they moved from Edmeston, Otsego Co., NY to Raisin Twp., Lenawee Co., Mich. by 1832. She was apparently deceased before 1850, as he was listed in the 1850 census of Raisin Twp. with son, ALBERT (preceding) and family in the household. Also in the household was CLARINDA, age 16, b. Ohio, possibly a granddaughter. Ref: P&BA-Len pg. 189-90. Note MASON W., following.

SOUTHWORTH, LYDIA L. (See William Montague b. 3 Oct. 1851, Raisin Twp.)

SOUTHWORTH, MARY JANE (See John Blackmar; note that they lived in Erie Co., Penn. ca. 1852). Note HARVEY, preceding.

SOUTHWORTH, MASON W. born ca. 1811, and wife, EMELINE, born ca. 1818, both in NY, were listed in the 1850 census of Raisin Twp., Lenawee Co., Mich. with JAMES, age 20; WALLACE, age 18, both b. NY; and HENRY, age 16; GEORGE, age 8; HERBERT, age 5, all b. Mich., in their household.

SOUTHWORTH, SIMEON S. born ca. 1799, VT, and wife, HARRIET, born ca. 1807, NY, were listed in the 1840 census index of Tecumseh Twp., Lenawee Co., Mich.; and in the 1850 census with GEORGE, age 20; CHARLES, age 17, both b. NY; and EDWARD, age 13; SAMUEL, age 6; CATHERINE, age 5; WILLIAM, age 1, all b. Mich., in their household.

SOUTHWORTH, THOMAS F. born ca. 1812, and wife, ALTHA W., born ca. 1814, both in NY, were listed in the 1840 census index of Fairfield Twp., Lenawee Co., Mich.; and in the 1850 census with NANCY, age 18; PORTER T., age 16; RUTH, age 14, all b. NY; and CLARK T., age 12; SALLY, age 11; THOMAS T., age 10; ALTHA W., age 9, all b. Mich., in their household.

SOUTHWORTH, WILLIAM Dr. of Avon Springs, NY was father of JOSEPHINE (m. William Seward Wilcox, also see).

SPAFFORD, ABNER and wife, BETSEY, were natives of New Hampshire, who had known daughter, CYNTHIA (m/1 Theodore Bissel; m/2 William W. Tilton, also see). Ref: P&BA-Len pg 878-881.

SPAFFORD, CHARLES born ca. 1800, New Hampshire, and wife, MARIA, born ca. 1803, NY, were listed in the 1840 census index of Tecumseh Twp., Lenawee Co., Mich. (adjacent to GEORGE; LUKE A.; & MARIAH L.); and in the 1850 census with CHARLES, age 16, b. NY; and GEORGE, age 65, b. NH (probably brother); Susan King, age 75, b. Conn. (possibly mother-in-law?); and Emily German, age 21, b. NY, in their household.

SPAFFORD, LUKE A. was listed in the 1840 census index of Tecumseh Twp., Lenawee Co., Mich., adjacent to CHARLES; GEORGE, & MARIAH L. In the 1850 census of Tecumseh Twp., there was MARY A., age 33, b. NY, listed as head of household, with VINCENT, age 13; ELISA, age 11; CYNTHIA, age 6, all b. Mich., in her household. Possibly this is family of Luke A.?

SPAFFORD, MARIAH L. was listed in the 1840 census index of Tecumseh Twp., Lenawee Co., Mich. near CHARLES; GEORGE; & LUKE A., all preceding.

SPAFFORD, SUMNER F. born ca. 1809, New Hampshire, and wife, EMELINE, born ca. 1816, Mass., were listed in the 1850 census of Adrian Twp., Lenawee Co., Mich. with CHARLES T., age 13, b. Mich., in their household.

SPALDING also see SPAULDING

SPALDING FAMILY - Gen. SIMON, son of SIMON and ANN (BILLINGS), born 16 Jan. 1742, Plainfield, Conn., was a descendant in the 6th generation from EDWARD who was the first to come to American. Gen. SIMON married in 1761 to RUTH (SHEPARD), and afterwards removed to the Wyoming Valley of Penn. He served in the Revolutiona as a Capt., and after the war as a General in the State Militia. He was a member of the Conn. Society of Cincinnati. In 1783, he helped establish the first settlement at Sheshequin, Bradford Co., Penn. He died there on 24 Jan. 1814, age 72; and she died 1 Oct. 1806, age 65. Children: 1. SARAH; 2. Col. JOHN (following); 3. RUTH; 4. REBECCA; 5. MARY; 6. ANNA; 7. GEORGE; 8. CHESTER PIERCE. Ref: Pioneer & Patriot Families of Bradford Co., Penn., by C. F. Heverly, 1913. Note: For further information on the members of this family who did not go to Michigan, please refer to this source.

SPALDING, AMOS P. (See Samuel Hoyt)

SPALDING, DAVID P., son of OBEDIAH GORE (following), born ca. 1827, Penn., and wife, ORRILLA T., born ca. 1830, NY, were listed in the 1850 census of Hudson Twp., Lenawee Co., Mich. with LAURA, age 9/12, b. Mich., in their household.

SPALDING, ELIZABETH (See George Whiting)

SPALDING, JOHN Col., son of Gen. SIMON (see Spalding family, preceding), born 14 Nov. 1765, was a Fifer during the Sullivan Expedition with his father's Company; and became a Colonel in the State Militia of Penn. He married in Sheshequin, Bradford Co. to

WEALTHY ANN (GORE), daughter of Obediah & Ann (Avery) Gore. He died there on 19 Feb. 1828; and she died 2 Jan. 1854, age 87. Of the children, following, only Obediah was said to have moved to Michigan, though others went to Illinois and Texas. HARRY; WILLIAM BELA; NOAH; OBEDIAH GORE (following); SIMON; SARAH; ULYSSES; WEALTHY ANN; GEORGE W.; JOHN AVERY; CHARLES M.; ZEBULON BUTLER; AVERY GORE; MARY ANN. Ref: Pioneer & Patriot Families of Bradford Co., Penn, by C. F. Heverly, 1913.

SPALDING, LYDIA (See Benjamin M. Stanley)

SPALDING, OBEDIAH GORE, son of Col. JOHN (preceding), born 11 Aug. 1780, Sheshequin, Penn., married there to CHLOTILDA (HOYT), daughter of Samuel (also see). About 1833, they removed to Monroe Co., Mich. He died there on 3 Dec. 1847; and she died 3 Sept. 1834. Of 9 children, 8 lived to maturity. 1. JANE (m. Kendall); 2. LAMIRA (m. Rodney; Buffalo, NY); 3. ELLEN (m. Kelly, Monroe Co., Mich.); 4. ELIZA (d. age 18); 5. JULIUS (Dundee, Mich.); 6. ULYSSES (Monroe Co., Mich.); 7. DAVID P. (preceding); 8. OBEDIAH G. (d. Calif.); 9. SUSAN CHLOTILDA b. 13 Mar. 1831, Athens, Bradford Co., Penn. (m. William M. Corbett, also see). Ref: P&BA-Len pg. 1178-80.

SPALDING, PARLEY J. Dr. born ca. 1806, NY, and ROMANDA, age 40, b. NY, were listed in the 1850 census of Adrian Twp., Lenawee Co., Mich. (with Romanda listed head of household?), and ELIZABETH R., age 8, b. Mich., in the household.

SPANGLE, CHARLES (See Ralph P. Baker)

SPANGLE, GEORGE born ca. 1813, and wife, MARY, born ca. 1813, both in Penn., were listed in the 1850 census of Rome Twp., Lenawee Co., Mich. with AARON, age 11; MARY, age 9; ALBERT, age 7; MYRON, age 4, all b. Penn.; and WILSON, age 3; GEORGE, age 7/12, both b. Mich., in their household.

SPARHAWK, EBEN and wife, FANNY (HUDSON), were natives of Vermont, who moved first to Summit Co., Ohio. In 1851, they removed to Madison Twp., Lenawee Co., Mich., where he died on 20 Apr. 1863, age 60. She afterwards went to Gratiot Co., Mich., where she died on 12 Apr. 1887, age 80. Children: 1. STEARNS; 2. ELI (following); 3. RACHEL (m. Silas Randolph; Gratiot Co., Mich.); 4. HENRY; 5. EMMA (m. Myron Livesay; Clinton Co., Mich.) Ref: P&BA-Len pg. 526.

SPARHAWK, ELI, son of EBEN (preceding), born 1 Dec. 1830, Summit Co., Ohio, moved to Madison Twp., Lenawee Co., Mich. with his parents. He married there on 29 Dec. 1853 to MARIAN (SERVICE), daughter of William (also see). Son, ELMER S. b. 1 Oct. 1865. Ref: P&BA-Len pg. 526.

SPARLING, JOSEPH and wife, FLORA (MEACHAM), were natives of NY who married in Summit Co., Ohio. In 1853, they moved to Franklin Twp., Lenawee Co., Mich. Children: 1. FRANCIS; 2. SARAH b. 14 Aug. 1846, Tallmadge, Ohio (m. Benjamin F. DePuy, also see). Joseph married again to PAULINE (LEE) of Summerfield, Monroe Co., Mich.; and they were living in Franklin Twp., Lenawee Co. in 1888. Ref: P&BA-Len pg. 894-6.

SPARROWS, SERENA (See Robert Morley)

SPAULDING also see SPALDING

SPAULDING, ADDIE (See Augustus W. Bradish)

SPAULDING, CHARLES, probably son of SUSAN (following), born ca. 1823, NY, with probably wife, JANE, age 18, born NY, were listed in the 1850 census of Palmyra Twp., Lenawee Co., Mich. next door to SUSAN.

SPAULDING, ELIZABETH born ca. 1815, Seneca Co., NY, went as a child to near Akron, Ohio; and afterwards to Macon Twp., Lenawee Co., Mich. (m. Nathaniel K. Bowen in 1842). Note WILLIAM, following, possibly her brother; and SAMUEL, following.

SPAULDING, ISAAC was listed in the 1840 census index of Adrian Twp., Lenawee Co., Mich.

SPAULDING, JENNIE (See Norman F. Bradish)

SPAULDING, P. J. was listed in the 1840 census index of Adrian Twp., Lenawee Co., Mich.; also note ISAAC, preceding.

SPAULDING, POLLY (See Jacob Rogers)

SPAULDING, SARAH (See Herbert B. Hathaway)

SPAULDING, SAMUEL born ca. 1789, NY, and wife, SARAH, born ca. 1793, Penn., were listed in the 1850 census of Macon Twp., Lenawee Co., Mich. with LOISA, age 20; SARAH J.. age 16, both b. Ohio, in their household. Note ELIZABETH, preceding; and WILLIAM (following).

SPAULDING, SAMUEL born ca. 1775, NY, and wife, HANNAH, born ca. 1783, VT, were probably they listed as "Saul" (Saml?) in the 1840 census index of Tecumseh Twp., Lenawee Co., Mich.; and in the 1850 census with probably grandchildren, ALMYRA, age 3; EDGAR? (male), age 1, both b. Mich., in their household.

SPAULDING, SUSAN born ca. 1790, Rhode Island, was listed head of household in the 1840 census index of Palmyra Twp., Lenawee Co., Mich. (near VOLNEY, following); and in the 1850 census with JAMES, age 20; JOHN, age 24, both b. NY; and possibly a grandson, CHARLES M., age 14, b. Mich., in her household. Next door was probably son, CHARLES (preceding).

SPAULDING, VOLNEY born ca. 1801, and wife, LORENA, born ca. 1806, both in NY, were listed in the 1840 census index of Palmyra Twp., Lenawee Co., Mich.; and in the 1850 census with Mary A. Alvord, age 65, b. Conn., in their household.

SPAULDING, WILLIAM born ca. 1825, Ohio (note ELIZABETH & SAMUEL, preceding.

SPEAR see SPEARS/SPEER

SPEARS, ALEXANDER born ca. 1778, Mass., and wife, ELIZABETH, born ca. 1788, NY, apparently lived in Penn. as early as 1820; and then were listed in the 1840 census index of Rome Twp., Lenawee Co., Mich.; and in the 1850 census next door to JAMES M.; & GEORGE W. (following). Also note HARVEY, following.

SPEARS, GEORGE W., probably son of ALEXANDER (preceding), born ca. 1822, Penn., and wife, LOUISA, born ca. 1822, NY, were listed in the 1850 census of Rome Twp., Lenawee Co., Mich. with JANE, age 4, b. Mich., in their household. GEORGE W. with wife, "JANE," of Rome Twp., Lenawee Co., Mich. were parents of IDA M. b. 26 Oct. 1856 (m. Jefferson R. Thomas, also see). Ref: P&BA-Len pg. 1085-6.

SPEARS, HARVEY born ca. 1820, Penn., and wife, LUCY A., born ca. 1828, NY, were listed in the 1850 census of Rollin Twp., Lenawee Co., Mich. with LOIS A., age 5; GEORGE G., age 2; ANDREW J., age 4/12, all b. Mich., in their household.

SPEARS, JAMES M., probably son of ALEXANDER (preceding), born ca. 1822, Penn., and wife, JUDAH, born ca. 1828, NY, were listed in the 1850 census of Rome Twp., Lenawee Co., Mich. with CLARISSA E., age 2, b. Mich., in their household.

SPEARS, MARY A. born 3 Feb. 1817, Penfield, Monroe Co., NY moved with parents to Erie Co., Ohio (m. Crowell Eddy, also see). Ref: P&BA-Len pg. 273-4.

SPEARS, NATHAN W. born ca. 1807, and wife, SUSAN, born ca. 1813, both in NY, were listed in the 1850 census of Tecumseh Twp., Lenawee Co., Mich. with JAMES, age 16; JESSE, age 14; CHARLES, age 12; JANE, age 10; FRANCES, age 9; MILES, age 7; MARY, age 5; HOBART, age 3; SARAH, age 2, all born Ohio, in their household. Also note WILLIAM, following.

SPEARS, STEPHEN P. born ca. 1810, and wife, LUCINDA, born ca. 1815, both in NY, were listed in the 1850 census of Seneca Twp., Lenawee Co., Mich. with PHILETUS, age 16; CORDELIA, age 14; CLINTON L., age 5, all b. Mich., in their household. Note: There was a STEPHEN SPEERS in Washtenaw Co., Mich. in 1840 census index.

SPEARS, WILLIAM born ca. 1829, Ohio, and wife, AMETTA, born ca. 1830, NY, were listed in the 1850 census of Tecumseh Twp., Lenawee Co., Mich. with no family. Note NATHAN W., preceding.

SPEARS, WILLIAM R. (spelled Speer) was listed in the 1840 census index of Madison Twp., Lenawee Co., Mich.

SPEED, CATHERINE (See Robert Smith)

SPEER also see SPEAR/SPEARS

SPEER, CHARLES was listed in the 1840 census index of Dover Twp., Lenawee Co., Mich.

SPEER, SARAH AMELIA born ca. 1832, NY, married John K Boies (also see) after 1850. In the 1850 census of Hudson Twp., Lenawee Co., Mich. she was listed in the household of Simeon Van Akin, and wife, Lydia, with probably siblings, MARVIN W., age 19, b. NY; and LORENZO, age 16, b. Mich., possibly all stepchildren of that household.

SPENCER, EPHRAIM and wife, CORDELIA (WOODING), were natives of Conn., who married in Mass. They removed to Camden, Oneida Co., NY; and he died there in 1853, age 60. She afterwards went to Grand Rapids, Mich. where she was still living in 1888, age 83. Eleven children, names not stated, except GEORGE W. (following); and SALLIE b. ca. 1826, Conn. (m. Oramon Tuttle, Jr., also see, on 12 Sept. 1844). Ref: P&BA-Lenpg. 873-4.

SPENCER, GEORGE W., son of EPHRAIM, born in Tolland Co., Conn., moved with his parents to Oneida Co., NY. He married there to ORICA (RAYMOND); and after her death, married again to SAPHRONIA (ROBINSON). He served in the Civil War in Co. H, 177th NY Inf. About 1866, they removed to Seneca Twp., Lenawee Co., Mich. In 1888, they lived in Milford, Oakland Co., Mich. Known daughter, IDA b. Camden, Oneida Co., NY (m. William H. Knox, also see, Lenawee Co., Mich.) Ref: P&BA-Len pg. 855-6.

SPENCER, HENRY born ca. 1801, Mass., and wife, SOPHIA, born ca. 1801, Conn., were listed in the 1850 census of Madison Twp., Lenawee Co., Mich. with ELIZA J., age 20; REWLEN P., age 19, both b. NY; and HANNAH B., age 16; WILLIAM H., age 14, both b. Canada; and SUSANNA, age 9, b. Mich., in their household.

SPENCER, ICHABOD J. born ca. 1800, Mass., and wife, JANE, born ca. 1807, NY, were listed in the 1840 census index of Rome Twp., Lenawee Co., Mich.; and in the 1850 census of Cambridge Twp. with JOHN, age 22, b. Ohio; ALMYRA, age 13, b. NY; and LAURA, age 10; POLLY, age 9, both b. Mich., in their household.

SPENCER, JAMES born ca. 1828, NY (See NATHAN, following).

SPENCER, NATHAN born ca. 1815, NY, and wife, ELIZA J., born ca. 1825, Mass., were listed in the 1850 census of Raisin Twp., Lenawee Co., Mich. with CHARLES U., age 2, b. Mich., and JAMES, age 22, b. NY, probably brother, in their household.

SPENCER, SIMEON born ca. 1801, VT, and wife, MAHITABLE, born ca. 1812, NY, were listed in the 1840 census index of Clinton Twp., Lenawee Co., Mich.; and in the 1850 census of Tecumseh Twp. with MARY, age 18; SARAH ANN, age 16 (may be she listed again in the household of John P. Silvers in the 1850 census); MARVIN, age 14; AMANDA, age 13; FIDELIA, age 7, all b. Mich., in their household.

SPENCER, URIEL born ca. 1796, and wife, ELIZABETH, born ca. 1804, both in NY, were listed in the 1850 census of Raisin Twp., Lenawee Co., Mich. with SARAH J., age 12; MARY E., age 9; MARTHA E., age 6, all b. Ohio, in their household.

SPENCER, WILLIAM, age 23, born NY, was listed in the 1850 census of Hudson Twp., Lenawee Co., Mich. in a Kenyon household.

SPERRY, ENOCH, son of JOSEPH (following), born 2 May 1801, New Haven, Conn., moved to Hudson, Summit Co., Ohio, where he married on 4 Aug. 1827 to LUCRETIA (JONES), daughter of Daniel (also see). In 1854, they moved to Ogden Twp., Lenawee Co., Mich. He died there 7 Nov. 1822; and she died in May 1881. Known daughter, CYNTHIA A. b. 30 Aug. 1828, Hudson, Ohio (m. James K. Crane, also see). Ref: P&BA-Len pg. 1204-6.

SPERRY, JOSEPH and wife, SARAH (BEECHER), were natives of Conn., where he died. She remained a widow for 40 years; and some time after his death went to Ohio and died at the home of a son in Parkman, Ohio. She was a cousin of Rev. Lyman Beecher, father of Henry Ward Beecher. There were 13 children, names not stated, except ENOCH (preceding). Ref: P&BA-Len pg. 1204-6.

SPOON, HENRY (See Henry Pontius)

SPOONER, AMOS B. born ca. 1821, and wife, EMELINE A., born ca. 1824, both in NY, were listed in the 1850 census of Dover Twp., Lenawee Co., Mich. with CONSTANT

C., age 3, b. NY; and FRANKLIN R., age 1, b. Ohio, in their household.

SPOONER, E. A. (See Edward Hodge)

SPOONER, JOHN B. (See John L. Hall)

SPRAGUE, AMASA and wife, PATIENCE, probably came to Jackson Co. Mich. from New York ca. 1847. Daughter, PATIENCE b. 4 July 1844, Schuyler Co., NY (m. John Cain, also see). Ref: P&BA-Len pg. 333-4.

SPRAGUE, BETSEY (See Samuel Russell)

SPRAGUE, CINTHIA born ca. 1804, NY (listed as a male?) was head of household in the 1850 census of Woodstock Twp., Lenawee Co., Mich. with ALBERT, age 9; ELI, age 29; EMMA, age 21, all b. NY, in the household.

SPRAGUE, DAVID Rev. born in Scotland was a Presbyterian Minister, who came to America at an early date. He lived in Saratoga Co., NY where known daughter, MARIAN was born (m. before 1800 to Jacob Hogaboom, also see, settled Harford, NY). David was married twice and had 21 children, names not stated. Ref: P&BA-Len pg. 1105-6.

SPRAGUE, DAVID and wife, MARY (JONES), were natives of Vermont, who had a known daughter, HARRIET b. VT (m. Guy C. Boughton, also see, in Lorain Co., Ohio before 1820). Ref: P&BA-Lenpg. 1139-40. Note DAVID F.; & EDMUND, following.

SPRAGUE, DAVID F. born ca. 1806, and wife, SARAH, born ca. 1806, both in NY, were listed in the 1850 census of Medina Twp., Lenawee Co., Mich. with HIRAM, age 20; ALFRED, age 17, both born Ohio, in their household. Note: EDMUND, following, was next door.

SPRAGUE, EDMUND born ca. 1815, and wife, JULIA, born ca. 1827, both in NY, were listed in the 1850 census of Medina Twp., Lenawee Co., Mich. with CELISTA, age 5; MARY, age 3; MARTHA, age 2; WILLIAM M., age 2/12; JANE, age 2/12, all b. Mich., in their household.

SPRAGUE, GIDEON R. born ca. 1798, NY, was listed in the 1840 census index of Fairfield Twp., Lenawee Co., Mich.; and in the 1850 census in a Fletcher household.

SPRAGUE, MARY H., age 16, born NY, was listed in the 1850 census of Ogden Twp., Lenawee Co., Mich. in a Cheeny household.

SPRAGUE, SAMUEL born ca. 1783, Conn., and wife, PHEBE, born ca. 1791, NJ, were listed in the 1850 census of Medina Twp., Lenawee Co., Mich. with SAMUEL, age 30; DANIEL, age 20; THEODORE, age 17; AMOS, age 15; JONAS, age 13 (prob. he who m. Helen Round, dau. of James E., also see; had dau., Theresa), all b. NY, in their household.

SPRAGUE, THOMAS J. born ca. 1802, and wife, BETSEY, born ca. 1799, both in NY, were listed in the 1850 census of Rome Twp., Lenawee Co., Mich. with WILLIAM, age 14; CHARLES, age 11; FRANKLIN, age 10, all b. Mich.; and Thurza Chandler, age 49, b. NY, in their household. Note: There was a THOMAS in the 1840 census index of Napoleon Twp., Jackson Co., Mich.

SPRING, AMOS was a native of Mass. who moved to LeRoy, Genesee Co., NY. He served in the War of 1812, and his brother, DENAS (DENNIS?), was killed in the war. He moved to Hermitage, Wyoming Co., NY where he died. Known daughter, LOIS A. (m. John J. Stark, also see). Ref: P&BA-Len pg. 446-7.

SPRING, CHARLES E. born ca. 1812, Mass., and wife, MARY, born ca. 1817, NY, were listed in the 1840 census index of Adrian Twp., Lenawee Co., Mich.; and in the 1850 census with ALICE C., age 4; JOHN H., age 4, both b. Mich.; and Silas Fox, age 45, b. NY, in their household.

SPRING, LEANDER born ca. 1818, Mass., and wife, MARY J., born ca. 1825, NY, were listed in the 1850 census of Medina Twp., Lenawee Co., Mich. with JAMES H., age 8; JEREMIAH, age 5; ALMERON, age 2; MARY L., age 1, all b. Mich., in their household.

SQUIRE, HANNAH (See Elijah Wing)

SQUIRES, LESLIE (See David M. Johnson)

STACK, MAURICE and wife, BRIDGET (SULLIVAN), of Co. Kerry, Ireland, were parents of 3 sons and 3 daughters, names not stated, except CATHERINE, born June 1830, came to the US at age 17 (m. John Moriarty, also see, Cayuga Co., NY). Maurice died in 1848, and Bridget died in 1865, both in Ireland. Ref: P&BA-Len pg. 1027-8.

STACY, CALVIN born ca. 1804, Mass., was listed in the 1850 census of Cambridge Twp., Lenawee Co., Mich. with no family.

STACY, CONSIDER A., son of Dr. CONSIDER H. (following), born 6 Jan. 1817, Hamilton, Madison Co., NY, married on 19 Aug. 1838 to MARY M. (WALKER), daughter of David Shapley (also see) of Broome Co., NY. Consider A. had come to Tecumseh Twp., Lenawee Co., Mich. in 1835; and settled there after his marriage. Children: (2 daughters, names not stated, died infancy) 1. SCOVEL CONSIDER b. 2 Aug. 1841; 2. LOANA b. ca. 1845; 3. GEORGE N.; 4. ALSPHONE S. (d. 16 Dec. 1876, killed by cars in Tecumseh); 5. JAMES A. (d. 9 Apr. 1881). Ref: P&BA-Len pg. 360-2.

STACY, CONSIDER H. Dr., son of RUFUS (following), born in New Salem, Mass., moved in 1814 to Hamilton, Madison Co., NY, where he married on 21 Aug. 1815 to POLLY (BASS) born ca. 1795, Mass. He died there in 1840. Polly died in 1876 in Tecumseh, Lenawee Co., Mich. Nine children, names not stated. Polly was listed in the 1850 census of Tecumseh Twp. head of household, with WEALTHY R., age 17, b. NY, in her household; and had a known son, CONSIDER A. (preceding); and GEORGE W., age 19, b. NY (was listed next door with wife, ANGELINE, age 20, b. NY). Ref: P&BA-Len pg. 360-2.

STACY, LOUISA, age 32, born NY, was listed in the 1850 census of Blissfield Twp., Lenawee Co., Mich. in a Marvin L. Stone household.

STACY, NATHANIEL was listed in the 1840 census index of Franklin Twp., Lenawee Co., Mich.

STACY, RUFUS born in New Salem, Mass., served in the Revolution directly under General Stark. (Note: Revolutionary War Pension Application #S33714, Rufus Stacey, Mass.) He was a descendant of a Stacy from Lincolnshire, England who had settled first at Cape Ann, Mass. The given name, Consider, was given the eldest son in serveral generations. Known son, Dr. CONSIDER H. (preceding).

STAHLER, HENRY of Niagara Co., NY was son of a family from Penn. He married by 1830 to SUSAN (HOOVER).

Pioneer Families of Southeastern Michigan

Known daughter, SUSAN M. (m. Abraham V. Dersham, also see, in Lockport, NY). Ref: P&BA-Len pg. 836-7.

STAIGER, ANNA (See Stephen Conger)

STALKER, W. D. married ALICE L. (MORSE), daughter of Charles C., born ca. 1840, in Medina Twp., Lenawee Co., Mich. Children: WILLIE M.; NINA A. They moved to Sacramento, CA by 1888.

STANDISH, MARY of Hadley, Mass. married Horace Seymour (also see); and was a descendant of Capt. Miles Standish.

STANDISH, WILLIAM was listed in the 1840 census index of Raisin Twp. Lenawee Co., Mich.

STANFIELD, ETTA (See Edward F. Muir)
STANFORD, ELIZABETH (See Samuel White)

STANLEY, ABNER born ca. 1811, and wife, ABIGAIL, born ca. 1812, were listed in the 1840 census index of Fairfield Twp., Lenawee Co., Mich.; and in the 1850 census with SAPHRONA, age 16; BRADLEY, age 13, both b. NY; and BENJAMIN F., age 11; PERMELIA E., age 8, both b. Mich.; and Hannah T. Cotton, age 31, in their household.

STANLEY, BENJAMIN M. and wife, LYDIA (SPALDING), were natives of New England, and were parents of ELIZABETH B. born 3 Nov. 1815, Jeffrey, New Hampshire (m/1 Charles Farnsworth; m/2 Charles Brown, see both). Ref: P&BA-Len pg. 780-1.

STANSELL, NICHOLAS was an early settler to Wayne Co., Mich.; and was a "brother-in-law of John Featherly."

STANTON, HIRAM was listed in the 1840 census index of Fairfield Twp., Lenawee Co., Mich.
STANTON, LUCRETIA (See William Bird)
STANTON, PATRICK born ca. 1812, and wife, MARY, born ca. 1810, both in Ireland, were listed in the 1840 census index of Macon Twp., Lenawee Co., Mich.; and in the 1850 census of Madison Twp. with THOMAS, age 14, b. NY; and DANIEL, age 12; EDWARD, age 9; WILLIAM, age 7; MARY, age 5; FRANCIS, age 3; ANN E., age 1, all b. Mich., in their household.

STARK, JOHN J., born in Oneida Co., NY, was a descendant to Gen. JOHN of Revolutionary fame. John J. married LOIS A. (SPRING), daughter of Amos (also see) in Leroy, Genesee Co., NY, where she was born. He was killed 30 June 1869 in a sawmill accident; and she afterwards went to the Dakota Territory. In 1888, she was living with her children. Known daughter, ELLA b. Middlebury, Wyoming Co., NY (m. Seth P. Sheldon, also see). Ref: P&BA-Len pg. 446-7.

STARM also see STORM
STARM, JAMES (See Moses Bowerman, Jr.)

STEARNES also see STEARNS
STEARNES, ALPHEUS born 1813, Mass., married in Raisin Twp., Lenawee Co., Mich. ca. 1840 to SUSAN (SISSON) born ca. 1817, NY. They moved to Tecumseh Twp. by the 1840 census. He died 4 July 1886; and she was still living in 1888. Known children (from 1850 census): ANNA, age 9; WILLIAM, age 7; JULIA A. b. 27 Feb. 1845 (m. M. E. Conklin, also see). Ref: P&BA-Len pg. 827. Also in their household in 1850 was Isaac Sisson, age 26, with probably wife, Emily, age 18, both b. NY, probably brother of Susan.
STEARNES, ELIZABETH, age 23, and OTIS, age 20, probably siblings, were listed in the 1850 census of Hudson Twp., Lenawee Co., Mich. in a Hamlin household.

STEARNS also see STEARNES
STEARNS, ALANSON and wife, ELIZA ANN, of Berkshire Co., Mass. were parents of known son, JAMES H. born 11 Mar. 1835, Mass. (m/1 Ellen Huise; m/2 E. L. Bliss; Leoni Twp., Jackson Co.). They moved to Norvell, Jackson Co., Mich. in 1854; and Alanson and another son, name not stated, were drowned in June 1870. Ref: History of Jackson Co., Mich., 1881, pg. 931.
STEARNS, ANSEL D. and wife, FRANCES, of Middlebury, VT, were parents of SARAH E. (m. Albert C. Huntington, also see). Ref: P&BA-Len pg. 1089.
STEARNS, CHARITY (PALMER) Mrs. married second to Andrew Taylor (also see).
STEARNS, CLARK born ca. 1815, Penn., and wife, AMANDA, born ca. 1816, NY, were listed in the 1850 census of Tecumseh Twp., Lenawee Co., Mich. with WILLIAM, age 15, b. Penn.; LEWIS, age 13; CHARLES, age 9, both b. Ohio; and ELISHA, age 5; and a male (ERNEST? or EME--), age 2, b. Mich., in their household.
STEARNS, CYRUS and wife, DIANTHA (ROCKWELL), daughter of Joshua (also see), moved from Laneboro, Berkshire Co., Mass. to Blissfield Twp., Lenawee Co., Mich. in 1834; and were listed there in the 1840 census index. They settled in 1852 in Columbia Twp., Jackson Co., Mich. (Note: They were not listed in the 1850 census of Blissfield Twp.) He died in 1863; and she died 1 May 1880, age 88. There were 4 sons and 2 daughters, and those mentioned were EDWIN b. 25 Aug. 1818, Lanesboro, Mass. (served in the Civil War); SARAH b. 27 Jan. 1823; MARY b. 18 Nov. 1828. Two sons, names not stated, were living in Blissfield Twp., Lenawee Co., in 1881. Ref: History of Jackson Co., Mich., 1881., pg. 814. Note MILO, following.
STEARNS, JACOB born ca. 1818, NY, was listed in the 1850 census of Medina Twp., Lenawee Co., Mich. in the household of Michael & Sarah Hoag.
STEARNS, JOSEPH had a wife, SARAH, who died 19 Oct. 1891, age 78 yrs, 3 mos., buried in the Mills Cemetery, Franklin Twp., Lenawee Co., Mich., located near the Ohio state line.
STEARNS, MILO born ca. 1826, Mass., was listed in the 1850 census of Palmyra Twp., Lenawee Co., Mich. in the household of Nelson and Ruth Goodrich.
STEARNS, WILLARD[1] married in January 1837 in Cherry Valley, Otsego Co., NY to LUCINDA (COUNROD), daughter of Peter (also see). He died 3 July 1838, Cherry Valley, NY leaving a known son, WILLARD[2] (following). Lucinda married again to Henry Bowen (also see). Ref: P&BA-Len pg. 615-6.
STEARNS, WILLARD[2], son of WILLARD[1] (preceding), born 3 Oct. 1838, Cherry Valley, NY, came to Franklin Twp., Lenawee Co., Mich. in 1851. He served as 1st Lt. in Co. H, 11th Mich. Cav., Civil War. He married on 5 May 1868 to MARTHA E. (PORTER), daughter of Philo (also

see). Children: 1. HARRY P. b. 23 Mar. 1869; 2. FANNIE L. b. 12 June 1871; 3. JENNIE b. 1 Aug. 1875; 4. VIRGINIA b. 10 Nov. 1884. Ref: P&BA-Len pg. 615-6.

STECK, J. F. (See Solomon Jeffords)

STEEL also see STEELE

STEEL, EBENEZER born ca. 1809, Mass., and wife, PHEBE, born ca. 1819, NY, were listed in the 1850 census of Hudson Twp., Lenawee Co., Mich. with ELLEN W., age 14, b Conn.; and JULIA A., age 7; VALENTILE A., age 2, both b. Mich., in their household.

STEEL, JOHN, age 19, born Mass., was listed in the 1850 census of Tecumseh Twp., Lenawee Co., Mich. in a Younger household.

STEEL, JOHN, son of SAMUEL (following), born ca. 1822 in the north of Ireland, came to New York City in 1850 with a sister (name not stated). He married on 17 Mar. 1857 to JANE (TAYLOR) born 26 Mar. 1826 in the north of Ireland. Probably by 1858, they moved to Livingston Co., NY; but were in New York City in 1861. About 1864, they removed to Macon Twp., Lenawee Co., Mich. She died 10 Mar. 1883. There were 6 children, but 4 died as infants. 1. SAMUEL (following); 2. JOHN b. 1861, New York City. Ref: P&BA-Len pg. 859-60.

STEEL, SAMUEL and wife were born and married in Ireland. She died there; and Samuel afterwards joined son, JOHN (preceding) in New York City. Samuel died in 1854. Ref: P&BA-Lenpg. 859-60.

STEEL, SAMUEL, son of JOHN (preceding), born 19 Aug. 1858, Livingston Co., NY, married ANNA (STEWART) who was born in Co. Antrim, Ireland, and had come to the US with her father and settled in Macon Twp., Lenawee Co., Mich. Known children: 1. IRA b. 3 Aug. 1885; 2. ROY b. 16 Nov. 1887. Ref: P&BA-Len pg. 859-60.

STEELE also see STEEL

STEELE, CAROLINE V., age 39, born NY, with MARGARET, age 16, b. NY, were listed in the 1850 census of Tecumseh Twp., Lenawee Co., Mich. in the household of Stephen Vanam?, perhaps father of Caroline V.

STEELE, JAMES R. married LUCY C. (UNDERWOOD), daughter of Edwin (also see).

STEELE, LOUISA (See William Burridge)

STEELE, POLLY (See Elias Gilbert²)

STEELE, SOLOMON and wife, LAURA (DOWNEY), moved from NY, possibly first to Ohio, and then to Palmyra Twp., Lenawee Co., Mich. Known daughters: MARGARETTA V. b. 27 Jan. 1845 (m. Dr. James H. Reynolds, also see); MARY b. Cayuga Co., NY (m. Samuel P. Whitmarsh, also see, in Oct. 1865). Ref: P&BA-Len pg. 425-6; 1135-6.

STEINHART, SARAH (See Joseph Marks)

STEPHENS also see STEVENS
STEPHENS, ADELINE (See Elias Dennis)
STEPHENS, ALEXANDER was listed in the 1840 census index of Lenawee Co., Mich.
STEPHENS, ALONSO S., probably son of LEWIS (following), born ca. 1798, and wife, MATILDA, born ca. 1795, both in New Hampshire, were listed in the 1850 census of Tecumseh Twp., Lenawee Co., Mich. with LEWIS, age 27; (MARY, age 25, wife of Lewis?); LUCINDA, age 19; JOEL, age 17; MARY, age 16, all b. NY; andd LESLIE, age 5/12 (possibly child of Lewis & Mary?); and HARRY, age 11, both b. Mich., in their household.

STEPHENS, CALEB W. (See John Johnson, son of Daniel)
STEPHENS, CHARLES born ca. 1812, Mass., and wife, THEODOSIA, born ca. 1810, NJ, were listed in the 1840 census index of Tecumseh Twp., Lenawee Co., Mich. with HARRIET, age 17, b. Mich., in their household, and in a neighboring household were ANGELINE, age 14; JAMES, age 11, both b. Mich., possibly related to this family.

STEPHENS, CHARLES D., age 19, born NY, was listed in the 1850 census of Tecumseh Twp., Lenawee Co., Mich. in a Hewitt household.

STEPHENS, DAVID STUBERT Rev. born 12 May 1847, Springfield, Ohio, President of Adrian College, was son of OLIVER PERRY and ANNA (BIDDLE) STEPHENS. Ref: P&BA-Len pg. 204-5.

STEPHENS, HENRY, age 35, born NY, was listed in the 1850 census of Tecumseh Twp., Lenawee Co., Mich. in an Inn.

STEPHENS, LEWIS, age 84, born Conn., was listed in the 1850 census of Tecumseh Twp., Lenawee Co., Mich. in the household of probably son, ALONSO S. (preceding).

STEPHENS, LYDIA born ca. 1792, New Hampshire, was listed in the 1850 census of Franklin Twp., Lenawee Co., Mich. in the household of Martha Young (age 30, b. NH).

STEPHENSON also see STEVENSON
STEPHENSON, ANDREW and wife, LYDIA (LAMPHERE), lived in Westmoreland, Oneida Co., NY as early as 1815. They may have moved to Chenango Co., NY; then in 1839 to Seneca Twp., Lenawee Co., Mich. They lived out their lives in Seneca Twp., except for about 1-1/2 years that they returned to Chenango Co. Eleven children, names not stated, known sons, ANDREW; & GEORGE W. (both following). Ref: P&BA-Len pg. 861-2; 884-5.

STEPHENSON, ANDREW, son of ANDREW, born ca. 1811, NY, came to Michigan first in 1838, then returned to Chenango Co., NY. He married POLLY (HAVEN), daughter of ASA; and in 1846, they returned to Morenci, Mich. In the 1850 census of Seneca Twp., Lenawee Co., his wife, OLIVE M., age 33 (probably this is "Polly"); and she died 23 Apr. 1877, Morenci. He married again on 5 Jan. 1879 to SUSAN (GEHRIG), daughter of George (also see). No children's names listed. Ref: P&BA-Len pg. 861-2.

STEPHENSON, GEORGE W., son of ANDREW (preceding), born 9 May 1815, Westmoreland, Oneida Co., NY, married in Chenango Co., HY to SALLIE (DAGGETT), daughter of Rufus (also see). He was listed in the 1840 census index of Seneca Twp., Lenawee Co., Mich.; and in the 1850 census listed the first 3 children following in his household. 1. ADELIA A., age 8 (m. Joseph Borton); 2. ROSELIA, age 5 (m. William Church); 3. ELLEN, age 2 (m. Brainard Greeley); 4. ADELBERT (m. Hattie Ingalls); 5. GERTRUDE (d. before 1888). George W. and Sallie moved to Morenci, Mich. in 1870. Ref: P&BA-Len pg. 884-5.

Pioneer Families of Southeastern Michigan

STEPHENSON, ISAAC born ca. 1820, England, was listed in the 1850 census of Cambridge Twp., Lenawee Co., Mich. in the household of JOHN (following).

STEPHENSON, JOHN born ca. 1811, Yorkshire, England, and wife, MARY (BREARS), born ca. 1813, England, came to the US in 1838; and were listed in the 1840 census index of Cambridge Twp., Lenawee Co., Mich. In the 1850 census, they listed WILLIAM, age 17, born England; and ELIZABETH, age 12; MARY, age 10; BREARS, age 7, all b. Mich.; and ISAAC (preceding), in their household. John died in Cambridge Twp. in 1875; and she died in 1881. Ref: P&BA-Len pg. 691-2.

STEPHENSON, JOHN, son of WILLIAM (following), born ca. 1828, Ireland, was listed in the 1850 census of Adrian Twp., Lenawee Co., Mich. with MARTHA, age 20; Dr. ROBERT, age 28, also born Ireland, in his household. A sister, ANN, had come to the US with JOHN. Ref: P&BA-Len pg. 363-4.

STEPHENSON, ROBERT Dr. (See WILLIAM, following).

STEPHENSON, SAMUEL of Hudson, Lenawee Co., Mich. was a partner in business with James Moreland (also see) who married ANN, daughter of WILLIAM (following). Ref: P&BA-Len pg. 363-4.

STEPHENSON, WILLIAM and wife, MARTHA (SMALL), lived in Co. Monaghan, Ireland. They were parents of JOHN (preceding); Dr. ROBERT (preceding, in household of JOHN in 1850 census); ANN b. 1829, Co. Monaghan, Ireland (m. James Moreland, also see). JANE, age 25, born Ireland, listed in household of James & Ann Moreland in 1850, probably another daughter. Ref: P&BA-Len pg. 363-4.

STEPHENSON, WILLIAM and wife, LYDIA (MORTON), were natives of Co. Antrim, Ireland, who came to the US in April 1866. They located in Clinton Twp., Lenawee Co., Mich. He died there in March 1878, age about 75; and she died on 28 May 1878, age about 71. They had 6 daughters and 4 sons, names not stated, except #9. JENNIE M. b. 12 July 1851, Ireland (m. John F. Schreder, also see). Ref: P&BA-Len pg. 641.

STERLING, SARAH ANN (See Abraham Cramer)

STEUERWALD, CHARLES (See James M. Scarritt)

STEVENS also see STEPHENS
STEVENS, ASHER (See James Whitney)
STEVENS, CALEB was a Revolutionary soldier, and was the father of LEVI (following). There was a Caleb in the Rev. War Pension applications, with Conn. service, with widow, MARY, Appl. #W19102, possibly this man.

STEVENS, CALEB, son of LEVI (following), born ca. 1818, and wife, SALLY, born ca. 1829, both in NY, were listed in the 1850 census of Rome Twp., Lenawee Co., Mich., with (male) REVO?, age 2/12, b. Mich., in their household; next door to ANNA. STEVENS, DANIEL was listed in the 1840 census index of Tecumseh Twp., Lenawee Co., Mich.

STEVENS, GEORGE was listed in the 1840 census index of Seneca Twp., Lenawee Co., Mich.

STEVENS, ISRAEL, son of PHINEAS (following), born Mass., married HANNAH (McDOWELL) in NY; and known daughter, ADELINE born 8 Feb. 1826 (m. Elias Sanford, also see), and lived in Sandusky Co., Ohio). Ref: P&BA-Len pg. 661-2.

STEVENS, LEVI, son of CALEB (preceding), and wife, ANNA (RAWSON), daughter of Silas (also see) settled in Rome Twp., Lenawee Co., Mich. in 1836; and were in the 1840 census index; and in the 1850 census ANNA, age 68, born NY, was head of household, with LEVI, age 26; NANCY, age 24, both b. NY, in her household; and listed next door was CALEB (preceding). Known daughter, MARIETTA b. 3 Dec. 1821, Sheldon, Wyoming Co., NY (m. George A. Stimson, also see).

STEVENS, ORLANDO S. was listed in the 1840 census index of TEcumseh Twp., Lenawee Co., Mich.

STEVENS, PHINEAS was a Revolutionary soldier, probably in Mass.; and was father of ISRAEL (preceding). There is a Phineas with a Revolutionary pension application #R10133 (rejected); and another with Conn. service, #S42411.

STEVENS, WARREN was listed in the 1840 census index of Tecumseh Twp., Lenawee Co., Mich.

STEVENSON also see STEPHENSON
STEVENSON, ALLEN born ca. 1833, NY, was listed in the 1850 census of Madison Twp., Lenawee Co., Mich. in a Treadwell household.

STEVENSON, ALONZO was listed in the 1840 census index of Medina Twp., Lenawee Co., Mich. Also note ELIZABETH; & JOSEPH (both following).

STEVENSON, E. J. married SARAH A. (HALL), daughter of Alfred (also see), born 27 Dec. 1854, Tecumseh Twp., Lenawee Co., Mich. Children: GEORGE; & ALFRED. Sarah A. married again to William H. Wiggins as his 3rd wife.

STEVENSON, ELIZABETH born ca. 1810, NY, was head of household in the 1850 census of Medina Twp., Lenawee Co., Mich. with CORNELIA, age 10, b. NY, in her household. Note ALONZO, preceding; and JOSEPH, following.

STEVENSON, HATTIE (See Eliza Coffin)
STEVENSON, JOHN born ca. 1822, and wife, LUCY A., born ca. 1821, both in NY, were listed in the 1850 census of Madison Twp., Lenawee Co., Mich. with CHARLES, age 5/12, b. Penn., in their household.

STEVENSON, JOHN R. Rev. born ca. 1820, Canada, and wife, CAROLINE, born ca. 1818, NY, were listed in the 1850 census of Seneca Twp., Lenawee Co., Mich. with LOUISA D., age 2; ARTHUR J., age 1, both b. Mich., in their household.

STEVENSON, OAKLEY born ca. 1810, and wife, REBECCA, born ca. 1814, both born New Jersey, were probably they listed in the 1840 census index of Macon Twp., Lenawee Co., Mich.; and in the 1850 census with SUSAN, age 15; DARWIN, age 12; MARTHA E., age 11; JEREMIAH, age 9; JOHN C., age 8; WILLIAM, age 4; MARY E., age 2, all shown born NY (please not that he was apparently in Mich. by 1840?)

STEVENSON, REBECCA (See Cornelius Polhemus)
STEVENSON, THOMAS, age 28, born Scotland, was listed in the 1850 census of Franklin Twp., Lenawee Co., Mich. in a Agnes Campbell household; and listed again in a Davenport household.

STEWARD also see STEWART
STEWARD, CAROLINE (See Caleb Parker)

STEWARD, HOMER L., son of IRA (following), born 3 Jan. 1835, Macon Twp., Lenawee Co., Mich., went in 1856 to California; but returned to Lenawee Co. He married FANNIE F. (BREWER), daughter of Joseph (also see) in 1864. They settled in Tecumseh village in 1872. Children: 1. ZELMA B.; 2. UENA M.; 3. FRANK K. Ref: P&BA-Len pg. 1110-1.

STEWARD, IRA born ca. 1802, Mass. (census said b. NY), went to near Utica, NY with parents as a child. He married ELIZABETH (CANFIELD) and they moved by 1828 to Plymouth, Wayne Co., Mich.; and in 1833 to Macon Twp., Lenawee Co. She died there in 1838. Children: 1. CHARLES D. b. ca. 1826, NY (to Livingston Co., Mich.); 2. OLIVER b. ca. 1828, Mich. (Nevada Co., CA); 3. LUCIAN b. ca. 1830 (to Calhoun Co., Mich.); 4. HELEN M. b. ca. 1833 (m. I. Scoles, Washington Co., Ark.); 5. HOMER L. (preceding). Apparently Ira married again, as in the 1850 census of Macon Twp., he had wife, ELISA, born ca. 1811, NY, and in addition to the children preceding, had EDWARD, age 10; SUSAN, age 8; LOUISA, age 5; MARY, age 3, in his household. Ref: P&BA-Len pg. 1110-1.

Note: The name was written "Steward" in the 1830, 1840, 1850 census; but the sketch was written "Stewart."

STEWART also see STEWARD & STUART
STEWART, ANNA (See Samuel Steel)
STEWART, ARSA S. born ca. 1811, and wife, DIANNE, born ca. 1815, NY, were listed in the 1850 census of Woodstock Twp., Lenawee Co., Mich. with HENRY, age 12; and HELEN, age 10; CLARK, age 6; MARY, age 9/12, all b. Mich., in their household.
STEWART, CATHARINE, age 17, born NY, was listed in the 1850 census of Macon Twp., Lenawee Co., Mich.
STEWART, CLYDE (See Nathaniel K. Bowen)
STEWART, DUNCAN J. born ca. 1812, and wife, MARY, age ?, both born NY, were listed in the 1850 census of Blissfield Twp., Lenawee Co., Mich. with MARGARET, age 17, b. NY, in their household.
STEWART, ELIZABETH of Co. Antrim, Ireland (See John H. Wilson).
STEWART, EUGENE, age 8, born Mich., was listed in the 1850 census of Fairfield Twp., Lenawee Co., Mich. in a Tenbrook household.
STEWART, GEORGE (See James L. Brown)
STEWART, HARRISON, age 28, born NY, was listed in the 1850 census of Tecumseh Twp., Lenawee Co., Mich. in a Bills household.
STEWART, HARRY W. born ca. 1813, and wife, LYDIA, born ca 1823, both in NY, were listed in the 1850 census of Madison Twp., Lenawee Co., Mich. with MARY, age 4/12, b. Mich., and PARLEY, age 40, b. NY (probably brother of Harry) in their household.
STEWART, JACOB born ca. 1788, New Jersey, and wife, PHOEBE, born ca. 1798, Penn., were listed in the 1840 census index of Cambridge Twp., Lenawee Co., Mich.; and in the 1850 census with WILLIAM, age 21, b. NY; and PHOEBE, age 14; SARAH, age 12; SYLVANUS, age 10, both b. Mich., in their household.
STEWART, JAMES A., son of WILLIAM (possibly from Scotland, who settled in Penn.), born ca. 1794, Cannonsburg, Washington Co., Penn., married there to MARY T. (STOKES), daughter of Joseph, supposedly born in Beaver Co., Penn. They moved to East Liverpool, Ohio in 1840; and then to Adrian, Lenawee Co., Mich. in 1846. She died 17 Aug. 1847. Known daughters: MARIE J. b. ca. 1826, Penn. (m. Edson Walker, also see, on 20 Dec. 1846); MARY E. b. ca. 1832, Penn. (in household in 1850). He was listed in the 1850 census of Madison Twp., Lenawee Co., with a wife, MARY M. born 1803, NY. He died 17 July 1882. Ref: P&BA-Len pg. 619-20.
STEWART, JOHN was listed in Seneca Twp., Lenawee Co., Mich., in the 1840 census index; and it is may be he in the 1850 census of Madison Twp., age 49, with wife, SARAH, age 42, both b. NY and ADALINE, age 13; JUSTINE?, age 5, both b. Mich. in their household. URIAL, age 10, b. Mich., in a Tenbrook household in the 1850 census of Madison Twp. may relate to this family.
STEWART, JOSEPH born ca. 1813, and wife, SUSAN A., born ca. 1822, both in NY, were listed in the 1850 census of Dover Twp., Lenawee Co., Mich. with no family in the household.
STEWART, MARY (See William Carter)
STEWART, NATHAN born ca. 1774, Mass., was listed in the 1850 census of Palmyra Twp., Lenawee Co., Mich. in household of son, RANSOM (following).
STEWART, PARLEY (See HARRY W., preceding)
STEWART, RACHEL (See Henry Moore)
STEWART, RANSOM, probably son of NATHAN (preceding), born ca. 1800, and wife, ALZORA, born ca. 1807, both in NY, were listed in the 1840 census index of Palmyra Twp., Lenawee Co., Mich.; and in the 1850 census with WILLIAM D., age 21, b. NY; aand ESTHER M., age 10, b. Mich.; Charlotte Foster, age 20, b. NY, and NATHAN, age 76, born Mass. (father?), in the household.
STEWART, ROBERT born ca. 1804, and wife, MARY, born ca. 1817, both in Ireland, were listed in the 1850 census of Tecumseh Twp., Lenawee Co., Mich. with Margaret Gillinett, age 40; Nancy Gillinett, age 30; Mary Gillinett, age 9, all b. Ireland, in their household.
STEWART, ROSANNA (See John Allen, Jr.)
STEWART, SAMUEL (See William Gregg)
STEWART, SAMUEL A. was listed in the 1830 census of Lenawee Co., Michigan Territory, with males: 2 und 5; 2 5-10; 1 10-15; 1 30-40; females: 1 30-40; in the household.
STEWART, THOMAS, age 13, born Ohio, was listed in the 1850 census of Seneca Twp., Lenawee Co., Mich. in a Penter? household.

STIGGINS, JOHN (See Thomas Chandler)

STILES, DELILAH (See Isaac Farst)

STILSON, ZADY (See Ichabod Taylor)

STIMPSON also see STIMSON & STINSON
STIMPSON, ELSEY was listed in the 1840 census index of Adrian Twp., Lenawee Co., Mich.

STIMSON also see STIMPSON & STINSON
STIMSON, GEORGE A., son of JOHN (following), born 19 Mar. 1820, Mendon, Monroe Co., NY, moved to Rome Twp., Lenawee Co., Mich. with his mother. He married

Pioneer Families of Southeastern Michigan

there on 27 Mar. 1846 to MARIETTA (STEVENS), daughter of Levi (also see). In 1849, they moved to Jackson Co., Mich., and lived first in Jackson Twp.; then Liberty Twp.; and last in Tompkins Twp. Son, SILAS R. (m. Maggie G. Snedeker; had dau: Mamie A.). History of Jackson Co., Mich., 1881, pg. 1126.

STIMSON, HENRY J., son of JOHN (following), born ca. 1818, NY, and wife, MARY, born ca. 1821, England, were listed in the 1840 census index of Rome Twp., Lenawee Co., Mich.; and in the 1850 census with THOMAS, age 11; EMILY, age 9; CYNTHIA, age 7; HENRY J., age 5; MARY A., age 2, all b. Mich., in their household.

STIMSON JOHN was born in Conn., and he was married twice and had a total of 12 children, names not all stated. Two sons, GILBERT; & LOVETT were said to have served in the War of 1812. He married second to SALLY (CLAFLIN), daughter of Increase (also see). They lived in Mendon, Monroe Co., NY ca. 1821; and John died in Orleans Co., NY in 1831. Sally afterwards moved to Rome Twp., Lenawee Co., Mich. The sketch stated she came there with her 3rd child, GEORGE A., preceding, and "3 of George's brothers." HENRY J. (preceding); & JOHN (following), are obviously two of these brothers. SALLY born ca. 1785, Mass., was listed head of household in the 1850 census of Rome Twp., Lenawee Co., Mich. with THEORON, age 23; DELAFAYETT, age 19, both b. NY, in her household; and HENRY J.; & JOHN listed next door

STIMSON, JOHN, son of JOHN (preceding), born ca. 1815, and wife, ISABELLA, born ca. 1821, Ohio, were listed in the 1850 census of Rome Twp., Lenawee Co., Mich. with GEORGE M., age 5; FRANCIS, age 4; SARAH J., age 2; MARY A., age 1, all b. Mich., in their household.

STINSON, HIRAM K. Rev. born ca. 1805, and wife, NANCY P., born ca. 1818, both in NY, were listed in the 1850 census of Adrian Twp., Lenawee Co., Mich. with MONTCALM, age 18; FRANCES E., age 16 (m. Charles Bigelow of Toledo, O. on 15 Apr. 1851); MARY L., age 11; ALMEDIA, age 9; CATHERINA M., age 5; GENEVIEVE, age 2, all b. NY, in their household. Note: Name called "Stimpson" in sketch naming Frances E.

STINSON, WILLIAM H. born ca. 1789, NY, and wife, ALICE, born ca. 1794, Conn., were listed in the 1840 census index of Rome Twp., Lenawee Co., Mich.; and in the 1850 census with JAMES, age 35; WILLIAM, age 21; WASHINGTON, age 18, all b. NY; and FRANCES, age 15; MARY A., age 12, both b. Mich., in their household.

STINE, MARY (See William Scout)

STITES, HARRIET (See Josiah Osgood)

STITT, JAMES born ca. 1800, and wife, MARY, born ca. 1793, Canada, were listed in the 1840 census index of Tecumseh Twp., Lenawee Co., Mich.; and in the 1850 census with JACKSON, age 17, b. NY, in their household. JOSEPH, age 20, b. NY, in another household, may relate to this family.

STOCK, GODFREY born Wurtemburg, Germany, came to the US and settled first in Lucas Co., Ohio. He married in Toledo to JULIA A. (HOUSEN) born Hanover, Germany, who had come to the US at age 21. They later moved to Riga Twp., Lenawee Co., Mich. Known daughters: CAROLINE (m. Eugene Johnson, son of William M., also see); LIBBIE (m. William M. Johnson, also see, on 10 Jan. 1882). Ref: P&BA-Len pg. 927-31.

STOCKWELL, CALABY? is listed in the 1840 census of Adrian Twp., Lenawee Co., Mich. not far from ELIATHAH (following).

STOCKWELL, CURTICE W. born ca. 1795, Mass., and wife, THERINA (FISHER) born 1799, NY, came to Rome Twp., Lenawee Co., Mich. in 1835. Known daughter, PHILURA b. 25 Mar. 1825, Yates, Orleans Co., NY (m. Dr. Alexander W. Seger, also see). In the 1850 census of Rome Twp., Curtice listed JULIA A. b. 3 July 1829, Orleans Co., NY (m. John S. Marks, also see); ELIJAH, age 23 (& CELIA, age 21, probably wife of ELIJAH?), all b. NY, in his household. Ref: P&BA-Len pg. 1114-7; 1209-10.

STOCKWELL, ELEAZER born 21 Apr. 1763, was a pioneer (before 1800) to Cayuga Co., NY, where he died. Known son, WILLIAM (following); & probably JOHN b. ca. 1809 (in household of William in 1850). Ref: P&BA-Len pg. 695-6. Note: In the 1800 census index of Cayuga Co., NY were ELEAZER; & DAVID, adjacent; and an ELEAZER B. also in Cayuga Co.

STOCKWELL, ELIATHAH born 19 May 1791, Whitehall, Washington Co., NY, moved in 1809 with his parents to Cato, Cayuga Co., NY. (Note: In the 1800 census index of Washington Co., NY were ABRAHAM; JOHN; & LEVI). He married on 8 Dec. 1814, Ira, NY to ESTHER (PERKINS), daughter of Christopher (also see); and removed to Java, Wyoming Co., NY. In 1837, they came to Adrian Twp., Lenawee Co., Mich. to join son, Martin P., and moved in 1849 to Dover Twp. She died 18 May 1856; and he died 23 Feb. 1867 (Note: Couldn't locate them in the 1850 census of Dover Twp.) Children: 1. BETSEY C. b. 1 Nov. 1815 (m. Peleg Varnold; d. Fulton Co., Ill.); 2. MARTIN P. (following); 3. CATHERINE ESTHER b. 1 Mar. 1821, Ira, NY (m. Aaron M. Phillips, also see); 4. LEVI L. b. 18 July 1823 (to Medina Twp.); 5. EZILDA b. 23 Oct. 1825 (m. D. S. Galloway, Dundee, Mich.); 6. HANNAH A. b. 5 Apr. 1828 (m. William Wildman, Coldwater, Mich.; in the 1850 census, she was listed in household of Aaron Phillips); 7. CHRISTOPHER P. b. 20 Jan. 1831 (in 1850 census in household of Davis Smith; later went "west."); 8. BENJAMIN F. b. 9 Apr. 1833 (d. 1835, NY); 9. HENRIETTA L. b. 13 Nov. 1835 (m. Stillwell Palmer; d. 12 June 1864, Dover Twp.) Ref: P&BA-Len pg. 215-7.

STOCKWELL, EMILY born ca. 1825, NY, was listed in the 1850 census of Hudson Twp., Lenawee Co., Mich. Note JOHN; & WILLIAM, following.

STOCKWELL, JOHN, probably son of ELEAZER (preceding), born ca. 1808, NY, was in household of WILLIAM (following).

STOCKWELL, LEVI L., son of ELIATHAH (preceding), was listed in the 1850 census of Medina Twp., Lenawee Co., Mich. in the same household as brother, CHRISTOPHER. He married on 3 July 1853 to HELEN (ATWOOD), daughter of Rodney (also see). They resided in Medina Twp. Children: 1. MARTIN R. (m. Lina Hause); 2. CORA E. (m. Edson Burroughs); 3. MARY A. (m. Wilbur McNair); 4. AMANDA L. (m. Fred

Herron); 5. ALMERON P.; 6. ESTHER M. (m. Frank Reeder); 7. ELMER E.; 8. NELLA H.; 9. LEWIS S. Ref: P&BA-Len pg. 727-8.

STOCKWELL, MARTIN P., son of ELIATHAH (preceding), was born 11 Feb. 1818, Cato, Cayuga Co., NY, and came to Lenawee Co. alone as a lad in 1838. He married LOUISA (BALEY), daughter of Joseph (also see) on 11 Aug. 1841. They were listed in the 1850 census of Dover Twp., Lenawee Co., Mich. Children: 1. OLIVE b. 11 July 1842 (m. Byron L. Shaw, Adrian); 2. CINDERELLA b. 15 Feb. 1844 (m. I. R. Gale; d. 15 Apr. 1884, Dover Twp.); 3. AGNES L. b. 26 Feb. 1846 (m. Aaron Van Ostrand; Dover Twp.); 4. JOSEPH B. b. 5 June 1848 (Dover Twp.); 5. ZAREFA b. 20 Sept. 1850 (m. Robert F. Pouley; Florida); 6. ANNA P. b. 12 Oct. 1852 (Cleveland, Ohio); 7. ALICE M. b. 7 Nov. 1854 (d. 8 Feb. 1864); 8. ESTHER M. b. 14 Dec. 1858 (d. 26 Mar. 1864); 9. ELMER E. b. 20 Oct. 1860 (d. 5 Oct. 1863); 10. MINNIE E. b. 14 July 1864; 11. M. LOUISE b. 26 July 1866. Ref: P&BA-Len pg. 215-7.

STOCKWELL, MARY (See Daniel Walker)

STOCKWELL, WILLIAM, son of ELEAZER (preceding), born 21 July 1809, Ira, Cayuga Co., NY, came to Hudson Twp., Lenawee Co., Mich. before 1839; but married in New York on 2 May 1839 to ELIZA A. (HORTON), born 1 Nov. 1811, Ulster Co., NY. They settled in Hudson Twp., Lenawee Co. He died 28 Nov. 1871; and she died 5 July 1882. Children: 1. STEPHEN WILLIAM b. 9 Nov. 1843; 2. SUSAN MADELINE b. 28 May 1846, Sterling, NY (while family was visiting there). In their household in the 1850 census of Hudson Twp., also was JOHN (preceding), age 41, b. NY.

STODARD also see STODDARD

STODARD, NATHAN born ca. 1793, Rhode Island, and wife, ZIMR--ODA?, born ca. 1796, NY, were listed in the 1840 census index of Adrian Twp., Lenawee Co., Mich.; and in the 1850 census with WILLIAM A., age 20; GEORGE S., age 18, both b. NY, in their household.

STODDARD also see STODARD

STODDARD, HENRY born ca. 1822, NY, and wife, CAROLINE, born ca. 1827, Ohio, were listed in the 1850 census of Rome Twp., Lenawee Co., Mich. with CORNELIA, age 3, b. Mich., in their household.

STODDARD, LEONARD born ca. 1803, Conn., and wife, CAROLINE, born ca. 1808, NY, were listed in the 1840 census index of Rome Twp., Lenawee Co., Mich.; and in the 1850 census with MARY A., age 19, b. NY; and EDWIN, age 10; ALPHONSO, age 4 (m. Mary E. Teachout, daughter of Welcome, also see), both b. Mich., in their household.

STODDARD, STEPHEN born ca. 1824, Conn., and wife, EUNICE, born ca. 1826, NY, were listed in the 1850 census of Riga Twp., Lenawee Co., Mich. with EUNICE A., age 4; BETSEY, age 2; SENECA, age 6/12, all b. Mich., in their household.

STODDARD, WHITMAN born ca. 1791, and ESTHER, born ca. 1794, both in Conn., were listed in the 1840 census index of Rome Twp., Lenawee Co., Mich. (adjacent to LEONARD); and in the 1850 census with SALLY, age 24; ABIGAIL, age 22, both b. NY; and WHITMAN JR., age 15, b. Mich., in their household.

STOEPEL, FREDERICK (See Welcome Teachout)

STOKES, JOSEPH died in Beaver Co., Penn. Known daughter, MARY T. b. Beaver Co., Penn. (m. James A. Stewart, also see; she d. 17 Aug. 1847, Adrian Twp., Lenawee Co., Mich.). Ref: P&BA-Len pg. 619-20.

STOKES, SOLOMON born ca. 1806, Penn., and wife, MARIAH, born ca. 1806, NY, were listed in the 1850 census of Medina Twp., Lenawee Co., Mich. with CAROLINE, age 14, b. NY; and Silas Bailey, age 7, b. NY, in their household.

STONE, AMOS, probably son of SAMUEL (following) was listed in the 1840 census index of Medina Twp., Lenawee Co., Mich.; and it is probably he, age 38, born NY, and possibly wife, ESTHER, age 37, b. VT; and CARMI, age 4, b. Mich., all in the household of SAMUEL in the 1850 census of Rome Twp.

STONE, ANNA (See Samuel Adams)

STONE, BLISS born ca. 1826, and wife, LUCY, born ca. 1829, married within the year, were listed in the 1850 census of Blissfield Twp., Lenawee Co., Mich. 2 doors from MARVIN L. (following). Note DANFORD M., following.

STONE, CHARLES born ca. 1814, Mass., and wife, MARIAH, born ca. 1816, NH, were listed in the 1850 census of Hudson Twp., Lenawee Co., Mich. with CHARLES H., age 11, LEANDER W., age 2/12; LYSANDER L., age 2/12, all b. Mich., in their household. Also note SETH, following.

STONE, DANFORD M. was listed in the 1840 census index of Blissfield Twp., Lenawee Co., Mich. Note BLISS, preceding, and MARVIN L., following.

STONE, DAVID born ca. 1825, and wife, ALVIRA, born ca. 1826, both in NY, were listed in the 1850 census of Medina Twp., Lenawee Co., Mich. with no family in their household. Note HANNAH, following.

STONE, HANNAH born ca. 1801, NY, was head of household in the 1850 census of Medina Twp., Lenawee Co., Mich. with MIRANDA, age 20; and John Rhinehart, age 21, both b. NY, in her household. They were about 5 doors from DAVID, preceding. Also note ROBERT, following.

STONE, ISAIAH born 1785, Mass., went to Vermont with parents as a child. He married MERCY (SAWYER) born Bradford, VT. In 1818, they removed to Royalton, Niagara Co., NY. In 1835, they moved to Knox Co., Ohio, where he died 2 Dec. 1843, age 58. There were 11 children, names not stated, except 4th child, & 2nd daughter, MEHITABLE b. 8 Nov. 1812, Bradford, Orange Co., Vt. (m. Eleazer Holdridge, also see, settled Raisin Twp., Lenawee Co., Mich.). Ref: P&BA-Len pg. 239-40.

STONE, JAMES B., age 6, born Mich., was listed in the 1850 census of Rollin Twp., Lenawee Co., Mich. in a Marlatt household.

STONE, LEWIS was a native of Saratoga Co., NY, and father of SALLIE b. 14 Oct. 1802 (m. Benajah Brown, also see).

STONE, MARIETTA, age 82, born New Jersey, was listed in the 1850 census of Cambridge Twp., Lenawee Co., Mich. in the household of Christopher Russ and wife, Olivia.

STONE, MARVIN L. born ca. 1820, NY, and HELEN M., born ca. 1829, Mass., were listed in the 1850 census of

Pioneer Families of Southeastern Michigan

Blissfield Twp., Lenawee Co., Mich. and it appears that LOUISA, age 2; CORNELIA, age 2/12, should be included in this household (written faintly between the lines), and possibly another name, age 2, not legible, all b. Mich. Louisa Stacy, age 32, b. NY; and Daniel S. Mead, age 17, b. Mass., were in the household. BLISS (preceding) was 2 doors away in the census. Note DANFORD M., preceding.

STONE, NAHUM, probably son of NATHANIEL S. (following), born ca. 1811, and wife, ELIZA A., born ca. 1821, both in NH, were listed in the 1850 census of Medina Twp., Lenawee Co., Mich. with AUGUSTA E., age 10; ADISON G., age 8; STACY M., age 2, all b. Mich., in their household (next door to NATHANIEL S.)

STONE, NATHANIEL S. born ca. 1781, New Hampshire, and wife, NANCY, born ca. 1782, Mass., were listed in the 1850 census of Medina Twp., Lenawee Co., Mich. next door to NAHUM (preceding).

STONE, POMEROY born ca. 1799, Conn., and wife, ELIZA, born ca. 1801, Mass., were listed in the 1840 census index of Adrian Twp., Lenawee Co., Mich.; and in the 1850 census with WILLIAM H., age 22, b. NY; and FRANCIS R., age 14; HELEN L., age 10, both b. Mich.; and Ann S. Richmond, age 48, b. Mass.; and (listed last) ANN M., age 22, b. NY, in their household.

STONE, ROBERT was listed in the 1840 census index of Medina Twp., Lenawee Co., Mich.

STONE, SAMUEL born ca. 1771, Vermont, and wife, REBECCA, born ca. 1781, Rhode Island were probably they listed in the 1840 census of Rome Twp., Lenawee Co., Mich.; and in the 1850 census with AMOS (preceding) and family; and Elvira Waggoner, age 11, b. Mich., in their household.

STONE, SARAH born 6 Apr. 1800, Bennington Co., VT, married in Mass. to Neley Bancroft (also see) and settled in Rome Twp., Lenawee Co. Mich.

STONE, SETH was listed in the 1840 census index of Hudson Twp., Lenawee Co., Mich. Note CHARLES, preceding.

STONE, WARREN was listed in the 1840 census index of Dover Twp., Lenawee Co., Mich.

STONE, WILLIAM T. born ca. 1795, New Hampshire, and wife, MARTHA, born ca. 1796, NY, were listed in the 1850 census of Ogden Twp., Lenawee Co., Mich. with AMANDA, age 25; ENOS, age 24; ALPHEUS, age 18, all b. NY; and MARGARET, age 13, b. Ohio; and Ellen Harrison, age 5, b. Mich., in their household.

STONE, ZIBA married ESTHER (SANFORD), daughter of Ezra (also see). They came possibly from Steuben Co., NY to Cohoctah Twp., Livingston Co., Mich., by 1835. Ref: <u>History of Livingston Co., Mich.</u>, 1880, pg. 442-3.

STONECKER, JOHN (See William Drake)

STONEHAM, ELIZABETH and sister, ?, were both wives of Rev. Henry Tripp (also see) in Bristol, England.

STOUT, CORNELIUS A. was listed in the 1830 census of Lenawee Co., Mich. Territory, with males: 1 und 5; 1 5-10; 1 30-40; 1 40-50; and females: 1 und 5; 1 5-10; 1 15-20, in the household. It is probaby they in the 1850 census of Adrian Twp., he age 52, born New Jersey, and wife, MARY G., age 46, b. NY, with SARAH E., age 21; JOHNSON, age 20; NARCISSA G., age 18; PHILURA J., age 16; JOSEPH B., age 14; JARED? C., age 13; ANN A., age 8, all b. Mich., in their household. Note that in the 1830 census there is a male older than Cornelius A. in his household, possibly RICHARD, following; also note GEORGE, following.

STOUT, DAVID born ca. 1796, and wife, PENELOPE, born ca. 1791, both in New Jersey, were listed in the 1840 census index of Macon Twp., Lenawee Co., Mich.; and in the 1850 census with ELISA A., age 25, b. NY; and AMOS, age 19; AUGUSTUS, age 14, both b. Mich., in their household. Note JOHN, following.

STOUT, ELIZABETH born New Jersey, believed to have married first to Waldron; and second to Joseph S. Hagaman (also see) in Seneca Co., NY. Ref: P&BA-Len pg. 1044-5.

STOUT, FRANCIS born ca. 1800, and wife, RHODA, born ca. 1805, both in NY, were listed in the 1840 census index of Franklin Twp., Lenawee Co., Mich.; and in the 1850 census with EUNICE, age 17; JULIA, age 24; MALAN, age 22; SUSANNAH, age 20; ARMINDA, age 19; MILTON, age 16, all b. NY; and MUNSON, age 15; FRANCES, age 13; ELIZABETH, age 11; SARAH, age 8; ALONSO, age 7; CLARINDA, age 8/12, all b. Mich., in their household.

STOUT, GEORGE was listed in the 1830 census of Lenawee Co., Mich. Territory, with males: 2 und 5; 1 20-30; and female: 1 15-20, in the household.

STOUT, ISAAC, probably son of JOHN (following), born ca. 1823, and wife, RACHEL, born ca. 1830, both born NY, were listed in the 1850 census of Franklin Twp., Lenawee Co., Mich. with LYDIA, age 3; ELLEN, age 4/12, both b. Mich., in their household.

STOUT, JOHN was listed in the 1840 census index of Fairfield Twp., Lenawee Co., Mich. and it may be he in the household of RICHARD, following, in the 1850 census.

STOUT, JOHN born ca. 1800, and wife, JANE, born ca. 1802, both in New Jersey, were listed in the 1840 census index of Franklin Twp., Lenawee Co., Mich.; and in the 1850 census with ZEBEDEE, age 25; JOHN, age 23; SALLY ANN, age 21; ESRALINE, age 17; GEORGE, age 18, all b. NY; and BENJAMIN, age 10; WILLIAM, age 6, both b. Mich., in their household; and ISAAC (preceding, listed next door in the census).

STOUT, JOHN, possibly son of DAVID (preceding), born ca. 1820, NJ, and wife, MARIETTA, born ca. 1828, NY, were listed in the 1850 census of Macon Twp., Lenawee Co., Mich. with no family.

STOUT, JOHNSON born ca. 1804, and wife, SARAH, born ca. 1804, both in NY, were listed in the 1840 census index of Franklin Twp., Lenawee Co., Mich.; and in the 1850 census with LEMUEL, age 22; ELIZABETH, age 16, both b. NY; and AUGUSTUS, age 14; RICHARD, age 9; MARY ANN, age 6, all b. Mich., in their household.

STOUT, RICHARD born ca. 1790, and wife, NANCY, born ca. 1780, both in New Jersey, were listed in the 1840 census index of Fairfield Twp., Lenawee Co., Mich.; and in the 1850 census with JOHN, age 36, b. NJ; RICHARD, age 23; CORNELIUS, age 19, both b. NY; and TUNIS, age 15, b. Mich.; and possibly the following are grandchildren, MARY J., age 7; WILLIAM, age 3, all b. Mich., in their household. Note: Between Stout households in the census were Julius Ayers (also see) and wife, MARY H., age 34, b. NJ, possibly a Stout. Also note RYNEAR & SAMUEL A., following.

LYMAN, age 10, b. Mich. in an Arnold household in the 1850 census of Fairfield Twp., may relate to this family.

STOUT, RYNEAR, probably son of RICHARD (preceding), born ca. 1822, and wife, ROSETTA C., born ca. 1830, both in NY, were listed in the 1850 census of Fairfield Twp., Lenawee Co., Mich. with ANN, age 1, b. Mich., in their household (2 doors from RICHARD).

STOUT, SAMUEL A., probably son of RICHARD (preceding), both ca. 1818, NY, and wife, ROSINA?, born ca. 1828, Mich., were listed in the 1850 census of Fairfield Twp., Lenawee Co., Mich. next to RYNEAR.

STOUT, WILSON H. born ca. 1821, and wife, SARAH, born ca. 1821, both in NY, were listed in the 1850 census of Tecumseh Twp., Lenawee Co., Mich. with HENRY, age 7; HERBAT, age 4; ISABELL, age 3; ANNETTA, age 3/12, all b. Mich., in their household.

STOWELL, CHARLES B., son of JOSIAH (following), born 25 Aug. 1843, Londonderry, VT, moved with his parents to Hudson Twp., Lenawee Co., Mich. He married on 27 Oct. 1868 to ELLEN C. (OLDS), daughter of Harley J. (also see) of Hillsdale Co., Mich. No children listed. Ref: P&BA-Len pg. 1072-3.

STOWELL, EZERIAH and wife, PHEBE A. (MYERS), were natives of NY who lived in Rochester in 1847, but moved later to Erie Co., NY. They were still living in 1888, ages 75 & 70, respectively. Known daughter, ADELL E. b. 9 Oct. 1847, Rochester, NY (m. Warren J. Parker, also see, on 20 Dec. 1865, Erie Co., NY). Ref: P&BA-Len pg. 889-90.

STOWELL, JOHN born ca. 1809, NY, and wife, MARTHA, born ca. 1815, England, were listed in the 1850 census of Ridgeway Twp., Lenawee Co., Mich. with EMORY A., age 11; FIDELIA, age 9; MARION, age 4, all b. Mich., in their household.

STOWELL, JOSIAH Gen., son of LUTHER (following), born 30 Apr. 1797, Petersham, Worcester Co., Mass., moved to Vermont with his parents. At age 20, he moved to Albany, NY, and after a year to Manchester, New Hampshire. He joined the NH militia, where he became a Brigadier General. He married 3 times and had 1 child by each marriage, first two names not stated. He married third to CHARLOTTE (BARR), daughter of Samuel (also see). About 1841, they returned to Londonderry, VT. In 1854, they moved to Hudson Twp., Lenawee Co., Mich. He died on 11 Dec. 1873; and she made her home with their son, CHARLES B. (preceding). Ref: P&BA-Len pg. 1072-3.

STOWELL, LUTHER born ca. 1772, Mass., moved before 1800 to Windham, and then to Londonderry, Windham Co., VT. He and wife, name not stated, died there, both at age 84. Mentioned was one son who remained on the farm; and known son, JOSIAH (preceding). Ref: P&BA-Len pg. 1072-3.

STOWERS, CHARLES G., son of JOHN (following), born 21 Dec. 1812, Chester, VT. He went with his parents to Jefferson Co., NY; and married at Watertown in 1844 to CLARA (ALLEN), daughter of Elisha (also see). They lived at Great Bend, Penn. at one time and then, in 1855, moved to Adrian, Lenawee Co., Mich. They lost a son at age 18, and an infant, names not stated. They adopted JULIA ANN (m. George H. Miller; Wyandotte, KS); & ALICE (m. Franklin Smith, Adrian). Ref: P&BA-Len pg. 384-5.

STOWERS, JOHN born 1785, VT, and wife, SARAH (MORRIS), daughter of Uriah (also see), born 1778, moved from Vermont to Pennsylvania; and then to Jefferson Co., NY. He died in Watertown, NY in 1844, and she died in 1875. Five children, and 3 sons were deceased before 1888 (names not stated). Known children: CHARLES G. (preceding); MARY S. (m. ? Mann; Watertown, NY). Ref: P&BA-Len pg. 384-5.

STRAIGHT, MARY (See Andrew Van Sickle)

STRAIGHT, WILLIAM born ca. 1820, and wife, MARYETTA, born ca. 1823, both in NY, were listed in the 1850 census of Woodstock Twp., Lenawee Co., Mich. with SARAH, age 9/12, b. Mich., in their household.

STRANAHAN, ARABELLA, age 14, born NY, was listed in the 1850 censu of Rome Twp., Lenawee Co., Mich. in a Schuereman household.

STRANAHAN, FARRAND Col. served in the War of 1812 from Columbia Co., NY, and was a brother of GEORGE S. (following).

STRANAHAN, GEORGE S. born 4 Oct. 1783, New Canaan, Columbia Co., NY, served in the War of 1812. He married there, wife's name not stated, and they moved to Erie Co., NY. About 1833, he and his son-in-law, Leonard Taylor, went to Jackson Co., Mich. and took up land. They returned to NY, and later moved to Napoleon Twp., Jackson Co., Mich. with their families. Children: 1. GEORGE; 2. MARANDA (m. Abram Sanford, also see, resided Brooklyn, Mich. in 1881); 3. JULIA A. (m. J. D. White, Columbia Twp., Jackson Co.); 4. MARIETTA (m. Stacy Clark, Liberty Twp.); 5. CORDELIA (m. George W. Lobdell; Jackson, Mich.); 6. CAROLINE (m. Leonard Taylor; to Branch Co., Mich.); 7. BETSEY (m. A. C. Clark, Columbia Twp.); 8. HIRAM (to Minnesota; deceased by 1881). Ref: History of Jackson Co., Mich., 1881, pg. 816.

STRANAHAN, MARGARET, age 7, born Mich., were listed in the 1850 census of Dover Twp., Lenawee Co., Mich. in a Robb household.

STRANAHAN, SAMUEL (spelled "Strinehan") was listed in the 1840 census index of Jackson Twp., Jackson Co., Mich.

STRANAHAN, WILLIAM H. was listed in the 1840 census index of Woodstock Twp., Lenawee Co., Mich.

STREET, ROBERT, son of ALFRED, born 23 July 1805, New York City, married ALMIRA (CLARK), daughter of George (also see) of Princeton, NJ. They settled in Palmyra Twp., Lenawee Co., Mich. by 1840. Known daughter, ELIZA C. (m. Arnold Pope, also see). Ref: P&BA-Len pg. 578-9.

STRETCH, JESSE born ca. 1814, married ANN (CHARLTON), born ca. 1821, both in England, and they were listed in the 1850 census of Palmyra Twp., Lenawee Co., Mich. with MARY E., age 5 (this is probably "ELIZABETH, dau. of Jesse," who m. George Holloway, also see); EMILY, age 3; EDWARD C., age 8/12, all b. Mich., and William Salkeld, age 28; Charles Salkeld, age 26; John Pepper, age 28, all b. England, in their household.

STRETCH, LYDIA P. (See R. S. Coggswell)

STRIKER, ABRAM born ca. 1821, Ohio, was listed in the 1850 census of Medina Twp., Lenawee Co., Mich.

STRIKER, CATHARINE (See James Carpenter)

STRIKER, DAVID was listed in the 1840 census index of Jackson Twp., Jackson Co., Mich.

STRIKER, WILLIAM born ca. 1791, and wife, ELIZABETH, born ca. 1806, both in NY, were listed in the 1850 census of Medina Twp., Lenawee Co., Mich. with DAVID, age 14; ELIZABETH, age 10; WILLIAM, age 8, all b. NY; and JAMES, age 6, b. Mich., in their household.

STRONG, ALVAH was the brother of SALLY born ca. 1811, VT (m. Wilson Wood, also see, and lived Orleans Co., NY; then Rollin Twp., Lenawee Co., Mich.) Alvah served in the Civil War.

STRONG, BENJAMIN G. born ca. 1822, Mass., and wife, CHARLOTTE, born ca. 1827, Conn., were listed in the 1850 census of Adrian Twp., Lenawee Co., Mich. with ERVILLA, age 5; EARL, age 3, both b. Mich., in their household.

STRONG, CHARLES born Conn., and wife, LORINDA (FISHER), born NY, settled first in Ontario Co., NY. In 1853, they moved to Tekonsha Twp., Calhoun Co., Mich. There were 9 children, and 7 were living in 1888 in NY, Ohio, & Michigan. Known son, NORMAN J. (following). Ref: P&BA-Len pg. 482-3.

STRONG, CHARLES born ca. 1814, and wife, MARTHA, born ca. 1822, both in Mass., were listed in the 1850 census of Tecumseh Twp., Lenawee Co., Mich. with MARY, age 7; CHARLES, age 4; FREDUS, age 1, all b. Mich.; and listed last was CORNELIA, age 12, b. Mich., who may not be a daughter of this household; and James Pocklington, age 16, b. England, in their household. Note: CHARLES F. was listed in the 1840 census index of Tecumseh Twp., may be this same man; also note RAWSEL, following.

STRONG, DANIEL was listed in the 1840 census index of Somerset Twp., Hillsdale Co., Mich., adjacent to DAVID.

STRONG, DAVID born ca. 1799, b. Conn.; and wife, SUSAN, born ca. 1800, Mass., were listed in the 1850 census of Adrian Twp., Lenawee Co., Mich. with OTIS W., age 19, b. Ohio; and ALMIRA, age 7, b. Mich., in their household. Note: There was a DAVID listed in the 1840 census index of Somerset Twp., Hillsdale Co., Mich., adjacent to DANIEL.

STRONG, JOHN S. born ca. 1820, and wife, DELIA, born ca. 1825, both in Ohio, were listed in the 1850 census of Tecumseh Twp., Lenawee Co., Mich. with HARRIET, age 1, b. Mich., all in the household of William and Delia Baldwin, probably parents of Delia.

STRONG, NORMAN J., son of CHARLES (preceding), born 1 Mar. 1824, West Bloomfield, Ontario Co., NY, was a teacher in Branch Co., Mich. for a time, then moved back to Calhoun Co., Mich. He married on 18 Oct. 1860 to BETSEY A. (MITCHELL), daughter of Charles (also see). In 1866, they moved to Lenawee Co., and in 1868 settled in Madison Twp. Children: 1. CHARLES M. (m. Ida L. Valentine, dau. of John B., also see); 2. EMMA A.; 3. DENNIS F.; 4. GRACE M.; 5. BENNIE; 6. CLARA (d. age 3-1/2); 7. RALPH B. (d. age 2 yrs). Ref: P&BA-Len pg. 482-3.

STRONG, RALPH B. born ca. 1812, and wife, ELECTA A., born ca. 1813, both in Conn., were listed in the 1850 census of Medina Twp., Lenawee Co., Mich. with JOSEPH T., age 12; FRANCIS, age 8, both b. Conn.; and GERTRUDE J., age 6; CHESTER W., age 5, both b. Ohio; and Emily Atwood, age 19, b. NY, in their household.

STRONG, RAWSEL (ROSWELL?) was listed in the 1840 census index of Tecumseh Twp., Lenawee Co., Mich., near CHARLES (preceding).

STRONG, ROBERT, and wife, OLIVE, came to Washtenaw Co., Mich. in 1832 from Lansingburg, Rensselaer Co., NY. Daughter, ELIZABETH (m/1 Yund, of Moscow, Hillsdale Co.; m/2 James Moreland, also see). Ref: P&BA-Len pg. 363-4.

STRONG, SABRA J. (See Calvin Town; also see Nicholas P. Houghtalin).

STRONG, SELDON of Mass., was father of JANE (m. Robert M. Bailey, as 2nd wife). LAURA M., a niece of Seldon, married Robert M. Bailey as his 3rd wife. Ref: P&BA-Len pg. 1168.

STRONG, WILLIAM born ca. 1828, Ohio, and wife, NANCY, born ca. 1832, NY, married within the year, were listed in the 1850 census of Adrian Twp., Lenawee Co., Mich. with no family.

STROUD, P. H. (See John C. Hogaboam)

STROUD, WILLIAM (See Ezra Sanford)

STUART also see STEWART

STUART, OLIVER, age 22, born NY, was listed in the 1850 census of Adrian Twp., Lenawee Co., Mich. in a boarding house.

STUCK, BENJAMIN born Penn., was son of a Revolutionary soldier who moved to Fayette, Seneca Co., NY at an early date and died in 1824. Benjamin married there to MARGARET born New Jersey; and he died 10 Feb. 1844; and she died in 1860, Seneca Co., NY. There were 5 daughters and 2 sons, and only named was LUCINDA M. b. 11 Nov. 1822, Fayette, NY (m. Amos A. Kinney, also see). Ref: P&BA-Len pg. 512-3. Note: There is a JOHN with Penn. service in Revolution, with widow, ELIZABETH, pension appl. #R10283.

STUCK, DAVID born ca. 1810, and wife, CATHARINE, born ca. 1813, both in NY, were listed in the 1850 census of Medina Twp., Lenawee Co., Mihc. with MARY E., age 5; RHODA A., age 2; and Jane J. June, age 1, all b. Mich., in their household.

STUCK, JOHN born ca. 1811, and wife, JANE, born ca. 1811, both in NY, were listed in the 1850 census of Raisin Twp., Lenawee Co., Mich. with LEVI, age 19; LEROY, age 16; CHAUNCEY, age 14; GEORGE, age 11; ELIZBETH, age 9, all b. NY; and CORDELIA, age 7; FRANCES, age 1, both b. Mich., in their household.

STUCK, LAVINA (See William Abbott)

STUCK, MARGARET (See John Cain)

STUMBAUGH, ELIZABETH, possibly daughter of JOHN (following), born ca. 1815, Penn. (m. Conrad Kiner, also see, and moved from Penn. to Seneca Twp., Lenawee Co., Mich.) Ref: P&BA-Len pg. 1009-10.

STUMBAUGH, JOHN born ca. 1787, and wife, SUSANNAH (MILLER), born ca. 1787, both in Penn., settled in

Seneca Twp., Lenawee Co., Mich. ca. 1844. Children: (possibly) ELIZABETH, preceding; & SAMUEL (following); and listed in John's household in 1850 were: SARAH, age 22; JOHN, age 21; LYDIA I., age 17; MATILDA b. ca. 1836 (m. John W. Tolford, also see), all b. Penn. Ref: P&BA-Len pg. 683.

STUMBAUGH, SAMUEL, possibly son of JOHN (preceding), born ca. 1823, and wife, SARAH, born ca. 1831, both in Penn., were listed in the 1850 census of Dover Twp., Lenawee Co., Mich. with HARRIET M., age 1, b. Ohio, in their household.

STURTEVANT, ELIAS L. born ca. 1813, and wife, OLIVE, born ca. 1819, both in NY, were listed in the 1850 census of Medina Twp., Lenawee Co., Mich. with CHARLOTTE, age 13; JOSEPH, age 11, both b. Penn.; and GEORGE W., age 10; WARREN, age 7; CYNTHIA, age 4, all b. NY, listed in their household. Note SCOTT, following.

STURTEVANT, SCOTT, probably born after 1850, married in Medina Twp. to SUSANNA (BAER), daughter of John A. (also see) and lived in Morenci, Lenawee Co., Mich.

STYTES, ELIZA (See Justus Cooley)

SULLEN, ALICE (See Justus Cooley)

SULLIVAN, BRIDGET (See Maurice Stack)

SUMNER, CLEMENT Rev. of Mass. had a daughter, ?, probably born in 1750s who married ca. 1780 to Greenwood Carpenter (See Ezra Carpenter).

SUNDERLIN, POLLY (See Elijah Wright)

SUTPHEN/SUTPHIN also see SUTFIN
SUTPHEN, ELEANOR see Eleanor Sutfin.

SUTFIN, AARON B., son of JOHN (following), born 1823, Yates Co., NY, came with his parents to Liberty Twp., Jackson Co., Mich.; and married there to SARAH (LEWIS), daughter of John (also see). She died in 1850 leaving daughters, CHRISTINA & AGNES. Aaron B. married second to her sister, ADALINE (LEWIS), who died in 1854 leaving a daughter, PHEBE (m. Charles Price). Aaron B. married in 1862 to M. A. (MARY ANN? CORNWELL), dau. of Ariel (also see) and they had children: BELLE B.; MATTIE A.; & GUY C. Ref: History of Jackson Co., Mich., 1881, pg. 956.

SUTFIN, ELEANOR born 3 July 1786, Seneca Co., NY (m. John A. Miller, also see). Note: There were PETER & WILLIAM listed in the 1800 census index index of Cayuga Co., NY (from which Seneca Co. was formed in 1804).

SUTFIN, ELEANOR, age 14, born NY, was listed in the 1850 census of Tecumseh Twp., Lenawee Co., Mich. in the household of Rev. Josiah Benton. Note JAMES, & WILLIAM, following.

SUTFIN, JAMES was listed in the 1840 census index of Tecumseh Twp., Lenawee Co., Mich. Note WILLIAM, following.

SUTFIN, JOHN and wife, POLLY (BAIRD), lived in Yates Co., NY ca. 1823, and came to Michigan in 1834; and it is probably they listed in the 1840 census index of Liberty Twp., Jackson Co., Mich. They had 12 children, names not stated, except AARON B. (preceding). She died at age 93. Ref: History of Jackson Co., Mich., 1881, pg. 956. Also note WILLIAM, following.

SUTFIN, PETER B., son of WILLIAM (following), born 18 Sept. 1845, Clinton Twp., Lenawee Co., Mich., married there to MARY (SERVICE), daughter of David (also see). Children: 1. BERTHA M.; 2. INA M.; 3. IVA M. Ref: P&BA-Len pg. 260-1.

SUTFIN, SARAH A. (See William Sickly)

SUTFIN, WILLIAM born ca. 1810, and wife, ALMIRA (BENNETT), possibly daughter of Reuben (also see), had 9 children, and those known were listed in their household in the 1850 census of Tecumseh Twp., Lenawee Co., Mich.: JOHN, age 19, b. NY; and ANTHONY, age 17; JAMES, age 15; LYDIA, age 10; LOUIS, age 9; PETER B. (preceding); GEORGE, age 3, all b. Mich. Almira died in Clinton Twp.; and William died in California. Note: In the 1840 census index, there was a WILLIAM in Jackson Twp., Jackson Co., Mich.; and another in Somerset Twp., Hillsdale Co., Mich. Note JOHN, preceding. Ref: P&BA-Len pg. 260-1.

SUTTON, ABIGAIL (See Robert Field)

SUTTON, ASA U. born ca. 1818, NY, and wife, SARAH A., born ca. 1820, NJ, were listed in the 1850 census of Raisin Twp., Lenawee Co., Mich. with HANNAH A., age 1, b. Mich., in their household.

SUTTON, BENJAMIN and wife, MARY, moved from New Jersey to Seneca Co., NY; and were parents of DEBORAH born 1796, Seneca Co. (m. Stephen Allen). It may be he listed in the 1800 census index of Cayuga Co., NY (from which Seneca was formed in 1804). Ref: P&BA-Len pg. 336-7. Note: Also see JOHN, following.

SUTTON, CHARLES (See William D. James)

SUTTON, CORNELIUS B. born ca. 1813, and wife, CHARLOTTE, born ca. 1813, both in NY, were listed in the 1840 census index of Ridgeway Twp., Lenawee Co., Mich.; and in the 1850 census with DEVILLA, age 13, b. Mich., in their household.

SUTTON, ISAAC, son of MOSES (following), born 3 May 1789, married in Oct. 1810 to SARAH (UNDERHILL), daughter of James (also see) and settled in Cayuga Co., NY. In 1836, they removed to Bedford Twp., Calhoun Co., Mich. (near Battle Creek). He died there on 30 Aug. 1861; and she afterwards came to Raisin Twp., Lenawee Co., Mich. She died in 1871/2 in Tecumseh Twp. Eight sons, and one daughter, and only named was the youngest, NEHEMIAH H. (following). Ref: P&BA-Len pg. 478-9.

SUTTON, JOHN and wife, SARAH (BLAINE) were natives of New Jersey, who lived variously in Onondaga, Wayne, and last in Seneca Co., NY, where they died. Known son, PHARIS (following). Ref: P&BA-Len pg. 250-1.

SUTTON, JOHN D. born ca. 1803, NY and wife, ABIGAIL (KNAPP), daughter of John (also see) came to Medina Twp., Lenawee Co., Mich. with their parents and were the first to marry in the township. In the 1850 census of Medina Twp., they listed children: 1. MAMARA, age 11; 2. WILLIAM M., age 9; 3. MARTHA J., b. 13 Oct. 1843 (m. Stephen W. Curtis, also see); 4. LEWIS, age 3; 5. MILLARD F., age 10/12. Ref: P&BA-Len pg. 696-7.

Pioneer Families of Southeastern Michigan

SUTTON, JOSEPH was the son of a man who had come from Lincolnshire, England to Massachusetts, and later settled in Northcastle, Westchester Co., NY. Joseph married MARY (SANDS), daughter of James & Sarah (Cornell) of Long Island. He died in Northcastle in 1765/70. Ref: P&BA-Len pg. 478-9. Note: This sketch called Joseph the father of MOSES (following), however, Westchester Patriarchs, by N. Davis, 1988, lists a different descent. The children of Joseph: JOSEPH; CALEB; JAMES; WILLIAM; RICHARDSON (following); ABIGAIL; MARY; SOPHIA; JERUSHA.

SUTTON, MOSES, son of RICHARDSON (following), born 15 Mar. 1756, probably in Westchester Co., NY, married REBECCA (UNDERHILL), daughter of Isaac (also see). Known son, ISAAC (preceding). Ref: P&BA-Len pg. 478-9. As noted above, this sketch called Moses son of JOSEPH, but Westchester Patriarchs states he was son of Richardson. Dates seem to indicate that this is correct, however further proof is welcome.

SUTTON, NEHEMIAH H., son of ISAAC (preceding), born 21 June 1829, Cayuga Co., NY, came to Michigan with his parents. He married on 13 Mar. 1854 to MARY E. (SATHERWAITE), daughter of Reuben (also see) and settled in Tecumseh Twp., Lenawee Co. Children: 1. ANNA R. (m. Frederick Stoepel, Detroit, Mich.); 2. MARY R. (m. James S. Wilson, Detroit, Mich.) Ref: P&BA-Len pg. 478-9.

SUTTON, PHARIS, son of JOHN (preceding), born 18 Oct. 1800, Onondaga Co., NY, went as an adult to Chautauqua Co., NY. He married HANNAH M. (FOOTE), daughter of Milton (also see), and in 1830 they removed to Adrian Twp., Lenawee Co., Mich.; and in 1837 to Hillsdale Co. In 1843, they removed to Rome Twp., Lenawee Co.; and in 1858 to Dover Twp. Children: 1. SARAH A. (d. infancy); 2. JULIA A. (d. infancy); 3. LOIS B. b. 2 Mar. 1833, Adrian Twp. (m. Hezekiah W. Hoxter, also see); 4. DEBORAH b. 6 July 1838, North Adams Twp., Hillsdale Co. (m. Jacob C. Gambee, also see); 5. MILTON F. (m. Charlotte E. Barkley, Hillsdale Co.); 6. ROBERT BENTON (following). Ref: P&BA-Len pg. 250-1.

SUTTON, RICHARDSON, son of JOSEPH (preceding), born 11 July 1732, Westchester co., NY, had a will proven on 16 Sept. 1775. He had married ELIZABETH (QUIMBY), daughter of Moses & Jane (Pellam), born 28 Feb. 1736, and had children: 1. ESTHER b. 15 Mar. 1752; 2. MOSES (preceding); 3. DANIEL b. 22 May 1758; 4. DEBORAH b. 17 June 1760; 5. ROBERT b. 5 Apr. 1762; 6. SAMUEL b. 22 Jan. 1764; 7. PHEBE b. 27 Aug. 1765; 8. JERUSHA b. 2 Sept. 1768; 9. ABIGAIL b. 12 Dec. 1770; 9. FRANCIS b. 13 Dec. 1772. Ref: Westchester Patriarchs, by N. Davis, 1988, pg. 231-2.

SUTTON, ROBERT B., son of PHARIS (preceding), born 22 Sept. 1841, Hillsdale Co., Mich., married ALICE C. (PONTIUS), daughter of David (also see). Children: 1. MAGGIE A.; 2. FLORENCE A. Ref: P&BA-Len pg. 250.

SWADERRER, FREDERICA (See Jacob Kurtz)

SWARTHOUT see SWARTOUT

SWARTOUT, ANDREW, possibly son of THOMAS (following), born ca. 1790, and wife, JUDAH, born ca. 1796, both in NY, were listed in the 1840 census index of Woodstock Twp., Lenawee Co., Mich.; and in the 1850 census with NOAH?/WEBB?, age 22; PHEBE, age 19; PETER, age 17; CORNELIUS, age 15; JUDAH, age 13, all b. NY; and ANDREW, age 11, b. Mich.; and THOMAS, age 55, b. NY, in their household.

SWARTOUT, BELLE (See Jabez Briggs)

SWARTOUT, EDWIN, age 13, born Indiana, was listed in the 1850 census of Tecumseh Twp., Lenawee Co., Mich. in a Young household.

SWARTOUT, ELIZA (See Garrett F. Harris)

SWARTOUT, FREEMAN, possibly son of ANDREW (preceding), born ca. 1813, NY, was listed in the 1840 census index of Woodstock Twp., Lenawee Co., Mich.; and in the 1850 census with the following in his household, relationships not known, though apparently more than one family: (possibly wife?) ABIGAIL, age 30; MARY, age 34; ELLEN, age 17; ELIZABETH, age 15; SCOTT, age 14, all b. NY; and FREDUS, age 12; ISAAC, age 9, both b. Mich.; and listed last, MARY, age 17, b. NY. Note: ANDREW was listed 2 doors away in the census.

SWARTOUT, GEORGE born ca. 1820, NY, was listed as head of household in the 1850 census of Woodstock Twp., Lenawee Co., Mich. with ANN, age 54, b. NY, probably his mother, and also MARGARET, age 34; ELIZABETH, age 23; WILLIAM, age 21; JAMES, age 19; THOMAS, age 15, all b. NY; and JOSEPH, age 12, b. Mich., in the household. Note JAMES, & SAMUEL, both following.

SWARTOUT, ISAAC, possibly son of ANDREW (preceding), born ca. 1815, and wife, MARY ANN, born ca. 1818, both in NY, were listed in the 1840 census index of Woodstock Twp., Lenawee Co., Mich.; and in the 1850 census with DANIEL, age 14; ALBERT, age 12; EMILY, age 9; NEWMAN, age 7; ABBY, age 3, all b. Mich., in their household (listed next door to ANDREW).

SWARTOUT, JAMES was listed in the 1840 census index of Woodstock Twp., Lenawee Co., Mich. Note THOMAS, following.

SWARTOUT, JOHN born ca. 1810, and wife, TRESA (THERESA?), born ca. 1818, both in NY, were listed in the 1850 census of Rome Twp., Lenawee Co., Mich. with MARGARET, age 17; MARY J., age 10; GODFREY, age 9; JACOB, age 8; ELIZABETH, age 7; WILLIAM H., age 5; BARBARY, age 3/12, and William Hutchins, age 5, all b. NY, in their household.

SWARTOUT, JOSEPH born ca. 1813, NY, and wife, POLLY, born ca. 1815, Conn., were listed in the 1850 census of Adrian Twp., Lenawee Co., Mich. with ALMARION (ALMERON?), age 15; NANCY, age 14; FLORINDA, age 12; ELIJAH, age 9; OLIVER, age 7, all b. NY; and JOSEPH, age 4, b. Mich., in their household.

SWARTOUT, LEWIS (See Israel Baker Maxwell)

SWARTOUT, LOIS (See Peter Van Vleet)

SWARTOUT, LYDIA (See Sanford Hause)

SWARTOUT, SAMUEL was listed in the 1840 census index of Woodstock Twp., Lenawee Co., Mich. Note THOMAS, following.

SWARTOUT, THOMAS was listed in the 1840 census index of Woodstock Twp., Lenawee Co., Mich., as a "pensioner, age 8(3)?," possibly Revolutionary War, listed adjacent to all of these families who were in Woodstock Twp. There was a man by this name listed in Ulster Co., NY in the 1800 census index. There was a

THOMAS with NY service in the Rev. War Pension Applications #S28490. Note ANDREW & JAMES; SAMUEL; & THOMAS, JR.

SWARTOUT, THOMAS JR., born ca. 1795, NY, probably son of THOMAS (preceding), was listed in the 1840 census index of Woodstock Twp., Lenawee Co., Mich.; and is probably he in the 1850 census in the household of ANDREW (preceding).

SWEET, B. G. was listed in the 1840 census index of Seneca Twp., Lenawee Co., Mich.

SWEET, HENRY born ca. 1822, NY, was listed head of household in the 1850 census of Dover Twp., Lenawee Co., Mich. with his mother, OBEDIENCE, age 63, born Conn., and probably siblings, TIMOTHY, age 31; GEORGE, age 26. both b. NY, in the household.

SWEET, JOHN born ca. 1805, and wife, MARIAH, born ca. 1815, both in NY, were listed in the 1850 census of Woodstock Twp., Lenawee Co., Mich. with JOHN, age 10; JAMES, age 8, both b. Mich.; and listed last, SALLY, age 17, b. NY, in their household.

SWEET, MARTHA of Wales, Maine (See David McFarland).

SWEET, PHILIP and wife, LYDIA (COLE), daughter of David (also see), moved in 1841 from Erie Co., NY to Coldwater, Branch Co., Mich., and he died there at age 65, and she at age 63. Fifteen children, names not stated, except #7. LUCINA b. 22 Jan. 1820 (m. Winslow Bates, also see, on 5 Apr. 1843). Ref: P&BA-Len pg. 554-5; 567-8.

SWEET, STEVEN was listed in the 1840 census index of Seneca Twp., Lenawee Co., Mich.

SWEET, WILLIAM born 23 Feb. 1783, NY, and wife, ABIGAIL, born 28 Apr. 1792, moved to Erie Co., Ohio before 1827. Both died there at age 76. Ten children, names not stated, except CAROLINE b. 23 Oct. 1827, New London, Erie Co., Ohio (m. James F. Munger, also see). Ref: P&BA-Len pg. 589-90.

SWICK, ARTEMUS married CLARA D. (RATHBUN), daughter of Lewis T. (also see); had known daughter, CORA. They lived in Ogden Twp., Lenawee Co., Mich.

SWICK, BARBARA of Seneca Co., NY married Alvah Coddington (also see) by 1830; and died 13 Mar. 1876, Tompkins Co., NY. Ref: P&BA-Len pg. 1012-5.

SWICK, ELIZABETH of Seneca Co., NY married George W. Brooks (also see).

SWICK, HARMON was listed in the 1840 census index of Macon Twp., Lenawee Co., Mich., adjacent to JOHN E. (following). In the 1850 census, there was a MARY, age 7, b. Mich., in the household of John H. & Phoebe A. Allen (possibly grandparents); and a RACHEL, age 11, b. Mich., in the household of Daniel & Annie Sones.

SWICK, J. CLARK (See Henry S. White)

SWICK, JOHN E. born ca. 1810, NY, and wife, SUSAN A., born ca. 1817, NJ, were listed in the 1840 census index of Macon Twp., Lenawee Co., Mich.; and in the 1850 census with MARY, age 15; PHOEBE, age 12; ALVENA b. 13 Nov. 1840, Macon Twp. (m/1 Albert Miller; m/2 Daniel Wiggins, see both); LOUIS? (LOIS? female), age 6; AGNES, age 4; WILLIAM, age 2, all b. Mich., and also in the household was Charity Covert, age 64, b. Penn., possibly mother-in-law?

SWIFT, MARY (See Bartlett Bump)

SWORD, JAMES born ca. 1795, England, and wife, RUTH, born ca. 1801, VT, were listed in the 1840 census index of Rome Twp., Lenawee Co., Mich.; and in the 1850 census of Adrian Twp. with HORATIO, age 27; PORTER L., age 20 (m. Rachel A. Todd, dau. of Gabriel H., also see); FRANCES, age 18; EDWIN, age 15; MARY, age 13, all b. NY, in their household.

SYKES, MERCY (See Obed Hervey, Sr.)

- T -

TABER also see TABOR
TABER B. of Virginia (See David E. Palmer)
TABER, THOMAS (See Philip S. DePuy)

TABOR also see TABER

TABOR, BENJAMIN F. and wife, ELIZABETH (HUMPHREY), natives of England, settled in Herkimer Co., NY (Note: In the 1800 census index, there were two men by this name in Columbia Co., NY). They removed to Wayne Co., NY, where she died. In 1844, Benjamin removed to Hillsdale Co., Mich. to live with son, Benjamin F. Jr., and died there on 11 May 1857, age 82y/1m/25d. Six of the children following lived to maturity: 1. PAMELIA; 2. SARAH A.; 3. GAYLORD G.; 4. CALISTIA; 5. HENRY H. (following); 6. ELIZABETH; 7. HARRIET; 8. BENJAMIN F. JR. Ref: P&BA-Len pg. 254-5. Note: There was a PHILIP B. in Litchfield Twp., Hillsdale Co., Mich. in the 1840 census index.

TABOR, BETSEY (See Luther Scott) Note: There was a BETSEY, age 4, born NY, in the 1850 census of Medina Twp., Lenawee Co., Mich. in a Haight household.

TABOR, GILES P. (Spelled "Jiles P.") in the 1840 census index of Madison Twp., Lenawee Co., Mich.

TABOR, HENRY H. son of BENJAMIN F. (preceding), born 29 Mar. 1815, Herkimer Co., NY, married on 25 Apr. 1839 to LUCY B. (UPTON), daughter of David (also see). They settled first in Wayne Co., NY, and then moved in 1842 to Washtenaw Co., Mich. Six months later, they moved to Wheatland Twp., Hillsdale Co. They remained there till 1856, then moved to Adrian Twp., Lenawee Co., Mich. Children: 1. NORMAN B.; 2. MARY E. (d. 18 mos); 3. ADELBERT (m. Ella Gunsolous; d. by 1888, had dau., Lena M.); 4. HENRY H. JR. Ref: P&BA-Len pg. 254-5.

TABOR, LORENZO, son of THOMAS (following), born 23 Feb. 1815, Bradford Co., VT, married on 13 May 1839 inSpringfield, VT to MARIA (ORMSBY) born 1811, VT. They came to Adrian Twp., Lenawee Co., Mich.; where he died 28 Apr. 1882. Children: 1. THOMAS W. (d. age 3); 2. LORENZO D. b. ca. 1846 (d. age 11); 3. CLARENCE L. (d. age 6 yrs); 4. MARIA S. In their household in the 1850 census also (probably mother of Maria) Susan Ormsby, age 63; Christiana Ormsby, age 39, both b. VT.

TABOR, PAUL born ca. 1784, Mass., and wife, WATY W., born ca. 1785, NH, were listed in the 1840 census index of Adrian Twp., Lenawee Co., Mich. (near to THOMAS, following); and in the 1850 census were in the

Pioneer Families of Southeastern Michigan

household of John and Mialma? (age 36, b. VT) Densmore, possibly she is their daughter.

TABOR, THOMAS born ca. 1786, Mass., and wife, **ABIGAIL (DREW)**, born ca. 1792, VT, moved from Vermont to Adrian Twp., Lenawee Co., Mich. before 1840; and were listed there in the 1850 census. He died in Hudson, Lenawee Co., Mich. Known son, **LORENZO** (preceding). Ref: P&BA-Len pg. 295-6.

TACKABERY, MIDDLETON born Ireland, and wife, **CLARISSA (CLARK)** born Vermont, apparently moved to Sherburn, Chenango Co., NY. Known daughter, **CLARISSA ALMEDA** (m. James M. Scarritt, also see, in Chenango Co., NY). Ref: P&BA-Len pg. 701-2.

TAFT, CYNTHIA (See Silas Wilcox)
TAFT, Rev. H. B. (See Aaron H. Cole)
TAFT, JAMES, age 50, born Ireland, was listed in the 1850 census of Medina Twp., Lenawee Co., Mich.
TAFT, STEPHEN J., age 22, born Mich., was head of household in the 1850 census of Medina Twp., Lenawee Co., Mich. with probably siblings, **RENSSELAER D.**, age 21; **LAURA A.**, age 19, also both b. Mich., in their household. Note: In the 1840 census index, there was a RENSSELAER "TEFT" listed in Jackson Twp., Jackson Co., Mich.

TAGSOLD, JOHN and wife, **CHRISTIANA**, came to Riga Twp., Lenawee Co., Mich. from Bavaria. Known daughter, **BARBARA** b. 19 Aug. 1847, Bavaria (m/1 John Miller; m/2 August Glaser, see both). Ref: P&BA-Len pg. 959-60.

TALBOT, BARTHOLOMEW was listed in the 1840 census index of Hudson Twp., Lenawee Co., Mich.
TALBOT, BENJAMIN I. was listed in the 1840 census index of Woodstock Twp., Lenawee Co., Mich.
TALBOT, JOHN born ca. 1790, Maryland, and wife, **RACHAEL**, born ca. 1791, Virginia, were listed in the 1850 census of Woodstock Twp., Lenawee Co., Mich. with **RACHAEL**, age 11, b. Mich., in their household.
TALBOT, JOHN, age 35, born Kentucky, was listed in the 1850 census of Macon Twp., Lenawee Co., Mich. in a Clarkson household.
TALBOT, SOPHIA (See E. W. Goheen)

TALMADGE ? of Dutchess Co., NY married Rufus Scofield (also see).
TALMADGE, JOSEPH J. born ca. 1807, and wife, **ABIGAIL**, born ca. 1808, both in Mass., were listed in the 1840 census index of Blissfield Twp., Lenawee Co., Mich.; and in the 1850 census with **HARRIET M.**, age 13; **GEORGE H.**, age 11; **MARY J.**, age 8; **GRACIA?**, age 6, all b. Mich., in their household.

TALMAN, GERTRUDE (See Jacob C. Winne)

TANSLEY, GEORGE H. (See John S. Kinney)

TARBELL, EMILY (See Wilber West)

TATOR, CATHERINE (See George I. Harder)

TAUTE, PETRONELLA (See Rudolph Heesen)

TAYER, BENJAMIN, probably born after 1850, married **NELLIE E. (PARSONS)**, daughter of Loss (also see). Ref: P&BA-Len pg. 698-9.
TAYER, PHOEBE A. (See Cornelius Osgood)
TAYER, REMINGTON was listed in the 1840 census index of Madison Twp., Lenawee Co., Mich.
TAYER, WILLIAM born ca. 1822, NY, was listed in the 1850 census of Madison Twp., Lenawee Co., Mich. with whom appears to be his wife, **JANE**, age 17, also born NY, both in the household of John A. Marshall, perhaps father of Jane?

TAYLOR, A. B. Rev. born ca. 1820, Penn., and wife, **ISABELLA**, born ca. 1826, NY, were listed in the 1850 census of Ridgeway Twp., Lenawee Co., Mich.
TAYLOR, ABIGAIL (See Nicholas Waggoner)
TAYLOR, ANDREW, son of **ICHABOD** (following), born 26 Mar. 1814, Delaware Co., NY, came to Rome Twp., Lenawee Co., Mich. in 1835. He married on 7 Mar. 1838 to **JEMIMA (ROGERS)** born ca. 1816, NY. Children (ages from the 1850 census): 1. **GEORGE G.**, age 11; 2. **EDWIN**, age 9 (note EDWIN A., following); 3. **JEANETTE**, age 7; 4. **MINERVA**, age 5; 5. **HIRAM**, age 2; 6. **FRANK**; 7. **CORNELIA**. Jemima died 23 Dec. 1857, age 40. Andrew married again to Mrs. **CHARITY M. (PALMER) STEARNS**. Child: 8. **BAIRD E.** Ref: P&BA-Len pg. 943.
TAYLOR, ASAHEL born ca. 1811, Mass., and wife, **HANNAH**, born ca. 1822, Penn., were listed in the 1840 census index of Tecumseh Twp., Lenawee Co., Mich.; and in the 1850 census with **JULIA**, age 17, b. Mass.; and **THEODORE**, age 6; **AUGUSTUS**, age 3; **FRANK**, age 1, all b. Mich., in their household.
TAYLOR, BETSEY (ELIZABETH?) born ca. 1779, Mass., was listed in the 1850 census of Rollin Twp., Lenawee Co., Mich. in the household of Linus and Mary (b. 1800, Mass.) Sutliff, just 2 doors from JOHN (following). Also note RUANY & SAMUEL, following.
TAYLOR, CHARLES H. was listed in the 1840 census index of Blissfield Twp., Lenawee Co., Mich.
TAYLOR, DORA (See Simon Shultis)
TAYLOR, DOROTHEA born New Jersey, married Joseph P. Lee (also see).
TAYLOR, EBENEZER born ca. 1821, and wife, **ARA? A.**, born ca. 1829, both in NY, were listed in the 1850 census of Raisin Twp., Lenawee Co., Mich. with **ELLEN M.**, age 3; **MARVIN J.**, age 2, both b. MIch., in their household.
TAYLOR, EDWIN A. married **SARAH (ONSTED)**, daughter of Peter (also see). Note EDWIN, son of ANDREW (preceding); and also son of JOSHUA (following).
TAYLOR, ELI was listed in the 1840 census index of Rome Twp., Lenawee Co., Mich.
TAYLOR, ELIZABETH (See ? Van Pelt)
TAYLOR, EMILY born Yorkshire, England, married John Scott, also see, and came to Ridgeway Twp., Lenawee Co., Mich. Note JOHN of Yorkshire, England (following).
TAYLOR, FRANCES (See George Sisson)
TAYLOR, GEORGE was listed in the 1840 census index of Tecumseh Twp., Lenawee Co., Mich. Also note ASAHEL, preceding.
TAYLOR, HANNAH born ca. 1780, Mass., was listed in the 1850 census of Adrian Twp., Lenawee Co., Mich. in the

household of daughter, SARAH S. b. ca. 1814, VT (m. George D. Bascom, also see). Note JOHN; RUANY; & SAMUEL, following.

TAYLOR, HENRY born ca. 1802, Conn., and wife, MARY, born ca. 1803, NY, may be they listed in the 1840 census index of Rome Twp., Lenawee Co., Mich.; and were in the 1850 census of Raisin Twp., with HENRY S., age 17, b. NY; and LAURA M., age 13, CHARLES H., age 11; JULIA E., age 9; LAVINA, age 7; GEORGE B., age 5, all b. Mich., in their household. Note ICHABOD, following.

TAYLOR, ICHABOD and wife, ZADY (STILSON), were natives of Conn., who went to Delaware Co., NY before 1815. He died there at age 57; and she had preceded him by 6 years at age 54. There were 15 children, names not stated, except ANDREW (preceding); and NORMAN (following). Ref: P&BA-Len pg. 943. Also note ELI; HENRY; PHINEAS; & WOOSTER.

TAYLOR, J. D. was listed in the 1840 census index of Adrian Twp., Lenawee Co., Mich.

TAYLOR, J. F. (See Bartlett Bump)

TAYLOR, JAMES (See James Wheeler)

TAYLOR, JANE (See John Steel)

TAYLOR, JOHN born ca. 1811, and wife, MARY, born ca. 1812, both in VT, may be they listed in the 1840 census index of Rollin Twp., Lenawee Co., Mich. (adjacent to RUANY & SAMUEL); and in the 1850 census with ISAAC, age 15, b. VT; ELIZABETH, age 14, b. Penn.; HARRIET, age 6, b. Ind., in their household.

TAYLOR, JOHN and wife, ANN (HARRISON) of Yorkshire, England, remained there; and he died at age 96, and she died at age 50. Known son, WILLIAM (following); and also note EMILY (preceding). Ref: P&BA-Len pg. 340-1.

TAYLOR, JOSHUA born ca. 1814, New Jersey, and wife, MARY C., born ca. 1820, Penn., were listed in the 1850 census of Raisin Twp., Lenawee Co., Mich. with EDWIN, age 6 (Note EDWIN A., preceding); MARTHANA, age 4; AARON C., age 1; JOHN, age 1/12, all b. Mich., in their household.

TAYLOR, LEONARD (See George S. Stranahan)

TAYLOR, LEWIS born ca. 1819, New Hampshire, and wife, EFELINDA, born ca. 1822, NY, were listed in the 1850 census of Madison Twp., Lenawee Co., Mich. with SARAH, age 8, b. NY; and LUCY, age 7/12, b. Mich.; STEWART, age 20, b. NY; and LUCY, age 60, probably mother of LEWIS & STEWART, b. Rhode Island, in their household.

TAYLOR, LOUISA Mrs. married second to George Daniels (See Augustus F. Daniels).

TAYLOR, MARY J. (See Peter M. Wheaton)

TAYLOR, NORMAN, possibly son of ICHABOD (preceding), born ca. 1818, NY, may be he listed in the 1840 census index as NORMAN P. in Cambridge Twp., Lenawee Co., Mich.; and in the 1850 census of Rome Twp. with wife, ARAMINTA, age 25, b. NY; and ELIZABETH, age 2, b. Mich., in his household.

TAYLOR, PHEBE born 23 Oct. 1792, New Jersey (m. John Benedict, also see). Ref: P&BA-Len pg. 300-1.

TAYLOR, PHINEAS was listed in the 1840 census index of Rome Twp., Lenawee Co., Mich. adjacent to ANDREW; ELI; HENRY; RUANY; SAMUEL & WOOSTER.

TAYLOR, RODMAN born ca. 1808, and wife, CYNTHIA, born ca. 1812, both in NY, were listed in the 1840 census index of Franklin Twp., Lenawee Co., Mich.; and in the 1850 census with LORAN? (male), age 15; LEVI, age 12; ALVIRA, age 7; MARY, age 1, all b. Mich., in their household.

TAYLOR, RUANY was listed in the 1840 census index of Rome Twp., Lenawee Co., Mich. Note PHINEAS, preceding.

TAYLOR, SALOME (See Ambrose Barnaby)

TAYLOR, SAMUEL was listed in the 1840 census index of Rome Twp., Lenawee Co., Mich. Note RUANY & JOHN.

TAYLOR, THEODORE born ca. 1816, Rhode Island, was listed in the 1850 census of Madison Twp., Lenawee Co., Mich. Note this given name in household of ASAHEL, preceding.

TAYLOR, WILLIAM was the son of ROBERT (a native of New Jersey of Scottish descent). William married MARY (CORSON) and they were pioneers to Lycoming Co., Penn. They later removed to Spencer, Lucas Co., Ohio. William died 18 Nov. 1884, Toledo, Ohio and she died 29 Dec. 1882. Known daughters: MARY J. b. 14 Sept. 1842 (m. Miner T. Cole, also see); & LUCRETIA (m. Pliny Van Fleet, also see). Ref: P&BA-Len pg. 228-30; 1147.

TAYLOR, WILLIAM, son of JOHN (preceding), born 1820, Yorkshire, England, married there to MARY (TODD), and remained until after the birth of 3 children. They moved to Ridgeway Twp., Lenawee Co., Mich. There were 6 children, and only named were the 4 surviving in 1888: 1. ROBERT (m. Elizabeth Lister); 2. FAITH (m. Thomas Loebster; Ridgeway Twp.); 3. FRANCIS (m. Helen Wilson); 4. JOHN (to Florida). Ref: P&BA-Len pg. 340-1.

TAYLOR, WOOSTER born ca. 1804, and wife, URSULA, born ca. 1807, both in Conn., were listed in the 1840 census of Rome Twp., Lenawee Co., Mich.; and in the 1850 census of Woodstock Twp. with HENRIETT, age 18; JANE, age 16, both b. NY; and ABNER, age 13; ADELAIDE, age 11, both b. Mich.; and also Thomas Marshall, age 19, b. NY, with wife, Emily, age 21, b. Conn., probably daughter of Wooster, and a child, Emily, age 9/12.

TEACHOUT, ALONZO[3], son of JACOB[2] (following), born 19 May 1819, Ontario Co., NY, married there in 1840 to ANNA (DEWEY), daughter of Col. Edmond B. (also see). Alonzo died in Manchester, NY in 1855. Children: 1. OSCAR L. (to Denison, TX); 2. SARAH A. (m. Samuel B. Gambee; d. 21 Nov. 1870, Rome Twp.); 3. FRANK D. (Rome Twp.). Anna married second to Joseph F. Baker (also see) of Rome Twp., Lenawee Co., Mich. Ref: P&BA-Len pg. 303-4.

TEACHOUT, CHAUNCEY born ca. 1813, and wife, LOUISA, born ca. 1828, both in NY, were listed in the 1850 census of Cambridge Twp., Lenawee Co., Mich. with JEMIMA, age 7; and ANG---? (female), age 5, both b. Mich., in their household. Note: There was a CHAUNCEY in the 1840 census index of Stockbridge Twp., Ingham Co., Mich.

TEACHOUT, CHARLES[3], son of WILLIAM[2] (following), born 2 Feb. 1837, Ontario Co., NY, came to Cambridge Twp., Lenawee Co., Mich. with his parents. He married in 1859 to HARRIET A. (BARRUS), daughter of Dellence (also see) of Rome Twp. They settled first in Rome Twp., then later to Adrian; and in 1876 to Rome

Pioneer Families of Southeastern Michigan

Center. In 1879, they moved to Adrian; and in 1880 to Tecumseh. Children: 1. FRED D. b. ca. 1860; 2. CLAUDE ELWOOD b. ca. 1868. Ref: P&BA-Len pg. 853-4.

TEACHOUT, DANIEL WEBSTER, son of WELCOME (following), b. 18 July 1844, served in Co. L, 11th Mich. Cav. during the Civil War. He married in Rome Twp., Lenawee Co., Mich. on 26 Dec. 1867 to CAROLINE M. (KIMBALL), daughter of Avery (also see). They lived in Rome Twp. until 1879, then moved to Adrian. Child: WELCOME A. b. 20 Apr. 1870. Ref: P&BA-Len pg. 847-8.

TEACHOUT, GEORGE W.^{3}, son of JACOB^2 (following), born 1 Feb. 1827, Ontario Co., NY, came to Mich. with his parents, and married in Sept. 1848 to HARRIET W. (TEACHOUT)^3, daughter of WILLIAM^2 (following). In 1852, they removed to Rome Twp., Lenawee Co., Mich. Children: 1. BENJAMIN F. b. 17 Jan. 1849 (m. Adel Sickles, dau. of John of Adrian; had dau., Florence W.); 2. HELEN E. b. 30 Sept. 1853 (m. F. A. Desermia, also see); 3. ELLEN A. (twin of Helen; m. John Sickles, Jr., also see); 4. WILLIAM A. (following). Ref: P&BA-Len pg. 303-4.

TEACHOUT, ISAIAH born ca. 1822, and wife, MARY, born ca. 1822, both in NY, were listed in the 1850 census of Rome Twp., Lenawee Co., Mich. with ADELIA A., age 3; CALISTA A., age 2, both b. Mich.; and Newman Curtis, age 26, with wife, Jane, age 20, both b. NY, in their household.

TEACHOUT, JACOB^1 came and wife, not named, came from Holland to America, and were living in Schuyler Co., NY ca. 1784. They probably moved to Ontario Co., NY. Known son, JACOB^2 (following). Ref: P&BA-Len pg. 961-2. Also note JOHN (following).

TEACHOUT, JACOB^2, son of JACOB^1 (preceding), born 1784, Schuyler Co., NY, married RACHEL (CURTIS), daughter of Elijah (also see) of Manchester, Ontario Co., NY. In 1864, they moved to Hillsdale Co., Mich. to live with a son. He died there in 1876, age 92. There were 12 children, names not stated, except ALONZO; & GEORGE (both preceding). Ref: P&BA-Len pg. 961-2. Note: There was a JACOB in the 1840 census index of Davison, Lapeer Co., Mich.; and WILLIAM in Rich Twp., Lapeer Co.

TEACHOUT, JOHN^1 (note JACOB^1, possibly father of John?) served in the War of 1812 in NY. He came to Cambridge Twp., Lenawee Co., Mich. from Ontario Co., NY after the death of his wife (name not stated) to live with known son, WILLIAM^2 (following). He died there at age 70. Ref: P&BA-Len pg. 961-2.

TEACHOUT, WELCOME born ca. 1812/16, probably in Ontario Co., NY, and married there to MELINDA (HOWLAND) born ca. 1820, NY. About 1843, they removed to Rome Twp., Lenawee Co., Mich.; and in 1860 moved to Adrian. He died in 1880, age 68 (1850 census said he was age 34?) Afterwards, Melinda made her home with son, DANIEL WEBSTER (preceding); and also had a known daughter, MARY E. (m. Alfonzo Stoddard, son of Leonard, also see; Rome Center). In the 1850 census of Rome Twp., they also listed last in their household JENETT, age 11, b. NY, possibly not their child. Ref: P&BA-Len pg. 847-8.

TEACHOUT, WILLIAM^2, son of JOHN^1 (preceding), born ca. 1805, NY, married in Ontario Co., NY to RACHEL (WELLS), daughter of Peter (also see). About 1853, they moved to Cambridge Twp., Lenawee Co., Mich. She died there in 1862, age 58; and he afterwards moved to Tecumseh, Mich., where he died in 1869. There were 2 sons and 4 daughters, names not stated, except CHARLES^3 (preceding); and HARRIET W.^{3} b. 7 Sept. 1830 (m. GEORGE W., preceding). Ref: P&BA-Len pg. 853-4; 961-2.

TEACHOUT, WILLIAM A.^{4}, son of GEORGE W.^{3} (preceding), married on 8 Feb. 1880 to MARY L. (CHRISTMAN), daughter of Henry C. (also see). Known children: 1. ZEDA L. b. 27 Jan. 1881; 2. CLARE W. b. 11 Dec. 1886. Ref: P&BA-Len pg. 200-1.

TEED, SARAH (See Samuel Lyke)

TEELING, ANNA C. (See Peter V. Smith)

TEEPLE, MARTHA (See John I. Voorhees)

TEEPLE, HENRY was said to be a Revolutionary soldier who was an early settler from Schoharie Co., NY to Genesee Co., NY. There was a GEORGE listed in the 1800 census index of Schoharie Co., NY. In the Rev. Pension Applications, there is a GEORGE with NJ service, with widow, HANNAH, #R10444; and JOHN with NJ service #R10445, both rejected; JACOB with Penn. service, #S16552. There was PETER in Kent Co., Mich. in the 1840 census index.

TEEPLE, PETER, son of HENRY (preceding), born Schoharie Co., NY, went to Genesee Co., NY with his parents. He served in the WAr of 1812. He married MARY (MURPHY), daughter of Isaac, born ca. 1795, New Jersey. They lived in Seneca Co., NY by 1813, where he later died. Known daughters: ELIZABETH b. 26 Feb. 1813, Seneca Co., NY; SARAH "SALLY" b. ca. 1823 (Sally m. Erastus Brockway, also see, as his second wife; and Elizabeth m. him as 3rd wife). Another daughter, name not stated, married and went to Waukegan, Ill. and Elizabeth was said to have accompanied them, then returned to Ogden Twp., and married Erastus Brockwasy in 1852. Peter's wife, Mary, after his death, married William Johnson (also see), and in the 1850 census of Ogden Twp., Lenawee Co., Mich., Elizabeth, preceding, age 34?, was listed in the household. Ref: P&BA-Len pg. 757-8.

TEETER, JOHN and wife, MARY, of Tompkins Co., NY were parents of FANNY b. 12 Jan. 1840 (m. Ansel P. Coddington, also see). In the 1850 census of Ulysses, Tompkins Co., NY were JOHN, age 53, and wife, MARY, age 52, with HARRIET, age 20; ALMY, age 16; and John Jones, age 13 (perhaps JOHN JONES TEETER?); and FANNY, age 11, in their household. Ref: P&BA-Len pg. 1012-5.

Note: JOHN probably had additional sons, JOSEPH E. (listed next door), age 27; JULIUS, age 33 (lived nearby); CHARLES, age 30, (also nearby).

TEMPLE, AMOS was listed in the 1840 census index of Jackson Twp., Jackson Co., Mich.

TEMPLE, MARY born England (See Thomas Farrah).

TEMPLE, NICHOLAS born ca. 1800, and wife, BETSEY, born ca. 1814, both in England, were listed in the 1840 census index of Raisin Twp., Lenawee Co., Mich.; and in the

1850 census with JOHN, age 15; AGNES, age 12, both b. England; and GEORGE, age 7; SARAH A., age 2, both b. Mich., in their household.

TEMPLE, ROBERT born ca. 1806, and wife, MARY, born ca. 1815, both in England, were listed in the 1840 census index of Rollin Twp., Lenawee Co., Mich.; and in the 1850 census with THOMAS, age 12, b. England; and JOSEPH, age 7; ALFRED, age 5; CHARLES, age 1, all b. Mich., in their household. HANNAH, age 16, b. England, a few doors away in a Marvin household, may relate to this family.

TENANT also see TENNENT

TENANT, ALFRED born ca. 1817, NY, and wife, FANNY J., born ca. 1826, Mich., were listed in the 1850 census of Blissfield Twp., Lenawee Co., Mich. with HARRIET, age 2; AUGUSTUS, age 1, both b. Mich., in their household.

TENANT, CONSTANT was a native of Rhode Island who moved to Saratoga Co., NY, where he remained. Known son, JOSEPH C. (following). Ref: P&BA-Len pg. 379-80. Also note ALFRED & WILLIAM, possibly additional sons.

TENANT, DANFORD, son of JOSEPH C. (following), born 14 Jan. 1841 (1839?), Edinburg, Saratoga Co., NY, came as an infant to Deerfield Twp. (then Blissfield Twp.) with his parents. He served in the Civil War. He married on 3 July 1871 to SARAH (DIVER), daughter of John (also see). Children: 1. HATTIE b. ca. 1875; 2. CLARENCE b. ca. 1880; 3. PERLEY (d. age 19 mos). Ref: P&BA-Len pg. 379-80.

TENANT, JOHN H., age 20, born NY, was listed in the 1850 census of Adrian Twp., Lenawee Co., Mich. in a Wheeler household.

TENANT, JOSEPH C., son of CONSTANT (preceding), born ca. 1808, married there to PHOEBE (ARMSTRONG) born ca. 1808, Saratoga Co. In 1841, they moved to Deerfield Twp. (then Blissfield Twp.), and she died there in 1857. They were listed in the 1850 census of Blissfield Twp. Children: 1. SEYMOUR b. ca. 1836; 2. WILLIAM C. b. ca. 1837 (d. age 15); 3. DANFORD b. 14 Jan. 1841 (was shown age 11 in the census - b. 1839?); 4. HARRIET C. b. ca. 1843 (m. Asa Diver); 5. THEODORE b. ca. 1848 (d. age 19); 6. EUGENE (to Monroe Co., Mich.) It is probably this Joseph who married again in Deerfield Twp. to Mrs. SARAH E. (KEENE) GOODALE, daughter of Samuel B., and widow of Hiram (see both). Joseph C. died in 1874. Ref: P&BA-Len pg. 379-80.

TENANT, WILLIAM born ca. 1800, and wife, BETSEY, born ca. 1799, both in NY, were listed in the 1840 census index of Blissfield Twp., Lenawee Co., Mich.; and in the 1850 census with PETER, age 18, b. NY; and JAMES A., age 15; ALIDA, age 9, both b. Mich., in their household.

TENBROOK, ALICE born ca. 1826, NY, was listed in the 1850 census of Adrian Twp., Lenawee Co., Mich. in the household of Alonzo Cummings, probably as an employee in Grocery store.

TENBROOK, ANNA born 1796, NY, married John Mead (also see) before 1820, probably in Tioga Co., NY, and moved in 1836 to Fairfield Twp., Lenawee Co., Mich. Note WILLIAM who was adjacent in 1840 census index, and 2 doors away in 1850 census; and JOHN (both following).

TENBROOK, CATHERINE born ca. 1797, Chemung Co., NY (then Tioga Co.), married Jabez Fisk (also see). Ref: P&BA-Len pg. 1041-2. Note JOHN, following.

TENBROOK, GARRETT, possibly son of JOHN (following), born in Chemung Co., NY (Tioga Co.) in 1803, married ca. 1826 to HANNAH (GANNON) born 1803, Orange Co., NY. They moved in 1831 to Madison Twp., Lenawee Co., Mich., where they both died in 1868. Nine children, and those known following, in their household in the 1850 census: 1. ALLA? (female), age 23; 2. WILLIAM, age 20; 3. PHEBE, age 18; 4. REBECCA, age 16; 5. CATHARINE, age 12 (m. Josiah J. Putnam, also see); 6. MARTHA, age 10 (prob. she who m. John W. Allen, also see); 7. HANNAH, age 6. Also in the household was Urial Stewart, age 10, b. Mich. Ref: P&BA-Len pg. 211. Note ALICE, preceding, possibly same as "ALLA."

TENBROOK, JOHN born 5 Aug. 1767, Somerset Co., NJ, married there to ALLIE (LOWE) and moved to Chemung Co. (then Tioga Co.), NY by 1801. She died there in 1832, and he died in 1843. Known son, JOHN (following). Ref: P&BA-Len pg. 1213-4. Also note ANNA; CATHERINE; GARRETT; & WILLIAM, possibly additional children.

TENBROOK, JOHN, son of JOHN (preceding), born 21 Nov. 1804, Chemung Co. (then Tioga Co.), NY. He came to Michigan, and married on 7 June 1838 in Ypsilanti, Washtenaw Co., Mich. to SARAH J. (ALLISON) born 22 June 1815, Orange Co., NY. Apparently were in NY 1839 to 1845. They settled first in Dover Twp., but settled by 1848 in Fairfield Twp., Lenawee Co., Mich. Listed in their household were WILLIAM L., age 11 (Served as Capt. in Co. A, 4th Mich. Inf., Civil War; m. Jane Cole of Fairfield; moved to Missouri); SUSAN, age 8 (m. Walker G. Porter, son of Asaph K., also see); HELEN, age 5 (m. John Tunison, Jr.); THOMAS, age 2 (d. 27 Jan. 1865, age 17); and not in household, JUDSON b. after 1850. Ref: P&BA-Len pg. 1213.

TENBROOK, SALLY A. (See John W. Tolford)

TENBROOK, WILLIAM born ca. 1801, and wife, NANCY, born ca. 1800, both in NY, were listed in the 1840 census index of Fairfield Twp., Lenawee Co., Mich.; and in the 1850 census with William French, age 18, b. NY; Jane Manger, age 11; Eugene Stewart, age 8, both b. Mich., in their household.

TEN EYCK spelled variously Ten Eyeck; Tenyek; Tenyck, etc.

TEN EYCK, JACOB born ca. 1804, NY, and wife, BETSEY, born ca. 1803, Penn., were listed in the 1850 census of Medina Twp., Lenawee Co., Mich. with GEORGE, age 20, b. NY; and SARAH A., age 18; CAROLINE, age 14; AMANDA, age 15; HANNAH, age 13; JANE, age 11; LUCRETIA, age 8; EDGAR, age 6; ANN A., age 3, all b. Mich., in their household.

TEN EYCK, POLLY (See Samuel Foster)

TEN EYCK, STEPHEN born ca. 1816, and HELEN, born ca. 1820, both in NY, were listed in the 1850 census of Seneca Twp., Lenawee Co., Mich.; and next door in another household was SARAH A., age 18, b. NY, probably related.

TENNENT also see TENANT
TENNENT, SARAH born 6 Oct. 1807, Warwick, Rhode Island, married Alfred D. Hall (also see). Ref: P&BA-Len pg. 1069-70.

TERPENEY see TERPENNING

TERPENNING was also spelled variously TERPNING; TERPENEY; TERPNER, in the census; but I have selected this spelling as the most correct. Researchers of this surname should check Ulster and Dutchess Co., NY records.
TERPENNING, EMILY, age 11, born Mich., was listed in the 1850 census of Adrian Twp., Lenawee Co., Mich. in the household of Abraham Perkins.
TERPENNING, EZEKIEL was listed in the 1840 census index of Hudson Twp., Lenawee Co., Mich.
TERPENNING, FREELOVE born ca. 1810, married on 23 Dec. 1819 to Stephen Perkins (also see) of Cayuga Co., NY.
TERPENNING, JAMES R., son of PETER S. (preceding), born 19 FEb. 1838, Cayuga Co., NY, served in Co. I, 1st Mich. Batt. Light Artl, Civil War. He married on 20 Dec. 1866 to LORETTA (PELHAM), daughter of Richard C. (also see). Children: 1. MARIA S. b. 27 Jan. 1868; 2. CLAUDE D. b. 26 May 1873. Ref: P&BA-Len pg. 206-7.
TERPENNING, JOHN born ca. 1817, and wife, NANCY, born ca. 1823, both in NY, were listed in the 1850 census of Adrian Twp., Lenawee Co., Mich. with WILLIAM H., age 6; HARRIET E., age 2; FRANCIS, age 3/12, all b. Mich., in their household.
TERPENNING, JULIA, age 18, born NY, was listed in the 1850 census of Adrian Twp., Lenawee Co., Mich. in the Voorhees household.
TERPENNING, PETER born ca. 1804, NY, and wife, LOVINA, born ca. 1806, Canada, were residents of Dover Twp., Lenawee Co., Mich. in 1835 (and neighbors of Henry F. Townsend). They were listed in the 1850 census of Dover Twp. with JOSEPH, age 22; WESLEY, age 18; JOHN S., age 15, all b. NY; and PHEBE, age 12; HENRY W., age 9; ELIZABETH, age 8; SARAH, age 6; GEORGE W., age 4, all b. Mich.; and listed last, JANETTE, age 18, b. Mich., probably not a daughter of this household.
TERPENNING, PETER S. born ca. 1806, and wife, LYDIA (HANNIBAL), born ca. 1807, were natives of Cayuga Co., NY. They remained there until about 1843, then moved to Eaton Co., Mich., and a few days later to Adrian, Lenawee Co., Mich. They lived in Rollin Twp. in the 1850 census; and later in Woodstock, Hillsdale Co.; and last in Addison, Lenawee Co., where he died. Lydia died 1 May 1884, age 77. There were 10 children, names not stated. In the 1850 census, they listed NEWTON, age 16; RUTH A., age 14; JAMES R. (following); SARAH M., age 10; OSRO? (male), age 8; MALISSA J., age 6, all b. NY. Ref: P&BA-Len pg. 206-7.

TERRELL also see TERRYL; TYRELL; TURRELL
TERRELL, CALVIN was listed in the 1840 census index of Palmyra Twp., Lenawee Co., Mich.
TERRELL, CHARLOTTE (See Thomas Williams)
TERRELL, HANNAH (See Ebenezer Fisk[2])
TERRELL, NELSON born ca. 1808, VT, and wife, EMILY, born ca. 1811, Conn., were listed in the 1850 census of Woodstock Twp., Lenawee Co., Mich. with MALISSA, age 19; DAVID, age 17, both b. Penn.; HORACE, age 15, b. Ohio; and ALVINA, age 13; CYNTHIA, age 11; ALONSO, age 8; EDGAR, age 6; EUGENE, age 4/12, all b. Mich., in their household. Also note Stephen Turrell.

TERWILLEYER also see TERWILLIGER
TERWILLEYER, JANE born Ulster Co., NY, married Aaron Palmer (also see).

TERWILLIGER, ABRAHAM of Ulster Co., NY was father of MARY b. ca. 1787 (m. JAMES[3], following). Ref: P&BA-Len pg. 868-9.
TERWILLIGER, BENJAMIN[1] and wife, ELSIE (FREER), of Ulster Co., NY, had known son, BENJAMIN[2] (following).
TERWILLIGER, BENJAMIN[2], son of BENJAMIN[1] (preceding), was baptized 3 Sept. 1758 in the Reformed Church of New Paltz, Ulster Co., NY. It is probably he who married EVA (HASBROUCK). In the records of this church, they listed the following children, possibly not a complete list: 1. DAVID bpt. 17 Nov. 1774; 2. JAMES[3] (James is "Jacobus" in Dutch records; following); 3. BENJAMIN HASBROUCK bpt. 23 Mar. 1777 (prob. d. young); 4. BENJAMIN bpt. 20 May 1783. Also note JOHN (following).
TERWILLIGER, BENJAMIN, probably son of JAMES[3] (following), born ca. 1806, and wife, SALLY, born ca. 1814, both in NY, were listed in the 1850 census of Hudson Twp., Lenawee Co., Mich. with THOMAS D., age 17, b. NY; and THEODORE, age 12; JAMES N., age 8; BENJAMIN F., age 6; CHARLES T., age 4, all b. Mich., in their household, next door to JAMES HARVEY (following).
TERWILLIGER, CATHERINE born ca. 1810, NY, married Gardner Robb (also see), and she may be daughter of JAMES[3], as her daughter, Amanda C. Robb, was listed in household of (brother?) HARVEY J. in the 1850 census.
TERWILLIGER, EUGENE (See John Forbes)
TERWILLIGER HARVEY J. See JAMES HARVEY (following)
TERWILLIGER, JAMES[3], son of BENJAMIN[2] (preceding), b. 28 Aug. 1778, Ulster Co., NY, married in 1821 to MARY (TERWILLIGER), daughter of ABRAHAM (also see) of Ulster Co., NY. They removed first to Cayuga Co., NY, and in 1825 to Ontario, Wayne Co., NY. In 1840, they moved to Ypsilanti, Washtenaw Co., Mich. where a brother (JOHN?) lived; and then moved to Hudson Twp., Lenawee Co. (probably he listed as "J. R." in the 1840 census index.) In the 1850 census, Mary, age 63, was residing in household of son, JAMES HARVEY (written Harvey J.), following. She died 13 Dec. 1874. BENJAMIN, preceding, is probably also a son; and CATHERINE (preceding), born ca. 1810, NY, a daughter.
TERWILLIGER, JAMES HARVEY, son of JAMES[3] (preceding), born 20 Aug. 1816, Waywarsing, Ulster Co., NY, married on 11 May 1869 to E. MATILDA (YOUNG), daughter of John (also see) of Seneca Co., NY. They adopted Lucian G. Lerch, son of her sister, Frances A. and husband, Frank Lerch. Ref: P&BA-Len pg. 868-9.
TERWILLIGER, JOHN was listed in the 1840 census index of Ypsilanti Twp., Washtenaw Co., Mich. Note JAMES[3] (preceding).

THACKRAY, JOSEPH, son of WILLIAM (following), born 17 July 1839, Albion, Yorkshire, England, came to

Ridgeway Twp., Lenawee Co., Mich. with his parents. He married on 19 Apr. 1859 to CHARLOTTE (PLUES), daughter of Moses (also see). Children: 1. MARY A. (m. Wesley Lester, Ridgeway Twp.); 2. ELIZABETH (m. William Niverson, Britton, Mich.) Ref: P&BA-Len pg. 481-2.

THACKRAY, MARY born ca. 1808, Yorkshire, England (m. George Exelby[1], also see).

THACKRAY, WILLIAM and wife, ELIZABETH (LOCKE), natives of Albion, Yorkshire, England, came to the US in 1842, and supposedly came directly to Ridgeway Twp., Lenawee Co., Mich. (Note: I did not locate them in the 1850 census of Lenawee Co.) Known son, JOSEPH (preceding). Ref: P&BA-Len pg. 481-2.

THATCHER, MICHAEL, born ca. 1798, New Jersey, went to Caneadea, Allegany Co., NY, and married there to HANNAH (SANFORD), daughter of Ezra (also see), born ca. 1799, NY. They moved to Cohoctah Twp., Livingston Co., Mich. to join the Sanford family. He died 9 Feb. 1854, and she died 29 Nov. 1878, age 79. In the 1850 census of Livingston Co., Mich., then Tuscola Twp. (now Cohoctah), they listed SARAH, age 25; MICHAEL, age 21 (m. Abigail P. Sears in 1875), both b. NY; and ESTHER, age 16, b. Mich., in their household. In 1881, two daughters were deceased, Ref: <u>History of Livingston Co., Mich.</u>, 1880, pg. 445.

THAYER, BETSEY of Taunton, Mass. married in 1818 to William Freeman, also see. She died in Palmyra Twp., Lenawee Co., Mich. in 1848. Ref: P&BA-Len pg. 668-9. Note RUEL; MOWRY; & SIMON D., following.

THAYER, CHLOE (See Luther C. Kilborn)

THAYER, DAVID B. born ca. 1823, and wife, CATHARINE, born ca. 1825, both in NY, were listed in the 1850 census of Adrian Twp., Lenawee Co., Mich. with ALBERT A., age 1, b. Mich.; and OLIVE, age 34, b. NY, in their household.

THAYER, HOSEA born 26 Nov. 1784, Springfield, Mass., married HANNAH (TORREY) born NY. Known daughter, DIANA b. 14 Apr. 1812, Hamilton, Madison Co., NY (m. Horatio G. Pope, also see). Hosea died 14 Jan. 1872; and Hannah died 6 Jan. 1874, Hamilton, NY.

THAYER, JERVIS L. "from Wayne Co., NY" purchased land in Jackson Co., Mich. in 1836; and there was a "J. L." in the 1840 census index of Henrietta Twp., Jackson Co.

THAYER, JESSE W. (spelled "Thaire" in census) born ca. 1808, Mass., and wife, MARY A., born ca. 1811, VT, were listed in the 1850 census of Medina Twp., Lenawee Co., Mich. with FANNY, age 5, b. NY, in their household. Note: It may be listed as "J. W." in the 1840 census index of Seneca Twp.

THAYER, JONAS born ca. 1820, NY, and wife, ELEANOR, born ca. 1827, Ohio, were listed in the 1850 census of Ogden Twp., Lenawee Co., Mich. with LOUISA A., age 6, b. Indiana; and CAROLINE A., age 3, b. Mich., in their household.

THAYER, JOSHUA "from Huron Co., Ohio" purchased in Napoleon Twp., Jackson Co., Mich. in 1836; and was listed there in the 1840 census index.

THAYER, MOWRY was listed in the 1840 census index of Palmyra Twp., Lenawee Co., Mich. adjacent to SIMON D., following.

THAYER, RUEL was listed in the 1840 census index of Ogden Twp., Lenawee Co., Mich. Note JONAS, preceding; and BETSEY (as she named a son Ruel), preceding.

THAYER, RUFUS born ca. 1798, New Hampshire, and wife, MARY, born ca. 1804, Mass., were listed in the 1850 census of Medina Twp., Lenawee Co., Mich. with SIMEON, age 25; WILLIAM, age 23; ELECTA, age 12, all b. NY; and JOHN, age 11; MARY, age 8, both b. Ohio, in their household.

THAYER, SIMON D. was listed in the 1840 census index of Palmyra Twp., Lenawee Co., Mich.

THEED, EDWARD (See John B. Clement)

THOMAS, ANN (See Eli Packer)

THOMAS, CHARLES L., son of RANSON (following), born ca. 1814, and wife, SALLY F. (BAKER), daughter of Joseph (also see),
born ca. 1819, both in NY, were listed in the 1840 census index of Adrian Twp., Lenawee Co., Mich. Children: 1. CLARISSA A. b. 14 June 1838 (m. Wesley Reynolds, also see); 2. MARCELLINE R. (d. age 5, before 1850); 3. STATIRA E. (d. child, before 1850); 4. JEFFERSON R. (following); 5. XARA F.; 6. FREDERICK. Ref: P&BA-Len pg. 1085-6.

THOMAS, DAVID born ca. 1820, and wife, SELINA, born ca. 1821, both in England, were listed in the 1850 census of Cambridge Twp., Lenawee Co., Mich. with SELINA, age 7; HARRIET, age 3, both b. Mich.; and William Palmer, age 26, b. England, in their household.

THOMAS, ELFA (See A. W. Ellis)

THOMAS, HARRIET (See William Dutton)

THOMAS, HENRY, probably son of RANSOM (following), born ca. 1826, and wife, LOISA, born ca. 1827, both in NY, were listed in the 1850 census of Adrian Twp., Lenawee Co., Mich. with MARY J., age 3/12, b. Mich., in their household (next door to RANSOM).

THOMAS, ISAAC born ca. 1818, and wife, ELIZABETH, born ca. 1821, both in Ohio, were listed in the 1850 census of Ogden Twp., Lenawee Co., Mich. with FRANKLIN, age 5, b. Ind; and ALFRED S., age 1, b. Mich.; and David Comstock, age 66, born Rhode Island, in their household.

THOMAS, JEFFERSON R., son of CHARLES L. (preceding), born ca. 1848, married on 9 Dec. 1877 to IDA M. (SPEAR), daughter o George W. (also see). They settled in Adrian Twp., Lenawee Co., Mich. Children: 1. BRUCE b. 12 Jan. 1881; 2. CHARLES L. b. 15 Sept. 1882; 3. GROVE C. b. 1 July 1885; 4. GENEVIEVE b. 26 Jan. 1887. Ref: P&BA-Len pg. 1085-6.

THOMAS, JOHN Rev. (See Hugh Tolford)

THOMAS, LEMUEL S. born ca. 1815, Mass., and wife, SARAH, born ca. 1823, NY, were listed in the 1850 census of Ridgeway Twp., Lenawee Co., Mich. with JAMES, age 6; WILMINA, age 4; SELAH, age 2, all b. Mich., in their household.

THOMAS, MARY (See Henry Hawley)

THOMAS, MARY, age 31, born NY, was listed in the 1850 census of Tecumseh Twp., Lenawee Co., Mich. in a Drew household.

THOMAS, RANSOM born ca. 1788, Conn., and wife, CATHARINE (CURE), born ca. 1793, NY, moved from Penfield, Monroe Co., NY to Adrian Twp., Lenawee Co., Mich. by 1840. There were 9 children, names not

Pioneer Families of Southeastern Michigan

stated, except #3. CHARLES L. (preceding); and listed next door in the 1850 census of Adrian Twp. was HENRY (preceding). Ransom died in 1850. Ref: P&BA-Len pg. 1085-6.

THOMPSON, ALEXANDER born ca. 1804, Penn., and wife, JANE, born ca. 1805, Conn., were listed in the 1850 census of Madison Twp., Lenawee Co., Mich. with George Edmonds, age 24, b. NY, in their household.

THOMPSON, BENJAMIN, age 20, born NY, was listed in the 1850 census of Madison Twp., Lenawee Co., Mich. Note JEREMIAH D., following.

THOMPSON, BENONA born ca. 1791, and wife, ANNA, born ca. 1795, both in NY, were listed in the 1840 census index of Dover Twp., Lenawee Co., Mich.; and in the 1850 census with WALTER, age 23; SMITH, age 21; JEREMIAH, age 16, all b. NY; and SARAH A., age 12, b. Mich., in their household. SIDNEY (following) was listed next door in the census.

THOMPSON, CAROLINE H. (See John H. Bates)

THOMPSON, CHARLES W. born ca. 1819, and wife, BETSEY J., born ca. 1829, both in NY, were listed in the 1850 census of Fairfield Twp., Lenawee Co., Mich. with HARLAM P., age 2; MARY A., age 4/12, both b. Ohio, in their household.

THOMPSON, CHAUNCEY born ca. 1812, Mass., and wife, MARGARET, born ca. 1814, NY, were listed in the 1840 census index of Seneca Twp., Lenawee Co., Mich. with ESTHER, age 14, b. NY; ERASTUS, age 12; CHAUNCEY, age 9, both b. Ohio; ALONZO S., age 4; ALPHONSO, age 4, both b. Mich., in their household; and HARRIET A., age 20, b. Mass., in the household next door probably is related.

THOMPSON, CYNTHIA (See Joseph Reed)

THOMPSON, DUDLEY (See Samuel Lewis)

THOMPSON, DUNREATH (See Robert M. Bailey)

THOMPSON, EBENEZER born 1825, NY, and wife, NANCY, born ca. 1832, Mich., were listed in the 1850 census of Palmyra Twp., Lenawee Co., Mich. with JOHN F., age 4/12, b. Mich., in their household. It is probably this EBENEZER called of Clayton, Lenawee Co. who had known daughter, EMMA L. (probably b. after 1856) who married William Bancroft, son of Cornelius (also see).

THOMPSON, ELIAS born ca. 1790, and wife, CATHARINE, born ca. 1792, both in Penn., were listed in the 1840 census index of Fairfield Twp., Lenawee Co., Mich.; and in the 1850 census with WILLIAM H., age 31, b. Penn., in their household.

THOMPSON, ELIHU and wife, DESIRE, of Burlington, Otsego Co., NY were parents of HANNAH b. 17 Mar. 1782 (m. Arnold Pope, also see). Ref: P&BA-Len pg. 578-9.

THOMPSON, ELISA, age 40, born NY, was listed in the 1850 census of Tecumseh Twp., Lenawee Co., Mich. with ELIZABETH, age 15; JAMES, age 13, both b. Mich., all in a Culbertson household. Note JOSEPH, following, in Tecumseh Twp. in 1840 census index.

THOMPSON, EPHIAS? born ca. 1788, Conn., and ABIGAIL, born ca. 1790, NJ, were listed in the 1850 census of Ogden Twp., Lenawee Co., Mich. with ORRIN, age 22, b. NY, in their household.

THOMPSON, GEORGE and wife, AMARILLA, had six children, names not stated, except SARAH b. 7 Feb. 1842 (m/1 Gilbert M Pettys; m/2 Marshall Blanchard; m/3 Roswell H. Hicks, see all). Ref: P&BA-Len pg. 1121-2.

THOMPSON, GEORGE, probably son of WALTER (following), born ca. 1825, and wife, MARCIA, born ca. 1827, both in NY, were listed in the 1850 census of Dover Twp., Lenawee Co., Mich. with GEORGE, age 1, b. Mich., in their household (next door to WALTER).

THOMPSON, GEORGE W., age 23, and HENRY, age 19, both born NY, were listed in the 1850 census of Tecumseh Twp., Lenawee Co., Mich. in an Inn.

THOMPSON, HENRY born ca. 1802, and wife, SARAH, born ca. 1815, both in NY, were listed in the 1840 census index of Clinton Twp., Lenawee Co., Mich.; and in the 1850 census of Tecumseh Twp. with WILLIAM, age 24; JOHN, age 23; GEORGE, age 21, all b. NY; and CHARLES, age 19; HENRY, age 17; MARY, age 16; MARTHA, age 15, all b. Ohio; and SOPHIA, age 13; ELIZABETH, age 11; JOSEPH, age 10; FRANCES, age 7, all b. Mich., in their household.

THOMPSON, JAMES H. born ca. 1816, and wife, PHILENA, born ca. 1826, both b. NY, were listed in the 1850 census of Madison Twp., Lenawee Co., Mich. with ERASMUS D., age 8; MARTHA, age 5, born b. Mich., in their household.

THOMPSON, JEREMIAH D. born ca. 1790, and wife, ELIZABETH, born ca. 1790, both in NY, were listed in the 1840 census index of Madison Twp., Lenawee Co., Mich.; and in the 1850 census with WALTER, age 29; SILAS, age 26 (note following); CALEB A., age 24; HULDAH, age 24 (wife of Caleb?), and Henry Cook, age 12, all b. NY, in their household.

THOMPSON, JOHN married after 1828 to Mrs. ORA (PHELPS) WARNER, daughter of Silas, and widow of Russell Warner (see both). They remained in Manchester, Ontario Co., NY.

THOMPSON, JOHN (See Jonathan Rowley)

THOMPSON, JOHN R. Col. (See Anthony McCurran)

THOMPSON, JOSEPH was listed in the 1840 census index of Tecumseh Twp., Lenawee Co., Mich. Note ELISA, preceding.

THOMPSON, JOSEPH^3 (son of JOB^2; JOSEPH^1) born England, was a descendant of a Lincolnshire family. He married in England to BETSEY (ATKINSON) and had 6 children. She died there; and he afterwards came alone in 1838 to America. He died in Pleasant Valley, NY. Known son, JOSEPH ATKINSON (also see) was the only child who came to the US. Ref: P&BA-Len pg. 270-1.

THOMPSON, JOSEPH ATKINSON Rev., son of JOSEPH^3 (preceding), was born Halifax, Yorkshire, England. He came alone to the US in 1853, settling first in Herkimer Co., NY, and later in Geauga Co., Ohio, then Lucas Co., Ohio. In 1873, he moved to Lenawee Co., Mich. He married first to HELEN (IRONSIDE), daughter of Alexander of Aberdeen, Scotland, who had come alone to the US at age 22. She died 11 Apr. 1883. There were 3 children: 1. CAROLINE (m. Peter Gillette, Riga Twp.); 2. JOSEPH (to Cloud Co., KS); 3. ELLEN (m. Albert Sanderson, Lucas Co., O.) Joseph Atkinson married again on 7 Jan. 1886 to NORA (JONES), daughter of John (also see). Ref: P&BA-Len pg. 270-1.

THOMPSON, LEVI H. born ca. 1813, and wife, ELIZA, born ca. 1822, both in NY, were listed in the 1850 census of

Dover Twp., Lenawee Co., Mich. with Samuel Vaughn, age 28, b. NY, in the household.

THOMPSON, MARVIN born ca. 1821, and wife, MARTHA, born ca. 1831, both in NY, were listed in the 1850 census of Adrian Twp., Lenawee Co., Mich. with WILLIAM, age 6/12, b. Mich., in their household.

THOMPSON, MARY (See Cornelius Gillespie)

THOMPSON, SELA born 5 Apr. 1794, Providence, RI, moved with his parents to West Bloomfield, Ontario Co., NY, where she married William Lawrence (also see). Ref: P&BA-Len pg. 917-8.

THOMPSON, SIDNEY, probably son of BENONA (preceding), born ca. 1814, and wife, CATHARINE, born ca. 1813, both in NY, were listed in the 1850 census of Dover Twp., Lenawee Co., Mich. with MARY E., age 7; JEREMIAH, age 5, both b. Mich.; and Henry Barrager, age 16, b. NY, in their household (next door to BENONA).

THOMPSON, SILAS married MARY M. (MAYNARD), daughter of John (also see) of Adrian, Lenawee Co., Mich. Note SILAS in household of JEREMIAH D. (preceding).

THOMPSON, THOMAS P. born ca. 1816, and wife, RUTH, born ca. 1820, both in NY, were listed in the 1850 census of Adrian Twp., Lenawee Co., Mich. with WALTER E., age 5; JAMES W., age 2, both b. Mich., in their household.

THOMPSON, WALTER B. born ca. 1800, and wife, AZUBAH, born ca. 1810, both in NY, were listed in the 1840 census index of Dover Twp., Lenawee Co., Mich.; and in the 1850 census with WALTER G., age 17, b. NY; and HARRIET A., age 8, born Mich., in their household; with GEORGE (preceding) listed next door.

THOMPSON, WARREN born ca. 1817, NY, and wife, ALMIRA, born ca. 1828, Ohio, were listed in the 1850 census of Fairfield Twp., Lenawee Co., Mich. with LAURA E., age 3, b. Mich.; and Betsey White, age 63, b. NY, in their household.

THOMS, LETITIA (WILSON) Mrs. married Anson Backus (also see).

THORN, JAMES HENRY born 20 Jan. 1816, Dutchess Co., NY, and came to Michigan in 1834; and lived Detroit, Ypsilanti, and Farmington, Mich. by 1835. He purchased land in 1835 in Jefferson Twp., Hillsdale Co.; and on 15 Oct. 1836 married MARY (MONROE). Mary died there in 1852. There were 6 children, and the 4 following were surviving in 1888. 1. WRAY T. (to Minden, Nebr.); 2. EUGENE W. (Iowa); 3. JOSEPH E. (Iowa); 4. JAMES B. (following). James Henry married again to SARAH (DILLON) and they had 3 children: 5. HENRY; 6. MARY (m. M. F. Tuck); 7. WALDO. Ref: P&BA-Len pg. 905-7.

THORN, JAMES B., son of JAMES HENRY (preceding), born 25 June 1846, Jefferson Twp., Hillsdale Co., Mich., married on 27 Aug. 1871 to ELLEN C. (KILBORN), daughter of Luther (also see). They lived in Pittsford Twp., Hillsdale Co. for about a year, then moved to Hudson, Lenawee Co. No children named in sketch. Ref: P&BA-Len pg. 905-7.

THORN, JANE A. (See James W. Bradner)

THORN, MARTIN M., son of WEBSTER (following), born ca. 1818, NY, was listed in the 1850 census of Raisin Twp., Lenawee Co., Mich. with (probably wife?) SARAH W., age 24, born NJ; WEBSTER (following); PHEBE G., age 29, b. NY, in the household.

THORN, WEBSTER born ca. 1771, New Jersey, was listed in the 1840 census index of Raisin Twp., Lenawee Co., Mich.; and in the 1850 census in the household of son, MARTIN M. (preceding). Note: It is probably this WEBSTER listed in the "exempts" in the Militia of Woodbridge Twp., Middlesex Co., NJ in 1793. In 1778-1780 in Woodbridge Twp. were listed BENJAMIN; ISAAC; JACOB; & JOHN; & in Piscataway, MARGARET. Ref: New Jersey in 1793, by Norton; Revolutionary Census of New Jersey, by K. Stryker-Rodda.

THORNTON, RICHARD (See ? Cochran)
THORNTON, ZUBA (See Abraham Kells)

THORP, JESSE and probably brother, WILLIAM, were in a party that went overland to California in 1852 (See Edgar Alonzo Perry).

THORP, LUCINDA born ca. 1799, VT, was listed head of household in the 1840 census index of Tecumseh Twp., Lenawee Co., Mich.; and again in the 1850 census with LYMAN, age 22, b. NY (noted as deaf & dumb) in her household.

THRAP, JOEL Rev., son of Rev. JOSEPH (following), born 9 Apr. 1820, Ohio, married on 15 July 1845 to HANNAH E. (ROGERS) of Bel Air, Harford Co., MD. He came to Lenawee Co., Mich. and was connected with Adrian College. Children: 1. CATHARINE A. (m. Dr. T. M. Lewis; Ker City, Fla.); 2. J. ROSE (m. H. B. Roberts); 3. JOHN R. (d. Mar. 1873, age 14). Ref: P&BA-Len pg. 892-3.

THRAP, JOSEPH Rev. born 16 Oct. 1776, married in 1803 to JEMIMA (CAMP), daughter of Isaac of Virginia. About 1804, they moved to Muskingum Co., Ohio; and in 1807 to Licking Co., Ohio. He died 1 May 1866, age 90; and she died in July 1867. Eleven children, names not stated, except #9. Rev. JOEL (preceding). Ref: P&BA-Len pg. 892-3.

THROOP, SARAH (See Grant Wickwire)
THROOP, LOREN was listed in the 1840 census index of Palmyra Twp., Lenawee Co., Mich.
THROOP, AURILLA, age 16, born NY, with probably siblings, ELIZA L, age 12; HENRY L., age 8, both b. Mich., were all listed in the household of John Willetts, age 51, b. NJ, and wife, Aurilla, age 41, b. NY. It appears that these may be children of Aurilla, and probably stepchildren of John Willetts. Note LOREN, preceding.

THROUP see THROOP

THUMB, LUCINDA (See Aaron Morehouse)

THURBER, CALEB and wife, LOUISA (HOUGHTON), had known daughter, MARY L. b. 22 Dec. 1852, Washtenaw Co., Mich. (m. John Woodford, also see); also had 5 more children not listed in the sketch. Ref: P&BA-Len pg. 1197.

THURBER, JOSHUA W., so of SAMUEL H. (following), born 11 Apr. 1814, NY. He settled in Madison Twp., Lenawee Co., Mich.; and married REBECCA (FISK), daughter of Jabez (also see). Children: 1. GERTRUDE G. (m. Dr. George W. Bowen; d. Arkansas, 1865, interred in Lenawee Co.: note: she was not listed in the 1850 census, and may be same as CATHARINE, age 8, in household who was not named in the sketch); 2. MARY J. b. ca. 1845 (m. Dr. George W. Bowen, as 2nd wife; d. Toledo, O. on 25 Mar. 1880); 3. ISABELLA b. ca. 1848 (m. Stephen P. Richardson; d. 1876); 4. AMOS b. ca. 1850, d. age 9 by drowning). Ref: P&BA-Len pg. 408-9.

THURBER, NORMAN H., son of SAMUEL H. (following), born 22 Feb. 1816, Unity, Cheshire Co., NY, moved with parents to Canandaigua, Ontario Co., NY, and lived there till 5 Oct. 1834, when he moved to Fairfield Twp., Lenawee Co., Mich. In 1839, he moved to Seneca Twp. He married on 6 Apr. 1843 in Fairfield Twp. to EUNICE N. (CARPENTER), daughter of John H. (also see); settled first in Seneca Twp., and to Fairfield Twp. in 1853, and to Seneca Twp. in 1856. Daughter, SARAH D. b. 8 Mar. 1844, Seneca Twp. (m. Ezra Abbott, also see, in Medina on 1 Jan. 1862). Ref: P&BA-Len pg. 248-9.

THURBER, SAMUEL H., son of SAMUEL W. (following), born in Cheshire Co., NH, married SALLY (GAGE), daughter of John, and lived first in Unity, NH. In 1820, they removed to Canandaigua, Ontario Co., NY, where she died in 1821. He died 5 Mar. 1837. Children: 1. JEFFERSON G.; 2. ALMIRA (d. 1837); 3. ROBERT G. (following); 4. HORACE C.; 5. MARY G.; 6. JOSHUA W. (preceding); 7. NORMAN H. (preceding); 8. BETSEY G.; 9. SARAH D. Ref: P&BA-Len pg. 248-9.

THURBER, SAMUEL W. born Wales, married ? (CHASE), and they moved to New Hampshire. Known son, SAMUEL H. (preceding). Ref: P&BA-Len pg. 248-9.

THURBER, ROBERT G., son of SAMUEL H. (preceding), born ca. 1808, New Hampshire, married in 1835 in Canandaigua, Ontario Co., NY to ISABELLA born ca. 1815, Scotland; and they moved to Fairfield Twp., Lenawee Co., Mich. by 1836. He died in Feb. 1859, age 51. Children: 1. JAMES H. b. ca. 1836; 2. JANE A., b. ca. 1838; 3. NANCY H. b. ca. 1840; 4. JENNETT S. b. ca. 1843; 5. ALMYRA b. ca. 1846 (m. Edgar S. Hagaman, also see); 6. HARRIET A. b. ca. 1849. Ref: P&BA-Len pg. 1044-5. Note: James Service, age 66, b. Scotland, was listed next door, possibly father of Isabella?

THURSTON, DANIEL was listed in the 1840 census index of Fairfield Twp., Lenawee Co., Mich.

THURSTON, LYDIA, age 68, born New Hampshire, was listed in the 1850 census of Adrian Twp., Lenawee Co., Mich. in the household of Benjamin F. Gouldsberry, and wife, Eliza who was age 41, also b. NH, probably daughter of Lydia.

THURSTON, STEPHEN (See Samuel King)

TIBBETS, BENJAMIN was listed in the 1840 census index of Blissfield Twp., Lenawee Co., Mich.
TIBBETS, DORCAS (See Nathan Rice)
TIBBETS, HENRY was listed in the 1840 census index of Hudson Twp., Lenawee Co., Mich.
TIBBETS, HENRY, age 6, b. Mich., was listed, in the 1850 census of Woodstock Twp., Lenawee Co., Mich. in the household of Israel and Anna Darlington.
TIBBETS, HENRY, age 18, born NY, was listed in the 1850 census of Madison Twp., Lenawee Co., Mich. in the household of Cyrus J. and Polly Dodge, and then dittoed after him were children who may be Dodge or Tibbets: LUCY, age 16; PERMELIA, age 12; SARAH, age 10; BETSEY, age 7; LYDIA A., age 4.
TIBBETS, LEVI, age 13?, born Mich., was listed in the 1850 census of Dover Twp., Lenawee Co., Mich. in the household of John M. and Sarah Bird.

TICHENOR, JOSEPH probably of Venice, Cayuga Co., NY had known daughter, ALMIRA (m. Bishop Ames, also see). Note: This surname was prevalent in Essex Co., NJ; and a number moved to the Finger Lakes area of NY.
TICHENOR, PHILENA, age 13; JEROME, age 10; HENRY, age 8, all b. Mich., probably siblings, spelled "Tickner" were listed in the 1850 census of Rome Twp., Lenawee Co., Mich. in the household of Benjamin Slocum.

TICKNER see TICHENOR

TIEDEN, THEDA (See Joel Osborn)

TIERNEY, MICHAEL (See Hugh Davitt)

TIFFANY, ALEXANDER, son of SYLVESTER (following), born 16 Oct. 1796, Niagara, Canada, married on 3 Sept. 1823 to ABIGAIL B. (ROBINSON), daughter of Dr. Gain (also see). They moved to NY, and then in 1832 to Palmyra Twp., Lenawee Co., Mich. He died 14 Jan. 1868, age 72. There were 11 children, names not stated, and known were from the 1850 census of Adrian Twp.: ALEXANDER R., age 24; FRANCES M., age 18, both b. NY; and GEORGE T., age 16; MARGARET T., age 5, both b. Mich., in their household. Ref: P&BA-Len pg. 407-8.

TIFFANY, BARTON was listed in the 1840 census index of Scipio Twp., Hillsdale Co., Mich. adjacent to OLNA, following.

TIFFANY, ERASTUS called a "native of Roxbury, Delaware Co., NY" married ELIZA J. (MACKEY), daughter of Elias (also see). They moved to Wisconsin in 1855; and later to Adrian, Lenawee Co., Mich. where he died in 1859. Known daughter, ELLA, bvorn 18 Feb. 1860 (m. J. Henry Uloth, also see). Eliza J. married again, husband's name not given, and died in Fairfield Twp., Lenawee Co. on 23 Dec. 1875. Ref: P&BA-Len pg. 783-4.

TIFFANY, FRED K. married CHARITY (DECKER), daughter of John of Pennsylvania. Fred K. died in Canada at age 67. Known daughter, ADDIE (m. GEORGE S., following). Ref: P&BA-Len pg. 407-8.

TIFFANY, GEORGE S., son of ALEXANDER (preceding), married ADDIE (TIFFANY), daughter of FRED K. (preceding). Children: 1. FREDERICK b. 12 Oct. 1867, Jackson, Mich.; 2. ABBIE G. b. 27 Apr. 1873 (d. age 5 wks); 3. GEORGE H. b. 12 Aug. 1874. Ref: P&BA-Len pg. 407-8.

TIFFANY, GIDEON Dr. and wife, SARAH (DEAN) came to America and settled first in Norton, Mass. They later moved to New Hampshire. About 1792, some sons moved to Canada. Known son, SYLVESTER (following). Ref: P&BA-Len pg. 407-8.

TIFFANY, OLNA was listed in the 1840 census index of Scipio Twp., Hillsdale Co., Mich. adjacent to BARTON, preceding.

TIFFANY, REUBEN was listed in the 1840 census index of Napoleon Twp., Jackson Co., Mich. adjacent to RUFUS F., following. Note ALEXANDER, preceding.

TIFFANY, RUFUS F. "of Lenawee Co., Mich." purchased land in Napoleon Twp., Jackson Co., Mich. in 1834; and was listed there in the 1840 census index adjacent to REUBEN, preceding. Note ALEXANDER, preceding.

TIFFANY, SYLVESTER, son of Dr. GIDEON (preceding), went to Niagara, Canada from New Hampshire ca. 1792. Known son, ALEXANDER (preceding), was born there. Ref: P&BA-Len pg. 407-8.

TIFFIN, D. (male; See William Davison)

TIFFIN, WILLIAM born ca. 1814, Kentucky, and wife, CATHARINE, born ca. 1829, Ohio, were listed in the 1850 census of Tecumseh Twp., Lenawee Co., Mich. with ALICE ANN, age 2, b. Mich., in their household.

TILDEN, JOSEPH born ca. 1809, and wife, DEBORAH, born ca. 1810, both in Mass., were listed in the 1840 census index of Raisin Twp., Lenawee Co., Mich.; and in the 1850 census of Tecumseh Twp. with JOSEPH, age 19, b. Mass.; and JULIA, age 9, b. Mich., in their household.

TILDEN, WALLACE (See Thomas Boyd)

TILFORD, JANE (See John Boyce)

TILLYAR, WILLIAM born 13 Oct. 1779, and wife, MARY (GRAY), born 22 Nov. 1782, lived in Seneca Co., NY. He died there on 11 Aug. 1833; and she died 17 Jan. 1836. Known daughter, CHARLOTTE b. 24 Aug. 1819, Ovid, NY (m/1 Richard Osborn; m/2 Edwin Cook, see both). Ref: P&BA-Len pg. 352-3.

TILSON, ALMENA Mrs. was the daughter of Ira Holloway (also see).

TILTON, ADELINE born ca. 1818, New Hampshire, was listed in the 1850 census of Tecumseh Twp., Lenawee Co., Mich. in a Baldwin household. Note JOSEPH, following.

TILTON, JOSEPH moved his family after 1803 from Cheshire Co., NH to Montgomery Co., NY. About 1831, they settled near Coldwater, Branch Co., Mich. He died there at age 64, and his wife died age 87. Known son, WILLIAM W. (following). Ref: P&BA-Len pg. 878-881. Also note ADELINE, preceding.

TILTON, JOSEPH B. was listed in the 1840 census index of Franklin Twp., Lenawee Co., Mich.; and it is probably he, age 45, born NY, in the 1850 census in the household of Almon Campburn and wife, Esther who was born ca. 1830, Mich., possibly his daughter.

TILTON, WILLIAM W., son of JOSEPH (preceding), born 21 July 1803, Cheshire Co., NH, moved to Montgomery Co., NY with his parents. When of age, he moved to Raisin Twp., Lenawee Co., Mich., and it is probably he listed in the 1830 census of Lenawee Co., Territory of Mich., age 20-30. He married in 1829 to MATILDA (SISSON), daughter of Thomas (also see) of Raisin Twp. Children: 1. ALBERT b. 8 Dec. 1830 (d. 18 Jan. 1870, leaving a wife & 3 children, who afterwards moved to Colorado); 2. HARRIET b. 6 Oct. 1832 (m. James B. Colvin, also see); 3. ABIGAIL b. 13 Mar. 1840 (m. Alonzo Bean, Raisin Twp.); 4. GEORGE W. b. 17 May 1842. Matilda died 27 May 1864, Tecumseh Twp. William W. married again in 1870 to Mrs. CYNTHIA (SPAFFORD) BISSEL, widow of Theodore Bissel, also see. They moved to Tecumseh, Mich. Ref: P&BA-Len pg. 878-81 with portrait.

TINGLEY, BENJAMIN was listed in the 1830 census of Oakland Co., Mich. Territory, with males: 1 15-20; 1 29-30; female: 1 15-20. There was a BENJAMIN in Rives Twp., Jackson Co., Mich. in 1840. Note REUBEN R. (following).

TINGLEY, DANIEL^1 came from Scotland "with 2 brothers" and settled in what is now Sussex Co., NY. (Note: In 1778-1780 there was a DANIEL listed in Mendham, Morris Co., NJ; and in 1783, there was an EBENEZER in Mendham). Daniel married MARGARET (VAN PELT) born NJ, and reared a family in Sussex Co.; resided in New York City for a time, but returned to Sussex Co. They moved to Seneca Co., NY where he died age 75/80. Afterwards, Margaret went to Adrian, Lenawee Co., Mich. to live with a son, and died there at age 88. Known son, SAMUEL^2 (following). Ref: P&BA-Len pg. 863-4.

TINGLEY, JOHN was listed in the 1830 census of Macomb Co., Mich. Terr. with males: 1 und 5; 1 20-30; 1 30-40; females; 1 und 5; 1 5-10; 1 20-30; 1 50-60.

TINGLEY, JOHN H.^{3}, son of SAMUEL^2 (following), b. 25 Dec. 1810, Sussex Co., NJ, came to Adrian Twp., Lenawee Co., Mich. from Seneca Co., NY about 1832/3. He sold to his brother, and moved to Rollin Twp. before the 1840 census. He married in 1837 to POLLY (LAMB), daughter of Roswell (also see). Children; 1. JANE E. b. 16 Aug. 1839 (d. 20 Mar. 1859, Rollin Twp.); 2. JOHN H. b. 8 June 1841 (m. Mary J. Rice; d. 30 Oct. 1868, leaving a child); 3. HOMER b. 1 Mar. 1845 (m. Helen Howd, dau. of Harvey; Hillsdale Co.); 4. ZACHARY T. b. 31 Mar. 1847 (m. L. Marlatt, Rollin Twp.); 5. NANCY b. 8 May 1849 (m. Marion Hare, Rollin Twp.); 6. SAMUEL D. (following); 7. MARY A. b. 7 Dec. 1853; 8. JOANNA b. 15 Nov. 1856. Ref: P&BA-Len pg. 728-9.

TINGLEY, REUBEN was listed in the 1840 census index of Macon Twp., Lenawee Co., Mich., adjacent to SAMUEL.

TINGLEY, REUBEN K. was listed in the 1840 census index of Moscow Twp., Hillsdale Co., Mich.

TINGLEY, REUBEN R. was born 18 Sept. 1828, Bloomfield Twp., Oakland Co., Mich. He moved to Jackson, Jackson Co., Mich. in 1841; and served in the Mexican War in 1848 in Co. H, Capt. Miles Co.; Col. Stockton's Regt; Gen. James Shields Div. He settled in Hanover, Jackson Co., Mich. Note BENJAMIN, preceding.

TINGLEY, SAMUEL^2, son of DANIEL^1 (preceding), born Sussex Co., NY, married in 1806 to REBECCA (HOLCOMB), daughter of John H. (also see). They moved to Seneca Co., NY; and then about 1833 to Adrian, Lenawee Co., Mich. She died in 1848 in Adrian Twp. Known children: 1. JULIA b. ca. 1808 (m. Jonathan Ball, also see); 2. JOHN H.^{3} (preceding); 3.

Pioneer Families of Southeastern Michigan

SAMUEL³ (following); 4. NANCY (m. Butler Treat, also see, on 15 Apr. 1840). Ref: P&BA-Len pg. 863-4; 1167-8.

TINGLEY, SAMUEL³, son of SAMUEL² (preceding), born 12 May 1818, Seneca Co., NY, married in 1844 in Adrian Twp., Lenawee Co., Mich. to JOHANNA (ENGELL), daughter of Jacob (also see) born 1823, NY. She died 23 Aug. 1883, Adrian Twp. Children: 1. ALFRED D. b. ca. 1845 (to Boston, Mass.); 2. CHARLES E. (Adrian Twp.); 3. SAMUEL O.; 4. ESTHER (twin of Ella); 5. ELLA. Ref: P&BA-Len pg. 863-4.

TINGLEY, SAMUEL, possibly son of REUBEN (preceding), born ca. 1801, NJ, and wife, MARY A., born ca. 1815, NY, may be they listed in the 1840 census index of Macon Twp., Lenawee Co., Mich. (adjacent to REUBEN); and in the 1850 census with JOHN, age 14; SARAH A., age 8; REUBEN, age 5; FRANCES A., age 2, all b. Mich., in their household. MARY A., age 13, b. Mich., in another household, may relate to this family.

TINGLEY, SAMUEL D.⁴, son of JOHN H.³ (preceding), married on 12 Feb. 1874 in Adrian Twp., Lenawee Co., Mich. to ELIZABETH ADELLE (McCURRAN), daughter of Anthony (also see), and settled in Rollin Twp.. Known children: 1. MARY A. b. 1 Mar. 1882; 2. STEPHEN S. b. 17 Sept. 1886. Ref: P&BA-Len pg. 876-7.

TINNEY, OLIVE (See Thomas Tobey)

TITUS, DEWIT C. was listed in the 1840 census index of Tecumseh Twp., Lenawee Co., Mich. adjacent to ISAAC (following).

TITUS, ELIZABETH was listed in the 1840 census index of Adrian Twp., Lenawee Co., Mich. Note FRANKLIN, following. Was Elizabeth Mapes originally Elizabeth Titus?

TITUS, FRANKLIN born ca. 1827, and wife, SARAH J., born ca. 1832, Mich., were listed in the 1850 census of Adrian Twp., Lenawee Co., Mich. with Elizabeth Mapes, age 51, b. NY, in their household.

TITUS, ISAAC was listed in the 1840 census index of Tecumseh Twp., Lenawee Co., Mich. adjacent to DEWIT C. (preceding).

TITUS, ISAAC was listed in the 1840 census index of Woodstock Twp., Lenawee Co., Mich.

TITUS, MAY (See Alonzo James)

TITUS, MINERVA (See Alonzo James)

TITUS, STEPHEN was listed in the 1840 census index of Raisin Twp., Lenawee Co., Mich.

TOBEY, EZRA, age 35, born NY, was listed in the 1850 census of Palmyra Twp., Lenawee Co., Mich. in the household of Lester P. Clark.

TOBEY, THOMAS born ca. 1779/81, and wife, OLIVE (TINNEY), born ca. 1783, both in Mass., moved to York, Livingston Co., NY; and about 1844 to Raisin Twp., Lenawee Co., Mich. They were listed in the 1850 census with THOMAS J., age 24; ELIZABETH A., age 18; JULIA H*., age 15, all b. NY, in their household. They later moved to Adrian. She died in 1857, age 64. He afterwards went to Ovid Twp., Shiawassee Co., Mich. where he died in Sept. 1865, age 86. Note: *The following sketch called her "Juliet H.," born ca. 1832, dau. of "Benjamin" & Olive (Tinney); and she m. Morgan M. Florance (also see); however the census does not bear out her age or father's name. Ref: P&BA-Len pg. 681.

TOBIAS, CHARLES M., son of MOSES (following), born 5 July 1827, Tompkins Co., NY, lived a number of states before settling in Dover Twp., Lenawee Co., Mich. in 1867. He married on 9 Feb. 1859 to ANGELINA (McLOUTH), a native of Dover Twp. Children: 1. ARTHUR W.; 2. ERNEST E.; 3. BURTON E.; 4. ELLA F. Ref: P&BA-Len pg. 222-3.

TOBIAS, EZRA born ca. 1813, NY, was listed in the 1850 census of Dover Twp., Lenawee Co., Mich. with probably wife (second?), FAYLINA?, age 19, b. VT; and in the household were LORENZO H., age 16; FREDERCIKA, age 15, both b. NY; and JOSHUA C., age 14; BETSEY A., age 12; EZRA H., age 4; FYLINA, age 1, all b. Ohio, in their household.

TOBIAS, MOSES, born Ulster Co., NY, and wife, JANE (MANNING), born Dutchess Co., NY, settled after their marriage in Tompkins Co., NY. In 1834, they removed to Ontario Co., NY; and in 1851 to Branch Co., Mich. Afterwards they settled in Calhoun Co., and finally to White Pigeon, St. Joseph Co., where they remained. There were 2 sons & 5 daughters, and only mentioned eldest child, CHARLES M. (preceding). Ref: P&BA-Len pg. 222-3.

TOBY see TOBEY

TODD, DANIEL MD, son of JAMES B. (following), born 17 Dec. 1827, Peterboro, New Hampshire, moved with his parents to Genesee Co., NY. As a young man, he went first to Wisconsin, then to Medina Twp., Lenawee Co., Mich. to visit a sister. He returned to NY where he married on 22 Mar. 1854 to JULIA S. (WELCH), daughter of James (also see), and they settled in Lenawee Co., Mich. In 1861, they moved to Canandaigua, Lenawee Co.; and in 1865 to Madison Twp.; and about 1870 into Adrian. Children: 1. JAMES FREDERICK b. 12 Sept. 1856, Madison Twp.; 2. HELEN J. b. 26 Feb. 1858; 3. EMMA L. b. 12 May 1861; 4. WILLIAM W. b. 6 May 1866. Ref: P&BA-Len pg. 857-8.

TODD, FREDERICK J. (See William TenBroeck Schermerhorn; also note JAMES FREDERICK in household of DANIEL, preceding).

TODD, GABRIEL H. born ca. 1805, Conn., and wife, MARY P. (IRELAND), born ca. 1806, NY, lived in New York City in 1830. About 1834, they moved to Adrian Twp., and by 1840 to Rome Twp., Lenawee Co., Mich. Children (with some ages from the 1850 census): 1. ELIZABETH (m. William Beecher); 2. JOHN H. (following); 3. RACHEL A., age 19 (m. Porter L. Sword, son of James, also see; lived Cleveland, O.); 4. JACOB W., age 16 (to Colorado); 5. OSCAR, age 13 (Los Angeles, CA); 6. GEORGE, age 11 (served Civil War); 7. CHARLES, age 10 (served Civil War); 8. ELBERT S., age 7 (Dr. of Divinity; Baltimore, MD); 9. HELEN A. "AMANDA," age 4 (prob. she who d. age 14). Ref: P&BA-Len pg. 901-2. Note: In the household in 1850 was Elizabeth Palmer, age 22, b. NY; & Alice Champenois, age 16, both b. NY.

TODD, HARVEY born ca. 1802, and wife, MARIA, born ca. 1803, both in Conn., were listed in Madison Twp., Lenawee Co., Mich. by 1840; and in the 1850 census with HANNAH, age 24, b. Conn.; and LYDIA J., age 12; ALMIRA H. b. 9 Nov. 1839, Adrian Twp. (m. John A. Townsend, also see); HARVEY H., age 8; WILLIAM A., age 6; MARY A., age 3, all b. Mich., in their household. Also in the household was Barbara Nash, age 78, b. Conn., possibly mother-in-law.

TODD, JAMES B., son of JOHN, born 25 Nov. 1787, Peterboro, NY, married on 8 Feb. 1816 to SARAH (APPLETON), daughter of Isaac (also see). In 1828, they removed to Byron, Genesee Co., NY. He died there 29 May 1863, and she died in Mar. 1884. Children: 1. ISAAC A. (Byron, NY); 2. RACHEL D. b. 3 May 1819, NH (m. Thomas F. Moore, also see); 3. SARAH; 4. EMILY A. (m. Alfred D. Hall, also see); 5. JOHN; 6. Dr. DANIEL (preceding); 7. SAMUEL; 8. JAMES F. Ref: P&BA-Len pg. 857-8; 915-6.

TODD, JOHN H., son of GABRIEL (preceding), born ca. 1830, NY, came to Lenawee Co., Mich. with his parents. He married ca. 1853 to SUSAN M. (HOXTER), daughter of William (also see). They lived in Rome Twp. until 1862, then moved to Rollin Twp. Children: 1. MARY b. 13 Sept. 1853 (m. Eugene Perkins); 2. IDA J. b. 22 July 1855 (m. Edwin Childs); 3. HEMAN H. b. 30 apr. 1858 (m. Rosa Chatfield); 4. CHARLES H. b. 17 Dec. 1876. Ref: P&BA-Len pg. 901-2.

TODD, LUCRETIA E. (See James B. Hood)

TODD, LUTHER born ca. 1824, NY, was listd in the 1850 census of Adrian Twp., Lenawee Co., Mich.

TODD, LUTHER L. (See Edward Hodge; also note name in family of RANSOM, following).

TODD, MARY of Yorkshire, England (See John Taylor).

TODD, MORRIS born ca. 1814, and wife, NANCY, born ca. 1821, both in NY, were listed in the 1850 census of Adrian Twp., Lenawee Co., Mich. with DAVID B., age 3; HOMER, age 1/12, both b. Mich., in their household.

TODD, RANSOM born ca. 1806, and wife, SALLY A., born ca. 1809, were listed in the 1840 census index of Adrian Twp., Lenawee Co., Mich. (adjacent to SAMUEL, following); and in the 1850 census with SARAH J., age 20; LUTHER L., age 18; HENRY J., age 16; ALVIRA, age 14; CYNTHIA L., age 12; SUSAN, age 10; MARTHA, age 7; NEWELL, age 4; ELMER E., age 1, all b. Mich., in their household. Note: They were listed in the 1830 census of Ypsilanti, Washtenaw Co., Mich. Territory.

TODD, SAMUEL was listed in the 1830 census of Lenawee Co., Mich. Territory with males: 1 5-10; 2 15-20; 1 30-40; 1 50-60; and female: 1 40-50 in the household. In the 1840 census index of Lenawee Co., Mich. there were 2 men by that name in Adrian Twp.

TOLCHARD, MARY (See Alpheus F. Haas)

TOLFORD, HUGH born ca. 1790, and wife, HANNAH (CURRIER), born ca. 1794, both in Grafton Co., NH, lived first in Danbury, NH, but in Apr. 1833 moved first to Madison Twp., Lenawee Co., Mich., and in 1834 to Dover Twp. He died 23 Jan. 1861; and she died 19 Mar. 1866. They were listed in the 1850 census of Dover Twp. with the children #3, 4 & 5 in their household. 1. PHILLIP b. ca. 1822 (lived Madison Twp. in 1850 census); 2. SARAH E. (m. Rev. John Thomas); 3. JOHN W. (following); 4. LYDIA J. (m. D. J. Furman, Dover Twp.); 5. JOSEPH P. b. ca. 1836, Mich. (m. Harriet Camp, dau. of Ambrose, also see); 6. THOMAS (deceased by 1888); 7. MARY (deceased by 1888). Ref: P&BA-Len pg. 683.

TOLFORD, JOHN W., son of HUGH (preceding), born 14 Jan. 1826, moved to Dover Twp., Lenawee Co., Mich. with his parents. He married first to SALLY (TENBROOK), who died 31 Oct. 1852, leaving a son: 1. FRANK (m. Jane Leacox). John W. married again to MATILDA (STUMBAUGH), daughter of John (also see). Children: 2. JOHN C. (m/1 Katie Ellis; m/2 Elizabeth McCabe); 3. HUGH P. (m. Anna Lucas; Weston, Mich.); 4. SARAH J. (m. R. A. McKnight); 5. MARY A. (m. E. T. Crowe; Butler Co., Ind.); 6. ROBERT J. (Dover Twp.); 7. GEORGE W. (d. age 2). Ref: P&BA-Len pg. 683.

TOLFORD, WILLIAM born ca. 1790, New Hampshire; and wife, MARY, born ca. 1805, NY, were listed in the 1840 census index of Madison Twp., Lenawee Co., Mich.; and in the 1850 census with HENRY W., age 20; SARAH J., age 18; both b. NY, in their household. Note WILLIAM D., following.

TOLFORD, WILLIAM D. born ca. 1825, NY, was listed in the 1850 census of Hudson Twp., Lenawee Co., Mich.

TOMER, CLARISSA born 1801, New Jersey (See Nathaniel Russ).

TOMER, NANCY, sister of CLARISSA, preceding (See Ira Rogers).

TOMPKINS, CHARLES born ca. 1810, and wife, BETSEY, born ca. 1807, both in NY, were listed in the 1840 census index of Woodstock Twp., Lenawee Co., Mich.; and in the 1850 census with THOMAS, age 13; POLLY, age 7; MARGARET, age 5; ALVIN, age 10/12, all b. Mich., in their household.

TOMPKINS, ELIJAH born ca. 1799, and wife, ABIGAIL, born ca. 1802, both in NY, were listed in the 1850 census of Medina Twp., Lenawee Co., Mich. with FANNY M., age 22, b. Ohio; and WILLIAM H., age 20; JAMES, age 18, both b. NY; and DAVID V., age 13; & GEORGE, age 5, both b. Ohio, in their household.

TOMPKINS, IDA (See Levi C. Richmond)

TOMPKINS, IRENE born 11 May 1793, Waterbury, Conn., married Dr. Nathan Town (also see). Ref: P&BA-Len pg. 874-5.

TOMPKINS, JOHN born ca. 1800, and wife, ELISA, born ca. 1801, both in New Jersey, were listed in the 1850 census of Tecumseh Twp., Lenawee Co., Mich. with MARY ANN, age 17; PHOEBE, age 13, both b. NY, in their household.

TOMPKINS, LEONARD P. Rev. born ca. 1822, and wife, EMILY S., born ca. 1825, both in NY, are listed in the 1850 census of Adrian Twp., Lenawee Co., Mich.

TOMPKINS, PRISCILLA (See John Iveson²)

TOOKER, IRA, son of REUBEN, born ca. 1816, NY, and wife, PHEBE, born ca. 1817, Mass., were listed in the 1850 census of Palmyra Twp., Lenawee Co., Mich. with HANNAH B., age 13, b. NY; and AMOS, age 12; JEROME, age 9, both b. Mich., in the household; and later had known daughter, CLARA (m. Theophilus Davis, also see).

TOOKER, REUBEN born ca. 1779, NY, and wife, REBECCA, born ca. 1782, Mass., were listed in the 1840 census index of Palmyra Twp., Lenawee Co., Mich.; and in the

Pioneer Families of Southeastern Michigan

1850 census with son, IRA (preceding), and family in their household. Note: There were 2 REUBEN listed in the 1800 census index of Orange Co., NY.

TORBIN see TORBRON

TORBRON, ANDREW born Scotland, and wife, HANNAH (HARE), born Dutchess Co., NY, settled first in Duanesburg, Schenectady Co., NY (which was Albany Co. till 1809). In 1829, they removed to Monroe Co., NY, where he died in 1831. She afterwards came to Dover Twp., Lenawee Co., Mich. where she made her home with her sons until her death ca. 1844. Sons: 1. WILLIAM (following(; 2. STEPHEN (following); 3. NICHOLAS; 4. GEORGE (following). Ref: P&BA-Len pg. 495-6.

TORBRON, GEORGE, son of ANDREW (preceding), born ca. 1815, and wife, AMANDA M., born ca. 1823, both in NY, were listed in the 1850 census of Madison Twp., Lenawee Co., Mich. with ALMA A., age 8; MARY E., age 1, both b. Mich.; then MATILDA, age 16, b. NY (too old to be child of Amanda); and listed last were Francis English, age 11; Eliza English, age 9; Mary English, age 6; Cynthia J. English, age 13, all b. Mich., in their household.

TORBRON, STEPHEN, son of ANDREW (preceding), born 18 Aug. 1805, Schenectady Co., NY, moved with his parents to Monroe Co., NY. He married there in Oct. 1832 to LYDIA (WELLS) born ca. 1810, Ontario Co., NY. In 1834, they removed to Madison Twp., Lenawee Co., but after a year settled in Dover Twp. In the 1850 census of Dover Twp., they listed GILBERT, age 14, b. Mich. (possibly the same who is listed in the household of WILLIAM, see following); and Newton McLouth, age 18, b. Mich., in their household. Lydia died 18 Jan. 1870. Stephen married again on 20 Mar. 1872 in Ypsilanti, Mich. to MARY E. (WHITMORE), daughter of Earl (also see). No children were listed in the sketch. Ref: P&BA-Len pg. 495-6.

TORBRON, WILLIAM, son of ANDREW (preceding), born ca. 1805, and wife, LUCY, born ca. 1809, both in NY, were listed in the 1840 census index of Dover Twp., Lenawee Co., Mich.; and in the 1850 census with JANE, age 19 (may be she listed again in a White household in 1850); ANDREW, age 18, both b. NY; and GILBERT, age 14 (may be he listed again in household of Stephen; m. Mary A. Wilber, dau. of William J., also see); RICHARD, age 10; LYDIA, age 8; WILLIAM, age 6; WILLARD, age 4, all b. Mich., in their household.

TORREY, CICERO, son of NORMAN (following), born 27 July 1837, Blissfield Twp., Lenawee Co., Mich., married on 1 Nov. 1883 to H. VIOLA (ANDERSON), born Wright Twp., Hillsdale Co., Mich. Son, NORMAN. Ref: P&BA-Len pg. 575-6.

TORREY, DAVID, son of WILLIAM (who had come from Conn. ca. 1750), born Williamstown, Berkshire Co., Mass., married ESTHER (WOODCOCK) in Williamstown. Known son, NORMAN (following). Ref: P&BA-Len pg. 575-6.

TORREY, GEORGE N., son of NOAH (following), born 1 Apr. 1835, Adrian Twp., Lenawee Co., Mich., was said to have lived in Rome Twp. in 1844, but was listed in Adrian Twp. in the 1850 census. He married on 15 Oct. 1862 to HARRIET L. (SELLECK), daughter of Ebenezer L. (also see), and settled in Rome Twp. Daughter: ETHEL I. b. 31 Aug. 1882. Ref: P&BA-Len pg. 1095-6.

TORREY, JOHN born Willimstown, Mass., and wife, RUTH (TYRELL), born Middletown, Conn., had known daughter, RUTH (m. Stephen Frazier who was born 8 Mar. 1773, also see). Ref: P&BA-Len pg. 948-50.

TORREY, NOAH, son of NOAH, born ca. 1809, Herkimer Co., NY, married THANKFUL (HOWES), daughter of Ezra (also see). In 1830, they moved to Adrian Twp., Lenawee Co., Mich.; and in 1844 to Rome Twp.; but returned to Adrian Twp. by the 1850 census. In that census, Thankful, age 32, was listed in the household of Thomas and Priscilla Jeffery; and Noah, age 41, and son, GEORGE N. (preceding), were listed in the household of Amos Howes (also see). Noah later went to Colorado and from there to California in 1851. He returned to Rome Twp., but went again to Colorado; and in 1880 returned to Rome Twp. to live with his son. He died 3 Jan. 1887, age 78. Ref: P&BA-Len pg. 1095-6.

TORREY, NORMAN, son of DAVID (preceding), born 24 June 1807, Williamstown, Berkshire Co., Mass., married there on 21 Sept. 1830 to ANN (KRIGER) born ca. 1805. They departed for Michigan, and settled in Blissfield Twp., Lenawee Co. In the 1850 census they listed: 1. CAROLINE, age 17 (deceased before 1888); 2. CICERO (preceding); 3. EVEREL b. 21 Mar. 1839 (lived Blissfield in 1888); 4. ELIZA, age 7 (deceased before 1888). Ref: P&BA-Len pg. 575-6.

TORREY, REUBEN was listed in the 1840 census index of Franklin Twp., Lenawee Co., Mich.

TOWER, CHESTER born ca. 1822, and wife, LOUISA, born ca. 1826, both in NY, were listed in the 1850 census of Cambridge Twp., Lenawee Co., Mich. with RHODOLPHUS, age 4, b. Mich., in their household (next door to PHOEBE, following).

TOWER, DEBORAH (See Ansel Ford)

TOWER, ERVIN see ERVIN TOWN

TOWER, JOSEPH P. and wife, CYNTHIA (PULLEN) born ca. 1794, Rhode Island, lived in Phelps, Ontario Co., NY in 1827. It may be they listed in the 1840 census index of Plymouth, Wayne Co., Mich. They apparently moved to Rollin Twp., Lenawee Co. before 1850, as son, JOSEPH H., age 38, b. NY, is listed head of household with CYNTHIA, age 56; and daughters, CORNELIA N., age 22; ANNA, age 20, born b. NY, in the household. Known daughter, ELIZABETH B. b. 22 Feb. 1827, Phelps, NY (m. George M. Lewis, also see). Ref: P&BA-Len pg. 1125-7.

TOWER, PHILO Rev. and wife, CYNTHIA D. (BEECHER) of Rochester, NY, were parents of MARY ADELIA BEECHER (m. Andrew Howell, also see). Ref: P&BA-Len pg. 1036-7.

TOWER, PHOEBE J., age 28, born NY, was listed head of household in the 1850 census of Cambridge Twp., Lenawee Co., Mich. (next door to CHESTER, preceding) with ANGELINE, age 9; ALBERT, age 7; CARLTON, age 4, all b. Mich., in her household.

TOWER, W. H. (See Enos Canniff)

TOWN also see TOWNE

TOWN, CALVIN, son of WILLIAM (following), born 17 June 1824, St. Lawrence Co., NY, moved with his parents to

Liberty Twp., Jackson Co., Mich. He married on 6 Jan. 1847 to SABRA J. (STRONG) born 13 July 1827. There were 7 children, one of whom did not survive (name not stated): 1. HELEN A. (m. G. M. Doty); 2. JAMES; 3. WILBUR W. (following); 4. INEZ I. (m. J. R. Newman); 5. EMELINE P.; 6. BERTIE A. Ref: History of Jackson Co., Mich., 1881, pg. 956-7. Note: It is probably this Mrs. Sabra Town who married on 16 Mar. 1869 to Nicholas P. Houghtalin (also see).

TOWN, ERVIN born ca. 1815, NY, may actually be ERVIN TOWER (as the handwriting is poor in the census), and wife, HANNAH, born ca. 1822, both in NY, were listed in the 1850 census of Madison Twp., Lenawee Co., Mich. with NANCY, age 2, b. Mich.; and Jesse Birdsall, age 29, and Diantha Birdall, age 19, both b. NY, in their household.

TOWN, GEORGE F., son of Dr. NATHAN (following), born ca. 1825, Canada, came to Lenawee Co., Mich. with his parents. He married ROSANNA born ca. 1828, NY. They were listed in the 1850 census of Rollin Twp. with ALPHONSE, age 3, b. Mich., in their household.

TOWN, HENRY and wife, moved in 1844 from Orleans Co., NY to Spring Arbor Twp., Jackson Co., Mich. He died there on 19 Dec. 1845. Children: 1. GEORGE W.; 2. KATE L. (m. Ambrose Crouch). Ref: History of Jackson Co., Mich., pg. 1063.

TOWN, NATHAN Dr. was born ca. 1798, Mass., and went to Herkimer Co., NY as a young man. He married on 25 Mar. 1813 to IRENE (TOMPKINS) who was born ca. 1793, Waterbury, Conn. After the War of 1812, they moved to Canada. They remained there until 1836, then removed to Rollin Twp., Lenawee Co., Mich. where they were listed in the 1840 census index. He died 28 Oct. 1854, age 62; and she died in July 1859, age 66. They were listed in the 1850 census of Rollin Twp. with only the last child in their household. Children: 1. ELIZA; 2. JULIA; 3. CORNELIA; 4. GEORGE F. (preceding); 5. MARY S. b. ca. 1828, Canada (prob. she who m. Thomas Alchin, also see); 6. Dr. WILLIAM B. b. 23 July 1830, Norwich, Oxford Co., Canada (m. Elmina C. Smith, dau. of Americus, also see, on 27 Oct. 1853). Ref: P&BA-Len pg. 874-5. Note resemblance to ROBERT, following.

TOWN, NATHAN was listed in the 1840 census index of Clinton Twp., Lenawee Co., Mich.

TOWN, ROBERT of Lee, Mass. was the father of HANNAH (m. Anson Backus, also see, before 1818, and went to Herkimer Co., NY).

TOWN, WILBUR W., son of CALVIN (preceding), born 13 May 1854, Jackson Co., Mich., married on 26 June 1875 to ROSE (HOUGHTALIN), probably daughter of Nicholas P. (also see) who was born 12 Apr. 1857. Known children: 1. FLOYD b. 4 Aug. 1876; 2. TRACEY b. 9 Sept. 1879. Ref: History of Jackson Co., Mich., 1881, pg. 956-7.

TOWN, WILLIAM and wife, MARY, were "natives of New Hampshire," who settled in Liberty Twp., Jackson Co., Mich. in 1846. Known son, CALVIN (preceding). Ref: History of Jackson Co., Mich., 1881, pg. 956-7.

TOWN, WILLIAM was listed in the 1840 census index of Rives Twp., Jackson Co., Mich.; and may be he who was called "William H. Town" of "Genesee Co., NY" who purchased in Jackson Co. in 1835.

TOWNE also see TOWN

TOWNE, SUSAN E. born near Keene, New Hampshire, married Edward A. Milliken (also see), and died in 1842 in Orleans Co., NY. Note WILLIAM & HENRY TOWN, preceding.

TOWNSEND, EDWIN F. born ca. 1798, and wife, HARRIET, born ca. 1797, both in NY, were listed in the 1850 census of Madison Twp., Lenawee Co., Mich. with ANN M., ag 27, b. Illinois; EMILY P., age 21, b. Wisconsin; and NELSON D., age 19; HELEN S., age 16; HARRIET, age 14, all b. NY, in their household.

TOWNSEND, HENRY F.^{3}, son of JOHN^2 (following), born 28 Aug. 1813, Westmoreland, Oneida Co., NY, married there on 16 June 1836 to LUCY R. (BENNETT), daughter of Jonathan (also see). In 1835, they removed to Adrian, Lenawee Co., Mich., and before 1837 to Dover Twp. They were listed in the 1850 census of Dover Twp. Children: 1. JOHN A. (following); 2. MILTON H. b. 3 Nov. 1841 (served in Civil War; settled in Dover Twp.); 3. LUCY A. b. ca. 1843, Mich. (m. A. B. Bedell; lived Clayton, Mich, and then Menominee, Mich.) Ref: P&BA-Len pg. 506-7.

TOWNSEND, HIRAM born ca. 1791, and wife, ELIZABETH, born ca. 1807, both in NY, were listed in the 1850 census of Medina Twp., Lenawee Co., Mich. with WILLIAM, age 16; FARNUM or VARNUM, age 14; CHARLES, age 12, all b. NY; and ALFRED, age 10; JOHN, age 8, both b. Mich., in their household.

TOWNSEND, JOHN^2, son of JOHN^1 (early settler of Oneida Co., NY), was born in Westmoreland, Oneida Co., NY. He married there to PARNEL (BISHOP), daughter of David (also see). He filed for land in Dover and Hudson Twps., Lenawee Co., Mich., but apparently returned to Whitesboro, Oneida Co., NY, where she died in May 1873; and he died later. There were 5 sons and 3 daughters, names not stated, except HENRY F. (preceding). Ref: P&BA-Len pg. 511-2.

TOWNSEND, JOHN A.^{4}, son of HENRY F.^{3} (preceding), born 11 July 1837, Dover Twp., Lenawee Co., Mich., married first on 21 May 1862 to ALMIRA H. (TODD), daughter of Harvey (also see). She died 12 Feb. 1874 in Madison Twp. Children: 1. WILLIAM H. b. 29 Aug. 1863, Rossville, Ill. (m. Mattie Anderson of Adrian Twp.); 2. LOUIS E. b. 23 July 1868, Palmyra Twp. (d. 29 Aug. 1869); 3. CHARLES H. b. 12 Sept. 1869, Madison Twp.; 4. MILTON b. 12 Apr. 1873, Madison Twp.; 5. ALMIRA B. b. 27 Nov. 1873, Madison Twp. John A. married again in Palmyra Twp. on 28 Oct. 1874 to SARAH L. (NASH), daughter of Samuel (also see). Ref: P&BA-Len pg. 506-7 & portrait of farm.

TRABEN, GEORGE and wife, CATHARINE (HECK), came to Adrian, Lenawee Co., Mich. in 1853 from Hesse-Darmstadt, Germany. Catharine died in 1857. Children: 1. MAGDALENA (m. William Arold); 2. JOHN (to California); 3. HENRY, twin of Margaret (to Louisville, KY); 4. MARGARET b. 18 Oct, 1850 (m. J. Hugo Smith, also see). Ref: P&BA-Len pg. 560-1.

TRACEY, HANNAH (See Stephen Hayward^1)

TRANN, JOHN L. (See George Heesen)

Pioneer Families of Southeastern Michigan

TRAVER, CHRISTIANA (See Jacob Finger[1])

TRAVIS, JEROME E. came to Macon Twp., Lenawee Co., Mich. as a young man, and married there to MATILDA (HARRIOTT). (Note: This may be Caroline M., daughter of Robert Harriott, also see). Known daughter, SARAH J. b. 23 June 1854, Macon Twp. (m. Charles A. Pocklington, also see). Ref: P&BA-Len pg. 385-6.

TREADWAY, CHRISTOPHER and wife, MARGARET (CASWELL), had known daughter, ABBIE b. 2 Mar. 1836, Jefferson Co., NY (m. James J. Jones, also see, Herkimer Co., NY). Ref: P&BA-Len pg. 995-6.

TREADWAY, REUBEN lived in Jefferson Co., Genesee Co., & Allegany Cos., NY, before moving to Riga Twp., Lenawee Co., Mich. in 1836. He was listed in the 1840 census index of Blissfield Twp. They later moved to Richfield Twp., Lucas Co., Ohio (probably by 1850); and was living there in 1888. Known children: MARTIN VAN BUREN (first white child b. Riga Twp.; d. in Civil War); SALLIE (m. Garrett Vrooman, also see, on 12 Nov. 1843). Ref: P&BA-Len pg. 792-3.

TREADWELL, BENJAMIN G. purchased land in Norvell, Jackson Co., Mich. in 1838. Also note SEYMOUR B. who was in Jackson Co. same year.

TREADWELL, JESSE born ca. 1813, and wife, CATHARINE M., born ca. 1823, both in NY, were listed in the 1840 census index of Madison Twp., Lenawee Co., Mich.; and in the 1850 census of Hudson Twp. with JERMAIN (male), age 9; NOAH H., age 6; GEORGE, age 4; JULIANN, age 2, all b. Mich., in their household. Also note THIRZA, following.

TREADWELL, LOUISA J. married in Niagara Co., NY to Frederick H. Corwin (also see).

TREADWELL, SEYMOUR B. purchased land in Jackson Co., Mich. in 1838, and is listed in Jackson Twp. in the 1840 census index. He had a known son, J. H. born 3 Apr. 1828 who came with his father to Jackson Co. (died Lake City, Colorado, 1880). Ref: History of Jackson Co. Mich., 1881, pg. 160. Note BENJAMIN G., preceding; and THIRZA (following).

TREADWELL, THIRZA Mrs., age 60, born NY, was listed head of household in the 1850 census of Madison Twp., Lenawee Co., Mich., with SEYMOUR, age 28; LYDIA, age 22, both b. NY, in her household. Note SEYMOUR B. (preceding).

TREADWELL, WILLIAM C. born ca. 1822, NY, and wife, ANN, born ca. 1826, England, were listed in the 1850 census of Hudson Twp., Lenawee Co., Mich.

TREAT FAMILY - RICHARD[1] was born ca. 1590, England, and died 1669, Wethersfield, Conn. He had 3 sons and 5 daughters, and known son, ROBERT[2], born ca. 1622, England, died 12 July 1710, Milford, Conn. Robert was Colonial Governor of Conn., and founder of Newark, NJ. He had 4 sons and 3 daughters, and known son, Capt. JOSEPH[3] born 17 Sept. 1662, Milford, Conn., died there 9 Aug. 1721. Joseph[3] had 7 sons and 5 daughters, and known son, STEPHEN[4] born 10 Oct. 1715, Milford, Conn., died 13 Nov. 1794, Middletown, Conn., had 3 sons and 6 daughters. Known son, STEPHEN JR.[5] born 26 May 1747, Middletown, Conn., was the father of 8 sons & 7 daughters. Known son, HOSEA[6] born 8 June 1781, Middletown, died 17 Sept. 1818, Holland Patent, NY. He married on 4 Apr. 1802 to HANNAH (BONFOEY), and had 8 children, among whom was BUTLER[7] (following). Hannah born ca. 1782, married again after Butler's death to Obediah Platt. Ref: P&BA-Len pg. 1167-8.

TREAT, ALANSON[8], son of BUTLER[7] (following), born 20 Jan. 1847, Adrian Twp., Lenawee Co., Mich., married in 1871 to CLARA M. (LINCOLN), daughter of Richard (also see) of Jackson Co., Mich. Six children, but only 3 surviving in 1888 were listed: 1. GRACE N. b. 27 Dec. 1875; 2. BUTLER b. 25 Nov. 1880; 3. HORACE b. 12 June 1885. Ref: P&BA-Len pg. 1167-8.

TREAT, ASAHEL B. born ca. 1804, Conn., and wife, LAURA born ca. 1803, NY, were listed in the 1840 census index of Adrian Twp., Lenawee Co., Mich. (adjacent to BUTLER, following); and in the 1850 census with HANNAH B., age 20; SARAH S., age 18, both b. NY, in their household.

TREAT, BUTLER[7], son of HOSEA[6] (See TREAT FAMILY, preceding), born 15 May 1818, Holland Patent, NY, married 15 Apr. 1840 in Adrian Twp., Lenawee Co., Mich. to NANCY (TINGLEY), daughter of Samuel (also see). She died before 1849; and the following children were listed in the household in the 1850 census: EUGENE A., age 8; HORACE T., age 6; ALANSON B., age 3, all b. Mich. Butler married again on 14 June 1849 to ANNA (EURITT), however, in the census she was called "LUCINA," age 21, born NY. They had 4 children, names not stated. In the 1850 census, his mother, Hannah Platt, age 68, b. Conn., was in the household. Butler married third to MARIETTA (VEDDER) on 6 Mar. 1861, and had 5 children by that marriage. He had a total of 3 daughters and 9 sons. Ref: P&BA-Len pg. 1167-8.

TREAT, DAVID B. born ca. 1812, NY, was listed in the 1850 census of Madison Twp., Lenawee Co., Mich. with no family.

TREAT, JOHN born ca. 1805, Conn., married CHARLOTTE (HOUGHTON) born ca. 1824, NY, and they were listed in the 1850 census of Adrian Twp., Lenawee Co., Mich. with no family. She married again after 1870 to Peter Onsted (also see). Ref: P&BA-Len pg. 1100-1.

TREAT, THOMAS S. was listed in the 1840 census index of Fairfield Twp., Lenawee Co., Mich.

TREAT, TITUS H. born ca. 1804, and wife, MARY, born ca 1814, were listed in the 1840 census index of Madison Twp., Lenawee Co., Mich.; and in the 1850 census with MARGARET A., age 18, b. NY; and ABIGAIL M., age 14; JOSEPH H., age 10; MARVIN P., age 7; CLARISSA A., age 5; FRANCIS H., age 3, all b. Mich., in their household.

TREXLER, ANNA (See Peter Hause)

TRIBOU, LESTER P. (See Lucius Lilley)

TRIM, IRA born 24 Dec. 1820, Owego Co., NY, settled in Rome Twp., Lenawee Co., Mich. where he was listed alone in the 1850 census (next door to Francis Howard). He married on 19 Feb. 1852 to LOVISA (HOWARD), note Francis Howard family. They had daughter, NANCY, born 4 Dec. 1852 (m. Seymour A. Colbath, also see). Ref: P&BA-Len pg. 862-3. Note SAMUEL, following.

TRIM, JOSEPH born ca. 1807, and wife, MALONEY, born ca. 1810, both in NY, were listed in the 1850 census of Rollin Twp., Lenawee Co., Mich. with MALVINA, age 12, b. NY; and MANDA, age 4, b. Mich., in their household.

TRIM, RICHARD was listed in the 1840 census index of Cambridge Twp., Lenawee Co., Mich.

TRIM, SAMUEL was listed in the 1840 census index of Rome Twp., Lenawee Co., Mich. Note IRA, preceding.

TRIPP, ALVIN, age 17, born NY, was listed in the 1850 census of Ridgeway Twp., Lenawee Co., Mich. in a Russell household.

TRIPP, HENRY Rev. born ca. 1784, Bristol, England, served in the British Navy. He married in Bristol to ? (STONEHAM) and they went to the West Indies as Missionaries, where she died of Yellow Fever leaving a son, HENRY JR. (following), Rev. Henry married again to her sister, ELIZABETH (STONEHAM) born ca. 1797, England. In 1831, after the birth of 3 children, they came to US and settled in Cambridge Twp., Lenawee Co., Mich.; and by 1840 in Franklin Twp. In the 1850 census they listed Dr. JOHN D. (following); JOSEPH, age 28; HANNAH, age 20, all b. England; and JULIANA, age 19, b. Ohio; and ROBERT, age 17; EMILY, age 12; and granddaughter, dau. of John, HARRIET, age 4/12, all b. Mich., in their household.

TRIPP, HENRY, JR., son of HENRY (preceding), born ca. 1820, West Indies, came to the US with his parents. He married SYLVIA, born ca. 1820, NY, and they were listed in the 1850 census of Franklin Twp., Lenawee Co., Mich. with HENRY, age 1, b. Mich., in their household.

TRIPP, JOHN D. Dr., son of Rev. HENRY (preceding), born 28 Nov. 1825, Bristol, England, married in Franklin Twp. to LUCRETIA (BEEBE) who was born in NY. She died 15 Feb. 1850 leaving daughter, HARRIET "HATTIE" L. born ca. 1850 (m. Allen Buck; Otsego, Mich.) Dr. Tripp married again on 17 Aug. 1851, Medina Twp., to LOIS (MANN), born NY, who had come to Mich. with her parents. They had 7 children (only 6 names were listed),: 2. WILLLIAM E. or ELBERT W. (following); 3. GEORGE J.; 4. LOTTA; 5. WILLIS J.; 6. ALMA; 7. NELLIE. Ref: P&BA-Len pg. 638-9.

TRIPP, WILLIAM E. Prof. (probably ELBERT W.), son of Dr. JOHN D. (preceding), born 27 Mar. 1853, Frnklin Twp., Lenawee Co., Mich., married on 1 Mar. 1884 to ISABELLA (AYERS), daughter of Dr. S. C. (also see). Known children: 1. LOIS A.; 2. JULIA G. Ref: P&BA-Len pg. 665.

TRUMBULL, EMMA Mrs. was the daughter of Albert Humphrey Bump (also see) and the Trumbulls resided in Hudson, Mich. in 1888.

TRUMBULL, SADIE (See James E. Rounds)

TRYON, ESTELLA (See Charles Chamberlain)

TUCK, M. F. (See James Henry Thorn)

TUCKER, BISHOP W. born ca. 1810, and wife, ELIZABETH J., age 22, both b. NY, married within the year, were listed in the 1850 census of Blissfield Twp., Lenawee Co., Mich. in a McKey household.

TUCKER, DANIEL was listed in the 1840 census index of Madison Twp., Lenawee Co., Mich.

TUCKER, JAMES B. born ca. 1818, and wife, SUSAN S., born ca. 1824, both in NY, were listed in the 1850 census of Madison Twp., Lenawee Co., Mich. with DELAVAN, age 4, b. Mich., and Albert Benedict, age 16, b. NY, in their household.

TUCKER, JOSEPH J. born ca. 1822, NY, and wife, MARY, born ca. 1822, Mich., were listed in the 1850 census of Tecumseh Twp., Lenawee Co., Mich. with SAMUEL (following) & CLEMENTINE in their household.

TUCKER, NANCY (See Isaac A. Colvin)

TUCKER, NANCY born ca. 1770, Mass., married Abel Foster, also see.

TUCKER, SAMUEL born ca. 1786, and wife, CLEMENTINE, born ca. 1788, both in NY, were listed in the 1840 census index of Clinton Twp., Lenawee Co., Mich.; and in the 1850 census of Tecumseh Twp. in the household of son, JOSEPH J. (preceding).

TUFTS, AARON born Mass., and wife, MARY, born Conn., had come with their parents to Genesee Co., NY and married there. He served in the War of 1812. She died ca. 1832; and he died in 1882, age 88. Known son, #4. AARON R. (following). Ref: P&BA-Len pg. 565-6.

TUFTS, AARON R., son of AARON (preceding), born 21 Apr. !825, Stafford, Genesee Co., NY, married there on 17 Jan. 1850 to MARGARET (PERRY), daughter of Roswell (also see), and settled in Seneca Twp., Lenawee Co., Mich. that year. Children: 1. FLORENCE B.; 2. EVA A. (m. Harvey Upton, also see); 3. MARY ANN (m. Thomas Clarson; he was killed 1883, Blissfield, in Railroad accident); 4. CHARLES L. (m. Ida M. Deline). Ref: P&BA-Len pg. 565-6.

TUNISON - This family were in Bridgewater, Somerset Co., NJ as early as 1778-1780, as FOLKERT was listed there with some of the following. In 1793, in the list of ratables, were Dr. GARRET; ANNA; JOHN P. (following); ABRAHAM; CORNELIUS; JAMES; WILLIAM; HENDRICK; DIRCK (RICHARD). Ref: Revolutionary Census of NJ, by K. Stryker-Rodda; and New Jersey in 1793, by Norton.

TUNISON, DANIEL COLE, son of THOMAS (following), born 17 Apr. 1828, came to Fairfield Twp., Lenawee Co., Mich. where he married on 21 Jan. 1858 to LUCY E. (HODGE), daughter of Edward (also see). They settled in Lucas Co., Ohio, and remained there till 1864 when they moved to Fairfield Twp., Lenawee Co., Mich. Children: 1. LURA C. (m. J. W. Mitchell; Brown Co., KS); 2. MARY E.; 3. ANNA C.; 4. ELLA H.; 5. OLIVE A. Ref: P&BA-Len pg. 514-5.

TUNISON, JOHN P. born in May 1762, NJ, note that it may be he in the list of ratables, preceding, in Bridgewater, Somerset Co., NJ ca. 1793. He married ELIZABETH (MILLER) in New Jersey in 1794. He had served in the Revolutionary War. Eight children, only known, THOMAS (following). Ref: P&BA-Len pg. 514-5.

TUNISON, PHILIP, and wife, MAGDALENE, of Seneca Co., NY, were parents of LYDIA who married Elvin C. Cole (also see) on 7 Mar. 1837, Covert, NY. Ref: P&BA-Len pg. 556-7; 610-11.

Pioneer Families of Southeastern Michigan

TUNISON, THOMAS, son of JOHN P. (preceding), born 10 Aug. 1797, NJ, married ANNA (COLE), daughter of Daniel (also see). After their marriage, they settled in Seneca Co., NY, and afterwards in Schuyler Co., NY. About 1849, they removed to Lucas Co., Ohio; and in 1864 to Fairfield Twp., Lenawee Co., Mich. She died there 26 Mar. 1886, and he died 30 Sept. 1886. Children: 1. ELIZABETH (m. Caleb Crissey; she d. 17 Mar. 1862, Lucas Co., O.); 2. SARAH (m. William Conklin; Syracuse, NY); 3. DANIEL COLE (preceding); 5. SUSAN S. (m. W. H. Williams; Lucas Co., O.); 6. JOHN P. (m/1 Helen TenBrook who d. 23 Sept. 1882; m/2 Mrs. Elvina Brown; Wood Co., O.) Ref: P&BA-Len pg. 514-5.

TURK, EUGENE (See Alvin Joslin)

TURNER, BENJAMIN born ca. 1822, VT, and wife, MELISSA L., born ca. 1828, NY, were listed in the 1850 census of Hudson Twp., Lenawee Co., Mich. with Hannah Grinell, age 21, b. NY, in their household.

TURNER, CALEB S. born ca. 1799, Delaware, and wife, LEAH, born ca. 1796, New Jersey, were listed in the 1840 census index of Adrian Twp., Lenawee Co., Mich.; and in the 1850 census with GEORGE, age 26; MARGARETT, age 19, both b. NY; and WILLIAM, age 17; ELIZABETH, age 15; JANE, age 13, all b. Mich., in their household.

TURNER, CARMI, born Mass., was a pioneer to Pierpont, Ashtabula Co., Ohio. Known daughter, MARTHA b. Mass. (m. Cornelius D. Seager, also see). Ref: P&BA-Len pg. 369-70.

TURNER, CAROLINE, age 23, b. NY, was listed in the 1850 census of Madison Twp., Lenawee Co., Mich. in a Harvey household.

TURNER, CHARLES B. was listed in the 1840 census index of Tecumseh Twp., Lenawee Co., Mich.; also note JETHRO (following).

TURNER, CYNTHIA (See Appolos Drown)

TURNER, EDWARD W. (See Edwin Cook)

TURNER, EDWIN Dr. (See Francis Brown)

TURNER, ELIZABETH Mrs., age 38, born NY, was listed head of household in the 1850 census of Ridgeway Twp., Lenawee Co., Mich. with WILLIAM, age 17; ALEXANDER, age 15, both b. NY; and ERASMUS D., age 11; MARY E., age 1, both b. Mich., in their household.

TURNER, EUGENE (See John A. Bennett)

TURNER, GILES born ca. 1807, Conn, and wife, MARIA, born ca. 1817, Mass., were listed in the 1840 census index of Franklin Twp., Lenawee Co., Mich.; and in the 1850 with WINFIELD, age 18, b. NY; THOMAS, age 10; ELIZABETH, age 6; EMMA, age 1, all b. Mich., in their household.

TURNER, HARVEY born ca. 1814, and wife, AMANDA, born ca. 1818, both in NY, were listed in the 1850 census of Medina Twp., Lenawee Co., Mich. with ISABELL, age 9, b. NY; and DAVID J., age 2/12, b. Mich., in their household.

TURNER, ISAAC F., son of REUBEN N. (following), born 27 Jan. 1833, St. Lawrence Co., NY, moved to Lenawee Co., Mich. with his parents. He married 15 Dec. 1864 to SARAH ELIZA (VAIL), daughter of Cornelius (also see). They lived first in Dover Twp.; and then in 1880 moved to Madison Twp. Children: 1. MARTHA E.; 2. CHARLOTTE A.; 3. REUBEN C.; 4. NELLIE; 5. ARTHUR I. Ref: P&BA-Len pg. 644.

TURNER, JAMES C. born ca. 1815, and wife, ALTHA, born ca. 1813, NY, were listed in the 1850 census of Madison Twp., Lenawee Co., Mich. with Vertice? F. Parsons, age 14, b. NY, in their household.

TURNER, JETHRO was listed in the 1840 census index of Tecumseh Twp., Lenawee Co., Mich., adjacent to CHARLES B. (preceding).

TURNER, JOHN born ca. 1799, and wife, FRANCES, born ca. 1790, both in NY, were listed in the 1850 census of Dover Twp., Lenawee Co., Mich. with MARY, age 12?, age & place of birth illegible. Note: It may be he in the 1840 census index of Macon Twp., Lenawee Co.

TURNER, JOSEPH - There were two listed in the 1840 census index of Lenawee Co., Mich., one in Palmyra Twp. & one in Blissfield Twp. Following may be one of these men.

TURNER, JOSEPH born ca. 1812, and wife, MARIA, born ca. 1916, both in NY, were listed in the 1850 census of Hudson Twp., Lenawee Co., Mich. with EDWIN, age 8; STEPHEN, age 6; HARRIET, age 2; BYRON, age 3/12, all b. Mich., in their household.

TURNER, JOSEPH was father of MARY born 25 Apr. 1865 (See Alvin Joslin).

TURNER, JOSHUA, son of CHARLES, was a native of Derbyshire, England, where he married MARIA (MORRIS) of Staffordshire, England. They remained in England. There were 7 children, 6 of whom lived to maturity, and the 3 named came to the US. WILLIAM (served in 5th NY Cav., died Andersonville Prison, Civil War); MARK (lived Riga Twp., Lenawee Co., Mich.; THOMAS O. (following). Ref: P&BA-Len pg. 951-2.

TURNER, LYDIA, age 61, born VT, was listed in the 1850 census of Tecumseh Twp., Lenawee Co., Mich. in the household of Nathaniel & Lucina Brackett.

TURNER, MARTHA, age 21, born NY, was listed in the 1850 census of Madison Twp., Lenawee Co., Mich. in the household Francis and Jane Hurlburt, possibly a stepdaughter? SALLIE, age 24, b. NY, dittoed after her may be either a Turner or Hurlburt?

TURNER, MARTHA (See Christian Kuney)

TURNER, MARTHA D. Mrs. was the daughter of Job Cook of Franklin Twp., Lenawee Co., Mich.

TURNER, MARY Mrs., age 26, born Canada, was listed head of household in the 1850 census of Adrian Twp., Lenawee Co., Mich. with NANCY, age 5; SARAH, age 3, both b. Ohio; and JOSEPH W., age 1, b. Mich.; and Hannah Walker, age 57, b. England, in her household.

TURNER, NANCY J. Mrs. was the daughter of Maj. Philo Mills (also see) of Franklin Twp., Lenawee Co., Mich.

TURNER, NELLIE (See Garrett F. Harris; also note ISAAC F., preceding.

TURNER, REUBEN N. born ca. 1807, and wife, PHEBE (FOSTER), born ca. 1809, both in NY, married in St. Lawrence Co., NY and moved afterwards to Westchester Co. In 1848, they removed to Seneca Twp., Lenawee Co., Mich.; and by 1850 to Madison Twp.; and last to Adrian Twp. He died 18 Aug. 1882; and she died 18 July 1878. In the 1850 census of Madison Twp. they listed in their household (all b. NY): 1. MARY E., age 19; 2. ISAAC F. (preceding); 3. CORNELIA F., age 12;

JAMES, age 10; CAROLINE, age 7; MARTHA A., age 5. Ref: P&BA-Len pg. 644.

TURNER, THOMAS O., son of JOSHUA (preceding), born 25 Mar. 1836, Derbyshire, England, came to the US in 1865. He went first in Cleveland, Ohio; and then to Berrien Co., Mich. In 1868, he settled in Riga Twp., Lenawee Co., Mich. He married there in 1870 to ELIZABETH (BROWN) who was also a native of Derbyshire, England. She died in 1873; and he married again on 6 Mar. 1876 to CHRISTINA (McCORMICK), daughter of William (also see). Children: 1. OLIVER 2. child d. infancy. Ref: P&BA-Len pg. 951-2.

TURRELL also see TERRELL & TERRYL

TURRELL, M. F. (See Archibald M. Sickly)

TURRELL, MARY J. Mrs. was the daughter of William Sickly (also see).

TURRELL, STEPHEN married Mrs. MARY (OSBORN) CLARK, widow of George W., by 1837, and he was listed in the 1840 census index of Woodstock Twp., Lenawee Co., Mich. Known son, NOBEL C. born ca. 1838. Stephen was apparently deceased by 1846, as Mary married by that year to Hiram Johnson (also see). Note: In the 1850 census, Noble was listed in their household as Noble Johnson. Ref: P&BA-Len pg. 1132-3.

TUTTLE, ABNER born ca. 1799, and wife, LAURA, born ca. 1808, both in NY, were listed in the 1850 census of Fairfield Twp., Lenawee Co., Mich. with SALLY, age 96?, born Conn., probably his mother, and Laura Wells, age 12, b. Mich., in their household. Note JOSEPH, following.

TUTTLE, ALBERT F. Dr. son of WILLIAM J. (following), born 9 Aug. 1827 near Niagara Falls, NY, located in Clinton, Lenawee Co., Mich. in 1850. He married LAURA L. (CLARK), daughter of John (also see). No children were listed in sketch. Ref: P&BA-Len pg. 342-3.

TUTTLE, DANIEL (See ORAMON, Sr.) was listed in the 1840 census index of Raisin Twp., Lenawee Co., Mich. It should also be noted that there were 2 men by this name in Washtenaw Co., Mich.; 1 in Calhoun Co.; and 1 in Wayne Co. in 1840.

TUTTLE, DAVID B. born ca. 1808, and wife, LUCY, born ca. 1816, both in NY, were listed in the 1840 census index of Rollin Twp., Lenawee Co., Mich.; and in the 1850 census with MARY, age 12, b. NY; and ALVIN, age 9; LYDIA A., age 7; LOVINA, age 5; JAMES H., age 4; GEORGE E., age 4/12, all b. Mich.; and LOVINA, age 73, b. VT, probably mother of David, in their household. JERRY, following, was listed next door.

TUTTLE, EDWIN (See Charles Wood)

TUTTLE, EMILY (See Ezra Abbott)

TUTTLE, HARRIET L. born ca. 1815, NY, married Albern H. Raymond (also see).

TUTTLE, JERRY born ca. 1819, NY, and wife, HARRIET, born ca. 1823, Maine, were listed in the 1850 census of Rollin Twp., Lenawee Co., Mich. with Ann Degorman, age 6, b. Mich., in their household (next door to DAVID B., preceding).

TUTTLE, JOHN[1] was a native of New Hampshire and remained there. He had known son, JOHN L. born 8 Feb. 1807, NH. Ref: P&BA-Len pg. 373-4. Note: WILLIAM J., following, probably another son, as his son, Dr. ALBERT F., was called a "cousin of Dr. JOHN L., son of JOHN L." (following).

TUTTLE, JOHN and wife, MARGARET, of Hillsdale Co., Mich., were parents of HARRIET who married Alonzo P. Rawson, son of Henry H. (also see).

TUTTLE, JOHN born ca. 1816, New Jersey, and wife, SARAH, born ca. 1820, NY, were listed in the 1850 census of Tecumseh Twp. (probably they in 1840 census index of Clinton Twp.), Lenawee Co., Mich. with GEORGE, age 12; JOHN, age 8; ALICE, age 1, all b. Mich.; and ANN, age 49, born New Jersey, and listed last, THEODORE, age 3, b. Mich., in their household.

TUTTLE, JOHN L.[2], son of JOHN[1] (preceding), born 8 Feb. 1807, New Hampshire, arrived in Green Oak Twp., Livingston Co., Mich. in 1832. He married in Ann Arbor, Mich. to DELIA JANE (CLEVELAND), daughter of David (also see). In the 1850 census of Green Oak Twp. they listed MARY, age 14, ELEANOR C., age 6 (m. Orrin P. Safford; Flint, Mich.); DELIA, age 4; Dr. JOHN L., age 1 (following), all b. Mich. He died in Livingston Co., Mich. in 1865; and she died in Clinton Twp., Lenawee Co. at home of their son, Dr. John L. Not named in the sketch were 1 deceased son and 3 deceased daughters, some possibly same ones listed in the census noted above. Ref: P&BA-Len pg. 373-4.

TUTTLE, JOHN L.[3] Dr., son of JOHN L.[2] (preceding), born 25 Mar. 1849, Green Oak Twp., Livingston Co., Mich., married in Flint, Mich. to JENNIE E. (SAFFORD), daughter of Orrin, Sr. (also see). They settled in Clinton, Lenawee Co., Mich. Children: 1. JOHN L.; 2. ELLA L. Ref: P&BA-Len pg. 373-4.

TUTTLE, JOSEPH was listed in the 1840 census index of Fairfield Twp., Lenawee Co., Mich. Also note ABNER, preceding.

TUTTLE, LILLIAN B. (See Alonzo Foster Bailey)

TUTTLE, NOAH, born Conn., was a direct descendant of WILLIAM who had come from England in 1636, and was founder of New Haven, Conn. Noah settled in Camden, Oneida Co., NY at an early date. (ANDREW settled with him, probably a brother). Noah had a known son, ORAMON, SR. (following); and probably also NOAH P. who was the first child born Camden, Oneida Co., NY. Ref: P&BA-Len pg. 873-4.

TUTTLE, ORAMON, Sr., son of NOAH (preceding), born ca. 1780, Conn., married there to ABBIE (BARNES) also born Conn. After their marriage, they settled near Camden, Oneida Co., NY, and later moved to Vienna, NY. She died 7 Nov. 1838, age 55; and he died in 1860, between 78-80 years old. Children: 1. EMILY; 2. SALLIE; 3. DANIEL; 4. LENT; 5. MARY; 6. ALMA; 7. THANKFUL; 8. SOPHIA; 9. NANCY C.; 10. ORAMON JR. (following); 11. MARY 2d; 12. NOAH. Two of these children, names not stated, settled in NY, and the rest moved to Michigan.

TUTTLE, ORAMON, Jr., son of ORAMON, Sr. (preceding), born 27 Apr. 1824, Oneida Co., NY, married on 12 Sept. 1844 in NY to SALLY A. (SPENCER), daughter of Ephraim (also see). They moved to Hillsdale Co., Mich. in 1855; and after a few months to Dover Twp., Lenawee Co., and later to Seneca Twp. Children: 1. CHARLES A.; 2. MARY (m. Charles Babcock, also see); 3. CAROLINE E. b. 22 Dec. 1847, Oneida Co., NY (m. Wallace Bryant, also see); 4. WILLIAM E. (m/1 Dorcas Hood, had son, Edwin;

Pioneer Families of Southeastern Michigan

m/2 Mrs. Hannah Rogers); 5. WILLARD (d. infancy); 6. JESSE M. (m. Nancy Wold, dau. of Solomon, had son, Floyd E.); 7. HERVEY (m. Mabel Austin, had dau., Eunice May); 8. IDA A. (m. Chester S. Bragg, also see); 9. HIRAM (m. Mary Carey, children: Meral R., & infant); 10. FREDERICK; 11. EDWIN (note preceding). Ref: P&BA-Len pg. 817-8; 872-3.

TUTTLE, WILLIAM J.[1] "of New England ancestry", possibly son of JOHN (preceding), and wife, MARY A. (CLEVELAND), moved from near Niagara Falls, NY to Ann Arbor, Mich. They resided there until about 10 years before his death, when he moved to Clinton, Lenawee Co., Mich. with his son, Dr. ALBERT F. (preceding); also had son, Dr. HENRY C. (Dr. in the Civil War, afterwards moved to Silver Lake, KS). William J. died at age 76, and she died at age 60 in Clinton. Ref: P&BA-Len pg. 342-3.

TUTTLE, WILLIAM (See John W. Ormsby)

TWISS, JEREMIAH was a native of New Hampshire, and father of ACHSAH born ca. 1815, NH (m. Lemuel C. P. Vaughn, also see). Ref: P&BA-Len pg. 1002-3.

TYRELL also see TYRREL; TURRELL

TYRELL, RUTH (See John Torrey)

TYRREL was spelled TERRYL in census; also see TYRELL.

TYRREL, WARREN born ca. 1817, Penn., and wife, CATHARINE, born ca. 1822, Ireland, were listed in the 1850 census of Woodstock Twp., Lenawee Co., Mich. with MARY, age 10; ADELAIDE, age 7; WILLIAM, age 5, all b. Mich., in their household. Also note Nelson Terrell, preceding.

- U -

ULOTH, ADAM H., son of GEORGE (following), born 2 Feb. 1852, married on 6 Mar. 1875 to ABBIE J. (SANTEE), daughter of James G. (also see). Children: 1. MILTON; 2. FLOYD.

ULOTH, GEORGE born ca. 1823, and wife, MAGDALENA (BURK), both born Germany, married there and in 1856, after the birth of 2 children, came to the US. They settled first in Lorain Co., Ohio; and about 1864 moved to Ogden Twp., Lenawee Co., Mich. He was killed 22 Oct. 1871 by a falling tree. Nine children, and listed were those surviving in 1888: 1. ADAM H. (preceding); 2. J. HENRY (following); 3. LIZZIE (m. Orrin Rugg; Kansas); 4. MINNIE (m. James Quinby; Lake Co., Mich.); 5. PETER; 6. CONRAD. Ref: P&BA-Len pg. 198; 783-4.

ULOTH, J. HENRY, son of GEORGE (preceding), born 5 July 1855, Germany, came with his parents to the US. He married on 26 Mar. 1877 to ELLA (TIFFANY), daughter of Erastus (also see). They resided in Ogden Twp., Lenawee Co., Mich. Known son, CLARENCE. Ref: P&BA-Len pg. 783-4.

UNANGST, REGINA (See H. N. McCarty)

UNDERHILL FAMILY - Westchester Patriarchs, by N. Davis, 1988, has a record of this family and the following is an excerpt. (Capt. JOHN[1]; NATHANIEL[2]; BENJAMIN[3]); DANIEL[4] was born 1730 & married ABIAH (CONKLIN), and moved from New Castle, Westchester Co., NY to Ulster Co., NY. Children: 1. SARAH (m. James Kniffen, moved to Scipio, Cayuga Co., NY); 2. AMY; 3. BENJAMIN (to Cayuga Co., NY).***ABRAHAM[2], also son of NATHANIEL[2], had son, ISAAC[4] born 21 June 1726, married SARAH (FIELD), daughter of Robert & Abigail (Sutton) Field of Long Island. Note the resemblance to ISAAC, following.

UNDERHILL, ISAAC had known daughter, REBECCA (m. Moses Sutton b. 1756, also see).

UNDERHILL, JAMES and wife, PHEBE, were parents of SARAH b. 6 Feb. 1790 (m. Isaac Sutton, also see, & settled in Cayuga Co., NY.) Ref: P&BA-Len pg. 478-9.

UNDERWOOD, CHARLES, age 27, and probably brothers, GEORGE, age 25; VANWYCK, age 23, all born NY, were listed in the household of Gideon Harkness in the 1850 census of Adrian Twp., Lenawee Co., Mich.

UNDERWOOD, DANIEL K. born ca. 1803, Mass., and wife, MARIAH A., born ca. 1810, NY, were listed in the 1850 census of Madison Twp., Lenawee Co., Mich. with WILLIAM A., age 3; CHARLES M., age 1, both b. Mich., in their household.

UNDERWOOD, E. E., son of SAMUEL (following), born 26 Aug. 1806, Berkshire Co., Mass., moved to Monroe Co., NY, then to Leoni Twp., Jackson Co., Mich. with his parents. He married MARGARET (AMMERMAN) and settled in Leoni Twp. Children: 1. HENRY b. 1846 (d. 1858); 2. MARY b. 1848; 3. LETTA b. 1851; 4. MARTHA b. 1852 (d. Apr. 1853); 5. DANIEL S. b. 1854; 6. IDA A. b. 1858; 7. FRED J. b. 1862. Ref: History of Jackson Co., Mich., 1881, pg. 933.

UNDERWOOD, EDGAR E., son of EDWIN (following), born 9 Nov. 1847, Palmyra Twp., Lenawee Co., Mich., married in 1867 to EMMA J. (BUTLER), born 1848, Genesee Co., NY. Child: CLARA C. b. 1874. Ref: P&BA-Len pg. 413-4.

UNDERWOOD, EDWARD, son of JOSEPH H. (following), born Feb. 1800, Dutchess Co., NY, moved ca. 1806 to Madison Co., NY with his parents. He married ANNA C. (MITCHELL), daughter of Joseph (also see) and settled first in Madison Co., NY, and later to Wayne Co., NY. In 1836, they removed to Palmyra Twp., Lenawee Co., Mich. She died 20 Feb. 1861; and he died 18 May 1878. Children: 1. MARY A. b. 29 June 1826/8, Williamson, Wayne Co., NY (m. John C. Harvey, also see); 2. THOMAS (following); 3. LYDIA b. ca. 1830 (d. age 27, unmarried); 4. CORNELIUS (d. age 7). Ref: P&BA-Len pg. 269-70; 415-6; 537-8.

UNDERWOOD, EDWARD F., son of THOMAS (following), married in Palmyra Twp., Lenawee Co., Mich. in 1875 to ALICE (WADE) born Litchfield, Hillsdale Co., Mich. Children: 1. ANNIE C.; 2. HATTIE; 3. METTA. Ref: P&BA-Len pg. 269-70.

UNDERWOOD, EDWIN, son of JOHN (following), born 12 May 1817, DeRuyter, Madison Co., NY, married on 22 Apr. 1841 to CHARLOTTE M. (COMSTOCK), daughter of Thomas (also see). In his household in the 1850 census of Palmyra Twp., Charlotte was listed as MARIA S. (?), age 32, with first two children: 1. LUCY C. b. 6 Apr. 1843 (m James R. Steele; she d. 10 Nov. 1873); 2. EDGAR E. (preceding); 3. JOHN T. b. 23 Jan. 1857 (m. Anna Martin, dau. of James, also see). Edwin died in May 1881. Ref: P&BA-Len pg. 401-2.

UNDERWOOD, EUNICE born 1781, Conn. (See Asa Bidwell).
UNDERWOOD, JAMES born ca. 1812, and wife, RACHEL, born ca. 1817, both in NY, were probably they listed as JAMES F. in the 1840 census index of Tecumseh Twp.; and in the 1850 census of Madison Twp. with LYDIA J., age 10; ELIZABETH R., age 8; ANN A., age 6; MARY A., age 3/12, all b. Mich.; and Nancy Linfield, age 17, b. NY; Samuel Jones, age 55, and wife, Lydia Jones, age 50 (probably parents of Rachel), both b. NY; Nelson H. Kimball, age 33, and wife, Abby J. Kimball, age 20, and Joseph Comstock, age 33, b. NY, in their household.
UNDERWOOD, JOHN born ca. 1810, Leicestershire, England, married there to ELIZABETH (PINER) born 1810, same place. After the birth of first 2 children, they immigrated ca. 1836 to the US, and lived for a few months in Toledo, Ohio, then moved to Ridgeway Twp., Lenawee Co. (may be he listed in the 1840 census index of Macon Twp.). John died Ridgeway Twp. on 13 Nov. 1886. Children: 1. CHARLES b. ca. 1835; 2. ANN b. ca. 1836, both in England; 3. MICHAEL (following, probably he listed as "JAMES," age 13, b. Mich., no Michael in household in 1850 census); 4. ELIZABETH b. ca. 1841; 5. WILLIAM (following); 6. JOHN b. ca. 1845; 7. SAMUEL (following); 8. GEORGE W. b. ca. 1847; 9. MARY E. b. ca. 1849. Ref: P&BA-Len pg. 329; 401-2.
UNDERWOOD, JOHN, born ca. 1789, NY, called "a native of Albany, NY," and wife, CATHARINE born ca. 1789, NY, had moved to Madison Co., NY, then Williamson, Monroe Co., NY. In 1833, they came to Ogden Twp., Lenawee Co., Mich., 1835 to Adrian Twp., and by 1840 to Palmyra Twp. In the 1850 census of Palmyra Twp., they listed JOHN H., age 14, b. Mich., in their household. Known son, EDWIN (preceding). Ref: P&BA-Len pg. 413-4. Note JOSEPH H., following.
UNDERWOOD, JOSEPH H. settled in Dutchess Co., NY before 1800 (he and ROBINSON were listed in the 1800 census index). He moved about 1806 to Madison Co., NY. There were 6 sons, and 1 daughter, names not stated, except, EDWARD (preceding). Ref: P&BA-Len pg. 537-8. Note CHARLES, with brothers GEORGE & VANWYCK, preceding.
UNDERWOOD, MICHAEL (JAMES?), son of JOHN (preceding), born ca. 1837, Ridgeway Twp., Lenawee Co., Mich., married there to ADELAIDE J. (PILBEAM), daughter of James (also see). He died 22 Sept. 1881. Children: 1. TRESSIE (d. age 2); 2. LIBBIE; 3. GLENN J.; 4. CLIFFORD I. Adelaide J. married again to WILLIAM, brother of MICHAEL, as his second wife. Ref: P&BA-Len pg. 401-2.
UNDERWOOD, PHENIE (SOPHRINA) - See WILLIAM, following.
UNDERWOOD, SAMUEL, son of JOHN (preceding), born 2 Sept. 1845, Ridgeway Twp., Lenawee Co., Mich., first went to Canada, but returned to Clinton, Mich. He married in Clinton on 30 May 1868 to MARY (MILLSON), daughter of John (also see). Children: 1. WEBSTER S.; 2. WARREN H. Ref: P&BA-Len pg. 329.
UNDERWOOD, SAMUEL and wife, JEMIMA (FLETCHER), moved from Berkshire Co., Mass. to Parma, Monroe Co., NY in 1814. (Note: There was a JONATHAN who settled in Parma, Monroe Co., NY in 1805, according to French's *Gazetteer of New York State*.) In 1832, they removed to Leoni Twp., Jackson Co., Mich. where they remained. Known son, E. E. (preceding). Ref: <u>History of Jackson Co., Mich.</u>, 1881, pg. 933.
UNDERWOOD, THOMAS, son of EDWARD (preceding), born 20 Oct. 1827, Williamson, Wayne Co., NY, married MARY (COMSTOCK), daughter of Jared (also see). They lived in Palmyra Twp., Lenawee Co., Mich. Children: 1. EDWARD F. (preceding); 2. ELLA b. 31 Jan. 1853 (m. Rev. Harvey Widney, also see); 3. WILLIAM b. 10 Aug. 1854 (to Pittsford, Hillsdale Co., Mich.) Ref: P&BA-Lenpg. 269-70; 537-8.
UNDERWOOD, WILLIAM, son of JOHN (preceding), born 8 Aug. 1843, Ridgeway Twp., Lenawee Co., Mich., married there to ELIZA J. (GETTY), daughter of James (also see). She died on 21 Aug. 1881. Children: 1. CHARLES W. (m. Nellie Cary, Ridgeway Twp.); 2. ARTHUR J. (m. Mary "Mamie" Boyce of Macon Twp.; settled Ridgeway); 3. ADDIE (m. Laban Babcock; Britton, Mich.); 4. SOPHRINA (m. Edgar Exelby, son of George, also see); 5. JOHN; 6. LOVIA; 7. AMOS; 8. CLAYBON; 9. CLARENCE. William married second to Mrs. ADELAIDE (PILBEAM) UNDERWOOD, widow of his brother, MICHAEL (also see). Ref: P&BA-Len pg. 401-2.

UNGEMACH, JOHN and wife, ANNA MARIA (ESKEL), were natives of Willersdorf, Hesse-Cassel, Germany. Known daughter, CATHARINE ELIZABETH, born 16 July 1836 (came to New York City in 1858, married there to Henry Finger[2], also see). Ref: P&BA-Len pg. 706-9.

UNGER, WILLIAM (See David Cochrane)

UPDIKE also see OPDYKE
UPDIKE, AARON was listed in the 1840 census index of Eas?, Jackson Co., Mich.
UPDIKE, ANSON, son of RALPH (following), born 15 July 1818, Ulysses, Tompkins Co., NY, moved with his father to Washtenaw Co., Mich in 1827, and in 1830 to Leoni, Jackson Co., Mich. He married there in 1839 to HARRIET S. (UPDIKE) also born Tompkins Co., NY. They went to California in 1850, but returned to Leoni Twp. in 1854. Eight children, only named were those surviving in 1881: 1. MONTGOMERY; 2. MATILDA; 3 HERMAN; 4. SIDNEY; 5. MILO K. Ref: <u>History of Jackson Co., Mich.</u>, 1881, pg. 933-4.
UPDIKE, CARRIE (See Philip S. DePuy)
UPDIKE, HENRY P. was buying in Leoni Twp., Jackson Co., Mich. in 1835.
UPDIKE, JACOB A., son of JOHN S. (following), born 19 Nov. 1821, New Jersey, moved as an infant to Tompkins Co., NY with his parents. He married CAROLINE (UPDIKE) on 19 Nov. 1845, and they were listed in the 1850 census of Ulysses, Tompkins Co., NY with ANN EDGA, age 5; AARON, age 2; and SAMUEL, age 1/12. They moved to Leoni Twp., Jackson Co., Mich. She died 25 Mar. 1863, Leoni Twp. Two of their children, names not stated, were still living in 1881. Jacob A. married again 16 July 1864 to ? (DELROW). Ref: <u>History of Jackson Co.,Mich.</u>, 1881, pg. 934.
UPDIKE, JAMES[1] born 1 Oct. 1803, and wife, BELINDA (HAUSE), born ca. 1807, both in NY, settled in Tecumseh Twp., Lenawee Co., Mich. by 1840. She died 30 Nov. 1873, Tecumseh, and he was living with son, Martin G. in 1888. In the 1850 census of Tecumseh

Pioneer Families of Southeastern Michigan

Twp., they listed ESTHER, age 18 (m. Rufus Keyser, as 2nd wife); CHESTER, age 19; ALMIRA, age 16; ALANSON, age 14; CATHERINE, age 12, all b. NY, and PHOEBE, age 10; MARTIN G., age 8; JAMES JR. (following); CAROLINE, age 4; MARY, age 2, all b. Mich., in their household. Known daughter, CHARITY b. ca. 1829, NY (m. Rufus Keyser, also see). Ref: P&BA-Len pg. 249-50. Note MARTIN G., following, brother?

UPDIKE, JAMES[2], son of JAMES[1] (preceding), born ca. 1844, TEcumseh Twp., Lenawee Co., Mich., married 2 Apr. 1873 to ATLANTA A. (BATES), daughter of John T. (also see) born 5 Nov. 1853, Cortland Co., NY. Sons: 1. EARL B. b. 7 Dec. 1876; 2. LUCIUS C. b. 29 Dec. 1878. Ref: P&BA-Len pg. 249-50.

UPDIKE, JOHN S. & MARGARET (APGER) of New Jersey moved to Ulysses, Tompkins Co., NY and were parents of JACOB A. (preceding). Also note AARON. Ref: History of Jackson Co., Mich., 1881, pg. 934.

UPDIKE, MARTIN G. born ca. 1820, and wife, ELIZABETH, born ca. 1826, both in NY, were listed in the 1850 census of Tecumseh Twp., Lenawee Co., Mich. with AUGUSTA, age 3; WILLIAM, age 2, both b. Mich., and Charles Hair, age 15, b. Penn., in their household. Note JOHN, preceding, brother?

UPDIKE, RALPH and wife, MARGARET (RITCHIE), lived in Ulysses, Tompkins Co., NY, then moved to Washtenaw Co., Mich. in 1827, and in 1830 to Grass Lake, Jackson Co., Mich. Known children: ANSON (preceding); PERLINA (d. 20 Jan. 1827, age 3y/7m/16d, buried in Old Log Meeting House Cemetery, Ulysses).

UPDIKE, SAMUEL purchased in Grass Lake Twp., Jackson Co., Mich. adjacent to RALPH, preceding, and was listed in the 1840 census index of Grass Lake Twp.

UPDIKE, THEODORE was an early settler of Leoni Twp., Jackson Co., Mich. where he was listed in the 1840 census index.

UPTON, ABIATHER born ca. 1808, NY, and wife, JANE, born ca. 1815, Scotland, were listed in the 1850 census of Rome Twp., Lenawee Co., Mich. with MARY, age 7; JANE, age 5, both b. NY; and JOANNA, age 1, b. Mich., in their household (next door to DAVID b. 1813, following).

UPTON, ADONIJAH born ca. 1820, Mass., was listed in the 1850 census of Adrian Twp., Lenawee Co., Mich. in a Moe household, next door to HENRY (following).

UPTON, DAVID, born ca. 1783, Charlemont, Mass., married MARY (MARSH), born ca. 1786, VT, resided by 1825 in Ontario, Wayne Co., NY. They moved to Wheatland, Hillsdale Co., Mich., later moving to Rollin Twp., Lenawee Co. He died in 1859. Three sons & seven daughters, names not stated, except LUCY B. (m. Henry H. Tabor, also see); & MARY ANN b. 27 Mar. 1825, Ontario, Wayne Co., NY (m/1 Nelson Wood; m/2 Thomas S. Weter, also see); and in their household in the 1850 census of Rollin Twp. were JAMES M., age 25; CORDELIA, age 21, both b. NY. Ref: P&BA-Len pg. 254-5; 283-4.

UPTON, DAVID born ca. 1813, NY, and wife, BARBARY, born ca. 1826, both in NY, were listed in the 1850 census of Rome Twp., Lenawee Co., Mich. with CAROLINE, age 3; OLIVE, age 1, both b. Mich., in their household (next door to ABIATHER, preceding).

UPTON, ELI born ca. 1816, New Hampshire, was listed in the 1840 census index of Hudson Twp., Lenawee Co., Mich.; and in the 1850 census with wife, ADALINE, born ca. 1826, NY, and ORRIN, age 4; WARREN, age 4, both b. Mich., in their household. Note JOSHUA, following.

UPTON, ELIZA, age 17, born Canada, was listed in the 1850 census of Raisin Twp., Lenawee Co., Mich. in a Laing household.

UPTON, HARVEY (note JOSHUA, following) married EVA A. (TUFTS), daughter of Aaron R. (also see) and settled in Madison Twp., Lenawee Co., Mich. Known children: WILLIE; & FLOYD. Ref: P&BA-Len pg. 565-6.

UPTON, HENRY born ca. 1804, Mass., and wife, CYNTHIA, born ca. 1808, Mass., were listed in the 1850 census of Adrian Twp., Lenawee Co., Mich. with OLIVE, age 18; ADONIJAH, age 12, LYDIA J., age 8, all b. Mich., in their household. Note ADONIJAH, preceding.

UPTON, JOSHUA born ca. 1821, New Hampshire, and wife, SARAH M., born ca. 1823, NY, were listed in the 1850 census of Medina Twp., Lenawee Co., Mich. with ELI, age 6; HARRIET, age 5; HARVEY (note preceding), age 4; NANCY, age 2, all b. Mich., in their household. Note ELI, preceding.

UPTON, NATHANIEL was listed in the 1840 census index of Medina Twp., Lenawee Co., Mich.

UPTON, NATHANIEL listed in the 1840 census index of Sandstone Twp., Jackson Co., Mich. may be father of EDMUND born 14 Mar. 1828, Dutchess Co., NY who came "with his father," name not stated, to Sandstone Twp. in 1835.

UPTON, WILLIAM born ca. 1805, and wife, CHARITY, born ca. 1807, both in Ireland, were listed in the 1850 census of Fairfield Twp., Lenawee Co., Mich. with ELEANOR, age 14, b. NY; and HUGH, age 11; JOSEPH, age 8; GILBERT, age 6; SUSAN, age 4; CHARITY, age 2, all b. Mich., in their household. ROBERT, age 17, b. NY, in another household may relate to this family. It may be this WILLIAM in the 1840 census index of Raisin Twp. Also note ELIZA, preceding.

- V -

VAARWERK, JANNA T. of Holland (See Frederick Nyland).

VADER, ELIZA (See William Louden)

VAIL, ALBERT was listed in the 1840 census index of Adrian Twp., Lenawee Co., Mich.

VAIL, CORNELIUS N., son of JOHN (following), born ca. 1815, and wife, PAMELIA (OUDEKIRK), born ca. 1818, both in NY, probably moved by 1840 to Madison Twp., Lenawee Co., Mich. with his father. He died there 17 Nov. 1871, and she died 10 Nov. 1884. Children (all b. Mich.): 1. ELLEN E. b. ca. 1842; 2. JENNIE E. b. ca. 1844; 3. SARAH ELIZA b. 26 Sept. 1845 (m. Isaac F. Turner, also see); 4. JOHN E. b. ca. 1849; 5. JAMES B.; 6. MARY A. Ref: P&BA-Len pg. 644.

VAIL, JOHN born ca. 1779, Conn., and wife, HANNAH, born ca. 1779, NY, were listed in the 1840 census index of Madison Twp., Lenawee Co., Mich.; and in the 1850 with probably son, ALMON, age 46, b. NY, in their household; and son, CORNELIUS N. (preceding) listed next door. Possibly a daughter, DELIA A., born ca. 1813,

NY (m. Isaac Warren, also see, Madison Twp. 7 Mar. 1838).

VAIL, MOSES born ca. 1801, and wife, AMANDA, born ca. 1804, both in NY, were listed in the 1840 census index of Seneca Twp., Lenawee Co., Mich.; and in the 1850 census with HIRAM, age 23; HENRY, age 19; HELEN, age 17, all b. NY; and HARVEY, age 9; HANNAH, age 11?; CELESTIA, age 7, all b. Mich., in their household.

VALENTINE, ANANIAS of Orange Co., NY married on 15 Oct. 1786 to ELIZABETH (MEEKER) in the Presbyterian Church of Goshen. He died 17 Jan. 1825, age 65; and she died 10 Sept. 1824, age 63, in Orange Co., NY. They listed in the following children in the records of this same church. 1. STEPHEN b. 12 Aug. 1787; 2. MARY b. 12 Sept. 1789; 3. KEZIAH (m. Richard S. Horton, also see); 4. HANNAH b. 10 July 1797; 5. PHEBE b. 10 Oct. 1799; 6. ELIZABETH b. 25 June 1802 (m. Moses Sawyer); 7. SARAH b. 29 Dec. 1804; 8. FLEMMON bpt. 8 Mar. 188; 9. WILLIAM b. 14 Dec. 1811.

VALENTINE, JOHN B. and wife, EVALINE (ALDRICH), were parents of IDA (m. Charles M. Strong, son of Norman J., also see, on 14 Sept. 1887). Ref: P&BA-Len pg. 482-3.

VAN AKEN also see VAN AKIN & VAN AUKEN

VAN AKEN, BENJAMIN H. born in New Jersey, and wife, RACHEL, born Penn., moved by 1821 to Detroit, Mich., and later to Fairfield Twp., Lenawee Co., Mich. It may be he spelled VAN AUKEN in the 1840 census index of Fairfield Twp., adjacent to ORIN. They later moved to Hillsdale Co., Mich. where they died "at an advanced age." Known daughter, PHEBE b. 14 Feb. 1814 (m. James J. Snedeker, also see). Ref: P&BA-Len pg. 372-3.

VAN AKIN also see VAN AKEN & VAN AUKEN

VAN AKIN FAMILY - Supposedly there were 3 brothers (always a rather doubtful claim) who came from Holland and settled first in Manhattan, and then one went to Kingston, NY and two went to Deer Park, Orange Co., NY (probably Machackameck, where Orange Co., NY, Sussex Co., NJ, and Penn. abut). Note: There was a MARINUS listed in the records of the Reformed Church of Kingston as early as 1690, listing the birth of a son, CORNELIUS. Researchers of this family should also see the records of the Machakameck Reformed Church of Orange Co., NY.

VAN AKIN, BENJAMIN born ca. 1820, NY, and wife, MARY A., born ca. 1823, Penn., were listed in the 1850 census of Adrian Twp., Lenawee Co., Mich. in a Cavaller household.

VAN AKIN, DUDLEY L., son of JOHN (following), born ca. 1811, and wife, BETSEY, born ca. 1810, both in NY, are probably they listed in the 1840 census index of Nankin Twp., Wayne Co., Mich. (adjacent to LAWSON A.); and in the 1850 census of Hudson Twp., Lenawee Co., Mich. with ALONZO R., age 18, b. NY; and LUCENA, age 16; SIMEON, age 14; FIDELIA? A., age 12 (may be she listed again next door in household of LUCENA, wife of John Belcher); MARY, age 9; HELEN, age 6; SARAH E., age 3, all b. Mich., in their household.

VAN AKIN, HIRAM, son of JOHN (following), born ca. 1807, was reared in Phelps, Ontario Co., NY. He married HANNAH (WILSON) who was born ca. 1803, NY. They moved in 1836, after the birth of 2 children, to Michigan, stopping first in Wayne Co., Mich. "where two brothers lived" (note DUDLEY L. & LAWSON A.); and then moved by 1837 to Hudson Twp., Lenawee Co., Mich. "where 2 brothers and his mother were living." Known children: 1. LUCENA b. 2 May 1831, Junius, NY (m/1 John Belcher; m/2 Samuel King, see both); 2. CORNELIA b. ca. 1836; 3. THOMAS b. ca. 1840, Mich. Hiram died in July 1887, and she died Apr. 1886. Ref: P&BA-Len pg. 987-8.

VAN AKIN, JACOBUS in Dutch Church records was also known as JAMES. Therefore, please note the following resemblance. In the baptismal records of the Reformed Church of Machackameck is the following: JACOBUS VAN AKIN, with wife, ELIZABETH (BUNSCHOTEN) listed the following children, perhaps not a complete list: 1. LEVI bpt. 19 Aug. 1759; 2. GERRITJE bpt. 14 June 1761; 3. JOHANNES bpt. 17 Nov. 1765 (may have d. young); 4. JOHANNES (JOHN) bpt. 13 Dec. 1767.

VAN AKIN, JAMES (note JACOBUS, preceding) moved from Orange Co., NY to Upper Smithfield, Penn. (then located in Pike Co. which adjoined Orange Co., NY). Known son, JOHN (following). Note: There was a JAMES VAN AUKEN/VAN AKIN of Monroe Co., Penn. (Monroe Co. formed in 1836, from Pike & Wayne Cos., Penn.) who married JANE (DECKER), daughter of Daniel. Among their children was son, CASPARUS (lived Harwick, NJ, then Sussex, now Warren Co.)

VAN AKIN, JOHN, son of JAMES (preceding), born in 1760s, Upper Smithfield, Penn., moved to Phelps, Ontario Co., NY ca. 1796 and was among the earliest settlers. He married MARGARET (WESTFALL), daughter of Simeon (also see). John died in 1854?, in NY, but his wife had gone as early as 1834 to Wayne Co., Mich. with a son. She died at the home of a son while visiting in 1854. Nine sons, and one daughter, and only known: DUDLEY L. (preceding); (probably) LAWSON A. (following); SIMEON (following); WILLIAM HENRY HARRISON (following); LUCINA (m. Henry Vandemark, also see); HIRAM (preceding). Ref: P&BA-Len pg. 607-8; 820-3; 987-8.

VAN AKIN, JOHN M. born ca. 1807, NY, and wife, HANNAH, born ca. 1811, VT?, were probably they listed in the 1840 census index of Dover Twp., Lenawee Co., Mich. as "J. W." adjacent to LEMUEL (following); and in the 1850 census with NATHANIEL, age 21; HARRISON, age 19; JAMES H., age 19, all b. NY; and SARAH M., age 17; DAVID M., age 14; MARTHA A., age 10; JOHN M., age 6; CHARLOTTE E., age 1, all b. Mich., in their household.

VAN AKIN, LAWSON A., probably son of JOHN (preceding), was listed in the 1840 census index of Nankin Twp., Wayne Co., Mich. with DUDLEY L. (preceding).

VAN AKIN, LEMUEL born ca. 1812 and wife, SALLY A., born ca. 1816, both in NY, were listed in the 1850 census of Dover Twp., Lenawee Co., Mich. with MARY S., age 13, b. NY; and ANSON S., age 5; JARED A., age 3, both b. Mich., in their household.

VAN AKIN, SIMEON, son of JOHN (preceding), born ca. 1790, Penn., was listed in the 1840 census of Hudson Twp., Lenawee Co., Mich.; and in the 1850 census with wife, LYDIA, born ca. 1805, NY, and CLARISSA, age 10; SIMEON, age 7; WILLIAM W., age 8/12, all b. Mich.,

Pioneer Families of Southeastern Michigan

and perhaps stepchildren: Marvin W. Speer, age 19; Sarah Amelia Speer, age 18 (m. John K, Boies, also see), both b. NY; and Lorenzo Speer, age 16, b. Mich., in their household.

VAN AKIN, WILLIAM H. born ca. 1814, and wife, ESTHER J., born ca. 1820, both born in NY, were listed in the 1850 census of Blissfield Twp., Lenawee Co., Mich. with HENRY, age 13; CHARLES J., age 8; SYLVESTER, age 6; CATHARINE, age 4; EDWIN, age 2, all b. Mich., in their household.

VAN AKIN, WILLIAM HENRY HARRISON, son of JOHN (preceding), born 2 July 1816, Phelps, Ontario Co., NY, went in 1834 to Wayne Co., Mich. He married on 19 Sept. 1839 to JULIA A. (FEATHERLY), daughter of Frederick (also see). It may be he listed as "HARRISON" in the 1840 census index of Hudson Twp., Lenawee Co., Mich. In 1848, they went to Pittsford, Hillsdale Co., Mich. In 1858 settled in Hudson, Lenawee Co., Mich. Children: 1. CHARLOTTE F. (m. Dr. H. Welch; Ann Arbor, Mich.); 2. CORNELIA A. (m. E. J. Smith; Union City, Mich.); 3. WILLIAM H. (Hudson, Mich.); 4. CHARLES H. (South Bend, Ind.); 5. LILLIE (m. A. J. Lawrence; Hudson Twp.) Ref: P&BA-Len pg. 607-8.

VAN ALSTINE, ABRAM born ca. 1815, and wife, PAMELA?, born ca. 1810, both in NY, were listed in the 1850 census of Madison Twp., Lenawee Co., Mich. with CLEVELAND, age 12; MARY J., age 8; HARRIETT?, age 6; GEORGE, age 5; HIRAM, age 3, all b. Mich., in their household.

VAN ALSTINE, H. (note Harriet, in family of Abram) married Peter Maxwell, son of Israel Baker Maxwell (also see).

VAN ALSTINE, LOVINA, age 14, born Ohio, was listed in the 1850 census of Dover Twp., Lenawee Co., Mich.

VAN ALSTINE, PETER born ca. 1782, and wife, ELIZABETH, born ca. 1792, both in NY, were listed in the 1850 census of Madison Twp., Lenawee Co., Mich. with ANDREW, age 39; JACKSON, age 19; JULIA, age 17, all b. NY, in their household.

VAN AUKEN also see VAN AKIN

VAN AUKEN FAMILY - From History of Sussex & Warren Co., NJ, by Snell, in a biography of ABRAM COLE VAN AUKIN, it details the following ancestry. DANIEL immigrated from Holland about 1750(??) and settled at Minisink, Orange Co., NY. He married LEAH (KETTLE) and they had 15 children, all of whom settled around Minisink. The sketch lists 8 of the children, and others are from records of Machackameck Reformed Church, and the will of Daniel probated 3 Feb. 1818 (Liber F., pg. 186). Children: 1. JEREMIAH 1st (killed by indians in 1779); 2. DANIEL JR.; 3. NATHANIEL b. 17 Dec. 1753 (served in Revolution); 4. CATHARINE bpt. 13 Feb. 1758 (m. Daniel Myers); 5. ELIJAH b. 23 Oct. 1759; 6. ABSALOM; 7. ISAIAH; 8. JANNETJE RACHEL b. 31 Oct. 1767; 9. JOSHUA b. 1 Dec. 1771; 10. LEAH b. 25 Dec. 1776 (m. Jacob Hornbeck); 11. JEREMIAH 2d b. 29 Oct. 1780; 12. LEDIA (LYDIA?) (m. Jacob Cole); 13. MARGERY (m. Cornelius Cuddeback); 14. NATHAN; 15. JANE (m. Evert Hornbeck). The will was dated 1810, and listed wife, LEAH; sons: JOSHUA; JEREMIAH; ELIJAH (then eldest); ISAIAH; NATHAN; NATHANIEL; DANIEL JR.; Daughters: LEDIA, wife of Jacob Cole; CATHERINE, wife of Daniel Myers; JANE, wife of Evert Hornbeck; MARGERY, wife of Cornelius Cuddeback, and a grandson, Daniel Van Inwagen. Others were apparently deceased.

VAN AUKEN, ANGELINE, born ca. 1802, Cayuga Co., NY, married Peter Loyster (also see). Ref: P&B-Len pg. 704-5.

VAN AUKEN, LEWIS and wife, JANE (WESTFALL), probably of Washtenaw Co., Mich., had 16 children. Known daughter, ELIZA, born 23 June 1816 (m. Austin Gillett, also see). Ref: P&BA-Len pg. 486-7.

VAN AUKEN, ORIN was listed in the 1840 census index of Fairfield Twp., Lenawee Co., Mich. adjacent to BENJAMIN (See Van Aken).

VAN BRUNT, HARRIET (See Otis Richmond)

VAN BRUNT, NICHOLAS N., age 30 b. NY, was listed in the 1850 census of Adrian Twp., Lenawee Co., Mich. in a hotel.

VAN BRUNT, W. N. (See Norman Geddes)

VAN BUREN, JANE (See John Payne)

VAN CAMPEN, ? Miss (See Ephraim Sanford)

VAN CUREN, LYDIA of Ulster Co., NY (See Jeremiah Bevier)

VAN CURLEY, MARY (See Jeremiah A. Gilson)

VANDEGRIFFE, ELIJAH born ca. 1807, Penn., and wife, SARAH R., born ca. 1808, NY, were listed in the 1850 census of Adrian Twp., Lenawee Co., Mich. with SARAH, age 21; WILLIAM, age 19; GILES, age 17; ANN, age 15; JANE, age 11, all b. NY; and Johnson Finch, age 9; Daniel Finch, age 8, both b Mich., in their household.

VANDEGRIFFE, JOHN born ca. 1811, Penn., and wife, ALMIRA, born ca. 1812, NY, were listed in the 1850 census of Adrian Twp., Lenawee Co., Mich. with JOHN W., age 1, b. Mich.; and Rosanna Osterhout, age 10, b. NY, in their household.

VANDEMARK, ADDIE M. (See James B. Wells)

VANDEMARK, HENRY, son of JOSEPH (following), born in Phelps, Ontario Co., NY, married there to LUCINA (VAN AKIN), daughter of John (also see). Known daughter, MARGARET (m. Calvin C. Colwell). Ref: P&BA-Len pg. 820-2.

VANDEMARK, JOSEPH born Pike Co., Penn., and he and LODEWICK were early settlers of Phelps, Ontario Co., NY in 1794 (per Gazeteer of New York State, by J. H. French). Joseph died there. Known son, HENRY (preceding). Ref: P&BA-Len pg. 820-2. Also note ORSON, following.

VANDEMARK, ORSON born ca. 1808, NY, and wife, JANE G. (BROOKS), moved from Ontario Co., NY to Clinton Twp., Lenawee Co., Mich. in 1845. He died in 1872; and she died in 1848. In the 1850 census of Tecumseh Twp. he listed (second wife?) LOUISA, age 21; LODEWICK, age 17; CHARLOTTE C. b. 7 Apr. 1835, Phelps, NY (m. William P. Silvers, also see); and possibly a grandson? FREDUS, age 9/12, b. Mich.

VANDERWERT, J. (See Valentine Wenzel²)

VANDEVENTER, MASA (See Henry McCarbery)

VANDEVENTER, PETER born ca. 1812, and wife, MARIA, born ca. 1820, both in NY, were listed in the 1850 census of Macon Twp., Lenawee Co., Mich. with JOHN, age 9; WILLIAM, age 7, both b. NY; and ANNA M., age 4; CATHARINE J., age 3; ELISA B., age 2/12, all b. Mich., in their household.

VAN DINE also see VAN DUYN & VAN DYNE

VAN DINE, JARED, age 2, born Mich., was listed in the 1850 census of Medina Twp., Lenawee Co., Mich. in a Jared Van Fleet household, probably a grandson.

VAN DOREN see VAN DORN (spelled both ways in census)

VAN DORN, ABRAM, possibly son of CORNELIUS (following), born ca. 1811, and wife, AURILLA, born ca. 1818, both in NY, were listed in the 1840 census index of Fairfield Twp., Lenawee Co., Mich.; and in the 1850 census with ANDREW J., age 11; ALMIRA, age 8; CHARLES S., age 7; LYDIA, age 4; FRANCIS C., age 3; CORNELIUS, age 1, all b. Mich., in their household.

VAN DORN, CORNELIUS born ca. 1785, and wife, ELLEN, born ca. 1791, both in New Jersey, were listed in the 1840 census index of Adrian Twp., Lenawee Co., Mich. (adjacent to JACOB, following); and in the 1850 census with WILLIAM, age 27; JOHN, age 19; LYDIA W., age 15, all b. NY, in their household. ABRAM C.; FRANCIS A.; ISAAC; & JACOB E. are probably additional sons.

VAN DORN, EDMUND B. born ca. 1826, and wife, ELIZABETH, born ca. 1831, both in NY, were listed in the 1850 census of Adrian Twp., Lenawee Co., Mich. in the Solomon Warren household, possibly in-laws.

VAN DORN, FRANCIS A., probably son of CORNELIUS (preceding), born ca. 1822, and wife, SARAH, born ca. 1825, both in NY, were listed in the 1850 census of Adrian Twp., Lenawee Co., Mich. with JULIUS C., age 9/12, b. Mich., in their household.

VAN DORN, ISAAC, probably son of CORNELIUS (preceding), born ca. 1815, and wife, ELIZA, born ca. 1820, both in NY, were listed in the 1850 census of Adrian Twp., Lenawee Co., Mich. with CORNELIUS, age 6; ELLEN, age 4, both b. NY; and MARY, age 3, b. Mich., in their household.

VAN DORN, JACOB E., probably son of CORNELIUS (preceding), born ca. 1814, and wife, DRUSILLA, born ca. 1813, both in NY, were listed in the 1840 census index of Adrian Twp., Lenawee Co., Mich. (adjacent to CORNELIUS); and in the 1850 census with CHESTER C., age 7 (prob. he who m. Sarah C. Whitacre, dau. of Aaron, also see), b. Mich., in their household.

VAN DORN, LYDIA (MILLER) Mrs., daughter of Isaiah C. Miller (also see), born ca. 1849, married a Van Dorn and had a daughter, SARAH.

VAN DORN, MARY (See James B. Hood; and note in household of ISAAC, preceding).

VAN DORN, WILLIAM, age 25, born NY, was listed in the 1850 census of Madison Twp., Lenawee Co., Mich. in a Van Sickle household. (Note that this may be same as he in household of CORNELIUS, preceding).

VAN DUYN also see VAN DYNE

VAN DUYN, DENNIS married ANNA (COVERT) possibly in Somerset Co., NJ, and about 1804 they removed to Seneca Co., NY. Known daughter, LUTETIA b. 19 Oct. 1803, NJ (m. Dr. Joseph Howell, also see). Ref: P&BA-Len pg. 1036-7; 1168-9. Note: There were Van Duyn & Covert surnames in the militia of Bridgewater, Somerset Co., NJ in 1793.

VAN DUZEN, ELIZABETH (SCHOFIELD) Mrs. (See Lewis Miller).

VAN DYNE also see VAN DINE; VAN DUYN

VAN DYNE, GEORGE, son of PETER (who had come from Germany to Ontario Co., NY), married in Ontario Co., NY to CATHARINE (MILLER); and they moved in 1854 to Blissfield Twp., Lenawee Co., Mich. She died in 1864. Known daughter, MARY E. (m. William Henry Colyer, also see). Ref: P&BA-Len pg. 1151.

VAN EVERY, CATHERINE (See Joseph H. Blaine)

VAN FLEET also see VAN VLEET

VAN FLEET, CORNELIUS, son of Col. MATHIAS (following), was born in Penn., and moved to Ohio with his parents. He married ca. 1840 to HANNAH (RUNYAN), daughter of William (also see), probably in Lucas Co., Ohio. There were 8 children, names not stated, except #8. PLINY (following). Ref: P&BA-Len pg. 1147.

VAN FLEET, JARED born ca. 1800, and wife, NANCY, born ca. 1801, both in Penn., were listed in the 1840 census index of Medina Twp., Lenawee Co., Mich.; and in the 1850 census with MARY, age 21, b. Penn.; and probably grandson, Jared Van Dine, age 2, b. Mich., in their household.

VAN FLEET, MATHIAS Col. was a native of Penn., and he moved to Dayton, then to Lucas Co., Ohio. He was a Col. in the State Militia. Known son, CORNELIUS (preceding). Ref: P&BA-Len pg. 1147.

VAN FLEET, PLINY, son of CORNELIUS (preceding), born 28 Apr. 1845, Westerville, Ohio, enlisted in Feb. 1864 in the 23rd NY Indep. Battery. Afterwards, he returned to Ohio. He married in Nov. 1871 to LUCRETIA (TAYLOR), daughter of William (also see). About 1882, they moved to Palmyra Twp., Lenawee Co., Mich. Children: 1. M. L.; 2. BLANCHE; 3. WILLIAM T.; 4. RALPH; 5. EDNA. Ref: P&BA-Len pg. 1147.

VAN NESS, JOSEPH B. (See Hudson W. Conkling)

VAN NOSTRAND also see VAN OSTRAND
VAN NOSTRAND, HANNAH E. (See Robert Wilson)

VAN NOY, WILLIAM (See Simeon Westfall)

VAN OSTRAND also see VAN NOSTRAND
VAN OSTRAND, AARON (See Martin P. Stockwell)
VAN OSTRAND, AMELIA (See Isaac Davis)

VAN PELT, ? and wife, ELIZABETH (TAYLOR), were natives of Penn., who moved to New Petersburg, Highland Co., Ohio in 1828. In 1850, they moved to Iowa, but came back to Sylvania, Lucas Co., Ohio, where he died in 1853, and she died later. Children: 1.

ISAAC (d. 1887); 2. SARAH JANE (m. Aaron Cleveland; Clermont, O.); 3. LEWIS (Ohio); 4. THOMAS (Ohio); 5. JOHN H. (following). Ref: P&BA-Len pg. 281-3.

VAN PELT, JOHN H., son of ? (preceding), born 20 July 1837, Highland Co., Ohio, married in Ohio in 1860 to CELESTIA (MERSEREAU), daughter of Cornelius (also see). They settled in Riga Twp., Lenawee Co., Mich. Children: 1. ALICE (m. Henry Gull; Riga Twp.); 2. LOUIS (Lima, Ohio); 3. GEORGE; 4. ARTHUR; 5. ERNEST; 6. JOHN; 7. CHARLES; 8. Infant deceased. Ref: P&BA-Len pg. 281-3.

VAN PELT, MARGARET born New Jersey (See Daniel Tingley[1])

VAN SCOY, LOVISA (See Edmund Burch)

VAN SICKLE, ANDREW born ca. 1802, and wife, MARY (STRAIGHT), born ca. 1806, both in New Jersey, married in Chemung Co., NY, after 1837 moved to Ohio. Before 1850, they moved to Seneca Twp., Lenawee Co., Mich. He died in May 1885; and she was still living in 1888, age 82. In the 1850 census of Seneca Twp., they listed in their household: 1. SOPHIA b. 27 Dec. 1827, Chemung Co., NY (m. Solomon Wolf, also see); 2. MARGARET, age 20; MARY A., age 18; HANNAH, age 17; LEAH, age 15; ISAAC, age 14; HIRAM, age 13, all b. NY. Ref: P&BA-Len pg. 1097. Note: Listed next door to JACOB, following, in 1850 census.

VAN SICKLE, ANDREW born ca. 1815, and wife, SARAH, born ca. 1820, both in NY, were listed in the 1850 census of Madison Twp., Lenawee Co., Mich. near to EDWIN (following) with William Van Dorn, age 25, b. NY, in the household.

VAN SICKLE, ANDREW J., son of ISAAC (following), born 22 Jan. 1834, married in 1855 to MATILDA (CHITTENDEN), daughter of Daniel (also see), born 20 Apr. 1836 in Mich. No children were listed in sketch. Ref: P&BA-Len pg. 208.

VAN SICKLE, EDWIN born ca. 1825, and wife, DELIA, born ca. 1826, both in NY, were listed in the 1850 census of Madison Twp., Lenawee Co., Mich. with ELLEN, age 1, b. Mich.; and WILLIAM, age 17, b. NY (brother?), in their household.

VAN SICKLE, IDA born after 1850, married William Wolf, son of Solomon (also see).

VAN SICKLE, ISAAC born ca. 1807, and wife, JANE (COX), born ca. 1812, both in New Jersey, moved to Chemung Co., NY after their marriage. They moved to Ohio for 8 years, then returned to NY; then again to Ohio, and about 1847 to Dover Twp., Lenawee Co., Mich. She died there in 1878, age 61. There were 3 sons, names not stated, residing in Seneca Co., NY. Isaac later resided with son, ANDREW J. (preceding); and the following were in the household in the 1850 census: JACOB b. ca. 1840, NY; GEORGE b. ca. 1844, Ohio. Ref: P&BA-Len pg. 208.

VAN SICKLE, JACOB born ca. 1804, and wife, MARGARET, born ca. 1812, both in NY, were listed in the 1850 census of Seneca Twp., Lenawee Co., Mich. with ISAIAH, age 21; JOHN, age 20; GEORGE, age 18; JONAS, age 16; PETER, age 13, all b. NY; and SUSAN, age 9; PERRY?, age 4, both b. Ohio; and WILSON?, age 7/12, b. Mich., in their household.

VAN SICKLE, MINA (probably born after 1850; see Elias Brower)

VAN SICKLE/SYCKLE, TILLIE (See Matthew H. Kerr)

VAN SICKLES, CORA (See Robert L. Rogers)

VANSTYKE, NANCY (See James P. Hawley)

VAN TUYL also see VAN TYLE

VAN TUYL, ADAM had come as a single man from Cayuga Co., NY to Clinton, Lenawee Co., Mich. He married there to SARAH (POLHEMUS), daughter of Cornelius (also see). They settled in Manchester, Washtenaw Co., Mich., and he died there in 1870. Of their 5 children, 2 were deceased before 1888 (names not stated): 1. JOHN A. (m. Annie Best; Manchester, Mich.); 2. GEORGE H. (m. Frances Sones); 3. WILLARD D. (m. Alta Silvers, dau. of William P., also see). After the death of Adam, Sarah married again to Rev. William Wastell (also see). Ref: P&BA-Len pg. 445-50.

VAN TUYL, CARRIE of Clinton Twp., Lenawee Co., Mich. (See David Woodward).

VAN TYLE also see VAN TUYL

VAN TYLE, THOMAS born ca. 1783, and wife, MARY, born ca. 1783, both in New Jersey, moved to Seneca Co., NY. In 1832, they moved to Lenawee Co., Mich. with known daughter, MARY (m. Henry Hoagland, also see, in 1824) and her husband. They were listed in the 1840 census index of Macon Twp.; but they were listed in the 1850 census of Ridgeway Twp. Thomas died in Ridgeway Twp. at age 73. Ref: P&BA-Len pg. 1127-8.

VAN VALKENBURG, HENRIETTA (See Jacob Crounse)

VAN VLECK, LUCRETIA (See Erastus Park)

VAN VLEET also see VAN FLEET

VAN VLEET, ANN (See Dr. William Brown)

VAN VLEET, GEORGE married in New Jersey to MARTHA (VOORHEES), and after the birth of 2 children, moved to Penn. It may be he listed in Amwell, Hunterdon Co., NJ in the Militia in 1793. Two children were born in Penn., and they moved to Seneca Co., NY (probably he listed in the 1800 census index of Cayuga Co., NY). She died there at age 50; and he died age 70. Known daughter, MAGGIE b. 17 May 1807, Seneca Co., NY (m. John Osgood, also see). Ref: P&BA-Len pg. 405-6.

VAN VLEET, JOHANNA probably born NJ, married Abraham Cadmus (also see). Ref: P&BA-Len pg. 331-3.

VAN VLEET, JOHN, son of PETER P. (following), born ca. 1842, Mich., married 12 Dec. 1867 to SARAH I. (LUCE), daughter of Samuel H. (also see). Son, JARED. Ref: P&BA-Len pg. 262-3.

VLEET, PETER was listed in the 1840 census index of Macon Twp., Lenawee Co., Mich. adjacent to PETER P. (following).

VAN VLEET, PETER JR. born in New Jersey, served in the Revolutionary War. It may be he listed in the Militia of Reading, Hunterdon, Co., NJ in 1793. He married MARY (BLUE), also born NJ, and they moved to Seneca Co., NY, where he died. It is probably he listed in the 1800 census index of Cayuga Co., NY. Nine sons, and three daughters, names not stated, except PETER P. (following).

VAN VLEET, PETER J. born ca. 1822, and wife, MARY, born ca. 1822, Conn., were listed in the 1850 census of Macon Twp., Lenawee Co., Mich. with EDWIN B., age 1, b. Mich., in their household.

VAN VLEET, PETER P., son of PETER JR. (preceding), born ca. 1799, NY, married in Seneca Co., NY to LOIS (SWARTHOUT), born ca. 1801, NY, and their first 8 children were born there. In 1832, they moved to Macon Twp.; and in 1834 to Ridgeway Twp., Lenawee Co., Mich., and was listed there in the 1840 census index. He died 31 June 1879. There were 7 sons and 6 daughters, names not stated. In the 1850 census of Ridgeway Twp., they listed SARAH A., age 26; EDGAR C., age 22 (m. Mary A. Waring, dau. of Joshua, also see); LOIS b. 10 Dec. 1830, Lodi, NY (m. Miles P. Morton, also see); SOPHIA, age 17; CATHARINE E., age 13, b. Mich.; JARED, age 11; #12. JOHN (preceding); EMMA J., age 4. Ref: P&BA-Len pg. 262-3; 580-1. Also note PETER J. & RALPH S.

VAN VLEET, RALPH S. born ca. 1821, and wife, HENRIETTA, borh ca. 1820, both in NY, were listed in the 1850 census of Tecumseh Twp., Lenawee Co., Mich. with SARAH, age 1; PETER, age 8/12; and William Miller, age 11, all b. Mich., in their household.

VAN VOORHEES also see VOORHEES
VAN VOORHEES, LUCRETIA (See Freeman Rice)

VAN WEY was spelled VAN WEE & VAN WYE in the census.
VAN WEY, DANIEL H., possibly son of HENRY (following), born ca. 1820, and wife, AMY, born ca. 1821, both in NY, were listed in the 1850 census of Hudson Twp., Lenawee Co., Mich. with GARRET F., age 1; DANIEL W., age 2/12, both b. Mich., and Peter B. Smith, age 27, b. NY, in their household.

VAN WEY, HENRY and wife, ELSIE (FREER), were natives of Ulster Co., NY, and moved to Palmyra Twp., Lenawee Co., Mich. He died there on 22 Oct. 1872. Known daughter, CATHERINE b. 5 Dec. 1811, Ulster Co. (m. Cornelius DeGraff, also see). Ref: P&BA-Len pg. 763. Note: They may also be parents of DANIEL C.; HENRY; PETER; & CORNELIUS (who was in household of Peter in 1850).

VAN WEY, HENRY, possibly son of HENRY (preceding), born ca. 1826, and wife, SOPHIA, born ca. 1825, both in NY, were listed in the 1850 census of Hudson Twp., Lenawee Co., Mich. with no family.

VAN WEY, PETER, possibly son of HENRY (preceding), born ca. 1817, and (probably) wife, MARGARET, born ca. 1832, both in NY, were listed with probably brother, CORNELIUS, age 18, b. NY; and Jane Covert, age 51, b. NY, in their household.

VAN WORT, GETTIE (See Henry G. Colegrove)

VAN WYAH see VAN WEY

VARNER, ANNE (See Wayne Kelley)

VARNEY, ANNA (See Elihu Carpenter)

VARNOLD, PELEG (See Eliathah Stockwell)

VARNUM, BENJAMIN was born ca. 1787, VT, and wife, MARY, born ca. 1800, NY, lived in Canada in 1821, and probably moved first to Washtenaw Co., Mich.; and then by the 1850 census to Seneca Twp., Lenawee Co., Mich., where they were listed with HENRIETTA, age 6, b. Mich., in their household. They were listed next door to probably daughter, STATIRA (VARNUM), b. 1821, Canada (and her husband, Abner P. Wilcox, also see). Also in Benjamin's household were Lorenzo Firman, age 18, and sister, Lucy Firman, age 15, both b. Canada; and next door in the Wilcox household was Lucinda Firman, age 16, b. Canada. These may be stepchildren of Benjamin?

VAUGHAN also see VAUGHN
VAUGHAN, JAMES was a native of Washington Co., NY, and he married ? (MOON). He died at age 60. Known son, LEMUEL C. P. (following). Ref: P&BA-Len pg. 1002-3. Note Henry Vaughn, following.

VAUGHAN, JULIUS Dr., son of LEMUEL C. P. (following), born 21 Mar. 1833, Concord, Erie Co., NY, got his medical degree in New York City. He afterwards in 1862 moved to Springville, Cambridge Twp., Lenawee Co., Mich. He married on 5 June 1866 to ANNA E. (WICKHAM), daugher of Thomas (also see) and remained in Springville. Son, CHARLES H. Ref: P&BA-Len pg. 1002-3.

VAUGHAN, LEMUEL C. P., son of JAMES (preceding), born ca. 1815, Washington Co., NY, married there to ACHSAH (TWISS), daughter of Jeremiah (also see). They moved to Concord, Erie Co., NY. He died there in Sept. 1879, age 64, and she was still living there in 1888, age 75. Children: 1. Dr. JULIUS (preceding); 2. RUSSELL J. (m. Theresa Green; Erie Co., NY); 3. ALONZO L. (m. Emma G. Smith); 4. JENNIE A. (in New York City); 5. C. L. DDS (Brooklyn, Jackson Co., Mich.); 6. LORENZO A. (m. Mary Potter; Erie Co., NY); 7. ACHSAH (m. Dr. Daniel Lewis; New York City). Ref: P&BA-Len pg. 1002-3.

VAUGHN also see VAUGHAN
VAUGHN, ELIZABETH (See John Hawkins)
VAUGHN, HENRY born ca. 1822, and wife, MARY C. (FELTON), born ca. 1830, Clarence Hollow, Erie Co., NY. Children (all b. after 1850): 1. MARY E. (m. Willis G. Mann; Newton, IA); 2. EVA C. (m. Charles M. Hinsdale; Newton, IA). They were listed in the 1850 census of Tecumseh Twp., Lenawee Co., Mich. with Welcome V. Fisk (also see) and wife, AMANDA (VAUGHN), in their household. After the death of Henry, Mary C. married second to Welcome V. Fisk. Ref: P&BA-Len pg. 339-40.

VAUGHN, JOSEPH was listed in the 1840 census index of Dover Twp., Lenawee Co., Mich.

VAUGHN, SAMUEL born ca. 1829, NY, was listed in the 1850 census of Dover Twp., Lenawee Co., Mich. in the household of Levi Thompson; and it may be he listed following as "S. D."

VAUGHN, S. D. married ELIZABETH (McMATH) who died in Dover Twp., Lenawee Co., Mich. on 26 Jan. 1857. He married second to her sister, LAURA A. (McMATH), both daughters of Fleming (also see). Ref: P&BA-Len PG. 409-10.

Pioneer Families of Southeastern Michigan

VAUGHN, WILLIAM born ca. 1818, and wife, ALMIRA (age illegible, 25?, possibly a 2nd wife, shown married within the year), both in NY, were listed in the 1850 census of Tecumseh Twp., Lenawee Co., Mich. with (ages illegible) WILLIAM, age 3?; & FREDUS? (male), ?/12? both b. Mich.; and also a MARIAN who appears older, born NY.

VEDDER, ALBERT, age 17, born NY, was listed in the 1850 census of Adrian Twp., Lenawee Co., Mich. in a Gurnee household.

VEDDER, CHAUNCEY married MARTHA H. (LANNING), daughter of James (also see). Note in household of JOHN, following.

VEDDER, HARMON born ca. 1806, NY, and wife, ANN(A) (BORDINE) born ca. 1816, Montgomery Co., NY, married in Orleans Co., NY, and moved by 1839 to Dover Twp., Lenawee Co., Mich. In the 1850 census of Dover Twp., they listed in their household: CORDELIA, age 11; AARON, age 10; SOPHRONIA b. 25 Apr. 1841, Dover Twp. (m. John Bryant, son of John, also see); RANSOM, age 5?; CLARK, age 6, all b. Mich., in their household.

VEDDER, JOHN born ca. 1809, and wife, ANNA, born ca. 1805, both in NY, were listed in the 1850 census of Adrian Twp., Lenawee Co., Mich. with MARIETTE, age 16, b. NY; and CLARISSA, age 13; LOREN, age 10; CHAUNCEY, age 8 (note preceding); SIMON, age 5; JOANNA, age 3, all b. Mich., in their household. Note ALBERT, preceding.

VEDDER, MARIETTA (See Butler Treat)

VELIE, MARIE (See John Munger)

VERGIL also see VIRGIL
VERGIL, ASEL was a Revolutionary soldier; and had known daughter, MALINDA born ca. 1789, Delaware Co., NY (m. Alvan Doty, also see). Asel died in Greene Co., NY. In the 1800 census index, there was an Asa Virgil in Columbia Co., NY.

VEST, ELI born ca. 1808, a "native of Seneca Co., NY," married ELIZA (WOOD), born ca. 1811, daughter of Barnabas (who was called a native of New England). They moved by 1840 to Tecumseh Twp., Lenawee Co., Mich. He died in 1855, age 47. Eliza was living in Clinton, Lenawee Co., Mich. in 1881. In the 1850 census of Tecumseh Twp., they listed MARY, age 16; JOHN, age 14; BENJAMIN, age 13, all b. NY; and GILBERT, age 11; CATHARINE b. 12 Sept. 1840, Tecumseh Twp. (m. Philip S. Howland, also see); CHARLOTTE, age 8; ANN, age 5; CHARLES, age 3, FRANCES, age 2/12, all b. Mich. Ref: History of Jackson Co., Mich., 1881, pg. 799-800.

VICKERY, NATHAN, son of ELI (born England, d. Rensselaer Co., NY), was born in Rensselaer Co., NY. He married JULIANA (RUSK), daughter of William (also see). In 1838, they settled in Richfield Twp., Lucas Co., Ohio, where they remained until "an advanced age." They moved to Riga Twp., Lenawee Co., Mich. to lived with daughter, MARY (m. Roberts). Known daughter, ANNA J. (m. Philo C. Seager, also see). Nathan died 27 July 1882; and she died 7 Aug. 1887, Riga Twp. Ref: P&BA-Len pg. 369-70.

VINCENT, CLARK born Rhode Island, appears to have married PARLY (GRAY) born Conn. who died in Allegany Co., NY (sketch was confusing). After his marriage, he moved to Rensselaer Co., NY. In 1830, he moved to Warren Co., Penn. where he died. Known daughter, PHILINDA (m. William Armitage, also see). Ref: P&BA-Len pg. 603-4.

VINCENT, JAMES Rev., son of JOHN & MARTHA (who both d. in England), born 22 Nov. 1812, Norfolk Co., England, married in Oct. 1843 to JANE E. (WELCH) of London. They came first to New Market, Canada, then Paris, Canada. In 1856, they moved to Warsaw, Wyoming Co., NY; and from there to churches in St. Clair, Mich.; and then to Illinois. He served in Albion, Muskegon, and Franklin, Mich. He retired to Tecumseh, Lenawee Co., Mich. Six children, but 3 died infancy (names not stated): 1. WILLIAM L. (d. 4th Mich. Cav., Civil War); 2. JAMES E. (Saginaw, Mich.); 3. FRANCES J. (m. Dr. Henry C. Wann; Chicago, Ill.) Ref: P&BA-Len pg. 609-10.

VINING, ELIZABETH (See William Ladd)

VIRGIL also see VERGIL
VIRGIL, PATIENCE (See Dr. Arba N. Moulton)

VIVIAN, WILLIAM (See Edwin A. Baker)

VOORHEES also see VAN VOORHEES
VOORHEES, FRANCIS born ca. 1811, NY, and wife, HOPE, born ca. 1824, Mass., were listed in the 1850 census of Madison Twp., Lenawee Co., Mich. with GEORGE, age 5; ELLIS, age 3; FRANCIS, age 1, all b. Mich.; and listed last in the household AUGUSTUS, age 17, b. NY.

VOORHEES, JOHN born ca. 1806, New Jersey, and wife, SUSAN, born ca. 1807, NY, are probably they listed in the 1840 census index of Ogden Twp., Lenawee Co., Mich.; and were listed in the 1850 census of Madison Twp. with JANE, age 21, b. NY; and JACOB, age 13; HENRY, age 8; EMELINE, age 8/12, all b. Mich., in their household.

VOORHEES, JOHN I, and wife, MARTHA (TEEPLE), probably born in New Jersey, were pioneers to Schoharie Co., NY. He came to Adrian Twp., Lenawee Co., Mich. at an advanced age to live with known daughter, MARY$_2$ b. ca. 1790, Schoharie Co. NY (m. Nathaniel Smith^2, also see). Ref: P&BA-Len pg. 704-5.; 1120-1.

VOORHEES, MARTHA born New Jersey (See George Van Vleet).

VOORHEES, ORLANDO, age 18, born NY, was listed in the 1850 census of Cambridge Twp., Lenawee Co., Mich. in the household of Charles and Samantha Winne.

VOORHEES, PETER T. born ca. 1805, and wife, REBECCA, born ca. 1809, both in NY (probably he listed "PETER A." in 1840 census index of Adrian Twp., Lenawee Co., Mich.); was listed in the 1850 census of Adrian Twp. with LEWIS, age 21; WARREN, age 18, both b. NY; and JAMES, age 16; CLINTON, age 14; STEPHEN T., age 7; ELTHERE M. (ESTHER M.?), age 5; EMERGINE, age 2, all b. Mich., in their household.

VOORHEES, RALPH born ca. 1811, Penn., and wife, PALMIRA, born ca. 1826, NY, were listed in the 1850 census of Adrian Twp., Lenawee Co., Mich. with EBIN, age 4; MATILDA, age 6/12, both b. Mich., in their household.

VOORHEES, SAMUEL born ca. 1810, and wife, ELEANOR, born ca. 1809, both in NY, were listed in the 1840 census index of Rome Twp., Lenawee Co., Mich.; and in the 1850 census with MARGARET, age 9; JOHN W., age 7, both b. Mich., in their household.

VREELAND, MICHAEL and wife, ELIZABETH, of Fayette, Seneca Co., NY, had known daughter, ELIZA (m. Hezekiah Knowles, Jr., also see).

VROOMAN, DANIEL came from Holland with his parents and they settled in the Mohawk Valley of NY where he remained. Known son, JOHN A. (following). Ref: P&BA-Lenpg. 792-3.

VROOMAN, GARRETT, son of JOHN A. (following), born 17 Jan. 1818, Lenox, Madison Co., NY, was a fur trader in the Michigan Territory before it was a state. He was living in 1842 in Richfield, Lucas Co., Ohio; and moved later to Raisinville, Mich. and afterwards to Riga Twp., Lenawee Co. He married on 12 Nov. 1843 to SALLIE (TREADWAY), daughter of Reuben (also see) of Riga Twp. Children: 1. F. HIRAM (to Alpena, Mich.); 2. A. ELEANOR (m. Henry E. Prentis; Metamora, Ohio). Ref: P&BA-Len pg. 792-3.

VROOMAN, JOHN A., son of DANIEL (preceding), born ca. 1792, Montgomery Co., NY, married ELIZABETH (BINGHAM), daugher of Rial (also see). They lived in Lenox, Madison Co., NY before 1818; and about 1837 moved to Lucas Co., Ohio. He died there in 1877, age 85. There were 10 children, and 8 lived to maturity (names not stated), except eldest, GARRETT (preceding); and ELECTA E. (m. Giles Comstock, also see). Ref: P&BA-Len pg. 792-3.

VROOMAN, JOSEPH born ca. 1823, Ohio, and wife ANN, born ca. 1830, NY, were listed in the 1850 census of Adrian Twp., Lenawee Co., Mich. with EMMA J., age 1, b. Ohio, in their household. Note JOHN A., preceding.

- W -

WADE, ALICE (See Edward F. Underwood)
WADE, GILBERT A. was listed in the 1840 census index of Rome Twp., Lenawee Co., Mich.
WADE, SILAS A. was listed in the 1840 census index of Rome Twp., Lenawee Co., Mich.

WADSWORTH, ALBERT born ca. 1802, and wife, POLLY, born ca. 1808, both in NY, were listed in the 1850 census of Hudson Twp., Lenawee Co., Mich. with SAMUEL W., age 17; CELESTIA M., age 14; ORSON, age 11; CHESTER, age 8, all b. NY; and BARRET, age 6, b. Mich., in their household.

WADSWORTH, CLARISSA, age 15, born Mich., was listed in the 1850 census of Hudson Twp., Lenawee Co., Mich. in a Harrington household. May belong to the family of ALBERT, preceding?

WADSWORTH, JOSEPH born 15 Feb. 1795, Bennington, VT, and he and his wife, POLLY, resided in Pittstown, Rensselaer Co., NY. They later moved to Rochester, NY where he died on 17 Aug. 1864 of Cholera. Known daughter, MARIAN born 27 Aug. 1829, Pittstown, NY (m. Willis Thompson Lawrence, also see). Ref: P&BA-Len pg. 917-8.

WADSWORTH, JOSEPH E. was born 19 Oct. 1801, Pompey, Onondaga Co., NY, and married in NY to ADELIA M. who was born 23 Nov. 1805, Conn. About 1837, they removed to Adrian Twp., Lenawee Co., Mich. In the 1850 census of Adrian Twp., only Adelia is listed in the household of her known daughter, EMILY E. born 23 Oct. 1825, Manchester, Ontario Co., NY (m. John R. Clark, also see). Apparently Adelia married again after 1850, as in the sketch she was called Mrs. Adelia M. Wheeler. Ref: P&BA-Len pg. 774-5.

WAGENLANDER, JOHN (See Jacob Kurtz)

WAGGONER also see WAGONER
WAGGONER, ADAM born ca. 1821, and wife, MARTHA, born ca. 1821, both in Germany, were listed in the 1850 census of Rome Twp., Lenawee Co., Mich. with LEWIS, age 2, b. Mich., in their household.

WAGGONER, ISRAEL born ca. 1790, New Jersey, lived for a time in Canada. His wife, LUCRETIA, born 1 Apr. 1787, Mass., went as a child to Vermont. Lucretia and a brother, Abel, went ca. 1807 from Vermont to Batavia, NY. Abel died, and she went to Buffalo, NY where she married first to ? Lake. They moved to NE Penn., and he served in the War of 1812. They afterwards moved to Ohio, and he died there in 1818. Lucretia married second to Israel in 1819, and they farmed in Huron Co., Ohio. He died in 1857, and she afterwards moved to Seneca Twp., Lenawee Co., Mich. and lived with a known daughter, MARY born 27 Aug. 1826 (m. Richard H. Kinney, also see). Known son, CLARK (went to Clyde, Ohio, had son, Ralph). Ref: P&BA-Len pg. 532-3.

WAGGONER, NICHOLAS, son of NICHOLAS (who d. age 65 in Montreal, Canada), was born 12 July 1803, Vermont, and moved at an early age to New York state. He married there to ABIGAIL (TAYLOR) born 7 Nov. 1821, NY. They moved to Rome Twp., Lenawee Co., Mich. in 1837, and she died 14 Dec. 1845. Known daughter, ALVIRA born 18 Jan. 1839, Rome Twp. (lived in household of Samuel Stone in 1850 census; m. Edmund Lapham, also see). ALBERT, age 6, born Mich. (listed in the 1850 census of Rome Twp. in the household of Jesse Fleming may be another son). Note: Nicholas was said to be living in Rome Twp. in 1888, but I was unable to locate him in the 1850 census.

WAGNER, BARBARA (See Christian Shultis)
WAGNER, JULIA (See John G. Heckert)

WAGONER see WAGGONER

WAIT see WAITE

WAITE, AUSTIN B. was listed in the 1840 census index of Tecumseh Twp., Lenawee Co., Mich.
WAITE, ELISHA W. born ca. 1797, NY, and wife, LYDIA, born ca. 1795, Conn., were listed in the 1840 census index of Dover Twp., Lenawee Co., Mich.; and in the 1850 census with MARY E., age 18; LOIZA, age 16, both b. NY; and HENRY M., age 3, b. Mich., in their household.

Pioneer Families of Southeastern Michigan

It is probably Elisha called "E. W." who married in Dover Twp. to Mrs. ASENATH (MACK) SHEPHERD, widow of Rev. Paul (also see).

WAITE, GEORGE L., son of HENRY (following), born 17 Sept. 1852, Palmyra Twp., married on 4 Jan. 1882 to IDA J. (KAYNER), daughter of Charles (also see). Children: CHARLES b. 26 Apr. 1883; 2. CORRINE b. 9 June 1884. Ref: P&BA-Len pg. 224-5.

WAITE, HENRY born Rochester, NY, married in 1850 to ADELINE (LUSK) born Monroe Co., NY. They moved to Madison Twp., Lenawee Co., Mich. where they were listed in the 1850 census with only child #2 in the household. They moved to Palmyra Twp. where he died 10 Dec. 1877; and she died in 1857. Children: 1. infant died; 2. WILLIAM A./or E. (Eaton Co., Mich.); 3. GEORGE L. (preceding); 4. JEROME B. (Palmyra Twp.) Henry married again, but name of wife not stated. Ref: P&BA-Len pg. 224-5.

WAITE, JULIA, age 35, born NY, was listed in the 1850 census of Adrian Twp., Lenawee Co., Mich. in a Morey household.

WAITE, MARY E. (See Fleming McMath)

WAITE, THOMAS, age 99?, born Conn., was listed in the 1850 census of Madison Twp., Lenawee Co., Mich. in a Meach household.

WAKEFIELD, CHARLES C., son of DENNIS (following), born 16 Feb. 1841, Seneca Twp., Lenawee Co., Mich.; lived in Pioneer, Ohio from 1862 to 1868, then returned to Morenci, Lenawee Co. He had married on 3 Nov. 1864 to JOSEPHINE O. (ROGERS) born 5 Apr. 1846, Pioneer, Ohio. Children: 1. CASSIUS E.; 2. ABBIE G.; 3. EVA E.; 4. LULU J.; 5. DENNIS K. Ref: P&BA-Len pg. 724-5.

WAKEFIELD, DENNIS, son of MOSES (following), born ca. 1810, Thompson, Windham Co., Conn., came to Lenawee Co., Mich. in 1834, and took up land in what is now Seneca & Medina Twps. He married in July 1839 to ABIGAIL (CROSBY), probably daughter of Charles (also see) who was also born in Thompson, Conn. She died in March, 1845. Children: 1. CHARLES C. (preceding); 2. LEIGH RICHMOND b. ca. 1843. Dennis married again in 1847 to CHARITY (SCOFIELD) born ca. 1825, NY. Children: 1. ANN AUGUSTA b. ca. 1848; 4. WILLIAM H. Charity died in March 1851; and Dennis married in Oct. 1853 to AMANDA (CROVER). He died 2 June 1886, Seneca Twp. Ref: P&BA-Len pg. 724-5.

WAKEFIELD, HIRAM, son of MOSES (following), born 6 Dec. 1807, and his wife, RACHEL (CROSBY), daughter of Charles (also see), were both born in Thompson, Conn. They married there in 1830, and in 1835 removed to Medina Twp., Lenawee Co., Mich. Known daughter, EMILY b. 29 June 1831, Thompson, Conn. (m. Silas A. Scofield, also see). Ref: P&BA-Len pg. 733-4.

WAKEFIELD, MOSES, born Conn., died in Thompson, Windham Co., Conn. in 1816. His wife, NANCY (KIMBALL), born ca. 1786, Conn., removed to Medina Twp., Lenawee Co., Mich. about 1835. In the 1850 census of Seneca Twp., Lenawee Co., she was listed in the household of Horatio N. Wilson (also see). Known sons: DENNIS (preceding); HIRAM (preceding); and probably daughter, PHEBE b. ca. 1815, Conn. (m. Horatio N. Wilson). Ref: P&BA-Len pg. 724-5.

WAKELY, SOPHRONIA (See Reuben Downs; Jacob Ward; & Charles Morgan).

WALDRON, AARON K., son of WILLIAM (following), born 23 Oct. 1823, Seneca Co., NY, married on 19 Sept. 1846 to SARAH M. (GUNDERMAN), daughter of Jacob (also see) probably in Seneca Co. They moved to Tecumseh Twp., Lenawee Co., Mich. by 1848 and were listed in the 1850 census. Children: 1. LEWIS M. b. ca. 1848; 2. WILLIAM J. b. 19 Dec. 1850 (m. Isabel F. Griswold, dau. of George, also see, on 30 Mar. 1881); 3. CHARLES A. (Raisin Twp.); 4. CLARA A.; 5. ADA E.; 6. SARAH H. Ref: P&BA-Len pg. 1066-7.

WALDRON, ELIZABETH Mrs., maiden name possibly (STOUT), apparently married first to a Waldron, and second to Joseph S. Hagaman (also see), possibly in Orleans Co., NY, and went afterwards to Seneca Co. One sketch called her Elizabeth Stout; and another called her Mrs. Elizabeth Waldron.

WALDRON, JOHN W. born ca. 1784, and wife, LYDIA, born ca. 1784, both in New Jersey, were listed in the 1850 census of Madison Twp., Lenawee Co., Mich. in the household of probably son, WILLIAM W. (following).

WALDRON, LEWIS W. (See I. H. Schreder)

WALDRON, POLLY (MARY?) born 23 Sept. 1776, Ulster Co., NY, married Abram Harris (also see). Ref: P&BA-Len pg. 739-40.

WALDRON, WILLIAM born in Jan. 1789, New Jersey, and wife, HESTER (MATTHEWS) born 2 July 1795, NY, settled in NY, possibly Seneca Co., where he died 14 Nov. 1833. They had 6 sons and 1 daughter, names not stated, except AARON K. (preceding). Ref: P&BA-Len pg. 978-81.

WALDRON, WILLIAM W., son of JOHN W. (preceding), born ca. 1828, and wife, HARRIET, born ca. 1830, both in NY, were listed in the 1850 census of Madison Twp., Lenawee Co., Mich. with father & mother, see JOHN W., preceding, in their household.

WALES, JACOB and wife, SYLVIA A. (RANSDELL), were natives of Mass. who went to New Hampshire. Four children, names not stated, except ESTHER I. (m. Luke N. Damon, also see, on 13 Nov. 1843). Ref: P&BA-Len pg. 460-1.

WALKER, ANDREW born ca. 1821, Mass., and probably wife, OLIVE A., born ca. 1826, NY, were listed in the 1850 census of Adrian Twp., Lenawee Co., Mich. with probably brother, SETH S. Jr. (following); and Rachel E. Tibbles, age 19, b. Mass., in their household.

WALKER, BENJAMIN G. born ca. 1813, and wife, MARY, born ca. 1818, both in NY, were listed in the 1840 census index of Adrian TWp., Lenawee Co., Mich.; and in the 1850 census of Tecumseh Twp. with MARY, age 11; SAMUEL, age 8; CAROLINE, age 5; EDWARD, age 2; LUCY, age 7/12, all b. Mich., in their household.

WALKER, DANIEL, son of JONAS (b. Mass., pioneer to Windham Co., VT where he remained), born Mass., moved to Windham Co., VT with his parents, and married there to MARY (STOCKWELL). He died near Pultney, VT. Ten children, names not stated, except #4. EDSON (following). Probably also JOEL, following. Ref: P&BA-Len pg. 619-20.

WALKER, DAVID, age 22, born NY, was listed in the 1850 census of Palmyra Twp., Lenawee Co., Mich. in a Crane household.

WALKER, DAVID SHAPELY and wife, LOIS, from Broome Co., NY were parents of MARY M. (m. Consider A. Stacy, also see, on 19 Aug. 1838, Tecumseh Twp., Lenawee Co., Mich.)

WALKER, EDSON, son of DANIEL (preceding), born 27 Oct. 1813, Dummerston, VT, moved in 1839 to Palmyra Twp.,Lenawee Co., Mich. (Note: He was not listed in 1840 census index of Palmyra Twp., but note JOEL, following). He married there on 1 Jan. 1842 to BETSEY (HOXSIE), daughter of John (also see), and she died the same year. He married again on 10 Dec. 1846 to MARIE J. (STEWART), daughter of James A. (also see). Children: 1. JAMES S. b. 17 Dec. 1847 (drowned in U.S. Marine Service, Civil War); 2. EDSON G. b. ca. 1850; 3. MARY L. (to Chicago, Ill.); 4. PLINY F. b. 9 Oct. 1855 (D. 14 Mar. 1873); 5. MATTIE J. Ref: P&BA-Len pg. 619-20.

WALKER, ELIZA W. born ca. 1810, NY (m. Alanson Phillips, also see, possibly in Ontario Co., NY).

WALKER, GEORGE, age 25, born NY, was listed in the 1850 census of Fairfield Twp., Lenawee Co., Mich. in a Hagaman household. Note STEPHEN, following. There was a GEORGE, age 22, b. NY, possibly same man, in the 1850 census of Madison Twp. in a Baker household.

WALKER, JOEL, probably son of DANIEL (preceding), born ca. 1811, VT, and wife, ARETHUSA, born ca. 1818, NH, were listed in the 1840 census index of Palmyra Twp., Lenawee Co., Mich.; and in the 1850 census with EMILY G., age 9; FREDERICK N., age 7; HARRIET H., age 4; GEORGE D., age 2, all b. Mich., in their household.

WALKER, MARY (See George Price)

WALKER, PAULINA (See Charles Brown)

WALKER, SAMUEL W. born ca. 1820, Penn., and wife, OTLINA?, born ca. 1819, Ohio, were listed in the 1850 census of Madison Twp., Lenawee Co., Mich. with HERBERT W., age 4; CLARENCE H., age 2, both b. Mich., in their household.

WALKER, SETH S., Jr. (son of SETH?), born ca. 1824, Mass., was listed in the 1850 census of Adrian Twp., Lenawee Co., Mich. in household of ANDREW (preceding). Seth married on 7 Apr. 1852 to AMELIA (LUTHER), daughter of Theodorick (also see) in Adrian. They were believed to have lived later in Fairfield Twp. Two sons and three daughters, names not stated, except HARRIET b. 9 Apr. 1854, Adrian (m. William H. Cheney, also see). Ref: P&BA-Len pg. 781-2. Note: It may be this same Seth, age 24, birthplace shown Ohio, in the 1850 census of Adrian Twp. in a hotel.

WALKER, STEPHEN born ca. 1801, NY, and wife, LYDIA, born ca. 1801, NH, were listed in the 1850 census of Fairfield Twp., Lenawee Co., Mich. with JOHN, age 19, b. NY; NATHANIEL, age 14; RANSOM, age 11, both b. Mich.; and Zedana? Stephenson, age 5, b. Canada, in their household. Note GEORGE, preceding.

WALKER, SYLVESTER, born ca. 1798, and wife, LUCY, born ca. 1799, were listed in the 1850 census of Cambridge Twp., Lenawee Co., Mich.

WALKER, WILLIAM (See Benjamin Reasoner)

WALLACE, IDA (See Peter McLouth)

WALLER, ASAHEL born ca. 1815, and wife, MANERVA, born ca. 1818, both in Ohio, were listed in the 1850 census of Raisin Twp., Lenawee Co., Mich. with EMORY, age 11; MARY, age 5; CORDELIA, age 2, all b. Ohio, in their household.

WALLER, DAVID moved from Tioga Co., Penn. to Palmyra, Ohio. He had known daughter, CORDELIA b. 1816, Ohio (m. Peter R. Adams, also see). Ref: P&BA-Len pg. 1063-4.

WALTER, CHRISTIAN, son of GEORGE (following), born 7 Feb. 1837, Schaffhausen, Switzerland, served in both the Italian and Swiss Armies. He came to the US in 1861. He enlisted in the 37th Ohio Inf., and served for 3 years during the Civil War. He married on 23 Mar. 1868 in Toledo, Ohio to MARGARET (FAELBECK), daughter of Phillip (also see), and settled in Toledo. About 1875, they removed to Riga Twp., Lenawee Co., Mich., and stayed 2 years, then returned to Ohio. In 1881, they returned to Lenawee Co., Mich. Children: 1. EDWARD; 2. JOHN; 3. FREDERICK; 4. MINA; 5. NETTIE; 6. FRANK; 7. CHARLES; 8. GEORGE 2d; 9. PHILLIP; 10. ROBERT. Ref: P&BA-Len pg. 626-7.

WALTER, GEORGE and wife, URSUAL (KUBLER), were natives of Schaffhausen, Switzerland, were he died 13 Dec. 1858, age 66; and she died in July 1862. Children: 1. SEBASTIAN; 2. MAGDELENA (came to US, lived Chicago); 3. JACOB (deceased by 1888); 4. BARBARA (came to US, lived Iowa); 5. GEORGE 1st (d. young); 6. CASPER; 7. CHRISTIAN (preceding); 8. GEORGE 2d (deceased by 1888); 9. URSULA. Ref: P&BA-Len pg. 626-7.

WALTER, REGINA (See Christian Schneirla)

WALTER, WILLIAM Prof. (See Franz Joseph Mitchell)

WALTERS, JOHN born in Worceser, Penn., moved with his parents to Richland Co., Ohio. He married ELIZA (LOWRY) also born Penn. Some years later, they moved to Hancock Co., Ohio; and in 1859 to Riga Twp., Lenawee Co., Mich. In 1864, they moved to Findlay, Ohio where they remained. Known daughter, SARAH J. (m. George F. Ford, also see). Ref: P&BA-Len pg. 809-10.

WALTERS, PHEBE (See Lorentus S. Calkins)

WALTZ, LYDIA (See Michael Wilt)

WALWORTH, CORNELIUS, possibly son of JOHN (following), born ca. 1808, and wife PAULINA, born ca. 1813, NY, were listed in the 1840 census of Adrian Twp., Lenawee Co., Mich.; and in the 1850 census of Rome Twp. with PHILANDER, age 14; EUGENE, age 12; WILLIAM, age 10; JOHN, age 3; AUGUSTUS, age 8/12, all b. Mich., in their household.

WALWORTH, JOHN born ca. 1780, NY, and wife, MARY, born ca. 1778, NH, were listed in the 1840 census index of Rome Twp., Lenawee Co., Mich.; and in the 1850 census in the household of son, JOHN, Jr. (following). Also note CORNELIUS, preceding.

WALWORTH, JOHN, Jr. was born ca. 1819, and wife, SARAH, was born ca. 1829, both in NY, married within the year, were listed in the 1850 census of Rome Twp., Lenawee

Co., Mich. with father, JOHN (preceding) & mother; and Edwin Maxfield, age 14, b. Mich., in his household.

WALWORTH, JOSEPH was listed in the 1840 census index of Rome Twp., Lenawee Co., Mich.

WALWORTH, POLLY (See Abraham A. Henion)

WAMBOLD, SUSAN (See John F. Schreder)

WANN, HENRY C. Dr. (See Rev. James Vincent)

WARD, CALEB was listed in the 1840 census index of Macon Twp., Lenawee Co., Mich.

WARD, DAVID Dr. born ca. 1798, NH, and wife, MARY, born ca. 1808, NY, were listed in the 1850 census of Adrian Twp., Lenawee Co., Mich. with BENJAMIN, age 13, b. NY; WILLIAM, age 8, b. Penn.; and FLORA, age 4, b. Mich., in their household. Note JOSIAH, following.

WARD, ENOCH, age 50, born NY, was listed in the 1850 census of Tecumseh Twp., Lenawee Co., Mich. in the household of George W. & Hepsibah Penros?

WARD, ISAAC born ca. 1824, and wife, MALVINA, born ca. 1827, both in NY, were listed in the 1850 census of Rollin Twp., Lenawee Co., Mich. with MARY J., age 1/12, b. NY, all in the household of Rufus & Abigail Herman (perhaps in-laws).

WARD, JACOB was the second husband of Mrs. SOPHRONIA (WAKELY) DOWNS, born ca. 1798, VT, widow of Reuben (also see). In the 1850 census of Macon Twp., Lenawee Co., Mich., in the household of Charles Morgan, the 3rd husband of Sophronia, were MARY A., age 13, and MARTHA A., age 12, both b. Mich., probably children of Jacob & Sophronia. Note JACOB, following; and also note CALEB & WARHAM, who were in Macon Twp. in 1840.

WARD, JACOB born ca. 1810, and wife, LYDIA, born ca. 1811, both in Penn., were listed in the 1840 census of Clinton Twp., Lenawee Co., Mich.; and in the 1850 census of Tecumseh Twp. with FRANCES, age 15, b. Penn.; and SABRINA, age 13; AUGUSTA, age 10; JULIA ANN, age 7; CHARLES, age 4, all b. Mich., in their household.

WARD, JOHN born ca. 1786, Conn., and wife, SALLY, born ca. 1787, NY, were listed in the 1850 census of Hudson Twp., Lenawee Co., Mich. with no family in their household.

WARD, JOHN born ca. 1798, and wife, MARY, born ca. 1808, were listed in the 1850 census of Hudson Twp., Lenawee Co., Mich. with Clarissa A. Brown, age 18, b. NY, in their household.

WARD, JOSIAH born ca. 1800, NH, and wife, ELIZA C., born ca. 1813, NY, were listed in the 1850 census of Adrian Twp., Lenawee Co., Mich. with JOSIAH L., age 16, b. NY; WILLIAM H., age 9; THOMAS, age 4; ESTELLA, age 2, all b. Mich., in their household. Note: It may be he listed as "JOSEPH" in the 1840 census index of Adrian Twp.

WARD, LEMON born ca. 1826, and wife, SUSAN, born ca. 1827, both in NY, were listed in the 1850 census of Hudson Twp., Lenawee Co., Mich. with ELLEN E., age 2, b. Mich.; and Edwin E. Barney, age 20, b. NY, in their household.

WARD, MARY, age 13, born Mich., was listed in the 1850 census of Tecumseh Twp., Lenawee Co., Mich. in Day household.

WARD, PETER was listed in the 1840 census index of Tecumseh Twp., Lenawee Co., Mich.

WARD, TROWBRIDGE born ca. 1816, and wife, NANCY N., born ca. 1826, both in NY, were listed in the 1850 census of Medina Twp., Lenawee Co., Mich. with ELVIRA, age 3; JOSEPHINE, age 2, both b. Ohio, in their household.

WARD, WARHAM was listed in the 1840 census index of Cambridge Twp., Lenawee Co., Mich.

WAREHAM, PHILIP[1] came to America from Germany before the Revolutionary War. He married BETSEY (HANES) and lived in Cumberland Co., Penn., where he died at age 79; and she preceded him by 15 years. Known son, PHILIP[2] (following). Ref: P&BA-Len pg. 939-40.

WAREHAM, PHILIP[2], son of PHILIP[1] (preceding), born Cumberland Co., Penn., married MARY (JOHNSON) born in Co. Fermanagh, Ireland. They remained in Cumberland Co., where he died at age 54, and she died at age 62. Known sons: JOHNSON (Carlisle, Penn.); and PHILIP[3] (following). Ref: P&BA-Len pg. 939-40.

WAREHAM, PHILIP[3], son of PHILIP[2] (preceding), born 12 Nov. 1807, Cumberland Co., Penn., married on 28 Oct. 1830 to RACHEL (DEWEY), daughter of Conrad (also see). They remained in Cumberland Co. until 1838, then moved to Wayne Co., Ohio. About 1848, they moved to Eaton Co., Mich.; and in 1860 to Woodstock Twp., Lenawee Co., Mich. She died there on 5 Mar. 1875. Children: 1. THEODORE b. 31 Oct. 1831, Penn. (m. Nancy Brown); 2. HAMILTON b. 7 Apr. 1834 (m. Julia E. Delaney); 3. PHILIP b. 28 Apr. 1836 (m. Catherine A. Casey); 4. JOHN b. 7 Oct. 1838 (m. Vina Holmes); 5. DAVID P. b. 23 May 1841 (d. 21 June 1861); 6. MARGARET C. b. 10 June 1843 (m. J. N. Mikesell; she d. 2 Mar. 1863); 7. JOHNSON b. 19 Sept. 1845 (m. Hattie Holland). Ref: P&BA-Len pg. 939-40.

WARING also see WARRING & WERRING

WARING, ALBERT, son of DANIEL (following), born 10 Feb. 1851, Tecumseh Twp., Lenawee Co., Mich., married on 3 Sept. 1879 to JULIA A. (SISSON), daughter of George (also see). No children were listed in sketch. Ref: P&BA-Len pg. 1052-3.

WARING, DANIEL born 24 Mar. 1806, Orange Co., NY, was listed in the 1830 census of Lenawee Co., Territory of Michigan, with 2 males 20-30 in the household. He married probably in Tecumseh Twp., Lenawee Co., Mich. to MARY ANN (HARRISON), daughter of John (also see), and about 1831 settled in Raisin Twp.; and afterwards in Tecumseh Twp. (In the 1840 census index, only WILLIAM, following, is listed in Tecumseh Twp., Daniel is not listed in Lenawee Co.) They were listed in the 1850 census of Tecumseh Twp. He died 18 May 1879, and she was still living in 1888, age 77, in the home of daughter, Sarah Eaton. There were 8 or 9 children, and the following are known: 1. JOHN H. b. ca. 1834 (to Van Buren Co., Mich.); 2. WILLIAM H. b. ca. 1838 (to Peoria Co., Ill.); 3. SARAH b. ca. 1840 (m. Horace B. Eaton, also see); 4. ALVAH M. b. ca. 1843 (to Ford Co., KS); 5. JOSEPH E. b. ca. 1847 (lived Tecumseh Twp.); 6. ALBERT (preceding); 7. ABIGAIL (twin of Albert; she d. 1877). Ref: P&BA-Len pg. 1052-3.

WARING, GUERNSEY P., son of JOSHUA (following), born 31 Aug. 1852, Ridgeway Twp., Lenawee Co., Mich., married first on 16 Sept. 1877 to "HANNAH"

AUGUSTA (CADMUS), daughter of Richard (also see). She died in 1883, age 35; and he married again to her sister, "ELLA" (HELEN A.) No children were listed in sketch. Ref: P&BA-Len pg. 630-2.

WARING, HARVEY was born ca. 1800 in NY, and was listed in the household of JOSHUA in the 1850 census of Ridgeway Twp., Lenawee Co., Mich., probably a brother.

WARING, JOSEPH (See Jairus P. Slayton)

WARING, JOSHUA born 3 Apr. 1803, Newburg, Orange Co., NY, married there in 1832 to RUTH A (LOCKWOOD), daughter of Gilbert (also see). In 1834, they came to Michigan, accompanied by her brothers, Daniel & William Lockwood. Joshua was listed in the 1840 census index of Macon Twp., Lenawee Co., Mich.; and they were in the 1850 census of Ridgeway Twp. In 1865, they moved to the village of Ridgeway; and he died 17 Mar. 1884. She was still living in 1888, age 72, with son, Guernsey. Children: 1. MARY A. b. ca. 1835 (m. Edgar C. Van Vleet, son of Peter P., also see; she d. 10 Oct. 1870, Ridgeway Twp.); 2. GILBERT L. b. 8 Feb. 1838 (m. Clara Clark, dau. of George W., also see; Gilbert d. 7 May 1874); 3. CORNELIUS L.; 4. GUERNSEY P. (preceding). Ref: P&BA-Len pg. 630-2.

WARING, WILLIAM was born ca. 1809, and wife, HANNAH, was born ca. 1800, both in NY, and they were listed in the 1840 census index of Tecumseh Twp., Lenawee Co., Mich.; and in the 1850 census with JOSHUA, age 19; LINDA, age 7, both b. Mich., in their household.

WARNER, ASENATH S. born 12 July 1813, Phelps, Ontario Co., NY, married Lyman W. Baker (also see). Ref: P&BA-Len pg. 541-2.

WARNER, CASSIUS P. born ca. 1812, Mass., and wife, CELIST, born ca. 1817, NY, were listed in the 1840 census index of Medina Twp. (as "C. P."); and in the 1850 census of Hudson Twp. with AMELIA, age 14; ELLEN, age 9, both b. Mich., in their household.

WARNER, CHARLES, age 3, born Mich., was listed in the 1850 census of Hudson Twp., Lenawee Co., Mich. in a Cady household.

WARNER, CLARISSA, age 68, born Mass., was listed head of household in the 1850 census of Palmyra Twp., Lenawee Co., Mich. with probably son, LUCIUS (following) and family in her household. Note STEPHEN of Palmyra Twp. in 1840 census index, possibly this is his family?

WARNER, CYRUS S. born ca. 1818, and wife, ELISA, born ca. 1821, both in NY, were listed in the 1850 census of Macon Twp., Lenawee Co., Mich. with SARAH, age 6/12, b. Mich., in their household.

WARNER, DAVID, born ca. 1726, from New England, was a pioneer to Walworth, Wayne Co., NY (formed in 1823 from part of Ontario Co., NY). He died in 1824, age 98. He had known son, RUSSELL (following). Ref: P&BA-Len pg. 932-3. Note: There was a DANIEL, probably from Mass., who was an early settler of Hopewell, Ontario Co., NY per French's Gazeteer of New York State.

WARNER, ELIZABETH (See John Gamber)

WARNER, ELIZABETH (COFFIN) Mrs. born ca. 1785, NY, married second to John Lagore (also see). Ref: P&BA-Len pg. 834-5.

WARNER, JOHN born 1 Jan. 1787, and wife, HANNAH (BROWN) born 3 Nov. 1794, both in NY, came to Adrian Twp., Lenawee Co., Mich. from Ontario Co., NY in 1834. They had 4 sons and 5 daughters, names not stated, except URSUAL A. b. 30 Mar. 1824, Ontario Co., NY (m. Van Rensselaer J. Osborn, also see); and the following were in the household in the 1850 census: ELIZA C., age 21; CHARLES A., age 16, both b. NY; and CAROLINE C., age 9; EMELINE, age 9 (probably twins), born Mich. Ref: P&BA-Len pg. 713-4.

WARNER, JOSEPH born ca. 1812, NY, and wife, CAROLINE, born ca. 1812, Mass., were listed in the 1850 census of Adrian Twp., Lenawee Co., Mich. with JARED, age 12; LUCIUS, age 5, both b. Mich., in their household. Note: Probably he in the 1840 census index of Raisin Twp., listed as JOSEPH C. Also note THOMAS C., following.

WARNER, LEMUEL born ca. 1814, and wife, SUSANNAH, born ca. 1815, both in Ohio, were listed in the 1850 census of Blissfield Twp., Lenawee Co., Mich. with LETA? A., age 12; EMORY, age 8; FRANKLIN, age 6, all b. Ohio; and JULIA A., age 5; JOHN W., age 1, both b. Mich., in their household.

WARNER, LUCIUS born ca. 1823, and wife, LYDIA, born ca. 1829, both in NY, were listed in the 1850 census of Palmyra Twp., Lenawee Co., Mich. with MARTHA, age 2/12, b. Mich., all in the household of CLARISSA (preceding). Also note STEPHEN, following.

WARNER, LUTHER, son of RUSSELL (following), born 14 Sept. 1818, Walworth (then Ontario Co., now Wayne Co.), after the death of his father in 1828, went to live with an Aunt in Monroe Co., NY. At age 14, he went alone to Oakland Co., Mich. to join his Aunt who had moved there. In 1839, he went to Hudson Twp., Lenawee Co., Mich.; and also lived for a time with a sister in Rome Twp. He married there in June 1841 to SARAH (CARPENTER), and they settled in Hudson Twp. She died in 1842. He married again in June 1845 to MELISSA (WILSON). She died leaving children: 1. BEATRICE A. b. ca. 1847; 2. MARK L. (In the 1850 census, they listed DELOS, age 10/12?; Mark was not listed.). Luther married third after 1850 to NANCY (BENNETT), daughter of Joel (also see) and had daughter: 3. JENNIE M. Ref: P&BA-Len pg. 932-3.

WARNER, MALINDA (See Gideon Bryan)

WARNER, NORTON D. born ca. 1809, and wife, SELINA?, born ca. 1811, both in Mass., were listed in the 1840 census index of Palmyra Twp., Lenawee Co., Mich.; and in the 1850 census with ALMON, age 16; GEORGE S., age 4, both b. Mich., in their household.

WARNER, RUSSELL, son of DAVID (preceding), married in Walworth, NY to ORA (PHELPS), daughter of Silas (also see). He died in 1828, and had known son, LUTHER (preceding). Ref: P&BA-Len pg. 932-3.

WARNER, SAMUEL and wife, ELIZABETH, came from Groveland, Ontario Co., NY to Freedom Twp., Washtenaw Co., Mich. ca. 1832. He died on 8 Oct. 1840, and she died years later. There were 6 children, names not stated, except #4. SARAH b. 9 Dec. 1817 (m. Levi C. Richmond, also see). Ref: P&BA-Len pg. 373.

WARNER, SAMUEL, probably son of SAMUEL, born ca. 1791, and wife, HANNAH, born ca. 1790, both in Conn., were listed in the 1840 census index of Medina Twp., Lenawee Co., Mich.; and in the 1850 census with

Pioneer Families of Southeastern Michigan

PHILANDER S., age 40, b. NY; and SAMUEL, age 81, born Conn., in their household.

WARNER, SETH Col. of Mass., had daughter, ?, who married Daniel Eldredge born 25 Feb. 1745, a Revolutionary soldier. Note: There was a Daniel "Eldridge," with Mass. service, and had widow, PHEBE, with Rev. Pension Appl. #W24116 (no proof it is same man). Ref: P&BA-Len pg. 937-8.

WARNER, SHELDON, son of CHESTER (who d. Ontario Co., NY), was born Phelps, Ontario Co., NY. Sheldon moved to Orleans Co., NY, where he married SARAH (PORTER), daughter of Allen (also see). Known daughter, ELECTA J. (m. Eugene Douglas Pierson, also see, on 12 Jan. 1881, Albion, NY). Ref: P&BA-Len pg. 858-9.

WARNER, SILAS P. born ca. 1823, and wife, NANCY, born ca. 1825, both in NY, were listed in the 1850 census of Hudson Twp., Lenawee Co., Mich. with RUSSELL, age 8; CECIL, age 6; ALYDA A., age 4; CELY? (male), age 2, all b. Mich., in their household.

WARNER, SOLOMON see Solomon Warren.

WARNER, STEPHEN was listed in the 1840 census index of Palmyra Twp., Lenawee Co., Mich. Note CLARISSA, preceding.

WARNER, THOMAS C. born ca. 1807, and wife, ELMINA, born ca. 1810, both in NY, were listed in the 1840 census index of Raisin Twp., Lenawee Co., Mich. (adjacent to JOSEPH C.); and in the 1850 census of Adrian Twp. with JOSEPH C., age 19; MARY C., age 17, both b. NY; and JAMES R., age 12; WILLIAM H., age 9; CHLOE E., age 1, all b. Mich., in their household.

WARNER, WILLIAM A. was listed in the 1840 census index of Medina Twp., Lenawee Co., Mich. Also note CASSIUS, P.

WARREN, ALBERT born ca. 1821, and wife, CLARISSA, born ca. 1824, were listed in the 1850 census of Adrian Twp., Lenawee Co., Mich. Note SOLOMON, following.

WARREN, ALLEN, probably son of SAMUEL (following), born ca. 1825, and wife, CYNTHIA S., born ca. 1823, both in NY, were listed in the 1850 census of Dover Twp., Lenawee Co., Mich. adjacent to SAMUEL. Later moved to St. Louis, Mich.

WARREN, DARWIN H., son of ISAAC (following), born ca. 1839, Dover Twp., Lenawee Co., Mich., served in the Civil War. He married in Dover Twp. on 5 Sept. 1865 to ANN M. (AUSTIN), daughter of Jonathan (also see). Children: 1. EVA E. (m. Levi J. Deline, Dover Twp.); 2. HARRIET E.; 3. DELIA L. Ref: P&BA-Len pg. 423-4.

WARREN, EDWIN born ca. 1821, NY, and wife, MARIA, born ca. 1821, Mich., were listed in the 1850 census of Tecumseh Twp., Lenawee Co., Mich. with no family.

WARREN, FRANCES MARIA born 20 Feb. 1818, Farmington, Ontario Co., NY, married on 28 Nov. 1838 to Pardon T. Davenport (also see) of Blissfield Twp. They were listed in the 1850 census with SUSANNAH, age 70, b. NJ, probably mother of Frances in their household. Ref: P&BA-Len pg. 984-5. Note SAMUEL, following.

WARREN, GEORGE, age 16, born Mich., was listed in the 1850 census of Raisin Twp., Lenawee Co., Mich. in a Cook household.

WARREN, ISAAC, son of SAMUEL (following) born 11 Sept. 1812, Farmington, Ontario Co., NY, came to Michigan in 1834 with his parents. He married on 7 Mar. 1838 to DELIA A. (VAIL), possibly daughter of John (also see) and they were listed in the 1850 census of Dover Twp., Lenawee Co. Children: 1. DARWIN H., age 11 (preceding); 2. HOMER, age 9 (d. Civil War, prisoner of war); 3. HARRIET L., age 7 (m. Milo Bovee, Dover Twp.); 4. ISAAC NEWTON (following); 5. MELVIN E. (d. Seneca Twp., 26 Dec. 1871). Ref: P&BA-Len pg. 423-4.

WARREN, ISAAC NEWTON, son of ISAAC (preceding), both 6 Nov. 1844, Dover Twp., Lenawee Co., Mich., married NANCY (HALSTEAD), daughter of Thompson (also see) on 9 Sept. 1876, Clayton, Mich. Known daughter, EDITH L. b. 26 Sept. 1882. Ref: P&BA-Len pg. 522-3.

WARREN, JESSE H., son of SAMUEL (following), born 5 May 1822, Farmington, Ontario Co., NY, came to Dover Twp., Lenawee Co., Mich. in 1834 with his parents. He married on 6 May 1848 in Madison Twp. to LUCINDA (HUTCHINSON), daughter of Chester (also see). They lived in Adrian Twp., and Dover Twp. Known children: 1. CHESTER H. b. ca. 1849; 2. EVELYN G. (m. Robert Carpenter, also see). Ref: P&BA-Len pg. 264-5.

WARREN, JOSEPH F. born ca. 1810, New Hampshire, and wife, HANNAH, born ca. 1810, NY, were listed in the 1850 census of Dover Twp., Lenawee Co., Mich. with ELVIRA, age 16, b. Ohio; and JONATHAN, age 11, b. Mich.; GEORGE, age 9, b. Ohio; JOSEPHUS, age 6, b. Ohio; and MARTHA, age 3; MARY, age 3, both Mich.; and Jonathan Wheeler, age 77, born NH, in their household.

WARREN, REBECCA (See William Bradish)

WARREN, SAMUEL (Note SAMUEL, following) born ca. 1783, New Jersey, was a descendant of Gen. JOSEPH of Revolutionary fame. Samuel married LUCINDA (DEWEY) born 1792 in Mass. They settled afterwards in Farmington, Ontario Co., NY; and in 1834 moved to Dover Twp., Lenawee Co., Mich. He died in Jan. 1858; and she died 11 May 1880. Children: 1. ISAAC (preceding); 2. MATILDA (drowned 23 Apr. 1835); 3. IRA; 4. MINERVA (lived Medina Twp.); 5. JESSE H. (preceding); 6. ALLEN (preceding); 7. AUSTIN b. ca. 1828 (lived Madison Twp.). Ref: P&BA-Len pg. 264-5.

WARREN, SAMUEL born in New Jersey, may be he in New Hanover, Burlington Co., NJ in 1778-80. Known daughter, AXIE b. NJ (m. John Archer, also see). Ref: P&BA-Len pg. 542-3. Note SAMUEL, preceding, son??

WARREN, SARAH (See Charles Wells)

WARREN, SOLOMON born ca. 1799, Conn., and wife, MARY, born ca. 1799, NY, were listed in the 1850 census of Adrian Twp., Lenawee Co., Mich. with HORACE, age 15, b. NY, in their household. Note: In the 1840 census index he was called Solomon Warner?

WARRING also see WARING & WERRING
WARRING, IDA (See Dr. Francis Grandy)

WASHBURNE, ALLEN (See Nehemiah Hall)

WASTELL, WILLIAM P. Rev., son of HENRY (who d. London, England), was born 17 Aug. 1804, England. He was a Congregational Minister who came to Quebec, and then St. Thomas, Canada. He also lived in St. Clair & Port Huron, Mich. He married SARAH S. (BRAMLEY), born ca. 1805, England, who died in St.

Clair, Mich. in 1870. There were 8 children living in 1888, names not stated. In the 1850 census of Tecumseh Twp., Lenawee Co., they listed ELISA, age 17; JOSEPH, age 15; MARY, age 13; HENRY, age 11, all b. England; and GEORGE, age 10?; JOHN, age 9; EDWARD, age 7, all b. Canada; and SAMUEL, age 1, b. Mich., in their household. He married second to Mrs. SARAH (POLHEMUS) VAN TUYLE. They lived in Clinton, Lenawee Co., Mich. Ref: P&BA-Len pg. 445-50.

WATERMAN, IRA born near Kinderhook, NY, married in Chenango Co., NY to FRANCES (HOLMES) who was born near Stonington, Conn. About 1820, they removed to Romulus, Seneca Co., NY. Children: 1. ELIZA A.; 2. MARY A.; 3. IRA D. (following); 4. DENNISON R.; 5. L. LOUISA; 6. CHARLES; 7. EMILY; 8. HARRIET. Ref: P&BA-Len pg. 802.

WATERMAN, IRA D., son of IRA (preceding), born 23 Nov. 1812, Chenonago Co., NY, moved to Seneca Co., NY with his parents. About 1840, he went to Lenawee Co., Mich., but returned to Seneca Co., NY. In 1842, he returned to Dover Twp., Lenawee Co. He married on 15 Mar. 1845, Adrian, to JANE (LOW), daughter of Stephen (also see), and settled in Dover Twp. Children: 1. MARGARET b. ca. 1846 (m. John D. Ramsdell, also see); 2. FRANCES b. ca. 1847 (m. William Judson, Ohio); 3. ISAAC (m. Jennie Ramsdell, dau. of David, also see; she d. 21 Oct. 1887, Clayton, Mich.). Ref: P&BA-Len pg. 802.

WATERMAN, MARY born 21 Apr. 1796, New Jersey (m. Jeremiah Brown).

WATERS also see WATTERS
WATERS, DANIEL was listed in the 1840 census index of Tecumseh Twp., Lenawee Co., Mich.
WATERS, HANNAH (See Asa Phetteplace)

WATKINS, ESTHER (See Reuben Slayton)
WATKINS, MARSHALL and wife, CAROLINE (INGERSOLL), of Ontario Co., NY died there in middle life. Known daughter, EMILY b. 24 Nov. 1835 (m. Homer Bickford, also see, Ontario Co., NY). Ref: P&BA-Len pg. 1158-9.

WATROUS, JOHN had known daughter, MARY (m. George H. Brooks, also see, in 1864).
WATROUS, REBECCA (See Levi Nichols)

WATSON, CAROLINE (See Benjamin Barrett)
WATSON, ENOCH T. born ca. 1807, New Hampshire, and wife, MARIA (HOXIE) born ca. 1805, NY, lived in Ontario Co., NY, then moved first to Ohio, and about 1838 to Madison Twp., Lenawee Co., Mich. He died 31 Jan. 1882; and she died 12 Feb. 1882. Children: 1. SARAH E. b. ca. 1835 (m. Ira S. Nickerson, also see); 2. SUSAN (d. infancy); 3. LAURA M. b. ca. 1842, Mich. (m. Curren Wilson, son of John, also see; went to Dakota); 4. SYLVESTER E. born ca. 1847 (d. age 3; was listed in the 1850 census). Ref: P&BA-Len pg. 422-3.
WATSON, CHARLES R. was listed in the 1840 census index of Adrian Twp., Lenawee Co., Mich., and is probably he in the 1850 census, listed as "C. R.," age 40, b. Penn., "blind." In his household were EDWARD M., age 10; CHARLES C., age 9; GEORGE, age 7, all b. Mich.; then listed last were probably siblings of Charles R.; ANN, age 35; ROBERT M., age 33; GEORGE, age 30, all b. Penn.; and JOHN B., age 28, b. NY.
WATSON, WILLIAM and wife, MARGARET, came to the US in 1828, and lived in Wheatland, Monroe co., NY; and afterwards in Huron Co., Ohio, where he died. They were parents of MARGARET born 1807/12, Perth, Scotland (m. John Bryant, also see). Ref: P&BA-Len pg. 766-7.
WATSON, WILLIAM and wife, ELECTA (COLE), lived near Batavia, Erie Co., NY in 1827. He died there a young man. She married again and moved to Rome Twp., Lenawee Co., Mich. In 1841, the family lived in Hillsdale Co., Mich., but returned to Lenawee Co. Known son, ZEBULON (following). Ref: P&BA-Len pg. 1124-5.
WATSON, ZDBULON, son of WILLIAM (preceding), born 16 Feb. 1827, near Batavia, NY, came with his mother and stepfather to Rome Twp., Lenawee Co., Mich. in 1835. He married PHEBE D. (BATES), daughter of Daniel (also see). They lived for 2 years in Branch Co., Mich., but returned to Rome Twp., Lenawee Co. No children named in sketch. Ref: P&BA-Len pg. 1124-5.

WATTERS also see WATERS
WATTERS, JOHN maried EDITH A. (BEDELL), daughter of Alva E. (also see), and had children: VEVIA; & LEILA B.

WEADHEAD, ELIZA (See Marvin Howard)

WEATHERBY, ANSON was listed in the 1840 census index of Seneca Twp., Lenawee Co., Mich. adjacent to "C" (CURTIS, following); and was in the 1850 census, age 55, with wife, HANNAH, age 48, both b. NY (this place of birth may be an error in "dittoing" in the census).
WEATHERBY, CURTIS, son of WILLIAM[1] (following), born ca. 1808, VT, and his wife, LOVINA, born ca. 1810, Conn., were listed in the 1840 census index of Seneca Twp., Lenawee Co., Mich. (near ANSON, preceding); and in the 1850 census with JANE, age 15; ESBAN, age 13; ELAM, age 10; WILLIAM, age 8; CURTIS, age 1, all b. Mich., in their household.
WEATHERBY, NATHAN, probably son of WILLIAM[1] (following), born ca. 1800, Mass., and his wife, SALLY, born ca. 1808, NY, were listed in the 1840 census index of Fairfield Twp., Lenawee Co., Mich.; and in the 1850 census with ANSON E., age 21, b. NY; and FRANCIS, age 18; SEYMOUR, age 16; HENRY, age 8; EMILY, age 13; MARY A., age 11; MARIA, age 7 (listed in that order in household), all b. Mich.
WEATHERBY, WILLIAM[1] born 22 July 1769, Mass., married on 8 Dec. 1797 to RELIEF (MILLER) born 20 Feb. 1775, Marlboro, Mass. They lived in Boston for about 36 years, then moved to Bennington Co., VT, where they remained until about 1823, then moved to Tioga Co., NY. In 1831, they moved to Fairfield Twp., Lenawee Co., Mich. He died 19 Aug. 1835; and she died 18 July 1835. There were 8 children, names not stated, except WILLIAM[2] (following). ANSON; CURTIS; & NATHAN, preceding, may all be additional sons.
WEATHERBY, WILLIAM[2], son of WILLIAM[1] (preceding), born 21 July 1813, Manchester, Bennington Co., VT, married on 31 Dec. 1835 to SARAH C. (CARPENTER), daughter of Rev. James (also see) of Fairfield Twp.,

Pioneer Families of Southeastern Michigan

Lenawee Co., Mich. They settled in Fairfield Twp. They were said to have had no children, but a foster son, William W. Wyman, son of Parker & Asenath (Carpenter) Wyman (also see). He was listed in their household in the 1850 census, age 6; and also in the household, relationship not known, was SARAH A., age 15, b. NY.

WEATHERWAX, HENRY, born ca. 1773, NY, was listed in the 1840 census index of Madison Twp., Lenawee Co., Mich. adjacent to HENRY H.; and in the 1850 census with Catharine Bowen, age 44, b. NY and her children, Henry, age 13 b. NY; George, age 12; Silas, age 10; Hiram, age 8, James A., age 4, perhaps these were daughter and grandchildren.

WEATHERWAX, HENRY H. was listed in the 1840 census index of Madison Twp., Lenawee Co., Mich. adjacent to HENRY (preceding).

WEATHERWAX, JACOB M. was listed in the 1840 census index of Raisin Twp., Lenawee Co., Mich.

WEATHERWAX, JANE A. (See Peter H. Bailey)

WEATHERWAX, JOHN born ca. 1790, NY, was listed in the 1850 census of Adrian Twp., Lenawee Co., Mich. with BETSEY, age 37; JOHN G., age 25; MARGARET, age 23, all b. NY; and George Armstead, age 34, b. VT; wife, Mary A. Armstead, age 34, b. NY; and Frances E. Armstaed, age 4, b. Mich., in his household.

WEATHERWAX, MARY ANN of Orleans Co., NY (See ? Wood).

WEAVER, C. M. (See Van Rensselaer J. Osborn)

WEBB, ADELIA born 4 Nov. 1812, Hackensack, NJ, daughter of a family who settled in Mich. in 1825 (note EZEKIEL, following, who was in Oakland Co., Mich. 1830 census, Mich. Territory). Adelia married Nathan H. Bassett (also see); and in the 1850 census of Hudson Twp., Lenawee Co., Mich., her birth place is given as NY? Ref: P&BA-Len pg. 1147-8.

WEBB, CHARLES, probably son of EZEKIEL (following), born ca, 1825, and wife, CHARLOTTE, age 20, both b. NY, were listed in the 1850 census of Raisin Twp., Lenawee Co., Mich. with no family listed.

WEBB, EZEKIEL born ca. 1782, NY, and wife, FANNY, born ca. 1791, Conn., may be they listed in the 1830 census of Oakland Co., Territory of Mich., with males: 2 und 5; 2 5-10; 1 15-20; 1 20-30; 1 40-50; females: 1 und 5; 1 5-10; 1 10-15; 2 15-20; 1 20-30; 1 40-50 in the household; and in the 1840 census index of Raisin Twp., Lenawee Co., Mich. In the 1850 census of Raisin Twp., they listed JAMES K., age 25, b. NY; and LOUISE, age 20, b. Mich., in their household.

WEBB, EZEKIEL D. born ca. 1821, NY, and wife, SARAH B., born ca. 1821, NH, were listed in the 1850 census of Adrian Twp., Lenawee Co., Mich. with SUSAN A., age 7; NATHAN H., age 8/12, both b. Mich., in their household.

WEBB, EZRA born ca. 1804, and wife, SYLVIA, born ca. 1813, both in NY, were listed in the 1850 census of Rome Twp., Lenawee Co., Mich. with WILLIAM H., age 13; ANN J., age 10; MARY A., age 7; EDWARD H., age 5, all b. Mich., in their household. Note: It is probably he listed in the 1840 census index of Exeter Twp., Monroe Co., Mich.

WEBB, HENRY B. born ca. 1800, and wife, EMILY, born ca. 1806, both in VT, were listed in the 1850 census of Blissfield Twp., Lenawee Co., Mich. with CARROLL C. (male), age 18; HARRIET, age 17; MARTHA, age 16; EDWARD, age 14; ELIZABETH, age 13; JANE, age 12; MARY, age 10; CHARLES, age 9, all b. NY, in their household. Note NELSON, following.

WEBB, ISAAC born ca. 1794, and (possibly second?) wife, PAULINA, born ca. 1811, both in NY, were listed in the 1850 census of Palmyra Twp., Lenawee Co., Mich. with JAMES, age 33; LUCY, age 15; EDWARD, age 12; LOVINA, age 9, all b. NY, in their household.

WEBB, MARTIN H. born ca. 1810, and wife, SUSAN, born ca. 1824, both in NY, were listed in the 1850 census of Hudson Twp., Lenawee Co., Mich. with EDWARD, age 7; EMMA A., age 3; EDGAR A., age 3; BLECKER, age 10/12, all b. Mich., in their household.

WEBB, NELSON, age 34, born VT, was listed in the 1850 census of Blissfield Twp., Lenawee Co., Mich. in the Alva North household. Note HENRY B., preceding.

WEBB, SIMEON born ca. 1795, NY, was listed in the 1850 census of Fairfield Twp., Lenawee Co., Mich. with ROXANNA, age 33, b. NY; and Eliza A. Burdick, age 10, b. Mich. in his household.

WEBB, STEPHEN born ca. 1806, Delaware, and wife, BETSEY, born ca. 1807, NY, may be they listed in the 1840 census index of Fairfield Twp., Lenawee Co., Mich.; and were listed in the 1850 census of Madison Twp. with PETER, age 20; JAMES, age 20; JOHN, age 19; JOEL, age 17, all b. NY; and another PETER, age 14; DOROTHY, age 13; LYDIA M., age 10; ELEANOR J., age 9; MARINDA, age 7; STEPHEN A., age 5, all b. Mich., in their household. It would appear that this is more than one family.

WEBBER, LUCY (See Thomas Hodge)

WEBSTER, JOHN came from New Hampshire to Adrian, Lenawee Co., Mich. prior to 1870. Known daughter, CLARA P. (m. Charles H. Raynor, also see).

WEDGE, SQUIRE was a native of Conn., and he married CATHERINE (HUSTED). They lived in NY; Luzerne Co., Penn.; and Ohio (possibly Huron Co.) He died age 68 in Ohio; and she afterwards went to Lenawee Co., and died at age 62 at home of known daughter, MARY E. b. 28 July 1825, Luzerne Co., Penn. (m. Isaac C. Gunn, also see, of Woodstock Twp.) Ref: P&BA-Len pg. 945-6.

WEEKS, JOHN, perhaps of Seneca Co., NY, had known daughter, E. P. (ELLEPHEE?) born ca. 1816, NY (m. Calvin Lawrence, also see).

WEIR, JOHN of Southport, Chemung Co., NY had known daughter, BETSEY b. 1798, Southport (m. Thomas Griswold, also see). Ref: P&BA-Len pg. 267-8.

WELCH, ALPHENE, age 15, born NY, was listed in the 1850 census of Adrian Twp., Lenawee Co., Mich. in a Hitchcock household.

WELCH, ANDREW and wife, MARY (RUTH), of Co. Carlow, Ireland, had 5 daughters and 1 son, JAMES (following). They both remained in Ireland where she died in 1827. Ref: P&BA-Len pg. 775-6.

WELCH, EDMUND born ca. 1819, VT, and wife, JANE R., born ca. 1820, NY, were listed in the 1850 census of

Rome Twp., Lenawee Co., Mich. with ALVIN C., age 7; JULIA M., age 3, both b. Mich., in their household.

WELCH, H. Dr. (See William H. H. Van Akin)

WELCH, JANE E. (See Rev. James Vincent)

WELCH, JAMES, son of ANDREW (preceding), born 25 Dec. 1814, Co. Carlow, Ireland, sailed from New Ross on 22 Apr. 1830, and landed in Quebec, Canada. He worked on the Erie Canal. He married on 20 Feb. 1836 to SUSAN (WORTHRING), daughter of George (also see). They moved to Akron, Summit Co., Ohio; and later to Portage Co., Ohio. About 1846, they moved to Seneca Twp., Lenawee Co., Mich. Children (first 5 b. Ohio; and rest in Mich.,per 1850 census): 1. MARY ANN b. ca. 1839 (m. E. R. Mason, also see); 2. ANDREW J. b. ca. 1840 (d. by 1888); 3. RUTH b. ca. 1841 (m. George Franklin, son of Amos, also see); 4. NANCY b. ca. 1843; 5. (MARIA) LYDIA b. ca. 1846 (m. Martin E. Baylor, also see); 6. EMMA b. ca. 1847; 7. CHARLES B. b. ca. 1849 (m. Nellie E. Barger; Fairfield Twp.); 8. VIOLA (m. Peter Marlott, also see); 9. HENRY (m. Mary B. Kellogg; had ch: Susie m.; Charles; Pearl E.; lived Seneca Twp.); 10. JOHN J. (d. by 1888); 11. JAMES B. (d. by 1888); 12. WILLIAM A.; 13. CARRIE E.; 14. EDMUND D.; 15. SUSAN I. (d. by 1888). Ref: P&BA-Len pg. 775-6.

WELCH, JAMES born 6 Mar. 1796, White Plains, NY, married LAURA H. (WHALEY), daughter of John (also see). They moved to Canandaigua, Mich., probably from Onondaga Co., NY. In 1852, they lived in Seneca Twp., Lenawee Co., Mich. Known daughter, JULIA S. b. 1 June 1833, Mandana, Onondaga Co., NY (m. Daniel Todd, MD, also see). Ref: P&BA-Lenpg. 857-8.

WELCH, JAMES born ca. 1811, NY, and wife, PANTHERE?, born ca. 1811, Mass., were listed in the 1850 census of Hudson Twp., Lenawee Co., Mich. with ALFRED, age 15, b. NY; and CYNTHIA, age 9; EMARILA, age 8; SPENCER, age 5; JUSTUS, age 3, all b. Mich., in their household.

WELCH, OLIVER born ca. 1798, and wife, ELIZA, born ca. 1804, both in NY, were listed in the 1850 census of Seneca Twp., Lenawee Co., Mich., with WILLIAM W., age 26; ALBERT D., age 23; GILMAN E., age 21; OLIVER O., age 16; BENJAMIN B., age 14, all b. NY; and CAROLINE, age 12; MARY, age 10; JOHN S., age 6, all b. Mich., in their household.

WELCH, PATRICK born ca. 1810, and wife, CATHARINE, born ca. 1810, both in Ireland, were listed in the 1850 census of Hudson Twp., Lenawee Co., Mich. with ELIZABETH, age 10, b. Ohio; and JAMES, age 8; MICHAEL, age 5; WILLIAM, age 3; MARY J., age 7/12, all b. Mich., in their household.

WELCH, PELEG born ca. 1813, VT, and wife, HANNAH, born ca. 1823, Canada, were listed in the 1850 census of Frankin Twp., Lenawee Co., Mich. (2 doors from WILLIAM, following), with ELISA, age 9, b. Mich.; and MATILDA, age 7; HARLOW, age 5 (prob. he who m. Mary Lovina Witherell, dau. of Ansel, also see); HA--(male), age 1, all b. Canada, in their household.

WELCH, SAMUEL born ca. 1797, NY, and wife, EUNICE, born ca. 1804, Mass., were listed in the 1850 census of Palmyra Twp., Lenawee Co., Mich. with SARAH A., age 22; EPHRAIM, age 18; EDWIN, age 15; WILLIAM H., age 14; EUNICE, age 11, all b. NY; and ROXANNE, age 9; JOHN, age 6; AMELIA J., age 3, all b. Ohio, in their household.

WELCH, WALTER (spelled "Weltch") was listed in the 1840 census index of Tecumseh Twp., Lenawee Co., Mich.

WELCH, WILLIAM was listed in the 1840 census index of Franklin Twp., Lenawee Co., Mich. It MAY be he listed in the 1850 census of Franklin Twp., spelled "Welsh," age 29, born NY, with wife, MARY, age 25, b. Canada, and ALONZO, age 3; HENRY, age 2/12, both b. Mich., in their household. Known daughter, EMMA b. 19 Dec. 1853, Franklin Twp. (m. Wesley B. Keyser, also see). In 1888, William was living in Clinton, Mich. Ref: P&BA-Len pg. 419-20.

WELLS, ABNER A. born ca. 1792, New Hampshire, and wife, MARY, born ca. 1815, VT, were listed in the 1850 census of Tecumseh Twp., Lenawee Co., Mich. with CHARLES, age 4, b. Mich. Note: There was an "A. A." in the 1840 census index of Ypsilanti Twp., Washtenaw Co., Mich.

WELLS, ALANSON was listed in the 1840 census index of Fairfield Twp., Lenawee Co., Mich. In the 1850 census of Fairfield Twp., there was a LAURA, age 12, b. Mich., listed in the household of Abner & Laura Tuttle.

WELLS, ALLEN G. born ca. 1823, and wife, LUCY, born ca. 1824, both in NY, were listed in the 1850 census of Raisin Twp., Lenawee Co., Mich. with no family.

WELLS, ANSON J. born ca. 1817, and wife, POLLY, born ca. 1805, both in NY, were listed in the 1850 census of Madison Twp., Lenawee Co., Mich. with NANCY, age 4, b. Mich.; George G. Downer, age 19, b. Mich.; Mary Hutchinson, age 24, b. NY, in their household.

WELLS, AUGUSTUS born ca. 1823, and wife, CHLOE A., born ca. 1830, were listed in the 1850 census of Madison Twp., Lenawee Co., Mich. with no family listed.

WELLS, BRIDGEMAN J., son of JAMES B. (following), born 16 June 1829, Richmond, Ontario Co., NY, moved to Lenawee Co., Mich. with his parents. He married on 16 Apr. 1856, Tecumseh, to ELIZABETH M. (OWEN), daughter of Henry (also see). Known daughter, ELLA K. Ref: P&BA-Len pg. 256-8.

WELLS, CHARLES and wife, SARAH (WARREN), were natives of Rhode Island who went to North Adams, Mass. at an early date. Known son, DANIEL P. (following). Ref: P&BA-Len pg. 675-6.

WELLS, CHARLES, born ca. 1809, Mass., and wife, DRUSILLA, borh ca. 1810, NY, were probably they listed in the 1840 census index of Farnklin Twp., Lenawee Co., Mich. (near JAMES, following); and were listed in the 1850 census with SARAH, age 9; GILES, age 8; ISBELL, age 8; LUTHERIA?, age 4; MARY, age 2, all b. Mich. This may be the CHARLES C. born 1808, Deerfield, Mass., who settled in Mich. in 1833.

WELLS, CYRUS went to Rutland Co., VT at an early age with his parents, where his father was slain by an Indian. They family had "New England origins." Cyrus married and moved to Richmond, Ontario Co., NY where he remained. His wife, name not stated, died in Franklin Twp., Lenawee Co., Mich. at the home of a son, JAMES B. (following). Ref: P&BA-Len pg. 256-8.

WELLS, DANIEL and his wife, MARY, were natives of North Adams, Mass., where they were said to have remained. They had a known daughter, NANCY K. b. ca. 1820, North Adams (m. Dr. Leonard G. Wells, also see, on 12 Oct. 1839, Lenawee Co., Mich. (Note: the 1850 census said she was b. NY). Ref: P&BA-Len pg. 918-20.

Pioneer Families of Southeastern Michigan

WELLS, DANIEL P., son of CHARLES (preceding), married SARAH (WELLS), probably in North Adams, Mass., and moved to Ontario Co., NY. She died there in 1825. About 1830, he removed to Battle Creek, Calhoun Co., Mich. where he remained. Known daughter, CLEMENZA EUNICE b. 4 Jan. 1823, Mass. (m. Edwin D. Pierson, also see). Ref: P&BA-Len pg. 675-6. Note: In the 1840 census index, Daniel P. is listed immediately adjacent to MARY; & SAMUEL P., all in Pennfield Twp., Calhoun Co., Mich.

WELLS, EDGAR R., son of RUSSELL (following), was born 28 Jan. 1840, Petersburg, Monroe Co., Mich. After the death of his mother, he made his home with his uncle, John Linn, in Ridgeway Twp., Lenawee Co. (where he was listed in the 1850 census). He married 12 Aug. 1863 to SARAH (EXELBY), born 4 Jan. 1844, Ridgeway (possibly daughter of George, also see). In 1884, they moved into Britton Station, Lenawee Co. No children were listed. Ref: P&BA-Len pg. 349-50.

WELLS, GABRIEL born ca. 1792, and wife, MARIA, born ca. 1798, both in NY, were listed in the 1840 census index of Raisin Twp., Lenawee Co., Mich.; and in the 1850 census with JANE, age 25; DANIEL, age 22; HARRIET E., age 19; SARAH M., age 16; JULIA, age 13; MARY, age 10. Note JOHN S., following.

WELLS, GIDEON L. was the father of JOHN H. (m. Mary E. Bancroft, dau. of Cornelius, also see). It may be this Gideon listed in the 1840 census index of Wheatland Twp., Hillsdale Co., Mich.

WELLS, HENRY W. born ca. 1822, and wife, EVELINA, BORN CA. 1822, both in NY, were listed in the 1850 census of Raisin Twp., Lenawee Co., Mich. with AGNES M., age 1, born Mich.

WELLS, IRA N. born ca. 1821, and wife, ANN, born ca. 1822, both in Conn., were listed in the 1850 census of Adrian Twp., Lenawee Co., Mich., with daughter, HENRIETTA, age 4, b. Mich., in their household.

WELLS, JAMES B., son of CYRUS (preceding), born 21 Sept. 1798, Rutland, VT, married on 24 Jan. 1822 in Richmond, Ontario Co., NY to SALLY (HARMON) who was born 6 July 1799, Richmond. In 1835, they moved to Franklin Twp., Lenawee Co., Mich. He died there 16 Dec. 1864; and she died 8 Sept. 1871. First 8 children were born NY, and last 5 born Mich.) 1. L. C. (m. Clara R. Allen); 2. EMILY G. (m. Joseph Estarbrook; d. 1859, Ypsilanti, Mich.); 3. MEHITABLE D. b. ca. 1825 (m. Robert C. McCollum, Franklin Twp.); 4. LOOMIS b. ca. 1827 (m. Emily C. Gregg, d. 12 Jan. 1860, Ypsilanti, Mich.); 5. BRIDGEMAN J. (preceding); 6. ELIZABETH L. (d. age 19 in 1850); 7. NATHANIEL H. b. ca. 1832 (m. Sarah Hemphill); 8. CYRUS 1st (d. infancy); 9. CYRUS W. b. ca. 1836 (m. Mattie C. Howard); 10. JULIA H. b. ca. 1838; 11. JAMES B. Jr. b. ca. 1839 (m. Addie M. Vandemark); 12. AMELIA B. b. ca. 1842 (m. C. E. Reed; Richmond, NY); 13. SAMUEL P. b. ca. 1846 (m. Grace E. Marshall; Lawrence, KS). Ref: P&BA-Len pg. 256-8.

WELLS, JOHN S born ca. 1790, NY, and wife, DEBORAH (GREEN), came to Raisin Twp., Lenawee Co., Mich. in 1838, possibly from Warren Co., NY. In the 1850 census of Raisin Twp., Deborah is not listed; but there is ELIZA, age 47, born NY, possibly a second wife. Children: 1. CONTENT (m. Reuben Hall; NY); 2. JOHN S. Jr.? (following); 3. JAMES (m. Mary Ann Patton; Adrian, Mich.); 4. COMFORT C. b. 4 June 1830, Warren Co., NY (m. Wilber West, also see). Ref: P&BA-Len pg. 454-5. Also note HENRY W., preceding.

WELLS, JOHN S. Jr., born ca. 1824, possibly son of JOHN S. (preceding), was not listed in the sketch, however appears to be of this family. In the 1850 census of Raisin Twp., Lenawee Co., Mich. he listed wife, SARAH A., age 29, b. NY; and ALLIS (ALICE?), age 2; LUCY A., age 1/12, both b. Mich., in his household.

WELLS, LAURA (See Henry Sanford)

WELLS, LUCINDA born 30 Apr. 1814, Marshfield, Washington Co., NY, married William C. Moore (also see). Ref: P&BA-Len pg. 738-9.

WELLS, LYDIA born Ontario Co., NY married Stephen Torbron (also see).

WELLS, PETER of Ontario Co., NY was the father of RACHEL (m. William Teachout, also see, and moved to Cambridge Twp., Lenawee Co., Mich. Ref: P&BA-Len pg. 961-2.

WELLS, ROBERT D. born ca. 1808, VT, and his wife, CELESTIA, born ca. 1809, Conn., were listed in the 1850 census of Ogden Twp., Lenawee Co., Mich. Note CYRUS, preceding.

WELLS, RUFUS was born ca. 1801, Mass. It may be he listed in the 1830 census of Wayne Co., Mich. Territory, with males: 1 5-10; 2 10-15; 1 15-20; 1 20-30; 1 50-60; and females: 1 und 5; 1 5-10; 1 15-20; 1 20-30; 1 40-50. He was listed in the 1850 census of Riga Twp., Lenawee Co., Mich. with ANNA, age 26, b. Canada, in his household. Note STILLMAN, following.

WELLS, RUSSELL born ca. 1810, NY, and wife, DELILAH (LINN), probably daughter of John (also see), came from NY to Ridgeway Twp., Lenawee Co., Mich. She died in 1842, and in the 1850 census of Madison Twp., he was living in another household. He died in Adrian in 1851. Son, EDGAR R. (preceding). Ref: P&BA-Len pg. 349-50.

WELLS, STELLA (See Eliza Coffin)

WELLS, STILLMAN, age 20, and probably siblings, PROCTOR, age 17; JERUSHA, age 14, all b. Mich., were listed in the 1850 census of Blissfield Twp., Lenawee Co., Mich. in a Gifford household. In other households were MARVIN, age 22; PROCTOR (again), age 18; DUDLEY, age 23, all b. Mich., relationships not known. Note RUFUS, preceding.

WELLS, THOMAS was listed in the 1840 census index of Hudson Twp., Lenawee Co., Mich. In the 1850 census, there was a HELEN, age 14, b. NY, listed in the household of Albert & Philancy Palmer.

WELLS, WALTER was listed in the 1840 census index of Madison Twp., Lenawee Co., Mich. Also note AUGUSTUS; & ANSON J., both preceding, of Madison Twp.

WELLS, WILLIAM born ca. 1821, NY, and wife, CAROLINE, born ca. 1823, Canada, were listed in the 1850 census of Cambridge Twp., Lenawee Co., Mich. with JAMES, age 9; GEORGE, age 6; ELEANOR, age 3; JANE, age 1, all b. Mich., in their household.

WELSH also see WELCH

WELSH, FRANK (See Benjamin S. Allen)

WEMPLE, JOHN, son of EPHRAIM (an early settler of Florida, NY where he remained), was born Florida, Montgomery Co., NY. He married JANE (ANTHONY) who was born Manhattan, NY. Known daughter,

HARRIET b. Montgomery Co., NY (m. Ramus Davis, also see). Ref: P&BA-Len pg. 268-9.

WEMPLE, JOHN born ca. 1814, and wife, CORNELIA, born ca. 1824, both in NY, were listed in the 1850 census of Cambridge Twp., Lenawee Co., Mich. with JOSEPHINE, age 9; WILLIAM, age 7; EUGENE, age 6/12, all b. Mich., in their household.

WENZEL, VALENTINE[1] and wife, MARY (HUTE), were natives of Hesse-Darmstadt, Germany, where they remained. Known sons: GEORGE (lived Baltimore, MD); VALENTINE[2] (following). Also, Frederick Foote, called "1/2 brother" of Valentine[2], probably son of Mary, came to Baltimore, MD. Ref: P&BA-Len pg. 847.

WENZEL, VALENTINE[2], son of VALENTINE[1] (preceding), born 25 Dec. 1822, Hesse-Darmstadt, Germany, arrived in New York City in August 1840, and went to Baltimore, NY to join his half-brother, Frederick Foote. He lived for a time in Harrisburg, Penn., and afterwards in Cumberland, Penn. He married in Oct. 1846 to CATHARINE (NEEDHEIMER) who was born Oct, 1828, Cumberland. In 1856, they came to Mich. and lived first in Adrian, Lenawee Co., and then to to Wright Twp., Hillsdale Co. About 1876, they moved to Hudson Twp., Lenawee Co. where he afterwards retired. Children: 1. ELEANORA (m. F. A. Smith, Minneapolis, MN); 2. CLARA P. (m. J. Vanderwert; Mankato, MN); 3. CHARLES E. (Minneapolis, MN); 4. WILLIAM H. (Clifford, Dakota); 5. MARY C. (m. Edward Jacobs; Butte City, Mont.); 6. FRANK J.; 7. CARRIE; 8. GEORGE A.; 9. STELLA I.; 10. EDWARD J. Ref: P&BA-Len pg. 847.

WERNER, CASPER, son of LEWIS, came with his parents from Gemany as a child, and settled in Alleghany Co., VA. He married in Penn. to JUDITH (SCHULTZ). In 1830, they settled in Preston Co., W. Va., where they remained. Known daughter, DELILAH (m. Jacob S. Rinehart, also see). Ref: P&BA-Len pg. 540-1.

WERNER, F. (See Solomon Jeffords)

WERRING also see WARING; WARRING

WERRING, HERBERT S. (See Robert L. Rogers)

WEST, ABRAHAM was born ca. 1787, NY, was listed in the 1830 census of Lenawee Co., Mich., Mich. Territory, with males: 1 und 5; 1 5-10; 1 30-40; and females: 2 und 5; 2 10-15; 1 30-40 in his household. He was listed in the 1840 census index of Adrian Twp.; and in the 1850 census of Adrian Twp., with wife, ANNA, age 51, b. NY; and GEORGE, age 20; SUSANNA, age 17; CORDELIA, age 15; SARAH, age 12; LYDIA A., age 7; and possibly another daughter?, Hulda W. Haviland, age 22, all b. Mich., in their household. Also note EDWIN C.; ELIJAH; JACOB, all following.

WEST, ABRAHAM, son of BENJAMIN (following), born ca. 1816, and wife, AMANDA (WESTGATE), born ca. 1828, both in Canada, were listed in the 1850 census of Raisin Twp., Lenawee Co., Mich. (next door to the household in which BENJAMIN was listed, with ALMON, age 5; BENJAMIN, age 3; ORRISON, age 1, all b. Mich., in their household.

WEST, BENJAMIN born 14 Nov. 1782, Dutchess Co., NY, married on 14 Aug. 1806 to POLLY (DISBROW) born 27 Sept. 1787, Elba, Greene Co., NY. They moved ca. 1813 to Oxford Co., Canada, where they remained until 1844, when they removed to Raisin Twp., Lenawee Co., Mich. arriving there on 28 May. She died on 31 Jan. 1849. In the 1850 census, he was listed in the household of John S. Wells, next door to Abraham. He died 6 Oct. 1858. There were 10 children, and only mentioned were: 1. MARY (m. Niles Bowerman); 2. ABRAHAM (preceding); 3. BRIGGS (following); 4. PHEBE b. 7 Mar. 1824 (m. Van R. Miller, also see); 5. WILBER (following); 6. HULETT (following). Ref: P&BA-Len pg. 454-4. Note LEVI, following; and see William Bowerman for possibly connection.

WEST, BRIGGS, son of BENJAMIN (preceding), born ca. 1814, Canada, and wife, POLLY (FARLING), (possibly daughter of John, also see) born ca. 1817, NY, were listed in the 1850 census of Raisin Twp., Lenawee Co., Mich. (2 doors from ABRAHAM) with REXFORD, age 8; MARY A., age 6, both b. Canada; and CAROLINE E., age 4; DELINDA E., age 8/12, both b. Mich., in their household.

WEST, C. D. (See Charles Mitchell)

WEST, EDWIN C. was listed in the 1840 census index of Adrian Twp., Lenawee Co., Mich. Note ABRAHAM & JACOB.

WEST, ELIJAH, possibly son of ABRAHAM (preceding), born ca. 1825, and wife, CYNTHIA, born ca. 1822, both in NY, were listed in the 1850 census of Adrian Twp., Lenawee Co., Mich. with ADELLA, age 1, b. Mich., in their household.

WEST, GIDEON was listed in the 1830 census of Lenawee Co., Mich. Territory with males: 2 10-15; 1 20-30; 1 50-60; females: 1 10-15; 1 50-60 in his household.

WEST, HULETT, youngest son of BENJAMIN (preceding), born 10 Feb. 1830, Norwich, Oxford Co., Canada, moved with his parents to Raisin Twp., Lenawee Co., Mich. In the 1850 census, he was listed with his father in the household of John S. Wells. He married in Raisin Twp. to Mrs. ELIZA (CHASE) COFFIN, probably daughter of Levi H. Chase, also see, and also see Eliza Coffin. No West children were listed in sketch. Ref: P&BA-Len pg. 504.

WEST, JACOB was listed in the 1840 census index of Adrian Twp., Lenawee Co., Mich. Note ABRAHAM & EDWIN C.

WEST, LEVI was listed in the 1840 census index of Raisin Twp., Lenawee Co., Mich.

WEST, LEVI of Palmyra, Wayne Co., NY, was father of MARY (m. Isaac Beagle Bowerman). See William Bowerman.

WEST, NATHAN and wife, SALLY, were pioneers to Richmond, Ontario Co., NY. Known daughter, OLIVE P. b. 9 July 1803, Richmond (m. Gardner P. Mason, also see). Ref: P&BA-Len pg. 198.

WEST, NORRIS born ca. 1825, and wife, FIDELIA, born ca. 1830, both in NY, were listed in the 1850 census of Palmyra Twp., Lenawee Co., Mich. with ANDREW M., age 3, b. Mich., in their household.

WEST, SEYMOUR was listed in the 1840 census index of Ogden Twp., Lenawee Co., Mich.

WEST, THOMAS (See Thomas Chandler)

WEST, WILBER, son of BENJAMIN (preceding), botn 23 Feb. 1827, Norwich, Oxford Co., Canada, came with his parents to Raisin Twp., Lenawee Co., Mich. He married on 3 July 1847 to COMFORT C. (WELLS),

Pioneer Families of Southeastern Michigan

daughter of John S. (also see). There were 8 children, of whom 2 died infancy (names not stated). Children: 1. DEBORAH b. ca. 1849 (m. Henry Fetterman; Blissfield, Mich.); 2. JAMES A. (m. Emily Tarbell; Fremont, Nebr.); 3. ANGELIA (m. E. R. Kemp; Palmyra Twp.); 4. IDA (m. David Bornois; Raisin Twp.); 5. ADELLA; 6. ALONZO. Ref: P&BA-Len pg. 454-5.

WESTBROOK (See Westfall)

WESTERMAN, JAMES[1] was born England, and came to America and settled in Butler Co., Penn. where he died. Known son, JAMES[2] (following). Ref: P&BA-Len pg. 276-7.

WESTERMAN, JAMES[2], son of JAMES[1] (preceding), born in Manchester, England, came at age 21 to Baltimore, MD where he married ELIZABETH (WILSON) of Maryland. They moved to Lowell, Mass.; then Allegheny City, and Pittsburgh, Penn. In 1840, they moved to Butler Co., Penn. In 1852, they removed to Riga Twp., Lenawee Co., Mich., and later to Adrian. He died in 1882, in Detroit, Mich. at the home of a daughter. She died 1883, Toledo, Ohio, at the home of a daughter. Known son: JESSIAH (following). Ref: P&BA-Len pg. 276-7.

WESTERMAN, JESSIAH, son of JAMES[2] (preceding), born 8 Aug. 1837, Allegheny City, Penn., served in the Civil War in an Ohio Infantry. He married on 23 Apr. 1865, Riga Twp., Lenawee Co., Mich. to BETTIE M. (GROVER), daughter of Leonard (also see). Children: 1. ALBERTA (m. George L. Bell); 2. ALLIE DELL; 3. MAUD; 4. MAY. Ref: P&BA-Len pg. 276-7.

WESTFALL - From History of Sussex & Warren Cos, NJ, by Snell, are some notes concerning this surname. Marriages: SIMON (or SIMEON) WESTFAEL born Dutchess Co., NY, probably son of JURIAN & BLANDINA (DeWITT) WESTVAAL, bapt. 30 July 1721, Reformed Chuch at Kingston, NY, dwelling in Smithfield, Bucks Co., Penn., married on 17 Apr. 1743 to JANNETJE (WESTBROEK), born at Normal, dwelling in "Mennissinck" (Minisink), Orange Co., NY. Known children: 1. JURY b. 23 Apr. 1744 (d. young?); 2. AELTJE b. 6 Oct. 1745; 3. JURY b. 24 Jan. 1748; 4. SIMEON b. 12 Feb. 1749 (note following); 5. JOHN DEWITT b. 19 May 1751; 6. WILHELMUS b. 8 July 1753; 7. SOLOMON b. 27 Jan. 1759; 8. BLANDINA b. 9 Nov. 1760; 9. RUBEN b. 8 Apr. 1764.*********DANIEL WESTFAEL born Machasmemeck (Orange Co., NY), is possibly he bpt. 1 Sept. 1723, son of JURIANN & MARIA (KODDEBEK) WESTVAAL, in the Reformed Church at Kingston, NY, married on 8 Apr. 1749 to MARIA (WESTBROEK). Daniel was said to have settled in Montague, Sussex Co., NJ, coming there with the Westbrook family. From the records of the Reformed church at Machackameck, known children: 1. ABRAM b. 29 Jan. 1749 (MAY be he who m. Antje Westbroeck); 2. ANTONY b. 2 Dec. 1750; 3. MARGARET b. 30 Mar. 1752; 4. AELTJE b. 10 Oct. 1754; 5. HANNATJE b. 10 Nov. 1761.*********Note: Researchers of this surname should see the records of the Reformed Church of Machackameck (NYG&BR, July 1911 thru Oct. 1913). In that record is a DANIEL bpt. 17 Oct. 1773, son of ABRAM & ANTJE (WESTBROECK) WESTFAEL, and sponsors were DANIEL & ANTJE (WESTBROECK) WESTFAEL (preceding). Note DANIEL, following.

WESTFALL, DANIEL and wife, POLLY (McKIBBY), were born in New Jersey. It may be he in the militia of Sandystone, Sussex Co., NJ in 1793. After their marriage, they moved to Niles, Cayuga Co., NY. She died in 1865, age 86, at Niles. Children from baptismal records of the Reformed church of Machackameck, which may not be a complete list: 1. ABRAHAM b. 27 Nov. 1800; 2. MATHHEW b. 4 Dec. 1802; 3. WILLIAM b. 26 Mar. 1803; 4. JOHN b. 9 Feb. 1806; 5. SOLOMON b. 6 Oct. 1807; 6. ALTIE b. 24 July 1809; and the following from the sketch: 7. LEWIS (following). Ref: P&BA-Len pg. 787-8.

WESTFALL, EUGENE (See Matthew B. McConnel)

WESTFALL, JANE (See Lewis Van Auken)

WESTFALL, LEWIS, son of DANIEL (preceding), born 16 Apr. 1818, Sussex Co., NJ, moved to Cayuga Co., NY with his parents. He moved to Skaneateles, NY for a time. He married H. LOUISE (MORRISON), daughter of Owen (also see). In 1852, they removed to Sandusky, Ohio; returned to Cayuga Co., NY for a time, and then in 1872, moved to Blissfield Twp., Lenawee Co., Mich. He died 25 Aug. 1885. No children were named in sketch. Ref: P&BA-Len pg. 787-8.

WESTFALL, SIMEON, possibly son of SIMEON (See WESTFALL, preceding), and wife, SALLIE (COLE), were born in Orange Co., NY, and moved to Upper Smithfield, then Pike Co., Penn. In the baptismal records of the Reformed Church of Machackameck were two of their children: 1. SIMEON bpt. 19 Feb. 1766 (sponsors, SIMEON & JANNETJE, see preceding); 2. JURRY bpt. 1 June 1777. Then from the History noted following: 3. MARGARET (m. John Van Akin, also see). Ref: P&BA-Len pg. 607-8.

WESTFALL, SIMEON - From History of Sussex & Warren Cos. NJ, by Snell. SIMEON was one of the first settlers of Westfall, Pike Co., Penn. He had a known son, DAVID who lived in Pike Co. David had children: 1. SIMEON; 2. CORNELIUS; 3. WILHELMUS; 4. ABRAHAM; 5. ESTHER (m. William Van Noy); 6. SARAH (m. James Bennett). Note resemblance to preceding.

WESTGATE, AMANDA born ca. 1828, Canada?, married Abraham West, also see, and resided in Raisin Twp., Lenawee Co., Mich.

WESTGATE, CHARLES H. was listed in the 1840 census index of Raisin Twp., Lenawee Co., Mich. near JEREMIAH & SYLVANUS. In the 1850 census of Raisin Twp., ESTHER J., age 17, b. Mich., listed in the household of Rufus Raymond; and HIRAM, age 14, b. Mich., listed in the household of James Reynolds, and MAY be children of this man?

WESTGATE, JEREMIAH born ca. 1793, NY, had known daughter, DORCAS (m. Samuel Bowerman, also see, in 1833); and probably son, JEREMIAH, Jr. (following). He married in Niagara Co., NY to Mrs. DORCAS (BOWMAN) KAYNER, born ca. 1813, NY, widow of Dr. George Kayner (also see), probably as a second wife. They moved by 1837 to Raisin Twp., Lenawee Co., Mich. In the 1850 census of Raisin Twp., they listed NELSON, age 13; ORLANDO, age 11 (probably he who m. Ellen J. Bowerman, dau. of Moses, Jr., also see); ALBERT, age 9; GEORGE, age 8; CORNELIUS, age 8;

ALZINA, age 3; ROBERT, age 3/12, all b. Mich.; and her children, Charles Kayner, age 16; Elizabeth Kayner, age 15, both b. NY, in their household.

WESTGATE, JEREMIAH, Jr., probably son of JEREMIAH (preceding), born ca. 1820, and wife, PHEBE R. (SLADE?), born ca. 1821, both in NY, were listed in the 1850 census of Raisin Twp., Lenawee Co., Mich. with FRANKLIN, age 7; WARREN, age 3, both b. Mich.; and probably in-laws, Lawton & Phebe Slade (also see), in their household.

WESTGATE, SYLVANUS born ca. 1797, and wife, ESTHER, born ca. 1802, both in NY, came from Royalton, Niagara Co., NY to Raisin Twp., Lenawee Co., Mich. in 1832. They had known daughter, ESTHER (m. William Ash, also see, she d. 1843); and in their household in the 1850 census were MARY, age 23; AUSTIN, age 19, both b. NY; and WILLIAM, age 17; SUSAN, age 7, both b. Mich.

WETER, JOSEPHUS born Oneida Co., NY, was son of man who had come from Germany and died in Oneida Co. at age 95. Josephus married ANNIE (BUCKLEY), daughter of John (also see). In 1849, they removed to Blissfield Twp., Lenawee Co., Mich., where he died in 1877, age 83. There were 5 sons and 2 daughters, names not stated, except #3. THOMAS SHEPHERD (following); RICHARD b. ca. 1833, NY, is probably another son, and was listed in household of THOMAS in 1850. Ref: P&BA-Len pg. 283-4. Note: Josephus was not listed in Blissfield Twp. in the 1850 census?

WETER, THOMAS SHEPHERD, son of JOSEPHUS (preceding), born 3 Mar. 1822, Floyd, Oneida Co., NY, moved in 1841 to Ross Co., Ohio; and married on 5 Nov. 1843 to MARY (POOLEY), daughter of Edward (also see). In 1845, they moved to Palmyra Twp., Lenawee Co., Mich. where he was listed as "SHEPARD," with first 2 children in their household. Mary died in Aug. 1851. 1. ANN MARIE b. 5 Jan. 1845, Jackson Co., O. (m. Wayne Roberts; Palmyra Twp.); 2. EDWARD b. 29 Aug. 1849, Palmyra Twp. (d. Aug. 1851). Thomas married again to Mrs. MARY ANN (UPTON) WOOD, daughter of David, and widow of Nelson (see both). Children: 3. SHEPHERD b. 4 Jan. 1854 (to Penn.); 4. ARABELL b. 16 July 1855 (m/1 Harrop Freeman; m/2 Thomas Fanning; Macomb Co., Mich.); 5. JAMES E. b. 9 apr. 1858 (to Macomb Co., Mich.); 6. NELSON C. b. 1 Apr. 1861 (to Antrim Co., Mich.); 7. DAVID E. b. 16 Nov. 1863; 8. CORA M. b. 4 Mar. 1865 (m. George Isley, son of Thomas C., also see). Ref: P&BA-Len pg. 283-4.

WETMORE also see WHITMORE

WETMORE, ELISHA and wife, CYNTHIA, were pioneers from New England to Oneida Co., NY where they remained. Known daughter, NANCY (m. Ebenezer L. Selleck, also see, in 1822 in Oneida Co.) Ref: P&BA-Len pg. 1094-5.

WEYLIE, EPHRAIM was a native of Alexandria, VA, whose father removed to Georgetown, Delaware, where he died. Ephraim moved to Tompkins Co., MY where he married JANE (DAVIS) who was born in Ludlowville, NY. They moved to Allegany Co., NY; and then in 1828, after the birth of 3 children, they moved to Elyria, Lorain Co., Ohio. She died there in June 1854; and he died in Dec. 1855. Seven sons and one daughter, names not stated, except PORTER M. (following). Ref: P&BA-Len pg. 577-8.

WEYLIE, PORTER M., son of EPHRAIM (preceding), born 24 Jan. 1824, Allegany Co., NY, moved with parents to Ohio. He married on 29 Dec. 1846, Elyria Twp., Lorain Co., Ohio to JULIA (BRADLEY), daughter of Thomas (also see). He servied in Co. E, 65th Ohio Inf. & Co. G, 60th Ohio Inf. during the Civil War.
In 1866, they moved to Blissfield Twp., Lenawee Co., Mich. Children: 1. CHARLES F.; 2. LOUISA C. (d. age 4); 3. JOHN K. Ref: P&BA-Len pg. 577-8.

WHALEY, CYRENUS born 31 Oct. 1816, Cato, Cayuga Co., NY, went to Onondaga Co. by 1827, and married there on 4 Feb. 1835 to SALLY (GORHAM), daughter of Shubael (also see). Before 1838, they moved to Jackson Co., Mich.; and then to Fulton Co., Ohio. They moved to Seneca Twp., Lenawee Co., Mich. by the 1850 census, and listed SQUIRE, age 12, b. NY; HELEN, age 12, b. Ohio (m. Henry Hayward?, also see); PHILETUS, age 7, b. Mich.; & ESTHER? (ESKRA?), age 4, b. NY, in their household. MARY, age 15, b. NY, listed in an Allen household may also relate to this family.

WHALEY, ELIZA (See Charles Negus)

WHALEY, JEROME, age 18, born NY, was listed in the 1850 census of Seneca twp., Lenawee Co., Mich.

WHALEY, JOHN and wife, NANCY, of Mandana, Onondaga Co., NY had known daughter, LAURA H. (m. James Welch, also see, before 1833 and settled in Seneca Twp., Lenawee Co., Mich.)

WHALEY, POLLY (See Zera Jennings)

WHALLEY, AMELIA (See James Smith)

WHEATON, ALFRED A., son of PETER M. (following), born 7 Jan. 1848, Woodstock Twp., Lenawee Co., Mich., married ELIZABETH (HEMINOVER) and had known children: WILLIAM H. b. 26 Dec. 1872; ARMINTHA H. b. 30 Oct. 1874; LYDIA b. 22 May 1886. Ref: P&BA-Len pg. 956-7.

WHEATON, CARPENTER born ca. 1814, NY, may be he listed as JOB C. in the 1840 census index of Franklin Twp., Lenawee Co., Mich., adjacent to WILBER, following. He married BETSEY (WHEATON), daughter of EGBERT (following); and they were listed in the 1850 census of Franklin Twp., Lenawee Co., Mich. with MARIA, age 14, b. NY; HARRIET, age 8; JAMES, age 6, both b. Mich., in their household.

WHEATON, EGBERT and wife, CATHERINE (JACKSON), were natives of Conn., who had settled in Cayuga Co., NY. They came to Mich. in 1836, and purchased land in Branch Co., but never resided there, and settled in Raisin Twp., Lenawee Co., Mich.; and later in Adrian Twp. He died in August 1840, age 57; and she died same month & year, age 53. There were 6 children, of whom 3 were surviving in 1888. 1. BETSEY b. ca. 1820, NY (m. CARPENTER, preceding); 2. LYDIA R. (m. H. Reed; Lapeer Co., Mich.); 3. DELILAH (m. Lewis Sanford, also see). Ref: P&BA-Len pg. 1129-30.

WHEATON, HORACE G., son of PETER M. (following), born 15 Nov. 1851, Woodstock Twp., Lenawee Co., Mich., married MARY (KANE) and had known children:

LeGRAND b. 30 May 1881; GEORGE b. 2 Nov. 1882. Ref: P&BA-Len pg. 956-7.

WHEATON, ICHABOD and wife, CATHERINE, moved ca. 1828 from Cayuga Co., NY to Victor, Ontario Co., NY. In 1836, they removed to Adrian Twp., Lenawee Co., Mich. where they were listed in the 1840 census index. They both died in August 1840, possibly of Ague. Known son, PETER M. (following). Also note JOB C. (CARPENTER?, preceding). Ref: P&BA-Len pg. 956-7.

WHEATON, JAMES O., son of PETER M. (following), born ca. 26 Dec. 1857, Woodstock Twp., Lenawee Co., Mich., married CORA (BRIGGS), daughter of Albert (also see), and had known son, JOHN M. b. 10 Jan. 1887. Ref: P&BA-Len pg. 956-7.

WHEATON, MALACHI S., son of PETER M. (following), born 30 Apr. 1846, Woodstock Twp., Lenawee Co., Mich., married LOUISE (HEMINOVER) and had children: 1. IDA R. b. 7 Oct. 1869 (d. 21 Apr. 1884); 2. LUTHER M. b. 9 Oct. 1871; 3. LORETTA E. b. 23 Jan. 1874. Lived in Jackson Co., Mich. Ref: P&BA-Len pg. 956-7.

WHEATON, PETER M., son of ICHABOD (preceding), born 14 Aug. 1822, Aurelius, Cayuga Co., NY, came to Adrian Twp., Lenawee Co., Mich. with his parents. He married on 25 June 1845 to LORETTA (SANFORD), daughter of Malachi (also see), and they settled in Woodstock Twp. Children: 1. MALACHI S. (preceding); 2. ALFRED A. (preceding); 3. ERASTUS M. b. 15 Sept. 1849 (d. 26 Aug. 1851); 4. HORACE G. (preceding); 5. BETSEY B. b. 3 Nov. 1853 (m. Alva E. Bedell, also see); 6. CATHARINE R. b. 29 Nov. 1844 (d. 27 Apr. 1862); 7. JAMES O. (preceding); 8. GEORGE b. 24 Jan. 1860 (d. 1 Mar. 1860); 9. ELMAR b. 3 Mar. 1861 (m. Mary J. Taylor, had known son, LaVerne b. 10 Oct. 1887); 10. ELLEN (twin of ELMAR); 11. ANNA H. M. b. 2 Apr. 1863; 12. IRA I. b. 17 Mary 1864; 13. JOB C. b. 13 Jan. 1871. Ref: P&BA-Len pg. 956-7.

WHEATON, WILBUR was listed in the 1840 census index of Franklin Twp., Lenawee Co., Mich. adjacent to JOB C.; and it may be he listed as WILLIAM in the 1850 census of Franklin Twp., age 62, b. Mass., with wife, LUCY, age 58, born NY, and MARGARETTA, age 15, and Harvey Parks, age 19, both b. NY, in their household.

WHEELER, A. P. was listed in the 1840 census index of Seneca Twp., Lenawee Co., Mich. Note MYRON, following.

WHEELER, ABEL was listed in the 1840 census index of Medina Twp., Lenawee Co., Mich.

WHEELER, ABRAHAM, son of JAMES (following), born 16 May 1803, Ovid, Seneca Co., NY, married there on 11 Nov. 1827 to AZUBA (YOUNG) born 1 Aug. 1805, Troy, NY. They removed in 1833 to Macon Twp., Lenawee Co., Mich. They remained there until 1863, the made their home with son, James K., in Rome Twp. She died 22 Sept. 1865. Children: 1. JAMES K. (following); 2. JOHN C. b. ca. 1833; 3. VELITTA b. ca. 1835, Mich. (deceased by 1888). Abraham married second to Mrs. CAROLINE HITCH, widow of Hubbard (note that this may be Hubbard Hicks, also see) of Rome Twp. Abraham died 6 Jan. 1874. Ref: P&BA-Len pg. 848-9.

WHEELER, ADELIA M. Mrs. (See Joseph E. Wadsworth)

WHEELER, ADOLPH, son of PROSPER (following), born 22 Mar. 1842, Manchester, Washtenaw Co., Mich., married ISABELLE (HATHEWAY), daughter of Gilbert (also see) of New Baltimore, Mich. They resided in Adrian, Lenawee Co., Mich. No children were listed in the sketch. Ref: P&BA-Len pg. 480-1.

WHEELER, ALTIE (See William Fitch)

WHEELER, CALEB born ca. 1781, Mass., and wife, SARAH, born ca. 1793, Conn. settled in Blissfield Twp., Lenawee Co., Mich. by 1830. In the 1830 census of Lenawee Co., Mich. Territory, they listed males: 1 und 5; 1 5-10; 1 10-15; 1 40-50; & females: 2 und 5; 1 5-10; 1 30-40 in their household. In the 1850 census of Blissfield Twp., they listed GEORGE, age 20; EMILY, age 22; LUTHER L., age 16, all b. Mich., in their household; and FRANCIS (following) was listed next door.

WHEELER, D. P. (See Frederick G. Beagle)

WHEELER, DAVID born ca. 1812, Mass., and wife, ROSILLA, born ca. 1818, New Hampshire, were listed in the 1850 census of Adrian Twp., Lenawee Co., Mich. with WILLIAM H., age 8, b. Mass., in their household. Note REUBEN, following, possibly brother?

WHEELER, FRANCIS, probably son of CALEB (preceding), born ca. 1820, and wife, SARAH, born ca. 1825, both in NY, were listed in the 1850 census of Blissfield Twp., Lenawee Co., Mich. with GEORGE, age 1, b. Mich., in their household (next door to CALEB).

WHEELER, JAMES and wife, ELIZABETH, were born and married in New Jersey. They moved to Ovid, Seneca Co., NY where they remained until 1833, then moved to what is now Adrian Twp., Lenawee Co., Mich. Known children: 1. JAMES, Jr. (following); 2. ABRAHAM (preceding); 3. EMELINE b. ca. 1813 (m. Charles White, also see). Ref: P&BA-Len pg. 848-9.

WHEELER, JAMES (Jr.), son of JAMES (preceding), born ca. 1797, New Jersey, and wife, SARAH, born ca. 1800, NY, were listed in the 1850 census of Macon Twp., Lenawee Co., Mich. with EMELINE, age 18, b. NY; and HENRY, age 14, b. Mich., in their household.

WHEELER, JAMES born ca. 1795, NY, and wife, MARY (ROSE), moved from NY to Raisin Twp., Lenawee Co., Mich. in 1831. It may be they listed in the 1840 census index of Tecumseh Twp. In the 1850 census of Tecumseh Twp., JULIA ANN, age 32; RUTH, age 27 (prob. she who m. James Taylor; Hart, Mich.), both b. NY, were listed in the household. Other known children: PHILURA (m. A. Hood; Detroit, Mich.); ELIZABETH "BETSEY" b. ca. 1822 (m. Joseph Collins, also see); JAMES H. (to Chicago, Ill.); SARAH J. b. Jan. 1818, Steuben Co., NY (m. James C. Eaton, also see). James was listed in the 1850 census of Tecumseh Twp. with probably a second wife, ANN, age 55, born NY. Ref: P&BA-Len pg. 471-2.

WHEELER, JAMES born ca. 1800, and wife, EMILY, born ca. 1815, both in NY, were listed in the 1850 census of Dover Twp., Lenawee Co., Mich. with CHARLES, age 7; POLLY, age 5; CLARISSA, age 4; SQUIRE, age 2, all b. Mich., in their household. Note JONATHAN, following.

WHEELER, JAMES born ca. 1823, Maine, was listed in the 1850 census of Palmyra Twp., Lenawee Co., Mich.

WHEELER, JAMES K., son of ABRAHAM (preceding), born 8 May 1829, Seneca Co., NY, came to Macon Twp., Lenawee Co., Mich. with his parents. He married on 12 Nov. 1851 to ELEANOR ANN (MILLER), daughter of John A. (also see). They lived in Woodstock Twp. from 1853 to 1865, then moved to Rome Twp. Children: 1.

FINETTA b. 2 Dec. 1852 (d. 5 July 1862, Woodstock Twp.); 2. JOHN A. b. 31 Jan. 1857 (m. Lizzie Slyter; Rollin Twp., dau: Veda b. 28 July 1883); 3. HERSHEL D. b. 28 Oct. 1860 (m Luella Myers on 13 Apr. 1886). Ref: P&BA-Len pg. 848-9.

WHEELER, JANE M. married David M. Johnson in Monroe Co., Mich. (also see).

WHEELER, JONATHAN born ca. 1773, New Hampshire, may be he listed as "JOHN" in the 1840 census index of Dover Twp., Lenawee Co., Mich. In the 1850 census of Dover Twp., he was listed in household of Joseph F. Warren, also b. NH, and wife, Hannah, age 40, b. NY. There was a FERNANDO, age 13, b. NY, listed in an Austin household, connection not known. Also note JAMES, preceding, in Dover Twp.

WHEELER, JOSIAH was listed in the 1830 census of Lenawee Co., Mich. Territoy, with males: 2 und 5; 1 5-10; 2 10-15; 1 30-40; and females; 1 5-10; 2 10-15; 1 15-20; 1 30-40 in the household. It is probably he listed in the 1840 census index of Tecumseh Twp., Lenawee Co., Mich. Also note JAMES; & SOLOMON.

WHEELER, JUDSON born ca. 1804, Conn., and wife, POLLY, born ca. 1805, VT, were listed in the 1850 census of Fairfield Twp., Lenawee Co., Mich. with ELIZABETH, age 20, b. NY; and CHARLOTTE F., age 16; SARAH A., age 11; EMMA M., age 9; CHARLES B., age 7, all b. Mich., in their household. HENRY, age 13, in the Zeba Miller, household may relate to this family.

WHEELER, LUTHER born ca. 1832, Mich., was listed in the 1850 census of Palmyra Twp., Lenawee Co., Mich.

WHEELER, MARTHA born ca. 1834, NY, was listed in the 1850 census of Medina Twp., Lenawee Co., Mich. in a Colegrove household. Also note ABEL & STEPHEN S.

WHEELER, MYRON born ca. 1816, Mass., was probably he listed in the 1840 census index of Seneca Twp., Lenawee Co., Mich.; and in the 1850 census of Madison Twp. with MARIA, age 18, b. NY; and JAMES H., age 8, b. Mich., in his household. Note that A. P., preceding, was in Seneca Twp.

WHEELER, PROSPER J. born Middletown, Conn., and wife, ZADIA B. (BENHAM) was born Dutchess Co., NY. They moved from NY to Washtenaw Co., Mich. about 1831, and by 1840 to Napoleon Twp., Jackson Co., Mich. where they remained for many years. They later moved to Manchester, Washtenaw Co., Mich.; and then to Lenawee Co. where he died in 1877. She was residing in Adrian in 1888. Six children, names not stated, except ADOLPH (preceding). PROSPER J., age 15, b. Mich., was listed in the 1850 census of Adrian, obviously related, in the household of John R. & Emily U. Clark.

WHEELER, REUBEN born in Gardner, Worcester co., Mass., moved to Adrian Twp., Lenawee Co., Mich. ca. 1840. He married on 9 June 1842 to SAMANTHA M. (BEALS), daughter of Caleb (also see). They lived in Adrian except for 2 years in California for his health. He died in Adrian in 1854. Children: 1. CHARLES H. (Co. C, 18th Mich. Inf., Civil War; d. in Confederate prison); 2. ALFRED R. (to Woonsocket, Dakotas). Samantha married again to Charles Dunham (also see) on 27 Oct. 1869. Ref: P&BA-Len pg. 842-3. Note: Reuben was not listed in the 1850 census, however, DAVID (preceding), shown as a Carpenter & Chair Maker, which was the business that Reuben established in Adrian, was listed adjacent to Kelly S. Beals, brother of Samantha. Reuben may have been in Calif. in 1850.

WHEELER, SAMUEL born ca. 1802, and wife, PHILENA, born ca. 1809, both in NY, were listed in the 1840 census index of Woodstock Twp., Lenawee Co., Mich. (adjacent to WILLIAM); and in the 1850 census with SIMON, age 21, b. NY; and ELISA, age 15; CAROLINE, age 12, both b. Mich., in their household.

WHEELER, SAMUEL born ca. 1810, and wife, CORNELIA, born ca. 1810, were listed in the 1850 census of Riga Twp., Lenawee Co., Mich. with MILTON, age 12; MARTHA, age 9, both b. NY; and HELEN, age 6; FLORENIA, age 3, both b. Mich., in their household.

WHEELER, SARAH (See William Baker)

WHEELER, SARAH B. married Dr. Increase S. Hamilton (also see) in NY in 1834. Ref: P&BA-Len pg. 1076-7.

WHEELER, SOLOMON born ca. 1813, NY, was listed in the 1840 census index of Tecumseh Twp., Lenawee Co., Mich. (adjacent to JOSIAH & JAMES of Tecumseh Twp.); and was listed in the 1850 census with (second?) wife, DELIA, born ca. 1826, NY, with JULIETT, age 12, HARVEY, age 10; JAMES, age 8; FRANKLIN, age 6, all b. Mich. in their household. Note that if age of Delia is correct, some of these children are too old to be hers. Also listed was Augusta Miller, age 26, b. NY.

WHEELER, STEPHEN S. born ca. 1821, NY, was listed head of household in the 1850 census of Medina Twp., Lenawee Co., Mich. with probably mother, ALMINA, age 43, b. NY, in the household. Note ABEL, preceding.

WHEELER, THOMAS born ca. 1785, NY, was listed in the 1840 census index of Cambridge Twp., Lenawee Co., Mich., and was listed in the 1850 census with W.? S., age 41, and possibly wife of W. S., ELISA ANN, age 40, both b. NY, in his household.

WHEELER, WILLIAM was listed in the 1840 census index of Woodstock Twp., Lenawee Co., Mich. Also note SAMUEL, preceding.

WHEELER, WILLIAM born ca. 1820, Mass., and wife, ELIZA J., born ca. 1825, NY, were listed in the 1850 census of Palmyra Twp., Lenawee Co., Mich.

WHELAN, ALVINZA, son of JOHN (following), born 16 Feb. 1835, Franklin Twp., Lenawee Co., Mich., married on 17 Jan. 1856, Adrian, to ADELIA J. (WITHERELL), daughter of Wilson (also see). They resided in Franklin Twp., Lenawee Co. Children: 1. JOHN B. (m. Myra Reynolds, dau. of B. F. of Tecumseh); 2. HOWARD. Ref: P&BA-Len pg. 664-5.

WHELAN, CYRUS, age 49, born NY, was listed in the 1850 census of Franklin Twp., Lenawee Co., Mich. in the household of John R. and Harriet Allen. Note ELI, following.

WHELAN, ELI born VT, and wife, DESIAH (BEEBE) born ca. 1772, Conn., lived first in Vermont, and then moved to Oneida Co., NY. They later moved to Clarkson, Monroe Co., NY. He died late in the War of 1812 leaving 7 sons and 3 daughters. She moved with children to Franklin Twp., Lenawee Co., Mich. and in the 1850 census, at age 78, was living in the household of Eli Knight and his wife, and probably her daughter, PEMILLIA b. ca. 1809, NY. Known son, WILLIAM (following); and ELI; ERI; & JOHN were all adjacent in the 1840 census index of Franklin Twp. IRENA b. ca.

Pioneer Families of Southeastern Michigan

1811, Monroe Co., NY (m. George W. Allen, Sr., also see) is probably another daughter. Ref: P&BA-Len pg. 458-9. Also note CYRUS, preceding.

WHELAN, ERI, probably son of ELI, born ca. 1800, NY, and wife, HANNAH, born ca. 1801, Mass., were listed in the 1840 census index of Franklin Twp., Lenawee Co., Mich.; and in the 1850 census with AISA?, age 21; ELISA, age 20, both b. NY; and HENRY, age 20; CYRUS, age 13; SEREPTA, age 9; ERVIN, age 8 (following); ELLEN, age 6, all b. Mich., and Joshua Seaton, age 69, in the household.

WHELAN, ERVIN, son of ERI (preceding), probably he called "Ervin Jr." who married on 11 Nov. 1867 to LAURA (BILLINGTON), daughter of Wilson (also see) in Coldwater, Mich. Known children: 1. ALTON; 2. ALMA; 3. HOYT. Ref: P&BA-Len pg. 637-8.

WHELAN, JOHN, probably son of ELI, born ca. 1802, NY, and wife, FREELOVE (RAYMOND) born ca. 1807, were called "natives of Livingston, Oswego Co., NY who settled in Clarkson, Monroe co., NY. In 1833, they moved to Franklin Twp., Lenawee Co., Mich. He died in Oct. 1867, and she was living in 1888, age 81. Five sons, and two daughters, names not stated. Known daughter, MARIAN N. b. 2 June 1831, Clarkson, NY (m. E. C. Wisner, also see); and in John's household in the 1850 census were : EMILINE, age 17, b. NY; and ALVINZA (preceding); MARTHA, age 13; JOHN, age 10; OTIS, age 8; HARLOW, age 6, all b. Mich. Ref: P&BA-Len pg. 528-9; 664-5.

WHELAN, JULIA (See Wilson Billington)

WHELAN, WILLIAM, son of ELI, born 6 Aug. 1806, Verona, Oneida Co., NY, married on 1 Jan. 1828, Clarkson, Monroe Co., NY to EMILY (JOSLIN/JOSLYN), daughter of Peleg (also see). In 1833, they moved to Franklin Twp., Lenawee Co., Mich. Children: 1. ELIZA ANN b. ca. 1829 (m. George W. Allen, son of Daniel, also see); 2. SARAH b. ca. 1831 (m. Fiske Beebe); 3. NANCY b. ca. 1835 (m. Francis Erkskine); 4. EMELINE b. 19 Mar. 1842, Franklin Twp. (m. William A/E Wisner, also see); 5. ROSETTA (m. Lorenzo Billington; Franklin Twp.); 6. JANE (deceased by 1888); 7. LETTIE (deceased in 1888, may be she listed as "Rosetta," age 3, in 1850 census). Thomas Van Wort, age 7, b. Mich. was in William's household in the 1850 census.

WHELE, JACOB (See Aaron Whitacre)

WHETMORE see WETMORE & WHITMORE

WHIPPO, PRISCILLA (See Sanford Smith)

WHITACRE also see WHITAKER

WHITACRE, AARON, son of JOSEPH (following), born 15 Sept. 1814, Muncie Twp., Lycoming Co., Penn., married on 22 Feb. 1838 to ANNA (CARSON) born 26 Oct. 1817, Shrewsbury Twp., Lycoming Co. They removed to Spencer Twp., Lucas Co., Ohio. She died there on 3 Apr. 1846. Children: 1. GEORGE (Nebraska); 2. JACOB (served Civil War from Illinois; & d. result of illness); 3. WILLIAM (Wichita, KS); 4. SARAH C. (m. Chester Van Dorn, son of Jacob E., also see). Aaron married again in Jan. 1847 to RACHEL (GARDNER), daughter of Robert (also see). They moved to Dover Twp., Lenawee Co., Mich. in 1853. Children (two d. infancy, names not stated): 5. ANN (m. Jacob Whele; Franklin Twp.); 6. ERASMUS (m. Elsie Hamlin; Dover Twp.); 7. NANCY A. (m. Franklin Allen; Dover Twp.); 8. JOSEPH G. (m. Eunice Hare; Clayton, Mich.) Ref: P&BA-Len pg. 476-7.

WHITACRE, JOSEPH, son of ROBERT (following), born 28 Dec. 1772, Wakefield, Bucks Co., Penn., married CATHARINE (ADLUM) born 29 Oct. 1770, Little York, York Co., Penn. They settled in Lycoming Co., Penn. where he died on 15 May 1844; and she died 31 Jan. 1851. Six sons & three daughters, names not stated, except youngest child, AARON (preceding). Ref: P&BA-Len pg. 476-7.

WHITACRE, ROBERT born 28 Dec. 1739, Bucks Co., penn., and wife, SARAH (WINDER) born 18 Oct. 1740, moved from Bucks Co. to Lycoming Co., Penn. where they remained. Known son, JOSEPH (preceding). Ref: P&BA-Len pg. 476-7.

WHITAKER also see WHITACRE

WHITAKER, J. WILLIAM, son of JOHN (following), born 10 Oct. 1822, Ulster Co., NY, moved to Ontario Co., NY and Sandusky Co., Ohio with his parents. He married on 28 Sept. 1847 to LOUISA A. (HAMILTON), daughter of Abram (also see). They moved a few years later to Hudson Twp., Lenawee Co., Mich. Children: 1. FRANK H. (Rollin Twp.); 2. ELEANOR H. Ref: P&BA-Len pg. 854-5.

WHITAKER, JOHN, son of WILLIAM (following), born probably in Ulster Co., NY, married there to ? who was born in Durham, NY (sketch said Durham Co.?, probably Greene Co.) They remained in Ulster Co. until 1824, then moved to Ontario Co., NY. In 1836, they moved to Sandusky Co., Ohio. About 1863, they came to Hudson Twp., Lenawee Co., Mich. to live with known son, J. WILLIAM (preceding). John died Sept. 1885. Ref: P&BA-Len pg. 854-5.

WHITAKER, WILLIAM moved from Ulster Co., NY to Ontario Co., NY ca. 1821. In 1831, he moved to York, Sandusky Co., Ohio. He died in 1835, and his wife, name not stated, died in Clyde, Ohio a few years later. Known son, JOHN (preceding). Ref: P&BA-Len pg. 854-5.

WHITE, ALIDA (See Orlando H. Alger)

WHITE, ALLEN born ca. 1828, and wife, CYNTHIA, born ca. 1832, both in NY, were married within the year, and living in the household of John Baker, probably father of Cynthia, in the 1850 census of Fairfield Twp., Lenawee Co., Mich.

WHITE, ALBERT, son of CHARLES, born 4 June 1839, Hillsdale Co., Mich., came to Adrian Twp., Lenawee Co., Mich. at age 16. He married on 1 Jan. 1862 to ANNA A. (HENION), daughter of Abraham A. (also see). They settled in Madison Twp., Lenawee Co., Mich. in 1885. Children: 1. HERBERT O.; 2. EMMA. Ref: P&BA-Len pg. 639-40.

WHITE, BART born ca. 1801, Mass., and wife, CYNTHIA, born ca. 1801, NY, were listed in the 1840 census index of Dover Twp., Lenawee Co., Mich. (adjacent to CURRAN; MYRON; ROBERT, following); and in the 1850 census with ORRIN, age 19; EDWIN, age 17, both b. NY; and MELVIN, age 6, b. Mich.; and Jane Torbron, age 20. b. NY, in their household.

WHITE, BETSEY born ca. 1787, NY, was listed in the 1850 census of Fairfield Twp., Lenawee Co., Mich. in the household of Warren Thompson, age 33, b. NY, and wife, Almira, age 22, b. Ohio, and daughter, Laura E., age 3, b. Mich.

WHITE, CELINDA born 25 Nov. 1817, Washington Co., NY, married in Niagara Co., NY to Alfred Bailey, also see. Ref: P&BA-Len pg. 985-6.

WHITE, CHARLES moved from Cayuga Co., NY to Adrian, Lenawee Co., Mich. and married there to EMELINE (WHEELER), daughter of James (also see), and settled in Hillsdale Co., Mich. He lived finally at Cutter's Corners, Mich. where he died in 1848. She was living in Minneapolis, Minn. at age 75, with a daughter. Children: 1. GEORGE; 2. ALBERT (preceding); 3. JAMES; 4. ANNA; 5. MORTAIN; 6. WILLIAM M. Ref: P&BA-Len pg. 639-40.

WHITE, CHARLOTTE (See John A. Baer)

WHITE, COMFORT (See Samuel B. Keene)

WHITE, CRAWFORD born ca. 1782, and wife, ANNA (TAYLOR), born ca. 1795, both in New Jersey, came to Raisin Twp., Lenawee Co., Mich. in 1836, probably from Monmouth Co., NJ. He died 1 Sept. 1854, age 73; and she died 19 Oct. 1870, age 76. Four children, names not stated, but the following were listed in their household in the 1850 census: DOROTHY b. ca. 1822; WILLIAM b. ca. 1828; ELWOOD T. (following), all b. New Jersey. Ref: P&BA-Len pg. 726. Note: Mary A. Winslow, age 11, b. Mich., was also in the household.

WHITE, CURRAN was listed in the 1840 census index of Dover Twp., Lenawee Co., Mich. adjacent to BART & ROBERT.

WHITE, DAVID born ca. 1806, VT, and wife, PHEBE C., born ca. 1814, Mass., were listed in the 1840 census index of Fairfield Twp., Lenawee Co., Mich.; and were in the 1850 census with LYSANDER M., age 16, b. NY; JEROME M., age 12; ALBERT W., age 2, both b. Mich., in their household.

WHITE, EDITH born ca. 1763, Mass., was listed in the 1850 census of Raisin Twp., Lenawee Co., Mich. in the household of James and Susanna Haviland (also see). Note that Susannah was age 55, b. NY, and may be a daughter of Edith?

WHITE, ELIZABETH of Mass., who was a direct descendant of PEREGRINE (the first white child born in New England), married Benjamin Lincoln (also see). Ref: P&BA-Len pg. 370-2.

WHITE, ELWOOD T., son of CRAWFORD (preceding), born 4 Oct. 1829, Monmouth Co., NJ, came to Raisin Twp., Lenawee Co., Mich. with his parents. He married on 15 Sept. 1857 at Mt. Morris to SARAH (NEWMAN) who was born 10 Mar. 1829, Chambersburg, Penn. (Sarah had lived in Maryland before moving to Mich.) Children: 1. ELWOOD P.; 2. KATIE; 3. ALVAH (to Kansas); 4. CHARLES (Raisin Twp.). Note: First 2 children were deceased by 1888. Ref: P&BA-Len pg. 726.

WHITE, ERASTUS born ca. 1808, and wife, ELIZA, born ca. 1812, both in NY, were listed in the 1840 census index of Ogden Twp., Lenawee Co., Mich.; and in the 1850 census with LYDIA A., age 17; RACHEL, age 14, both b. NY; and JANE, age 12; WILLIAM, age 9; DIADAMA, age 7; JOSEPH, age 4; LINA, age 3; AMELIA, age 1/12, all b. Mich., in their household.

WHITE, FAYETTE, probably son of WALTER (following), born ca. 1825, and wife, MELINDA, born ca. 1829, both in NY, were listed in the 1850 census of Woodstock Twp., Lenawee Co., Mich. with HELEN, age 2, b. Mich., in their household.

WHITE, GEORGE was listed in the 1840 census index of Tecumseh Twp., Lenawee Co., Mich.

WHITE, GEORGE H., age 25, born VT, was listed in the 1850 census of Hudson Twp., Lenawee Co., Mich. in an Ames household.

WHITE, HANNAH Mrs. (See Benjamin West)

WHITE, HENRY S., son of ZEBINA (following), born 4 June 1833, Niagara Co., NY, came with his parents to Fairfield Twp., Lenawee Co., Mich. He married on 3 Sept. 1854 to JERUSHA S. (LOWE), daughter of Isaiah (also see) of Jasper, Mich. They settled in Fairfield Twp. Children: 1. LUCIUS T. (m. Mary E. Clark); 2. ZEBINA (d. 11 July 1876, age 18); 3. MABEL G. (m. J. Clark Swick; Fairfield Twp.); 4. NELLIE. Ref: P&BA-Len pg. 859.

WHITE, J. D. (See George S. Stranahan)

WHITE, JEFFERSON (See Merchant Brooks)

WHITE, JOEL, age 29, born NY, was listed in the 1850 census of Tecumseh Twp., Lenawee Co., Mich. in a Daniel Hyatt household.

WHITE, JOHN born ca. 1781, and wife, POLLY, born ca. 1781, both in New Hampshire, were listed in the 1850 census of Fairfield Twp., Lenawee Co., Mich. with JOHN, age 48, b. VT, in their household. ZEBINA (following) is probably another son. Ref: P&BA-Len pg. 859. Also note DAVID, preceding, & WILLIAM (following). Note: There was a JOHN in the 1840 census index of Blissfield Twp.

WHITE, JOHN T. (See William Wilber)

WHITE, JOSEPH born ca. 1815, and wife, SARAH, borh ca. 1825, both in NY, were listed in the 1850 census of Ogden Twp., Lenawee Co., Mich. with FRANCIS, age 8, b. NY; and SARAH A., age 6; CELINDA, age 2, both b. Mich., in their household. Note ERASTUS, preceding.

WHITE, JOSEPHUS born 5 Aug. 1808 near Canandaigua, Ontario Co., NY, married in New York to SARAH (BIDDLE) born 24 Oct. 1806, New Jersey. He was an ordained Minister for a time. They lived in Monroe Co., NY, and then moved in 1839 to Erie Co., NY, and afterwards to Camden, Lorain Co., Ohio. In 1846, they moved to Ogden Twp., Lenawee Co., Mich. He died there 4 Oct. 1880; and she died 2 May 1878. They were listed in the 1850 census and their place of birth was shown as Ohio; and the following were in their household. Children: 1. CAROLINE E. b. 7 July 1836, Brighton, Monroe Co., NY (m. L. T. Rathbun, also see); 2. DEMARIS C. b. 9 Mar. 1840, Concord, Erie Co., NY (m. James Hodges; Ogden Twp.); 3, JAY W. b. ca. 1847, Mich. Also in their household was Sydney Biddle?, age 12, b. Ohio. Ref: P&BA-Len pg. 802-3.

WHITE, LOW of Sherburne, Chenango Co., NY, had known daughter, HANNAH born 23 May 1785, Orwell, VT (m. Joseph Southworth, also see, and died in Raisin Twp., Lenawee Co., Mich. on 13 Sept. 1849).

WHITE, M. L. (See George H. Back)

WHITE, MARGARET (See Andrew Clement; & Thomas Campbell)

WHITE, MEHALA (See Joseph Patterson)

Pioneer Families of Southeastern Michigan

WHITE, MYRON was listed in the 1840 census index of Dover Twp., Lenawee Co., Mich. adjacent to BART; CURRAN; & ROBERT.

WHITE, NEHEMIAH was listed in the 1840 census index of Clinton Twp., Lenawee Co., Mich.

WHITE, ROBERT born ca. 1803, and wife, HULDAH, born ca. 1811, both in NY, were listed in the 1840 census index of Dover Twp., Lenawee Co., Mich. (adjacent to BART, & CURRAN, preceding); and in the 1850 census with MARVIN, age 17, b. NY; and ROMINA, age 8; MENLY?, age 4; CURRAN, age 3, all b. Mich., in their household.

WHITE, SAMUEL, son of JOHN & ELIZABETH (STANDFORD) of England, was born 20 July 1810, Suffolkshire, England. His father, JOHN, died in England, age 44; and mother died there at agae 85. Samuel married in England to ANN (SMITH), born 1810, and in 1830 they immigrated to Wayne Co., NY. In 1836, they moved to Cambridge Twp., Lenawee Co., Mich., and she died there at age 66. Eight children, names not stated, but the following were listed in the 1850 census of Cambridge Twp.: 1. MARY, age 17, b. NY; 2. WILLIAM B. (following); 3. HICKS?, age 12; 4. GEORGE, age 10; 5. CAROLINE, age 6; 6. LYDIA, age 2/12, last 3 born Mich. Samuel married again in 1879 to Mrs. LOSINA S. (PARKER) ARCHER, daughter of Joshua (also see); and widow of William D. Archer. Ref: P&BA-Len pg. 1076-7.

WHITE, THERON born ca. 1800, and wife, LOUIS (LOIS?), born ca. 1802, both shown born Ohio? (Note JOSEPHUS, preceding), were listed in the 1840 census index of Medina Twp., Lenawee Co., Mich.; and were listed in the 1850 census of Seneca Twp., Lenawee Co., Mich. with RHODA, age 9, b. Mich., in their household.

WHITE, THOMAS and wife, SOPHRINA, were parents of ANN E. who married Dr. Increase S. Hamilton (also see) in Tecumseh, Lenawee Co., Mich. in 1873, as his 3rd wife.

WHITE, W. (See Eli E. Munn)

WHITE, WALTER, son of EBENEZER, born 8 Dec. 1801, Tapson, Orange Co., VT, married in 1823 to MALANY (ROTNOUR), daughter of George of Lenox, Madison Twp., NY. In 1835, they removed to Brooklyn, Jackson Co., Mich.; and in 1838 to Columbia Twp., Jackson Co. Children: 1. FAYETTE (preceding); 2. GEORGE A.; 3. JEFFERSON T. (prob. he who m. Angeleck Brooks, dau. of Merchant, also see); 4. AMOS W. Ref: <u>History of Jackson Co., Mich.</u>, 1881, pg. 819.

WHITE, WARREN S. born ca. 1821, and wife, ELIZA (FOOT), born ca. 1829, both in NY, were listed in the 1850 census of Fairfield Twp., Lenawee Co., Mich. with LEWIS S., age 2/12, b. Mich., in their housheold. Also in their household was Phebe Foot, age 60, b. Ohio. Warren apparently died by 1865, as Eliza married again after 1865 to Seth B. Sayres (also see) of Seneca Twp.

WHITE, WILLIAM Rev. born in Rensselaerville, Albany Co., NY, of Quaker parentage, became a Baptist Minister. He married PRUDENCE (WICKES), daughter of Israel P., who was born in Cayuga Co., NY. They eventually settled in Ithaca, Tompkins Co., NY; and then moved to Ohio in 1842. In 1852, they moved to Wright Twp. (Hillsdale Co.?), Mich.; and then to Linden, Genesee Co., Mich., where he died. She was still living there in 1888 with a son & daughter, names not stated. Known daughter HARRIET A. "of Jacksonville, Tompkins Co., NY," born 28 May 1832 (m/1 ? Robinson; m/2 John M. Osborn, also see, on 5 Apr. 1870). Ref: P&BA-Len pg. 1180-5.

WHITE, WILLIAM born ca. 1801, and wife, REBECCA, born ca. 1820, both in Canada, were listed in the 1850 census of Blissfield Twp., Lenawee Co., Mich. with Jesse Fletcher, age 11; Virtue P. Blunt, age 4, both b. Mich., in their household.

WHITE, WILLIAM of Conn. was the father of HANNAH M. (m. Benjamin Ingraham, also see; and were pioneers to Ottawa Co., Ohio). Ref: P&BA-Len pg. 723-4.

WHITE, WILLIAM moved from Maine to Wayne Co., NY. He had known daughter, MARY b. ca. 1805, Maine (m. Nathaniel Crockett, also see, in Wayne Co., NY). Ref: P&BA-Len pg. 672&5; 993.

WHITE, WILLIAM and wife, ARMENIA (SAWYER), moved from Niagara Co., NY to Michigan on 25 June 1860. She died 10 July 1874, Ionia Co., Mich.; and he was still living in 1888 in Fairfield Twp., Lenawee Co., Mich. Known daughter, LORETTA A. b. 18 Sept. 1841, Niagara Co., NY (m. Warren A. Bailey, also see). Ref: P&BA-Len pg. 985-6.

WHITE, WILLIAM B., son of SAMUEL (preceding), born 25 Dec. 1834, Palmyra, Wayne Co., NY, came to Cambridge Twp., Lenawee Co., Mich. with his parents. He married on 31 Oct. 1860 to ELLEN (LEWIS), daughter of Calvin (also see). They settled in Cambridge Twp. Children: 1. MARY I. b. 13 Dec. 1861 (m. Frank W. Gilbert, Rome Twp.); 2. ANN M. b. 1 May 1864; 3. ARTHUR E. b. 21 Nov. 1870. Ref: P&BA-Len pg. 786-7.

WHITE, ZEBINA, probably son of JOHN (preceding), born 1809, VT, went to Niagara Co., NY. He married POLLY (SHELDON) born ca. 1811, NY. In 1837, they moved from Niagara Co., NY to Fairfield Twp., Lenawee Co., Mich. The sketch named 4 children: LIVONA b. ca. 1831 (m. L. Q. Munn; Madison Twp.); MELVINA (d. Infancy); CORDELIA (m. Ezra Smith; Berrien Co., Mich.); HENRY S. (preceding). However, the 1850 census of Fairfield Twp., does not list Cordelia, but does list PHILENA, age 13; and also lists ABRAM, age 8, not listed in the sketch. Ref: P&BA-Len pg. 859.

WHITEMAN, ANNA (See George I. Harder)

WHITFIELD, ANN (See Daniel Baker)

WHITING, ALANSON and wife, ANNA, of Seneca Co., NY had known daughter, ELIZABETH b. 22 May 1813, Seneca Co. (m. David T. Maynard, also see). Ref: P&BA-Len pg. 576-7.

WHITING, EMMA, age 56, born Mass., was listed in the 1850 census of Tecumseh Twp., Lenawee Co., Mich. in the household of John & Mary Osborn.

WHITING, FRANCIS H., son of GEORGE (following), born 27 Aug. 1837, Monroe Co., Mich., married VIANA (BERDAN), daughter of David (also see) in Tecumseh, Lenawee Co., Mich. on 29 Dec. 1859. They located first in Saline, Washtenaw Co., Mich.; and then moved to Tecumseh Twp., Lenawee Co.; and later settled in Macon Twp. Children: 1. WILLIAM W. (to Pratt, KS); 2. ELLA; 3. ROY J. Ref: P&BA-Len pg. 353-4.

WHITING, GEORGE born ca. 1810, Penn Yan, Yates Co., NY married there to ELIZABETH (SPALDING), a native of Vermont. They moved to Monroe, Monroe Co., Mich.

by 1837. George went to Califoria in the Gold Rush, and remained until 1852, then returned to York Twp., Washtenaw Co., Mich. He died in 1873, age 63. She was still living in 1888, over age 70, with eldest daughter, Fidelia, in Milan, Monroe Co., Mich. Known children: FRANCIS H. (preceding); FIDELIA (m. Burhan; Milan, Mich.) Ref: P&BA-Len pg. 353-4.

WHITING, HIRAM S. married ELMIRA (WOOLSEY), daughter of Nathaniel W. (also see). He died in Washtenaw Co., Mich. Children: 1. MATILDA b. ca. 1838 (to St. Louis, MO); 2. AMANDA b. ca. 1840 (Bloomville, Seneca Co., O.); 3. MARY A. b. ca. 1840 (m. Oscar Holcomb; Bloomville, O.); 4. LOUVISA (m/1 Benjamin Baer, son of Peter, also see; m/2 Henry Mull; m/3 John D. Smith); 5. MARIA (d. age 19); 6. LUCINDA b. ca. 1847 (to Anoka, MN); 7. LOUIS b. ca. 1850 (d. 18 Mar. 1886, age 36). Elmira married again to Peter Baer (also see). Ref: P&BA-Len pg. 841-2.

WHITMARSH, ALVIN was born 1796, Cummington, Hampshire Co., Mass., and he married first to LYDIA (CLARK) who died in Mass. leaving 4 children, names not stated. He married again to her sister, NAOMI (CLARK), also born Hampshire Co., Mass. About 1834, they removed to Brooklyn, NY; and then to Newburg, NY. In 1839, they were in Cold Springs, NY, and in 1841 moved to Chicago, Ill. From there, they went to Princeton, Bureau Co., Ill., where he died in 1862, age 66. She was still living there in 1888, age 85. They had 4 children, names not stated, and the eldest was SAMUEL P. (following). Ref: P&BA-Len pg. 1135-6.

WHITMARSH, HORACE was listed in the 1840 census index of Palmyra Twp., Lenawee Co., Mich. adjacent to NAHUM, following.

WHITMARSH, NAHUM born ca. 1795, and wife, MARGARET, born ca. 1805, both in Mass., were listed in the 1840 census index of Palmyra Twp., Lenawee Co., Mich. (adjacent to HORACE, preceding); and in the 1850 census with CHARLES C., age 20; CLARISSA W., age 17, both b. Mass.; and LEWIS, age 11, b. Mich., in their household.

WHITMARSH, RUTH (See Hezekiah Ford[1])

WHITMARSH, SAMUEL P., son of ALVIN (preceding), born 8 July 1831, Springfield, Mass., moved with his parents to NY and then to Princeton, Ill. He came to Lenawee Co., Mich. in 1848/9, but returned to Princeton. In 1852, he went to California and Mexico. In 1865, he went to Ohio. He married MARY (STEELE), daughter of Solomon (also see) in Oct. 1865, and in 1867 settled in Palmyra Twp., Lenawee Co., Mich. Children: 1. ROLLIN H.; 2. OLIVE. Ref: P&BA-Len pg. 1135-6.

WHITMORE also see WETMORE

WHITMORE, EARL, native of western NY, married Mrs. ELBRA (PATTEE) EMERSON, widow of Jesse. They moved to Cleveland, Ohio before 1832; and then, before 1872, moved to Blissfield Twp., Lenawee Co., Mich., and afterwards to Ypsilanti, Mich. Known children: 1. GEORGE; 2. MARY E. b. 20 Sept. 1837, Cleveland (m. Stephen Torbron (also see). Ref: P&BA-Len pg. 495-6.

WHITMORE, STEPHEN D. Rev. married EMMA M. (BENNETT), daughter of Gershom B. (also see), born 19 Jan. 1852. Stephen died 6 Mar. 1881. Children: 1. EDSON G. b. 3 Aug. 1873; 2. LULU b. 24 Dec. 1877. Ref: P&BA-Len pg. 649-50.

WHITNEY, ABEL, son of JAMES (following), born ca. 1817, NY, married on 27 Oct. 1836 to SARAH ANN (BUDLONG), daughter of Daniel (also see) of Adrian. They were listed in the 1850 census of Adrian Twp., Lenawee Co., Mich. with AUGUSTUS H., age 9, b. Mich., and her sister, Almira M. Budlong, age 36, b. NY, in their household. Ref: P&BA-Len pg. 187.

WHITNEY, DANIEL S. born ca. 1808, and wife, LOISA L., born ca. 1815, both in NY, were listed in the 1850 census of Adrian Twp., Lenawee Co., Mich. with MAGDALENE, probably mother, age 73, born NJ, in their household (next door to VOLNEY B.) Note JOHN, following.

WHITNEY, DAVID born ca. 1817, and wife, HARRIET, born ca. 1820, both in NY, were listed in the 1850 census of Rollin Twp., Lenawee Co., Mich. with JABEZ, age 5, b. Mich., in their household.

WHITNEY, HANNAH (See Eber Bradley)

WHITNEY, JAMES was born 10 Feb. 1783, Warwick, Orange Co., NY; and at age 18 moved to Romulus, NY. He married there on 9 Nov. 1806 to MARY (FRISBIE). They moved in 1814 to Shelby, Orleans Co., NY; and in 1828 to Adrian, Lenawee Co., Mich.; and 1833 to Nottawa, St. Joseph Co., Mich. They afterwards moved to Moulton, Allen Co., Ohio where he died 11 Aug. 1851; and she died 28 Aug. 1851, both buried in Ft. Amanda, Ohio. Children: 1. MARIAN b. 1 July 1808, Romulus, NY (m. 18 Nov. 1829 to Asher Stevens; she d. 7 Mar. 1863; he d. 18 Nov. 1847, Ft. Amanda, O.); 2. RUSSELL (following); 3. ABEL (preceding); 4. REBECCA b. 22 July 1815, Shelby, NY (m/1 Edmund Burris Brown; m/2 Cornelius Cline; lived Nottawa, Mich.); 5. JAMES b. 30 Jan. 1818 (d. 1850, unmarried); 6. WILLIAM AUGUSTUS (following); 7. BENJAMIN b. 10 Aug. 1822, Shelby, NY (m/1 Minerva Daniels 5 Nov. 1845; m/2 1 Mar. 1857 Margaret Josephine Armstrong; lived Duchauquet, O.; he d. 14 Apr. 1883, bur. Shawnee Cem.); 8. SARAH b. 17 May 1825 (m. William V. R. Layton on 1 May 1851; lived Wapakoneta, O.) Ref: P&BA-Len pg. 183-186 (with complete pedigree).

WHITNEY, JANE (See Levi Jennings)

WHITNEY, JOEL, probably son of JONATHAN (from Conway, Franklin Co., Mass. to Seneca, Ontario Co., NY 1788-9), was born in Conway. He died in Seneca, NY. Known son, JOEL (following). Ref: P&BA-Len pg. 823-4.

WHITNEY, JOEL, son of JOEL (preceding), born in Seneca Castle, Ontario Co., NY, served in the War of 1812. He married ESTHER (BELDING), daughter of Consider (also see). Known daughter, SYBIL (m. Oliver S. Colwell, also see, on 2 Sept. 1841.) Ref: P&BA-Len pg. 823-4.

WHITNEY, JOHN was listed in the 1840 census index of Adrian Twp., Lenawee Co., Mich. Note DANIEL S.; & VOLNEY B.

WHITNEY, NATHAN of Seneca Castle, Ontario Co., NY married Mrs. THANKFUL (PAYNE) COLWELL, widow of Daniel[2] (also see), and he died there.

WHITNEY, ORLANDO was listed in the 1840 census index of Medina Twp., Lenawee Co., Mich.

Pioneer Families of Southeastern Michigan

WHITNEY, RICHARD H. born ca. 1809, and wife, NANCY F., born ca. 1813, both in Mass., were listed in the 1850 census of Madison Twp., Lenawee Co., Mich. with SARAH, age 12; EDWARD S., age 9; CHANNING, age 6; CHARLES C., age 4; AARON, age 5/12, all b. Mich., in their household. Note: It may be this Richard listed as "R. M." in the 1840 census index of Madison Twp.

WHITNEY, RUSSELL, son of JAMES (preceding), born 30 Aug. 1810, NY, married on 16 Nov. 1831 to ANGELINE (ROGERS), born ca. 1817, NY, and settled in Rome Twp., Lenawee Co., Mich. before 1840. They were listed in the 1850 census of Rome Twp. with SALLY A., age 16; HELEN, age 15; ANDREW J., age 14; EMELINE, age 12; SAMPSON, age 9; ELEANOR, age 11; MARTIN V., age 8; ROME, age 7; CHARLES, age 5; DALLAS, age 3; AUGUSTA, age 2, all b. Mich., in their household.

WHITNEY, SAMUEL P. born ca. 1820, and wife, ALMYRA, born ca. 1812, both in NY, were listed in the 1850 census of Hudson Twp., Lenawee Co., Mich. with JOEL C., age 7; DAVID, age 4/12, both b. Mich., in their household.

WHITNEY, VOLNEY B. was born ca. 1811. and wife, FANNY, born ca. 1825, both b. NY, were listed in the 1850 census of Adrian Twp., Lenawee Co., Mich. with MARY, age 1, b. Mich., in their household (next door to DANIEL S.)

WHITNEY, WILLIAM AUGUSTUS, son of JAMES (preceding), born 21 Apr. 1820, Shelby, NY married on 14 Sept. 1847 to ELLEN MARIE (BIXBY), daughter of David (also see). They were listed in the 1850 census of Adrian Twp., Lenawee Co., Mich. with only the first child in their household. William died 23 Jan. 1884, buried in Oakwood Cem., Adrian, Lenawee Co., Mich. Children: 1. DWIGHT AVERY b. 21 June 1848, Adrian (m. 25 Jan. 1870 to Marian Sela Lawrence, dau. of Willis T., also see, and had dau., Lena B.); 2. FANNY LEE b. 16 July 1859, Adrian (m. O. F. Berdan; lived Adrian & Detroit). Ref: P&BA-Len pg. 187. Note: In the 1850 census, Caroline Beagle, age 14, b. MD, was in their household.

WHITNEY, WILLIAM B. born ca. 1813, and wife, ABIGAIL, born ca. 1814, both in NY, were listed in the 1850 census of Madison Twp., Lenawee Co., Mich. with WILLIAM M., age 8, b. NY; and ELLEN G., age 5; EDGAR B., age 2, both b. Mich., in their household.

WHITTIER, DELIA (See Clark Ames)

WICKES, ISRAEL P. of Cayuga Co., NY was the father of PRUDENCE (m. Rev. William White, also see).

WICKHAM, ANNA Mrs. born ca. 1807, NY, was listed head of household in the 1850 census of Rome Twp., Lenawee Co., Mich. with HARVEY, age 6, b. Mich.; and children, George Ashdown, age 14; James Ashdown, age 12, both b. Mich. Note: There was a (Miss) ? "Ashtown" listed in the 1840 census index of Rome Twp., which may be she; and she afterwards married a Wickham?

WICKHAM, EMMA (See James B. Hood)

WICKHAM, HANNAH Mrs. born ca. 1823, Canada, was listed in the 1850 census of Adrian Twp., Lenawee Co., Mich. in the household of John O'Brien, age 81, born Ireland, with Wickham children: JOHN, age 8; ROBERT, age 6; WILLIAM, age 4; MARGARET, age 7/12, all b. Mich. Note: The census was taken on 21 Sept. 1850; and then in the census of Madison Twp., Lenawee Co., taken 27 Sept., these 3 boys were listed in the "Poor House," possibly because the mother could not longer care for them.

WICKHAM, THOMAS of Co. Wexford, Ireland married there to ELLEN (HAYS), and he died there. Ellen came to the US in 1851, living first in New York City, and then Buffalo, NY where she remained. Known daughters who also came to the US: 1. MARY (lived Monmouth, Ill.); 2. MARGARET "MAGGIE" (Central Park, Chicago, Ill.); and youngest daughter, ANNA E. b. 15 Nov. 1844, Ireland (came to Cambridge Twp., Lenawee Co., Mich. and lived with William & Caroline Geddes; then married on 5 June 1866 to Dr. Julius Vaughn, also see). Ref: P&BA-Len pg. 1002-3.

WICKHAM, W. married JULIA (ORAM), daughter of George (also see) born 8 Mar. 1842; d. 3 July 1869, leaving a son, WALTER H. Ref: P&BA-Len pg. 645-6.

WICKWIRE, FREDERICK W., son of GRANT (following), born 7 Mar. 1807, Litchfield, Conn., married there on 4 Apr. 1830 to SUSAN A. (KING), daughter of David C. (also see). They moved to Raisin Twp., Lenawee Co., Mich. in 1832. He died there on 23 Dec. 1887, age 80. Children: 1. CHARLOTTE M. b. 2 Jan. 1831, Conn. (m. Edwin S. Mudgett; Villajo, CA); 2. HENRY G. b. 25 Sept. 1832, Raisin Twp. (to Duvall's Bluff, Ark.); 3. MARY E. b. 5 Mar. 1835 (m. Homer E. Wilson, Raisin Twp.); 4. WILLIAM K. b. 14 June 1838 (lived Hudson Twp.); 5. SUSAN JANE b. 11 Feb. 1847 (m. John W. Niles; Brooklyn, NY). Ref: P&BA-Len pg. 258-9.

WICKWIRE, GRANT born Colchester, Conn., settled in Litchfield in 1788. He served in the Revolutionary War; and married in 1789 to SARAH (THROOP). He died in 1847; and she had died in 1821. Thirteen children, of whom ten grew to maturity; and only mentioned was FREDERICK W. (preceding). Ref: P&BA-len pg. 258-9.

WIDNEY, CHARLES (See Moses Bowerman, Jr.)

WIDNEY, HARVEY Rev. born 11 Mar. 1849, DeKalb Co., Ind., married ELLA (UNDERWOOD), daughter of Thomas (also see) of Palmyra Twp., Lenawee Co., Mich. They lived in LaHarpe, Ill. and Excelsior, Minn. where he died 25 Aug. 1887. Children: 1. HALLIE M.; 2. EDWARD U.; 3. ELIZABETH. Ref: P&BA-Len pg. 537-8.

WIEMANS, ELIZABETH (See Uric Winegar)

WIES, STEPHEN and wife, KATHERINE, were natives of Germany. Known daughter, LOUISE (m. Henry C. Bowen, also see, in 1883 in Adrian, Lenawee Co., Mich.) Ref: P&BA-Len pg. 514.

WIGGINS, ANNIN born 9 Oct. 1805, NY, and wife, SARAH (TENNENT) born 6 Oct. 1807, Warwick, Rhode Island, lived in Floyd, Oneida Co., NY; and afterwards in Wyoming Co., NY. There were 4 sons and 6 daughters, names not stated, except WILLIAM H. (following). Ref: P&BA-Len pg. 1069-70.

WIGGINS, DANIEL, son of JOHN (following), born 16 Feb. 1828, Yorkshire, England, married there in Dec. 1849 to JANE (BRITTON), probably daughter of John, Sr. (also see). In 1850, they came to NY, then to Macon Twp., Lenawee Co., Mich.; and were listed in the 1850 census of Ridgeway Twp. (next door to John Britton, Sr.). She died 17 July 1876, age 50. Children: 1. EDDIE C. (d. 21 Dec. 1859, age 2); 2. JOHN T. (m. Martha Cheever, dau. of John, also see; Macon Twp.); 3. DANIEL R.; 4. FRANCIS A.; 5. HANNAH M.; 6. IDA M. (prob. she who m. Joseph E. Exelby, also see); 7. HATTIE L.; 8. JOSEPH. Daniel married again on 22 Nov. 1871 to Mrs. ALVENA (SWICK) MILLER, daughter of John E.; and widow of Albert (see both). Child: 9. MARY b. 4 Aug. 1879. Ref: P&BA-Len pg. 963-4.

WIGGINS, DANIEL, age 20, born England, was listed in the 1850 census of Raisin Twp., Lenawee Co., Mich. in a Lovett household.

WIGGINS, JOHN and wife, ANNA (SILVERSIDE), were born and remained in Yorkshire, England. There were 7 children, and only named in sketch was DANIEL (preceding). Ref: P&BA-Len pg. 963-4.

WIGGINS, RICHARD born ca. 1811, NY, was listed in the 1850 census of Rome Twp., Lenawee Co., Mich. with WILLIAM H., age 10; CHARLES, age 8; JOHN W., age 6, all b. NY; and HANNAH E., age 2, b. Mich., in his household.

WIGGINS, WILLIAM H., son of ANNIN (preceding), born 8 Apr. 1839, Floyd, Oneida Co., NY, moved with his parents to Wyoming Co., NY. He married ELLEN M. (SHIPMAN), daughter of Stephen (also see) at Warsaw, Wyoming Co. In 1861, they removed to Bridgewater, Washtnenaw Co., Mich.; and afterwards to Manchester, where she died 9 Nov. 1870, leaving 2 children: 1. MARY O.; 2. WILLIAM. William H. married again on 16 Aug. 1871 to CLARISSA A. (RUSS), daughter of Silas H. (also see). They settled in Adrian Twp., Lenawee Co. in 1873. She died 29 Dec. 1885, leaving 2 children: 3. MINNIE B. b. ca. 1876; 4. LAVERNA b. ca. 1882. William H. married third to SARAH A. (HALL), daughter of Alfred D. (also see). Ref: P&BA-Len pg. 1069-70.

WILBER also see WILBUR

WILBER, DAVID S. born ca. 1801, and wife, SAPHRONA, born ca. 1801, were listed in the 1850 census of Medina Twp., Lenawee Co., Mich. with HARRIET, age 16; ALBERT, age 13; JAMES A., age 8, all b. NY, in their household. Listed in 2 other households in Medina Twp. were MARY A., age 20; and GEORGE, age 21, both b. NY, who may relate to this family.

WILBER, JOHN was listed in the 1840 census index of Rome Twp., Lenawee Co., Mich.; he was called an uncle to John S. Marks (also see).

WILBER, LEMUEL born ca. 1818, and wife, PERMELIA, born ca. 1822, were listed in the 1850 census of Fairfield Twp., Lenawee Co., Mich. a few doors from WILLIAM, following.

WILBER, RACHEL (See George Conger)

WILBER, RACHEL died in Cayuga Co., NY (See Isaac Sanford).

WILBER, WILLIAM born ca. 1789, and wife, SARAH M., born ca. 1794, both in Rhode Island, were listed in the 1840 census index of Fairfield Twp., Lenawee Co., Mich.; and in the 1850 census with ABIGAIL, age 24; DAVID, age 22; BUEL?, age 19, all b. NY, in their household. Also note LEMUEL; & WILLIAM J. of Fairfield Twp., probably additional sons.

WILBER, WILLIAM and wife, RUTH (BRIGGS), were natives of Rhode Island, and they married in Schoharie Co., NY, and later settled in Knox, Albany Co., NY. He died there in 1812; and she died in May 1813. Children: 1. JUDITH (m/1 David Parks who d. Johnstown, NY; m/2 David Carpenter, also see); 2. ABISHA b. ca. 1805 (m. Gilbert Gage, also see); 3. AMANDA b. ca. 1809 (m/1 Elias Richardson who d. Victor, NY; m/2 Samuel Jordan, also see); 4. WILLIAM J. (following, of Dover Twp.); 5. SALLY (m. John T. White, Wayne Co., NY). Ref: P&BA-Len pg. 875-6.

WILBER, WILLIAM J., son of WILLIAM & RUTH (preceding), born 16 Jan. 1810, Albany, NY, married on 28 Oct. 1833, Schenectady Co., NY to LUCRETIA B. (GALE) of Duanesburg, NY. In 1851, they sold out and moved to Dover Twp., Lenawee Co., Mich. Lucretia died 17 Oct. 1867. Children: 1. JAMES GALE (to Florida); 2. MARY A. (m. Gilbert Torbron, son of William, also see; she d. 20 sept. 1885, Clayton, Mich.); 3. JOSEPH OSCAR (Adrian, Mich.); 4. WALTER B. (Buena Vista, Colo.); 5. ERNEST (Buena Vista, Colo.); 6. JOHN (Buena Vista, Colo.) William J. married again to Mrs. FIDELIA A. (SHAW) McLOUTH, daughter of Bradley, Sr.; and widow of Peter see both). Son: 7. WILLIAM E. (d. age 8 mos). Ref: P&BA-Len pg. 875-6.

WILBER, WILLIAM J., son of WILLIAM & SARAH M. (preceding), born ca. 1822, and wife, CATHARINE, born ca. 1826, both in NY, were listed in the 1850 census of Fairfield Twp., Lenawee Co., Mich. with SARAH M., age 3, b. Mich., and George Shirts, age 3, b. Mich., in their household.

WILBERHAM, CLARA (See George W. Clark)

WILBUR also see WILBER
WILBUR, ELIZABETH (See Caleb Slocum)
WILBUR, HANNAH (See Levi Pitts)
WILBUR, REBECCA (See Joseph Pratt)
WILBUR, SILAS (See John Ladd)
WILBUR, THOMAS and wife, JANE (DUNBAR), were natives of NY who moved to Fairfield Twp., Lenawee Co., Mich. in 1855. She died in the Fall of 1868; and he died 22 May 1875, Fairfield Twp. Only child, PHOEBE L. b. 22 May 1857, Fairfield Twp. (m. Hiram D. Arnold, also see). Ref: P&BA-Len pg. 583-4. Note William Wilber of Fairfield Twp.

WILCOX, AARON born ca. 1804, and wife, AZUBA, born ca. 1804, both in NY, were listd in the 1840 census index of Ogden Twp., Lenawee Co., Mich.; and were in the 1850 census of Palmyra Twp. with MILES, age 21; SARAH, age 17, both b. NY; and LEWIS, age 15; LUTHER, age 15; FRANKLIN, age 12; HORACE, age 8, all b. Mich., in their household.

WILCOX, ABNER P., son of JOHN (following), born ca. 1805, NY, remained there until after the death of his wife, name not stated. He removed to Washtenaw Co., Mich. where he married again to STATIRA (VARNUM), probably daughter of Benjamin (also see). In 1848, they moved to Seneca Twp., Lenawee Co., Mich. He died June 1866, and she was still living there in 1888. In the 1850 census, they listed JOSEPHINE, age 6; and EMILY J., age 2, both b. Mich. Emily J. may be same as known daughter, JULIA b. 16 Mar. 1846, Washtenaw Co., Mich.

Pioneer Families of Southeastern Michigan

(m. Alpheus J. Robertson, also see). Ref: P&BA-Len pg. 591-2. Note: CHESTER was listed a few doors away.

WILCOX, ALBERT born ca. 1806, Mass., and wife, ELIZA, born ca. 1812, NY, may be they listed in the 1840 census index of Cambridge Twp., Lenawee Co., Mich.; and were listed in the 1850 census of Dover Twp. with HARRIET, age 21,; THOMAS A., age 17, both b. NY; and MARYETTE, age 10; GERTRUDE, age 5, both b. Mich.; and George Miller, age 10, b. Mich., in their household.

WILCOX, AUSTIN, son of EDMUND & ELIZABETH (SCRANTON), was born 28 Aug. 1779, Madison, Conn. He married CLARISSA (NETTLETON), and they moved to Bergen, Genesee Co., NY, where he died 18 Aug. 1856; and she had died 10 June 1829. There were 3 sons and 5 daughters, of whom 3 daughters were deceased by 1888 (names not stated); those mentioned: 1. AUSTIN SCRANTON (following); 2. WILLIAM SEWARD (following); 3. HENRY HAMILTON (following); 4. HARRIET (m. Samuel Church, Bergen, NY). Ref: P&BA-Len pg. 485-6.

WILCOX, AUSTIN SCRANTON, son of AUSTIN (preceding), born ca, 1812, Conn., and wife, HANNAH, born ca. 1814, NY, were listed in the 1840 census index of Adrian Twp., Lenawee Co., Mich.; and were in the 1850 census with HENRY, age 11; FRANCES, age 8; LOUISA, age 3, all b. Mich., in their household. He was deceased before 1888. Ref: P&BA-Len pg. 485-6.

WILCOX, BETSEY, age 62, born NY, was listed head of household in the 1850 census of Palmyra Twp., Lenawee Co., Mich. with Lucretia Wood, age 19, b. NY, and Ann E. Randall, age 5, b. Mich., in her household.

WILCOX, CATHARINE was listed in the 1840 census index of Palmyra Twp., Lenawee Co., Mich.

WILCOX, CHESTER born ca. 1812, and wife, SARAH, born ca. 1823, both in NY, were listed in the 1850 census of Seneca Twp., Lenawee Co., Mich. with FRANCIS, age 12; MARIAN, age 9; CHARLES, age 4, all b. NY, in their household. Note that Sarah may be too young to be mother of Francis. They were listed a few doors from ABNER P. in the census. Note: There was a CHESTER in Milan, Monroe Co., Mich. in the 1840 census index.

WILCOX, EDWIN J., and wife, NANCY (DEWITT), came first to Hudson Twp., Lenawee Co., Mich., then moved to Adrian, where she died in 1866. He died Oct. 1886 in Calhoun Co., Mich. Children: 1. IDA (m. Charles I. Holmes, also see); 2. ELIZA (m. John Jacobs; Branch Co., Mich.) Note: There was an EDWIN in the 1840 census index of Cambridge Twp., Lenawee Co., Mich. adjacent to ALBERT & HENRY.

WILCOX, FELIX born ca. 1815, NY, and wife, ELIZABETH, born ca. 1814, England, were listed in the 1850 census of Rollin Twp., Lenawee Co., Mich. with DAVID H., age 7; THOMAS, age 4; LOIS A., age 1/12, and Maria Smith, age 22, b. Ohio, in their household.

WILCOX, GEORGE A., son of WILLIAM SEWARD (following), born 12 Oct. 1848, Adrian, Lenawee Co., Mich., married there in July 1874 to SUSETTE R. (BERRY), daughter of James (also see) of Adrian. Children: 1. S. FANNY; 2. WILLIAM SEWARD. Ref: P&BA-Len pg. 1210-11.

WILCOX, GUY C. B. born ca. 1817, NY, and wife, NANCY, born ca. 1818, VT, were listed in the 1850 census of Fairfield Twp., Lenawee Co., Mich. with OPHILIA, age 12; ANGELINE, age 10; SILAS, age 7; ALFRED, age 5; FLORA, age 4; VILETTA, age 2; MARY C., age 3/12, all b. Mich., in their household. Note: There was a GUY listed in Bloomfield Twp., Oakland Co., Mich. in 1840 census index.

WILCOX, HARVEY, age 18, born NY, was listed in the 1850 census of Blissfield Twp., Lenawee Co., Mich. Note ISAAC, following.

WILCOX, HENRY, age 35, born NY, may be he listed in the 1840 census index of Cambridge Twp., Lenawee Co., Mich., adjacent to ALBERT; & EDWIN, preceding.; and he was listed in the 1850 census in an Isaac Miner household.

WILCOX, HENRY HAMILTON, son of AUSTIN (preceding), born 28 Oct. 1822, Bergen, NY, moved with his parents to Genesee Co., NY; and in 1843 came to Adrian, Lenawee Co., Mch. He married on 28 Oct. 1845 to EUNICE J. (SMITH), daughter of Hervey of Northampton, Mass., born 28 Sept. 1825. Children: 1. MARY E. (m. Dr. C. W. Butler; Mont Clair, NJ); 2. LILLIAN E.; 3. AUSTIN. Ref: P&BA-Len pg. 485-6.

WILCOX, HIRAM born ca. 1819, and wife, LOISA, born ca. 1819, both in NY, were listed in the 1850 census of Rollin Twp., Lenawee Co., Mich. with FRANCES L., age 5, b. NY; and CLARA, age 5/12, b. Mich., in their household.

WILCOX, IRA (See Eli E. Munn; also note in household of ISAAC, following).

WILCOX, ISAAC born ca. 1806, and wife, EMELINE, born ca. 1809, were listed in the 1840 census index of Blissfield Twp., Lenawee Co., Mich.; and in the 1850 census with JOHN, age 18; DAVID, age 16, both b. NY; and IRA, age 13; MARGARET, age 11; GEORGE, age 8; SARAH, age 5; FRANKLIN, age 3; MARY, age 2, all b. Mich., in their household.

WILCOX, JANE ANN (See Abraham Cramer)

WILCOX, JOEL born ca. 1830, and wife, LOVISA, born ca. 1833, VT, married within the year, were listed in the 1850 census of Adrian Twp., Lenawee Co., Mich.

WILCOX, JOHN came from NY to Seneca Twp., Lenawee Co., Mich. where he died. Known son, ABNER P. (preceding). Ref: P&BA-Len pg. 591-2.

WILCOX, LIBBIE (See Benjamin Hornbeck)

WILCOX, LYMAN born ca. 1799, NY, and wife, FLORINDA, born ca. 1801, Mass., were probably they listed in the 1840 census of Seneca Twp., Lenawee Co., Mich.; and in the 1850 census listed ELIZABETH J., age 15; EDWIN, age 11, both b. NY, in their household.

WILCOX, LYMAN born ca. 1815, and wife, MARGARET, born ca. 1818, both in NY, were listed in the 1850 census of Hudson Twp., Lenawee Co., Mich. with MARTHA W., age 12; HARRISON H., age 8; SIMEON?/SIMSON? T., age 6; OLIVE J., age 4, all b. Mich., in their household.

WILCOX, SILAS born 13 Feb. 1787, Rhode Island, and wife, CYNTHIA (TAFT) born 1 Jan. 1790, Chesterfield, Mass., lived in Wayne Co., NY; and probably Orleans Co., NY before moving to Fairfield Twp, Lenawee Co., Mich., where he died 5 Aug. 1837. In the 1850 census of Fairfield Twp, Cynthia, age 58, b. Mass., was listed in the household of John Rizigler?, and wife, HARRIET, age 19, b. NY, probably daughter of Cynthia. Known daughter, ELIZA M. b. 2 May 1812, Palmyra, NY (m.

Benjamin Carpenter, also see). Ref: P&BA-Len pg. 523-4.

WILCOX, WILLIAM SEWARD, son of AUSTIN (preceding), born 25 Apr. 1819, Riga, Monroe Co., NY, went to Milan, Ohio in 1836, then moved to Adrian, Lenawee Co., Mich. He married SARAH F. (CLAY) born ca. 1824, NY. Son, GEORGE A. (preceding). Sarah F. died 12 Feb. 1852; and he married again to JOSEPHINE (SOUTHWORTH), daughter of Dr. William (also see). Ref: P&BA-Len pg. 1210-11.

WILDER, ARTEMUS born ca. 1796 (census said ca. 1807) was reared near Attica, NY. His wife, FANNY (COOLEY), was born ca. 1801 (census said ca. 1808), also in NY. They were listed in the 1840 census index of Palmyra Twp., Lenawee Co., Mich.; and were in the 1850 census with CHARLES M., age 21; ANGELINE, age 20; CAROLINE, age 20; DENSEY (female), age 16; DEBORAH, age 16, all b. NY; and LAURA A., age 10 (m. Austin G. Hall, also see); FRANCES, age 2; ELLEN, age 1, EDWARD, age 1, all b. Mich., in their household. Artemus died in 1866, age 70; and she died in 1869, age 68. Ref: P&BA-Len pg. 967-8.

WILDER, DAVID was listed in the 1840 census index of Rome Twp., Lenawee Co., Mich.

WILDER, EPHRAIM, son of JOHN O. (following), born Sept. 1814, probably in Ontario Co., NY, married CATHARINE (CASE) in NY. They moved to Adrian Twp., Lenawee Co., Mich., where he died in 1869. Children: 1. MARTHA (m. T. J. Batterson; Buffalo, NY); 2. HENRY J. (following); 3. ERASTUS M.; 4. OZRO (deceased bef. 1888). Ref: P&BA-Len pg. 305-6.

WILDER, ERASTUS born ca. 1775, Mass., was listed in the 1850 census of Medina Twp., Lenawee Co., Mich. in the household of son, LEVI B. (following).

WILDER, HENRY J., son of EPHRAIM (preceding), born 7 Feb. 1844, Bristol, Ontario Co., NY, moved to Adrian Twp., Lenawee Co., Mich. in 1863. He married on 24 Aug. 1880 to JOSEPHINE P. (MARSHALL) born 18 Feb. 1847, daughter of Charles M. (also see) of Adrian. Children: 1. MARY L. b. 15 July 1882; 2. child d. 14 Oct. 1887, infancy. Ref: P&BA-Len pg. 305-6.

WILDER, JOHN O. born 1798, NY, died in Bristol, Ontario Co., NY at age 63. Known son, EPHRAIM (preceding). Ref: P&BA-Len pg. 305-6.

WILDER, LEVI B., son of ERASTUS (preceding), born ca. 1809, and wife, CHARLOTTE, born ca. 1813, both born NY, were listed in the 1840 census index of Medina Twp., Lenawee Co., Mich., and in the 1850 census with ELECTA, age 16, b. NY; and CORDELIA, age 13; ERASTUS H., age 5, both b. Mich.; and father, ERASTUS, preceding, in their household.

WILDER, NANCY (CRAMER) Mrs. was the daughter of Abraham Cramer (also see) and resided in Perryville, (Madison Co.?), NY. Ref: P&BA-Len pg. 1152-5.

WILDEY also see WILEY

WILDEY, AUGUSTUS born ca. 1820, NY, came to Lenawee Co., Mich. with his parents, names not stated, before his marriage to LUCRETIA (PACKARD) born ca. 1830, NY. They had 3 sons and 3 daughters, names not stated, but they were listed in the 1850 census of Seneca Twp., Lenawee Co., Mich. with SARAH A., age 2; WILLIAM M. (following), both b. Mich. He died in Mar. 1885, age 54; and she died in 1881. Ref: P&BA-Len pg. 1091-2. Note: He was written as "Wildey" in the census; but as "Wiley" in the sketch.

WILDEY, JAMES born ca. 1796, and wife, SUBMIT, born ca. 1796, both in NY, were listed in the 1850 census of Medina Twp., Lenawee Co., Mich. with CUTTING B., age 23; OSCAR, age 18, both b. NY, in their household. Note AUGUSTUS, preceding.

WILDEY, WILLIAM, son of AUGUSTUS B. (preceding), born 30 Apr. 1850, Seneca Twp., Lenawee Co., Mich., married in 1874 to EFFA J. (HAYWARD), daughter of Micajah (also see). Children: 1. FLOYD A. b. 22 Oct. 1882; 2, DAVID RAY b. 13 Sept. 1885. Ref: P&BA-Len pg. 913-4.

WILDMAN, WILLIAM (See Eliathah Stockwell)

WILEY also see WILDEY

WILEY, AUGUSTUS see Augustus Wildey

WILEY, DAVID born ca. 1793?, and wife, CATHARINE, born ca. 1800, NY, were listed in the 1830 census of Lenawee Co., Mich. Territory with males: 1 und 5; 1 40-50; females: 2 und 5; 2 5-10; 1 30-40. They were listed as "Wilder" in the 1840 census index of Rome Twp., Lenawee Co., Mich.; and in the 1850 census listed EDWIN T., age 20; SARAH, age 17; MARVIN, age 7; AMELIA, age 3, all b. Mich.

WILKINS, CHARLES probably born after 1850 (See Thomas A. Liddel; and note GEORGE A. & JAMES R., following).

WILKINS, GEORGE A. born ca. 1813, and wife, HANNAH, born ca. 1814, both in NY, were listed in the 1840 census index of Macon Twp., Lenawee Co., Mich.; and in the 1850 census with JAMES, age 6, b. Mich., and Samuel Winters, age 80, born NJ, in their household.

WILKINS, JAMES R. born ca. 1814, and wife, MARIA, born ca. 1823, Canada, were listed in the 1850 census of Macon Twp., Lenawee Co., Mich. with LOUISA, age 8; ANN M., age 6; MALINDA H., age 4; JAMES H., age 1, all b. Mich., in their household.

WILKINSON, DANIEL S. born ca. 1820, NY, was mentioned as a business partner of Daniel D. Sinclair (also see) of Adrian, Lenawee Co., Mich. In the 1850 census of Adrian, he is listed in the household of SMITH S., following.

WILKINSON, ELIZABETH (See John Penoyer)

WILKINSON, SMITH S. born ca. 1825, NY, and wife, HELEN, born ca. 1829, VT, were listed in the 1850 census of Adrian Twp., Lenawee Co., Mich. with HELEN A., age 6/12, b. Mich.; and DANIEL S. (preceding), in their household.

WILLETT, AGNES (See William R. Wilson)

WILLETT, CORNELIUS born ca. 1798, and wife, CLARISSA, born ca. 1798, both in NJ, were listed in the 1840 census index of Medina Twp., Lenawee Co., Mich.; and in the 1850 census with SALLY R., age 26?, b. NY; and MARSHALL, age 14; MELISSA, age 9, both b. Mich., in their household. Note MARTIN, & WILLIAM, following.

WILLETT, DARIUS born ca. 1818, and wife, ELIZA A., born ca. 1827, both in NY, were listed in the 1850 census of Adrian Twp., Lenawee Co., Mich. with WARREN, age

Pioneer Families of Southeastern Michigan

2, b. Mich.; and listed last, SARAH A., age 15, b. NY, in their household.

WILLETT, ICHABOD born ca. 1804, NY, and wife, CATHARINE, born ca. 1805, Canada, were listed in the 1840 census of Macon Twp., Lenawee Co., Mich. (spelled "Willits"); and in the 1850 census with NATHAN, age 25; MILES, age 21; SALLY A., age 23, all b. Canada; and ISAAC, age 18; CATHARINE, age 15; HANNAH, age 13; JOHN, age 11; ADELBERT, age 9; JAMES, age 3, all b. Mich., in their household.

WILLETT, JOHN born ca. 1799, NJ, was listed in the 1840 census index of Rome Twp., Lenawee Co., Mich.; and was listed in the 1850 census with wife, AURILLA, born ca. 1809, NY, and POSSIBLY stepchildren, Aurilla C. Throup, age 16, b. NY; and

Elizabeth Throup, age 12; Henry L. Throup, age 8, both b. Mich., in their household. WILLIAM F., following, probably his son.

WILLETT, JOHN born ca. 1822, and wife, CAROLINE, born ca. 1829, both in NY, were listed in the 1850 census of Ogden Twp., Lenawee Co., Mich. with no family.

WILLETT, JOHN P. born ca. 1803, NJ, and wife, MARY, born ca. 1803, NY, were listed in the 1850 census of Fairfield Twp., Lenawee Co., Mich. with JOSEPH W., age 19; SARAH M., age 17; THOMAS H., age 13, all b. NY, in their household.

WILLETT, JOSEPH C. born ca. 1785, and wife, CHRISTIAN, borh ca. 1795, both in New Jersey, were listed in the 1850 census of Seneca Twp., Lenawee Co., Mich. with NATHAN B., age 18; NANCY B., age 24; JESSE C., age 19, all b. NY; and ELIZABETH H., age 7, b. Mich., in their household. Note MICAJAH, following.

WILLETT, JOSEPH born ca. 1809, and wife, ABIGAIL, born ca. 1808, both in NY, were listed in the 1850 census of Fairfield Twp., Lenawee Co., Mich. with MARCY, age 18; EMELINE, age 16, both b. NY, in their household.

WILLETT, MARGARET of Hunterdon Co., NJ (See Julius Dalley).

WILLETT, MARTIN was listed in the 1840 census index of Medina Twp., Lenawee Co., Mich. adjacent to CORNELIUS, preceding; & WILLIAM, following.

WILLETT, MICAJAH and wife, JUDITH (CRAMER), were pioneers from New Jersey to Ontario Co., NY. Known daughter, ELIZABETH b. 26 Feb. 1782, NJ (m. Henry Hayward^2, also see). Ref: P&BA-Len pg. 998-9.

WILLETT, MICAJAH was listed in the 1840 census index of Seneca Twp., Lenawee Co., Mich.

WILLETT, WILLIAM waas listed in the 1840 census index of Medina twp., Lenawee Co., Mich. Note CORNELIUS & MARTIN, preceding.

WILLETT, WILLIAM F., probably son of JOHN (preceding), was born ca. 1824, NY, and his wife, ELIZA (JEFFERY), daughter of JAMES K. (also see), were listed in the 1850 census of Rome Twp., Lenawee Co., Mich., next door to JOHN. They later moved to Ingham Co., Mich.

WILLEY also see WILEY

WILLEY, CORNELIA (See Oramel Sackett)

WILLEY, HENRICK born ca. 1789, Conn., and wife, LORRIS, borh ca. 1795, Mass., were listed in the 1840 census index of Blissfield Twp., Lenawee Co., Mich.; and were in the 1850 census with ELLEN, age 22, b. NY; and Alice Worth, age 5; Arthur Worth, age 3, both b. Mich., in their household.

WILLEY, MARIETTA (See John Maynard)

WILLEY, SUSAN T. born ca. 1831, NY, was listed in the 1850 census of Medina Twp., Lenawee Co., Mich. in household of J. M. Burroughs. Note that she may be a Wildey or Wiley.

WILLIAMS, ADELINE (See Abram Hamilton)

WILLIAMS, ALBERT born ca. 1828, and wife, NANCY, born ca. 1830, both in NY, were listed in the 1850 census of Adrian Twp., Lenawee Co., Mich.

WILLIAMS, ALEXANDER born ca. 1810, and wife, ANNA, born ca. 1812, were listd in the 1850 census of Adrian Twp., Lenawee Co., Mich. with CATHARINE, age 19; DAVID, age 15; DARIUS, age 14; LEMUEL, aage 11; SILAS, age 9; ALEXANDER V., age 7, all b. Ohio; and LUCINDA, age 5; BETSEY, age 3; NANCY, age 3/12, all b. Mich., in their household. Note WOODWARD, following.

WILLIAMS, ALPHONSO, age 26, born NY, was listed in the 1850 census of Seneca Twp., Lenawee Co., Mich. in a Barnes household. Also note THOMAS B., following.

WILLIAMS, BENJAMIN F. born ca. 1815, and wife, SALLY A., born ca. 1824, both in NY, were listed in the 1850 census of Hudson Twp., Lenawee Co., Mich. with no family.

WILLIAMS, DANIEL born ca. 1809, and wife, EMILY, born ca. 1817, both in Conn., were listed in the 1840 census index of Tecumseh Twp., Lenawee Co., Mich.; and in the 1850 census with MARY, age 14; JOHN, age 12, both b. NY; and CHARLES, age 8, b. Mich., in their household.

WILLIAMS, E. D. Mrs. was daughter of William W. Luck (also see).

WILLIAMS, E. GEORGINA (See Daniel Root)

WILLIAMS, ERASTUS was listed in the 1840 census index of Macon Twp., Lenawee Co., Mich.

WILLIAMS, F. L. (See Hugh McConnell)

WILLIAMS, G. G. (See Sylvester Kenyon)

WILLIAMS, GEORGE M. born ca. 1801, and wife, HARRIET, born ca. 1824, Illinois, were listed in the 1850 census of Blissfield Twp., Lenawee Co., Mich. with MARY, age 3; LLOYD, age 2, both b. Mich., in their household.

WILLIAMS, LESNOR? L. born ca. 1821, and wife, MARY J., born ca. 1822, both in NY, were listed in the 1850 census of Fairfield Twp., Lenawee Co., Mich. with LORD G., age 4; SAABRINA M., age 1, both b. Mich., in their household.

WILLIAMS, LLOYD, son of SHIRLEY B. (following), born ca. 1822, NY, and wife, MARY, born ca. 1826, Canada, were listed in the 1850 census of Hudson Twp., Lenawee Co., Mich. with SHIRLEY B., age 9/12, b. Mich., in their household.

WILLIAMS, LYDIA, age 78, born New Jersey, was listed in the 1850 census of Raisin Twp., Lenwee Co., Mich. in the household of Elizbeth Lovett, age 49, born NJ.

WILLIAMS, MARTHA (See John Roberts)

WILLIAMS, MARTIN born ca. 1828, and wife, AGNES, born ca. 1828, both in Mich.?, married within the year, were listed in the 1850 census of Blissfield Twp., Lenawee Co., Mich.

WILLIAMS, MEHITABLE married first to Allen Pierce, also see, possibly in Cayuga Co., NY; and she came to Lenawee Co., Mich. where she married Constant Rowley as his 3rd wife (also see).

WILLIAMS, MORGAN born ca. 1802, NY, and wife, MARY, born ca. 1802, VT, were listed in the 1840 census index of Adrian Twp., Lenawee Co., Mich. with SARAH, age 23 (may be she listed again in a Gore household); ALFRED, age 17, both b. NY; and CATHARINE, age 13, b. Mich., in their household. Also note ALBERT, preceding.

WILLIAMS, NELLIE E. (See Dr. Henry P. Combs)

WILLIAMS, PETER born ca. 1813, and wife, MARY ANN, born ca. 1821, both in NY, were listed in the 1850 census of Tecumseh Twp., Lenawee Co., Mich. with SOPHRONIA, age 11; DAVID, age 5, both b. Mich., in their household. Note: There was a PETER in Washtenaw Co., Mich. in the 1840 census index.

WILLIAMS, RUSSELL E. born ca. 1807, Mass., was listed in the 1840 census index of Blissfield Twp., Lenawee Co., Mich.; and was listed in the 1850 census with wife, NANCY, born ca. 1820, NY, who seems too young to be mother of some of following in the household: ALMIRA, age 22; EUNICE, age 17; DRAYTON B., age 15, all b. NY; and JEWETT, age 12; CLINTON, age 10; JANE, age 7, all b. Mich.

WILLIAMS, SAMUEL born ca. 1805, Canada, and wife, JUDITH, borh ca. 1806, NY, were listed in the 1840 census index of Medina Twp., Lenawee Co., Mich. (near THOMAS, following); and were in the 1850 census with JOSEPH, age 14; MARTHA J., age 12; PHEBE, age 11; MARY, age 9; SAMUEL, age 5; JUDITH, age 3, all b. Mich., in their housheold. Note: In the 1850 census of Medina Twp. is HENRY, age 20, b. NY; MARY, age 18, b. NY; ELIZABETH, age 17, b. Mich., all in different households, whom may relate to this family??

WILLIAMS, SHIRLEY B. born ca. 1797, Conn., and wife, HANNAH, borh ca. 1799, NY, were listed in the 1850 census of Hudson Twp., Lenawee Co., Mich. with SILAS O., age 17, b. NY, in their household. Note son, LLOYD (preceding).

WILLIAMS, THOMAS born ca. 1798, Penn., and wife, CHARLOTTE (TERRELL), born ca. 1804, NY, were called "natives of Genesee Co., NY," who lived in Bennington (now in Wyoming Co.), before moving to Medina Twp., Lenawee Co., Mich. There were 5 children, 4 mentioned were still living in 1888. 1. WILLIAM W. (may be he, age 26, b. NY, in a Blake household in 1850 census of Medina Twp.; he went to Canada); 2. MARY L. b. ca. 1830, NY (m/1 David Edwards; m/2 Benjamin D. Osborn, see both); 3. JANE C. b. ca. 1833 (m. ? Allen; Seneca Twp.); 4. THOMAS C. b. ca. 1838 (to Oakland Co., Mich.) Ref: P&BA-Len pg. 1077-8.

WILLIAMS, THOMAS B. born ca. 1825, and wife, BETSEY A., born ca. 1833, both in NY, were listed in the 1850 census of Seneca Twp., Lenawee Co., Mich. with DECATUR?, age 6/12, b. Mich., in their household. Note ALPHONSO, preceding.

WILLIAMS, THOMAS J. born ca. 1805, and wife, EUNICE, born ca. 1810, both in VT, were listed in the 1850 census of Rollin Twp., Lenawee Co., Mich. with ESTHER, age 19; EUNICE, age 16; EDWARD, age 8, all b. VT; and DANIEL, age 6; WILLET, age 4; MARY, age 2, all b. Mich., in their household.

WILLIAMS, W. H. (See Thomas Tunison)

WILLIAMS, WILLIAM born ca. 1806, VT, and wife, JANE M., born ca. 1814, Penn., were listed in the 1850 census of Madison Twp., Lenawee Co., Mich. with ELLA A., age 12; WINTER?, age 10; FLORA, age 8; HENRIETT, age 4; FLORENCE, age 2, all b. Mich., in their household. Note: There was a WILLIAM in the 1840 census index of Clinton Twp., Lenawee Co., Mich.

WILLIAMS, WOODWARD, age 20, born Ohio, was listed in the 1850 census of Medina Twp., Lenawee Co., Mich. in a Pratt household. Note ALEXANDER, preceding.

WILLIAMSON, CHARLES born ca. 1822, and wife, PHEBE, born ca. 1816, both in NY, were listed in the 1850 census of Tecumseh Twp., Lenawee Co., Mich. with GEORGE, age 2, b. Mich.; and possibly a stepdaughter, Helen Ketcham, age 6, b. Mich.; and Jacob Ketcham, age 70, b. NY, in their household.

WILLIAMSON, EDWARD, age 25, b. NY, was listed in the 1850 census of Tecumseh Twp., Lenawee Co., Mich. in a Wm. Pecher? household.

WILLIAMSON, HENRY and wife, MARY A. (COTTRELL), of Palmyra, Wayne Co., NY were parents of MARY born Palmyra, NY (m. Orrin R. Pierce, also see; 1875 in Hudson Twp., Lenawee Co., Mich.) Ref: P&BA-Len pg. 646-7.

WILLIAMSON, ISAAC born ca. 1791, Conn., and wife, MARTHA, borh ca. 1791, NY, were listed in the 1850 census of Tecumseh Twp., Lenawee Co., Mich. Note ISAAC H., following.

WILLIAMSON, ISAAC H. born ca. 1811, Conn., and wife, POLLY, born ca. 1813, Mass., were listed in the 1850 census of Woodstock Twp., Lenawee Co., Mich. with EDGAR, age 8, b. NY; and WARREN, age 1, b. Mich,., in their household. Note ISAAC, preceding.

WILLIAMSON, JOHN born ca. 1820, and wife, MARY, born ca. 1821, both in NY, were listed in the 1850 census of Tecumseh Twp., Lenawee Co., Mich.

WILLIAMSON, JOHN (See John A. Baer)

WILLIS, SAMUEL married after 1851 to Mrs. AMANDA (GODDARD) HOAGLAND, daughter of Lyman, and widow of Henry (see both). Ref: P&BA-Len pg. 377-8.

WILLIT/WILLITS also see WILLETT

WILLITS, C. MAUDE (See Marshall Reed)

WILLSEY see WILSEY

WILLSON see WILSON

WILSEY, ABRAHAM born ca. 1817, NY, and wife, RULINA?, born ca. 1812, Conn., were listed in the 1840 census index of Adrian Twp., Lenawee Co., Mich.; and in the 1850 census of Franklin Twp. with LUCY, age 14; HULDAH, age 11; JAMES, age 9; ELIZABETH, age 8; AMANDA, age 8/12, all b. Mich., in their household.

WILSEY, ELIZABETH born ca. 1782, NJ, was head of household in the 1850 census of Franklin Twp., Lenawee Co., Mich.; and then it appears to be she listed again in the 1850 census of Adrian Twp. in the household of William Armstrong and wife, Eliza (age 34, b. NY). Note WILLIAM, and JAMES, both following.

Pioneer Families of Southeastern Michigan

WILSEY, HANNAH born ca. 1832, NY, was listed in the 1850 census of Tecumseh Twp., Lenawee Co., Mich.

WILSEY, HENRY[1] and wife, SABRINA, moved from Dutchess Co., NY to Troy, Bradford Co., Penn. ca. 1806. Known son, JEREMIAH[2] (following). Ref: P&BA-Len pg. 752-3.

WILSEY, JAMES born ca. 1817, and wife, MARGARET, born ca. 1822, both in NY, were listed in the 1850 census of Adrian Twp., Lenawee Co., Mich. with JOHN, age 10; CHARLES, age 8; WILLIAM, age 5, all b. NY; and MARY, age 3, b. Mich., in their household (2 doors from ELIZABETH, preceding).

WILSEY, JEREMIAH[2], son of JEREMIAH[1] (preceding), born 15 Feb. 1801, Dutchess Co., NY, moved with his parents to Bradford Co., Penn. He married MARTHA (BAXTER) of Troy, Penn., and she died in 1829, leaving children: 1. MARTHA b. ca. 1825, Penn. (m. John Gates, also see); 2. JESHURON (d. age 21). Jeremiah married again on 4 Mar. 1830 to Mrs. BETSEY (SANDERS) LUCAS, daughter of Loudwick, and widow of George (see both) in Penn. They moved about 1832 to Huron Co., Ohio; and about 1837 to Woodstock Twp., Lenawee Co., Mich. He died 9 Apr. 1876; and she died 6 Jan. 1885. Children: 3. JANE b. ca. 1832, Penn. (m. Ira Reynolds; Fremont, Nebr.); 4. ELIZA b. ca. 1834, Ohio (m. James A. Parkhurst, also see); 5. BETAEY b. ca. 1836, Ohio (m. Henry W. Kane, also known as Wilson H. Kane, also see); 6. ANN b. ca. 1838, Mich. (m. Lyman Griffith; she d. 11 Sept. 1873, Fremont, Nebr.); 7. JEREMIAH (following); 8. HENRY b. ca. 1842 (served Co. I, 4th Mich., d. in prison in Civil War); 9. WILLIAM b. 20 Apr. 1844 (unmarried in 1888, Woodstock Twp.). Ref: P&BA-Len pg. 752-3. Note: In the 1850 census of Woodstock Twp., listed in their household was an ISAIAH, age 22, b. NY, not identified in sketch.

WILSEY, JEREMIAH[3], son of JEREMIAH[2] (preceding), born 17 June 1839, served in Co. I, 4th Mich. during the Civil War, and was in Belle Isle and Andersonville prisons for 21 months. He married on 30 Apr. 1868 to ELIZA J. (BABCOCK), daughter of Harry (also see) and settled in Woodstock Twp. Children: 1. MAY D. b. 24 July 1873; 2. HUGH H. b. 27 Sept. 1875; 3. INA B. b. 9 Feb. 1878; 4. GRACE E. b. 25 Sept. 1884; 5. LUCY A. b. 3 June 1887. Ref: P&BA-Len pg. 752-3.

WILSEY, WILLIAM was listed in the 1840 census index of Franklin Twp., Lenawee Co., Mich. Also note ELIZABETH; & JAMES preceding.

WILSON, ABIGAIL (See William Cairns)

WILSON, ABNER born ca. 1788?, and wife, RACHEL, born ca. 1805, both in NY, were listed in the 1840 census index of Frankin Twp., Lenawee Co., Mich.; and in the 1850 census with HELEN?, age 18, b. NY, in their household. The entry was badly written over, so was almost illegible. ANDREW, age 28, following, was next door.

WILSON, ANDREW, age 87, born NY, was listed in the 1850 census of Ridgeway Twp., Lenawee Co., Mich. in the household of son, ROBERT (following) who was reared in Wayne Co., NY.

WILSON, ANDREW, probably son of ABNER, born ca. 1822, and wife, FRANCES, born ca. 1828, both in NY, were listed in the 1850 census of Franklin Twp. (next door to ABNER), Lenawee Co., Mich. with ABNER, age 1; HENRY, age 1/12, both b. Mich., in their household.

WILSON, ANDREW was a native of New York state. He married Mrs. MARY A. (ALLEN) COLLINS, widow of Isaac (also see) of Macon Twp., Lenawee Co., Mich. They retired to Tecumseh, Lenawee Co.. Ref: P&BA-Len pg. 192.

WILSON, CARRIE (See Cyrenus Sanford)

WILSON, CHARLES A. and wife, LUCY J. (REED), settled in Madison Twp., Lenawee Co., Mich. by 1855. She died there at age 35; and he was still living there in 1888. Children: 1. HORATIO L. (following); 2. HATTIE S.; 3. GEORGE A.; 4. ELLA. Ref: P&BA-Len pg. 1006-7.

WILSON, CHARLES B., son of SIMON D. (following), born 17 Apr. 1833, Thompson, Conn., moved to Seneca Twp., Lenawee Co., Mich. with his parents. He married there 25 Aug. 1858 to ROSA M. (HILL), daughter of Rollin R. (also see). She died 1 Feb. 1885. Children: 1. CLARENCE A.; 2. LUELLA (m. Frank B. Smith); 3. CHARLES W. (Kansas). Ref: P&BA-Len pg. 568-9.

WILSON, DANIEL born ca. 1801, Mass., and wife, ANN, born ca. 1801, NY, were listed in the 1850 census of Adrian Twp., Lenawee Co., Mich. with RHODA M., age 21; JANE E., age 19; MELISSA M., age 17; WILLIAM W., age 14, all b. NY, in their household.

WILSON, DAVID S. born ca. 1825, and wife, SARAH, borh ca. 1803, both in NY, were listed in the 1850 census of Seneca Twp., Lenawee Co., Mich. with DELILAH, age 8/12, b. Mich., in their household.

WILSON, EDWIN (See Richard DeGreene)

WILSON, ELIZABETH (See James Westerman[2])

WILSON, EMMA (See Justus Cooley)

WILSON, ENOCH born ca. 1803, NY, and wife, MARGARET, borh ca. 1806, NJ, were probably they listed in the 1840 census index of Franklin Twp., Lenawee Co., Mich. (adjacent to ABNER & SAMUEL); and in the 1850 census of Cambridge Twp. with ZILLEY? (female), age 20; ZENAS, age 18; CHARITY, age 17; NANCY, age 15, all b. NY; and BETSEY, ag 13; HANNAH, age 11; ADELINE, age 9; JANE, age 6; ENOCH, age 3, all b. Mich., in their household.

WILSON, FANNIE (ELLIS) Mrs. (See Benjamin B. Fisk)

WILSON, G. W. came to Seneca Twp., Lenwee Co., Mich. in 1836 with Dennis Wakefield (who had come from Thompson, Conn.) Note SIMON D. from Thompson, Conn.

WILSON, HANNAH married Hiram Van Akin, also see, in Phelps, Ontario Co., NY by 1831. Ref: P&BA-Len pg. 987-8.

WILSON, HARPER R. born ca. 1809, VT, and PROBABLY second wife, ALICE, born ca. 1821, NY, were listed in the 1850 census of Rome Twp., Lenawee Co., Mich. with HARRIET E., age 17; LAVINA A., age 15; PRUDENCE, age 9, all b. NY; and EMILY, age 7; WILLIAM H., age 5; JOSEPH N., age 4; ELIZA, age 3, all b. Mich., in their household.

WILSON, HARRIET, daughter of CORNELIUS, of NY state, married Theron L. Burr (also see).

WILSON, HELEN (See William Taylor)

WILSON, HOMER E. (See Frederick W. Wickwire)

WILSON, HORATIO L., son of CHARLES A. (preceding), born 15 Oct. 1855, Madison Twp., Lenawee Co., Mich., married on 8 Sept. 1875 to MARTHA A. (CRANE), daughter of Alford (also see). Children: 1. EDDIE L. b. 23 Sept. 1879 (d. 8 mos); 2. CHARLES A. b. 12 Feb. 1882;

3. FREDDIE A. b. 1 Sept. 1884. Ref: P&BA-Len pg. 1006-7.

WILSON, HORATIO N. born ca. 1811, Conn., and wife, HARRIET, borh ca. 1815, Conn., were listed in the 1840 census index of Seneca Twp., Lenawee Co., Mich.; and in the 1850 census with JOSEPHINE, age 13; GEORGE, age 9; MARY, age 7, all b. Mich., and Nancy Wakefield (also see), probably mother of Harriet, in their household. Note: They were listed next door to SIMON D., following.

WILSON, JAMES born ca. 1786, and wife, SUSANNAH, born ca. 1790, both in Mass., were probably they listed in the 1840 census index of Clinton Twp., Lenawee Co., Mich.; and were listed in the 1850 census of Tecumseh Twp. with GEORGE, age 37; JAMES, age 25, both b. NY, and probably a grandson, THOMAS, age 1, b. Mich., in their household.

WILSON, JAMES born ca. 1807, Conn., and wife, HARRIET, borh ca. 1817, NY, were listed in the 1850 census of Seneca Twp., Lenawee Co., Mich. with P---(male), age 11, b. Conn.; and LOVISA, age 7, b. Mich., in their household. Note SIMON D. & HORATIO N.

WILSON, JAMES S. (See Nehemiah Sutton)

WILSON, JESSE born ca. 1803, and wife, EMILY, born ca. 1806, both in VT, were listed in the 1850 census of Adrian Twp., Lenawee Co., Mich. with JOHN P., age 21; EMILY M., age 17; CELIA K., age 10, all b. NY, in their household; and JESSE M. (following) listed next door.

WILSON, JESSE M., probably son of JESSE (preceding), born ca. 1826, and wife, DEBORAH J., born ca. 1827, both in NY, were listed in the 1850 census of Adrian Twp., Lenawee Co., Mich. with FRANCIS H., age 1, b. Mich., in their household.

WILSON, JOEL born ca. 1813, VT, and wife, PHEBE, born ca. 1810, NJ, were listed in the 1850 census of Rollin Twp., Lenawee Co., Mich. with perhaps stepchildren: Joseph Perkins, age 16, b. NY; Anthony Perkins, age 13; Susan A. Perkins, age 10; John Perkins, age 7, all b. Mich., in their household.

WILSON, JOHN born ca. 1787, and wife, HARRIET (LANGS), born ca. 1796, both in Penn., moved from Northumberland Co., Penn. to Livingston Co., NY before 1832; and in 1835, moved to Woodstock Twp., Lenawee Co., Mich. He died there at age 68, and she died at age 62. There were 8 children, names not stated, except MARIETTA b. 16 Jan. 1832, NY (m. James H. Rogers, also see); MINERVA (m. R. P. Darling; Woodstock Twp.); and in the household in 1850 was OSCAR, age 15, b. NY. Ref: P&BA-Len pg. 677-8. Note PHILEMON, following.

WILSON, JOHN born ca. 1796, NY, and wife, SOPHIA, born ca. 1797, Mass., may be they listed in the 1840 census index of Adrian Twp., Lenwee Co., Mich.; and in the 1850 census of Madison Twp. with SAMUEL, age 26; CHARLES A., age 24; HIRAM T., age 19, all b. NY; and CURRAN, age 14 (m. Laura M. Watson, dau. of E T., also see); MARY, age 12, both b. Mich., in their household. Next door was NELSON D., age 28, b. NY with wife, MARY A., age 23, b. NY.

WILSON, JOHN born ca. 1800, and wife, AMY, born ca. 1805, NY, were listed in the 1850 census of Hudson Twp., Lenawee Co., Mich. with MARY M., age 19; CHARLOTTE, age 15, both b. NY; and LLEWELLYN, age 5, b. Mich., in their household.

WILSON, JOHN born ca. 1816, NY, and wife, MALVINA, born ca. 1826, Ohio, were listed in the 1850 census of Blissfield Twp., Lenawee Co., Mich. with ARTHUR, age 2, b. Mich., in their household.

WILSON, JOHN H. born 1825, Co. Antrim, Ireland, married there to ELIZABETH (STEWART) who died there leaving 6 children, 2 of whom were deceased before 1888, names not stated: 1. FRANCIS (m. SARAH WILSON; Los Angeles, CA); 2. WILLIAM (m. SARAH L. WILSON, Tecumseh); 3. JAMES (m. Anna Lane; Los Angeles, CA); 4. JOHN (Meadow Creek, Madison Co., Mont.) John H. married again to ROSA (CRAIG). Children: 5. THOMAS b. Ireland; 6. ROBERT b. Ireland; 7. MAGGIE b. Macon Twp. (m. John Smith; Tecumseh). About 1863, the family had moved from Ireland to Quebec, Canada; and then to Macon Twp., Lenawee Co., Mich., and afterwards to Ridgeway Twp. They returned to Macon Twp. by 1877. Ref: P&BA-Len pg. 1055-6.

WILSON, LETITIA married first to ? Thoms; and second to Anson Backus (also see).

WILSON, MARIA born ca. 1826, NY, was listed in the 1850 census of Madison Twp., Lenawee Co., Mich. in the Lewis Dodge household.

WILSON, MATTHEW of Cleveland, Ohio (See William Isley).

WILSON, MELISSA (See Luther Warner; note in household of DANIEL, preceding).

WILSON, PHEBE born 1803, Rockland Co., NY, married in Sodus, Wayne Co., NY on 8 May 1828 to Nelson Bradish (also see). Note ROBERT, following.

WILSON, PHILEMON born ca. 1819, and wife, ESTHER, born ca. 1828, both in NY, were listed in the 1850 census of Woodstock Twp., Lenawee Co., Mich. with FRANCES, age 3, b. Mich., in their household. Note JOHN, preceding.

WILSON, PHILO born ca. 1806, and wife, SUBMIT, born ca. 1809, both in Conn., were listed in the 1840 census index of Medina Twp., Lenawee Co., Mich.; and in the 1850 census with ANNA M., age 7; GEORGE D., age 5, both b. Mich.; and next door was HANNAH, age 19, b. Conn., in the household of Joseph Russell whose wife, Alvira, was age 20, born Conn. (another daughter?)

WILSON, R. S. (See James R. Cairns)

WILSON, REBECCA (See Henry Nichols)

WILSON, RICHARD born ca. 1801, England, and wife, JULIA A., born ca. 1805, Penn., were listed in the 1850 census of Raisin Twp., Lenawee Co., Mich. with ELIJAH, age 15, b. NY; and CAROLINE, age 12; JANE, age 6; SAMUEL, age 4, all b. Mich., in their household.

WILSON, ROBERT born ca. 1800, son of ANDREW (preceding), was reared in Wayne Co., NY, but married in Genesee Co., NY to PHOEBE (ROBERTSON) born ca. 1805, NJ. They were listed in the 1840 census index of Macon Twp., Lenawee Co., Mich., but moved to Ridgeway Twp. She died there in 1855. Known son, WILLIAM R. (following). In their household in the 1850 census of Ridgeway Twp. was father, ANDREW (preceding). Robert married again to HANNAH E. (VAN NOSTRAND); and he died 8 Oct. 1866. Hannah was still living in 1888 in Clinton Twp. Ref: P&BA-Len pg. 313.

WILSON, SAMUEL born ca. 1818, and wife, ELIZABETH, born ca. 1822, were probably they listed in the 1840 census index of Franklin Twp., Lenawee Co., Mich.;

Pioneer Families of Southeastern Michigan

and in the 1850 census with SARAH, age 7; ELMA, age 3; CHARLES, age 1, all b. Mich., in their household.

WILSON, SARAH & SARAH L. (See JOHN H., preceding)

WILSON, SIMON D. born ca. 1806, Conn., and wife, MILLICENT (BALDWIN), born ca. 1805, Mass., married in Windsor, Berkshire Co., Mass. They lived there first, then moved to Thompson, Conn. before 1833. In 1834, they removed to Seneca Twp., Lenawee Co., Mich. He died in 1887, age 82; and she had died in 1864. Children: 1. ELIZA A. b. ca. 1831, Conn. (m. W. H. Clarke; College Springs, IA; she d. 1864); 2. CHARLES B. (preceding); 3. LUCY D. b. ca. 1841, Conn. (m. Royal Hamlin, son of Luman, also see; he d. 1882). Ref: P&BA-Len pg. 568-9. Note: In the 1850 census, were next door to HORATIO N.

WILSON, THOMAS born ca. 1809, England, came to Raisin Twp., Lenawee Co., Mich. by 1840, where he married LYDIA B. (HOAG) born ca. 1811, NY. He died 5 Dec. 1882, age 73; and she died 31 Aug. 1863. They were Quakers. Known children in 1850 census: EDWIN, age 13; FRANCES A. b. 23 May 1844, Palmyra Twp. (m. Charles E. Bowerman, also see). Ref: P&BA-Len pg. 195.

WILSON, WILLIAM, son of WILLIAM (who was born in Penn, and died near Lancaster, O.), was born in Ohio. He moved to Lucas Co., Ohio, near Sylvania, where he married MARY A. (LATHROP), daughter of Col. Lucina D. of Lucas Co. They settled in Litchfield Twp., Lucas Co. Known dauger, PAMELIA b. 3 Feb. 1846 (m. Eugene F. Ford, also see). Ref: P&BA-Len pg. 871-2.

WILSON, WILLIAM R., son of ROBERT (preceding), born ca. 1828, NY, married on 5 May 1852 in Raisin Twp., Lenawee Co., Mich. to MARY A. (KELLEY), daughter of Wayne (also see). They settled in Ridgeway Twp. Children: 1. JULIA E. b. 12 Dec. 1862 (d. 30 Aug. 1864); 2. HENRY C. (m. Agnes Willett of Blissfield Twp.; went to Constantine, St. Joseph Co.); 3. EUGENE A. (m. Kittie E. Fessenden; Petoskey, Emmet Co., Mich.) Ref: P&BA-Len pg. 313.

WILT, GEORGE W.[4] (See MICHAEL[1], following) was born in Preston Co., W. Va. He served in the Civil War in Co I, 3rd Maryland Inf. He came to Ogden Twp., Lenawee Co., Mich. in 1868; and married on 21 Dec. 1871 to SARAH (ROBERTSON), daughter of James (also see). No children were listed in sketch. Ref: P&BA-Len pg. 1092.

WILT, JEREMIAH born ca 1817, Penn, and wife, ELIZA A., born ca. 1817, NY, were listed in the 1850 census of Adrian Twp., Lenawee Co., Mich. with MOSES, age 9; MARY E., age 5, both b. Ohio in their household. Note that this may be WITT.

WILT, M. L. married SARAH P. (HARSH), daughter of George Frederick (also see) of a family from Aurora, W. Va.

WILT, MICHAEL[1] was born in Bedford Co., Penn., and was an early settler to near what is now Aurora, Preston Co., W. VA. He had a known son, MICHAEL[2], born either in Penn. or W. Va., who married LYDIA (WALTZ). They had a son ?[3] (possibly Michael?) who maried in Preston Co., W. Va. to MARIA (MARTIN), daughter of Peter (also see) of Garrett Co., MD. She died in 1863, and he afterwards went to Elkins, Garrett Co., MD. Known son, #2. GEORGE W. (preceding). Ref: P&BA-Len pg. 1092. Also note M. L., preceding.

WILTSE also see WILSEY

WILTSE, HENRY (See William Ladd)

WILTSIE see WILSEY

WITLESY, HANNAH (See Joseph Marks)

WIMPLE, ABIAL (See Andrew J. Hunter)

WIMPLE, JACOB A. born ca. 1782, and wife, TEMPERANCE, born ca. 1794, both in NY, were listed in the 1850 census of Franklin Twp., Lenawee Co., Mich. with Martha Roberts, age 22; Amelia Roberts, age 16, both b. Mich., in their household.

WINCHELL, WILLIAM F. and wife, SUBMIT, were natives of Grafton, Conn., and it may be he listed in the 1800 census index of Chenango Co., NY. They were pioneer settlers to Sangerfield, Oneida Co., NY. Known daughter, HARRIET (m. Eri Jewett, also see). Ref: P&BA-Len pg. 800-1.

WINDER, SARAH (See Robert Whitacre)

WINDLE, G. C. (See Jabez Briggs)

WINEGAR, ULRIC and wife, ELIZABETH (WIEMANS), were parents of JANE born 22 Dec. 1811 (m. John Hicks, also see, on 25 Oct. 1833, Rensselaer Co., NY). Ref: P&BA-Len pg. 1121-2.

WINES, SURRAJAH, son of JAMES (of NY), was born ca. 1803, NY, and he married JANE A. (PHILLIPS), daughter of Nicholas (also see) and was living in Wolcott, Wayne Co., NY in 1833. They moved to Blissfield Twp., Lenawee Co., Mich. ca. 1846. He died in Kalamazoo, Mich.; and she died in Tecumseh Twp. at the "home of a daughter." They were listed in the 1850 census of Blissfield Twp. with CHARITY A. b. 2 May 1833, Wolcott, NY (m. Lagrange H. Dewey, also see); JAMES, age 15; DAVID A., age 13; HETTY A., age 11; JOTHAM F., age 8, all b. NY, and MARY, age 4; IRENA, age 1, both b. Mich., in their household. Ref: P&BA-Len pg. 846-7.

WING, ABRAM, son of WILLIAM (following), born 28 July 1836, Ypsilanti Twp., Washtenaw Co., Mich., moved in 1848 to Rockford, Ill. and lived with an uncle. He afterwards went to Madison, Wisc. and lived with an uncle, David Gardner, and returned from there to Ypsilanti. He enlistsed in Co. B, 47th Ohio Inf. during the Civil War, and became a 2nd Lt. He married in 1863, to ALICE E. (SIZER) of Adrian, Lenawee Co., Mich. and settled there. Children: 1. HENRY A.; 2. ADELIA A. Ref: P&BA-Len pg. 1156-7.

WING, ELIJAH and wife, HANNAH (SQUIRE), were born in Conn., lived in Berkshire Co., Mass. in 1814; and in 1826, removed to Steuben Co., NY. He died there at age 66; and she came to Rollin Twp., Lenawee Co., Mich. where she died at home of son, Spencer. There were 6 sons and 6 daughters, and only mentioned were SPENCER; & WALDEN (following). Ref: P&BA-Len pg. 946-7.

WING, FREDERICK A. probably born after 1850 (See John K. Boies).

WING, WALDEN, son of ELIJAH (preceding), born 12 Apr. 1814, Berkshire Co., Mass., moved with his parents to Steuben Co., NY. He married 12 Jan. 1837 to ALVIRA (RAYMOND) born ca. 1814, NY. In 1838, they moved to Rollin Twp., Lenawee Co., Mich. She died there at age 59. Children: 1. STEPHEN C. b. 9 June 1838 (d. 7 June 1846); 2. OSCAR L. b. 3 Jan. 1841 (d. 14 Sept. 1842); 3. PHILURA H. b. 25 Aug. 1843; 4. HENRY S. b. 8 Aug. 1845 (d. 17 Mar. 1846)l\; 5. MARY L. b. 1 Oct. 1848 (m. Thomas Maloney, 4 Nov. 1875, went to Wash. Terr.); 6. CROSBY W. b. 11 Aug. 1851 (m. Harriet M. Wood, dau. of Charles, also see; d. in R.R. accident 9 June 1875); 7. CLARENCE O. b. 19 June 1858 (m. Martha Beal). Walden married again on 27 Oct. 1875 to HELEN (MOREHOUSE), daughter of Aaron (also see). A child died infancy. Ref: P&BA-Len pg. 946-7.

WING, WILLIAM born in NY, came to Washtenaw Co., Mich. at a young age and married in Ypsilanti Twp. to MARIA (SOOP), probably daughter of Abram (also see), who was born in the Mohawk Valley of NY. He died in 1857. There were at least 2 daughters, names not stated, and son, ABRAM (preceding). Ref: P&BA-Len pg. 1156-7. Note: In the 1840 census index of Washtenaw Co., Mich., there was an ALSON in Saline Twp.; and a NELSON H.; & "P." with no township noted.

WINKLER, ELIZABETH "BETSEY" (See Rev. Moses Bennett; also see John Greenleaf).

WINKLER, JOHN of Elmira, NY was father of MERCY who married Joel Bennett, also see. Note: He may also be father of ELIZABETH, preceding, as Rev. Moses Bennett was a brother of Joel.

WINNIE also see WINNE
WINNIE, SUSAN (See George Sheeler)

WINSLOW, MARVIN L. and wife, LUCINDA E. (DELANO), were reared and married in Jefferson Co., NY (Jefferson formed from Oneida Co., NY ca. 1802). Their known daughter, child #7., MARIAN M. was born 5 July 1842, Hermon, NY (St. Lawrence Co.?) They removed to Fairfield Twp., Lenawee Co., Mich.; but in 1855 moved to Portage Co., Wisc. Lucinda died there on 16 July 1874; and he died in Edna, Minn. on 5 Jan. 1883. Marian married in Portage Co., Wisc to Urson Bumpus (also see) on 19 Mar. 1858; and she married second to Peter Gussenbauer of Fairfield Twp., Lenawee Co., Mich. (also see). Ref: P&BA-Len pg. 566-7.

WINTER also see WINTERS
WINTER, ASA was listed in the 1840 census index of Adrian Twp., Lenawee Co., Mich. near E. C. (following). AMELIA, age 71, born Conn., was listed in the 1850 census of Adrian Twp., possibly widow of Asa. Listed with her was MARSHA, age 31, b. Penn., and they were listed in the household of Russell and Eunice (age 46, b. VT) Lyman...Is she a daughter? Zuba Follett, age 44, b. VT, also in the household may be related.

WINTER, E. C., possibly son of ASA (preceding), born ca. 1802, VT, and wife, MARY A., born ca. 1814, NY, were listed in the 1850 census of Adrian Twp., Lenawee Co., Mich. with WILLIAM, age 14, b. Mich. in their household.

WINTER, WILLIAM born ca. 1815, Penn. was probably he listed in the 1840 census index of Raisin Twp., Lenawee Co., Mich. He was listed in the 1850 census with possibly second wife, MARY, born ca. 1828, Mich., and ZINA, age 11, b. Mich., in his household.

WINTERS also see WINTER
WINTERS, ALPHONSO was listed in the 1840 census index of Tecumseh Twp., Lenawee Co., Mich.

WINTERS, JAMES and wife, CHRISTINA (HAM), were natives of Rensselaer Co., NY, who later moved to Schenectady Co., NY. Children: 1. ANN; 2. DANIEL; 3. CLARISSA b. 11 Aug. 1831, Schenectady Co., NY (m. John M. Payne, also see); 4. SENECA; 5. WILLIAM; 6. SARAH; 7. JUDSON; 8. THEODOCIA; 9. ABBY. Ref: P&BA-Lenpg. 292.

WINTERS, SAMUEL born ca. 1770, NJ, was listed in the 1850 census of Macon Twp., Lenawee Co., Mich. in the household og George Wilkins (also see) and wife, Hannah (daughter of Samuel?). Note SAMUEL S., following. It may this SAMUEL or SAMUEL S. listed in the 1840 census index of Franklin Twp.

WINTERS, SAMUEL S. born ca. 1818, Penn., and wife, ELSY, borh ca. 1823, NY, were listed in the 1850 census of Macon Twp., Lenawee Co., Mich. with MYRON S., age 8; PHILETA A., age 4; EMERETTA, age 2; ALONZO F., age 5/12, all b. Mich., in their household.

WIRT, HENRY J., son of JAMES (following), born 6 May 1829, Chautauqua Co., NY, came to Medina Twp., Lenawee Co., Mich. in 1857 with his brother. He married first to MARY M. (SALSBURY), and she died 2 Nov. 1873. Children: 1. MINNIE (m. Gerry Acker); 2. NETTIE; 3. HATTIE. Henry J. married again to CLARA or CLARISSA A. (FOX), daughter of Thomas (also see). Daughter, 4. MARY E. Ref: P&BA-Len pg. 718-9.

WIRT, JAMES and wife, RACHEL (RATHBURN), were both born in NY, and lived in Chautauqua Co., NY, and then in Orleans Co., NY. In 1856, they removed to Lenawee Co., Mich., and he died in Medina Twp. ca. 1858. She died 28 Dec. 1885. Sons: WILLIAM F. (Medina Twp.); 2. HENRY J. (preceding). Ref: P&BA-Len pg. 718-9.

WISNER, ABRAHAM, son of JEHIEL (following), born 1799, Orange Co., NY, was reared in Orange and Seneca Cos., NY. He married in Niagara Co., NY to SARAH (WISNER), born ca. 1807, NY, a distant relative, and stayed there until after the birth of first 6 children. In 1833, they moved via Canada to Franklin, Lenawee Co., Mich., where the rest of the children were born. He died in Nov. 1865, age 68; and she died May 1865, age 59. Known children: 1. JEHIEL (following); 2. ALPHEUS (following); 3. EDWARD C. (following); and the following were in their household in the 1850 census of Franklin Twp.: 4. RUFUS, age 19, b. NY; 5. HULDAH, age 16; 6. HANNAH, age 13; then he called "9th child," 9. WILLIAM E./A.? (following); 10. ADORIAH? (female), age 8; 11. SARAH, age 4; 12. SAMUEL, age 1, last 6 b. Mich. Ref: P&BA-Len pg. 274-5; 528-9.

WISNER, ALPHEUS, son of ABRAHAM (preceding), born ca. 1824, and wife, JULIA, born ca. 1827, both in NY, were

Pioneer Families of Southeastern Michigan

listed in the 1850 census of Franklin Twp., Lenawee Co., Mich. with MARY ANN, age 2/12, b. Mich., in their household.

WISNER, EDWARD C., son of ABRAHAM (preceding), born ca. 1827, NY, married 1 Jan. 1850 to MARIAN M. (WHELAN), daughter of John (also see) and settled in Franklin Twp., Lenawee Co., Mich. No children listed in sketch. Ref: P&BA-Len pg. 528-9.

WISNER, JEHIEL was a Revolutionary soldier. It may be he in the Rev. Pension Applications with NJ and NY service, Appl. #S29546. Jehiel and wife, SUSAN (called LUANNA in one sketch, probably meant to be "Susanna" CHANDLER), lived in Orange & Seneca Cos., NY. It may be he listed in the 1800 census index of Cayuga Co., NY. They moved from Niagara Co., NY to Franklin Twp., Lenawee Co., Mich. to make their home with eldest son, ABRAHAM (preceding). There were 9 children, names not stated. Jehiel died in 1839, and she a little later. Ref: P&BA-Lenpg. 274-5; 528-9. Also note Rev. WILLIAM G. (following).

WISNER, JEHIEL, son of ABRAHAM (preceding) born ca. 1823, and wife, HARRIET, borh ca. 1825, both in NY, were listed in the 1850 census of Franklin Twp., Lenawee Co., Mich. with EMILY, age 4; CLARISSA, age 2; SARAH, age 2/12, all b. Mich., in their household.

WISNER, WILLIAM E. (or A.), son of ABRAHAM (preceding), born 14 Jan. 1839, Franklin Twp., Lenawee Co., Mich.married on 1 Jan. 1862 in Franklin Twp. to EMELINE (WHELAN), daughter of William (also see). Children: 1. MAUD (d. age 9 mos); 2. ERNEST (to Logan Co., Nebr.); 3. OWEN (Logan Co., Nebr.); 4. GRACE; 5. MINNIE; 6. STELLA; 7. DEWEY; 8. EMILY; 9. SCOTT. Ref: P&BA-Lenpg. 274-5.

WISNER, WILLIAM G. Rev. born 9 Dec. 1802, Aurelius, Cayuga Co., NY (note JEHIEL, preceding), married ELIZABETH (HUDNUTT), daughtero fo Nathaniel. They lived in Castile, Wyoming Co., NY; and later moved to Manchester, Washtenaw Co., Mich. Known daughter, SARAH b. 7 Aug. 1832, Castile, NY (m. Dr. Edwin P. Andrews, also see). Ref: P&BA-Len pg. 1118-9.

WISNER, ZEPPINAH?, age 23, born NY, was listed in the 1850 census of Dover Twp., Lenawee Co., Mich. in a Sabins household.

WITHAM, ? married in Boston, Mass. to FRANCES M. (SHAW) who was born in Lynn, Mass. Known daughter, EMMIE (m. Frank Prebbles of Lynn). Frances married again to Henry P. Downs (also see) of Macon Twp., Lenawee Co., Mich. Ref: P&BA-Len pg. 347-8.

WITHERELL, ANSEL married LOVINA (CHAPMAN), in Mass. or Conn., and he died in 1817 in Deerfield, Mass.; and she died there in 1838. They had 5 children, and only names were LAURA b. 1810, Mass. (m. Job Graves, also see); ANSEL (following); and probably WILSON (following). Ref: P&BA-Len pg. 886-7.

WITHERELL, ANSEL, son of ANSEL (preceding), born 22 Apr. 1814, Chatham, Conn., married on 9 July 1844, Franklin Twp., Lenawee Co., Mich. to MARY S. (CLARK), daughter of Noah (also see). Children: 1. ADELIA S. (d. infancy); 2. MARY LOVINA b. ca. 1847 (m. Harlow Welch, prob. son of Peleg, also see; Manchester, Mich.); 3. JEHIEL A. (d. infancy); 4. EDGAR A. (d. age 4); 5. CLARA E. (d. 1880, age 24). Ref: P&BA-Len pg. 886-7.

WITHERELL, WILSON, probably son of ANSEL, was born ca. 1812, Conn. (census said Mass.), and his wife, ELIZABETH (CHEESEMAN) was born ca. 1813, NY. They married in Jefferson Co., NY, where daughter, Adelia and 2 sons were born. They located first in Franklin Twp., Lenawee Co., Mich,; and then after 1850 moved to Manchester, Washtenaw Co., Mich. He died there 21 Nov. 1885; and she died age 73. Children: 1. ADELIA J. (written " Cordelia,: in 1850 census) b. ca. 1837 (m. Alvinza Whelan, also see); 2. ROWLEY, b. ca. 1845, NY; 3. DUDLEY b. ca. 1847. Ref: P&BA-Len pg. 664-5.

WITT, JEREMIAH see Jeremiah Wilt

WITT, MARY ANN of Westphalia, Germany (See John P. Schwab).

WIXSON, REUBEN and wife, HANNAH, were parents of ANNA b. 20 Jan. 1824, Steuben Co., NY (m. Jehial H. Bramble, also see). They were said to have come to Michigan.

WOIMPLE, JOHN (See William Bradley; also see John J. Adams)

WOLCOTT, KALEP and wife, RHODE (HEDGES), of Steuben Co., NY were parents of LAURINDA b. 17 Jan. 1825, Steuben Co. (m. John W. Benedict, also see). Ref: P&BA-Len pg. 300-1.

WOLF, GEORGE, born in Cumberland Co., Penn., went to Ohio with his parents. He married there to NANCY (GERWELL) born Virginia. They settled in Ashland Co., Ohio. He died 11 June 1864, age 69; and she was living in 1888, age 83. There were 6 sons and 4 daughters, names not stated, some of whom went to Iowa, Missouri, Ohio and Michigan. Known son, SOLOMON (following). Ref: P&BA-Len pg. 1097-8.

WOLF, SOLOMON, son of GEORGE (preceding), born 12 Jan. 1826, Wayne Co., Ohio (an area now in Ashland Co.), married on 1 Nov. 1849? (probably 1850, as she was listed in her father's home in the 1850 census?) to SOPHIA (VAN SICKLE), daughter of Andrew (also see). They settled in Seneca Twp., Lenawee Co., Mich. She died 5 June 1885. Children: 1. GEORGE (m. Estella Camburn); 2. NANCY (m. Jesse Tuttle, son of Oramon, Jr., also see); 3. WILLIAM (m. Ida Van Sickle). Ref: P&BA-Len pg. 1097-8.

WOOD, ? moved from Livingston Co., NY to Orleans Co., NY ca. 1824. Known children: 1. WILSON (following); 2. JONATHAN (Orleans Co., NY); 3. MELINDA (m. Burtis Hoyt; she d. Jackson Co., Mich.); 4. LORETTA (m. Abram Miller; Orleans Co., NY); 5. WILLIAM (m. Mary Ann Weatherwax; Orleans Co., NY). Ref: P&BA-Len pg. 719-20. Also note SQUIRE, following.

WOOD, A. F. (See Isaac C. Gunn)

WOOD, ALFRED H., son of LEANDER (following), born 13 Oct. 1829, Shelby, Orleans Co., NY, came to Rome Twp., Lenawee Co., Mich. in 1833 with his parents; and married on 15 Feb. 1855 to ALMIRA S. (COMSTOCK), daughter of Warner (also see). Children: 1. ALFRED

WILLIS b. 6 Jan. 1857; 2. GERTRUDE M. b. 26 July 1859; 3. MARY (d. infancy); 4. ELOISE b. 12 June 1866. Ref: P&BA-Len pg. 494-5.

WOOD, BARNABAS was a "native of New England," and had a known daughter, ELIZA (m. Eli Vest, also see, who was b. ca. 1808, probably in Seneca Co., NY, and moved to Tecumseh, Lenawee Co., Mich.)

WOOD, BERTHA (See Levi Jennings)

WOOD, CALVIN born ca. 1801, and wife, HARRIET, born ca. 1811, both in NY, were listed in the 1840 census index of Tecumseh Twp., Lenawee Co., Mich.; and were in the 1850 census with IRENE, age 16, b. Mich., in their household.

WOOD, CHARLES married MARIA (NEWITT), daughter of John (also see) of Madison Co., NY, dates not given. He died in Rollin Twp., Lenawee Co., Mich. by 1862. Children: 1. HARRIET M. b. 22 Sept. 1852 (m. Crosby Wing, son of Walden, also see; Jackson Co., Mich.); 2. ELIZABETH b. 8 Feb. 1855 (m. Edwin Tuttle); 3. ORILLA b. 25 Nov. 1858 (m. Hiram Babcock; Rollin Twp.) Maria married again on 10 Sept. 1862 to William Derbyshire (also see) whose first wife was ROSANNA (WOOD). Ref: P&BA-Len pg. 642-3. Note CHARLES in household of SQUIRE, following?

WOOD, CHARLES D., son of WILSON (following), born 4 Dec. 1845 (shown age 7 in 1850 census?), married 3 Dec. 1871 to ADA A. (COOK), daughter of Samuel (also see) of St. Joseph Co., Mich. Known child: 1. LELA OLIVE b. 9 Sept. 1875. Ref: P&BA-Len pg. 719-20.

WOOD, CHARLES P. born ca. 1824, and wife, SARAH born ca. 1826, both in Ohio, were listed in the 1850 census of Rollin Twp., Lenawee Co., Mich. with no family. Note: They were listed next door to James Carr, age 46, b. Ohio, and wife, Elizabeth, age 46, b. MD, possibly parents of Sarah??

WOOD, CHARLES S. born ca. 1827, and wife, JANE, born ca. 1828, both in NY, were listed in the 1850 census of Tecumseh Twp., Lenawee Co., Mich. with LEVI B., age 9, b. Mich., whom seems to old to be their child, in their household. Note CALVIN & ELIPHALET.

WOOD, DAVID was a "native of NY," and his wife, ELIZA (BRIGGS), was a "native of New England." They married in NY, and settled in Lake Co., Ohio, then moved to Fulton Co., Ohio. She died 26 June 1882, and he was still living there in 1888. Children: 1. JULIETTE (m. Hiram B. Abbott, also see); 2. ELIZA b. ca. 1832, NY (m. Perry Hamlin, also see); 3. MINERVA A. (deceased before 1888); 4. JOHN B. (Ohio); 5. SUSAN A. (m. S. Clarke, Ohio); 6. GEORGE (deceased before 1888); 7. JEROME (Ohio). Ref: P&BA-Len pg. 354-7.

WOOD, EDWIN B., age 24, born Ohio, was listed in the 1850 census of Tecumseh Twp., Lenawee Co., Mich. in a Stacy household.

WOOD, ELIZABETH (See Robert Cairns; also see David Smith, Jr.)

WOOD, ELIZABETH (ORAM) Mrs., born 9 Jan. 1840, England, was the daughter of George Oram, also see, husband's name not stated. She died July 1875, Adrian Twp., Lenawee Co., Mich. There were 4 children, names not stated.

WOOD, ELIPHALET born ca. 1792, New Hampshire, and wife, SALLY, born ca. 1795, Mass., were probably they listed in the 1840 census of Tecumseh Twp., Lenawee Co., Mich.; and were in the 1850 census with the following in their household. (Please note the places of birth shown. IF CORRECT, they were in Mich. as early as 1828, but went back to NH for a time?) Listed were: PERRY, age 26; ALMIRA, age 28, both b. NH; DAVIS, age 22, b. Mich.; JOSEPHINE, age 10, b. NH.

WOOD, GEORGE was listed in the 1840 census index of Blissfield Twp., Lenawee Co., Mich.

WOOD, GEORGE and wife, AZUBAH (RANSOM), probably from Ontario Co., NY, settled in Toledo, Ohio. She died in 1840. He lived for a time in Toledo, then returned to NY, where he died 7 Dec. 1884. Four children, names not stated, except SARAH E. b. 19 Feb. 1836, Geneva, NY (m. Henry J. Carlton, also see). Ref: P&BA-Len pg. 447-8.

WOOD, GEORGE born ca. 1819, NY, and wife, ELIZABETH, born ca. 1822, England, were listed in the 1850 census of Cambridge Twp., Lenawee Co., Mich. with ELLEN, age 7. b. NY; and ANGELIA, age 2, b. Mich., in their household.

WOOD, HARRIET, age 19, born NY, was listed in the 1850 census of Adrian Twp., Lenawee Co., Mich. in the household of Charles Smith. Note HARRY, following.

WOOD, HARRY born ca. 1789, NY, was a resident of Adrian Twp., Lenwee Co., Mich. in 1831. He was listed in the 1840 census index (adjacent to WHITING, following); and also in the 1850 census of Adrian Twp. with wife, HESTER A., age 44, b. NY; and the following, some of whom seem too old to be children of Hester. It appears that the household was probably two families. Listed were: LEANDER, age 30; JOHN, age 26; LYMAN, age 25; ALEXANDER, age 23; JACKSON, age 21, all b. NY; and then CYNTHIA, age 31, b. NY with the following children: NOAH, age 8; CHARLES, age 5; FRANCES A., age 2, all b. Mich., all listed in this order in the household. Note LEANDER, following.

WOOD, J. J. (See Oliver S. Colwell)

WOOD, JACKSON M. born ca. 1820, and wife, LOUISA M., born ca. 1824, both in NY, were listed in the 1850 census of Hudson Twp., Lenawee Co., Mich. with JEROME, age 4; DARWIN, age 5/12, both b. Mich., in their household. Also note HARRY, following.

WOOD, JAMES born ca. 1810, and wife, ADALINE, born ca. 1813, both in NY, were listed in the 1850 census of Adrian Twp., Lenawee Co., Mich. with SARAH, age 14; LUTHER, age 12, both b. NY; and MYRON, age 11; HENRY, age 9; HARRISON, age 7, all b. Mich., in their household. Note: It may be this JAMES in the 1840 census index of Rome Twp. Also note LEANDER.

WOOD, JANE, age 56, born Penn., was listed in the 1850 census of Adrian Twp., Lenawee Co., Mich. in the household of Joseph and Catherine Little.

WOOD, JOHN was listed in the 1830 census of Lenawee Co., Mich. Territory, with males: 1 und 5; 1 5-10; 1 30-40; females: 1 und 5; 1 5-10; 1 30-40 in his household. Note HARRY, preceding.

WOOD, JOHN born ca. 1804, and wife, CAROLINE, bornca. 1814, both in NY, were listed in the 1850 census of Macon Twp., Lenawee Co., Mich. with MELVIN, age 21; CYNTHIA, age 18; LOANNA, age 16, all b. NY; and ELMYRA, age 5, b. Mich., in their household.

WOOD, LEANDER born 22 June 1804, Onondaga Co., NY, married on 25 Sept. 1825 to MARIA (CURE) born 4 Oct. 1806, Saratoga Co., NY. They settled first in Orleans Co., NY. In 1833, they removed to Rome Twp.,

Pioneer Families of Southeastern Michigan

Lenawee Co., Mich. She died there in Jan. 1852. He removed to Adrian, where he died 10 Sept. 1863. Eight children, those known were from the 1850 census, except Alfred: 1. WILLIAM (following); 2. ALFRED H. (preceding); 3. SAPHRONA b. ca. 1833, NY; 4. POLLY A. b. ca. 1835, Mich.; 5. MARTIN L. b. ca. 1837; 6. HANNAH M. b. ca. 1842. Ref: P&BA-len pg. 494-5.

WOOD, LEVI and wife, BETHANY, were natives of New England who were pioneers to Orleans, Ontario Co., NY. Known daughter, PAMELIA (m. John Phillips, also see). Ref: P&BA-Len pg. 699-700.

WOOD, LUCY (See Christian Kuney)

WOOD, LUKE born ca. 1802, and wife, DELIA, born ca. 1805, were probably they listed in the 1840 census index of Franklin Twp., Lenawee Co., Mich.; and were in the 1850 census with SABRINA, age 25, b. NY; and MELLVILLE, age 20; JAMES, age 17; HARVEY, age 14; AMY, age 10, all b. Mich., in their household.

WOOD, MEHITABLE (See Aaron Dumham)

WOOD, NATHAN N. was listed in the 1840 census index of Palmyra Twp., Lenawee Co., Mich. Note NOAH, following. There was a LUCRETIA, age 19, b. NY, in the 1850 census of Palmyra Twp. in the household of Betsey Wilcox.

WOOD, NELSON married MARY ANN (UPTON), daughter of David (also see) in Sept. 1847; and he died 16 Sept. 1849, Rollin Twp., Lenawee Co., Mich. Ref: P&BA-Len pg. 283-4. Note SQUIRE, following.

WOOD, NOAH born ca. 1815, Ohio, and wife, HANNAH, born ca. 1812, NY, were listed in the 1850 census of Palmyra Twp., Lenawee Co., Mich. with MARY, age 13, b. NY; and WILLIAM, age 10; LABAN, age 8; IRA, age 5, all b. Mich. in their household. Note: NATHAN N. listed in the 1840 census index of Palmyra Twp., possibly is same man.

WOOD, ROSANNA born 20 Dec. 1820, Madison Co., NY, married William Derbyshire (also see) and she died 19 Dec. 1861, Rollin Twp., Lenawee Co., Mich. William married second to the widow of CHARLES, preceding. Note SQUIRE, following.

WOOD, ROSWELL born ca. 1804, and wife, ANNA, borh ca. 1806, both in NY, were listed in the 1850 census of Rollin Twp., Lenawee Co., Mich. with DELOSS, age 12, b. NY, in their household. Note this same given name, DELOSS, in household of WILSON, following.

WOOD, SQUIRE born ca. 1798, and wife, POLLY, born ca. 1783, both in NY, were listed in the 1840 census index of Rolin Twp., Lenawee Co., Mich. (adjacent to WILSON, following); and were in the 1850 census with CHARLES, age 32 (note preceding); DYER, age 28; JAMES, age 17; TRIPHENA, age 15; NEPHI? (male), age 14, all b. NY; and JOEL, age 12, b. Mich., in their household. Also note ROSANNA, born ca. 1820, Madison Co., NY, preceding.

WOOD, WARREN born ca. 1804, and wife, HENRIETTA, born ca. 1817, both in NY, were listed in the 1850 census of Tecumseh Twp., Lenawee Co., Mich. with WILLIAM, age 18; ELLEN, age 13, both b. NY; and William Frost, age 65, b. Mass.; Mary Frost, age 42, b. NY; and Sarah Tompkins, age 18, b. NY in their household.

WOOD, WEALTHY (See George Hare)

WOOD, WHITING was listed in the 1840 census index of Adrian Twp. Lenawee Co., Mich. adjacent to HARRY, preceding. Note the family listed in the household of Harry, who might be family of Whiting??

WOOD, WILLIAM, son of LEANDER (preceding), born 21 June 1826, Onondaga Co., NY, moved with his parents ot Rome Twp., Lenawee Co., Mich. He married 14 Oct. 1847 to SALLY ADELINE (DECKER), daugher of Uriah (also see). They settled in Rome Twp. Children: 1. ELIZABETH J. b. 15 Mar. 1849 (m. William H. Smith); 2. ALBERT H. b. 27 Sept. 1850 (d. age 1); 3. WILLIAM H. (following); 4. CLARK L. b. 30 June 1864. Ref: P&BA-Len pg. 1146-7.

WOOD, WILLIAM H., son of WILLIAM (preceding), born 25 Sept. 1854, Rome Twp., Lenawee Co., Mich., married MARY (LEWIS), daughter of Adolphus (also see). Children: 1. EDWARD L. b. 11 Dec. 1877; 2. EDWIN A. b. 6 Oct. 1879; 3. EMMETT H. b. 14 Jan. 1881. Ref: P&BA-Len pg. 1146-7.

WOOD, WILSON, son of ? (preceding) of Livingston & Orleans Co., NY, born ca. 1811, NY, married SALLY (STRONG), born ca. 1811, VT. They removed to Rollin Twp., Lenawee Co., Mich. by 1836. He died 4 Sept. 1884, age 72; and she died 24 Feb. 1885, age 74. Children (all b. Mich.): 1. LUCY JANE b. ca. 1836; 2. DAN M. b. ca. 1838 (served Civil War; resided Rollin Twp.); 3. CHARLES D. (preceding); 4. DELOS S. (d. age 6). Ref: P&BA-Len pg. 719-20. Note: In the 1840 census index was adjacent to SQUIRE, also see.

WOODARD also see WOODWARD

WOODARD, BETSEY (See Benjamin Sanger)

WOODARD, HENRY was born ca. 1785, and his wife, POLLY, born ca. 1789, were listed in the 1840 census index of Fairfield Twp., Lenawee Co., Mich.; and were in the 1850 census with MARY A., age 14, b. Mich., in their household. They were listed 2 doors from son?, JOSEPH, following.

WOODARD, JACOB born ca. 1800, and wife, JULIA, born ca. 1805, both in NY, were listed in the 1850 census of Medina Twp., Lenawee Co., Mich. in the household of son, JERRY?, age 27, b. NY, and also listed were JOHN, age 21; NANCY, age 19; MARY A., age 15, all b. NY. Note JOHN, following.

WOODARD, JOHN born ca. 1773, and wife, LYDIA, born ca. 1790, NY, were listed in the 1850 census of Medina Twp., Lenawee Co., Mich. with no fammily.

WOODARD, JOSEPH born ca. 1809, and wife, ABIGAIL, born ca. 1808, both in NY, were listed in the 1840 census index of Fairfield Twp., Lenawee Co., Mich. (adjacent to HENRY, preceding); and in the 1850 census with SARAH M., age 21; WILLIAM, age 18, both b. NY; and CHARLES A., age 6; JEROME F., age 4, both b. Mich., in their household.

WOODARD, SAMUEL was listed in the 1840 census index of Adrian Twp., Lenawee Co., Mich.

WOODARD, STEPHEN born ca. 1808, England, and wife, ELIZABETH, born ca. 1813, NY, were listed in the 1850 census of Palmyra Twp., Lenawee Co., Mich. with MATILDA, age 17; MARTIN, age 14; LYDIA, age 12; SARAH, age 10, all b. NY, in their household.

WOODCOCK, ESTHER (See David Torrey of Mass.)

WOODFORD, JOHN, son of NOAH N. (following), born 18 May 1846, Hillsdale Co., Mich., married on 22 Sept. 1868 to MARY L. (THRUBER), daughter of Caleb (also see) in Lansing, Mich. They settled in Madison Twp., Lenawee Co. Children: 1. CHARLIE C. (d. age 16); 2. FRANK H. Ref: P&BA-Len pg. 1197.

WOODFORD, NOAH N. born ca. 1812, and wife, CHARLOTTE, born ca. 1814, both in NY, married in Adrian, Lenawee Co., Mich. They lived in Hillsdale Co., MIch. for a time, but by the 1850 census were in Madison Twp., Lenawee Co., Mich. He went to California in 1853, but returned to Lenawee Co., then went to California again in 1859. He returned about 1862, and by 1866 was living in Madison Twp. Children in household in 1850: 1. WILLIAM, age 13; CHARLES, age 11; GEORGE, age 9; JOHN (preceding). Also listed was Lucinda Marcy, age 5. Ref: P&BA-Len pg. 1197.

WOODING, CORDELIA (See Ephraim Spencer)

WOODWARD also see WOODARD

WOODWARD, DAVID, son of LEWIS (following), was born probably in Ontario Co., NY, and came with his parents to Clinton Twp., Lenawee Co., Mich. in 1835. He lived in Clinton Twp., but also had a fruit farm in Bridgewater, Washtenaw Co., Mich. He married LOIS (HEMPHALE), born Saratoga Co., NY, who had come as a child to Michigan. Known son, FRANK L. (m. Carrie Van Tuyle, had dau., Donna). Ref: P&BA-Len pg. 488-91.

WOODWARD, EBENEZER was a Revolutionary soldier and he removed from Vermont to Ontario Co., NY at an early date. He died there in 1832. It may be he in the Rev. pension application records, written Ebenezer "Woodord" with VT service. Known son, LEWIS (following). Ref: P&BA-Len pg. 488-91.

WOODWARD, EUGENE (See George M. Lewis)

WOODWARD, LEWIS, son of EBENEZER (preceding), born in VT, removed to Ontario Co., NY with his parents. He served in the War of 1812. He removed to Clinton Twp., Lenawee Co., Mich. where he was listed in the 1840 census index as "Woodard." There were at least 4 sons, and known was DAVID (preceding). Ref: P&BA-Len pg. 488-91.

WOODWARD, LUCY born ca. 1829, VT, was listed with MINERVA, age 10, b. MIch, both in the 1850 census of Adrian Twp., Lenawee Co., Mich. in housheold of L. R. Mapes, whose wife, Samantha, was age 31, also born VT. Note LEWIS, preceidng.

WOODWARD, JOHN and wife, SARAH, came from London, England, and eventually settled in Hector, Tompkins Co., NY. In the 1850 census of Hector, NY, Sarah is listed head of household, age 64, born England. Known daughter, ANN HEX b. 1820, London (m. William H. Osborne, also see). Ref: P&BA-Len pg. 421-2.

WOODWARD, SAMUEL H. born ca. 1822, VT, MAY be he listed in the 1840 census index of Adrian Twp., Lenawee Co., Mich.; and he was listed in the 1850 census with wife, EMMA, born ca. 1825, NY, with no family. Note LEWIS, preceding.

WOODWORTH, ALATHEAR (See Samuel Niles)

WOODWORTH, GEORGE was born ca. 1826, NY, and was listed in the 1850 census of Madison Twp., Lenawee Co., Mich. in a French household.

WOODWORTH, GEORGE W., son of ORVILLE (following), born 28 June 1840, Medina Twp., Lenawee Co., Mich., married on 23 Feb. 1863 to SUSAN M. (HALL), daughter of Abel (also see). She died 25 Sept. 1865, Medina Twp. George W. married again on 8 Dec. 1879, Lansing, Mich. to ALICE (MASON), daughter of W. S. G. (also see). Ref: P&BA-Len pg. 622-5.

WOODWORTH, JOSEPH was listed in the 1840 census index of Adrian Twp., Lenawee Co., Mich.

WOODWORTH, ORVILLE born 1 Feb. 1807, Columbia Co., NY, married in 1830 to AMANDA (BENNETT), born Norwich, Chenango Co., NY on 11 Apr. 1812. They lived in Sennett, Cayuga Co., NY. One reference stated that they "came from New Jersey to Medina Twp., Lenawee Co., Mich. in 1835." He died 3 Oct. 1870; and she died 17 Dec. 1875. Known children (in the household in 1850 census of Medina Twp.): 1. MARY b. ca. 1833, NY (m. John Johnson; Hudson Mich.); 2. SARAH b. ca. 1837, Mich.; 3. GEORGE W. (preceding); 4. WILLIAM b. ca. 1843; 5. JANETTE b. ca. 1846. Ref: P&BA-Len pg. 622-5.

WOODWORTH, SARAH (See Willard Joslin)

WOOLRIDGE, JOHN served in the War of 1812. He married SALLY (GILBERT); and they moved from Dutchess Co., NY to Smyrna, Chenango Co., NY where they remained. Known daughter, POLLY b. Poughkeepsie, NY (m. James Scarritt[4], also see).

WOOLSEY, ALANSON, son of RICHARD (following), born 5 Feb. 1813, Columbia Co., NY, moved with his parents to Ontario Co., NY. He married at Victor, NY on 29 Nov. 1837 to MAHALA (LADD), daughter of John (also see). They moved in 1838 to Dover Twp. Lenawee Co., Mich.; and a few months later to Madison Twp. Children: 1. JOHN WELLINGTON b. ca. 1840; 2. WILLIAM (d. age 5); 3. CALISTA b. ca. 1846 (m. P. B. Chase); 4. CHARLES b. ca. 1849 (to Chicago, Ill.); 5. RUDOLPH A. (m. Elizabeth Douglas; Madison Twp.). Ref: P&BA-Len pg. 1037-8.

WOOLSEY, NATHANIEL W. and wife, MARY (JONES), were parents of ELMIRA born 13 Nov. 1808, Seneca, Ontario Co., NY (m/1 Hiram S. Whiting; m/2 Peter Baer, see both). Ref: P&BA-Len pg. 841-2.

WOOLSEY, RICHARD and wife, MERCY (MOSHER), were natives of Columbia Co., NY who resided in Monroe and Ontario Cos., NY. Children: 1. HANNAH; 2. LEMUEL; 3. HENRY; 4. AMBROSE; 5. SALLY; 6. WHITING; 7. JAMES J.; 8. DANIEL; 9. JASON; 10. AUGUSTUS; 11. ALANSON (preceding); 12. ALONZO. Ref: P&BA-Len pg. 1037-8.

WOOSTER, DAVID (See Levi Jennings)

WORDEN, ASA was listed in the 1840 census index of Pittsford Twp., Hillsdale Co., Mich. Note DUDLEY & ROBERT, following.

WORDEN, DUDLEY and wife, LUCRETIA (GILLETT), settled in Hudson Twp., Lenawee Co., Mich. in 1831; and resided there in the 1840 census. They moved later to Pittsford, Hillsdale Co., Mich. where he died in 1858. There were 2 sons, names not stated, and known daughter, STELLA b. 1 Oct. 1855, Pittsford (m. George H. Lockwood, also see). Ref: P&BA-Len pg. 1035-6.

Pioneer Families of Southeastern Michigan

WORDEN, JANE (See Jared Reynolds)

WORDEN, JOHN born ca. 1801, and wife, POLLY, born ca. 1810, both in NY, were listed in the 1850 census of Rollin Twp., Lenawee Co., Mich. with WILLIAM H., age 15; PHEBE E., age 14, both b. NY; and JOHN B., age 9; AMANDA A., age 3, both b. Ohio, in their household. SEAMOUR (SEYMOUR), age 21 and family (following) were in the household.

WORDEN, NEWMAN (See Lewis Ganun)

WORDEN, ROBERT was listed in the 1840 census index of Pittsford Twp., Hillsdale Co., Mich. Note ASA & DUDLEY, preceding.

WORDEN, SEYMOUR, probably son of JOHN (preceding), born ca. 1829, NY, and wife, FRANCES A., born ca. 1830, Ohio, were listed in the 1850 census of Rollin Twp., Lenawee Co., Mich. with GEORGE W., age 9/12, b. Ohio, all in the household of JOHN.

WORDEN, SILAS born ca. 1813, NY, and wife, FANNY, born ca. 1816, NH, were listed in the 1850 census of Dover Twp., Lenawee Co., Mich. with MARY, age 14, b. NH; and SUSAN M., age 12; WILLIAM H., age 10; NELSON, age 7; ALEXANDER, age 5; LAURA, age 2, all b. Mich., in their household.

WORDEN, W. H. and wife, NAOMI (MERRILL), moved after 1851 from Fulton Co., Ohio to Ogden Twp., Lenawee Co., Mich.; and then to Fairfield Twp. Known daughter, EMMA E. b. 6 Mar. 1851, Fulton Co., Ohio (m. Bruen E. Peebles, also see). Ref: P&BA-Len pg. 637.

WORKMAN, CHARLES was listed in the 1840 census index of Tecumseh Twp., Lenawee Coc., Mich.

WORKMAN, MARY A. Mrs. was the daughter of Maj. Philo Mills (also see).

WORTH, ALICE (See Henrick Willey)

WORTH, ALVA born ca. 1806, Conn., and wife, ORESSA E.?, born ca. 1818, NY, were listed in the 1850 census of Blissfield Twp., Lenawee Co., Mich. with GUY, age 14, b. NY, in their household.

WORTH, ARTHUR (See Henrick Willey)

WORTH, COMINS was listed in the 1840 census index of Adrian Twp., Lenawee Co., Mich.

WORTH, JOHN[1] settled in Nantucket, Mass. in Colonial times, and married there to SARAH (HOAG). They had a son, RICHARD[2] who married ANNA (MACEY), and had a son, RICHARD[3]. Richard[3] married ELIZABETH (FOLGER) of a Quaker family, who was a sister of Walter Folger, and a grandniece of Benjamin Franklin. They had a son, ?[4] (name not stated) born in 1782, possibly another Richard. Richard[3] in his later years moved to DeRuyter, Madison Co., NY. ?[4] grew up in Mass., but went first to Ghent, Columbia Co., NY, where he married ELIZABETH (CRANDALL). They later moved to near Lincklean, Chenango Co., NY. He died 2 May 1854 while visiting some of his children near Royalton, Ohio. Known daughter, HEPSIBETH b. ca. 1825, DeRuyter, NY (m. David Carpenter, also see, of Blissfield Twp., Lenawee Co., Mich., on 16 Aug. 1848, as his 3rd wife). Ref: P&BA-Len pg. 837.

WORTH, MOSES S. born ca. 1822, and wife, MARIA, born ca. 1824, both in NY, were listed in the 1850 census of Blissfield Twp., Lenawee Co., Mich. with BLANCHE C., age 1, b. Mich., in their household.

WORTH, OBED T. born ca. 1815, and with him was DAVID, age 18, both b. NY, in the 1850 census of Seneca Twp., Lenawee Co., Mich.

WORTH, SETH born ca. 1798, and wife, MARTHA?, born ca. 1805, both in Mass., were listed in the 1840 census index of Clinton Twp., Lenawee Co., Mich.; and were listed in the 1850 census with LYDIA, age 12; WILLIAM HENRY, age 10. both b. Mich., in their household.

WORTHRING, GEORGE and wife, MAHALA (BIRGGS), of Shelby, Orleans Co., NY had known daughter, SUSAN born ca. 1821, Orleans Co. (m. James Welch, also see). Ref: P&BA-Len pg. 775-6.

WOTRING, ABRAM[1] was believed to have come from Germany and settled first in Maryland; and then moved to what is now Preson Co., W. Va. Known son, ABRAM[2] born Maryland, married in W. Va. to MARY (SMITH) who was born on the line between Maryland and Virginia. Known sons: JACOB[3] (following); ABRAM S.[3] (following). WOTRING, ABRAM S.[3], son of ABRAM[2] (Note ABRAM[1], preceding), born in Mar. 1810, Preston Co., W. Va., married there to RUTH (HOOD), daughter of Julius (also see). They remained there until about 1840, they moved to Taylor Co., where they founded the village of Aurora (first named West Union). They were both still living there in 1888, at advanced ages. Nine children, names not stated, except Capt. JEHU F. (following); & #6. SAMUEL G. (following). Ref: P&BA-Len pg. 720-1; 1107-8.

WOTRING, FREDERICK[4], son of JACOB[3] (following), born 1808, Preston Co., W. Va., married there to CATHERINE (RINEHART) and remained until 1874, when they moved to Ogden Twp., Lenawee Co., Mich. He died in Apr. 1875; but she was surviving in 1888. Ten children, of whom 9 grew to maturity, names not stated, except GEORGE F.[5] (following). Ref: P&BA-Len pg. 1104-5.

WOTRING, GEORGE F.[5], son of FREDERICK[4] (preceding), born 13 Aug. 1860, Preston Co., W. Va., married on 17 Oct. 1886 to EVA (CHENEY), daughter of Alpheus (also see). They settled in Ogden Twp., Lenawee Co., Mich. Son, CLARK OTIS. Ref: P&BA-Len pg. 1104-5.

WOTRING, JACOB[3], son of ABRAM[2] (Note ABRAM[1], preceding), born Hagerstown, MD, married SARAH (HARSH), daughter of Frederick (also see). She died in Aurora, W. Va. Children: 1. PETER (d. Preson Co.); 2. FREDERICK (preceding); 3. ELIZABETH (d. Preston Co., W. VA.); 4. NICHOLAS (following). Ref: P&BA-Len pg. 734-5.

WOTRING, JEHU F.[4] Capt., son of ABRAHAM S.[3] (preceding), born 18 Mar. 1834, Preston Co., W. Va., married on 1 July 1855 to MARY A. (CRANE), daughter of Calvin (also see). He served in the Civil War in 6th W. Va. Cavalry (Union forces); and was captured and was in Libby & Danville Prisons. In 1866, they moved to Morgan Co., W. Va.; and in 1870 to Ogden Twp., Lenawee Co., Mich. Children: 1. ALICE BELLE (m. William McComb; Ogden Twp.); 2. ARTHUR C. (Ogden Twp.); 3. ARTEMIS O. (Palmyra Twp.); 4. DORA (d. age 4); 5. IDA M. (d. age 2-1/2); 6. RUTH O.; 7. BRUCE B.; 8. MARY E.; 9. MAUD. Ref: P&BA-Len pg. 1107-8.

WOTRING, NICHOLAS[4], son of JACOB[3] (preceding), born 3 Jan. 1820, Preston Co., W. Va., married on 21 Apr. 1842 to

SUSANNA (RINEHART), daughter of Thomas (also see) in Preston Co. They removed to Ogden Twp., Lenawee Co., Mich. in 1865. No children were mentioned. Ref: P&BA-Len pg. 734-5.

WOTRING, NICHOLAS probably born after 1850 (See Frederick H. Corwin).

WOTRING, SAMUEL[4], son of ABRAM S.[3] (preceding), born 4 May 1840, W. Union, W. Va., served in the Civil War in Co. B, 2nd VA Inf. (later formed into 2d VA Cav.) He married on 18 Jan. 1866 to MARY (SMELL), daughter of George (also see). They resided in Grafton, W. VA. until 1872, then moved to Ogden Twp., Lenawee Co., Mich. Children: 1. GEORGE L.; 2. JAMES W.; 3. SARAH E.; 4. EDNA E.; 5. PERRY (d. infancy); 6. EUGENE F.; 7. HARRY L. Ref: p&ba-IEN PG. 720-1.

WRIGHT, AARON H. was listed in the 1840 census index of Macon Twp., Lenawee Co., Mich.

WRIGHT, ALVIN was listed in the 1840 census index of Tecumseh Twp., Lenawee Co., Mich.

WRIGHT, ANN born ca. 1815, South Caroline, noted as "black," was listed in the household of an Innkeeper in the 1850 census of Tecumseh Twp., Lenawee Co., Mich.

WRIGHT, ANN born ca. 1832, NY, was listed in the 1850 census of Madison Twp., Lenawee Co., Mich. in a Hunt household.

WRIGHT, ANNA L. born ca. 1831, NY, was listted in the 1850 census of Raisin Twp., Lenawee Co., Mich. in an Aldridge household.

WRIGHT, CHARLES born ca. 1813, Ohio, and wife, MARYET (MARGARET?), born ca. 1820, England, were listed in the 1850 census of Blissfield Twp., Lenawee Co., Mich, with CHARLOTTE, age 7, b. Ohio; and HARRIET, age 4; OR--(female), age 2, both b. Mich., in their household.

WRIGHT, ELIJAH born 26 Jan. 1793, and wife, POLLY (SUNDERLIN), born 25 Sept. 1796, both in NY, moved from Yates Co., NY in 1830 to Clinton Twp., Lenawee Co., Mich. He died 4 Dec. 1863; and she died 28 Apr. 1857 at the home of only child, SALLIE A. b. 1818, Barrington, NY (m/1 Belden Booth who d. before 1842; m/2 Rancelier Mills, also see, as his 2nd wife). Ref: P&BA-Len pg. 1086-7. In the 1850 census of Tecumseh Twp., they listed grandson, Wright Mills, age 4, b. Mich.; and Mary Quick, age 19, b. NY, in their household.

WRIGHT, EPHRAIM of Mass. had daughter, ? (See Joshua Knight).

WRIGHT, F. F. (See Richard H. Osborn)

WRIGHT, GEORGE A. born ca. 1812, and wife, HARRIET, born ca. 1817, both in NY, were listed in the 1850 census of Dover Twp., Lenawee Co., Mich. with ANDALUSIA, age 8, born NY, in their household.

WRIGHT, IRA born ca. 1786, New Hampshire, and wife, MARY, born ca. 1786, NY, were listed in the 1840 census index of Madison Twp., Lenawee Co., Mich.; and in the 1850 census with SAMANTHA, age 26. b. NY; and HENRY, age 8, b. Mich., in their household.

WRIGHT, MARY (See Simon Oliver)

WRIGHT, MOSES, probably son of THOMAS (following), born ca. 1815, Mass., and wife, HARRIET, born ca. 1815, Conn., were listed in the 1840 census of Tecumseh Twp., Lenawee Co., Mich. with CHARLES, age 3; JULIA, age 1, both b. Mich. Note THOMAS & IRENA, following, who were also in household.

WRIGHT, NANCY (See Henry Lybarker)

WRIGHT, NANCY born ca. 1826, Mich., and LEVI E., age 4, born Ohio, were listed in the 1850 census of Medina Twp., Lenawee Co., Mich. in the household of Levi Goss.

WRIGHT, PETER had known daughter, LUCY (m. John Richardson, also see, in Ohio, poss. Lorain Co.) Ref: P&BA-Len pg. 1203-4.

WRIGHT, ROSWELL born ca. 1824, Mass., and wife, EMILY, borh ca. 1826, England, were listed in the 1850 census of Tecumseh Twp., Lenawee Co., Mich. with WILLIAM, age 1, b. Mich., in their household.

WRIGHT, SARAH born England (See John Harrison).

WRIGHT, SOLOMON H. born ca. 1816, and wife, LUCY, born ca. 1822, both in Ohio, were listed in the 1850 census of Blissfield Twp., Lenawee Co., Mich. with EUNICE, age 8; ELVIN, age 6, both b. Ohio, in their household.

WRIGHT, SPAFFORD was listed in the 1840 census index of Tecumseh Twp., Lenawee Co., Mich.

WRIGHT, THOMAS and wife, SALLIE (MURPHY), of Nichols, Tioga Co., NY, were parents of FRANCES b. 13 Mar. 1806, Nichols (m/1 Horace Corbin; m/2 Eben Dunham, see both.) Ref: P&BA-Len pg. 375-6.

WRIGHT, THOMAS born ca. 1784, and wife, IRENA, born ca. 1785, both in Mass., were listed in the 1840 census index of Tecumseh Twp., Lenawee Co., Mich. (spelled "Right"); and in the 1850 census were in the household of probably son, MOSES (preceding).

WRIGHT, WALTER born ca. 1801, and wife, FRANCES, born ca. 1807, both in NY, were listed in the 1850 census of Madison Twp., Lenawee Co., Mich. with ELIZABETH, age 22, b. NY, in their household.

WRIGHT, WALTER (See Hugh Davitt)

WRIGHT, WILLIAM and wife, ADDIE, born Erie Co., NY, were parents of GERTIE O. b. 12 Dec. 1864, Erie Co., NY (m. Seth W. Joslin, son of Alvin, also see). Ref: P&BA-Len pg. 547-8.

WRIGHT, WILLIAM born ca. 1815, and wife, ELIZABETH, born ca. 1823, both in England, were listed in the 1850 census of Tecumseh Twp., Lenawee Co., Mich. with WILLIAM, age 2, b. Mich., in their household.

WYMAN, HENRY Dr., son of JONATHAN (following), born 2 Apr. 1803, Keene, NH, moved to Jefferson Co., NY with his parents. In 1831, he moved to Anderson, Madison Co., Ind. He married first in 1835 to PRUDENCE (BERRY) born in Clark Co., Ind. She died in 1837, leaving a son: 1. OLIVER (to Minneapolis, MN). He moved to Mississippi from 1841 to 1843, then moved to Blissfield Twp., Lenawee Co., Mich. He married again in 1844 to ZELINDA (CARPENTER), daughter of Clement (also see) and lived in Blissfield Twp. She died there 14 Nov. 1877. Children: 2. Dr. HAL C. (Detroit, Mich.); 3. Dr. HUGH S. (Alaska); 4. CARRIE S. (m. F. B. Lamb; Blissfield, Mich.). Ref: P&BA-Len pg. 794&7.

WYMAN, JONAS was a native of Orleans Co., NY who moved to Lansing, Ingham Co., Mich. where known daughter, DELIA was born (m. Chauncey M. Crego, also see).

WYMAN, JONATHAN, son of a man who died at the Battle of Concord on 19 Apr. 1775, was born ca. 1769, Concord, Mass. His mother died, and he was raised by a married sister. He went as a young man to Cheshire Co., NH.

Pioneer Families of Southeastern Michigan

He married there to ABIGAIL (ADAMS) who was born in Nelson, NH. About 1840, they moved to Rodman, Jefferson Co., NY. She died there. Known son, Dr. HENRY (preceding). Ref: P&BA-Len pg. 794&7.

WYMAN, PARKER married ASENATH (CARPENTER) probably in Fairfield Twp., Lenawee Co., Mich., and they were parents of known son, WILLIAM W. (following). They may have been deceased by 1850, as William W. was raised by William Weatherby (also see) in whose home he was listed in the census. Ref: P&BA-Len pg. 1020-1. Note SHELDON, following.

WYMAN, PETER, son of SHELDON (following), born 23 June 1837/9, married on 18 Oct. 1860 to LYDIA D. (PAUL), daughter of William (also see). Son, OTIS F. (d. age 3 wks).

WYMAN, SHELDON born 20 Mar. 1814, Rupert, Bennington Co., VT, moved with his parents to Shelby, Orleans Co., NY; and then to Medina Co., Ohio. He came to Fairfield Twp., Lenawee Co., Mich. in 1834. He married on 3 Nov. 1836 to LYDIA (CARPENTER), daughter of James (also see). There were 9 children, 2 dying infancy, names not stated. 1. JAMES M. b. ca. 1837; 2. THOMAS J. b. ca. 1837 (twin?); 3. PETER (preceding); 4. CANDACE b. ca. 1842 (m. D. W. Hickman; Delaware Co., Ind.); 5. SARAH b. ca. 1845 (m. John E. Mason); 6. ALONZO b. ca. 1849; 7. MARY (m. Isaiah Reynolds). Ref: P&BA-Len pg. 459-60.

WYMAN, WILLIAM W., son of PARKER (preceding), born 1 Feb. 1844, Fairfield Twp., Lenawee Co., Mich. was reared by William and Sarah C. (Carpenter) Weatherby, probably his Aunt. He married on 3 July 1865 to SALINA (DELAND), daughter of Joseph (also see). Children: CORA S. (d. age 12); DELIGHT (d. age 5); LAURA (m. George B. Schomp); BLOND; WARREN B. Ref: P&BA-Len pg. 1020-1.

WYRILL, MARY (See George L. Oliver)

- Y -

YAUTZ, ELIZABETH born Hagerstown, MD (See Levi Hopkins).

YEATON, STEPHEN from England settled in Maine. It is probably he with marriage intentions published on 6 Apr. 1761 in Poland, Maine to MARY (SAWYER), daughter of Joseph, born 6 Apr. 1741. He lived out his life in Minot, ME. They were probably parents of STEPHEN; and a daughter who m. John Goodwin (also see). Ref: P&BA-Lenpg. 1011-12.

YEATTEN see YEATON

YOST, WILLIAM (written "Youst") born ca. 1808, and wife, MARY, born ca. 1808, both in NY, were listed in the 1850 census of Hudson Twp., Lenawee Co., Mich. with THEODORE, age 16; MILAN, age 14; ADALINE, age 12; WILLIAM H., age 10 (note W. H., following); MARTIN, age 8, all b. NY, in their household.

YOST, W. H. (See Charles Dunham)

YOUNG, ALFRED married MARTHA (JOHNSON), daughter of William (also see). Note JOHN, following, as Martha's brother, William M. Johnson, married SARAH, daughter of JOHN.

YOUNG, AZUBA (See Abraham Wheeler)

YOUNG, JOSEPH came from England to America and settled in Seneca Co., NY. After the death of his wife, name not stated, he returned to England. Known son, JOHN (following). Ref: P&BA-Len pg. 868-9.

YOUNG, JOHN, son of JOSEPH (preceding), born 1796, England, came to Seneca Co., NY with his parents. He married in Romulus, Seneca Co., NY to PAULINA (SCHOOLEY), daughter of William H. (also see). They lived variously in Romulus & Ovid, NY; went to Maryland; returned to Varick, NY, then lived in McGregor Co., Iowa; Highland Park, Ill.; and then in 1864 to Marion Co., Ill. He died near Kinmundy, Ill. in Sept. 1877. She died in Sept. 1868. Children: 1. LAZETTA (m. William C. Barker; Watkins, NY, where she d.); 2. FRANCES A. (m. Frank Lerch; Waukegan, Ill.; where she d.); 3. Dr. WILLIAM T. (Vineland, NJ); 4. JOSEPH (Vineland, NJ); 5. E. MATILDA b. 8 June 1833 (m. James Harvey Terwilliger, also see); Ref: P&BA-Len pg. 868-9.

YOUNG, JOHN and wife, BETSEY, of Penn., were parents of SARAH (m. William M. Johnson, also see, as his second wife). Note that ALFRED (preceding) married Martha Johnson, sister of William M. Ref: P&BA-Len pg. 927-31.

YOUNG, LUCRETIA (See Daniel Jones)

YOUNG, LYDIA (See David Cochrane)

YOUNG, REBECCA (See Joseph Ritchey)

YOUNG, SAMUEL moved after 1805 from New Jersey to Ilion (German Flats), and then Russia, Herkimer Co., NY. Known daughter, LYDIA b. ca. 1805 (sketch said b. NJ, but 1850 census of Hudson Twp., Lenawee Co., Mich. census said b. Rhode Island) married Samuel Frazier (also see). Ref: P&BA-Len pg. 948-50.

YOUNGLOVE, CHARLOTTE (See George W. Clark)

YOUNGS, DAVIS born ca. 1798, NY, and wife, AMA (SMITH), born ca. 1800, Rhode Island, settled first in McKean Co., Penn.; and then about 1850 moved to Seneca Twp., Lenawee Co., Mich. They had 4 sons and 4 daughters, names not stated. SYLVESTER, following, was adjacent in the 1850 census. In their household were ALMINA, age 21; ORRIN, age 18; ROYAL A. (following); JAMES, age 9, all b. Penn. Ref: P&BA-LEn pg. 781. Note: SARAH, following, probably another daughter.

YOUNGS, ROYAL A., son of DAVIS (preceding), born 12 Dec. 1835, McKean Co., Penn., moved with his parents to Seneca Twp., Lenawee Co., Mich. He married on 4 Sept. 1859 to CLARINDA (PLETCHER), daughter of Andrew (also see). Of their 8 children, 5 died infancy. 1. FRED (m. Mary Scott; Seneca Twp.); 2. IRVING; 3. HERBERT. Ref: P&BA-Len pg. 781.

YOUNGS, SARAH born ca. 1824, Penn. (See Ebenezer Capron).

YOUNGS, SYLVESTER, possibly son of DAVIS (preceding), born ca. 1818, and wife, ANGELINE, born ca. 1822, both in Penn., were listed in the 1850 census of Seneca Twp., Lenawee Co., Mich. with RHODA E., age 10; FAYETTE C., age 7, both b. Penn.; and WILLIAM H., age 5; ANSON C., age 1, both b. Mich., in their household.

YOUST see YOST

YUND, ELIZABETH (STRONG) Mrs. (See James Moreland[3]; also see Robert Strong).

- Z -

ZALER, BARBARA (See James L. Brown)

ZELUFF, BENJAMIN was listed in the 1840 census index of Dundee, Monroe Co., Mich. Also note ZEBEDIAH.

ZELUFF, DAVID, born NJ, came to Monroe Co., Mich. as a young man and married LOIZA (RUSSELL) born in NY. In 1840, he is listed as "David H." in the census index of Milan Twp., Monroe Co., Mich. In 1850, they moved to Utica, MIch.; and to Ridgeway Twp., Lenawee Co. by 1865. Known son, JOHN H. (following). Known daughter, ELIZABETH (m. William H. Curtiss, son of Hiram A., also see). Note: This surname appears in Essex Co., NJ in the militia in 1793.

ZELUFF, JOHN H., son of DAVID (preceding), born 12 Sept. 1844, Dundee, Monroe Co., Mich., married in Ridgeway Twp., Lenawee Co. on 21 Mar. 1867 to ELIZA J. (POCKLINGTON), daughter of William (also see). Children: 1. EUGENE; 2. SERENE; 3. CASS; 4. FRANK; 5. FLORA; 6. LINAS. Ref: P&BA-Len pg. 378-9.

ZELUFF, ZEBEDIAH was listed in the 1840 census index of Dundee Twp., Monroe Co., Mich. Note BENJAMIN; & DAVID, preceding.

ZIBBLE, MARY A. (See Herman Morsman)